Lecture Notes in Artificial Intelligence   4539

Edited by J. G. Carbonell and J. Siekmann

Subseries of Lecture Notes in Computer Science

T0189095

Nader H. Bshouty   Claudio Gentile (Eds.)

Learning
Theory

20th Annual Conference on Learning Theory, COLT 2007
San Diego, CA, USA, June 13-15, 2007
Proceedings

 Springer

Series Editors

Jaime G. Carbonell, Carnegie Mellon University, Pittsburgh, PA, USA
Jörg Siekmann, University of Saarland, Saarbrücken, Germany

Volume Editors

Nader H. Bshouty
Department of Computer Science
Technion, Haifa, 32000, Israel
E-mail: bshouty@cs.technion.ac.il

Claudio Gentile
Dipartimento di Informatica e Comunicazione
Università dell'Insubria, Varese, Italy
E-mail: claudio.gentile@uninsubria.it

Library of Congress Control Number: 2007927819

CR Subject Classification (1998): I.2.6, I.2.3, I.2, F.4.1-2, F.2, F.1.1

LNCS Sublibrary: SL 7 – Artificial Intelligence

ISSN   0302-9743
ISBN-10   3-540-72925-9 Springer Berlin Heidelberg New York
ISBN-13   978-3-540-72925-9 Springer Berlin Heidelberg New York

Springer is a part of Springer Science+Business Media

springer.com

© Springer-Verlag Berlin Heidelberg 2007
Printed in Germany

Typesetting: Camera-ready by author, data conversion by Scientific Publishing Services, Chennai, India
Printed on acid-free paper   SPIN: 12073375   06/3180   5 4 3 2 1 0

Preface

This volume contains papers presented at the 20th Annual Conference on Learning Theory (previously known as the Conference on Computational Learning Theory) held in San Diego, USA, June 13-15, 2007, as part of the 2007 Federated Computing Research Conference (FCRC).

The Technical Program contained 41 papers selected from 92 submissions, 5 open problems selected from among 7 contributed, and 2 invited lectures. The invited lectures were given by Dana Ron on "Property Testing: A Learning Theory Perspective," and by Santosh Vempala on "Spectral Algorithms for Learning and Clustering." The abstracts of these lectures are included in this volume.

The Mark Fulk Award is presented annually for the best paper co-authored by a student. The student selected this year was Samuel E. Moelius III for the paper "U-Shaped, Iterative, and Iterative-with-Counter Learning" co-authored with John Case. This year, student awards were also granted by the *Machine Learning Journal*. We have therefore been able to select two more student papers for prizes. The students selected were Lev Reyzin for the paper "Learning Large-Alphabet and Analog Circuits with Value Injection Queries" (co-authored with Dana Angluin, James Aspnes, and Jiang Chen), and Jennifer Wortman for the paper "Regret to the Best vs. Regret to the Average" (co-authored with Eyal Even-Dar, Michael Kearns, and Yishay Mansour).

The selected papers cover a wide range of topics, including unsupervised, semisupervised and active learning, statistical learning theory, regularized learning, kernel methods and SVM, inductive inference, learning algorithms and limitations on learning, on-line and reinforcement learning. The last topic is particularly well represented, covering alone more than one-fourth of the total.

The large number of quality submissions placed a heavy burden on the Program Committee of the conference: Jose Balcazar (UPC Barcelona), Shai Ben David (University of Waterloo), Avrim Blum (Carnegie Mellon University), John Case (University of Delaware), Michael Collins (MIT), Ran El-Yaniv (Technion), Paul Goldberg (Liverpool University), Peter Grunwald (CWI, The Netherlands), Mark Herbster (University College London), Marcus Hutter (ANU/NICTA, Australia), Adam Kalai (Georgia Tech), Roni Khardon (Tufts University), Adam Klivans (University of Texas), John Lafferty (Carnegie Mellon University), Phil Long (Google), Gabor Lugosi (ICREA and Pompeu Fabra University), Yishay Mansour (Tel Aviv University), Partha Niyogi (University of Chicago), Rocco Servedio (Columbia University), John Shawe-Taylor (University College London), Hans Ulrich Simon (University of Bochum), Frank Stephan (National University of Singapore), Gilles Stoltz (CNRS and ENS, France), Csaba Szepesvari (University of Alberta), Alexandre Tsybakov (Univ. Paris VI).

We are extremely grateful for their careful and thorough reviewing, and for the detailed and active discussions that ensured the very high quality of the final program. We would like to have mentioned the sub-reviewers who assisted the Programme Committee in reaching their assessments, but unfortunately space constraints do not permit us to include this long list of names and we must simply ask them to accept our thanks anonymously.

We are particularly grateful to Sanjoy Dasgupta, the conference Local Chair, for handling all the local arrangements to ensure a successful event, and for maintaining the learningtheory.org Web site. Many thanks to Marco Tarini for assisting us in designing the conference Web site, to Cissy Liu for the photo of San Diego therein, and to Samory Kpotufe for designing the conference T-shirt.

Special thanks to Nicolò Cesa-Bianchi and Yishay Mansour for selecting exciting and thought-provoking open problems for the open problems session.

The COLT Steering Committee members assisted us throughout the organization of the conference, and we would like to thank them all. We would also like to thank Microsoft for providing the software used in the Program Committee deliberations. Finally, we would like to thank the *Machine Learning Journal,* Google Inc., and IBM for their sponsorship of the conference.

April 2007   Nader Bshouty
                                                    Claudio Gentile

Organization

Sponsored by:

Table of Contents

Learning Algorithms and Limitations on Learning

Online and Reinforcement Learning III

Online and Reinforcement Learning IV

Dimensionality Reduction

Other Approaches

Open Problems

Property Testing:
A Learning Theory Perspective

Dana Ron

Department of EE – Systems, Tel-Aviv University Ramat Aviv, Israel
`danar@eng.tau.ac.il`

Property testing [15,9] is the study of the following class of problems.

> *Given the ability to perform local queries concerning a particular object (e.g., a function, or a graph), the problem is to determine whether the object has a predetermined global property (e.g., linearity or bipartiteness), or differs significantly from any object that has the property. In the latter case we say it is* far *from (having) the property. The algorithm is allowed a probability of failure, and typically it inspects only a small part of the whole object.*

Property testing problems are usually viewed as relaxations of decision problems. Namely, instead of requiring that the algorithm decide whether the object has the property or does not have the property, the algorithm is required to decide whether the object has the property or is far from having the property. As such, we are interested in testing algorithms that are much more efficient than the corresponding decision algorithms, and in particular have complexity that is sublinear in the size of the object.

Another view of property testing is as a relaxation of learning (with queries and under the uniform distribution)[1]. Namely, instead of asking that the algorithm output a good approximation of the function (object) from within a particular family of functions F, we only require that it decide whether the function belongs to F or is far from any function in F. Given this view, a natural motivation for property testing is to serve as a preliminary step before learning (and in particular, agnostic learning (e.g., [12]): We can first run the testing algorithm to decide whether to use a particular family of functions as our hypothesis class. Here too we are interested in testing algorithms that are more efficient than the corresponding learning algorithms. As observed in [9], property testing is no harder than *proper* learning. Namely, if we have a proper learning algorithm for a family of functions F then we can use it as a subroutine to test the property: "does the function belong to F".

The choice of which of the aforementioned views to take is typically determined by the type of objects and properties in question. Much of property testing

---

[1] Testing under non-uniform distributions (e.g., [10,1]) and testing with random examples (e.g., [11]) have been considered, but most of the work in property testing deals with testing under the uniform distributions and with queries.

N. Bshouty and C. Gentile (Eds.): COLT 2007, LNAI 4539, pp. 1–2, 2007.

deals with combinatorial objects and in particular graphs (e.g., [9,3]). For such objects it is usually more natural to view property testing as a relaxation of exact decision. Indeed, there are many combinatorial properties for which there are testing algorithms that are much more efficient than the corresponding decision problems. On the other hand, when the objects are functions, then it is usually more natural to look at property testing from a learning theory perspective. In some cases, both viewpoints are appropriate.

This talk will focus on several results that hopefully will be of interest from a learning theory perspective. These include: linearity testing [4] and low-degree testing (e.g., [15]), testing basic Boolean formula [13,7], testing monotonicity (e.g., [8,5]), testing of clustering (e.g., [2]), and distribution-free testing (e.g., [10,1]).

For surveys on property testing see [6,14], and for an online bibliography see: www.cs.princeton.edu/courses/archive/spring04/cos5987/bib.html.

References

1. Ailon, N., Chazelle, B.: Information theory in property testing and monotonicity testing in higher dimensions. Information and Computation 204, 1704–1717 (2006)
2. Alon, N., Dar, S., Parnas, M., Ron, D.: Testing of clustering. SIAM Journal on Discrete Math. 16(3), 393–417 (2003)
3. Alon, N., Fischer, E., Newman, I., Shapira, A.: A combinatorial characterization of the testable graph properties: It's all about regularity. In: Proceedings of the Thirty-Eighth Annual ACM Symposium on the Theory of Computing (2006)
4. Blum, M., Luby, M., Rubinfeld, R.: Self-testing/correcting with applications to numerical problems. Journal of the ACM 47, 549–595 (1993)
5. Ergun, F., Kannan, S., Kumar, S.R., Rubinfeld, R., Viswanathan, M.: Spot-checkers. Journal of Computer and System Sciences 60(3), 717–751 (2000)
6. Fischer, E.: The art of uninformed decisions: A primer to property testing. Bulletin of the European Association for Theoretical Computer Science 75, 97–126 (2001)
7. Fischer, E., Kindler, G., Ron, D., Safra, S., Samorodnitsky, S.: Testing juntas. Journal of Computer and System Sciences 68(4), 753–787 (2004)
8. Goldreich, O., Goldwasser, S., Lehman, E., Ron, D., Samordinsky, A.: Testing monotonicity. Combinatorica 20(3), 301–337 (2000)
9. Goldreich, O., Goldwasser, S., Ron, D.: Property testing and its connection to learning and approximation. Journal of the ACM 45(4), 653–750 (1998)
10. Halevy, S., Kushilevitz, E.: Distribution-free property testing. In: Arora, S., Jansen, K., Rolim, J.D.P., Sahai, A. (eds.) RANDOM 2003 and APPROX 2003. LNCS, vol. 2764, pp. 341–353. Springer, Heidelberg (2003)
11. Kearns, M., Ron, D.: Testing problems with sub-learning sample complexity. Journal of Computer and System Sciences 61(3), 428–456 (2000)
12. Kearns, M.J., Schapire, R.E., Sellie, L.M.: Toward efficient agnostic learning. Machine Learning 17(2-3), 115–141 (1994)
13. Parnas, M., Ron, D., Samorodnitsky, A.: Testing boolean formulae. SIAM Journal on Discrete Math. 16(1), 20–46 (2002)
14. Ron, D.: Property testing. In: Rajasekaran, S., Pardalos, P. M., Reif, J. H., Rolim, J. D. P.(eds.) Handbook on Randomization, Volume II, pp. 597–649 (2001)
15. Rubinfeld, R., Sudan, M.: Robust characterization of polynomials with applications to program testing. SIAM Journal on Computing 25(2), 252–271 (1996)

Spectral Algorithms for Learning and Clustering

Santosh S. Vempala

Georgia Tech, Atlanta GA 30332, USA
vempala@cc.gatech.edu
http://www.cc.gatech.edu/~vempala

1 Summary

Roughly speaking, spectral algorithms are methods that rely on the principal components (typically singular values and singular vectors) of an input matrix (or graph). The spectrum of a matrix captures many interesting properties in surprising ways. Spectral methods are already used for unsupervised learning, image segmentation, to improve precision and recall in databases and broadly for information retrieval. The common component of these methods is the subspace of a small number of singular vectors of the data, by means of the Singular Value Decomposition (SVD). We describe SVD from a geometric perspective and then focus on its central role in efficient algorithms for (a) the classical problem of "learning" a mixture of Gaussians in $\mathbf{R}^n$ and (b) clustering a set of objects from pairwise similarities.

2 Mixture Models

A finite mixture model for an unknown distribution is a weighted combination of a finite number of distributions of a known type. The problem of learning or estimating a mixture model is formulated as follows. We assume that we get samples from a distribution F on $\Re^n$ which is a mixture (convex combination) of unknown distributions $F_1, F_2, \ldots, F_k$, with (unknown) mixing weights $w_1, w_2, \ldots, w_k > 0$, i.e., $F = \sum_{i=1}^{k} w_i F_i$ and $\sum_{i=1}^{k} w_i = 1$. The goal is to (a) classify the sample points according to the underlying distributions and (b) estimate essential parameters of the components, such as the mean and covariance matrix of each component. This problem has been widely studied, particularly for the special case when each F_i is a Gaussian.

There has been substantial progress on this problem over the past decade (initiated by Dasgupta, FOCS 1999) leading to rigorous algorithms under the assumption that the means of the components are sufficiently separated. While the known separation bound is near-optimal for mixtures of spherical Gaussians (and more generally, mixtures of weakly isotropic components), it is far from the best possible for general Gaussians and the following fundamental problem remains wide open: classify a sample from a mixture of Gaussians with arbitrary covariance matrices, under the assumptions that for any pair of Gaussians, their projections to the line joining their means are well-separated (i.e., the overlap in measure is negligible).

N. Bshouty and C. Gentile (Eds.): COLT 2007, LNAI 4539, pp. 3–4, 2007.

The method to prove the current best bounds is the SVD (Vempala and Wang, JCSS 2004). We illustrate the power of the SVD in this context via the following observation for *any* mixture model (Kannan et al COLT 2005).

Theorem 1. *Let F be a mixture with k components $F_1, \ldots, F_k$ and mixing weights $w_1, \ldots, w_k$. Let W be the k-dimensional SVD subspace of F. For each i, let μ_i be the mean of F_i, $d(\mu_i, W)$ denote the orthogonal distance of μ_i to the subspace W and $\sigma_{i,W}^2$ be the maximum variance of F_i along any direction in W. Then,*

$$\sum_{i=1}^{k} w_i d(\mu_i, W)^2 \leq k \sum_{i=1}^{k} w_i \sigma_{i,W}^2.$$

3   Clustering from Similarities

Clustering a set of objects given a pairwise similarity function is a problem with many applications. There are many approaches to the problem. A popular approach is to formulate an explicit objective function and then give an algorithm to find a clustering that (approximately) optimizes the objective function. There are two difficulties with this approach (a) the right objective function seems to differ widely based on the context of the application (b) the optimization problem is typically NP-hard and proposed solutions, even if polytime, are not efficient in practice.

We describe the following approach (Kannan et al JACM 2004, Cheng et al ACM Trans. Database Sys. 2006): first form a tree by recursively partitioning the given set (the root is the set of all objects, the leaves are singletons), then find the best *tree-respecting* clustering, where each cluster is a subtree, for the objective function of choice. The recursive partitioning is done by a spectral algorithm while the tree clustering is via dynamic programming and is efficient for a large class of functions. We discuss the performance of the method both theoretically and empirically on multiple data sets.

Minimax Bounds for Active Learning

Rui M. Castro[1,2] and Robert D. Nowak[1]

[1] University of Wisconsin, Madison WI 53706, USA
rcastro@cae.wisc.edu, nowak@engr.wisc.edu
[2] Rice University, Houston TX 77005, USA

Abstract. This paper aims to shed light on achievable limits in active learning. Using minimax analysis techniques, we study the achievable rates of classification error convergence for broad classes of distributions characterized by decision boundary regularity and noise conditions. The results clearly indicate the conditions under which one can expect significant gains through active learning. Furthermore we show that the learning rates derived are tight for "boundary fragment" classes in d-dimensional feature spaces when the feature marginal density is bounded from above and below.

1 Introduction

The interest in active learning in the machine learning community has increased greatly in the last few of years, in part due to the dramatic growth of data sets and the high cost of labeling all the examples in such sets. There are several empirical and theoretical results suggesting that in certain situations active learning can be significantly more effective than passive learning [1,2,3,4,5]. Many of these results pertain to the "noiseless" setting, in which the labels are deterministic functions of the features. In certain noiseless scenarios it has been shown that the number of labeled examples needed to achieve a desired classification error rate is much smaller than what would be need using passive learning. In fact for some of those scenarios, active learning requires only $O(\log n)$ labeled examples to achieve the same performance that can be achieved through passive learning with n labeled examples [3,6,7,8]. This exponential speed-up in learning rates is a tantalizing example of the power of active learning.

Although the noiseless setting is interesting from a theoretical perspective, it is very restrictive, and seldom relevant for practical applications. Some active learning results have been extended to the "bounded noise rate" setting. In this setting labels are no longer a deterministic function of the features, but for a given feature the probability of observing a particular label is significantly higher than the probability of observing any other label. In the case of binary classification this means that if $(\boldsymbol{X}, Y)$ is a feature-label pair, where $Y \in \{0,1\}$, then $|\Pr(Y = 1|\boldsymbol{X} = \boldsymbol{x}) - 1/2| > c$ for every $\boldsymbol{x}$ in the feature space, with $c > 0$. In other words, $\Pr(Y = 1|\boldsymbol{X} = \boldsymbol{x})$ "jumps" at the decision boundary, providing a very strong cue to active learning procedures. Under this assumption it can be

N. Bshouty and C. Gentile (Eds.): COLT 2007, LNAI 4539, pp. 5–19, 2007.

shown that results similar to the ones for the noiseless scenario can be achieved [4,9,10,11]. These results are intimately related to adaptive sampling techniques in regression problems [12,13,14,10,15], where similar performance gains have been reported. Furthermore the active learning algorithm proposed in [9] in addition to provide improvements in certain bounded noise conditions is shown to perform no worse than passive learning in general settings.

In this paper, we expand the theoretical investigation of active learning to include cases in which the noise is unbounded. In the case of binary classification this means that $\Pr(Y = 1|\boldsymbol{X} = \boldsymbol{x})$ is not bounded away from $1/2$. Notice that in this case there is no strong cue that active learning procedures can follow, since as sampling approaches the decision boundary the conditional probability $\Pr(Y = 1|\boldsymbol{X} = \boldsymbol{x})$ approaches $1/2$. Since situations like this seem very likely to arise in practice (e.g., simply due to feature measurement errors if nothing else), it is important to identify the potential of active learning in such cases.

Our main result can be summarized as follows. Following Tsybakov's formulation of distributional classes [16], the complexity of the Bayes decision boundary can in many cases be characterized by a parameter $\rho = (d - 1)/\alpha$, where d is the dimension of the feature space and α is the Hölder regularity of the boundary. Furthermore, the behavior of $\Pr(Y = 1|\boldsymbol{X} = \boldsymbol{x})$ in the vicinity of the boundary can be characterized by a parameter $\kappa \geq 1$. The value $\kappa = 1$ corresponds to the noiseless or bounded noise situation and $\kappa > 1$ corresponds to unbounded noise conditions. We derive lower bounds on active learning performance. In particular, it is shown that the fastest rate of classification error decay using active learning is $n^{-\frac{\kappa}{2\kappa+\rho-2}}$, where n is the number of collect examples, whereas the fastest decay rate possible using passive learning is $n^{-\frac{\kappa}{2\kappa+\rho-1}}$. Note that the active learning rate is always superior to that of passive learning. Tsybakov has shown that in certain cases ($\kappa \to 1$ and $\rho \to 0$) passive learning can achieve "fast" rates approaching n^{-1} (faster than the usual $n^{-1/2}$ rate). In contrast, our results show that in similar situations active learning can achieve much faster rates (in the limit decaying as fast as any negative power of n). Also note that the passive and active rates are essentially the same as $\kappa \to \infty$, which is the case in which $\Pr(Y = 1|\boldsymbol{X} = \boldsymbol{x})$ is very flat near the boundary and consequently there is no cue that can efficiently drive an active learning procedure. Furthermore we show that the learning rates derived are tight for "boundary fragment" classes in d-dimensional feature spaces when the density of the marginal distribution $P_{\boldsymbol{X}}$ (over features) is bounded from above and below on $[0, 1]^d$.

The paper is organized as follows. In Section 2 we formally state the active learning problem and define the probability classes under consideration. Section 3 presents the basic results on lower bounds for active learning rates and in Section 4 we provide corresponding upper bounds, which match the lower bounds up to a logarithmic factor. Together, this demonstrates the bounds are tight and hence near minimax optimal. Final remarks are made in Section 5 and the main proofs are given in the Appendix.

2   Problem Formulation

Let $(\boldsymbol{X}, Y) \in [0,1]^d \times \{0,1\}$ be a random vector, with *unknown* distribution $P_{\boldsymbol{X}Y}$. Our goal is to construct a "good" classification rule, that is, given $\boldsymbol{X}$ we want to predict Y as accurately as possible, where our classification rule is a measurable function $f : [0,1]^d \to \{0,1\}$. The performance of the classifier is evaluated in terms of the expected 0/1-loss. With this choice the risk is simply the probability of classification error,

$$R(f) \overset{\Delta}{=} \mathbb{E}[\mathbf{1}\{f(\boldsymbol{X}) \neq Y\}] = \Pr(f(\boldsymbol{X}) \neq Y) ,$$

where $\mathbf{1}\{\cdot\}$ denotes the indicator function. Since we are considering only binary classification (two classes) there is a one-to-one correspondence between classifiers and sets: Any reasonable classifier is of the form $f(\boldsymbol{x}) = \mathbf{1}\{\boldsymbol{x} \in G\}$, where G is a measurable subset of $[0,1]^d$. We use the term classifier interchangeably for both f and G. Define the optimal risk as

$$R^* \overset{\Delta}{=} \inf_{G \text{ measurable}} R(G) .$$

R^* is attained by the *Bayes Classifier* $G^* \overset{\Delta}{=} \{\boldsymbol{x} \in [0,1]^d : \eta(\boldsymbol{x}) \geq 1/2\}$, where

$$\eta(\boldsymbol{x}) = \mathbb{E}[Y|\boldsymbol{X} = \boldsymbol{x}] = \Pr(Y = 1|\boldsymbol{X} = \boldsymbol{x}) ,$$

is called the *conditional probability* (we use this term only if it is clear from the context). In general $R(G^*) > 0$ unless the labels are a deterministic function of the features, and therefore even the optimal classifier misclassifies sometimes. For that reason the quantity of interest for the performance evaluation of a classifier G is the *excess risk*

$$R(G) - R(G^*) = d(G, G^*) \overset{\Delta}{=} \int_{G \Delta G^*} |2\eta(\boldsymbol{x}) - 1| \mathrm{d}P_{\boldsymbol{X}}(\boldsymbol{x}) , \tag{1}$$

where Δ denotes the symmetric difference between two sets[1], and $P_{\boldsymbol{X}}$ is the marginal distribution of $\boldsymbol{X}$.

Suppose that $P_{\boldsymbol{X}Y}$ is unknown, but that we have a large (infinite) pool of feature examples we can select from, large enough so that we can choose any feature point $\boldsymbol{X}_i \in [0,1]^d$ and observe its label Y_i. The data collection operation has a temporal aspect to it, namely we collect the labeled examples one at the time, starting with $(\boldsymbol{X}_1, Y_1)$ and proceeding until $(\boldsymbol{X}_n, Y_n)$ is observed. One can view this process as a query learning procedure, where one queries the label of a feature vector. Formally we have:

A1 - Y_i, $i \in \{1, \dots, n\}$ are distributed as

$$Y_i = \begin{cases} 1 \text{ , with probability } \eta(\boldsymbol{X}_i) \\ 0 \text{ , with probability } 1 - \eta(\boldsymbol{X}_i) \end{cases} .$$

---

[1] $A \Delta B \overset{\Delta}{=} (A \cap B^c) \cup (A^c \cap B)$, where A^c and B^c are the complement of A and B respectively.

The random variables $\{Y_i\}_{i=1}^{n}$ are conditionally independent given $\{X_i\}_{i=1}^{n}$.

A2.1 - Passive Sampling: X_i is independent of $\{Y_j\}_{j\neq i}$.

A2.2 - Active Sampling: X_i depends only on $\{X_j, Y_j\}_{j<i}$. In other words

$$X_i | X_1 \ldots X_{i-1}, X_{i+1}, \ldots, X_n, Y_1 \ldots Y_{i-1}, Y_{i+1}, \ldots, Y_n$$
$$\overset{\text{a.s.}}{=} X_i | X_1 \ldots X_{i-1}, Y_1 \ldots Y_{i-1} .$$

The conditional distribution on the right hand side (r.h.s) of the above expression is called the *sampling strategy* and is denoted by S_n. It completely defines our sampling procedure. After collecting the n examples, that is after collecting $\{X_i, Y_i\}_{i=1}^{n}$, we construct a classifier $\widehat{G}_n$ that is desired to be close to G^*. The subscript n denotes dependence on the data set, instead of writing it explicitly.

Under the passive sampling scenario (A2.1) the sample locations do not depend on the labels (except for the trivial dependence between X_j and Y_i), and therefore the collection of sample points $\{X_i\}_{i=1}^{n}$ may be chosen before any observations are collected. On the other hand, the active sampling scenario (A2.2) allows for the ith sample location to be chosen using all the information collected up to that point (the previous $i-1$ samples).

In this paper we are interested in a particular class of distributions, namely scenarios where the Bayes decision set is a boundary fragment. That is, the Bayes decision boundary is the graph of function. We consider Hölder smooth boundary functions. Throughout the paper assume that $d \geq 2$, the dimension of the feature space.

Definition 1. *A function* $f : [0,1]^{d-1} \to \mathbb{R}$ *is* Hölder smooth *if it has continuous partial derivatives up to order* $k = \lfloor \alpha \rfloor$ *(k is the maximal integer such that* $k < \alpha$*) and*

$$\forall \, z, x \in [0,1]^{d-1} : \quad |f(z) - TP_x(z)| \leq L\|z - x\|^\alpha ,$$

where $L, \alpha > 0$*, and* $TP_x(\cdot)$ *denotes the degree* k *Taylor polynomial approximation of* f *expanded around* x*. Denote this class of functions by* $\Sigma(L, \alpha)$*.*

For any $g \in \Sigma(L, \alpha)$ let $\text{epi}(g) = \{(x,y) \in [0,1]^{d-1} \times [0,1] : y \geq g(x)\}$, that is, $\text{epi}(g)$ is epigraph of g. Define

$$\mathcal{G}_{\text{BF}} \overset{\Delta}{=} \{\text{epi}(g) : g \in \Sigma(L, \alpha)\} .$$

In other words $\mathcal{G}_{\text{BF}}$ is a collection of sets indexed by Hölder smooth functions of the first $d-1$ coordinates of the feature domain $[0,1]^d$. Therefore G^* and the corresponding boundary function g^* are equivalent representations of the Bayes classifier.

In order to get a better understanding of the potential of active learning we impose further conditions on the distribution P_{XY}. We assume that P_X is uniform on $[0,1]^d$. The results in this paper can easily be generalized to the case where the marginal density of X with respect to the Lebesgue measure is not uniform, but bounded above and below, yielding the same rates of error convergence. We require also $\eta(\cdot)$ to have a certain behavior around the decision boundary. Let $\boldsymbol{x} = (\tilde{\boldsymbol{x}}, x_d)$ where $\tilde{\boldsymbol{x}} = (x_1, \ldots, x_{d-1})$. Let $\kappa \geq 1$ and $c > 0$ then

$$|\eta(\boldsymbol{x}) - 1/2| \geq c|x_d - g^*(\tilde{\boldsymbol{x}})|^{\kappa-1}, \quad \text{if } |x_d - g^*(\tilde{\boldsymbol{x}})| \leq \epsilon_0 , \tag{2}$$

$$|\eta(\boldsymbol{x}) - 1/2| \geq c\epsilon_0^{\kappa-1}, \quad \text{if } |x_d - g^*(\tilde{\boldsymbol{x}})| > \epsilon_0 , \tag{3}$$

for some $\epsilon_0 > 0$. The condition above is very similar to the so-called margin condition (or noise-condition) introduced by Tsybakov [16]. If $\kappa = 1$ then the $\eta(\cdot)$ function "jumps" across the Bayes decision boundary, that is $\eta(\cdot)$ is bounded away from the value $1/2$. If $\kappa > 1$ then $\eta(\cdot)$ crosses the value $1/2$ at the Bayes decision boundary. Condition (2) indicates that $\eta(\cdot)$ cannot be arbitrarily "flat" around the decision boundary (e.g., for $\kappa = 2$ the function $\eta(\cdot)$ behaves linearly around $1/2$). This means that the noise affecting observations that are made close to the decision boundary is roughly proportional to the distance to the boundary. We also assume a reverse-sided condition on $\eta(\cdot)$, namely

$$|\eta(\boldsymbol{x}) - 1/2| \leq C|x_d - g^*(\tilde{\boldsymbol{x}})|^{\kappa-1} , \tag{4}$$

for all $\boldsymbol{x} \in [0,1]^d$, where $C > c$. This condition, together with (2) and (3) provides a two-sided characterization of the "noise" around the decision boundary. Similar two-sided conditions have been proposed for other problems [17,18]. Let $BF(\alpha, \kappa, L, C, c)$ be the class of distributions satisfying the noise conditions above with parameter κ and whose Bayes classifiers are boundary fragments with smoothness α.

3 Lower Bounds

In this section we present lower bounds on the performance of active and passive sampling methods. We start by characterizing active learning for the boundary fragment classes.

Theorem 1. *Let $\rho = (d-1)/\alpha$. Then*

$$\liminf_{n \to \infty} \inf_{\widehat{G}_n, S_n} \sup_{P \in BF(\alpha, \kappa, L, C, c)} \mathbb{E}[R(\widehat{G}_n)] - R(G^*) \geq c_{\min} n^{-\frac{\kappa}{2\kappa + \rho - 2}} ,$$

where $\inf_{\widehat{G}_n, S_n}$ denotes the infimum over all possible classifiers and sampling strategies S_n, and $c_{\min} > 0$ is a constant.

The proof of Theorem 1 is presented in Appendix A. An important remark is that condition (4) does not play a role in the rate of the lower bound, therefore dropping that assumption (equivalently taking $C = \infty$) does not alter the result of the theorem.

Contrast this result with the one attained for passive sampling: under the passive sampling scenario it is clear that the sample locations $\{\boldsymbol{X}_i\}_{i=1}^n$ must be scattered around the interval $[0,1]^d$ in a somewhat uniform manner. These can be deterministically placed, for example over a uniform grid, or simply taken uniformly distributed over $[0,1]^d$. The results in [16] imply that, under (A1), (A2.1), and $\kappa \geq 1$,

$$\inf_{\widehat{G}_n, S_n} \sup_{P \in \mathrm{BF}(\alpha, \kappa, L, C, c)} \mathbb{E}[R(\widehat{G}_n)] - R(G^*) \geq c_{\min} n^{-\frac{\kappa}{2\kappa + \rho - 1}} \tag{5}$$

where the samples $\{X_i\}_{i=1}^n$ are independent and identically distributed (i.i.d.) uniformly over $[0,1]^d$. Furthermore this bound is tight, in the sense that it is possible to devise classification strategies attaining the same asymptotic behavior. We notice that under the passive sampling scenario the excess risk decays at a strictly slower rate than the lower bound for the active sampling scenario, and the rate difference can be dramatic, specially for large smoothness α (equivalently low complexity ρ). The active learning lower bound is also tight (as shown in the next section), which demonstrates that active learning has the potential to improve significantly over passive learning. Finally the result of Theorem 1 is a lower bound, and it therefore applies to the broader classes of distributions introduced in [16], characterized in terms of the metric entropy of the class of Bayes classifiers.

The proof of Theorem 1 employs relatively standard techniques, and follows the approach in [19]. The key idea is to reduce the original problem to the problem of deciding among a finite collection of representative distributions. The determination of an appropriate collection of such distributions and careful managing assumption (A2.2) are the key aspects of the proof. Notice also that the result in (5) can be obtained by modifying the proof of Theorem 1 slightly.

4   Upper Bounds

In this section we construct an active learning procedure and upper bound its error performance. The upper bound achieves the rates of Theorem 1 to within a logarithmic factor. This procedure yields a classifier $\widehat{G}_n$ that has boundary fragment structure, although the boundary is no longer a smooth function. It is instead a piecewise polynomial function. This methodology proceeds along the lines of [20,21], extending one-dimensional active sampling methods to this higher dimensional setting. For this methodology we use some results reported in [22] addressing the problem of one-dimensional change-point detection under the noise conditions imposed in this paper. The ideas in that work were motivated by the work of Burnashev and Zigangirov [12], pertaining a change-point detection problem under the bounded noise rate condition (equivalent to $\kappa = 1$).

We begin by constructing a grid over the first $d - 1$ dimensions of the feature domain, namely let M be an integer and $\tilde{l} \in \{0, \ldots, M\}^{d-1}$. Define the line segments $\mathcal{L}_{\tilde{l}} \triangleq \{(M^{-1}\tilde{l}, x_d) : x_d \in [0, 1]\}$. We collect N samples along each line, yielding a total of NM^{d-1} samples (where $n \geq NM^{d-1}$). Our goal is to estimate $g(M^{-1}\tilde{l})$, for all $\tilde{l}$, using these samples. We will then interpolate the estimates of g at these points to construct a final estimate of the decision boundary. The correct choices for M and N will arise from the performance analysis; for now we point out only that both M and N are growing with the total number of samples n.

When restricting ourselves to the line segment $\mathcal{L}_{\tilde{l}}$ the estimation problem boils down to a one-dimensional change-point detection problem. Consider first the case $\kappa = 1$. In [12] an active sampling methodology was developed and analyzed, with the following property: using N sample points actively chosen yields an estimator $\hat{g}(M^{-1}\tilde{l})$ of $g(M^{-1}\tilde{l})$ such that

$$\Pr\left(|\hat{g}(M^{-1}\tilde{l}) - g^*(M^{-1}\tilde{l})| > t\right) \leq \frac{1}{t}\exp(-c^2 N) \ ,$$

therefore it is possible to estimate $g^*(M^{-1}\tilde{l})$ accurately with a very small number of samples. It was shown in [22] (and further detailed in [23]) that, when $\kappa > 1$, using N sample points in $\mathcal{L}_{\tilde{l}}$ chosen actively based on knowledge of κ, yields an estimate $\hat{g}(M^{-1}\tilde{l})$ of $g(M^{-1}\tilde{l})$ such that

$$\Pr(|\hat{g}(M^{-1}\tilde{l}) - g^*(M^{-1}\tilde{l})| > t) \leq \frac{2}{t}\exp\left(-\frac{N}{3}c^2\left(\frac{t}{6}\right)^{2\kappa-2}\right) \ . \qquad (6)$$

Taking

$$t = t_N \stackrel{\Delta}{=} c_1\left(\log N/N\right)^{\frac{1}{2\kappa-2}} \qquad (7)$$

guarantees that $\Pr(|\hat{g}(M^{-1}\tilde{l}) - g^*(M^{-1}\tilde{l})| > t_N) = O\left(N^{-\gamma}\right)$, where $\gamma > 0$ can be arbitrarily large provided c_1 is sufficiently large.

Let $\{\hat{g}(M^{-1}\tilde{l})\}$ be the estimates obtained using this method at each of the points indexed by $\tilde{l}$. We use these estimates to construct a piecewise polynomial fit to approximate g^*. In what follows assume $\alpha > 1$. The case $\alpha = 1$ can be handled in a very similar way. Begin by dividing $[0,1]^{d-1}$ (that is, the domain of g^*) into cells. Let M_0 be the largest integer such that $M_0 \leq M/\lfloor\alpha\rfloor$. Let $\tilde{q} \in \{0, \ldots, M_0\}^{d-1}$ index the cells

$$I_{\tilde{q}} \stackrel{\Delta}{=} \left[\tilde{q}_1\lfloor\alpha\rfloor M^{-1}, (\tilde{q}_1+1)\lfloor\alpha\rfloor M^{-1}\right] \times \cdots \times \left[\tilde{q}_{d-1}\lfloor\alpha\rfloor M^{-1}, (\tilde{q}_{d-1}+1)\lfloor\alpha\rfloor M^{-1}\right] \ .$$

Note that these cells almost partition the domain $[0,1]^{d-1}$ entirely. If $M/\lfloor\alpha\rfloor$ is not an integer there is a small region on the edge of the domain that is not covered by these cells, with volume $O(M^{-1})$. In each of these cells we perform a polynomial interpolation using the estimates of g^* at points within the cell. We consider a tensor product polynomial fit $\hat{L}_{\tilde{q}}$, that can be written as

$$\hat{L}_{\tilde{q}}(\tilde{x}) = \sum_{\tilde{l}:M^{-1}\tilde{l}\in I_{\tilde{q}}} \hat{g}(M^{-1}\tilde{l})Q_{\tilde{q},\tilde{l}}(\tilde{x}) \ ,$$

where $\tilde{x} \in [0,1]^d$. The functions $Q_{\tilde{q},\tilde{l}}$ are the tensor-product Lagrange polynomials [24]. The final estimate of g^* is therefore given by

$$\hat{g}(\tilde{x}) = \sum_{\tilde{q}\in\{0,\ldots,M_0\}^{d-1}} \hat{L}_{\tilde{q}}(\tilde{x})\mathbf{1}\{\tilde{x} \in I_{\tilde{q}}\}$$

which defines a classification rule $\hat{G}_n$.

Theorem 2. *Consider the classification methodology described above, using* $M = \left\lfloor n^{\frac{1}{\alpha(2\kappa-2)+d-1}} \right\rfloor$ *and* $N = \lfloor n/(M-1)^{d-1} \rfloor$. *Let* $\rho = (d-1)/\alpha$, *then*

$$\limsup_{n\to\infty} \sup_{P \in BF_{(\alpha,\kappa,L,C,c)}} \mathbb{E}[R(\widehat{G}_n)] - R(G^*) \leq c_{\max} (\log n/n)^{\frac{\kappa}{2\kappa+\rho-2}} .$$

The proof of Theorem 2 is given in Appendix B. One sees that this estimator achieves the rate of Theorem 1 to within a logarithmic factor. It is not clear if the logarithmic factor is an artifact of our construction, or if it is unavoidable. One knows [20] that if $\kappa, \alpha = 1$ the logarithmic factor can be eliminated by using a slightly more sophisticated interpolation scheme.

5   Final Remarks

Since the upper and lower bounds agree up to a logarithmic factor, we may conclude that lower bound is near minimax optimal. That is, for the distributional classes under consideration, no active or passive learning procedure can perform significantly better in terms of error decay rates. Our upper bounds were derived constructively, based on an active learning procedure originally developed for one-dimensional change-point detection [12]. In principle, the methodology employed in the upper bound calculation could be applied in practice in the case of boundary fragments and with knowledge of the key regularity parameters κ and ρ. Unfortunately this is not a scenario one expects to have in practice, and thus a key open problem is the design of active learning algorithms that are adaptive to unknown regularity parameters and capable of handling arbitrary boundaries (not only fragments). A potential approach is a multiscale technique as used in [10]. The results of this paper do indicate what we should be aiming for in terms of performance. Moreover, the bounds clarify the situations in which active learning may or may not offer a significant gain over passive learning, and it may be possible to assess the conditions that might hold in a given application in order to gauge the merit of pursuing an active learning approach.

Acknowledgements. Supported by NSF grants CCR-0350213 and CNS-0519824.

References

1. Mackay, D.J.C.: Information-based objective functions for active data selection. Neural Computation 4, 698–714 (1991)
2. Cohn, D., Ghahramani, Z., Jordan, M.: Active learning with statistical models. Journal of Artificial Intelligence Research, pp. 129–145 (1996)
3. Freund, Y., Seung, H.S., Shamir, E., Tishby, N.: Selective sampling using the query by committee algorithm. Machine Learning 28(2-3), 133–168 (1997)
4. Cesa-Bianchi, N., Conconi, A., Gentile, C.: Learning probabilistic linear-threshold classifiers via selective sampling. In: Schölkopf, B., Warmuth, M.K. (eds.) COLT/Kernel 2003. LNCS (LNAI), vol. 2777, Springer, Heidelberg (2003)

5. Blanchard, G., Geman, D.: Hierarchical testing designs for pattern recognition. The Annals of Statistics 33(3), 1155–1202 (2005)
6. Dasgupta, S., Kalai, A., Monteleoni, C.: Analysis of perceptron-based active learning. In: Auer, P., Meir, R. (eds.) COLT 2005. LNCS (LNAI), vol. 3559, Springer, Heidelberg (2005)
7. Dasgupta, S.: Coarse sample complexity bounds for active learning. In: Advances in Neural Information Processing (NIPS) (2005)
8. Dasgupta, S.: Analysis of a greedy active learning strategy. In: Advances in Neural Information Processing (NIPS) (2004)
9. Balcan, N., Beygelzimer, A., Langford, J.: Agostic active learning. In: 23rd International Conference on Machine Learning, Pittsburgh, PA, USA (2006)
10. Castro, R., Willett, R., Nowak, R.: Faster rates in regression via active learning. In: Proceedings of Neural Information Processing Systems (NIPS), extended version (2005), available at http://homepages.cae.wisc.edu/~rcastro/ECE-05-3.pdf
11. Kääriäinen, M.: On active learning in the non-realizable case. NIPS Workshop on Foundations of Active Learning (2005)
12. Burnashev, M.V., Zigangirov, K.S.: An interval estimation problem for controlled observations. Problems in Information Transmission 10, 223–231 (1974) (Translated from Problemy Peredachi Informatsii, 10(3),51–61, July-September, 1974). Original article submitted (June 25, 1973)
13. Hall, P., Molchanov, I.: Sequential methods for design-adaptive estimation of discontinuities in regression curves and surfaces. The Annals of Statistics 31(3), 921–941 (2003)
14. Golubev, G., Levit, B.: Sequential recovery of analytic periodic edges in the binary image models. Mathematical Methods of Statistics 12, 95–115 (2003)
15. Bryan, B., Schneider, J., Nichol, R.C., Miller, C.J., Genovese, C.R., Wasserman, L.: Active learning for identifying function threshold boundaries. In: Advances in Neural Information Processing (NIPS) (2005)
16. Tsybakov, A.: Optimal aggregation of classifiers in statistical learning. The Annals of Statistics 32(1), 135–166 (2004)
17. Cavalier, L.: Nonparametric estimation of regression level sets. Statistics 29, 131–160 (1997)
18. Tsybakov, A.B.: On nonparametric estimation of density level sets. The Annals of Statistics 25, 948–969 (1997)
19. Tsybakov, A.B.: Introduction à l'estimation non-paramétrique. In: Mathématiques et Applications, vol. 41, Springer, Heidelberg (2004)
20. Korostelev, A.P.: On minimax rates of convergence in image models under sequential design. Statistics & Probability Letters 43, 369–375 (1999)
21. Korostelev, A., Kim, J.C.: Rates of convergence for the sup-norm risk in image models under sequential designs. Statistics & probability Letters 46, 391–399 (2000)
22. Castro, R., Nowak, R.: Upper and lower bounds for active learning. In: 44th Annual Allerton Conference on Communication, Control and Computing (2006)
23. Castro, R.M., Nowak, R.D.: Minimax bounds for active learning. Technical report, ECE Dept. University of Wisconsin - Madison (2007), available at http://homepages.cae.wisc.edu/~rcastro/ECE-07-3.pdf
24. de Boor, C.: The error in polynomial tensor-product and chung-yao, interpolation. In: LeMéhauté, A., Rabut, C., Schumaker, L., (eds.): Surface Fitting and Multiresolution Methods, Vanderbilt University Press, 35–50 (1997)

A   Proof of Theorem 1

The proof strategy follows the basic idea behind standard minimax analysis methods, and consists in reducing the problem of classification in the large class $\mathrm{BF}(\alpha, \kappa, L, C, c)$ to a test of a finite set of hypothesis. These are distributions $P_{XY} \in \mathrm{BF}(\alpha, \kappa, L, C, c)$ chosen carefully. The main tool is the following theorem, adapted from [19] (page 85, theorem 2.5).

Theorem 3 (Tsybakov, 2004). *Let $\mathcal{F}$ be a class of models. Associated with each model $f \in \mathcal{F}$ we have a probability measure P_f defined on a common probability space. Let $M \geq 2$ be an integer and let $d_f(\cdot, \cdot) : \mathcal{F} \times \mathcal{F} \to \mathbb{R}$ be a collection of semi-distances (indexed by $f \in \mathcal{F}$). Suppose we have $\{f_0, \ldots, f_M\} \in \mathcal{F}$ such that*

i) $d_{f_k}(f_j, f_k) \geq 2\,a > 0, \quad \forall_{0 \leq j, k \leq M}$,
ii) $P_{f_0} \ll P_{f_j}, \quad \forall_{j=1,\ldots,M}$, (see footnote[2])
iii) $\frac{1}{M} \sum_{j=1}^{M} KL(P_{f_j} \| P_{f_0}) \leq \gamma \log M$,

where $0 < \gamma < 1/8$. The following bound holds.

$$\inf_{\widehat{f}} \sup_{f \in \mathcal{F}} P_f \left(d_f(\widehat{f}, f) \geq a \right) \geq \frac{\sqrt{M}}{1 + \sqrt{M}} \left(1 - 2\gamma - 2\sqrt{\frac{\gamma}{\log M}} \right) > 0 \ ,$$

where the infimum is taken with respect to the collection of all possible estimators of f (based on a sample from P_f), and KL denotes the Kullback-Leibler divergence[3] .

Note that in final statement of Theorem 3 the semi-distance between the estimate $\widehat{f}_n$ and f might depend on f. This is a critical feature in our setup, since the excess risk depends on the underlying unknown distribution (1).

To apply the theorem we need to construct a subset of $\mathrm{BF}(\alpha, \kappa, L, C, c)$ with the desired characteristics. These elements are distributions P_{XY} and therefore uniquely characterized by the conditional probability $\eta(x) = \Pr(Y = 1 | X = x)$ (since we are assuming that P_X is uniform over $[0,1]^d$). Let $x = (\tilde{x}, x_d)$ with $\tilde{x} \in [0,1]^{d-1}$. As a notational convention we use a tilde to denote a vector of dimension $d-1$. Define

$$m = \left\lceil c_0 n^{\frac{1}{\alpha(2\kappa - 2) + d - 1}} \right\rceil \ , \qquad \tilde{x}_{\tilde{l}} = \frac{\tilde{l} - 1/2}{m} \ ,$$

---

[2] Let P and Q be two probability measures defined on a common probability space $(\Omega, \mathcal{B})$. Then $P \ll Q$ if and only if for all $B \in \mathcal{B}$, $Q(B) = 0 \Rightarrow P(B) = 0$.

[3] Let P and Q be two probability measures defined on a common probability space. The Kullback-Leibler divergence is defined as

$$KL(P\|Q) = \begin{cases} \int \log \frac{\mathrm{d}P}{\mathrm{d}Q} \mathrm{d}P \ , & \text{if } P \ll Q, \\ +\infty & , \text{ otherwise.} \end{cases}$$

where $\mathrm{d}P/\mathrm{d}Q$ is the Radon-Nikodym derivative of measure P with respect to measure Q.

where $\tilde{l} \in \{1, \ldots, m\}^{d-1}$. Define also $\varphi_{\tilde{l}}(\tilde{x}) = Lm^{-\alpha}h(m(\tilde{x} - \tilde{x}_{\tilde{l}}))$, with $h \in \Sigma(1, \alpha)$, $\text{supp}(h) = (-1/2, 1/2)^{d-1}$ and $h \geq 0$. It is easily shown that such a function exists, for example

$$h(\tilde{x}) = a \prod_{i=1}^{d-1} \exp\left(-\frac{1}{1 - 4x_i^2}\right) \mathbf{1}\{|x_i| < 1/2\} ,$$

with $a > 0$ sufficiently small. The functions $\varphi_{\tilde{l}}$ are little "bumps" centered at the points $\tilde{x}_{\tilde{l}}$. The collection $\{\tilde{x}_{\tilde{l}}\}$ forms a regular grid over $[0, 1]^{d-1}$.

Let $\Omega = \{\omega = (\omega_1, \ldots, \omega_{m^{d-1}}), \ \omega_i \in \{0, 1\}\} = \{0, 1\}^{m^{d-1}}$, and define

$$\mathcal{G} = \left\{ g_\omega(\cdot) : g_\omega(\cdot) = \sum_{\tilde{l} \in \{1, \ldots, m\}^{d-1}} \omega_{\tilde{l}} \varphi_{\tilde{l}}(\cdot), \ \omega \in \Omega \right\} .$$

The set $\mathcal{G}$ is a collection of boundary functions. The binary vector ω is an indicator vector: if $\omega_{\tilde{l}} = 1$ then "bump" $\tilde{l}$ is present, otherwise that "bump" is absent. Note that $\varphi_{\tilde{l}} \in \Sigma(L, \alpha)$ and these functions have disjoint support, therefore $\mathcal{G} \subseteq \Sigma(L, \alpha)$. Let $g \in \mathcal{G}$ and construct the conditional distribution

$$\eta_\omega(x) = \begin{cases} \min\left(\frac{1}{2} + c \cdot \text{sign}(x_d - g(\tilde{x}))|x_d - g(\tilde{x})|^{\kappa-1}, 1\right), & \text{if } x_d \leq A \\ \min\left(\frac{1}{2} + c \cdot x_d^{\kappa-1}, 1\right), & \text{if } x_d > A \end{cases} ,$$

$$A = \max_{\tilde{x}} \varphi(\tilde{x}) \left(1 + \frac{1}{(C/c)^{1/(\kappa-1)} - 1}\right) = Lm^{-\alpha}h_{\max}\left(1 + \frac{1}{(C/c)^{1/(\kappa-1)} - 1}\right) ,$$

with $h_{\max} = \max_{\tilde{x} \in \mathbb{R}^{d-1}} h(\tilde{x})$. The choice of A is done carefully, in order to ensure that the functions η_ω are similar, but at the same time satisfy the margin conditions. It is easily checked that conditions (2), (3) and (4) are satisfied for the distributions above. By construction the Bayes decision boundary for each of these distributions is given by $x_d = g(\tilde{x})$ and so these distributions belong to the class $\text{BF}(\alpha, \kappa, L, C, c)$. Note also that these distributions are all identical if $x_d > A$. As n increases m also increases and therefore A decreases, so the conditional distributions described above are becoming more and more similar. This is key to bound the Kullback-Leibler divergence between these distributions.

The above collection of distributions, indexed by $\omega \in \Omega$, is still too large for the application of Theorem 3. Recall the following lemma.

Lemma 1 (Varshamov-Gilbert bound, 1962). *Let $m^{d-1} \geq 8$. There exists a subset $\{\omega^{(0)}, \omega^{(1)}, \ldots, \omega^{(M)}\}$ of Ω such that $M \geq 2^{m^{d-1}/8}$, $\omega^{(0)} = (0, \ldots, 0)$ and*

$$\rho(\omega^{(j)}, \omega^{(k)}) \geq m^{d-1}/8, \quad \forall \ 0 \leq j < k \leq M ,$$

where ρ denotes the Hamming distance.

For a proof of the Lemma 1 see [19](page 89, lemma 2.7). To apply Theorem 3 we use the M distributions $(\eta_{\boldsymbol{\omega}^{(0)}}, \dots, \eta_{\boldsymbol{\omega}^{(M)}}\}$ given by the lemma. For each distribution $\eta_{\boldsymbol{\omega}^{(i)}}$ we have the corresponding Bayes classifier G_i^*. Define the semidistances

$$d_i(G, G') = \int_{G \Delta G'} |2\eta_{\boldsymbol{\omega}^{(i)}}(\boldsymbol{x}) - 1| \mathrm{d}\boldsymbol{x} \ .$$

The next step of the proof is to lower-bound $d_i(G_j^*, G_i^*) = R_i(G_j^*) - R_i(G_i^*)$ for all $j \neq i$. Note that

$$d_i(G_j^*, G_i^*) = \int_{[0,1]^{d-1}} \int_0^{|g_i^*(\tilde{\boldsymbol{x}}) - g_j^*(\tilde{\boldsymbol{x}})|} |2\eta_{\boldsymbol{\omega}^{(i)}}(\boldsymbol{x}) - 1| \mathrm{d}x_d \mathrm{d}\tilde{\boldsymbol{x}}$$

$$= \sum_{\tilde{l} \in \{1, \dots, m\}^{d-1}} |\omega_{\tilde{l}}^{(i)} - \omega_{\tilde{l}}^{(j)}| \int_{[0,1]^{d-1}} \int_0^{Lm^{-\alpha} h(m(\tilde{\boldsymbol{x}} - \tilde{\boldsymbol{x}}_{\tilde{l}}))} |2\eta_{\boldsymbol{\omega}^{(i)}}(\boldsymbol{x}) - 1| \mathrm{d}x_d \mathrm{d}\tilde{\boldsymbol{x}} \ .$$

To bound the double-integral we just need to consider the two possible values of $\omega_{\tilde{l}}^{(i)}$. We display here case $\omega_{\tilde{l}}^{(i)} = 1$, but exactly the same result can be shown for $\omega_{\tilde{l}}^{(i)} = 0$.

$$\int_{[0,1]^{d-1}} \int_0^{Lm^{-\alpha} h(m(\tilde{\boldsymbol{x}} - \tilde{\boldsymbol{x}}_{\tilde{l}}))} |2\eta_{\boldsymbol{\omega}^{(i)}}(\boldsymbol{x}) - 1| \mathrm{d}x_d \mathrm{d}\tilde{\boldsymbol{x}}$$

$$= \int_{[0,1]^{d-1}} \int_0^{Lm^{-\alpha} h(m(\tilde{\boldsymbol{x}} - \tilde{\boldsymbol{x}}_{\tilde{l}}))} 2c(x_d - Lm^{-\alpha} h(m(\tilde{\boldsymbol{x}} - \tilde{\boldsymbol{x}}_{\tilde{l}})))^{\kappa-1} \mathrm{d}x_d \mathrm{d}\tilde{\boldsymbol{x}}$$

$$= 2cm^{-(d-1)} \int_{[-1/2, 1/2]^{d-1}} \int_0^{Lm^{-\alpha} h(\tilde{\boldsymbol{z}})} (x_d - Lm^{-\alpha} h(\tilde{\boldsymbol{z}})^{\kappa-1} \mathrm{d}x_d \mathrm{d}\tilde{\boldsymbol{z}}$$

$$= \frac{2cm^{-(d-1)}}{\kappa} \int_{[-1/2, 1/2]^{d-1}} L^\kappa m^{-\alpha\kappa} h^\kappa(\tilde{\boldsymbol{z}}) \mathrm{d}\tilde{\boldsymbol{z}}$$

$$= \frac{2c}{\kappa} L^\kappa m^{-\alpha\kappa-(d-1)} \|h\|_\kappa^\kappa \sim m^{-\alpha\kappa-(d-1)} \ ,$$

where $\|h\|_\kappa$ denotes the κ norm of h. Taking into account Lemma 1 we have that, for n large enough

$$d_i(G_j^*, G_i^*) \geq \rho(\omega_{\tilde{l}}^{(i)}, \omega_{\tilde{l}}^{(j)}) \frac{2c}{\kappa} L^\kappa m^{-\alpha\kappa-(d-1)} \|h\|_\kappa^\kappa$$

$$\geq \frac{2c}{8\kappa} L^\kappa \|h\|_\kappa^\kappa m^{-\alpha\kappa} \stackrel{\Delta}{=} a_n \sim m^{-\alpha\kappa} \ .$$

We are ready for the final step of the proof. We need the following straightforward result.

Lemma 2. *Let P and Q be Bernoulli random variables with parameters respectively p and q, such that $p, q \to 1/2$. Then $KL(P\|Q) = 2(p-q)^2 + o((p-q)^2)$.*

Now let P_i be the distribution of $(\boldsymbol{X}_1, Y_1, \ldots, \boldsymbol{X}_n, Y_n)$ assuming the underlying conditional distribution is $\eta_{\boldsymbol{\omega}^{(i)}}$. Use the notation $\boldsymbol{Z}_j^X \triangleq (\boldsymbol{X}_1, \ldots, \boldsymbol{X}_j)$ and $\boldsymbol{Z}_j^Y \triangleq (Y_1, \ldots, Y_j)$. Then

$$
\begin{aligned}
\mathrm{KL}(P_i \| P_0) &= \mathbb{E}_i \left[\log \frac{P_{\boldsymbol{Z}_n^X, \boldsymbol{Z}_n^Y; i}(\boldsymbol{Z}_n^X, \boldsymbol{Z}_n^Y)}{P_{\boldsymbol{Z}_n^X, \boldsymbol{Z}_n^Y; 0}(\boldsymbol{Z}_n^X, \boldsymbol{Z}_n^Y)} \right] \\
&= \mathbb{E}_i \left[\log \frac{\prod_{j=1}^n P_{Y_j | \boldsymbol{X}_j; i}(Y_j | \boldsymbol{X}_j) \, P_{\boldsymbol{X}_j | \boldsymbol{Z}_{j-1}^X, \boldsymbol{Z}_{j-1}^Y; i}(\boldsymbol{X}_j | \boldsymbol{Z}_{j-1}^X, \boldsymbol{Z}_{j-1}^Y)}{\prod_{j=1}^n P_{Y_j | \boldsymbol{X}_j; 0}(Y_j | \boldsymbol{X}_j) \, P_{\boldsymbol{X}_j | \boldsymbol{Z}_{j-1}^X, \boldsymbol{Z}_{j-1}^Y; 0}(\boldsymbol{X}_j | \boldsymbol{Z}_{j-1}^X, \boldsymbol{Z}_{j-1}^Y)} \right] \quad (8) \\
&= \mathbb{E}_j \left[\log \frac{\prod_{j=1}^n P_{Y_j | \boldsymbol{X}_j; i}(Y_j | \boldsymbol{X}_j)}{\prod_{j=1}^n P_{Y_j | \boldsymbol{X}_j; 0}(Y_j | \boldsymbol{X}_j)} \right] \\
&= \mathbb{E}_j \left[\mathbb{E}_j \left[\log \frac{\prod_{j=1}^n P_{Y_j | \boldsymbol{X}_j; i}(Y_j | \boldsymbol{X}_j)}{\prod_{j=1}^n P_{Y_j | \boldsymbol{X}_j; 0}(Y_j | \boldsymbol{X}_j)} \, \middle| \, \boldsymbol{X}_1, \ldots, \boldsymbol{X}_n \right] \right] \\
&\leq 2n(cA^{\kappa-1})^2 + o(n(cA^{\kappa-1})^2) \leq \text{const} \cdot nm^{-\alpha(2\kappa-2)} ,
\end{aligned}
$$

where the last inequality holds provided n is large enough and const is chosen appropriately. In (8) note that the distribution of $\boldsymbol{X}_j$ conditional on $\boldsymbol{Z}_{j-1}^X, \boldsymbol{Z}_{j-1}^Y$ depends only on the sampling strategy S_n, and therefore does not change with the underlying distribution, hence those terms in the numerator and denominator cancel out. Finally

$$
\frac{1}{M} \sum_{i=1}^M \mathrm{KL}(P_i \| P_0) \leq \text{const} \cdot nm^{-\alpha(2\kappa-2)} \leq \text{const} \cdot c_0^{-(\alpha(2\kappa-2)+d-1)} m^{d-1} .
$$

From Lemma 1 we also have $\frac{\gamma}{8} m^{d-1} \log 2 \leq \gamma \log M$ therefore choosing c_0 large enough in the definition of m guarantees the conditions of Theorem 3 and so

$$
\inf_{\widehat{G}_n, S_n} \sup_{P \in \mathrm{BF}(\alpha, \kappa, L, C, c)} P(R(\widehat{G}_n) - R(G^*) \geq a_n) \geq c_{\min} ,
$$

where $c_{\min} > 0$, for n large enough. An application of Markov's inequality yields the original statement of the theorem, concluding the proof.

B   Proof of Theorem 2

The proof methodology aims at controlling the excess risk for an event that happens with high probability. To avoid carrying around cumbersome constants we use the 'big-O' [4] notation for simplicity. We show the proof only for the case $\kappa > 1$, since the proof when $\kappa = 1$ is almost analogous.

Define the event $\Omega_n = \left\{ \forall \tilde{\boldsymbol{l}} \in \{0, \ldots, M\}^{d-1} \quad |\widehat{g}(M^{-1}\tilde{\boldsymbol{l}}) - g^*(M^{-1}\tilde{\boldsymbol{l}})| \leq t_N \right\}$.

In words, Ω_n is the event that the M^{d-1} point estimates of g do not deviate very much from the true values. Using a union bound, taking into account (6)

---

[4] Let u_n and v_n be two real sequences. We say $u_n = O(v_n)$ if and only if there exists $C > 0$ and $n_0 > 0$ such that $|u_n| \leq Cv_n$ for all $n \geq n_0$.

and the choice t_N in (7) one sees that $1 - \Pr(\Omega_n) = O(N^{-\gamma}M^{d-1})$, where γ can be chosen arbitrarily large. With the choice of M in the theorem and choosing c_1 wisely in the definition of t_N (7) we have $1 - \Pr(\Omega_n) = O\left(n^{-\frac{\alpha\kappa}{\alpha(2\kappa-2)+d-1}}\right)$.

The excess risk of our classifier is given by

$$
\begin{aligned}
R(\widehat{G}_n) - R(G^*) &= \int_{\widehat{G}_n \Delta G^*} |2\eta(\boldsymbol{x}) - 1|\mathrm{d}\boldsymbol{x} \\
&= \int_{[0,1]^{d-1}} \int_{\min(\widehat{g}(\tilde{\boldsymbol{x}}),g^*(\tilde{\boldsymbol{x}}))}^{\max(\widehat{g}(\tilde{\boldsymbol{x}}),g^*(\tilde{\boldsymbol{x}}))} |2\eta((\tilde{\boldsymbol{x}},x_d)) - 1|\mathrm{d}x_d\mathrm{d}\tilde{\boldsymbol{x}} \\
&\leq \int_{[0,1]^{d-1}} \int_{\min(\widehat{g}(\tilde{\boldsymbol{x}}),g^*(\tilde{\boldsymbol{x}}))}^{\max(\widehat{g}(\tilde{\boldsymbol{x}}),g^*(\tilde{\boldsymbol{x}}))} C|x_d - g(\tilde{\boldsymbol{x}})|^{\kappa-1}\mathrm{d}x_d\mathrm{d}\tilde{\boldsymbol{x}} \\
&= \int_{[0,1]^{d-1}} \int_0^{|\widehat{g}(\tilde{\boldsymbol{x}})-g^*(\tilde{\boldsymbol{x}})|} Cz^{\kappa-1}\mathrm{d}z\mathrm{d}\tilde{\boldsymbol{x}} \\
&= \frac{C}{\kappa} \int_{[0,1]^{d-1}} |\widehat{g}(\tilde{\boldsymbol{x}}) - g^*(\tilde{\boldsymbol{x}})|^\kappa \mathrm{d}\tilde{\boldsymbol{x}} = O\left(\|\widehat{g} - g^*\|_\kappa^\kappa\right) ,
\end{aligned}
$$

where the inequality follows from condition (4).

Let $L_{\tilde{\boldsymbol{q}}}$, $\tilde{\boldsymbol{q}} \in \{0,\ldots,M_0\}^{d-1}$ be the clairvoyant version of $\widehat{L}_{\tilde{\boldsymbol{q}}}$, that is,

$$
L_{\tilde{\boldsymbol{q}}}(\tilde{\boldsymbol{x}}) = \sum_{\tilde{\boldsymbol{l}}:M^{-1}\tilde{\boldsymbol{l}}\in I_{\tilde{\boldsymbol{q}}}} g^*(M^{-1}\tilde{\boldsymbol{l}})Q_{\tilde{\boldsymbol{q}},\tilde{\boldsymbol{l}}}(\tilde{\boldsymbol{x}}) .
$$

It is well known that these interpolating polynomials have good local approximation properties for Hölder smooth functions, namely we have that

$$
\sup_{g\in\Sigma(L,\alpha)} \max_{\tilde{\boldsymbol{x}}\in I_{\tilde{\boldsymbol{q}}}} |L_{\tilde{\boldsymbol{q}}}(\tilde{\boldsymbol{x}}) - g^*(\tilde{\boldsymbol{x}})| = O(M^{-\alpha}) . \tag{9}
$$

This result is proved in [23]. We have almost all the pieces we need to conclude the proof. The last fact we need is a bound on the variation of the tensor-product Lagrange polynomials, namely it is easily shown that

$$
\max_{\tilde{\boldsymbol{x}}\in I_{\tilde{\boldsymbol{q}}}} \left|Q_{\tilde{\boldsymbol{q}},\tilde{\boldsymbol{l}}}(\tilde{\boldsymbol{x}})\right| \leq \lfloor\alpha\rfloor^{(d-1)\lfloor\alpha\rfloor} . \tag{10}
$$

We are now ready to show the final result. Assume for now that Ω_n holds, therefore $|\widehat{g}(M^{-1}\tilde{\boldsymbol{l}}) - g^*(M^{-1}\tilde{\boldsymbol{l}})| \leq t_N$ for all $\tilde{\boldsymbol{l}}$. Note that t_N is decreasing as n (and consequently N) increase.

$$
R(\widehat{G}_n) - R(G^*) = O\left(\|\widehat{g} - g^*\|_\kappa^\kappa\right)
$$

$$
= O\left(\sum_{\tilde{\boldsymbol{q}}\in\{0,\ldots,M_0\}^{d-1}} \left\|(\widehat{L}_{\tilde{\boldsymbol{q}}} - g^*)\mathbf{1}\{\tilde{\boldsymbol{x}}\in I_{\tilde{\boldsymbol{q}}}\}\right\|_\kappa^\kappa\right) + O(M^{-1})
$$

$$
= O\left(\sum_{\tilde{\boldsymbol{q}}} \left\|(L_{\tilde{\boldsymbol{q}}} - g^*)\mathbf{1}\{\tilde{\boldsymbol{x}}\in I_{\tilde{\boldsymbol{q}}}\} + (\widehat{L}_{\tilde{\boldsymbol{q}}} - L_{\tilde{\boldsymbol{q}}})\mathbf{1}\{\tilde{\boldsymbol{x}}\in I_{\tilde{\boldsymbol{q}}}\}\right\|_\kappa^\kappa\right) + O(M^{-1})
$$

$$
= O\left(\sum_{\tilde{\boldsymbol{q}}} \left(\left\|(L_{\tilde{\boldsymbol{q}}} - g^*)\mathbf{1}\{\tilde{\boldsymbol{x}}\in I_{\tilde{\boldsymbol{q}}}\}\right\|_\kappa + \left\|(\widehat{L}_{\tilde{\boldsymbol{q}}} - L_{\tilde{\boldsymbol{q}}})\mathbf{1}\{\tilde{\boldsymbol{x}}\in I_{\tilde{\boldsymbol{q}}}\}\right\|_\kappa\right)^\kappa\right) + O(M^{-1}) ,
$$

where the term $O(M^{-1})$ corresponds to the error in the area around the edge of $[0,1]^{d-1}$, not covered by any cells in $\{I_{\tilde{q}}\}$. The volume of this region is $O(M^{-1})$. Note now that

$$\|(L_{\tilde{q}} - g^*)\mathbf{1}\{\tilde{x} \in I_{\tilde{q}}\}\|_{\kappa} = \left(\int_{I_{\tilde{q}}} (L_{\tilde{q}}(\tilde{x}) - g^*(\tilde{x}))^{\kappa}\, d\tilde{x}\right)^{1/\kappa}$$

$$= O\left(\left(\int_{I_{\tilde{q}}} M^{-\alpha\kappa} d\tilde{x}\right)^{1/\kappa}\right) = O\left(M^{-\alpha} M^{-\frac{d-1}{\kappa}}\right).$$

Where we used (9). We have also

$$\left\|(\widehat{L}_{\tilde{q}} - L_{\tilde{q}})\mathbf{1}\{\tilde{x} \in I_{\tilde{q}}\}\right\|_{\kappa} = \sum_{\tilde{l}:M^{-1}\tilde{l}\in I_{\tilde{q}}} \left|\widehat{g}(M^{-1}\tilde{l}) - g^*(M^{-1}\tilde{l})\right| \left\|Q_{\tilde{q},\tilde{l}}\right\|_{\kappa}$$

$$\leq \sum_{\tilde{l}:M^{-1}\tilde{l}\in I_{\tilde{q}}} t_N \left(\int_{I_{\tilde{q}}} \left|Q_{\tilde{q},\tilde{l}}(\tilde{x})\right|^{\kappa} d\tilde{x}\right)^{1/\kappa}$$

$$\leq \sum_{\tilde{l}:M^{-1}\tilde{l}\in I_{\tilde{q}}} t_N \left(\int_{I_{\tilde{q}}} \lfloor\alpha\rfloor^{(d-1)\lfloor\alpha\rfloor\kappa} d\tilde{x}\right)^{1/\kappa} = O\left(t_N M^{-(d-1)/\kappa}\right).$$

Using these two facts we conclude that

$$R(\widehat{G}_n) - R(G^*) =$$

$$O\left(\sum_{\tilde{q}} \left(\|(L_{\tilde{q}} - g^*)\mathbf{1}\{\tilde{x} \in I_{\tilde{q}}\}\|_{\kappa} + \left\|(\widehat{L}_{\tilde{q}} - L_{\tilde{q}})\mathbf{1}\{\tilde{x} \in I_{\tilde{q}}\}\right\|_{\kappa}\right)^{\kappa}\right) + O(M^{-1})$$

$$= O\left(\sum_{\tilde{q}\in\{0,\ldots,M_0\}^{d-1}} \left(M^{-\alpha} M^{-\frac{d-1}{\kappa}} + t_N M^{-(d-1)/\kappa}\right)^{\kappa}\right) + O(M^{-1})$$

$$= O\left(M^{d-1}\left(M^{-\alpha} M^{-\frac{d-1}{\kappa}} + t_N M^{-(d-1)/\kappa}\right)^{\kappa}\right) + O(M^{-1})$$

$$= O\left((M^{-\alpha} + t_N)^{\kappa} + M^{-1}\right).$$

Plugging in the choices of M and N given in the theorem statement we obtain

$$R(\widehat{G}_n) - R(G^*) = O\left((\log n/n)^{\frac{\alpha\kappa}{\alpha(2\kappa-2)+d-1}}\right).$$

Finally, noticing that $1 - \Pr(\Omega_n) = O\left(n^{-\frac{\alpha\kappa}{\alpha(2\kappa-2)+d-1}}\right)$ we have

$$\mathbb{E}[R(\widehat{G}_n)] - R(G^*) \leq O\left((\log n/n)^{\frac{\alpha\kappa}{\alpha(2\kappa-2)+d-1}}\right)\Pr(\Omega_n) + 1\cdot(1-\Pr(\Omega_n))$$

$$= O\left((\log n/n)^{\frac{\alpha\kappa}{\alpha(2\kappa-2)+d-1}}\right),$$

concluding the proof.

Stability of k-Means Clustering

Shai Ben-David[1], Dávid Pál[1], and Hans Ulrich Simon[2],[*]

[1] David R. Cheriton School of Computer Science,
University of Waterloo,
Waterloo, Ontario, Canada
{shai,dpal}@cs.uwaterloo.ca
[2] Ruhr-Universität Bochum, Germany
simon@lmi.rub.de

Abstract. We consider the stability of k-means clustering problems. Clustering stability is a common heuristics used to determine the number of clusters in a wide variety of clustering applications. We continue the theoretical analysis of clustering stability by establishing a complete characterization of clustering stability in terms of the number of optimal solutions to the clustering optimization problem. Our results complement earlier work of Ben-David, von Luxburg and Pál, by settling the main problem left open there. Our analysis shows that, for probability distributions with finite support, the stability of k-means clusterings depends solely on the number of optimal solutions to the underlying optimization problem for the data distribution. These results challenge the common belief and practice that view stability as an indicator of the validity, or meaningfulness, of the choice of a clustering algorithm and number of clusters.

1   Introduction

Clustering is one of the most widely used techniques for exploratory data analysis. Across all disciplines, from social sciences over biology to computer science, people try to get a first intuition about their data by identifying meaningful groups among the data points. Despite this popularity of clustering, distressingly little is known about theoretical properties of clustering [11]. In particular, two central issues, the problem of assessing the meaningfulness of a certain cluster structure found in the data and the problem of choosing k—the number of clusters—which best fits a given data set are basically unsolved.

A common approach to provide answers to these questions has been the notion of *clustering stability*. The intuitive idea behind that method is that if we repeatedly sample data points and apply the clustering algorithm, then a "good" algorithm should produce clusterings that do not vary much from one sample to another. In other words, the algorithm is stable with respect to input randomization. In particular, stability is viewed as an indication whether the model

---

[*] This work was supported in part by the IST Programme of the European Community, under the PASCAL Network of Excellence, IST-2002-506778. This publication only reflects the authors' views.

N. Bshouty and C. Gentile (Eds.): COLT 2007, LNAI 4539, pp. 20–34, 2007.

proposed by some algorithm fits the data or not. For example, if our data contains three "true" clusters, but we use a clustering algorithm which looks for four clusters, the algorithm wrongly needs to split one of the clusters into two clusters. Which of the three true clusters are split might change from sample to sample, and thus the result will not be very stable. Based on such intuitive considerations, stability is being widely used in practical applications as a heuristics for tuning parameters of clustering algorithms, like the number of clusters, or various stopping criteria, see for example [7], [4], [5], [6].

Aiming to provide theoretical foundations to such applications of stability, Ben-David et al. [3] have set forward formal definitions for stability and some related clustering notions and used this framework to embark on mathematical analysis of stability. Their results challenge these heuristics by showing that stability is determined by the structure of the set of optimal solutions to the risk minimization objective. They postulate that stability is fully determined by the number of distinct clusterings that minimize the risk objective function. They show that the existence of a unique minimizer implies stability. As for the reverse implication, they show that if the probability distribution generating the data has multiple minimizing clusterings, *and is symmetric with respect to these clusterings* then it is unstable. They conjecture that their symmetry condition is not necessary, and that the mere existence of multiple minimizers already implies instability. The main result in this paper is proving this conjecture for k-means clustering over finite-support probability distributions. We believe that our proofs, and therefore our main result, can be generalized to other risk minimization clustering problems.

These results indicate that, contrary to common belief and practice, stability may *not* reflect the validity or meaningfulness of the choice of the number of clusters. Instead, the parameters it measures are rather independent of clustering parameters. Our results reduce the problem of stability estimation to concrete geometric properties of the data distribution.

Using our characterization of stability, one can readily construct many example data distributions in which bad choices of the number of clusters result in stability while, on the other hand, domain partitions reflecting the true basic structure of a data set result in instability. As an illustration of these phenomena, consider the following simple data probability distribution P over the unit interval: For some large enough N, the support of P consists of $2N$ equally weighted points, N of which are equally spaced over the sub-interval $A = [0, 2a]$ and N points are equally spaced over the sub-interval $B = [1 - a, 1]$, where $a < 1/3$. First, let us consider k, the number of target centers, to be 2. It is not hard to see that for some value of $a < 1/3$ two partitions, one having the points in A as one cluster and the points in B as its second cluster, and the other having as one cluster only the points in some sub-interval $[0, 2a - \epsilon]$ and the remaining points as its second cluster, must have the same 2-means cost. It follows from our result that although 2 is the 'right' number of clusters for this distribution, the choice of $k = 2$ induces instability (note that the value of ϵ and a remain practically unchanged for all large enough N). On the other hand, if one considers, for the same value of a, $k = 3$, 3-means will have a unique minimizing solution (having the points in the intervals $[0, a]$, $[a, 2a]$ and $[1 - a, 1]$ as its clusters) and therefore be stable, leading the common heuristics to the conclusion that 3 is a good choice as the number of clusters for our data distributions (and, in particular, a better choice than 2). Note that, in this example, the data distribution is not symmetric, therefore, its instability for 2-means could not be detected by the previously known stability analysis.

The question of the practical value of stability as a clustering evaluation paradigm is intriguing and complex, we shall discuss it some more (without claiming to resolve it) in the Conclusion (Section 6 below).

The term "stability" is used for a variety of meanings in the clustering literature, not all of which are equivalent to our use of the term. In particular, note that the recent work of Rakhlin et al [10], considers a different notion of stability (examining the effect of replacing a small fraction of a clustering sample, as opposed to considering a pair of independent samples, as we do here). They investigate the relative size of a sub-sample that may be replaced without resulting in a big change of the sample clustering and show a bound to that size. Smaller sub-samples are proven to have small effect on the resulting clustering, and for larger fractions, they show an example of "instability".

Here, we analyze the expected distance between clusterings resulting form two independent samples. We define stability as having this expected distance converge to zero as the sample sizes grow to infinity.

Our main result is Theorem 4, in which we state that the existence of multiple optimal-cost clusterings implies instability. We formally state it in Section 3. Since its proof is lengthy, we first outline it, in Section 4. The technical lemmas are stated formally, and some of them are proved in Section 5. Proofs of the rest of the lemmas can be found in the extended version [1] available online. Section 2 is devoted to setting the ground in terms of definitions notation and basic observations.

2   Definitions

In the rest of the paper we use the following standard notation. We consider a data space X endowed with probability measure P. A finite multi-set $S = \{x_1, x_2, \ldots, x_m\}$ of X is called a *sample*. When relevant, we shall assume that samples are drawn i.i.d from (X, P). We denote by $\hat{S}$ the uniform probability distribution over the sample S.

A *clustering* $\mathcal{C}$ of a set X is a finite partition $\mathcal{C}$, of X (namely, an equivalence relation over X with a finite number of equivalence classes). The equivalence classes of a clustering are called clusters. We introduce the notation $x \sim_{\mathcal{C}} y$ whenever x and y lie in the same cluster of $\mathcal{C}$, and $x \nsim_{\mathcal{C}} y$ otherwise. If the clustering is clear from the context we drop the subscript and simply write $x \sim y$ or $x \nsim y$.

A function A, that for any given finite sample $S \subset X$ computes a clustering of X, is called a *clustering algorithm* (in spite of the word 'algorithm', we ignore any computability considerations). Note that this definition differs slightly from some common usage of "clustering algorithms" in which it is assumed that the algorithm outputs only a partition of the input sample.

In order to define the stability of a clustering algorithm we wish to measure by how much two clusterings differ. Given a probability distribution P over X, we define the *P-Hamming clustering distance* between two clusterings $\mathcal{C}$ and $\mathcal{D}$ as

$$d_P(\mathcal{C}, \mathcal{D}) = \Pr_{\substack{x \sim P \\ y \sim P}} [(x \sim_{\mathcal{C}} y) \oplus (x \sim_{\mathcal{D}} y)],$$

where $\oplus$ denotes the logical XOR operation. In other words, $d_P(\mathcal{C}, \mathcal{D})$ is the P-probability of drawing a pair of points on which the equivalence relation defined by $\mathcal{C}$ differs from the one defined by $\mathcal{D}$. Other definitions of clustering distance may also be used, see [3] and [8]. However, the Hamming clustering distance is conceptually the simplest, universal, and easy to work with. For a probability distribution P with a finite support, the Hamming distance has the additional property that two clusterings have zero distance if and only if they induce the same partitions of the support of P. We shall thus treat clusterings with zero Hamming clustering distance as equal.

The central notion of this paper is *instability*:

Definition 1 (Instability). *The* instability *of a clustering algorithm A with respect to a sample size m and a probability distribution P is*

$$\text{Instability}(A, P, m) = \mathbb{E}_{\substack{S_1 \sim P^m \\ S_2 \sim P^m}} d_P(A(S_1), A(S_2)).$$

The instability *of A with respect to P is*

$$\text{Instability}(A, P) = \lim_{m \to \infty} \text{Instability}(A, P, m).$$

We say that an algorithm A is stable *on P, if* $\text{Instability}(A, P) = 0$, *otherwise we say that A is* unstable.

A large class of clustering problems aim to choose the clustering by minimizing some risk function. We call these clustering optimization problems.

Definition 2 (Risk Minimization Clustering Problems)

- *A clustering* risk minimization problem *is a quadruple $(X, \mathcal{L}, \mathcal{P}, R)$, where X is some domain set, $\mathcal{L}$ is a set of legal clusterings of X, $\mathcal{P}$ is a set of probability distributions over X, and $R : \mathcal{P} \times \mathcal{L} \to \mathbb{R}_+$ [1] is an objective function (or risk) that the clustering algorithm aims to minimize.*
- *An* instance *of the risk minimizing problem is a concrete probability distribution P from $\mathcal{P}$. The optimal cost $\text{opt}(P)$ for an instance P, is defined as $\text{opt}(P) = \inf_{\mathcal{C} \in \mathcal{L}} R(P, \mathcal{C})$.*

---

[1] We denote by $\mathbb{R}_+$ the set of non-negative real numbers, and by $\mathbb{R}_{++}$ the set of positive real numbers.

– For a sample $S \subseteq X$, we call $R(\hat{S}, \mathcal{C})$ the empirical risk of $\mathcal{C}$ with respect to the sample S.
– A risk-minimizing (or R-minimizing) clustering algorithm is an algorithm that for any sample S, has $R(\hat{S}, A(S)) = opt(\hat{S})$. For all practical purposes this requirement defines A uniquely. We shall therefore refer to the risk-minimizing algorithm.

Given a probability distribution P over some Euclidean space $X \subseteq \mathbb{R}^d$ and a clustering $\mathcal{C}$ of X with clusters $C_1, C_2, \ldots, C_k$, let $c_1, c_2, \ldots, c_k$ be the P-centers of mass of the clusters C_i. Namely, $c_i = \mathbb{E}_{x \sim P}[x | x \in C_i]$, and, for every $x \in X$, let c_x denote the center of mass of the class to which x belongs. The k-means risk R is defined as

$$R(P, \mathcal{C}) = \mathop{\mathbb{E}}_{x \sim P} \|x - c_x\|_2^2 . \tag{1}$$

In many cases, risk minimizing algorithms converge to the true risk as sample sizes grow to infinity. For the case of k-mean and k-medians on bounded subset of $\mathbb{R}^d$ with the Euclidean metric, such convergence was proved by Pollard [9], and uniform, finite-sample rates of convergence were shown in [2].

Definition 3 (Uniform Convergence). *Let P be a probability distribution. The risk function R converges uniformly if for any positive ϵ and δ, there exists sample size m_0 such that for all $m > m_0$*

$$\mathop{\Pr}_{S \sim P^m} \left[\forall \mathcal{C} \in \mathcal{S} \quad |R(\hat{S}, \mathcal{C}) - R(P, \mathcal{C})| < \epsilon \right] > 1 - \delta \;.^2$$

3   Stability of Risk Optimizing Clustering Algorithms

Informally speaking, our main claim is that the stability of the risk minimizing algorithm with a uniformly converging risk function is fully determined by the number of risk optimal clusterings. More concretely, a risk-minimizing algorithm is stable on an input data distribution P, if and only if P has a unique risk minimizing clustering. We prove such a result for the k-means clustering problem

The first step towards such a characterization follows from Pollard [9]. He proves that the existence of a unique k-means minimizing clustering (for a P's with bounded support over Euclidean spaces) implies stability. Ben-David et al, [3] extended this result to a wider class of clustering problems.

As for the reverse implication, [3] shows that if P has multiple risk-minimizing clusterings, and is *symmetric* with respect to these clusterings, then it is unstable. Where symmetry is defined as an isometry $g : X \to X$ of the underlying metric space (X, ℓ) which preserves P (that is, for any measurable set A, $\Pr_{x \sim P}[x \in A] = \Pr_{x \sim P}[g(x) \in A]$), and the clustering distance and the risk function are invariant under g. Note that the k-means risk function and the

---

^{2} Here m_0 can also depend on P, and not only on ϵ and δ. The uniform convergence bound proved in [2] is a stronger in this sense, since it expresses m_0 as a function of ϵ and δ only and holds for any P.

Hamming clustering distance are invariant under any such symmetry. See [3] for details.

Ben-David et al [3] conjecture that symmetry is not a necessary condition. Namely, that the mere existence of multiple risk-minimizing clusterings suffices for instability. In this paper we prove that this conjecture holds for k-means clustering over finite-support probability distributions.

Theorem 4. *Let P be a probability distribution over the Euclidean space $\mathbb{R}^d$ with a finite support. Then, the k-means risk-minimizing algorithm is stable on P if and only if there exist unique clustering minimizing the k-means risk function $R(P, \cdot)$.*

The next section outlines the proof. In Section 5 we follow that outline with precise statements of the needed technical lemmas and some proofs. Some of the proofs are omitted and can be found in the extended version [1] available online.

4   Proof Outline

A finite-support probability distribution may be viewed as a vector of weights. Similarly, any finite sample over such a domain can be also described by a similar relative frequency vector. We view the clustering problem as a function from such vectors to partitions of the domain set. Loosely speaking, having multiple optimal clusterings for some input distribution, P, say, $\mathcal{C}_1, \mathcal{C}_2, \ldots \mathcal{C}_h$, we consider the decision function that assigns each sample-representing vector to the index $i \in \{1, \ldots h\}$ of its optimal solution. (Note that due to the uniform convergence property, for large enough samples, with high probability, these sample based partitions are among the actual input optimal clusterings.) We analyze this decision function and show that, for large enough sample sizes, none of its values is obtained with probability 1. This implies instability, since having two different partitions, each with non-zero probability, implies a non-zero expectation of the distance between sample-generated clustering solutions.

To allow a more detailed discussion we need some further notation.

Let $F = \{x_1, x_2, \ldots, x_n\}$ be the support of P with $P(\{x_i\}) = \mu_i > 0$ for all $i = 1, 2, \ldots, n$ and $\mu_1 + \mu_2 + \cdots + \mu_n = 1$. Let

$$\mu = (\mu_1, \mu_2, \ldots, \mu_n).$$

If $n \leq k$ or $k \leq 1$ there is a trivial unique minimizer. Hence we assume that $n > k \geq 2$.

For a sample S of size m, we denote the number of occurrences of the point x_i in S by m_i, and use $w_i = m_i/m$ to denote the empirical frequency (*weight*) of the point x_i in the sample. The sample is completely determined by the vector of weights

$$w = (w_1, w_2, \ldots, w_n).$$

Since the support of P is finite, there are only finitely many partitions of F.

A partition, $\mathcal{C}$, is called *optimal* if its risk, $R(P, \mathcal{C})$ equals $opt(P)$. A partition is called *empirically optimal* for a sample S, if its empirical risk, $R(\hat{S}, \mathcal{C})$ equals $opt(\hat{S})$. We shall freely replace $\hat{S}$ with its weight vector w, in particular, we overload the notation and write $R(w, \mathcal{C}) = R(\hat{S}, \mathcal{C})$.

Consider a pair of distinct optimal partitions $\mathcal{C}$ and $\mathcal{D}$. For weights w consider the empirical risk, $R(w, \mathcal{C})$, of the partition $\mathcal{C}$ on a sample with weights w. Likewise, consider the empirical risk $R(w, \mathcal{D})$. The k-means risk minimizing algorithm "prefers" $\mathcal{C}$ over $\mathcal{D}$ when $R(w, \mathcal{C}) < R(w, \mathcal{D})$. We consider the set of weights

$$Q = \{w \in \mathbb{R}^n_{++} \mid R(w, \mathcal{C}) < R(w, \mathcal{D})\},$$

where, $\mathbb{R}_{++}$ denotes the set of (strictly) positive real numbers. We allow Q to contain weight vectors w having arbitrary positive sum of weights, $w_1 + w_2 + \cdots + w_n$, not necessarily equal to one. Due to the homogeneity of the k-means risk as a function of the weights, weight vectors of arbitrary total weight can be rescaled to probability weights without effecting the risk preference between two clusterings (for details see the proof Lemma 13). This relaxation simplifies the analysis.

Step 1: We analyze the set Q in a small neighborhood of μ. In Lemma 12, we show that Q contains an *open cone T with peak at μ*. The proof of the Lemma consists of several smaller steps.

(a) We first define the function $f : \mathbb{R}^n \to \mathbb{R}$, $f(w) = R(w, \mathcal{D}) - R(w, \mathcal{C})$. In this notation $Q = \{w \mid f(w) > 0\}$. Note the important fact that $f(\mu) = 0$. We analyze the behavior of f near μ.

(b) From Observation 5 it follows that $R(w, \mathcal{C})$ is a rational function of w. Then, in Lemma 6, we compute the Taylor expansion of $R(w, \mathcal{C})$ at the point μ.

(c) In Lemma 10 we show that the first non-zero term in the Taylor expansion of f attains both positive and negative values, and thus f itself attains both positive and negative values arbitrarily close to μ.

(d) We show that, since f is rational and hence analytic in the neighborhood of μ, it follows that Q contains a cone T whose peak is at μ.

Step 2: Consider the hyperplane

$$H = \{w \in \mathbb{R}^n \mid w_1 + w_2 + \cdots + w_n = 1\}$$

in which the weights actually lie. In Lemma 13 we show that $Q \cap H$ contains an $(n-1)$-dimensional open cone Y.

Step 3: The distribution of the random vector w describing the sample is a multinomial distribution with m trials. From central limit theorem it follows that as the sample size m approaches infinity the probability distribution of w can be approximated by a multivariate Gaussian distribution lying in H. The Gaussian distribution concentrates near its mean value μ as the sample size increases. The shape of Q near μ determines the probability that the algorithm prefers partition $\mathcal{C}$ over $\mathcal{D}$. Formally, in Lemma 14 we show that $\lim_{m \to \infty} \Pr[w \in Y] > 0$; hence $\lim_{m \to \infty} \Pr[w \in Q] > 0$.

Step 4: For sufficiently large sample sizes the partition of F output by the algorithm is, with high probability, one of the optimal partitions. From the previous step it follows that with non-zero probability any optimal partition has lower empirical risk than any other optimal partition. Hence, there exist at least two optimal partitions of F, such that each of them is empirically optimal for a sample with non-zero probability. These two partitions cause instability of the algorithm. A precise argument is presented in Lemma 15.

5   The Technical Lemmas

Observation 5 (Explicit Risk Formula). *For a partition $\mathcal{C}$ and a weight vector w,*

$$R(w,\mathcal{C}) = \sum_{i=1}^{k}\sum_{x_t\in C_i} w_t \left\| x_t - \frac{\sum_{x_s\in C_i} w_s x_s}{\sum_{x_s\in C_i} w_s}\right\|_2^2 , \tag{2}$$

where $C_1, C_2,\ldots, C_k$ are the clusters of $\mathcal{C}$. Therefore $R(w,\mathcal{C})$ is a rational function of w.

Proof. This is just a rewriting of the definition of the k-means cost function for the case of a finite domain. We use weighted sums expressions for the expectations and

$$c_i = \frac{\sum_{x_s\in C_i} w_s x_s}{\sum_{x_s\in C_i} w_s}$$

to calculate the centers of mass of the clusters.   □

Lemma 6 (Derivatives of f). *Let $\mathcal{C}$ be a partition of the support of P. The first two derivatives of the risk function $R(w,\mathcal{C})$ with respect to w at μ are as follows.*

1. *The gradient is*

$$(\nabla R(\mu,\mathcal{C}))_p = \left.\frac{\partial R(w,\mathcal{C})}{\partial w_p}\right|_{w=\mu} = \|c_\ell - x_p\|_2^2 ,$$

   assuming that x_p lies in the cluster C_ℓ.
2. *The (p,q)-th entry of the Hessian matrix*

$$(\nabla^2 R(\mu))_{p,q} = \left.\frac{\partial^2 R(w,\mathcal{C})}{\partial w_p \partial w_q}\right|_{w=\mu}$$

   equals to

$$-2\frac{(c_\ell - x_p)^T(c_\ell - x_q)}{\sum_{x_s\in C_\ell}\mu_s}$$

if x_p, x_q lie in a common cluster C_ℓ, and is zero otherwise.

Here, $c_1, c_2, \ldots, c_k$ are the optimal centers $c_i = \left(\sum_{x_s \in C_i} \mu_s x_s \right) / \left(\sum_{x_s \in C_i} \mu_s \right)$, and $C_1, C_2, \ldots, C_k \subseteq F$ are the clusters of $\mathcal{C}$.

Proof. Straightforward but long calculation, starting with formula (2). See the extended version paper [1] available online.   □

Lemma 7 (Weights of Clusters). *Let $\mathcal{C}$ and $\mathcal{D}$ be two partitions of F. Consider the weights μ assigned to points in F. Then, either for every point in F the weight of its cluster in $\mathcal{C}$ is the same as the weight of its cluster in $\mathcal{D}$. Or, there are two points in F, such that the weight of the cluster of the first point in $\mathcal{C}$ is strictly larger than in $\mathcal{D}$, and the weight of the cluster of the second point in $\mathcal{C}$ is strictly smaller than in $\mathcal{D}$.*

Proof. For any point $x_t \in F$ let $a_t = \sum_{x_s \in C_i} \mu_s$ be the weight of the cluster C_i in which x_t lies in the partition $\mathcal{C}$. Likewise, let $b_t = \sum_{x_s \in D_j} \mu_s$ be the weight of the cluster D_j in which x_t lies in the clustering $\mathcal{D}$. Consider the two sums $\sum_{t=1}^{n} \frac{\mu_t}{a_t}$ and $\sum_{t=1}^{n} \frac{\mu_t}{b_t}$. It easy to see that the sums are equal, $\sum_{t=1}^{n} \frac{\mu_t}{a_t} = \sum_{i=1}^{k} \sum_{x_t \in C_i} \frac{\mu_t}{a_t} = k = \sum_{i=1}^{k} \sum_{x_t \in D_i} \frac{\mu_t}{b_t} = \sum_{t=1}^{n} \frac{\mu_t}{b_t}$. Either all the corresponding summands μ_t / a_t and μ_t / b_t in the two sums are equal and hence $a_t = b_t$ for all t. Or, there exist points x_t and x_s such that $\mu_t / a_t < \mu_t / b_t$ and $\mu_s / a_s > \mu_s / b_s$, and hence $a_t > b_t$ and $a_s < b_s$.   □

Lemma 8 (No Ties). *Let $\mathcal{C}$ be an optimal partition and let $c_1, c_2, \ldots, c_k$ be the centers of mass of the clusters of $\mathcal{C}$ computed with respect to the weight vector μ. Then, for a point x of the support lying in a cluster C_i of $\mathcal{C}$, the center of mass c_i is strictly closer to x than any other center.*

Proof. Suppose that the distance $\|c_j - x\|_2$, $j \neq i$, is smaller or equal to the distance $\|c_i - x\|$. Then, we claim that moving the point x to the cluster C_j decreases the risk. After the move of x, recompute the center of C_i. As a result the risk strictly decreases. Then recompute the center of mass of C_j, the risk decreases even more.   □

Lemma 9 (Hessian determines Clustering). *For partitions $\mathcal{C}, \mathcal{D}$ of the support of P, the following holds. If the Hesse matrices of the risk functions $R(w, \mathcal{C})$ and $R(w, \mathcal{D})$, respectively, coincide at μ, then $\mathcal{C} = \mathcal{D}$.*

Proof. For sake of brevity, let

$$A_{p,q} := \left. \frac{\partial^2 R(w, \mathcal{C})}{\partial w_p \partial w_q} \right|_{w=\mu}.$$

It suffices to show that centers $c_1, c_2, \ldots, c_k$ of partition $\mathcal{C}$ are uniquely determined by matrix A. To this end, we view A as the adjacency matrix of a graph G with nodes $x_1, x_2, \ldots, x_n$, where nodes x_p, x_q are connected by an edge if and only if $A_{p,q} \neq 0$. Let $K_1, K_2, \ldots, K_\ell$ be the connected components of G. Note that there is an edge between x_p and x_q only if p and q belong to the same cluster in $\mathcal{C}$. Thus, the connected components of G represent a refinement of partition $\mathcal{C}$. Consider a fixed cluster C_j in $\mathcal{C}$ with center c_j. Recall that

$$c_j = \sum_{x_i \in C_j} \mu_i x_i \ . \tag{3}$$

Let $K \subseteq C_j$ be any connected component of G that is contained in C_j and define, for sake of brevity, $\mu(K) := \sum_{x_i \in C} \mu_i$ and $K' = C_j \setminus K$. We claim that

$$c_j = \frac{1}{\mu(K)} \sum_{x_i \in K} \mu_i x_i \ , \tag{4}$$

that is, c_j is determined by any component $K \subseteq C_j$. Since this is obvious for $K = C_j$, we assume that $K \subsetneq C_j$. We can rewrite (3) as

$$0 = \left(\sum_{x_i \in K} \mu_i(x_i - c_j) \right) + \left(\sum_{x_{i'} \in K'} \mu_{i'}(x_{i'} - c_j) \right) \ . \tag{5}$$

Pick any pair i, i' such that $x_i \in K$ and $x_{i'} \in K'$. Since x_i and $x_{i'}$ are not neighbors in G, $A_{i,i'} = 0$, which means that $x_i - c_j$ is orthogonal to $x_{i'} - c_j$. Thus the vector represented by the first sum in (5) is orthogonal on the vector represented by the second sum. It follows that both sums yield zero, respectively. Rewriting this for the first sum, we obtain (4). □

Lemma 10 (Indefinitness). *Let $\mathcal{C}$ and $\mathcal{D}$ be any two optimal partitions. Let $f(w) = R(w, \mathcal{D}) - R(w, \mathcal{C})$. Consider the Taylor expansion of f around μ. Then, $\nabla f(\mu) \neq 0$ or the Hessian, $\nabla^2 f(\mu)$, is indefinite.*[3]

Proof. We denote by $C_1, C_2, \ldots, C_k \subseteq F$ the clusters of $\mathcal{C}$ and by $D_1, D_2, \ldots, D_k \subseteq F$ the clusters of $\mathcal{D}$. We denote by $c_1, c_2, \ldots, c_k$ the optimal centers for $\mathcal{C}$, and by $d_1, d_2, \ldots, d_k$ the optimal centers for $\mathcal{D}$. That is, the center c_i is the center of mass of C_i, and d_j is the center of mass of D_j.

Consider the Taylor expansion of f at μ. Lemma 9 implies that the Hessian, $\nabla^2 f(\mu)$, is not zero. Assuming $\nabla f(\mu) = 0$ i.e. $\nabla R(\mu, \mathcal{C}) = \nabla R(\mu, \mathcal{D})$, we need to show that $\nabla^2 f(\mu)$ is indefinite.

For any point $x_p \in F$ we define three numbers e_p, a_p and b_p as follows. Suppose $x_p \in C_\ell$ and $x_p \in D_{\ell'}$. The first part of the Lemma 6 and $\nabla R(\mu, \mathcal{C}) = \nabla R(\mu, \mathcal{D})$ imply that the distance between x_p and c_ℓ equals to the distance between x_p and $d_{\ell'}$; denote this distance by e_p. Denote by a_p the weight of the cluster C_ℓ, that is, $a_p = \sum_{x_t \in C_\ell} \mu_t$. Likewise, let b_p be the weight of the cluster $D_{\ell'}$, that is, $b_p = \sum_{x_t \in D_{\ell'}} \mu_t$.

Consider the diagonal entries of Hessian matrix of f. Using the notation we had just introduced, by the second part of the Lemma 6 the (p, p)-th entry is

$$(\nabla^2 f(\mu))_{p,p} = \left(\frac{\partial^2 R(w, \mathcal{D})}{\partial w_p^2} - \frac{\partial^2 R(w, \mathcal{C})}{\partial w_p^2} \right) \Bigg|_{w=\mu} = 2e_p^2 \left(\frac{1}{a_p} - \frac{1}{b_p} \right) \ .$$

---

[3] A matrix is *indefinite* if it is neither positively semi-definite, nor negatively semi-definite.

We claim that if $e_p = 0$, then $a_p = b_p$. Let $x_p \in C_\ell \cap D_{\ell'}$, and suppose without loss of generality that $a_p > b_p$. Since $e_p = 0$ it is $x_p = c_\ell = d_{\ell'}$. Since $a_p > b_p$ there is another point x_q that causes the decrease of the weight the cluster C_ℓ. Formally, $x_q \in C_\ell$, $x_q \notin D_{\ell'}$, but $x_q \in D_{\ell''}$. This means that in $\mathcal{D}$ the point x_q is closest to both $d_{\ell'}$ and $d_{\ell''}$. By Lemma 8, a tie can not happen in an optimal partition, which is a contradiction.

By Lemma 7, either (a) for all indices p, $a_p = b_p$, or (b) there are indices i, j such that $a_i > b_i$ and $a_j < b_j$. In the subcase (a), all the diagonal entries of Hessian matrix are zero. Since the Hessian matrix is non-zero, there must exist a non-zero entry off the diagonal making the matrix is indefinite. In the subcase (b), the above claim implies that the indices i, j for which $a_i > b_i$ and $a_j < b_j$ are such that $e_i, e_j > 0$. Hence, the (i, i)-th diagonal entry of the Hessian matrix is negative, and the (j, j)-the diagonal entry of the Hessian matrix is positive. Therefore the Hessian matrix is indefinite.   □

Corollary 11. *There exists arbitrarily small $\delta \in \mathbb{R}^n$, $f(\mu + \delta) > 0$ (and similarly, there exists arbitrarily small δ', $f(\mu + \delta') < 0$).*

Proof. Consider the Taylor expansion of f at μ and its lowest order term $T(x - \mu)$. that does not vanish (according to Lemma 10, either the gradient or the Hessian). Since T can take values of positive and of negative sign (obvious for the gradient, and obvious from Lemma 10 for the Hessian), we can pick a vector $x = \mu + \delta$ such that $T(x - \mu) = T(\delta) > 0$. Since T is homogeneous in δ, $T(\lambda \delta) > 0$ for every $\lambda > 0$. If λ is chosen sufficiently small, then $f(\mu + \lambda \delta)$ has the same sign as $T(\lambda \delta)$. The considerations for negative sign are symmetric.   □

Lemma 12 (Existence of a Positive Open Cone). *There exist positive real numbers ϵ and δ, and a unit vector $u \in \mathbb{R}^n$ such that the open cone*

$$T = \left\{ w \in \mathbb{R}^n_{++} \ \middle| \ 0 < \|w - \mu\|_2 < \epsilon, \ \frac{u^T(w - \mu)}{\|w - \mu\|_2} > 1 - \delta \right\}$$

is contained in Q, the set of weights for which $R(w, \mathcal{C}) < R(w, \mathcal{D})$.

Proof. Let h be the order of the first non-zero term in the Taylor expansion of $f(\mu + u)$ around μ (as a multi-variate polynomial in u). Using Corollary 11, pick a vector u so that $f(\mu + u) > 0$ and, for some $\eta > 0$, for every v in the η-ball around u, that term of the Taylor expansion of $f(\mu + u)$ dominates the higher order terms. The existence of such a ball follows from the smoothness properties of f. Note that this domination holds as well for any $f(\mu + \lambda v)$ such that $0 < \lambda \leq 1$.

Let δ be the supremum, over the vectors v in the η-ball, of the expression $1 - (u^T v)/\|v\|_2$. (That is, $1 - \delta$ is the infimum of the cosines of the angles between u and v's varying over the η-ball.) And let $\epsilon = \eta$.

For the vectors v, by the Taylor expansion formula, λv, $\text{sign}(f(\mu + \lambda v)) = \text{sign}(f(\mu + v)) = \text{sign}(f(\mu + u)) > 0$. Hence, all the points of the form $w = \mu + \lambda v$ contain the cone sought.   □

Lemma 13 (Existence of a Positive Open Cone II). *There exists positive real numbers ϵ, δ and a unit vector $u \in \mathbb{R}^n$ with sum of coordinates, $u_1 + u_2 + \cdots + u_n$, equal to zero, such that the $(n-1)$-dimensional open cone*

$$Y = \left\{ w \in H \cap \mathbb{R}^n_{++} \;\middle|\; 0 < \|w - \mu\|_2 < \epsilon, \; \frac{u^T(w - \mu)}{\|w - \mu\|_2} > 1 - \delta \right\}$$

is contained in $Q \cap H$.

Proof. We use the projection $\phi : \mathbb{R}^n_{++} \to H$, $\phi(w) = w/(w_1 + w_2 + \cdots + w_n)$. Note that for the k-means cost function, for every clustering $\mathcal{C}$ and every positive constant λ, $R(\lambda w, \mathcal{C}) = \lambda R(w, \mathcal{C})$. It follows that the projection ϕ does not affect the sign of f. That is, $\text{sign}(f(w)) = \text{sign}(f(\phi(w)))$. Therefore $Q \cap H = \phi(Q) \subset Q$. The projection $\phi(T)$ clearly contains an $(n-1)$-dimensional open cone Y of the form as stated in the Lemma. More precisely, there exists positive numbers ϵ, δ and unit vector u (the direction of the axis of the cone), such that the cone

$$Y := Y_{\epsilon,\delta,u} = \left\{ w \in H \cap \mathbb{R}^n_{++} \;\middle|\; 0 < \|w - \mu\|_2 < \epsilon, \; \frac{u^T(w - \mu)}{\|w - \mu\|_2} > 1 - \delta \right\}$$

is contained in $\phi(T)$. Since the cone Y lies in H, the direction of the axis, u, can be picked in such way that the sum of its coordinates $u_1 + u_2 + \cdots + u_n$ is zero. Since $T \subseteq Q$, we get $Y \subset \phi(T) \subset \phi(Q) = Q \cap H$. $\qquad\square$

Lemma 14 (Instability). *Let $\mathcal{C}$ and $\mathcal{D}$ be distinct optimal partitions. Let Q be the set of weights where the k-means clustering algorithm prefers $\mathcal{C}$ over $\mathcal{D}$. Then, $\lim_{m \to \infty} \Pr[w \in Q] > 0$.*

Proof. Let $Y \subset (Q \cap H)$ be an $(n-1)$-dimensional open cone (as implied by lemma 13) lying in the hyperplane H defined by the equation $w_1 + w_2 + \cdots + w_n = 1$. We show that,

$$\lim_{m \to \infty} \Pr[w \in Y] > 0 \,,$$

which implies the claim.

We have

$$\Pr[w \in Y] = \Pr\left[\frac{u^T(w - \mu)}{\|w - \mu\|_2} > 1 - \delta, \; 0 < \|w - \mu\|_2 < \epsilon \right]$$

$$= \Pr\left[\frac{u^T(\sqrt{m}(w - \mu))}{\sqrt{m}\|w - \mu\|_2} > 1 - \delta, \; 0 < \sqrt{m}\|w - \mu\|_2 < \epsilon\sqrt{m} \right] .$$

By the central limit theorem $\sqrt{m}(w - \mu)$ weakly converges to a normally distributed random variable $Z \sim N(0, \Sigma)$, where Σ is the covariance matrix.[4] In particular this means that there is a sequence $\{\zeta_m\}_{m=1}^{\infty}$, $\zeta_m \to 0$, such that

---

[4] $\Sigma = \text{diag}(\mu_1, \mu_2, \ldots, \mu_n) - \mu\mu^T$, the rank of Σ is $n - 1$, and its rows (or columns) span the $(n-1)$-dimensional vector space $\{u \in \mathbb{R}^n \mid u_1 + u_2 + \cdots + u_n = 0\}$.

$$\left| \Pr\left[\frac{u^T(\sqrt{m}(w-\mu))}{\sqrt{m}\|w-\mu\|_2} > 1-\delta,\ 0 < \sqrt{m}\|w-\mu\|_2 < \epsilon\sqrt{m} \right] \right.$$

$$\left. -\Pr\left[\frac{u^T Z}{\|Z\|_2} > 1-\delta,\ 0 < \|Z\|_2 < \epsilon\sqrt{m} \right] \right| < \zeta_m$$

Consequently, we can bound the probability $\Pr[w \in Y]$ as

$$\Pr[w \in Y] \geq \Pr\left[\frac{u^T Z}{\|Z\|_2} > 1-\delta,\ 0 < \|Z\|_2 < \epsilon\sqrt{m} \right] - \zeta_m$$

$$\geq 1 - \Pr\left[\frac{u^T Z}{\|Z\|_2} < 1-\delta \right] - \Pr\left[\|Z\|_2 \geq \epsilon\sqrt{m} \right] - \Pr\left[\|Z\|_2 = 0 \right] - \zeta_m\ .$$

Take the limit $m \to \infty$. The last three terms in the last expression vanish. Since u has sum of its coordinates zero and $Z \sim N(0, \Sigma)$ is normally distributed, the term $\lim_{m\to\infty} \Pr\left[\frac{u^T Z}{\|Z\|_2} < 1-\delta \right]$ lies in $(0,1)$. $\square$

Lemma 15 (Multiple Optimal Partitions). *If there are at least two optimal partitions of the support F, then the k-means algorithm is unstable.*

Proof. Let $\mathcal{C}_1, \mathcal{C}_2, \ldots, \mathcal{C}_h$, $h \geq 2$, be the optimal partitions. Suppose that

$$\lim_{m\to\infty} \Pr[A(S) = \mathcal{C}_i] = \pi_i\ ,$$

where by the event $A(S) = \mathcal{C}_i$ we mean that the k-means algorithm on the sample S outputs the partition $\mathcal{C}_i$ of the support.

Claim: Each number π_i is strictly less than one.

Proof of the Claim:

$$\Pr_{S\sim P^m}[A(S) = \mathcal{C}_i] \leq \Pr\left[R(w, \mathcal{C}_i) \leq \min_{\substack{\ell=1,2,\ldots,h \\ \ell \neq i}} R(w, \mathcal{C}_\ell) \right]$$

$$\leq \Pr[R(w, \mathcal{C}_i) \leq R(w, \mathcal{C}_j)]$$

$$= 1 - \Pr[R(w, \mathcal{C}_i) > R(w, \mathcal{C}_j)]$$

Taking limit $m \to \infty$ on both sides of the inequality and applying Lemma 14, $\lim_{m\to\infty} \Pr[R(w, \mathcal{C}_i) > R(w, \mathcal{C}_j)] > 0$ the claim follows.

Since k-means is risk converging, as sample size increases with probability approaching one, $A(S)$ outputs an optimal partition, and hence $\pi_1 + \pi_2 + \cdots + \pi_h = 1$. Necessarily at least two numbers π_i, π_j are strictly positive. That is, the algorithm outputs two different partitions $\mathcal{C}_i, \mathcal{C}_j$ with non-zero probability for arbitrarily large sample size. The algorithm will be switching between these two partitions. Formally, Instability$(A, P) \geq d_P(\mathcal{C}_i, \mathcal{C}_j)\pi_i\pi_j$ is strictly positive. $\square$

6 Conclusions and Discussion

Stability reflects a relation between clustering algorithms and the data sets (or data generating probability distributions) they are applied to. Stability is commonly viewed as a necessary condition for the suitability of the clustering algorithm, and its parameter setting, to the input data, as well as to the meaningfulness of the clustering the algorithm outputs. As such, stability is often used for model selection purposes, in particular for choosing the number of clusters for a given data. While a lot of published work demonstrates the success of this approach, the stability paradigm is mainly a heuristic and is not supported by clear theoretical guarantees. We embarked on the task of providing theoretical analysis of clustering stability. The results of Ben-David el al [3] and this paper challenge the common interpretation of stability described above. We show that the stability of risk-minimizing clustering algorithms over data generating distributions is just an indicator of weather the objective function (the risk) that the algorithm is set to minimize has one or more optimal solutions over the given input. This characterization is orthogonal to the issues of model selection to which stability is commonly applied. Based on our characterization, it is fairly simple to come up with examples of data sets (or data generating distributions) for which a 'wrong' choice of the number of clusters results in stability, whereas a 'correct' number of clusters results in instability (as well as examples for any of the other combinations of 'wrong/correct number of clusters' and 'stable/unstable'). The results of this paper apply to k-means over finite domains, but we believe that they are extendable to wider classes of clustering tasks.

How can that be? How can a paradigm that works in many practical applications be doomed to failure when analyzed theoretically? The answers should probably reside in the differences between what is actually done in practice and what our theory analyzes. The first suspect in that domain is the fact that, while in practice every stability procedure is based on some finite sample, our definition of stability refers to the limit behavior, as sample sizes grow to infinity. In fact, it should be pretty clear that, for any reasonable clustering risk function, an overwhelming majority of realistic data sets should have a unique optimal clustering solution. It is unlikely that for a real data set two different partitions will result in *exactly* the same k-means cost. It therefore follows that for large enough samples, these differences in the costs of solutions will be detected by the samples and the k means clustering will stabilize. On the other hand, sufficiently small samples may fail to detect small cost differences, and therefore look stable. It may very well be the case that the practical success will breakdown if stability tests would take into account larger and larger samples. If that is the case, it is a rather unusual occasion where working with larger samples obscures the 'truth' rather than crystalizes it.

At this point, this is just a speculation. The most obvious open questions that we see ahead is determining whether this is indeed the case by coming up with a useful non-asymptotic characterization of stability. Can our work be extended to predicting the behavior of stability over finite sample sizes?

Other natural questions to answered include extending the results of this paper to arbitrary probability distributions (doing away with our finite support assumption), as well as extending our analysis to other risk-minimizing clustering tasks.

Acknowledgments

We are happy to express our gratitude to Shalev Ben-David (Shai's son) for his elegant proof of Lemma 7.

References

1. Extended version of this paper. Availabe at http://www.cs.uwaterloo.ca/~dpal/papers/stability/stability.pdf or at http://www.cs.uwaterloo.ca/~shai/publications/stability.pdf
2. Ben-David, S.: A framework for statistical clustering with a constant time approximation algorithms for k-median clustering. In: Proceedings of the Conference on Computational Learning Theory, pp. 415–426 (2004)
3. Ben-David, S., von Luxburg, U., Pál, D.: A sober look at clustering stability. In: Proceedings of the Conference on Computational Learning Theory, pp. 5–19 (2006)
4. Ben-Hur, A., Elisseeff, A., Guyon, I.: A stability based method for discovering structure in clustered data. Pacific Symposium on Biocomputing 7, 6–17 (2002)
5. Dudoit, S., Fridlyand, J.: A prediction-based resampling method for estimating the number of clusters in a dataset. Genome Biology, 3(7) (2002)
6. Lange, T., Braun, M.L., Roth, V., Buhmann, J.: Stability-based model selection. Advances in Neural Information Processing Systems 15, 617–624 (2003)
7. Levine, E., Domany, E.: Resampling method for unsupervised estimation of cluster validity. Neural Computation 13(11), 2573–2593 (2001)
8. Meila, M.: Comparing clusterings. In: Proceedings of the Conference on Computational Learning Theory, pp. 173–187 (2003)
9. Pollard, D.: Strong consistency of k-means clustering. The Annals of Statistics 9(1), 135–140 (1981)
10. Rakhlin, A., Caponnetto, A.: Stability of k-means clustering. In: Schölkopf, B., Platt, J., Hoffman, T. (eds.) Advances in Neural Information Processing Systems 19, MIT Press, Cambridge, MA (2007)
11. von Luxburg, U., Ben-David, S.: Towards a statistical theory of clustering. In: PASCAL workshop on Statistics and Optimization of Clustering (2005)

Margin Based Active Learning

Maria-Florina Balcan[1], Andrei Broder[2], and Tong Zhang[3]

[1] Computer Science Department, Carnegie Mellon University, Pittsburgh, PA
ninamf@cs.cmu.edu
[2] Yahoo! Research, Sunnyvale, CA 94089, USA
broder@yahoo-inc.com
[3] Yahoo! Research, New York, 100111, USA
tzhang@yahoo-inc.com

Abstract. We present a framework for margin based active learning of linear separators. We instantiate it for a few important cases, some of which have been previously considered in the literature. We analyze the effectiveness of our framework both in the realizable case and in a specific noisy setting related to the Tsybakov small noise condition.

1 Introduction

There has recently been substantial interest in using unlabeled data together with labeled data for machine learning. The motivation is that unlabeled data can often be much cheaper and more plentiful than labeled data, and so if useful information can be extracted from it that reduces dependence on labeled examples, this can be a significant benefit.

There are currently two settings that have been considered to incorporate unlabeled data in the learning process. The first one is the so-called *Semi-supervised Learning* [3,5], where, in addition to a set of labeled examples drawn at random from the underlying data distribution, the learning algorithm can also use a (usually larger) set of unlabeled examples from the same distribution. In this setting, unlabeled data becomes informative under *additional* assumptions and beliefs about the learning problem. Examples of such assumptions are the one used by Transductive SVM (namely, that the target function should cut through low density regions of the space), or by Co-training (namely, that the target should be self-consistent in some way). Unlabeled data is then potentially useful in this setting because it allows one to reduce search space from the whole set of hypotheses, down to the set of *a-priori* reasonable with respect to the underlying distribution.

The second setting, an increasingly popular one for the past few years, is *Active Learning* [2,6,8]. Here, the learning algorithm has both the capability of drawing random unlabeled examples from the underlying distribution and that of asking for the labels of *any* of these examples, and the hope is that a good classifier can be learned with significantly fewer labels by *actively* directing the queries to *informative* examples. As opposed to the Semi-supervised learning setting, and similarly to the classical supervised learning settings (PAC and Statistical Learning Theory settings) the only prior belief about the learning problem in the Active Learning setting is that the target function

N. Bshouty and C. Gentile (Eds.): COLT 2007, LNAI 4539, pp. 35–50, 2007.

(or a good approximation of it) belongs to a given concept class. Luckily, it turns out that for simple concept classes such as linear separators on the line one can achieve an *exponential* improvement (over the usual supervised learning setting) in the labeled data sample complexity, under no additional assumptions about the learning problem [2,6].[1] In general, however, for more complicated concept classes, the speed-ups achievable in the active learning setting depend on the match between the distribution over example-label pairs and the hypothesis class, and therefore on the target hypothesis in the class. Furthermore, there are simple examples where active learning does not help at all, even if there in the realizable case (see, for example, [8]). Recent interesting work of Dasgupta [8] gives a nice generic characterization of the sample complexity aspect of active learning in the realizable case.

A few variants and restrictions of the general active learning setting have also been considered lately. For instance the Query by Committee analysis [10] assumes realizability (i.e., there exists a perfect classifier in a known set) and a correct Bayesian prior on the set of hypotheses [10]. The analysis of the active Perceptron algorithm described in [9] relies on an even stronger assumption, of known and fixed distribution.

In the general active learning setting, for the realizable case, Cohen, Atlas and Ladner have introduced in [6] a *generic* active learning algorithm. This algorithm is a sequential algorithm that keeps track of two spaces — the current *version space* H_i, defined as the set of hypotheses in H consistent with all labels revealed so far, and the current *region of uncertainty* R_i, defined as the set of all x in the instance space X, for which there exists a pair of hypotheses in H_i that disagrees on x. In round i, the algorithm picks a random unlabeled example from R_i and queries it, eliminating all hypotheses in H_i inconsistent with the received label. The algorithm then eliminates those $x \in R_i$ on which all surviving hypotheses agree, and recurses. This algorithm was later analyzed and generalized to the non-realizable case in [2], and it was shown that in certain cases it does provide a significant improvement in the sample complexity.

In this paper we analyze a generic margin based active learning algorithm for learning linear separators and instantiate it for a few important cases, some of which have been previously considered in the literature. Specifically, the generic procedure we analyze is presented in Figure 1. To simplify calculation, we will present and analyze a few modifications of the algorithm as well.

Our Contributions: We present and analyze a framework for margin based active learning and also instantiate it for a few important cases. Specifically:

- We point out that in order to obtain a *significant* improvement in the labeled data sample complexity we have to use a strategy which is more *aggressive* than the one proposed by Cohen, Atlas and Ladner in [6] and later analyzed in [2]. We point out that this is true even in the special case when the data instances are drawn uniformly from the the unit ball in R^d, and when the labels are consistent with a linear separator going through the origin. Indeed, in order to obtain a truly exponential improvement, and to be able to learn with only $\tilde{O}\left(d \log\left(\frac{1}{\epsilon}\right)\right)$ labeled examples, we need, in each iteration, to sample our examples from a subregion carefully chosen,

---

[1] For this simple concept class one can achieve a pure exponential improvement [6] in the realizable case, while in the agnostic case the improvement depends upon the noise rate [2].

and not from the entire region of uncertainty, which would imply a labeled data sample complexity of $\tilde{O}\left(d^{\frac{3}{2}}\log\left(\frac{1}{\epsilon}\right)\right)$.

- We show that our algorithm and argument extend to the non-realizable case. A specific case we analyze here is again the setting where the data instances are drawn uniformly from the the unit ball in R^d, and a linear classifier w^* is the Bayes classifier. We additionally assume that our data satisfies the popular Tsybakov small noise condition along the decision boundary [14]. We consider both a simple version which leads to *exponential* improvement similar to the item 1 above, and a setting where we get only a polynomial improvement in the sample complexity, and where this is provably the best we can do [4].
- We analyze a "large margin" setting and show how active learning can dramatically improve (the supervised learning) sample complexity; the bounds we obtain here *do not depend* on the dimensionality d.
- We provide a general and unified analysis of our main algorithm – Algorithm 1.

Structure of this paper: For clarity, we start by analyzing in Section 3 the special case where the data instances are drawn uniformly from the the unit ball in R^d, and when the labels are consistent with a linear separator w^* going through the origin. We then analyze the noisy setting in Section 4, and give dimension independent bounds in a large margin setting in Section 5. We present our generic Margin Based learning algorithm and analysis in Section 6 and finish with a discussion and in Section 7.

2   Definitions and Notation

Consider the problem of predicting a binary label y based on its corresponding input vector x. As in the standard machine learning formulation, we assume that the data points (x, y) are drawn from an unknown underlying distribution P over $X \times Y$; X is called the *instance space* and Y is the *label space*. In this paper we assume that $Y = \{\pm 1\}$.

Our goal is to find a classifier f with the property that its expected true loss of $\text{err}(f)$ is as small as possible. Here we assume $\text{err}(f) = E_{(x,y)\sim P}[\ell(f(x), y)]$, where we use $E_{(x,y)\sim P}$ to denote the expectation with respect to the true (but unknown) underlying distribution P. Throughout the paper, without loss of generality, we assume that $f(x)$ is a real-valued function, which induces a classification rule $2I(f(x) \geq 0) - 1$, where $I(\cdot)$ is the set indicator function. The decision at $f(x) = 0$ is not important in our analysis. We consider in the following the classification error loss, defined as $\ell(f(x), y) = 1$ if $f(x)y \leq 0$ and $\ell(f(x), y) = 0$ otherwise. We denote by $\text{d}(f, g)$ the probability that the two classifiers f and g predict differently on an example coming at random from P. Furthermore, for $\alpha \in [0, 1]$ we denote by $\text{B}(f, \alpha)$ the set $\{g \mid \text{d}(f, g) \leq \alpha\}$.

In this paper, we are interested in linear classifiers of the form $f(x) = w \cdot x$, where w is the weight vector which we need to learn from training data. We are interested in using active learning (selective sampling) algorithms to improve the performance of linear classification methods under various assumptions. In particular, we are interested in margin based selective sampling algorithms which have been widely used in practical applications (see e.g. [13]). A general version of the type of algorithm we analyze here

Input: unlabeled data set $\mathcal{U} = \{x_1, x_2, \ldots, \}$
         a learning algorithm $\mathcal{A}$ that learns a weight vector from labeled data
         a sequence of sample sizes $0 < \tilde{m}_1 < \tilde{m}_2 < \ldots < \tilde{m}_s = \tilde{m}_{s+1}$
         a sequence of cut-off values $b_k > 0$ $(k = 1, \ldots, s)$
Output: classifier $\hat{w}_s$.
Label data points $x_1, \ldots, x_{\tilde{m}_1}$ by a human expert
iterate $k = 1, \ldots, s$
     use $\mathcal{A}$ to learn weight vector $\hat{w}_k$ from the first $\tilde{m}_k$ labeled samples.
     for $j = \tilde{m}_k + 1, \ldots, \tilde{m}_{k+1}$
     if $|\hat{w}_k \cdot x_j| > b_k$ **then** let $y_j = \text{sign}(\hat{w}_k \cdot x_j)$
     else label data point x_j by a human expert
     end for
end iterate

Fig. 1. Margin-based Active Learning

is described in Figure 1. Specific choices for the learning algorithm $\mathcal{A}$, sample sizes m_k, and cut-off values b_k depends on various assumptions we will make about the data, which we will investigate in details in the following sections.

3   The Realizable Case Under the Uniform Distribution

We consider here a commonly studied setting in the active learning literature [7,8,9]. Specifically, we assume that the data instances are drawn uniformly from the the unit ball in R^d, and that the labels are consistent with a linear separator w^* going through the origin (that is $P(w^* \cdot xy \leq 0) = 0$). We assume that $\|w^*\|_2 = 1$. It is worth noting that even in this seemingly simple looking scenario, there exists an $\Omega\left(\frac{1}{\epsilon}\left(d + \log\frac{1}{\delta}\right)\right)$ lower bound on the PAC learning sample complexity [12].

We start by informally presenting why active learning is in principle possible, at least when d is constant. We show it is not difficult to improve the labeled data sample complexity from $\tilde{O}(\frac{d}{\epsilon})$ to $\tilde{O}\left(d^{\frac{3}{2}} \log\left(\frac{1}{\epsilon}\right)\right)$. Specifically, let us consider Procedure 1, where $\mathcal{A}$ is a learning algorithm for finding a linear classifier consistent with the training data. Assume that in each iteration k, $\mathcal{A}$ finds a linear separator $\hat{w}_k$, $\|\hat{w}_k\|_2 = 1$ which is consistent with the first $\tilde{m}_k$ labeled examples. We want to ensure that $\text{err}(\hat{w}_k) \leq \frac{1}{2^k}$ (with large probability), which (by standard VC bounds) requires a sample of size $\tilde{m}_k = \tilde{O}(2^k d)$; note that this implies we need to add in each iteration about $m_k = \tilde{m}_{k+1} - \tilde{m}_k = \tilde{O}(2^k d)$ new labeled examples. The desired result will follow if we can show that by choosing appropriate b_k, we only need to ask the human expert to label $\tilde{O}(d^{3/2})$ out of the $m_k = \tilde{O}(2^k d)$ data points and ensure that all m_k data points are correctly labeled (i.e. the examples labeled automatically are in fact correctly labeled).

Note that given our assumption about the data distribution the error rate of any given separator w is $\text{err}(w) = \frac{\theta(w,w^*)}{\pi}$, where $\theta(w, w^*) = \arccos(w \cdot w^*)$. Therefore $\text{err}(\hat{w}_k) \leq 2^{-k}$ implies that $\|\hat{w}_k - w^*\|_2 \leq 2^{-k}\pi$. This implies we can *safely* label all the points with $|\hat{w}_k \cdot x| \geq 2^{-k}\pi$ because w^* and $\hat{w}_k$ predict the same on those examples. The probability of x such that $|\hat{w}_k \cdot x| \leq 2^{-k}\pi$ is $\tilde{O}(2^{-k}\sqrt{d})$ because in high dimensions, the 1-dimensional projection of uniform random variables in the unit ball is approximately a Gaussian variable with variance $1/d$. Therefore if we let $b_k = 2^{-k}\pi$ in the k-th iteration, and draw $m_{k+1} - m_k = \tilde{O}(2^k d)$ new examples to achieve an error rate of $2^{-(k+1)}$ for $\hat{w}_{k+1}$, the expected number of human labels needed is at most $\tilde{O}(d^{\frac{3}{2}})$. This essentially implies the desired result. For a high probability statement, we can use Procedure 2, which is a modification of Procedure 1.

Input: allowed error rate ϵ, probab. of failure δ, a sampling oracle for P_X, a labeling oracle
a sequence of sample sizes $m_k > 0$, $k \in Z^+$; a sequence of cut-off values $b_k > 0$, $k \in Z^+$
Output: weight vector $\hat{w}_s$ of error at most ϵ with probability $1 - \delta$
Draw m_1 examples from P_X, label them and put into a working set $W(1)$.
iterate $k = 1, \ldots, s$
    find a hypothesis $\hat{w}_k$ ($\|\hat{w}_k\|_2 = 1$) consistent with all labeled examples in $W(k)$.
    let $W(k + 1) = W(k)$.
    until m_{k+1} additional data points are labeled, draw sample x from P_X
    if $|\hat{w}_k \cdot x| \geq b_k$, reject x
    otherwise, ask for label of x, and put into $W(k + 1)$
end iterate

Fig. 2. Margin-based Active Learning (separable case)

Note that we can apply our favorite algorithm for finding a consistent linear separator (e.g., SVM for the realizable case, linear programming, etc.) at each iteration of Procedure 2, and the overall procedure is *computationally efficient*.

Theorem 1. *There exists a constant C, s. t. for any $\epsilon, \delta > 0$, using Procedure 2 with $b_k = \frac{\pi}{2^{k-1}}$ and $m_k = Cd^{\frac{1}{2}} \left(d \ln d + \ln \frac{k}{\delta} \right)$, after $s = \lceil \log_2 \frac{1}{\epsilon} \rceil$ iterations, we find a separator of error at most ϵ with probability $1 - \delta$.*

Proof. The proof is a rigorous version of the informal one given earlier. We prove by induction on k that at the k'th iteration, with probability $1 - \delta(1 - 1/(k+1))$, we have $\text{err}(\hat{w}) \leq 2^{-k}$ for all separators $\hat{w}$ consistent with data in the set $W(k)$; in particular, $\text{err}(\hat{w}_k) \leq 2^{-k}$.

For $k = 1$, according to Theorem 7 in Appendix A, we only need $m_1 = O(d + \ln(1/\delta))$ examples to obtain the desired result. In particular, we have $\text{err}(\hat{w}_1) \leq 1/2$ with probability $1 - \delta/2$. Assume now the claim is true for $k - 1$. Then at the k-th iteration, we can let $S_1 = \{x : |\hat{w}_{k-1} \cdot x| \leq b_{k-1}\}$ and $S_2 = \{x : |\hat{w}_{k-1} \cdot x| > b_{k-1}\}$. Using the notation $\text{err}(w|S) = \text{Pr}_x((w \cdot x)(w^* \cdot x) < 0 | x \in S)$, for all $\hat{w}$ we have:

$$\text{err}(\hat{w}) = \text{err}(\hat{w}|S_1) \text{Pr}(S_1) + \text{err}(\hat{w}|S_2) \text{Pr}(S_2).$$

Consider an arbitrary $\hat{w}$ consistent with the data in $W(k - 1)$. By induction hypothesis, we know that with probability at least $1 - \delta(1 - 1/k)$, both $\hat{w}_{k-1}$ and $\hat{w}$ have errors at most 2^{1-k} (because both are consistent with $W(k - 1)$). As discussed earlier, this implies that $\|\hat{w}_{k-1} - w^*\|_2 \leq 2^{1-k}\pi$ and $\|\hat{w} - w^*\|_2 \leq 2^{1-k}\pi$. So, $\forall x \in S_2$, we have $(\hat{w}_{k-1} \cdot x)(\hat{w} \cdot x) > 0$ and $(\hat{w}_{k-1} \cdot x)(w^* \cdot x) > 0$. This implies that $\text{err}(\hat{w}|S_2) = 0$. Now using the estimate provided in Lemma 4 with $\gamma_1 = b_{k-1}$ and $\gamma_2 = 0$, we obtain $\text{Pr}_x(S_1) \leq b_{k-1}\sqrt{4d/\pi}$. Therefore $\text{err}(\hat{w}) \leq 2^{2-k}\sqrt{4\pi d} \cdot \text{err}(\hat{w}|S_1)$, for all $\hat{w}$

consistent with $W(k-1)$. Now, since we are labeling m_k data points in S_1 at iteration $k-1$, it follows from Theorem 7 that we can find C s. t. with probability $1-\delta/(k^2+k)$, for all $\hat{w}$ consistent with the data in $W(k)$, $\text{err}(\hat{w}|S_1)$, the error of $\hat{w}$ on S_1, is no more than $1/(4\sqrt{4\pi d})$. That is we have $\text{err}(\hat{w}) \le 2^{-k}$ with probability $1-\delta((1-1/k)+1/(k^2+k)) = 1-\delta(1-1/(k+1))$ for all $\hat{w}$ consistent with $W(k)$, and in particular $\text{err}(\hat{w}_k) \le 2^{-k}$, as desired. $\square$

The choice of rejection region in Theorem 1 essentially follows the idea in [6]. It was suggested there that one should not sample from a region (S_2 in the proof) in which all classifiers in the current version space (in our case, classifiers consistent with the labeled examples in $W(k)$) predict the same label. A more general version, with theoretical analysis, was considered in [2]. Here we have used a more a refined VC-bound for the realizable case, e.g., Theorem 7, to get a better bound. However, the strategy of choosing b_k in Theorem 1 (thus the idea of [6]) is not optimal. This can be seen from the proof, in which we showed $\text{err}(\hat{w}_s|S_2) = 0$. If we enlarge S_2 (using a smaller b_k), we can still ensure that $\text{err}(\hat{w}_s|S_2)$ is small; furthermore, $\text{Pr}(S_1)$ becomes smaller, which allows us to use fewer labeled examples to achieve the same reduction in error. Therefore in order to show that we can achieve an improvement from $\tilde{O}\left(\frac{d}{\epsilon}\right)$ to $\tilde{O}\left(d\log\left(\frac{1}{\epsilon}\right)\right)$ as in [9], we need a more *aggressive* strategy. Specifically, at round k we set as margin parameter $b_k = \tilde{O}\left(\frac{\log(k)}{2^k\sqrt{d}}\right)$, and in consequence use fewer examples to transition between rounds. In order to prove correctness we need to refine the analysis as follows:

Theorem 2. *There exists a constant C s. t. for $d \ge 4$, and for any $\epsilon, \delta > 0$, $\epsilon < 1/4$, using Procedure 2 with $m_k = C\sqrt{\ln(1+k)}\left(d\ln(1+\ln k) + \ln\frac{k}{\delta}\right)$ and $b_k = 2^{1-k}\pi d^{-1/2}\sqrt{5+\ln(1+k)}$, after $s = \lceil\log_2\frac{1}{\epsilon}\rceil - 2$ iterations, we find a separator of error $\le \epsilon$ with probability $1-\delta$.*

Proof. As in Theorem 1, we prove by induction on k that at the k's iteration, for $k \le s$, with probability at least $1-\delta(1-1/(k+1))$, we $\text{err}(\hat{w}) \le 2^{-k-2}$ for all choices of $\hat{w}$ consistent with data in the working set $W(k)$; in particular $\text{err}(\hat{w}_k) \le 2^{-k-2}$.

For $k = 1$, according to Theorem 7, we only need $m_k = O(d+\ln(1/\delta))$ examples to obtain the desired result; in particular, we have $\text{err}(\hat{w}_1) \le 2^{-k-2}$ with probability $1-\delta/(k+1)$. Assume now the claim is true for $k-1$ ($k > 1$). Then at the k-th iteration, we can let $S_1 = \{x : |\hat{w}_{k-1} \cdot x| \le b_{k-1}\}$ and $S_2 = \{x : |\hat{w}_{k-1} \cdot x| > b_{k-1}\}$. Consider an arbitrary $\hat{w}$ consistent with the data in $W(k-1)$. By induction hypothesis, we know that with probability $1-\delta(1-1/k)$, both $\hat{w}_{k-1}$ and $\hat{w}$ have errors at most 2^{-k-1}, implying $\theta(\hat{w}_{k-1}, w^*) \le 2^{-k-1}\pi$ and $\theta(\hat{w}, w^*) \le 2^{-k-1}\pi$. Therefore $\theta(\hat{w}, \hat{w}_{k-1}) \le 2^{-k}\pi$. Let $\tilde{\beta} = 2^{-k}\pi$ and using $\cos\tilde{\beta}/\sin\tilde{\beta} \le 1/\tilde{\beta}$ and $\sin\tilde{\beta} \le \tilde{\beta}$ it is easy to verify that $b_{k-1} \ge 2\sin\tilde{\beta}d^{-1/2}\sqrt{5+\ln\left(1+\sqrt{\ln\max(1,\cos\tilde{\beta}/\sin\tilde{\beta})}\right)}$. By Lemma 7, we have both

$$\text{Pr}_x\left[(\hat{w}_{k-1} \cdot x)(\hat{w} \cdot x) < 0, x \in S_2\right] \le \frac{\sin\tilde{\beta}}{e^5\cos\tilde{\beta}} \le \frac{\sqrt{2}\tilde{\beta}}{e^5} \quad \text{and}$$
$$\text{Pr}_x\left[(\hat{w}_{k-1} \cdot x)(w^* \cdot x) < 0, x \in S_2\right] \le \frac{\sin\tilde{\beta}}{e^5\cos\tilde{\beta}} \le \frac{\sqrt{2}\tilde{\beta}}{e^5}.$$

Taking the sum, we obtain $\Pr_x \left[(\hat{w} \cdot x)(w^* \cdot x) < 0, x \in S_2 \right] \leq \frac{2\sqrt{2}\tilde{\beta}}{e^5} \leq 2^{-(k+3)}$. Using now Lemma 4 we get that for all $\hat{w}$ consistent with the data in $W(k-1)$ we have:

$$\text{err}(\hat{w}) \leq \text{err}(\hat{w}|S_1)\Pr(S_1) + 2^{-(k+3)} \leq \text{err}(\hat{w}_k|S_1)b_{k-1}\sqrt{4d/\pi} + 2^{-(k+3)}$$

$$\leq 2^{-(k+2)}\left(\text{err}(\hat{w}|S_1)16\sqrt{4\pi}\sqrt{5+\ln(1+k)}+1/2\right).$$

Since we are labelling m_k points in S_1 at iteration $k-1$, we know from Theorem 7 that $\exists C$ s. t. with probability $1 - \delta/(k+k^2)$ we have $\text{err}(\hat{w}_k|S_1)16\sqrt{4\pi}\sqrt{5+\ln(1+k)} \leq 0.5$ for all $\hat{w}$ consistent with $W(k)$; so, with probability $1-\delta((1-1/k)+1/(k+k^2)) = 1 - \delta(1 - 1/(k+1))$, we have $\text{err}(\hat{w}) \leq 2^{-k-2}$ for all $\hat{w}$ consistent with $W(k)$. □

The bound in Theorem 2 is generally better than the one in Theorem 1 due to the improved dependency on d in m_k. However, m_k depends on $\sqrt{\ln k}\ln\ln k$, for $k \leq \lceil \log_2 \frac{1}{\epsilon} \rceil - 2$. Therefore when $d \ll \ln k(\ln\ln k)^2$, Theorem 1 offers a better bound. Note that the strategy used in Theorem 2 is more aggressive than the strategy used in the selective sampling algorithm of [2,6]. Indeed, we do not sample from the entire region of uncertainty – but we sample just from a subregion carefully chosen. This helps us to get rid of the undesired $d^{1/2}$. Clearly, our analysis also holds with very small modifications when the input distribution comes from a high dimensional Gaussian.

4   The Non-realizable Case Under the Uniform Distribution

We show that a result similar to Theorem 2 can be obtained even for non-separable problems. The non-realizable (noisy) case for active learning in the context of classification was recently explored in [2,4]. We consider here a model which is related to the simple one-dimensional problem in [4], which assumes that the data satisfy the increasingly popular Tsybakov small noise condition along the decision boundary[14]. We first consider a simple version which still leads to exponential convergence similar to Theorem 2. Specifically, we still assume that the data instances are drawn uniformly from the the unit ball in R^d, and a linear classifier w^* is the Bayes classifier. However, we do not assume that the Bayes error is zero. We consider the following low noise condition: there exists a known parameter $\beta > 0$ such that:

$$P_X(|P(Y=1|X) - P(Y=-1|X)| \geq 4\beta) = 1.$$

In supervised learning, such a condition can lead to fast convergence rates. As we will show in this section, the condition can also be used to quantify the effectiveness of active-learning. The key point is that this assumption implies the stability condition required for active learning:

$$\beta \min\left(1, \frac{4\theta(w,w^*)}{\pi}\right)^{1/(1-\alpha)} \leq \text{err}(w) - \text{err}(w^*) \tag{1}$$

with $\alpha = 0$. We analyze here a more general setting with $\alpha \in [0, 1)$. As mentioned already, the one dimensional setting was examined in [4]. We call $\text{err}(w) - \text{err}(w^*)$ the *excess error* of w. In this setting, Procedure 2 needs to be slightly modified, as in Figure 3.

Input: allowed error rate ϵ, probab. of failure δ, a sampling oracle for P_X, and a labeling oracle
   a sequence of sample sizes $m_k > 0$, $k \in Z^+$; a sequence of cut-off values $b_k > 0$, $k \in Z^+$
   a sequence of hypothesis space radii $r_k > 0$, $k \in Z^+$;
   a sequence of precision values $\epsilon_k > 0$, $k \in Z^+$
Output: weight vector $\hat{w}_s$ of excess error at most ϵ with probability $1 - \delta$
Pick random $\hat{w}_0$: $\|\hat{w}_0\|_2 = 1$.
Draw m_1 examples from P_X, label them and put into a working set W.
iterate $k = 1, \ldots, s$
   find $\hat{w}_k \in B(\hat{w}_{k-1}, r_k)$ ($\|\hat{w}_k\|_2 = 1$) to approximately minimize training error:
   $\sum_{(x,y) \in W} I(\hat{w}_k \cdot xy) \leq \min_{w \in B(\hat{w}_{k-1}, r_k)} \sum_{(x,y) \in W} I(w \cdot xy) + m_k \epsilon_k$.
   clear the working set W
   until m_{k+1} additional data points are labeled, draw sample x from P_X
   if $|\hat{w}_k \cdot x| \geq b_k$, reject x
   otherwise, ask for label of x, and put into W
end iterate

Fig. 3. Margin-based Active Learning (non-separable case)

Theorem 3. *Let $d \geq 4$. Assume there exists a weight vector w^* s. t. the stability condition (1) holds. Then there exists a constant C, s. t. for any $\epsilon, \delta > 0$, $\epsilon < \beta/8$, using Procedure 3 with $b_k = 2^{-(1-\alpha)k} \pi d^{-1/2} \sqrt{5 + \alpha k \ln 2 - \ln \beta + \ln(2 + k)}$, $r_k = 2^{-(1-\alpha)k-2}\pi$ for $k > 1$, $r_1 = \pi$, $\epsilon_k = 2^{-\alpha(k-1)-4} \beta / \sqrt{5 + \alpha k \ln 2 - \ln \beta + \ln(1+k)}$, and $m_k = C \epsilon_k^{-2} \left(d + \ln \frac{k}{\delta}\right)$, after $s = \lceil \log_2(\beta/\epsilon) \rceil$ iterations, we find a separator with excess error $\leq \epsilon$ with probability $1 - \delta$.*

Proof. The proof is similar to that of Theorem 2. We prove by induction on k that after $k \leq s$ iterations, $\mathrm{err}(\hat{w}_k) - \mathrm{err}(w^*) \leq 2^{-k}\beta$ with probability $1 - \delta(1 - 1/(k+1))$.

For $k = 1$, according to Theorem 8, we only need $m_k = \beta^{-2} O(d + \ln(k/\delta))$ examples to obtain $\hat{w}_1$ with excess error $2^{-k}\beta$ with probability $1 - \delta/(k+1)$. Assume now the claim is true for $k - 1$ ($k \geq 2$). Then at the k-th iteration, we can let $S_1 = \{x : |\hat{w}_{k-1} \cdot x| \leq b_{k-1}\}$ and $S_2 = \{x : |\hat{w}_{k-1} \cdot x| > b_{k-1}\}$. By induction hypothesis, we know that with probability at least $1 - \delta(1 - 1/k)$, $\hat{w}_{k-1}$ has excess errors at most $2^{-k+1}\beta$, implying $\theta(\hat{w}_{k-1}, w^*) \leq 2^{-(1-\alpha)(k-1)}\pi/4$. By assumption, $\theta(\hat{w}_{k-1}, \hat{w}_k) \leq 2^{-(1-\alpha)k-2}\pi$. Let $\tilde{\beta} = 2^{-(1-\alpha)k-2}\pi$ and using $\cos \tilde{\beta} / \sin \tilde{\beta} \leq 1/\tilde{\beta}$ and $\sin \tilde{\beta} \leq \tilde{\beta}$, it is easy to verify

that $b_{k-1} \geq 2 \sin \tilde{\beta} d^{-1/2} \sqrt{5 + \alpha k \ln 2 - \ln \beta + \ln \left(1 + \sqrt{\ln(\cos \tilde{\beta} / \sin \tilde{\beta})}\right)}$. From

Lemma 7, we have both
$$\Pr_x \left[(\hat{w}_{k-1} \cdot x)(\hat{w}_k \cdot x) < 0, x \in S_2\right] \leq \frac{\sin \tilde{\beta}}{e^5 \beta^{-1} 2^{\alpha k} \cos \tilde{\beta}} \leq \frac{\sqrt{2}\tilde{\beta}\beta}{2^{\alpha k} e^5} \quad \text{and}$$
$$\Pr_x \left[(\hat{w}_{k-1} \cdot x)(w^* \cdot x) < 0, x \in S_2\right] \leq \frac{\sin \tilde{\beta}}{e^5 \beta^{-1} 2^{\alpha k} \cos \tilde{\beta}} \leq \frac{\sqrt{2}\tilde{\beta}\beta}{2^{\alpha k} e^5}.$$

Taking the sum, we obtain $\Pr_x \left[(\hat{w}_k \cdot x)(w^* \cdot x) < 0, x \in S_2\right] \leq \frac{2\sqrt{2}\tilde{\beta}\beta}{2^{\alpha k} e^5} \leq 2^{-(k+1)}\beta$. Therefore we have (using Lemma 4):

$$\mathrm{err}(\hat{w}_k) - \mathrm{err}(w^*) \leq (\mathrm{err}(\hat{w}_k|S_1) - \mathrm{err}(w^*|S_1)) \Pr(S_1) + 2^{-(k+1)}\beta$$
$$\leq (\mathrm{err}(\hat{w}_k|S_1) - \mathrm{err}(w^*|S_1)) b_{k-1} \sqrt{4d/\pi} + 2^{-(k+1)}\beta$$
$$\leq 2^{-k}\beta \left((\mathrm{err}(\hat{w}_k|S_1) - \mathrm{err}(w^*|S_1))\sqrt{\pi}/(4\epsilon_k) + 1/2\right).$$

By Theorem 7, we can choose C s. t. with m_k samples, we obtain $\text{err}(\hat{w}_k|S_1) - \text{err}(w^*|S_1) \leq 2\epsilon_k/\sqrt{\pi}$ with probability $1-\delta/(k+k^2)$. Therefore $\text{err}(\hat{w}_k) - \text{err}(w^*) \leq 2^{-k}\beta$ with probability $1 - \delta((1 - 1/k) + 1/(k + k^2)) = 1 - \delta(1 - 1/(k+1))$. □

If $\alpha = 0$, then we can achieve exponential convergence similar to Theorem 2, even for *noisy* problems. However, for $\alpha \in (0, 1)$, we must label $\sum_k m_k = O(\epsilon^{-2\alpha} \ln(1/\epsilon)(d + \ln(s/\delta))$ examples[2] to achieve an error rate of ϵ That is, we only get a polynomial improvement compared to the batch learning case (with sample complexity between $O(\epsilon^{-2})$ and $O(\epsilon^{-1})$). In general, one *cannot* improve such polynomial behavior – see [4] for some simple one-dimensional examples.

Note: Instead of rejecting x when $|\hat{w}_k \cdot x| \geq b_k$, we can add them to W using the automatic labels from $\hat{w}_k$. We can then remove the requirement $\hat{w}_k \in B(\hat{w}_{k-1}, r_k)$ (thus removing the parameters r_k). The resulting procedure will have the same convergence behavior as Theorem 3 because the probability of making error by $\hat{w}_k$ when $|\hat{w}_k \cdot x| \geq b_k$ is no more than $2^{-(k+2)}\beta$.

5   Dimension Independent Bounds

Although we showed that active learning can improve sample complexity, the bounds depend on the dimensionality d. In many practical problems, such dependency can be removed if the classifier can separate the data with large margin. We consider the following simple case, with x drawn from a d-dimensional Gaussian with bounded total variance: $x \sim N(0, \Sigma)$, $\Sigma = \text{diag}(\sigma_1^2, \ldots, \sigma_d^2)$ and $\sigma_1 \geq \cdots \geq \sigma_d > 0$. Note that $\mathbf{E}_x\|x\|_2^2 = \sum_j \sigma_j^2$. The Gaussian assumption can also be replaced by other similar assumptions such as uniform distribution in an ellipsoid. We employ the Gaussian assumption for computational simplicity. We assume further that the label is consistent with a weight vector w^* with $\|w^*\|_2 = 1$. However, if we do not impose any restrictions on w^*, then it is not possible to learn w^* without the d-dependence. A standard assumption that becomes popular in recent years is to assume that w^* achieves a good margin distribution. In particular, we may impose the following margin distribution condition $\forall \gamma > 0$:

$$P_x(|w^* \cdot x| \leq \gamma) \leq \frac{2\gamma}{\sqrt{2\pi}\sigma} \tag{2}$$

Condition (2) says that the probability of small margin is small. Since the projection $w^* \cdot x$ is normal with variance $\sigma^2 = \sum_j \sigma_j^2 (w_j^*)^2$, the margin condition (2) can be replaced by

$$\|w^*\|_\Sigma \geq \sigma \tag{3}$$

where $\|\xi\|_\Sigma = \sqrt{\sum_j \xi_j^2 \sigma_j^2}$, which says that the variance of x projected to w^* is at least σ. This condition restricts the hypothesis space containing w^* so that we may develop a learning bound that is independent of d. Although one can explicitly impose a margin constraint based on (3), for simplicity, we shall consider a different method here that

---

[2] We are ignoring dependence on β here.

approximates w^* with a vector in a small dimensional space. Lemma 1 shows that it is possible. For $w, w' \in R^d$, we define $\theta_\Sigma(w, w') = \arccos \frac{\sum_j \sigma_j^2 w_j w_j'}{\|w\|_\Sigma \|w'\|_\Sigma}$.

Lemma 1. *If w^* with $\|w^*\|_2 = 1$ satisfies (3) and let $w^*[k] = [w_1^*, \ldots, w_k^*, 0, \ldots, 0]$, then $\sin \theta_\Sigma(w^*, w^*[k]) \leq \sigma_{k+1}/\sigma$.*

Proof. By assumption, we have:
$$\sin(\theta_\Sigma(w^*, w^*[k]))^2 = \frac{\sum_{j=k+1}^d \sigma_j(w_j^*)^2}{\sum_{j=1}^d \sigma_j^2(w_j^*)^2} \leq \sigma_{k+1}^2 \frac{\sum_{j=k+1}^d (w_j^*)^2}{\sum_{j=1}^d \sigma_j^2(w_j^*)^2} \leq \sigma_{k+1}^2 \frac{\sum_j (w_j^*)^2}{\sum_j \sigma_j^2(w_j^*)^2} =$$
$(\sigma_{k+1}/\sigma)^2$, as desired. $\qquad\qquad\qquad\qquad\qquad\qquad\qquad\qquad\qquad\qquad\qquad\qquad\qquad\qquad\square$

Note that the error of classifier w is given by $\mathrm{err}(w) = \frac{\theta_\Sigma(w, w^*)}{\pi}$. Therefore Lemma 1 shows that under the margin distribution condition (2), it is possible to approximate w^* using a low dimensional $w^*[k]$ with small error. We can now prove that:

Theorem 4. *Assume that the true separator w^* with $\|w^*\|_2 = 1$ satisfies (3). There exists C s. t. $\forall \epsilon, \delta > 0$, $\epsilon < 1/8$, using Procedure 4 with $b_k = 2^{1-k}\pi\sqrt{5 + \ln(1 + k)}$, $b_0 = 0$, $d_k = \inf\{\ell : \sin(2^{-(k+4)}e^{-b_{k-1}^2/2}\pi \geq \sigma_{\ell+1}/\sigma\}$, $r_k = 2^{-k}\pi$ for $k > 1$, $r_1 = \pi$, $\epsilon_k = 2^{-5}/\sqrt{5 + \ln(1 + k)}$, and $m_k = C\epsilon_k^{-2}\left(d_k + \ln\frac{k}{\delta}\right)$, after $s = \lceil \log_2\left(\frac{1}{\epsilon}\right)\rceil - 2$ iterations, we find a separator with excess error $\leq \epsilon$ with probability $1 - \delta$.*

Proof. We prove by induction on k that after $k \leq s$ iterations, $\mathrm{err}(\hat{w}_k) - \mathrm{err}(w^*) \leq 2^{-(k+2)}$ with probability $1 - \delta(1 - 1/(k + 1))$. Note that by Lemma 1, the choice of d_k ensures that $\theta_\Sigma(w^*, w^*[d_k]) \leq 2^{-(k+3)}\pi$, and thus $\mathrm{err}(w^*[d_k]) \leq 2^{-(k+3)}$.

For $k = 1$, according to Theorem 7, we only need $m_k = O(d_k + \ln(k/\delta))$ examples to obtain $\hat{w}_1 \in \mathcal{H}[d_k]$ with excess error $2^{-(k+2)}$ with probability $1 - \delta/(k+1)$. Assume now the claim is true for $k - 1$ ($k \geq 2$). Then at the k-th iteration, we can let $S_1 = \{x : |\hat{w}_{k-1} \cdot x| \leq b_{k-1}\}$ and $S_2 = \{x : |\hat{w}_{k-1} \cdot x| > b_{k-1}\}$. By induction hypothesis, we know that with probability at least $1 - \delta(1 - 1/k)$, $\hat{w}_{k-1}$ has excess errors at most $2^{-(k+1)}$, implying $\theta(\hat{w}_{k-1}, w^*) \leq 2^{-(k+1)}\pi$. By assumption, $\theta(\hat{w}_{k-1}, \hat{w}_k) \leq 2^{-k}\pi$. Let $\tilde{\beta} = 2^{-k}\pi$ and use $\cos\tilde{\beta}/\sin\tilde{\beta} \leq 1/\tilde{\beta}$ and $\sin\tilde{\beta} \leq \tilde{\beta}$, it is easy to verify that the following inequality holds $b_{k-1} \geq \sqrt{2}\sin\tilde{\beta}\sqrt{5 + \ln\left(1 + \sqrt{\ln(\cos\tilde{\beta}/\sin\tilde{\beta})}\right)}$.

Let $P = \mathrm{Pr}_x\left[(\hat{w}_{k-1} \cdot x)(\hat{w}_k \cdot x) < 0, x \in S_2\right]$, and let $(\xi_1, \xi_2) \sim N(0, I_{2\times 2})$ and $\theta = \theta_\Sigma(\hat{w}_k, \hat{w}_{k-1})$. By Lemma 3, we have
$$P = 2\Pr_x[\xi_1 \leq 0, \xi_1 \cos(\theta) + \xi_2 \sin(\theta) \geq b_{k-1}]$$
$$\leq 2\Pr_x\left[\xi_1 \leq 0, \xi_1 + \xi_2 \sin(\tilde{\beta})/\cos(\tilde{\beta}) \geq b_{k-1}/\cos(\tilde{\beta})\right]$$
$$\leq \frac{\sin\tilde{\beta}}{\cos\tilde{\beta}}\left(1 + \sqrt{\ln(\cos(\tilde{\beta})/\sin(\tilde{\beta}))}\right)e^{-b_{k-1}^2/(2\sin(\tilde{\beta})^2)} \leq \frac{\sqrt{2}\tilde{\beta}}{e^5}.$$

Similarly, we also have $\mathrm{Pr}_x\left[(\hat{w}_{k-1} \cdot x)(w^* \cdot x) < 0, x \in S_2\right] \leq \frac{\sqrt{2}\tilde{\beta}}{e^5}$. This implies that $\mathrm{Pr}_x\left[(\hat{w}_k \cdot x)(w^* \cdot x) < 0, x \in S_2\right] \leq \frac{2\sqrt{2}\tilde{\beta}}{e^5} \leq 2^{-(k+3)}$. Now using Lemma 2, we have
$$\mathrm{err}(\hat{w}_k) \leq \mathrm{err}(\hat{w}_k|S_1)\Pr(S_1) + 2^{-(k+3)} \leq \mathrm{err}(\hat{w}_k|S_1)b_{k-1}/\sqrt{2\pi} + 2^{-(k+3)}$$
$$\leq 2^{-(k+2)}\left(\mathrm{err}(\hat{w}_k|S_1)8\sqrt{5 + \ln(1 + k)} + 1/2\right).$$

Our choice of d_k ensures that $\mathrm{err}(w^*[d_k]|S_1) \leq 2^{-6}/\sqrt{5 + \ln k}$. From Theorem 8, we know it is possible to choose a constant C such that with m_k samples we have $\mathrm{err}(\hat{w}_k|S_1)8\sqrt{5 + \ln(1 + k)} \leq 0.5$ with probability $1 - \delta/(k + k^2)$. Hence $\mathrm{err}(\hat{w}_k) \leq 2^{-k-2}$ with probability $1 - \delta((1 - 1/k) + 1/(k + k^2)) = 1 - \delta(1 - 1/(k + 1))$. $\square$

Input: allowed error rate ϵ, probab. of failure δ, a sampling oracle for P_X, and a labeling oracle
  $\Sigma = \mathrm{diag}(\sigma_1^2, \ldots, \sigma_d^2)$, a sequence of sample sizes $m_k > 0$, $k \in Z^+$
  a sequence of cut-off values $b_k > 0$, $k \in Z^+$ and one of hypothesis space radii $r_k > 0$, $k \in Z^+$
  a sequence of hypothesis space dimensions $d_k > 0$, $k \in Z^+$
  a sequence precision values $\epsilon_k > 0$, $k \in Z^+$.
Output: weight vector $\hat{w}_s$ of excess error at most ϵ with probability $1 - \delta$
Pick random $\hat{w}_0$: $\|\hat{w}_0\|_\Sigma = 1$.
Draw m_1 examples from P_X, label them and put into a working set W.
iterate $k = 1, \ldots, s$
  find $\hat{w}_k \in \mathcal{H}[d_k]$ ($\|\hat{w}_k\|_\Sigma = 1$, $\|\hat{w}_k - \hat{w}_{k-1}\|_\Sigma \leq 2(1 - \cos(r_k))$) such that
    $\sum_{(x,y) \in W} I(\hat{w}_k \cdot xy) \leq m_k \epsilon_k$,
    where $\mathcal{H}[d_k] = \{w \in R^d : w_{d_k+1} = \cdots = w_d = 0\}$
  clear the working set W
  until m_{k+1} additional data points are labeled, draw sample x from P_X
  if $|\hat{w}_k \cdot x| \geq b_k$, reject x
  otherwise, ask for label of x, and put into W
end iterate

Fig. 4. Margin-based Active Learning (with low-dimensional approximation)

Using a more refined ratio VC-bound, one can easily improve the choice of $m_k = C\epsilon_k^{-2}(d_k + \ln(k/\delta))$ to $m_k = C\epsilon_k^{-1}(d_k \ln \epsilon^{-1} + \ln(k/\delta))$ in Theorem 4. In Algorithm 4, instead of putting constraint of $\hat{w}_k$ using r_k, one can also use $\hat{w}_{k-1}$ to label data x and put them into the working set W such that $|\hat{w}_{k-1} \cdot x| \geq b_{k-1}$, which introduces error at most $2^{-(k+3)}$. One may then train a $\hat{w}_k$ using labeled data in W without the constraint $\|\hat{w}_k - \hat{w}_{k-1}\|_\Sigma \leq 2(1 - \cos(r_k))$; the results will be similar.

The sample complexity of Procedure 4 depends on d_k which is determined by the decay of σ_k instead of d. In particular we can consider a few possible decays with $d = \infty$:

- Assume $\sigma_k \leq O(2^{-\beta k})$ with constant $\beta > 0$, which is the eigenvalue decaying behavior for exponential kernels. In this case d_k is $O(k/\beta)$. Therefore we only need $m_k = O(k^2 \ln k)$ examples at each iteration k.
- Assume $\sigma_k \leq O(k^{-\beta})$ with constant $\beta > 0$, which is the eigenvalue decaying behavior for spline kernels. In this case d_k is $O(2^{k/\beta})$. Therefore we need $m_k = \tilde{O}(2^{k/\beta})$ examples at each iteration k. The total samples needed to achieve accuracy ϵ is $\tilde{O}(\epsilon^{-1/\beta})$. Note that when $\beta > 1$, we achieve faster than $O(1/\epsilon)$.
- When the total variation is bounded: $\sum_j \sigma_j^2 \leq 1$, which means that $\|x\|_2$ is bounded on average (corresponding to standard large margin kernel methods with bounded $\|x\|_2$), then $\sigma_k \leq 1/\sqrt{k}$. Therefore we can take $d_k = O(2^{2k})$ and $m_k = \tilde{O}(2^{2k})$. The total sample size needed to achieve accuracy ϵ is $\tilde{O}(\epsilon^{-2})$. The constant will

depend on the margin $\sigma/\sqrt{\sum_j \sigma_j^2}$ but independent of the dimensionality d which is infinity.

6 A General Analysis for Margin Based Active Learning

We show here a general bound for Algorithm 1 based on assumptions about the algorithm $\mathcal{A}$, the sample sizes m_k, and the thresholds b_k. This is a more abstract version of the same underlying idea used in proving the results presented earlier in the paper.

Theorem 5. *Consider Algorithm 1. Let $\mathcal{A}$ be empirical risk minimization algorithm with respect to the hypothesis space $\mathcal{H}$ and assume that given $\epsilon, \delta > 0$, with $m \geq M(\mathcal{H}, \epsilon, \delta)$ samples, we have distribution free uniform convergence bound. I.e.:*

$$P\left[\sup_{w \in \mathcal{H}} \left| \mathbf{E} I(w \cdot xy \leq 0) - \tfrac{1}{m} \sum_{i=1}^{m} I(w \cdot x_i y_i \leq 0) \right| \leq \epsilon\right] \geq 1 - \delta. \quad (4)$$

Let $\delta \in (0,1)$ be the probability of failure. Assume that we ensure that at each stage k:

- *Choose margin threshold b_{k-1} such that with probability $1 - 0.5\delta/(k+k^2)$, $\exists \hat{w}_*$:* $P((\hat{w}_{k-1} \cdot x)(\hat{w}_* \cdot x) \leq 0, |\hat{w}_{k-1} \cdot x| > b_{k-1}) \leq 2^{-(k+2)}$ *and* $P(\hat{w}_* \cdot xy \leq 0) \leq \inf_{w \in \mathcal{H}} \mathrm{err}(w) + 2^{-(k+2)}$.
- *Take $m_k = \tilde{m}_k - \tilde{m}_{k-1} = M(\mathcal{H}, 2^{-(k+3)}, 0.5\delta/(k+k^2))$.*

Then after s iterations, $\mathrm{err}(\hat{w}_s) \leq \inf_{w \in \mathcal{H}} \mathrm{err}(w) + 2^{-s}$ with probability at least $1 - \delta$.

Proof Sketch: By the assumption on m_k, with probability $1 - \delta/(k+k^2)$, we have: $\mathrm{err}(\hat{w}_k) \leq P(\hat{w}_k \cdot xy \leq 0, x \in S_1) + P((\hat{w}_k \cdot x)(\hat{w}_* \cdot x) \leq 0, x \in S_2) + P(\hat{w}_* \cdot xy \leq 0, x \in S_2) \leq P(\hat{w}_k \cdot xy \leq 0, x \in S_1) + P((\hat{w}_k \cdot x)(\hat{w}_{k-1} \cdot x) \leq 0, x \in S_2) + P(\hat{w}_* \cdot xy \leq 0, x \in S_2) + 2^{-(k+2)} \leq P(\hat{w}_* \cdot xy \leq 0, x \in S_1) + P((\hat{w}_* \cdot x)(\hat{w}_{k-1} \cdot x) \leq 0, x \in S_2) + P(\hat{w}_* \cdot xy \leq 0, x \in S_2) + 2 \cdot 2^{-(k+2)} \leq \mathrm{err}(\hat{w}_*) + 3 \cdot 2^{-(k+2)} \leq \inf_{w \in \mathcal{H}} \mathrm{err}(w) + 2^{-k}$. $\quad\square$

In order to obtain a robust active learning algorithm that does not depend on the underlying data generation assumptions, one can estimate $M(\mathcal{H}, \epsilon, \delta)$ using sample complexity bounds. For example, we have used standard bounds such as Theorem 8 in earlier sections. A similar approach is taken in [2]. One can also replace (4) with a ratio uniform convergence bound such similar to the realizable case VC bound in Theorem 7. For some problems, this may lead to improvements.

In principle, it is also possible to estimate b_k using theoretical analysis. We only need to find b_k such that when $\hat{w}_k \cdot x > b_k$, no weight vector w can disagree with $\hat{w}_k$ with probability more than $2^{-(k+3)}$ if $\mathrm{err}(w)$ is within 2^{-k} of the optimal value. However, the computation is more complicated, and requires that we know the underlying distribution of x. Note that in the theorems proved in earlier sections, we were able to estimate b_k because specific distributions of x were considered. Without such knowledge, practitioners often pick b_k by heuristics. Picking the right b_k is necessary for achieving good performance in our analysis. One practical solution is to perturb $\hat{w}_k$ (e.g. using bootstrap samples) and find b_k such that the perturbed vectors agrees with $\hat{w}_k$ with large probability when $\hat{w}_k \cdot x > b_k$. Another possibility is to use a procedure that tests for the best b_k. This is relatively easy to do for realizable problems, as shown in Figure 5. We can then prove that:

Theorem 6. *Consider Algorithm 5. Let $\mathcal{A}$ be the empirical risk minimization algorithm with respect to the hypothesis space $\mathcal{H}$, and assume that $\forall \epsilon, \delta > 0$, with $m \geq M(\mathcal{H}, \epsilon, \delta)$ samples we have distribution free uniform convergence bound: i.e. with probability $1 - \delta$, $\forall w \in \mathcal{H}$, we have both*

$$\mathbf{E}I(w \cdot xy \leq 0) \leq \tfrac{2}{m} \sum_{i=1}^{m} I(w \cdot x_i y_i \leq 0) + \epsilon \quad \text{and}$$

$$\tfrac{1}{m} \sum_{i=1}^{m} I(w \cdot x_i y_i \leq 0) \leq 2\mathbf{E}I(w \cdot xy \leq 0) + \epsilon.$$

Let $N(\epsilon, \delta)$ be a distribution free convergence bound for the binary random variables $\xi \in \{0, 1\}$: i. e. for $m \geq N(\epsilon, \delta)$ with probability $1 - \delta$ we have both

$$\mathbf{E}\xi \leq \tfrac{1.5}{m} \sum_{i=1}^{m} \xi_i + \epsilon \text{ and } \tfrac{1}{m} \sum_{i=1}^{m} \xi_i \leq 1.5\mathbf{E}\xi + \epsilon.$$

Let $m_k = M(\mathcal{H}, 2^{-(k+5)}, 0.5\delta/(k+k^2))$, $n_k = N(2^{-(k+3)}, 0.25\delta/(\ell_k(k+k^2)))$, and $\epsilon_k = 2^{-(k+1)}$. Assume also we take b_{k,ℓ_k} s.t. $P(\hat{w}_{k-1} \cdot x \geq b_{k,\ell_k}) \leq 2^{-(k+5)}$.

If $\inf_{w \in \mathcal{H}} I(w \cdot xy \leq 0) = 0$, then after s iterations, with probability $1 - \delta$, we have:

- *At each iteration $k \leq s$, before the for loop over q stops: $\forall \hat{w}_* \in \mathcal{H}$ such that $P(\hat{w}_* \cdot xy \leq 0) > 2^{-(k+6)}$: $P((\hat{w}_{k-1} \cdot x)(\hat{w}_* \cdot x) \leq 0, |\hat{w}_{k-1} \cdot x| > b_{k,q}) > 2^{-(k+6)}$.*
- *The final error is $\mathrm{err}(\hat{w}_s) \leq 2^{-s}$.*

We omit the proof here due to lack of space. Note that Theorem 6 implies that we only need to label a portion of data, with margins b_{k,q_k}, where q_k is the smallest q such that $\exists \hat{w}_* \in \mathcal{H}$ with $P(\hat{w}_* \cdot xy \leq 0) \leq 2^{-(k+6)}$ and $P((\hat{w}_{k-1} \cdot x)(\hat{w}_* \cdot x) \leq 0, |\hat{w}_{k-1} \cdot x| > b_{k,q}) \leq 2^{-(k+6)}$. It does not require us to estimate b_k as in earlier theorems. However, it requires an extra n_k labeled data at each iteration to select the optimal margin $b_{k,q}$. This penalty is usually small because the testing sample size n_k is often significantly smaller than m_k. For example, for d dimensional linear classifiers consider earlier, m_k needs to

Input: a learning algorithm $\mathcal{A}$ that learns a weight vector from labeled data
   a sequence of training sample sizes $m_1, \ldots, m_s$;
   a sequence of validation sample sizes $n_1, \ldots, n_s$ and one of acceptance thresholds $\epsilon_1, \ldots, \epsilon_s$
   a sequence of cut-off points $\{-1 = b_{k,0} < b_{k,1} < \cdots < b_{k,\ell_k}\}$ $(k = 1, \ldots, s)$
Output: classifier $\hat{w}_s$
label data points $x_1, \ldots, x_{m_1}$ by a human expert and use $\mathcal{A}$ to learn weight vector $\hat{w}_1$.
iterate $k = 2, \ldots, s$
   generate and label n_k samples $(x'_1, y'_1), \ldots, (x'_{n_k}, y'_{n_k})$
   generate m_k samples x_j with labels $y_j = \mathrm{sign}(\hat{w}_{k-1} \cdot x_j)$ $(j = 1, \ldots, m_k)$
   for $q = 1, \ldots, \ell_k$
     label y_j by a human expert if $|\hat{w}_{k-1} \cdot x_j| \in (b_{k,q-1}, b_{k,q}]$ $(j = 1, \ldots, m_k)$
     use $\mathcal{A}$ to learn weight vector $\hat{w}_k$ from examples (x_j, y_j) $(j = 1, \ldots, m_k)$
     if (error of $\hat{w}_k$ on (x'_j, y'_j) $(j = 1, \ldots, n_k)$ is less than ϵ_k) **break**
   end for
end iterate

Fig. 5. Margin-based Active Learning with Testing

depend on d but n_k can be d-independent. Therefore it is possible to achieve significant improvement with this testing procedure. Its advantage is that we can choose b_k based on data, and thus the procedure can be applied to distributions that are not uniform.

7   Discussion and Open Problems

While our procedure is computationally efficient in the realizable case, it remains an open problem to make it efficient in the general case. It is conceivable that for some special cases (e.g. the marginal distribution over the instance space is uniform, as in section 4) one could use the recent results of Kalai et. al. for Agnostically Learning Halfspaces [11]. In fact, it would be interesting to derive precise bounds for the more general of class of log-concave distributions.

Acknowledgements. We thank Alina Beygelzimer, Sanjoy Dasgupta, Adam Kalai, and John Langford for a number of useful discussions. Part of this work was done while the first author was visiting Yahoo! Research.

References

1. Anthony, M., Bartlett, P.: Neural Network Learning: Theoretical Foundations. Cambridge University Press, Cambridge (1999)
2. Balcan, M.-F., Beygelzimer, A., Langford, J.: Agnostic active learning. In: ICML (2006)
3. Balcan, M.-F., Blum, A.: A PAC-style model for learning from labeled and unlabeled data. In: Proceedings of the Annual Conference on Computational Learning Theory (2005)
4. Castro, R.M., Nowak, R.D.: Upper and lower error bounds for active learning. In: The 44th Annual Allerton Conference on Communication, Control and Computing (2006)
5. Chapelle, O., Schölkopf, B., Zien, A. (eds.): Semi-Supervised Learning. MIT Press, Cambridge, MA (2006)
6. Cohen, D., Atlas, L., Ladner, R.: Improving generalzation with active learning. 15(2), 201–221 (1994)
7. Dasgupta, S.: Analysis of a greedy active learning strategy. In: Advances in Neural Information Processing Systems (2004)
8. Dasgupta, S.: Coarse sample complexity bounds for active learning. In: Advances in Neural Information Processing Systems (2005)
9. Dasgupta, S., Kalai, A., Monteleoni, C.: Analysis of perceptron-based active learning. In: Proceedings of the Annual Conference on Computational Learning Theory (2005)
10. Freund, Y., Seung, H., Shamir, E., Tishby, N.: Selective sampling using the query by committee algorithm. Machine Learning 28(2-3), 133–168 (1997)
11. Kalai, A., Klivans, A., Mansour, Y., Servedio, R.: Agnostically learning halfspaces. In: Proceedings of the 46th Annual Symposium on the Foundations of Computer Science (2005)
12. Long, P.M.: On the sample complexity of PAC learning halfspaces against the uniform distribution. IEEE Transactions on Neural Networks 6(6), 1556–1559 (1995)
13. Tong, S., Koller, D.: Support vector machine active learning with applications to text classification. Journal of Machine Learning Research 4, 45–66 (2001)
14. Tsybakov, A.: Optimal aggregation of classifiers in statistical learning. Annals of Statistics (2004)

A   Useful Facts

We state here two standard Sample Complexity bounds [1] and a few useful probability bounds for standard normal variable.

Theorem 7. *Let H be a set of functions from X to $\{-1,1\}$ with finite VC-dimension $V \geq 1$. Let P be an arbitrary, but fixed probability distribution over $X \times \{-1,1\}$. For any $\epsilon, \delta > 0$, if we draw a sample from P of size $N(\epsilon,\delta) = \frac{1}{\epsilon}\left(4V\log\left(\frac{1}{\epsilon}\right) + 2\log\left(\frac{2}{\delta}\right)\right)$, then with probability $1 - \delta$, all hypotheses with error $\geq \epsilon$ are inconsistent with the data.*

Theorem 8. *Let H be a set of functions from X to $\{-1,1\}$ with finite VC-dimension $V \geq 1$. Let P be an arbitrary, but fixed probability distribution over $X \times \{-1,1\}$. There exists a universal constant C, such that for any $\epsilon, \delta > 0$, if we draw a sample $((x_i, y_i))_i$ from P of size $N = N(\epsilon,\delta) = \frac{C}{\epsilon^2}\left(V + \log\left(\frac{1}{\delta}\right)\right)$, then with probability $1 - \delta$, for all $h \in H$, we have $\left|\frac{1}{N}\sum_{i=1}^{N} I(h(x_i) \neq y_i) - \mathbf{E}_{(X,Y)}I(h(X) \neq Y)\right| \leq \epsilon.$*

Lemma 2. *Assume $x = [x_1, x_2] \sim N(0, I_{2\times2})$, then any given $\gamma_1, \gamma_2 \geq 0$, we have $\Pr_x((x_1, x_2) \in [0, \gamma_1] \times [\gamma_2, 1]) \leq \frac{\gamma_1}{2\sqrt{2\pi}}e^{-\gamma_2^2/2}.$*

Lemma 3. *Assume $x = [x_1, x_2] \sim N(0, I_{2\times2})$. For any given $\gamma, \beta > 0$, the following holds: $\Pr_x(x_1 \leq 0, x_1 + \beta x_2 \geq \gamma) \leq \frac{\beta}{2}\left(1 + \sqrt{-\ln[\min(1,\beta)]}\right)e^{-\gamma^2/(2\beta^2)}.$*

B   Probability Estimation in High Dimensional Ball

Consider $x = [x_1, \ldots, x_d] \sim P_x$ uniformly distributed on unit ball in R^d. Let A be an arbitrary set in R^2; we are interested in estimating the probability $\Pr_x((x_1, x_2) \in A)$. Let V_d be the volume of d-dimensional ball; we know $V_d = \pi^{d/2}/\Gamma(1 + d/2)$ where Γ is the Gamma-function. In particular $V_{d-2}/V_d = d/(2\pi)$. It follows:

$$\Pr_x((x_1, x_2) \in A) = \frac{V_{d-2}}{V_d}\int_{(x_1,x_2)\in A}(1 - x_1^2 - x_2^2)^{(d-2)/2}dx_1dx_2 =$$

$$\frac{d}{2\pi}\int_{(x_1,x_2)\in A}(1 - x_1^2 - x_2^2)^{(d-2)/2}dx_1dx_2 \leq \frac{d}{2\pi}\int_{(x_1,x_2)\in A}e^{-(d-2)(x_1^2+x_2^2)/2}dx_1dx_2.$$

where we use the inequality $(1 - z) \leq e^{-z}$.

Lemma 4. *Let $d \geq 2$ and let $x = [x_1, \ldots, x_d]$ be uniformly distributed in the d-dimensional unit ball. Given $\gamma_1 \in [0, 1]$, $\gamma_2 \in [0, 1]$, we have:*

$$\Pr_x((x_1, x_2) \in [0, \gamma_1] \times [\gamma_2, 1]) \leq \frac{\gamma_1\sqrt{d}}{2\sqrt{\pi}}e^{-(d-2)\gamma_2^2/2}.$$

Proof. Let $A = [0, \gamma_1] \times [\gamma_2, 1]$. We have
$\Pr_x((x_1, x_2) \in A) \leq \frac{d}{2\pi}\int_{(x_1,x_2)\in A}e^{-(d-2)(x_1^2+x_2^2)/2}dx_1dx_2 \leq \frac{\gamma_1 d}{2\pi}\int_{x_2\in[\gamma_2,1]}e^{-(d-2)x_2^2/2}dx_2$

$\leq \frac{\gamma_1 d}{2\pi}e^{-(d-2)\gamma_2^2/2}\int_{x\in[0,1-\gamma_2)}e^{-(d-2)x^2/2}dx \leq \frac{\gamma_1 d}{2\pi}e^{-(d-2)\gamma_2^2/2}\min\left[1 - \gamma_2, \sqrt{\frac{\pi}{2(d-2)}}\right].$

Note that when $d \geq 2$, $\min(1, \sqrt{\pi/(2(d - 2))}) \leq \sqrt{\pi/d}$. $\square$

Lemma 5. *Assume $x = [x_1, \ldots, x_d]$ is uniformly distributed in the d-dimensional unit ball. Given $\gamma_1 \in [0,1]$, we have $\Pr_x(x_1 \geq \gamma_1) \leq \frac{1}{2}e^{-d\gamma_1^2/2}$.*

Proof. Let $A = [\gamma_1, 1] \times [-1, 1]$. Using a polar coordinate transform, we have:
$\Pr_x((x_1, x_2) \in A) = \frac{d}{2\pi} \int_{(x_1,x_2)\in A}(1 - x_1^2 - x_2^2)^{(d-2)/2}dx_1 dx_2 =$
$\frac{d}{2\pi}\int_{(r, r\cos\theta)\in[0,1]\times[\gamma_1,1]}(1-r^2)^{\frac{d-2}{2}}r\,dr d\theta = \frac{1}{2\pi}\int_{(r,r\cos\theta)\in[0,1]\times[\gamma_1,1]}d\theta d(1-r^2)^{\frac{d}{2}}$
$\leq \frac{1}{2\pi}\int_{(r,\theta)\in[\gamma_1,1]\times[-\pi/2,\pi/2]}d\theta d(1-r^2)^{d/2} = 0.5(1-\gamma_1^2)^{d/2} \leq \frac{1}{2}e^{-d\gamma_1^2/2}.$ □

Lemma 6. *Let $d \geq 4$ and let $x = [x_1, \ldots, x_d]$ be uniformly distributed in the d-dimensional unit ball. Given $\gamma, \beta > 0$, we have:*

$$\Pr_x(x_1 \leq 0, x_1 + \beta x_2 \geq \gamma) \leq \frac{\beta}{2}(1 + \sqrt{-\ln\min(1,\beta)})e^{-d\gamma^2/(4\beta^2)}.$$

Proof. Let $\alpha = \beta\sqrt{-2d^{-1}\ln\min(1,\beta)}$, we have:
$\Pr_x(x_1 \leq 0, x_1 + \beta x_2 \geq \gamma)$
$\leq \Pr_x(x_1 \leq -\alpha, x_1 + \beta x_2 \geq \gamma) + \Pr_x(x_1 \in [-\alpha, 0], x_1 + \beta x_2 \geq \gamma)$
$\leq \Pr_x(x_1 \leq -\alpha, x_2 \geq (\alpha+\gamma)/\beta) + \Pr_x(x_1 \in [-\alpha, 0], x_2 \geq \gamma/\beta)$
$\leq \frac{1}{2}\Pr_x(x_2 \geq (\alpha+\gamma)/\beta) + \Pr_x(x_1 \in [0, \alpha], x_2 \geq \gamma/\beta)$
$\leq \frac{1}{4}e^{-d(\alpha+\gamma)^2/(2\beta^2)} + \frac{\alpha\sqrt{d}}{2\sqrt{\pi}}e^{-d\gamma^2/(4\beta^2)}$
$\leq \left[\frac{1}{4}e^{-\frac{d\alpha^2}{2\beta^2}} + \frac{\alpha\sqrt{d}}{2\sqrt{\pi}}\right]e^{-\frac{d\gamma^2}{4\beta^2}} = \left[\frac{\min(1,\beta)}{4} + \frac{\beta\sqrt{-2\ln\min(1,\beta)}}{2\sqrt{\pi}}\right]e^{-\frac{d\gamma^2}{4\beta^2}}.$ □

Lemma 7. *Let u and w be two unit vectors in R^d, and assume that $\theta(u, w) \leq \tilde{\beta} < \pi/2$. Let $d \geq 4$ and let $x = [x_1, \ldots, x_d]$ be uniformly distributed in the d-dimensional unit ball. Consider $C > 0$, let $\gamma = \frac{2\sin\tilde{\beta}}{\sqrt{d}}\sqrt{\ln C + \ln\left(1 + \sqrt{\ln\max(1, \cos\tilde{\beta}/\sin\tilde{\beta})}\right)}$. Then $\Pr_x\left[(u \cdot x)(w \cdot x) < 0, |w \cdot x| \geq \gamma\right] \leq \frac{\sin\tilde{\beta}}{C\cos\tilde{\beta}}.$*

Proof. We rewrite the desired probability as $2\Pr_x[w \cdot x \geq \gamma, u \cdot x < 0]$. W.l.g., let $u = (1, 0, 0, \ldots, 0)$ and $w = (\cos(\theta), \sin(\theta), 0, 0, \ldots, 0)$. For $x = [x_1, x_2, \ldots, x_d]$ we have $u \cdot x = x_1$ and $w \cdot x = \cos(\theta)x_1 + \sin(\theta)x_2$. Using this representation and Lemma 6, we obtain $\Pr_x[w \cdot x \geq \gamma, u \cdot x < 0] = \Pr_x[\cos(\theta)x_1 + \sin(\theta)x_2 \geq \gamma, x_1 < 0] \leq \Pr_x\left[x_1 + \frac{\sin(\tilde{\beta})}{\cos(\tilde{\beta})}x_2 \geq \frac{\gamma}{\cos(\tilde{\beta})}, x_1 < 0\right] \leq \frac{\sin\tilde{\beta}}{2\cos\tilde{\beta}}\left(1 + \sqrt{\ln\max(1, \frac{\cos\tilde{\beta}}{\sin\tilde{\beta}})}\right)e^{-\frac{d\gamma^2}{4\sin^2\tilde{\beta}}} = \frac{\sin\tilde{\beta}}{2\cos\tilde{\beta}}C^{-1}$, as desired. □

Learning Large-Alphabet and Analog Circuits with Value Injection Queries

Dana Angluin[1], James Aspnes[1,*], Jiang Chen[2,**], and Lev Reyzin[1,***]

[1] Computer Science Department, Yale University
{angluin,aspnes}@cs.yale.edu, lev.reyzin@yale.edu
[2] Center for Computational Learning Systems, Columbia University
criver@cs.columbia.edu

Abstract. We consider the problem of learning an acyclic discrete circuit with n wires, fan-in bounded by k and alphabet size s using value injection queries. For the class of transitively reduced circuits, we develop the Distinguishing Paths Algorithm, that learns such a circuit using $(ns)^{O(k)}$ value injection queries and time polynomial in the number of queries. We describe a generalization of the algorithm to the class of circuits with shortcut width bounded by b that uses $(ns)^{O(k+b)}$ value injection queries. Both algorithms use value injection queries that fix only $O(kd)$ wires, where d is the depth of the target circuit. We give a reduction showing that without such restrictions on the topology of the circuit, the learning problem may be computationally intractable when $s = n^{\Theta(1)}$, even for circuits of depth $O(\log n)$. We then apply our large-alphabet learning algorithms to the problem of approximate learning of analog circuits whose gate functions satisfy a Lipschitz condition. Finally, we consider models in which behavioral equivalence queries are also available, and extend and improve the learning algorithms of [5] to handle general classes of gates functions that are polynomial time learnable from counterexamples.

1 Introduction

We consider learning large-alphabet and analog acyclic circuits in the value injection model introduced in [5]. In this model, we may inject values of our choice on any subset of wires, but we can only observe the one output of the circuit. However, the value injection query algorithms in that paper for boolean and constant alphabet networks do not lift to the case when the size of the alphabet is polynomial in the size of the circuit.

One motivation for studying the boolean network model includes gene regulatory networks. In a boolean model, each node in a gene regulatory network can represent a gene whose state is either active or inactive. However, genes may have a large number of states of activity. Constant-alphabet network models

---

[*] Supported in part by NSF grant CNS-0435201.
[**] Supported in part by a research contract from Consolidated Edison.
[***] Supported by a Yahoo! Research Kern Family Scholarship.

N. Bshouty and C. Gentile (Eds.): COLT 2007, LNAI 4539, pp. 51–65, 2007.
© Springer-Verlag Berlin Heidelberg 2007

may not adequately capture the information present in these networks, which motivates our interest in larger alphabets.

Akutsu et al. [2] and Ideker, Thorsson, and Karp [9] consider the discovery problem that models the experimental capability of gene disruption and over-expression. In such experiments, it is desirable to manipulate as few genes as possible. In the particular models considered in these papers, node states are fully observable – the gene expression data gives the state of every node in the network at every time step. Their results show that in this model, for bounded fan-in or sufficiently restricted gene functions, the problem of learning the structure of a network is tractable.

In contrast, there is ample evidence that learning boolean circuits solely from input-output behaviors may be computationally intractable. Kearns and Valiant [12] show that specific cryptographic assumptions imply that **NC1** circuits and **TC0** circuits are not PAC learnable in polynomial time. These negative results have been strengthened to the setting of PAC learning with membership queries [6], even with respect to the uniform distribution [13]. Furthermore, positive learnability results exist only for fairly limited classes, including propositional Horn formulas [3], general read once Boolean formulas [4], and decision trees [7], and those for specific distributions, including **AC0** circuits [14], DNF formulas [10], and **AC0** circuits with a limited number of majority gates [11].[1]

Thus, Angluin et al. [5] look at the relative contributions of full observation and full control of learning boolean networks. Their model of value injection allows full control and restricted observation, and it is the model we study in this paper. Interestingly, their results show that this model gives the learner considerably more power than with only input-output behaviors but less than the power with full observation. In particular, they show that with value injection queries, **NC1** circuits and **AC0** circuits are exactly learnable in polynomial time, but their negative results show that depth limitations are necessary.

A second motivation behind our work is to study the relative importance of the parameters of the models for learnability results. The impact of alphabet size on learnability becomes a natural point of inquiry, and ideas from fixed parameter tractability are very relevant [8,15].

2   Preliminaries

2.1   Circuits

We give a general definition of acyclic circuits whose wires carry values from a set Σ. For each nonnegative integer k, a **gate function** of arity k is a function from Σ^k to Σ. A **circuit** C consists of a finite set of wires $w_1, \ldots, w_n$, and for each wire w_i, a gate function g_i of arity k_i and an ordered k_i-tuple $w_{\sigma(i,1)}, \ldots, w_{\sigma(i,k_i)}$ of wires, the **inputs** of w_i. We define w_n to be the **output wire** of the circuit. We may think of wires as outputs of gates in C.

---

[1] Algorithms in both [14] and [11] for learning **AC0** circuits and their variants run in quasi-polynomial time.

The **unpruned graph** of a circuit C is the directed graph whose *vertices* are the wires and whose *edges* are pairs (w_i, w_j) such that w_i is an input of w_j in C. A wire w_i is **output-connected** if there is a directed path in the unpruned graph from that wire to the output wire. Wires that are not output-connected cannot affect the output value of a circuit. The **graph** of a circuit C is the subgraph of its unpruned graph induced by the output-connected wires.

A circuit is **acyclic** if its graph is acyclic. In this paper we consider only acyclic circuits. If u and v are vertices such that $u \neq v$ and there is a directed path from u to v, then we say that u is an **ancestor** of v and that v is a **descendant** of u. The **depth** of an output-connected wire w_i is the length of a longest path from w_i to the output wire w_n. The depth of a circuit is the maximum depth of any output-connected wire in the circuit. A wire with no inputs is an **input wire**; its **default value** is given by its gate function, which has arity 0 and is constant.

We consider the property of being transitively reduced [1] and a generalization of it: bounded shortcut width. Let G be an acyclic directed graph. An edge (u, v) of G is a **shortcut edge** if there exists a directed path in G of length at least two from u to v. G is **transitively reduced** if it contains no shortcut edges. A circuit is transitively reduced if its graph is transitively reduced.

The **shortcut width** of a wire w_i is the number of wires w_j such that w_j is both an ancestor of w_i and an input of a descendant of w_i. (Note that we are counting wires, not edges.) The **shortcut width** of a circuit C is the maximum shortcut width of any output-connected wire in C. A circuit is transitively reduced if and only if it has shortcut width 0. A circuit's shortcut width turns out to be a key parameter in its learnability by value injection queries.

2.2   Experiments on Circuits

Let C be a circuit. An **experiment** e is a function mapping each wire of C to $\Sigma \cup \{*\}$, where $*$ is not an element of Σ. If $e(w_i) = *$, then the wire w_i is **free** in e; otherwise, w_i is **fixed** in e. If e is an experiment that assigns $*$ to wire w, and $\sigma \in \Sigma$, then $e|_{w=\sigma}$ is the experiment that is equal to e on all wires other than w, and fixes w to σ. We define an ordering $\preceq$ on $\Sigma \cup \{*\}$ in which all elements of Σ are incomparable and precede $*$, and lift this to the componentwise ordering on experiments. Then $e_1 \preceq e_2$ if every wire that e_2 fixes is fixed to the same value by e_1, and e_1 may fix some wires that e_2 leaves free.

For each experiment e we inductively define the value $w_i(e) \in \Sigma$, of each wire w_i in C under the experiment e as follows. If $e(w_i) = \sigma$ and $\sigma \neq *$, then $w_i(e) = \sigma$. Otherwise, if the values of the input wires of w_i have been defined, then $w_i(e)$ is defined by applying the gate function g_i to them, that is, $w_i(e) = g_i(w_{\sigma(i,1)}(e), \ldots, w_{\sigma(i,k_i)}(e))$. Because C is acyclic, this uniquely defines $w_i(e) \in \Sigma$ for all wires w_i. We define the value of the circuit to be the value of its output wire, that is, $C(e) = w_n(e)$ for every experiment e.

Let C and C' be circuits with the same set of wires and the same value set Σ. If $C(e) = C'(e)$ for every experiment e, then we say that C and C' are **behaviorally equivalent**. To define approximate equivalence, we assume that there is a metric d on Σ mapping pairs of values from Σ to a real-valued distance between them. If $d(C(e), C'(e)) \leq \epsilon$ for every experiment e, then we say that C and C' are ϵ-**equivalent**.

We consider two principal kinds of circuits. A **discrete circuit** is a circuit for which the set Σ of wire values is a finite set. An **analog circuit** is a circuit for which $\Sigma = [0, 1]$. In this case we specify the distance function as $d(x, y) = |x - y|$.

2.3   The Learning Problems

We consider the following general learning problem. There is an unknown target circuit C^* drawn from a known class of possible target circuits. The set of wires $w_1, \ldots, w_n$ and the value set Σ are given as input. The learning algorithm may gather information about C^* by making calls to an oracle that will answer value injection queries. In a **value injection query**, the algorithm specifies an experiment e and the oracle returns the value of $C^*(e)$. The algorithm makes a value injection query by listing a set of wires and their fixed values; the other wires are assumed to be free, and are not explicitly listed. The goal of a learning algorithm is to output a circuit C that is either exactly or approximately equivalent to C^*.

In the case of learning discrete circuits, the goal is behavioral equivalence and the learning algorithm should run in time polynomial in n. In the case of learning analog circuits, the learning algorithm has an additional parameter $\epsilon > 0$, and the goal is ϵ-equivalence. In this case the learning algorithm should run in time polynomial in n and $1/\epsilon$. In Section 5.1, we consider algorithms that may use **equivalence queries** in addition to value injection queries.

3   Learning Large-Alphabet Circuits

In this section we consider the problem of learning a discrete circuit when the alphabet Σ of possible values is of size $n^{O(1)}$. In Section 4 we reduce the problem of learning an analog circuit whose gate functions satisfy a Lipschitz condition to that of learning a discrete circuit over a finite value set Σ; the number of values is $n^{\Theta(1)}$ for an analog circuit of depth $O(\log n)$. Using this approach, in order to learn analog circuits of even moderate depth, we need learning algorithms that can handle large alphabets.

The algorithm Circuit Builder [5] uses value injection queries to learn acyclic discrete circuits of unrestricted topology and depth $O(\log n)$ with constant fan-in and constant alphabet size in time polynomial in n. However, the approach of [5] to building a sufficient set of experiments does not generalize to alphabets of size $n^{O(1)}$ because the total number of possible settings of side wires along a test path grows superpolynomially. In fact, we give evidence in Section 3.1 that this problem becomes computationally intractable for an alphabet of size $n^{\Theta(1)}$.

In turn, this negative result justifies a corresponding restriction on the topology of the circuits we consider. We first show that a natural top-down algorithm using value-injection queries learns transitively reduced circuits with arbitrary depth, constant fan-in and alphabet size $n^{O(1)}$ in time polynomial in n. We then give a generalization of this algorithm to circuits that have a constant bound on their shortcut width. The topological restrictions do not result in trivial classes; for example, every levelled graph is transitively reduced.

3.1   Hardness for Large Alphabets with Unrestricted Topology

We give a reduction that turns a large-alphabet circuit learning algorithm into a clique tester. Because the clique problem is complete for the complexity class $W[1]$ (see [8,15]), this suggests the learning problem may be computationally intractable for classes of circuits with large alphabets and unrestricted topology.

The Reduction. Suppose the input is (G, k), where $k \geq 2$ is an integer and $G = (V, E)$ is a simple undirected graph with $n \geq 3$ vertices, and the desired output is whether G contains a clique of size k. We construct a circuit C of depth $d = \binom{k}{2}$ as follows. The alphabet Σ is V; let v_0 be a particular element of V. Define a gate function g with three inputs s, u, and v as follows: if (u, v) is an edge of G, then the output of g is equal to the input s; otherwise, the output is v_0. The wires of C are $s_1, \ldots, s_{d+1}$ and $x_1, x_2, \ldots, x_k$. The wires x_j have no inputs; their gate functions assign them the default value v_0. For $i = 1, \ldots, d$, the wire s_{i+1} has corresponding gate function g, where the s input is s_i, and the u and v inputs are the i-th pair (x_ℓ, x_m) with $\ell < m$ in the lexicographic ordering. Finally, the wire s_1 has no inputs, and is assigned some default value from $V - \{v_0\}$. The output wire is s_{d+1}.

To understand the behavior of C, consider an experiment e that assigns values from V to each of $x_1, \ldots, x_k$, and leaves the other wires free. The gates g pass along the default value of s_1 as long as the values $e(x_\ell)$ and $e(x_m)$ are an edge of G, but if any of those checks fail, the output value will be v_0. Thus the default value of s_1 will be passed all the way to the output wire if and only if the vertex values assigned to $x_1, \ldots, x_k$ form a clique of size k in G.

We may use a learning algorithm as a clique tester as follows. Run the learning algorithm using C to answer its value-injection queries e. If for some queried experiment e, the values $e(x_1), \ldots, e(x_k)$ form a clique of k vertices in G, stop and output the answer "yes." If the learning algorithm halts and outputs a circuit without making such a query, then output the answer "no." Clearly a "yes" answer is correct, because we have a witness clique. And if there is a clique of size k in G, the learning algorithm must make such a query, because in that case, the default value assigned to s_1 cannot otherwise be learned correctly; thus, a "no" answer is correct. Then we have the following.

Theorem 1. *If for some nonconstant computable function $d(n)$ an algorithm using value injection queries can learn the class of circuits of at most n wires, alphabet size s, fan-in bound 3, and depth bound $d(n)$ in time polynomial in n and s, then there is an algorithm to decide whether a graph on n vertices has a clique of size k in time $f(k)n^\alpha$, for some function f and constant α.*

Because the clique problem is complete for the complexity class $W[1]$, a polynomial time learning algorithm as hypothesized in the theorem for any nonconstant computable function $d(n)$ would imply fixed-parameter tractability of all the problems in $W[1]$ [8,15]. However, we show that restricting the circuit to be transitively reduced (Theorem 2), or more generally, of bounded shortcut width (Theorem 3), avoids the necessity of a depth bound at all.[2]

3.2 Distinguishing Paths

This section develops some properties of distinguishing paths, making no assumptions about shortcut width. Let C^* be a circuit with n wires, an alphabet Σ of cardinality s, and fan-in bounded by a constant k. An arbitrary gate function for such a circuit can be represented by a **gate table** with s^k entries, giving the value of the gate function for each possible k-tuple of input symbols.

Experiment e **distinguishes** σ from τ for w if e sets w to $*$ and $C^*(e|_{w=\sigma}) \neq C^*(e|_{w=\tau})$. If such an experiment exists, the values σ and τ are **distinguishable** for wire w; otherwise, σ and τ are **indistinguishable** for w.

A **test path** π for a wire w in C^* consists of a directed path of wires from w to the output wire, together with an assignment giving fixed values from Σ to some set S of other wires; S must be disjoint from the set of wires in the path, and each element of S must be an input to some wire beyond w along the path. The wires in S are the **side wires** of the test path π. The **length** of a test path is the number of edges in its directed path. There is just one test path of length 0, consisting of the output wire and no side wires.

We may associate with a test path π the partial experiment p_π that assigns $*$ to each wire on the path, and the specified value from Σ to each wire in S. An experiment e **agrees with** a test path π if e extends the partial experiment p_π, that is, p_π is a subfunction of e. We also define the experiment e_π that extends p_π by setting all the other wires to $*$.

If π is a test path and V is a set of wires disjoint from the side wires of π, then V is **functionally determining** for π if for any experiment e agreeing with π and leaving the wires in V free, for any experiment e' obtained from e by setting the wires in V to fixed values, the value of $C^*(e')$ depends only on the values assigned to the wires in V. That is, the values on the wires in V determine the output of the circuit, given the assignments specified by p_π. A test path π for w is **isolating** if $\{w\}$ is functionally determining for π.

Lemma 1. *If π is an isolating test path for w then the set V of inputs of w is functionally determining for π.*

We define a **distinguishing path** for wire w and values $\sigma, \tau \in \Sigma$ to be an isolating test path π for w such that e_π distinguishes between σ and τ for w. The significance of distinguishing paths is indicated by the following lemma, which is analogous to Lemma 10 of [5].

Lemma 2. *Suppose σ and τ are distinguishable for wire w. Then for any minimal experiment e distinguishing σ from τ for w, there is a distinguishing path π for wire w and values σ and τ such that the free wires of e are exactly the wires of the directed path of π, and e agrees with π.*

---

[2] The target circuit C constructed in the reduction is of shortcut width $k - 1$.

Conversely, a shortest distinguishing path yields a minimal distinguishing experiment, as follows. This does not hold for circuits of general topology without the restriction to a shortest path.

Lemma 3. *Let π be a shortest distinguishing path for wire w and values σ and τ. Then the experiment e obtained from p_π by setting every unspecified wire to an arbitrary fixed value is a minimal experiment distinguishing σ from τ for w.*

3.3   The Distinguishing Paths Algorithm

In this section we develop the Distinguishing Paths Algorithm.

Theorem 2. *The Distinguishing Paths Algorithm learns any transitively reduced circuit with n wires, alphabet size s, and fan-in bound k, with $O(n^{2k+1}s^{2k+2})$ value injection queries and time polynomial in the number of queries.*

Lemma 4. *If C^* is a transitively reduced circuit and π is a test path for w in C^*, then none of the inputs of w is a side wire of π.*

The Distinguishing Paths Algorithm builds a directed graph G whose vertices are the wires of C^*, in which an edge (v, w) represents the discovery that v is an input of w in C^*. The algorithm also keeps for each wire w a **distinguishing table** T_w with $\binom{s}{2}$ entries, one for each unordered pair of values from Σ. The entry for (σ, τ) in T_w is 1 or 0 according to whether or not a distinguishing path has been found to distinguish values σ and τ on wire w. Stored together with each 1 entry is a corresponding distinguishing path and a bit marking whether the entry is processed or unprocessed.

At each step, for each distinguishing table T_w that has unprocessed 1 entries, we try to extend the known distinguishing paths to find new edges to add to G and new 1 entries and corresponding distinguishing paths for the distinguishing tables of inputs of w. Once every 1 entry in every distinguishing table has been marked processed, the construction of distinguishing tables terminates. Then a circuit C is constructed with graph G by computing gate tables for the wires; the algorithm outputs C and halts.

To extend a distinguishing path for a wire w, it is necessary to find an input wire of w. Given a distinguishing path π for wire w, an input v of w is **relevant** with respect to π if there are two experiments e_1 and e_2 that agree with π, that set the inputs of w to fixed values, that differ only by assigning different values to v, and are such that $C^*(e_1) \neq C^*(e_2)$. Let $V(\pi)$ denote the set of all inputs v of w that are relevant with respect to π. It is only relevant inputs of w that need be found, as shown by the following.

Lemma 5. *Let π be a distinguishing path for w. Then $V(\pi)$ is functionally determining for π.*

Given a distinguishing path π for wire w, we define its corresponding **input experiments** E_π to be the set of all experiments e that agree with π and set up to $2k$ additional wires to fixed values and set the rest of the wires free. Note that each of these experiments fix at most $2k$ more values than are already fixed in the distinguishing path. Consider all pairs (V, Y) of disjoint sets of wires not set by p_π such that $|V| \leq k$ and $|Y| \leq k$; for every possible way of setting $V \cup Y$ to fixed values, there is a corresponding experiment in E_π.

Find-Inputs. We now describe a procedure, Find-Inputs, that uses the experiments in E_π to find all the wires in $V(\pi)$. Define a set V of at most k wires not set by p_π to be **determining** if for every disjoint set Y of at most k wires not set by p_π and for every assignment of values from Σ to the wires in $V \cup Y$, the value of C^* on the corresponding experiment from E_π is determined by the values assigned to wires in V, independent of the values assigned to wires in Y. Find-Inputs finds all determining sets V and outputs their intersection.

Lemma 6. *Given a distinguishing path π for w and its corresponding input experiments E_π, the procedure Find-Inputs returns $V(\pi)$.*

Find-Paths. We now describe a procedure, Find-Paths, that takes the set $V(\pi)$ of all inputs of w relevant with respect to π, and searches, for each triple consisting of $v \in V(\pi)$ and $\sigma, \tau \in \Sigma$, for two experiments e_1 and e_2 in E_π that fix all the wires of $V(\pi) - \{v\}$ in the same way, but set v to σ and τ, respectively, and are such that $C^*(e_1) \neq C^*(e_2)$. On finding such a triple, the distinguishing path π for w can be extended to a distinguishing path π' for v by adding v to the start of the path, and making all the wires in $V(\pi) - \{v\}$ new side wires, with values fixed as in e_1. If this gives a new 1 for entry (σ, τ) in the distinguishing paths table T_v, then we change the entry, add the corresponding distinguishing path for v to the table, and mark it unprocessed. We have to verify the following.

Lemma 7. *Suppose π' is a path produced by Find-Paths for wire v and values σ and τ. Then π' is a distinguishing path for wire v and values σ, τ.*

The Distinguishing Paths Algorithm initializes the simple directed graph G to have the set of wires of C^* as its vertex set, with no edges. It initializes T_w to all 0's, for every non-output wire w. Every entry in T_{w_n} is initialized to 1, with a corresponding distinguishing path of length 0 with no side wires, and marked as unprocessed. The Distinguishing Paths Algorithm is summarized in Algorithm 1; the procedure Construct-Circuit is described below.

We now show that when processing of the tables terminates, the tables T_w are correct and complete. We first consider the correctness of the 1 entries.

Lemma 8. *After the initialization, and after each new 1 entry is placed in a distinguishing table, every 1 entry in a distinguishing table T_w for (σ, τ) has a corresponding distinguishing path π for wire w and values σ and τ.*

A distinguishing table T_w is **complete** if for every pair of values $\sigma, \tau \in \Sigma$ such that σ and τ are distinguishable for w, T_w has a 1 entry for (σ, τ).

Lemma 9. *When the Distinguishing Paths Algorithm terminates, T_w is complete for every wire w in C^*.*

Algorithm 1. Distinguishing Paths Algorithm

Initialize G to have the wires as vertices and no edges.
Initialize T_{w_n} to all 1's, marked unprocessed.
Initialize T_w to all 0's for all non-output wires w.
while there is an unprocessed 1 entry (σ, τ) in some T_w **do**
    Let π be the corresponding distinguishing path.
    Perform all input experiments E_π.
    Use Find-Inputs to determine the set $V(\pi)$.
    Add any new edges (v, w) for $v \in V(\pi)$ to G.
    Use Find-Paths to find extensions of π for elements of $V(\pi)$.
    for each extension π' that gives a new 1 entry in some T_v **do**
        Put the new 1 entry in T_v with distinguishing path π'.
        Mark this new 1 entry as unprocessed.
    Mark the 1 entry for (σ, τ) in T_w as processed.
Use Construct-Circuit with G and the tables T_w to construct a circuit C.
Output C and halt.

Construct-Circuit. Now we show how to construct a circuit C behaviorally equivalent to C^* given the graph G and the final distinguishing tables. G is the graph of C, determining the input relation between wires. Note that G is a subgraph of the graph of C^*, because edges are added only when relevant inputs are found.

Gate tables for wires in C will keep different combinations of input values and their corresponding output. Since some distinguishing tables for wires may have 0 entries, we will record values in gate tables up to equivalence, where σ and τ are in the same equivalence class for w if they are indistinguishable for w. We process one wire at a time, in arbitrary order. We first record, for one representative σ of each equivalence class of values for w, the outputs $C^*(e_\pi | w = \sigma)$ for all the distinguishing paths π in T_w. Given a setting of the inputs to w (in C), we can tell which equivalence class of values of w it should map to as follows. For each distinguishing path π in T_w, we record the output of C^* for the experiment equal to e_π with the inputs of w set to the given fixed values and $w = *$. The value of σ with recorded outputs that match these outputs for all π is written in w's gate table as the output for this setting of the inputs. Repeating this for every setting of w's inputs completes w's gate table, and we continue to the next gate.

Lemma 10. *Given the graph G and distinguishing tables as constructed in the Distinguishing Paths Algorithm, the procedure Construct-Circuit constructs a circuit C behaviorally equivalent to C^*.*

We analyze the total number of value injection queries used by the Distinguishing Paths Algorithm; the running time is polynomial in the number of queries. To construct the distinguishing tables, each 1 entry in a distinguishing table is processed once. The total number of possible 1 entries in all the tables is bounded by ns^2. The processing for each 1 entry is to take the corresponding distinguishing path π and construct the set E_π of input experiments, each of which consists of choosing up to $2k$ wires and setting them to arbitrary values from Σ, for a total of $O(n^{2k}s^{2k})$ queries to construct E_π. Thus, a total of $O(n^{2k+1}s^{2k+2})$ value injection queries are used to construct the distinguishing tables.

To build the gate tables, for each of n wires, we try at most s^2 distinguishing path experiments for at most s values of the wire, which takes at most s^3 queries. We then run the same experiments for each possible setting of the inputs to the wire, which takes at most $s^k s^2$ experiments. Thus Construct-Circuit requires a total of $O(n(s^3 + s^{k+2}))$ experiments, which are already among the ones made in constructing the distinguishing tables. Note that every experiment fixes at most $O(kd)$ wires, where d is the depth of C^*. This concludes the proof of Theorem 2.

3.4 The Shortcuts Algorithm

In this section we sketch the Shortcuts Algorithm, which generalizes the Distinguishing Paths Algorithm to circuits with bounded shortcut width.

Theorem 3. *The Shortcuts Algorithm learns the class of circuits having n wires, alphabet size s, fan-in bound k, and shortcut width bounded by b using a number of value injection queries bounded by $(ns)^{O(k+b)}$ and time polynomial in the number of queries.*

When C^* is not transitively reduced, there may be edges of its graph that are important to the behavior of the circuit, but are not completely determined by the behavior of the circuit. For example, three circuits given in [5] are behaviorally equivalent, but have different topologies; a behaviorally correct circuit cannot be constructed with just the edges that are common to the three circuit graphs. Thus, the Shortcuts Algorithm focuses on finding a **sufficient** set of experiments for C^*, and uses Circuit Builder [5] to build the output circuit C.

On the positive side, we can learn quite a bit about the topology of a circuit C^* from its behavior. An edge (v, w) of the graph of C^* is **discoverable** if it is the initial edge on some minimal distinguishing experiment e for v and some values σ_1 and σ_2. This is a behaviorally determined property; all circuits behaviorally equivalent to C^* must contain all the discoverable edges of C^*.

We generalize the definition of a distinguishing path to a **distinguishing path with shortcuts**, which has an additional set of **cut wires** K, which is disjoint from the path wires and the side wires, and is such that every wire in K is an input to some wire beyond w on the path (where w is the initial wire.) Moreover, $\{w\} \cup K$ is functionally determining for the path.

Like the Distinguishing Paths Algorithm, the Shortcuts Algorithm maintains a directed graph G containing known edges (v, w) of the graph of C^*, and a set of distinguishing tables T_w indexed by triples (B, a_1, a_2), where B is a set of at most b wires not containing w, and a_1 and a_2 are assignments of fixed values to the wires in $\{w\} \cup B$. If there is an entry for (B, a_1, a_2) in T_w, it is a distinguishing path with shortcuts π such that $K \subseteq B$ and $K \cap S = \emptyset$ and it distinguishes a_1 from a_2. Each entry is marked as processed or unprocessed.

The algorithm processes an entry by using the distinguishing path π for (w, B) to find new edges (v, w) in G, and to find new or updated entries in the tables

T_v such that (v, w) is in G. An entry is updated if a new distinguishing path for the entry is shorter than the current one, which it then replaces. When an entry is created or updated, it is marked as unprocessed. All entries in T_w are also marked as unprocessed when a new edge (v, w) is added to G.

We show that when processing of the tables T_w is complete, G contains every discoverable edge of C^* and for every wire w and the shortcut wires $B(w)$ of w in C^*, if the assignments a_1 and a_2 are distinguishable for $(w, B(w))$, then there is a correct entry for $(B(w), a_1, a_2)$ in T_w. The final tables T_w are used to create experiments for Circuit Builder. To guarantee a sufficient set of experiments, this procedure is iterated for every restriction of C^* obtained by selecting at most k possible input wires and assigning arbitrary fixed values to them.

4   Learning Analog Circuits Via Discretization

We show how to construct a discrete approximation of an analog circuit, assuming its gate functions satisfy a Lipschitz condition with constant L, and apply the large-alphabet learning algorithm of Theorem 3.

4.1   A Lipschitz Condition

An analog function g of arity k satisfies a Lipschitz condition with constant L if for all $x_1, \ldots, x_k$ and $x'_1, \ldots, x'_k$ from $[0, 1]$ we have

$$|g(x_1, \ldots, x_k) - g(x'_1, \ldots, x'_k)| \leq L \max_i |x_i - x'_i|.$$

Let m be a positive integer. We define a discretization function D_m from $[0, 1]$ to the m points $\{1/2m, 3/2m, \ldots, (2m - 1)/2m\}$ by mapping x to the closest point in this set (choosing the smaller point if x is equidistant from two of them.) Then $|x - D_m(x)| \leq 1/2m$ for all $x \in [0, 1]$. We extend D_m to discretize analog experiments e by defining $D_m(*) = *$ and applying it componentwise to e.

Lemma 11. *If g is an analog function of arity k, satisfying a Lipschitz condition with constant L and m is a positive integer, then for all $x_1, \ldots, x_k$ in $[0, 1]$, $|g(x_1, \ldots, x_k) - g(D_m(x_1), \ldots, D_m(x_k))| \leq L/2m$.*

4.2   Discretizing Analog Circuits

We describe a discretization of an analog gate function in which the inputs and the output may be discretized differently. Let g be an analog function of arity k and r, s be positive integers. The (r, s)-**discretization** of g is g', defined by

$$g'(x_1, \ldots, x_k) = D_r(g(D_s(x_1), \ldots, D_s(x_k))).$$

Let C be an analog circuit of depth d_{max} and let L and N be positive integers. Define $m_d = N(3L)^d$ for all nonnegative integers d. We construct a particular discretization C' of C by replacing each gate function g_i by its (m_d, m_{d+1})-discretization, where d is the depth of wire w_i. We also replace the value set $\Sigma = [0, 1]$ by the value set Σ' equal to the union of the ranges of D_{m_d} for $0 \leq d \leq d_{max}$. Note that the wires and tuples of inputs remain unchanged. The resulting discrete circuit C' is termed the (L, N)-**discretization** of C.

Lemma 12. *Let L and N be positive integers. Let C be an analog circuit of depth d_{max} whose gate functions all satisfy a Lipschitz condition with constant L. Let C' denote the (L, N)-discretization of C and let $M = N(3L)^{d_{max}}$. Then for any experiment e for C, $|C(e) - C'(D_M(e))| \leq 1/N$.*

This lemma shows that if every gate of C satisfies a Lipschitz condition with constant L, we can approximate C's behavior to within ϵ using a discretization with $O((3L)^d/\epsilon)$ points, where d is the depth of C. For $d = O(\log n)$, this bound is polynomial in n and $1/\epsilon$.

Theorem 4. *There is a polynomial time algorithm that approximately learns any analog circuit of n wires, depth $O(\log n)$, constant fan-in, gate functions satisfying a Lipschitz condition, and shortcut width bounded by a constant.*

5   Learning with Experiments and Counterexamples

In this section, we consider the problem of learning circuits using both value injection queries and counterexamples. In a **counterexample query**, the algorithm proposes a hypothesis C and receives as answer either the fact that C exactly equivalent to the target circuit C^*, or a **counterexample**, that is, an experiment e such that $C(e) \neq C^*(e)$. In [5], polynomial-time algorithms are given that use value injection queries and counterexample queries to learn (1) acyclic circuits of arbitrary depth with arbitrary gates of constant fan-in, and (2) acyclic circuits of arbitrary depth with NOT gates and AND, OR, NAND, and NOR gates of arbitrary fan-in.

The algorithm that we now develop generalizes both previous algorithms by permitting any class of gates that is polynomial time learnable with counterexamples. It also guarantees that the depth of the output circuit is no greater than the depth of the target circuit and the number of additional wires fixed in value injection queries is bounded by $O(kd)$, where k is a bound on the fan-in and d is a bound on the depth of the target circuit.

5.1   The Learning Algorithm

The algorithm proceeds in a cycle of proposing a hypothesis, getting a counterexample, processing the counterexample, and then proposing a new hypothesis. Whenever we receive a counterexample e, we process the counterexample so that we can "blame" at least one gate in C; we find a witness experiment e^* eliminating a gate g in C. In effect, we reduce the problem of learning a circuit to the problem of learning individual gates with counterexamples.

An experiment e^* is a **witness experiment** eliminating g, if and only if e^* fixes all inputs of g but sets g free and $C(e^*|_{w=g(e^*)}) \neq C(e^*)$. It is important that we require e^* fix all inputs of g, because then we know it is g and not its ancestors computing wrong values. The main operation of the procedure that processes counterexamples is to fix wires.

Given a counterexample e, let procedure **minimize** fix wires in e while preserving the property that $C(e) \neq C'(e)$ until it cannot fix any more. Therefore, $e^* = minimize(e)$ is a minimal counterexample for C' under the partial order $\preceq$ defined in Sect. 2.2. The following lemma is a consequence of Lemma 10 in [5].

Lemma 13. *If e^* is a minimal counterexample for C', there exists a gate g in C' such that e^* is a witness experiment for g.*

Now we run a separate counterexample learning algorithm for each individual wire. Whenever C' receives a counterexample, at least one of the learning algorithms will receive one. However, if we run all the learning algorithms simultaneously and let each learning algorithm propose a gate function, the hypothesis circuit may not be acyclic. Instead we will use Algorithm 2 to coordinate them, which can be viewed as a generalization of the circuit building algorithm for learning AND/OR circuits in [5]. Conflicts are defined below.

Algorithm 2. Learning with experiments and counterexamples

Run an individual learning algorithm for each wire w. Each learning algorithm takes as candidate inputs only wires that have fewer conflicts.
Let C be the hypothesis circuit.
while there is a counterexample for C **do**
  Process the counterexample to obtain a counterexample for a wire w.
  Run the learning algorithm for w with the new counterexample.
  if there is a conflict for w **then**
    Restart the learning algorithms for w and all wires whose candidate inputs have changed.

The algorithm builds an acyclic circuit C because each wire has as inputs only wires that have fewer conflicts. At the start, each individual learning algorithm runs with an empty candidate input set since there is yet no conflict. Thus, each of them tries to learn each gate as a constant gate, and some of them will not succeed. A **conflict** for w happens when there is no hypothesis in the hypothesis space that is consistent with the set of counterexamples received by w. For constant gates, there is a conflict when we receive a counterexample for each of the $|\Sigma|$ possible constant functions. We note that there will be no conflict for a wire w if the set of candidate inputs contains the set of true inputs of w in the target circuit C^*, because then the hypothesis space contains the true gate.

Whenever a conflict occurs for a wire, it has a chance of having more wires as candidate inputs. Therefore, our learning algorithm can be seen as repeatedly rebuilding a partial order over wires based on their numbers of conflicts. Another natural partial order on wires is given by the **level** of a wire, defined as the length of a longest directed path in C^* from a constant gate to the wire. The following lemma shows an interesting connection between levels and numbers of conflicts.

Lemma 14. *The number of conflicts each wire receives is bounded by its level.*

Corollary 1. *The depth of C is at most the depth of C^*.*

In fact, the depth of C is bounded by the minimum depth of any circuit behaviorally equivalent to C^*.

Theorem 5. *Circuits whose gates are polynomial time learnable with counterexamples are learnable in polynomial time with experiments and counterexamples.*

Proof. By the learnability assumption of each gate, Algorithm 2 will receive only polynomially many counterexamples between two conflicts, because the candidate inputs for every wire are unchanged. (A conflict can be detected when the number of counterexamples exceeds the polynomial bound.) Lemma 14 bounds the number of conflicts for each wire by its level, which then bounds the total number of counterexamples of Algorithm 2 by a polynomial. It is clear that we use $O(n)$ experiments to process each counterexample. Thus, the total number of experiments is bounded by a polynomial as well.

5.2   A New Diagnosis Algorithm

A shortcoming of **minimize** is that it fixes many wires, which may be undesirable in the context of gene expression experiments. In this section, we propose a new diagnosis algorithm to find a witness experiment e^* for some gate g in C. If the hypothesis circuit C has depth d and fan-in bound k, the new algorithm fixes only $O(dk)$ more gates than the number fixed in the original counterexample.

Given a counterexample e, we first gather a list of potentially wrong wires. Let $w_C(e)$ be the value of wire w in C under experiment e. We can compute $w_C(e)$ given e because we know C. The **potentially wrong** wires are those w's such that $C^*(e|_{w=w_C(e)}) \neq C^*(e)$. It is not hard to see that a potentially wrong wire must be a free wire in e. We can gather all **potentially wrong** wires by conducting n experiments, each fixing one more wire than e does.

Now, pick an arbitrary potentially wrong wire w and let g be its gate function in C. If g's inputs are fixed in e, then e is a witness experiment for g, and we are done. Otherwise, fix all g's free input wires to their values in C, and let e' be the resulting experiment. There are two cases: either g is wrong or one of g's inputs computes a wrong value.

1. If $C^*(e'|_{w=w_C(e)}) \neq C^*(e')$, then e' is a witness experiment for g.
2. Otherwise, we have $C^*(e'|_{w=w_C(e)}) = C^*(e')$. Because $C^*(e|_{w=w_C(e)}) \neq C^*(e)$, we have either $C^*(e') \neq C^*(e)$ or $C^*(e'|_{w=w_C(e)}) \neq C^*(e|_{w=w_C(e)})$. Note that the only difference between e and e' is that e' fixes free inputs of g to their values in C. So either e or $e|_{w=w_C(e)}$ is an experiment in which fixing all g's free inputs gives us a change in the circuit outputs. We then

start from whichever experiment gives us such a change and fix free inputs of g in C one after another, until the circuit output changes. We will find an experiment e'', for which one of g's inputs is potentially wrong. We then restart the process with e'' and this input of g.

At each iteration, we go to a deeper gate in C. The process will stop within d iterations. If C has fan-in at most k, the whole process will fix at most $d(k-1)+1$ more gates than were fixed in the original experiment e.

References

1. Aho, A.V., Garey, M.R., Ullman, J.D.: The transitive reduction of a directed graph. SIAM J. Comput. 1, 131–137 (1972)
2. Akutsu, T., Kuhara, S., Maruyama, O., Miyano, S.: Identification of gene regulatory networks by strategic gene disruptions and gene overexpressions. In: SODA '98: Proceedings of the Ninth Annual ACM-SIAM Symposium on Discrete Algorithms, pp. 695–702, Philadelphia, PA, USA, Society for Industrial and Applied Mathematics (1998)
3. Angluin, D., Frazier, M., Pitt, L.: Learning conjunctions of Horn clauses. Machine Learning 9, 147–164 (1992)
4. Angluin, D., Hellerstein, L., Karpinski, M.: Learning read-once formulas with queries. J. ACM 40, 185–210 (1993)
5. Angluin, D., Aspnes, J., Chen, J., Wu, Y.: Learning a circuit by injecting values. In: Proceedings of the Thirty-Eighth Annual ACM Symposium on Theory of Computing, pp. 584–593. ACM Press, New York, USA (2006)
6. Angluin, D., Kharitonov, M.: When won't membership queries help? J. Comput. Syst. Sci. 50(2), 336–355 (1995)
7. Bshouty, N.H.: Exact learning boolean functions via the monotone theory. Inf. Comput. 123(1), 146–153 (1995)
8. Downey, R.G., Fellows, M.R.: Parameterized Complexity. Springer, Heidelberg (1999)
9. Ideker, T., Thorsson, V., Karp, R.: Discovery of regulatory interactions through perturbation: Inference and experimental design. In: Pacific Symposium on Biocomputing 5, 302–313 (2000)
10. Jackson, J.C.: An efficient membership-query algorithm for learning DNF with respect to the uniform distribution. J. Comput. Syst. Sci. 55(3), 414–440 (1997)
11. Jackson, J.C., Klivans, A.R., Servedio, R.A.: Learnability beyond AC0. In: STOC '02: Proceedings of the thirty-fourth annual ACM symposium on Theory of computing, pp. 776–784. ACM Press, New York, USA (2002)
12. Kearns, M., Valiant, L.: Cryptographic limitations on learning boolean formulae and finite automata. J. ACM 41(1), 67–95 (1994)
13. Kharitonov, M.: Cryptographic hardness of distribution-specific learning. In: STOC '93: Proceedings of the twenty-fifth annual ACM symposium on Theory of computing, pp. 372–381. ACM Press, New York, USA (1993)
14. Linial, N., Mansour, Y., Nisan, N.: Constant depth circuits, Fourier transform, and learnability. Journal of the ACM 40(3), 607–620 (1993)
15. Niedermeier, R. (ed.): Invitation to Fixed-Parameter Algorithms. Oxford University Press, Oxford (2006)

Teaching Dimension and the Complexity of Active Learning

Steve Hanneke

Machine Learning Department
Carnegie Mellon University
Pittsburgh, PA 15213 USA
shanneke@cs.cmu.edu

Abstract. We study the label complexity of pool-based active learning in the PAC model with noise. Taking inspiration from extant literature on Exact learning with membership queries, we derive upper and lower bounds on the label complexity in terms of generalizations of *extended teaching dimension*. Among the contributions of this work is the first nontrivial general upper bound on label complexity in the presence of persistent classification noise.

1 Overview of Main Results

In supervised machine learning, it is becoming increasingly apparent that well-designed interactive learning algorithms can provide valuable improvements over passive algorithms in learning performance while reducing the amount of effort required of a human annotator. In particular, there is presently much interest in the pool-based active learning setting, in which a learner can request the label of any example in a large pool of unlabeled examples. In this case, one crucial quantity is the number of label requests required by a learning algorithm: the *label complexity*. This quantity is sometimes significantly smaller than the sample complexity of passive learning. A thorough theoretical understanding of these improvements seems essential to fully exploit the potential of active learning.

In particular, active learning is formalized in the PAC model as follows. The pool of m unlabeled examples are sampled i.i.d. according to some distribution $\mathcal{D}$. A binary label is assigned to each example by a (possibly randomized) oracle, but is hidden from the learner unless it requests the label. The *error rate* of a classifier h is defined as the probability of h disagreeing with the oracle on a fresh example $X \sim \mathcal{D}$. A learning algorithm outputs a classifier $\hat{h}$ from a *concept space* $\mathbb{C}$, and we refer to the infimum error rate over classifiers in $\mathbb{C}$ as the *noise rate*, denoted ν. For $\epsilon, \delta, \eta \in (0,1)$, we define the *label complexity*, denoted $\#LQ(\mathbb{C}, \mathcal{D}, \epsilon, \delta, \eta)$, as the smallest number q such that there is an algorithm that outputs a classifier $\hat{h} \in \mathbb{C}$, and for sufficiently large m, for any oracle with $\nu \leq \eta$, with probability at least $1 - \delta$ over the sample and internal randomness, the algorithm makes at most q label requests and $\hat{h}$ has error rate at most $\nu + \epsilon$.[1]

---

[1] Alternatively, if we know q ahead of time, we can have the algorithm halt if it ever tries to make more than q queries. The analysis is nearly identical in either case.

N. Bshouty and C. Gentile (Eds.): COLT 2007, LNAI 4539, pp. 66–81, 2007.

The careful reader will note that this definition does not require the algorithm to be successful if $\nu > \eta$, distinguishing this from the fully agnostic setting [1]; we discuss possible methods to bridge this gap in later sections.

Kulkarni [2] has shown that if there is no noise, and one is allowed arbitrary binary valued queries, then $O\left(\log N(\epsilon)\right) \leq O\left(d \log \frac{1}{\epsilon}\right)$ queries suffice to PAC learn, where $N(\epsilon)$ denotes the size of a minimal ϵ-cover of $\mathbb{C}$ with respect to $\mathcal{D}$, and d is the VC dimension of $\mathbb{C}$. This bound often has exponentially better dependence on $\frac{1}{\epsilon}$, compared to the sample complexity of passive learning. However, many binary valued queries are unnatural and difficult to answer in practice. One of the driving motivations for research on the label complexity of active learning is identifying, in a general way, which concept spaces and distributions allow us to obtain this exponential improvement using only label requests for examples in the unlabeled sample. A further question is whether such improvements can be sustained in the presence of classification noise. In this paper, we investigate these questions from the perspective of a general analysis.

On the subject of learning through interaction, there is a rich literature concerning the complexity of Exact learning with membership queries [3, 4]. The interested reader should consult the limpid survey by Angluin [4]. The essential distinction between that setting and the setting we are presently concerned with is that, in Exact learning, the learning algorithm is required to *identify* the oracle's actual target function, rather than *approximating* it with high probability; on the other hand, in the Exact setting there is no classification noise and the algorithm can ask for the label of *any* example. In a sense, Exact learning with membership queries is a limiting case of PAC active learning. As such, we may hope to draw inspiration from the extant work on Exact learning when formulating an analysis for the PAC setting.

To quantify $\#MQ(\mathbb{C})$, the worst-case number of membership queries required for Exact learning with concept space $\mathbb{C}$, Hegedüs [3] defines a quantity called the *extended teaching dimension* of $\mathbb{C}$, based on the *teaching dimension* of Goldman & Kearns [5]. Letting t_0 denote this quantity, Hegedüs proves that

$$\max\{t_0, \log_2 |\mathbb{C}|\} \leq \#MQ(\mathbb{C}) \leq t_0 \log_2 |\mathbb{C}|,$$

where the upper bound is achieved by a version of the Halving algorithm.

Inspired by these results, we generalize the extended teaching dimension to the PAC setting, adding dependences on ϵ, δ, η, and $\mathcal{D}$. Specifically, we define two quantities, t and $\tilde{t}$, both of which have t_0 as a limiting case. We show that

$$\Omega\left(\max\left\{\frac{\eta^2}{\epsilon^2}, \tilde{t}, \log N(2\epsilon)\right\}\right) \leq \#LQ(\mathbb{C}, \mathcal{D}, \epsilon, \delta, \eta) \leq \tilde{O}\left(\left(\frac{\eta^2}{\epsilon^2}+1\right) t \log N(\epsilon/2)\right)$$

where $\tilde{O}$ hides factors logarithmic in $\frac{1}{\epsilon}, \frac{1}{\delta}$, and d. The upper bound is achieved by an active learning algorithm inspired by the Halving algorithm, which uses $\tilde{O}\left(d\frac{\eta+\epsilon}{\epsilon^2}\right)$ unlabeled examples. With these tools in hand, we analyze the label complexity of axis-aligned rectangles with respect to product distributions, showing improvements over known passive learning results in dependence on η when positive examples are not too rare.

The rest of the paper is organized as follows. In Section 2, we briefly survey the related literature on the label complexity of active learning. This is followed in Section 3 with the introduction of definitions and notation, and a brief discussion of known results for Exact learning in Section 4. In Section 5, we move into results for the PAC setting, beginning with the noise-free case for simplicity. Then, in Section 6, we describe the general setting, and prove an upper bound on the label complexity of active learning with noise; to the author's knowledge, this is the first general result of its kind, and along with lower bounds on label complexity presented in Section 7, represents the primary contribution of this work. We continue in Section 8, with an application of these bounds to describe the label complexity of axis-aligned rectangles with product distributions. We conclude with some enticing open problems in Section 9.

2   Context and Related Work

The recent literature studying general label complexity can be coarsely partitioned by the measure of progress used in the analysis. Specifically, there are at least three distinct ways to measure the progress of an active learning algorithm: *diameter* of the version space, *measure* of the region of disagreement, and *size* of the version space. By the *version space* at a time during the algorithm execution, we mean the set of concepts in $\mathbb{C}$ that have not yet been ruled out as a possible output. One approach to studying label complexity is to summarize in a single quantity how easy it is to make progress in terms of one of these progress metrics. This quantity, apart from itself being interesting, can then be used to derive upper and lower bounds on the label complexity.

To study the ease of reducing the diameter of the version space in active learning, Dasgupta [6] defines a quantity ρ he calls the *splitting index*. ρ is dependent on $\mathbb{C}$, $\mathcal{D}$, ϵ, and another parameter τ he defines, as well as the oracle itself. Dasgupta finds that when the noise rate is zero, roughly $\tilde{O}(\frac{d}{\rho})$ label requests are sufficient, and $\Omega(\frac{1}{\rho})$ are necessary for learning (for respectively appropriate τ values). However, Dasgupta's analysis is restricted to the noise-free case, and there are no known extensions addressing the noisy case.

In studying ways to enable active learning in the presence of noise, Balcan et al. [1] propose the A^2 algorithm. This algorithm is able to learn in the presence of arbitrary classification noise. The strategy behind A^2 is to induce confidence intervals for the differences of error rates of concepts in the version space. If an estimated difference is statistically significant, the algorithm removes the worst of the two concepts. The key observation is that, since the algorithm only estimates error *differences*, there is no need to request the label of any example that all remaining concepts agree on. Thus, the number of label requests made by A^2 is largely controlled by how quickly the *region of disagreement* collapses as the algorithm progresses. However, apart from fall-back guarantees and a few special cases, there is presently no published general analysis of the number of label requests made by A^2, and no general index of how easy it is to reduce the region of disagreement.

The third progress metric is reduction in the *size* of the version space. If the concept space is infinite, an ϵ'-cover of $\mathbb{C}$ can be substituted for $\mathbb{C}$, for some suitable ϵ'.[2] This paper presents the first general study of the ease of reducing the size of the version space. The corresponding index summarizing the potential for progress in this metric remains informative in the presence of noise, given access to an upper bound on the noise rate.

In addition to the above studies, Kääriäinen [7] presents an interesting analysis of active learning with various types of noise. Specifically, he proves that under noise that is not persistent (in that requesting the same label twice may yield different responses) and where the Bayes optimal classifier is in $\mathbb{C}$, any algorithm that is successful for the zero noise setting can be transformed into a successful algorithm for the noisy setting with only a small increase in the number of label requests. However, these positive results do not carry into our present setting (*arbitrary persistent* classification noise). In fact, in addition to these positive results, Kääriäinen [7] presents negative results in the form of a general lower bound on the label complexity of active learning with arbitrary (persistent) classification noise. Specifically, he finds that for most nontrivial distributions $\mathcal{D}$, one can force any algorithm to make $\Omega\left(\frac{\nu^2}{\epsilon^2}\right)$ label requests.

3   Notation

We begin by introducing some notation. Let $\mathcal{X}$ be a set, called the *instance space*, and $\mathcal{F}$ be a corresponding σ-algebra. Let $\mathcal{D}_{XY}$ be a probability measure on $\mathcal{X} \times \{-1, 1\}$. We use $\mathcal{D}$ to denote the marginal distribution of $\mathcal{D}_{XY}$ over $\mathcal{X}$. $\mathbb{C}_{\mathcal{F}}$ is the set of all $\mathcal{F}$-measurable $f : \mathcal{X} \to \{-1, 1\}$. $\mathbb{C} \subseteq \mathbb{C}_{\mathcal{F}}$ is a concept space on $\mathcal{X}$, and we use d to denote the VC dimension of $\mathbb{C}$; to focus on nontrivial learning, we assume $d > 0$. For any $h, h' \in \mathbb{C}_{\mathcal{F}}$, define $er_{\mathcal{D}}(h, h') = \mathcal{P}r_{X \sim \mathcal{D}}\{h(X) \neq h'(X)\}$. If $\mathcal{U} \in \mathcal{X}^m$, define $er_{\mathcal{U}}(h, h') = \frac{1}{m}\sum_{x \in \mathcal{U}} I[h(x) \neq h'(x)]$.[3] If $\mathcal{L} \in (\mathcal{X} \times \{-1, 1\})^m$, define $er_{\mathcal{L}}(h) = \frac{1}{m}\sum_{(x,y) \in \mathcal{L}} I[h(x) \neq y]$. For any $h \in \mathbb{C}_{\mathcal{F}}$, define $er(h) = \mathcal{P}r_{(X,Y) \sim \mathcal{D}_{XY}}\{h(X) \neq Y\}$. Define the *noise rate* $\nu = \inf_{h \in \mathbb{C}} er(h)$. An α-cover of $\mathbb{C}$ is any $V \subseteq \mathbb{C}$ s.t. $\forall h \in \mathbb{C}, \exists h' \in V$ with $er_{\mathcal{D}}(h, h') \leq \alpha$.

Generally, in this setting data is sampled i.i.d. according to $\mathcal{D}_{XY}$, but the labels are hidden from the learner unless it asks the oracle for them individually. In particular, requesting the same example's label twice gives the same label both times (though if the data sequence contains two identical examples, requesting

---

[2] An alternative, but very similar progress metric is the size of an ϵ-cover of the version space. The author suspects the analysis presented in this paper can be extended to describe that type of progress as well.

[3] We overload the standard set-theoretic notation to also apply to sequences. In particular, $\sum_{x \in \mathcal{U}}$ indicates a sum over entries of the sequence $\mathcal{U}$ (not necessarily all distinct). Similarly, we use $|\mathcal{U}|$ to denote length of the sequence $\mathcal{U}$, $S \subseteq \mathcal{U}$ to denote a subsequence of $\mathcal{U}$, $S \cup \mathcal{U}$ to denote concatenation of two sequences, and for any particular $x \in \mathcal{U}$, $\mathcal{U} \setminus \{x\}$ indicates the subsequence of $\mathcal{U}$ with all entries except the single occurrence of x that is implicitly referenced in the statement. It may help to think of each instance x in a sample as having a unique identifier.

both labels might give two different values). However, for notational simplicity, we often abuse this notation by stating that $X \sim \mathcal{D}$ and later stating that the algorithm requests the label of X, denoted $Oracle(X)$; by this, we implicitly mean that $(X, Y) \sim \mathcal{D}_{XY}$, and the oracle reveals the value of Y upon request. In particular, for $\mathcal{U} \sim \mathcal{D}^m$, $h \in \mathbb{C}_{\mathcal{F}}$, define $er_{\mathcal{U}}(h) = \frac{1}{m}\sum_{x \in \mathcal{U}} I[h(x) \neq Oracle(x)]$.

Definition 1. *For $V \subseteq \mathbb{C}$ with finite $|V|$, the majority vote concept $h_{maj} \in \mathbb{C}_{\mathcal{F}}$ is defined by $h_{maj}(x) = 1$ iff $|\{h \in V : h(x) = 1\}| \geq \frac{1}{2}|V|$.*

Definition 2. *For $\mathcal{U} \in \mathcal{X}^m$, $h \in \mathbb{C}_{\mathcal{F}}$, we overload notation to define the sequence of labels $h(\mathcal{U}) = \{h(x)\}_{x \in \mathcal{U}}$ assigned to entries of $\mathcal{U}$ by h. For $V \subseteq \mathbb{C}_{\mathcal{F}}$, $V[\mathcal{U}]$ denotes any subset of V such that $\forall h \in V, |\{h' \in V[\mathcal{U}] : h'(\mathcal{U}) = h(\mathcal{U})\}| = 1$. $V[\mathcal{U}]$ represents the labelings of $\mathcal{U}$ realizable by V.*

4   Extended Teaching Dimension

Definition 3. *(Extended Teaching Dimension [3]) Let $V \subseteq \mathbb{C}$, $m \geq 0$, $\mathcal{U} \in \mathcal{X}^m$.*

$$\forall f \in \mathbb{C}_{\mathcal{F}}, XTD(f, V, \mathcal{U}) = \inf\{t | \exists R \subseteq \mathcal{U} : |\{h \in V : h(R) = f(R)\}| \leq 1 \wedge |R| \leq t\}.$$
$$XTD(V, \mathcal{U}) = \sup_{f \in \mathbb{C}_{\mathcal{F}}} XTD(f, V, \mathcal{U}).$$

For a given f, we call any $R \subseteq \mathcal{U}$ such that $|\{h \in V : h(R) = f(R)\}| \leq 1$ a specifying set for f on $\mathcal{U}$ with respect to V.[4]

The goal of Exact learning with membership queries is to ask for the labels $f(x)$ of individual examples $x \in \mathcal{X}$ until the only concept in $\mathbb{C}$ consistent with the observed labels is the target $f \in \mathbb{C}$. Hegedüs [3] presents the following algorithm.

Algorithm: MembHalving
Output: The target concept $f \in \mathbb{C}$
0. $V \leftarrow \mathbb{C}$
1. Repeat until $|V| = 1$
2.   Let h_{maj} be the majority vote of V
3.   Let $R \subseteq \mathcal{X}$ be a minimal specifying set for h_{maj} on $\mathcal{X}$ with respect to V
4.   Ask for the label $f(x)$ of every $x \in R$
5.   Let $V \leftarrow \{h \in V | \forall x \in R, f(x) = h(x)\}$
6. Return the remaining element of V

Theorem 1. *(Exact Learning: Hegedüs [3]). Letting $\#MQ(\mathbb{C})$ denote the Exact learning query complexity of $\mathbb{C}$ with membership queries on any examples in $\mathcal{X}$, and $t_0 = XTD(\mathbb{C}, \mathcal{X})$, then the following inequalities are valid if $|\mathbb{C}| > 2$.*

$$\max\{t_0, \log_2 |\mathbb{C}|\} \leq \#MQ(\mathbb{C}) \leq t_0 \log_2 |\mathbb{C}|.$$

Furthermore, this upper bound is achieved by the MembHalving algorithm.[5]

---

[4] We also overload all of these definitions in the obvious way for sets $\mathcal{U} \subseteq \mathcal{X}$.

[5] By a slight alteration to choose queries in a particular greedy order, Hegedüs is able to reduce this upper bound to $2\frac{t_0}{\log_2 t_0} \log_2 |\mathbb{C}|$. However, it is the simpler form of the algorithm (presented here) that we draw inspiration from in the following sections.

The upper bound of Theorem 1 is clear when we view MembHalving as a version of the Halving algorithm [8]. That is, querying all examples in a specifying set for h guarantees either h makes a mistake or we identify f. Thus, querying a specifying set for h_{maj} guarantees that we at least halve the version space.

The following definitions represent natural extensions of XTD to the PAC setting. The relation of these quantities to the complexity of active learning is our primary focus.

Definition 4. *(XTD Growth Function)* For $m \geq 0$, $V \subseteq \mathbb{C}$, $\delta \in [0, 1]$,

$$XTD(V, \mathcal{D}, m, \delta) = \inf\{t | \forall f \in \mathbb{C}_{\mathcal{F}}, \mathcal{P}r_{\mathcal{U} \sim \mathcal{D}^m}\{XTD(f, V[\mathcal{U}], \mathcal{U}) > t\} \leq \delta\}.$$
$$XTD(V, m) = \sup_{\mathcal{U} \in \mathcal{X}^m} XTD(V[\mathcal{U}], \mathcal{U}).$$

$XTD(\mathbb{C}, \mathcal{D}, m, \delta)$ plays an important role in distribution-dependent bounds on the label complexity, while $XTD(\mathbb{C}, m)$ plays an analogous role in distribution-free bounds. Clearly $0 \leq XTD(\mathbb{C}, \mathcal{D}, m, \delta) \leq XTD(\mathbb{C}, m) \leq m$.

As a simple example, consider the space of thresholds on the line. That is, suppose $\mathcal{X} = \mathbb{R}$ and $\mathbb{C} = \{h_\theta : \theta \in \mathbb{R}, h_\theta(x) = +1 \text{ iff } x \geq \theta\}$. In this case, $XTD(\mathbb{C}, m) = 2$, since for any set $\mathcal{U}$ of m points, and any $f \in \mathbb{C}_{\mathcal{F}}$, we can form a specifying set with the points $\min\{x \in \mathcal{U} : f(x) = +1\}$ and $\max\{x \in \mathcal{U} : f(x) = -1\}$, (if they exist).

5   The Complexity of Realizable Active Learning

Before discussing the general setting, we begin with realizable learning ($\eta = 0$), because the analysis is quite simple, and clearly highlights the relationship to the MembHalving algorithm. We handle noisy labels in the next section.

Based on Theorem 1, it should be clear that for $m \geq \Omega\left(\frac{1}{\epsilon}\left(d\log\frac{1}{\epsilon} + \log\frac{1}{\delta}\right)\right)$, $\#LQ(\mathbb{C}, \mathcal{D}, \epsilon, \delta, 0) \leq XTD(\mathbb{C}, m)d\log_2\frac{em}{d}$. Roughly speaking, this is achieved by drawing m unlabeled examples $\mathcal{U}$ and executing MembHalving with concept space $\mathbb{C}[\mathcal{U}]$ and instance space $\mathcal{U}$. This gives a *data-dependent* bound of $XTD(\mathbb{C}[\mathcal{U}], \mathcal{U})\log_2|\mathbb{C}[\mathcal{U}]| \leq XTD(\mathbb{C}, m)d\log_2\frac{em}{d}$. We can also obtain a related *distribution-dependent* result as follows. Consider the following algorithm.

Algorithm: ActiveHalving
Input: $V \subseteq \mathbb{C}_{\mathcal{F}}$, values $\epsilon, \delta \in (0, 1)$, $\mathcal{U} = \{x_1, x_2, \ldots, x_m\} \in \mathcal{X}^m$, constant $n \in \mathbb{N}$
Output: Concept $\hat{h} \in V$
0. Let $i \leftarrow 0$
1. Repeat
2. $i \leftarrow i + 1$
3.   Let $\mathcal{U}_i = \{x_{1+n(i-1)}, x_{2+n(i-1)}, \ldots, x_{ni}\}$
4.   Let h_{maj} be the majority vote of V
5.   Let $R \subseteq \mathcal{U}_i$ be a minimal specifying set for h_{maj} on $\mathcal{U}_i$ w.r.t. $V[\mathcal{U}_i]$
6.   Ask for the label $f(x)$ of every $x \in R$
7.   Let $V \leftarrow \{h \in V | f(R) = h(R)\}$
8.   If $\exists h \in V$ s.t. $h_{maj}(\mathcal{U}_i) = h(\mathcal{U}_i)$, Return $\arg\min_{\hat{h} \in V} er_{\mathcal{U}}(\hat{h}, h_{maj})$

Theorem 2. *Let* $m = \left\lceil \frac{256d}{\epsilon} \left(\ln \frac{92d}{\epsilon\delta} \right)^2 \right\rceil$, *and* $n = \left\lceil \frac{4}{\epsilon} \ln \frac{12d \log_2 \frac{4em}{\delta}}{\delta} \right\rceil$. *Let* $\hat{t} = XTD \left(\mathbb{C}, \mathcal{D}, n, \frac{\delta}{12d \log_2 \frac{4em}{\delta}} \right)$. *If* $N(\delta/(2m))$ *is the size of a minimal* $\frac{\delta}{2m}$-*cover of* $\mathbb{C}$, *then*

$$\#LQ(\mathbb{C}, \mathcal{D}, \epsilon, \delta, 0) \le \hat{t} \log_2 N(\delta/(2m)) \le O\left(\hat{t}d \log \frac{d}{\epsilon\delta} \right).$$

Proof. The bound is achieved by ActiveHalving$(V, \epsilon, \delta, \mathcal{U}, n)$, where $\mathcal{U} \sim \mathcal{D}^m$, and V is a minimal $\frac{\delta}{2m}$-cover of $\mathbb{C}$. Let $f \in \mathbb{C}$ have $er(f) = 0$. Let $\hat{f} = \arg\min_{h \in V} er(h)$. With probability $\ge 1 - \delta/2$, $f(\mathcal{U}) = \hat{f}(\mathcal{U})$. Suppose this happens. In each iteration, if the condition in step 8 does not obtain, then either $\exists x \in R : h_{maj}(x) \ne f(x)$ or else $V[\mathcal{U}_i] = \{h\}$ for some $h \in V$ such that $\exists x \in \mathcal{U}_i : h_{maj}(x) \ne h(x) = f(x)$. Either way, we must have eliminated at least half of V in step 7, so the condition in step 8 fails at most $\log_2 N(\delta/(2m)) < 2d \log_2 \frac{4em}{\delta} - 1$ times.

On the other hand, suppose the condition in step 8 obtains. This happens only when $h_{maj}(\mathcal{U}_i) = f(\mathcal{U}_i)$. $Pr_{\mathcal{U}_i} \left\{ er_{\mathcal{U}_i}(h_{maj}, f) = 0 \wedge er_{\mathcal{U}}(h_{maj}, f) > \frac{\epsilon}{4} \right\} \le \frac{\delta}{12d \log_2 \frac{4em}{\delta}}$. By a union bound, the probability that an h_{maj} with $er_{\mathcal{U}}(h_{maj}, f) > \frac{\epsilon}{4}$ satisfies the condition in step 8 on any iteration is at most $\frac{\delta}{6}$. If this does not happen, then the $\hat{h} \in V$ we return has $er_{\mathcal{U}}(\hat{h}, f) \le er_{\mathcal{U}}(\hat{h}, h_{maj}) + er_{\mathcal{U}}(h_{maj}, f) \le er_{\mathcal{U}}(f, h_{maj}) + er_{\mathcal{U}}(h_{maj}, f) \le \frac{\epsilon}{2}$. By Chernoff and union bounds, m is large enough so that with probability at least $1 - \frac{\delta}{6}$, $er_{\mathcal{U}}(\hat{h}, f) \le \frac{\epsilon}{2} \Rightarrow er_{\mathcal{D}}(\hat{h}, f) \le \epsilon$. So with probability $1 - \frac{5\delta}{6}$, we return an $\hat{h} \in \mathbb{C}$ with $er_{\mathcal{D}}(\hat{h}, f) \le \epsilon$.

On the issue of number of queries, each iteration queries a minimal specifying set for h_{maj} on a set of size n. The probability the size of this set is larger than $\hat{t}$ for a particular set $\mathcal{U}_i$ is at most $\frac{\delta}{12d \log_2 \frac{4em}{\delta}}$. By a union bound, the probability it is larger than $\hat{t}$ on any iteration is at most $\frac{\delta}{6}$. Thus, the total probability of success (in learning and obtaining the query bound) is at least $1 - \delta$. $\qquad\square$

Note that we can obtain a worst-case label bound for ActiveHalving by replacing $\hat{t}$ above with $XTD(\mathbb{C}, n)$. Theorem 2 highlights the relationship to known results in Exact learning with membership queries [3]. In particular, if $\mathbb{C}$ and $\mathcal{X}$ are finite, and $\mathcal{D}$ has support everywhere on $\mathcal{X}$, then as $\epsilon \to 0$ and $\delta \to 0$, the bound converges to $XTD(\mathbb{C}, \mathcal{X}) \log_2 |\mathbb{C}|$, the upper bound in Theorem 1.

6 The Complexity of Active Learning with Noise

The following algorithm can be viewed as a noise-tolerant version of ActiveHalving. Significant care is needed to ensure we do not discard the best concept, and that the final classifier is near-optimal. The main trick is to use subsamples of size $< \frac{1}{16\eta}$. Since the probability of such a subsample containing a noisy example is small, the specifying sets for h_{maj} will often be noise-free. Therefore, if $h \in V$ is contradicted in many such specifying sets, we can be confident h is suboptimal. Likewise, if for a particular unqueried x, there are many such subsamples containing x where h_{maj} is *not* contradicted, and where there is a consistent h, then more often than not, $h(x) = h^*(x)$, where $h^* = \arg\min_{h' \in V} er(h')$.

Algorithm: $ReduceAndLabel(V, \mathcal{U}, \epsilon, \delta, \hat{\eta})$

Input: Finite $V \subseteq \mathbb{C}_\mathcal{F}$, $\mathcal{U} = \{x_1, x_2, \ldots, x_m\} \in \mathcal{X}^m$, values $\epsilon, \delta, \hat{\eta} \in (0, 1]$.

Output: Concept $h \in V$.

0. Let $u = \lfloor |\mathcal{U}|/(5 \ln |V|) \rfloor$
1. Let $V_0 \leftarrow V$, $i \leftarrow 0$
2. Do
3. $i \leftarrow i + 1$
4.   Let $\mathcal{U}_i = \{x_{1+u(i-1)}, x_{2+u(i-1)}, \ldots, x_{ui}\}$
5. $V_i \leftarrow Reduce\left(V_{i-1}, \mathcal{U}_i, \frac{\delta}{48 \ln |V|}, \hat{\eta} + \frac{\epsilon}{2}\right)$
6. Until $|V_i| > \frac{3}{4}|V_{i-1}|$ or $|V_i| \leq 1$
7. Let $\bar{\mathcal{U}} = \{x_{ui+1}, x_{ui+2}, \ldots, x_{ui+\ell}\}$, where $\ell = \left\lceil 12\frac{\hat{\eta}}{\epsilon^2} \ln \frac{12|V|}{\delta} \right\rceil$
8. $\mathcal{L} \leftarrow Label\left(V_{i-1}, \bar{\mathcal{U}}, \frac{\delta}{12}, \hat{\eta} + \frac{\epsilon}{2}\right)$
9. Return $h \in V_i$ having smallest $er_\mathcal{L}(h)$, (or any $h \in V$ if $V_i = \varnothing$)

Subroutine: $Reduce(V, \mathcal{U}, \delta, \hat{\eta})$

Input: Finite $V \subseteq \mathbb{C}_\mathcal{F}$, unlabeled sequence $\mathcal{U}$, values $\delta, \hat{\eta} \in (0, 1]$

Output: Concept space $V' \subseteq V$

0. Let $m = |\mathcal{U}|$, $n = \left\lfloor \frac{1}{16\hat{\eta}} \right\rfloor$, $r = \left\lceil 397 \ln \frac{2}{\delta} \right\rceil$, $\theta = \frac{27}{320}$
1. Let h_{maj} be the majority vote of V
2. For $i \in \{1, 2, \ldots, r\}$
3.   Sample a subsequence S_i of size n uniformly without replacement from $\mathcal{U}$
4.   Let R_i be a minimal specifying set for h_{maj} in S_i with respect to $V[S_i]$
5.   Ask for the label of every example in R_i
6.   Let $\bar{V}_i$ be the concepts $h \in V$ s.t. $h(R_i) \neq Oracle(R_i)$
7. Let $\bar{V}$ be the set of $h \in V$ that appear in $> \theta \cdot r$ of the sets $\bar{V}_i$
8. Return $V' = V \setminus \bar{V}$

Subroutine: $Label(V, \mathcal{U}, \delta, \hat{\eta})$

Input: Finite $V \subseteq \mathbb{C}_\mathcal{F}$, unlabeled sequence $\mathcal{U}$, values $\delta, \hat{\eta} \in (0, 1]$

Output: Labeled sequence $\mathcal{L}$

0. Let $\ell = |\mathcal{U}|$, $n = \left\lfloor \frac{1}{16\hat{\eta}} \right\rfloor$, $k = \left\lceil 167\frac{\ell}{n} \ln \frac{3\ell}{\delta} \right\rceil$
1. Let h_{maj} be the majority vote of V, and let $\mathcal{L} \leftarrow \{\}$
2. For $i \in \{1, 2, \ldots, k\}$
3.   Sample a subsequence S_i of size n uniformly without replacement from $\mathcal{U}$
4.   Let R_i be a minimal specifying set for h_{maj} in S_i with respect to $V[S_i]$
5.   For each $x \in R_i$, ask the oracle for its label y_x and let $\mathcal{L} \leftarrow \mathcal{L} \cup \{(x, y_x)\}$
6. Let $\hat{\mathcal{U}} \subseteq \mathcal{U}$ be the subsequence of examples we did not ask for the label of
7. For each $x \in \hat{\mathcal{U}}$
8.   Let $\hat{I}_x = \{i : x \in S_i \text{ and } \exists h \in V \text{ s.t. } h(R_i) = h_{maj}(R_i) = Oracle(R_i)\}$
9.   For each $i \in \hat{I}_x$, let $h_i \in V$ be s.t. $h_i(R_i) = Oracle(R_i)$
10.   Let y be the majority value of $\{h_i(x) : i \in \hat{I}_x\}$ (breaking ties arbitrarily)
11.   Let $\mathcal{L} \leftarrow \mathcal{L} \cup \{(x, y)\}$
12. Return $\mathcal{L}$

Lemma 1. *(Reduce) Suppose $h^* \in V$ is a concept such that $er_{\mathcal{U}}(h^*) \leq \hat{\eta} < \frac{1}{32}$. Let V' be the set returned by $Reduce(V, \mathcal{U}, \epsilon, \delta, \hat{\eta})$. With probability at least $1 - \delta$, $h^* \in V'$, and if $er_{\mathcal{U}}(h_{maj}, h^*) \geq 10\hat{\eta}$ then $|V'| \leq \frac{3}{4}|V|$.*

Proof. By a *noisy example*, in this context we mean any $x \in \mathcal{U}$ for which $h^*(x)$ disagrees with the oracle's label. Let $n = \left\lfloor \frac{1}{16\hat{\eta}} \right\rfloor$ and $r = \left\lceil 397 \ln \frac{2}{\delta} \right\rceil$, $\theta = \frac{27}{320}$. By a Chernoff bound, sampling r subsequences of size n, each without replacement from $\mathcal{U}$, guarantees with probability $\geq 1 - \frac{\delta}{2}$ that at most θr of the subsequences contain any noisy examples. In particular, this would imply $h^* \in V'$.

Now suppose $er_{\mathcal{U}}(h_{maj}, h^*) \geq 10\hat{\eta}$. For any particular subsampled sequence S_i, $Pr_{S_i \sim U_n(\mathcal{U})} \{h_{maj}(S_i) = h^*(S_i)\} \leq (1 - 10\hat{\eta})^n \leq 0.627$. So the probability there is some $x \in S_i$ with $h_{maj}(x) \neq h^*(x)$ is at least 0.373. By a Chernoff bound, with probability at least $1 - \frac{\delta}{2}$, at least $4\theta r$ of the r subsamples contain some $x \in \mathcal{U}$ such that $h_{maj}(x) \neq h^*(x)$.

By a union bound, the total probability the above two events succeed is at least $1 - \delta$. Suppose this happens. Any sequence S_i containing no noisy examples but $\exists x \in S_i$ such that $h_{maj}(x) \neq h^*(x)$ necessarily has $|\bar{V}_i| \geq \frac{1}{2}|V|$. Since there are at least $3\theta r$ such subsamples S_i, we have $|\bar{V}| \geq \left(3\theta r \cdot \frac{1}{2}|V| - \theta r \cdot |V|\right) / (2\theta r) = \frac{1}{4}|V|$, so that $|V'| \leq \frac{3}{4}|V|$. $\square$

Lemma 2. *(Label) Let $\mathcal{U} \in \mathcal{X}^\ell$, $\ell > n$. Suppose $h^* \in V$ has $er_{\mathcal{U}}(h^*) \leq \hat{\eta} < \frac{1}{32}$. Let h_{maj} be the majority vote of V, and suppose $er_{\mathcal{U}}(h_{maj}, h^*) \leq 12\hat{\eta}$. Let $\mathcal{L}$ be the sequence returned by $Label(V, \mathcal{U}, \delta, \hat{\eta})$. With probability at least $1 - \delta$, for every $(x, y) \in \mathcal{L}$, y is either the oracle's label for x or $y = h^*(x)$. In any case, $\forall x \in \mathcal{U}, |\{y : (x, y) \in \mathcal{L}\}| = 1$.*

Proof. As above, a *noisy example* is any $x \in \mathcal{U}$ such that $h^*(x)$ disagrees with the oracle. For any x we ask for the label of, the entry $(x, y) \in \mathcal{L}$ has y equal to the oracle's label, so the focus of the proof is on $\hat{\mathcal{U}}$. For each $x \in \hat{\mathcal{U}}$, let $I_x = \{i : x \in S_i\}$, $A = \{i : \exists x' \in R_i, h^*(x') \neq Oracle(x')\}$, and $B = \{i : \exists x' \in R_i, h_{maj}(x') \neq h^*(x')\}$. $\forall x \in \hat{\mathcal{U}}$, if $|I_x \cap A| < |(I_x \setminus B) \setminus A|$, we have that $|\{i \in I_x : h^*(R_i) = h_{maj}(R_i) = Oracle(R_i)\}| > \frac{1}{2}|\hat{I}_x| > 0$. In particular, this means the majority value of $\{h_i(x) : i \in \hat{I}_x\}$ is $h^*(x)$. The remainder of the proof bounds the probability this fails to happen.

For $x \in \hat{\mathcal{U}}$, for $i \in \{1, 2, \ldots, k\}$ let $\bar{S}_{i,x}$ of size n be sampled uniformly without replacement from $\mathcal{U} \setminus \{x\}$, $\bar{A}_x = \{i : \exists x' \in \bar{S}_{i,x}, h^*(x') \neq Oracle(x')\}$, and $\bar{B}_x = \{i : \exists x' \in \bar{S}_{i,x}, h_{maj}(x') \neq h^*(x')\}$.

$$Pr\left\{\exists x \in \hat{\mathcal{U}} : |I_x \cap A| \geq |(I_x \setminus B) \setminus A|\right\}$$

$$\leq \sum_{x \in \mathcal{U}} Pr\left\{|I_x| < \frac{nk}{2\ell}\right\} + Pr\left\{|I_x \cap \bar{A}_x| \geq \frac{\sqrt{96}-1}{80}|I_x| \wedge |I_x| \geq \frac{nk}{2\ell}\right\} +$$

$$Pr\left\{|(I_x \setminus \bar{B}_x) \setminus \bar{A}_x| \leq \frac{\sqrt{96}-1}{80}|I_x| \wedge |I_x| \geq \frac{nk}{2\ell}\right\} \leq \ell\left[e^{-\frac{kn}{8\ell}} + 2e^{-\frac{nk}{167\ell}}\right] \leq \delta.$$

The second inequality is due to Chernoff and Hoeffding bounds. $\square$

Lemma 3. *Suppose $\nu = \inf_{h \in \mathbb{C}} er(h) \leq \eta$ and $\eta + \frac{3}{4}\epsilon < \frac{1}{32}$. Let V be an $\frac{\epsilon}{2}$-cover of $\mathbb{C}$. Let $\mathcal{U} \sim \mathcal{D}^m$, with $m = \left\lceil 224\frac{\eta + \epsilon/2}{\epsilon^2} \ln \frac{48 \ln |V|}{\delta} \right\rceil \lceil 5 \ln |V| \rceil$. Let $n = \left\lfloor \frac{1}{16(\eta + 3\epsilon/4)} \right\rfloor$, $\ell = \left\lceil 48\frac{\eta + \epsilon/2}{\epsilon^2} \ln \frac{12|V|}{\delta} \right\rceil$, $s = \left\lceil 397 \ln \frac{96 \ln |V|}{\delta} \right\rceil (4 \ln |V|) + \left\lceil 167 \frac{\ell}{n} \ln \frac{36\ell}{\delta} \right\rceil$, and $t = XTD\left(V, \mathcal{D}, n, \frac{\delta}{2s}\right)$. With probability $\geq 1 - \delta$, ReduceAndLabel $\left(V, \mathcal{U}, \frac{\epsilon}{2}, \delta, \eta + \frac{\epsilon}{2}\right)$ makes at most ts label queries and returns a concept h with $er(h) \leq \nu + \epsilon$.*

Proof. Let $h^* \in V$ have $er(h^*) \leq \nu + \frac{\epsilon}{2}$. Suppose the value of i is ι when we reach step 7. Clearly $\iota \leq \log_{4/3} |V| \leq 4 \ln |V|$. Let h^i_{maj} denote the majority vote of V_i. We proceed by bounding the probability that any of six specific events fail to happen. The first event is

$$\left[\forall i \in \{1, 2, \ldots, \iota\}, er_{\mathcal{U}_i}(h^*) \leq \eta + \frac{3}{4}\epsilon \right].$$

The probability this fails is $\leq (4 \ln |V|)e^{-\left\lfloor \frac{m}{5 \ln |V|} \right\rfloor \frac{\epsilon^2}{\eta + \epsilon/2} \frac{1}{48}} \leq \frac{\delta}{12}$ (by Chernoff and union bounds). The next event we consider is

$$\left[\forall i \in \{1, 2, \ldots, \iota\}, h^* \in V_i \text{ and (if } |V_\iota| > 1) \ er_{\mathcal{U}_\iota}\left(h^{\iota-1}_{maj}, h^*\right) < 10\left(\eta + \frac{3}{4}\epsilon\right) \right].$$

By Lemma 1 and a union bound, the previous event succeeds but this one fails with probability $\leq \frac{\delta}{12}$. Next, note that the event

$$\left[\forall i \in \{1, 2, \ldots, \iota\}, er_{\mathcal{U}_i}\left(h^{i-1}_{maj}, h^*\right) < 10\left(\eta + \frac{3}{4}\epsilon\right) \Rightarrow er_{\mathcal{D}}\left(h^{i-1}_{maj}, h^*\right) \leq \frac{21}{2}\left(\eta + \frac{3}{4}\epsilon\right) \right]$$

fails with probability $\leq (4 \ln |V|)e^{-\left\lfloor \frac{m}{5 \ln |V|} \right\rfloor (\eta + \frac{3}{4}\epsilon)\frac{1}{84}} \leq \frac{\delta}{12}$. The fourth event is

$$\left[er_{\bar{\mathcal{U}}}\left(h^{\iota-1}_{maj}, h^*\right) \leq 12\left(\eta + \frac{3}{4}\epsilon\right) \right].$$

By a Chernoff bound, the probability this fails when the previous three events succeed is $\leq e^{-\frac{\ell}{14}(\eta + \frac{3}{4}\epsilon)} \leq \frac{\delta}{12}$. The fifth event is

$$[er_{\bar{\mathcal{U}}}(h^*) \leq er(h^*) + \frac{\epsilon}{4} \text{ and } \forall h \in V_{\iota-1}, er(h) > er(h^*) + \frac{\epsilon}{2} \Rightarrow er_{\bar{\mathcal{U}}}(h) > er_{\bar{\mathcal{U}}}(h^*)].$$

By Chernoff and union bounds, the probability the previous events succeed but this fails is $\leq |V|e^{-\frac{\ell}{48}\frac{\epsilon^2}{\eta + \epsilon/2}} \leq \frac{\delta}{12}$. Finally, consider the event

$$[\forall (x, y) \in \mathcal{L}, y = h^*(x) \text{ or } y = Oracle(x)].$$

By Lemma 2, this fails when the other five succeed with probability $\leq \frac{\delta}{12}$. Thus the probability all of these events succeed is $\geq 1 - \frac{\delta}{2}$. If they succeed, then any $h' \in V_\iota$ with $er(h') > \nu + \epsilon \geq er(h^*) + \frac{\epsilon}{2}$ has $er_{\mathcal{L}}(h') > er_{\mathcal{L}}(h^*) \geq \min_{h \in V_\iota} er_{\mathcal{L}}(h)$. Thus the h we return has $er(h) \leq \nu + \epsilon$.

In each call to *Reduce*, we ask for the labels of a minimal specifying set for $r = \left\lceil 397 \ln \frac{96 \ln |V|}{\delta} \right\rceil$ sequences of length n. For each, we make at most t label requests with probability $\geq 1 - \frac{\delta}{2s}$, so the probability any call to *Reduce* makes more than tr label requests is $\leq \frac{4\delta r \ln |V|}{2s}$. Similarly, in *Label* we request the labels of a minimal specifying set for $\leq k = \left\lceil 167 \frac{\ell}{n} \ln \frac{36\ell}{\delta} \right\rceil$ sequences of length n. So we make at most tk queries in *Label* with probability $\geq 1 - \frac{\delta k}{2s}$. Thus, the total probability we make more than $t(k + 4r \ln |V|) = ts$ queries is $\leq \frac{4\delta r \ln |V|}{2s} + \frac{\delta k}{2s} = \frac{\delta}{2}$. The total probability either the query or error bound is violated is at most δ. $\square$

Theorem 3. *Let* $n = \left\lfloor \frac{1}{16(\eta+3\epsilon/4)} \right\rfloor$, *and let* N *be the size of a minimal* $\frac{\epsilon}{2}$-*cover of* $\mathbb{C}$. *Let* $\ell = \left\lceil 48 \frac{\eta+\epsilon/2}{\epsilon^2} \ln \frac{12N}{\delta} \right\rceil$. *Let* $s = \left\lceil (397 \ln \frac{96 \ln N}{\delta}) \right\rceil (4 \ln N) + \left\lceil 167 \frac{\ell}{n} \ln \frac{36\ell}{\delta} \right\rceil$, *and* $t = XTD\left(\mathbb{C}, \mathcal{D}, n, \frac{\delta}{2s}\right)$.

$$\#LQ(\mathbb{C}, \mathcal{D}, \epsilon, \delta, \eta) \leq ts = O\left(t\left(\frac{\eta^2}{\epsilon^2}+1\right)\left(d\log\frac{1}{\epsilon} + \log\frac{1}{\delta}\right)\left(\log\frac{d}{\epsilon\delta}\right)\right).$$

Proof. It is known that $N < 2\left(\frac{4e}{\epsilon} \ln \frac{4e}{\epsilon}\right)^d$ [9]. If $\eta + \frac{3}{4}\epsilon \geq \frac{1}{32}$, the bound exceeds the passive sample complexity, so it clearly holds. Otherwise, the result follows from Lemma 3 and the fact that $XTD\left(V, \mathcal{D}, n, \frac{\delta}{2s}\right) \leq XTD\left(\mathbb{C}, \mathcal{D}, n, \frac{\delta}{2s}\right)$. $\qquad\square$

Generally, if we do not know an upper bound η on the noise rate ν, then we can perform a guess-and-double procedure using a labeled validation set, which grows to size at most $\tilde{O}\left(\frac{\nu+\epsilon}{\epsilon^2}\right)$. See Section 9 for more discussion of this matter.

We can create a general algorithm, independent of $\mathcal{D}$, by using unlabeled examples to (with probability $\geq 1 - \delta/2$) construct the $\frac{\epsilon}{2}$-cover. It is possible to do this while maintaining $|V| \leq N' = 2\left(\frac{16e}{\epsilon} \ln \frac{16e}{\epsilon}\right)^d$ using $O\left(\frac{1}{\epsilon^2}\left(d\log\frac{1}{\epsilon} + \log\frac{1}{\delta}\right)\right)$ unlabeled examples. Thus, replacing t in Theorem 3 with $XTD(\mathbb{C}, n)$ and increasing N to N' gives an upper bound on the *distribution-free* label complexity.

7 Lower Bounds

In this section, we prove lower bounds on the label complexity.

Definition 5. *(Extended Partial Teaching Dimension) Let* $V \subseteq \mathbb{C}$, $m \geq 0$, $\delta \geq 0$. $\forall f \in \mathbb{C}_\mathcal{F}, \mathcal{U} \in \mathcal{X}^{\lceil m \rceil}$,

$XPTD(f, V, \mathcal{U}, \delta) = \inf\{t | \exists R \subseteq \mathcal{U} : |\{h \in V : h(R) = f(R)\}| \leq \delta|V| + 1 \wedge |R| \leq t\}.$

$XPTD(V, \mathcal{D}, \delta) = \inf\{t | \forall f \in \mathbb{C}_\mathcal{F}, \lim_{n\to\infty} \mathcal{P}r_{\mathcal{U}\sim\mathcal{D}^n}\{XPTD(f, V, \mathcal{U}, \delta) > t\} = 0\}.$

$XPTD(V, m, \delta) = \sup_{f\in\mathbb{C}_\mathcal{F}} \sup_{\mathcal{U}\in\mathcal{X}^{\lceil m \rceil}} XPTD(f, V[\mathcal{U}], \mathcal{U}, \delta).$

Theorem 4. *Let* $\epsilon \in [0, 1/2)$, $\delta \in [0, 1)$. *For any* 2ϵ-*separated set* $V \subseteq \mathbb{C}$ *with respect to* $\mathcal{D}$,

$$\max\{\log\left[(1-\delta)|V|\right], XPTD(V, \mathcal{D}, \delta)\} \leq \#LQ(\mathbb{C}, \mathcal{D}, \epsilon, \delta, 0).$$

If $0 < \delta < 1/16$ *and* $0 < \epsilon/2 \leq \eta < 1/2$, *and there are* $h_1, h_2 \in \mathbb{C}$ *such that* $er_\mathcal{D}(h_1, h_2) > 2(\eta + \epsilon)$, *then*

$$\Omega\left(\left(\frac{\eta^2}{\epsilon^2}+1\right)\log\frac{1}{\delta}\right) \leq \#LQ(\mathbb{C}, \mathcal{D}, \epsilon, \delta, \eta).$$

Also, the following distribution-free lower bound applies. If $\forall x \in \mathcal{X}, \{x\} \in \mathcal{F}$,[6] *then letting* $\mathfrak{D}$ *denote the set of all probability distributions on* $\mathcal{X}$, *for any* $V \subseteq \mathbb{C}$,

$$XPTD(V, (1-\epsilon)/\epsilon, \delta) \leq \sup_{\mathcal{D}'\in\mathfrak{D}} \#LQ(\mathbb{C}, \mathcal{D}', \epsilon, \delta, 0).$$

---

[6] This condition is not necessary, but simplifies the proof.

Proof. The $\log\left[(1-\delta)|V|\right]$ lower bound is due to Kulkarni [2].

We prove the $XPTD(V,\mathcal{D},\delta)$ lower bound by the probabilistic method as follows. If $\delta|V|+1 \geq |V|$, the bound is trivially true, so assume $\delta|V|+1 < |V|$ (and in particular, $|V| < \infty$). Let $m \geq 0$, $\tilde{t} = XPTD(V,\mathcal{D},\delta)$. By definition of $\tilde{t}$, $\exists f' \in \mathbb{C}_\mathcal{F}$ such that $\lim_{n\to\infty} \mathcal{P}r_{\mathcal{U}\sim\mathcal{D}^n}\{XPTD(f',V,\mathcal{U},\delta) \geq \tilde{t}\} > 0$. By the Dominated Convergence Theorem and Kolmogorov's Zero-One Law, this implies $\lim_{n\to\infty} \mathcal{P}r_{\mathcal{U}\sim\mathcal{D}^n}\{XPTD(f',V,\mathcal{U},\delta) \geq \tilde{t}\} = 1$. Since this probability is nonincreasing in n, this means $\mathcal{P}r_{\mathcal{U}\sim\mathcal{D}^m}\{XPTD(f',V,\mathcal{U},\delta) \geq \tilde{t}\} = 1$. Suppose $\mathcal{A}$ is a learning algorithm. For $\mathcal{U} \in \mathcal{X}^m$, $f \in \mathbb{C}_\mathcal{F}$, define random quantities $R_{\mathcal{U},f} \subseteq \mathcal{U}$ and $h_{\mathcal{U},f} \in \mathbb{C}$, denoting the examples queried and classifier returned by $\mathcal{A}$, respectively, when the oracle answers consistent with f and the input unlabeled sequence is $\mathcal{U} \sim \mathcal{D}^m$. If we sample f uniformly at random from V,

$$\mathbb{E}_f\left[\mathcal{P}r_{\mathcal{U},R_{\mathcal{U},f},h_{\mathcal{U},f}}\left\{er_\mathcal{D}(f,h_{\mathcal{U},f}) > \epsilon \vee |R_{\mathcal{U},f}| \geq \tilde{t}\right\}\right]$$
$$\geq \mathcal{P}r_{f,\mathcal{U},R_{\mathcal{U},f},h_{\mathcal{U},f}}\left\{f(R_{\mathcal{U},f}) = f'(R_{\mathcal{U},f}) \wedge er_\mathcal{D}(f,h_{\mathcal{U},f}) > \epsilon \vee |R_{\mathcal{U},f}| \geq \tilde{t}\right\}$$
$$\geq \mathbb{E}_\mathcal{U}\left[\inf_{h\in\mathbb{C},R\subseteq\mathcal{U}:|R|<\tilde{t}}\mathcal{P}r_f\left\{f(R) = f'(R) \wedge er_\mathcal{D}(h,f) > \epsilon\right\}\right] > \delta.$$

Therefore, there must be some fixed target $f \in \mathbb{C}$ such that the probability that $er_\mathcal{D}(f,h_{\mathcal{U},f}) > \epsilon$ or $|R_{\mathcal{U},f}| \geq XPTD(V,\mathcal{D},\delta)$ is $> \delta$, proving the lower bound.

Kääriäinen [7] proves a distribution-free version of the $\Omega\left(\left(\frac{\eta^2}{\epsilon^2}+1\right)\log\frac{1}{\delta}\right)$ bound, and also mentions its extendibility to the distribution-dependent setting. Since the distribution-dependent claim and proof thereof are only implicit in that reference, for completeness we present a brief proof here. Let $\Delta = \{x : h_1(x) \neq h_2(x)\}$. Suppose h^* is chosen from $\{h_1, h_2\}$ by an adversary. Given $\mathcal{D}$, we construct a distribution $\mathcal{D}_{XY}$ with the following property[7]. $\forall A \in \mathcal{F}, \mathcal{P}r_{(X,Y)\sim\mathcal{D}_{XY}}\{Y = h^*(X)|X \in A \cap \Delta\} = \frac{1}{2} + \frac{\epsilon}{2(\eta+\epsilon)}$, and $\mathcal{P}r_{(X,Y)\sim\mathcal{D}_{XY}}\{Y = h_1(X)|X \in A\backslash\Delta\} = 1$. Any concept $h \in \mathbb{C}$ with $er(h) \leq \eta+\epsilon$ has $\mathcal{P}r\{h(X) = h^*(X)|h_1(X) \neq h_2(X)\} > \frac{1}{2}$. Since this probability can be estimated to arbitrary precision with arbitrarily high probability using unlabeled examples, we have a reduction to active learning from the task of determining with probability $\geq 1-\delta$ whether h_1 or h_2 is h^*. Examining the latter task, since every subset of Δ in $\mathcal{F}$ yields the same conditional distribution, any optimal strategy is based on samples from this distribution. It is known (e.g., [10,11]) that this requires expected number of samples at least

$$\frac{(1-8\delta)\log\frac{1}{8\delta}}{8D_{KL}\left(\frac{1}{2}+\frac{\epsilon}{2(\eta+\epsilon)}\|\frac{1}{2}-\frac{\epsilon}{2(\eta+\epsilon)}\right)} > \frac{1}{40}\frac{(\eta+\epsilon)^2}{\epsilon^2}\ln\frac{1}{8\delta},$$

where $D_{KL}(p\|q) = p\log\frac{p}{q} + (1-p)\log\frac{1-p}{1-q}$.

We prove the $XPTD(V,(1-\epsilon)/\epsilon,\delta)$ bound as follows. Let $n = \frac{1-\epsilon}{\epsilon}$. For $S \in \mathcal{X}^{\lceil n\rceil}$, let $\mathcal{D}_S$ be the uniform distribution on the entries of S. Let $f'' \in \mathbb{C}_\mathcal{F}$ be such that $XPTD(f'',V[S],S,\delta) = \max_{f\in V[S]} XPTD(f,V[S],S,\delta)$, and define

---

[7] Although this proof relies on stochasticity of the oracle, with additional assumptions on $\mathcal{D}$ and Δ similar to Kääriäinen's [7], a similar result holds for deterministic oracles.

$t'' = XPTD(f'', V[S], S, \delta)$. Let $m \geq 0$. Let $R_{\mathcal{U},f}$ and $h_{\mathcal{U},f}$ be defined as above, for $\mathcal{U} \sim \mathcal{D}_S^m$. As above, we use the probabilistic method, this time by sampling the target function f uniformly from $V[S]$.

$$\mathbb{E}_f \left[\mathcal{P}r_{\mathcal{U}, R_{\mathcal{U},f}, h_{\mathcal{U},f}} \{ er_{\mathcal{D}_S}(h_{\mathcal{U},f}, f) > \epsilon \vee |R_{\mathcal{U},f}| \geq t'' \} \right]$$
$$\geq \mathbb{E}_{\mathcal{U}} \left[\mathcal{P}r_{f, R_{\mathcal{U},f}, h_{\mathcal{U},f}} \{ f(R_{\mathcal{U},f}) = f''(R_{\mathcal{U},f}) \wedge h_{\mathcal{U},f}(S) \neq f(S) \vee |R_{\mathcal{U},f}| \geq t'' \} \right]$$
$$\geq \min_{h \in \mathbb{C}, R \subseteq S : |R| < t''} \mathcal{P}r_f \{ f(R) = f''(R) \wedge h(S) \neq f(S) \} > \delta.$$

Taking the supremum over $S \in \mathcal{X}^{\lceil n \rceil}$ completes the proof. □

8 Example: Axis-Aligned Rectangles

As an application, we analyze axis-aligned rectangles, when $\mathcal{D}$ is a product density. An axis-aligned rectangle in $\mathbb{R}^n$ is defined by a sequence $\{(a_i, b_i)\}_{i=1}^n$, such that $a_i \leq b_i$, and the examples labeled $+1$ are $\{x \in \mathcal{X} : \forall i, a_i \leq x \leq b_i\}$. Throughout this section, we assume $\mathcal{F}$ is the standard Borel σ-algebra on $\mathbb{R}^n$.

Lemma 4. *(Balanced Axis-Aligned Rectangles) If $\mathcal{D}$ is a product distribution on $\mathbb{R}^n$ with continuous CDF, and $\mathbb{C}$ is the set of axis-aligned rectangles such that $\forall h \in \mathbb{C}, \mathcal{P}r_{X \sim \mathcal{D}}\{h(X) = +1\} \geq \lambda$, then*

$$XTD(\mathbb{C}, \mathcal{D}, m, \delta) \leq O\left(\frac{n^2}{\lambda} \log \frac{nm}{\delta} \right).$$

Proof. If G_i is the CDF of X_i for $X \sim \mathcal{D}$, then $G_i(X_i)$ is uniform in $(0,1)$, and for any $h \in \mathbb{C}$, the function $h'(x) = h(\{\min\{y : x_i = G_i(y)\}\}_{i=1}^n)$ (for $x \in (0,1)^n$) is an axis-aligned rectangle. This mapping of the problem into $(0,1)^n$ is equivalent to the original, so for the rest of this proof, we assume $\mathcal{D}$ is uniform on $(0,1)^n$.

If m is smaller than the bound, the result clearly holds, so assume $m \geq 2n + \frac{4n}{\lambda} \left(\ln \frac{8n}{\delta} + 2n \ln \frac{2nm^2}{\delta} \right)$. Our first step is to discretize the concept space. Let S be the set of concepts h such that the region $\{x : h(x) = +1\}$ is specified by the interior of some rectangle $\{(a_i, b_i)\}_{i=1}^n$ with $a_i, b_i \in \left\{ 0, \frac{\delta}{2nm^2}, 2\frac{\delta}{2nm^2}, ..., \left\lceil \frac{2nm^2}{\delta} \right\rceil \frac{\delta}{2nm^2} \right\}$, $a_i < b_i$. By a union bound, with probability $\geq 1 - \delta/2$ over the draw of $\mathcal{U} \sim \mathcal{D}^m$, $\forall x, y \in \mathcal{U}, \forall i \in \{1, 2, ..., n\}, |x_i - y_i| > \frac{\delta}{2nm^2}$. In particular, this would imply there are valid choices of $S[\mathcal{U}]$ and $\mathbb{C}[\mathcal{U}]$ so that $\mathbb{C}[\mathcal{U}] \subseteq S[\mathcal{U}]$. As such, $XTD(\mathbb{C}, \mathcal{D}, m, \delta) \leq XTD(S \cap \mathbb{C}, \mathcal{D}, m, \delta/2)$.

Let $f \in \mathbb{C}_{\mathcal{F}}$. If $\mathcal{P}r_{X \sim \mathcal{D}} \{f(X) = +1\} < \frac{3}{4}\lambda$, then with probability $\geq 1 - \delta/2$, for each $h \in S \cap \mathbb{C}$, there is at least one $x \in \mathcal{U}$ s.t. $h(x) = +1 \neq f(x)$. Thus $\mathcal{P}r_{\mathcal{U} \sim \mathcal{D}^m} \left\{ XTD(f, (\mathbb{C} \cap S)[\mathcal{U}], \mathcal{U}) > \frac{4}{\lambda} \ln \frac{2|S|}{\delta} \right\} \leq \delta/2$.

For any set of examples R, let $CLOS(R)$ be the smallest axis-aligned rectangle $h \in S$ that labels all of R as $+1$. This is known as the *closure* of R. Additionally, let $A \subseteq R$ be a smallest set such that $CLOS(A) = CLOS(R)$. This is known as a minimal spanning set of R. Clearly $|A| \leq 2n$, since the extreme points in each direction form a spanning set.

Let $h \in S$ be such that $Pr_{X \sim \mathcal{D}}\{h(X) = +1\} \geq \frac{1}{2}$. Let $\{(a_i, b_i)\}_{i=1}^{n}$ define the rectangle. Let $x^{(ai)}$ be the example in $\mathcal{U}$ with largest $x_i^{(ai)}$ component such that $x_i^{(ai)} < a_i$ and $\forall j \neq i, a_j \leq x_j^{(ai)} \leq b_j$, or if no such example exists, $x^{(ai)}$ is defined as the $x \in \mathcal{U}$ with smallest x_i. Let $x^{(bi)}$ be defined similarly, except having the smallest $x_i^{(bi)}$ component with $x_i^{(bi)} > b_i$, and again $\forall j \neq i, a_j \leq x_j^{(bi)} \leq b_j$. If no such example exists, then $x^{(bi)}$ is defined as the $x \in \mathcal{U}$ with largest x_i. Let $A_{h,\mathcal{U}} \subseteq \mathcal{U}$ be the subsequence of all examples $x \in \mathcal{U}$ such that $\exists i \in \{1, 2, \dots, n\}$ with $x_i^{(ai)} \leq x_i < a_i$ or $b_i < x_i \leq x_i^{(bi)}$. The surface volume of each face of the rectangle is at least $\lambda/2$. By a union bound over the $2n$ faces of the rectangle, with probability at least $1 - \delta/(4|S|)$, $|A_{h,\mathcal{U}}| \leq \frac{4n}{\lambda} \ln \frac{8n|S|}{\delta}$. With probability $\geq 1 - \delta/4$, this is satisfied for every $h \in S$ with $Pr_{X \sim \mathcal{D}}\{h(X) = +1\} \geq \frac{\lambda}{2}$.

Now suppose $f \in \mathbb{C}_{\mathcal{F}}$ satisfies $Pr_{X \sim \mathcal{D}}\{f(X) = +1\} \geq \frac{3\lambda}{4}$. Let $\mathcal{U}_+ = \{x \in \mathcal{U} : f(x) = +1\}$, $h_{clos} = CLOS(\mathcal{U}_+)$. If any $x \in \mathcal{U} \setminus \mathcal{U}_+$ has $h_{clos}(x) = +1$, we can form a specifying set for f on $\mathcal{U}$ with respect to $S[\mathcal{U}]$ using a minimal spanning set for $\mathcal{U}_+$ along with this x. If there is no such x, then $h_{clos}(\mathcal{U}) = f(\mathcal{U})$, and we use a minimal specifying set for h_{clos}. With probability $\geq 1 - \delta/4$, for every $h \in S$ such that $Pr_{X \sim \mathcal{D}}\{h(X) = +1\} < \frac{\lambda}{2}$, there is some $x \in \mathcal{U}_+$ such that $h(x) = -1$. If this happens, since $h_{clos} \in S$, this implies $Pr_{X \sim \mathcal{D}}\{h_{clos}(X) = +1\} \geq \frac{\lambda}{2}$. In this case, for a specifying set, we use $A_{h_{clos}, \mathcal{U}}$ along with a minimal spanning set for $\{x \in \mathcal{U} : f(x) = +1\}$. So $Pr_{\mathcal{U} \sim \mathcal{D}^m} \left\{ XTD(f, (\mathbb{C} \cap S)[\mathcal{U}], \mathcal{U}) > 2n + \frac{4n}{\lambda} \ln \frac{8n|S|}{\delta} \right\}$ $\leq \delta/2$. Noting that $|S| \leq \left(\frac{2nm^2}{\delta} \right)^{2n}$ completes the proof. $\square$

Note that we can obtain an estimate $\hat{p}$ of $p = Pr_{(X,Y) \sim \mathcal{D}_{XY}} \{Y = +1\}$ that, with probability $\geq 1 - \delta/2$, satisfies $p/2 \leq \hat{p} \leq 2p$, using at most $O\left(\frac{1}{p} \log \frac{1}{p\delta}\right)$ labeled examples (by guess-and-halve). Since clearly $Pr_{X \sim \mathcal{D}}\{h^*(X) = +1\} \geq p - \eta$, we can take $\lambda = (\hat{p}/2) - \eta$, giving the following oracle-dependent bound.

Theorem 5. *If $\mathcal{D}$ is as in Lemma 4 and $\mathbb{C}$ is the set of all axis-aligned rectangles, then if $p = Pr_{(X,Y) \sim \mathcal{D}_{XY}} \{Y = +1\} > 4\eta$, we can, with probability $\geq 1 - \delta$, find an $h \in \mathbb{C}$ with $er(h) \leq \nu + \epsilon$ without the number of label requests exceeding*

$$\tilde{O}\left(\frac{n^3}{(p/4) - \eta} \left(\frac{\eta^2}{\epsilon^2} + 1 \right) \right).$$

This result is somewhat encouraging, since if $\eta < \epsilon$ and p is not too small, the label bound represents an exponential improvement in $\frac{1}{\epsilon}$ compared to known results for passive learning, while maintaining polylog dependence on $\frac{1}{\delta}$ and polynomial dependence on n, though the degree increases from 1 to 3. We might wonder whether the property of being balanced is sufficient for these improvements. However, as the following theorem shows, balancedness alone is insufficient for guaranteeing polylog dependence on $\frac{1}{\epsilon}$. The proof is omitted for brevity.

Theorem 6. *If $n \geq 2$, there is a distribution $\mathcal{D}'$ on $\mathbb{R}^n$ such that, if $\mathbb{C}$ is the set of axis-aligned rectangles h with $Pr_{X \sim \mathcal{D}'}\{h(X) = +1\} \geq \lambda$, then there is a $V \subset \mathbb{C}$ 2ϵ-separated with respect to $\mathcal{D}'$ such that $\Omega\left(\frac{(1-\delta)(1-\lambda)}{\epsilon}\right) \leq XPTD(V, \mathcal{D}', \delta)$.*

9 Open Problems

There are a number of possibilities for tightening these bounds. The upper bound of Theorem 3 contains a $O\left(\log \frac{d}{\epsilon\delta}\right)$ factor, which does not appear in any known lower bounds. In the worst case, when $XTD(\mathbb{C}, \mathcal{D}, n, \delta) = O(n)$, this factor clearly does not belong, since the bound exceeds the passive learning sample complexity in that case. It may be possible to reduce or remove this factor. On a related note, Hegedüs [3] introduces a modified MembHalving algorithm, which makes queries in a particular greedy order. By doing so, the bound decreases to $2\frac{t_0}{\log t_0} \log_2 |\mathbb{C}|$ instead of $t_0 \log_2 |\mathbb{C}|$. A similar technique might be possible here, though the effect seems more difficult to quantify. Additionally, a more careful treatment of the constants in these bounds may yield significant improvements.

The present analysis requires access to an upper bound η on the noise rate. As mentioned, it is possible to remove this assumption by a guess-and-double procedure, using a labeled validation set of size $\Omega(1/\epsilon)$. In practice, this may not be too severe, since we often use a validation set to tune parameters or estimate the final error rate anyway. Nonetheless, it would be nice to remove this requirement without sacrificing anything in dependence on $\frac{1}{\epsilon}$. In particular, it may sometimes be possible to determine whether a classifier is near-optimal using only a few carefully chosen queries.

As a final remark, exploring the connections between the present analysis and the related approaches discussed in Section 2 could prove fruitful. Thorough study of these approaches and their interrelations seems essential for a complete understanding of the label complexity of active learning.

References

1. Balcan, M.-F., Beygelzimer, A., Langford, J.: Agnostic active learning. In: Proc. of the 23rd International Conference on Machine Learning (2006)
2. Kulkarni, S.R., Mitter, S.K., Tsitsiklis, J.N.: Active learning using arbitrary binary valued queries. Machine Learning 11, 23–35 (1993)
3. Hegedüs, T.: Generalized teaching dimension and the query complexity of learning. In: Proc. of the 8th Annual Conference on Computational Learning Theory (1995)
4. Angluin, D.: Queries revisited. Theoretical Computer Science 313, 175–194 (2004)
5. Goldman, S.A., Kearns, M.J.: On the complexity of teaching. Journal of Computer and System Sciences 50, 20–31 (1995)
6. Dasgupta, S.: Coarse sample complexity bounds for active learning. In: Advances in Neural Information Processing Systems 18 (2005)

7. Käariäinen, M.: Active learning in the non-realizable case. In: Proc. of the 17th International Conference on Algorithmic Learning Theory (2006)
8. Littlestone, N.: Learning quickly when irrelevant attributes abound: A new linear-threshold algorithm. Machine Learning 2, 285–318 (1988)
9. Haussler, D.: Decision theoretic generalizations of the PAC model for neural net and other learning applications. Information and Computation 100, 78–150 (1992)
10. Wald, A.: Sequential tests of statistical hypotheses. The Annals of Mathematical Statistics 16(2), 117–186 (1945)
11. Bar-Yossef, Z.: Sampling lower bounds via information theory. In: Proc. of the 35th Annual ACM Symposium on the Theory of Computing, pp. 335–344 (2003)

Multi-view Regression Via Canonical Correlation Analysis

Sham M. Kakade[1] and Dean P. Foster[2]

[1] Toyota Technological Institute at Chicago
Chicago, IL 60637
[2] University of Pennsylvania
Philadelphia, PA 19104

Abstract. In the multi-view regression problem, we have a regression problem where the input variable (which is a real vector) can be partitioned into two different views, where it is assumed that either view of the input is sufficient to make accurate predictions — this is essentially (a significantly weaker version of) the co-training assumption for the regression problem.

We provide a semi-supervised algorithm which first uses unlabeled data to learn a norm (or, equivalently, a kernel) and then uses labeled data in a ridge regression algorithm (with this induced norm) to provide the predictor. The unlabeled data is used via canonical correlation analysis (CCA, which is a closely related to PCA for two random variables) to derive an appropriate norm over functions. We are able to characterize the intrinsic dimensionality of the subsequent ridge regression problem (which uses this norm) by the correlation coefficients provided by CCA in a rather simple expression. Interestingly, the norm used by the ridge regression algorithm is derived from CCA, unlike in standard kernel methods where a special apriori norm is assumed (i.e. a Banach space is assumed). We discuss how this result shows that unlabeled data can decrease the sample complexity.

1 Introduction

Extracting information relevant to a task in an unsupervised (or semi-supervised) manner is one of the fundamental challenges in machine learning — the underlying question is how unlabeled data can be used to improve performance. In the "multi-view" approach to semi-supervised learning [Yarowsky, 1995, Blum and Mitchell, 1998], one assumes that the input variable x can be split into two different "views" $(x^{(1)}, x^{(2)})$, such that good predictors based on each view tend to agree. Roughly speaking, the common underlying multi-view assumption is that the best predictor from either view has a low error — thus the best predictors tend to agree with each other.

There are many applications where this underlying assumption is applicable. For example, object recognition with pictures form different camera angles — we expect a predictor based on either angle to have good performance. One

N. Bshouty and C. Gentile (Eds.): COLT 2007, LNAI 4539, pp. 82–96, 2007.

can even consider multi-modal views, e.g. identity recognition where the task might be to identify a person with one view being a video stream and the other an audio stream — each of these views would be sufficient to determine the identity. In NLP, an example would be a paired document corpus, consisting of a document and its translation into another language. The motivating example in Blum and Mitchell [1998] is a web-page classification task, where one view was the text in the page and the other was the hyperlink structure.

A characteristic of many of the multi-view learning algorithms [Yarowsky, 1995, Blum and Mitchell, 1998, Farquhar et al., 2005, Sindhwani et al., 2005, Brefeld et al., 2006] is to force agreement between the predictors, based on either view. The idea is to force a predictor, $h^{(1)}(\cdot)$, based on view one to agree with a predictor, $h^{(2)}(\cdot)$, based on view two, i.e. by constraining $h^{(1)}(x^{(1)})$ to usually equal $h^{(2)}(x^{(2)})$. The intuition is that the complexity of the learning problem should be reduced by eliminating hypothesis from each view that do not agree with each other (which can be done using unlabeled data).

This paper studies the multi-view, linear regression case: the inputs $x^{(1)}$ and $x^{(2)}$ are real vectors; the outputs y are real valued; the samples $((x^{(1)}, x^{(2)}), y)$ are jointly distributed; and the prediction of y is *linear* in the input x. Our first contribution is to explicitly formalize a multi-view assumption for regression. The multi-view assumption we use is a *regret* based one, where we assume that the best linear predictor from each view is roughly as good as the best linear predictor based on both views. Denote the (expected) squared loss of a prediction function $g(x)$ to be loss(g). More precisely, the multi-view assumption is that

$$\mathrm{loss}(f^{(1)}) - \mathrm{loss}(f) \le \epsilon$$
$$\mathrm{loss}(f^{(2)}) - \mathrm{loss}(f) \le \epsilon$$

where $f^{(\nu)}$ is the *best linear predictor* based on view $\nu \in \{1, 2\}$ and f is the *best linear predictor* based on both views (so $f^{(\nu)}$ is a linear function of $x^{(\nu)}$ and f is a linear function of $x = (x^{(1)}, x^{(2)})$). This assumption implies that (only on average) the predictors must agree (shown in Lemma 1). Clearly, if the both optimal predictors $f^{(1)}$ and $f^{(2)}$ have small error, then this assumption is satisfied, though this precondition is not necessary. This (average) agreement is explicitly used in the "co-regularized" least squares algorithms of Sindhwani et al. [2005], Brefeld et al. [2006], which directly constrain such an agreement in a least squares optimization problem.

This assumption is rather weak in comparison to previous assumptions [Blum and Mitchell, 1998, Dasgupta et al., 2001, Abney, 2004]. Our assumption can be viewed as weakening the original co-training assumption (for the classification case). First, our assumption is stated in terms of expected errors only and implies only expected approximate agreement (see Lemma 1). Second, our assumption is only in terms of regret — we do *not* require that the loss of any predictor be small. Lastly, we make no further distributional assumptions (aside from a bounded second moment on the output variable), such as the commonly used, overly-stringent assumption that the distribution of the views be conditionally independent given the label [Blum and Mitchell, 1998, Dasgupta et al.,

2001, Abney, 2004]. In Balcan and Blum [2006], they provide a compatibility notion which also relaxes this latter assumption, though it is unclear if this compatibility notion (defined for the classification setting) easily extends to the assumption above.

Our main result provides an algorithm and an analysis under the above multi-view regression assumption. The algorithm used can be thought of as a ridge regression algorithm with regularization based on a norm that is determined by *canonical correlation analysis* (CCA). Intuitively, CCA [Hotelling, 1935] is an unsupervised method for analyzing jointly distributed random vectors. In our setting, CCA can be performed with the unlabeled data.

We characterize the expected regret of our multi-view algorithm, in comparison to the best linear predictor, as a sum of a bias and a variance term: the bias is 4ϵ so it is small if the multi-view assumption is good; and the variance is $\frac{d}{n}$, where n is the sample size and d is the *intrinsic dimensionality* which we show to be the sum of the squares of the correlation coefficients provided by CCA. The notion of intrinsic dimensionality we use is the related to that of Zhang [2005], which provides a notion of intrinsic dimensionality for kernel methods.

An interesting aspect to our setting is that no apriori assumptions are made about any special norm over the space of linear predictions, unlike in kernel methods which *apriori* impose a Banach space over predictors. In fact, our multi-view assumption is co-ordinate free — the assumption is stated in terms of the best linear predictor for the given linear *subspaces*, which has no reference to any coordinate system. Furthermore, no apriori assumptions about the dimensionality of our spaces are made — thus being applicable to infinite dimensional methods, including kernel methods. In fact, kernel CCA methods have been developed in Hardoon et al. [2004].

The remainder of the paper is organized as follows. Section 2 formalizes our multi-view assumption and reviews CCA. Section 3 presents the main results, where the bias-variance tradeoff and the intrinsic dimensionality are characterized. The Discussion expands on a number of points. The foremost issue addressed is how the multi-view assumption, with unlabeled data, could potentially allow a significant reduction in the sample size. Essentially, in the high (or infinite) dimensional case, the multi-view assumption imposes a norm which could coincide with a much lower intrinsic dimensionality. In the Discussion, we also examine two related multi-view learning algorithms: the SVM-2K algorithm of Farquhar et al. [2005] and the co-regularized least squares regression algorithm of Sindhwani et al. [2005].

2   Preliminaries

This first part of this section presents the multi-view regression setting and formalizes the multi-view assumption. As is standard, we work with a distribution $D(x, y)$ over input-output pairs. To abstract away the difficulties of analyzing the use of a *random* unlabeled set sampled from $D(x)$, we instead assume that the second order statistics of x are known. The transductive setting and the fixed design setting (which we discuss later in Section 3) are cases where this assumption is satisfied. The second part of this section reviews CCA.

2.1   Regression with Multiple Views

Assume that the input space X is a subset of a real linear space, which is of either finite dimension (i.e. $X \subset \mathbb{R}^d$) or countably infinite dimension. Also assume that each $x \in X$ is in ℓ_2 (i.e. x is a squared summable sequence). In the multi-view framework, assume each x has the form $x = (x^{(1)}, x^{(2)})$, where $x^{(1)}$ and $x^{(2)}$ are interpreted as the two views of x. Hence, $x^{(1)}$ is an element of a real linear space $X^{(1)}$ and $x^{(2)}$ is in a real linear space $X^{(2)}$ (and both $x^{(1)}$ and $x^{(2)}$ are in ℓ_2). Conceptually, we should think of these spaces as being high dimensional (or countably infinite dimensional).

We also have outputs y that are in $\mathbb{R}$, along with a joint distribution $D(x, y)$ over $X \times \mathbb{R}$. We assume that the second moment of the output is bounded by 1, i.e. $\mathbb{E}[y^2|x] \le 1$ — it is not required that y itself be bounded. No boundedness assumptions on $x \in X$ are made, since these assumptions would have no impact on our analysis as it is only the subspace defined by X that is relevant.

We also assume that our algorithm has knowledge of the second order statistics of $D(x)$, i.e. we assume that the covariance matrix of x is known. In both the transductive setting and the fixed design setting, such an assumption holds. This is discussed in more detail in Section 3.

The loss function considered for $g : X \to \mathbb{R}$ is the average squared error. More formally,

$$\text{loss}(g) = \mathbb{E}\left[(g(x) - y)^2\right]$$

where the expectation is with respect to (x, y) sampled from D. We are also interested in the losses for predictors, $g^{(1)} : X^{(1)} \to \mathbb{R}$ and $g^{(2)} : X^{(2)} \to \mathbb{R}$, based on the different views, which are just $\text{loss}(g^{(\nu)})$ for $\nu \in \{1, 2\}$.

The following assumption is made throughout the paper.

Assumption 1. *(Multi-View Assumption) Define $L(Z)$ to be the space of linear mappings from a linear space Z to the reals and define:*

$$f^{(1)} = \text{argmin}_{g \in L(X^{(1)})} \text{loss}(g)$$
$$f^{(2)} = \text{argmin}_{g \in L(X^{(2)})} \text{loss}(g)$$
$$f = \text{argmin}_{g \in L(X)} \text{loss}(g)$$

which exist since X is a subset of ℓ_2. The multi-view assumption is that

$$\text{loss}(f^{(\nu)}) - \text{loss}(f) \le \epsilon$$

for $\nu \in \{1, 2\}$.

Note that this assumption makes no reference to any coordinate system or norm over the linear functions. Also, it is not necessarily assumed that the losses, themselves are small. However, if loss($f^{(\nu)}$) is small for $\nu \in \{1, 2\}$, say less than ϵ, then it is clear that the above assumption is satisfied.

The following Lemma shows that the above assumption implies that $f^{(1)}$ and $f^{(2)}$ tend to agree on average.

Lemma 1. *Assumption 1 implies that:*

$$\mathbb{E}\left(f^{(1)}(x^{(1)}) - f^{(2)}(x^{(2)})\right)^2 \le 4\epsilon$$

where the expectation is with respect to x sampled from D.

The proof is provided in the Appendix. As mentioned in the Introduction, this agreement is explicitly used in the co-regularized least squares algorithms of Sindhwani et al. [2005], Brefeld et al. [2006].

2.2   CCA and the Canonical Basis

A useful basis is that provided by CCA, which we define as the *canonical basis*.

Definition 1. *Let $B^{(1)}$ be a basis of $X^{(1)}$ and $B^{(2)}$ be a basis of $X^{(2)}$. Let $x_1^{(\nu)}, x_2^{(\nu)}, \ldots$ be the coordinates of $x^{(\nu)}$ in $B^{(\nu)}$. The pair of bases $B^{(1)}$ and $B^{(2)}$ are the canonical bases if the following holds (where the expectation is with respect to D):*

1. Orthogonality Conditions:

$$\mathbb{E}[x_i^{(\nu)} x_j^{(\nu)}] = \begin{cases} 1 & \text{if } i = j \\ 0 & \text{else} \end{cases}$$

2. Correlation Conditions:

$$\mathbb{E}\left[x_i^{(1)} x_j^{(2)}\right] = \begin{cases} \lambda_i & \text{if } i = j \\ 0 & \text{else} \end{cases}$$

where, without loss of generality, it is assumed that $1 \ge \lambda_i \ge 0$ and that

$$1 \ge \lambda_1 \ge \lambda_2 \ge \ldots$$

The i-th canonical correlation coefficient is defined as λ_i.

Roughly speaking, the joint covariance matrix of $x = (x^{(1)}, x^{(2)})$ in the canonical basis has a particular structured form: the individual covariance matrices of $x^{(1)}$ and $x^{(2)}$ are just identity matrices and the cross covariance matrix between $x^{(1)}$ and $x^{(2)}$ is diagonal. CCA can also be specified as an eigenvalue problem[1] (see Hardoon et al. [2004] for review).

---

[1] CCA finds such a basis is as follows. The correlation coefficient between two real values (jointly distributed) is defined as $\mathrm{corr}(z, z') = \frac{\mathbb{E}[zz']}{\sqrt{\mathbb{E}[z^2]\mathbb{E}[z'^2]}}$ Let $\Pi_a x$ be the projection operator, which projects x onto direction a. The first canonical basis vectors $b_1^{(1)} \in B^{(1)}$ and $b_1^{(2)} \in B^{(2)}$ are the unit length directions a and b which maximize $\mathrm{corr}(\Pi_a x^{(1)}, \Pi_b x^{(2)})$ and the corresponding canonical correlation coefficient λ_1 is this maximal correlation. Inductively, the next pair of directions can be found which maximize the correlation subject to the pair being orthogonal to the previously found pairs.

3   Learning

Now let us assume we have observed a training sample $T = \{(x_m^{(\nu)}, y_m)\}_{m=1}^n$ of size n from a view ν, where the samples drawn independently from D. We also assume that our algorithm has access to the covariance matrix of x, so that the algorithm can construct the canonical basis.

Our goal is to construct an estimator $\widehat{f}^{(\nu)}$ of $f^{(\nu)}$ — recall $f^{(\nu)}$ is the best linear predictor using only view ν — such that the regret

$$\text{loss}(\widehat{f}^{(\nu)}) - \text{loss}(f^{(\nu)})$$

is small.

Remark 1. (The Transductive and Fixed Design Setting) There are two natural settings where this assumption of knowledge about the second order statistics of x holds — the *random transductive* case and the *fixed design* case. In both cases, X is a known finite set. In the random transductive case, the distribution D is assumed to be uniform over X, so each x_m is sampled uniformly from X and each y_m is sampled from $D(y|x_m)$. In the fixed design case, assume that each $x \in X$ appears exactly once in T and again y_m is sampled from $D(y|x_m)$. The fixed design case is commonly studied in statistics and is also referred to as signal reconstruction.[2] The covariance matrix of x is clearly known in both cases.

3.1   A Shrinkage Estimator (Via Ridge Regression)

Let the representation of our estimator $\widehat{f}^{(\nu)}$ in the canonical basis $B^{(\nu)}$ be

$$\widehat{f}^{(\nu)}(x^{(\nu)}) = \sum_i \widehat{\beta}_i^{(\nu)} x_i^{(\nu)} \tag{1}$$

where $x_i^{(\nu)}$ is the i-th coordinate in $B^{(\nu)}$. Define the canonical shrinkage estimator of $\widehat{\beta}^{(\nu)}$ as:

$$\widehat{\beta}_i^{(\nu)} = \lambda_i \widehat{\mathbb{E}}[x_i y] \equiv \frac{\lambda_i}{n} \sum_m x_{m,i}^{(\nu)} y_m \tag{2}$$

Intuitively, the shrinkage by λ_i down-weights directions that are less correlated with the other view. In the extreme case, this estimator ignores the uncorrelated coordinates, those where $\lambda_i = 0$. The following remark shows how this estimator has a natural interpretation in the fixed design setting — it is the result of ridge regression with a specific norm (induced by CCA) over functions in $L(X^{(\nu)})$.

Remark 2. (Canonical Ridge Regression). We now specify a ridge regression algorithm for which the shrinkage estimator is the solution. Define the *canonical*

---

[2] In the fixed design case, one can view each $y_m = f(x_m) + \eta$, where η is 0 mean noise so $f(x_m)$ is the conditional mean. After observing a sample $\{(x_m^{(\nu)}, y_m)\}_{m=1}^{|X|}$ for *all* $x \in X$ (so $n = |X|$), the goal is to reconstruct $f(\cdot)$ accurately.

norm for a linear function in $L(X^{(\nu)})$ as follows: using the representation of $\widehat{f}^{(\nu)}$ in $B^{(\nu)}$ as defined in Equation 1, the canonical norm of $\widehat{f}^{(\nu)}$ is defined as:

$$||\widehat{f}^{(\nu)}||_{\text{CCA}} = \sqrt{\sum_i \frac{1 - \lambda_i}{\lambda_i} \left(\widehat{\beta}_i^{(\nu)}\right)^2} \tag{3}$$

where we overload notation and write $||\widehat{f}^{(\nu)}||_{\text{CCA}} = ||\widehat{\beta}^{(\nu)}||_{\text{CCA}}$. Hence, functions which have large weights in the less correlated directions (those with small λ_i) have larger norms. Equipped with this norm, the functions in $L(X^{(\nu)})$ define a Banach space. In the fixed design setting, the ridge regression algorithm with this norm chooses the $\widehat{\beta}^{(\nu)}$ which minimizes:

$$\frac{1}{|X|} \sum_{m=1}^{|X|} \left(y_m - \widehat{\beta}^{(\nu)} \cdot x_m^{(\nu)}\right)^2 + ||\widehat{\beta}^{(\nu)}||_{\text{CCA}}^2$$

Recall, that in the fixed design setting, we have a training example for each $x \in X$, so the sum is over all $x \in X$.

It is straightforward to show (by using orthogonality) that the estimator which minimizes this loss is the canonical shrinkage estimator defined above. In the more general transductive case, it is not quite this estimator, since the sampled points $\{x_m^{(\nu)}\}_m$ may not be orthogonal in the training sample (they are only orthogonal when summed over all $x \in X$). However, in this case, we expect that the estimator provided by ridge regression is approximately equal to the shrinkage estimator.

We now state the first main theorem.

Theorem 1. *Assume that $\mathbb{E}[y^2|x] \leq 1$ and that Assumption 1 holds. Let $\widehat{f}^{(\nu)}$ be the estimator constructed with the canonical shrinkage estimator (Equation 2) on training set T. For $\nu \in 1, 2$, then*

$$\mathbb{E}_T[\text{loss}(\widehat{f}^{(\nu)})] - \text{loss}(f^{(\nu)}) \leq 4\epsilon + \frac{\sum_i \lambda_i^2}{n}$$

where expectation is with respect to the training set T sampled according to D^n.

We comment on obtaining high probability bounds in the Discussion. The proof (presented in Section 3.3) shows that the 4ϵ results from the bias in the algorithm and $\frac{\sum_i \lambda_i^2}{n}$ results from the variance. It is natural to interpret $\sum_i \lambda_i^2$ as the intrinsic dimensionality.

Note that Assumption 1 implies that:

$$\mathbb{E}_T[\text{loss}(\widehat{f}^{(\nu)})] - \text{loss}(f) \leq 5\epsilon + \frac{\sum_i \lambda_i^2}{n}$$

where the comparison is to the best linear predictor f over both views.

Remark 3. (Intrinsic Dimensionality) Let $\widehat{\beta}^{(\nu)}$ be a linear estimator in the vector of sampled outputs, $Y = (y_1, y_2, \ldots y_m)$. Note that the previous thresholded estimator is such a linear estimator (in the fixed design case). We can write $\widehat{\beta}^{(\nu)} = PY$ where P is a linear operator. Zhang [2005] defines $tr(P^T P)$ as the intrinsic dimensionality, where $tr(\cdot)$ is the trace operator. This was motivated by the fact that in the fixed design setting the error drops as $\frac{tr(P^T P)}{n}$, which is bounded by $\frac{d}{n}$ in a finite dimensional space. Zhang [2005] then goes on to analyze the intrinsic dimensionality of kernel methods in the random design setting (obtaining high probability bounds). In our setting, the sum $\sum_i \lambda_i^2$ is precisely this trace, as P is a diagonal matrix with entries λ_i.

3.2   A (Possibly) Lower Dimensional Estimator

Consider the thresholded estimator:

$$\widehat{\beta}_i^{(\nu)} = \begin{cases} \widehat{\mathbb{E}}[x_i y] & \text{if } \lambda_i \geq 1 - \sqrt{\epsilon} \\ 0 & \text{else} \end{cases} \tag{4}$$

where again $\widehat{\mathbb{E}}[x_i y]$ is the empirical expectation $\frac{1}{n} \sum_m x_{m,i}^{(\nu)} y_m$. This estimator uses an unbiased estimator of $\beta_i^{(\nu)}$ for those i with large λ_i and thresholds to 0 for those i with small λ_i. Hence, the estimator lives in a finite dimensional space (determined by the number of λ_i which are greater than $1 - \sqrt{\epsilon}$).

Theorem 2. *Assume that $\mathbb{E}[y^2|x] \leq 1$ and that Assumption 1 holds. Let d be the number of λ_i for which $\lambda_i \geq 1 - \sqrt{\epsilon}$. Let $\widehat{f}^{(\nu)}$ be the estimator constructed with the threshold estimator (Equation 4) on training set T. For $\nu \in 1, 2$, then*

$$\mathbb{E}_T[\text{loss}(\widehat{f}^{(\nu)})] - \text{loss}(f^{(\nu)}) \leq 4\sqrt{\epsilon} + \frac{d}{n}$$

where expectation is with respect to the training set T sampled according to D^n.

Essentially, the above increases the bias to $4\sqrt{\epsilon}$ and (potentially) decreases the variance. Such a bound may be useful if we desire to explicitly keep $\widehat{\beta}^{(\nu)}$ in a lower dimensional space — in contrast, the explicit dimensionality of the shrinkage estimator could be as large as $|X|$.

3.3   The Bias-Variance Tradeoff

This section provides lemmas for the proofs of the previous theorems. We characterize the bias-variance tradeoff in this error analysis. First, a key technical lemma is useful, for which the proof is provided in the Appendix.

Lemma 2. *Let the representation of the best linear predictor $f^{(\nu)}$ (defined in Assumption 1) in the canonical basis $B^{(\nu)}$ be*

$$f^{(\nu)}(x^{(\nu)}) = \sum_i \beta_i^{(\nu)} x_i^{(\nu)} \tag{5}$$

Assumption 1 implies that

$$\sum_i (1 - \lambda_i) \left(\beta_i^{(\nu)}\right)^2 \le 4\epsilon$$

for $\nu \in \{1, 2\}$.

This lemma shows how the weights (of an optimal linear predictor) cannot be too large in coordinates with small canonical correlation coefficients. This is because for those coordinates with small λ_i, the corresponding β_i must be small enough so that the bound is not violated. This lemma provides the technical motivation for our algorithms.

   Now let us review some useful properties of the square loss. Using the representations of $f^{(\nu)}$ and f defined in Equations 1 and 5, a basic fact for the square loss with linear predictors is that

$$\text{loss}(\widehat{f}^{(\nu)}) - \text{loss}(f^{(\nu)}) = ||\widehat{\beta}^{(\nu)} - \beta^{(\nu)}||_2^2$$

where $||x||_2 = \sqrt{\sum_i x_i^2}$. The expected regret can be decomposed as follows:

$$\mathbb{E}_T \left[||\widehat{\beta}^{(\nu)} - \beta^{(\nu)}||_2^2\right] = ||\mathbb{E}_T[\widehat{\beta}^{(\nu)}] - \beta^{(\nu)}||_2^2 + \mathbb{E}_T \left[||\widehat{\beta}^{(\nu)} - \mathbb{E}_T[\widehat{\beta}^{(\nu)}]||_2^2\right] \quad (6)$$

$$= ||\mathbb{E}_T[\widehat{\beta}^{(\nu)}] - \beta^{(\nu)}||_2^2 + \sum_i \text{Var}(\widehat{\beta}_i^{(\nu)}) \quad (7)$$

where the first term is the bias and the second is the variance.

   The proof of Theorems 1 and 2 follow directly from the next two lemmas.

Lemma 3. *(Bias-Variance for the Shrinkage Estimator) Under the preconditions of Theorem 1, the bias is bounded as:*

$$||\mathbb{E}_T[\widehat{\beta}^{(\nu)}] - \beta^{(\nu)}||_2^2 \le 4\epsilon$$

and the variance is bounded as:

$$\sum_i \text{Var}(\widehat{\beta}_i^{(\nu)}) \le \frac{\sum_i \lambda_i^2}{n}$$

Proof. It is straightforward to see that:

$$\beta_i^{(\nu)} = \mathbb{E}[x_i y]$$

which implies that

$$\mathbb{E}_T[\widehat{\beta}_i^{(\nu)}] = \lambda_i \beta_i^{(\nu)}$$

Hence, for the bias term, we have:

$$||\mathbb{E}_T[\widehat{\beta}^{(\nu)}] - \beta^{(\nu)}||_2^2 = \sum_i (1 - \lambda_i)^2 (\beta_i^{(\nu)})^2$$

$$\le \sum_i (1 - \lambda_i)(\beta_i^{(\nu)})^2$$

$$\le 4\epsilon$$

We have for the variance

$$\text{Var}(\widehat{\beta}_i^{(\nu)}) = \frac{\lambda_i^2}{n} \text{Var}(x_i^{(\nu)} y)$$

$$\leq \frac{\lambda_i^2}{n} \mathbb{E}[(x_i^{(\nu)} y)^2]$$

$$= \frac{\lambda_i^2}{n} \mathbb{E}[(x_i^{(\nu)})^2 \mathbb{E}[y^2|x]]$$

$$\leq \frac{\lambda_i^2}{n} \mathbb{E}[(x_i^{(\nu)})^2]$$

$$= \frac{\lambda_i^2}{n}$$

The proof is completed by summing over i.   □

Lemma 4. *(Bias-Variance for the Thresholded Estimator) Under the preconditions of Theorem 2, the bias is bounded as:*

$$||\mathbb{E}_T[\widehat{\beta}^{(\nu)}] - \beta^{(\nu)}||_2^2 \leq 4\sqrt{\epsilon}$$

and the variance is bounded as:

$$\sum_i \text{Var}(\widehat{\beta}_i^{(\nu)}) \leq \frac{d}{n}$$

Proof. For those i such that $\lambda_i \geq 1 - \sqrt{\epsilon}$,

$$\mathbb{E}_T[\widehat{\beta}_i^{(\nu)}] = \beta_i^{(\nu)}$$

Let j be the index at which the thresholding begins to occur, i.e. it is the smallest integer such that $\lambda_j < 1 - \sqrt{\epsilon}$. Using that for $i \geq j$, we have $1 < (1 - \lambda_j)/\sqrt{\epsilon} \leq (1 - \lambda_i)/\sqrt{\epsilon}$, so the bias can be bounded as follows:

$$||\mathbb{E}_T[\widehat{\beta}^{(\nu)}] - \beta^{(\nu)}||_2^2 = \sum_i \left(\mathbb{E}_T[\widehat{\beta}_i^{(\nu)}] - \beta_i^{(\nu)} \right)^2$$

$$= \sum_{i \geq j} (\beta_i^{(\nu)})^2$$

$$\leq \sum_{i \geq j} \frac{1 - \lambda_i}{\sqrt{\epsilon}} (\beta_i^{(\nu)})^2$$

$$\leq \frac{1}{\sqrt{\epsilon}} \sum_i (1 - \lambda_i)(\beta_i^{(\nu)})^2$$

$$\leq 4\sqrt{\epsilon}$$

where the last step uses Lemma 2.

Analogous to the previous proof, for each $i < j$, we have:

$$\text{Var}(\widehat{\beta}_i^{(\nu)}) \leq 1$$

and there are d such i.   □

4   Discussion

Why does unlabeled data help? Theorem 1 shows that the regret drops at a uniform rate (down to ϵ). This rate is the intrinsic dimensionality, $\sum_i \lambda_i^2$, divided by the sample size n. Note that this intrinsic dimensionality is only a property of the input distribution. Without the multi-view assumption (or working in the single view case), the rate at which our error drops is governed by the extrinsic dimensionality of x, which could be large (or countably infinite), making this rate very slow without further assumptions. It is straightforward to see that the intrinsic dimensionality is no greater than the extrinsic dimensionality (since λ_i is bounded by 1), though it could be much less. The knowledge of the covariance matrix of x allows us to compute the CCA basis and construct the shrinkage estimator which has the improved converge rate based on the intrinsic dimensionality. Such second order statistical knowledge can be provided by the unlabeled data, such as in the transductive and fixed design settings.

Let us compare to a ridge regression algorithm (in the single view case), where one apriori chooses a norm for regularization (such as an RKHS norm imposed by a kernel). As discussed in Zhang [2005], this regularization governs the bias-variance tradeoff. The regularization can significantly decrease the variance — the variance drops as $\frac{d}{n}$ where d is a notion of intrinsic dimensionality defined in Zhang [2005]. However, the regularization also biases the algorithm to predictors with small norm — there is no apriori reason that there exists a good predictor with a bounded norm (under the pre-specified norm). In order to obtain a reasonable convergence rate, it must also be the case that the best predictor (or a good one) has a small norm under our pre-specified norm. In contrast, in the multi-view case, the multi-view assumption implies that the bias is bounded — recall that Lemma 3 showed that the bias was bounded by 4ϵ. Essentially, our proof shows that the bias induced by using the special norm induced by CCA (in Equation 3) is small.

Now it may be the case that we have apriori knowledge of what a good norm is. However, learning the norm (or learning the kernel) is an important open question. The multi-view setting provides one solution to this problem.

Can the bias be decreased to 0 asymptotically? Theorem 1 shows that the error drops down to 4ϵ for large n. It turns out that we can not drive this bias to 0 asymptotically without further assumptions, as the input space could be infinite dimensional.

On obtaining high probability bounds. Clearly, stronger assumptions are needed than just a bounded second moment to obtain high probability bounds with concentration properties. For the fixed design setting, if y is bounded, then it is straightforward to obtain high probability bounds through standard Chernoff arguments. For the random transductive case, this assumption is not sufficient — this is due to the additional randomness from x. Note that we cannot artificially impose a bound on x as the algorithm only depends on the subspace spanned by X, so upper bounds have no meaning — note the algorithm scales X such that it has an identity covariance matrix (e.g. $E[x_i^2] = 1$). However, if we have a higher moment bound, say on the ratio of $E[x_i^4]/E[x_i^2]$, then one could use the Bennett bound can be used to obtain data dependent high probability bounds, though providing these is beyond the scope of this paper.

Related Work. The most closely related multi-view learning algorithms are the SVM-2K algorithm of Farquhar et al. [2005] and the co-regularized least squares regression algorithm of Sindhwani et al. [2005]. Roughly speaking, both of these algorithms try to find two hypothesis — $h^{(1)}(\cdot)$, based on view one, and $h^{(2)}(\cdot)$, based on view two — which both have low training error and which tend to agree with each other on unlabeled error, where the latter condition is enforced by constraining $h^{(1)}(x^{(1)})$ to usually equal $h^{(2)}(x^{(2)})$ on an unlabeled data set.

The SVM-2K algorithm considers a classification setting and the algorithm attempts to force agreement between the two hypothesis with slack variable style constraints, common to SVM algorithms. While this algorithm is motivated by kernel CCA and SVMs, the algorithm does not directly use kernel CCA, in contrast to our algorithm, where CCA naturally provides a coordinate system. The theoretical analysis in [Farquhar et al., 2005] argues that the Rademacher complexity of the hypothesis space is reduced due to the agreement constraint between the two views.

The multi-view approach to regression has been previously considered in Sindhwani et al. [2005]. Here, they specify a co-regularized least squares regression algorithm, which is a ridge regression algorithm with an additional penalty term which forces the two predictions, from both views, to agree. A theoretical analysis of this algorithm is provided in Rosenberg and Bartlett [2007], which shows that the Rademacher complexity of the hypothesis class is reduced by forcing agreement.

Both of these previous analysis do not explicitly state a multi-view assumption, so it hard to directly compare the results. In our setting, the multi-view regret is explicitly characterized by ϵ. In a rather straightforward manner (without appealing to Rademacher complexities), we have shown that the rate at which the regret drops to 4ϵ is determined by the intrinsic dimensionality. Furthermore, both of these previous algorithms use an apriori specified norm over their class of functions (induced by an apriori specified kernel), and the Rademacher complexities (which are used to bound the convergence rates) depend on this norm. In contrast, our framework assumes no norm — the norm over functions is imposed by the correlation structure between the two views.

We should also note that their are close connections to those unsupervised learning algorithms which attempt to maximize relevant information. The Imax framework of Becker and Hinton [1992], Becker [1996] attempts to maximize information between two views $x^{(1)}$ and $x^{(2)}$, for which CCA is a special case (in a continuous version). Subsequently, the information bottleneck provided a framework for capturing the mutual information between two signals [Tishby et al., 1999]. Here, the goal is to compress a signal $x^{(1)}$ such that it captures relevant information about another signal $x^{(2)}$. The framework here is unsupervised as there is no specific supervised task at hand. For the case in which the joint distribution of $x^{(1)}$ and $x^{(2)}$ is Gaussian, Chechik et al. [2003] completely characterizes the compression tradeoffs for capturing the mutual information between these two signals — CCA provides the coordinate system for this compression.

In our setting, we do not explicitly care about the mutual information between $x^{(1)}$ and $x^{(2)}$ — performance is judged only by performance at the task at hand, namely our loss when predicting some other variable y. However, as we show, it turns out that these unsupervised mutual information maximizing algorithms provide appropriate intuition for multi-view regression, as they result in CCA as a basis.

Acknowledgements

We thank the anonymous reviewers for their helpful comments.

References

Abney, S.: Understanding the Yarowsky Algorithm. Comput. Linguist. 30(3), 365–395 (2004) ISSN 0891-2017.
Balcan, M.-F., Blum, A.: A PAC-Style Model for Learning from Labeled and Unlabeled Data. In: Semi-Supervised Learning, pp. 111–126. MIT Press, Cambridge (2006)
Becker, S.: Mutual information maximization: Models of cortical self-organization. Network: Computation in Neural Systems (1996)
Becker, S., Hinton, G.-E.: Self-organizing neural network that discovers surfaces in random-dot stereograms. 1992 355(6356), 161–163 (1992), doi:10.1038/355161a0
Blum, A., Mitchell, T.: Combining labeled and unlabeled data with co-training. In: COLT' 98: Proceedings of the eleventh annual conference on Computational learning theory, Madison, Wisconsin, United States, pp. 92–100. ACM Press, New York, NY, USA (1998) ISBN 1-58113-057-0.
Brefeld, U., Gartner, T., Scheffer, T., Wrobel, S.: Efficient co-regularised least squares regression. In: ICML '06: Proceedings of the 23rd international conference on Machine learning, Pittsburgh, Pennsylvania, pp. 137–144. ACM Press, New York, NY, USA (2006) ISBN 1-59593-383-2.
Chechik, G., Globerson, A., Tishby, N., Weiss, Y.: Information bottleneck for gaussian variables, URL (2003), citeseer.ist.psu.edu/article/chechik03information.html
Dasgupta, S., Littman, M.-L., Mcallester, D.: Pac generalization bounds for co-training (2001)
Farquhar, J. D. R., Hardoon, D. R., Meng, H., Shawe-Taylor, J., Szedmák, S.: Two view learning: Svm-2k, theory and practice. In: NIPS, 2005.
Hardoon, D.R., Szedmak, S.R., Shawe-Taylor, J.R.: Canonical Correlation Analysis: An Overview with Application to Learning Methods. Neural Comput. 16(12), 2639–2664 (2004) ISSN 0899-7667.
Hotelling, H.: The most predictable criterion. Journal of Educational Psychology (1935)
Rosenberg, D., Bartlett, P.: The rademacher complexity of co-regularized kernel classes. submitted. In: Proceedings of the Eleventh International Conference on Artificial Intelligence and Statistics (2007)

Sindhwani, V., Niyogi, P., Belkin, M.: A co-regularized approach to semi-supervised learning with multiple views. In: Proceedings of the ICML Workshop on Learning with Multiple Views (2005)

Tishby, N., Pereira, F., Bialek, W.: The information bottleneck method. In: Proceedings of the 37-th Annual Allerton Conference on Communication, Control and Computing, pp. 368–377, URL (1999), citeseer.ist.psu.edu/tishby99information.html

Yarowsky, D.: Unsupervised word sense disambiguation rivaling supervised methods. In: Proceedings of the 33rd annual meeting on Association for Computational Linguistics, pp. 189–196, Morristown, NJ, USA, Association for Computational Linguistics (1995)

Zhang, T.: Learning Bounds for Kernel Regression Using Effective Data Dimensionality. Neural Comput. 17(9), 2077–2098 (2005) ISSN 0899-7667.

Appendix

We now provide the proof of Lemma 1

Proof (of Lemma 1). Let $\beta^{(\nu)}$ be the weights for $f^{(\nu)}$ and let β be the weights of f in some basis. Let $\beta^{(\nu)} \cdot x^{(\nu)}$ and $\beta \cdot x$ be the representation of $f^{(\nu)}$ and f in this basis. By Assumption 1

$$
\begin{aligned}
\epsilon &\geq \mathbb{E}(\beta^{(\nu)} \cdot x^{(\nu)} - y)^2 - \mathbb{E}(\beta \cdot x - y)^2 \\
&= \mathbb{E}(\beta^{(\nu)} \cdot x^{(\nu)} - \beta \cdot x + \beta \cdot x - y)^2 - \mathbb{E}(\beta \cdot x - y)^2 \\
&= \mathbb{E}(\beta^{(\nu)} \cdot x^{(\nu)} - \beta \cdot x)^2 - 2\mathbb{E}[(\beta^{(\nu)} \cdot x^{(\nu)} - \beta \cdot x)(\beta \cdot x - y)]
\end{aligned}
$$

Now the "normal equations" for β (the first derivative conditions for the optimal linear predictor β) states that for each i:

$$
\mathbb{E}[x_i(\beta \cdot x - y)] = 0
$$

where x_i is the i component of x. This implies that both

$$
\mathbb{E}[\beta \cdot x(\beta \cdot x - y)] = 0
$$
$$
\mathbb{E}[\beta^{(\nu)} \cdot x^{(\nu)}(\beta \cdot x - y)] = 0
$$

where the last equation follows since $x^{(\nu)}$ has components in x.
    Hence,
$$
\mathbb{E}[(\beta^{(\nu)} \cdot x^{(\nu)} - \beta \cdot x)(\beta \cdot x - y)] = 0
$$

and we have shown that:

$$
\mathbb{E}(\beta^{(1)} \cdot x^{(1)} - \beta \cdot x)^2 \leq \epsilon
$$
$$
\mathbb{E}(\beta^{(2)} \cdot x^{(2)} - \beta \cdot x)^2 \leq \epsilon
$$

The triangle inequality states that:

$$\mathbb{E}(\beta^{(1)} \cdot x^{(1)} - \beta^{(2)} \cdot x)^2$$
$$\leq \left(\sqrt{\mathbb{E}(\beta^{(1)} \cdot x^{(1)} - \beta \cdot x)^2} + \sqrt{\mathbb{E}(\beta^{(2)} \cdot x^{(2)} - \beta \cdot x)^2} \right)^2$$
$$\leq (2\sqrt{\epsilon})^2$$

which completes the proof.   □

Below is the proof of Lemma 2.

Proof (of Lemma 2). From Lemma 1, we have:

$$4\epsilon \geq \mathbb{E}\left[(\beta^{(1)} \cdot x^{(1)} - \beta^{(2)} \cdot x^{(2)})^2 \right]$$
$$= \sum_i \left((\beta_i^{(1)})^2 + (\beta_i^{(2)})^2 - 2\lambda_i \beta_i^{(1)} \beta_i^{(2)} \right)$$
$$= \sum_i \left((1-\lambda_i)(\beta_i^{(1)})^2 + (1-\lambda_i)(\beta_i^{(2)})^2 + \lambda_i((\beta_i^{(1)})^2 + (\beta_i^{(2)})^2 - 2\beta_i^{(1)}\beta_i^{(2)}) \right)$$
$$= \sum_i \left((1-\lambda_i)(\beta_i^{(1)})^2 + (1-\lambda_i)(\beta_i^{(2)})^2 + \lambda_i(\beta_i^{(1)} - \beta_i^{(2)})^2 \right)$$
$$\geq \sum_i \left((1-\lambda_i)(\beta_i^{(1)})^2 + (1-\lambda_i)(\beta_i^{(2)})^2 \right)$$
$$\geq \sum_i (1-\lambda_i)(\beta_i^{(\nu)})^2$$

where the last step holds for either $\nu = 1$ or $\nu = 2$.   □

Aggregation by Exponential Weighting and Sharp Oracle Inequalities

Arnak S. Dalalyan and Alexandre B. Tsybakov

University of Paris 6,
4, Place Jussieu, 75252 Paris cedex 05, France

Abstract. In the present paper, we study the problem of aggregation under the squared loss in the model of regression with deterministic design. We obtain sharp oracle inequalities for convex aggregates defined via exponential weights, under general assumptions on the distribution of errors and on the functions to aggregate. We show how these results can be applied to derive a sparsity oracle inequality.

1 Introduction

Consider the regression model

$$Y_i = f(x_i) + \xi_i, \quad i = 1, \ldots, n, \tag{1}$$

where $x_1, \ldots, x_n$ are given elements of a set $\mathcal{X}$, $f : \mathcal{X} \to \mathbb{R}$ is an unknown function, and ξ_i are i.i.d. zero-mean random variables on a probability space $(\Omega, \mathcal{F}, P)$ where $\Omega \subseteq \mathbb{R}$. The problem is to estimate the function f from the data $D_n = ((x_1, Y_1), \ldots, (x_n, Y_n))$.

Let $(\Lambda, \mathcal{A})$ be a probability space and denote by $\mathscr{P}_\Lambda$ the set of all probability measures defined on $(\Lambda, \mathcal{A})$. Assume that we are given a family $\{f_\lambda, \lambda \in \Lambda\}$ of functions $f_\lambda : \mathcal{X} \to \mathbb{R}$ such that the mapping $\lambda \mapsto f_\lambda$ is measurable, $\mathbb{R}$ being equipped with the Borel σ-field. Functions f_λ can be viewed either as weak learners or as some preliminary estimators of f based on a training sample independent of $\mathbf{Y} \triangleq (Y_1, \ldots, Y_n)$ and considered as frozen.

We study the problem of aggregation of functions in $\{f_\lambda, \lambda \in \Lambda\}$ under the squared loss. Specifically, we construct an estimator $\hat{f}_n$ based on the data D_n and called *aggregate* such that the expected value of its squared error

$$\|\hat{f}_n - f\|_n^2 \triangleq \frac{1}{n} \sum_{i=1}^n \left(\hat{f}_n(x_i) - f(x_i) \right)^2$$

is approximately as small as the oracle value $\inf_{\lambda \in \Lambda} \|f - f_\lambda\|_n^2$.

In this paper we consider aggregates that are mixtures of functions f_λ with exponential weights. For a measure π from $\mathscr{P}_\Lambda$ and for $\beta > 0$ we set

$$\hat{f}_n(x) \triangleq \int_\Lambda \theta_\lambda(\beta, \pi, \mathbf{Y}) f_\lambda(x) \, \pi(d\lambda), \quad x \in \mathcal{X}, \tag{2}$$

N. Bshouty and C. Gentile (Eds.): COLT 2007, LNAI 4539, pp. 97–111, 2007.

with

$$\theta_\lambda(\beta, \pi, \mathbf{Y}) = \frac{\exp\left\{-n\|\mathbf{Y} - f_\lambda\|_n^2/\beta\right\}}{\int_\Lambda \exp\left\{-n\|\mathbf{Y} - f_w\|_n^2/\beta\right\}\pi(dw)} \tag{3}$$

where $\|\mathbf{Y} - f_\lambda\|_n^2 \triangleq \frac{1}{n}\sum_{i=1}^n \left(Y_i - f_\lambda(x_i)\right)^2$ and we assume that π is such that the integral in (2) is finite.

Note that $\hat{f}_n$ depends on two tuning parameters: the prior measure π and the "temperature" parameter β. They have to be selected in a suitable way.

Using the Bayesian terminology, $\pi(\cdot)$ is a prior distribution and $\hat{f}_n$ is the posterior mean of f_λ in a "phantom" model $Y_i = f_\lambda(x_i) + \xi_i'$, where ξ_i' are iid normally distributed with mean 0 and variance $\beta/2$.

The idea of mixing with exponential weights has been discussed by many authors apparently since 1970-ies (see [27] for a nice overview of the subject). Most of the work focused on the important particular case where the set of estimators is finite, i.e., w.l.o.g. $\Lambda = \{1, \ldots, M\}$, and the distribution π is uniform on Λ. Procedures of the type (2)–(3) with general sets Λ and priors π came into consideration quite recently [9,8,3,29,30,1,2,25], partly in connection to the PAC-Bayesian approach. For finite Λ, procedures (2)–(3) were independently introduced for prediction of deterministic individual sequences with expert advice. Representative work and references can be found in [24,17,11]; in this framework the results are proved for cumulative loss and no assumption is made on the statistical nature of the data, whereas the observations Y_i are supposed to be uniformly bounded by a known constant. This is not the case for the regression model that we consider here.

We mention also related work on cumulative exponential weighting methods: there the aggregate is defined as the average $n^{-1}\sum_{k=1}^n \hat{f}_k$. For regression models with random design, such procedures are introduced and analyzed in [8], [9] and [26]. In particular, [8] and [9] establish a sharp oracle inequality, i.e., an inequality with leading constant 1. This result is further refined in [3] and [13]. In addition, [13] derives sharp oracle inequalities not only for the squared loss but also for general loss functions. However, these techniques are not helpful in the framework that we consider here, because the averaging device cannot be meaningfully adapted to models with non-identically distributed observations.

Aggregate $\hat{f}_n$ can be computed on-line. This, in particular, motivated its use for on-line prediction with finite Λ. Papers [13], [14] point out that $\hat{f}_n$ and its averaged version can be obtained as a special case of mirror descent algorithms that were considered earlier in deterministic minimization. Finally, [10] establishes an interesting link between the results for cumulative risks proved in the theory of prediction of deterministic sequences and generalization error bounds for the aggregates in the stochastic i.i.d. case.

In this paper we establish sharp oracle inequalities for the aggregate $\hat{f}_n$ under the squared loss, i.e., oracle inequalities with leading constant 1 and optimal rate of the remainder term. For a particular case, such an inequality has been pioneered in [16]. The result of [16] is proved for a finite set Λ and Gaussian errors. It makes use of Stein's unbiased risk formula, and gives a very precise constant in the remainder term of the inequality. The inequalities that we prove below are valid for general Λ and arbitrary functions f_λ satisfying some mild conditions. Furthermore, we treat non-Gaussian errors. We introduce new techniques of the proof based on dummy randomization which allows us to obtain the result for "n-divisible" distributions of errors ξ_i. We then apply the Skorokhod embedding to cover the class of all symmetric error distributions with finite exponential moments. Finally, we consider the case where f_λ is a linear combination of M known functions with the vector of weights $\lambda \in \mathbb{R}^M$. For this case, as a consequence of our main result we obtain a sparsity oracle inequality (SOI). We refer to [22] where the notion of SOI is introduced in a general context. Examples of SOI are proved in [15,5,4,6,23]. In particular, [5] deals with the regression model with fixed design that we consider here and proves approximate SOI for BIC type and Lasso type aggregates. We show that the aggregate with exponential weights satisfies a sharp SOI, i.e., a SOI with leading constant 1.

2 Risk Bounds for n-Divisible Distributions of Errors

The assumptions that we need to derive our main result concern essentially the probability distribution of the i.i.d. errors ξ_i.

(A) There exist i.i.d. random variables $\zeta_1, \ldots, \zeta_n$ defined on an enlargement of the probability space $(\Omega, \mathcal{F}, P)$ such that:

(A1) the random variable $\xi_1 + \zeta_1$ has the same distribution as $(1 + 1/n)\xi_1$,

(A2) the vectors $\boldsymbol{\zeta} = (\zeta_1, \ldots, \zeta_n)$ and $\boldsymbol{\xi} = (\xi_1, \ldots, \xi_n)$ are independent.

Note that (A) is an assumption on the distribution of ξ_1. If ξ_1 satisfies (A1), then we will say that its distribution is n-*divisible*. We defer to Section 4 the discussion about how rich is the class of n-divisible distributions.

Hereafter, we will write for brevity θ_λ instead of $\theta_\lambda(\beta, \pi, \mathbf{Y})$. Denote by $\mathscr{P}'_\Lambda$ the set of all the measures $\mu \in \mathscr{P}_\Lambda$ such that $\lambda \mapsto f_\lambda(x)$ is integrable w.r.t. μ for $x \in \{x_1, \ldots, x_n\}$. Clearly $\mathscr{P}'_\Lambda$ is a convex subset of $\mathscr{P}_\Lambda$. For any measure $\mu \in \mathscr{P}'_\Lambda$ we define

$$\bar{f}_\mu(x_i) = \int_\Lambda f_\lambda(x_i)\, \mu(d\lambda), \quad i = 1, \ldots, n.$$

We denote by $\theta \cdot \pi$ the probability measure $A \mapsto \int_A \theta_\lambda\, \pi(d\lambda)$ defined on $\mathcal{A}$. With the above notation, we have $\hat{f}_n = \bar{f}_{\theta \cdot \pi}$.

We will need one more assumption. Let $L_\zeta : \mathbb{R} \to \mathbb{R} \cup \{\infty\}$ be the moment generating function of the random variable ζ_1, i.e., $L_\zeta(t) = E(e^{t\zeta_1})$, $t \in \mathbb{R}$.

(B) There exist a functional $\Psi_\beta : \mathscr{P}'_\Lambda \times \mathscr{P}'_\Lambda \to \mathbb{R}$ and a real number $\beta_0 > 0$ such that

$$\begin{cases} e^{(\|f - \bar{f}_{\mu'}\|_n^2 - \|f - \bar{f}_\mu\|_n^2)/\beta} \prod_{i=1}^n L_\zeta\left(\frac{2(\bar{f}_\mu(x_i) - \bar{f}_{\mu'}(x_i))}{\beta}\right) \le \Psi_\beta(\mu, \mu'), \\ \mu \mapsto \Psi_\beta(\mu, \mu') \text{ is concave and continuous in the total} \\ \text{variation norm for any } \mu' \in \mathscr{P}'_\Lambda, \\ \Psi_\beta(\mu, \mu) = 1, \end{cases} \qquad (4)$$

for any $\beta \ge \beta_0$.

Simple sufficient conditions for this assumption to hold in particular cases are given in Section 4.

The next theorem presents a "PAC-Bayesian" type bound.

Theorem 1. *Let π be an element of $\mathscr{P}_\Lambda$ such that $\theta \cdot \pi \in \mathscr{P}'_\Lambda$ for all $\mathbf{Y} \in \mathbb{R}^n$ and $\beta > 0$. If assumptions (A) and (B) are fulfilled, then the aggregate $\hat{f}_n$ defined by (2) with $\beta \geq \beta_0$ satisfies the oracle inequality*

$$E\left(\|\hat{f}_n - f\|_n^2\right) \leq \int \|f_\lambda - f\|_n^2 \, p(d\lambda) + \frac{\beta \, \mathcal{K}(p, \pi)}{n+1}, \quad \forall \, p \in \mathscr{P}_\Lambda, \qquad (5)$$

where $\mathcal{K}(p, \pi)$ stands for the Kullback-Leibler divergence between p and π.

Proof. Define the mapping $\mathbf{H} : \mathscr{P}'_\Lambda \to \mathbb{R}^n$ by

$$\mathbf{H}_\mu = (\bar{f}_\mu(x_1) - f(x_1), \ldots, \bar{f}_\mu(x_n) - f(x_n))^\top, \quad \mu \in \mathscr{P}'_\Lambda.$$

For brevity, we will write

$$\mathbf{h}_\lambda = \mathbf{H}_{\delta_\lambda} = (f_\lambda(x_1) - f(x_1), \ldots, f_\lambda(x_n) - f(x_n))^\top, \quad \lambda \in \Lambda,$$

where δ_λ is the Dirac measure at λ (that is $\delta_\lambda(A) = \mathbb{1}(\lambda \in A)$ for any $A \in \mathcal{A}$ where $\mathbb{1}(\cdot)$ denotes the indicator function).

Since $E(\xi_i) = 0$, assumption (A1) implies that $E(\zeta_i) = 0$ for $i = 1, \ldots, n$. On the other hand, (A2) implies that $\boldsymbol{\zeta}$ is independent of θ_λ. Therefore, we have

$$E\left(\|\bar{f}_{\theta \cdot \pi} - f\|_n^2\right) = \beta E \log \exp \left\{ \frac{\|\bar{f}_{\theta \cdot \pi} - f\|_n^2 - 2\boldsymbol{\zeta}^\top \mathbf{H}_{\theta \cdot \pi}}{\beta} \right\} = S + S_1$$

where

$$S = -\beta E \log \int_\Lambda \theta_\lambda \exp \left\{ -\frac{\|f_\lambda - f\|_n^2 - 2\boldsymbol{\zeta}^\top \mathbf{h}_\lambda}{\beta} \right\} \pi(d\lambda),$$

$$S_1 = \beta E \log \int_\Lambda \theta_\lambda \exp \left\{ \frac{\|\bar{f}_{\theta \cdot \pi} - f\|_n^2 - \|f_\lambda - f\|_n^2 + 2\boldsymbol{\zeta}^\top (\mathbf{h}_\lambda - \mathbf{H}_{\theta \cdot \pi})}{\beta} \right\} \pi(d\lambda).$$

The definition of θ_λ yields

$$S = -\beta E \log \int_\Lambda \exp \left\{ -\frac{n\|\mathbf{Y} - f_\lambda\|_n^2 + \|f_\lambda - f\|_n^2 - 2\boldsymbol{\zeta}^\top \mathbf{h}_\lambda}{\beta} \right\} \pi(d\lambda)$$

$$+ \beta E \log \int_\Lambda \exp \left\{ -\frac{n\|\mathbf{Y} - f_\lambda\|_n^2}{\beta} \right\} \pi(d\lambda). \qquad (6)$$

Since $\|\mathbf{Y} - f_\lambda\|_n^2 = \|\boldsymbol{\xi}\|_n^2 - 2n^{-1}\boldsymbol{\xi}^\top \mathbf{h}_\lambda + \|f_\lambda - f\|_n^2$, we get

$$S = -\beta E \log \int_\Lambda \exp \left\{ -\frac{(n+1)\|f_\lambda - f\|_n^2 - 2(\boldsymbol{\xi} + \boldsymbol{\zeta})^\top \mathbf{h}_\lambda}{\beta} \right\} \pi(d\lambda)$$

$$+ \beta E \log \int_\Lambda \exp \left\{ -\frac{n\|f - f_\lambda\|_n^2 - 2\boldsymbol{\xi}^\top \mathbf{h}_\lambda}{\beta} \right\} \pi(d\lambda)$$

$$= \beta E \log \int_\Lambda e^{-n\rho(\lambda)} \pi(d\lambda) - \beta E \log \int_\Lambda e^{-(n+1)\rho(\lambda)} \pi(d\lambda), \qquad (7)$$

where we used the notation $\rho(\lambda) = (\|f - f_\lambda\|_n^2 - 2n^{-1}\boldsymbol{\xi}^\top \boldsymbol{h}_\lambda)/\beta$ and the fact that $\boldsymbol{\xi} + \boldsymbol{\zeta}$ can be replaced by $(1 + 1/n)\boldsymbol{\xi}$ inside the expectation. The Hölder inequality implies that $\int_\Lambda e^{-n\rho(\lambda)}\pi(d\lambda) \leq (\int_\Lambda e^{-(n+1)\rho(\lambda)}\pi(d\lambda))^{\frac{n}{n+1}}$. Therefore,

$$S \leq -\frac{\beta}{n+1} E \log \int_\Lambda e^{-(n+1)\rho(\lambda)} \, \pi(d\lambda). \tag{8}$$

Assume now that $p \in \mathscr{P}_\Lambda$ is absolutely continuous with respect to π. Denote by ϕ the corresponding Radon-Nikodym derivative and by Λ_+ the support of p. Using the concavity of the logarithm and Jensen's inequality we get

$$-E \log \int_\Lambda e^{-(n+1)\rho(\lambda)}\pi(d\lambda) \leq -E \log \int_{\Lambda_+} e^{-(n+1)\rho(\lambda)}\pi(d\lambda)$$

$$= -E \log \int_{\Lambda_+} e^{-(n+1)\rho(\lambda)}\phi^{-1}(\lambda) \, p(d\lambda)$$

$$\leq (n+1)E \int_{\Lambda_+} \rho(\lambda) \, p(d\lambda) + \int_{\Lambda_+} \log \phi(\lambda) \, p(d\lambda).$$

Noticing that the last integral here equals to $\mathcal{K}(p, \pi)$ and combining the resulting inequality with (8) we obtain

$$S \leq \beta E \int_\Lambda \rho(\lambda) \, p(d\lambda) + \frac{\beta \mathcal{K}(p, \pi)}{n+1}.$$

Since $E(\xi_i) = 0$ for every $i = 1, \ldots, n$, we have $\beta E(\rho(\lambda)) = \|f_\lambda - f\|_n^2$, and using the Fubini theorem we find

$$S \leq \int_\Lambda \|f_\lambda - f\|_n^2 \, p(d\lambda) + \frac{\beta \mathcal{K}(p, \pi)}{n+1}. \tag{9}$$

Note that this inequality also holds in the case where p is not absolutely continuous with respect to π, since in this case $\mathcal{K}(p, \pi) = \infty$.

To complete the proof, it remains to show that $S_1 \leq 0$. Let $E_{\boldsymbol{\xi}}(\cdot)$ denote the conditional expectation $E(\cdot|\boldsymbol{\xi})$. By the concavity of the logarithm,

$$S_1 \leq \beta E \log \int_\Lambda \theta_\lambda E_{\boldsymbol{\xi}} \exp \left\{ \frac{\|\bar{f}_{\theta \cdot \pi} - f\|_n^2 - \|f_\lambda - f\|_n^2 + 2\boldsymbol{\zeta}^\top (\boldsymbol{h}_\lambda - \boldsymbol{H}_{\theta \cdot \pi})}{\beta} \right\} \pi(d\lambda).$$

Since $f_\lambda = \bar{f}_{\delta_\lambda}$ and $\boldsymbol{\zeta}$ is independent of θ_λ, the last expectation on the right hand side of this inequality is bounded from above by $\Psi_\beta(\delta_\lambda, \theta \cdot \pi)$. Now, the fact that $S_1 \leq 0$ follows from the concavity and continuity of the functional $\Psi_\beta(\cdot, \theta \cdot \pi)$, Jensen's inequality and the equality $\Psi_\beta(\theta \cdot \pi, \theta \cdot \pi) = 1$.

REMARK. Another way to read the result of Theorem 1 is that, if the probabilistic "phantom" Gaussian error model is used to construct $\hat{f}_n$, with variance taken larger than a certain threshold value, then the Bayesian posterior mean under the true model is close in expectation to the best prediction, even when the true data generating distribution does not have Gaussian errors, but errors of more general type.

3   Model Selection with Finite or Countable Λ

Consider now the particular case where Λ is countable. W.l.o.g. we suppose that $\Lambda = \{1, 2, \ldots\}$, $\{f_\lambda, \lambda \in \Lambda\} = \{f_j\}_{j=1}^{\infty}$ and we set $\pi_j \triangleq \pi(\lambda = j)$. As a corollary of Theorem 1 we get the following sharp oracle inequalities for model selection type aggregation.

Theorem 2. *Assume that π is an element of $\mathscr{P}_\Lambda$ such that $\theta \cdot \pi \in \mathscr{P}'_\Lambda$ for all $\mathbf{Y} \in \mathbb{R}^n$ and $\beta > 0$. Let assumptions (A) and (B) be fulfilled and let Λ be countable. Then for any $\beta \geq \beta_0$ the aggregate $\hat{f}_n$ satisfies the inequality*

$$E\left(\|\hat{f}_n - f\|_n^2\right) \leq \inf_{j \geq 1}\left(\|f_j - f\|_n^2 + \frac{\beta \log \pi_j^{-1}}{n+1}\right).$$

In particular, if $\pi_j = 1/M$, $j = 1, \ldots, M$, we have

$$E\left(\|\hat{f}_n - f\|_n^2\right) \leq \min_{j=1,\ldots,M}\|f_j - f\|_n^2 + \frac{\beta \log M}{n+1}. \tag{10}$$

Proof. For a fixed integer $j_0 \geq 1$ we apply Theorem 1 with p being the Dirac measure: $p(\lambda = j) = \mathbb{1}(j = j_0)$, $j \geq 1$. This gives

$$E\left(\|\hat{f}_n - f\|_n^2\right) \leq \|f_{j_0} - f\|_n^2 + \frac{\beta \log \pi_{j_0}^{-1}}{n+1}.$$

Since this inequality holds for every j_0, we obtain the first inequality of the proposition. The second inequality is an obvious consequence of the first one.

REMARK. The rate of convergence $(\log M)/n$ obtained in (10) is optimal rate of model selection type aggregation when the errors ξ_i are Gaussian [21,5].

4   Checking Assumptions (A) and (B)

In this section we give some sufficient conditions for assumptions (A) and (B). Denote by $\mathcal{D}_n$ the set of all probability distributions of ξ_1 satisfying assumption (A1). First, it is easy to see that all zero-mean Gaussian or double-exponential distributions belong to $\mathcal{D}_n$. Furthermore, $\mathcal{D}_n$ contains all stable distributions. However, since non-Gaussian stable distributions do not have second order moments, they do not satisfy (4). One can also check that the convolution of two distributions from $\mathcal{D}_n$ belongs to $\mathcal{D}_n$. Finally, note that the intersection $\mathcal{D} = \cap_{n \geq 1}\mathcal{D}_n$ is included in the set of all infinitely divisible distributions and is called the L-class (see [19], Theorem 3.6, p. 102).

However, some basic distributions such as the uniform or the Bernoulli distribution do not belong to $\mathcal{D}_n$. To show this, let us recall that the characteristic function of the uniform on $[-a, a]$ distribution is given by $\varphi(t) = \sin(at)/(\pi a t)$. For this function, $\varphi((n+1)t)/\varphi(nt)$ is equal to infinity at the points where

$\sin(nat)$ vanishes (unless $n = 1$). Therefore, it cannot be a characteristic function. Similar argument shows that the centered Bernoulli and centered binomial distributions do not belong to $\mathcal{D}_n$.

We now discuss two important cases of Theorem 1 where the errors ξ_i are either Gaussian or double exponential.

Proposition 1. *Assume that* $\sup_{\lambda \in \Lambda} \|f - f_\lambda\|_n \leq L < \infty$. *If the random variables* ξ_i *are i.i.d. Gaussian* $\mathcal{N}(0, \sigma^2)$, $\sigma^2 > 0$, *then for every* $\beta \geq (4 + 2/n)\sigma^2 + 2L^2$ *the aggregate* $\hat{f}_n$ *satisfies inequality (5).*

Proof. If $\xi_i \sim \mathcal{N}(0, \sigma^2)$, assumption (A) is fulfilled with random variables ζ_i having the Gaussian distribution $\mathcal{N}(0, (2n + 1)\sigma^2/n^2)$. Using the Laplace transform of the Gaussian distribution we get $L_\zeta(u) = \exp(\sigma^2 u^2(2n+1)/(2n^2))$. Therefore, take

$$\Psi_\beta(\mu, \mu') = \exp\left(\frac{\|f - \bar{f}_{\mu'}\|_n^2 - \|f - \bar{f}_\mu\|_n^2}{\beta} + \frac{2\sigma^2(2n+1)\|\bar{f}_\mu - \bar{f}_{\mu'}\|_n^2}{n\beta^2}\right).$$

This functional satisfies $\Psi_\beta(\mu, \mu) = 1$, and it is not hard to see that the mapping $\mu \mapsto \Psi_\beta(\mu, \mu')$ is continuous in the total variation norm. Finally, this mapping is concave for every $\beta \geq (4 + 2/n)\sigma^2 + 2\sup_\lambda \|f - f_\lambda\|_n^2$ by virtue of Lemma 3 in the Appendix. Therefore, assumption (B) is fulfilled and the desired result follows from Theorem 1.

Assume now that ξ_i are distributed with the double exponential density

$$f_\xi(x) = \frac{1}{\sqrt{2\sigma^2}} \, e^{-\sqrt{2}|x|/\sigma}, \quad x \in \mathbb{R}.$$

Aggregation under this assumption is discussed in [28] where it is recommended to modify the shape of the aggregate in order to match the shape of the distribution of the errors. The next proposition shows that sharp risk bounds can be obtained without modifying the algorithm.

Proposition 2. *Assume that* $\sup_{\lambda \in \Lambda} \|f - f_\lambda\|_n \leq L < \infty$ *and* $\sup_{i,\lambda} |f_\lambda(x_i)| \leq \bar{L} < \infty$. *Let the random variables* ξ_i *be i.i.d. double exponential with variance* $\sigma^2 > 0$. *Then for any* β *larger than*

$$\max\left(\left(8 + \frac{4}{n}\right)\sigma^2 + 2L^2, \; 4\sigma\left(1 + \frac{1}{n}\right)\bar{L}\right)$$

the aggregate $\hat{f}_n$ *satisfies inequality (5).*

Proof. We apply Theorem 1. The characteristic function of the double exponential density is $\varphi(t) = 2/(2 + \sigma^2 t^2)$. Solving $\varphi(t)\varphi_\zeta(t) = \varphi((n+1)t/n)$ we get the characteristic function φ_ζ of ζ_1. The corresponding Laplace transform L_ζ in this case is $L_\zeta(t) = \varphi_\zeta(-it)$, which yields

$$L_\zeta(t) = 1 + \frac{(2n+1)\sigma^2 t^2}{2n^2 - (n+1)^2\sigma^2 t^2}.$$

Therefore

$$\log L_\zeta(t) \leq (2n+1)(\sigma t/n)^2, \quad |t| \leq \frac{n}{(n+1)\sigma} \,.$$

We now use this inequality to check assumption (B). For all $\mu, \mu' \in \mathscr{P}_\Lambda$ we have

$$2\big|\bar{f}_\mu(x_i) - \bar{f}_{\mu'}(x_i)\big|/\beta \leq 4\bar{L}/\beta, \quad i = 1, \dots, n.$$

Therefore, for $\beta > 4\sigma\big(1 + 1/n\big)\bar{L}$ we get

$$\log L_\zeta\left(2\big|\bar{f}_\mu(x_i) - \bar{f}_{\mu'}(x_i)\big|/\beta\right) \leq \frac{4\sigma^2(2n+1)(\bar{f}_\mu(x_i) - \bar{f}_{\mu'}(x_i))^2}{n\beta^2} \,.$$

Thus, we get the functional Ψ_β of the same form as in the proof of Proposition 1, with the only difference that σ^2 is now replaced by $2\sigma^2$. Therefore, it suffices to repeat the reasoning of the proof of Proposition 1 to complete the proof.

5   Risk Bounds for General Distributions of Errors

As discussed above, assumption (A) restricts the application of Theorem 1 to models with "n-divisible" errors. We now show that this limitation can be dropped. Recall that the main idea of the proof of Theorem 1 consists in an artificial introduction of the dummy random vector ζ independent of ξ. However, the independence property is too strong as compared to what we really need in the proof of Theorem 1. Below we come to a weaker condition invoking a version of Skorokhod embedding (a detailed survey on this subject can be found in [18]).

For simplicity we assume that the errors ξ_i are symmetric, i.e., $P(\xi_i > a) = P(\xi_i < -a)$ for all $a \in \mathbb{R}$. The argument can be adapted to the asymmetric case as well, but we do not discuss it here.

We now describe a version of Skorokhod's construction that will be used below, cf. [20, Proposition II.3.8].

Lemma 1. *Let $\xi_1, \dots, \xi_n$ be i.i.d. symmetric random variables on $(\Omega, \mathcal{F}, P)$. Then there exist i.i.d. random variables $\zeta_1, \dots, \zeta_n$ defined on an enlargement of the probability space $(\Omega, \mathcal{F}, P)$ such that*

(a) $\xi + \zeta$ has the same distribution as $(1 + 1/n)\xi$.
(b) $E(\zeta_i|\xi_i) = 0$, $i = 1, \dots, n$,
(c) for any $\lambda > 0$ and for any $i = 1, \dots, n$, we have

$$E(e^{\lambda\zeta_i}|\xi_i) \leq e^{(\lambda\xi_i)^2(n+1)/n^2}.$$

Proof. Define ζ_i as a random variable such that, given ξ_i, it takes values ξ_i/n or $-2\xi_i - \xi_i/n$ with conditional probabilities $P(\zeta_i = \xi_i/n|\xi_i) = (2n+1)/(2n+2)$ and $P(\zeta_i = -2\xi_i - \xi_i/n|\xi_i) = 1/(2n+2)$. Then properties (a) and (b) are straightforward. Property (c) follows from the relation

$$E(e^{\lambda\zeta_i}|\xi_i) = e^{\frac{\lambda\xi_i}{n}}\left(1 + \frac{1}{2n+2}\left(e^{-2\lambda\xi_i(1+1/n)} - 1\right)\right)$$

and Lemma 2 in the Appendix with $x = \lambda\xi_i/n$ and $\alpha = 2n+2$.

We now state the main result of this section.

Theorem 3. *Fix some $\alpha > 0$ and assume that $\sup_{\lambda \in \Lambda} \|f - f_\lambda\|_n \leq L$ for a finite constant L. If the errors ξ_i are symmetric and have a finite second moment $E(\xi_i^2)$, then for any $\beta \geq 4(1 + 1/n)\alpha + 2L^2$ we have*

$$E\left(\|\hat{f}_n - f\|_n^2 \right) \leq \int_\Lambda \|f_\lambda - f\|_n^2 \, p(d\lambda) + \frac{\beta \, \mathcal{K}(p, \pi)}{n + 1} + R_n, \quad \forall \, p \in \mathscr{P}_\Lambda, \quad (11)$$

where the residual term R_n is given by

$$R_n = E^* \left(\sup_{\lambda \in \Lambda} \sum_{i=1}^n \frac{4(n+1)(\xi_i^2 - \alpha)(f_\lambda(x_i) - \bar{f}_{\theta \cdot \pi}(x_i))^2}{n^2 \beta} \right)$$

and E^* denotes expectation with respect to the outer probability P^*.

Proof. In view of Lemma 1(b) the conditional expectation of random variable ζ_i given θ_λ vanishes. Therefore, with the notation of the proof of Theorem 1, we get $E(\|\hat{f}_n - f\|_n^2) = S + S_1$. Using Lemma 1(a) and acting exactly as in the proof of Theorem 1 we get that S is bounded as in (9). Finally, as shown in the proof of Theorem 1 the term S_1 satisfies

$$S_1 \leq \beta E \log \int_\Lambda \theta_\lambda E_{\boldsymbol{\xi}} \exp \left\{ \frac{\|\bar{f}_{\theta \cdot \pi} - f\|_n^2 - \|f_\lambda - f\|_n^2 + 2 \boldsymbol{\zeta}^\top (\boldsymbol{h}_\lambda - \boldsymbol{H}_{\theta \cdot \pi})}{\beta} \right\} \pi(d\lambda).$$

According to Lemma 1(c),

$$E_{\boldsymbol{\xi}} \left(e^{2 \boldsymbol{\zeta}^T (\boldsymbol{h}_\lambda - \boldsymbol{H}_{\theta \cdot \pi})/\beta} \right) \leq \exp \left\{ \sum_{i=1}^n \frac{4(n+1)(f_\lambda(x_i) - \bar{f}_{\theta \cdot \pi}(x_i))^2 \xi_i^2}{n^2 \beta^2} \right\}.$$

Therefore, $S_1 \leq S_2 + R_n$, where

$$S_2 = \beta E \log \int_\Lambda \theta_\lambda \exp \left(\frac{4\alpha(n+1)\|f_\lambda - \bar{f}_{\theta \cdot \pi}\|_n^2}{n\beta^2} - \frac{\|f - f_\lambda\|_n^2 - \|f - \bar{f}_{\theta \cdot \pi}\|_n^2}{\beta} \right) \pi(d\lambda).$$

Finally, we apply Lemma 3 with $s^2 = 4\alpha(n+1)$ and Jensen's inequality to get that $S_2 \leq 0$.

Corollary 1. *Let the assumptions of Theorem 3 be satisfied and let $|\xi_i| \leq B$ almost surely where B is a finite constant. Then the aggregate $\hat{f}_n$ satisfies inequality (5) for any $\beta \geq 4B^2(1 + 1/n) + 2L^2$.*

Proof. It suffices to note that for $\alpha = B^2$ we get $R_n \leq 0$.

Corollary 2. *Let the assumptions of Theorem 3 be satisfied and suppose that $E(e^{t|\xi_i|^\kappa}) \leq B$ for some finite constants $t > 0$, $\kappa > 0$, $B > 0$. Then for any $n \geq e^{2/\kappa}$ and any $\beta \geq 4(1 + 1/n)(2(\log n)/t)^{1/\kappa} + 2L^2$ we have*

$$E\left(\|\hat{f}_n - f\|_n^2 \right) \leq \int_\Lambda \|f_\lambda - f\|_n^2 \, p(d\lambda) + \frac{\beta \, \mathcal{K}(p, \pi)}{n + 1} \quad (12)$$

$$+ \frac{16BL^2(n+1)(2 \log n)^{2/\kappa}}{n^2 \beta \, t^{2/\kappa}}, \quad \forall \, p \in \mathscr{P}_\Lambda.$$

In particular, if $\Lambda = \{1, \ldots, M\}$ and π is the uniform measure on Λ we get

$$E\left(\|\hat{f}_n - f\|_n^2\right) \leq \min_{j=1,\ldots,M} \|f_j - f\|_n^2 + \frac{\beta \log M}{n+1} \tag{13}$$
$$+ \frac{16BL^2(n+1)(2\log n)^{2/\kappa}}{n^2 \beta \, t^{2/\kappa}}.$$

Proof. Set $\alpha = (2(\log n)/t)^{1/\kappa}$ and note that

$$R_n \leq \frac{4(n+1)}{n^2 \beta} \sup_{\lambda \in \Lambda, \mu \in \mathscr{P}'_\Lambda} \|f_\lambda - \bar{f}_\mu\|_n^2 \sum_{i=1}^n E(\xi_i^2 - \alpha)_+ \leq \frac{16L^2(n+1)}{n\beta} E(\xi_1^2 - \alpha)_+$$

where $a_+ = \max(0, a)$. For any $x \geq (2/(t\kappa))^{1/\kappa}$ the function $x^2 e^{-tx^\kappa}$ is decreasing. Therefore, for any $n \geq e^{2/\kappa}$ we have $x^2 e^{-tx^\kappa} \leq \alpha^2 e^{-t\alpha^\kappa} = \alpha^2/n^2$, as soon as $x \geq \alpha$. Hence, $E(\xi_1^2 - \alpha)_+ \leq B\alpha^2/n^2$ and the desired inequality follows.

REMARK. Corollary 2 shows that if the tails of the errors have exponential decay and β is of the order $(\log n)^{1/\kappa}$ which minimizes the remainder term, then the rate of convergence in the oracle inequality (13) is of the order $(\log n)^{\frac{1}{\kappa}}(\log M)/n$. In the case $\kappa = 1$, comparing our result with the risk bound obtained in [13] for averaged algorithm in random design regression, we see that an extra $\log n$ multiplier appears. We conjecture that this deterioration is due to the technique of the proof and probably can be removed.

6   Sparsity Oracle Inequality

Let $\phi_1, \ldots, \phi_M$ be some functions from $\mathcal{X}$ to $\mathbb{R}$. Consider the case where $\Lambda \subseteq \mathbb{R}^M$ and $f_\lambda = \sum_j \lambda_j \phi_j$, $\lambda = (\lambda_1, \ldots, \lambda_M)$. For $\lambda \in \mathbb{R}^M$ denote by $J(\lambda)$ the set of indices j such that $\lambda_j \neq 0$, and set $M(\lambda) \triangleq Card(J(\lambda))$. For any $\tau > 0$, $0 < L_0 \leq \infty$, define the probability densities

$$q_0(t) = \frac{3}{2(1+|t|)^4}, \quad \forall t \in \mathbb{R},$$

$$q(\lambda) = \frac{1}{C_0} \prod_{j=1}^M \tau^{-1} q_0(\lambda_j/\tau) \mathbb{1}(\|\lambda\| \leq L_0), \quad \forall \lambda \in \mathbb{R}^M,$$

where $C_0 = C_0(\tau, M, L_0)$ is the normalizing constant and $\|\lambda\|$ stands for the Euclidean norm of $\lambda \in \mathbb{R}^M$.

Sparsity oracle inequalities (SOI) are oracle inequalities bounding the risk in terms of the sparsity index $M(\lambda)$ or similar characteristics. The next theorem provides a general tool to derive SOI from the "PAC-Bayesian" bound (5). Note that in this theorem $\hat{f}_n$ is not necessarily defined by (2). It can be any procedure satisfying (5).

Theorem 4. *Let $\hat{f}_n$ satisfy (5) with $\pi(d\lambda) = q(\lambda)\,d\lambda$ and $\tau \le \delta L_0/\sqrt{M}$ where $0 < L_0 \le \infty$, $0 < \delta < 1$. Assume that Λ contains the ball $\{\lambda \in \mathbb{R}^M : \|\lambda\| \le L_0\}$. Then for all λ^* such that $\|\lambda^*\| \le (1-\delta)L_0$ we have*

$$E\left(\|\hat{f}_n - f\|_n^2\right) \le \|f_{\lambda^*} - f\|_n^2 + \frac{4\beta}{n+1}\sum_{j\in J(\lambda^*)}\log(1 + \tau^{-1}|\lambda_j^*|) + R(M,\tau,L_0,\delta),$$

where the residual term is

$$R(M,\tau,L_0,\delta) = \tau^2 e^{2\tau^3 M^{5/2}(\delta L_0)^{-3}}\sum_{j=1}^M \|\phi_j\|_n^2 + \frac{2\beta\tau^3 M^{5/2}}{(n+1)\delta^3 L_0^3}$$

for $L_0 < \infty$ and $R(M,\tau,\infty,\delta) = \tau^2 \sum_{j=1}^M \|\phi_j\|_n^2$.

Proof. We apply Theorem 1 with $p(d\lambda) = C_{\lambda^*}^{-1}q(\lambda - \lambda^*)\mathbb{1}(\|\lambda - \lambda^*\| \le \delta L_0)\,d\lambda$, where C_{λ^*} is the normalizing constant. Using the symmetry of q and the fact that $f_\lambda - f_{\lambda^*} = f_{\lambda-\lambda^*} = -f_{\lambda^*-\lambda}$ we get

$$\int_\Lambda \langle f_{\lambda^*} - f, f_\lambda - f_{\lambda^*}\rangle_n\,p(d\lambda) = C_{\lambda^*}^{-1}\int_{\|w\|\le\delta L_0}\langle f_{\lambda^*} - f, f_w\rangle_n\,q(w)\,dw = 0.$$

Therefore $\int_\Lambda \|f_\lambda - f\|_n^2\,p(d\lambda) = \|f_{\lambda^*} - f\|_n^2 + \int_\Lambda \|f_\lambda - f_{\lambda^*}\|_n^2\,p(d\lambda)$. On the other hand, bounding the indicator $\mathbb{1}(\|\lambda - \lambda^*\| \le \delta L_0)$ by one and using the identities $\int_\mathbb{R} q_0(t)\,dt = \int_\mathbb{R} t^2 q_0(t)\,dt = 1$, we obtain

$$\int_\Lambda \|f_\lambda - f_{\lambda^*}\|_n^2\,p(d\lambda) \le \frac{1}{C_0 C_{\lambda^*}}\sum_{j=1}^M \|\phi_j\|_n^2 \int_\mathbb{R} \frac{w_j^2}{\tau}q_0\left(\frac{w_j}{\tau}\right)dw_j = \frac{\tau^2 \sum_{j=1}^M \|\phi_j\|_n^2}{C_0 C_{\lambda^*}}.$$

Since $1 - x \ge e^{-2x}$ for all $x \in [0, 1/2]$, we get

$$C_{\lambda^*}C_0 = \frac{1}{\tau^M}\int_{\|\lambda\|\le\delta L_0}\left\{\prod_{j=1}^M q_0\left(\frac{\lambda_j}{\tau}\right)\right\}d\lambda \ge \frac{1}{\tau^M}\prod_{j=1}^M\left\{\int_{|\lambda_j|\le\frac{\delta L_0}{\sqrt{M}}}q_0\left(\frac{\lambda_j}{\tau}\right)d\lambda_j\right\}$$

$$= \left(\int_0^{\delta L_0/\tau\sqrt{M}}\frac{3dt}{(1+t)^4}\right)^M = \left(1 - \frac{1}{(1+\delta L_0\tau^{-1}M^{-1/2})^3}\right)^M$$

$$\ge \exp\left(-\frac{2M}{(1+\delta L_0\tau^{-1}M^{-1/2})^3}\right) \ge \exp(-2\tau^3 M^{5/2}(\delta L_0)^{-3}).$$

On the other hand, in view of the inequality $1 + |\lambda_j/\tau| \le (1 + |\lambda_j^*/\tau|)(1 + |\lambda_j - \lambda_j^*|/\tau)$ the Kullback-Leibler divergence between p and π is bounded as follows:

$$\mathcal{K}(p,\pi) = \int_{\mathbb{R}^M}\log\left(\frac{C_{\lambda^*}^{-1}q(\lambda - \lambda^*)}{q(\lambda)}\right)p(d\lambda) \le 4\sum_{j=1}^M\log(1 + |\tau^{-1}\lambda_j^*|) - \log C_{\lambda^*}.$$

Easy computation yields $C_0 \le 1$. Therefore $C_{\lambda^*} \ge C_0 C_{\lambda^*} \ge \exp(-\frac{2\tau^3 M^{5/2}}{(\delta L_0)^3})$ and the desired result follows.

We now discuss a consequence of the obtained inequality in the case where the errors are Gaussian. Let us denote by Φ the Gram matrix associated to the family

$(\phi_j)_{j=1,\ldots,M}$, i.e., $M \times M$ matrix with entries $\Phi_{j,j'} = n^{-1}\sum_{i=1}^{n}\phi_j(x_i)\phi_{j'}(x_i)$ for every $j, j' \in \{1, \ldots, M\}$. We denote by $\lambda_{\max}(\Phi)$ the maximal eigenvalue of Φ. In what follows, for every $x > 0$, we write $\log_+ x = (\log x)_+$.

Corollary 3. *Let $\hat{f}_n$ be defined by (2) with $\pi(d\lambda) = q(\lambda)\,d\lambda$ and let $\tau = \frac{\delta L_0}{M\sqrt{n}}$ with $0 < L_0 < \infty$, $0 < \delta < 1$. Let ξ_i be i.i.d. Gaussian $\mathcal{N}(0, \sigma^2)$ with $\sigma^2 > 0$, $\lambda_{max}(\Phi) \le K^2$, $\|f\|_n \le \bar{L}$ and let $\beta \ge (4 + 2n^{-1})\sigma^2 + 2L^2$ with $L = \bar{L} + L_0 K$. Then for all $\lambda^* \in \mathbb{R}^M$ such that $\|\lambda^*\| \le (1-\delta)L_0$ we have*

$$E\big[\|\hat{f}_n - f\|_n^2\big] \le \|f_{\lambda^*} - f\|_n^2 + \frac{4\beta}{n+1}\Big[M(\lambda^*)\Big(1 + \log_+\big\{\frac{M\sqrt{n}}{\delta L_0}\big\}\Big) + \sum_{J(\lambda^*)}\log_+|\lambda_j^*|\Big]$$

$$+ \frac{C}{nM^{1/2}\min(M^{1/2}, n^{3/2})},$$

where C is a positive constant independent of n, M and λ^*.

Proof. We apply Theorem 4 with $\Lambda = \{\lambda \in \mathbb{R}^M : \|\lambda\| \le L_0\}$. We need to check that $\hat{f}_n$ satisfies (5). This is indeed the case in view of Proposition 1 and the inequalities $\|f_\lambda - f\|_n \le \|f\|_n + \sqrt{\lambda^\top\Phi\lambda} \le \bar{L} + K\|\lambda\| \le L$. Thus we have

$$E\Big(\|\hat{f}_n - f\|_n^2\Big) \le \|f_{\lambda^*} - f\|_n^2 + \frac{4\beta}{n+1}\sum_{j\in J(\lambda^*)}\log(1 + \tau^{-1}|\lambda_j^*|) + R(M, \tau, L_0, \delta),$$

with $R(M, \tau, L_0, \delta)$ as in Theorem 4. One easily checks that $\log(1 + \tau^{-1}|\lambda_j^*|) \le 1 + \log_+(\tau^{-1}|\lambda_j^*|) \le 1 + \log_+(\tau^{-1}) + \log_+(|\lambda_j^*|)$. Hence, the desired inequality follows from

$$
\begin{aligned}
R(M, \tau, L_0, \delta) &= \frac{(\delta L_0)^2}{M^2 n}e^{2M^{-3}n^{-3/2}M^{5/2}}\sum_{j=1}^{M}\|\phi_j\|_n^2 + \frac{2\beta M^{5/2}}{(n+1)M^3 n^{3/2}} \\
&\le \frac{(\delta L_0)^2 M K^2 e^2}{M^2 n} + \frac{2\beta}{(n+1)M^{1/2}n^{3/2}} \le \frac{C}{nM^{1/2}\min(M^{1/2}, n^{3/2})}.
\end{aligned}
$$

REMARK. The result of Corollary 3 can be compared with the SOI obtained for other procedures [5,6,7]. These papers impose heavy restrictions on the Gram matrix Φ either in terms of the coherence introduced in [12] or analogous local characteristics. Our result is not of that kind: we need only that the maximal eigenvalue of Φ were bounded. On the other hand, we assume that the oracle vector λ^* belongs to a ball of radius $< L_0$ in ℓ_2 with known L_0. This assumption is not very restrictive in the sense that the ℓ_2 constraint is weaker than the ℓ_1 constraint that is frequently imposed. Moreover, the structure of our oracle inequality is such that we can consider slowly growing L_0, without seriously damaging the result.

References

1. Audibert, J.-Y.: Une approche PAC-bayésienne de la théorie statistique de l'apprentissage. PhD Thesis. University of Paris 6 (2004)
2. Audibert, J.-Y.: A randomized online learning algorithm for better variance control. In: COLT 2006. Proceedings of the 19th Annual Conference on Learning Theory. LNCS (LNAI), vol. 4005, pp. 392–407. Springer, Heidelberg (2006)

3. Bunea, F., Nobel, A.B.: Sequential Procedures for Aggregating Arbitrary Estimators of a Conditional Mean. Preprint Florida State University (2005), http://www.stat.fsu.edu/~flori
4. Bunea, F., Tsybakov, A.B., Wegkamp, M.H.: Aggregation and sparsity via ℓ_1-penalized least squares. In: Lugosi, G., Simon, H.U. (eds.) COLT 2006. LNCS (LNAI), vol. 4005, pp. 379–391. Springer, Heidelberg (2006)
5. Bunea, F., Tsybakov, A.B., Wegkamp, M.H.: Aggregation for gaussian regression. Annals of Statistics, to appear (2007), http://www.stat.fsu.edu/~wegkamp
6. Bunea, F., Tsybakov, A.B., Wegkamp, M.H.: Sparsity oracle inequalities for the Lasso, Submitted (2006)
7. Candes, E., Tao, T.: The Dantzig selector: statistical estimation when p is much larger than n. Annals of Statistics, to appear (2007)
8. Catoni, O.: Universal. aggregation rules with exact bias bounds. Preprint n.510, Laboratoire de Probabilités et Modèles Aléatoires, Universités Paris 6 and Paris 7 (1999), http://www.proba.jussieu.fr/mathdoc/preprints/index.html#1999
9. Catoni, O.: Statistical Learning Theory and Stochastic Optimization. In: Ecole d'été de Probabilités de Saint-Flour 2001. Lecture Notes in Mathematics, Springer, Heidelberg (2004)
10. Cesa-Bianchi, N., Conconi, A., Gentile, G.: On the generalization ability of on-line learning algorithms. IEEE Trans. on Information Theory 50, 2050–2057 (2004)
11. Cesa-Bianchi, N., Lugosi, G.: Prediction, Learning, and Games. Cambridge University Press, New York (2006)
12. Donoho, D.L., Elad, M., Temlyakov, V.: Stable Recovery of Sparse Overcomplete Representations in the Presence of Noise. IEEE Trans. on Information Theory 52, 6–18 (2006)
13. Juditsky, A., Rigollet, P., Tsybakov, A.: Learning by mirror averaging. Preprint n, Laboratoire de Probabilités et Modèle aléatoires, Universités Paris 6 and Paris 7, (2005). n. 1034, https://hal.ccsd.cnrs.fr/ccsd-00014097
14. Juditsky, A.B., Nazin, A.V., Tsybakov, A.B., Vayatis, N.: Recursive aggregation of estimators via the Mirror Descent Algorithm with averaging. Problems of Information Transmission 41, 368–384 (2005)
15. Koltchinskii, V.: Sparsity in penalized empirical risk minimization, Submitted (2006)
16. Leung, G., Barron, A.: Information theory and mixing least-square regressions. IEEE Transactions on Information Theory 52, 3396–3410 (2006)
17. Littlestone, N., Warmuth, M.K.: The weighted majority algorithm. Information and Computation 108, 212–261 (1994)
18. Obloj, J.: The Skorokhod embedding problem and its offspring. Probability Surveys 1, 321–392 (2004)
19. Petrov, V.V.: Limit Theorems of Probability Theory. Clarendon Press, Oxford (1995)
20. Revuz, D., Yor, M.: Continuous Martingales and Brownian Motion. Springer, Heidelberg (1999)
21. Tsybakov, A.B.: Optimal rates of aggregation. In: Schölkopf, B., Warmuth, M. (eds.) Computational Learning Theory and Kernel Machines. LNCS (LNAI), vol. 2777, pp. 303–313. Springer, Heidelberg (2003)
22. Tsybakov, A.B.: Regularization, boosting and mirror averaging. Comments on "Regularization in Statistics", by Bickel, P., Li, B., Test 15, 303–310 (2006)
23. van de Geer, S.A.: High dimensional generalized linear models and the Lasso. Research report No.133. Seminar für Statistik, ETH, Zürich (2006)

24. Vovk, V.: Aggregating Strategies. In: Proceedings of the 3rd Annual Workshop on Computational Learning Theory, COLT1990, pp. 371–386. Morgan Kaufmann, San Francisco, CA (1990)
25. Vovk, V.: Competitive on-line statistics. International Statistical Review 69, 213–248 (2001)
26. Yang, Y.: Combining different procedures for adaptive regression. Journal of Multivariate Analysis 74, 135–161 (2000)
27. Yang, Y.: Adaptive regression by mixing. Journal of the American Statistical Association 96, 574–588 (2001)
28. Yang, Y.: Regression with multiple candidate models: selecting or mixing? Statist. Sinica 13, 783–809 (2003)
29. Zhang, T.: From epsilon-entropy to KL-complexity: analysis of minimum information complexity density estimation. Annals of Statistics, to appear (2007)
30. Zhang, T.: Information theoretical upper and lower bounds for statistical estimation. IEEE Transactions on Information Theory, to appear (2007)

A   Appendix

Lemma 2. *For any $x \in \mathbb{R}$ and any $\alpha > 0$, $x + \log\left(1 + \frac{1}{\alpha}\left(e^{-x\alpha} - 1\right)\right) \leq \frac{x^2\alpha}{2}$.*

Proof. On the interval $(-\infty, 0]$, the function $x \mapsto x + \log\left(1 + \frac{1}{\alpha}\left(e^{-x\alpha} - 1\right)\right)$ is increasing, therefore it is bounded by its value at 0, that is by 0. For positive values of x, we combine the inequalities $e^{-y} \leq 1 - y + y^2/2$ (with $y = x\alpha$) and $\log(1 + y) \leq y$ (with $y = 1 + \frac{1}{\alpha}(e^{-x\alpha} - 1)$).

Lemma 3. *For any $\beta \geq s^2/n + 2\sup_{\lambda \in \Lambda} \|f - f_\lambda\|_n^2$ and for every $\mu' \in \mathscr{P}_\Lambda'$, the function*

$$\mu \mapsto \exp\left(\frac{s^2\|\bar{f}_{\mu'} - \bar{f}_\mu\|_n^2}{n\beta^2} - \frac{\|f - \bar{f}_\mu\|_n^2}{\beta}\right)$$

is concave.

Proof. Consider first the case where $Card(\Lambda) = m < \infty$. Then every element of $\mathscr{P}_\Lambda$ can be viewed as a vector from $\mathbb{R}^m$. Set

$$Q(\mu) = (1 - \gamma)\|f - f_\mu\|_n^2 + 2\gamma\langle f - f_\mu, f - f_{\mu'}\rangle_n$$
$$= (1 - \gamma)\mu^T H_n^T H_n \mu + 2\gamma\mu^T H_n^T H_n \mu',$$

where $\gamma = s^2/(n\beta)$ and H_n is the $n \times m$ matrix with entries $(f(x_i) - f_\lambda(x_i))/\sqrt{n}$. The statement of the lemma is equivalent to the concavity of $e^{-Q(\mu)/\beta}$ as a function of $\mu \in \mathscr{P}_\Lambda$, which holds if and only if the matrix $\beta\nabla^2 Q(\mu) - \nabla Q(\mu)\nabla Q(\mu)^T$ is positive-semidefinite. Simple algebra shows that $\nabla^2 Q(\mu) = 2(1-\gamma)H_n^T H_n$ and $\nabla Q(\mu) = 2H_n^T[(1 - \gamma)H_n\mu + \gamma H_n\mu']$. Therefore, $\nabla Q(\mu)\nabla Q(\mu)^T = H_n^T \mathbf{M} H_n$, where $\mathbf{M} = 4H_n\tilde{\mu}\tilde{\mu}^T H_n^T$ with $\tilde{\mu} = (1 - \gamma)\mu + \gamma\mu'$. Under our assumptions, β is larger than s^2/n, ensuring thus that $\tilde{\mu} \in \mathscr{P}_\Lambda$. Clearly, $\mathbf{M}$ is a symmetric and positive-semidefinite matrix. Moreover,

$$\lambda_{max}(\mathbf{M}) \leq \mathrm{Tr}(\mathbf{M}) = 4\|H_n\tilde{\mu}\|^2 = \frac{4}{n}\sum_{i=1}^{n}\left(\sum_{\lambda\in\Lambda}\tilde{\mu}_\lambda(f - f_\lambda)(x_i)\right)^2$$

$$\leq \frac{4}{n}\sum_{i=1}^{n}\sum_{\lambda\in\Lambda}\tilde{\mu}_\lambda(f(x_i) - f_\lambda(x_i))^2 = 4\sum_{\lambda\in\Lambda}\tilde{\mu}_\lambda\|f - f_\lambda\|_n^2$$

$$\leq 4\max_{\lambda\in\Lambda}\|f - f_\lambda\|_n^2$$

where $\lambda_{max}(\mathbf{M})$ is the largest eigenvalue of $\mathbf{M}$ and $\mathrm{Tr}(\mathbf{M})$ is its trace. This estimate yields the matrix inequality

$$\nabla Q(\mu)\nabla Q(\mu)^T \leq 4\max_{\lambda\in\Lambda}\|f - f_\lambda\|_n^2\, H_n^T H_n.$$

Hence, the function $e^{-Q(\mu)/\beta}$ is concave as soon as $4\max_{\lambda\in\Lambda}\|f - f_\lambda\|_n^2 \leq 2\beta(1 - \gamma)$. The last inequality holds for every $\beta \geq n^{-1}s^2 + 2\max_{\lambda\in\Lambda}\|f - f_\lambda\|_n^2$.

The general case can be reduced to the case of finite Λ as follows. The concavity of the functional $G(\mu) = \exp\left(\frac{s^2\|\bar{f}_\mu - \bar{f}_\mu\|_n^2}{n\beta^2} - \frac{\|f - \bar{f}_\mu\|_n^2}{\beta}\right)$ is equivalent to the validity of the inequality

$$G\left(\frac{\mu + \tilde{\mu}}{2}\right) \geq \frac{G(\mu) + G(\tilde{\mu})}{2}, \qquad \forall\, \mu, \tilde{\mu} \in \mathscr{P}'_\Lambda. \tag{14}$$

Fix now arbitrary $\mu, \tilde{\mu} \in \mathscr{P}'_\Lambda$. Take $\tilde{\Lambda} = \{1, 2, 3\}$ and consider the set of functions $\{\tilde{f}_\lambda, \lambda \in \tilde{\Lambda}\} = \{\bar{f}_\mu, \bar{f}_{\tilde{\mu}}, \bar{f}_{\mu'}\}$. Since $\tilde{\Lambda}$ is finite, $\mathscr{P}'_{\tilde{\Lambda}} = \mathscr{P}_{\tilde{\Lambda}}$. According to the first part of the proof, the functional

$$\tilde{G}(\nu) = \exp\left(\frac{s^2\|\bar{f}_{\mu'} - \bar{\bar{f}}_\nu\|_n^2}{n\beta^2} - \frac{\|f - \bar{\bar{f}}_\nu\|_n^2}{\beta}\right), \quad \nu \in \mathscr{P}_{\tilde{\Lambda}},$$

is concave on $\mathscr{P}_{\tilde{\Lambda}}$ as soon as $\beta \geq s^2/n + 2\max_{\lambda\in\tilde{\Lambda}}\|f - \tilde{f}_\lambda\|_n^2$, and therefore for every $\beta \geq s^2/n + 2\sup_{\lambda\in\Lambda}\|f - f_\lambda\|_n^2$ as well. (Indeed, by Jensen's inequality for any measure $\mu \in \mathscr{P}'_\Lambda$ we have $\|f - \bar{f}_\mu\|_n^2 \leq \int \|f - f_\lambda\|_n^2 \mu(d\lambda) \leq \sup_{\lambda\in\Lambda}\|f - f_\lambda\|_n^2$.) This leads to

$$\tilde{G}\left(\frac{\nu + \tilde{\nu}}{2}\right) \geq \frac{\tilde{G}(\nu) + \tilde{G}(\tilde{\nu})}{2}, \qquad \forall\, \nu, \tilde{\nu} \in \mathscr{P}_{\tilde{\Lambda}}.$$

Taking here the Dirac measures ν and $\tilde{\nu}$ defined by $\nu(\lambda = j) = \mathbb{1}(j = 1)$ and $\tilde{\nu}(\lambda = j) = \mathbb{1}(j = 2)$, $j = 1, 2, 3$, we arrive at (14). This completes the proof of the lemma.

Occam's Hammer

Gilles Blanchard[1] and François Fleuret[2]

[1] Fraunhofer FIRST.IDA, Berlin, Germany
`blanchar@first.fraunhofer.de`
[2] EPFL, CVLAB, Lausanne, Switzerland
`francois.fleuret@epfl.ch`

Abstract. We establish a generic theoretical tool to construct probabilistic bounds for algorithms where the output is a subset of objects from an initial pool of candidates (or more generally, a probability distribution on said pool). This general device, dubbed "Occam's hammer", acts as a meta layer when a probabilistic bound is already known on the objects of the pool taken individually, and aims at controlling the *proportion* of the objects in the set output not satisfying their individual bound. In this regard, it can be seen as a non-trivial generalization of the "union bound with a prior" ("Occam's razor"), a familiar tool in learning theory. We give applications of this principle to randomized classifiers (providing an interesting alternative approach to PAC-Bayes bounds) and multiple testing (where it allows to retrieve exactly and extend the so-called Benjamini-Yekutieli testing procedure).

1 Introduction

In this paper, we establish a generic theoretical tool allowing to construct probabilistic bounds for algorithms which take as input some (random) data and return as an output a set A of objects among a pool $\mathcal{H}$ of candidates (instead of a single object $h \in \mathcal{H}$ in the classical setting). Here the "objects" could be for example classifiers, functions, hypotheses... according to the setting. One wishes to predict that each object h in the output set A satisfies a property $R(h, \alpha)$ (where α is an ajustable level parameter); the purpose of the probabilistic bound is to guarantee that the proportion of objects in A for which the prediction is false does not exceed a certain value, and this with a prescribed statistical confidence $1 - \delta$. Our setting also covers the more general case where the algorithm returns a (data-dependent) probability density over $\mathcal{H}$.

Such a wide scope can appear dubious in its generality at first and even seem to border with abstract nonsense, so let us try to explain right away what is the nature of our result, and pinpoint a particular example to fix ideas. The reason we encompass such a general framework is that our result acts as a 'meta' layer: we will pose that we already have at hand a probabilistic bound for single, fixed elements $h \in \mathcal{H}$. Assuming the reader is acquainted with classical learning theory, let us consider the familiar example where $\mathcal{H}$ is a set of classifiers and we observe an i.i.d. labeled sample of training data as an input. For each fixed

N. Bshouty and C. Gentile (Eds.): COLT 2007, LNAI 4539, pp. 112–126, 2007.
© Springer-Verlag Berlin Heidelberg 2007

classifier $h \in \mathcal{H}$, we can predict with success probability at least $1-\delta$ the property $R(h,\delta)$ that the generalization error of h is bounded by the training error up to a quantity $\varepsilon(\delta)$, for example using the Chernoff bound. In the classical setting, a learning method will return a single classifier $h \in \mathcal{H}$. If nothing is known about the algorithm, we have to resort to worst-case analysis, that is, obtain a uniform bound over $\mathcal{H}$; or in other terms, ensure that the probability that the predicted properties hold for *all* $h \in \mathcal{H}$ is at least $1 - \delta$. The simplest way to achieve this is to apply the union bound, combined with a prior Π on $\mathcal{H}$ (assumed to be countable in this situation) prescribing how to distribute the failure probability δ over $\mathcal{H}$. In the folklore, this is generally referred to as *Occam's razor* bound, because the quantity $- \log(\Pi(h))$, which can be interpreted as a coding length for objects $h \in \mathcal{H}$, appears in some explicit forms of the bound. This can be traced back to [4] where the motivations and framework were somewhat different. The formulation we use here seems to have first appeared explicitly in [9].

The goal of the present work is to put forward what can be seen as an analogue of the above "union bound with a prior" for the set output (or probability output) case, which we call *Occam's hammer* by remote analogy with the principle underlying Occam's razor bound. Occam's hammer relies on *two* priors: a complexity prior similar to the razor's (except it can be continuous) and a second prior over the output set size or inverse output density. We believe that Occam's hammer is not as immediately straightforward as the classical union bound, and hope to show that it has potential for interesting applications. For reasons of space, we will cut to the chase and first present Occam's hammer in an abstract setting in the next section (the reader should keep in mind the classifiers example to have a concrete instance at hand) then proceed to some applications in Section 3 (including a detailed treatment of the classifiers example in Section 3.1) and a discussion about tightness in Section 4. A natural application field is *multiple testing*, where we want to accept or reject (in the classical statistical sense) hypotheses from a pool $\mathcal{H}$; this will be developed in section 3.2. The present work was motivated by the PASCAL theoretical challenge [6] on this topic.

2   Main Result

2.1   Setting

Assume we have a pool of objects which is a measurable space $(\mathcal{H}, \mathfrak{H})$ and observe a random variable X (which can possibly represent an entire data sample) from a probability space $(\mathcal{X}, \mathfrak{X}, P)$. Our basic assumption is:

Assumption A: for every $h \in \mathcal{H}$, and $\delta \in [0, 1]$, we have at hand a set $\mathcal{B}(h, \delta) \in \mathfrak{X}$ such that $\mathbb{P}_{X \sim P}[X \in \mathcal{B}(h, \delta)] \leq \delta$. We call $\mathcal{B}(h, \delta)$ "bad event at level δ for h". Moreover, we assume that the function $(x, h, \delta) \in \mathcal{X} \times \mathcal{H} \times [0, 1] \mapsto \mathbf{1}\{x \in \mathcal{B}(h, \delta)\}$ is jointly measurable in its three variables (this amounts to say that the set defined by this indicator function is measurable in the product space). Finally, we assume that for any $h \in \mathcal{H}$ we have $\mathcal{B}(h, 0) = \emptyset$.

It should be understood that "bad events" represent regions where a certain desired property does not hold, such as the true error being larger than the empirical error plus $\varepsilon(\delta)$ in the classification case. Note that this 'desirable property' implicitly depends on the assigned confidence level $1 - \delta$. We should keep in mind that as δ decreases, the set of observations satisfying the corresponding property grows larger, but the property itself loses significance (as is clear once again in the generalization error bound example). Of course, the 'properties' corresponding to $\delta = 0$ or 1 will generally be trivial ones, i.e. $\mathcal{B}(h, 0) \equiv \emptyset$ and $\mathcal{B}(h, 1) \equiv \mathcal{X}$. Let us reformulate the union bound in this setting:

Proposition 2.1 (Abstract Occam's razor). *Let Π be a prior probability distribution on $\mathcal{H}$ and assume* (**A**) *holds. Then*

$$\mathbb{P}_{X \sim P} \left[\exists h \in \mathcal{H}, X \in \mathcal{B}(h, \delta \Pi(\{h\})) \right] \leq \delta. \tag{1}$$

The following formulation is equivalent: for any rule taking X as an input and returning $h_X \in \mathcal{H}$ as an output (in a measurable way as a function of X), we have

$$\mathbb{P}_{X \sim P} \left[X \in \mathcal{B}(h_X, \delta \Pi(\{h_X\})) \right] \leq \delta. \tag{2}$$

Proof. In the first inequality we want to bound the probability of the event

$$\bigcup_{h \in \mathcal{H}} \mathcal{B}(h, \delta \Pi(\{h\})) \, .$$

Since we assumed $B(h, 0) = \emptyset$ the above union can be reduced to a countable union over the set $\{h \in \mathcal{H} : \Pi(\{h\}) > 0\}$. It is in particular measurable. Then, we apply the union bound over the sets in this union. The event in the second inequality can be written as

$$\bigcup_{h \in \mathcal{H}} \left(\{X : h_X = h\} \cap \mathcal{B}(h, \delta \Pi(\{h\})) \right) \, .$$

It is measurable by the same argument as above, and a subset of the first considered event. Finally, from the second inequality we can recover the first one by considering a rule that for any X returns an element of $\{h \in \mathcal{H} | X \in \mathcal{B}(h, \delta \Pi(\{h\}))\}$ if this set is non empty, and some arbitrary fixed h_0 otherwise. It is possible to do so in a measurable way again because the set of atoms of Π is countable.   □

Note that Occam's razor is obviously only interesting for *atomic* priors, and therefore essentially only useful for a countable object space $\mathcal{H}$.

2.2   False Prediction Rate

Let us now assume that we have an algorithm or "rule" taking X as an input and returning as an output a subset $A_X \subset \mathcal{H}$; we assume the function $(X, h) \in \mathcal{X} \times \mathcal{H} \mapsto \mathbf{1}\{h \in A_X\}$ is jointly measurable in its two variables. What we are interested in is upper bounding the proportion of objects in A_X falling in a "bad event". Here the word 'proportion' refers to a volume ratio, where volumes are measured through a reference measure Λ on $(\mathcal{H}, \mathfrak{H})$. Like in Occam's razor, we want to allow the set level to depend on h and possibly on A_X. Here is a formal definition for this:

Definition 2.2 (False prediction rate, FPR). *Pose assumption* **(A)**. *Fix a function* $\Delta : \mathcal{H} \times \mathbb{R}_+ \rightarrow [0,1]$, *jointly measurable in its two parameters, called the* level function. *Let* Λ *be a volume measure on* $\mathcal{H}$; *we adopt the notation* $|S| \equiv \Lambda(S)$ *for* $S \in \mathfrak{H}$. *Define the* false prediction rate *for level function* Δ *as*

$$\rho_\Delta(X, A) = \frac{|A \cap \{h \in \mathcal{H} : X \in \mathcal{B}(h, \Delta(h, |A|))\}|}{|A|}, \ \textit{if } |A| \in (0, \infty); \qquad (3)$$

and $\rho_\Delta(X, A) = 0$, *if* $|A| = 0$ *or* $|A| = \infty$.

The name *false prediction rate* was chosen by reference to the notion of *false discovery rate* (FDR) for multiple testing (see below Section 3.2). We will drop the index Δ to lighten notation when it is unambiguous. The pointwise false prediction rate for a specific algorithm $X \mapsto A_X$ is therefore $\rho(X, A_X)$. In what follows, we will actually upper bound the *expected value* $\mathbb{E}_X[\rho(X, A_X)]$ over the drawing of X. In some cases, controlling the averaged FPR is a goal of its own right. Furthermore, if we have a bound on $\mathbb{E}_X[\rho]$, then we can apply straightforwardly Markov's inequality to obtain a confidence bound over ρ:

$$\mathbb{E}_X[\rho(X, A_X)] \leq \gamma \Rightarrow \rho(X, A_X) \leq \gamma\delta^{-1} \text{ with probability at least } 1 - \delta.$$

2.3   Warming Up: Algorithm with Constant Volume Output

To begin with, let us consider the easier case where the set ouput given by the algorithm has a fixed size, i.e. $|A_X| = a$ is a constant instead of being random.

Proposition 2.3. *Suppose assumption* **(A)** *holds and that* $(X, h) \in \mathcal{X} \times \mathcal{H} \mapsto \mathbf{1}\{h \in A_X\}$ *is jointly measurable in its two variables. Assume* $|A_X| = \Lambda(A_X) \equiv a$ *a.s. Let* π *be a probability density function on* $\mathcal{H}$ *with respect to the measure* Λ. *Then putting* $\Delta(h, |A|) = \min(\delta a \pi(h), 1)$, *it holds that*

$$\mathbb{E}_{X \sim P}[\rho(X, A_X)] \leq \delta.$$

Proof: Obviously, Δ is jointly measurable in its two variables, and by the composition rule so is the function $X \mapsto \rho(X, A_X)$. We then have

$$\mathbb{E}_{X \sim P}[\rho(X, A_X)] = \mathbb{E}_{X \sim P}\left[a^{-1}|A_X \cap \{h \in \mathcal{H}, X \in \mathcal{B}(h, \Delta(h, |A_X|))\}|\right]$$

$$\leq \mathbb{E}_{X \sim P}[|\{h \in \mathcal{H} : X \in \mathcal{B}(h, \min(\delta a \pi(h), 1))\}|]\, a^{-1}$$

$$= \mathbb{E}_{X \sim P}\left[\int_h \mathbf{1}\{X \in \mathcal{B}(h, \min(\delta a \pi(h), 1))\}d\Lambda(h)\right] a^{-1}$$

$$= \int_h \mathbb{P}_{X \sim P}[X \in \mathcal{B}(h, \min(\delta a \pi(h), 1))]\, d\Lambda(h)a^{-1}$$

$$\leq \delta \int_h \pi(h)d\Lambda(h) = \delta. \qquad \square$$

As a sanity check, consider a countable set $\mathcal{H}$ with Λ the counting measure, and an algorithm returning only singletons, $A_X = \{h_X\}$, so that $|A_X| \equiv 1$. Then in this case $\rho \in \{0, 1\}$, and with the above choice of Δ, we get $\rho(X, \{h\}) = \mathbf{1}\{X \in \mathcal{B}(h, \delta\pi(h))\}$. Therefore, $\mathbb{E}_X[\rho(X, A_X)] = \mathbb{P}_X[X \in \mathcal{B}(h_X, \delta\pi(h_X))] \leq \delta$, i.e., we have recovered version (2) of Occam's razor.

2.4   General Case

The previous section might let us hope that $\Delta(h, |A|) = \delta|A|\pi(h)$ would be a suitable level function in the more general situation where the size $|A_X|$ is also variable; but things get more involved. The observant reader might have noticed that, in Proposition 2.3, the weaker assumption $|A_X| \geq a$ a.s. is actually sufficient to ensure the conclusion. This thefore suggests the following strategy to deal with variable size of A_X: (1) consider a discretization of sizes through a decreasing sequence (a_k) converging to zero; and a prior Γ on the elements of the sequence; (2) apply Proposition 2.3 for all k with $(a_k, \Gamma(a_k)\delta)$ in place of (a, δ); (3) define $\Delta(h, |A|) = \delta\pi(h)a_k\Gamma(a_k)$ whenever $|A| \in [a_k, a_{k-1})$; then by summation over k (or, to put it differently, the union bound) it holds that $\mathbb{E}[\rho] \leq \delta$ for this choice of Δ.

This is a valid approach, but we will not enter into more details concerning it; rather, we propose what we consider to be an improved and more elegant result below, which will additionally allow to handle the more general case where the algorithm returns a probability density over $\mathcal{H}$ instead of just a subset. However, we will require a slight strengthening of assumption (**A**):

Assumption A': like assumption (**A**), but we additionaly require that for any $h \in \mathcal{H}$, $\mathcal{B}(h, \delta)$ is a nondecreasing sequence of sets as a function of δ, i.e., $\mathcal{B}(h, \delta) \subset \mathcal{B}(h, \delta')$ for $\delta \leq \delta'$.

The assumption of nondecreasing bad events as a function of their probability seems quite natural and is satisfied in the applications we have in mind; in classification for example, bounds on the true error are nonincreasing in the parameter δ (so the set of samples where the bound is violated is nondecreasing). We now state our main result (proof found in the appendix):

Theorem 2.4 (Occam's hammer). *Pose assumption* (**A'**) *satisfied. Let:*

(i) Λ be a nonnegative reference measure on $\mathcal{H}$ (the volumic measure);

(ii) Π be a probability distribution on $\mathcal{H}$ absolutely continuous wrt Λ (the complexity prior), and denote $\pi = \frac{d\Pi}{d\Lambda}$;

(iii) Γ be a probability distribution on $(0, +\infty)$ (the inverse density prior). Put $\beta(x) = \int_0^x u \, d\Gamma(u)$ for $x \in (0, +\infty)$. Define the level function

$$\Delta(h, u) = \min(\delta\pi(h)\beta(u), 1).$$

Then for any algorithm $X \mapsto \theta_X$ returning a probability density θ_X over $\mathcal{H}$ with respect to Λ, and such that $(X, h) \mapsto \theta_X(h)$ is jointly measurable in its two variables, it holds that

$$\mathbb{P}_{X \sim P, h \sim \Theta_X}\left[X \in \mathcal{B}(h, \Delta(h, \theta_X(h)^{-1}))\right] \leq \delta,$$

where Θ_X is the distribution on $\mathcal{H}$ such that $\frac{d\Theta_X}{d\Lambda} = \theta_X$.

Comments: The conclusion of the above theorem is a probabilistic statement over the *joint* draw of the input variable X and the object h, where the conditional distribution of h given X is Θ_X.

Note that a rule returning a probability density distribution over $\mathcal{H}$ is more general than a rule returning a set, as the latter case can be cast into the former by considering a constant density over the set, $\theta_A(h) = |A|^{-1}\mathbf{1}\{h \in A\}$; in this case the inner probability over $h \sim \Theta_{A_X}$ is exactly the false prediction rate $\rho_\Delta(X, A_X)$ introduced previously. This specialization gives a maybe more intuitive interpretation of the inverse density prior Γ, which then actually becomes a prior on the volume of the set output. We can thus recover the case of constant set volume a of Proposition 2.3 by using the above specialization and taking a Dirac distribution for the inverse density prior, $\Gamma = \delta_a$. In particular, version (2) of Occam's razor is a specialization of Occam's hammer (up to the minor strengthening in assumption (**A'**)).

To compare with the "naive" strategy described earlier based on a size discretization sequence (a_k), we get the following advantages: Occam's hammer also works with the more general case of a probability output; it avoids any discretization of the prior; finally, if even we take the discrete prior $\Gamma = \sum_k \gamma_k \delta_{a_k}$ in Occam's hammer, the level function for $|A| \in [a_k, a_{k-1})$ will be proportional to the partial sum $\sum_{j \leq k} \gamma_j a_j$, instead of only the term $\gamma_k a_k$ in the naive approach (remember that the higher the level function, the better, since the corresponding 'desirable property' is more significant for higher levels).

3 Applications

3.1 Randomized Classifiers: An Alternate Look at PAC-Bayes Bounds

Our first application is concerned with our running example, classifiers. More precisely, assume the input variable is actually an i.i.d. sample $S = (X_i, Y_i)_{i=1}^n$, and $\mathcal{H}$ is a set of classifiers. Let $\mathcal{E}(h)$, resp. $\widehat{\mathcal{E}}(h, S)$, denote the generalization, resp. training, error. We assume that generalization and training error are measurable in their respective variables, which is a tame assumption for all practical purposes. We consider a randomized classification algorithm, consisting in selecting a probability density function θ_S on $\mathcal{H}$ based on the sample (again, jointly measurable in (x, h)), then drawing a classifier at random from $\mathcal{H}$ using the distribution Θ_S such that $\frac{d\Theta_S}{d\Lambda} = \theta_S$, where Λ is here assumed to be a reference *probability* measure. For example, we could return the uniform density on the set of classifiers $A_S \subset \mathcal{H}$ having their empirical error less than a (possibly data-dependent) threshold. Combining Occam's Hammer with the Chernoff bound, we obtain the following result:

Proposition 3.1. *Let Λ be a probability measure over $\mathcal{H}$; consider an algorithm $S \mapsto \theta_S$ returning a probability density θ_S over $\mathcal{H}$ (wrt. Λ). Let $\delta \in (0,1)$ and $k > 0$ be fixed. If h_S is a randomized classifier drawn according to Θ_S, the following inequality holds with probability $1 - \delta$ over the joint draw of S and h_S:*

$$D_+\left(\widehat{\mathcal{E}}(h_S, S) \| \mathcal{E}(h_S)\right) \leq \frac{1}{n}\left(\log\left((k+1)\delta^{-1}\right) + \left(1 + \frac{1}{k}\right)\log_+ \theta_S(h_S)\right), \quad (4)$$

where $\log_+$ *is the positive part of the logarithm; and* $D_+(q\|p) = q\log\frac{q}{p} + (1 - q)\log\frac{1-q}{1-p}$ *if* $q < p$ *and 0 otherwise.*

Proof. Define the bad events $\mathcal{B}(h,\delta) = \left\{S : D_+(\widehat{\mathcal{E}}(h,S)\|\mathcal{E}(h)) \leq \frac{\log\delta^{-1}}{n}\right\}$, satisfying assumption (**A'**) by Chernoff's bound (see, e.g., [7]), including the measurability assumptions of (**A**) by the composition rule. Choose $\Pi = \Lambda$, i.e., $\pi \equiv 1$, and Γ the probability distribution on $[0,1]$ having density $\frac{1}{k}x^{-1+\frac{1}{k}}$, so that $\beta(x) = \frac{1}{k+1}\min(x^{1+\frac{1}{k}}, 1)$, and apply Occam's hammer. Replacing δ by the level function given by Occam's hammer gives rise to the following factor:

$$
\begin{aligned}
\log(\min(\delta\pi(h_S)\beta(\theta_S(h_S)^{-1}), 1)^{-1}) &= \log_+(\delta^{-1}\min((k+1)^{-1}\theta_S(h_S)^{-\frac{k+1}{k}}, 1)^{-1}) \\
&= \log_+(\delta^{-1}\max((k+1)\theta_S(h_S)^{\frac{k+1}{k}}, 1)) \\
&\leq \log_+((k+1)\delta^{-1}\max(\theta_S(h_S)^{\frac{k+1}{k}}, 1)) \\
&\leq \log((k+1)\delta^{-1}) + \log_+(\theta_S(h_S)^{\frac{k+1}{k}}) \\
&= \log((k+1)\delta^{-1}) + \left(1 + \frac{1}{k}\right)\log_+(\theta_S(h_S)).
\end{aligned}
$$

$\square$

Comparison with PAC-Bayes bounds. The by now quite well-established PAC-Bayes bounds ([9], see also [7] and references therein, and [5,1,10] for recent developments) deal with a similar setting of randomized classifiers. One important difference is that PAC-Bayes bounds are generally concerned with bounding the *averaged error* $\mathbb{E}_{h\sim\Theta_S}[\mathcal{E}(h)]$ of the randomized procedure. Occam's hammer, on the other hand, bounds $\mathcal{E}(h)$ directly the true error of a single randomized output: this is particularly relevant in practice since the information given to the user by Occam's hammer bound concerns precisely the classifier returned by the rule. In other words, Proposition 3.1 appears as a *pointwise* version of the PAC-Bayes bound. It is important to understand that a pointwise version is a stronger statement, as we can recover a traditional PAC-Bayes bound as a consequence of Proposition 3.1 (the proof is found in the appendix):

Corollary 3.2. *Provided the conclusion of Proposition 3.1 holds, for any* $k > 0$ *the following holds with probability* δ *over the the draw of* S:

$$
\begin{aligned}
D_+\left(\mathbb{E}_{h_S\sim\Theta_S}\left[\widehat{\mathcal{E}}(h_S,S)\right]\middle\|\mathbb{E}_{h_S\sim\Theta_S}[\mathcal{E}(h_S)]\right) \\
\leq \frac{1}{n}\left(\log\left((k+1)\delta^{-1}\right) + \frac{k+1}{k}KL(\Theta_S\|\Lambda) + 3.5 + \frac{1}{2k}\right),
\end{aligned}
$$

where KL *denotes the Kullback-Leibler divergence.*

It is interesting to compare this to an existing version of the PAC-Bayes bound: if we pick $k = n - 1$ in the above corollary, then we recover almost exactly a tight version of the PAC-Bayes bound given in [7], Theorem 5.1 (the differences are: a $(n-1)^{-1}$ instead of n^{-1} factor in front of the KL divergence term, and the additional trailing terms bounded by $\frac{4}{n}$). Hence, Proposition 3.1 proves a stronger property than the latter cited PAC-Bayes bound (admittedly up to the very minor loosening just mentioned).

Note that pointwise results for randomized procedures using the PAC-Bayes approach have already appeared in recent work [1,5], using a Bernstein type bound rather than Chernoff. It is not clear to us however whether the methodology developed there is precise enough to obtain a Chernoff type bound and recover a pointwise version of [7], Theorem 5.1, which is what we do here.

At any rate, we believe the Occam's hammer approach should turn out more precise for pointwise results. To give some support to this claim, we note that all existing PAC-Bayes bounds up to now structurally rely on Chernoff's method (i.e. using the Laplace transform) via two main ingredients: (1) the entropy extremal inequality $\mathbb{E}_P[X] \geq \log \mathbb{E}_Q[e^X] + D(P\|Q)$ and (2) inequalities on the Laplace transform of i.i.d. sums. Occam's hammer is, in a sense, less sophisticated since it only relies on simple set measure manipulations and contains no intrinsic exponential moment inequality argument. On the other hand, it acts as a 'meta' layer into which any other bound family can be plugged in. These could be bounds based on the Laplace transform (Chernoff method) as above, or not: in the above example, we have used Chernoff's bound for the sake of comparison with earlier work, but we could as well have plugged in the tighter binomial tail inversion bound (which is the most accurate deterministic bound possible for estimating a Bernoulli parameter), and this is clearly a potential improvement for finite size training sets. To this regard, we plan to make an extensive comparison on simulations in future work. In classical PAC-Bayes, there is no such clear separation between the bound and the randomization; they are intertwined in the analysis.

3.2   Multiple Testing: A Family of "Step-Up" Algorithms with Distribution-Free FDR Control

We now change gears and switch to the context of multiple testing. $\mathcal{H}$ is now a set of *null hypotheses* concerning the distribution P. In this section we will assume for simplicity that $\mathcal{H}$ is finite and the volume measure Λ is the counting measure, although this could be obviously extended. The goal is, based on oberved data, to discover a subset of hypotheses which are predicted to be *false* (or "*rejected*"). To have an example in mind, think of microarray data, where we observe a small number of i.i.d. repetitions of a variable in very high dimension d (the total number of genes), corresponding to the expression level of said genes, and we want to find a set of genes having average expression level bigger than some fixed threshold t. In this case, there is one null hypothesis h per gene, namely that the average expression level for this gene is *lower* than t.

We assume that we already have at hand a family of tests $T(X, h, \alpha)$ of level α for each individual h. That is, $T(X, h, \alpha)$ is a measurable function taking values in $\{0, 1\}$ (the value 1 corresponds to "null hypothesis rejected") such that for all $h \in \mathcal{H}$, for all distributions P such that h is true, $\mathbb{P}_{X \sim P}[T(X, h, \alpha) = 1] \leq \alpha$. To apply Occam's hammer, we suppose that the family $T(X, h, \alpha)$ is increasing, i.e.

$\alpha \geq \alpha' \Rightarrow T(X, h, \alpha) \geq T(X, h, \alpha')$. This is generally statisfied, as typically tests have the form $T(X, h, \alpha) = \mathbf{1}\{F(h, X) > \phi(\alpha)\}$, where F is some test statistic and $\phi(\alpha)$ is a nonincreasing threshold function (as, for example, in a one-sided T-test).

For a fixed, but unknown, data distribution P, let us define

$$\mathcal{H}_0 = \{h \in \mathcal{H} : P \text{ satisfies hypothesis } h\}$$

the set of true null hypotheses, and $\mathcal{H}_1 = \mathcal{H} \setminus \mathcal{H}_0$ its complementary. An important and relatively recent concept in multiple testing is that of *false discovery rate* (FDR) introduced in [2]. Let $A : X \mapsto A_X \subset \mathcal{H}$ be a rule returning a set of rejected hypotheses based on the data. The FDR of such a procedure is defined as

$$FDR(A) = \mathbb{E}_{X \sim P} \left[\frac{|A_X \cap \mathcal{H}_0|}{|A_X|} \right]. \tag{5}$$

Note that, in contrast to our notion of FPR introduced in Section 2.2, the FDR is already an averaged quantity. A desirable goal is to design testing procedures where it can be ensured that the FDR is controlled by some fixed level α. The rationale behind this is that, in practice, one can afford that a small proportion of rejected hypotheses are actually true. Before this notion was introduced, in most cases one would instead bound the probability that *at least one* hypothesis was falsely rejected: this is typically achieved using the (uniform) union bound, known as "Bonferroni's correction" in the multitesting literature. The hope is that, by allowing a little more slack in the acceptable error by controlling only the FDR, one obtains less conservative testing procedures as a counterpart. We refer the reader to [2] for a more extended discussion on these issues.

Let us now describe how Occam's hammer can be put to use here. Let Π be a probability distribution over $\mathcal{H}$, Γ be a probability distribution over the integer inteval $[1 \ldots |\mathcal{H}|]$, and $\beta(k) = \sum_{i \leq k} i\Gamma(i)$. Define the procedure returning the following set of hypotheses :

$$A : X \mapsto A_X = \bigcup \{G \subset \mathcal{H} : \forall h \in G,\ T(X, h, \alpha\Pi(h)\beta(|G|)) = 1\}. \tag{6}$$

This type of procedure is called "step-up" and can be implemented through a simple water-emptying type algorithm. Namely, it is easy to see that if we define

$$B_\gamma = \{h : T(X, h, \alpha\Pi(h)\gamma) = 1\},\ \text{ and } \gamma(X) = \sup\{\gamma \geq 0 : \beta(|B_\gamma|) \geq \gamma\},$$

then $A_X = B_{\gamma(X)}$. The easiest way to construct this is to sort the hypotheses $h \in \mathcal{H}$ by increasing order of their "weighted p-values"

$$p(h, X) = \Pi(h) \inf \{\gamma \geq 0 : T(X, h, \gamma) = 1\},$$

and to return the $k(X)$ first hypotheses for this order, where $k(X)$ is the largest integer such that $p^{(k)}(X) \leq \alpha\beta(k)$ (where $p^{(k)}(X)$ is the k-th ordered p-value as defined above).

We have the following property for this procedure:

Proposition 3.3. *The set of hypotheses returned by the procedure defined by* (6) *has its false discovery rate bounded by* $\Pi(\mathcal{H}_0)\alpha \leq \alpha$.

Proof. It can be checked easily that $(x, h) \mapsto |A_X|^{-1} \mathbf{1}\{h \in A_X\}$ is measurable in its two variables (this is greatly simplified by the fact that $\mathcal{H}$ is assumed to be finite here). Define the collection of "bad events" $B(h, \delta) = \{X : T(X, h, \delta) = 1\}$ if $h \in \mathcal{H}_0$, and $B(h, \delta) = \emptyset$ otherwise. It is an increasing family by the assumption on the test family. Obviously, for any $G \subset \mathcal{H}$, and any level function Δ:

$$G \cap \{h \in \mathcal{H} : X \in \mathcal{B}(h, \Delta(h, |G|))\} = G \cap \mathcal{H}_0 \cap \{h \in \mathcal{H} : T(X, h, \Delta(h, |G|)) = 1\} \; ;$$

therefore, for any G satifying

$$G \subset \{h \in \mathcal{H} : T(X, h, \Delta(h, |G|)) = 1\} \; , \tag{7}$$

it holds that $|G \cap \{h \in \mathcal{H} : X \in \mathcal{B}(h, \Delta(h, |G|))\}| = |G \cap \mathcal{H}_0|$, so that the averaged (over the draw of X) FPR (3) for level function Δ coincides with the FDR (5). When Δ is nondecreasing in its second parameter, it is straightforward that the union of two sets satisfying (7) also satisfies (7), hence A_X satisfies the above condition for the level function given by Occam's Hammer. Define the modified prior $\widetilde{\Pi}(h) = \mathbf{1}\{h \in \mathcal{H}_0\} \Pi(\mathcal{H}_0)^{-1} \Pi(h)$. Apply Occam's hammer with the reference measure Λ being the counting measure; priors $\widetilde{\Pi}$, Γ as defined above and $\delta = \Pi(\mathcal{H}_0)\alpha$ to conclude. □

Interestingly, the above result specialized to the case where Π is uniform on $\mathcal{H}$ and $\Gamma(i) = \kappa^{-1}i^{-1}$, $\kappa = \sum_{i \leq |\mathcal{H}|} i^{-1}$ results in $\beta(i) = \kappa^{-1}i$, and yields exactly what is known as the *Benjamini-Yekutieli (BY) step-up procedure* [3]. Unfortunately, the interest of the BY procedure is mainly theoretical, because the more popular *Benjamini-Hochberg* (BH) step-up procedure [2] is generally preferred in practice. The BH procedure is in all points similar to BY, except the above constant κ is replaced by 1. The BH procedure was shown to result in controlled FDR at level α *if the test statistics are independent or satisfy a certain form of positive dependency* [3]. In contrast, the BY procedure is distribution-free. Practitioners usually favor the less conservative BH, although the underlying statistical assumption is disputable. For example, in the interesting case of microarray data analysis, it is reported that the amplification of genes during the process can be very unequal as genes "compete" for the amount of polymerase available. A few RNA strands can "take over" early in the RT-PCR process, and, due to the exponential reaction, can let other strands non-amplified because of a lack of polymerase later in the process. Such an effect creates strong statistical dependencies between individual gene amplifications, in particular *negative* dependencies in the oberved expression levels.

This dicussion aside, we think there are several interesting added benefits in retrieving the BY procedure via Occam's hammer. First, in our opinion Occam's hammer sheds a totally new light on this kind of multi-testing procedure as the proof method followed in [3] was different and very specific to the framework and properties of statistical testing. Secondly, Occam's hammer allows us to generalize straightforwardly this procedure to an entire family by playing with the prior Π and more importantly the size prior Γ. In particular, it is clear that if something is known *a priori* over the expected size of the output, then this should be taken into account in the size prior Γ, possibly leading to a more powerful testing procedure. Further, there is a significant hope that we can improve the accuracy of the procedure by considering priors depending on unknown quantities, but which can be suitably approximated in view of the data, thereby following the general principle of "self-bounding" algorithms that has proved to be quite powerful ([8], see also [5,1] where this idea is used as well under a different form, called "localization"). This is certainly an exciting direction for future developments.

4   Tightness of Occam's Hammer Bound

It is of interest to know whether Occams' hammer is accurate in the sense that equality in the bound can be achieved in some (worst case) situations. A simple argument is that Occam's hammer is a generalization of Occam's razor: and since the razor is sharp [7], so is the hammer... This is somewhat unsatisfying since this ignores the situation Occam's hammer was designed for. In this section, we address this point by imposing an (almost) arbitrary inverse density prior ν and exhibiting an example where the bound is tight. Furthermore, in order to represent a "realistic" situation, we want the "bad sets" $B(h, \alpha)$ to be of the form $\{X_h > t(h, \alpha)\}$ where X_h is a certain real random variable associated to h. This is consistent with situations of interest described above (confidence intervals and hypothesis testing). We have the following result:

Proposition 4.1. *Let* $\mathcal{H} = [0,1]$ *with interval extremities identified (i.e. the unit circumference circle). Let* ν *be a probability distribution on* $[0,1]$, *and* $\alpha_0 \in [0,1]$ *be given. Put* $\beta(x) = \int_0^x u d\nu(u)$. *Assume that* β *is a continuous, increasing function. Then there exists a family of real random variables* $(X_h)_{h \in \mathcal{H}}$, *having identical marginal distributions* P *and a random subset* $A \subset [0,1]$ *such that, if* $t(\alpha)$ *is the upper* α-*quantile of* P *(i.e.,* $P(X > t(\alpha)) = \alpha$), *then*

$$\mathbb{E}_{(X_h)} \left[\frac{|\{h \in A \text{ and } X_h > t(\alpha_0 \beta(|A|))\}|}{|A|} \right] = \alpha_0 \,.$$

Furthermore, P *can be made equal to any arbitrary distribution without atoms.*

Comments. In the proposed construction (see proof in the appendix), the FPR is a.s. equal to α_0, and the marginal distribution of $|A|$ is precisely ν. This example shows that Occam's hammer can be sharp for the type of situation it was crafted for (set output procedures), and it reinforces the interpretation of ν as a "prior", since the bound is sharp precisely when the output distribution corresponds to the chosen prior. However, this example is still not entirely satisfying because in the above construction, we are basically oberving a single sample of (X_h), while in most interesting applications we have statistics based on averages of i.i.d. samples. If we could construct an example in which (X_h) is a Gaussian process, it would be fine, since observing an i.i.d. sample and taking the average would amount to a variance rescaling of the original process. In the above, although we can choose each X_h to have a marginal Gaussian distribution, the whole family is unfortunately not jointly Gaussian (inspecting the proof, it appears that for $h \neq h'$ there is a nonzero probability that $X_h = X_{h'}$, as well as $X_h \neq X_{h'}$, so that $(X_h, X_{h'})$ cannot be jointly Gaussian). Finding a good sharpness example using a Gaussian process (the most natural candidate would be a stationary process on the circle with some specific spectral structure) is an interesting open problem.

5 Conclusion

We hope to have shown convincingly that Occam's hammer is a powerful and versatile theoretical device. It allows an alternate, and perhaps unexpected, approach to PAC-Bayes type bounds, as well as to multiple testing procedures. For the application to PAC-Bayes type bounds, an interesting feature of Occam's hammer approach is to provide a bound that is valid for the particular classifier returned by the randomization procedure and not just on average performance over the random output, and the former property is stronger. Furthermore, the tightest bounds available for a single classifier (i.e. by binomial tail inversion) can be plugged in without further ado. For multiple testing, the fact that we retrieve exactly the BY distribution-free multitesting procedure and extend it to a whole family shows that Occam's hammer has a strong potential for producing *practically useful* bounds and procedures. In particular, a very interesting direction for future research is to include in the priors knowledge about the typical behavior of the output set size. At any rate, a significant feat of Occam's hammer is to provide a strong first bridging between the worlds of learning theory and multiple hypothesis testing.

Finally, we want to underline once again that, like Occam's razor, Occam's hammer is a *meta* device that can apply on top of other bounds. This feature is particularly nice and leads us to expect that this tool will prove to have meaningful uses for other applications.

References

1. Audibert, J.-Y.: Data-dependent generalization error bounds for (noisy) classification: a PAC-Bayesian approach. Technical Report PMA-905, Laboratoire de Probabilités et Modèles Aléatoires, Universités Paris 6 and Paris 7 (2004)
2. Benjamini, Y., Hochberg, Y.: Controlling the false discovery rate – a practical and powerful approach to multiple testing. J. Roy. Stat. Soc. B 57(1), 289–300 (1995)
3. Benjamini, Y., Yekutieli, D.: The control of the false discovery rate in multiple testing under dependency. Annals of Statistics 29(4), 1165–1188 (2001)
4. Blumer, A., Ehrenfeucht, A., Haussler, D., Warmuth, M.: Occam's razor. Information processing letters 24, 377–380 (1987)
5. Catoni, O.: A PAC-Bayesian approach to adaptive classification. Technical report, LPMA, Université Paris 6 (submitted to Annals of Statistics) (2004)
6. Gavin, G., Gelly, S., Guermeur, Y., Lallich, S., Mary, J., Sebag, M., Teytaud, O.: PASCAL theoretical challenge. Type I and type II errors for multiple simultaneous hypothesis testing, `http://www.lri.fr/~teytaud/risq`

7. Langford, J.: Tutorial on practical prediction theory for classification. Journal of Machine Learning Research 6, 273–306 (2005)
8. Langford, J., Blum, A.: Microchoice bounds and self bounding learning algorithms. Machine Learning, (First communicated at COLT'99) 51(2), 165–179 (2003)
9. McAllester, D.: Bayesian stochastic model selection. Machine Learning, (First communicated at COLT'98 and '99) 51(1), 5–21 (2003)
10. Zhang, T.: Information theoretical upper and lower bounds for statistical estimation. IEEE Transaction on Information Theory 52(4), 1307–1321 (2006)

A   Appendix – Additional Proofs

Proof of Theorem 2.4. The proof of Occam's hammer is in essence an integration by parts argument, where the "parts" are level sets over $\mathcal{X} \times \mathcal{H}$ of the output density $\theta_X(h)$. We prove a slightly more general result than announced: let us consider a level function of the form

$$\Delta(h, u) = \min(\delta G(h, u), 1),$$

where $G : \mathcal{H} \times \mathbb{R}_+ \to \mathbb{R}_+$ is a measurable function which is nondecreasing in its second parameter, and satisfying

$$\int_{h \in \mathcal{H}} \int_{t \geq 0} G(h, t) t^{-2} d\Lambda(h) dt \leq 1.$$

Then the announced conclusion holds for this level function. First, note that the function $(X, h) \mapsto \mathbf{1}\{X \in \mathcal{B}(h, \Delta(h, \theta_X(h)^{-1}))\}$ is jointly measurable in its two variables by the composition rule using the measurability assumption in **(A)**; on $\theta_X(h)$ in the statement of the theorem; and on G above. We then have

$$\mathbb{P}_{X \sim P, h \sim \Theta_X} \left[X \in \mathcal{B}(h, \Delta(h, \theta_X(h)^{-1})) \right]$$

$$= \int_{(X,h)} \mathbf{1}\{X \in \mathcal{B}(h, \Delta(h, \theta_X(h)^{-1}))\} \theta_X(h) d\Lambda(h) dP(X)$$

$$= \int_{(X,h)} \mathbf{1}\{X \in \mathcal{B}(h, \Delta(h, \theta_X(h)^{-1}))\} \int_{y>0} y^{-2} \mathbf{1}\{y \geq \theta_X(h)^{-1}\} dy dP(X) d\Lambda(h)$$

$$= \int_{y>0} y^{-2} \int_{(X,h)} \mathbf{1}\{X \in \mathcal{B}(h, \Delta(h, \theta_X(h)^{-1}))\} \mathbf{1}\{\theta_X(h)^{-1} \leq y\} dP(X) d\Lambda(h) dy$$

$$\leq \int_{y>0} y^{-2} \int_{(X,h)} \mathbf{1}\{X \in \mathcal{B}(h, \Delta(h, y))\} dP(x) d\Lambda(h) dy$$

$$= \int_{y>0} y^{-2} \int_{h} \mathbb{P}_{X \sim P} \left[X \in \mathcal{B}(h, \min(\delta G(h, y), 1)) \right] d\Lambda(h) dy$$

$$\leq \int_{y=0}^{\infty} \int_{h} y^{-2} \delta G(h, y) d\Lambda(h) dy \leq \delta.$$

For the first inequality, we have used assumption **(A')** that $B(h, \delta)$ is an increasing family and the fact $\Delta(h, u)$ is a nondecreasing function in u (by assumption on G). In the second inequality we have used the assumption on the probability of bad events. The other equalities are obtained using Fubini's theorem.

Now, it is easy to check that $G(h,t) = \pi(h)\beta(t)$ satisfies the above requirements, since it is obviously measurable, β is a nondecreasing function, and

$$\int_{h \in \mathcal{H}} \int_{t \geq 0} \pi(h)\beta(t)t^{-2}d\Lambda(h)dt = \int_h \pi(h)d\Lambda(h) \int_{t \geq 0} \int_{u \geq 0} ut^{-2}\mathbf{1}\{u \leq t\}d\Gamma(u)dt$$

$$= \int_{u \geq 0} d\Gamma(u) = 1 \,.$$

Note that in a more general case, if we have a joint prior probability distribution Γ on the product space $\mathcal{H} \times \mathbb{R}_+$, and if $\mathcal{H}$ is a Polish space, then there exists a regular conditional probability distribution $\Gamma(t|h)$, and the function $G(h,t) = \int_{u=0}^{t} ud\Gamma(u|h)$ is measurable and has the required properties by an obvious extension of the above argument. We opted to state our main result only in the case of a product prior for the sake of simplicity, but this generalization might be relevant for future applications. □

Proof of Corollary 3.2. Let us denote by $A_\delta \subset \mathcal{H} \times \mathcal{S}$ (here $\mathcal{S}$ denotes the set of samples S) the event where inequality (4) is violated; Proposition 3.1 states that $\mathbb{E}_{S \sim P}[\mathbb{P}_{h \sim \Theta_S}[(h,S) \in A_\delta]] \leq \delta$, hence by Markov's inequality, for any $\gamma \in (0,1)$ it holds with probability $1 - \delta$ over the drawing of $S \sim P$ that

$$\mathbb{P}_{h \sim \Theta_S}[(h,S) \in A_{\delta\gamma}] \leq \gamma \,.$$

Let us consider the above statement for $(\delta_i, \gamma_i) = (\delta 2^{-i}, 2^{-i})$, and perform the union bound over the δ_i for integers $i \geq 1$. Since $\sum_{i \geq 1} \delta_i = \delta$, we obtain that with probability $1 - \delta$ over the drawing of $S \sim P$, it holds that for all integers $i \geq 0$ (the case $i = 0$ is trivial):

$$\mathbb{P}_{h \sim \Theta_S}[(h,S) \in A_{\delta 2^{-2i}}] \leq 2^{-i} \,.$$

From now on, consider a fixed sample S such that the above is satisfied. Let us denote

$$F(h,S) = nD_+(\widehat{\mathcal{E}}(h,S)\|\mathcal{E}(h_S)) - \log\left((k+1)\delta^{-1}\right) - \left(1 + \frac{1}{k}\right)\log_+ \theta_S(h) \,.$$

By the assumption on S, for all integers $i \geq 0$: $\mathbb{P}_{h \sim \Theta_S}[F(h,S) \geq 2i\log 2] \leq 2^{-i}$; so that

$$\mathbb{E}_{h \sim \Theta_S}[F(h,S)] \leq \int_{t > 0} \mathbb{P}_{h \sim \Theta_S}[F(h,S) \geq t]\, dt$$

$$\leq 2\log 2 \sum_{i \geq 0} \mathbb{P}_{h \sim \Theta_S}[F(h,S) \geq 2i\log 2] \leq 3 \,.$$

Now let us detail specific terms entering in the expectation $\mathbb{E}_{h \sim \Theta_S}[F(h,S)]$: we have

$$\mathbb{E}_{h_S \sim \Theta_S}\left[D_+(\widehat{\mathcal{E}}(h,S)\|\mathcal{E}(h_S))\right] \geq D_+\left(\mathbb{E}_{h_S \sim \Theta_S}\left[\widehat{\mathcal{E}}(h_S,S)\right]\Big\|\mathbb{E}_{h_S \sim \Theta_S}[\mathcal{E}(h_S)]\right) \,,$$

because the function D_+ is convex in is two joint parameters. Finally,

$$\mathbb{E}_{hs\sim\Theta_S}\left[\log_+\theta_S(h)\right] = \mathbb{E}_{hs\sim\Lambda}\left[\theta_S(h)\log_+\theta_S(h)\right]$$
$$\leq \mathbb{E}_{hs\sim\Lambda}\left[\theta_S(h)\log\theta_S(h)\right] - \min_{0\leq x<1} x\log x$$
$$= KL(\Theta_S\|\Lambda) + e^{-1}.$$

Bounding e^{-1} by $1/2$ and gathering the terms leads to the conclusion.   □

Proof of Proposition 4.1. Let ν and α_0 be fixed. We will construct explicitly the family $(X_h)_{h\in\mathcal{H}}$. Now, let U be a random variable uniformly distributed in $[0,1]$ and V an independent variable with distribution ν. We now define the family (X_h) given (U,V) the following way:

$$X_h = \begin{cases} g(V) & \text{if } h \in [U, U+\alpha_0 V], \\ Y & \text{otherwise}, \end{cases}$$

where $g(v)$ is a decreasing real function $[0,1] \to [t_0, +\infty)$, and Y is a random variable independent of (U,V), and with values in $(-\infty, t_0]$. We will show that it is possible to choose g, Y, t_0 to satisfy the claim of the proposition. In the above construction, remember that since we are working on the circle, the interval $[U, U+\alpha_0 V]$ should be "wrapped around" if $U + \alpha_0 > 1$.

First, let us compute explicitly the upper quantile $t(\alpha)$ of X_h for $\alpha \leq \alpha_0$. We have assumed that $Y < t_0$ a.s., so that for any $h \in \mathcal{H}$, $t \geq t_0$,

$$\mathbb{P}\left[X_h > t\right] = \mathbb{E}_V\left[\mathbb{P}\left[X_h > t|V\right]\right] = \mathbb{E}_V\left[\mathbb{P}\left[g(V) > t; h \in [U, U+\alpha_0 V]|V\right]\right]$$
$$= \int_0^{g^{-1}(t)} \alpha_0 v d\nu(v) = \alpha_0\beta(g^{-1}(t)).$$

Setting the above quantity equal to α, entails that $t(\alpha) = g(\beta^{-1}(\alpha_0^{-1}\alpha))$. Now, let us choose $A = [U, U+V]$ (note that due to the simplified structure of this example, the values of U and V can be inferred by looking at the family (X_h) alone since $[U, U+\alpha_0 V] = \{h : X_h \geq t_0\}$, hence A can really be seen as a function of the observed data alone). Then $|A| = V$, hence

$$t(\alpha_0\beta(|A|)) = g(\beta^{-1}(\alpha_0^{-1}\alpha_0\beta(V))) = g(V).$$

This entails that we have precisely $A \cap \{h : X_h \geq t(\alpha_0(\beta(|A|)))\} = [U, U+\alpha_0 V]$, so that $|\{h \in A \text{ and } X_h \geq t(\alpha_0\beta(|A|)\}| \, |A|^{-1} = \alpha_0$ a.s. Finally, if we want a prescribed marginal distribution P for X_h, we can take t_0 as the upper α_0-quantile of P, Y a variable with distribution the conditional of $P(x)$ given $x < t_0$, and, since β is continuous increasing, we can choose g so that $t(\alpha)$ matches the upper quantiles of P for $\alpha \leq \alpha_0$.   □

Resampling-Based Confidence Regions and Multiple Tests for a Correlated Random Vector

Sylvain Arlot[1,2], Gilles Blanchard[3], and Étienne Roquain[4]

[1] Univ Paris-Sud, Laboratoire de Mathématiques d'Orsay, Orsay Cedex, F-91405;
CNRS, Orsay cedex, F-91405
sylvain.arlot@math.u-psud.fr
[2] INRIA Futurs, Projet Select
[3] Fraunhofer FIRST.IDA, Berlin, Germany
blanchar@first.fraunhofer.de
[4] INRA Jouy-en-Josas, unité MIG, 78 352 Jouy-en-Josas Cedex, France
etienne.roquain@jouy.inra.fr

Abstract. We study generalized bootstrapped confidence regions for the mean of a random vector whose coordinates have an unknown dependence structure, with a non-asymptotic control of the confidence level. The random vector is supposed to be either Gaussian or to have a symmetric bounded distribution. We consider two approaches, the first based on a concentration principle and the second on a direct bootstrapped quantile. The first one allows us to deal with a very large class of resampling weights while our results for the second are restricted to Rademacher weights. However, the second method seems more accurate in practice. Our results are motivated by multiple testing problems, and we show on simulations that our procedures are better than the Bonferroni procedure (union bound) as soon as the observed vector has sufficiently correlated coordinates.

1 Introduction

In this work, we assume that we observe a sample $\mathbf{Y} := (\mathbf{Y}^1, \ldots, \mathbf{Y}^n)$ of $n \geq 2$ i.i.d. observations of an integrable random vector $\mathbf{Y}^i \in \mathbb{R}^K$ with a dimension K possibly much larger than n. Let $\mu \in \mathbb{R}^K$ denote the common mean of the $\mathbf{Y}^i$; our main goal is to find a non-asymptotic $(1 - \alpha)$-confidence region for μ, of the form:

$$\left\{ x \in \mathbb{R}^K \text{ s.t. } \phi\left(\overline{\mathbf{Y}} - x\right) \leq t_\alpha(\mathbf{Y}) \right\}, \tag{1}$$

where $\phi : \mathbb{R}^K \to \mathbb{R}$ is a measurable function fixed in advance by the user (measuring a kind of distance), $\alpha \in (0,1), t_\alpha : \left(\mathbb{R}^K\right)^n \to \mathbb{R}$ is a measurable data-dependent threshold, and $\overline{\mathbf{Y}} = \frac{1}{n} \sum_{i=1}^n \mathbf{Y}^i$ is the empirical mean of the sample $\mathbf{Y}$.

The form of the confidence region (1) is motivated by the following multiple testing problem: if we want to test simultaneously for all $1 \leq k \leq K$ the hypotheses $H_{0,k} = \{\mu_k \leq 0\}$ against $H_{1,k} = \{\mu_k > 0\}$, we propose to reject the $H_{0,k}$ corresponding to

$$\{1 \leq k \leq K \text{ s.t. } \overline{\mathbf{Y}}_k > t_\alpha(\mathbf{Y})\}.$$

N. Bshouty and C. Gentile (Eds.): COLT 2007, LNAI 4539, pp. 127–141, 2007.
© Springer-Verlag Berlin Heidelberg 2007

The error of this multiple testing procedure can be measured by the family-wise error rate defined by the probability that at least one hypothesis is wrongly rejected. Here, this error will be strongly (i.e. for any value of μ) controlled by α as soon as the confidence region (1) for μ with $\phi = \sup(\cdot)$ is of level at least $1 - \alpha$. Indeed, for all μ,

$$\mathbb{P}\left(\exists k \text{ s.t. } \overline{\mathbf{Y}}_k > t_\alpha(\mathbf{Y}) \text{ and } \mu_k \leq 0\right) \leq \mathbb{P}\left(\exists k \text{ s.t. } \overline{\mathbf{Y}}_k - \mu_k > t_\alpha(\mathbf{Y})\right)$$

$$= \mathbb{P}\left(\sup_k \left\{\overline{\mathbf{Y}}_k - \mu_k\right\} > t_\alpha(\mathbf{Y})\right).$$

The same reasoning with $\phi = \sup |\cdot|$ allows us to test $H_{0,k} = \{\mu_k = 0\}$ against $H_{1,k} = \{\mu_k \neq 0\}$, by choosing the rejection set $\{1 \leq k \leq K \text{ s.t. } |\overline{\mathbf{Y}}_k| > t_\alpha(\mathbf{Y})\}$.

While this goal is statistical in motivation, to tackle it we want to follow a point of view inspired from learning theory, in the following sense: first, we want a non-asymptotical result valid for any fixed K and n; secondly, we do not want to make any assumptions on the dependency structure of the coordinates of $\mathbf{Y}^i$ (although we will consider some general assumptions over the distribution of $\mathbf{Y}$, for example that it is Gaussian). Since the dimensionality K is possibly larger than the number of observations n, it is not appropriate here to estimate the dependency structure (e.g. the covariance matrix) via classical parametric procedures to construct a confidence region.

The ideal threshold t_α in (1) is obviously the $1 - \alpha$ quantile of the distribution of $\phi\left(\overline{\mathbf{Y}} - \mu\right)$. However, this quantity depends on the unknown dependency structure of the coordinates of $\mathbf{Y}^i$ and is therefore itself unknown.

We propose here to approach t_α by some resampling scheme: the heuristics of the resampling method (introduced by Efron [1], generalized to exchangeable weighted bootstrap by Mason and Newton [2] and Praestgaard and Wellner [3]) is that the distribution of $\overline{\mathbf{Y}} - \mu$ is "close" to the one of

$$\overline{\mathbf{Y}}_{[W-\overline{W}]} := \frac{1}{n}\sum_{i=1}^n (W_i - \overline{W})\mathbf{Y}^i = \frac{1}{n}\sum_{i=1}^n W_i(\mathbf{Y}^i - \overline{\mathbf{Y}}) = \overline{(\mathbf{Y} - \overline{\mathbf{Y}})}_{[W]},$$

conditionally to $\mathbf{Y}$, where $(W_i)_{1 \leq i \leq n}$ are real random variables independent of $\mathbf{Y}$ called the *resampling weights*, and $\overline{W} = n^{-1}\sum_{i=1}^n W_i$. We emphasize that the family $(W_i)_{1 \leq i \leq n}$ itself *need not be independent*.

Following this idea, we propose two different approaches to obtain non-asymptotic confidence regions:

1. The expectations of $\phi\left(\overline{\mathbf{Y}} - \mu\right)$ and $\phi\left(\overline{\mathbf{Y}}_{[W-\overline{W}]}\right)$ can be precisely compared, and the processes $\phi\left(\overline{\mathbf{Y}} - \mu\right)$ and $\mathbb{E}\left[\phi\left(\overline{\mathbf{Y}}_{[W-\overline{W}]}\right)|\mathbf{Y}\right]$ concentrate well around their expectations.

2. The $1 - \alpha$ quantile of the distribution of $\phi\left(\overline{\mathbf{Y}}_{[W-\overline{W}]}\right)$ conditionally to $\mathbf{Y}$ is close to the one of $\phi\left(\overline{\mathbf{Y}} - \mu\right)$.

Method 1 above is closely related to the Rademacher complexity approach in learning theory, and our results in this direction are heavily inspired by the work of Fromont [4], who studies general resampling schemes in a learning theoretical setting. It may also be seen as a generalization of cross-validation methods. For method 2, we will restrict ourselves specifically to Rademacher weights in our analysis, because we use a symmetrization trick.

Using resampling to construct confidence regions or tests is a vast field of study in statistics (see *e.g.* [1,2,3,5,6,7,8,9] and the references therein). Roughly speaking, we can mainly distinguish between two types of results: asymptotic results which are not adapted to the goals we have fixed here, and exact randomized tests. The latter are based on an invariance of the null distribution under a given transformation. In the setting considered in this paper, we will consider symmetric distributions, allowing us to use symmetrization techniques. However, because our first goal is to derive a confidence region, the vector of the means is unknown and we cannot use directly exact randomized tests (this argument applies to the one-sided test setting as well where the mean is also unknown). Our method 2 uses a symmetrization argument after having empirically recentred the data. To our knowledge, this gives the first non-asymptotic approximation result on resampled quantiles.

Finally, following [8], we note that all our multiple testing procedures can be transformed into step-down procedures (this will be detailed in the long version of this paper).

Let us now define a few notations that will be useful throughout this paper.

- Vectors, such as data vectors $\mathbf{Y}^i = (\mathbf{Y}^i_k)_{1 \leq k \leq K}$, will always be column vectors. Thus, $\mathbf{Y}$ is a $K \times n$ data matrix.
- If $\mu \in \mathbb{R}^K$, $\mathbf{Y} - \mu$ is the matrix obtained by subtracting μ from each (column) vector of $\mathbf{Y}$. If $c \in \mathbb{R}$ and $W \in \mathbb{R}^n$, $W - c = (W_i - c)_{1 \leq i \leq n} \in \mathbb{R}^n$.
- If X is a random variable, $\mathcal{D}(X)$ is its distribution and $\mathrm{Var}(X)$ is its variance.
- The vector $\sigma = (\sigma_k)_{1 \leq k \leq K}$ is the vector of the standard deviations of the data: $\forall k, 1 \leq k \leq K, \sigma_k = \mathrm{Var}^{1/2}(\mathbf{Y}^1_k)$.
- $\overline{\Phi}$ is the standard Gaussian upper tail function.

Several properties may be assumed for the function $\phi : \mathbb{R}^K \to \mathbb{R}$:

- Subadditivity: $\forall x, x' \in \mathbb{R}^K, \quad \phi(x + x') \leq \phi(x) + \phi(x')$.
- Positive-homogeneity: $\forall x \in \mathbb{R}^K, \forall \lambda \in \mathbb{R}_+, \quad \phi(\lambda x) = \lambda \phi(x)$.
- Bounded by the p-norm, $p \in [1, \infty]$: $\forall x \in \mathbb{R}^K, |\phi(x)| \leq \|x\|_p$, where $\|x\|_p$ is equal to $(\sum_{k=1}^K |x_k|^p)^{1/p}$ if $p < \infty$ and $\max_k\{|x_k|\}$ otherwise.

Finally, different assumptions on the generating distribution of $\mathbf{Y}$ can be made:

(GA) The Gaussian assumption: the $\mathbf{Y}^i$ are Gaussian vectors
(SA) The symmetric assumption: the $\mathbf{Y}^i$ are symmetric with respect to μ i.e. $\mathbf{Y}^i - \mu \sim \mu - \mathbf{Y}^i$.
(BA)(p, M) The bounded assumption: $\|\mathbf{Y}^i - \mu\|_p \leq M$ a.s.

In this paper, our primary focus is on the Gaussian framework (GA), because the corresponding results will be more accurate. In addition, we will always assume that we know some upper bound on a p-norm of σ for some $p > 0$.

The paper is organized as follows: Section 2 deals with the concentration method with general weights. In Section 3, we propose an approach based on resampling quantiles, with Rademacher weights. We illustrate our methods in Section 4 with a simulation study. The proofs of our results are given in Section 5.

2   Confidence Region Using Concentration

In this section, we consider a general $\mathbb{R}^n$-valued *resampling weight vector* W, satisfying the following properties: W is independent of $\mathbf{Y}$, for all $i \in \{1, \dots, n\}$ $\mathbb{E}\left[W_i^2\right] < \infty$, the $(W_i)_{1 \leq i \leq n}$ have an exchangeable distribution (*i.e.* invariant under any permutation of the indices) and the coordinates of W are not a.s. equal, *i.e.* $\mathbb{E}\left|W_1 - \overline{W}\right| > 0$. Several examples of resampling weight vectors are given in Section 2.3, where we also tackle the question of choosing a resampling.

Four constants that depend only on the distribution of W appear in the results below (the fourth one is defined only for a particular class of weights). They are defined as follows and computed for classical resamplings in Tab. 1:

$$A_W := \mathbb{E}\left|W_1 - \overline{W}\right| \tag{2}$$

$$B_W := \mathbb{E}\left[\left(\frac{1}{n}\sum_{i=1}^{n}\left(W_i - \overline{W}\right)^2\right)^{\frac{1}{2}}\right] \tag{3}$$

$$C_W := \left(\frac{n}{n-1}\mathbb{E}\left[\left(W_1 - \overline{W}\right)^2\right]\right)^{\frac{1}{2}} \tag{4}$$

$$D_W := a + \mathbb{E}\left|\overline{W} - x_0\right| \quad \text{if } \forall i, |W_i - x_0| = a \text{ a.s. (with } a > 0, x_0 \in \mathbb{R}). \tag{5}$$

Note that under our assumptions, these quantities are positive. Moreover, if the weights are i.i.d., $C_W = \mathrm{Var}(W_1)^{\frac{1}{2}}$. We can now state the main result of this section:

Theorem 2.1. *Fix $\alpha \in (0,1)$ and $p \in [1, \infty]$. Let $\phi : \mathbb{R}^K \to \mathbb{R}$ be any function subadditive, positive-homogeneous and bounded by the p-norm, and let W be a resampling weight vector.*

1. *If $\mathbf{Y}$ satisfies (GA), then*

$$\phi\left(\overline{\mathbf{Y}} - \mu\right) < \frac{\mathbb{E}\left[\phi\left(\overline{\mathbf{Y}}_{[W-\overline{W}]}\right)|\mathbf{Y}\right]}{B_W} + \|\sigma\|_p \overline{\Phi}^{-1}(\alpha/2)\left[\frac{C_W}{nB_W} + \frac{1}{\sqrt{n}}\right] \tag{6}$$

holds with probability at least $1 - \alpha$. The same bound holds for the lower deviations, i.e. with inequality (6) reversed and the additive term replaced by its opposite.

2. *If $\mathbf{Y}$ satisfies (BA)(p, M) and (SA), then*

$$\phi\left(\overline{\mathbf{Y}} - \mu\right) < \frac{\mathbb{E}\left[\phi\left(\overline{\mathbf{Y}}_{[W-\overline{W}]}\right)|\mathbf{Y}\right]}{A_W} + \frac{2M}{\sqrt{n}}\sqrt{\log(1/\alpha)}$$

holds with probability at least $1 - \alpha$. *If moreover the weights satisfy the assumption of* (5), *then*

$$\phi \left(\overline{\mathbf{Y}} - \mu \right) > \frac{\mathbb{E} \left[\phi \left(\overline{\mathbf{Y}}_{[W - \overline{W}]} \right) | \mathbf{Y} \right]}{D_W} - \frac{M}{\sqrt{n}} \sqrt{1 + \frac{A_W^2}{D_W^2}} \sqrt{2 \log(1/\alpha)}$$

holds with probability at least $1 - \alpha$.

If there exists a deterministic threshold t_α such that $\mathbb{P}(\phi \left(\overline{\mathbf{Y}} - \mu \right) > t_\alpha) \leq \alpha$, the following corollary establishes that we can combine the above concentration threshold with t_α to get a new threshold almost better than both.

Corollary 2.2. *Fix* $\alpha, \delta \in (0, 1)$, $p \in [1, \infty]$ *and take* ϕ *and* W *as in Theorem 2.1. Suppose that* $\mathbf{Y}$ *satisfies* (GA) *and that* $t_{\alpha(1-\delta)}$ *is a real number such that* $\mathbb{P} \left(\phi \left(\overline{\mathbf{Y}} - \mu \right) > t_{\alpha(1-\delta)} \right) \leq \alpha(1 - \delta)$. *Then with probability at least* $1 - \alpha$, $\phi \left(\overline{\mathbf{Y}} - \mu \right)$ *is upper bounded by the minimum between* $t_{\alpha(1-\delta)}$ *and*

$$\frac{\mathbb{E} \left[\phi \left(\overline{\mathbf{Y}}_{[W - \overline{W}]} \right) | \mathbf{Y} \right]}{B_W} + \frac{\|\sigma\|_p}{\sqrt{n}} \overline{\Phi}^{-1} \left(\frac{\alpha(1 - \delta)}{2} \right) + \frac{\|\sigma\|_p C_W}{n B_W} \overline{\Phi}^{-1} \left(\frac{\alpha \delta}{2} \right). \quad (7)$$

Remark 2.3. 1. Corollary 2.2 is a consequence of the proof of Theorem 2.1, rather than of the theorem itself. The point here is that $\mathbb{E} \left[\phi \left(\overline{\mathbf{Y}}_{[W - \overline{W}]} \right) | \mathbf{Y} \right]$ is almost deterministic, because it concentrates at the rate $n^{-1} (= o(n^{-1/2}))$.
   2. For instance, if $\phi = \sup(\cdot)$ (resp. $\sup|\cdot|$), Corollary 2.2 may be applied with t_α equal to the classical Bonferroni threshold for multiple testing (obtained using a simple union bound over coordinates)

$$t_{\mathrm{Bonf},\alpha} := \frac{1}{\sqrt{n}} \|\sigma\|_\infty \overline{\Phi}^{-1} \left(\frac{\alpha}{K} \right) \left(\text{resp. } t'_{\mathrm{Bonf},\alpha} := \frac{1}{\sqrt{n}} \|\sigma\|_\infty \overline{\Phi}^{-1} \left(\frac{\alpha}{2K} \right) \right).$$

We thus obtain a confidence region almost equal to Bonferroni's for small correlations and better than Bonferroni's for strong correlations (see simulations in Section 4).

The proof of Theorem 2.1 involves results which are of self interest: the comparison between the expectations of the two processes $\mathbb{E} \left[\phi \left(\overline{\mathbf{Y}}_{[W - \overline{W}]} \right) | \mathbf{Y} \right]$ and $\phi \left(\overline{\mathbf{Y}} - \mu \right)$ and the concentration of these processes around their means. This is examined in the two following subsections. The last subsection gives some elements for a wise choice of resampling weight vectors among several classical examples.

2.1   Comparison in Expectation

In this section, we compare $\mathbb{E} \left[\phi \left(\overline{\mathbf{Y}}_{[W - \overline{W}]} \right) \right]$ and $\mathbb{E} \left[\phi \left(\overline{\mathbf{Y}} - \mu \right) \right]$. We note that these expectations exist in the Gaussian and the bounded case provided that ϕ is measurable and bounded by a p-norm. Otherwise, in particular in Propositions 2.4 and 2.6, we assume that these expectations exist. In the Gaussian case, these quantities are equal up to a factor that depends only on the distribution of W:

Proposition 2.4. *Let* $\mathbf{Y}$ *be a sample satisfying (GA) and* W *a resampling weight vector. Then, for any measurable positive-homogeneous function* $\phi : \mathbb{R}^K \to \mathbb{R}$, *we have the following equality*

$$B_W \mathbb{E}\left[\phi\left(\overline{\mathbf{Y}} - \mu\right)\right] = \mathbb{E}\left[\phi\left(\overline{\mathbf{Y}}_{[W-\overline{W}]}\right)\right]. \tag{8}$$

Remark 2.5. 1. In general, we can compute the value of B_W by simulation. For some classical weights, we give bounds or exact expressions in Tab. 1.
  2. In a non-Gaussian framework, the constant B_W is still relevant, at least asymptotically: in their Theorem 3.6.13, Van der Vaart and Wellner [10] use the limit of B_W when n goes to infinity as a normalizing constant.

When the sample is only symmetric we obtain the following inequalities :

Proposition 2.6. *Let* $\mathbf{Y}$ *be a sample satisfying (SA),* W *a resampling weight vector and* $\phi : \mathbb{R}^K \to \mathbb{R}$ *any subadditive, positive-homogeneous function.*

(i) We have the general following lower bound :

$$A_W \mathbb{E}\left[\phi\left(\overline{\mathbf{Y}} - \mu\right)\right] \leq \mathbb{E}\left[\phi\left(\overline{\mathbf{Y}}_{[W-\overline{W}]}\right)\right]. \tag{9}$$

(ii) Moreover, if the weights satisfy the assumption of (5), we have the following upper bound

$$D_W \mathbb{E}\left[\phi\left(\overline{\mathbf{Y}} - \mu\right)\right] \geq \mathbb{E}\left[\phi\left(\overline{\mathbf{Y}}_{[W-\overline{W}]}\right)\right]. \tag{10}$$

Remark 2.7. 1. The bounds (9) and (10) are tight for Rademacher and Random hold-out ($n/2$) weights, but far less optimal in some other cases like Leave-one-out (see Section 2.3).
  2. When $\mathbf{Y}$ is not assumed to be symmetric and $\overline{W} = 1$ a.s., Proposition 2 in [4] shows that (9) holds with $\mathbb{E}(W_1 - \overline{W})_+$ instead of A_W. Therefore, the symmetry of the sample allows us to get a tighter result (for instance twice sharper with Efron or Random hold-out (q) weights).

2.2   Concentration Around the Expectation

In this section we present concentration results for the two processes $\phi\left(\overline{\mathbf{Y}} - \mu\right)$ and $\mathbb{E}\left[\phi\left(\overline{\mathbf{Y}}_{[W-\overline{W}]}\right) \big| \mathbf{Y}\right]$ in the Gaussian framework.

Proposition 2.8. *Let* $p \in [1, +\infty]$, $\mathbf{Y}$ *a sample satisfying (GA) and* $\phi : \mathbb{R}^K \to \mathbb{R}$ *be any subadditive function, bounded by the p-norm.*

(i) For all $\alpha \in (0,1)$, with probability at least $1 - \alpha$ the following holds:

$$\phi\left(\overline{\mathbf{Y}} - \mu\right) < \mathbb{E}\left[\phi\left(\overline{\mathbf{Y}} - \mu\right)\right] + \frac{\|\sigma\|_p \overline{\Phi}^{-1}(\alpha/2)}{\sqrt{n}}, \tag{11}$$

and the same bound holds for the corresponding lower deviations.

(ii) Let W be some exchangeable resampling weight vector. does not depend on $(i,j), i \neq j$ and $\mathbb{E}(W_i - \overline{W})^2$ do not depend on i. Then, for all $\alpha \in (0,1)$, with probability at least $1 - \alpha$ the following holds:

$$\mathbb{E}\left[\phi\left(\overline{\mathbf{Y}}_{[W-\overline{W}]}\right) | \mathbf{Y}\right] < \mathbb{E}\left[\phi\left(\overline{\mathbf{Y}}_{[W-\overline{W}]}\right)\right] + \frac{\|\sigma\|_p C_W \overline{\Phi}^{-1}(\alpha/2)}{n}, \tag{12}$$

and the same bound holds for the corresponding lower deviations.

The first bound (11) with a remainder in $n^{-1/2}$ is classical. The last one (12) is much more interesting since it enlights one of the key properties of the resampling idea: the "stabilization". Indeed, the resampling quantity $\mathbb{E}\left[\phi\left(\overline{\mathbf{Y}}_{[W-\overline{W}]}\right) | \mathbf{Y}\right]$ concentrates around its expectation at the rate $C_W n^{-1} = o\left(n^{-1/2}\right)$ for most of the weights (see Section 2.3 and Tab. 1 for more details). Thus, compared to the original process, it is almost deterministic and equal to $B_W \mathbb{E}\left[\phi\left(\overline{\mathbf{Y}} - \mu\right)\right]$.

Remark 2.9. Combining expression (8) and Proposition 2.8 (ii), we derive that for a Gaussian sample $\mathbf{Y}$ and any $p \in [1, \infty]$, the following upper bound holds with probability at least $1 - \alpha$:

$$\mathbb{E}\left\|\overline{\mathbf{Y}} - \mu\right\|_p < \frac{\mathbb{E}\left[\left\|\overline{\mathbf{Y}}_{[W-\overline{W}]}\right\|_p | \mathbf{Y}\right]}{B_W} + \frac{\|\sigma\|_p C_W}{n B_W} \overline{\Phi}^{-1}(\alpha/2), \tag{13}$$

and a similar lower bound holds. This gives a control with high probability of the L^p-risk of the estimator $\overline{\mathbf{Y}}$ of the mean $\mu \in \mathbb{R}^K$ at the rate $C_W B_W^{-1} n^{-1}$.

2.3   Resampling Weight Vectors

In this section, we consider the question of choosing some appropriate resampling weight vector W when using Theorem 2.1 or Corollary 2.2. We define the following classical resampling weight vectors:

1. **Rademacher:** W_i i.i.d. Rademacher variables, i.e. $W_i \in \{-1, 1\}$ with equal probabilities.
2. **Efron:** W has a multinomial distribution with parameters $(n; n^{-1}, \ldots, n^{-1})$.
3. **Random hold-out** (q) (R. h.-o.), $q \in \{1, \ldots, n\}$: $W_i = \frac{n}{q}\mathbb{1}_{i \in I}$, where I is uniformly distributed on subsets of $\{1, \ldots, n\}$ of cardinality q. These weights may also be called cross validation weights, or leave-$(n - q)$-out weights. A classical choice is $q = n/2$ (when $2|n$). When $q = n - 1$, these weights are called **leave-one-out** weights.

Table 1. Resampling constants for classical resampling weight vector

Efron	$2\left(1-\frac{1}{n}\right)^n = A_W \leq B_W \leq \sqrt{\frac{n-1}{n}}$ $\quad C_W = 1$
Efr., $n \to +\infty$	$\frac{2}{e} = A_W \leq B_W \leq 1 = C_W$
Rademacher	$1 - \frac{1}{\sqrt{n}} \leq A_W \leq B_W \leq \sqrt{1-\frac{1}{n}}$ $\quad C_W = 1$ $\quad D_W \leq 1 + \frac{1}{\sqrt{n}}$
Rad., $n \to +\infty$	$A_W = B_W = C_W = D_W = 1$
R. h.-o. (q)	$A_W = 2\left(1-\frac{q}{n}\right)$ $\quad B_W = \sqrt{\frac{n}{q}-1}$ $C_W = \sqrt{\frac{n}{n-1}}\sqrt{\frac{n}{q}-1}$ $\quad D_W = \frac{n}{2q} + \left|1 - \frac{n}{2q}\right|$
R. h.-o. $(n/2)$ $(2\|n)$	$A_W = B_W = D_W = 1$ $\quad C_W = \sqrt{\frac{n}{n-1}}$
Leave-one-out	$\frac{2}{n} = A_W \leq B_W = \frac{1}{\sqrt{n-1}}$ $\quad C_W = \frac{\sqrt{n}}{n-1}$ $\quad D_W = 1$

For these classical weights, exact or approximate values for the quantities A_W, B_W, C_W and D_W (defined by equations (2) to (5)) can be easily derived (see Tab. 1). Now, to use Theorem 2.1 or Corollary 2.2, we have to choose a particular resampling weight vector. In the Gaussian case, we propose the following accuracy and complexity criteria: first, relations (6), (7) and (8) suggest that the quantity $C_W B_W^{-1}$ can be proposed as *accuracy* index for W. Secondly, an upper bound on the computational burden to compute exactly the resampling quantity is given by the cardinality of the support of $\mathcal{D}(W)$, thus providing a *complexity* index.

These two criteria are estimated in Tab. 2 for classical weights. Since for any exchangeable weight vector W, we have $C_W B_W^{-1} \geq [n/(n-1)]^{1/2}$ and the cardinality of the support of $\mathcal{D}(W)$ is greater than n, the *leave-one-out weights* satisfy the best accuracy-complexity trade-off among exchangeable weights.

Remark 2.10. Of course, for general weights (complex or not), the computation of resampling quantities can be done by Monte-Carlo simulations, *i.e.* drawing randomly a small number of independent weight vectors (see [9], appendix II for a discussion). We did not yet investigate the analysis of the corresponding approximation.

Remark 2.11. When the leave-one-out weights are too complex (if n is large), we can use "piece-wise exchangeable" weights instead: consider a regular partition $(B_j)_{1 \leq j \leq V}$ of $\{1, \ldots, n\}$ (where $V \in \{2, \ldots, n\}$ and $V|n$), and define the weights $W_i = \frac{V}{V-1}\mathbb{1}_{i \notin B_J}$ with J uniformly distributed on $\{1, \ldots, V\}$. These weights are called the **(regular) V-fold cross validation** weights (V-f. c.v.). Considering the process $(\widetilde{\mathbf{Y}}^j)_{1 \leq j \leq K}$ where $\widetilde{\mathbf{Y}}^j = \frac{V}{n}\sum_{i \in B_j} \mathbf{Y}^i$ is the empirical mean of $\mathbf{Y}$ on block B_j, we can show that Theorem 2.1 can be extended to (regular) V-fold cross validation weights with the following resampling constants [1]: $A_W = 2/V$, $B_W = (V-1)^{-1/2}$, $C_W = \sqrt{n}(V-1)^{-1}$, $D_W = 1$. Thus, while the complexity index of V-f. c.v. weights is only V, we lose a factor $[(n-1)/(V-1)]^{1/2}$ in the accuracy index.

---

[1] When V does not divide n and the blocks are no longer regular, Theorem 2.1 can also be generalized, but the constants have more complex expressions.

Remark 2.12 (Link to leave-one-out prediction risk estimation). Consider us-
ing $\overline{\mathbf{Y}}$ for *predicting* a new data point $\mathbf{Y}^{n+1} \sim \mathbf{Y}^1$ (independent on $\mathbf{Y} =$
$(Y^1, \ldots, Y^n))$. The corresponding L^p-prediction risk is given by $\mathbb{E} \left\| \overline{\mathbf{Y}} - \mathbf{Y}^{n+1} \right\|_p$.
For Gaussians, this prediction risk is proportional to the L^p-risk: $\mathbb{E} \left\| \overline{\mathbf{Y}} - \mu \right\|_p =$
$(n+1)^{\frac{1}{2}} \mathbb{E} \left\| \overline{\mathbf{Y}} - \mathbf{Y}^{n+1} \right\|_p$, so that the estimator of the L^p-risk proposed in
Remark 2.9 leads to an estimator of the prediction risk. In particular, using
leave-one-out weights and noting $\overline{\mathbf{Y}}^{(-i)}$ the mean of the $(\mathbf{Y}^j, j \neq i, 1 \leq j \leq n)$,
we have then established that the leave-one-out estimator $\frac{1}{n} \sum_{i=1}^{n} \left\| \overline{\mathbf{Y}}^{(-i)} - \mathbf{Y}^i \right\|_p$
correctly estimates the prediction risk (up to the factor $(1 - 1/n^2)^{\frac{1}{2}} \sim 1$).

Table 2. Choice of the resampling weight vectors : accuracy-complexity tradeoff

Resampling	$C_W B_W^{-1}$ (accuracy)	Card (supp $\mathcal{L}(W)$) (complexity)
Efron	$\leq \frac{1}{2} \left(1 - \frac{1}{n}\right)^{-n} \xrightarrow[n\to\infty]{} \frac{e}{2}$	$\binom{2n-1}{n-1} \propto n^{-\frac{1}{2}} 4^n$
Rademacher	$\leq \left(1 - n^{-1/2}\right)^{-1} \xrightarrow[n\to\infty]{} 1$	2^n
R. h.-o. $(n/2)$	$= \sqrt{\frac{n}{n-1}} \xrightarrow[n\to\infty]{} 1$	$\binom{n}{n/2} \propto n^{-1/2} 2^n$
Leave-one-out	$= \sqrt{\frac{n}{n-1}} \xrightarrow[n\to\infty]{} 1$	n

3   Confidence Region Using Resampled Quantiles

In this section, we present a different approach: we approximate the quantiles of
the variable $\phi\left(\overline{\mathbf{Y}} - \mu\right)$ by the quantiles of the corresponding resampled distri-
bution $\mathcal{D}\left(\phi\left(\overline{\mathbf{Y}}_{[W-\overline{W}]}\right) \mid \mathbf{Y}\right)$, in the particular Rademacher resampling scheme.
Let us define for a function ϕ the resampled empirical quantile:

$$q_\alpha(\phi, \mathbf{Y}) = \inf \left\{ x \in \mathbb{R} \text{ s.t. } \mathbb{P}_W \left[\phi(\overline{\mathbf{Y}}_{[W]}) > x \right] \leq \alpha \right\} ,$$

where in W is an i.i.d Rademacher weight vector. We now state the main technical result of this section:

Proposition 3.1. *Fix $\delta, \alpha \in (0,1)$. Let $\mathbf{Y}$ be a data sample satisfying assumption (SA). Let $f : \left(\mathbb{R}^K\right)^n \to [0, \infty)$ be a nonnegative (measurable) function on the
set of data samples. Let ϕ be a nonnegative, subadditive, positive-homogeneous
function. Denote $\widetilde{\phi}(x) = \max\left(\phi(x), \phi(-x)\right)$. Finally, for $\eta \in (0,1)$, denote*

$$\overline{\mathcal{B}}(n, \eta) = \min \left\{ k \in \{0, \ldots, n\} \text{ s.t. } 2^{-n} \sum_{i=k+1}^{n} \binom{n}{i} < \eta \right\} ,$$

the upper quantile function of a binomial $(n, \frac{1}{2})$ variable. Then we have:

$$\mathbb{P}\left[\phi(\overline{\mathbf{Y}} - \mu) > q_{\alpha(1-\delta)}\left(\phi, \mathbf{Y} - \overline{\mathbf{Y}}\right) + f(\mathbf{Y})\right]$$

$$\leq \alpha + \mathbb{P}\left[\widetilde{\phi}(\overline{\mathbf{Y}} - \mu) > \frac{n}{2\overline{\mathcal{B}}\left(n, \frac{\alpha\delta}{2}\right) - n} f(\mathbf{Y})\right]$$

Remark 3.2. By Hoeffding's inequality, $\frac{n}{2\overline{\mathcal{B}}(n,\frac{\alpha\delta}{2})-n} \geq \left(\frac{n}{2\ln\left(\frac{2}{\alpha\delta}\right)}\right)^{1/2}$.

By iteration of this proposition we obtain the following corollary:

Corollary 3.3. *Fix J a positive integer, $(\alpha_i)_{i=0,\ldots,J-1}$ a finite sequence in $(0,1)$ and $\beta, \delta \in (0,1)$. Let $\mathbf{Y}$ be a data sample satisfying assumption (SA). Let $\phi : \mathbb{R}^K \to \mathbb{R}$ be a nonnegative, subadditive, positive-homogeneous function and $f : \left(\mathbb{R}^K\right)^n \to [0,\infty)$ be a nonnegative function on the set of data samples. Then the following holds:*

$$\mathbb{P}\left[\phi(\overline{\mathbf{Y}} - \mu) > q_{(1-\delta)\alpha_0}(\phi, \mathbf{Y} - \overline{\mathbf{Y}}) + \sum_{i=1}^{J-1} \gamma_i q_{(1-\delta)\alpha_i}(\widetilde{\phi}, \mathbf{Y} - \overline{\mathbf{Y}}) + \gamma_J f(\mathbf{Y})\right]$$

$$\leq \sum_{i=0}^{J-1} \alpha_i + \mathbb{P}\left[\widetilde{\phi}(\overline{\mathbf{Y}} - \mu) > f(\mathbf{Y})\right], \quad (14)$$

where, for $k \geq 1$, $\gamma_k = n^{-k} \prod_{i=0}^{k-1} \left(2\overline{\mathcal{B}}\left(n, \frac{\alpha_i \delta}{2}\right) - n\right)$.

The rationale behind this result is that the sum appearing inside the probability in (14) should be interpreted as a series of corrective terms of decreasing order of magnitude, since we expect the sequence γ_k to be sharply decreasing. Looking at Hoeffding's bound, this will be the case if the levels are such that $\alpha_i \gg \exp(-n)$.

Looking at (14), we still have to deal with the trailing term on the right-hand side to obtain a useful result. We did not succeed in obtaining a self-contained result based on the symmetry assumption (SA) alone. However, to upper-bound the trailing term, we can assume some additional regularity assumption on the distribution of the data. For example, if the data are Gaussian or bounded, we can apply the results of the previous section (or apply some other device like Bonferroni's bound (8)). We want to emphasize that the bound used in this last step does not have to be particularly sharp: since we expect (in favorable cases) γ_J to be very small, the trailing probability term on the right-hand side as well as the contribution of $\gamma_J f(\mathbf{Y})$ to the left-hand side should be very minor. Therefore, even a coarse bound on this last term should suffice.

Finally, we note as in the previous section that, for computational reasons, it might be relevant to consider a block-wise Rademacher resampling scheme.

4   Simulations

For simulations we consider data of the form $Y_t = \mu_t + G_t$, where t belongs to an $m \times m$ discretized 2D torus of $K = m^2$ "pixels", identified with $\mathbb{T}_m^2 = (\mathbb{Z}/m\mathbb{Z})^2$, and G is a centered Gaussian vector obtained by 2D discrete convolution of an i.i.d. standard Gaussian field ("white noise") on $\mathbb{T}_m^2$ with a function $F : \mathbb{T}_m^2 \to \mathbb{R}$ such that $\sum_{t \in \mathbb{T}_m^2} F^2(t) = 1$. This ensures that G is a stationary Gaussian process on the discrete torus, it is in particular isotropic with $\mathbb{E}\left[G_t^2\right] = 1$ for all $t \in \mathbb{T}_m^2$.

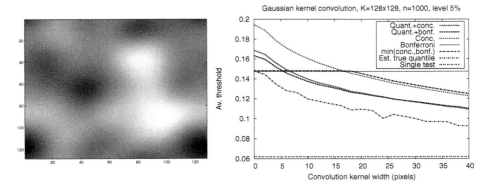

Fig. 1. Left: example of a 128x128 pixel image obtained by convolution of Gaussian white noise with a (toroidal) Gaussian filter with width $b = 18$ pixels. Right: average thresholds obtained for the different approaches, see text.

In the simulations below we consider for the function F a "Gaussian" convolution filter of bandwidth b on the torus:

$$F_b(t) = C_b \exp\left(-d(0, t)^2/b^2\right) ,$$

where $d(t, t')$ is the standard distance on the torus and C_b is a normalizing constant. Note that for actual simulations it is more convenient to work in the Fourier domain and to apply the inverse DFT which can be computed efficiently. We then compare the different thresholds obtained by the methods proposed in this work for varying values of b. Remember that the only information available to the algorithm is the bound on the marginal variance; the form of the function F_b itself is of course unknown.

On Fig. 1 we compare the thresholds obtained when $\phi = \sup|\cdot|$, which corresponds to the two-sided multiple testing situation. We use the different approaches proposed in this work, with the following parameters: the dimension is $K = 128^2 = 16384$, the number of data points per sample is $n = 1000$ (much smaller than K, so that we really are in a non-asymptotic framework), the width b takes even values in the range $[0, 40]$, the overall level is $\alpha = 0.05$. For the concentration threshold (6) ('conc.'), we used Rademacher weights. For the "compound" threshold of Corollary 2.2 ('min(conc.,bonf.)'), we used $\delta = 0.1$ and the Bonferroni threshold $t'_{\text{Bonf},0.9\alpha}$ as the deterministic reference threshold. For the quantile approach (14), we used $J = 1$, $\alpha_0 = 0.9\alpha$, $\delta = 0.1$, and the function f is given either by the Bonferroni threshold ('quant.+bonf.') or the concentration threshold ('quant.+conc.'), both at level 0.1α. Each point represents an average over 50 experiments. Finally, we included in the figure the Bonferroni threshold $t'_{\text{Bonf},\alpha}$, the threshold for a single test for comparison, and an estimation of the true quantile (actually, an empirical quantile over 1000 samples).

The quantiles or expectation with Rademacher weights were estimated by Monte-Carlo with 1000 draws. On the figure we did not include standard deviations: they are quite low, of the order of 10^{-3}, although it is worth noting that the quantile threshold has a standard deviation roughly twice as large as the concentration threshold (we did not investigate at this point what part of this variation is due to the MC approximation).

The overall conclusion of this preliminary experiment is that the different thresholds proposed in this work are relevant in the sense that they are smaller than the Bonferroni threshold provided the vector has strong enough correlations. As expected, the quantile approach appears to lead to tighter thresholds. (However, this might not be always the case for smaller sample sizes.) One advantage of the concentration approach is that the 'compound' threshold (7) can "fall back" on the Bonferroni threshold when needed, at the price of a minimal threshold increase.

5   Proofs

Proof (Proof of Prop. 2.4). Denoting by $\boldsymbol{\Sigma}$ the common covariance matrix of the $\mathbf{Y}^i$, we have $\mathcal{D}(\overline{\mathbf{Y}}_{[W-\overline{W}]}|W) = \mathcal{N}\big(0, (n^{-1}\sum_{i=1}^n (W_i - \overline{W})^2)n^{-1}\boldsymbol{\Sigma}\big)$, and the result follows because $\mathcal{D}(\overline{\mathbf{Y}} - \mu) = \mathcal{N}(0, n^{-1}\boldsymbol{\Sigma})$ and ϕ is positive-homogeneous. $\qquad\square$

Proof (Proof of Prop. 2.6). (i). By independence between W and $\mathbf{Y}$, using the positive homogeneity, then convexity of ϕ, for every realization of $\mathbf{Y}$ we have:

$$
A_W \phi\left(\overline{\mathbf{Y}} - \mu\right) = \phi\left(\mathbb{E}\left[\frac{1}{n}\sum_{i=1}^n |W_i - \overline{W}|\left(\mathbf{Y}^i - \mu\right)\,\Big|\,\mathbf{Y}\right]\right)
$$

$$
\leq \mathbb{E}\left[\phi\left(\frac{1}{n}\sum_{i=1}^n |W_i - \overline{W}|\left(\mathbf{Y}^i - \mu\right)\right)\,\Big|\,\mathbf{Y}\right].
$$

We integrate with respect to $\mathbf{Y}$, and use the symmetry of the $\mathbf{Y}^i$ with respect to μ and again the independence between W and $\mathbf{Y}$ to show finally that

$$
A_W \mathbb{E}\left[\phi\left(\overline{\mathbf{Y}} - \mu\right)\right] \leq \mathbb{E}\left[\phi\left(\frac{1}{n}\sum_{i=1}^n |W_i - \overline{W}|\left(\mathbf{Y}^i - \mu\right)\right)\right]
$$

$$
= \mathbb{E}\left[\phi\left(\frac{1}{n}\sum_{i=1}^n (W_i - \overline{W})\left(\mathbf{Y}^i - \mu\right)\right)\right] = \mathbb{E}\left[\phi\left(\overline{\mathbf{Y}}_{[W-\overline{W}]}\right)\right].
$$

We obtain (ii) via the triangle inequality and the same symmetrization trick. $\square$

Proof (Proof of Prop. 2.8). We denote by $\mathbf{A}$ a square root of the common covariance matrix of the $\mathbf{Y}^i$ and by $(a_k)_{1\leq k\leq K}$ the rows of $\mathbf{A}$. If $\mathbf{G}$ is a $K \times m$ matrix with standard centered i.i.d. Gaussian entries, then $\mathbf{A}\mathbf{G}$ has the same distribution as $\mathbf{Y} - \mu$. We let for all $\zeta \in \left(\mathbb{R}^K\right)^n$, $T_1(\zeta) := \phi\left(\frac{1}{n}\sum_{i=1}^n \mathbf{A}\zeta_i\right)$

and $T_2(\zeta) := \mathbb{E}\left[\phi\left(\frac{1}{n}\sum_{i=1}^{n}(W_i - \overline{W})\mathbf{A}\zeta_i\right)\right]$. From the Gaussian concentration theorem of Cirel'son, Ibragimov and Sudakov (see for example [11], Thm. 3.8), we just need to prove that T_1 (resp. T_2) is a Lipschitz function with constant $\|\sigma\|_p/\sqrt{n}$ (resp. $\|\sigma\|_p C_W/n$), for the Euclidean norm $\|\cdot\|_{2,Kn}$ on $\left(\mathbb{R}^K\right)^n$. Let $\zeta, \zeta' \in \left(\mathbb{R}^K\right)^n$. Using firstly that ϕ is 1-Lipschitz (since it is subadditive and bounded by the p-norm), and secondly Cauchy-Schwartz's inequality coordinate-wise and $\|a_k\|_2 \leq \sigma_k$, we deduce

$$|T_1(\zeta) - T_1(\zeta')| \leq \left\|\frac{1}{n}\sum_{i=1}^{n}\mathbf{A}\left(\zeta_i - \zeta_i'\right)\right\|_p \leq \|\sigma\|_p\left\|\frac{1}{n}\sum_{i=1}^{n}\left(\zeta_i - \zeta_i'\right)\right\|_2.$$

Therefore, we get $|T_1(\zeta) - T_1(\zeta')| \leq \frac{\|\sigma\|_p}{\sqrt{n}}\|\zeta - \zeta'\|_{2,Kn}$ by convexity of $x \in \mathbb{R}^K \to \|x\|_2^2$, and we obtain (i). For T_2, we use the same method as for T_1 :

$$|T_2(\zeta) - T_2(\zeta')| \leq \|\sigma\|_p \mathbb{E}\left\|\frac{1}{n}\sum_{i=1}^{n}(W_i - \overline{W})(\zeta_i - \zeta_i')\right\|_2$$

$$\leq \frac{\|\sigma\|_p}{n}\sqrt{\mathbb{E}\left\|\sum_{i=1}^{n}(W_i - \overline{W})(\zeta_i - \zeta_i')\right\|_2^2}. \qquad (15)$$

We now develop $\left\|\sum_{i=1}^{n}(W_i - \overline{W})(\zeta_i - \zeta_i')\right\|_2^2$ in the Euclidean space $\mathbb{R}^K$ (note that from $\left(\sum_{i=1}^{n}(W_i - \overline{W})\right)^2 = 0$, we have $\mathbb{E}(W_1 - \overline{W})(W_2 - \overline{W}) = -C_W^2/n$):

$$\mathbb{E}\left\|\sum_{i=1}^{n}(W_i - \overline{W})(\zeta_i - \zeta_i')\right\|_2^2 = C_W^2\sum_{i=1}^{n}\|\zeta_i - \zeta_i'\|_2^2 - \frac{C_W^2}{n}\left\|\sum_{i=1}^{n}(\zeta_i - \zeta_i')\right\|_2^2.$$

Consequently,

$$\mathbb{E}\left\|\sum_{i=1}^{n}(W_i - \overline{W})(\zeta_i - \zeta_i')\right\|_2^2 \leq C_W^2\sum_{i=1}^{n}\|\zeta_i - \zeta_i'\|_2^2 \leq C_W^2\|\zeta - \zeta'\|_{2,Kn}^2. \qquad (16)$$

Combining expression (15) and (16), we find that T_2 is $\|\sigma\|_p C_W/n$-Lipschitz. $\quad\square$

Proof (Proof of Thm. 2.1). The case (BA)(p, M) and (SA) is obtained by combining Prop. 2.6 and McDiarmid's inequality (see for instance [4]). The (GA) case is a straightforward consequence of Prop. 2.4 and the proof of Prop. 2.8. $\quad\square$

Proof (Proof of Cor. 2.2). From Prop. 2.8 (i), with probability at least $1 - \alpha(1 - \delta)$, $\phi\left(\overline{\mathbf{Y}} - \mu\right)$ is upper bounded by the minimum between $t_{\alpha(1-\delta)}$ and $\mathbb{E}\left[\phi\left(\overline{\mathbf{Y}} - \mu\right)\right] + \frac{\|\sigma\|_p\overline{\Phi}^{-1}(\alpha(1-\delta)/2)}{\sqrt{n}}$ (because these thresholds are deterministic). In addition, Prop. 2.4 and Proposition 2.8 (ii) give that with probability at least $1 - \alpha\delta$, $\mathbb{E}\left[\phi\left(\overline{\mathbf{Y}} - \mu\right)\right] \leq \frac{\mathbb{E}[\phi(\overline{\mathbf{Y}}-\mu)|\mathbf{Y}]}{B_W} + \frac{\|\sigma\|_p C_W}{B_W n}\overline{\Phi}^{-1}(\alpha\delta/2)$. The result follows by combining the two last expressions. $\quad\square$

Proof (Proof of Prop. 3.1). Remember the following inequality coming from the definition of the quantile q_α: for any fixed $\mathbf{Y}$

$$\mathbb{P}_W\left[\phi\left(\overline{\mathbf{Y}}_{[W]}\right) > q_\alpha(\phi, \mathbf{Y})\right] \le \alpha \le \mathbb{P}_W\left[\phi\left(\overline{\mathbf{Y}}_{[W]}\right) \ge q_\alpha(\phi, \mathbf{Y})\right], \qquad (17)$$

which will be useful in this proof. We have

$$\begin{aligned}
\mathbb{P}_{\mathbf{Y}}\left[\phi(\overline{\mathbf{Y}} - \mu) > q_\alpha(\phi, \mathbf{Y} - \mu)\right] &= \mathbb{E}_W\left[\mathbb{P}_{\mathbf{Y}}\left[\phi(\overline{(\mathbf{Y} - \mu)}_{[W]}) > q_\alpha(\phi, (\mathbf{Y} - \mu)_{[W]})\right]\right] \\
&= \mathbb{E}_{\mathbf{Y}}\left[\mathbb{P}_W\left[\phi\left(\overline{(\mathbf{Y} - \mu)}_{[W]}\right) > q_\alpha(\phi, \mathbf{Y} - \mu)\right]\right] \\
&\le \alpha.
\end{aligned} \qquad (18)$$

The first equality is due to the fact that the distribution of $\mathbf{Y}$ satisfies assumption (SA), hence the distribution of $(\mathbf{Y} - \mu)$ invariant by reweighting by (arbitrary) signs $W \in \{-1, 1\}^n$. In the second equality we used Fubini's theorem and the fact that for any arbitrary signs W as above $q_\alpha(\phi, (\mathbf{Y} - \mu)_{[W]}) = q_\alpha(\phi, \mathbf{Y} - \mu)$; finally the last inequality comes from (17). Let us define the event

$$\Omega = \left\{\mathbf{Y} \text{ s.t. } q_\alpha(\phi, \mathbf{Y} - \mu) \le q_{\alpha(1-\delta)}(\phi, \mathbf{Y} - \overline{\mathbf{Y}}) + f(\mathbf{Y})\right\};$$

then we have using (18):

$$\begin{aligned}
\mathbb{P}\left[\phi(\overline{\mathbf{Y}} - \mu) > q_{\alpha(1-\delta)}(\phi, \mathbf{Y} - \overline{\mathbf{Y}}) + f(\mathbf{Y})\right] & \\
&\le \mathbb{P}\left[\phi(\overline{\mathbf{Y}} - \mu) > q_\alpha(\phi, \mathbf{Y} - \mu)\right] + \mathbb{P}\left[\mathbf{Y} \in \Omega^c\right] \\
&\le \alpha + \mathbb{P}\left[\mathbf{Y} \in \Omega^c\right].
\end{aligned} \qquad (19)$$

We now concentrate on the event Ω^c. Using the subadditivity of ϕ, and the fact that $\overline{(\mathbf{Y} - \mu)}_{[W]} = \overline{(\mathbf{Y} - \overline{\mathbf{Y}})}_{[W]} + \overline{W}(\overline{\mathbf{Y}} - \mu)$, we have for any fixed $\mathbf{Y} \in \Omega^c$:

$$\begin{aligned}
\alpha &\le \mathbb{P}_W\left[\phi(\overline{(\mathbf{Y} - \mu)}_{[W]}) \ge q_\alpha(\phi, \mathbf{Y} - \mu)\right] \\
&\le \mathbb{P}_W\left[\phi(\overline{(\mathbf{Y} - \mu)}_{[W]}) > q_{\alpha(1-\delta)}(\phi, \mathbf{Y} - \overline{\mathbf{Y}}) + f(\mathbf{Y})\right] \\
&\le \mathbb{P}_W\left[\phi(\overline{(\mathbf{Y} - \overline{\mathbf{Y}})}_{[W]}) > q_{\alpha(1-\delta)}(\phi, \mathbf{Y} - \overline{\mathbf{Y}})\right] + \mathbb{P}_W\left[\phi(\overline{W}(\overline{\mathbf{Y}} - \mu)) > f(\mathbf{Y})\right] \\
&\le \alpha(1 - \delta) + \mathbb{P}_W\left[\phi(\overline{W}(\overline{\mathbf{Y}} - \mu)) > f(\mathbf{Y})\right].
\end{aligned}$$

For the first and last inequalities we have used (17), and for the second inequality the definition of Ω^c. From this we deduce that

$$\Omega^c \subset \left\{\mathbf{Y} \text{ s.t. } \mathbb{P}_W\left[\phi(\overline{W}(\overline{\mathbf{Y}} - \mu)) > f(\mathbf{Y})\right] \ge \alpha\delta\right\}.$$

Now using the homogeneity of ϕ, and the fact that both ϕ and f are nonnegative:

$$\mathbb{P}_W\left[\phi(\overline{W}(\overline{\mathbf{Y}}-\mu)) > f(\mathbf{Y})\right] = \mathbb{P}_W\left[|\overline{W}| > \frac{f(\mathbf{Y})}{\phi(\mathrm{sign}(\overline{W})(\overline{\mathbf{Y}}-\mu))}\right]$$

$$\leq \mathbb{P}_W\left[|\overline{W}| > \frac{f(\mathbf{Y})}{\widetilde{\phi}(\overline{\mathbf{Y}}-\mu)}\right]$$

$$= 2\mathbb{P}\left[\frac{1}{n}(2B_{n,\frac{1}{2}}-n) > \frac{f(\mathbf{Y})}{\widetilde{\phi}(\overline{\mathbf{Y}}-\mu)}\bigg|\mathbf{Y}\right],$$

where $B_{n,\frac{1}{2}}$ denotes a binomial $(n,\frac{1}{2})$ variable (independent of $\mathbf{Y}$). From the two last displays we conclude

$$\Omega^c \subset \left\{\mathbf{Y}\ \text{s.t.}\ \widetilde{\phi}(\overline{\mathbf{Y}}-\mu) > \frac{n}{2\overline{\mathcal{B}}\left(n,\frac{\alpha\delta}{2}\right)-n}f(\mathbf{Y})\right\},$$

which, put back in (19), leads to the desired conclusion.   □

Acknowledgements

We want to thank Pascal Massart for his particulary relevant suggestions.

References

1. Efron, B.: Bootstrap methods: another look at the jackknife. Ann. Statist. 7(1), 1–26 (1979)
2. Mason, D.M., Newton, M.A.: A rank statistics approach to the consistency of a general bootstrap. Ann. Statist. 20(3), 1611–1624 (1992)
3. Præstgaard, J., Wellner, J.A.: Exchangeably weighted bootstraps of the general empirical process. Ann. Probab. 21(4), 2053–2086 (1993)
4. Fromont, M.: Model selection by bootstrap penalization for classification. In: Shawe-Taylor, J., Singer, Y. (eds.) COLT 2004. LNCS (LNAI), vol. 3120, pp. 285–299. Springer, Heidelberg (2004)
5. Westfall, P.H., Young, S.S.: Resampling-Based Multiple Testing. Wiley, Examples and Methods for P- Value Adjustment (1993)
6. Ge, Y., Dudoit, S., Speed, T.P.: Resampling-based multiple testing for microarray data analysis (With comments and a rejoinder by the authors). Test. 12(1), 1–77 (2003)
7. Hall, P., Mammen, E.: On general resampling algorithms and their performance in distribution estimation. Ann. Statist. 22(4), 2011–2030 (1994)
8. Romano, J.P., Wolf, M.: Exact and approximate stepdown methods for multiple hypothesis testing. J. Amer. Statist. Assoc. 100(469), 94–108 (2005)
9. Hall, P.: The bootstrap and Edgeworth expansion. Springer Series in Statistics. Springer-Verlag, New York (1992)
10. Van der Vaart, A.W., Wellner, J.A.: Weak convergence and empirical processes (With applications to statistics). Springer Series in Statistics, p. 508. Springer-Verlag, New York (1996)
11. Massart, P.: Concentration inequalities and model selection (lecture notes of the St-Flour probability summer school 2003). (2005) Available online at http://www.math.u-psud.fr/~massart/stf2003_massart.pdf

Suboptimality of Penalized Empirical Risk Minimization in Classification

Guillaume Lecué*

Laboratoire de Probabilités et Modèles Aléatoires (UMR CNRS 7599)
Université Paris VI
4 pl.Jussieu, BP 188, 75252 Paris, France
lecue@ccr.jussieu.fr

Abstract. Let $\mathcal{F}$ be a set of M classification procedures with values in $[-1, 1]$. Given a loss function, we want to construct a procedure which mimics at the best possible rate the best procedure in $\mathcal{F}$. This fastest rate is called optimal rate of aggregation. Considering a continuous scale of loss functions with various types of convexity, we prove that optimal rates of aggregation can be either $((\log M)/n)^{1/2}$ or $(\log M)/n$. We prove that, if all the M classifiers are binary, the (penalized) Empirical Risk Minimization procedures are suboptimal (even under the margin/low noise condition) when the loss function is somewhat more than convex, whereas, in that case, aggregation procedures with exponential weights achieve the optimal rate of aggregation.

1 Introduction

Consider the problem of binary classification. Let $(\mathcal{X}, \mathcal{A})$ be a measurable space. Let (X, Y) be a couple of random variables, where X takes its values in $\mathcal{X}$ and Y is a random label taking values in $\{-1, 1\}$. We denote by π the probability distribution of (X, Y). For any function $\phi : \mathbb{R} \longmapsto \mathbb{R}$, define the $\phi-$risk of a real valued classifier $f : \mathcal{X} \longmapsto \mathbb{R}$ by

$$A^\phi(f) = \mathbb{E}[\phi(Y f(X))].$$

Many different losses have been discussed in the literature along the last decade (cf. [10,13,26,14,6]), for instance:

$\phi_0(x) = \mathbb{1}_{(x \leq 0)}$ classical loss or $0 - 1$ loss
$\phi_1(x) = \max(0, 1 - x)$ hinge loss (SVM loss)
$x \longmapsto \log_2(1 + \exp(-x))$ logit-boosting loss
$x \longmapsto \exp(-x)$ exponential boosting loss
$x \longmapsto (1 - x)^2$ squared loss
$x \longmapsto \max(0, 1 - x)^2$ 2-norm soft margin loss

We will be especially interested in losses having convex properties as it is considered in the following definition (cf. [17]).

---

* Paper to be considered for the Mark Fulk Award for the "best student paper".

N. Bshouty and C. Gentile (Eds.): COLT 2007, LNAI 4539, pp. 142–156, 2007.
© Springer-Verlag Berlin Heidelberg 2007

Definition 1. *Let $\phi : \mathbb{R} \longmapsto \mathbb{R}$ be a function and β be a positive number. We say that ϕ is $\beta-$**convex on** $[-1, 1]$ when*

$$[\phi'(x)]^2 \leq \beta \phi''(x), \quad \forall |x| \leq 1.$$

For example, logit-boosting loss is $(e/\log 2)-$convex, exponential boosting loss is $e-$convex, squared and $2-$norm soft margin losses are $2-$convex.

We denote by f_ϕ^* a function from $\mathcal{X}$ to $\mathbb{R}$ which minimizes A^ϕ over all real-valued functions and by $A_*^\phi \overset{\text{def}}{=} A^\phi(f_\phi^*)$ the minimal $\phi-$risk. In most of the cases studied f_ϕ^* or its sign is equal to the Bayes classifier

$$f^*(x) = \text{sign}(2\eta(x) - 1),$$

where η is the conditional probability function $x \longmapsto \mathbb{P}(Y = 1 | X = x)$ defined on $\mathcal{X}$ (cf. [3,26,34]). The Bayes classifier f^* is a minimizer of the ϕ_0-risk (cf. [11]).

Our framework is the same as the one considered, among others, by [27,33,7] and [29,17]. We have a family $\mathcal{F}$ of M classifiers $f_1, \ldots, f_M$ and a loss function ϕ. Our goal is to mimic the oracle $\min_{f \in \mathcal{F}}(A^\phi(f) - A_*^\phi)$ based on a sample D_n of n i.i.d. observations $(X_1, Y_1), \ldots, (X_n, Y_n)$ of (X, Y). These classifiers may have been constructed from a previous sample or they can belong to a dictionary of simple prediction rules like decision stumps. The problem is to find a strategy which mimics as fast as possible the best classifier in $\mathcal{F}$. Such strategies can then be used to construct efficient adaptive estimators (cf. [27,22,23,9]). We consider the following definition, which is inspired by the one given in [29] for the regression model.

Definition 2. *Let ϕ be a loss function. The remainder term $\gamma(n, M)$ is called* **optimal rate of aggregation for the** $\phi-$**risk**, *if the following two inequalities hold.*

i) *For any finite set $\mathcal{F}$ of M functions from $\mathcal{X}$ to $[-1, 1]$, there exists a statistic $\tilde{f}_n$ such that for any underlying probability measure π and any integer $n \geq 1$,*

$$\mathbb{E}[A^\phi(\tilde{f}_n) - A_*^\phi] \leq \min_{f \in \mathcal{F}}\left(A^\phi(f) - A_*^\phi\right) + C_1 \gamma(n, M). \tag{1}$$

ii) *There exists a finite set $\mathcal{F}$ of M functions from $\mathcal{X}$ to $[-1, 1]$ such that for any statistic $\tilde{f}_n$ there exists a probability distribution π such that for all $n \geq 1$*

$$\mathbb{E}\left[A^\phi(\tilde{f}_n) - A_*^\phi\right] \geq \min_{f \in \mathcal{F}}\left(A^\phi(f) - A_*^\phi\right) + C_2 \gamma(n, M). \tag{2}$$

Here C_1 and C_2 are absolute positive constants which may depend on ϕ. Moreover, when the above two properties i) and ii) are satisfied, we say that the procedure $\tilde{f}_n$, appearing in (1), is an **optimal aggregation procedure for the** $\phi-$**risk**.

The paper is organized as follows. In the next Section we present three aggregation strategies that will be shown to attain the optimal rates of aggregation.

Section 3 presents performance of these procedures. In Section 4 we give some proofs of the optimality of these procedures depending on the loss function. In Section 5 we state a result on suboptimality of the penalized Empirical Risk Minimization procedures and of procedures called selectors. In Section 6 we give some remarks. All the proofs are postponed to the last Section.

2   Aggregation Procedures

We introduce procedures that will be shown to achieve optimal rates of aggregation depending on the loss function $\phi : \mathbb{R} \longmapsto \mathbb{R}$. All these procedures are constructed with the empirical version of the $\phi-$risk and the main idea is that a classifier f_j with a small empirical $\phi-$risk is likely to have a small $\phi-$risk. We denote by

$$A_n^\phi(f) = \frac{1}{n} \sum_{i=1}^n \phi(Y_i f(X_i))$$

the empirical $\phi-$risk of a real-valued classifier f.

The Empirical Risk Minimization (**ERM**) procedure, is defined by

$$\tilde{f}_n^{ERM} \in \operatorname{Arg}\min_{f \in \mathcal{F}} A_n^\phi(f). \tag{3}$$

This is an example of what we call a **selector** which is an aggregate with values in the family $\mathcal{F}$. Penalized ERM procedures are also examples of selectors.

The Aggregation with Exponential Weights (**AEW**) procedure is given by

$$\tilde{f}_n^{AEW} = \sum_{f \in \mathcal{F}} w^{(n)}(f)f, \tag{4}$$

where the weights $w^{(n)}(f)$ are defined by

$$w^{(n)}(f) = \frac{\exp\left(-nA_n^\phi(f)\right)}{\sum_{g \in \mathcal{F}} \exp\left(-nA_n^\phi(g)\right)}, \quad \forall f \in \mathcal{F}. \tag{5}$$

The Cumulative Aggregation with Exponential Weights (**CAEW**) procedure, is defined by

$$\tilde{f}_{n,\beta}^{CAEW} = \frac{1}{n} \sum_{k=1}^n \tilde{f}_{k,\beta}^{AEW}, \tag{6}$$

where $\tilde{f}_{k,\beta}^{AEW}$ is constructed as in (4) based on the sample $(X_1,Y_1),\ldots,(X_k,Y_k)$ of size k and with the 'temperature' parameter $\beta > 0$. Namely,

$$\tilde{f}_{k,\beta}^{AEW} = \sum_{f \in \mathcal{F}} w_\beta^{(k)}(f)f, \text{ where } w_\beta^{(k)}(f) = \frac{\exp\left(-\beta^{-1}kA_k^\phi(f)\right)}{\sum_{g \in \mathcal{F}} \exp\left(-\beta^{-1}kA_k^\phi(g)\right)}, \quad \forall f \in \mathcal{F}.$$

The idea of the ERM procedure goes to Le Cam and Vapnik. Exponential weights have been discussed, for example, in [2,15,19,33,7,25,35,1] or in [32,8] in the on-line prediction setup.

3   Exact Oracle Inequalities

We now recall some known upper bounds on the excess risk. The first point of the following Theorem goes to [31], the second point can be found in [18] or [9] and the last point, dealing with the case of a $\beta-$convex loss function, is Corollary 4.4 of [17].

Theorem 1. *Let $\phi : \mathbb{R} \longmapsto \mathbb{R}$ be a bounded loss function. Let $\mathcal{F}$ be a family of M functions $f_1, \ldots, f_M$ with values in $[-1, 1]$, where $M \geq 2$ is an integer.*

i) The Empirical Risk Minimization procedure $\tilde{f}_n = \tilde{f}_n^{ERM}$ satisfies

$$\mathbb{E}[A^\phi(\tilde{f}_n) - A_*^\phi] \leq \min_{f \in \mathcal{F}}(A^\phi(f) - A_*^\phi) + C\sqrt{\frac{\log M}{n}}, \qquad (7)$$

where $C > 0$ is a constant depending only on ϕ.
ii) If ϕ is convex, then the CAEW procedure $\tilde{f}_n = \tilde{f}_n^{CAEW}$ with "temperature parameter" $\beta = 1$ and the AEW procedure $\tilde{f}_n = \tilde{f}_n^{AEW}$ satisfy (7).
iii) If ϕ is $\beta-$convex for a positive number β, then the CAEW procedure with "temperature parameter" β, satisfies

$$\mathbb{E}[A^\phi(\tilde{f}_{n,\beta}^{CAEW}) - A_*^\phi] \leq \min_{f \in \mathcal{F}}(A^\phi(f) - A_*^\phi) + \beta\frac{\log M}{n}.$$

4   Optimal Rates of Aggregation

To understand how behaves the optimal rate of aggregation depending on the loss we introduce a "continuous scale" of loss functions indexed by a non negative number h,

$$\phi_h(x) = \begin{cases} h\phi_1(x) + (1 - h)\phi_0(x) & \text{if } 0 \leq h \leq 1 \\ (h - 1)x^2 - x + 1 & \text{if } h > 1, \end{cases}$$

defined for any $x \in \mathbb{R}$, where ϕ_0 is the $0 - 1$ loss and ϕ_1 is the hinge loss.

This set of losses is representative enough since it describes different type of convexity: for any $h > 1$, ϕ_h is $\beta-$convex on $[-1, 1]$ with $\beta \geq \beta_h \stackrel{\text{def}}{=} (2h - 1)^2/(2(h - 1)) \geq 2$, for $h = 1$ the loss is linear and for $h < 1$, ϕ_h is non-convex. For $h \geq 0$, we consider

$$A_h(f) \stackrel{\text{def}}{=} A^{\phi_h}(f), f_h^* \stackrel{\text{def}}{=} f_{\phi_h}^* \text{ and } A_h^* \stackrel{\text{def}}{=} A_*^{\phi_h} = A^{\phi_h}(f_h^*).$$

Theorem 2. *Let $M \geq 2$ be an integer. Assume that the space $\mathcal{X}$ is infinite.*
If $0 \leq h < 1$, then the optimal rate of aggregation for the ϕ_h-risk is achieved by the ERM procedure and is equal to

$$\sqrt{\frac{\log M}{n}}.$$

For $h = 1$, *the optimal rate of aggregation for the ϕ_1−risk is achieved by the ERM, the AEW and the CAEW (with 'temperature' parameter $\beta = 1$) procedures and is equal to*

$$\sqrt{\frac{\log M}{n}}.$$

If $h > 1$ *then, the optimal rate of aggregation for the ϕ_h−risk is achieved by the CAEW, with 'temperature' parameter β_h and is equal to*

$$\frac{\log M}{n}.$$

5   Suboptimality of Penalized ERM Procedures

In this Section we prove a lower bound under the margin assumption for any selector and we give a more precise lower bound for penalized ERM procedures. First, we recall the definition of the margin assumption introduced in [30].

Margin Assumption(MA): *The probability measure π satisfies the margin assumption $MA(\kappa)$, where $\kappa \geq 1$ if we have*

$$\mathbb{E}[|f(X) - f^*(X)|] \leq c(A_0(f) - A_0^*)^{1/\kappa}, \tag{8}$$

for any measurable function f with values in $\{-1, 1\}$
We denote by $\mathcal{P}_\kappa$ the set of all probability distribution π satisfying $MA(\kappa)$.

Theorem 3. *Let $M \geq 2$ be an integer, $\kappa \geq 1$ be a real number, $\mathcal{X}$ be infinite and $\phi : \mathbb{R} \longmapsto \mathbb{R}$ be a loss function such that $a_\phi \stackrel{\text{def}}{=} \phi(-1) - \phi(1) > 0$. There exists a family $\mathcal{F}$ of M classifiers with values in $\{-1, 1\}$ satisfying the following.*
   Let $\tilde{f}_n$ be a selector with values in $\mathcal{F}$. Assume that $\sqrt{(\log M)/n} \leq 1/2$. There exists a probability measure $\pi \in \mathcal{P}_\kappa$ and an absolute constant $C_3 > 0$ such that $\tilde{f}_n$ satisfies

$$\mathbb{E}\left[A^\phi(\tilde{f}_n) - A_*^\phi\right] \geq \min_{f \in \mathcal{F}} \left(A^\phi(f) - A_*^\phi\right) + C_3 \left(\frac{\log M}{n}\right)^{\frac{\kappa}{2\kappa - 1}}. \tag{9}$$

Consider the penalized ERM procedure $\tilde{f}_n^{pERM}$ associated with $\mathcal{F}$, defined by

$$\tilde{f}_n^{pERM} \in \text{Arg}\min_{f \in \mathcal{F}}(A_n^\phi(f) + \text{pen}(f))$$

where the penalty function $\text{pen}(\cdot)$ satisfies $|\text{pen}(f)| \leq C\sqrt{(\log M)/n}, \forall f \in \mathcal{F}$, with $0 \leq C < \sqrt{2}/3$. Assume that $1188\pi C^2 M^{9C^2} \log M \leq n$. If $\kappa > 1$ then, there exists a probability measure $\pi \in \mathcal{P}_\kappa$ and an absolute constant $C_4 > 0$ such that the penalized ERM procedure $\tilde{f}_n^{pERM}$ satisfies

$$\mathbb{E}\left[A^\phi(\tilde{f}_n^{pERM}) - A_*^\phi\right] \geq \min_{f \in \mathcal{F}} \left(A^\phi(f) - A_*^\phi\right) + C_4\sqrt{\frac{\log M}{n}}.$$

Remark 1. *Inspection of the proof shows that Theorem 3 is valid for any family $\mathcal{F}$ of classifiers $f_1, \ldots, f_M$, with values in $\{-1, 1\}$, such that there exist points $x_1, \ldots, x_{2^M}$ in $\mathcal{X}$ satisfying $\{(f_1(x_j), \ldots, f_M(x_j)) : j = 1, \ldots, 2^M\} = \{-1, 1\}^M$.*

Remark 2. *If we use a penalty function such that $|\mathrm{pen}(f)| \leq \gamma n^{-1/2}, \forall f \in \mathcal{F}$, where $\gamma > 0$ is an absolute constant (i.e. $0 \leq C \leq \gamma(\log M)^{-1/2}$), then the condition "$1188\pi C^2 M^{9C^2} \log M \leq n$" of Theorem 3 is equivalent to "n greater than a constant".*

Theorem 3 states that the ERM procedure (and even penalized ERM procedures) cannot mimic the best classifier in $\mathcal{F}$ with rates faster than $((\log M)/n)^{1/2}$ if the basis classifiers in $\mathcal{F}$ are different enough, under a very mild condition on the loss ϕ. If there is no margin assumption (which corresponds to the case $\kappa = +\infty$), the result of Theorem 3 can be easily deduced from the lower bound in Chapter 7 of [11]. The main message of Theorem 3 is that such a negative statement remains true even under the margin assumption $MA(\kappa)$. Selectors aggregate cannot mimic the oracle faster than $((\log M)/n)^{1/2}$ in general. Under $MA(\kappa)$, they cannot mimic the best classifier in $\mathcal{F}$ with rates faster than $((\log M)/n)^{\kappa/(2\kappa-1)}$ (which is greater than $(\log M)/n$ when $\kappa > 1$). We know, according to Theorem 1, that the CAEW procedure mimics the best classifier in $\mathcal{F}$ at the rate $(\log M)/n$ if the loss is $\beta-$convex. Thus, penalized ERM procedures (and more generally, selectors) are suboptimal aggregation procedures when the loss function is $\beta-$convex even if we add the constraint that π satisfies $MA(\kappa)$.

We can extend Theorem 3 to a more general framework [24] and we obtain that, if the loss function associated with a risk is somewhat more than convex then it is better to use aggregation procedures with exponential weights instead of selectors (in particular penalized ERM or pure ERM). We do not know whether the lower bound (9) is sharp, i.e., whether there exists a selector attaining the reverse inequality with the same rate.

6   Discussion

We proved in Theorem 2 that the ERM procedure is optimal only for non-convex losses and for the borderline case of the hinge loss. But, for non-convex losses, the implementation of the ERM procedure requires minimization of a function which is not convex. This is hard to implement and not efficient from a practical point of view. In conclusion, the ERM procedure is theoretically optimal only for non-convex losses but in that case it is practically inefficient and it is practically efficient only for the cases where ERM is theoretically suboptimal.

For any convex loss ϕ, we have $\frac{1}{n} \sum_{k=1}^{n} A^\phi(\tilde{f}_{k,\beta}^{AEW}) \leq A^\phi(\tilde{f}_\beta^{CAEW})$. Next, less observations are used for the construction of $\tilde{f}_{k,\beta}^{AEW}, 1 \leq k \leq n - 1$, than for the construction of $\tilde{f}_{n,\beta}^{AEW}$. We can therefore expect the $\phi-$risk of $\tilde{f}_{n,\beta}^{AEW}$ to be smaller than the $\phi-$risk of $\tilde{f}_{k,\beta}^{AEW}$ for all $1 \leq k \leq n - 1$ and hence smaller than the $\phi-$risk of $\tilde{f}_{n,\beta}^{CAEW}$. Thus, the AEW procedure is likely to be an optimal aggregation procedure for the convex loss functions.

The hinge loss happens to be really hinge for different reasons. For losses "between" the $0-1$ loss and the hinge loss ($0 \le h \le 1$), the ERM is an optimal aggregation procedure and the optimal rate of aggregation is $\sqrt{(\log M)/n}$. For losses "over" the hinge loss ($h > 1$), the ERM procedure is suboptimal and $(\log M)/n$ is the optimal rate of aggregation. Thus, there is a breakdown point in the optimal rate of aggregation just after the hinge loss. This breakdown can be explained by the concept of margin : this argument has not been introduced here by the lack of space, but can be found in [24]. Moreover for the hinge loss we get, by linearity

$$\min_{f \in \mathcal{C}} A_1(f) - A_1^* = \min_{f \in \mathcal{F}} A_1(f) - A_1^*,$$

where $\mathcal{C}$ is the convex hull of $\mathcal{F}$. Thus, for the particular case of the hinge loss, "model selection" aggregation and "convex" aggregation are identical problems (cf. [21] for more details).

7   Proofs

Proof of Theorem 2: The optimal rates of aggregation of Theorem 2 are achieved by the procedures introduced in Section 2. Depending on the value of h, Theorem 1 provides the exact oracle inequalities required by the point (1) of Definition 2. To show optimality of these rates of aggregation, we need only to prove the corresponding lower bounds. We consider two cases: $0 \le h \le 1$ and $h > 1$. Denote by $\mathcal{P}$ the set of all probability distributions on $\mathcal{X} \times \{-1,1\}$.

Let $0 \le h \le 1$. It is easy to check that the Bayes rule f^* is a minimizer of the ϕ_h−risk. Moreover, using the inequality $A_1(f) - A_1^* \ge A_0(f) - A_0^*$, which holds for any real-valued function f (cf. [34]), we have for any prediction rules $f_1, \ldots, f_M$ (with values in $\{-1,1\}$) and for any finite set $\mathcal{F}$ of M real valued functions,

$$\inf_{\hat{f}_n} \sup_{\pi \in \mathcal{P}} \left(\mathbb{E}\left[A_h(\hat{f}_n) - A_h^* \right] - \min_{f \in \mathcal{F}}(A_h(f) - A_h^*) \right) \tag{10}$$

$$\ge \inf_{\hat{f}_n} \sup_{\substack{\pi \in \mathcal{P} \\ f^* \in \{f_1,\ldots,f_M\}}} \left(\mathbb{E}\left[A_h(\hat{f}_n) - A_h^* \right] \right) \ge \inf_{\hat{f}_n} \sup_{\substack{\pi \in \mathcal{P} \\ f^* \in \{f_1,\ldots,f_M\}}} \left(\mathbb{E}\left[A_0(\hat{f}_n) - A_0^* \right] \right).$$

Let N be an integer such that $2^{N-1} \le M$, $x_1, \ldots, x_N$ be N distinct points of $\mathcal{X}$ and w be a positive number satisfying $(N-1)w \le 1$. Denote by P^X the probability measure on $\mathcal{X}$ such that $P^X(\{x_j\}) = w$, for $j = 1, \ldots, N-1$ and $P^X(\{x_N\}) = 1 - (N-1)w$. We consider the cube $\Omega = \{-1,1\}^{N-1}$. Let $0 < \mathfrak{h} < 1$. For all $\sigma = (\sigma_1, \ldots, \sigma_{N-1}) \in \Omega$ we consider

$$\eta_\sigma(x) = \begin{cases} (1 + \sigma_j \mathfrak{h})/2 & \text{if } x = x_1, \ldots, x_{N-1}, \\ 1 & \text{if } x = x_N. \end{cases}$$

For all $\sigma \in \Omega$ we denote by π_σ the probability measure on $\mathcal{X} \times \{-1,1\}$ defined by its marginal P^X on $\mathcal{X}$ and its conditional probability function η_σ.

We denote by ρ the Hamming distance on Ω. Let $\sigma, \sigma' \in \Omega$ such that $\rho(\sigma, \sigma') = 1$. Denote by H the Hellinger's distance. Since $H^2\left(\pi_\sigma^{\otimes n}, \pi_{\sigma'}^{\otimes n}\right) = 2\left(1 - \left(1 - H^2(\pi_\sigma, \pi_{\sigma'})/2\right)^n\right)$ and $H^2(\pi_\sigma, \pi_{\sigma'}) = 2w(1 - \sqrt{1 - \mathfrak{h}^2})$, then, the Hellinger's distance between the measures $\pi_\sigma^{\otimes n}$ and $\pi_{\sigma'}^{\otimes n}$ satisfies

$$H^2\left(\pi_\sigma^{\otimes n}, \pi_{\sigma'}^{\otimes n}\right) = 2\left(1 - (1 - w(1 - \sqrt{1 - \mathfrak{h}^2}))^n\right).$$

Take w and $\mathfrak{h}$ such that $w(1 - \sqrt{1 - \mathfrak{h}^2}) \leq n^{-1}$. Then, $H^2\left(\pi_\sigma^{\otimes n}, \pi_{\sigma'}^{\otimes n}\right) \leq 2(1 - e^{-1}) < 2$ for any integer n.

Let $\sigma \in \Omega$ and $\hat{f}_n$ be an estimator with values in $\{-1, 1\}$ (only the sign of a statistic is used when we work with the $0 - 1$ loss). For $\pi = \pi_\sigma$, we have

$$\mathbb{E}_{\pi_\sigma}[A_0(\hat{f}_n) - A_0^*] \geq \mathfrak{h}w\mathbb{E}_{\pi_\sigma}\left[\sum_{j=1}^{N-1} |\hat{f}_n(x_j) - \sigma_j|\right].$$

Using Assouad's Lemma (cf. Lemma 1), we obtain

$$\inf_{\hat{f}_n} \sup_{\sigma \in \Omega} \left(\mathbb{E}_{\pi_\sigma}\left[A_0(\hat{f}_n) - A_0^*\right]\right) \geq \mathfrak{h}w\frac{N-1}{4e^2}. \tag{11}$$

Take now $w = (n\mathfrak{h}^2)^{-1}$, $N = \lceil \log M / \log 2 \rceil$, $\mathfrak{h} = \left(n^{-1}\lceil \log M / \log 2 \rceil\right)^{1/2}$. We complete the proof by replacing w, $\mathfrak{h}$ and N in (11) and (10) by their values.

For the case $h > 1$, we consider an integer N such that $2^{N-1} \leq M$, $N - 1$ different points $x_1, \ldots, x_N$ of $\mathcal{X}$ and a positive number w such that $(N-1)w \leq 1$. We denote by P^X the probability measure on $\mathcal{X}$ such that $P^X(\{x_j\}) = w$ for $j = 1, \ldots, N - 1$ and $P^X(\{x_N\}) = 1 - (N - 1)w$. Denote by Ω the cube $\{-1, 1\}^{N-1}$. For any $\sigma \in \Omega$ and $h > 1$, we consider the conditional probability function η_σ in two different cases. If $2(h - 1) \leq 1$ we take

$$\eta_\sigma(x) = \begin{cases} (1 + 2\sigma_j(h - 1))/2 & \text{if } x = x_1, \ldots, x_{N-1} \\ 2(h - 1) & \text{if } x = x_N, \end{cases}$$

and if $2(h - 1) > 1$ we take

$$\eta_\sigma(x) = \begin{cases} (1 + \sigma_j)/2 & \text{if } x = x_1, \ldots, x_{N-1} \\ 1 & \text{if } x = x_N. \end{cases}$$

For all $\sigma \in \Omega$ we denote by π_σ the probability measure on $\mathcal{X} \times \{-1, 1\}$ with the marginal P^X on $\mathcal{X}$ and the conditional probability function η_σ of Y knowing X.
Consider

$$\rho(h) = \begin{cases} 1 & \text{if } 2(h - 1) \leq 1 \\ (4(h - 1))^{-1} & \text{if } 2(h - 1) > 1 \end{cases} \text{ and } g_\sigma^*(x) = \begin{cases} \sigma_j & \text{if } x = x_1, \ldots, x_{N-1} \\ 1 & \text{if } x = x_N. \end{cases}$$

A minimizer of the ϕ_h-risk when the underlying distribution is π_σ is given by

$$f_{h,\sigma}^* \overset{\text{def}}{=} \frac{2\eta_\sigma(x) - 1}{2(h - 1)} = \rho(h)g_\sigma^*(x), \quad \forall x \in \mathcal{X},$$

for any $h > 1$ and $\sigma \in \Omega$.

When we choose $\{f^*_{h,\sigma} : \sigma \in \Omega\}$ for the set $\mathcal{F} = \{f_1, \ldots, f_M\}$ of basis functions, we obtain

$$\sup_{\{f_1,\ldots,f_M\}} \inf_{\hat{f}_n} \sup_{\pi \in \mathcal{P}} \left(\mathbb{E}\left[A_h(\hat{f}_n) - A^*_h \right] - \min_{j=1,\ldots,M} (A_h(f_j) - A^*_h) \right)$$

$$\geq \inf_{\hat{f}_n} \sup_{\substack{\pi \in \mathcal{P}: \\ f^*_h \in \{f^*_{h,\sigma}:\sigma\in\Omega\}}} \left(\mathbb{E}\left[A_h(\hat{f}_n) - A^*_h \right] \right).$$

Let σ be an element of Ω. Under the probability distribution π_σ, we have $A_h(f) - A^*_h = (h-1)\mathbb{E}[(f(X) - f^*_{h,\sigma}(X))^2]$, for any real-valued function f on $\mathcal{X}$. Thus, for a real valued estimator $\hat{f}_n$ based on D_n, we have

$$A_h(\hat{f}_n) - A^*_h \geq (h-1)w \sum_{j=1}^{N-1} (\hat{f}_n(x_j) - \rho(h)\sigma_j)^2.$$

We consider the projection function $\psi_h(x) = \psi(x/\rho(h))$ for any $x \in \mathcal{X}$, where $\psi(y) = \max(-1, \min(1, y)), \forall y \in \mathbb{R}$. We have

$$\mathbb{E}_\sigma[A_h(\hat{f}_n) - A^*_h] \geq w(h-1) \sum_{j=1}^{N-1} \mathbb{E}_\sigma(\psi_h(\hat{f}_n(x_j)) - \rho(h)\sigma_j)^2$$

$$\geq w(h-1)(\rho(h))^2 \sum_{j=1}^{N-1} \mathbb{E}_\sigma(\psi(\hat{f}_n(x_j)) - \sigma_j)^2$$

$$\geq 4w(h-1)(\rho(h))^2 \inf_{\hat{\sigma}\in[0,1]^{N-1}} \max_{\sigma\in\Omega} \mathbb{E}_\sigma \left[\sum_{j=1}^{N-1} |\hat{\sigma}_j - \sigma_j|^2 \right],$$

where the infimum $\inf_{\hat{\sigma}\in[0,1]^{N-1}}$ is taken over all estimators $\hat{\sigma}$ based on one observation from the statistical experience $\{\pi_\sigma^{\otimes n}|\sigma \in \Omega\}$ and with values in $[0,1]^{N-1}$.

For any $\sigma, \sigma' \in \Omega$ such that $\rho(\sigma, \sigma') = 1$, the Hellinger's distance between the measures $\pi_\sigma^{\otimes n}$ and $\pi_{\sigma'}^{\otimes n}$ satisfies

$$H^2\left(\pi_\sigma^{\otimes n}, \pi_{\sigma'}^{\otimes n}\right) = \begin{cases} 2\left(1 - (1 - 2w(1 - \sqrt{1-h^2}))^n\right) & \text{if } 2(h-1) < 1 \\ 2\left(1 - (1 - 2w(1 - \sqrt{3/4}))^n\right) & \text{if } 2(h-1) \geq 1 \end{cases}.$$

We take

$$w = \begin{cases} (2n(h-1)^2) & \text{if } 2(h-1) < 1 \\ 8n^{-1} & \text{if } 2(h-1) \geq 1. \end{cases}$$

Thus, we have for any $\sigma, \sigma' \in \Omega$ such that $\rho(\sigma, \sigma') = 1$,

$$H^2\left(\pi_\sigma^{\otimes n}, \pi_{\sigma'}^{\otimes n}\right) \leq 2(1 - e^{-1}).$$

To complete the proof we apply Lemma 1 with $N = \lceil (\log M)/n \rceil$.

Proof of Theorem 3: Consider $\mathcal{F}$ a family of classifiers $f_1, \ldots, f_M$, with values in $\{-1, 1\}$, such that there exist 2^M points $x_1, \ldots, x_{2^M}$ in $\mathcal{X}$ satisfying $\{(f_1(x_j), \ldots, f_M(x_j)) : j = 1, \ldots, 2^M\} = \{-1, 1\}^M \stackrel{\text{def}}{=} \mathcal{S}_M$.

Consider the lexicographic order on $\mathcal{S}_M$:

$$(-1, \ldots, -1) \preccurlyeq (-1, \ldots, -1, 1) \preccurlyeq (-1, \ldots, -1, 1, -1) \preccurlyeq \ldots \preccurlyeq (1, \ldots, 1).$$

Take j in $\{1, \ldots, 2^M\}$ and denote by x'_j the element in $\{x_1, \ldots, x_{2^M}\}$ such that $(f_1(x'_j), \ldots, f_M(x'_j))$ is the j-th element of $\mathcal{S}_M$ for the lexicographic order. We denote by φ the bijection between $\mathcal{S}_M$ and $\{x_1, \ldots, x_{2^M}\}$ such that the value of φ at the j-th element of $\mathcal{S}_M$ is x'_j. By using the bijection φ we can work independently either on the set $\mathcal{S}_M$ or on $\{x_1, \ldots, x_{2^M}\}$. Without any assumption on the space $\mathcal{X}$, we consider, in what follows, functions and probability measures on $\mathcal{S}_M$. Remark that for the bijection φ we have

$$f_j(\varphi(x)) = x^j, \quad \forall x = (x^1, \ldots, x^M) \in \mathcal{S}_M, \forall j \in \{1, \ldots, M\}.$$

With a slight abuse of notation, we still denote by $\mathcal{F}$ the set of functions $f_1, \ldots, f_M$ defined by $f_j(x) = x^j$, for any $j = 1, \ldots, M$.

First remark that for any f, g from $\mathcal{X}$ to $\{-1, 1\}$, using $\mathbb{E}[\phi(Yf(X))|X] = \mathbb{E}[\phi(Y)|X]\mathbb{I}_{(f(X)=1)} + \mathbb{E}[\phi(-Y)|X]\mathbb{I}_{(f(X)=-1)}$, we have

$$\mathbb{E}[\phi(Yf(X))|X] - \mathbb{E}[\phi(Yg(X))|X] = a_\phi(1/2 - \eta(X))(f(X) - g(X)).$$

Hence, we obtain $A^\phi(f) - A^\phi(g) = a_\phi(A_0(f) - A_0(g))$. So, we have for any $j = 1, \ldots, M$,

$$A^\phi(f_j) - A^\phi(f^*) = a_\phi(A_0(f_j) - A_0^*).$$

Moreover, for any $f : \mathcal{S}_M \longmapsto \{-1, 1\}$ we have $A_n^\phi(f) = \phi(1) + a_\phi A_n^{\phi_0}(f)$ and $a_\phi > 0$ by assumption, hence,

$$\tilde{f}_n^{pERM} \in \text{Arg} \min_{f \in \mathcal{F}}(A_n^{\phi_0}(f) + \text{pen}(f)).$$

Thus, it suffices to prove Theorem 3, when the loss function ϕ is the classical $0-1$ loss function ϕ_0.

We denote by $\mathcal{S}_{M+1}$ the set $\{-1, 1\}^{M+1}$ and by $X^0, \ldots, X^M$, $M+1$ independent random variables with values in $\{-1, 1\}$ such that X^0 is distributed according to a Bernoulli $\mathcal{B}(w, 1)$ with parameter w (that is $\mathbb{P}(X^0 = 1) = w$ and $\mathbb{P}(X^0 = -1) = 1 - w$) and the M other variables $X^1, \ldots, X^M$ are distributed according to a Bernoulli $\mathcal{B}(1/2, 1)$. The parameter $0 \leq w \leq 1$ will be chosen wisely in what follows.

For any $j \in \{1, \ldots, M\}$, we consider the probability distribution $\pi_j = (P^X, \eta^{(j)})$ of a couple of random variables (X, Y) with values in $S_{M+1} \times \{-1, 1\}$, where P^X is the probability distribution on $\mathcal{S}_{M+1}$ of $X = (X^0, \ldots, X^M)$ and $\eta^{(j)}(x)$ is the regression function at the point $x \in \mathcal{S}_{M+1}$, of $Y = 1$ knowing that $X = x$, given by

$$\eta^{(j)}(x) = \begin{cases} 1 & \text{if } x^0 = 1 \\ 1/2 + h/2 & \text{if } x^0 = -1, x^j = -1 \\ 1/2 + h & \text{if } x^0 = -1, x^j = 1 \end{cases}, \quad \forall x = (x^0, x^1, \ldots, x^M) \in \mathcal{S}_{M+1},$$

where $h > 0$ is a parameter chosen wisely in what follows. The Bayes rule f^*, associated with the distribution $\pi_j = (P^X, \eta^{(j)})$, is identically equal to 1 on $\mathcal{S}_{M+1}$.

If the probability distribution of (X, Y) is π_j for a $j \in \{1, \ldots, M\}$ then, for any $0 < t < 1$, we have $\mathbb{P}[|2\eta(X) - 1| \leq t] \leq (1 - w)\mathbb{I}_{h \leq t}$. Now, we take

$$1 - w = h^{\frac{1}{\kappa - 1}},$$

then, we have $\mathbb{P}[|2\eta(X) - 1| \leq t] \leq t^{\frac{1}{\kappa - 1}}$ and so $\pi_j \in \mathcal{P}_\kappa$.

We extend the definition of the f_j's to the set $\mathcal{S}_{M+1}$ by $f_j(x) = x^j$ for any $x = (x^0, \ldots, x^M) \in \mathcal{S}_{M+1}$ and $j = 1, \ldots, M$. Consider $\mathcal{F} = \{f_1, \ldots, f_M\}$. Assume that (X, Y) is distributed according to π_j for a $j \in \{1, \ldots, M\}$. For any $k \in \{1, \ldots, M\}$ and $k \neq j$, we have

$$A_0(f_k) - A_0^* = \sum_{x \in \mathcal{S}_{M+1}} |\eta(x) - 1/2||f_k(x) - 1|\mathbb{P}[X = x] = \frac{3h(1 - w)}{8} + \frac{w}{2}$$

and the excess risk of f_j is given by $A_0(f_j) - A_0^* = (1 - w)h/4 + w/2$. Thus, we have

$$\min_{f \in \mathcal{F}} A_0(f) - A_0^* = A_0(f_j) - A_0^* = (1 - w)h/4 + w/2.$$

First, we prove the lower bound for any selector. Let $\tilde{f}_n$ be a selector with values in $\mathcal{F}$. If the underlying probability measure is π_j for a $j \in \{1, \ldots, M\}$ then,

$$\mathbb{E}_n^{(j)}[A_0(\tilde{f}_n) - A_0^*] = \sum_{k=1}^{M} (A_0(f_k) - A_0^*)\pi_j^{\otimes n}[\tilde{f}_n = f_k]$$

$$= \min_{f \in \mathcal{F}}(A_0(f) - A_0^*) + \frac{h(1 - w)}{8}\pi_j^{\otimes n}[\tilde{f}_n \neq f_j],$$

where $\mathbb{E}_n^{(j)}$ denotes the expectation w.r.t. the observations D_n when (X, Y) is distributed according to π_j. Hence, we have

$$\max_{1 \leq j \leq M} \{\mathbb{E}_n^{(j)}[A_0(\tilde{f}_n) - A_0^*] - \min_{f \in \mathcal{F}}(A_0(f) - A_0^*)\} \geq \frac{h(1 - w)}{8} \inf_{\hat{\phi}_n} \max_{1 \leq j \leq M} \pi_j^{\otimes n}[\hat{\phi}_n \neq j],$$

where the infimum $\inf_{\hat{\phi}_n}$ is taken over all tests valued in $\{1, \ldots, M\}$ constructed from one observation in the model $(\mathcal{S}_{M+1} \times \{-1, 1\}, \mathcal{A} \times \mathcal{T}, \{\pi_1, \ldots, \pi_M\})^{\otimes n}$, where $\mathcal{T}$ is the natural σ−algebra on $\{-1, 1\}$. Moreover, for any $j \in \{1, \ldots, M\}$, we have

$$K(\pi_j^{\otimes n} | \pi_1^{\otimes n}) \le \frac{nh^2}{4(1 - h - 2h^2)},$$

where $K(P|Q)$ is the Kullback-Leibler divergence between P and Q (that is $\int \log(dP/dQ)dP$ if $P << Q$ and $+\infty$ otherwise). Thus, if we apply Lemma 2 with $h = ((\log M)/n)^{(\kappa-1)/(2\kappa-1)}$, we obtain the result.

Second, we prove the lower bound for the pERM procedure $\hat{f}_n = \tilde{f}_n^{pERM}$. Now, we assume that the probability distribution of (X, Y) is π_M and we take

$$h = \left(C^2 \frac{\log M}{n}\right)^{\frac{\kappa-1}{2\kappa}}. \tag{12}$$

We have $\mathbb{E}[A_0(\hat{f}_n) - A_0^*] = \min_{f \in \mathcal{F}}(A_0(f) - A_0^*) + \frac{h(1-w)}{8}\mathbb{P}[\hat{f}_n \ne f_M]$. Now, we upper bound $\mathbb{P}[\hat{f}_n = f_M]$, conditionally to $\mathcal{Y} = (Y_1, \ldots, Y_n)$. We have

$$\mathbb{P}[\hat{f}_n = f_M | \mathcal{Y}]$$
$$= \mathbb{P}[\forall j = 1, \ldots, M - 1, A_n^{\phi_0}(f_M) + \text{pen}(f_M) \le A_n^{\phi_0}(f_j) + \text{pen}(f_j) | \mathcal{Y}]$$
$$= \mathbb{P}[\forall j = 1, \ldots, M - 1, \nu_M \le \nu_j + n(\text{pen}(f_j) - \text{pen}(f_M)) | \mathcal{Y}],$$

where $\nu_j = \sum_{i=1}^n \mathbb{1}_{(Y_i X_i^j \le 0)}, \forall j = 1, \ldots, M$ and $X_i = (X_i^j)_{j=0,\ldots,M} \in \mathcal{S}_{M+1}, \forall i = 1, \ldots, n$. Moreover, the coordinates $X_i^j, i = 1, \ldots, n; j = 0, \ldots, M$ are independent, $Y_1, \ldots, Y_n$ are independent of $X_i^j, i = 1, \ldots, n; j = 1, \ldots, M - 1$ and $|\text{pen}(f_j)| \le h^{\kappa/(\kappa-1)}, \forall j = 1, \ldots, M$. So, we have

$$\mathbb{P}[\hat{f}_n = f_M | \mathcal{Y}] = \sum_{k=0}^n \mathbb{P}[\nu_M = k | \mathcal{Y}] \prod_{j=1}^{M-1} \mathbb{P}[k \le \nu_j + n(\text{pen}(f_j) - \text{pen}(f_M)) | \mathcal{Y}]$$

$$\le \sum_{k=0}^n \mathbb{P}[\nu_M = k | \mathcal{Y}] \left(\mathbb{P}[k \le \nu_1 + 2nh^{\kappa/(\kappa-1)} | \mathcal{Y}]\right)^{M-1}$$

$$\le \mathbb{P}[\nu_M \le \bar{k} | \mathcal{Y}] + \left(\mathbb{P}[\bar{k} \le \nu_1 + 2nh^{\kappa/(\kappa-1)} | \mathcal{Y}]\right)^{M-1},$$

where

$$\bar{k} = \mathbb{E}[\nu_M | \mathcal{Y}] - 2nh^{\kappa/(\kappa-1)}$$
$$= \frac{1}{2} \sum_{i=1}^n \left(\frac{2 - 4h}{2 - 3h} \mathbb{1}_{(Y_i=-1)} + \frac{1 + h^{1/(\kappa-1)}(h/2 - 1/2)}{1 + h^{1/(\kappa-1)}(3h/4 - 1/2)} \mathbb{1}_{(Y_i=1)}\right) - 2nh^{\kappa/(\kappa-1)}.$$

Using Einmahl and Masson's concentration inequality (cf. [12]), we obtain

$$\mathbb{P}[\nu_M \le \bar{k} | \mathcal{Y}] \le \exp(-2nh^{2\kappa/(\kappa-1)}).$$

Using Berry-Esséen's theorem (cf. p.471 in [4]), the fact that $\mathcal{Y}$ is independent of $(X_i^j; 1 \le i \le n, 1 \le j \le M-1)$ and $\bar{k} \ge n/2 - 9nh^{\kappa/(\kappa-1)}/4$, we get

$$\mathbb{P}[\bar{k} \le \nu_1 + 2nh^{\frac{\kappa}{\kappa-1}}|\mathcal{Y}] \le \mathbb{P}\left[\frac{n/2 - \nu_1}{\sqrt{n/2}} \le 6h^{\frac{\kappa}{\kappa-1}}\sqrt{n}\right] \le \Phi(6h^{\frac{\kappa}{\kappa-1}}\sqrt{n}) + \frac{66}{\sqrt{n}},$$

where Φ stands for the standard normal distribution function. Thus, we have

$$\mathbb{E}[A_0(\hat{f}_n) - A_0^*] \ge \min_{f \in \mathcal{F}}(A_0(f) - A_0^*) \tag{13}$$

$$+\frac{(1-w)h}{8}\left(1 - \exp(-2nh^{2\kappa/(\kappa-1)}) - \left(\Phi(6h^{\kappa/(\kappa-1)}\sqrt{n}) + 66/\sqrt{n}\right)^{M-1}\right).$$

Next, for any $a > 0$, by the elementary properties of the tails of normal distribution, we have

$$1 - \Phi(a) = \frac{1}{\sqrt{2\pi}}\int_a^{+\infty}\exp(-t^2/2)dt \ge \frac{a}{\sqrt{2\pi}(a^2+1)}e^{-a^2/2}. \tag{14}$$

Besides, we have for $0 < C < \sqrt{2}/6$ (a modification for $C = 0$ is obvious) and $(3376C)^2(2\pi M^{36C^2}\log M) \le n$, thus, if we replace h by its value given in (12) and if we apply (14) with $a = 16C\sqrt{\log M}$, then we obtain

$$\left(\Phi(6h^{\kappa/(\kappa-1)}\sqrt{n}) + 66/\sqrt{n}\right)^{M-1} \le \exp\left[-\frac{M^{1-18C^2}}{18C\sqrt{2\pi\log M}} + \frac{66(M-1)}{\sqrt{n}}\right]. \tag{15}$$

Combining (13) and (15), we obtain the result with $C_4 = (C/4)\left(1-\exp(-8C^2)-\exp(-1/(36C\sqrt{2\pi\log 2}))\right) > 0$. ∎

The following lemma is used to establish the lower bounds of Theorem 2. It is a version of Assouad's Lemma (cf. [28]). Proof can be found in [24].

Lemma 1. *Let $(\mathcal{X}, \mathcal{A})$ be a measurable space. Consider a set of probability $\{P_\omega/\omega \in \Omega\}$ indexed by the cube $\Omega = \{0,1\}^m$. Denote by $\mathbb{E}_\omega$ the expectation under P_ω. Let $\theta \ge 1$ be a number. Assume that:*

$$\forall \omega, \omega' \in \Omega/\rho(\omega, \omega') = 1, \ H^2(P_\omega, P_{\omega'}) \le \alpha < 2,$$

then we have

$$\inf_{\hat{w}\in[0,1]^m}\max_{\omega\in\Omega}\mathbb{E}_\omega\left[\sum_{j=1}^m|\hat{w}_j - w_j|^\theta\right] \ge m2^{-3-\theta}(2-\alpha)^2$$

where the infimum $\inf_{\hat{w}\in[0,1]^m}$ is taken over all estimator based on an observation from the statistical experience $\{P_\omega|\omega \in \Omega\}$ and with values in $[0,1]^m$.

We use the following lemma to prove the weakness of selector aggregates. A proof can be found p. 84 in [28].

Lemma 2. *Let* $\mathbb{P}_1, \ldots, \mathbb{P}_M$ *be* M *probability measures on a measurable space* $(\mathcal{Z}, \mathcal{T})$ *satisfying* $\dfrac{1}{M} \sum_{j=1}^{M} K(\mathbb{P}_j | \mathbb{P}_1) \leq \alpha \log M$, *where* $0 < \alpha < 1/8$. *We have*

$$\inf_{\hat{\phi}} \max_{1 \leq j \leq M} \mathbb{P}_j(\hat{\phi} \neq j) \geq \frac{\sqrt{M}}{1 + \sqrt{M}} \left(1 - 2\alpha - 2\sqrt{\frac{\alpha}{\log 2}} \right),$$

where the infimum $\inf_{\hat{\phi}}$ *is taken over all tests* $\hat{\phi}$ *with values in* $\{1, \ldots, M\}$ *constructed from one observation in the statistical model* $(\mathcal{Z}, \mathcal{T}, \{\mathbb{P}_1, \ldots, \mathbb{P}_M\})$.

References

1. Audibert, J.-Y.: A randomized online learning algorithm for better variance control. In: Lugosi, G., Simon, H.U. (eds.) COLT 2006. LNCS (LNAI), vol. 4005, pp. 392–407. Springer, Heidelberg (2006)
2. Barron, A., Li, J.: Mixture density estimation. Biometrics 53, 603–618 (1997)
3. Bartlett, P.L., Jordan, M.I., McAuliffe, J.D.: Convexity, classification, and risk bounds. Journal of the American Statistical Association 101(473), 138–156 (2006)
4. Bickel, P., Doksum, K.: Mathematical Statistics: Basic Ideas and Selected Topics, vol. 1. Prentice-Hall, Englewood Cliffs (2001)
5. Boucheron, S., Bousquet, O., Lugosi, G.: Theory of classification: some recent advances. ESAIM Probability and Statistics 9, 323–375 (2005)
6. Bühlmann, P., Yu, B.: Analyzing bagging. Ann. Statist. 30(4), 927–961 (2002)
7. Catoni, O.: Statistical Learning Theory and Stochastic Optimization. Ecole d'été de Probabilités de Saint-Flour 2001. Lecture Notes in Mathematics. Springer, Heidelberg (2001)
8. Cesa-Bianchi, N., Lugosi, G.: Prediction, Learning, and Games. Cambridge University Press, New York (2006)
9. Chesneau, C., Lecué, G.: Adapting to unknown smoothness by aggregation of thresholded wavelet estimators. Submitted (2006)
10. Cortes, C., Vapnik, V.: Support-vector networks. Machine Learning 20(3), 273–297 (1995)
11. Devroye, L., Györfi, L., Lugosi, G.: A Probabilistic Theory of Pattern Recognition. Springer, Heidelberg (1996)
12. Einmahl, U., Mason, D.: Some Universal Results on the Behavior of Increments of Partial Sums. Ann. Probab. 24, 2626–2635 (1996)
13. Freund, Y., Schapire, R.: A decision-theoric generalization of on-line learning and an application to boosting. Journal of Computer and System Sciences 55, 119–139 (1997)
14. Friedman, J., Hastie, T., Tibshirani, R.: Additive logistic regression: a statistical view of boosting. Ann. Statist. 28, 337–407 (2000)
15. Haussler, D., Kivinen, J., Warmuth, M.K.: Sequential prediction of individual sequences under general loss functions. IEEE Trans. on Information Theory 44(5), 1906–1925
16. Hartigan, J.: Bayesian regression using akaike priors. Yale University, New Haven, Preprint (2002)
17. Juditsky, A., Rigollet, P., Tsybakov, A.: Learning by mirror averaging. Preprint n.1034, LPMA

18. Juditsky, A., Nazin, A., Tsybakov, A.B., Vayatis, N.: Recursive Aggregation of Estimators by Mirror Descent Algorithm with averaging. Problems of Information Transmission 41(4), 368–384
19. Kivinen, J., Warmuth, M.K.: Averaging expert predictions. In: Fischer, P., Simon, H.U. (eds.) EuroCOLT 1999. LNCS (LNAI), vol. 1572, pp. 153–167. Springer, Heidelberg (1999)
20. Koltchinskii, V.: Local Rademacher Complexities and Oracle Inequalities in Risk Minimization (IMS Medallion Lecture). Ann. Statist. 34(6), 1–50 (2006)
21. Lecué, G.: Optimal rates of aggregation in classification. Submitted (2005)
22. Lecué, G.: Simultaneous adaptation to the margin and to complexity in classification. To appear in Ann. Statist (2005)
23. Lecué, G.: Optimal oracle inequality for aggregation of classifiers under low noise condition. In: Lugosi, G., Simon, H.U. (eds.) COLT 2006. LNCS (LNAI), vol. 4005, pp. 364–378. Springer, Heidelberg (2006)
24. Lecué, G.: Suboptimality of Penalized Empirical Risk Minimization. Manuscript (2006)
25. Leung, G., Barron, A.: Information theory and mixing least-square regressions. IEEE Transactions on Information Theory 52(8), 3396–3410 (2006)
26. Lugosi, G., Vayatis, N.: On the Bayes-risk consistency of regularized boosting methods. Ann. Statist. 32(1), 30–55 (2004)
27. Nemirovski, A.: Topics in Non-parametric Statistics, Ecole d'été de Probabilités de Saint-Flour 1998. Lecture Notes in Mathematics, vol. 1738. Springer, Heidelberg (2000)
28. Tsybakov, A.: Introduction à l'estimation non-paramétrique. Springer, Heidelberg (2004)
29. Tsybakov, A.B.: Optimal rates of aggregation. In: Schölkopf, B., Warmuth, M. (eds.) Computational Learning Theory and Kernel Machines. LNCS (LNAI), vol. 2777, pp. 303–313. Springer, Heidelberg (2003)
30. Tsybakov, A.B.: Optimal aggregation of classifiers in statistical learning. Ann. Statist. 32(1), 135–166 (2004)
31. Vapnik, V.N., Chervonenkis, A.Y.: Necessary and sufficient conditions for the uniform convergence of empirical means to their true values. Teor. Veroyatn. Primen. 26, 543–563 (1981)
32. Vovk, V.: Aggregating Strategies. In: Proceedings of the 3rd Annual Workshop on Computational Learning Theory, COLT1990, pp. 371–386. Morgan Kaufmann, San Francisco, CA (1990)
33. Yang, Y.: Mixing strategies for density estimation. Ann. Statist. 28(1), 75–87 (2000)
34. Zhang, T.: Statistical behavior and consistency of classification methods based on convex risk minimization. Ann. Statist. 32(1), 56–85 (2004)
35. Zhang, T.: Adaptive estimation in Pattern Recognition by combining different procedures. Statistica Sinica 10, 1069–1089 (2000)
36. Zhang, T.: From epsilon-entropy to KL-complexity: analysis of minimum information complexity density estimation, To appear in Ann. Statist (2006)

Transductive Rademacher Complexity and Its Applications

Ran El-Yaniv and Dmitry Pechyony

Computer Science Department
Technion - Israel Institute of Technology
{rani,pechyony}@cs.technion.ac.il

Abstract. We present data-dependent error bounds for transductive learning based on transductive Rademacher complexity. For specific algorithms we provide bounds on their Rademacher complexity based on their "unlabeled-labeled" decomposition. This decomposition technique applies to many current and practical graph-based algorithms. Finally, we present a new PAC-Bayesian bound for mixtures of transductive algorithms based on our Rademacher bounds.

1 Introduction

Transductive learning was already proposed and briefly studied more than thirty years ago [19], but only lately has it been empirically recognized that transduction can often facilitate more efficient or accurate learning than the traditional supervised learning approach (see, e.g., [8]). This recognition has motivated a flurry of recent activity focusing on transductive learning, with many new algorithms and heuristics being proposed. Nevertheless, issues such as the identification of "universally" effective learning principles for transduction remain unresolved. Statistical learning theory provides a principled approach to attack such questions through the study of error bounds. For example, in inductive learning such bounds have proven instrumental in characterizing learning principles and deriving practical algorithms.

So far, several general error bounds for transductive inference have been developed [20,6,9,12]. In this paper we continue this fruitful line of research and develop tight, high probability data-dependent error bounds for transduction based on the Rademacher complexity. Inspired by [16] (Theorem 24), our main result in this regard is Theorem 2, offering a sufficient condition for transductive learning. While this result is syntactically similar to known inductive Rademacher bounds (see, e.g., [3]), it is fundamentally different in the sense that the transductive Rademacher averages are taken with respect to hypothesis spaces that can depend on the unlabeled training and test examples. This opportunity is unavailable in the inductive setting where the hypothesis space must be fixed before any example is observed.

Our second contribution is a technique for establishing Rademacher bounds for specific algorithms based on their *unlabeled-labeled decomposition (ULD)*. In

N. Bshouty and C. Gentile (Eds.): COLT 2007, LNAI 4539, pp. 157–171, 2007.

this decomposition we present the algorithm as sgn($K\alpha$), where K is a matrix that depends on the unlabeled data and α is a vector that may depend on all given information including the labeled training set. We show that many state-of-the-art algorithms have non-trivial ULD leading to tight error bounds. In particular, we provide such bounds for the Gaussian random field transductive algorithm of [23], the "consistency method" of [22], the spectral graph transducer (SGT) algorithm of [15], the eigenmap algorithm of [5] and the Tikhonov regularization algorithm of [4].

We also show a simple Monte-Carlo scheme for bounding the Rademacher complexity of any transductive algorithm using its ULD. We demonstrate the efficacy of this scheme for the "consistency method" of [22]. Experimental evidence from [8] (Chapter 21) indicates that the SGT algorithm of [15] is amongst the better transductive algorithms currently known. Motivated by this fact we derived a specific error bound for this algorithm. Our final contribution is a PAC-Bayesian bound for transductive mixture algorithms. This result, which is stated in Theorem 3, is obtained as a consequence of Theorem 2 using the techniques of [17]. This result motivates the use of ensemble methods in transduction that are yet to be explored in this setting.

Related Work. Vapnik [20] presented the first general 0/1 loss bounds for transduction. His bounds are implicit in the sense that tail probabilities are specified in the bound as the outcome of a computational routine. Vapnik's bounds can be refined to include prior "beliefs" as noted in [9]. Similar implicit but somewhat tighter bounds were developed in [6] for the 0/1 loss case. Explicit PAC-Bayesian transductive bounds for any bounded loss function were presented in [9]. The bounds of [1] for semi-supervised learning also hold in the transductive setting, making them conceptually similar to some transductive PAC-Bayesian bounds. General error bounds based on stability were developed in [12].

Effective applications of the general bounds mentioned above to particular algorithms or "learning principles" is not automatic. In the case of the PAC-Bayesian bounds several such successful applications are presented in terms of appropriate "priors" that promote various structural properties of the data [9,11,13]. Ad-hoc bounds for particular algorithms were developed in [4,21].

Error bounds based on the Rademacher complexity are a well-established topic in induction (see [3] and references therein). The first Rademacher transductive risk bound was presented in [16]. This bound, which is a straightforward extension of the inductive Rademacher techniques of [3], is limited to the special case when training and test sets are of equal size. The bound presented here overcomes this limitation.

2   Transductive Rademacher Complexity

We begin with some definitions. Consider a fixed set $S_{m+u} = (\langle x_i, y_i \rangle)_{i=1}^{m+u}$ of $m + u$ points x_i in some space together with their labels y_i. The learner is provided with the (unlabeled) *full-sample* $X_{m+u} = \{x_i\}_{i=1}^{m+u}$. A set consisting of m points is selected from X_{m+u} uniformly at random among all subsets of size m. These m points together with their labels are given to the learner as a *training set*. Re-numbering the points we denote the training set points by $X_m = \{x_1, \ldots, x_m\}$ and the labeled training set by $S_m = (\langle x_i, y_i \rangle)_{i=1}^m$. The set $X_u \triangleq \{x_{m+1}, \ldots, x_{m+u}\} = X_{m+u} \setminus X_m$ is called the *test set*. The learner's goal is to predict the labels of the test points in X_u based on $S_m \cup X_u$.

This paper focuses on binary learning problems where labels $y \in \{\pm 1\}$. The learning algorithms we consider generate "soft classification" vectors $\mathbf{h} = (h(1), \ldots h(m+u)) \in \mathbb{R}^{m+u}$, where $h(i)$ (or $h(x_i)$) is the soft, or confidence-rated, label of example x_i given by the "hypothesis" $\mathbf{h}$. For actual (binary) classification of x_i the algorithm outputs $\mathrm{sgn}(h(i))$.

Based on the full-sample X_{m+u} the algorithm selects an hypothesis space $\mathcal{H}$ of such soft classification hypotheses. Then, given the labels of training points the algorithm selects one hypothesis from $\mathcal{H}$ for classification. The goal is to minimize its *test error* $\mathcal{L}_u(\mathbf{h}) \triangleq \frac{1}{u} \sum_{i=m+1}^{m+u} \ell(h(x_i), y_i)$ w.r.t. the $0/1$ loss function ℓ. In this work we use also the margin loss function ℓ_γ. For a positive real γ, $\ell_\gamma(y_1, y_2) = 0$ if $y_1 y_2 \geq \gamma$ and $\ell_\gamma(y_1, y_2) = \min\{1, \ 1 - y_1 y_2/\gamma\}$ otherwise. The *empirical (margin) error* of $\mathbf{h}$ is $\widehat{\mathcal{L}}_m^\gamma(\mathbf{h}) \triangleq \frac{1}{m} \sum_{i=1}^m \ell_\gamma(h(x_i), y_i)$. We denote by $\mathcal{L}_u^\gamma(\mathbf{h})$ the *test margin error*.

We adapt the inductive Rademacher complexity to our transductive setting but generalize it a bit to include "neutral" Rademacher values also.

Definition 1 (Transductive Rademacher Complexity). *Let* $\mathcal{V} \subseteq \mathbb{R}^{m+u}$ *and* $p \in [0, 1/2]$. *Let* $\boldsymbol{\sigma} = (\sigma_1, \ldots, \sigma_{m+u}\}$ *be a vector of i.i.d. random variables such that*

$$\sigma_i \triangleq \begin{cases} 1 & w.p. \quad p; \\ -1 & w.p. \quad p; \\ 0 & w.p. \quad 1 - 2p. \end{cases} \tag{1}$$

The Transductive Rademacher Complexity *with parameter p is* $R_{m+u}(\mathcal{V}, p) \triangleq (\frac{1}{m} + \frac{1}{u}) \cdot \mathbf{E}_{\boldsymbol{\sigma}} \{\sup_{\mathbf{v} \in \mathcal{V}} \boldsymbol{\sigma} \cdot \mathbf{v}\}$.

For the case $p = 1/2$ and $m = u$ the resulting transductive complexity coincides with the standard inductive definition (see, e.g., [3]) up to the normalization factor $(\frac{1}{m} + \frac{1}{u})$. Whenever $p < 1/2$, some Rademacher variables will obtain (neutral) zero values and reduce the complexity (see Lemma 1). We use this parameterized version of the complexity to tighten our bounds. Notice that the transductive complexity is an empirical quantity that does not depend on any underlying distribution. Also, the transductive complexity depends on the test points whereas the inductive complexity only depends on the (unlabeled) training points.

The following lemma states that $R_{m+u}(\mathcal{V}, p)$ is monotone increasing with p. The proof of the lemma is omitted and will appear in the full version. The proof of Lemma 1 is based on the technique used in the proof of Lemma 5 in [17].

Lemma 1. *For any* $\mathcal{V} \subseteq \mathbb{R}^{m+u}$ *and* $0 \leq p_1 < p_2 \leq 1/2$, $R_{m+u}(\mathcal{V}, p_1) < R_{m+u}(\mathcal{V}, p_2)$.

The statements that follow utilize the Rademacher complexity with $p_0 \triangleq \frac{mu}{(m+u)^2}$. We abbreviate $R_{m+u}(\mathcal{V}) \triangleq R_{m+u}(\mathcal{V}, p_0)$. By Lemma 1, all our bounds apply also to $R_{m+u}(\mathcal{V}, p)$ for all $p > p_0$.

3   Uniform Concentration Inequality for a Set of Vectors

Denote by I_r^s for the set of natural numbers $\{r, \ldots, s\}$ $(r < s)$. Let $\mathbf{Z} \triangleq \mathbf{Z}_1^{m+u} \triangleq (Z_1, \ldots, Z_{m+u})$ be a *random permutation vector* where the variable Z_k, $k \in I_1^{m+u}$, is the kth component of a permutation of I_1^{m+u} that is chosen uniformly at random. Let $\mathbf{Z}^{ij}$ be a perturbed permutation vector obtained by exchanging Z_i and Z_j in $\mathbf{Z}$. Any function f on permutations of I_1^{m+u} is called (m, u)-*permutation symmetric* if $f(\mathbf{Z}) \triangleq f(Z_1, \ldots, Z_{m+u})$ is symmetric on $Z_1, \ldots, Z_m$ as well as on $Z_{m+1}, \ldots, Z_{m+u}$.

The following lemma (that will be utilized in the proof of Theorem 1) presents a concentration inequality that is a slight extension of Lemma 2 from [12]. The argument relies on the Hoeffding-Azuma inequality for martingales (the proof will appear in the full version). Note that a similar but weaker statement can be extracted using the technique of [16] (Claim 2 of the proof of Theorem 24).[1]

Lemma 2 ([12]). *Let $\mathbf{Z}$ be a random permutation vector over I_1^{m+u}. Let $f(\mathbf{Z})$ be an (m, u)-permutation symmetric function satisfying $\left| f(\mathbf{Z}) - f(\mathbf{Z}^{ij}) \right| \leq \beta$ for all $i \in I_1^m$, $j \in I_{m+1}^{m+u}$. Then*

$$\mathbf{P_Z}\left\{ f(\mathbf{Z}) - \mathbf{E_Z}\left\{ f(\mathbf{Z}) \right\} \geq \epsilon \right\} \leq \exp\left(-\frac{\epsilon^2(m+u)}{2\beta^2 mu} \right). \qquad (2)$$

Let $\mathcal{V}$ be a set of vectors in $[B_1, B_2]^{m+u}$, $B_1 \leq 0$, $B_2 \geq 0$ and set $B \triangleq B_2 - B_1$, $B_{\max} = \max(|B_1|, |B_2|)$. Consider two independent permutations of I_1^{m+u}, $\mathbf{Z}$ and $\mathbf{Z}'$. For any $\mathbf{v} \in \mathcal{V}$ denote by $\mathbf{v}(\mathbf{Z}) \triangleq (v(Z_1), v(Z_2), \ldots, v(Z_{m+u}))$ the vector $\mathbf{v}$ permuted according to $\mathbf{Z}$. We use the following abbreviations for averages of $\mathbf{v}$ over subsets of its components: $\mathbf{H}_k\{\mathbf{v}(\mathbf{Z})\} \triangleq \frac{1}{m} \sum_{i=1}^k v(Z_i)$, $\mathbf{T}_k\{\mathbf{v}(\mathbf{Z})\} \triangleq \frac{1}{u} \sum_{i=k+1}^{m+u} v(Z_i)$ (note that $\mathbf{H}$ stands for 'head' and $\mathbf{T}$, for 'tail'). In the special case where $k = m$ we set $\mathbf{H}\{\mathbf{v}(\mathbf{Z})\} \triangleq \mathbf{H}_m\{\mathbf{v}(\mathbf{Z})\}$, and $\mathbf{T}\{\mathbf{v}(\mathbf{Z})\} \triangleq \mathbf{T}_m\{\mathbf{v}(\mathbf{Z})\}$. Finally, the average component of $\mathbf{v}$ is denoted $\bar{\mathbf{v}} \triangleq \frac{1}{m+u} \sum_{i=1}^{m+u} v(i)$.

---

[1] The idea in [16] is to represent a function of the permutation of $m + u$ indices as a function of independent random variables and use McDiarmid's bounded difference inequality for *independent* random variables. It is not hard to extend the result of [16] for $m = u$ to the general case of $m \neq u$, but the resulting concentration inequality would have a $1/(m + u)$ term instead of the $(m + u)/(mu)$ term as in our Lemma 2. We achieve this advantage by exploiting the (m, u)-symmetry. The resulting sharper bound is critical for obtaining converging error bounds using our techniques.

For any $\mathbf{v} \in \mathcal{V}$ and any permutation $\mathbf{Z}$ of I_1^{m+u} we have

$$\mathbf{T}\{\mathbf{v}(\mathbf{Z})\} = \mathbf{H}\{\mathbf{v}(\mathbf{Z})\} + \mathbf{T}\{\mathbf{v}(\mathbf{Z})\} - \mathbf{H}\{\mathbf{v}(\mathbf{Z})\}$$

$$\leq \mathbf{H}\{\mathbf{v}(\mathbf{Z})\} + \sup_{\mathbf{v} \in \mathcal{V}} \left[\mathbf{T}\{\mathbf{v}(\mathbf{Z})\} - \bar{\mathbf{v}} + \bar{\mathbf{v}} - \mathbf{H}\{\mathbf{v}(\mathbf{Z})\} \right]$$

$$= \mathbf{H}\{\mathbf{v}(\mathbf{Z})\} + \sup_{\mathbf{v} \in \mathcal{V}} \left[\mathbf{T}\{\mathbf{v}(\mathbf{Z})\} - \mathbf{E}_{\mathbf{Z}'}\mathbf{T}\{\mathbf{v}(\mathbf{Z}')\} + \mathbf{E}_{\mathbf{Z}'}\mathbf{H}\{\mathbf{v}(\mathbf{Z}')\} - \mathbf{H}\{\mathbf{v}(\mathbf{Z})\} \right]$$

$$\leq \mathbf{H}\{\mathbf{v}(\mathbf{Z})\} + \mathbf{E}_{\mathbf{Z}'} \underbrace{\sup_{\mathbf{v} \in \mathcal{V}} \left[\mathbf{T}\{\mathbf{v}(\mathbf{Z})\} - \mathbf{T}\{\mathbf{v}(\mathbf{Z}')\} + \mathbf{H}\{\mathbf{v}(\mathbf{Z}')\} - \mathbf{H}\{\mathbf{v}(\mathbf{Z})\} \right]}_{\triangleq g(\mathbf{Z})}.$$

The function $g(\mathbf{Z})$ is (m, u)-permutation symmetric in $\mathbf{Z}$. It can be verified that $|g(\mathbf{Z}) - g(\mathbf{Z}^{ij})| \leq B\left(\frac{1}{m} + \frac{1}{u}\right)$. Therefore, we can apply Lemma 2 with $\beta \triangleq B\left(\frac{1}{m} + \frac{1}{u}\right)$ to $g(\mathbf{Z})$. Since $\mathbf{T}\{\mathbf{v}(\mathbf{Z})\} - \mathbf{H}\{\mathbf{v}(\mathbf{Z})\} \leq g(\mathbf{Z})$, we obtain, with probability of at least $1 - \delta$ over random permutation $\mathbf{Z}$ of I_1^{m+u}, for all $\mathbf{v} \in \mathcal{V}$:

$$\mathbf{T}\{\mathbf{v}(\mathbf{Z})\} \leq \mathbf{H}\{\mathbf{v}(\mathbf{Z})\} + \mathbf{E}_{\mathbf{Z}}\{g(\mathbf{Z})\} + B\left(\frac{1}{m} + \frac{1}{u}\right)\sqrt{\frac{2mu}{m+u}\ln\frac{1}{\delta}}$$

$$= \mathbf{H}\{\mathbf{v}(\mathbf{Z})\} + \mathbf{E}_{\mathbf{Z}}\{g(\mathbf{Z})\} + B\sqrt{2\left(\frac{1}{m} + \frac{1}{u}\right)\ln\frac{1}{\delta}}. \tag{3}$$

Our goal is to bound the expectation $\mathbf{E}_{\mathbf{Z}}\{g(\mathbf{Z})\}$. For technical convenience we use the following definition of the Rademacher complexity with pairwise Rademacher variables. This definition is equivalent to Def. 1 with $p = \frac{mu}{(m+u)^2}$.

Definition 2. *Let* $\mathbf{v} = (v(1), \dots, v(m + u)) \in \mathbb{R}^{m+u}$. *Let* $\mathcal{V}$ *be a set of vectors from* $\mathbb{R}^{m+u}$. *Let* $\tilde{\boldsymbol{\sigma}} = \{\tilde{\sigma}_i\}_{i=1}^{m+u}$ *be a vector of i.i.d. random variables defined as:*

$$\tilde{\sigma}_i = (\tilde{\sigma}_{i,1}, \tilde{\sigma}_{i,2}) = \begin{cases} \left(-\frac{1}{m}, -\frac{1}{u}\right) & \text{with prob. } \frac{mu}{(m+u)^2} , \\ \left(-\frac{1}{m}, \frac{1}{m}\right) & \text{with prob. } \frac{m^2}{(m+u)^2} , \\ \left(\frac{1}{u}, \frac{1}{m}\right) & \text{with prob. } \frac{mu}{(m+u)^2} , \\ \left(\frac{1}{u}, -\frac{1}{u}\right) & \text{with prob. } \frac{u^2}{(m+u)^2} . \end{cases} \tag{4}$$

The "pairwise" transductive Rademacher complexity is defined to be

$$\tilde{R}_{m+u}(\mathcal{V}) \triangleq \mathbf{E}_{\tilde{\boldsymbol{\sigma}}} \left\{ \sup_{\mathbf{v} \in \mathcal{V}} \sum_{i=1}^{m+u} (\tilde{\sigma}_{i,1} + \tilde{\sigma}_{i,2})v(i) \right\}. \tag{5}$$

It is not hard to see from the definition of $\boldsymbol{\sigma}$ and $\tilde{\boldsymbol{\sigma}}$ that $R_{m+u}(\mathcal{V}) = \tilde{R}_{m+u}(\mathcal{V})$.

Lemma 3. *Let* $\mathbf{Z}$ *be a random permutation of* I_1^{m+u}. *Let* $c_0 = \sqrt{\frac{32\ln(4e)}{3}} < 5.05$. *Then*

$$\mathbf{E}_{\mathbf{Z}}\{g(\mathbf{Z})\} \leq \tilde{R}_{m+u}(\mathcal{V}) + c_0 B\left(\frac{1}{u} + \frac{1}{m}\right)\sqrt{\min(m, u)}. \tag{6}$$

Proof: The proof of Lemma 3 is based on ideas from the proof of Lemma 3 in [3]. Let n_1, n_2 and n_3 be the number of random variables $\tilde{\sigma}_i$ realizing the value

$\left(-\frac{1}{m}, -\frac{1}{u}\right)$, $\left(-\frac{1}{m}, \frac{1}{m}\right)$, $\left(\frac{1}{u}, \frac{1}{m}\right)$, respectively. Set $N_1 \triangleq n_1 + n_2$ and $N_2 \triangleq n_2 + n_3$. Note that the n_i's and N_i's are random variables. Denote by R the distribution of $\tilde{\boldsymbol{\sigma}}$ defined by (4) and by $\mathtt{R}(N_1, N_2)$, the distribution R conditioned on the events $n_1 + n_2 = N_1$ and $n_2 + n_3 = N_2$. We define

$$s(N_1, N_2) \triangleq \mathbf{E}_{\tilde{\boldsymbol{\sigma}} \sim \mathtt{R}(N_1, N_2)} \left\{ \sup_{\mathbf{v} \in \mathcal{V}} \sum_{i=1}^{m+u} (\tilde{\sigma}_{i,1} + \tilde{\sigma}_{i,2}) v(i) \right\}. \tag{7}$$

The rest of the proof is based on the following three claims:

Claim 1. $\tilde{R}_{m+u}(\mathcal{V}) = \mathbf{E}_{N_1, N_2} \{ s(N_1, N_2) \}$.
Claim 2. $\mathbf{E}_{\mathbf{Z}} g(\mathbf{Z}) \} = s \left(\mathbf{E}_{\tilde{\boldsymbol{\sigma}}} N_1, \mathbf{E}_{\tilde{\boldsymbol{\sigma}}} N_2 \right)$.
Claim 3. $s \left(\mathbf{E}_{\tilde{\boldsymbol{\sigma}}} N_1, \mathbf{E}_{\tilde{\boldsymbol{\sigma}}} N_2 \right) - \mathbf{E}_{N_1, N_2} \{ s(N_1, N_2) \} \leq c_0 B \left(\frac{1}{u} + \frac{1}{m} \right) \sqrt{m}$.

Having established these three claims we immediately obtain

$$\mathbf{E}_{\mathbf{Z}} \{ g(\mathbf{Z}) \} \leq \tilde{R}_{m+u}(\mathcal{V}) + c_0 B \left(\frac{1}{u} + \frac{1}{m} \right) \sqrt{m}. \tag{8}$$

The entire development is symmetric in m and u and, therefore, we also obtain the same result but with $\sqrt{u}$ instead of $\sqrt{m}$. By taking the minimum of (8) and the symmetric bound (with $\sqrt{u}$) we establish the theorem. It remains to prove the three claims.

Proof of Claim 1. Note that N_1 and N_2 are random variables whose distribution is induced by the distribution of $\tilde{\boldsymbol{\sigma}}$. We have

$$\tilde{R}_{m+u}(\mathcal{V}) = \mathbf{E}_{N_1, N_2} \mathbf{E}_{\tilde{\boldsymbol{\sigma}} \sim \mathtt{Rad}(N_1, N_2)} \sup_{\mathbf{v} \in \mathcal{V}} \sum_{i=1}^{m+u} (\tilde{\sigma}_{i,1} + \tilde{\sigma}_{i,2}) v(i) = \mathbf{E}_{N_1, N_2} s(N_1, N_2).$$

Proof of Claim 2. (Sketch) By the definitions of $\mathbf{H}_k$ and $\mathbf{T}_k$ (appearing just after Lemma 2), for any $N_1, N_2 \in I_1^{m+u}$ we have

$$\mathbf{E}_{\mathbf{Z}, \mathbf{Z}'} \sup_{\mathbf{v} \in \mathcal{V}} \left[\mathbf{T}_{N_1} \{ \mathbf{v}(\mathbf{Z}) \} - \mathbf{T}_{N_2} \{ \mathbf{v}(\mathbf{Z}') \} + \mathbf{H}_{N_2} \{ \mathbf{v}(\mathbf{Z}') \} - \mathbf{H}_{N_1} \{ \mathbf{v}(\mathbf{Z}) \} \right] =$$

$$\mathbf{E}_{\mathbf{Z}, \mathbf{Z}'} \sup_{\mathbf{v} \in \mathcal{V}} \left[\frac{1}{u} \sum_{i=N_1+1}^{m+u} v(Z_i) - \frac{1}{u} \sum_{i=N_2+1}^{m+u} v(Z_i') + \frac{1}{m} \sum_{i=1}^{N_2} v(Z_i') - \frac{1}{m} \sum_{i=1}^{N_1} v(Z_i) \right]. \tag{9}$$

The values of N_1 and N_2, and the distribution of $\mathbf{Z}$ and $\mathbf{Z}'$, with respect to which we take the expectation in (9), induce a distribution of assignments of coefficients $\{ \frac{1}{m}, -\frac{1}{m}, \frac{1}{u}, -\frac{1}{u} \}$ to the components of $\mathbf{v}$. For any N_1, N_2 and realizations of $\mathbf{Z}$ and $\mathbf{Z}'$, each component $v(i)$, $i \in I_1^{m+u}$, is assigned to exactly two coefficients, one for each of the two permutations ($\mathbf{Z}$ and $\mathbf{Z}'$). Let $\mathbf{a} \triangleq (a_1, \dots, a_{m+u})$, where $a_i \triangleq (a_{i,1}, a_{i,2})$. For any $i \in I_1^{m+u}$, the pair $(a_{i,1}, a_{i,2})$ takes the values of the coefficients of $v(i)$, where the first component is induced by the realization $\mathbf{Z}$ (i.e., $a_{i,1}$ is either $-\frac{1}{m}$ or $\frac{1}{u}$) and the second component by the realization of $\mathbf{Z}'$ (i.e., $a_{i,2}$ is either $\frac{1}{m}$ or $-\frac{1}{u}$).

Let $\mathtt{A}(N_1, N_2)$ be the distribution of vectors $\mathbf{a}$, induced by the distribution of $\mathbf{Z}$ and $\mathbf{Z}'$, for particular N_1, N_2. Using this definition we can write

$$(9) = \mathbf{E}_{\mathbf{a} \sim \mathtt{A}(N_1, N_2)} \sup_{v \in \mathcal{V}} \left[\sum_{i=1}^{m+u} (a_{i,1} + a_{i,2}) v(i) \right]. \tag{10}$$

We argue (the full proof will appear in the full version) that the distributions $\mathtt{R}(N_1, N_2)$ and $\mathtt{A}(N_1, N_2)$ are identical. Therefore, it follows from (10) that

$$(9) = \mathbf{E}_{\tilde{\sigma} \sim \mathtt{R}(N_1, N_2)} \left\{ \sup_{v \in \mathcal{V}} \left[\sum_{i=1}^{m+u} (\tilde{\sigma}_{i,1} + \tilde{\sigma}_{i,2}) v(i) \right] \right\} = s(N_1, N_2). \tag{11}$$

Note that $\mathbf{E}_{\tilde{\sigma}} N_1 = \mathbf{E}_{\tilde{\sigma}} \{n_1 + n_2\} = m$ and $\mathbf{E}_{\tilde{\sigma}} N_2 = \mathbf{E}_{\tilde{\sigma}} \{n_2 + n_3\} = m$. Hence

$$\mathbf{E}_{\mathbf{Z}} \{g(\mathbf{Z})\} = \mathbf{E}_{\tilde{\sigma} \sim \mathtt{Rad}(m,m)} \left\{ \sup_{v \in \mathcal{V}} \left[\sum_{i=1}^{m+u} (\tilde{\sigma}_{i,1} + \tilde{\sigma}_{i,2}) \, v(i) \right] \right\} = s\left(\mathbf{E}_{\tilde{\sigma}} N_1, \mathbf{E}_{\tilde{\sigma}} N_2 \right).$$

Proof of Claim 3. (Sketch) Abbreviate $Q \triangleq \frac{1}{m} + \frac{1}{u}$. For any $1 \leq N_1, N_2, N_1', N_2' \leq m + u$ we have (the technical proof will appear in the full version),

$$|s(N_1, N_2) - s(N_1', N_2)| \leq B_{\max} |N_1 - N_1'| Q \,, \tag{12}$$

$$|s(N_1, N_2) - s(N_1, N_2')| \leq B_{\max} |N_2 - N_2'| Q \,. \tag{13}$$

We use the following Bernstein-type concentration inequality (see [10], Problem 8.3) for the Binomial random variable $X \sim \mathrm{Bin}(p, n)$: $\mathbf{P}_X \{|X - \mathbf{E}X| > t\} < 2 \exp\left(-\frac{3t^2}{8np}\right)$. Noting that $N_1, N_2 \sim \mathrm{Bin}\left(\frac{m}{m+u}, m+u\right)$, we use (12), (13) and the Bernstein-type inequality (applied with $n \triangleq m + u$ and $p \triangleq \frac{m}{m+u}$) to obtain

$$\mathbf{P}_{N_1, N_2} \{|s(N_1, N_2) - s(\mathbf{E}_{\tilde{\sigma}} \{N_1\}, \mathbf{E}_{\tilde{\sigma}} \{N_2\})| \geq \epsilon\}$$

$$\leq \mathbf{P}_{N_1, N_2} \{|s(N_1, N_2) - s(N_1, \mathbf{E}_{\tilde{\sigma}} N_2)| + |s(N_1, \mathbf{E}_{\tilde{\sigma}} N_2) - s(\mathbf{E}_{\tilde{\sigma}} N_1, \mathbf{E}_{\tilde{\sigma}} N_2)| \geq \epsilon\}$$

$$\leq \mathbf{P}_{N_1, N_2} \left\{|s(N_1, N_2) - s(N_1, \mathbf{E}_{\tilde{\sigma}} N_2)| \geq \frac{\epsilon}{2}\right\}$$

$$+ \mathbf{P}_{N_1, N_2} \left\{|s(N_1, \mathbf{E}_{\tilde{\sigma}} N_2) - s(\mathbf{E}_{\tilde{\sigma}} N_1, \mathbf{E}_{\tilde{\sigma}} N_2)| \geq \frac{\epsilon}{2}\right\}$$

$$\leq \mathbf{P}_{N_2} \left\{|N_2 - \mathbf{E}_{\tilde{\sigma}} N_2| B_{\max} Q \geq \frac{\epsilon}{2}\right\} + \mathbf{P}_{N_1} \left\{|N_1 - \mathbf{E}_{\tilde{\sigma}} N_1| B_{\max} Q \geq \frac{\epsilon}{2}\right\}$$

$$\leq 4 \exp\left(-\frac{3\epsilon^2}{32(m+u)\frac{m}{m+u} B_{\max}^2 Q^2}\right) = 4 \exp\left(-\frac{3\epsilon^2}{32m B_{\max}^2 Q^2}\right).$$

Next we use the following fact (see [10], Problem 12.1): if a nonnegative random variable X satisfies $\mathbf{P}\{X > t\} \leq c \cdot \exp(-kt^2)$, then $\mathbf{E}X \leq \sqrt{\ln(ce)/k}$. Using this fact with $c \triangleq 4$ and $k \triangleq 3/(32mQ^2)$ we have

$$|\mathbf{E}_{N_1, N_2} \{s(N_1, N_2)\} - s(\mathbf{E}_{\tilde{\sigma}} N_1, \mathbf{E}_{\tilde{\sigma}} N_2)| \leq \mathbf{E}_{N_1, N_2} |s(N_1, N_2) - s(\mathbf{E}_{\tilde{\sigma}} N_1, \mathbf{E}_{\tilde{\sigma}} N_2)|$$

$$\leq \sqrt{\frac{32 \ln(4e)}{3} m B_{\max}^2 Q^2}. \tag{14}$$

$\square$

By combining (3) and Lemma 3 we obtain the next concentration inequality, which is the main result of this section.

Theorem 1. *Let $B_1 \leq 0$, $B_2 \geq 0$ and $\mathcal{V}$ be a (possibly infinite) set of real-valued vectors in $[B_1, B_2]^{m+u}$. Let $B \triangleq B_2 - B_1$ and $B_{\max} \triangleq \max(|B_1|, |B_2|)$. Let $Q \triangleq \left(\frac{1}{u} + \frac{1}{m}\right)$. Then with probability of at least $1-\delta$ over random permutation $\mathbf{Z}$ of I_1^{m+u}, for all $\mathbf{v} \in \mathcal{V}$,*

$$\mathbf{T}\{\mathbf{v}(\mathbf{Z})\} \leq \mathbf{H}\{\mathbf{v}(\mathbf{Z})\} + R_{m+u}(\mathcal{V}) + B_{\max} c_0 Q \sqrt{\min(m, u)} + B\sqrt{2Q \ln \frac{1}{\delta}}. \quad (15)$$

4   Uniform Rademacher Error Bound

Our goal now is to utilize the concentration inequality of Theorem 1 to derive a uniform error bound for all soft labelings $\mathbf{h} \in \mathcal{H}$ of the full-sample. The idea is to apply Theorem 1 with an appropriate instantiation of the set $\mathcal{V}$ so that $\mathbf{T}\{\mathbf{v}(\mathbf{Z})\}$ will correspond to the test error and $\mathbf{H}\{\mathbf{v}(\mathbf{Z})\}$ to the empirical error. The following lemma will be used in this analysis. The lemma is an adaptation, which accommodates the transductive Rademacher variables, of Lemma 5 from [17]. The proof is omitted (but will be provided in the full version).

Lemma 4. *Let $\mathcal{H} \subseteq \mathbb{R}^{m+u}$ be a set of vectors. Let f and g be real-valued functions. Let $\boldsymbol{\sigma} = \{\sigma_i\}_{i=1}^{m+u}$ be Rademacher variables, as defined in (1). If for all $1 \leq i \leq m+u$ and any $\mathbf{h}, \mathbf{h}' \in \mathcal{H}$, $|f(h(i)) - f(h'(i))| \leq |g(h(i)) - g(h'(i))|$, then*

$$\mathbf{E}_{\boldsymbol{\sigma}} \sup_{\mathbf{h} \in \mathcal{H}} \left[\sum_{i=1}^{m+u} \sigma_i f(h(i))\right] \leq \mathbf{E}_{\boldsymbol{\sigma}} \sup_{\mathbf{h} \in \mathcal{H}} \left[\sum_{i=1}^{m+u} \sigma_i g(h(i))\right]. \quad (16)$$

Let $Y \in \{\pm 1\}^{m+u}$, and denote by $Y(i)$ the ith component of Y. For any Y define $\ell_\gamma^Y(h(i)) \triangleq \ell_\gamma(h(i), Y(i))$. Noting that ℓ_γ^Y satisfies the Lipschitz condition $|\ell_\gamma^Y(h(i)) - \ell_\gamma^Y(h'(i))| \leq \frac{1}{\gamma}|h(i) - h'(i)|$, we apply Lemma 4 with the functions $f(h(i)) = \ell_\gamma^Y(h(i))$ and $g(h(i)) = h(i)/\gamma$, to get

$$\mathbf{E}_{\boldsymbol{\sigma}} \left\{\sup_{\mathbf{h} \in \mathcal{H}} \sum_{i=1}^{m+u} \sigma_i \ell_\gamma^Y(h(i))\right\} \leq \frac{1}{\gamma} \mathbf{E}_{\boldsymbol{\sigma}} \left\{\sup_{\mathbf{h} \in \mathcal{H}} \sum_{i=1}^{m+u} \sigma_i h(i)\right\}. \quad (17)$$

For any Y, define $\boldsymbol{\ell}_\gamma^Y(\mathbf{h}) \triangleq (\ell_\gamma^Y(h(1)), \ldots, \ell_\gamma^Y(h(m+u)))$. Taking Y to be the true (unknown) labeling of the full-sample, we set $L_{\mathcal{H}}^\gamma = \{\mathbf{v} \,:\, \mathbf{v} = \boldsymbol{\ell}_\gamma^Y(\mathbf{h}), \mathbf{h} \in \mathcal{H}\}$. It follows from (17) that $R_{m+u}(L_{\mathcal{H}}^\gamma) \leq \frac{1}{\gamma} R_{m+u}(\mathcal{H})$. Applying Theorem 1 with $\mathbf{v} \triangleq \boldsymbol{\ell}_\gamma(\mathbf{h})$, $\mathcal{V} \triangleq L_{\mathcal{H}}^\gamma$, $B_{\max} = B = 1$, and using the last inequality we obtain:[2]

---

[2] This bound holds for any *fixed* margin parameter γ. Using the technique of the proof of Theorem 18 in [7] we can also obtain a bound that is uniform in γ.

Theorem 2. *Let $\mathcal{H}$ be any set of full-sample soft labelings. The choice of $\mathcal{H}$ can depend on the full-sample X_{m+u}. Let $c_0 = \sqrt{\frac{32 \ln(4e)}{3}} < 5.05$ and $Q \stackrel{\Delta}{=} \left(\frac{1}{u} + \frac{1}{m}\right)$. For any fixed γ, with probability of at least $1 - \delta$ over the choice of the training set from X_{m+u}, for all $\mathbf{h} \in \mathcal{H}$,*

$$\mathcal{L}_u(\mathbf{h}) \leq \mathcal{L}_u^{\gamma}(\mathbf{h}) \leq \widehat{\mathcal{L}}_m^{\gamma}(\mathbf{h}) + \frac{R_{m+u}(\mathcal{H})}{\gamma} + c_0 Q \sqrt{\min(m, u)} + \sqrt{2Q \ln \frac{1}{\delta}}. \quad (18)$$

5   Bounds for Unlabeled-Labeled Decompositions (ULDs)

Let r be any natural number and let K be an $(m + u) \times r$ matrix depending only on X_{m+u}. Let $\boldsymbol{\alpha}$ be an $r \times 1$ vector that may depend on both S_m and X_u. The soft classification output $\mathbf{y}$ of any transductive algorithm can be represented by

$$\mathbf{y} = K \cdot \boldsymbol{\alpha}. \quad (19)$$

We refer to (19) as an *unlabeled-labeled decomposition (ULD)*. In this section we develop bounds on the Rademacher complexity of algorithms based on their ULDs. We note that any transductive algorithm has a trivial ULD, for example, by taking $r = m + u$, setting K to be the identity matrix and assigning $\boldsymbol{\alpha}$ to any desired (soft) labels. We are interested in "non-trivial" ULDs and provide useful bounds for such decompositions.[3]

In a "vanilla" ULD, K is an $(m + u) \times (m + u)$ matrix and $\boldsymbol{\alpha} = (\alpha_1, \ldots, \alpha_{m+u})$ simply specifies the given labels in S_m (where $\alpha_i \in \{\pm 1\}$ for labeled points, and $\alpha_i = 0$ otherwise). From our point of view any vanilla ULD is not trivial because $\boldsymbol{\alpha}$ does not encode the final classification of the algorithm. For example, the algorithm of Zhou et al. [22] straightforwardly admits a vanilla ULD. On the other hand, the natural (non-trivial) ULD of the algorithms of Zhu et al. [23] and of Belkin and Niyogi [5] is not of the vanilla type. For some algorithms it is not necessarily obvious how to find non-tirivial ULDs. Later we mention such cases – in particular, the algorithms of Joachims [15] and of Belkin et al. [4].

We now present a bound on the transductive Rademacher complexity of any transductive algorithm basing on their ULD. Let $\{\lambda_i\}_{i=1}^r$ be the singular values of K. We use the well-known fact that $\|K\|_{\text{Fro}} = \sqrt{\sum_{i=1}^r \lambda_i^2}$, where $\|K\|_{\text{Fro}} \stackrel{\Delta}{=} \sqrt{\sum_{i,j}(K(i,j))^2}$ is the Frobenius norm of K. Suppose that $\|\boldsymbol{\alpha}\|_2 \leq \mu_1$ for some μ_1. Let $\mathcal{H} \stackrel{\Delta}{=} \mathcal{H}(K)$ be the transductive hypothesis space induced by the matrix K; that is, $\mathcal{H}$ is the set of all possible outputs of the algorithm corresponding to a fixed full-sample X_{m+u}, all possible training/test partitions and all possible labelings of the training set. Using the abbreviation $K(i, \cdot)$ for the ith row of K and following the proof idea of Lemma 22 in [3], we obtain (the complete derivation will appear in the full version),

---

[3] For the trivial decomposition where K is the identity matrix it can be shown that the risk bound (18), combined with the forthcoming Rademacher complexity bound (20), is greater than 1 (the proof will be provided in the full version).

$$R_{m+u}(\mathcal{H}) = \mathbf{E}_\sigma \left\{ \sup_{h \in \mathcal{H}} \sum_{i=1}^{m+u} \sigma_i h(x_i) \right\} = \mathbf{E}_\sigma \left\{ \sup_{\alpha : \|\alpha\|_2 \leq \mu_1} \sum_{i=1}^{m+u} \sigma_i \langle \alpha, K(i, \cdot) \rangle \right\}$$

$$\leq \mu_1 \sqrt{ \sum_{i=1}^{m+u} \frac{2}{mu} \langle K(i, \cdot), K(i, \cdot) \rangle } = \mu_1 \sqrt{ \frac{2}{mu} \|K\|_{\mathrm{Fro}}^2 } = \mu_1 \sqrt{ \frac{2}{mu} \sum_{i=1}^{r} \lambda_i^2 } , \quad (20)$$

where the inequality is obtained using the Cauchy-Schwartz and Jensen inequalities. Using the bound (20) in conjunction with Theorem 2 we get a data-dependent error bound for any algorithm, that can be computed once we derive an upper bound on the maximal length of possible values of the α vector, appearing in its ULD. Notice that for any vanilla ULD, $\mu_1 = \sqrt{m}$. Later on we derive a tight μ_1 for non-trivial ULDs of SGT [15] and of the "consistency method" [22].

The bound (20) is syntactically similar in form to a corresponding inductive Rademacher bound of kernel machines [3]. However, as noted above, the fundamental difference is that in induction, the choice of the kernel (and therefore $\mathcal{H}$) must be *data-independent* in the sense that it must be selected before the training examples are observed. In our transductive setting, K and $\mathcal{H}$ can be selected based on the unlabeled full-sample.

5.1   Example: Analysis of SGT

We now exemplify the use of the ULD Rademacher bound (20) and analyze the SGT algorithm [15]. We start with a description of a simplified version of SGT that captures the essence of the algorithm.[4] Let W be a symmetric $(m + u) \times (m + u)$ similarity matrix of the full-sample X_{m+u}. The matrix W can be built in various ways, for example, it can be a k-nearest neighbors graph. Let D be a diagonal matrix, whose (i, i)th entry is the sum of the ith row in W. An unnormalized Laplacian of W is $L = D - W$. Let $\tau = (\tau_1, \ldots, \tau_{m+u})$ be a vector that specifies the given labels in S_m; that is, $\tau_i \in \{\pm 1\}$ for labeled points, and $\tau_i = 0$ otherwise. Let c be a fixed constant and $\mathbf{1}$ be an $(m + u) \times 1$ vector whose entries are 1 and let C be a diagonal matrix such that $C(i, i) = 1$ iff example i is in the training set (and zero otherwise). The soft classification $\mathbf{h}^*$ produced by the SGT algorithm is the solution of the following optimization problem:

$$\min_{\mathbf{h} \in \mathbb{R}^{m+u}} \mathbf{h}^T L \mathbf{h} + c(\mathbf{h} - \tau)^T C(\mathbf{h} - \tau) \quad (21)$$

$$s.t. \; \mathbf{h}^T \mathbf{1} = 0, \qquad \mathbf{h}^T \mathbf{h} = m + u. \quad (22)$$

It is shown in [15] that $\mathbf{h}^* = K\alpha$, where K is an $(m+u) \times r$ matrix[5] whose columns are orthonormal eigenvectors corresponding to non-zero eigenvalues of the Laplacian L and α is an $r \times 1$ vector. While α depends on both the training and test sets, the matrix K depends only on the unlabeled full-sample. Substituting $\mathbf{h}^* = K\alpha$ to the second constraint in (22) and using the orthonormality of the columns of

---

[4] We omit some heuristics that are optional in SGT. Their inclusion does not affect the error bound we derive.

[5] r is the number of non-zero eigenvalues of L, after performing spectral transformations. Joachims set the default r to 80.

K, we get $m + u = \mathbf{h}^T\mathbf{h} = \boldsymbol{\alpha}^T K^T K \boldsymbol{\alpha} = \boldsymbol{\alpha}^T \boldsymbol{\alpha}$. Hence, $\|\boldsymbol{\alpha}\|_2 = \sqrt{m+u}$ and we can take $\mu_1 = \sqrt{m+u}$. Since K is an $(m + u) \times r$ matrix with orthonormal columns, $\|K\|_{\mathrm{Fro}}^2 = r$. Consequently, by (20) the transductive Rademacher complexity of SGT is upper bounded by $\sqrt{2r\left(\frac{1}{m} + \frac{1}{u}\right)}$, where r is the number of non-zero eigenvalues of L. Notice that this bound is oblivious to the magnitude of these eigenvalues.

5.2 Kernel ULD

If $r = m + u$ and K is a kernel matrix (this holds if K is positive semidefinite), then we say that the decomposition is a *kernel-ULD*. Let $\mathcal{H} \subseteq \mathbb{R}^{m+u}$ be the reproducing kernel Hilbert space (RKHS), corresponding to K. We denote by $\langle \cdot, \cdot \rangle_{\mathcal{H}}$ the inner product in $\mathcal{H}$. Since K is a kernel matrix, by the reproducing property[6] of $\mathcal{H}$, $K(i,j) = \langle K(i,\cdot), K(j,\cdot) \rangle_{\mathcal{H}}$. Suppose that the vector $\boldsymbol{\alpha}$ satisfies $\sqrt{\boldsymbol{\alpha}^T K \boldsymbol{\alpha}} \leq \mu_2$ for some μ_2. Let $\{\lambda_i\}_{i=1}^{m+u}$ be the eigenvalues of K. By similar arguments used to derive (20) we have (details will appear in the full version):

$$R_{m+u}(\mathcal{H}) = \mathbf{E}_{\boldsymbol{\sigma}}\left\{\sup_{h\in\mathcal{H}}\sum_{i=1}^{m+u}\sigma_i h(x_i)\right\} = \mathbf{E}_{\boldsymbol{\sigma}}\left\{\sup_{\boldsymbol{\alpha}:\sqrt{\boldsymbol{\alpha}^T K\boldsymbol{\alpha}}\leq\mu_2}\sum_{i,j=1}^{m+u}\sigma_i\alpha_j K(i,j)\right\}$$

$$\leq \mu_2\sqrt{\sum_{i=1}^{m+u}\frac{2}{mu}K(i,i)} = \mu_2\sqrt{\frac{2\cdot\mathrm{trace}(\mathrm{K})}{mu}} = \mu_2\sqrt{\frac{2}{mu}\sum_{i=1}^{m+u}\lambda_i}. \quad (23)$$

By defining the RKHS induced by the unnormalized Laplacian, as in [14], and using a generalized representer theorem [18], it can be shown that the algorithm of Belkin et al. [4] has a kernel-ULD (the details will appear in the full version).

5.3 Monte-Carlo Rademacher Bounds

We now show how to compute Monte-Carlo Rademacher bounds with high confidence for any transductive algorithm using its ULD. Our empirical examination of these bounds shows that they are tighter than the analytical bounds (20) and (23). The technique, which is based on a simple application of Hoeffding's inequality, is made particularly simple for vanilla ULDs.

Let $\mathcal{V} \subseteq \mathbb{R}^{m+u}$ be a set of vectors, $\boldsymbol{\sigma} \in \mathbb{R}^{m+u}$ to be a Rademacher vector (1), and $g(\boldsymbol{\sigma}) = \sup_{\mathbf{v}\in\mathcal{V}} \boldsymbol{\sigma}\cdot\mathbf{v}$. By Def. 1, $R_{m+u}(\mathcal{V}) = \mathbf{E}_{\boldsymbol{\sigma}}\{g(\boldsymbol{\sigma})\}$. Let $\boldsymbol{\sigma}_1, \ldots, \boldsymbol{\sigma}_n$ be an i.i.d. sample of Rademacher vectors. We estimate $R_{m+u}(\mathcal{V})$ with high-confidence by applying the Hoeffding inequality on $\sum_{i=1}^n \frac{1}{n}g(\boldsymbol{\sigma}_i)$. To apply the Hoeffding inequality we need a bound on $\sup_{\boldsymbol{\sigma}}|g(\boldsymbol{\sigma})|$, which is derived for the case where $\mathcal{V}$ is all possible outputs of the algorithm (for a fixed X_{m+u}). Specifically, suppose that $\mathbf{v} \in \mathcal{V}$ is an output of the algorithm, $\mathbf{v} = K\boldsymbol{\alpha}$, and assume that $\|\boldsymbol{\alpha}\|_2 \leq \mu_1$. By Def. 1, for all $\boldsymbol{\sigma}$, $\|\boldsymbol{\sigma}\|_2 \leq b \overset{\Delta}{=} \sqrt{m+u}\left(\frac{1}{m} + \frac{1}{u}\right)$. Using elementary linear algebra we have $\sup_{\boldsymbol{\sigma}}|g(\boldsymbol{\sigma})| \leq \sup_{\|\boldsymbol{\sigma}\|_2\leq b,\ \|\boldsymbol{\alpha}\|_2\leq\mu_1}|\boldsymbol{\sigma} K\boldsymbol{\alpha}| \leq b\mu_1\lambda_{\max}$, where $\lambda_{\max}$

---

[6] This means that $\forall \mathbf{h} \in \mathcal{H}$ and $i \in I_1^{m+u}$, $h(i) = \langle K(i,\cdot), \mathbf{h} \rangle_{\mathcal{H}}$.

is a maximal singular value of K. Applying the one-sided Hoeffding inequality on n samples of $g(\boldsymbol{\sigma})$ we have, for any given δ, that with probability of at least $1 - \delta$ over the random i.i.d. choice of the vectors $\boldsymbol{\sigma}_1, \ldots, \boldsymbol{\sigma}_n$,

$$R_{m+u}(\mathcal{V}) \leq \frac{1}{n} \sum_{i=1}^{n} \sup_{\boldsymbol{\alpha}: \|\boldsymbol{\alpha}\|_2 \leq \mu_1} \boldsymbol{\sigma}_i K \boldsymbol{\alpha} + \mu_1 \sqrt{m + u} \left(\frac{1}{m} + \frac{1}{u} \right) \lambda_{\max} \sqrt{\frac{2 \ln \frac{1}{\delta}}{n}}. \quad (24)$$

To use the bound (24), the value of $\sup_{\boldsymbol{\alpha}: \|\boldsymbol{\alpha}\|_2 \leq \mu} \boldsymbol{\sigma}_i K \boldsymbol{\alpha}$ should be computed for each randomly drawn $\boldsymbol{\sigma}_i$. This computation is algorithm-dependent and below we show how to compute it for the algorithm of [22].[7] In cases where we can compute the supremum exactly (as in vanilla ULDs; see below) we can also get a lower bound using the symmetric Hoeffding inequality.

Example: Application to the CM algorithm. We start with a brief description of the Consistency Method (CM) algorithm of [22]. The algorithm has a natural vanilla ULD (see definition at the beginning of Sec. 5), where the matrix K is computed as follows. Let W and D be matrices as in SGT (see Sec. 5.1). A normalized Laplacian of W is $L = D^{-1/2} W D^{-1/2}$. Let β be a parameter in $(0, 1)$. Then, $K \overset{\Delta}{=} (1 - \beta)(I - \beta L)^{-1}$ and the output of CM is $\mathbf{y} = K \cdot \boldsymbol{\alpha}$, where $\boldsymbol{\alpha}$ specifies the given labels. Consequently $\|\boldsymbol{\alpha}\|_2 \leq \sqrt{m}$. Moreover, it can be verified that K is a kernel matrix, and therefore, the decomposition is a kernel-ULD. It turns out that for CM, the exact value of the supremum in (24) can be analytically derived. The vectors $\boldsymbol{\alpha}$, that induce the CM hypothesis space for a particular K, have exactly m components with values in $\{\pm 1\}$; the rest of the components are zeros. Let Ψ be the set of all possible such $\boldsymbol{\alpha}$'s. Let $\mathbf{t}(\boldsymbol{\sigma}_i) = (t_1, \ldots, t_{m+u}) \overset{\Delta}{=} \boldsymbol{\sigma}_i K \in \mathbb{R}^{1 \times (m+u)}$ and $|\mathbf{t}(\boldsymbol{\sigma}_i)| \overset{\Delta}{=} (|t_1|, \ldots, |t_{m+u}|)$. Then, for any fixed $\boldsymbol{\sigma}_i$, $\sup_{\boldsymbol{\alpha} \in \Psi} \boldsymbol{\sigma}_i K \boldsymbol{\alpha}$ is the sum of the m largest elements in $|\mathbf{t}(\boldsymbol{\sigma}_i)|$. This derivation holds for any vanilla ULD.

To demonstrate the Rademacher bounds discussed in this paper we present an empirical comparison of the bounds over two datasets (Voting, and Pima) from the UCI repository. For each dataset we took $m + u$ to be the size of the dataset (435 and 768, respectively) and we took m to be 1/3 of the full-sample size. The matrix W is the 10-nearest neighbor graph computed with the cosine similarity metric. We applied the CM algorithm with $\beta = 0.5$. The Monte-Carlo bounds (both upper and lower) were computed with $\delta = 0.05$ and $n = 10^5$.

We compared the Mote-Carlo bounds with the ULD bound (20), named here "the SVD bound", and the kernel-ULD bound (23), named here "the eigenvalue bound". The graphs in Figure 1 compare these four bounds for each of the datasets as a function of the number of non-zero eigenvalues of K (trimmed to maximum 430 eigenvalues). Specifically, each point t on the x-axis corresponds to bounds computed with a matrix K_t that approximates K using only the smallest t eigenvalues of K. In both examples the lower and upper Monte-Carlo bounds tightly "sandwich" the true Rademacher complexity. It is striking that

---

[7] An application of this approach in induction seems to be very hard, if not impossible. For example, in the case of RBF kernel machines we will need to optimize over (typically) infinite-dimensional vectors in the feature space.

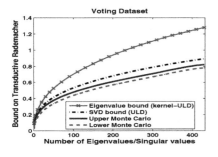
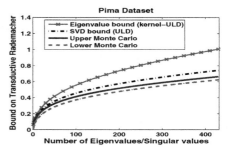

Fig. 1. A comparison of transductive Rademacher bounds

the SVD bound is very close to the true Rademacher complexity. In principle, with our simple Monte-Carlo method we can approximate the true Rademacher complexity up to any desired accuracy (with high confidence) at the cost of drawing sufficiently many Rademacher vectors.

6   PAC-Bayesian Bound for Transductive Mixtures

In this section we adapt part of the results of [17] to transduction. The proofs of all results presented in this section will appear in the full version of the paper.

Let $\mathcal{B} = \{\mathbf{h}_i\}_{i=1}^{|\mathcal{B}|}$ be a finite set of *base-hypotheses*. The class $\mathcal{B}$ can be formed after observing the full-sample X_{m+u}, but before obtaining the training/test set partition and the labels. Let $\mathbf{q} = (q_1, \ldots, q_{|\mathcal{B}|}) \in \mathbb{R}^{|\mathcal{B}|}$. Our goal is to construct a useful *mixture hypothesis*, $\widetilde{\mathbf{h}}_{\mathbf{q}} \triangleq \sum_{i=1}^{|\mathcal{B}|} q_i \mathbf{h}_i$. We assume that $\mathbf{q}$ belongs to a domain $\Omega_{g,A} = \{\mathbf{q} \mid g(\mathbf{q}) \leq A\}$, where $g : \mathbb{R}^{|\mathcal{B}|} \to \mathbb{R}$ is a predefined function and $A \in \mathbb{R}$ is a constant. The domain $\Omega_{g,A}$ and the set $\mathcal{B}$ induce the class $\widetilde{\mathcal{B}}_{g,A}$ of all possible mixtures $\widetilde{\mathbf{h}}_{\mathbf{q}}$. Recalling that $Q \triangleq (1/m + 1/u)$ and $c_0 = \sqrt{32\ln(4e)/3} < 5.05$, we apply Theorem 2 with $\mathcal{H} \triangleq \widetilde{\mathcal{B}}_{g,A}$ and obtain that with probability of at least $1 - \delta$ over the training/test partition of X_{m+u}, for all $\widetilde{\mathbf{h}}_{\mathbf{q}} \in \widetilde{\mathcal{B}}_{g,A}$,

$$\mathcal{L}_u(\widetilde{\mathbf{h}}_{\mathbf{q}}) \leq \widehat{\mathcal{L}}_m^{\gamma}(\widetilde{\mathbf{h}}_{\mathbf{q}}) + \frac{R_{m+u}(\widetilde{\mathcal{B}}_{g,A})}{\gamma} + c_0 Q\sqrt{\min(m,u)} + \sqrt{2Q\ln\frac{1}{\delta}}. \quad (25)$$

Let $Q_1 \triangleq \sqrt{2Q\left(\ln(1/\delta) + 2\ln\log_s\left(s\tilde{g}(\mathbf{q})/g_0\right)\right)}$. It is straightforward to apply the technique used in the proof of Theorem 10 in [17] and obtain the following bound, which eliminates the dependence on A.

Corollary 1. *Let $g_0 > 0$, $s > 1$ and $\tilde{g}(\mathbf{q}) = s\max(g(\mathbf{q}), g_0)$. For any (fixed) g, with probability of at least $1 - \delta$ over the training/test set partition, for all[8] $\widetilde{\mathbf{h}}_{\mathbf{q}}$,*

$$\mathcal{L}_u(\widetilde{\mathbf{h}}_{\mathbf{q}}) \leq \widehat{\mathcal{L}}_m^{\gamma}(\widetilde{\mathbf{h}}_{\mathbf{q}}) + \frac{R_{m+u}(\widetilde{\mathcal{B}}_{g,\tilde{g}(\mathbf{q})})}{\gamma} + c_0 Q\sqrt{\min(m,u)} + Q_1. \quad (26)$$

---

[8] In the bound (26) the meaning of $R_{m+u}(\widetilde{\mathcal{B}}_{g,\tilde{g}(\mathbf{q})})$ is as follows. For any $\mathbf{q}$ let $A = \tilde{g}(\mathbf{q})$ and $R_{m+u}(\widetilde{\mathcal{B}}_{g,\tilde{g}(\mathbf{q})}) \triangleq R_{m+u}(\widetilde{\mathcal{B}}_{g,A})$.

We now instantiate Corollary 1 for $g(\mathbf{q})$ being the KL-divergence and derive a PAC-Bayesian bound. To this end, we restrict $\mathbf{q}$ to be a probability vector. Let $\mathbf{p} \in \mathbb{R}^{|\mathcal{B}|}$ be a *"prior"* probability vector. The vector $\mathbf{p}$ can only depend on the unlabeled full-sample X_{m+u}. For a particular prior $\mathbf{p}$ let $g(\mathbf{q}) \triangleq D(\mathbf{q}\|\mathbf{p}) = \sum_{i=1}^{|\mathcal{B}|} q_i \ln\left(\frac{q_i}{p_i}\right)$. Adopting Lemma 11 of [17] to the transductive Rademacher variables, defined in (1), we obtain the following bound.

Theorem 3. *Let $g_0 > 0$, $s > 1$. Let $\mathbf{p}$ and $\mathbf{q}$ be any prior and posterior distribution over $\mathcal{B}$, respectively. Set $g(\mathbf{q}) \triangleq D(\mathbf{q}\|\mathbf{p})$ and $\tilde{g}(\mathbf{q}) \triangleq s \max(g(\mathbf{q}), g_0)$. Then, with prob. of at least $1 - \delta$ over the training/test set partition, for all $\widetilde{\mathbf{h}}_{\mathbf{q}}$,*

$$\mathcal{L}_u(\widetilde{\mathbf{h}}_{\mathbf{q}}) \leq \widehat{\mathcal{L}}_m^{\gamma}(\widetilde{\mathbf{h}}_{\mathbf{q}}) + \frac{Q}{\gamma}\sqrt{2\tilde{g}(\mathbf{q}) \sup_{\mathbf{h} \in \mathcal{B}} \|\mathbf{h}\|_2^2} + c_0 Q\sqrt{\min(m, u)} + Q_1. \qquad (27)$$

Theorem 3 is a PAC-Bayesian result, where the prior $\mathbf{p}$ can depend on X_{m+u} and the posterior can be optimized adaptively, based also on S_m.

7   Concluding Remarks

We have studied the use of Rademacher complexity analysis in the transductive setting. Our results include the first general Rademacher bound for soft classification algorithms, the unlabeled-labeled decomposition (ULD) technique for bounding Rademacher complexity of any transductive algorithm and a bound for Bayesian mixtures.

It would be nice to further improve our bounds using, for example, the local Rademacher approach [2]. However, we believe that the main advantage of these transductive bounds is the possibility of selecting a hypothesis space based on the full-sample. A clever data-dependent choice of this space should provide sufficient flexibility to achieve a low training error with low Rademacher complexity. In our opinion this opportunity can be explored and exploited much further.

This work opens up new avenues for future research. For example, it would be interesting to optimize the matrix K in the ULD representation explicitly (to fit the data) under a constraint of low Rademacher complexity. Also, it would be nice to find "low-Rademacher" approximations of particular K matrices. The PAC-Bayesian bound for mixture algorithms motivates the development and use of transductive mixtures, an area that has yet to be investigated.

Acknowledgement. We thank Yair Wiener for useful comments.

References

1. Balcan, M.F., Blum, A.: An Augmented PAC Model for Semi-Supervised Learning (chapter 22). In: Chapelle, O., Schölkopf, B., Zien, A. (eds.) Semi-Supervised Learning, pp. 383–404. MIT Press, Cambridge (2006)
2. Bartlett, P., Bousquet, O., Mendelson, S.: Local Rademacher complexities. Annals of Probability 33(4), 1497–1537 (2005)

3. Bartlett, P., Mendelson, S.: Rademacher and Gaussian complexities: risk bounds and structural results. Journal of Machine Learning Research 3, 463–482 (2002)
4. Belkin, M., Matveeva, I., Niyogi, P.: Regularization and semi-supervised learning on large graphs. In: Shawe-Taylor, J., Singer, Y. (eds.) COLT 2004. LNCS (LNAI), vol. 3120, pp. 624–638. Springer, Heidelberg (2004)
5. Belkin, M., Niyogi, P.: Semi-supervised learning on Riemannian manifolds. Machine Learning 56, 209–239 (2004)
6. Blum, A., Langford, J.: PAC-MDL Bounds. In: COLT, pp. 344–357. Springer, Heidelberg (2003)
7. Bousquet, O., Elisseeff, A.: Stability and generalization. Journal of Machine Learning Research 2, 499–526 (2002)
8. Chapelle, O., Schölkopf, B., Zien, A.: Semi-Supervised Learning. MIT Press, Cambridge, MA (2006), http://www.kyb.tuebingen.mpg.de/ssl-book
9. Derbeko, P., El-Yaniv, R., Meir, R.: Explicit learning curves for transduction and application to clustering and compression algorithms. Journal of Artificial Intelligence Research 22, 117–142 (2004)
10. Devroye, L., Gyorfi, L., Lugosi, G.: A Probabilistic Theory of Pattern Recognition. Springer, Heidelberg (1996)
11. El-Yaniv, R., Gerzon, L.: Effective transductive learning via objective model selection. Pattern Recognition Letters 26, 2104–2115 (2005)
12. El-Yaniv, R., Pechyony, D.: Stable transductive learning. In: Lugosi, G., Simon, H.U. (eds.) Proceedings of the 19th Annual Conference on Learning Theory, pp. 35–49 (2006)
13. Hanneke, S.: An analysis of graph cut size for transductive learning. In: ICML, pp. 393–399 (2006)
14. Herbster, M., Pontil, M., Wainer, L.: Online learning over graphs. In: ICML, pp. 305–312 (2005)
15. Joachims, T.: Transductive learning via spectral graph partitioning. In: Proceedings of the 20th International Conference on Machine Learning, pp. 290–297 (2003)
16. Lanckriet, G., Cristianini, N., Bartlett, P., Ghaoui, L.E., Jordan, M.: Learning the Kernel Matrix with Semidefinite Programming. Journal of Machine Learning Research 5, 27–72 (2004)
17. Meir, R., Zhang, T.: Generalization error bounds for Bayesian Mixture Algorithms. Journal of Machine Learning Research 4, 839–860 (2003)
18. Scholkopf, B., Herbrich, R., Smola, A.: A generalized representer theorem. In: Helmbold, D., Williamson, B. (eds.) COLT 2001 and EuroCOLT 2001. LNCS (LNAI), vol. 2111, pp. 416–426. Springer, Heidelberg (2001)
19. Vapnik, V., Chervonenkis, A.: The theory of pattern recognition. Moscow: Nauka (1974)
20. Vapnik, V.N.: Estimation of Dependences Based on Empirical Data. Springer, Heidelberg (1982)
21. Zhang, T., Ando, R.: Analysis of spectral kernel design based semi-supervised learning. In: NIPS, pp. 1601–1608 (2005)
22. Zhou, D., Bousquet, O., Lal, T.N., Weston, J., Scholkopf, B.: Learning with local and global consistency. In: NIPS, pp. 321–328 (2003)
23. Zhu, X., Ghahramani, Z., Lafferty, J.D.: Semi-supervised learning using gaussian fields and harmonic functions. In: ICML, pp. 912–919 (2003)

U-Shaped, Iterative,
and Iterative-with-Counter Learning

John Case and Samuel E. Moelius III

Department of Computer & Information Sciences
University of Delaware
103 Smith Hall
Newark, DE 19716
{case,moelius}@cis.udel.edu

Abstract. This paper solves an important problem left open in the literature by showing that *U-shapes* are *un*necessary in *iterative learning*. A *U-shape* occurs when a learner first *learns*, then *unlearns*, and, finally, *relearns*, some target concept. *Iterative learning* is a Gold-style learning model in which each of a learner's output conjectures depends *only* upon the learner's just previous conjecture and upon the most recent input element. Previous results had shown, for example, that U-shapes are *un*necessary for explanatory learning, but *are* necessary for behaviorally correct learning.

Work on the aforementioned problem led to the consideration of an iterative-like learning model, in which each of a learner's conjectures may, *in addition*, depend upon the number of elements so far presented to the learner. Learners in this new model are strictly more powerful than traditional iterative learners, yet not as powerful as full explanatory learners. Can any class of languages learnable in this new model be learned without U-shapes? For now, *this* problem is left open.

1 Introduction

U-Shapes. A *U-shape* occurs when a learner first *learns*, then *unlearns*, and, finally, *relearns*, some target concept. This phenomenon has been observed, for example, in children learning the use of regular and irregular verbs, e.g., a child first correctly learns that the past tense of "speak" is "spoke"; then, the child overregularizes and *in*correctly uses "speaked"; finally, the child returns to correctly using "spoke" [18,20,23].

Important questions regarding U-shapes are the following. Are U-shapes an *un*necessary accident of human evolution, *or*, are there classes of tasks that can be learned *with* U-shapes, but *not* otherwise? That is, are there classes of tasks that are learnable *only* by returning to some *abandoned* correct behavior?

There have been mathematical attempts to answer these questions in the context of Gold-style language learning [12,14].[1] Models of Gold-style language

---

[1] In this paper, we focus exclusively on language learning, as opposed to, say, function learning [14].

N. Bshouty and C. Gentile (Eds.): COLT 2007, LNAI 4539, pp. 172–186, 2007.

learning differ from one another in ways described hereafter, however, the following is common to all. Infinitely often, a *learner* is fed successively longer finite, initial sequences of an *infinite* sequence of numbers and, possibly, pauses (#). The set of all such numbers represents a *language*, and, the infinite sequence, itself, is called a *text* for the language. For each such initial sequence, the learner outputs a *conjecture* (i.e., grammar) for the language contained in the text.

One way in which Gold models differ from one another is in the criteria used to judge the *success* of a learner. Examples of models with differing criteria are *explanatory learning* (**Ex**-learning) [12,14][2] and *behaviorally correct learning* (**Bc**-learning) [8,14]. In both models, for a learner to be successful, all but finitely many of the learner's conjectures must correctly (semantically) identify the input language. However, **Ex**-learning has the additional requirement that a learner converge *syntactically* to a single conjecture.

In Gold-style learning, a U-shape is formalized as: outputting a semantically correct conjecture, then outputting a semantically incorrect conjecture, and, finally, returning to a semantically correct conjecture [3,4,1]. As it turns out, U-shapes are *un*necessary for **Ex**-learning, i.e., every class of languages that can be **Ex**-learned can be **Ex**-learned with*out* U-shapes [1, Theorem 20]. On the other hand, U-shapes *are* necessary for **Bc**-learning, i.e., there are classes of languages that *can* be **Bc**-learned *with* U-shapes, but *not* with*out* [11, proof of Theorem 4]. Thus, in at least some contexts, this *seemingly* inefficient behavior can actually increase one's learning power.[3]

Iterative Learning. For both **Ex**-learning and **Bc**-learning, a learner is free to base a conjecture upon *every* element presented to the learner up to that point. Thus, in a sense, an **Ex**-learner or **Bc**-learner can *remember* every element presented to it. One could argue that such an ability is beyond that possessed by (most) humans. This calls into question the applicability of **Ex**-learning and **Bc**-learning to modeling human learning. That is, it would seem that any model of human learning should be *memory limited* in some respect.

Iterative learning (**It**-learning) [25,16,7] is a straightforward variation of the **Ex**-learning model that *is* memory limited.[4] In this model, each of a learner's conjectures can depend *only* upon the learner's just previous conjecture and upon the most recent input element. An **It**-learner can remember elements that it has seen by *coding* them into its conjectures. However, like an **Ex**-learner, an **It**-learner is required to converge syntactically to a single conjecture. Thus, on any given text, an **It**-learner can perform such a coding-trick for only finitely many elements.

There have been previous attempts to determine whether U-shapes are necessary in **It**-learning [4,13]. The memory limited aspect of **It**-learning makes it more nearly applicable than **Ex**-learning or **Bc**-learning to modeling human learning.

---

[2] **Ex**-learning is the model that was actually studied by Gold [12].
[3] There exist Gold models that lie strictly between **Ex** and **Bc** [5]. For nearly every such model considered, U-shapes are necessary [3].
[4] Other memory limited models are considered in [19,11,7,4].

Herein (Theorem 2 in Section 3), we solve this important open problem by showing that U-shapes are *un*necessary in **It**-learning, i.e., any class of languages that can be **It**-learned can be **It**-learned with*out* U-shapes.

Other Restricted Forms of Learning. Two other restricted forms of learning that have been well studied are *set-driven learning* (**SDEx**-learning) and *partly set-driven learning* (**PSDEx**-learning) [24,22,10,17].[5] The **SDEx**-learning model requires that a learner output syntactically identical conjectures when fed two different initial sequences with the same content, i.e., listing the same set of numbers. So, for example, when forming a conjecture, an **SDEx**-learner can*not* consider the number of elements so far presented to it, or the order in which those elements were presented. The **PSDEx**-learning model is similar, except that a learner is required to output identical conjectures when fed initial sequences with the same content *and length*. Thus, when forming a conjecture, a **PSDEx**-learner can*not* consider the order in which elements were presented to it, but *can* consider the number of such elements.

SDEx-learners and **It**-learners are alike in that neither can consider the number of elements so far presented to it when forming a conjecture. Furthermore, **PSDEx**-learners are like **SDEx**-learners with *just this one* restriction lifted. Herein, we consider a similar counterpart to **It**-learners. That is, we consider a model in which each of a learner's output conjectures can depend *only* upon the learner's just previous conjecture, the most recent input element, *and a counter* indicating the number of elements so far presented to the learner. We call this model *iterative-with-counter* learning (**ItCtr**-learning). In Section 4, we show that **ItCtr**-learning and **SDEx**-learning are incomparable (Theorems 3 and 4), i.e., for each, there is a class of languages learnable by that one, but *not* the other. It follows that **ItCtr**-learning is strictly more powerful than **It**-learning, yet not as powerful as full **Ex**-learning.

In an early attempt at showing that U-shapes are unnecessary in **It**-learning, we obtained the partial result that U-shapes are unnecessary in **It**-learning of classes of *infinite* languages. Independently, Sanjay Jain obtained the same (partial) result [13]. Thus, we hypothesize: learning without U-shapes is easier when the learner has access to some source of *infinitude*, e.g., the cardinality of the input language. This belief is what led us to consider the **ItCtr**-learning model, as every learner in this model has access to a source of infinitude, i.e., the counter, even when fed a text for a *finite* language.

Assuming our above hypothesis is correct, it should be easy to show that U-shapes are unnecessary in **ItCtr**-learning. Unfortunately, however, this problem has turned out to be more difficult than we had anticipated. So, for now, it is left open.

Organization. The remainder of this paper is organized as follows. Section 2, just below, gives notation and preliminaries. Section 3 proves our main result,

---

[5] **PSDEx**-learning is also called *rearrangement independent learning* in the literature (e.g., [17]).

namely, that U-shapes are *unnecessary* in **It**-learning. Section 4 explores **ItCtr**-learning, and, restates, formally, the problem that this paper leaves open.

2 Notation and Preliminaries

Computability-theoretic concepts not explained below are treated in [21].

$\mathbb{N}$ denotes the set of natural numbers, $\{0, 1, 2, \ldots\}$. Lowercase Roman letters, with or without decorations, range over elements of $\mathbb{N}$, unless stated otherwise. A and L, with or without decorations, range over subsets of $\mathbb{N}$. $\mathcal{L}$ ranges over collections of subsets of $\mathbb{N}$. For all finite, nonempty A, $\max A$ denotes the maximum element of A. $\max \emptyset \stackrel{\text{def}}{=} -1$.

ψ ranges over one-argument partial functions. For all ψ and x, $\psi(x)\downarrow$ denotes that $\psi(x)$ converges; $\psi(x)\uparrow$ denotes that $\psi(x)$ diverges.[6] For all ψ, $\text{dom}(\psi) \stackrel{\text{def}}{=} \{x : \psi(x)\downarrow\}$ and $\text{rng}(\psi) \stackrel{\text{def}}{=} \{y : (\exists x)[\psi(x) = y]\}$. We use $\uparrow$ to denote the value of a divergent computation. λ denotes the empty function.

$\varphi_0, \varphi_1, \ldots$ denotes any fixed, acceptable numbering of all one-argument partial computable functions [21]. Φ denotes a fixed Blum complexity measure for φ [2]. For all p, $W_p \stackrel{\text{def}}{=} \text{dom}(\varphi_p)$. Thus, for all p, W_p is the pth recursively enumerable set [21]. $W_\uparrow \stackrel{\text{def}}{=} \emptyset$.

$(\mathbb{N} \cup \{\#\})^*$ denotes the set of all finite initial segments of total functions of type $\mathbb{N} \to (\mathbb{N} \cup \{\#\})$. $(\mathbb{N} \cup \{\#\})^{\leq \omega}$ denotes the set of *all* (finite and infinite) initial segments of total functions of type $\mathbb{N} \to (\mathbb{N} \cup \{\#\})$. α, β, ϱ, σ, and τ, with or without decorations, range over elements of $(\mathbb{N} \cup \{\#\})^*$. T, with or without decorations, ranges over total functions of type $\mathbb{N} \to (\mathbb{N} \cup \{\#\})$.

For all $f \in (\mathbb{N} \cup \{\#\})^{\leq \omega}$, $\text{content}(f) \stackrel{\text{def}}{=} \text{rng}(f) - \{\#\}$. For all T and L, T *is a text for* $L \stackrel{\text{def}}{=} \text{content}(T) = L$. For all σ, $|\sigma|$ (pronounced: the *length* of σ) $\stackrel{\text{def}}{=} |\text{dom}(\sigma)|$. For all $f \in (\mathbb{N} \cup \{\#\})^{\leq \omega}$, and all σ, n, and i, (1) and (2) below.

$$f[n](i) \stackrel{\text{def}}{=} \begin{cases} f(i), & \text{if } i < n; \\ \uparrow, & \text{otherwise.} \end{cases} \tag{1}$$

$$(\sigma \diamond f)(i) \stackrel{\text{def}}{=} \begin{cases} \sigma(i), & \text{if } i < |\sigma|; \\ f(i - |\sigma|), & \text{otherwise.} \end{cases} \tag{2}$$

M, with or without decorations, ranges over partial computable functions of type $(\mathbb{N} \cup \{\#\})^* \to (\mathbb{N} \cup \{?\})$.[7]

The following are the Gold-style learning models considered in this paper.

Definition 1. For all **M** and L, (a)-(e) below.

(a) **M** *Ex-identifies* $L \Leftrightarrow$ for all texts T for L, there exist i and p such that $(\forall j \geq i)[\mathbf{M}(T[j]) = p]$ and $W_p = L$.

---

[6] For all one-argument partial functions ψ and x, $\psi(x)$ *converges* iff there exists y such that $\psi(x) = y$; $\psi(x)$ *diverges* iff there is *no* y such that $\psi(x) = y$. If ψ is partial computable, and x is such that $\psi(x)$ diverges, then one can imagine that a program associated with ψ *goes into an infinite loop* on input x.

[7] Such an **M** is often called an *inductive inference machine* [14].

(b) **M SDEx**-*identifies* L $\Leftrightarrow$ **M Ex**-identifies L, *and*, for all ϱ and σ, if content(ϱ) = content(σ), then $\mathbf{M}(\varrho) = \mathbf{M}(\sigma)$.

(c) **M PSDEx**-*identifies* L $\Leftrightarrow$ **M Ex**-identifies L, *and*, for all ϱ and σ, if $|\varrho| = |\sigma|$ and content(ϱ) = content(σ), then $\mathbf{M}(\varrho) = \mathbf{M}(\sigma)$.

(d) **M It**-*identifies* L $\Leftrightarrow$ **M Ex**-identifies L, *and*, for all ϱ, σ, and τ such that content$(\varrho) \cup$ content$(\sigma) \cup$ content$(\tau) \subseteq L$, (i) and (ii) below.[8]

  (i) $\mathbf{M}(\varrho)\!\downarrow$.
  (ii) $\mathbf{M}(\varrho) = \mathbf{M}(\sigma) \Rightarrow \mathbf{M}(\varrho \diamond \tau) = \mathbf{M}(\sigma \diamond \tau)$.

(e) **M ItCtr**-*identifies* L $\Leftrightarrow$ **M Ex**-identifies L, *and*, for all ϱ, σ, and τ such that content$(\varrho) \cup$ content$(\sigma) \cup$ content$(\tau) \subseteq L$, (i) and (ii) below.

  (i) $\mathbf{M}(\varrho)\!\downarrow$.
  (ii) $[|\varrho| = |\sigma| \wedge \mathbf{M}(\varrho) = \mathbf{M}(\sigma)] \Rightarrow \mathbf{M}(\varrho \diamond \tau) = \mathbf{M}(\sigma \diamond \tau)$.

Ex, **SD**, **PSD**, **It**, and **ItCtr** are mnemonic for *explanatory, set-driven, partly set-driven, iterative,* and *iterative-with-counter,* respectively.

Definition 2. For all $\mathcal{I} \in \{\mathbf{Ex}, \mathbf{SDEx}, \mathbf{PSDEx}, \mathbf{It}, \mathbf{ItCtr}\}$, (a) and (b) below.

(a) For all $\mathbf{M}$, $\mathcal{I}(\mathbf{M}) = \{L : \mathbf{M}\ \mathcal{I}\text{-identifies}\ L\}$.
(b) $\mathcal{I} = \{\mathcal{L} : (\exists \mathbf{M})[\mathcal{L} \subseteq \mathcal{I}(\mathbf{M})]\}$.

Definition 3. For all $\mathcal{I} \in \{\mathbf{Ex}, \mathbf{SDEx}, \mathbf{PSDEx}, \mathbf{It}, \mathbf{ItCtr}\}$, (a) and (b) below.

(a) For all $\mathbf{M}$, L, and texts T for L, **M** *exhibits a U-shape on* T $\Leftrightarrow$ there exist i, j, and k such that $i < j < k$, $\{\mathbf{M}(T[i]), \mathbf{M}(T[j]), \mathbf{M}(T[k])\} \subset \mathbb{N}$, and

$$W_{\mathbf{M}(T[i])} = L \ \wedge \ W_{\mathbf{M}(T[j])} \neq L \ \wedge \ W_{\mathbf{M}(T[k])} = L. \tag{3}$$

(b) $\mathbf{NU}\mathcal{I} = \big\{\mathcal{L} : (\exists \mathbf{M})\big[\mathcal{L} \subseteq \mathcal{I}(\mathbf{M}) \wedge\ (\forall L \in \mathcal{L})[\mathbf{M}\ \text{does}\ not\ \text{exhibit a}$
                                            U-shape on any text for $L]\big]\big\}$.

NU is mnemonic for *non-U-shaped.* Clearly, for all $\mathcal{I}$ as above, $\mathbf{NU}\mathcal{I} \subseteq \mathcal{I}$.

---

[8] In some parts of the literature (e.g., [4]), an iterative learner is defined as a partial computable function of type $((\mathbb{N} \cup \{?\}) \times (\mathbb{N} \cup \{\#\})) \rightarrow (\mathbb{N} \cup \{?\})$ satisfying certain conditions. An advantage to typing an iterative learner in this way is that it makes explicit the fact that each of the learner's conjectures is based upon another conjecture and an input element. However, we prefer the type given in Definition 1(d), as it is consistent with that of a learner in other models, e.g., **Ex**.

There is some similarity between an iterative learner and an *automaton* with a potentially infinite set of states, corresponding to the learner's conjectures. It was thinking of iterative learners in this way, and the Myhill-Nerode Theorem [9], that led us to formulate iterative learners as in Definition 1(d). A proof that this formulation is equivalent to that of [4] can be found in [6].

3 It = NUIt

In this section, we prove our main result (Theorem 2), namely, that U-shapes are *unnecessary* in **It**-learning.

Definition 4, below, introduces a notion that we call *canniness*. Intuitively, an **It**-learner that is canny does *not* change its mind excessively, and is, therefore, much easier to reason about. Theorem 1, below, shows that, for any $\mathcal{L} \in$ **It**, there exists a canny learner that **It**-identifies every language in $\mathcal{L}$. This fact is used in the proof of Theorem 2.

Proving Theorem 1 does not appear to be trivial. However, due to space constraints, its proof omitted. A proof of Theorem 1 can be found in [6].

Definition 4. For all **M**, **M** is *canny* $\Leftrightarrow$ for all σ, (a)-(c) below.

(a) $\mathbf{M}(\sigma)\!\downarrow \; \Rightarrow \; \mathbf{M}(\sigma) \in \mathbb{N}$, i.e., **M** never outputs ?.
(b) $\mathbf{M}(\sigma \diamond \#) = \mathbf{M}(\sigma)$.
(c) For all $x \in \mathbb{N}$, if $\mathbf{M}(\sigma \diamond x) \neq \mathbf{M}(\sigma)$, then, for all $\tau \supseteq \sigma \diamond x$, $\mathbf{M}(\tau \diamond x) = \mathbf{M}(\tau)$.

Theorem 1. For all $\mathcal{L} \in$ **It**, there exists $\mathbf{M}'$ such that $\mathcal{L} \subseteq$ **It**$(\mathbf{M}')$ and $\mathbf{M}'$ is canny.

Definition 5. For all **M** and σ, (a)-(d) below.

(a) $C_{\mathbf{M}}(\sigma) = \{x \in \mathbb{N} \cup \{\#\} : \mathbf{M}(\sigma \diamond x)\!\downarrow = \mathbf{M}(\sigma)\!\downarrow\}$.
(b) $B_{\mathbf{M}}(\sigma) = \{x \in \mathbb{N} \cup \{\#\} : \mathbf{M}(\sigma \diamond x)\!\downarrow \neq \mathbf{M}(\sigma)\!\downarrow\}$.
(c) $B_{\mathbf{M}}^{\cap}(\sigma) = \bigcap_{0 \leq i \leq |\sigma|} B_{\mathbf{M}}(\sigma[i])$.
(d) $CB_{\mathbf{M}}(\sigma) = \left(\bigcup_{0 \leq i < |\sigma|} C_{\mathbf{M}}(\sigma[i])\right) \cap B_{\mathbf{M}}(\sigma)$.

C is mnemonic for *cycle*. B is mnemonic for *branch*.

Lemma 1. Suppose that **M** and $\mathcal{L}$ are such that $\mathcal{L} \subseteq$ **It**$(\mathbf{M})$ and **M** is canny. Suppose that L and σ are such that $L \in \mathcal{L}$ and content$(\sigma) \subseteq L$. Suppose, finally, that $L \cap B_{\mathbf{M}}^{\cap}(\sigma) = \emptyset$ and that $L \cap CB_{\mathbf{M}}(\sigma)$ is finite. Then, $W_{\mathbf{M}(\sigma)} = L$.

Proof (Sketch). Suppose the hypotheses. Let $A = L \cap CB_{\mathbf{M}}(\sigma)$. Clearly,

$$(\forall x \in A)(\exists \varrho \subset \sigma)[x \in C_{\mathbf{M}}(\varrho)]. \tag{4}$$

Furthermore, since $L \cap B_{\mathbf{M}}^{\cap}(\sigma) = \emptyset$,

$$L - A \subseteq C_{\mathbf{M}}(\sigma). \tag{5}$$

Consider a text T for L described, informally, as follows. T looks, initially, like σ with the elements of A interspersed. The elements of A are positioned in T in such a way that **M** does *not* make a mind-change when encountering these elements. The ϱ in (4) make this possible. Beyond this initial sequence resembling σ, T consists of the elements of $L - A$ and, possibly, pauses ($\#$), in any order. Clearly, by (5) and the fact the **M** is canny, **M** converges to $\mathbf{M}(\sigma)$ on such a text T. Thus, it must be the case that $W_{\mathbf{M}(\sigma)} = L$. $\approx \square$ (*Lemma 1*)

Lemma 2. Suppose that $\mathbf{M}$, $\mathcal{L}$, L, and σ are as in Lemma 1. Suppose, *in addition*, that L *is finite*. Then, for all τ such that $[\sigma \subseteq \tau \ \wedge \ \text{content}(\tau) \subseteq L]$, $W_{\mathbf{M}(\tau)} = L$.

Proof. Suppose the hypotheses, and let τ be such that $\sigma \subseteq \tau$ and $\text{content}(\tau) \subseteq L$. Since $L \cap B_{\mathbf{M}}^{\cap}(\sigma) = \emptyset$ and $\sigma \subseteq \tau$, clearly, $L \cap B_{\mathbf{M}}^{\cap}(\tau) = \emptyset$. Furthermore, since L is finite, $L \cap CB_{\mathbf{M}}(\tau)$ is finite. Thus, by Lemma 1, $W_{\mathbf{M}(\tau)} = L$. $\square$ (*Lemma 2*)

Lemma 3. Suppose that $\mathbf{M}$ and $\mathcal{L}$ are such that $\mathcal{L} \subseteq \mathbf{It}(\mathbf{M})$. Suppose that L and σ are such that $L \in \mathcal{L}$ and $\text{content}(\sigma) \subseteq L$. Suppose, finally, that $L \cap B_{\mathbf{M}}(\sigma)$ is infinite. Then, for all texts T for L, and all i, there exists $j \geq i$ such that $T(j) \in B_{\mathbf{M}}(\sigma)$.

Proof. Suppose the hypotheses. By way of contradiction, let T and i be such that, for all $j \geq i$, $T(j) \notin B_{\mathbf{M}}(\sigma)$. Then it must be the case that $L \cap B_{\mathbf{M}}(\sigma) \subseteq \{T(0), ..., T(i-1)\} \cap B_{\mathbf{M}}(\sigma)$. But since $L \cap B_{\mathbf{M}}(\sigma)$ is infinite and $\{T(0), ..., T(i-1)\} \cap B_{\mathbf{M}}(\sigma)$ is finite, this is a contradiction. $\square$ (*Lemma 3*)

Theorem 2. It = NUIt.

Proof. Clearly, $\mathbf{NUIt} \subseteq \mathbf{It}$. Thus, it suffices to show that $\mathbf{It} \subseteq \mathbf{NUIt}$. Let $\mathcal{L} \in \mathbf{It}$ be fixed. A machine $\mathbf{M}'$ is constructed such that $\mathcal{L} \subseteq \mathbf{It}(\mathbf{M}')$ and $\mathbf{M}'$ does *not* exhibit a U-shape on any text for a language in $\mathcal{L}$.

Let $\mathbf{M}$ be such that $\mathcal{L} \subseteq \mathbf{It}(\mathbf{M})$. Without loss of generality, assume that $\mathbf{M}$ is canny. Let $p_{\mathbf{M}}$ be such that

$$\varphi_{p_{\mathbf{M}}} = \mathbf{M}. \tag{6}$$

Let $e : (\mathbb{N} \cup \{\#\})^* \times \mathbb{N} \to \mathbb{N}$ be a partial computable function such that, for all σ, (a)-(c) below.

(a) $\text{dom}(e(\sigma, \cdot))$ is an initial segment of $\mathbb{N}$.
(b) $e(\sigma, \cdot)$ is 1-1.
(c) $\text{rng}(e(\sigma, \cdot)) = W_{\mathbf{M}(\sigma)}$.

Clearly, such an e exists. Let $f : (\mathbb{N} \cup \{\#\})^* \times \mathbb{N} \times (\mathbb{N} \cup \{\#\})^* \to \mathbb{N}$ be a 1-1, computable function such that, for all σ, m, α, and q, if $f(\sigma, m, \alpha) = q$, then W_q is the least fixpoint of the following recursive definition.[9]

> STAGE $s \geq 0$. If $e(\sigma, s)\downarrow$, then let $x = e(\sigma, s)$, and let $A = W_q^s \cup \{x\}$. If *each* of (a)-(d) below is satisfied, then set $W_q^{s+1} = A$ and proceed to stage $s+1$; otherwise, go into an infinite loop thereby making W_q finite.
> (a) $e(\sigma, s)\downarrow$.
> (b) $\mathbf{M}(\sigma \diamond x)\downarrow$.
> (c) $x \in C_{\mathbf{M}}(\sigma) \cup CB_{\mathbf{M}}(\sigma)$.
> (d) $(\forall w \in A)[w \in CB_{\mathbf{M}}(\sigma) \Rightarrow w \leq m]$
> $\vee \ (\forall \tau)[[\sigma \subset \tau \ \wedge \ \text{content}(\tau) \subseteq A \ \wedge \ |\tau| \leq |A|] \Rightarrow A \subseteq W_{f(\tau,0,\lambda)}]$.

---

[9] The requirement that the programs produced by f witness least fixpoints of this definition is, in fact, not necessary for the proof of the theorem. The requirement is here simply to make the definition of $W_{f(\cdot,\cdot,\cdot)}$ unambiguous.

Clearly, such an f exists.

Claim 1.

(a) For all σ, m, and α, $W_{f(\sigma,m,\alpha)} \subseteq W_{\mathbf{M}(\sigma)}$.
(b) For all σ, m, n, and α, if $m \leq n$, then $W_{f(\sigma,m,\alpha)} \subseteq W_{f(\sigma,n,\alpha)}$.
(c) For all σ, m, α, and β, $W_{f(\sigma,m,\alpha)} = W_{f(\sigma,m,\beta)}$.

Proof of Claim. Easily verifiable from the definition of f. $\square$ (*Claim 1*)

Let P be such that, for all σ and m, and all $x \in \mathbb{N} \cup \{\#\}$, $P(\sigma, m, x) \Leftrightarrow x \neq \#$ and

$$(\exists w)[\Phi_{\mathbf{M}(\sigma)}(w) \leq x \ \wedge \ \Phi_{p\mathbf{M}}(\sigma \diamond w) \leq x \ \wedge \ w \in CB_{\mathbf{M}}(\sigma) \ \wedge \ m < w \leq x]. \quad (7)$$

Note that P is a computable predicate. Let $\mathbf{M}'$ be such that $\mathbf{M}'(\lambda) = f(\lambda, 0, \lambda)$, and, for all ϱ, σ, m, and α, and all $x \in \mathbb{N} \cup \{\#\}$, if $\mathbf{M}'(\varrho)\uparrow$, then $\mathbf{M}'(\varrho \diamond x)\uparrow$; furthermore, if $\mathbf{M}'(\varrho) = f(\sigma, m, \alpha)$, then $\mathbf{M}'(\varrho \diamond x)$ is:

$$
\begin{aligned}
&\uparrow, &&\text{if } \text{(i) } \mathbf{M}(\sigma)\uparrow \vee \mathbf{M}(\sigma \diamond x)\uparrow \vee \mathbf{M}(\sigma \diamond \alpha)\uparrow \vee \mathbf{M}(\sigma \diamond \alpha \diamond x)\uparrow; \\
&f(\sigma \diamond \alpha \diamond x, 0, \ \lambda \ \ ), &&\text{if } \text{(ii) } \neg\text{(i)} \ \wedge \ \big[x \in B_{\mathbf{M}}^{\cap}(\sigma) \ \vee \ [x \in CB_{\mathbf{M}}(\sigma) \ \wedge \ x > m]\big]; \\
&f(\sigma, \ \ \ \ \ \ m, \alpha \diamond x), &&\text{if } \text{(iii) } \neg\text{(i)} \ \wedge \ x \in CB_{\mathbf{M}}(\sigma \diamond \alpha) \ \wedge \ x \leq m; \\
&f(\sigma, \ \ \ \ \ \ x, \ \lambda \ \ ), &&\text{if } \text{(iv) } \neg\text{(i)} \ \wedge \ x \in C_{\mathbf{M}}(\sigma \diamond \alpha) \ \wedge \ P(\sigma, m, x) \ \wedge \ \alpha = \lambda; \\
&f(\sigma \diamond \alpha, \ \ \ \ 0, \ \lambda \ \ ), &&\text{if } \text{(v) } \neg\text{(i)} \ \wedge \ x \in C_{\mathbf{M}}(\sigma \diamond \alpha) \ \wedge \ P(\sigma, m, x) \ \wedge \ \alpha \neq \lambda; \\
&f(\sigma, \ \ \ \ \ \ m, \alpha \ \ ), &&\text{if } \text{(vi) } \neg\text{(i)} \ \wedge \ x \in C_{\mathbf{M}}(\sigma \diamond \alpha) \ \wedge \ \neg P(\sigma, m, x).
\end{aligned}
$$

Let $L \in \mathcal{L}$ be fixed, and let T be a fixed text for L.

Claim 2. For all i, $\mathbf{M}'(T[i])\downarrow$.

Proof of Claim. Clearly, for all i, σ, m, and α, if $\mathbf{M}'(T[i]) = f(\sigma, m, \alpha)$, then content($\sigma$) $\cup$ content(α) $\subseteq$ content($T[i]$) $\subseteq L$. It follows that condition (i) *never* applies as $\mathbf{M}'$ is fed T, and, thus, for all i, $\mathbf{M}'(T[i])\downarrow$. $\square$ (*Claim 2*)

For all i, let σ_i, m_i, and α_i be such that

$$\mathbf{M}'(T[i]) = f(\sigma_i, m_i, \alpha_i). \quad (8)$$

By Claim 2, such σ_i, m_i, and α_i exist.

Claim 3. For all i, (a)-(e) below.

(a) $\sigma_i \diamond \alpha_i \subseteq \sigma_{i+1} \diamond \alpha_{i+1} \subseteq \sigma_i \diamond \alpha_i \diamond T(i)$.
(b) If $T(i) \in B_{\mathbf{M}}(\sigma_i \diamond \alpha_i)$, then $\sigma_{i+1} \diamond \alpha_{i+1} = \sigma_i \diamond \alpha_i \diamond T(i)$.
(c) If $T(i) \in B_{\mathbf{M}}^{\cap}(\sigma_i)$, then $\sigma_{i+1} = \sigma_i \diamond \alpha_i \diamond T(i)$.
(d) If $\sigma_i = \sigma_{i+1}$, then $m_i \leq m_{i+1}$.
(e) $\mathbf{M}(T[i])\downarrow = \mathbf{M}(\sigma_i \diamond \alpha_i)\downarrow$.

Proof of Claim. (a)-(d) are easily verifiable from the definition of $\mathbf{M}'$. (e) follows from (a) and (b). $\square$ (*Claim 3*)

Claim 4. There exists i such that, for all $j \geq i$, condition (vi) applies in calculating $\mathbf{M}'(T[j+1])$.

Proof of Claim. Suppose, by way of contradiction, that one or more of conditions (i)-(v) applies infinitely often as $\mathbf{M}'$ is fed T. By Claim 2, condition (i) *never* applies as $\mathbf{M}'$ is fed T. Also, note that, for all i, if condition (v) applies in calculating $\mathbf{M}'(T[i+1])$, then $\alpha_i \neq \lambda$ and $\alpha_{i+1} = \lambda$. Furthermore, for all i, if $\alpha_i = \lambda$ and $\alpha_{i+1} \neq \lambda$, then condition (iii) applies in calculating $\mathbf{M}'(T[i+1])$. Thus, if condition (v) applies infinitely often, then it must also be the case that condition (iii) applies infinitely often. Therefore, it suffices to consider the following cases.

CASE condition (iii) applies infinitely often. Then, for infinitely many i, $T(i) \in B_{\mathbf{M}}(\sigma_i \diamond \alpha_i)$. Furthermore, by Claim 3(e), for infinitely many i, $T(i) \in B_{\mathbf{M}}(T[i])$. Thus, $\mathbf{M}$ does *not* converge on T — a contradiction.

CASE condition (ii) applies infinitely often, but condition (iii) applies only finitely often. Let i be such that, for all $j \geq i$, condition (iii) does *not* apply in calculating $\mathbf{M}'(T[j+1])$. Let j be such that $j \geq i$ and $\alpha_j = \lambda$. Since condition (ii) applies infinitely often, such a j must exist. Clearly, by the definition of $\mathbf{M}'$,

$$(\forall k \geq j)[\alpha_k = \lambda]. \tag{9}$$

Since condition (ii) applies infinitely often, for infinitely many $k \geq j$,

$$
\begin{aligned}
T(k) &\in B_{\mathbf{M}}(\sigma_k) \\
&= B_{\mathbf{M}}(\sigma_k \diamond \alpha_k) \text{ \{by (9)\}}, \\
&= B_{\mathbf{M}}(T[k]) \quad \text{\{by Claim 3(e)\}}.
\end{aligned}
$$

Thus, $\mathbf{M}$ does *not* converge on T — a contradiction.

CASE condition (iv) applies infinitely often, but conditions (ii) and (iii) apply only finitely often. Let i be such that, for all $j \geq i$, neither condition (ii) nor (iii) applies in calculating $\mathbf{M}'(T[j+1])$. Let j be such that $j \geq i$ and $\alpha_j = \lambda$. Since condition (iv) applies infinitely often, such a j must exist. Clearly, by the definition of $\mathbf{M}'$,

$$(\forall k \geq j)[\sigma_k = \sigma_j \ \wedge \ \alpha_k = \lambda]. \tag{10}$$

Furthermore, for all $k \geq j$,

$$
\begin{aligned}
\mathbf{M}(T[k]) &= \mathbf{M}(\sigma_k \diamond \alpha_k) \text{ \{by Claim 3(e)\}} \\
&= \mathbf{M}(\sigma_j) \quad \text{\{by (10)\}}.
\end{aligned}
$$

Thus, $\mathbf{M}$ converges to $\mathbf{M}(\sigma_j)$ on T, and, therefore, $W_{\mathbf{M}(\sigma_j)} = L$. Since condition (iv) applies infinitely often, it must be the case that $W_{\mathbf{M}(\sigma_j)} \cap CB_{\mathbf{M}}(\sigma_j)$ is infinite. Thus, $L \cap CB_{\mathbf{M}}(\sigma_j)$ is infinite. By Lemma 3, there exists $k \geq j$ such that $T(k) \in B_{\mathbf{M}}(\sigma_j)$. Thus, there exists $k \geq j$ such that $T(k) \in B_{\mathbf{M}}(\sigma_k \diamond \alpha_k)$. But then, clearly, condition (ii) or (iii) applies in calculating $\mathbf{M}'(T[k+1])$ — a contradiction.   □ *(Claim 4)*

Henceforth, let k_1 be *least* such that

$$(\forall i \geq k_1)[\text{condition (vi) applies in calculating } \mathbf{M}'(T[i+1])]. \tag{11}$$

By Claim 4, such a k_1 exists.

Claim 5. For all $i \geq k_1$, (a)-(g) below.

(a) $\sigma_i = \sigma_{k_1}$.
(b) $m_i = m_{k_1}$.
(c) $\alpha_i = \alpha_{k_1}$.
(d) $T(i) \in C_{\mathbf{M}}(\sigma_{k_1}) \cup CB_{\mathbf{M}}(\sigma_{k_1})$.
(e) $T(i) \in CB_{\mathbf{M}}(\sigma_{k_1}) \Rightarrow T(i) \leq m_{k_1}$.
(f) $\neg P(\sigma_{k_1}, m_{k_1}, T(i))$.
(g) $\mathbf{M}'(T[i]) = \mathbf{M}'(T[k_1])$.

Proof of Claim. (a)-(f) follow from the definition of $\mathbf{M}'$ and the choice of k_1. (g) follows from (a)-(c). □ (*Claim 5*)

Claim 6. $L \cap B_{\mathbf{M}}^{\cap}(\sigma_{k_1}) = \emptyset$.

Proof of Claim. By way of contradiction, let x be such that $x \in L \cap B_{\mathbf{M}}^{\cap}(\sigma_{k_1})$. By Claim 5(d), there exists $i < k_1$ such that $T(i) = x$. Clearly, $x \in B_{\mathbf{M}}^{\cap}(\sigma_i)$. Thus, by Claim 3(c), it must be the case that $x \in \text{content}(\sigma_{k_1})$. But this contradicts the assumption that $\mathbf{M}$ is canny. □ (*Claim 6*)

Henceforth, let k_0 be *least* such that

$$L \cap B_{\mathbf{M}}^{\cap}(\sigma_{k_0}) = \emptyset. \tag{12}$$

By Claim 6, such a k_0 exists.

Claim 7. For all $i < k_0$, $L \not\subseteq W_{\mathbf{M}'(T[i])}$.

Proof of Claim. Let i be such that $i < k_0$. By the choice of k_0, there exists x such that $x \in L \cap B_{\mathbf{M}}^{\cap}(\sigma_i)$. Since $x \in B_{\mathbf{M}}^{\cap}(\sigma_i)$, clearly, by the definition of f, $x \notin W_{\mathbf{M}'(T[i])}$. □ (*Claim 7*)

Claim 8. If L is finite, then, for all σ' such that $[\sigma_{k_0} \subseteq \sigma' \wedge \text{content}(\sigma') \subseteq L]$, (a) and (b) below.

(a) $W_{\mathbf{M}(\sigma')} = L$.
(b) $W_{\mathbf{M}(\sigma')} \cap B_{\mathbf{M}}^{\cap}(\sigma') = \emptyset$.

Proof of Claim. (a) is immediate by Lemma 2. (b) follows from (a) and the choice of k_0. □ (*Claim 8*)

Let Q be such that, for all σ', $Q(\sigma') \Leftrightarrow$ for all τ,

$$[\sigma' \subset \tau \wedge \text{content}(\tau) \subseteq W_{\mathbf{M}(\sigma')} \wedge |\tau| \leq |W_{\mathbf{M}(\sigma')}|] \Rightarrow W_{\mathbf{M}(\sigma')} \subseteq W_{f(\tau,0,\lambda)}. \tag{13}$$

Claim 9. If L is finite, then, for all σ' such that $[\sigma_{k_0} \subseteq \sigma' \wedge \text{content}(\sigma') \subseteq L \wedge Q(\sigma')]$, $L \subseteq W_{f(\sigma',0,\lambda)}$.

Proof of Claim. Suppose that L is finite. Let σ' be such that $\sigma_{k_0} \subseteq \sigma'$, content($\sigma'$) $\subseteq L$, and $Q(\sigma')$. By Claim 8(a), $W_{\mathbf{M}(\sigma')} = L$. Consider the calculation of $f(\sigma', 0, \lambda)$. Clearly, if it can be shown that, for each stage s in which $e(\sigma', s)\downarrow$, conditions (b)-(d) are satisfied, then $L \subseteq W_{f(\sigma', 0, \lambda)}$.

Let s be such that $e(\sigma', s)\downarrow$. Let x and A be as in stage s of the calculation of $f(\sigma', 0, \lambda)$. Since $x \in W_{\mathbf{M}(\sigma')} = L$, clearly, $\mathbf{M}(\sigma' \diamond x)\downarrow$. Furthermore, by Claim 8(b), $W_{\mathbf{M}(\sigma')} \cap B_{\mathbf{M}}^{\cap}(\sigma') = \emptyset$. Thus, since $x \in W_{\mathbf{M}(\sigma')}$, $x \in C_{\mathbf{M}}(\sigma') \cup CB_{\mathbf{M}}(\sigma')$. Finally, since $Q(\sigma')$ and $A \subseteq W_{\mathbf{M}(\sigma')}$,

$$(\forall \tau)\big[[\sigma' \subset \tau \ \wedge \ \text{content}(\tau) \subseteq A \ \wedge \ |\tau| \leq |A|] \ \Rightarrow \ A \subseteq W_{f(\tau, 0, \lambda)}\big]. \tag{14}$$

$\square$ (*Claim 9*)

Claim 10. If L is finite, then, for all σ' such that $[\sigma_{k_0} \subseteq \sigma' \ \wedge \ \text{content}(\sigma') \subseteq L]$, $Q(\sigma')$.

Proof of Claim. Suppose that L is finite. Let σ' be such that $\sigma_{k_0} \subseteq \sigma'$ and content(σ') $\subseteq L$. By Claim 8(a), $W_{\mathbf{M}(\sigma')} = L$. Thus, if $|\sigma'| \geq |L|$, then $Q(\sigma')$ holds vacuously. So, suppose, inductively, that

$$(\forall \sigma'')\big[[\sigma_{k_0} \subseteq \sigma'' \ \wedge \ \text{content}(\sigma'') \subseteq L \ \wedge \ |\sigma'| < |\sigma''|] \ \Rightarrow \ Q(\sigma'')\big]. \tag{15}$$

Let τ be such that $\sigma' \subset \tau$ and content(τ) $\subseteq W_{\mathbf{M}(\sigma')}$. Clearly, $\sigma_{k_0} \subseteq \tau$, content($\tau$) $\subseteq L$, and $|\sigma'| < |\tau|$. Thus, by (15), $Q(\tau)$. Furthermore,

$$\begin{aligned} W_{f(\tau, 0, \lambda)} &\supseteq L && \{\text{by Claim 9}\} \\ &= W_{\mathbf{M}(\sigma')} && \{\text{by Claim 8(a)}\}. \end{aligned}$$

$\square$ (*Claim 10*)

Claim 11. If L is finite, then, for all σ' such that $[\sigma_{k_0} \subseteq \sigma' \ \wedge \ \text{content}(\sigma') \subseteq L]$, $L \subseteq W_{f(\sigma', 0, \lambda)}$.

Proof of Claim. Immediate by Claims 9 and 10. $\square$ (*Claim 11*)

Claim 12. If L is finite, then, for all $i \geq k_0$, $W_{\mathbf{M}'(T[i])} = L$.

Proof of Claim. Suppose that L is finite, and let i be such that $i \geq k_0$. Clearly, by the definition of $\mathbf{M}'$, $\sigma_{k_0} \subseteq \sigma_i$. Thus,

$$\begin{aligned} L &\subseteq W_{f(\sigma_i, 0, \lambda)} && \{\text{by Claim 11}\} \\ &\subseteq W_{\mathbf{M}'(T[i])} && \{\text{by (b) and (c) of Claim 1}\} \\ &\subseteq W_{\mathbf{M}(\sigma_i)} && \{\text{by Claim 1(a)}\} \\ &= L && \{\text{by Claim 8(a)}\}. \end{aligned}$$

$\square$ (*Claim 12*)

Claim 13. If L is finite, then, for all i, $W_{\mathbf{M}'(T[i])} = L \Leftrightarrow i \geq k_0$.

Proof of Claim. Immediate by Claims 7 and 12. $\square$ (*Claim 13*)

Claim 14. If L is finite, then $\mathbf{M}'$ **It**-identifies L from T, and, furthermore, $\mathbf{M}'$ does *not* exhibit a U-shape on T.

Proof of Claim. Immediate by Claims 5(g) and 13. $\square$ (*Claim 14*)

Claim 15. For all i such that $k_0 \leq i < k_1$, if $\sigma_i \neq \sigma_{i+1}$, then there exists $w \in (L \cup W_{\mathbf{M}(\sigma_i)}) \cap CB_{\mathbf{M}}(\sigma_i)$ such that $w > m_i$.

Proof of Claim. Let i be such that $k_0 \leq i < k_1$ and $\sigma_i \neq \sigma_{i+1}$. Clearly, one of the following cases must apply.

CASE condition (ii) applies in calculating $\mathbf{M}'(T[i+1])$. Then, clearly, $T(i) \in L \cap CB_{\mathbf{M}}(\sigma_i)$ and $T(i) > m_i$.

CASE condition (v) applies in calculating $\mathbf{M}'(T[i+1])$. Then, since $P(\sigma_i, m_i, T(i))$, clearly, there exists $w \in W_{\mathbf{M}(\sigma_i)} \cap CB_{\mathbf{M}}(\sigma_i)$ such that $w > m_i$. □ *(Claim 15)*

Claim 16. For all i such that $k_0 \leq i < k_1$, if there exists j such that $i < j \leq k_1$ and $\sigma_i \neq \sigma_j$, then there exists $w \in (L \cup W_{\mathbf{M}(\sigma_i)}) \cap CB_{\mathbf{M}}(\sigma_i)$ such that $w > m_i$.

Proof of Claim. Let i be such that $k_0 \leq i < k_1$, and let j be *least* such that $i < j \leq k_1$ and $\sigma_i \neq \sigma_j$. By Claim 15, there exists $w \in (L \cup W_{\mathbf{M}(\sigma_{j-1})}) \cap CB_{\mathbf{M}}(\sigma_{j-1}) = (L \cup W_{\mathbf{M}(\sigma_i)}) \cap CB_{\mathbf{M}}(\sigma_i)$ such that $w > m_{j-1}$. Furthermore, by Claim 3(d), $m_{j-1} \geq m_i$, and, thus, $w > m_i$. □ *(Claim 16)*

Claim 17. If L is infinite, then, for all i and j such that $k_0 \leq i < j \leq k_1$, if $L \subseteq W_{\mathbf{M}'(T[i])}$, then $W_{\mathbf{M}'(T[i])} \subseteq W_{\mathbf{M}'(T[j])}$.

Proof of Claim. By way of contradiction, suppose that L is infinite, and let i and j be such that $k_0 \leq i < j \leq k_1$, $L \subseteq W_{\mathbf{M}'(T[i])}$, and $W_{\mathbf{M}'(T[i])} \not\subseteq W_{\mathbf{M}'(T[j])}$. By Claim 1(a), $L \subseteq W_{\mathbf{M}(\sigma_i)}$. By (b) and (c) of Claim 1, it must be the case that $\sigma_i \subset \sigma_j$. Thus, by Claim 16, there exists $w \in (L \cup W_{\mathbf{M}(\sigma_i)}) \cap CB_{\mathbf{M}}(\sigma_i) = W_{\mathbf{M}(\sigma_i)} \cap CB_{\mathbf{M}}(\sigma_i)$ such that $w > m_i$.

For all s, let x^s denote the value of x during stage s of the calculation of $f(\sigma_i, m_i, \alpha_i)$, and let A^s denote the contents of the set A during stage s of the calculation of $f(\sigma_i, m_i, \alpha_i)$. Choose s such that (a)-(f) below.

(a) $\mathbf{M}(\sigma_i \diamond x^s)\!\downarrow$.
(b) $x^s \in C_{\mathbf{M}}(\sigma_i) \cup CB_{\mathbf{M}}(\sigma_i)$.
(c) $w \in A^s$.
(d) content$(\sigma_j) \subseteq A^s$.
(e) $|\sigma_j| \leq |A^s|$.
(f) $A^s \not\subseteq W_{\mathbf{M}'(T[j])}$.

Clearly, such an s exists. However, since $A^s \not\subseteq W_{\mathbf{M}'(T[j])}$, by (b) and (c) of Claim 1, $A^s \not\subseteq W_{f(\sigma_j, 0, \lambda)}$. Thus, by the definition of f, it must be the case that $W_{\mathbf{M}'(T[i])}$ is finite. But this contradicts $L \subseteq W_{\mathbf{M}'(T[i])}$. □ *(Claim 17)*

Claim 18. $L \cap CB_{\mathbf{M}}(\sigma_{k_1})$ is finite.

Proof of Claim. By Claim 5(e), $L \cap CB_{\mathbf{M}}(\sigma_{k_1}) \subseteq$ content$(T[k_1]) \cup \{0, ..., m_{k_1}\}$. □ *(Claim 18)*

Claim 19. $W_{\mathbf{M}(\sigma_{k_1})} = L$.

Proof of Claim. Immediate by Claims 6 and 18, and by Lemma 1. □ *(Claim 19)*

Claim 20. If L is infinite, then $\max\big(L \cap CB_{\mathbf{M}}(\sigma_{k_1})\big) \leq m_{k_1}$.

Proof of Claim. By way of contradiction, suppose that L is infinite, and let x be such that $x \in L \cap CB_{\mathbf{M}}(\sigma_{k_1})$ and $x > m_{k_1}$. Choose $i \geq k_1$ such that (a)-(c) below.

(a) $\Phi_{\mathbf{M}(\sigma_{k_1})}(x) \leq T(i)$.
(b) $\Phi_{p\mathbf{M}}(\sigma_{k_1} \diamond x) \leq T(i)$.
(c) $x \leq T(i)$.

By Claim 19 and the fact that L is infinite, such an i exists. Clearly, $P\big(\sigma_{k_1}, m_{k_1}, T(i)\big)$. But this contradicts Claim 5(f). $\square$ *(Claim 20)*

Claim 21. If L is infinite, then $W_{\mathbf{M}'(T[k_1])} = L$.

Proof of Claim. Follows from Claims 6, 19, and 20, and from the definition of f. $\square$ *(Claim 21)*

Claim 22. If L is infinite, then there exists i such that, for all j, $W_{\mathbf{M}'(T[j])} = L$ $\Leftrightarrow$ $j \geq i$.

Proof of Claim. Immediate by Claims 7, 17, and 21. $\square$ *(Claim 22)*

Claim 23. If L is infinite, then $\mathbf{M}'$ **It**-identifies L from T, and, furthermore, $\mathbf{M}'$ does *not* exhibit a U-shape on T.

Proof of Claim. Immediate by Claims 5(g) and 22. $\square$ *(Claim 23)*

$\square$ *(Theorem 2)*

4   Iterative-with-Counter Learning

This section explores a learning model that we call *iterative-with-counter learning* (**ItCtr**-learning) (Definition 6, below). In this model, each of a learner's output conjectures can depend *only* upon the learner's just previous conjecture, the most recent input element, *and a counter* indicating the number of elements so far presented to the learner. Theorems 3 and 4, together, show that **ItCtr**-learning and **SDEx**-learning are incomparable, i.e., for each, there is a class of languages learnable by that one, but *not* the other. It follows that **ItCtr**-learning is strictly more powerful than **It**-learning, yet not as powerful as full **Ex**-learning. Finally, Problem 1, below, restates, formally, the problem that this paper leaves open.

Due to space constraints, the proofs of Theorems 3 and 4 are omitted. Proofs of these theorems can be found in [6].

ItCtr-learning was introduced in Definition 1(e) in Section 2, but is repeated here for convenience.

Definition 6.

(a) For all $\mathbf{M}$ and L, $\mathbf{M}$ **ItCtr**-*identifies* L $\Leftrightarrow$ $\mathbf{M}$ **Ex**-identifies L, *and*, for all ϱ, σ, and τ such that $\text{content}(\varrho) \cup \text{content}(\sigma) \cup \text{content}(\tau) \subseteq L$, (i) and (ii) below.
   (i) $\mathbf{M}(\varrho)\downarrow$.
   (ii) $[|\varrho| = |\sigma| \wedge \mathbf{M}(\varrho) = \mathbf{M}(\sigma)] \Rightarrow \mathbf{M}(\varrho \diamond \tau) = \mathbf{M}(\sigma \diamond \tau)$.

(b) For all $\mathbf{M}$, $\mathbf{ItCtr}(\mathbf{M}) = \{L : \mathbf{M}\ \mathbf{ItCtr}\text{-identifies } L\}$.
(c) $\mathbf{ItCtr} = \{\mathcal{L} : (\exists \mathbf{M})[\mathcal{L} \subseteq \mathbf{ItCtr}(\mathbf{M})]\}$.

Theorem 3 (Based on [15, remark on page 238]). Let $\mathcal{L}$ be such that

$$\mathcal{L} = \{\{0, ..., m\} : m \in \mathbb{N}\} \cup \{\mathbb{N} - \{0\}\}. \tag{16}$$

Then, $\mathcal{L} \in \mathbf{SDEx} - \mathbf{ItCtr}$.

Theorem 4. Let $\langle \cdot, \cdot \rangle : \mathbb{N} \times \mathbb{N} \to \mathbb{N}$ be any 1-1, onto, computable function [21], and let $\mathcal{L}$ be such that

$$\mathcal{L} = \{\{\langle e, i \rangle : i \in \mathbb{N}\} : \varphi_e(0)\uparrow\} \cup \{\{\langle e, i \rangle : i \leq \varphi_e(0)\} : \varphi_e(0)\downarrow\}. \tag{17}$$

Then, $\mathcal{L} \in \mathbf{ItCtr} - \mathbf{SDEx}$.

Kinber, *et al.* [15, Theorem 7.7 and remark on page 238] showed that $\mathbf{It} \subset \mathbf{SDEx}$. Schäfer-Richter [22] and Fulk [10], independently, showed that $\mathbf{SDEx} \subset \mathbf{PSDEx}$ and that $\mathbf{PSDEx} = \mathbf{Ex}$. Clearly, $\mathbf{It} \subseteq \mathbf{ItCtr} \subseteq \mathbf{Ex}$. From these observations and Theorems 3 and 4, above, it follows that the *only* inclusions (represented by arrows) among $\mathbf{It}$, $\mathbf{SDEx}$, $\mathbf{ItCtr}$, and $\mathbf{PSDEx} = \mathbf{Ex}$ are the following.

Problem 1. Is it the case that $\mathbf{ItCtr} = \mathbf{NUItCtr}$?

Acknowledgments. We would like to thank Lorenzo Carlucci, Sanjay Jain, Timo Kötzing, and Frank Stephan for reviewing early versions of the proof of Theorem 2. We would also like to thank Timo Kötzing for answering technical questions about [25], which is in German. Finally, we would like to thank several anonymous referees for their useful comments.

References

1. Baliga, G., Case, J., Merkle, W., Stephan, F., Wiehagen, W.: When unlearning helps, Submitted (2007)
2. Blum, M.: A machine independent theory of the complexity of recursive functions. Journal of the ACM 14, 322–336 (1967)
3. Carlucci, L., Case, J., Jain, S., Stephan, F.: Non U-shaped vacillatory and team learning. In: ALT 2005. Lecture Notes in Artificial Intelligence, Springer, Heidelberg (2005)
4. Carlucci, L., Case, J., Jain, S., Stephan, F.: Memory-limited U-shaped learning (Journal version conditionally accepted for Information and Computation). In: COLT 2006. LNCS (LNAI), vol. 4005, pp. 244–258. Springer, Heidelberg (2006)

5. Case, J.: The power of vacillation in language learning. SIAM Journal on Computing 28(6), 1941–1969 (1999)
6. Case, J., Moelius III, S.E.: U-shaped, iterative, and iterative-with-counter learning (expanded version). Technical report, University of Delaware, (2007) Available at http://www.cis.udel.edu/~moelius/publications
7. Case, J., Jain, S., Lange, S., Zeugmann, T.: Incremental concept learning for bounded data mining. Information and Computation 152, 74–110 (1999)
8. Case, J., Lynes, C.: Machine inductive inference and language identification. In: Nielsen, M., Schmidt, E.M. (eds.) Proceedings of the 9th International Colloquium on Automata, Languages and Programming. LNCS, vol. 140, pp. 107–115. Springer, Heidelberg (1982)
9. Davis, M., Sigal, R., Weyuker, E.: Computability, Complexity, and Languages, 2nd edn. Academic Press, San Diego (1994)
10. Fulk, M.: Prudence and other conditions on formal language learning. Information and Computation 85, 1–11 (1990)
11. Fulk, M., Jain, S., Osherson, D.: Open problems in Systems That Learn. Journal of Computer and System Sciences 49(3), 589–604 (1994)
12. Gold, E.: Language identification in the limit. Information and Control 10, 447–474 (1967)
13. Jain, S.: Private communication (2006)
14. Jain, S., Osherson, D., Royer, J., Sharma, A.: Systems that Learn: An Introduction to Learning Theory. MIT Press, Cambridge, Mass (1999)
15. Kinber, E., Stephan, F.: Language learning from texts: mind changes, limited memory, and monotonicity. Information and Computation 123, 224–241 (1995)
16. Lange, S., Zeugmann, T.: Incremental learning from positive data. Journal of Computer and System Sciences 53, 88–103 (1996)
17. Lange, S., Zeugmann, T.: Set-driven and rearrangement-independent learning of recursive languages. Mathematical Systems Theory 6, 599–634 (1996)
18. Marcus, G., Pinker, S., Ullman, M., Hollander, M., Rosen, T.J., Xu, F.: Overregularization in Language Acquisition. Monographs of the Society for Research in Child Development, vol. 57, no. 4. University of Chicago Press, Includes commentary by Clahsen, H. (1992)
19. Osherson, D., Stob, M., Weinstein, S.: Systems that Learn: An Introduction to Learning Theory for Cognitive and Computer Scientists. MIT Press, Cambridge, Mass (1986)
20. Plunkett, K., Marchman, V.: U-shaped learning and frequency effects in a multilayered perceptron: implications for child language acquisition. Cognition 38, 43–102 (1991)
21. Rogers, H.: Theory of Recursive Functions and Effective Computability. McGraw Hill, New York, 1967. Reprinted, MIT Press (1987)
22. Schäfer-Richter, G.: Über Eingabeabhängigkeit und Komplexität von Inferenzstrategien. PhD thesis, Rheinisch-Westfälische Technische Hochschule Aachen, Germany (1984)
23. Taatgen, N.A., Anderson, J.R.: Why do children learn to say broke? A model of learning the past tense without feedback. Cognition 86, 123–155 (2002)
24. Wexler, K., Culicover, P.: Formal Principles of Language Acquisition. MIT Press, Cambridge, Mass (1980)
25. Wiehagen, R.: Limes-erkennung rekursiver funktionen durch spezielle strategien. Electronische Informationverarbeitung und Kybernetik 12, 93–99 (1976)

Mind Change Optimal Learning of Bayes Net Structure

Oliver Schulte[1], Wei Luo[1], and Russell Greiner[2]

[1] Simon Fraser University, Vancouver-Burnaby, BC V5A 1S6, Canada
{oschulte,wluoa}@cs.sfu.ca
[2] University of Alberta, Edmonton, Alberta T6G 2E8, Canada
greiner@cs.ualberta.ca

Abstract. This paper analyzes the problem of learning the structure of a Bayes net (BN) in the theoretical framework of Gold's learning paradigm. Bayes nets are one of the most prominent formalisms for knowledge representation and probabilistic and causal reasoning. We follow constraint-based approaches to learning Bayes net structure, where learning is based on observed conditional dependencies between variables of interest (e.g., "X is dependent on Y given any assignment to variable Z"). Applying learning criteria in this model leads to the following results. (1) The mind change complexity of identifying a Bayes net graph over variables $\mathbf{V}$ from dependency data is $\binom{|\mathbf{V}|}{2}$, the maximum number of edges. (2) There is a unique fastest mind-change optimal Bayes net learner; convergence speed is evaluated using Gold's dominance notion of "uniformly faster convergence". This learner conjectures a graph if it is the unique Bayes net pattern that satisfies the observed dependencies with a minimum number of edges, and outputs "no guess" otherwise. Therefore we are using standard learning criteria to define a natural and novel Bayes net learning algorithm. We investigate the complexity of computing the output of the fastest mind-change optimal learner, and show that this problem is NP-hard (assuming P = RP). To our knowledge this is the first NP-hardness result concerning the existence of a uniquely optimal Bayes net structure.

1 Introduction

One of the goals of computational learning theory is to analyze the complexity of practically important learning problems, and to design optimal learning algorithms for them that meet performance guarantees. In this paper, we model learning the structure of a Bayes net as a language learning problem in the Gold paradigm. We apply identification criteria such as mind change bounds [9, Ch. 12.2][20], mind-change optimality [11,12], and text-efficiency (minimizing time or number of data points before convergence) [16,8]. Bayes nets, one of the most prominent knowledge representation formalisms [18,19], are widely used to define probabilistic models in a graphical manner, with a directed acyclic graph (DAG) whose edges link the variables of interest.

We base our model of BN structure learning on an approach known as "constraint-based" learning [5]. Constraint-based learning views a BN structure as a specification of conditional dependencies of the form $X \not\!\perp Y | \mathbf{S}$, where X and Y are variables of interest and $\mathbf{S}$ is a set of variables disjoint from $\{X, Y\}$. (Read $X \not\!\perp Y | \mathbf{S}$ as "variable X is dependent on variable Y given values for the variables in the set $\mathbf{S}$".) For example,

N. Bshouty and C. Gentile (Eds.): COLT 2007, LNAI 4539, pp. 187–202, 2007.

a conditional dependence statement represented by a Bayes net may be "father's eye colour is dependent on mother's eye colour given child's eye colour". In this view, a BN structure is a syntactic representation of a dependency relation [18, Sec.3.3]. It is possible for distinct BN structures to represent the same dependency relation; in that case the equivalent BN structures share a partially directed graph known as a *pattern* (defined below), so a BN pattern is a unique syntactic representation of a dependency relation. A dependency relation meets the mathematical definition of a language in the sense of Gold's paradigm, where the basic "strings" are dependence statements of the form "$X \not\!\perp Y | \mathbf{S}$". We show that in this learning model, the mind change complexity of learning a Bayes net graph for a given set of variables $\mathbf{V}$ is $\binom{|\mathbf{V}|}{2}$—the maximum number of edges in a graph with node set $\mathbf{V}$. Our analysis leads to a characterization of BN learning algorithms that are mind-change optimal. A learner is mind-change optimal if it minimizes the number of mind changes not only globally in the entire learning problem, but also locally in subproblems encountered after receiving some evidence [11,12]; see Section 5. Mind-change optimal BN learners are exactly those that conjecture a BN pattern G only if the pattern is the unique one that satisfies the observed dependencies *with a minimum number of edges*.

Applying Gold's notion of dominance in convergence time [8, p.462], we show that there is a fastest mind-change optimal learner whose convergence time dominates that of all other mind-change optimal learners. The fastest learner is defined as follows: If there is more than one BN pattern G that satisfies the observed dependencies with a minimum number of edges, output "?" (for "no guess"). If there is a unique pattern G that satisfies the observed dependencies with a minimum number of edges, output G. Thus standard identification criteria in Gold's paradigm lead to a natural and novel algorithm for learning BN structure. The technically most complex result of the paper examines the computational complexity of the fastest mind-change optimal BN learner: we show that computing its conjectures is NP-hard (assuming that $P = RP$).

Related Work. Many BN learning systems follow the "search and score" paradigm, and seek a structure that optimizes some numeric score [5]. Our work is in the alternative constraint-based paradigm. Constraint-based (CB) algorithms for learning Bayes net structure are a well-developed area of machine learning. Introductory overviews are provided in [5], [15, Ch.10]. The Tetrad system [6] includes a number of CB methods for different classes of Bayes nets. A fundamental difference between existing CB approaches and our model is that the existing methods assume access to an oracle that returns an answer for every query of the form "does $X \not\!\perp Y | \mathbf{S}$ hold?" In contrast, our model corresponds to the situation of a learner whose evidence (in the form of dependency assertions) grows incrementally over time. Another difference is that existing CB methods assume that their oracle indicates *both* whether two variables are conditionally dependent and whether they are conditionally independent. In language learning terms, the CB method has access to both positive data (dependencies) and negative data (independencies). In our analysis, the learner receives only positive data (dependencies). To our knowledge, our work is the first application of Gold's language learning paradigm to Bayes net learning.

A Bayes net that satisfies a set of given dependencies $\mathcal{D}$ is said to be an I-map for $\mathcal{D}$. We show the NP-hardness of the following problem: for a given set of dependencies $\mathcal{D}$

represented by an oracle O (Section 6), decide whether there is a unique edge minimal I-map G for $\mathcal{D}$, and if so, output G. Bouckaert proved that the problem is NP-hard without the uniqueness condition [2, Lm. 4.5]. However, Bouckaert's proof cannot be adapted for our uniqueness problem, which requires a much more complex reduction. To our knowledge, this is the first NP-hardness result for deciding the existence of a uniquely optimal Bayes net structure for any optimality criterion.

We introduce concepts and results from both learning theory and Bayes net theory in the next section. Section 3 presents and discusses our model of BN structure learning as a language learning problem. Section 4 analyzes the mind change complexity of BN structure learning. Section 5 characterizes the mind-change optimal learning algorithms for this problems and describes the fastest mind-change optimal learner. The final two sections define the problem of computing the output of the fastest mind-change optimal learner and show that the problem is NP-hard.

2 Preliminaries: Language Identification and Bayes Nets

We first introduce general concepts from learning theory, followed by basic definitions from Bayes net theory.

2.1 Language Identification with Bounded Mind Changes

We employ notation and terminology from [10], [13, Ch.1], [16], and [8]. We write $\mathbb{N}$ for the set of natural numbers $\{0, 1, 2, ...\}$. The symbols $\subseteq, \supseteq, \subset, \supset$, and $\emptyset$ respectively stand for subset, superset, proper subset, proper superset, and the empty set. We assume that there is an at most countable set $\mathbb{E}$ of potential evidence items (strings in language learning). A **language** is a subset of $\mathbb{E}$; we write L for a generic language [8, p.449]. A **language learning problem** is a collection of languages; we write $\mathcal{L}$ for a generic collection of languages. A **text** T is a mapping of $\mathbb{N}$ into $\mathbb{E} \cup \{\#\}$, where $\#$ is a symbol not in $\mathbb{E}$. (The symbol $\#$ models pauses in data presentation.) We write content(T) for the intersection of $\mathbb{E}$ and the range of T. A text T is **for** a language L iff $L = $ content(T). The initial sequence of text T of length n is denoted by $T[n]$. The set of all finite initial sequences over $\mathbb{E} \cup \{\#\}$ is denoted by SEQ. We also use SEQ$(\mathcal{L})$ to denote finite initial sequences consistent with languages in $\mathcal{L}$. Greek letters σ and τ range over SEQ. We write content(σ) for the intersection of $\mathbb{E}$ and the range of σ. We write $\sigma \subset T$ to denote that text T extends initial sequence σ; similarly for $\sigma \subset \tau$. A **learner** Ψ **for** a collection of languages $\mathcal{L}$ is a mapping of SEQ$(\mathcal{L})$ into $\mathcal{L} \cup \{?\}$. Our term "learner" corresponds to the term "scientist" in [13, Ch.2.1.2]. We say that a learner Ψ **identifies** a language L on a text T for L, if $\Psi(T[n]) = L$ for all but a finitely many n. Next we define identification of a language collection relative to some evidence.

Definition 1. *A learner Ψ for $\mathcal{L}$ **identifies** $\mathcal{L}$ given $\sigma \iff$ for every language $L \in \mathcal{L}$, and for every text $T \supset \sigma$ for L, the learner Ψ identifies L on T.*

Thus a learner Ψ identifies a language collection $\mathcal{L}$ if Ψ identifies $\mathcal{L}$ given the empty sequence Λ. A learner Ψ **changes its mind** at some nonempty finite sequence $\sigma \in$ SEQ if $\Psi(\sigma) \neq \Psi(\sigma^-)$ and $\Psi(\sigma^-) \neq ?$, where σ^- is the initial segment of σ with σ's last element removed [9, Ch.12.2]. (No mind changes occur at the empty sequence Λ.).

Definition 2. *Let* $\mathrm{MC}(\Psi, T, \sigma)$ *denote the total number of mind changes of* Ψ *on text* T *after sequence* σ *(i.e.,* $\mathrm{MC}(\Psi, T, \sigma) = |\{\tau : \sigma \subset \tau \subset T : \Psi$ *changes its mind at* $\tau\}|$*).*

1. Ψ *identifies* $\mathcal{L}$ *with **mind-change bound** k given* $\sigma \iff \Psi$ *identifies* $\mathcal{L}$ *given* σ *and* Ψ *changes its mind at most k times on any text $T \supset \sigma$ for a language in $\mathcal{L}$ after σ (i.e., if $T \supset \sigma$ extends data sequence σ and T is a text for any language $L \in \mathcal{L}$, then* $\mathrm{MC}(\Psi, T, \sigma) \leq k$*).*
2. *A language collection* $\mathcal{L}$ *is **identifiable with mind change bound** k given* $\sigma \iff$ *there is a learner* Ψ *such that* Ψ *identifies* $\mathcal{L}$ *with mind change bound k given* σ*.*

2.2 Bayes Nets: Basic Concepts and Definitions

We employ notation and terminology from [19], [18] and [22]. A **Bayes net structure** is a directed acyclic graph $G = (\mathbf{V}, E)$. Two nodes X, Y are **adjacent** in a BN if G contains an edge $X \to Y$ or $Y \to X$. The **pattern** $\pi(G)$ of DAG G is the partially directed graph over $\mathbf{V}$ that has the same adjacencies as G, and contains an arrowhead $X \to Y$ if and only if G contains a triple $X \to Y \leftarrow Z$ where X and Z are not adjacent. A node W is a **collider on undirected path** p in DAG G if and only if the left and right neighbours of W on p point into W. Every BN structure defines a separability relation between a pair of nodes X, Y relative to a set of nodes $\mathbf{S}$, called **d-separation**. If X, Y are two variables and $\mathbf{S}$ is a set of variables disjoint from $\{X, Y\}$, then $\mathbf{S}$ d-separates X and Y if along every (undirected) path between X and Y there is a node W satisfying one of the following conditions: (1) W is a collider on the path and neither W nor any of its descendants is in $\mathbf{S}$, or (2) W is not a collider on the path and W is in $\mathbf{S}$. We write $(X \perp\!\!\!\perp Y|\mathbf{S})_G$ if X and Y are d-separated by $\mathbf{S}$ in graph G. If two nodes X and Y are not d-separated by $\mathbf{S}$ in graph G, then X and Y are **d-connected** by $\mathbf{S}$ in G, written $(X \not\perp\!\!\!\perp Y|\mathbf{S})_G$. The d-connection relation, or **dependency relation**, for a graph is denoted by $\mathcal{D}_G$, that is, $\langle X, Y, \mathbf{S} \rangle \in \mathcal{D}_G$ iff $(X \not\perp\!\!\!\perp Y|\mathbf{S})_G$. Verma and Pearl proved that two Bayes nets G_1 and G_2 represent the same dependency relation iff they have the same pattern (i.e., $\mathcal{D}_{G_1} = \mathcal{D}_{G_2}$ iff $\pi(G_1) = \pi(G_2)$ [24, Thm. 1]). Thus we use a pattern as a syntactic representation for a Bayes net dependency relation and write G to denote both graphs and patterns unless there is ambiguity. The **statement space** over a set of variables $\mathbf{V}$, denoted by $\mathcal{U}_{\mathbf{V}}$, contains all conditional dependency statements of the form $(X \not\perp\!\!\!\perp Y|\mathbf{S})$, where X, Y are distinct variables in $\mathbf{V}$ and $\mathbf{S} \subseteq \mathbf{V} \setminus \{X, Y\}$.

Fig. 1 shows a Bayes net from [19, p.15]. In this network, node wet is an unshielded collider on the path sprinkler $-$ wet $-$ rain; node wet is not a collider on the path sprinkler $-$ wet $-$ slippery. The pattern of the network has the same skeleton, but contains only two edges that induce the collider wet. From d-separation we have (sprinkler $\perp\!\!\!\perp$ rain|{season})$_G$ and (sprinkler $\not\perp\!\!\!\perp$ rain|{season, wet})$_G$. Next we introduce our model of BN structure learning, which associates a language collection $\mathcal{L}_{\mathbf{V}}$ with a given set of variables $\mathbf{V}$; the language collection $\mathcal{L}_{\mathbf{V}}$ comprises all dependency relations defined by Bayes net structures.

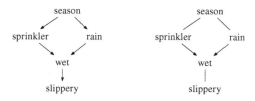

Fig. 1. Sprinkler network and its pattern

Table 1. The correspondence between constraint-based learning of Bayes Nets from conditional dependency data and Gold's language learning model

General Language Learning	Bayes Net Structure Learning
string	conditional dependency statement $X \not\perp Y|\mathbf{S}$
language	conditional dependency relation
index	pattern
text	complete dependency sequence

3   Bayes Net Learning with Bounded Mind Changes

This section defines our model of BN structure learning. We discuss the assumptions in the model and compare them to assumptions made in other constraint-based BN learning approaches.

3.1   Definition of the Learning Model

Fix a set of variables $\mathbf{V}$. The evidence item set $\mathbb{E}$ is the statement space $\mathcal{U}_{\mathbf{V}}$. Let $\mathcal{L}_{\mathbf{V}}$ be the **set of BN-dependency relations over variables** $\mathbf{V}$ (i.e., $\mathcal{L}_{\mathbf{V}} = \{\mathcal{D}_G :$ G is a pattern over $\mathbf{V}\}$). A **complete dependency sequence** T is a mapping of $\mathbb{N}$ into $\mathcal{U}_{\mathbf{V}} \cup \{\#\}$. A dependency sequence T is **for** a dependency relation $\mathcal{D}$ iff $\mathcal{D} = $ content (T). A Bayes net learning algorithm Ψ maps a finite data sequence σ over $\mathcal{U}_{\mathbf{V}} \cup \{\#\}$ to a pattern G. As Table 1 illustrates, this defines a language learning model, with some changes in terminology that reflect the Bayes net context.

Example. Let G be the DAG in Figure 1. The dependency relation for the graph $\mathcal{D}_G$ contains $\{\ \langle \texttt{season}, \texttt{sprinkler}, \emptyset \rangle, \langle \texttt{season}, \texttt{sprinkler}, \{\texttt{rain}\} \rangle, \ldots, \langle \texttt{sprinkler},$ $\texttt{rain}, \{\texttt{season}, \texttt{wet}\} \rangle, \langle \texttt{sprinkler}, \texttt{rain}, \{\texttt{season}, \texttt{slippery}\} \rangle \}$. Any text enumerating $\mathcal{D}_G$ is a dependency sequence for $\mathcal{D}_G$.

3.2   Discussion

A Bayes net defines a dependency relation via the d-separation criterion. The motivation for this criterion stems from how a Bayes net represents a probability distribution P. Let P be a joint distribution over variables $\mathbf{V}$. If $\mathbf{X}, \mathbf{Y}$ and $\mathbf{Z}$ are three disjoint sets of variables, then $\mathbf{X}$ and $\mathbf{Y}$ are **stochastically independent given S**, denoted by

$(\mathbf{X} \perp\!\!\!\perp \mathbf{Y}|\mathbf{S})_P$, if $P(\mathbf{X}, \mathbf{Y}|\mathbf{S}) = P(\mathbf{X}|\mathbf{S}) P(\mathbf{Y}|\mathbf{S})$ whenever $P(\mathbf{S}) > 0$. If $\mathbf{X}$, $\mathbf{Y}$, and $\mathbf{S}$ are disjoint sets of nodes in G and $\mathbf{X}$ and $\mathbf{Y}$ are not empty, then $\mathbf{X}$ and $\mathbf{Y}$ are d-separated by $\mathbf{S}$ if and only if every pair $\langle X, Y \rangle$ in $\mathbf{X} \times \mathbf{Y}$ is d-separated by $\mathbf{S}$. In constraint-based BN learning, it is common to assume that the probability distribution generating the data of interest has a faithful BN representation [22, Thm.3.2], [19, Ch.2.4].

Definition 3. *Let* $\mathbf{V}$ *be a set of variables,* G *a Bayes net over* $\mathbf{V}$, *and* P *a joint distribution over* $\mathbf{V}$. *Then* G *is **faithful to** P if* $(\mathbf{X} \not\perp\!\!\!\perp \mathbf{Y}|\mathbf{S})_P$ *in* P $\iff$ $(\mathbf{X} \not\perp\!\!\!\perp \mathbf{Y}|\mathbf{S})_G$ *in* G.

Assuming faithfulness, the dependencies in the data can be exactly represented in a Bayes net or a pattern, which is the assumption in our language learning model. It is easy to see that a graph G is faithful to a distribution P if and only if G is faithful with respect to variable pairs, that is, if $(X \not\perp\!\!\!\perp Y|\mathbf{S})_P$ in P $\iff$ $(X \not\perp\!\!\!\perp Y|\mathbf{S})_G$ in G for all variables X, Y. Therefore CB methods focus on conditional dependencies of the form $X \not\perp\!\!\!\perp Y|\mathbf{S}$, which is the approach we follow throughout the paper.

As Gold's paradigm does not specify how linguistic data are generated for the learner, our model does not specify how the observed dependencies are generated. In practice, a BN learner obtains a random sample $\mathbf{d}$ drawn from the operating joint distribution over the variables $\mathbf{V}$, and applies a suitable statistical criterion to decide if a dependency $X \not\perp\!\!\!\perp Y|\mathbf{S}$ holds. One way in which data for our model can be generated from random samples is the following: For every triple $X \not\perp\!\!\!\perp Y|\mathbf{S}$ with $\{X, Y\} \cap \mathbf{S} = \emptyset$, a statistical test is performed with $X \perp\!\!\!\perp Y|\mathbf{S}$ as the null hypothesis. (For small numbers of variables, this is a common procedure in statistics called "all subsets variable selection" [25, p.59].) If the test rejects the null hypothesis, the dependency $X \not\perp\!\!\!\perp Y|\mathbf{S}$ is added to the dependency data; otherwise no conclusion is drawn. Many CB systems also use a statistical test to answer queries to a dependency oracle: given a query "Does $X \not\perp\!\!\!\perp Y|\mathbf{S}$ hold?", the system answers "yes" if the test rejects the hypothesis $X \perp\!\!\!\perp Y|\mathbf{S}$, and "no" otherwise. The assumption that this procedure yields correct results is called the assumption of valid statistical testing [5, Sect.6.2]. Our model is more realistic in two respects. First, the model assumes only that *dependency information* is available, but does not rely on independence data. In fact, many statisticians hold that no independence conclusion should be drawn when a statistical significance test fails to reject an independence hypothesis [7]. Second, our model does not assume that the dependency information is supplied by an oracle all at once, but explicitly considers learning in a setting where more information becomes available as the sample size increases.

Since the set of dependency relations $\mathcal{L}_{\mathbf{V}}$ constitutes a language collection in the sense of the Gold paradigm, we can employ standard identification criteria to analyze this learning problem. We begin by applying a fundamental result in Bayes net theory to determine the mind change complexity of the problem.

4   The Mind Change Complexity of Learning Bayes Net Structure

Following Angluin [1, Condition 3] and Shinohara [21], we say that a class of languages $\mathcal{L}$ has **finite thickness** if the set $\{L \in \mathcal{L} : s \in L\}$ is finite for every string or evidence item $s \in \bigcup \mathcal{L}$. For language collections with finite thickness, their mind change complexity is determined by a structural feature called the inclusion depth [12, Def.6.1].

Definition 4. *Let $\mathcal{L}$ be a language collection and L be a language in $\mathcal{L}$. The **inclusion depth** of L in $\mathcal{L}$ is the size n of the largest index set $\{L_i\}_{1 \leq i \leq n}$ of distinct languages in $\mathcal{L}$, such that $L \subset L_1 \subset \cdots \subset L_i \subset \cdots \subset L_n$. The **inclusion depth** of $\mathcal{L}$ is the maximum of the inclusion depths of languages in $\mathcal{L}$.*

The next proposition establishes the connection between inclusion depth and mind change complexity. It follows immediately from the general result for ordinal mind change bounds established in [12, Prop. 6.1].

Proposition 1. *Let $\mathcal{L}$ be a language collection with finite thickness. Then there is a learner Ψ that identifies $\mathcal{L}$ with mind change bound $k \iff$ the inclusion depth of $\mathcal{L}$ is at most k.*

Since we are considering Bayes nets with finitely many variables, the statement space $\mathcal{U}_{\mathbf{V}}$ is finite, so the language collection $\mathcal{L}_{\mathbf{V}}$ containing all BN-dependency relations is finite and therefore $\mathcal{L}_{\mathbf{V}}$ has finite thickness. Hence we have the following corollary.

Corollary 1. *Let $\mathbf{V}$ be a set of variables. There exists a learner Ψ that identifies $\mathcal{L}_{\mathbf{V}}$ with mind change bound $k \iff$ the inclusion depth of $\mathcal{L}_{\mathbf{V}}$ is at most k.*

A fundamental result in Bayes net theory allows us to determine the inclusion depth of a dependency relation in $\mathcal{L}_{\mathbf{V}}$. An edge $A \to B$ is **covered** in a DAG G if the parents of B are exactly the parents of A plus A itself (see Figure 2). The operation that reverses the direction of the arrow between A and B is a **covered edge reversal**. The following theorem was conjectured by Meek [14] and proven by Chickering [3, Thm.4].

Fig. 2. Edge $A \to B$ is covered, whereas $D \to A$ is not covered

Theorem 1 (Meek-Chickering). *Let G and H be two DAGs over the same set of variables $\mathbf{V}$. Then $\mathcal{D}_G \subseteq \mathcal{D}_H \iff$ the DAG H can be transformed into the DAG G by repeating the following two operations: (1) covered edge reversal, and (2) single edge deletion.*

The next corollary characterizes the inclusion depth of the BN dependence relation $\mathcal{D}_G$ for a graph G in terms of a simple syntactic feature of G, namely the number of missing adjacencies.

Corollary 2. *Let $G = (\mathbf{V}, E)$ be a Bayes net structure. Then the inclusion depth of the BN-dependence relation $\mathcal{D}_G$ equals $\binom{|\mathbf{V}|}{2} - |E|$, the number of adjacencies not in G. In particular, the totally disconnected network has inclusion depth $\binom{|\mathbf{V}|}{2}$; a complete network has inclusion depth 0.*

Proof. We use downward induction on the number of edges n in graph G. Let $N = \binom{|\mathbf{V}|}{2}$. Base case: $n = N$. Then G is a complete graph, so $\mathcal{D}_G$ contains all dependency statements in the statement space $\mathcal{U}_\mathbf{V}$, and therefore has 0 inclusion depth. Inductive step: Assume the hypothesis for $n + 1$ and consider a graph G with n edges. Add an edge to G to obtain a BN G' with $n + 1$ edges that is a supergraph of G'. The definition of d-separation implies that $\mathcal{D}_G \subset \mathcal{D}_{G'}$. By inductive hypothesis, there is an inclusion chain $\mathcal{D}_{G'} \subset \mathcal{D}_{G_1} \cdots \subset \mathcal{D}_{G_{N-(n+1)}}$ consisting of BN dependency relations. Hence the inclusion depth of G is at least $N - (n + 1) + 1 = N - n$.

To show that the inclusion depth of G is exactly $N - n$, suppose for contradiction that it is greater than $N - n$. Then there is an inclusion chain $\mathcal{D}_G \subset \mathcal{D}_{H_1} \subset \mathcal{D}_{H_2} \subset \cdots \subset \mathcal{U}_\mathbf{V}$ of length greater than $N - n$. So the inclusion depth of $\mathcal{D}_{H_2}$ is at least $N - (n+1)$ and the inclusion depth of $\mathcal{D}_{H_1}$ is at least $N - n$. Hence by inductive hypothesis, the number of edges in H_2 is at most $n+1$ and in H_1 at most n. So at least two of the graphs G, H_1, H_2 have the same number of edges. Without loss of generality, assume that H_1 and H_2 have the same number of edges. Since $\mathcal{D}_{H_1} \subset \mathcal{D}_{H_2}$, Theorem 1 implies that H_1 can be obtained from H_2 with covered edge reversals. But covered edge reversals are symmetric, so we also have $\mathcal{D}_{H_2} \subseteq \mathcal{D}_{H_1}$, which contradicts the choice of H_1 and H_2. So the inclusion depth of $\mathcal{D}_G$ is $N - n$, which completes the inductive proof.

Together with Proposition 1, the corollary implies that the mind change complexity of identifying a Bayes Net structure over variables $\mathbf{V}$ is given by the maximum number of edges over $\mathbf{V}$.

Theorem 2. *For any set of variables* $\mathbf{V}$*, the inclusion depth of* $\mathcal{L}_\mathbf{V}$ *is* $\binom{|\mathbf{V}|}{2}$*. So the mind change complexity of identifying the correct Bayes Net structure from dependency data is* $\binom{|\mathbf{V}|}{2}$*.*

The next section characterizes the BN learning algorithms that achieve optimal mind change performance.

5   Mind-Change Optimal Learners for Bayes Net Structure

We analyze mind-change optimal algorithms for identifying Bayes net structure. The intuition underlying mind-change optimality is that a learner that is efficient with respect to mind changes minimizes mind changes not only globally in the entire learning problem, but also locally in subproblems after receiving some evidence [12,11]. We formalize this idea as in [12, Def.2.3]. If a mind change bound exists for $\mathcal{L}$ given σ, let $\mathrm{MC}_\mathcal{L}(\sigma)$ be the least k such that $\mathcal{L}$ is identifiable with k mind changes given σ. For example, given a sequence σ of dependencies, let $G = (\mathbf{V}, E)$ be a BN that satisfies the dependencies in σ with a minimum number of edges. Then the mind change complexity $\mathrm{MC}_{\mathcal{L}_\mathbf{V}}(\sigma)$ is $\binom{|\mathbf{V}|}{2} - |E|$. Mind change optimality requires that a learner should succeed with $\mathrm{MC}_\mathcal{L}(\sigma)$ mind changes after each data sequence σ.

Definition 5 (based on Def.2.3 of [12]). *A learner* Ψ *is strongly mind-change optimal (SMC-optimal) for* $\mathcal{L}$ *if for all data sequences* σ *the learner* Ψ *identifies* $\mathcal{L}$ *given* σ *with at most* $\mathrm{MC}_\mathcal{L}(\sigma)$ *mind changes.*

The next proposition characterizes SMC-optimal learners for language collections with finite inclusion depth. It follows from the general characterization of SMC-optimal learners for all language collections established in [12, Prop.4.1].

Proposition 2. *Let Ψ be a learner that identifies a language collection $\mathcal{L}$ with finite inclusion depth. Then Ψ is SMC-optimal for $\mathcal{L}$ if and only if for all data sequences σ: if $\Psi(\sigma) \neq ?$, then $\Psi(\sigma)$ is the unique language with the largest inclusion depth for σ.*

Applying the proposition to Bayes net learners yields the following corollary.

Corollary 3. *Let Ψ be a Bayes net learner that identifies the correct Bayes net pattern for a set of variables $\mathbf{V}$. The learner Ψ is SMC-optimal for $\mathcal{L}_{\mathbf{V}} \iff$ for all dependency sequences σ, if the output of Ψ is not $?$, then Ψ outputs a uniquely edge-minimal pattern for the dependencies $\mathcal{D} = \mathrm{content}(\sigma)$.*

It is easy to implement a slow SMC-optimal BN learner. For example, for a given set of dependencies $\mathcal{D}$ it is straightforward to check if there is a pattern G that covers exactly those dependencies (i.e., $\mathcal{D}_G = \mathcal{D}$). So an SMC-optimal learner could output a pattern G if there is one that matches the observed dependencies exactly, and output $?$ otherwise. But such a slow learner requires exponentially many dependency statements as input. There are SMC-optimal learners that produce a guess faster; in fact, using Gold's notion of "uniformly faster", we can show that there is a unique fastest SMC-optimal learner. Gold proposed the following way to compare the convergence speed of two learners [8, p. 462].

Definition 6. *Let $\mathcal{L}$ be a language collection.*

1. *The convergence time of a learner Ψ on text T is defined as $\mathrm{CP}(\Psi, T) \equiv$ the least time m such that $\Psi(T[m]) = \Psi(T[m'])$ for all $m' \geq m$.*
2. *A learner Ψ identifies $\mathcal{L}$ uniformly faster than learner $\Phi \iff$*
   (a) for all languages $L \in \mathcal{L}$ and all texts T for L, we have $\mathrm{CP}(\Psi, T) \leq \mathrm{CP}(\Phi, T)$, and
   (b) for some language $L \in \mathcal{L}$ and some text T for L, we have $\mathrm{CP}(\Psi, T) < \mathrm{CP}(\Phi, T)$.

For a language collection $\mathcal{L}$ with finite inclusion depth, Proposition 2 implies that if there is no language L that uniquely maximizes inclusion depth given σ, then a learner that is SMC-optimal outputs $?$ on σ. Intuitively, the fastest SMC-optimal learner delays making a conjecture no longer than is necessary to meet this condition. Formally, this learner is defined as follows for all sequences $\sigma \in \mathrm{SEQ}(\mathcal{L})$:

$$\Psi^{\mathcal{L}}_{\mathrm{fast}}(\sigma) = \begin{cases} ? & \text{if no language uniquely maximizes inclusion depth given } \sigma \\ L & \text{if } L \in \mathcal{L} \text{ uniquely maximizes inclusion depth given } \sigma. \end{cases}$$

The next observation asserts that $\Psi^{\mathcal{L}}_{\mathrm{fast}}$ is the fastest SMC-optimal method for $\mathcal{L}$.

Observation 1. *Let $\mathcal{L}$ be a language collection with finite inclusion depth. Then $\Psi^{\mathcal{L}}_{\mathrm{fast}}$ is SMC-optimal and identifies $\mathcal{L}$ uniformly faster than any other SMC-optimal learner for $\mathcal{L}$.*

Proof. The proof is a variant of standard results on text-efficiency (e.g., [13, Ch.2.3.3]) and is omitted for space reasons.

Observation 1 leads to the following algorithm for identifying a BN pattern.

Corollary 4. *Let* **V** *be a set of variables. For a given sequence of dependencies σ, the learner $\Psi_{\text{fast}}^{\mathbf{V}}$ outputs ? if there is more than one edge-minimal pattern that covers the dependencies in σ, and otherwise outputs a uniquely edge-minimal pattern for the dependencies $\mathcal{D} = \text{content}(\sigma)$. The learner $\Psi_{\text{fast}}^{\mathbf{V}}$ is SMC-optimal and identifies the correct pattern uniformly faster than any other SMC-optimal BN structure learner.*

The remainder of the paper analyzes the run-time complexity of the $\Psi_{\text{fast}}^{\mathbf{V}}$ method; we show that computing the output of the learner is NP-hard (assuming that $P = RP$).

6   Computational Complexity of Fast Mind-Change Optimal Identification of Bayes Net structure

This section considers the computational complexity of implementing the fastest SMC-optimal learner $\Psi_{\text{fast}}^{\mathbf{V}}$. We describe the standard approach of analyzing the complexity of constraint-based learners in the Bayes net literature and state some known results from complexity theory for background.

As with any run-time analysis, an important issue is the representation of the input to the algorithm. The most straightforward approach for our learning model would be to take the input as a list of dependencies, and the input size to be the size of that list. However, in practice CB learners do not receive an explicitly enumerated list of dependencies, but rather they have access to a dependency oracle (cf. Section 3.2). Enumerating relevant dependencies through repeated queries is part of the computational task of a CB learner. Accordingly, the standard complexity analysis takes a dependency oracle and a set of variables as the input to the learning algorithm (e.g., [4, Def.12],[2]).

Definition 7. *A dependency oracle O for a variable set* **V** *is a function that takes as input dependency queries from the statement space $\mathcal{U}_{\mathbf{V}}$ and returns, in constant time, either "yes" or "?".*

The dependency relation associated with oracle O is given by $\mathcal{D}_O = \{X \not\perp Y | \mathbf{S} \in \mathcal{U}_{\mathbf{V}} : O$ returns "yes" on input $X \not\perp Y | \mathbf{S}\}$. We note that our model of learning Bayes net structure can be reformulated in terms of a sequence of oracles: Instead of a complete sequence of dependency statements for a dependence relation $\mathcal{D}_G$, the learner could be presented with a sequence of dependency oracles $O_1, O_2, \ldots, O_n, \ldots$ such that $\mathcal{D}_{O_i} \subseteq \mathcal{D}_{O_{i+1}}$ and $\bigcup_{i=1}^{\infty} \mathcal{D}_{O_i} = \mathcal{D}_G$. The mind change and convergence time results remain the same in this model.

We will reduce the problem of computing the output of the fastest mind change optimal learner $\Psi_{\text{fast}}^{\mathbf{V}}$ to deciding the existence of a unique exact cover by 3-sets.

UEC3SET
Instance A finite set X with $|X| = 3q$ and a collection C of 3-element subsets of X.
Question Does C contain a unique *exact cover* for X, that is, a unique subcollection $C' \subseteq C$ such that every element of X occurs in exactly one member of C'?

We apply the following well-known result. The class RP comprises the decision problems that can be decided in polynomial time with a randomized algorithm [17, Def.11.1].

Proposition 3. *A polynomial time algorithm for* UEC3SET *yields a polynomial time algorithm for the satisfiability problem* SAT *provided that* $P = RP$. *So* UEC3SET *is NP-hard under that assumption.*

The proposition follows from the famous theorem of Valiant and Vazirani that gives a probabilistic reduction of SAT to UNIQUE SAT [23]. Standard reductions show that UNIQUE SAT reduces to UEC3SET. Computing the conjectures of the learner $\Psi_{\text{fast}}^{\mathbf{V}}$ poses the following computational problem.

UNIQUE MINIMAL I-MAP
Input A set of variables $\mathbf{V}$ and a dependency oracle O for $\mathbf{V}$.
Output If there is a *unique* DAG pattern G that covers the dependencies in O with a minimal number of edges, output G. Otherwise output ?.

This is a function minimization problem; the corresponding decision problem is the following.

UNIQUE I-MAP
Instance A set of variables $\mathbf{V}$, a dependency oracle O for $\mathbf{V}$, and a bound k.
Question Is there a DAG pattern G such that: G covers the dependencies in O, every other DAG pattern G' covering the dependencies in O has more edges than G, and G has at most k edges?

Clearly an efficient algorithm for the function minimization problem yields an efficient algorithm for UNIQUE I-MAP. We will show that UNIQUE I-MAP is NP-hard, assuming that $P = RP$. Let $\leq_P$ denote polynomial-time many-one reducibility.

Theorem 3. UEC3SET $\leq_P$ UNIQUE I-MAP $\leq_P$ UNIQUE MINIMAL I-MAP. *So* UNIQUE MINIMAL I-MAP *is NP-hard provided that* $P = RP$.

Proof. We give a reduction from UEC3SET to UNIQUE I-MAP. Consider an instance of UEC3SET with sets universe U of size $|U| = 3m$, and $c_1, .., c_p$, where $|c_i| = 3$ for $i = 1, .., p$ and $U = \cup_{i=1}^m c_i$. Define the following set V of variables.

1. For every set c_i, a *set variable* C_i.
2. For every element x_j of the universe U, a *member variable* X_j.
3. A *root variable* R.

Set the bound $k = 3p + m$. The following program M implements a dependency oracle O over the variables V, in time polynomial in the size of the given UEC3SET instance.

Definition of Dependency Oracle
Input A dependency query $V_1 \not\perp V_2 | \mathbf{S}$.
Output Oracle Clauses
    1. If $V_1 = C_i, V_2 = X_j$, and $x_j \in c_i$, then return "dependent".

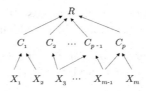

Fig. 3. The basic graph for the NP-hardness proof. A set cover of size m corresponds to m edges of the form $C \rightarrow R$.

2. If $V_1 = X_i, V_2 = X_j$, and there is a set $c_k \supseteq \{x_i, x_j\}$ such that $C_k \in \mathbf{S}$, then return "dependent".
3. If $V_1 = R, V_2 = X_j, \mathbf{S} = \emptyset$ then return "dependent".
4. If $V_1 = R, V_2 = X_j, |\mathbf{S}| = 1$, and $\mathbf{S} \neq \{C\}$ where $x_j \in c$, then return "dependent".
5. In all other cases, return ?.

We argue that there is a unique exact set cover for an instance $\langle U, \{c_i\} \rangle$ iff there is a unique I-map with at most k edges for O. So if there were a polynomial time algorithm A for UNIQUE I-MAP, we could solve the UEC3SET instance in polynomial time by using the program M to "simulate" the oracle O and use A to solve the corresponding instance of UNIQUE I-MAP. Our proof strategy is as follows. The *basic graph* for O is the following DAG B: (1) for every two variables X_j, C_i, the graph contains an arrow $X_j \rightarrow C_i$ iff $x_j \in c_i$, and (2) for every variable C_i, there is an arrow $C_i \rightarrow R$. The basic graph is also a pattern because all arrows correspond to unshielded colliders; see Figure 3. We show that if there is a unique I-map G for O with at most k edges, then G is a subgraph of the basic graph, with possibly edges $C_i \rightarrow R$ missing for some sets c_i, such that the set of variables $\{C_1, C_2, ..., C_m\}$ with the edge $C_i \rightarrow R$ in G corresponds to an exact cover $\{c_1, .., c_m\}$. Conversely, any unique exact cover corresponds to a subgraph of the basic graph in the same manner. For reasons of space, we just illustrate most of the following assertions rather than giving full proofs. It is easiest to consider separately the constraints imposed by each clause of M. Let $\mathcal{D}_i$ be the set of dependencies corresponding to Clause i. For example, $\mathcal{D}_1 = \{\langle C_i, X_j, \mathbf{S} \rangle : x_j \in c_i\}$.

Assertion 1. *Let DAG G be an I-map for $\mathcal{D}_1$. Then any two variables X and C are adjacent whenever $x \in c$.*

Assertion 2. *Let DAG G be an I-map for $\mathcal{D}_1 \cup \mathcal{D}_2$, and suppose that x_i, x_j are two elements of a set c. Then X_i and X_j are adjacent in G, or G contains a component $X_i \rightarrow C \leftarrow X_j$.*

Clause 3 requires that every member variable X be d-connected to the root variable. The intuition is that the basic graph B contains the most edge-efficient way to achieve the connection because with just one edge $C \rightarrow R$ the graph d-connects three member variables at once. We show that any I-map for $\mathcal{D}_3$ can be transformed into a subgraph of B without increasing the number of edges. We begin by establishing that in an I-map

G of $\mathcal{D}_3$, all arcs originating in the root variable R can be reversed with the result G' still an I-map of $\mathcal{D}_3$.

Assertion 3. *Let DAG G be an I-map of $\mathcal{D}_3$. Let G' be the graph obtained by reversing all edges of the form $R \to V$. Then G' is an I-map of $\mathcal{D}_3$.*

Illustration: Suppose G contains a component $R \to X \to X'$. Reverse the edge $R \to X$ to obtain G'. Consider the d-connecting path $R \to X \to X'$ in G. We can replace the edge $R \to X$ by $R \leftarrow X$ in G' without introducing additional colliders, so d-connection still holds. The next assertion shows that inductively, all nodes can be oriented towards R.

Assertion 4. *Let DAG G be an I-map of $\mathcal{D}_3$, with some node A an ancestor of R. Let G' be the graph obtained by reversing all edges of the form $A \to V$ where V is not an ancestor of R. Then G' is an I-map of $\mathcal{D}_3$.*

Illustration: Suppose G contains a component $X' \leftarrow X \to C \to R$. Reverse the edge $X' \leftarrow X$ to obtain G'. Consider the d-connecting path $X' \leftarrow X \to C \to R$ in G. In any such directed path in G' we can replace the edge $X' \leftarrow X$ by $X' \to X$ in G' without introducing additional colliders, so d-connection still holds.

Assertion 5. *Let DAG G be an I-map of $\mathcal{D}_3$. Suppose that for some node V, there are two directed paths $V \to U_1 \to \cdots \to U_p \to R$ and $V \to W_1 \to \cdots \to W_q \to R$. Let G' be the graph obtained from G by deleting the edge $V \to U_1$. Then G' is an I-map of $\mathcal{D}_3$.*

Illustration: Suppose G contains two paths $X \to C \to R$ and $X \to X' \to R$. Delete the edge $X \to X'$ to obtain G'. Then X remains d-connected to R. In general, a d-connecting path to R in G using the edge $X \to X'$ can be "rerouted" via either X or X'.

For a DAG G, let $\mathrm{sets}(G) = \{C : C$ is adjacent to R in $G\}$ comprise all set variables adjacent to R; these set variables are *covered*. A member variable X is *covered* in G if there is a covered set variable C such that $x \in c$. The *covered component* of G consists of the root variable R, and the covered set and member variables of G (so the covered component is $\{R\} \cup \mathrm{sets}(G) \cup \{X : \exists C \in \mathrm{sets}(G)$ s.t. $x \in c\}$). A DAG G is *normally directed* if all covered components of G are ancestors of the root variable R. By Assertion 4 we can normally direct every DAG G and still satisfy the dependencies in $\mathcal{D}_3$.

Assertion 6. *Let DAG G be a normally directed I-map of $\mathcal{D}_1 \cup \mathcal{D}_2 \cup \mathcal{D}_3$. Suppose that G contains an adjacency $V - V'$ where V is covered in G and V' is not. Unless $V - V' = X \to C$ for $x \in c$, there is a normally directed I-map G' of $\mathcal{D}_1 \cup \mathcal{D}_2 \cup \mathcal{D}_3$ such that V' is covered in G', all covered variables in G are covered in G', and G' has no more edges than G.*

Illustration: Suppose G contains an edge $X \to C$ where X is not covered, and a path $X \to X' \to C' \to R$. Add the edge $C \to R$ and delete the edge $X \to X'$ to obtain G'. Then X is d-connected to R via C. In general, a d-connecting path in G using the edge $X \to X'$ can be "rerouted" via either X or X'.

Assertion 7. *Suppose that DAG G is an I-map of $\mathcal{D}_1 \cup \mathcal{D}_2 \cup \mathcal{D}_3$ and not all member variables X are covered in G. Then there is an I-map G' of $\mathcal{D}_1 \cup \mathcal{D}_2 \cup \mathcal{D}_3$ that covers all member variables such that G' has no more edges than G, and $\text{sets}(G') \supset \text{sets}(G)$.*

Illustration: Suppose that X is uncovered, and that G contains an edge $X \to C$. Since X is not covered, the edge $C \to R$ is not in G. Since G covers $\mathcal{D}_3$, the variable X must be d-connected to the root variable R; suppose that G contains an edge $X \to R$. We can add an edge $C \to R$ to obtain G^* without losing any d-connection. Now there are two directed paths connecting X to R, so by Assertion 5 deleting the edge $X \to R$ yields a graph G' with the same number of edges as G that is still an I-map of $\mathcal{D}_1 \cup \mathcal{D}_2 \cup \mathcal{D}_3$.

Assertion 8. *No I-map of $\mathcal{D}_1 \cup \mathcal{D}_2 \cup \mathcal{D}_3$ has fewer than k edges.*

Proof: Let G be an I-map of $\mathcal{D}_1 \cup \mathcal{D}_2 \cup \mathcal{D}_3$. By Assertion 1, every I-map G of $\mathcal{D}_1 \cup \mathcal{D}_2$ contains $3p$ edges connecting each member variable with the set variables for the sets containing it. By Assertion 6 we can transform G into a graph G' such that G' is an I-map of $\mathcal{D}_1 \cup \mathcal{D}_2 \cup \mathcal{D}_3$, covers all its member variables, and has the same number of edges as G. Thus $\text{sets}(G')$ is a set cover for U, and so the size of $\text{sets}(G')$ is at least m, which means that we have at least m edges connecting the root variable R to set variables. Hence overall G' and hence G has $k = 3p + m$ edges.

Assertion 9. *Let DAG G be an I-map of $\mathcal{D}_1 \cup \mathcal{D}_2 \cup \mathcal{D}_3$ with k edges. Then for every uncovered member variable X of G, there is exactly one undirected path from X to R in G.*

Illustration: Suppose that G contains an edge $X \to R$ and a path $X \to X' \to C' \to R$ where X is not covered. Then as in Assertion 5, we can delete the edge $X \to R$ to obtain a graph with fewer than k edges that is still an I-map of $\mathcal{D}_1 \cup \mathcal{D}_2 \cup \mathcal{D}_3$. But this contradicts Assertion 8. The final assertion adds the constraints of Clause 4.

Assertion 10. *Let DAG G be an I-map of O with k edges. Then G is normally directed, every member variable in G is covered, and $\text{sets}(G)$ is an exact set cover of U.*

An exact set cover corresponds to a unique normally directed I-map for the dependency oracle O with $k = 3p + m$ edges (the I-map contains m edges $C \to R$ for each set c in the cover). Conversely Assertion 10 implies that every I-map for O with k edges corresponds to a unique exact set cover. Hence there is a 1-1 and onto correspondence between exact set covers and I-maps for O.

7   Conclusion

This paper applied learning-theoretic analysis to a practically important learning problem: identifying a correct Bayes net structure. We presented a model of this task in which learning is based on conditional dependencies between variables of interest. This model fits Gold's definition of a language learning problem, so identification criteria from Gold's paradigm apply. We considered mind-change optimality and text efficiency. The mind change complexity of identifying a Bayes net over variable set $\mathbf{V}$ is $\binom{|\mathbf{V}|}{2}$, the maximum number of edges in a graph with node set $\mathbf{V}$. There is a unique mind-change optimal learner $\Psi_{\text{fast}}^{\mathbf{V}}$ whose convergence time dominates that of all other mind-change optimal learners. This learner outputs a BN pattern G if G is the unique graph satisfying the observed dependencies with a minimum number of edges; otherwise $\Psi_{\text{fast}}^{\mathbf{V}}$ outputs ? for "no guess". In many language learning problems, it is plausible to view the mind change complexity of a language as a form of simplicity [12, Sec.4]. Our results establish that the mind-change based notion of simplicity for a Bayes net graph G is the inclusion depth of G, which is measured by the number of edges absent in G. Using the number of edges as a simplicity criterion to guide learning appears to be a new idea in Bayes net learning research.

The technically most complex result of the paper shows that an exact implementation of the unique mind-change optimal learner $\Psi_{\text{fast}}^{\mathbf{V}}$ is NP-hard because determining whether there is a uniquely simplest (edge-minimal) Bayes net for a given set of dependencies is NP-hard. To our knowledge, this is the first NP-hardness result for deciding the existence of a uniquely optimal Bayes net structure by any optimality criterion.

Acknowledgements

This research was supported by NSERC discovery grants to the first and third author. We are indebted to Josh Buresh-Oppenheim for discussions of complexity theory. Kevin T. Kelly suggested considering Bayes net learning based on conditional dependencies rather than independencies. We are indebted to the anonymous COLT reviewers for helpful comments. The Alberta Ingenuity Centre for Machine Learning provided valuable support.

References

1. Angluin, D.: Inductive inference of formal languages from positive data. I&C 45, 117–135 (1980)
2. Bouckaert, R.: Bayesian belief networks: from construction to inference. PhD thesis, U. Utrecht (1995)
3. Chickering, D.: Optimal structure identification with greedy search. JMLR 3, 507–554 (2003)
4. Chickering, D., Heckerman, D., Meek, C.: Large-sample learning of bayesian networks is NP-hard. JMLR 5, 1287–1330 (2004)
5. Cooper, G.: An overview of the representation and discovery of causal relationships using bayesian networks. In: Computation, Causation, and Discovery, pp. 4–62 (1999)
6. Scheines, R., et al.: TETRAD 3 User's Manual. CMU (1996)
7. Giere, R.: The significance test controversy. BJPS 23(2), 170–181 (1972)
8. Gold, E.M.: Language identification in the limit. Info. and Cont. 10(5), 447–474 (1967)
9. Jain, S., Osherson, D., Royer, J., Sharma, A.: Systems That Learn, 2nd edn. MIT Press, Cambridge (1999)
10. Jain, S., Sharma, A.: Mind change complexity of learning logic programs. TCS 284, 143–160 (2002)
11. Luo, W., Schulte, O.: Mind change efficient learning. In: Auer, P., Meir, R. (eds.) COLT 2005. LNCS (LNAI), vol. 3559, pp. 398–412. Springer, Heidelberg (2005)

12. Luo, W., Schulte, O.: Mind change efficient learning. Info. & Comp. 204, 989–1011 (2006)
13. Martin, E., Osherson, D.N.: Elements of Scientific Inquiry. MIT Press, Cambridge (1998)
14. Meek, C.: Graphical Models: Selecting causal and stat. models. PhD thesis, CMU (1997)
15. Neapolitan, R.E.: Learning Bayesian Networks. Pearson Education (2004)
16. Osherson, D., Stob, M., Weinstein, S.: Systems that learn. MIT Press, Cambridge (1986)
17. Papadimitriou, C.H.: Computational complexity. Addison-Wesley, London (1994)
18. Pearl, J.: Probabilistic Reasoning in Intelligent Systems. Morgan Kauffmann, San Francisco (1988)
19. Pearl, J.: Causality: Models, Reasoning, and Inference. Cambridge University Press, Cambridge (2000)
20. Putnam, H.: Trial and error predicates and the solution to a problem of mostowski. JSL 30(1), 49–57 (1965)
21. Shinohara, T.: Inductive inference of monotonic formal systems from positive data. New Gen. Comp. 8(4), 371–384 (1991)
22. Spirtes, P., Glymour, C., Scheines, R.: Causation, prediction, and search. MIT Press, Cambridge (2000)
23. Valiant, L., Vazirani, V.: NP is as easy as detecting unique solutions. TCS 47, 85–93 (1986)
24. Verma, T., Pearl, J.: Equiv. and synth. of causal models. In: UAI'90, pp. 220–227 (1990)
25. Zucchini, W.: An introduction to model selection. J. Math. Psyc. 44, 41–61 (2000)

Learning Correction Grammars

Lorenzo Carlucci[1], John Case[2], and Sanjay Jain[3,*]

[1] Via Elea 8, 00183, Roma, Italy
carlucci5@unisi.it
[2] Department of Computer and Information Sciences, University of Delaware,
Newark, DE 19716-2586, U.S.A.
case@cis.udel.edu
[3] Department of Computer Science,
National University of Singapore, Singapore 117543, Republic of Singapore
sanjay@comp.nus.edu.sg

Abstract. We investigate a new paradigm in the context of learning in the limit: learning *correction grammars* for classes of *r.e.* languages. Knowing a language may feature a representation of the target language in terms of *two* sets of rules (two grammars). The second grammar is used to make corrections to the first grammar. Such a pair of grammars can be seen as a single description of (or grammar for) the language. We call such grammars *correction grammars*. Correction grammars capture the observable fact that people *do* correct their linguistic utterances during their usual linguistic activities.

We show that learning correction grammars for classes of r.e. languages in the **TxtEx**-model (i.e., converging to a single correct correction grammar in the limit) is sometimes more powerful than learning ordinary grammars even in the **TxtBc**-model (where the learner is allowed to converge to infinitely many syntactically distinct but correct conjectures in the limit). For each $n \geq 0$, there is a similar learning advantage, where we compare learning correction grammars that make $n + 1$ corrections to those that make n corrections.

The concept of a correction grammar can be extended into the constructive transfinite, using the idea of counting-down from notations for transfinite constructive ordinals. For u a notation in Kleene's general system $(O, <_o)$ of ordinal notations, we introduce the concept of an u-correction grammar, where u is used to bound the number of corrections that the grammar is allowed to make. We prove a general hierarchy result: if u and v are notations for constructive ordinals such that $u <_o v$, then there are classes of r.e. languages that can be **TxtEx**-learned by conjecturing v-correction grammars but not by conjecturing u-correction grammars.

Surprisingly, we show that — above "ω-many" corrections — it is not possible to strengthen the hierarchy: **TxtEx**-learning u-correction grammars of classes of r.e. languages, where u is a notation in O for *any* ordinal, can be simulated by **TxtBc**-learning w-correction grammars, where w is any notation for the smallest infinite ordinal ω.

* Lorenzo Carlucci and John Case were supported in part by NSF Grant Number CCR-0208616 at the University of Delaware. Sanjay Jain was supported in part by NUS grant number R252-000-212-112.

N. Bshouty and C. Gentile (Eds.): COLT 2007, LNAI 4539, pp. 203–217, 2007.
© Springer-Verlag Berlin Heidelberg 2007

1   Introduction and Motivation

We investigate a new model in the context of Gold-style computability-theoretic learning theory (see [19,21]): learning "correction grammars". Burgin [5] suggested that knowing a language may feature a representation of the language in terms of *two* sets of rules, i.e., two grammars, say g_1 and g_2: g_2 is used to "edit" errors of (make corrections to) g_1. In set-theoretic terms, the language L is represented as the difference $(L_1 - L_2)$, where L_i is the language generated by the grammar g_i. The pair $\langle g_1, g_2 \rangle$ can thus be seen as a single description of (or "grammar" for) the language L. Burgin called these grammars *grammars with prohibition*. We call them *correction grammars*. It is quite natural to generalize the idea to include descriptions of a language in terms of finitely many differences, i.e., to "grammars" that are allowed up to a fixed finite number of corrections: $p = \langle i_1, \ldots, i_n \rangle$ is an *n-correction grammar* for L if and only if $L = L_{i_1} - (L_{i_2} - \cdots (L_{i_{n-1}} - L_{i_n}) \cdots)$.

Correction grammars can be seen as capturing the observable fact that people *do* correct their linguistic utterances. The idea of correction grammars explores the theoretical possibility that the cause of self-correcting behaviour depends on the form of the rules themselves, rather than, e.g., on an error in the rule or in rule application.

Is there some *learning* gain, in using correction grammars, that compensates for the need of self-corrections? We investigate a formal version of this question, in the context of computability-theoretic learning theory [19,21]: a learning machine (an algorithmic device) receives as input a sequence $e_1, e_2, \ldots$ of all and only the elements of an r.e. language L (any such sequence is called a *text* for L) and outputs a corresponding infinite sequence $g_1, g_2, \ldots$ of standard type-0 grammars [20] (or, equivalently, r.e. indices [28]) that *may* generate L. Several criteria of successful learning of a language can and have been studied. The most basic one is *Explanatory Learning from Text* (**TxtEx**-learning): the machine is required to output, past some point, one and the same correct grammar for the input language. A more liberal (and more powerful) criterion is *Behaviourally Correct Learning from Text* (**TxtBc**-learning): the machine is required to output, past some point, only correct grammars, though possibly infinitely many syntactically distinct ones. Both criteria feature learning *in the limit* (the machine does not know if and when it has converged) and require success of the learner on *any* order of presentation of the data. Since learning a single r.e. language is trivial in this model, the simultaneous learning of *classes* of r.e. languages is studied. The formal version of the above question is now: what is the power of an algorithmic learning machine that outputs correction grammars instead of r.e. indices for *r.e.* languages?

One of the main results of the present paper (Theorem 12) implies that learning correction grammars for classes of r.e. languages is more powerful than learning ordinary r.e. indices in the **TxtEx**-model. The increase in power is so strong that there are classes of *recursive* languages that are **TxtEx**-learnable by a machine that outputs correction grammars but not by any **TxtBc**-learner conjecturing r.e. indices — and this even if the learner is presented with full graphs of characteristic functions of the languages in the class. Theorem 12 in fact is stronger: it shows the advantages of learning $(n+1)$-correction grammars over learning n-correction grammars for recursive languages.

The next, mathematically natural step is to extend the concept of a correction grammar into the *constructive transfinite*. The *constructive ordinals* are those ordinals that have a program (called a *notation*) in some system which specifies how to build them. We use ordinal notations to bound the number of corrections allowed to a correction grammar (see [18] and [1] for other uses of ordinal notations in the context of inductive inference). *For example*, counting down corrections allowed from any notation w for the smallest infinite ordinal $\omega = 0 < 1 < 2 < \ldots$ is equivalent to declaring algorithmically, at the time a first correction is made, the *finite* number of *further* corrections to be allowed. This is more powerful than just initially setting the finite number of corrections allowed.

We use Kleene's general notation system $(O, <_o)$ [24,25,26] and concepts from the Ershov Hierarchy [13,14,15] to rigorously formalize the concept of a u-correction grammar, where u is a notation in O for some constructive ordinal.

O has at least one notation for each constructive ordinal, and the order relation $<_o$ on notations in O naturally embeds into the ordering of the corresponding ordinals.

The Ershov Hierarchy is based on effective iteration of set-theoretic difference on r.e. sets including up into the constructive transfinite. A correction grammar for an r.e. set will be a "description" of the r.e. set *as belonging to some level of the Ershov Hierarchy*.

We use particular acceptable programming systems from [10] for the relevant classes of the Ershov Hierarchy. Our results are independent of which acceptable programming systems is used. The *acceptable* programming systems for a class are those which contain a universal simulator and into which all other universal programming systems for the class can be compiled. Acceptable systems are characterized as universal systems with an algorithmic substitutivity principle called S-m-n, and also satisfy self-reference principles such as Recursion Theorems [28,29,10].

Let u and v be notations in O for constructive ordinals α and β, respectively, such that $u <_o v$ (which implies $\alpha < \beta$). Corollary 11 implies that there are classes of *recursive* languages that can be **TxtEx**-learned by conjecturing correction grammars that count-down from v but not by conjecturing correction grammars that count-down from u — and this even if the learner is required to be successful only on the full graphs of the characteristic functions of the languages in the class, instead of on arbitrary texts for those languages.

Surprisingly, Theorem 16 and Theorem 20 show that the following collapse occurs: any class of r.e. languages that is **TxtEx**-learnable or **TxtBc**-learnable by a learner outputting u-correction grammars, for any notation u for a transfinite ordinal, is already **TxtBc**-learnable by a learner outputting w-correction grammars, where w is a notation for the smallest infinite ordinal ω. Hence, there is a learning power tradeoff between, on the one hand, employing u-corrections, where u is a notation for a very large transfinite ordinal, with **TxtEx**-learning which nicely features only *one* correct correction grammar in the limit and, on the other hand, stopping at "ω" corrections but, then, paying the price of infinitely many distinct correction grammars in the limit. Several other similar collapsing results are proved.

Proofs which are omitted here due to space restrictions are given in [6].

2   Preliminaries

2.1   Notation and Recursion Theory Background

Any unexplained recursion theoretic notation is from [28]. The symbol **N** denotes the set of natural numbers, $\{0, 1, 2, 3, \ldots\}$. The symbols $\emptyset$, $\subseteq$, $\subset$, $\supseteq$, $\supset$, and Δ denote empty set, subset, proper subset, superset, proper superset, and symmetric difference, respectively. The cardinality of a set S is denoted by $\text{card}(S)$. $\text{card}(S) \leq *$ denotes that S is finite. We use the convention $n < *$ for all $n \in \mathbf{N}$. The maximum and minimum of a set are denoted by $\max(\cdot), \min(\cdot)$, respectively, where $\max(\emptyset) = 0$ and $\min(\emptyset) = \infty$. $L_1 =^n L_2$ means that $\text{card}(L_1 \Delta L_2) \leq n$ and L_1 and L_2 are called n-variants. $L_1 =^* L_2$ means that $\text{card}(L_1 \Delta L_2) \leq *$, i.e., is finite; in this case L_1 and L_2 are called finite-variants.

We let $\langle \cdot, \cdot \rangle$ stand for Cantor's computable, bijective mapping $\langle x, y \rangle = \frac{1}{2}(x+y)$ $(x+y+1)+x$ from $\mathbf{N} \times \mathbf{N}$ onto $\mathbf{N}$ [28]. Note that $\langle \cdot, \cdot \rangle$ is monotonically increasing in both of its arguments. We define $\pi_1(\langle x, y \rangle) = x$ and $\pi_2(\langle x, y \rangle) = y$.

By φ we denote a fixed *acceptable* programming system for the partial-recursive functions mapping **N** to **N**. By φ_i we denote the partial-recursive function computed by the program number i in the φ-system. We assume that multiple arguments are coded in some standard way [28] and suppress the explicit coding. By Φ we denote an arbitrary fixed Blum complexity measure [4,20] for the φ-system. By convention we use Φ_i to denote the partial recursive function $x \to \Phi(i, x)$. Intuitively, $\Phi_i(x)$ may be thought as the number of steps it takes to compute $\varphi_i(x)$. $\varphi_{i,s}$ denotes the complexity-bounded version of φ_i, that is, $\varphi_{i,s}(x) = \varphi_i(x)$, if $x < s$ and $\Phi_i(x) < s$; $\varphi_{i,s}(x)$ is undefined otherwise.

W_i denotes $\text{domain}(\varphi_i)$. That is, W_i is the set of all numbers on which the φ-program i halts. This treats i as an *acceptor* program for W_i [20]. By $W_{i,s}$ we denote the set $\text{domain}(\varphi_{i,s}) = \{x < s \mid \Phi_i(x) < s\}$. χ_L denotes the characteristic function of L. We say that p is a limiting recursive program for a total function f if φ_p is a total function, and for all x, $\lim_{t \to \infty} \varphi_p(x, t) = f(x)$.

The symbol $\mathcal{E}$ will denote the set of all r.e. languages. The symbol L ranges over $\mathcal{E}$. The symbol $\mathcal{L}$ ranges over subsets of $\mathcal{E}$.

2.2   Constructive Ordinals and Kleene's O

We proceed informally (for a detailed treatment see [28,2]). A *system of notation* S is a collection of (numerical codes of) programs (*S-notations*) each of which specifies a structured algorithmic description of some ordinal. A system of notation S will consist of a subset N_S of **N** (the set of S-notations), and a mapping

$S[\cdot]$ from N_S to an initial segment of the ordinals. The notations are (codes of) programs for building, or laying down end-to-end, the denoted ordinal. An ordinal is called *constructive* when it has a notation in some system of notation.

A system of notation S is *acceptable* if any other system is recursively order-preservingly embeddable in it. Each acceptable system of notation assigns *at least one* notation to every constructive ordinal. A system of notation S is *univalent* if $S[\cdot]$ is injective. It is known that every acceptable system *fails* to be univalent (see [28]).

Kleene [24,25,26,28] developed a general acceptable system of notation O. Every constructive ordinal has at least one notation in O. O is endowed with a relation $<_o$ on notations that naturally embeds in the ordering of the corresponding constructive ordinals. We define '$x =_o y$' to mean '$x, y \in O$ and $x = y$'. '$x \leq_o y$', '$x \geq_o y$', and '$x >_o y$' have the obvious meaning. For all $x, y \in O$, it is true that, if $x <_o y$ then $O[x] < O[y]$. It is also true that, for all $y \in O$, if $O[y] = \beta$, then for every $\alpha < \beta$, there is an x such that $x <_o y$ and $O[x] = \alpha$. If $u \in O$ and $O[u] = \alpha$, then we say that u is *for* α.

We shall use the following basic properties of O in later proofs.

Lemma 1 (Some properties of O, [28])

1. *For every $n \in \mathbf{N}$ there exists a unique O-notation for n. This notation will be denoted by $\underline{n}$.*
2. *For every $v \in O$, $\{u \mid u <_o v\}$ is a univalent system of notations for the corresponding initial segment of the ordinals.*
3. *There exists an r.e. set Z such that $\{u \mid u <_o v\} = \{u \mid \langle u, v \rangle \in Z\}$, for each $v \in O$.*
4. *There exists a computable mapping $+_o : \mathbf{N} \times \mathbf{N} \longrightarrow \mathbf{N}$ such that, for every $u, v \in O$, (i) $u +_o v \in O$, (ii) $O[u +_o v] = O[u] + O[v]$, and (iii) if $v \neq 0$ then $u <_o u +_o v$.*

In the rest of this paper, u, v, w denote elements in O.

2.3   The Ershov Hierarchy

We introduce the Ershov Hierarchy [13,14,15], and give the definition of a *particular* acceptable universal programming system W^u — due to Case and Royer [10] — for each level of the hierarchy (this system was created in part to make sure there *is* such an acceptable system; the construction of the W^u's is also nicely uniform in $u \in O$). Our presentation of the Ershov Hierarchy is in terms of count-down functions from O-notations for constructive ordinals. For a similar presentation, see [2].

Definition 2 (Count-Down Function). A computable function $F : \mathbf{N} \times \mathbf{N} \to O$ is a *count-down function* if for all x and t, $F(x, t+1) \leq_o F(x, t)$.

For a binary function h we write $h(x, \infty)$ for the limit $\lim_{t \to \infty} h(x, t)$.

Definition 3 (Ershov Hierarchy). $A \in \Sigma_u^{-1}$ if and only if there exists a computable function $h : \mathbf{N} \times \mathbf{N} \to \{0,1\}$ and a count-down function F such that, for all $x, t \in \mathbf{N}$,

(i) $\chi_A(x) = h(x, \infty)$,
(ii) $h(x,0) = 0$ and $F(x,0) \leq_o u$,
(iii) $h(x, t+1) \neq h(x,t) \Rightarrow F(x, t+1) <_o F(x,t)$.

In this case we say that h and F *witness* $A \in \Sigma_u^{-1}$.

Note that $\Sigma_0^{-1} = \{\emptyset\}$. Definition 3 immediately implies that $u <_o v \Rightarrow \Sigma_u^{-1} \subseteq \Sigma_v^{-1}$. The containment is in fact proper, so that one speaks of the Ershov Hierarchy.

Every set X in $\Sigma_{u+_o 1}^{-1}$ is equal to $Y - Z$ for some $Y \in \mathcal{E}$, $Z \in \Sigma_u^{-1}$, such that $Z \subseteq Y$. In particular, X in $\Sigma_{\underline{n}}^{-1}$ is a difference of n r.e. sets.

Let us denote by φ^{TM} an acceptable programming system for the partial computable functions based on a coding of deterministic multi-tape Turing Machines [28]. For each x and i in $\mathbf{N}$, let $\Phi_i^{\mathrm{TM}}(x)$ be the runtime of Turing Machine i on input x. $\Phi_i^{\mathrm{TM}}(x)$ is a Blum Complexity Measure [4] for φ^{TM} and $\{\langle x, i, t\rangle \mid \Phi_i^{\mathrm{TM}}(x) \leq t\}$ is primitive recursively decidable (see, e.g., [29]).

Let z_0 be a fixed φ^{TM}-program for accepting Z, where Z is as in part 3 of Lemma 1.

Definition 4 (Convenient Function). Let F be a count-down function. Then F is *convenient* (relative to z_0) if

$$(\forall x)(\forall t)[F(x, t+1) <_o F(x,t) \Rightarrow \Phi_{z_0}^{\mathrm{TM}}(\langle F(x, t+1), F(x,t)\rangle) \leq t].$$

We say that h and F *conveniently witness* $A \in \Sigma_u^{-1}$ when h and F witness $A \in \Sigma_u^{-1}$ and F is convenient.

Let ψ be a *standard* programming system for the primitive recursive functions, (i.e., one for which the S-m-n Theorem, Recursion Theorems, etc. all hold) [29].

Definition 5. Let $u \in O$. We say that i, j, x are *u-consistent through* t when $\psi_i(x,0) = 0$, $\psi_j(x,0) =_o u$ and for each $t' < t$

(i) $\psi_i(x, t'+1) \in \{0,1\}$,
(ii) $\psi_j(x, t'+1) \neq \psi_j(x, t') \Leftrightarrow \Phi_{z_0}^{\mathrm{TM}}(\psi_j(x, t'+1), \psi_j(x, t')) \leq t'$,
(iii) $\psi_i(x, t'+1) \neq \psi_i(x, t') \Rightarrow \psi_j(x, t'+1) <_o \psi_j(x, t')$.

Definition 6. Let $u \in O$. For each i, j, x, t let

$$h^u(i, j, x, t) = \begin{cases} 0 & \text{if } i, j, x \text{ are not } u\text{-consistent through } 0; \\ \psi_i(x, t') & \text{otherwise, where} \\ & t' \text{ is the greatest number } \leq t \\ & \text{such that } i, j, x \text{ are } u\text{-consistent through } t'. \end{cases}$$

For each $i, j \in \mathbf{N}$, let

$$W_{\langle i,j\rangle}^u = \{x : h^u(i, j, x, \infty) = 1\}.$$

We call $p = \langle i, j \rangle$ a *u-correction grammar* for W_p^u, and we are herein interested in such grammars for r.e. languages. We abbreviate $h^u(\pi_1(p), \pi_2(p), x, t)$ as $\theta_p^u(x, t)$.

Case and Royer [10] proved that W^u is an acceptable universal programming system for Σ_u^{-1}. In particular, the Kleene Recursion Theorem holds in the W^u-system: given a W^u-system task p, there exists an e such that program e in the W^u-system makes a self-copy (i.e., computes a copy of its own code) and applies that task p to this self-copy (and, of course, to its external input). In proofs below, for convenience, we will give the description of what such an e does with its self-copy in an *informal* system. We will describe task-relevant functions h and F, *each informally in terms of e*, such that F is a count-down function and h and F witness that $\{x \mid h(x, \infty) = 1\} \in \Sigma_u^{-1}$ (Definition 3). We then invoke the acceptability of W^u to obtain a formal translation into the W^u-system of the informal description involving h and F. In practice, though, we will merely describe informally what such a formal e does with its self-copy, and only implicitly invoke the acceptability of the W^u-systems.

2.4   Learning Criteria

We present concepts from language learning theory (see [21]) and then formally define learning correction grammars.

A *sequence* σ is a mapping from an initial segment of $\mathbf{N}$ into $(\mathbf{N} \cup \{\#\})$. The empty sequence is denoted by λ. The *content* of a sequence σ, denoted content(σ), is the set of natural numbers in the range of σ. The *length* of σ, denoted $|\sigma|$, is the number of elements in σ. So, $|\lambda| = 0$. For $n \leq |\sigma|$, the initial sequence of σ of length n is denoted by $\sigma[n]$. So, $\sigma[0]$ is λ.

Intuitively, the pause-symbol $\#$ represents a pause in the presentation of data. We let σ, τ and γ range over finite sequences. Concatenation of σ and τ is denoted by $\sigma\tau$. Sometimes we abuse the notation and use σx to denote the concatenation of sequence σ and the sequence of length 1 which contains the element x.

A *text* T for a language L is a mapping from $\mathbf{N}$ into $(\mathbf{N} \cup \{\#\})$ such that L is the set of natural numbers in the range of T. $T(i)$ represents the $(i+1)$-st element in the text. The *content* of a text T, denoted content(T), is the set of natural numbers in the range of T; that is, the language which T is a text for. $T[n]$ denotes the finite initial sequence of T with length n.

A *learning machine* (or just *learner*) is an algorithmic device which computes a mapping from the set of all finite sequences into $\mathbf{N}$. We let $\mathbf{M}$ range over learning machines. We note that, without loss of generality, for all criteria of learning discussed in this paper, a learner $\mathbf{M}$ may be assumed to be total. $\mathbf{M}(T[n])$ denotes the hypothesis of the learner $\mathbf{M}$ after it has seen the first n members of T. $\mathbf{M}(T) = e$ denotes that $\mathbf{M}$ converges on T to e, that is $\mathbf{M}(T[n]) = e$, for all but finitely many n.

There are several criteria for a learning machine to be successful on a language. We now define Explanatory [9,19] and Behaviourally Correct [9,27] learning.

Definition 7. [9,19,27] Suppose $a \in \mathbf{N} \cup \{*\}$.

(a) **M TxtEx**^{a}-*identifies a text* T just in case $(\exists i \mid W_i =^a \text{content}(T))$ $(\forall^\infty n)[\mathbf{M}(T[n]) = i]$.

(b) **M TxtBc**^{a}-*identifies a text* T just in case $(\forall^\infty n \in \mathbf{N})[W_{\mathbf{M}(T[n])} =^a \text{content}(T)]$.

For $\mathbf{I} \in \{\mathbf{Ex}, \mathbf{Bc}\}$, **TxtI**^{a}, we say that a machine **M TxtI**^{a}-identifies a language if **M TxtI**^{a}-identifies each text for the language. A machine **M** is said to **TxtI**^{a}-identify a class of languages if **M TxtI**^{a}-identifies each language in the class. **TxtI**^{a} denotes the collection of all classes of languages that can be **TxtI**^{a}-identified by some machine.

For $a = 0$, we often write **I** instead of **I**^{a}. It is well-known that **TxtEx**$^a \subset$ **TxtBc**^{a} (see [21]).

For results about learning with anomalies, we refer to [21] and only recall that for both **TxtEx**- and **TxtBc**-learning allowing more anomalies in the limit increases learning power, and that **TxtEx*** and **TxtBc** are incomparable.

When we only require that a learner is successful when fed the graph of the characteristic function of the language instead of any text, we obtain the concept of *learning from informant* (see [19]). For an informant I, we denote by $I[n]$, the first n elements of I. A canonical informant for a language L is $(0, \chi_L(0)), (1, \chi_L(1)), (2, \chi_L(2)), \ldots$. For a characteristic function f, we use $f[n]$ to denote the initial segment $(0, f(0)), (1, f(1)), \ldots, (n-1, f(n-1))$.

Using **Inf** instead of **Txt** in the name of any learning criterion indicates that the requirement of learning *from texts* is substituted by the requirement of learning *from informant*. It is well-known that more can be learned from informant than from text (see [21]).

We can now formally introduce learning by correction grammars. Intuitively, a **Cor**^{u}**I**-learner, where **I** is any learning criterion, is a successful **I**-learner when its conjectures are interpreted as u-correction grammars.

Definition 8 (Learning Correction Grammars). Let $u \in O$, $a \in \mathbf{N} \cup \{*\}$.

(a) **Cor**^{u}**TxtEx**^{a} is the collection of all classes $\mathcal{L}$ of r.e. languages such that there exists an **M** such that $(\forall L \in \mathcal{L})(\forall \text{ texts } T \text{ for } L)(\exists i)[W_i^u =^a L \wedge (\forall^\infty n)[\mathbf{M}(T[n]) = i]]$ — in this case we say that $\mathcal{L}$ is **Cor**^{u}**TxtEx**^{a}-identified by **M**.

(b) **Cor**^{u}**TxtBc**^{a} is the collection of all classes $\mathcal{L}$ of r.e. languages such that there exists an **M** such that $(\forall L \in \mathcal{L})(\forall \text{ texts } T \text{ for } L)(\forall^\infty n)[W_{\mathbf{M}(T[n])}^u =^a L]$ — in this case we say that $\mathcal{L}$ is **Cor**^{u}**TxtBc**^{a}-identified by **M**.

It is important to note that, while the Ershov Hierarchy goes well beyond the r.e. languages, we are herein interested in the r.e. languages and their learnability with respect to u-correction grammars.

The following result shows the advantages of allowing more anomalies in the final conjectures. It can be proved using techniques for similar results featuring learning standard r.e. grammars.

Theorem 9. *For all $u \in O$, for all $n \in \mathbf{N}$,*

(a) $\mathbf{TxtEx}^{2n+1} - \mathbf{Cor}^u\mathbf{TxtBc}^n \neq \emptyset$.
(b) $\mathbf{TxtBc}^{n+1} - \mathbf{Cor}^u\mathbf{TxtBc}^n \neq \emptyset$.
(c) $\mathbf{TxtEx}^{n+1} - \mathbf{Cor}^u\mathbf{TxtEx}^n \neq \emptyset$.
(d) $\mathbf{Cor}^u\mathbf{InfEx}^* \subseteq \mathbf{Cor}^u\mathbf{InfBc}$.
(e) *For w an O-notation for ω, $\mathcal{E} \in \mathbf{Cor}^w\mathbf{InfBc}$.*

3   Hierarchy Results

In this section we prove some hierarchy results about learning correction grammars. Each of the separation results is witnessed by a class of recursive languages.

Our first main result (Corollary 11) shows that an increase in learning power is obtained — in the context of **TxtEx**-learning correction grammars — when the number of corrections allowed is counted by (notations for) larger and larger constructive transfinite ordinals.

Next (Theorem 12) we prove a strengthening of this hierarchy for all finite levels: for all $n \in \mathbf{N}$, there are classes of *recursive* languages that can be **TxtEx**-learned by a learner conjecturing $\underline{n+1}$-correction grammars that cannot be **TxtBc**-learned by any learner conjecturing $\underline{n}$-correction grammars (not even from informant). We will show in Section 4 that this strengthening is best possible: it cannot be extended beyond the ω-th level of the hierarchy.

We now prove that for all $u, v \in O$ such that $u <_o v$ there exist classes of recursive languages that are learnable by a **TxtEx**-learner that outputs v-correction grammars but such that no **TxtEx**-learner can learn those classes using u-correction grammars, even if presented with informants instead of texts.

Notation: We use $h(\cdot, s)$ to denote the function which maps x to $h(x,s)$.

Theorem 10. *For all $n \in \mathbf{N}$, $u \in O$, $\mathbf{Cor}^{u+_o\underline{1}}\mathbf{TxtEx} - \mathbf{Cor}^u\mathbf{InfEx}^n \neq \emptyset$.*

Proof. Let $\mathcal{L} = \{L \text{ recursive} \mid L \neq \emptyset \wedge W_{\min(L)}^{u+_o\underline{1}} = L\}$. Clearly $\mathcal{L} \in \mathbf{Cor}^{u+_o\underline{1}}\mathbf{TxtEx}$. Suppose by way of contradiction that $\mathbf{M} \ \mathbf{Cor}^u\mathbf{InfEx}^n$-identifies $\mathcal{L}$.

By the Kleene Recursion Theorem in the system $W^{u+_o\underline{1}}$ there exists an e such that $W_e^{u+_o\underline{1}} = \{x \mid h(x,\infty) = 1\}$, where h is a function informally defined in stages below (we will have that $e = \min(\{x \mid h(x,\infty) = 1\})$). Along with h we informally define another function F, such that F is a count-down function and h and F witness that $\{x \mid h(x,\infty) = 1\} \in \Sigma_{u+_o\underline{1}}^{-1}$ (Definition 3).

Initially, $h(x,0) = 0$ for all x; $h(y,1) = 0$, for $y < e$, and $h(y,1) = 1$, for $y \geq e$. $F(y,0) = u +_o 1$ and $F(y,1) = u$, for all y. Let $x_1 = e + 1$. Go to stage 1 (we start with stage 1 for ease of notation).

We will have the invariants that, at the start of stage s,

(1) for $x > x_s + n$, $h(x,s) = 1$ and $F(x,s) = u$.
(2) for $x < x_s$, for all $t > s$, $h(x,t) = h(x,s)$.
(3) For all $x_s \leq x \leq x_s + n$, either

(3a) for $i = \mathbf{M}(h(\cdot, s)[x_s])$,
$$h(x, s) = 1 - \theta_i^u(x, s), \text{ and}$$
$$F(x, s) = \psi_{\pi_2(i)}(x, s), \text{ or}$$
(3b) $h(x, s) = 1$, $F(x, s) = u$ (in this case $x_s \neq x_{s-1}$, where we take $x_0 = 0$).

Stage s
1. If there exists a z, $x_s + n < z \leq s$, such that $\mathbf{M}(h(\cdot, s)[z]) \neq \mathbf{M}(h(\cdot, s)[x_s])$,
    then
    Let $x_{s+1} = z$.
    For all x, let $h(x, s+1) = h(x, s)$ and $F(x, s+1) = F(x, s)$.
    Go to stage $s + 1$.
2. Else,
    2.1 Let $i = \mathbf{M}(h(\cdot, s)[x_s])$.
    2.2 For $x_s \leq x \leq x_s + n$, let
    $$h(x, s+1) = 1 - \theta_i^u(x, s+1), \text{ and}$$
    $$F(x, s+1) = \psi_{\pi_2(i)}(x, s+1).$$
    (Note that above change is valid, based on invariant 3 above).
    2.3 For $x < x_s$ or $x > x_s + n$, let
    $$h(x, s+1) = h(x, s), \text{ and}$$
    $$F(x, s+1) = F(x, s).$$
    2.4 Let $x_{s+1} = x_s$.
    Go to stage $s + 1$.
End stage s

It is easy to see that the invariants are satisfied. We now consider two cases.
Case 1: $\lim_{s \to \infty} x_s$ is infinite.
In this case, clearly, the function mapping x to $\lim_{t \to \infty} h(x, t)$ is a recursive function, and on this function $\mathbf{M}$ makes infinitely many mind-changes. Furthermore, clearly, $\lim_{t \to \infty} h(x, t)$ is a characteristic function for a language in $\mathcal{L}$.
Case 2: $\lim_{s \to \infty} x_s$ is finite.
Suppose $\lim_{t \to \infty} x_t = z = x_s$. In this case, clearly, the function mapping x to $\lim_{t \to \infty} h(x, t)$ is a recursive function, and a characteristic function for a language (say L) in $\mathcal{L}$. Let χ_L denote the characteristic function of L and let $\mathbf{M}(\chi_L)$ denote $\mathbf{M}$'s final conjecture when the input informant is χ_L. We have that $\mathbf{M}(\chi_L) = \mathbf{M}(\chi_L[z])$, as the condition in step 1 did not succeed beyond stage s. Furthermore, using invariant (3), $\mathbf{M}(\chi_L[z])$ makes errors on inputs x, for $x_s \leq x \leq x_s + n$.
From both the above cases, we have that e is a $(u +_o \mathbf{1})$-correction grammar for a language in $\mathcal{L}$ which is not $\mathbf{Cor}^u\mathbf{InfEx}^n$-identified by $\mathbf{M}$.   □

Corollary 11. *For all $u, v \in O$, if $u <_o v$ then for all $n \in \mathbf{N}$*
(a) $\mathbf{Cor}^v\mathbf{TxtEx} - \mathbf{Cor}^u\mathbf{InfEx}^n \neq \emptyset$.
(b) $\mathbf{Cor}^u\mathbf{TxtEx}^n \subset \mathbf{Cor}^v\mathbf{TxtEx}^n$.
(c) $\mathbf{Cor}^u\mathbf{InfEx}^n \subset \mathbf{Cor}^v\mathbf{InfEx}^n$.

We show that for finite levels the results of the previous section can be strengthened considerably. We will show in Section 4 that it is *impossible* to obtain the analogous strengthening for transfinite levels.

Theorem 12. *For $k \in \mathbf{N}$, $\mathbf{Cor}^{k+1}\mathbf{TxtEx} - \mathbf{Cor}^k\mathbf{InfBc} \neq \emptyset$.*

Proof. Let $\mathcal{L} = \{L \text{ recursive} \mid L \neq \emptyset \wedge W^{k+1}_{\min(L)} = L\}$. Clearly, $\mathcal{L} \in \mathbf{Cor}^{k+1}\mathbf{TxtEx}$. Now suppose by way of contradiction that $\mathcal{L} \in \mathbf{Cor}^k\mathbf{TxtBc}$ as witnessed by $\mathbf{M}$.

By the Kleene Recursion Theorem in the system W^{k+1}, there exists an e such that $W^{k+1}_e = \{x \mid h(x, \infty) = 1\}$, where h can be informally defined in stages as follows. We will ensure that $h(x, \cdot)$ changes its mind for any x at most $k + 1$-times. Thus, the definition of a function F such that h and F witness $\{x \mid h(x, \infty) = 1\} \in \Sigma^{-1}_{k+1}$ is implicit in our construction.

We will also define finite sets $S^0 \subseteq S^1 \ldots$. These sets denote the values of x whose membership in $L = W^{k+1}_e$ has been frozen: for all s, for all $x \in S^s$, for all $t \geq s$, $h(x, t) = h(x, s)$.

Let $MC(h, x, s) = \operatorname{card}(\{t < s \mid h(x, t) \neq h(x, t + 1)\})$ (the number of mind changes in the sequence $h(x, 0), h(x, 1), \ldots, h(x, s)$). Similarly, let $MCP(i, x, s) = \operatorname{card}(\{t < s \mid \theta^k_i(x, t) \neq \theta^k_i(x, t + 1)\})$.

We will have the following invariants for each s.

(1) For all $x \notin S^{s+1}$, $MC(h, x, s+1) \leq 1 + MCP(i, x, s)$, where $i = \mathbf{M}(h(\cdot, s + 1)[x])$.

(2) For all $x \in S^{s+1}$, $MC(h, x, s + 1) \leq k + 1$.

(3) If $x \notin S^{s+1}$ and $x \leq s$, then $h(x, s + 1) \neq \theta^k_{\mathbf{M}(h(\cdot, s+1)[x])}(x, s)$.

Initially, $h(x, 0) = 0$, for all x; $h(x, 1) = 0$, for $x < e$ and $h(x, 1) = 1$ for all $x \geq e$. Let $S^1 = \{x \mid x \leq e\}$. Clearly, the invariants are satisfied in the beginning. Go to stage $s = 1$ (we start with stage 1, for ease of notation).

Begin Stage s:

1. If there exists an $x \leq s$, $x \notin S^s$ such that $\theta^k_{\mathbf{M}(h(\cdot,s)[x])}(x, s) = h(x, s)$, then pick the least such x and go to step 2. Otherwise, go to step 3.
    (* For $i = \mathbf{M}(h(\cdot, s)[x])$, note that invariant (1) implies that $MC(h, x, s) \leq 1 + MCP(i, x, s-1) \leq 1 + MCP(i, x, s)$. Thus, $\theta^k_{\mathbf{M}(h(\cdot,s)[x])}(x, s) = h(x, s)$, implies, $MC(h, x, s) \leq MCP(i, x, s)$. Thus, step 2 modification of $h(x, s + 1)$ preserves invariant (1). *)

2. Let $h(x, s + 1) = 1 - h(x, s)$. For $y \neq x$, let $h(y, s + 1) = h(y, s)$.
    Let $S^{s+1} = S^s \cup \{y < x \mid MC(h, y, s+1) < MC(h, x, s+1)\} \cup \{y \mid x < y \leq s\}$.
    (* Intuitively, $\{y < x \mid MC(h, y, s+1) < MC(h, x, s+1)\}$ is added to S^{s+1}, as these y's had too few mind changes, and we need to freeze them to maintain recursiveness of W^{k+1}_e. Set $\{y \mid x < y \leq s\}$, is added to S^{s+1} as the diagonalizations done up to now for these y are no longer valid due to a change in the membership of x; thus, to maintain invariant (1) and (3) we need to place such y into S^{s+1}. *)
    Go to stage $s + 1$.

3. For all x, let $h(x, s + 1) = h(x, s)$, and let $S^{s+1} = S^s$.
    Go to stage $s + 1$.

End Stage s

It is easy to verify that the invariants are satisfied. Also, using invariants (1), (2) we have that $h \in \Sigma_{k+1}^{-1}$. Let L be the language for which h is the limiting characteristic function. We will show below that L is recursive. Thus, $L \in \mathcal{L}$. We now argue that L is not $\mathbf{Cor}^k\mathbf{TxtBc}$-identified by $\mathbf{M}$.

Let $k' \leq k + 1$ be maximal such that there are infinitely many inputs x for which $MC(h, x, \infty) = \lim_{t\to\infty} MC(h, x, t) = k'$. Let s be the largest stage such that $MC(h, z, s+1) > MC(h, z, s) \geq k'$ for some z. Such a largest stage s exists by the maximality of k'.

Note that if $x > z$, and $MC(h, x, t+1) = k' > MC(h, x, t)$, for some $t > s$, then for all $y < x$, for all $t' > t$, $h(y, t') = h(y, t)$, as either $MC(h, y, t) \geq k'$, or y will be placed in S^{t+1} at stage t. It follows that all such x are not in $\bigcup_{s' \in \mathbf{N}} S^{s'}$, and thus $\theta_{\mathbf{M}(\chi_L[x])}^k(x) \neq h(x, \infty)$, by invariant (3).

Recursiveness of $L = W_e^{k+1}$ follows because — except for finitely many elements on which h has $> k'$ mind-changes — once we find an element x on which h has k' mind-changes, we know the membership in W_e^{k+1} for all $y \leq x$. $\qquad \square$

We note that the proof of Theorem 12 essentially also shows that for all $n \in \mathbf{N}$, $\mathbf{Cor}^{n+1}\mathbf{TxtEx} - \mathbf{Cor}^n\mathbf{InfEx}^* \neq \emptyset$. Also, the proof can be modified to yield that for $n \in \mathbf{N}$, for all $m \in \mathbf{N}$, $\mathbf{Cor}^{n+1}\mathbf{TxtEx} - \mathbf{Cor}^n\mathbf{InfBc}^m \neq \emptyset$.

For $\mathbf{TxtBc}^*$-learning, we can show that $\mathbf{Cor}^2\mathbf{TxtBc}^* - \mathbf{Cor}^1\mathbf{TxtBc}^* \neq \emptyset$, but the existence of a hierarchy is open in general (in Section 4 we show that there is no hierarchy for $\mathbf{Cor}^u\mathbf{TxtBc}^*$-learning above any notation for ω).

4   Collapsing Results

In this section we show some surprising collapsing results: every $\mathbf{Cor}^u\mathbf{TxtEx}$-learnable class is already *behaviourally* learnable by a learner outputting grammars that make at most ω mind-changes. We show analogous collapsing results for $\mathbf{TxtEx}^*$, $\mathbf{TxtBc}^a$, for $a \in \mathbf{N} \cup \{*\}$.

Lemma 13. *Suppose $L \in \mathcal{E}$. Given a program p for limiting recursively computing χ_L, one can effectively (in p, i, t) define g_i^t, such that*

(a) *for all but finitely many t, for all but finitely many i, g_i^t is the minimal φ-grammar for L, and*

(b) *for all t, the sequence $g_0^t, g_1^t, \ldots$ is a non-increasing sequence starting with t.*

Proof. Given a limiting recursive program p, let $g_0^t = t$ and let $g_{r+1}^t = \min(\{g_r^t\} \cup \{i < g_r^t \mid W_{i,t} \subseteq \{x \mid \varphi_p(x, t+r) = 1\}$ and $\{x < t \mid \varphi_p(x, t+r) = 1\} \subseteq W_{i,r}\})$.

Now suppose p is a limiting recursive program for χ_L and j is the minimal grammar for L. Let $t > j$ be a large enough number such that for all $i < j$, there exists an $x < t$, such that (i) $\varphi_p(x, \cdot)$ does not make a mind-change beyond t (that is for all $t' > t$, $\varphi_p(x, t') = \varphi_p(x, t)$), and (ii) $x \in W_i$ if and only if $x \in W_{i,t}$ and (iii) W_i and L differ at x.

It is then easy to verify that for all $t' > t$, $\lim_{r\to\infty} g_r^{t'}$ converges to j. $\qquad \square$

Corollary 14. *Let w be any O-notation for ω, and $u \in O$. There exists a recursive function $h(\cdot, \cdot)$ such that, for any W^u-grammar q for an r.e. language L, for all but finitely many n, $h(q, n)$ is a W^w-grammar for L.*

Proof. $h(q, n)$ is defined as follows. Let p be such that p is a limiting recursive program for χ_L. Note that p can be obtained effectively from q. Let g_i^t be as defined in Lemma 13 for p.

Let e_n be such that $\varphi_{e_n}(x, 0) = 0$ and $\varphi_{e_n}(x, s + 1) = 1$, if and only if $x \in W_{g_s^n, s}$. Thus, by Lemma 13, for all but finitely many n, e_n is a limiting recursive program for χ_L, and $\varphi_{e_n}(x, \cdot)$ changes its mind at most $2n + 2$ times.

By acceptability of W^w, one can effectively get a W^w grammar i_n (from e_n, and thus from q, n) for $\{x \mid \lim_{t \to \infty} \varphi_{e_n}(x, t) = 1\}$. We are now done by defining $h(q, n) = i_n$ as above. $\qquad\square$

Corollary 15. *Let w be any O-notation for ω, and $u \in O$. There exists a recursive function $h(\cdot)$ such that, for any W^u-grammar q for an r.e. language L, $h(q)$ is a W^w-grammar for a finite variant of L.*

Proof. $h(q)$ is defined as follows. Let p be such that p is a limiting recursive program for χ_L. Note that p can be obtained effectively from q. Let g_i^t be as defined in Lemma 13 for p.

Let e be such that $\varphi_e(x, 0) = 0$ and $\varphi_e(x, s + 1) = 1$, if and only if $x \in W_{g_s^x, s}$. Thus, by Lemma 13, for all but finitely many x, $\varphi_e(x, \infty) = \chi_L(x)$, and $\varphi_e(x, \cdot)$ changes its mind at most $2x + 2$ times.

By acceptability of W^w, one can effectively get a W^w-grammar i (from e, and thus from q) for $\{x \mid \lim_{t \to \infty} \varphi_e(x, t) = 1\}$. We are now done by defining $h(q) = i$ as above. $\qquad\square$

Theorem 16. *For all $u \in O$, for all O-notation w for ω, $\mathbf{Cor}^u\mathbf{TxtEx} \subseteq \mathbf{Cor}^w\mathbf{TxtBc}$.*

Proof. Let h be as defined in Corollary 14. Let $\mathbf{M}$ be $\mathbf{Cor}^u\mathbf{TxtEx}$-learner for $\mathcal{L}$. Let $\mathbf{M}'(T[n]) = h(\mathbf{M}(T[n]), n)$. Theorem now follows from Corollary 14. $\quad\square$

The above theorem can be generalized to show that for all $u \in O$, for all O-notation w for ω, for all $m \in \mathbf{N}$, $\mathbf{Cor}^u\mathbf{TxtEx}^{2m} \subseteq \mathbf{Cor}^w\mathbf{TxtBc}^m$. One can also show the following.

Theorem 17. *For all $u \in O$, $\mathbf{Cor}^u\mathbf{TxtEx}^* \subseteq \mathbf{TxtBc}^*$.*

The next result shows that the hierarchy $\mathbf{Cor}^1\mathbf{TxtEx}^* \subset \mathbf{Cor}^2\mathbf{TxtEx}^* \subset \ldots$ (see Section 3) collapses at level ω.

Theorem 18. *For all $u \in O$, for all O-notation w for ω, $\mathbf{Cor}^u\mathbf{TxtEx}^* \subseteq \mathbf{Cor}^w\mathbf{TxtEx}^*$.*

Proof. Let h be as defined in Corollary 15. Let $\mathbf{M}$ be $\mathbf{Cor}^u\mathbf{TxtEx}$-learner for $\mathcal{L}$. Let $\mathbf{M}'(T[n]) = h(\mathbf{M}(T[n]))$. Theorem now follows from Corollary 15. $\quad\square$

The same proof as above gives the following:

Theorem 19. *For all* $u \in O$, *for all* O*-notation* w *for* ω, $\mathbf{Cor}^u\mathbf{TxtBc}^* \subseteq \mathbf{Cor}^w\mathbf{TxtBc}^*$.

It is open whether there exists a hierarchy of learning $\underline{n}$-correction grammars, for $n \in \mathbf{N}$, with respect to the $\mathbf{TxtBc}^*$-model.

Theorem 20. *For all* $u \in O$, *for all* O*-notation* w *for* ω, *for all* $m \in \mathbf{N}$, $\mathbf{Cor}^u\mathbf{TxtBc}^m \subseteq \mathbf{Cor}^w\mathbf{TxtBc}^m$.

5   Learning Succinct Correction Grammars

In scientific inference, parsimony of explanations is considered highly desirable. Grammar size is one of many ways to measure parsimony of grammars [16,22]. For r.e. L, let $\mathrm{MinGram}(L)$ be the minimal i such that $W_i = L$. For $\mathcal{L} \in \mathbf{TxtEx}$ as witnessed by $\mathbf{M}$, if there is a computable function g such that, for every $L \in \mathcal{L}$, for all texts T for L, $\mathbf{M}(T) \leq g(\mathrm{MinGram}(L))$, then we say $\mathcal{L} \in \mathbf{TxtMEx}$ (as witnessed by $\mathbf{M}$ and g). In this setting we call g a *parsimony factor*. The final grammars of a $\mathbf{TxtMEx}$-learner are *nearly minimal-size*: they are within a computable factor of minimal size grammars. Kinber [23] proved that requiring nearly-minimal size final conjectures limits learning power: the class Zero* = $\{\{\langle x, f(x)\rangle \mid x \in \mathbf{N}\} \mid f \text{ is a recursive function and } (\forall^\infty x)[f(x) = 0]\}$ witnesses $\mathbf{TxtMEx} \subset \mathbf{TxtEx}$. Chen [12] later showed that Zero* is not even in $\mathbf{TxtMEx}^n$ for every $n \in \mathbf{N}$. By contrast, we have the following theorem. Thus, one can learn *very succinct* correction grammars, when compared to ordinary grammars.

Theorem 21. *There exists a learner* $\mathbf{M}$ *which* $\mathbf{Cor}^2\mathbf{TxtEx}$*-identifies* Zero*, *and for some recursive function* g, *for all texts* T *for* $L \in$ Zero*, $\mathbf{M}(T) \leq g(\mathrm{MinGram}(L))$.

Acknowledgements. We thank the referees for several helpful comments.

References

1. Ambainis, A., Case, J., Jain, S., Suraj, M.: Parsimony Hierarchies for Inductive Inference. Journal of Symbolic Logic 69(1), 287–327 (2004)
2. Ash, J., Knight, J.F.: Recursive Structures and Ershov's Hierarchy. Mathematical Logic Quarterly 42, 461–468 (1996)
3. Blum, L., Blum, M.: Toward a mathematical theory of inductive inference. Information and Control 28, 125–155 (1975)
4. Blum, M.: A machine-independent theory of the complexity of recursive functions. Journal of the ACM 14, 322–336 (1967)
5. Burgin, M.: Grammars with prohibition and human-computer interaction. In: Proceedings of the 2005 Business and Industry Symposium and the 2005 Military, Government, and Aerospace Simulation Symposium, pp. 143–147. Society for Modeling and Simulation (2005)
6. Carlucci, L., Case, J., Jain, S.: Learning correction grammars. TR12/06, National University of Singapore (December 2006)

7. Case, J.: The power of vacillation in language learning. SIAM Journal on Computing 28(6), 1941–1969 (1999)
8. Case, J., Jain, S., Sharma, A.: On learning limiting programs. International Journal of Foundations of Computer Science 3(1), 93–115 (1992)
9. Case, J., Lynes, C.: Machine inductive inference and language identification. In: Nielsen, M., Schmidt, E.M. (eds.) Automata, Languages, and Programming. LNCS, vol. 140, pp. 107–115. Springer, Heidelberg (1982)
10. Case, J., Royer, J.: Program size complexity of correction grammars. Preprint (2006)
11. Case, J., Smith, C.: Comparison of identification criteria for machine inductive inference. Theoretical Computer Science 25, 193–220 (1983)
12. Chen, K.: Tradeoffs in inductive inference of nearly minimal sized programs. Information and Control 52, 68–86 (1982)
13. Ershov, Y.L.: A hierarchy of sets I. Algebra and Logic 7, 23–43 (1968)
14. Ershov, Y.L.: A hierarchy of sets II. Algebra and Logic 7, 212–232 (1968)
15. Ershov, Y.L.: A hierarchy of sets III. Algebra and Logic 9, 20–31 (1970)
16. Freivalds, R.: Minimal Gödel numbers and their identification in the limit. LNCS, vol. 32, pp. 219–225. Springer, Heidelberg (1975)
17. Freivalds, R.: Inductive inference of minimal programs. In: Fulk, M., Case, J. (eds.) Proceedings of the Third Annual Workshop on Computational Learning Theory, pp. 3–20. Morgan Kaufmann Publishers, Inc. San Francisco (1990)
18. Freivalds, R., Smith, C.: On the role of procrastination in machine learning. Information and Computation 107(2), 237–271 (1993)
19. Gold, E.M.: Language identification in the limit. Information and Control 10, 447–474 (1967)
20. Hopcroft, J., Ullman, J.: Introduction to Automata Theory, Languages and Computation. Addison-Wesley, London (1979)
21. Jain, S., Osherson, D., Royer, J., Sharma, A.: Systems that Learn: An Introduction to Learning Theory, 2nd edn. MIT Press, Cambridge (1999)
22. Jain, S., Sharma, A.: Program Size Restrictions in Computational Learning. Theoretical Computer Science 127, 351–386 (1994)
23. Kinber, E.: On the synthesis in the limit of almost minimal Gödel numbers. Theory Of Algorithms and Programs, LSU, Riga. 1, 221–223 (1974)
24. Kleene, S.C.: On notation for ordinal numbers. Journal of Symbolic Logic 3, 150–155 (1938)
25. Kleene, S.C.: On the forms of predicates in the theory of constructive ordinals. American Journal of Mathematics 66, 41–58 (1944)
26. Kleene, S.C.: On the forms of predicates in the theory of constructive ordinals (second paper). American Journal of Mathematics 77, 405–428 (1955)
27. Osherson, D., Weinstein, S.: Criteria for language learning. Information and Control 52, 123–138 (1982)
28. Rogers, H.: Theory of Recursive Functions and Effective Computability. McGraw-Hill, 1967. Reprinted by MIT Press in (1987)
29. Royer, J., Case, J.: Subrecursive Programming Systems: Complexity & Succinctness. Birkhäuser (1994)
30. Schaefer, M.: A guided tour of minimal indices and shortest descriptions. Archive for Mathematical Logic 18, 521–548 (1998)

Mitotic Classes

Sanjay Jain[1],* and Frank Stephan[2],*

[1] Department of Computer Science,
National University of Singapore, Singapore 117543, Republic of Singapore
sanjay@comp.nus.edu.sg
[2] Department of Computer Science and Department of Mathematics,
National University of Singapore, Singapore 117543, Republic of Singapore
fstephan@comp.nus.edu.sg

Abstract. For the natural notion of splitting classes into two disjoint subclasses via a recursive classifier working on texts, the question is addressed how these splittings can look in the case of learnable classes. Here the strength of the classes is compared using the strong and weak reducibility from intrinsic complexity. It is shown that, for explanatorily learnable classes, the complete classes are also mitotic with respect to weak and strong reducibility, respectively. But there is a weak complete class which cannot be split into two classes which are of the same complexity with respect to strong reducibility. It is shown that for complete classes for behaviourally correct learning, one half of each splitting is complete for this learning notion as well. Furthermore, it is shown that explanatorily learnable and recursively enumerable classes always have a splitting into two incomparable classes; this gives an inductive inference counterpart of Sacks Splitting Theorem from recursion theory.

1 Introduction

A well-known observation is that infinite sets can be split into two parts of the same cardinality as the original set, while finite sets cannot be split in such a way; for example, the integers can be split into the sets of the even and odd numbers while splitting a set of 5 elements would result in subsets of unequal sizes. In this sense, infinite sets are more perfect than finite ones. The corresponding question in complexity and recursion theory is the following: which sets can be split into two sets of the same complexity as the orginal set [1,9,10,14].

Ambos-Spies [1] defined one of the variants of mitocity using many-one reducibilities. Here a set A is many-one reducible to a set B iff there is a recursive function f such that $A(x) = B(f(x))$. That is, one translates every input x for A into an input $f(x)$ for B, takes the solution provided by B (in the set or out of the set) and then copies this to obtain the solution for A. Similarly one considers also complexity-theoretic counterparts of many-one reductions; for example one can translate an instance (G_1, G_2) of the Graph-Isomorphism problem into an instance ϕ of the Satisfiability problem in polynomial time, where G_1 is isomorphic to G_2 iff ϕ is satisfiable. Here, one can choose the reduction such that one

---

* Supported in part by NUS grant number R252-000-212-112.

N. Bshouty and C. Gentile (Eds.): COLT 2007, LNAI 4539, pp. 218–232, 2007.
© Springer-Verlag Berlin Heidelberg 2007

does not only test membership, but can also translate a solution of ψ into an isomorphism between G_1 and G_2 whenever such a solution exists for ψ. Indeed, NP-complete problems are characterized as those into which every NP problem can be translated. This general method of reducing problems and translating solutions (although here the translation of the solution is just the identity) occurs quite frequently in other fields of mathematics. In inductive inference, intrinsic complexity is based on the notion of reducing one learning problem $\mathcal{L}$ to another problem $\mathcal{H}$: first an operator translates a text T for a set L in $\mathcal{L}$ into a text $\Theta(T)$ for a set H in $\mathcal{H}$ and then another operator translates a solution E, which is a sequence converging to an index e of H, into a solution for L given as a sequence converging to an index e' of L. Before explaining this in more detail, some terminology is necessary to make it precise.

- A partial recursive function is a partial function computed by a Turing machine, where the machine does not halt on inputs on which the function is undefined. A recursively enumerable (r.e.) set is the domain or the range of a partial-recursive function. There is an acceptable numbering $W_0, W_1, W_2, \ldots$ of all r.e. sets [15, Section II.5] which is kept fixed from now on.
- A general recursive operator Θ is a mapping from total functions to total functions such that there is a recursively enumerable set E of triples which satisfies the following: for every total function f and every x, y, $\Theta(f)(x) = y$ iff there is an n such that $(f(0)f(1)\ldots f(n), x, y) \in E$.
- A language is a recursively enumerable subset of the natural numbers.
- A class $\mathcal{L}$ is a set of languages. A family $L_0, L_1, L_2, \ldots$ is an indexing for $\mathcal{L}$ iff $\{(e, x) : x \in L_e\}$ is r.e. and $\mathcal{L} = \{L_0, L_1, L_2, \ldots\}$.
- A text T for a set $L \in \mathcal{L}$ is a mapping from the set $\mathbb{N}$ of natural numbers to $\mathbb{N} \cup \{\#\}$ such that $L = \{T(n) \mid n \in \mathbb{N} \wedge T(n) \in \mathbb{N}\}$. The latter set on the right hand side of the equation is called the content of T, in short, content(T). $T[n]$ denotes the first n elements of sequence T, that is $T[n] = T(0), T(1) \ldots, T(n-1)$.
- A learner is a general recursive operator (see [20]) which translates T into another sequence E. The learner converges on T iff there is a single e such that $E(n) = e$ for almost all n — in this case one says that the learner converges on T to e. The learner identifies (see [11]) T iff it converges to some e such that $W_e = $ content(T). A learner identifies L iff it identifies every text for L and it identifies $\mathcal{L}$ iff it identifies every $L \in \mathcal{L}$. Note that, in some cases, learning algorithms can also be described such that they use the indices from a given indexing for $\mathcal{L}$; such indices can always be translated into indices of the acceptable numbering $W_0, W_1, \ldots$ of all r.e. sets.
- A classifier [19] is a general recursive operator which translates texts to sequences over $\{0, 1\}$. A classifier C converges on a text T to a iff $C(T[n]) = a$ for almost all n.
- For the learning criteria considered in this paper, one can assume without loss of generality that the learner M computes $E(n)$ from input $T[n]$. $M(T[n])$ denotes this hypothesis. A similar convention holds for classifiers.

Freivalds, Kinber and Smith [6] consider reductions between learnability problems for function classes. Jain and Sharma [13] carried this idea over to the field of learning languages from positive data and formalized the following two reducibilities for learnability problems. The main difference between these two notions is that Θ can be one-to-many in the case of the weak reducibility, as different texts for the same language can go to texts for different languages, while for the strong reducibility this is not allowed, at least for languages in the given class.

- A class $\mathcal{L}$ is weakly reducible to $\mathcal{H}$ iff there are general recursive operators Θ and Ψ such that
  - Whenever T is a text for a language in $\mathcal{L}$, $\Theta(T)$ is a text for a language in $\mathcal{H}$;
  - Whenever E is a sequence which converges to an index e with $W_e =$ content($\Theta(T)$) for some text T of a language in $\mathcal{L}$, $\Psi(E)$ is a sequence converging to an e' with $W_{e'} =$ content(T).

  One writes $\mathcal{L} \leq_{weak} \mathcal{H}$ in this case.
- A class $\mathcal{L}$ is strongly reducible to $\mathcal{H}$ iff there are general recursive operators Θ, Ψ as above with the following additional constraint. Whenever T, T' are texts for the same language in $\mathcal{L}$, $\Theta(T), \Theta(T')$ are texts for the same language in $\mathcal{H}$. One writes $\mathcal{L} \leq_{strong} \mathcal{H}$ in this case. Furthermore, $\Theta(L)$ denotes the language content($\Theta(T)$), where T is a text for L.

Jain, Kinber, Sharma and Wiehagen investigated these concepts in several papers [12,13]. They found that there are complete classes with respect to $\leq_{weak}$ and $\leq_{strong}$. Here a class $\mathcal{H}$ is complete with respect to $\leq_{weak}$ ($\leq_{strong}$) iff $\mathcal{H}$ can be learned in the limit from text and for every learnable class $\mathcal{L}$ it holds that $\mathcal{L} \leq_{weak} \mathcal{H}$ ($\mathcal{L} \leq_{strong} \mathcal{H}$). If $\sqsubseteq$ is a recursive dense linear ordering on $\mathbb{N}$ without least and greatest element (which makes $\mathbb{N}$ an order-isomorphic copy of the rationals) then

$$\mathcal{Q} = \{\, \{y \in \mathbb{N} \mid y \sqsubseteq x\} \mid x \in \mathbb{N} \}$$

is a class which is complete for both, $\leq_{weak}$ and $\leq_{strong}$. The following classes are complete for $\leq_{weak}$ but not for $\leq_{strong}$:

$$\mathcal{I} = \{\, \{0, 1, \ldots, x\} \mid x \in \mathbb{N}\};$$
$$\mathcal{CS} = \{\mathbb{N} - \{x\} \mid x \in \mathbb{N}\}$$

If one looks at $\mathcal{CS}$, one can easily see that it is the disjoint union of two classes of equivalent intrinsic complexity, namely the class $\{\mathbb{N} - \{x\} \mid x \text{ is even}\}$ and $\{\mathbb{N} - \{x\} \mid x \text{ is odd}\}$. All three classes can be translated into each other and a classifier can witness the splitting: if T is a text for a member of $\mathcal{CS}$, then the classifier converges in the limit to the remainder of x divided by 2 for the unique $x \notin$ content(T). This type of splitting can be formalized to the notion of a mitotic class.

Definition 1. Two infinite classes $\mathcal{L}_0$ and $\mathcal{L}_1$ are called a *splitting* of a class $\mathcal{L}$ iff $\mathcal{L}_0 \cup \mathcal{L}_1 = \mathcal{L}$, $\mathcal{L}_0 \cap \mathcal{L}_1 = \emptyset$ and there exists a classifier C such that, for all $a \in \{0,1\}$ and for all texts T with content$(T) \in \mathcal{L}_a$, C converges on T to a.

A class $\mathcal{L}$ is *strong mitotic* (*weak mitotic*) iff there is a splitting $\mathcal{L}_0, \mathcal{L}_1$ of $\mathcal{L}$ such that $\mathcal{L} \equiv_{strong} \mathcal{L}_0 \equiv_{strong} \mathcal{L}_1$ ($\mathcal{L} \equiv_{weak} \mathcal{L}_0 \equiv_{weak} \mathcal{L}_1$).

The study of such notions is motivated from recursion theory [15,20] where a recursively enumerable set is called mitotic iff it is the disjoint union of two other recursively enumerable sets which have the same Turing degree. The importance of this notion is reflected by Ladner's result that an r.e. set is mitotic iff it is autoreducible, that is, iff there is an oracle Turing machine M such that $A(x) = M^{A \cup \{x\}}(x)$ for all x [14]. Furthermore the notion had been carried over to complexity theory where it is still an important research topic [1,9,10].

Although intrinsic complexity is not the exact counterpart of Turing degrees in recursion theory, it is the only type of complexity which is defined via reducibilities and not via measures such as counting mind changes or the size of long term memory in inductive inference. Therefore, from the viewpoint of inductive inference, the above defined version of mitotic classes is reasonable. Indeed, there are some obvious parallels: in recursion theory, any r.e. cylinder is mitotic, where a cylinder A is a set of the form $\{(x,y) \mid x \in B, y \in \mathbb{N}\}$ for some set $B \subseteq \mathbb{N}$. A corresponding cylindrification of a class $\mathcal{L}$ would be the class

$$\{ \{(x,y) \mid y \in L\} \mid x \in \mathbb{N}, L \in \mathcal{L}\}.$$

It can easily be seen that this class is strong mitotic and thus also weak mitotic. Indeed, two constraints are placed in Definition 1 in order to be as near to the original definition of mitoticity in recursion theory as possible:

- If A is split into two r.e. sets A_0, A_1 with $A_0 \equiv_T A_1$ then $A \equiv_T A_0 \equiv_T A_1$. Thus all three classes involved are required to have the same intrinsic complexity degree.
- There is a partial-recursive function with domain A mapping the elements of A_a to a for all $a \in \{0,1\}$. This is taken over by requiring the existence of a classifier which works correctly on all texts of the class. It is not required to converge on every text as then many naturally strong mitotic classes, like $\mathcal{CS}$, would no longer be mitotic. This has a parallel in recursion theory: if one splits a maximal set (as defined in Remark 8 below) into two r.e. sets A_0 and A_1, which are both not recursive, then the sets A_0 and A_1 are recursively inseparable.

Besides the reducibilities $\leq_{weak}$ and $\leq_{strong}$ considered here, other reducibilities have also been considered [12,13]. This paper deals only with $\leq_{weak}$ and $\leq_{strong}$, as these two are the most natural and representative.

One emphasis of the current work is on the search for natural classes which split or do not split. Therefore it is always required that the class under consideration is learnable in the limit. Furthermore, one tries to show properties for complete classes, recursively enumerable classes and indexed families. Angluin

[2] defined that $\{L_0, L_1, L_2, \ldots\}$ is an indexed family iff the function $e, x \mapsto L_e(x)$ is recursive. For indexed families $\{L_0, L_1, L_2, \ldots\}$ one can assume, without loss of generality, that $L_n \neq L_m$ whenever $n \neq m$. A learner for this family is called exact iff it converges on every text for L_n to n. The following remark is important for several proofs.

Remark 2. One says that a learner M or a classifier C converges on T to a value a iff $M(T[n]) = a$ or $C(T[n]) = a$ for almost all n, respectively. But it does not matter – in the framework of inductive inference – how fast this convergence is; the machine can be slowed down by starting with an arbitrary guess and later repeating hypotheses, if needed. Similarly, if one translates one text of a language L into a text of a language H, it is not important how fast the symbols of H show up in the translated text, it is only important that they show up eventually. Therefore the translator can put into the translated text pause symbols until more data is available or certain simulated computations have terminated.

Therefore, learners, operators translating texts and classifiers can be made primitive recursive by the just mentioned delaying techniques. Thus one can have recursive enumerations $\Theta_0, \Theta_1, \Theta_2, \ldots$ of translators from texts to texts, $M_0, M_1, M_2, \ldots$ of learners and $C_0, C_1, C_2, \ldots$ of classifiers such that, for every given translator, learner or classifier, this list contains an equivalent one. These lists can be used in proofs where diagonalizations are needed.

Given a text T and a number n, one denotes by $\Theta(T[n])$ the initial part $\Theta(T)[m]$ for the largest $m \leq n$ such that $\Theta(T)[m]$ is produced without accessing any datum in T beyond the n-th position. Note that, for every m, there is an n such that $\Theta(T[n])$ extends $\Theta(T)[m]$ and $\Theta(T[n])$ can be computed from $T[n]$.

2   Complete Classes

The two main results are that classes which are complete for $\leq_{strong}$ are strong mitotic and classes which are complete for $\leq_{weak}$ are weak mitotic. This stands in contrast to the situation in recursion theory where some Turing-complete r.e. sets are not mitotic [14]. Note that certain classes which are complete only for $\leq_{weak}$ fail to be strong mitotic; thus the main results cannot be improved.

Theorem 3. *Every class which is complete for $\leq_{strong}$ is also strong mitotic.*

Proof. Let $\mathcal{L}$ and $\mathcal{H}$ be any classes which are complete for $\leq_{strong}$. Then the class $\mathcal{K}$ consisting of the sets $I = \{1, 3, 5, 7, \ldots\}$, $J = \{0\} \cup I$, $\{2x + 3 : x \in H\}$ and $J \cup \{2x + 2 : x \in H\}$ for every $H \in \mathcal{H}$ is also complete for $\leq_{strong}$. Since $\mathcal{L}$ is complete for $\leq_{strong}$, there is a translation Θ which maps languages in $\mathcal{K}$ to languages in $\mathcal{L}$ such that proper inclusion is preserved. Thus there is some $e \in \Theta(J) - \Theta(I)$. As $\mathcal{H}$ is complete for $\leq_{strong}$, the subclasses $\{\Theta(\{2x + 3 : x \in H\}) : H \in \mathcal{H}\}$ and $\{\Theta(J \cup \{2x + 2 : x \in H\}) : H \in \mathcal{H}\}$ of $\mathcal{L}$ are also complete for $\leq_{strong}$. All members of the first class do not contain e while all members of the second class contain e as an element. It follows that the subclasses

$\mathcal{L}_0 = \{L \in \mathcal{L} : e \notin L\}$ and $\mathcal{L}_1 = \{L \in \mathcal{L} : e \in L\}$ are complete and disjoint and can be classified by a C, which conjectures 1 if e has shown up in the text so far and 0 otherwise. Therefore, $\mathcal{L}$ is strong mitotic. □

The following notion is used to formulate Proposition 6 which is a central ingredient of Theorem 7. Furthermore, learners with certain properties are needed.

Definition 4. For any sequence T of symbols, let all(T) be the length of the shortest prefix of T containing all symbols which show up in T, that is, let

$$\text{all}(T) = \sup\{n + 1 : \text{content}(T[n]) \subset \text{content}(T)\}.$$

Note that all$(T) < \infty$ iff content(T) is a finite set.

The following remark combines some ideas of Blum and Blum [4] and Fulk [8].

Remark 5. Let $\mathcal{L}$ be a learnable class. Then there is a learner M for $\mathcal{L}$ with the following properties:

- M is prudent, that is, whenever M outputs an index e on some input data, then M learns W_e;
- M is order independent, that is, for every set L, either M diverges on all texts for L or M converges on all texts for L to the same index;
- for every text T and index e, if $M(T[n]) = e$ for infinitely many n, then $M(T[n]) = e$ for almost all n.

Proposition 6. *Suppose $\mathcal{I} \leq_{weak} \mathcal{L}$ and M is a learner for $\mathcal{L}$ which satisfies the conditions in Remark 5. Then there is a reduction (Θ, Ψ) from $\mathcal{I}$ to $\mathcal{L}$ such that, for all texts T for a language in $\mathcal{I}$, M converges on $\Theta(T)$ to an index $e > \text{all}(T)$.*

Proof. Assume that (Θ'', Ψ'') witnesses that $\mathcal{I} \leq_{weak} \mathcal{L}$. Now a reduction (Θ', Ψ') from $\mathcal{I}$ to $\mathcal{I}$ is constructed such that Θ can be taken to be the composition of Θ' and Θ''.

The key idea for this is the following: one constructs (Θ', Ψ') from $\mathcal{I}$ to $\mathcal{I}$ such that, for every text T of a set in $\mathcal{I}$, M converges on $\Theta''(\Theta'(T))$ to an index $e > \text{all}(T)$. Note that all(T) is finite for all texts for members of $\mathcal{I}$. By Remark 2, assume without loss of generality that Θ'' is primitive recursive. The idea is that Θ' translates a text T for $I_n = \{0, 1, \ldots, n\}$ to a text for $I_{2^n(1+2m)}$ for some m; Ψ' translates any sequence converging to an index of the set $I_{2^n(1+2m)}$ into a sequence converging to an index of I_n.

Given a sequence E of indices, $\Psi'(E)(s)$ is computed as follows. Let k be the least number such that $W_{E(s),s} \subseteq I_k$. Choose m, n such that $2^n(1+2m) = k$ and output the canonical index for I_n. It is easy to see that this translation works whenever E converges to an index of some set in $\mathcal{I}$.

Construction of Θ'. The construction of Θ' is more involved. For the construction, the special properties of M from Remark 5 are important. The most adequate way to describe $\Theta'(T)$ is to build longer and longer finite prefixes

$\tau_0, \tau_1, \tau_2, \ldots$ of this target $\Theta'(T)$. The construction starts with $\tau_0 = 0\#$ and in stage s, the extension τ_{s+1} of τ_s be defined according to the first case which applies:

Case 1: $M(\Theta''(\tau_s)) \leq \text{all}(T[s])$. Then let τ_{s+1} be the first extension of τ_s found such that $M(\Theta''(\tau_{s+1})) \neq M(\Theta''(\tau_s))$;

Case 2: Case 1 does not hold but $\text{content}(\tau_s) \neq I_{2^n(1+2m)}$ for all m, where n is the least number with $\text{content}(T[s]) \subseteq I_n$. Then let $\tau_{s+1} = \tau_s a$ for the least nonelement a of $\text{content}(\tau_s)$;

Case 3: Case 1 and Case 2 do not hold. Then $\tau_{s+1} = \tau_s\#$.

Here $\Theta''(\tau_s)$ and $\Theta''(\tau_{s+1})$ are defined as in Remark 2 and can be computed from τ_s and τ_{s+1}, respectively.

Verification. For the verification, assume that a set $I_n = \{0, 1, 2, \ldots, n\} \in \mathcal{I}$ and a text T for I_n are given.

First note that, in Case 1 of the construction, the extension τ_{s+1} of τ_s can always be found. To see this, note that there are two texts T_1, T_2 extending τ_s for different sets in $\mathcal{I}$. It follows that $\Theta''(T_1)$ and $\Theta''(T_2)$ are texts of different sets and thus M converges on them to different indices. Thus one can take a sufficiently long prefix of one of T_1, T_2 in order to get the desired τ_{s+1}.

Second, it can be shown by induction that $|\tau_s| > s$ in all stages s; this guarantees that Θ' is indeed a general recursive operator.

Third, one shows that M does not converge on $\Theta''(\Theta'(T))$ to any index less than or equal to $\text{all}(T)$. By Case 1 in the construction, M cannot converge on $\Theta''(\Theta'(T))$ to an index $e \leq \text{all}(T)$. Thus, by Remark 5, there is a stage s_0 such that Case 1 of the construction is never taken after stage s_0 and $\text{content}(T[s_0]) = I_n$.

Fourth, one shows that $\Theta'(T)$ is a text for some language in $\mathcal{I}$. There is a least m such that $\text{content}(\tau_{s_0}) \subseteq I_{2^n(1+2m)}$. For all stages $s > s_0$, if $\text{content}(\tau_s) \subset I_{2^n(1+2m)}$, then τ_{s+1} is chosen by Case 2, else τ_{s+1} is chosen by Case 3. One can easily see that the resulting text $\Theta'(T) = \lim_{s \to \infty} \tau_s$ is a text for $I_{2^n(1+2m)}$. Indeed, $\Theta'(T) = \tau_{s_1}\#^\infty$ for $s_1 = s_0 + 2^n(1 + 2m) + 2$.

So it follows that Θ' maps every text of a set I_n to a text for some set $I_{2^n(1+2m)}$ as desired. So, for all texts T of sets in $\mathcal{I}$, M converges on $\Theta''(\Theta'(T))$ to some index $e > \text{all}(T)$.   □

Theorem 7. *Let $\mathcal{L}$ be a learnable class which is complete for $\leq_{weak}$. Then $\mathcal{L}$ is weak mitotic.*

Proof. Let $I_n = \{0, 1, \ldots, n\}$. By Proposition 6 there is a reduction (Θ, Ψ) from $\mathcal{I}$ to $\mathcal{L}$ and a learner M such that M satisfies the conditions outlined in Remark 5 and, for every text T of a member of $\mathcal{I}$, M converges on $\Theta(T)$ to an index $e > \text{all}(T)$. For this reason, using oracle K for the halting problem, one can check, for every index e, whether there is a text T for a language in $\mathcal{I}$ such that M on $\Theta(T)$ converges to e. This can be seen as follows: One can assume, without loss of generality, that, besides $\#$, no data-item in a text is repeated. Also, among the texts for sets in $\mathcal{I}$, only the texts of the sets $\{0\}$, $\{0,1\}$, $\{0,1,2\}$, …, $\{0,1,2,\ldots,e\}$ can satisfy all$(T) \leq e$. Thus, one has just to check the behaviour of the given learner M for the class $\mathcal{L}$ on the texts in the class

$$\mathcal{T}_e = \{\Theta(T') \mid T' \in \{0,1,\ldots,e,\#\}^e \cdot \#^\infty \wedge \text{content}(T) \in \mathcal{I}\}.$$

Now, define a classifier C such that on a text T, the n-th guess of C is 1 iff there is an odd number $m \leq M(T[n])$ and a text $T'' \in \mathcal{T}_{M(T[n])}$ for I_m such that $M(\Theta(T''))[n]) = M(T[n])$.

For the verification that C is a classifier, assume that M converges on T to some index e. Then C converges on T to 1 iff there is a an odd number m and a text T' for I_m in $\mathcal{T}_e$ such that M converges on the texts T and $\Theta(T')$ to the same number. Otherwise C converges on T to 0. If M does not converge on T, then T is not a text for a set in $\mathcal{L}$ and the behaviour of C on T is irrelevant. Thus C is a classifier which splits $\mathcal{L}$ into two classes $\mathcal{L}_0$ and $\mathcal{L}_1$. These classes $\mathcal{L}_0$ and $\mathcal{L}_1$ contain the images of repetition-free texts of sets in the classes $\{I_0, I_2, I_4, \ldots\}$ and $\{I_1, I_3, I_5, \ldots\}$, respectively. Thus both classes are complete for $\leq_{weak}$ and the splitting of $\mathcal{L}$ into $\mathcal{L}_0$ and $\mathcal{L}_1$ witnesses that $\mathcal{L}$ is weak mitotic. □

As several proofs use known properties of maximal sets, the following remark summarizes some of these properties.

Remark 8. A set A is *maximal* iff (a) A is recursively enumerable, (b) A has an infinite complement and (c) every recursively enumerable set B satisfies that either $B - A$ is finite or the complement of $A \cup B$ is finite.

A maximal set is dense simple, that is, if $a_0, a_1, a_2, \ldots$ gives the complement in ascending order and f is a recursive function, then $f(a_n) < a_{n+1}$ for almost all n.

For any partial-recursive function ψ and maximal set A, the following statements hold.

- Either $\psi(x)$ is defined for almost all $x \in \overline{A}$ or for only finitely many $x \in \overline{A}$.
- The set $\{x \notin A \mid \psi(x) \in A\}$ is either finite or contains almost all elements of $\overline{A}$.
- If, for every x, there is some $y > x$ such that $y \notin A$, $\psi(y)$ is defined, $\psi(y) > x$ and $\psi(y) \notin A$, then $\psi(z)$ is defined and $\psi(z) = z$ for almost all $z \in \overline{A}$.

These basic facts about maximal sets will be used in several proofs. Odifreddi [15, Pages 288–294] provides more information on maximal sets including the proof of the existence by Friedberg [7].

Theorem 9. *There exists an indexed family* $\{L_0, L_1, L_2, \ldots\}$ *which is weak mitotic and complete for* $\leq_{weak}$, *but not strong mitotic.*

Proof. Let A be a maximal set with complement $\{a_0, a_1, \ldots\}$ where $a_n < a_{n+1}$ for all n. Now let $\mathcal{L}$ consist of the sets

- $\{x, x+1, x+2, \ldots, x+y\}$ for all $x \in A$ and $y \in \mathbb{N}$;
- $\{x, x+1, x+2, \ldots\}$ for all $x \notin A$.

As A is r.e., $\mathcal{L}$ can be represented as an indexed family. Learnability is also clear as the learner, on input σ, first determines $x = \min(\text{content}(\sigma))$ and then conjectures $\text{content}(\sigma)$ if $x \in A_{|\sigma|}$, and conjectures $\{x, x+1, x+2, \ldots\}$ otherwise. Without loss of generality, it can be assumed that $a_0 > 0$ and thus $\mathcal{L}$ is a superclass of $\mathcal{I}$ and therefore $\mathcal{L}$ is complete for $\leq_{weak}$. By Theorem 7, $\mathcal{L}$ is weak mitotic.

Let $\mathcal{L}_0$ and $\mathcal{L}_1$ be two disjoint classes with union $\mathcal{L}$. Without loss of generality, $\{a_0, a_0 + 1, a_0 + 2, \ldots\} \in \mathcal{L}_1$. Assume now by way of contradiction that $\mathcal{L} \leq_{strong} \mathcal{L}_0$ as witnessed by (Θ, Ψ). As Θ has to preserve the proper subset relation on the content of the texts while translating, every text of a set of the form $\{a_n, a_n + 1, a_n + 2, \ldots\}$ has to be translated into a text for a set of the form $\{a_m, a_m + 1, a_m + 2, \ldots\}$ (to preserve the property that translation of $\{a_n, a_n + 1, a_n + 2, \ldots\}$ has infinitely many subsets in the class).

Now consider the function f which outputs, on input x, the first element found to be in the range of the image $\Theta(\sigma)$ for some σ with $x = \min(\text{content}(\sigma))$. The function f is recursive, but by Remark 8 and A being maximal, the relation $f(a_n) < a_{n+1}$ holds for almost all n. It follows that if n is sufficiently large, then some text of $\{a_n, a_n + 1, a_n + 2, \ldots\}$ is translated to a text of one of the sets $\{a_k, a_k + 1, a_k + 2, \ldots\}$ with $k \leq n$. Now fix a text T for $\{a_n, a_n + 1, a_n + 2, \ldots\}$. One can then inductively define a sequence of strings $\sigma_n, \sigma_{n-1}, \ldots, \sigma_0$ such that each sequence $\sigma_n \sigma_{n-1} \ldots \sigma_m T$ is a text for $\{a_m, a_m + 1, a_m + 2, \ldots\}$ and

$$\text{content}(\Theta(\sigma_n \sigma_{n-1} \ldots \sigma_m \sigma_{m-1})) \not\subseteq \text{content}(\Theta(\sigma_n \sigma_{n-1} \ldots \sigma_m T))$$

for each $m \leq n$. As Θ maps texts of infinite sets in $\mathcal{L}$ to texts of infinite sets in $\mathcal{L}$, one can conclude that

$$\text{content}(\Theta(\sigma_n \sigma_{n-1} \ldots \sigma_m T)) = \{a_m, a_m + 1, a_m + 2, \ldots\}.$$

Thus, for every m, some text of the set $\{a_m, a_m + 1, a_m + 2, \ldots\}$ is mapped to a text for the same set in contradiction to the assumption that Θ does not have $\{a_0, a_0 + 1, a_0 + 2, \ldots\}$ in its range. Therefore $\mathcal{L}$ is not strong mitotic. $\qquad\square$

3 Incomplete Learnable Classes

Finite classes are not mitotic and thus every nonempty class has a subclass which is not mitotic. For infinite classes, one can get that the corresponding subclass is also infinite. The proof is a standard application of Ramsey's Theorem: Given classifiers $C_0, C_1, C_2, \ldots$ one selects a subclass $\{H_0, H_1, H_2, \ldots\}$ of $\{L_0, L_1, L_2, \ldots\}$ such that each classifier C_n classifies $H_n, H_{n+1}, H_{n+2}, \ldots$ in the same way. The class $\{H_0, H_1, H_2, \ldots\}$ may not be an indexed family but be a very thin class in the sense that the indices of H_n with respect to $L_0, L_1, L_2, \ldots$ are growing very fast. Alternatively, one can also take the $H_0, H_1, H_2, \ldots$ such that, for a given enumeration of primitive recursive operators, the text $\Theta_n(T_m)$ of the ascending text T_m of H_m is not a text for any H_k with $k > \max(\{n, m\})$. The latter method gives the following result.

Theorem 10. *Every infinite class $\mathcal{L}$ has an infinite subclass $\mathcal{H}$ such that $\mathcal{H}$ is not weakly isomorphic to any proper subclass of $\mathcal{H}$. In particular, $\mathcal{H}$ is not weak mitotic.*

There is an easier example of a class which is not weak mitotic. It is even an indexed family of finite sets.

Example 11. *Assume that $\{L_0, L_1, L_2, \ldots\}$ is given as $L_0 = \{0,1\}$ and $L_n = \{n\}$ for all $n \in \mathbb{N} - \{0\}$. Then $\{L_0, L_1, L_2, \ldots\}$ is not weak mitotic.*

Proof. Given any splitting $\mathcal{L}_0, \mathcal{L}_1$ of $\{L_0, L_1, L_2, \ldots\}$, one of these classes, say $\mathcal{L}_0$, contains at most one of the sets L_0, L_1. Then, for any given reduction (Θ, Ψ) from $\{L_0, L_1, L_2, \ldots\}$ to $\mathcal{L}_0$, $\Theta(\sigma)$ produces some string of nonempty content for some $\sigma \in 1\#^*$. Thus there are texts T_0, T_1 extending σ for L_0 and L_1, respectively, such that $\Theta(T_0)$ and $\Theta(T_1)$ are texts for different sets in $\mathcal{L}_0$ with a nonempty intersection. However, such sets do not exist, by choice of $\mathcal{L}_0$.   □

Note that the class

$$\{\{0,1,2\}, \{1,2\}, \{2\}, \{3\}, \{4\}, \{5\}, \ldots, \{n\}, \ldots\}$$

compared with the class from Example 11 has the following slight improvement. For any splitting $\mathcal{L}_0, \mathcal{L}_1$ of the class, one half of the splitting contains an ascending chain of two or three sets, while the other half contains only disjoint sets. Thus the two halves are not equivalent with respect to $\leq_{weak}$.

As these two examples show, it is more adequate to study the splitting of more restrictive classes like the inclusion-free classes. A special case of such classes are the finitely learnable classes. Here a class is finitely learnable [11] iff there is a learner which, on every text for a language to be learnt, outputs only one hypothesis, which must be correct. For technical reasons, the learner keeps outputting a special symbol denoting the absence of a reasonable conjecture until it outputs its only hypothesis.

Theorem 12. $\{L_0, L_1, L_2, \ldots\} \equiv_{strong} \{H_0, H_1, H_2, \ldots\}$ *whenever both classes are infinite indexed families which are finitely learnable. In particular, every such class is strong mitotic.*

Proof. As $\{L_0, L_1, L_2, \ldots\}$ and $\{H_0, H_1, H_2, \ldots\}$ are infinite, one can without loss of generality assume that the underlying enumerations are one-to-one. Furthermore, they have exact finite learners M and N, respectively, which use the corresponding indexing. Now one translates $\{L_0, L_1, L_2, \ldots\}$ to $\{H_0, H_1, H_2, \ldots\}$ by mapping L_n to H_n; thus Ψ is the identity mapping, where in the domain the n stands for H_n and in the range the n stands for L_n. $\Theta(T) = \#^k T_n$ where k is the least number such that M outputs a hypothesis n on input $T[k]$ (that is, first position where M conjectures a hypothesis) and T_n is the ascending text of H_n. This completes the proof of the first statement.

Given now an infinite finitely learnable class $\{L_0, L_1, L_2, \ldots\}$, one can split it into $\{L_0, L_2, L_4, \ldots\}$ and $\{L_1, L_3, L_5, \ldots\}$ which are the subclasses of languages with even and odd index, respectively. Both classes are also infinite indexed families which are finitely learnable. Thus they are all equivalent by the above result. Furthermore, a classifier for splitting can be obtained by simulating the learner M on the input text, and then converging to 0 if the (only) grammar output by M on the input text is even, and to 1 if the (only) grammar output by M on the input text is odd. □

4   Further Splitting Theorems

Another question is whether classes can be split into incomparable classes. So one would ask whether there is a parallel result to Sacks Splitting Theorem [18]: Every nonrecursive r.e. set A is the disjoint union of two r.e. sets A_0 and A_1 such that the Turing degrees of A_0 and A_1 are incomparable and strictly below the one of A. The next example shows that there are classes where every splitting is of this form; so these classes are not weak mitotic. Furthermore, splittings exist, so the result is not making use of a pathological diagonalization against all classifiers.

Example 13. *Let A be a maximal set. If $a \notin A$, then let $L_a = \{a\}$, else let $L_a = A$. Then $\{L_0, L_1, L_2, \ldots\}$ is recursively enumerable and finitely learnable, but any splitting $\mathcal{L}_0, \mathcal{L}_1$ of $\{L_0, L_1, L_2, \ldots\}$ satisfies $\mathcal{L}_0 \not\leq_{weak} \mathcal{L}_1$ and $\mathcal{L}_1 \not\leq_{weak} \mathcal{L}_0$.*

Proof. Let $T_0, T_1, T_2, \ldots$ be a recursive enumeration of recursive texts for $L_0, L_1, L_2, \ldots$, respectively. Let $F(a)$ be the cardinality of $\{b < a \mid b \notin A\}$. It is easy to see that one can split $\{L_0, L_1, L_2, \ldots\}$ into $\{L_a \mid a \in A \vee F(a)$ is even$\}$ and $\{L_a \mid a \notin A \wedge F(a)$ is odd$\}$. Thus this class has a splitting; in fact there are infinitely many of them. Furthermore, $\{L_0, L_1, L_2, \ldots\}$ is finitely learnable by outputting an index for L_a for the first a occurring in a given text.

Assume now by way of contradiction that there is a splitting $\mathcal{L}_0, \mathcal{L}_1$ with $\mathcal{L}_0 \leq_{weak} \mathcal{L}_1$ via a reduction (Θ, Ψ). Now one defines the partial-recursive function f which outputs on input a the first number occurring in $\Theta(T_a)$; if there occurs no number then $f(a)$ is undefined. As $\mathcal{L}_0$ is infinite, there are infinitely many $a \notin A$ with $L_a \in \mathcal{L}_0$. For all but one of these, $\Theta(T_a)$ has to be a text for some set $L_b \neq A$ in $\mathcal{L}_1$. Then $L_b = \{b\}$ and $f(a) = b \notin A$ for these a. It follows that, for every x, there is an $a > x$ with $a \notin A \wedge f(a) \notin A \wedge f(a) > x$. Then, by Remark 8, $f(a) = a$ for almost all $a \notin A$. As infinitely many of these a belong to an $L_a \in \mathcal{L}_0$, one has that $\Theta(T_a)$ is a text for L_a and Θ translates some text for a set in $\mathcal{L}_0$ into a text for a set in $\mathcal{L}_0$ and not into a text for a set in $\mathcal{L}_1$. Thus $\mathcal{L}_0 \not\leq_{weak} \mathcal{L}_1$. By symmetry of the argument, $\mathcal{L}_1 \not\leq_{weak} \mathcal{L}_0$. □

While the previous example showed that there are classes for which every splitting is a Sacks splitting, the next result shows that every learnable recursively enumerable class has a Sacks splitting; but it might also have other splittings.

Theorem 14. *Every infinite recursively enumerable and learnable class $\{L_0, L_1, L_2, \ldots\}$ has a splitting into two infinite subclasses $\mathcal{L}_0, \mathcal{L}_1$ such that $\mathcal{L}_0 \not\leq_{weak} \mathcal{L}_1$ and $\mathcal{L}_1 \not\leq_{weak} \mathcal{L}_0$.*

For this reason, one cannot give a recursively enumerable class where all splittings $\mathcal{L}_0, \mathcal{L}_1$ satisfy either $\mathcal{L}_0 \leq_{strong} \mathcal{L}_1$ or $\mathcal{L}_1 \leq_{strong} \mathcal{L}_0$. Furthermore, complete classes have comparable splittings like before as they are mitotic and have even equivalent splittings. The next example gives a class where some splittings are comparable but where they are never equivalent.

Example 15. *Let A be a maximal set. For all $a \in \mathbb{N}$ and $b \in \{0,1,2\}$, let $L_{3a+b} = \{3a + b\}$ if $a \notin A$ and $L_{3a+b} = \{3c + b \mid c \in A\}$ if $a \in A$. Then $\{L_0, L_1, L_2, \ldots\}$ is not weak mitotic but has a splitting $\mathcal{L}_0, \mathcal{L}_1$ with $\mathcal{L}_0 \leq_{strong} \mathcal{L}_1$.*

Proof. If one takes the splitting $\mathcal{L}_0 = \{L_0, L_3, L_6, \ldots\}$ and $\mathcal{L}_1 = \{L_1, L_2, L_4, L_5, L_7, L_8, \ldots\}$ then it is easy to see that $\mathcal{L}_0 \leq_{strong} \mathcal{L}_1$ via (Θ, Ψ) such that Θ is based on translating every datum $3x$ to $3x + 1$ and Ψ is based on transforming every index e into an index for $\{3x \mid 3x + 1 \in W_e\}$. The details are left to the reader.

Given now a further splitting $\mathcal{L}_2, \mathcal{L}_3$ of $\{L_0, L_1, L_2, \ldots\}$, one of these two classes, say $\mathcal{L}_2$, must contain at least two of the sets $L_{3a}, L_{3a+1}, L_{3a+2}$ for infinitely many $a \notin A$. Assume by way of contradiction that (Θ, Ψ) would witness $\mathcal{L}_2 \leq_{weak} \mathcal{L}_3$. Now one defines the following functions f_b for $b = 0, 1, 2$ by letting $f_b(a)$ to be the first number x found such that $3x$ or $3x + 1$ or $3x + 2$ occurs in the text $\Theta((3a + b)^\infty)$. Now choose two different $b, b' \in \{0, 1, 2\}$ such that there are infinitely many $a \in \mathbb{N} - A$ with $L_{3a+b}, L_{3a+b'} \in \mathcal{L}_2$. Then one knows that, for every bound c, there are infinitely many $a \in \mathbb{N} - A$ such that $L_{3a+b} \in \mathcal{L}_2$ and $\Theta((3a + b)^\infty)$ is a text for some language in $\mathcal{L}_3 - \{L_0, L_1, L_2, \ldots, L_c\}$. It follows by Remark 8 that $f_b(a) = a$ for almost all $a \notin A$. The same applies to $f_{b'}$. So there is an $a \notin A$ such that $L_{3a+b}, L_{3a+b'}$ are both in $\mathcal{L}_2$ and that Θ maps texts of both languages to texts of the sets $L_{3a}, L_{3a+1}, L_{3a+2}$. As only one of these sets can be in $\mathcal{L}_3$, Θ has to map texts of different languages to texts of the same language, a contradiction. Thus $\mathcal{L}_2 \not\leq_{weak} \mathcal{L}_3$ and the class cannot be weak mitotic. □

5   Beyond Explanatory Learning

One could, besides classes which are complete for (explanatorily) learning, also consider classes which are complete for behaviourally correct learning [3,5,16] with respect to $\leq_{strong}$. Note that such a class $\mathcal{L}$ is no longer explanatorily learnable, but $\mathcal{L}$ satisfies the following two properties:

- The class $\mathcal{L}$ is behaviourally correct learnable, that is, there is a learner which outputs, on every text T for a language in $\mathcal{L}$, an infinite sequence $e_0, e_1, e_2, \ldots$ of hypotheses such that $W_{e_n} = \text{content}(T)$ for almost all n;
- Every behaviourally correct learnable class $\mathcal{H}$ satisfies $\mathcal{H} \leq_{strong} \mathcal{L}$.

Note that the reduction $\leq_{strong}$ considered in this paper is always the same as defined for explanatory learning; reducibilities more adapted to behaviourally correct learning had also been studied [12,13].

It is easy to show that such complete classes exist. Consider as an example the class $\mathcal{L}$ of all sets $\{x\} \cup \{x+y+1 \mid y \in L\}$, where the x-th behaviourally correct learner learns the set L. So given any behaviourally correct learnable class and an index x of its learner, the translation $L \mapsto \{x\} \cup \{x+y+1 \mid y \in L\}$ would translate all the sets learnt by this learner into sets in $\mathcal{L}$.

In the following let $\mathcal{L}$ be any class which is complete for behaviourally correct learning with respect to $\leq_{strong}$. Note that methods similar to those in Theorem 3 show that $\mathcal{L}$ is strong mitotic. The next result shows that for any splitting $\mathcal{L}_0, \mathcal{L}_1$ of $\mathcal{L}$, one of these two classes is complete for behaviourally correct learning as well and therefore this class cannot be split into two incomparable subclasses.

Theorem 16. *If $\mathcal{L}_0, \mathcal{L}_1$ are a splitting of a class which is complete for behaviourally correct learning with respect to $\leq_{strong}$, then either $\mathcal{L}_0 \equiv_{strong} \mathcal{L}_0 \cup \mathcal{L}_1$ or $\mathcal{L}_1 \equiv_{strong} \mathcal{L}_0 \cup \mathcal{L}_1$.*

As just seen, any splitting $\mathcal{L}_0, \mathcal{L}_1$ of a class which is complete for behaviourally correct learning satisfies either $\mathcal{L}_0 \equiv_{strong} \mathcal{L}_1$ or $\mathcal{L}_0 <_{strong} \mathcal{L}_1$ or $\mathcal{L}_1 <_{strong} \mathcal{L}_0$. As the class is strong mitotic, it can happen that the two halves of a split are equivalent although this is not always the case. The next result gives a class where the two halves of a splitting are always comparable but never equivalent.

Theorem 17. *There is a recursively enumerable and behaviourally correctly learnable class, which is not weak mitotic, such that every splitting $\mathcal{L}_0, \mathcal{L}_1$ of the class satisfies either $\mathcal{L}_0 \leq_{strong} \mathcal{L}_1$ or $\mathcal{L}_1 \leq_{strong} \mathcal{L}_0$, but not $\mathcal{L}_0 \equiv_{weak} \mathcal{L}_1$.*

6   Autoreducibility

Trakhtenbrot [21] defined that a set A is autoreducible iff one can reduce A to A such that $A(x)$ is obtained by accessing A only at places different to x. Ladner [14] showed that a recursively enumerable set is mitotic iff it is autoreducible. Ambos-Spies pointed this result out to the authors and asked whether the same holds in the setting of inductive inference. Unfortunately, this characterisation fails for both of the major variants of autoreducibility. These variants are the ones corresponding to strong and weak reducibility.

Definition 18. *A class $\mathcal{L}$ is strong (weak) autoreducible iff there is a strong (weak) reduction (Θ, Ψ) from $\mathcal{L}$ to $\mathcal{L}$ such that, for all sets $L \in \mathcal{L}$ and all texts T for L, $\Theta(T)$ is a text for a language in $\mathcal{L} - \{L\}$.*

Example 19. *Let A be a maximal set and $\mathcal{L}$ contain the following sets:*

- *$\{3x\}, \{3x+1\}, \{3x+2\}$ for all $x \notin A$;*
- *$\{3y : y \in A\}, \{3y+1 : y \in A\}, \{3y+2 : y \in A\}$.*

Then the class $\mathcal{L}$ is neither strong mitotic nor weak mitotic. But $\mathcal{L}$ is autoreducible via some (Θ, Ψ) where Θ maps any text T to a text T' such that all *elements of the form $3y$ in T have the form $3y+1$ in T', all elements of the form $3y+1$ in T have the form $3y+2$ in T' and all elements of the form $3y+2$ have the form $3y$ in T'.*

So even the implication "strong autoreducible $\Rightarrow$ weak mitotic" fails. The remaining question is whether at least the converse direction is true in inductive inference. This is still unknown, but there is some preliminary result on sets which are complete for $\leq_{weak}$.

Theorem 20. *If a class $\mathcal{L}$ is weak complete, then it is weak autoreducible.*

Proof. Let $\mathcal{L}$ be weak complete and M be a learner for $\mathcal{L}$ which satisfies the conditions from Remark 5. As $\mathcal{L}$ is weak complete, by Proposition 6, there is a reduction (Θ, Ψ) from the class $\mathcal{I}$ to $\mathcal{L}$ such that, for any set $I_x = \{0, 1, \ldots, x\} \in \mathcal{I}$ and any text T for I_x, $\Theta(T)$ is a text for a set on which M does not converge to an index less than or equal to x. Now, an autoreduction (Θ', Ψ') is constructed.

For this, one first defines Θ'' as follows and then concatenates it with Θ. The operator Θ'' translates every text T for a set L into a text for $I_{2^n(1+2m)}$ where m, n are chosen such that n is the value to which M converges on T and m is so large that all the elements put into $\Theta''(T)$, when following intermediate hypotheses of M on T, are contained in the set $I_{2^n(1+2m)}$. It is easy to verify that this can be done. Then Θ' is given as $\Theta'(T) = \Theta(\Theta''(T))$. The sequence $\Theta'(T)$ is a text for a set in $\mathcal{L}$ with the additional property that M converges on it to an index larger than $2^n(1 + 2m)$; this index is therefore different from n and content($\Theta'(T)$) $\neq$ content(T).

The reverse operator Ψ' can easily be generated from Ψ. If E converges to an index for content($\Theta'(T)$), then $\Psi(E)$ converges to some index for $I_{2^n(1+2m)}$. The number $2^n(1 + 2m)$ can be determined in the limit from this index by enumerating the corresponding finite set; thus Ψ' can translate E via $\Psi(E)$ to a sequence which converges to n. □

Example 21. *The class $\mathcal{L}$ from Theorem 9 is weak complete and weak autoreducible but not strong autoreducible.*

Proof. Let $\mathcal{L}$ and $a_0, a_1, a_2, \ldots$ be as in Theorem 9. Assume that (Θ, Ψ) witness that $\mathcal{L}$ is strong autoreducible. Then Θ has to preserve inclusions and therefore map infinite sets in $\mathcal{L}$ to infinite sets. So, content($\Theta(a_0 (a_0 + 1) (a_0 + 2) \ldots)$) is an infinite set in $\mathcal{L}$ different from $\{a_0, a_0 + 1, a_0 + 2, \ldots\}$. By induction, one can show that

content($\Theta(a_n (a_n + 1) (a_n + 2) \ldots)$) $\subseteq \{a_{n+1}, a_{n+1} + 1, a_{n+1} + 2, \ldots\}$ and

content($\Theta(a_n (a_n + 1) (a_n + 2) \ldots)$) $\subset \{a_n, a_n + 1, a_n + 2, \ldots\}$.

But in Theorem 9 it was shown that no recursive operator has these properties. That $\mathcal{L}$ is weak complete was shown in Theorem 9 and that $\mathcal{L}$ is weak autoreducible follows from Theorem 20. □

References

1. Ambos-Spies, K.: P-mitotic sets. In: Logic and Machines. LNCS, vol. 177, pp. 1–23. Springer, Heidelberg (1984)
2. Angluin, D.: Inductive inference of formal languages from positive data. Information and Control 45, 117–135 (1980)
3. Bārzdiņš, J.: Two theorems on the limiting synthesis of functions. In *Theory of Algorithms and Programs*, Vol. 1, Latvian State University, Riga, 210, 82–88 (1974)
4. Blum, L., Blum, M.: Toward a mathematical theory of inductive inference. Information and Control 28, 125–155 (1975)
5. Case, J., Lynes, C.: Inductive inference and language identification. In: Ninth International Colloquium on Automata, Languages and Programming (ICALP), Aarhus, Denmark, July 12-16. LNCS, vol. 140, pp. 107–115. Springer, Heidelberg (1982)
6. Freivalds, R., Kinber, E., Smith, C.: On the intrinsic complexity of learning. Information and Computation 123, 64–71 (1995)
7. Friedberg, R.: Three theorems on recursive enumeration. The. Journal of Symbolic Logic 23, 309–316 (1958)
8. Fulk, M.: Prudence and other conditions on formal language learning. Information and Computation 85, 1–11 (1990)
9. Glaßer, C., Pavan, A., Selman, A., Zhang, L.: Mitosis in computational complexity. In: Theory and Applications of Models of Computation. Third International Conference, TAMC 2006, Beijing, China, May 15-20. LNCS, vol. 3959, pp. 61–67. Springer, Heidelberg (2006)
10. Glaßer, C., Ogihara, M., Pavan, A., Selman, A., Zhang, L.: Autoreducibility, mitoticity and immunity. In: Mathematical Foundations of Computer Science. Thirtieth International Symposium, MFCS 2005, Gdansk, Poland, August 29 - September 2. LNCS, vol. 3618, pp. 387–398. Springer, Heidelberg (2005)
11. Gold, E.M.: Language identification in the limit. Information and Control 10, 447–474 (1967)
12. Jain, S., Kinber, E., Wiehagen, R.: Language learning from texts: degrees of intrinsic complexity and their characterizations. Journal of Computer and System Sciences 63, 305–354 (2001)
13. Jain, S., Sharma, A.: The intrinsic complexity of language identification. Journal of Computer and System Sciences 52, 393–402 (1996)
14. Ladner, R.: Mitotic recursively enumerable sets. The. Journal of Symbolic Logic 38, 199–211 (1973)
15. Odifreddi, P.: Classical Recursion Theory. North-Holland, Amsterdam (1989)
16. Osherson, D.N., Weinstein, S.: Criteria of language learning. Information and Control 52, 123–138 (1982)
17. Post, E.: Recursively enumerable sets of positive integers and their decision problems. Bulletin of the American Mathematical Society 50, 284–316 (1944)
18. Sacks, G.E.: On the degrees less than $\mathbf{0}'$. Annals of Mathematics 77, 211–231 (1977)
19. Smith, C.H., Wiehagen, R., Zeugmann, T.: Classifying predicates and languages. International Journal of Foundations of Computer Science 8, 15–41 (1997)
20. Soare, R.: Recursively Enumerable Sets and Degrees. Springer-Verlag, Heidelberg (1987)
21. Trakhtenbrot, B.A.: On autoreducibility. Soviet Mathematics, Doklady (Doklady Akademii Nauk. SSSR) 11, 814–817 (1970)

Regret to the Best vs. Regret to the Average

Eyal Even-Dar[1], Michael Kearns[1], Yishay Mansour[2,*], and Jennifer Wortman[1]

[1] Department of Computer and Information Science, University of Pennsylvania
[2] School of Computer Science, Tel Aviv University

Abstract. We study online regret minimization algorithms in a bicriteria setting, examining not only the standard notion of regret to the best expert, but also the regret to the average of all experts, the regret to any fixed mixture of experts, and the regret to the worst expert. This study leads both to new understanding of the limitations of existing no-regret algorithms, and to new algorithms with novel performance guarantees. More specifically, we show that *any* algorithm that achieves only $O(\sqrt{T})$ cumulative regret to the best expert on a sequence of T trials must, in the worst case, suffer regret $\Omega(\sqrt{T})$ to the average, and that for a wide class of update rules that includes many existing no-regret algorithms (such as Exponential Weights and Follow the Perturbed Leader), the product of the regret to the best and the regret to the average is $\Omega(T)$. We then describe and analyze a new multi-phase algorithm, which achieves cumulative regret only $O(\sqrt{T} \log T)$ to the best expert and has only *constant* regret to any fixed distribution over experts (that is, with no dependence on either T or the number of experts N). The key to the new algorithm is the gradual increase in the "aggressiveness" of updates in response to observed divergences in expert performances.

1 Introduction

Beginning at least as early as the 1950s, the long and still-growing literature on no-regret learning has established the following type of result. On any sequence of T trials in which the predictions of N "experts" are observed, it is possible to maintain a dynamically weighted prediction whose cumulative regret to the best single expert *in hindsight* (that is, after the full sequence has been revealed) is $O(\sqrt{T \log N})$, with absolutely no statistical assumptions on the sequence. Such results are especially interesting in light of the fact that even in known *stochastic* models, there is a matching lower bound of $\Omega(\sqrt{T \log N})$. The term "no-regret" derives from the fact that the per-step regret is only $O(\sqrt{\log N / T})$, which approaches zero as T becomes large.

In this paper we revisit no-regret learning, but with a bicriteria performance measure that is of both practical and philosophical interest. More specifically,

* Y. Mansour was supported in part by grant no. 1079/04 from the Israel Science Foundation, a grant from BSF, an IBM faculty award, and the IST Programme of the European Community, under the PASCAL Network of Excellence, IST-2002-506778. This paper reflects only the authors' views.

N. Bshouty and C. Gentile (Eds.): COLT 2007, LNAI 4539, pp. 233–247, 2007.

in addition to looking at the cumulative regret to the *best* expert in hindsight, we simultaneously analyze the regret to the *average* gain of all experts (or more generally, any fixed weighting of the experts). For comparisons to the average, the gold standard will be only *constant* regret (independent of T and N). Note that considering regret to the average in isolation, *zero* regret is easily achieved by simply leaving the weights uniform at all times.

We consider a setting in which each expert receives a (bounded) gain at each time step. The gain of the algorithm on a given time step is then a weighted average of these expert gains. The regret of the algorithm is measured in terms of cumulative gains over time. Our results establish hard trade-offs between regret to the best expert and the regret to the average in this setting, demonstrate that most known algorithms manage this trade-off poorly, and provide new algorithms with near optimal bicriteria performance. On the practical side, our new algorithms augment traditional no-regret results with a "safety net": while still managing to track the best expert near-optimally, they are guaranteed to never underperform the average (or any other fixed weighting of experts) by more than just constant regret. On the philosophical side, the bicriteria analyses and lower bounds shed new light on prior no-regret algorithms, showing that the unchecked aggressiveness of their updates can indeed cause them to badly underperform simple benchmarks like the average.

Viewed at a suitably high level, many existing no-regret algorithms have a similar flavor. These algorithms maintain a distribution over the experts that is adjusted according to performance. Since we would like to compete with the best expert, a "greedy" or "momentum" algorithm that rapidly adds weight to an outperforming expert (or set of experts) is natural. Most known algorithms shift weight between competing experts at a rate proportional to $1/\sqrt{T}$, in order to balance the tracking of the current best expert with the possibility of this expert's performance suddenly dropping. Updates on the scale of $1/\sqrt{T}$ can be viewed as "aggressive", at least in comparison to the minimal average update of $1/T$ required for any interesting learning effects. (If updates are $o(1/T)$, the algorithm cannot make even a constant change to any given weight in T steps.)

How poorly can existing regret minimization algorithms perform with respect to the average? Consider a sequence of gains for two experts where the gains for expert 1 are $1, 0, 1, 0, \cdots$, while the gains for expert 2 are $0, 1, 0, 1, \cdots$. Typical regret minimization algorithms (such as Exponential Weights [1,2], Follow the Perturbed Leader [3], and the Prod algorithm [4]) will yield a gain of $T/2 - O(\sqrt{T})$, meeting their guarantee of $O(\sqrt{T})$ regret with respect to the best expert. However, this performance leaves something to be desired. Note that in this example the performance of the best expert, worst expert, and average of the experts is identically $T/2$. Thus all of the algorithms mentioned above actually suffer a regret to the average (and to the worst expert) of $\Omega(\sqrt{T})$. The problem stems from the fact that in all even time steps the probability of expert 1 is exactly $1/2$; after expert 1 observes a gain of 1 we increase its probability by $c/\sqrt{T}$; and therefore in odd steps the probability of expert 2 is only $(1/2 - c/\sqrt{T})$

Summary of Lower Bounds		
Algorithm:	If Regret to Best Is:	Then Regret to Average Is:
Any Algorithm	$O(\sqrt{T})$	$\Omega(\sqrt{T})$
Any Algorithm	$\leq \sqrt{T \log T}/10$	$\Omega(T^{\epsilon})$
Any Difference Algorithm	$O(T^{\frac{1}{2}+\alpha})$	$\Omega(T^{\frac{1}{2}-\alpha})$

Summary of Algorithmic Results			
Algorithm:	Regret to Best:	Regret to Average:	Regret to Worst:
Phased Aggression	$O(\sqrt{T \log N}(\log T + \log\log N))$	$O(1)$	$O(1)$
BestAverage	$O(\sqrt{TN \log T})$	$O(1)$	$O(1)$
BestWorst	$O(N\sqrt{T \log N})$	$O(\sqrt{T \log N})$	0
EW	$O(T^{\frac{1}{2}+\alpha} \log N)$	$O(T^{\frac{1}{2}-\alpha})$	$O(T^{\frac{1}{2}-\alpha})$

Fig. 1. Summary of lower bounds and algorithmic results presented in this paper

(where the value of c depends on the specific algorithm). Note that adding a third expert, which is the average, would not change this.[1]

This paper establishes a sequence of results that demonstrates the inherent tension between regret to the best expert and the average, illuminates the problems of existing algorithms in managing this tension, and provides new algorithms that enjoy optimal bicriteria performance guarantees.

On the negative side, we show that *any* algorithm that has a regret of $O(\sqrt{T})$ to the best expert must suffer a regret of $\Omega(\sqrt{T})$ to the average. We also show that any regret minimization algorithm that achieves at most $\sqrt{T \log T}/10$ regret to the best expert, must, in the worst case, suffer regret $\Omega(T^{\epsilon})$ to the average, for some constant $\epsilon \geq 0.02$. These lower bounds are established even when $N = 2$.

On the positive side, we describe a new algorithm, *Phased Aggression*, that almost matches the lower bounds above. Given any algorithm whose cumulative regret to the best expert is at most R (which may be a function of T and N), we can use it to derive an algorithm whose regret to the best expert is $O(R \log R)$ with only constant regret to the average (or any fixed distribution over the experts). Using an $O(\sqrt{T \log N})$ regret algorithm, this gives regret to the best of $O(\sqrt{T \log N}(\log T + \log \log N))$. In addition, we show how to use an R-regret algorithm to derive an algorithm with regret $O(NR)$ to the best expert and *zero* regret to the worst expert. These algorithms treat the given R-regret algorithm as a black box. Remaining closer to the specifics of existing algorithms, we also show that by restarting the Exponential Weights algorithm with progressively more aggressive learning rates (starting initially at the most conservative rate of $1/T$), we achieve a somewhat inferior tradeoff of $O(\sqrt{TN} \log T)$ regret to the best expert and constant regret to the average.

---

[1] The third expert would clearly have a gain of $1/2$ at every time step. At odd time steps, the weight of the first expert would be $1/3 + c/\sqrt{T}$, while that of the second expert would be $1/3 - c/\sqrt{T}$, resulting in a regret of $\Omega(\sqrt{T})$ to the average.

Our algorithms are somewhat different than many of the traditional regret minimization algorithms, especially in their apparently essential use of *restarts* that are driven by observed differences in expert performance. We show that this is no coincidence. For a wide class of update rules that includes many existing algorithms (such as Weighted Majority/Exponential Weights, Follow the Perturbed Leader, and Prod), we show that the product of the regret to the best and the regret to the average is $\Omega(T)$. This establishes a frontier from which such algorithms inherently cannot escape. Furthermore, any point on this frontier can in fact be achieved by such an algorithm (i.e., a standard multiplicative update rule with an appropriately tuned learning rate).

It is worth noting that it is not possible in general to guarantee $o(\sqrt{T})$ regret to any arbitrary *pair* of distributions, D_1 and D_2. Suppose D_1 places all weight on one expert, while D_2 places all weight on a second. Competing simultaneously with both distributions is then equivalent to competing with the best expert.

Finally, we remark that our lower bounds on the trade-off between best and average regret *cannot* be circumvented by simply adding an "average expert" and running standard no-regret algorithms, even with the use of a prior distribution with a significant amount of weight on the average.[2]

Related Work: Previous work by Auer et al. [5] considered adapting the learning rate of expert algorithms gradually. However, the goal of their work was to get an any-time regret bound without using the standard doubling technique. Vovk [6] also considered trade-offs in best expert algorithms. His work examined for which values of a and b it is possible for an algorithm's gain to be bounded by $aG_{best,T} + b \log N$, where $G_{best,T}$ is the gain of the best expert.

2   Preliminaries

In the classic experts framework, each expert $i \in \{1, \cdots, N\}$ receives a gain $g_{i,t} \in [0,1]$ at each time step t.[3] The cumulative gain of expert i up to time t is $G_{i,t} = \sum_{t'=1}^{t} g_{i,t'}$. We denote the average cumulative gain of the experts at time t as $G_{avg,t} = (1/N) \sum_{i=1}^{N} G_{i,t}$, and the gain of the best and worst expert as $G_{best,t} = \max_i G_{i,t}$ and $G_{worst,t} = \min_i G_{i,t}$. For any fixed distribution D over the experts, we define the gain of this distribution to be $G_{D,t} = \sum_{i=1}^{N} D(i) G_{i,t}$.

At each time t, an algorithm A assigns a weight $w_{i,t}$ to each expert i. These weights are normalized to probabilities $p_{i,t} = w_{i,t}/W_t$ where $W_t = \sum_i w_{i,t}$. Algorithm A then receives a gain $g_{A,t} = \sum_{i=1}^{N} p_{i,t} g_{i,t}$. The cumulative gain of algorithm A up to time t is $G_{A,t} = \sum_{t'=1}^{t} g_{A,t'} = \sum_{t'=1}^{t} \sum_{i=1}^{N} p_{i,t'} g_{i,t'}$.

The standard goal of an algorithm in this setting is to minimize the regret to the best expert at a fixed time T. In particular, we would like to

---

[2] Achieving a constant regret to the average would require a prior of $1 - O(1/T)$ on this artificial expert and a learning rate of $O(1/T)$. Putting this much weight on the average results in $\Omega(T)$ regret to each of the original experts.

[3] All results presented in this paper can be generalized to hold for instantaneous gains in any bounded region.

minimize the regret $R_{best,A,T} = \max\{G_{best,T} - G_{A,T}, 1\}$.[4] In this work, we are simultaneously concerned with minimizing both this regret and the regret to the average and worst expert, $R_{avg,A,T} = \max\{G_{avg,T} - G_{A,T}, 1\}$ and $R_{worst,A,T} = \max\{G_{worst,T} - G_{A,T}, 1\}$ respectively, in addition to the regret $R_{D,A,T}$ to an arbitrary distribution D, which is defined similarly.

3 The $\Theta(T)$ Frontier for Difference Algorithms

We begin our results with an analysis of the trade-off between regret to the best and average for a wide class of existing algorithms, showing that the product between the two regrets for this class is $\Theta(T)$.

We call an algorithm A a *difference algorithm* if, when $N = 2$ and instantaneous gains are restricted to $\{0, 1\}$, the normalized weights A places on each of the two experts depend only on the difference between the experts' cumulative gains. In other words, A is a difference algorithm if there exists a function f such that when $N = 2$ and $g_{i,t} \in \{0, 1\}$ for all i and t, $p_{1,t} = f(d_t)$ and $p_{2,t} = 1 - f(d_t)$ where $d_t = G_{1,t} - G_{2,t}$. Exponential Weights [1,2], Follow the Perturbed Leader [3], and the Prod algorithm [4] are all examples of difference algorithms.[5] While a more general definition of the class of difference algorithms might be possible, this simple definition is sufficient to show the lower bound.

3.1 Difference Frontier Lower Bound

Theorem 1. *Let A be any difference algorithm. Then*

$$R_{best,A,T} \cdot R_{avg,A,T} \geq R_{best,A,T} \cdot R_{worst,A,T} = \Omega(T).$$

Proof. For simplicity, assume that T is an even integer. We will consider the behavior of the difference algorithm A on two sequences of expert payoffs. Both sequences involve only two experts with instantaneous gains in $\{0, 1\}$. (Since the theorem provides a lower bound, it is sufficient to consider an example in this restricted setting.) Assume without loss of generality that initially $p_{1,1} \leq 1/2$.

In the first sequence, S_1, Expert 1 has a gain of 1 at every time step while Expert 2 always has a gain 0. Let ρ be the first time t at which A has $p_{1,t} \geq 2/3$. A must have regret $R_{best,A,T} \geq \rho/3$ since it loses at least $1/3$ to the best expert on each of the first ρ time steps and cannot compensate for this later.[6]

Since the probability of Expert 1 increases from $p_{1,1} \leq 1/2$ to at least $2/3$ in ρ time steps in S_1, there must be one time step $\tau \in [2, \rho]$ in which the probability of Expert 1 increased by at least $1/(6\rho)$, i.e., $p_{1,\tau} - p_{1,\tau-1} \geq 1/(6\rho)$. The second sequence S_2 we consider is as follows. For the first τ time steps, Expert 1 will have a gain of 1 (as in S_1). For the last τ time steps, Expert 1 will have a gain of 0. For the remaining $T - 2\tau$ time steps (in the range $[\tau, T - \tau]$), the gain

---

[4] This minimal value of 1 makes the presentation of the trade-off "nicer" (for example in the statement of Theorem 1), but has no real significance otherwise.

[5] For Prod, this follows from the restriction on the instantaneous gains to $\{0, 1\}$.

[6] If such a ρ does not exists, then $R_{best,A,T} = \Omega(T)$ and we are done.

of Expert 1 will alternate $0, 1, 0, 1, \cdots$. Throughout the sequence, Expert 2 will have a gain of 1 whenever Expert 1 has a gain of 0 and a gain of 0 every time Expert 1 has a gain of 1. This implies that each expert has a gain of exactly $T/2$ (and hence $G_{best,T} = G_{avg,T} = G_{worst,T} = T/2$).

During the period $[\tau, T - \tau]$, consider a pair of consecutive times such that $g_{1,t} = 0$ and $g_{1,t+1} = 1$. Since A is a difference algorithm we have that $p_{1,t} = p_{1,\tau}$ and $p_{1,t+1} = p_{1,\tau-1}$. The gain of algorithm A in time steps t and $t + 1$ is $(1 - p_{1,\tau}) + p_{1,\tau-1} \leq 1 - 1/(6\rho)$, since $p_{1,\tau} - p_{1,\tau-1} \geq 1/(6\rho)$. In every pair of time steps t and $T - t$, for $t \leq \tau$, the gain of A in those times steps is exactly 1, since the difference between the experts is identical at times t and $T - t$, and hence the probabilities are identical. This implies that the total gain of the algorithm A is at most

$$\tau + \frac{T - 2\tau}{2}\left(1 - \frac{1}{6\rho}\right) \leq \frac{T}{2} - \frac{T - 2\tau}{12\rho}$$

On sequence S_1, the regret of algorithm A with respect to the best expert is $\Omega(\rho)$. On sequence S_2, the regret with respect to the average and worst is $\Omega(T/\rho)$. The theorem follows. $\square$

3.2   A Difference Algorithm Achieving the Frontier

We now show that the standard Exponential Weights (EW) algorithm with an appropriate choice of the learning rate parameter η [2] is a difference algorithm achieving the trade-off described in Section 3.1, thus rendering it tight for this class. Recall that for all experts i, EW assigns initial weights $w_{i,1} = 1$, and at each subsequent time t, updates weights with $w_{i,t+1} = e^{\eta G_{i,t}} = w_{i,t} e^{\eta g_{i,t}}$. The probability with which expert i is chosen at time t is then given by $p_{i,t} = w_{i,t}/W_t$ where $W_t = \sum_{j=1}^{N} w_{j,t}$.

Theorem 2. *Let $G^* \leq T$ be an upper bound on G_{max}. For any α such that $0 \leq \alpha \leq 1/2$, let $EW = EW(\eta)$ with $\eta = (G^*)^{-(1/2+\alpha)}$. Then $R_{best,EW,T} \leq (G^*)^{1/2+\alpha}(1 + \ln N)$ and $R_{avg,EW,T} \leq (G^*)^{1/2-\alpha}$.*

Proof. These bounds can be derived using a series of bounds on the quantity $\ln(W_{T+1}/W_1)$. First we bound this quantity in terms of the gain of the best expert. This piece of the analysis is standard (see, for example, Theorem 2.4 in [7]), and gives us the following: $G_{best,T} - G_{EW,T} \leq \eta G_{EW,T} + \ln N/\eta$.

Next we bound the same quantity in terms of the average cumulative gain, using the fact that the arithmetic mean of a set of numbers is always greater than or equal to the geometric mean.

$$\ln\left(\frac{W_{T+1}}{W_1}\right) = \ln\left(\frac{\sum_{i=1}^{N} w_{i,T+1}}{N}\right) \geq \ln\left(\left(\prod_{i=1}^{N} w_{i,T+1}\right)^{\frac{1}{N}}\right) \tag{1}$$

$$= \frac{1}{N}\sum_{i=1}^{N} \ln w_{i,T+1} = \frac{1}{N}\sum_{i=1}^{N} \eta G_{i,T} = \eta G_{avg,T}$$

Together with the analysis in [7], this gives us $G_{avg,T} - G_{EW,T} \leq \eta G_{EW,T}$.

Note that if $G_{best,T} \leq G_{EW,T}$, both the regret to the best expert and the regret to the average will be minimal, so we can assume this is not the case and replace the term $G_{EW,T}$ on the right hand side of these bounds with $G_{best,T}$ which is in turn bounded by G^*. This yields the following pair of bounds.

$$G_{best,T} - G_{EW,T} \leq \eta G^* + \ln N / \eta, \qquad\qquad G_{avg,T} - G_{EW,T} \leq \eta G^*$$

By changing the value of η, we can construct different trade-offs between the two bounds. Setting $\eta = (G^*)^{-(1/2+\alpha)}$ yields the desired result.   □

This trade-off can be generalized to hold when we would like to compete with an arbitrary distribution D by initializing $w_{i,1} = D(i)$ and substituting an alternate inequality into (1). The $\ln(N)$ term in the regret to the best expert will be replaced by $max_{i \in N} \ln(1/D(i))$, making this practical only for distributions that lie inside the probability simplex and not too close to the boundaries.

4   Breaking the Difference Frontier Via Restarts

The results so far have established a $\Theta(T)$ frontier on the product of regrets to the best and average experts for difference algorithms. In this section, we will show how this frontier can be broken by non-difference algorithms that gradually increase the aggressiveness of their updates via a series of restarts invoked by observed differences in performance so far. As a warm-up, we first show how a very simple algorithm that is not a difference algorithm can enjoy standard regret bounds compared to the best expert in terms of T (though worse in terms of N), while having *zero* cumulative regret to the worst.

4.1   Regret to the Best and Worst Experts

Using a standard regret-minimization algorithm as a black box, we can produce a very simple algorithm that achieves a clear trade-off between regret to the best expert and regret to the worst expert. Let A be a regret minimization algorithm such that $R_{best,A,T} \leq R$ for some R which may be a function of T and N. We define the modified algorithm *BestWorst(A)* as follows. While the difference between the cumulative gains of the best and worst experts is smaller than NR, *BestWorst(A)* places equal weight on each expert, playing the average. After the first time τ at which this condition is violated, it begins running a fresh instance of algorithm A and continues to use A until the end of the sequence.

Until time τ, this algorithm must be performing at least as well as the worst expert since it is playing the average. At time τ, the algorithm's gain must be R more than that of the worst expert since the gain of the best expert is NR above the gain of the worst. Now since from time τ algorithm A is run, we know that the gain of *BestWorst(A)* in the final $T - \tau$ time steps will be within R of the gain of the best expert. Therefore, *BestWorst(A)* will maintain a lead over the worst expert. In addition, the regret of the algorithm to the best expert will be bounded by NR, since up to time τ it will have a regret of at most $(N-1)R$ with respect to the best expert. This establishes the following theorem.

BestAverage (G^*)
Let $k^* = \frac{1}{2} \log G^* - 3$ and $\ell = 8\sqrt{NG^*}$
for $k = 1 : k^* - 1$ **do**

    Reset weights and run a new instance of EW(η) with $\eta = \eta_k = \frac{2^k}{G^*}$ until a time t such that $(G^p_{best,t} - G^p_{avg,t}) \geq \ell$

end

Reset and run EW(η) with $\eta = \eta_{k^*} = \frac{2^{k^*}}{G^*}$ until time T

Fig. 2. The *BestAverage* algorithm for N experts

Theorem 3. *Let A be a regret minimization algorithm with regret at most R to the best expert and let BW be* BestWorst(A). *Then $R_{best,BW,T} = O(NR)$ and $G_{BW,T} \geq G_{worst,T}$.*

It follows immediately that using a standard regret minimization algorithm with $R = O(\sqrt{T \log N})$ as the black box, we can achieve a regret of $O(N\sqrt{T \log N})$ to the best expert while maintaining a lead over the worst.

4.2   An EW-Based Algorithm with Restarts

In Section 4.3 below we will give a general algorithm whose specialization will produce our best bicriteria regret bounds to the best and average. For pedagogical purposes, in this section we first present an algorithm for which we can prove inferior bicriteria bounds, but which works by directly applying restarts with increasingly aggressive learning rates to an existing difference algorithm. This multi-phase algorithm, which we shall call *BestAverage*, competes with the best expert while maintaining only constant regret to the average.

The algorithm is given in Figure 2. In each phase, a new instance of EW is run with a new, increasingly large value for the learning rate η. In the pseudocode and throughout the remainder of this paper, we will use the notation $G^p_{i,t}$ to mean the cumulative gain of expert i at time t only from the current phase of the algorithm, i.e. the amount that expert i has gained since the last time the learning rate η was reset. Similarly we will use $G^p_{best,t}$, $G^p_{avg,t}$, and $G^p_{BA,t}$ to be the gain of the best expert, average, and the *BestAverage* algorithm in the current phase through time t.

The following theorem states that *BestAverage* can guarantee a regret to the best expert that is "almost" as low as a standard no-regret algorithm while maintaining a constant regret to the average. The proof, which involves an analysis of the algorithm's gain compared to the gain of the best expert and the average both in the middle and at the end of each phase, has been omitted due to lack of space. The main insight of the proof is that whenever *BestAverage* exits a phase, it must have a quantifiable gain over the average. While the algorithm may lose to the average during the next phase, it will never lose much more than the gain it has already acquired. At the same time, we can bound how far the average is behind the best expert at any given phase and use this to bound the regret of the algorithm to the best expert.

PhasedAggression (A, R, D)
for $k = 1 : \log(R)$ **do**
    Let $\eta = 2^{k-1}/R$
    Reset and run a new instance of A
    while $(G^p_{best,t} - G^p_{D,t} < 2R)$ **do**
        Feed A with the previous gains g_{t-1} and let q_t be it distribution
        Use $p_t = \eta q_t + (1 - \eta)D$
    end
end
Reset and run a new instance of A until time T

Fig. 3. The *Phased Aggression* algorithm for N experts

Theorem 4. *Let $G^* \leq T$ be an upper bound on G_{max}. Then $R_{best,BA,T} = O(\sqrt{G^*N}\log G^*)$ and $R_{avg,BA,T} \leq 2$.*

This theorem can be extended to hold when we would like to compete with arbitrary distributions D by using the generalized version of EW with prior D. The term $\sqrt{N}$ in the regret to the best expert will be replaced by max $(\sqrt{N}, \max_{i \in N} \ln(1/D(i)))$.

4.3   Improved Dependence on N and Fixed Mixtures

Figure 3 shows *Phased Aggression*, an algorithm that achieves similar guarantees to *BestAverage* with a considerably better dependence on the number of experts. This algorithm has the added advantage that it can achieve a constant regret to *any* specified distribution D, not only the average, with no change to the bounds. The name of the algorithm refers to the fact that it operates in distinct phases separated by restarts, with each phase more aggressive than the last.

The idea behind the algorithm is rather simple. We take a regret minimization algorithm A, and mix between A and the target distribution D. As the gain of the best expert exceeds the gain of D by larger amounts, we put more and more weight on the regret minimization algorithm A, "resetting" A to its initial state at the start of each phase. Once the weight on A has been increased, it is never decreased again. We note that this algorithm (or reduction) is similar in spirit to the EW-based approach above, in the sense that each successive phase is moving weight from something that is not learning at all (the fixed distribution D) to an algorithm that is implicitly learning aggressively (the given algorithm A). As before, new phases are invoked only in response to greater and greater outperformance by the current best expert.

Theorem 5. *Let A be any algorithm with regret R to the best expert, D be any distribution, and PA be an instantiation of PhasedAggression(A, R, D). Then $R_{best,PA,T} \leq 2R(\log R + 1)$ and $R_{D,PA,T} \leq 1$.*

Proof. We will again analyze the performance of the algorithm compared to the best expert and the distribution D both during and at the end of any phase k.

First consider any time t during phase k. The regret of the algorithm is split between the regret of the fixed mixture and the regret of the no-regret algorithm according to their weights. Since A is an R-regret algorithm its regret to both the best expert and to the distribution D is bounded by R, and thus the regret of the algorithm due to the weight on A is $2^{k-1}/R$ times R. With the remaining $1 - (2^{k-1}/R)$ weight, the regret to the best expert is bounded by $2R$ since $G^p_{best,t} - G^p_{D,t} < 2R$ during the phase, and its regret to distribution D is 0. Thus at any time t during phase k we have

$$ G^p_{best,t} - G^p_{PA,t} < R\left(\frac{2^{k-1}}{R}\right) + 2R\left(1 - \frac{2^{k-1}}{R}\right) < 2R $$

and

$$ G^p_{D,t} - G^p_{PA,t} \le R\left(\frac{2^{k-1}}{R}\right) = 2^{k-1} $$

Now consider what happens when the algorithm exits phase k. A phase is only exited at some time t such that $G^p_{best,t} - G^p_{D,t} > 2R$. Since A is R-regret, its gain (in the current phase) will be within R of the gain of the best expert, resulting in the algorithm PA gaining a *lead* over distribution D for the phase: $G^p_{PA,t} - G^p_{D,t} \ge R(2^{k-1}/R) = 2^{k-1}$.

Combining these inequalities, it is clear that if the algorithm ends in phase k at time T, then

$$ G_{best,T} - G_{PA,T} \le 2Rk \le 2R(\log R + 1) $$

and

$$ G_{D,T} - G_{PA,T} \le 2^{k-1} - \sum_{j=1}^{k-1} 2^{j-1} = 2^{k-1} - (2^{k-1} - 1) = 1 $$

These inequalities hold even when the algorithm reaches the final phase and has all of its weight on A, thus proving the theorem.   □

5   A General Lower Bound

So far we have seen that a wide class of existing algorithms (namely all difference algorithms) is burdened with a stark best/average regret trade-off, but that this frontier can be obliterated by simple algorithms that tune how aggressively they update, in phases modulated by the observed payoffs so far. What is the limit of what can be achieved in our bicriteria regret setting?

In this section we show a pair of general lower bounds that hold for *all* algorithms. The bounds are stated and proved for the average but once again hold for any fixed distribution D. These lower bounds come close to the upper bound achieved by the *Phased Aggression* algorithm described in the previous section.

Theorem 6. *Any algorithm with regret $O(\sqrt{T})$ to the best expert must have regret $\Omega(\sqrt{T})$ to the average. Furthermore, any algorithm with regret at most $\sqrt{T \log T}/10$ to the best expert must have regret $\Omega(T^\epsilon)$ to the average for some positive constant $\epsilon \ge 0.02$.*

More specifically, we will show that for any constant $\alpha > 0$, there exists a constant $\beta > 0$ such that for sufficiently large values of T (i.e. $T > (150\alpha)^2$), for any algorithm A, there exists a sequence of gains g of length T such that if $R_{best,A,T} \leq \alpha\sqrt{T}$ then $R_{avg,A,T} \geq \beta\sqrt{T}$. Additionally, for any constant $\alpha' > 1/10$ there exist constants $\beta' > 0$ and $\epsilon > 0$ such that for sufficiently large values of T (i.e. $T > 2^{(10\alpha)^2}$), for any algorithm A, there exists a sequence of gains of length T such that if $R_{best,A,T} \leq \alpha'\sqrt{T \log T}$ then $R_{avg,A,T} \geq \beta'T^\epsilon$.

The proof of this theorem begins by defining a procedure for creating a "bad" sequence g of expert gains for a given algorithm A. This sequence can be divided into a number of (possibly noncontiguous) segments. By first analyzing the maximum amount that the algorithm can gain over the average and the minimum amount it can lose to the average in each segment, and then bounding the total number of segments possible under the assumption that an algorithm is no-regret, we can show that it is not possible for an algorithm to have $O(\sqrt{T})$ regret to the best expert without having $\Omega(\sqrt{T})$ regret to the average. The full proof is rather technical and appears in a separate subsection below.

5.1   Proof of Theorem 6

Fix a constant $\alpha > 0$. Given an algorithm A, we will generate a sequence of expert gains g of length $T > (150\alpha)^2$ such that g will be "bad" for A. In Figure 4, we show how to generate such a sequence. Here d_t is the difference between the gains of the two experts at time t, and ϵ_t is the increase in the probability that the algorithm assigns to the current best expert since the last time the d_t was smaller. This is used to ensure that the best expert will only do well when the algorithm does not have "too much" weight on it. The function f and parameter γ will be defined later in the analysis.

We say that an algorithm A is f-compliant if at any time t we have $\epsilon_t = f(d_{t-1}) \pm \delta$, for an arbitrarily small δ, and if for any time t in which $d_t = 0$, we have $p_{1,t} = p_{2,t} = 1/2$. For the sake of this analysis, it is more convenient to think of ϵ_t as being exactly equal to $f(d_{t-1})$ and to allow the algorithm to "choose" whether it should be considered larger or smaller. Lemma 1 states that given the sequence generation process in Figure 4, we can concentrate only on the class of f-compliant algorithms. Due to space constraints, the proof is omitted.

Lemma 1. *Consider any algorithm A and let $g = GenerateBadSeq(A, f, \gamma)$. There exists an f-compliant algorithm A' such that $GenerateBadSeq(A', f, \gamma) = g$ and at any time t, $g_{A',t} \geq g_{A,t}$.*

Given an f-compliant algorithm, we can write its probabilities as a function of the difference between expert gains d_t. We define a function $F(d) = 1/2 + \sum_{i=1}^{|d|} f(i)$, where $F(0) = 1/2$. It is easy to verify that an algorithm A that sets the probability of the best expert at time t to $F(d_t)$ is an f-compliant algorithm.

We are now ready to define the function f used in the sequence generation.

$$f(d) = \frac{2^{m(d)-1}}{\gamma\sqrt{T}} \quad \text{where} \quad m(d) = \left\lceil \frac{16\alpha}{\sqrt{T}}|d| \right\rceil$$

244   E. Even-Dar et al.

```
GenerateBadSeq(A, f, γ)
t = 1; G_{avg,0} = G_{A,0} = d_0 = 0;
while (G_{avg,t-1} − G_{A,t-1} ≤ 0.115√T/γ) do
    p_{1,t} = A(g); p_{2,t} = 1 − A(g);
    if (d_{t-1} = 0) then
        if (p_{1,t} ≤ ½) then
            g_{1,t} = 1; g_{2,t} = 0; last(|d_{t-1}|) = p_{1,t};
        else
            g_{1,t} = 0; g_{2,t} = 1; last(|d_{t-1}|) = p_{2,t};
        end
    else
        i_t = argmax_i G_{i,t}; j_t = argmin_j G_{j,t};
        last(|d_{t-1}|) = p_{i_t,t};
        ε_t = p_{i_t,t} − last(|d_{t-1} − 1|);
        if (ε_t ≤ f(|d_{t-1}|)) then
            g_{i_t,t} = 1; g_{j_t,t} = 0;
        else
            g_{i_t,t} = 0; g_{j_t,t} = 1;
        end
    end
    G_{A,t} = G_{A,t-1} + p_{1,t}g_{1,t} + p_{2,t}g_{2,t};
    G_{avg,t} = G_{avg,t-1} + (g_{1,t} + g_{2,t})/2;
    d_t = d_{t-1} + g_{1,t} − g_{2,t};
    t = t + 1;
end
g_{1,t} = g_{2,t} = ½ for the rest of the sequence
```

Fig. 4. Algorithm for creating a bad sequence for any algorithm A

The following fact is immediate from this definition and will be useful many times in our analysis.

$$F(d) \le \frac{1}{2} + \sum_{i=1}^{m(d)} \frac{2^{i-1}}{\gamma\sqrt{T}} \left(\frac{\sqrt{T}}{16\alpha}\right) \le \frac{1}{2} + \frac{2^{m(d)}}{16\gamma\alpha} \tag{2}$$

We define the (possibly noncontiguous) m segment to be the set of all times t for which $m(d_t) = m$, or more explicitly, all times t for which $(m-1)(\sqrt{T}/(16\alpha))$ $\le |d_t| < m(\sqrt{T}/(16\alpha))$. We denote this set of times by $\mathcal{T}_m$.

We now introduce the notion of *matched times* and *unmatched times*. We define a pair of matched times as two times t_1 and t_2 such that the difference between the cumulative gains the two experts changes from d to $d+1$ at time t_1 and stays at least as high as $d+1$ until changing from $d+1$ back to d at time t_2. More formally, for some difference d, $d_{t_1-1} = d$, $d_{t_1} = d+1$, $d_{t_2} = d$, and for all t such that $t_1 < t < t_2$, $d_t > d$ (which implies that $d_{t_2-1} = d+1$). Clearly each pair of matched times consists of one time step in which the gain of one expert is 1 and the other 0 while at the other time step the reverse holds. We refer to any time at which one expert has gain 1 while the other has gain 0 that is *not* part of a pair of matched times as an unmatched time. If at any time t

we have $d_t = d$, then there must have been d unmatched times. We denote by $\mathcal{M}_m$ and $\mathcal{UM}_m$ the matched and unmatched times in $\mathcal{T}_m$, respectively. These concepts will become important due to the fact that an algorithm will generally lose with respect to the average for every pair of matched times, but will gain with respect to the average on every unmatched time.

The following lemma quantifies the algorithm's regret to the best expert and the average of all experts for each pair of matched times.

Lemma 2. *For any f-compliant algorithm A and any pair of matched times t_1 and t_2 in the m segment, the algorithm's gain from times t_1 and t_2 is $1 - 2^{m-1}/(\gamma\sqrt{T})$, while the gain of the average and the best expert is 1.*

Proof. Let $d = d_{t_1} - 1$. Without loss of generality assume that the leading expert is expert 1, i.e., $d \geq 0$. The gain of the algorithm at time t_1 is $p_{1,t_1} = F(d)$, while the gain at t_2 is $p_{2,t_2} = 1 - p_{1,t_2} = 1 - F(d+1) = 1 - (F(d) + f(d))$. Thus the algorithm has a total gain of $1 - f(d) = 1 - 2^{m-1}/(\gamma\sqrt{T})$ for these time steps.   □

Our next step is to provide an upper bound for the gain of the algorithm over the average expert from the unmatched times only.

Lemma 3. *The gain of any f-compliant algorithm A in only the unmatched times in the m segment of the algorithm is at most $2^m\sqrt{T}/(256\gamma\alpha^2)$ larger than the gain of the average expert in the unmatched times in segment m, i.e.,* $\sum_{t \in \mathcal{UM}_m} g_{A,t} - 1/2 \leq 2^m\sqrt{T}/(256\gamma\alpha^2)$.

Proof. Since the leading expert does not change in the unmatched times (in retrospect), we can assume w.l.o.g. that it is expert 1. From (2), it follows that

$$\sum_{t \in \mathcal{UM}_m} g_{A,t} - 1/2 \leq \sum_{i=0}^{\frac{\sqrt{T}}{16\alpha}} \left(F(d+i) - \frac{1}{2} \right) \leq \frac{2^m}{16\gamma\alpha} \frac{\sqrt{T}}{16\alpha} \leq \frac{2^m\sqrt{T}}{256\gamma\alpha^2}$$

□

Combining lemmas 2 and 3, we can compute the number of matched times needed in the m segment in order for the loss of the algorithm to the average from matched times to cancel the gain of the algorithm over the average from unmatched times.

Lemma 4. *For any given x, if there are at least $T/(128\alpha^2) + x$ pairs of matched times in the m segment, then the gain of any f-compliant algorithm A in the m segment is bounded by the gain of the average expert in the m segment minus $x2^{m-1}/(\gamma\sqrt{T})$, i.e. $\sum_{t \in \mathcal{T}_m} g_{A,t} \leq \sum_{t \in \mathcal{T}_m} (1/2) - 2^{m-1}x/(\gamma\sqrt{T})$.*

Proof. From Lemma 2, the loss of A with respect to the average for each pair of matched times is $2^{m-1}/(\gamma\sqrt{T})$. From Lemma 3, A could not have gained more than $2^m\sqrt{T}/(256\alpha^2\gamma)$ over the average in the m segment. Since there are at least $2T/(128\alpha^2) + 2x$ matched times, the *total* amount the algorithm loses to the average in the m segment is at least $2^{m-1}x/(\gamma\sqrt{T})$.   □

The next lemma bounds the number of segments in the sequence using the fact that A is $\alpha\sqrt{T}$-regret algorithm.

Lemma 5. *For any f-compliant algorithm A such that $R_{best,A,T} < \alpha\sqrt{T}$ and for $\gamma = 2^{48\alpha^2}/\alpha$, there are at most $48\alpha^2$ segments in $\boldsymbol{g} = GenerateBadSeq(A, f, \gamma)$.*

Proof. Once again we assume that leading expert is expert 1. Setting $\gamma = 2^{48\alpha^2}/\alpha$ in (2), ensures that $F(d)$ is bounded by $2/3$ as long as m remains below $48\alpha^2$. Thus $F(d)$ is bounded by $2/3$ for all unmatched times until we reach segment $48\alpha^2$. This implies that if the sequence reaches segment $48\alpha^2$, then the regret with respect to the best expert will be at least $48\alpha^2\sqrt{T}/(16\alpha)(1/3) = \alpha\sqrt{T}$ which contradicts the fact that A is a $\alpha\sqrt{T}$-regret algorithm, so it cannot be the case that the sequence has $48\alpha^2$ or more segments.   □

The following observation will be useful in simplifying the main proof, allowing us to further restrict our attention to the class of *monotone f-compliant* algorithms, where an algorithm is *monotone* if it never returns to a segment m after moving on to segment $m+1$. A lower bound on the performance of monotone algorithms will imply the general lower bound.

Lemma 6. *Suppose $d_t = d > 0$, $d_{t+1} = d + 1$, $d_{t+2} = d + 2$, and $d_{t+3} = d + 1$. The gain of an f-compliant algorithm will not decrease if we instead let $d_{t+2} = d$.*

We are now ready to prove the main lower bound theorem.

Proof. (Theorem 6) First, consider the case in which the main `while` loop of $GenerateBadSeq(A, f, \gamma)$ terminates before time T. It must be the case that $G_{avg,t-1} - G_{A,t-1} > 0.115\sqrt{T}/\gamma = \Omega(\sqrt{T})$ and there is nothing more to prove.

Throughout the rest of the proof, assume that the main `while` loop is never exited while generating the sequence $\boldsymbol{g}$. From Lemma 4 we know that if there are at least $T/(128\alpha^2)$ pairs of matched times in the ℓ segment, then the loss to the average from these times will cancel the gain from unmatched times in this segment. By Lemma 5 there are at most $48\alpha^2$ segments. If the algorithm has *exactly* $T/(128\alpha^2)$ pairs of matched times at each segment, it will have at most a total of $T/(128\alpha^2)(48\alpha^2) = (3/8)T$ pairs of matched times and will cancel all of its gain over the average from the unmatched times in all segments. Note that there are at most $48\alpha^2\sqrt{T}/(16\alpha) = 3\alpha\sqrt{T}$ unmatched times. Since we have chosen T such that $\alpha < \sqrt{T}/150$, we can bound this by $0.02T$. This implies that there are at least $0.49T$ pairs of matched times. We define the following quantity for algorithm A: $x_m = |\mathcal{M}_m|/2 - T/(128\alpha^2)$. We have that

$$\sum_{m=1}^{48\alpha^2} x_m = \left(\sum_{m=1}^{48\alpha^2} \frac{|\mathcal{M}_m|}{2} \right) - \frac{3T}{8} \geq 0.49T - (3/8)T = 0.115T$$

Let m^* be the first segment for which we have $\sum_{i=1}^{m} x_i \geq 0.115T$ (since we consider only monotone algorithms we need not worry about timing issues). For every k, $1 \leq k \leq m^*$, we have $z_k = \sum_{i=k}^{m^*} x_i > 0$ (otherwise m^* would not be the first segment). Note that we can bound the regret to the average as follows.

$$
\sum_{i=1}^{m^*} x_i \frac{2^{i-1}}{\gamma\sqrt{T}} = \frac{1}{\gamma\sqrt{T}} x_1 + \frac{1}{\gamma\sqrt{T}} \sum_{i=2}^{m^*} x_i \left(1 + \sum_{j=1}^{i-1} 2^{j-1} \right)
$$

$$
= \frac{1}{\gamma\sqrt{T}} \sum_{i=1}^{m^*} x_i + \frac{1}{\gamma\sqrt{T}} \sum_{i=2}^{m^*} \sum_{j=2}^{i} 2^{j-2} x_i
$$

$$
= \frac{1}{\gamma\sqrt{T}} z_1 + \frac{1}{\gamma\sqrt{T}} \sum_{i=2}^{m^*} 2^{i-2} z_i \geq \frac{0.115T}{\gamma\sqrt{T}} = \frac{0.115\sqrt{T}}{\gamma}
$$

This shows that the regret to the average must be at least $0.115\sqrt{T}/\gamma = \beta\sqrt{T}$ where $\beta = 0.115\alpha/2^{48\alpha^2}$, yielding the first result of the theorem.

If we now let T be large enough that $\alpha \leq \sqrt{\log T}/10$, this regret must be at least $(0.115\alpha/2^{(48/100)\log T})\sqrt{T} = 0.115\alpha T^{1/2-48/100} = O(T^{1/50})$, which proves the last part of the theorem. □

Acknowledgments

We are grateful to Manfred Warmuth and Andrew Barron for their thought-provoking remarks on the results presented here.

References

1. Littlestone, N., Warmuth, M.K.: The weighted majority algorithm. Information and Computation 108(2), 212–261 (1994)
2. Freund, Y.: Predicting a binary sequence almost as well as the optimal biased coin. Information and Computation 182(2), 73–94 (2003)
3. Kalai, A., Vempala, S.: Efficient algorithms for on-line optimization. Journal of Computer and System Sciences 71(3), 291–307 (2005)
4. Cesa-Bianchi, N., Mansour, Y., Stoltz, G.: Improved second-order bounds for prediction with expert advice. In: COLT, pp. 217–232 (2005)
5. Auer, P., Cesa-Bianchi, N., Gentile, C.: Adaptive and self-confident on-line learning algorithms. Journal of Computer and System Sciences 64, 48–75 (2002)
6. Vovk, V.: A game of prediction with expert advice. Journal of Computer and System Sciences 56(2), 153–173 (1998)
7. Cesa-Bianchi, N., Lugosi, G.: Prediction, learning, and games. Cambridge University Press, Cambridge (2006)

Strategies for Prediction Under Imperfect Monitoring[*]

Gábor Lugosi[1], Shie Mannor[2], and Gilles Stoltz[3]

[1] ICREA and Department of Economics, Universitat Pompeu Fabra, Ramon Trias Fargas 25-27, 08005 Barcelona, Spain
lugosi@upf.es
[2] Department of Electrical & Computer Engineering, McGill University, 3480 University Street, Montreal, Québec, Canada H3A-2A7
shie.mannor@mcgill.ca
[3] CNRS and Département de mathématiques et applications, Ecole normale supérieure, 45 rue d'Ulm, 75005 Paris, France
gilles.stoltz@ens.fr

Abstract. We propose simple randomized strategies for sequential prediction under imperfect monitoring, that is, when the forecaster does not have access to the past outcomes but rather to a feedback signal. The proposed strategies are consistent in the sense that they achieve, asymptotically, the best possible average reward. It was Rustichini [11] who first proved the existence of such consistent predictors. The forecasters presented here offer the first constructive proof of consistency. Moreover, the proposed algorithms are computationally efficient. We also establish upper bounds for the rates of convergence. In the case of deterministic feedback, these rates are optimal up to logarithmic terms.

1 Introduction

Sequential prediction of arbitrary (or "individual") sequences has received a lot of attention in learning theory, game theory, and information theory; see [3] for an extensive review. In this paper we focus on the problem of prediction of sequences taking values in a finite alphabet when the forecaster has limited information about the past outcomes of the sequence.

The randomized prediction problem is described as follows. Consider a sequential decision problem where a forecaster has to predict the environment's action. At each round, the forecaster chooses an action $i \in \{1, \ldots, N\}$, and the environment chooses an action $j \in \{1, \ldots, M\}$ (which we also call an "outcome"). The forecaster's reward $r(i,j)$ is the value of a reward function $r :$

---

[*] S. M. was partially supported by the Canada Research Chairs Program and by the Natural Sciences and Engineering Research Council of Canada. G.L. acknowledges the support of the Spanish Ministry of Science and Technology grant MTM2006-05650. G.S. was partially supported by the French "Agence Nationale pour la Recherche" under grant JCJC06-137444 "From applications to theory in learning and adaptive statistics." G.L. and G.S. acknowledge the PASCAL Network of Excellence under EC grant no. 506778.

N. Bshouty and C. Gentile (Eds.): COLT 2007, LNAI 4539, pp. 248–262, 2007.

$\{1, \ldots, N\} \times \{1, \ldots, M\} \to [0, 1]$. Now suppose that, at the t-th round, the forecaster chooses a probability distribution $\boldsymbol{p}_t = (p_{1,t}, \ldots, p_{N,t})$ over the set of actions, and plays action i with probability $p_{i,t}$. We denote the forecaster's action at time t by I_t. If the environment chooses action $J_t \in \{1, \ldots, M\}$, the reward of the forecaster is $r(I_t, J_t)$. The prediction problem is defined as follows:

RANDOMIZED PREDICTION WITH PERFECT MONITORING

Parameters: number N of actions, cardinality M of outcome space, reward function r, number n of game rounds.

For each round $t = 1, 2, \ldots, n$,

(1) the environment chooses the next outcome J_t;
(2) the forecaster chooses $\boldsymbol{p}_t$ and determines the random action I_t, distributed according to $\boldsymbol{p}_t$;
(3) the environment reveals J_t;
(4) the forecaster receives a reward $r(I_t, y_t)$.

The goal of the forecaster is to minimize the average regret

$$\max_{i=1,\ldots,N} \frac{1}{n} \sum_{t=1}^{n} r(i, J_t) - \frac{1}{n} \sum_{t=1}^{n} r(I_t, J_t) \, ,$$

that is, the realized difference between the cumulative reward of the best strategy $i \in \{1, \ldots, N\}$, in hindsight, and the reward of the forecaster. Denoting by $r(\boldsymbol{p}, j) = \sum_{i=1}^{N} p_i r(i, j)$ the linear extension of the reward function r, the Hoeffding-Azuma inequality for sums of bounded martingale differences (see [8], [1]), implies that for any $\delta \in (0, 1)$, with probability at least $1 - \delta$,

$$\frac{1}{n} \sum_{t=1}^{n} r(I_t, J_t) \geq \frac{1}{n} \sum_{t=1}^{n} r(\boldsymbol{p}_t, J_t) - \sqrt{\frac{1}{2n} \ln \frac{1}{\delta}} \, ,$$

so it suffices to study the average expected reward $(1/n) \sum_{t=1}^{n} r(\boldsymbol{p}_t, J_t)$. Hannan [7] and Blackwell [2] were the first to show the existence of a forecaster whose regret is $o(1)$ for all possible behaviors of the opponent. Here we mention one of the simplest, yet quite powerful forecasting strategies, the *exponentially weighted average* forecaster. This forecaster selects, at time t, an action I_t according to the probabilities

$$p_{i,t} = \frac{\exp\left(\eta \sum_{s=1}^{t-1} r(i, J_s)\right)}{\sum_{k=1}^{N} \exp\left(\eta \sum_{s=1}^{t-1} r(k, J_s)\right)} \quad i = 1, \ldots, N,$$

where $\eta > 0$ is a parameter of the forecaster. One of the basic well-known results in the theory of prediction of individual sequences states that the regret of the exponentially weighted average forecaster is bounded as

$$\max_{i=1,\ldots,N} \frac{1}{n} \sum_{t=1}^{n} r(i, J_t) - \frac{1}{n} \sum_{t=1}^{n} r(\boldsymbol{p}_t, J_t) \leq \frac{\ln N}{n\eta} + \frac{\eta}{8} . \tag{1}$$

With the choice $\eta = \sqrt{8 \ln N / n}$ the upper bound becomes $\sqrt{\ln N/(2n)}$. Different versions of this result have been proved by several authors; see [3] for a review.

In this paper we are concerned with problems in which the forecaster does not have access to the outcomes J_t. The information available to the forecaster at each round is called the *feedback*. These feedbacks may depend on the outcomes J_t only or on the action–outcome pairs (I_t, J_t) and may be deterministic or drawn at random. In the simplest case when the feedback is deterministic, the information available to the forecaster is $s_t = h(I_t, J_t)$, given by a fixed (and known) deterministic feedback function $h : \{1, \ldots, N\} \times \{1, \ldots, M\} \to \mathcal{S}$ where $\mathcal{S}$ is the finite set of signals. In the most general case, the feedback is governed by a random feedback function of the form $H : \{1, \ldots, N\} \times \{1, \ldots, M\} \to \mathcal{P}(\mathcal{S})$ where $\mathcal{P}(\mathcal{S})$ is the set of probability distributions over the signals. The received feedback s_t is then drawn at random according to the probability distribution $H(I_t, J_t)$ by using an external independent randomization.

To make notation uniform throughout the paper, we identify a deterministic feedback function $h : \{1, \ldots, N\} \times \{1, \ldots, M\} \to \mathcal{S}$ with the random feedback function $H : \{1, \ldots, N\} \times \{1, \ldots, M\} \to \mathcal{P}(\mathcal{S})$ which, to each pair (i, j), assigns $\delta_{h(i,j)}$ where δ_s is the probability distribution over the set of signals $\mathcal{S}$ concentrated on the single element $s \in \mathcal{S}$.

We will see that the prediction problem becomes significantly simpler in the special case when the feedback distribution depends only on the outcome, that is, when for all $j = 1, \ldots, M$, $H(\cdot, j)$ is constant. In other words, H depends on the outcome J_t but not on the forecaster's action I_t. To simplify notation in this case, we write $H(J_t) = H(I_t, J_t)$ for the feedback at time t ($h(J_t) = h(I_t, J_t)$ in case of deterministic feedback). This setting encompasses, for instance, the full-information case (when the outcomes J_t are revealed) and the setting of noisy observations (when a finite random variable with distribution depending only on J_t is observed).

The sequential prediction problem under imperfect monitoring is formalized in Figure 1.

Next we describe a reasonable goal for the forecaster and define the appropriate notion of consistency. To this end, we introduce some notation. If $\boldsymbol{p} = (p_1, \ldots, p_N)$ and $\boldsymbol{q} = (q_1, \ldots, q_M)$ are probability distributions over $\{1, \ldots, N\}$ and $\{1, \ldots, M\}$, respectively, then, with a slight abuse of notation, we write

$$r(\boldsymbol{p}, \boldsymbol{q}) = \sum_{i=1}^{N} \sum_{j=1}^{M} p_i q_j r(i, j)$$

RANDOMIZED PREDICTION UNDER IMPERFECT MONITORING

Parameters: number N of actions, number M of outcomes, reward function r, random feedback function H, number n of rounds.

For each round $t = 1, 2 \dots, n$,

1. the environment chooses the next outcome $J_t \in \{1, \dots, M\}$ without revealing it;
2. the forecaster chooses a probability distribution $\boldsymbol{p}_t$ over the set of N actions and draws an action $I_t \in \{1, \dots, N\}$ according to this distribution;
3. the forecaster receives reward $r(I_t, J_t)$ and each action i gets reward $r(i, J_t)$, where none of these values is revealed to the forecaster;
4. a feedback s_t drawn at random according to $H(I_t, J_t)$ is revealed to the forecaster.

Fig. 1. The game of randomized prediction under imperfect monitoring

for the linear extension of the reward function r. We also extend linearly the random feedback function in its second argument: for a probability distribution $\boldsymbol{q} = (q_1, \dots, q_M)$ over $\{1, \dots, M\}$, define the vector in $\mathbb{R}^{|\mathcal{S}|}$

$$H(i, \boldsymbol{q}) = \sum_{j=1}^{M} q_j H(i, j) , \qquad i = 1, \dots, N.$$

Denote by $\mathcal{F}$ the convex set of all the N-vectors $H(\cdot, \boldsymbol{q}) = (H(1, \boldsymbol{q}), \dots, H(N, \boldsymbol{q}))$ of probability distributions obtained this way when $\boldsymbol{q}$ varies. ($\mathcal{F} \subset \mathbb{R}^{|\mathcal{S}|N}$ is the set of feasible distributions over the signals). In the case where the feedback only depends on the outcome, all components of this vector are equal and we denote their common value by $H(\boldsymbol{q})$. We note that in the general case, the set $\mathcal{F}$ is the convex hull of the M vectors $H(\cdot, j)$. Therefore, performing a Euclidean projection on $\mathcal{F}$ can be done efficiently using quadratic programming.

To each probability distribution $\boldsymbol{p}$ over $\{1, \dots, N\}$ and probability distribution $\Delta \in \mathcal{F}$, we may assign the quantity

$$\rho(\boldsymbol{p}, \Delta) = \min_{\boldsymbol{q}: H(\cdot, \boldsymbol{q}) = \Delta} r(\boldsymbol{p}, \boldsymbol{q}) .$$

Note that $\rho \in [0, 1]$, and ρ is concave in $\boldsymbol{p}$ and convex in Δ.

To define the goal of the forecaster, let $\overline{\boldsymbol{q}}_n$ denote the empirical distribution of the outcomes $J_1, \dots, J_n$ up to round n. This distribution may be unknown to the forecaster since the forecaster observes the signals rather than the outcomes. The best the forecaster can hope for is an average reward close to $\max_{\boldsymbol{p}} \rho(\boldsymbol{p}, H(\cdot, \overline{\boldsymbol{q}}_n))$. Indeed, even if $H(\cdot, \overline{\boldsymbol{q}}_n)$ was known beforehand, the maximal expected reward for the forecaster would be $\max_{\boldsymbol{p}} \rho(\boldsymbol{p}, H(\cdot, \overline{\boldsymbol{q}}_n))$, simply because without any additional information the forecaster cannot hope to do better than against the worst element which is equivalent to $\boldsymbol{q}$ as far as the signals are concerned.

Based on this argument, the (per-round) regret R_n is defined as the averaged difference between the obtained cumulative reward and the target quantity described above, that is,

$$R_n = \max_{\boldsymbol{p}} \rho(\boldsymbol{p}, H(\cdot, \overline{\boldsymbol{q}}_n)) - \frac{1}{n} \sum_{t=1}^{n} r(I_t, J_t) \ .$$

Rustichini [11] proves the existence of a forecasting strategy whose per-round regret is guaranteed to satisfy $\limsup_{n\to\infty} R_n \leq 0$ with probability one, for all possible imperfect monitoring problems. However, Rustichini's proof is not constructive and it seems unlikely that his proof method can give rise to computationally efficient prediction algorithms.

Several partial solutions had been proposed so far. Piccolboni and Schindelhauer [10] and Cesa-Bianchi, Lugosi, and Stoltz [4] study the case when $\max_{\boldsymbol{p}} \rho(\boldsymbol{p}, H(\cdot, \overline{\boldsymbol{q}}_n)) = \max_{i=1,\ldots,N} r(i, \overline{\boldsymbol{q}}_n) = \max_{i=1,\ldots,N} (1/n) \sum_{t=1}^{n} r(i, J_t)$. In this case strategies with a vanishing per-round regret are called *Hannan consistent*. This case turns out to be considerably simpler than the general case and computationally tractable explicit algorithms have been derived. Also, it is shown in [4] that in this case it is possible to construct strategies whose regret decreases as $O_p(n^{-1/3})$. (Note that Hannan consistency is achievable, for example, in the adversarial multi-armed bandit problem, as shown in [4].)

The general case was considered by Mannor and Shimkin [9] who construct an approachability based algorithm with vanishing regret in the case when the feedback depends only on the outcome. In addition, Mannor and Shimkin discuss the more general case of feedback that depends on both the action and the outcome and provide an algorithm that attains a relaxed goal comparing to the goal attained in this work.

In this paper we construct simple and computationally efficient strategies whose regret vanishes with probability one. In Section 2 we consider the simplest special case when the actions of the forecaster do not influence the feedback which is, moreover, deterministic. This case is basically as easy as the full information case and we obtain a regret bound of the order of $n^{-1/2}$ (with high probability). In Section 3 we study random feedback but still with the restriction that it is only determined by the outcome. Here we are able to obtain a regret of the order of $n^{-1/4}\sqrt{\log n}$. The most general case is dealt with in Section 4. The forecaster introduced there has a regret of the order of $n^{-1/5}\sqrt{\log n}$. Finally, in Section 5 we show that this may be improved to $n^{-1/3}$ in the case of deterministic feedback, which is known to be optimal (see [4]).

2   Deterministic Feedback Only Depends on Outcome

We start with the simplest case when the feedback signal is deterministic and it does not depend on the action I_t of the forecaster. In other words, after making the prediction at time t, the forecaster observes $h(J_t)$.

In this case, we group the outcomes according to the deterministic feedback they are associated to. Each signal s is uniquely associated to a group of outcomes. This situation is very similar to the case of full monitoring except that rewards are measured by ρ and not by r. This does not pose a problem since r is lower bounded by ρ in the sense that for all $\boldsymbol{p}$ and j,

$$r(\boldsymbol{p}, j) \geq \rho(\boldsymbol{p}, \delta_{h(j)}) .$$

We introduce a forecaster that resembles the gradient-based strategies described, for example, in Cesa-Bianchi and Lugosi [3, Section 2.5]. The forecaster uses any sub-gradient of $\rho(\cdot, \delta_{h(J_t)})$ at time t. (Recall that if f is a concave function defined over a convex subset of $\mathbb{R}^d$, any vector $\boldsymbol{b}(\boldsymbol{x}) \in \mathbb{R}^d$ is a sub-gradient of f at $\boldsymbol{x}$ if $f(\boldsymbol{y}) - f(\boldsymbol{x}) \leq \boldsymbol{b}(\boldsymbol{x}) \cdot (\boldsymbol{y} - \boldsymbol{x})$ for all $\boldsymbol{y}$ in the domain of f. Sub-gradients always exist in the interior of the domain of a concave function. Here, in view of the exponentially weighted update rules, we only evaluate them in the interior of the simplex.) The forecaster requires a tuning parameter $\eta > 0$. The i-th component of $\boldsymbol{p}_t$ is

$$p_{i,t} = \frac{e^{\eta \sum_{s=1}^{t-1} \left(\widetilde{r}(\boldsymbol{p}_s, \delta_{h(J_s)}) \right)_i}}{\sum_{j=1}^{N} e^{\eta \sum_{s=1}^{t-1} \left(\widetilde{r}(\boldsymbol{p}_s, \delta_{h(J_s)}) \right)_j}} ,$$

where $\left(\widetilde{r}(\boldsymbol{p}_s, \delta_{h(J_s)}) \right)_i$ is the i-th component of any sub-gradient $\widetilde{r}(\boldsymbol{p}_s, \delta_{h(J_s)}) \in \nabla \rho(\boldsymbol{p}_s, \delta_{h(J_s)})$ of the concave function $f(\cdot) = \rho(\cdot, \delta_{h(J_s)})$.

The computation of a sub-gradient is trivial whenever $\rho(\boldsymbol{p}_s, \delta_{h(J_s)})$ is differentiable because it is then locally linear and the gradient equals the column of the reward matrix corresponding to the outcome y_s for which $r(\boldsymbol{p}_s, y_s) = \rho(\boldsymbol{p}_s, \delta_{h(J_s)})$. Note that $\rho(\cdot, \delta_{h(J_s)})$ is differentiable exactly at those points at which it is locally linear. Since it is concave, the Lebesgue measure of the set where it is non-differentiable equals zero. To avoid such values, one may add a small random perturbation to $\boldsymbol{p}_t$ or just calculate a sub-gradient using the simplex method. Note that the components of the sub-gradients are always bounded by a constant that depends on the game parameters. This is the case since $\rho(\cdot, \delta_{h(J_s)})$ is concave and continuous on a compact set and is therefore Lipschitz leading to a bounded sub-gradient. Let K denote a constant such that $\sup_{\boldsymbol{p}} \max_j \|\widetilde{r}(\boldsymbol{p}, \delta_{h(j)})\|_\infty \leq K$. This constant depends on the specific parameters of the game. The regret is bounded as follows. Note that the following bound (and the considered forecaster) coincide with those of (1) in case of perfect monitoring. (In that case, $\rho(\cdot, \delta_{h(j)}) = r(\cdot, j)$, the subgradients are given by r, and therefore, are bounded between 0 and 1.).

Proposition 1. *For all $\eta > 0$, for all strategies of the environment, for all $\delta > 0$, the above strategy of the forecaster ensures that, with probability at least $1 - \delta$,*

$$R_n \leq \frac{\ln N}{\eta n} + \frac{K^2 \eta}{2} + \sqrt{\frac{1}{2n} \ln \frac{1}{\delta}} .$$

In particular, choosing $\eta \sim \sqrt{(\ln N)/n}$ yields $R_n = O(n^{-1/2} \sqrt{\ln(N/\delta)})$.

Proof. Note that since the feedback is deterministic, $H(\overline{q}_n)$ takes the simple form $H(\overline{q}_n) = \frac{1}{n} \sum_{t=1}^{n} \delta_{h(J_t)}$. Now, for any p,

$$n\rho(p, H(\overline{q}_n)) - \sum_{t=1}^{n} r(p_t, J_t)$$

$$\leq n\rho(p, H(\overline{q}_n)) - \sum_{t=1}^{n} \rho(p_t, \delta_{h(J_t)}) \quad \text{(by the lower bound on r in terms of ρ)}$$

$$\leq \sum_{t=1}^{n} \left(\rho(p, \delta_{h(J_t)}) - \rho(p_t, \delta_{h(J_t)}) \right) \quad \text{(by convexity of ρ in the second argument)}$$

$$\leq \sum_{t=1}^{n} \widetilde{r}(p_t, \delta_{h(J_t)}) \cdot (p - p_t) \quad \text{(by concavity of ρ in the first argument)}$$

$$\leq \frac{\ln N}{\eta} + \frac{nK^2\eta}{2} \quad \text{(by (1), after proper rescaling)},$$

where at the last step we used the fact that the forecaster is just the exponentially weighted average predictor based on the rewards $(\widetilde{r}(p_s, \delta_{h(J_s)}))_i$ and that all these reward vectors have components between $-K$ and K. The proof is concluded by the Hoeffding-Azuma inequality, which ensures that, with probability at least $1 - \delta$,

$$\sum_{t=1}^{n} r(I_t, J_t) \geq \sum_{t=1}^{n} r(p_t, J_t) - \sqrt{\frac{n}{2} \ln \frac{1}{\delta}} . \tag{2}$$

3   Random Feedback Only Depends on Outcome

Next we consider the case when the feedback does not depend on the forecaster's actions, but, at time t, the signal s_t is drawn at random according to the distribution $H(J_t)$. In this case the forecaster does not have a direct access to

$$H(\overline{q}_n) = \frac{1}{n} \sum_{t=1}^{n} H(J_t)$$

anymore, but only observes the realizations s_t drawn at random according to $H(J_t)$. In order to overcome this problem, we group together several consecutive time rounds (m of them) and estimate the probability distributions according to which the signals have been drawn.

To this end, denote by Π the Euclidean projection onto $\mathcal{F}$ (since the feedback depends only on the outcome we may now view the set $\mathcal{F}$ of feasible distributions over the signals as a subset of $\mathcal{P}(\mathcal{S})$, the latter being identified with a subset of $\mathbb{R}^{|\mathcal{S}|}$ in a natural way). Let m, $1 \leq m \leq n$, be a parameter of the algorithm. For $b = 0, 1, \ldots$, we denote

$$\widehat{\Delta}^b = \Pi \left(\frac{1}{m} \sum_{t=bm+1}^{(b+1)m} \delta_{s_t} \right) . \tag{3}$$

Parameters: Integer $m \geq 1$, real number $\eta > 0$.
Initialization: $w^0 = (1, \ldots, 1)$.
For each round $t = 1, 2, \ldots$

1. If $bm + 1 \leq t < (b+1)m$ for some integer b, choose the distribution $\boldsymbol{p}_t = \boldsymbol{p}^b$ given by

$$p_{k,t} = p_k^b = \frac{w_k^b}{\sum_{j=1}^{N} w_j^b}$$

   and draw an action I_t from $\{1, \ldots, N\}$ according to it;
2. if $t = (b+1)m$ for some integer b, perform the update

$$w_k^{b+1} = w_k^b \, e^{\eta \left(\tilde{r}(\boldsymbol{p}^b, \widehat{\Delta}^b) \right)_k} \qquad \text{for each } k = 1, \ldots, N,$$

   where for all Δ, $\tilde{r}(\cdot, \Delta)$ is a sub-gradient of $\rho(\cdot, \Delta)$ and $\widehat{\Delta}^b$ is defined in (3).

Fig. 2. The forecaster for random feedback depending only on outcome

For the sake of the analysis, we also introduce

$$\Delta^b = \frac{1}{m} \sum_{t=bm+1}^{(b+1)m} H(J_t) \, .$$

The proposed strategy is described in Figure 2. Observe that the practical implementation of the forecaster only requires the computation of (sub)gradients and of ℓ^2 projections, which can be done in polytime. The next theorem bounds the regret of the strategy which is of the order of $n^{-1/4}\sqrt{\log n}$. The price we pay for having to estimate the distribution is thus a deteriorated rate of convergence (from the $O(n^{-1/2})$ obtained in the case of deterministic feedback). We do not know whether this rate can be improved significantly as we do not know of any nontrivial lower bound in this case.

Theorem 1. *For all integers $m \geq 1$, for all $\eta > 0$, and for all $\delta > 0$, the regret against any strategy of the environment is bounded, with probability at least $1 - (n/m + 1)\delta$, by*

$$R_n \leq 2\sqrt{2}\, L \, \frac{1}{\sqrt{m}} \sqrt{\ln \frac{2}{\delta}} + \frac{m \ln N}{n\eta} + \frac{K^2 \eta}{2} + \frac{m}{n} + \sqrt{\frac{1}{2n} \ln \frac{1}{\delta}} \, ,$$

where K, L are constants which depend only on the parameters of the game. The choices $m = \lceil \sqrt{n} \rceil$ and $\eta \sim \sqrt{(m \ln N)/n}$ imply $R_n = O(n^{-1/4}\sqrt{\ln(nN/\delta)})$ with probability of at least $1 - \delta$.

The proof of the theorem relies on the following Lipschitzness property of ρ, which we state without a proof in this extended abstract.

Proposition 2. *The function $(\boldsymbol{p}, \Delta) \mapsto \rho(\boldsymbol{p}, \Delta)$ is uniformly Lipschitz in its second argument.*

Proof (of Theorem 1). We start by grouping time rounds m by m. For simplicity, we assume that $n = (B+1)m$ for some integer B (this accounts for the m/n term in the bound). For all $\boldsymbol{p}$,

$$n\,\rho(\boldsymbol{p}, H(\overline{\boldsymbol{q}}_n)) - \sum_{t=1}^{n} r(\boldsymbol{p}_t, J_t) \leq \sum_{b=0}^{B} \left(m\,\rho\left(\boldsymbol{p}, \Delta^b\right) - m\,r\left(\boldsymbol{p}^b, \frac{1}{m}\sum_{t=bm+1}^{(b+1)m} \delta_{J_t}\right) \right)$$

$$\leq m \sum_{b=0}^{B} \left(\rho\left(\boldsymbol{p}, \Delta^b\right) - \rho\left(\boldsymbol{p}^b, \Delta^b\right) \right) ,$$

where we used the definition of the algorithm, convexity of ρ in its second argument, and finally, the definition of ρ as a minimum. We proceed by estimating Δ^b by $\widehat{\Delta}^b$. By a version of the Hoeffding-Azuma inequality in Hilbert spaces proved by Chen and White [5, Lemma 3.2], and since the ℓ^2 projection can only help, for all b, with probability at least $1 - \delta$,

$$\left\| \Delta^b - \widehat{\Delta}^b \right\|_2 \leq \sqrt{\frac{2 \ln \frac{2}{\delta}}{m}} .$$

By Proposition 2, ρ is uniformly Lipschitz in its second argument (with constant L), and therefore we may further bound as follows. With probability $1 - (B+1)\delta$,

$$m \sum_{b=0}^{B} \left(\rho\left(\boldsymbol{p}, \Delta^b\right) - \rho\left(\boldsymbol{p}^b, \Delta^b\right) \right)$$

$$\leq m \sum_{b=0}^{B} \left(\rho\left(\boldsymbol{p}, \widehat{\Delta}^b\right) - \rho\left(\boldsymbol{p}^b, \widehat{\Delta}^b\right) \right) + 2\,L(B+1)\sqrt{2m \ln \frac{2}{\delta}} .$$

The term containing $(B+1)\sqrt{m} = n/\sqrt{m}$ is the first term in the upper bound. The remaining part is bounded by using the same slope inequality argument as in the previous section (recall that $\widetilde{r}$ denotes a sub-gradient),

$$m \sum_{b=0}^{B} \left(\rho\left(\boldsymbol{p}, \widehat{\Delta}^b\right) - \rho\left(\boldsymbol{p}^b, \widehat{\Delta}^b\right) \right) \leq m \sum_{b=0}^{B} \widetilde{r}\left(\boldsymbol{p}^b, \widehat{\Delta}^b\right) \cdot (\boldsymbol{p} - \boldsymbol{p}^b)$$

$$\leq m \left(\frac{\ln N}{\eta} + \frac{(B+1)K^2\eta}{2} \right) = \frac{m \ln N}{\eta} + \frac{nK^2\eta}{2}$$

where we used Theorem 1 and the boundedness of the function $\widetilde{r}$ between $-K$ and K. The proof is concluded by the Hoeffding-Azuma inequality which, as in (2), gives the final term in the bound. The union bound indicates that the obtained bound holds with probability at least $1 - (B+2)\delta \geq 1 - (n/m + 1)\delta$.

4   Random Feedback Depends on Action–Outcome Pair

We now turn to the most general case, where the feedback is random and depends on the action–outcome pairs (I_t, J_t). The key is, again, to exhibit efficient estimators of the (unobserved) $H(\cdot, \overline{q}_n)$.

Denote by Π the projection, in the Euclidian distance, onto $\mathcal{F}$ (where $\mathcal{F}$, as a subset of $(\mathcal{P}(\mathcal{S}))^N$, is identified with a subset of $\mathbb{R}^{|\mathcal{S}|N}$). For $b = 0, 1, \ldots$, denote

$$\widehat{\Delta}^b = \Pi \left(\frac{1}{m} \sum_{t=bm+1}^{(b+1)m} \left[\widehat{h}_{i,t} \right]_{i=1,\ldots,N} \right) \tag{4}$$

where the distribution $H(i, J_t)$ of the random signal s_t received by action i at round t is estimated by

$$\widehat{h}_{i,t} = \frac{\delta_{s_t}}{p_{i,t}} \mathbb{1}_{I_t=i} \ .$$

We prove that the $\widehat{h}_{i,t}$ are conditionally unbiased estimators. Denote by $\mathbb{E}_t$ the conditional expectation with respect to the information available to the forecaster at the beginning of round t. This conditioning fixes the values of p_t and J_t. Thus,

$$\mathbb{E}_t \left[\widehat{h}_{i,t} \right] = \frac{1}{p_{i,t}} \mathbb{E}_t \left[\delta_{s_t} \mathbb{1}_{I_t=i} \right] = \frac{1}{p_{i,t}} \mathbb{E}_t \left[H(I_t, J_t) \mathbb{1}_{I_t=i} \right] = \frac{1}{p_{i,t}} H(i, J_t) p_{i,t}$$

$$= H(i, J_t) \ .$$

For the sake of the analysis, introduce $\Delta^b = \dfrac{1}{m} \displaystyle\sum_{t=bm+1}^{(b+1)m} H(\cdot, J_t)$. The proposed forecasting strategy is sketched in Figure 3. Here again, the practical implementation of the forecaster only requires the computation of (sub)gradients and of ℓ^2 projections, which can be done efficiently. The next theorem states that the regret in this most general case is at most of the order of $n^{-1/5}\sqrt{\log n}$. Again, we do not know whether this bound can be improved significantly.

Theorem 2. *For all integers $m \geq 1$, for all $\eta > 0$, $\gamma \in (0, 1)$, and $\delta > 0$, the regret against any strategy of the environment is bounded, with probability at least $1 - (n/m + 1)\delta$, as*

$$R_n \leq L N \sqrt{\frac{2|\mathcal{S}|}{\gamma m} \ln \frac{2N|\mathcal{S}|}{\delta}} + L \frac{N^{3/2}\sqrt{|\mathcal{S}|}}{3\gamma m} \ln \frac{2N|\mathcal{S}|}{\delta}$$

$$+ \frac{m \ln N}{n\eta} + \frac{K^2\eta}{2} + \gamma + \frac{m}{n} + \sqrt{\frac{1}{2n} \ln \frac{1}{\delta}} \ ,$$

where L and K are constants which depend on the parameters of the game. The choices $m = \lceil n^{3/5} \rceil$, $\eta \sim \sqrt{(m \ln N)/n}$, and $\gamma \sim n^{-1/5}$ ensure that, with probability at least $1 - \delta$, $R_n = O\left(n^{-1/5}N\sqrt{\ln \frac{Nn}{\delta}} + n^{-2/5}N^{3/2} \ln \frac{Nn}{\delta}\right)$.

Parameters: Integer $m \geq 1$, real numbers $\eta, \gamma > 0$.
Initialization: $\boldsymbol{w}^0 = (1, \ldots, 1)$.

For each round $t = 1, 2, \ldots$

1. if $bm + 1 \leq t < (b+1)m$ for some integer b, choose the distribution $\boldsymbol{p}_t = \boldsymbol{p}^b = (1 - \gamma)\widetilde{\boldsymbol{p}}^b + \gamma\boldsymbol{u}$, where $\widetilde{\boldsymbol{p}}^b$ is defined component-wise as

$$\widetilde{p}_k^b = \frac{w_k^b}{\sum_{j=1}^N w_j^b}$$

and $\boldsymbol{u}$ denotes the uniform distribution, $\boldsymbol{u} = (1/N, \ldots, 1/N)$;
2. draw an action I_t from $\{1, \ldots, N\}$ according to it;
3. if $t = (b+1)m$ for some integer b, perform the update

$$w_k^{b+1} = w_k^b \, e^{\eta \left(\widetilde{r}(\boldsymbol{p}^b, \widehat{\Delta}^b)\right)_k} \qquad \text{for each } k = 1, \ldots, N,$$

where for all $\Delta \in \mathcal{F}$, $\widetilde{r}(\cdot, \Delta)$ is a sub-gradient of $\rho(\cdot, \Delta)$ and $\widehat{\Delta}^b$ is defined in (4).

Fig. 3. The forecaster for random feedback depending on action–outcome pair

Proof. The proof is similar to the one of Theorem 1. A difference is that we bound the accuracy of the estimation of the Δ^b via a martingale analog of Bernstein's inequality due to Freedman [6] rather than the Hoeffding-Azuma inequality. Also, the mixing with the uniform distribution of Step 1 needs to be handled.

We start by grouping time rounds m by m. Assume, for simplicity, that $n = (B+1)m$ for some integer B (this accounts for the m/n term in the bound). As before, we get that, for all $\boldsymbol{p}$,

$$n \, \rho(\boldsymbol{p}, H(\cdot, \overline{\boldsymbol{q}}_n)) - \sum_{t=1}^n r(\boldsymbol{p}_t, J_t) \leq m \sum_{b=0}^B \left(\rho\left(\boldsymbol{p}, \Delta^b\right) - \rho\left(\boldsymbol{p}^b, \Delta^b\right)\right) \qquad (5)$$

and proceed by estimating Δ^b by $\widehat{\Delta}^b$. Freedman's inequality [6] (see, also, [4, Lemma A.1]) implies that for all $b = 0, 1, \ldots, B$, $i = 1, \ldots, N$, $s \in \mathcal{S}$, and $\delta > 0$,

$$\left| \Delta_i^b(s) - \frac{1}{m} \sum_{t=bm+1}^{(b+1)m} \widehat{h}_{i,t}(s) \right| \leq \sqrt{2\frac{N}{\gamma m} \ln \frac{2}{\delta}} + \frac{1}{3}\frac{N}{\gamma m} \ln \frac{2}{\delta}$$

where $\widehat{h}_{i,t}(s)$ is the probability mass put on s by $\widehat{h}_{i,t}$ and $\Delta_i^b(s)$ is the i-th component of Δ^b. This is because the sums of the conditional variances are bounded as

$$\sum_{t=bm+1}^{(b+1)m} \mathrm{Var}_t \left(\frac{\mathbb{1}_{I_t=i, s_t=s}}{p_{i,t}}\right) \leq \sum_{t=bm+1}^{(b+1)m} \frac{1}{p_{i,t}} \leq \frac{mN}{\gamma} \, .$$

Summing (since the ℓ^2 projection can only help), the union bound shows that for all b, with probability at least $1 - \delta$,

$$\left\| \Delta^b - \widehat{\Delta}^b \right\|_2 \le d \stackrel{\text{def}}{=} \sqrt{N\,|S|} \left(\sqrt{2\frac{N}{\gamma m} \ln \frac{2N\,|S|}{\delta}} + \frac{1}{3}\frac{N}{\gamma m} \ln \frac{2N\,|S|}{\delta} \right).$$

By using uniform Lipschitzness of ρ in its second argument (with constant L; see Proposition 2), we may further bound (5) with probability $1 - (B+1)\delta$ by

$$m \sum_{b=0}^{B} \left(\rho\left(\boldsymbol{p}, \Delta^b\right) - \rho\left(\boldsymbol{p}^b, \Delta^b\right) \right) \le m \sum_{b=0}^{B} \left(\rho\left(\boldsymbol{p}, \widehat{\Delta}^b\right) - \rho\left(\boldsymbol{p}^b, \widehat{\Delta}^b\right) + L\,d \right)$$

$$= m \sum_{b=0}^{B} \left(\rho\left(\boldsymbol{p}, \widehat{\Delta}^b\right) - \rho\left(\boldsymbol{p}^b, \widehat{\Delta}^b\right) \right) + m(B+1)L\,d.$$

The terms $m(B+1)L\,d = nL\,d$ are the first two terms in the upper bound of the theorem. The remaining part is bounded by using the same slope inequality argument as in the previous section (recall that $\widetilde{r}$ denotes a sub-gradient bounded between $-K$ and K):

$$m \sum_{b=0}^{B} \left(\rho\left(\boldsymbol{p}, \widehat{\Delta}^b\right) - \rho\left(\boldsymbol{p}^b, \widehat{\Delta}^b\right) \right) \le m \sum_{b=0}^{B} \widetilde{r}\left(\boldsymbol{p}^b, \widehat{\Delta}^b\right) \cdot (\boldsymbol{p} - \boldsymbol{p}^b) .$$

Finally, we deal with the mixing with the uniform distribution:

$$m \sum_{b=0}^{B} \widetilde{r}\left(\boldsymbol{p}^b, \widehat{\Delta}^b\right) \cdot (\boldsymbol{p} - \boldsymbol{p}^b) \le (1-\gamma)m \sum_{b=0}^{B} \widetilde{r}\left(\boldsymbol{p}^b, \widehat{\Delta}^b\right) \cdot \left(\boldsymbol{p} - \widetilde{\boldsymbol{p}}^b\right) + \gamma m(B+1)$$

$$\text{(since, by definition, } \boldsymbol{p}^b = (1-\gamma)\widetilde{\boldsymbol{p}}^b + \gamma \boldsymbol{u})$$

$$\le (1-\gamma)m \left(\frac{\ln N}{\eta} + \frac{(B+1)K^2\eta}{2} \right) + \gamma m(B+1)$$

$$\text{(by (1))}$$

$$\le \frac{m \ln N}{\eta} + \frac{nK^2\eta}{2} + \gamma n .$$

The proof is concluded by the Hoeffding-Azuma inequality which, as in (2), gives the final term in the bound. The union bound indicates that the obtained bound hold with probability at least $1 - (B+2)\delta \ge 1 - (n/m+1)\delta$.

5   Deterministic Feedback Depends on Action–Outcome Pair

In this last section we explain how in the case of deterministic feedback the fore-caster of the previous section can be modified so that the order of magnitude of the per-round regret improves to $n^{-1/3}$. This relies on the linearity of ρ in its second argument. In the case of random feedback, ρ may not be linear which required grouping rounds of size m. If the feedback is deterministic, such grouping is not needed and the $n^{-1/3}$ rate is obtained as a trade-off between an exploration term (γ) and the cost payed for estimating the feedbacks ($\sqrt{1/(\gamma n)}$). This rate of convergence has been shown to be optimal in [4] even in the Hannan consistent case. The key property is summarized in the next technical lemma whose proof is omitted for the lack of space.

Lemma 1. *For every fixed p, the function $\rho(p, \cdot)$ is linear on $\mathcal{F}$.*

Next we describe the modified forecaster. Denote by $\mathcal{H}$ the vector space generated by $\mathcal{F} \subset \mathbb{R}^{|S|N}$ and Π the linear operator which projects any element of $\mathbb{R}^{|S|N}$ onto $\mathcal{H}$. Since the $\rho(p, \cdot)$ are linear on $\mathcal{F}$, we may extend them linearly to $\mathcal{H}$ (and with a slight abuse of notation we write ρ for the extension). As a consequence, the functions $\rho(p, \Pi(\cdot))$ are linear defined on $\mathbb{R}^{|S|N}$ and coincide with the original definition on $\mathcal{F}$. We denote by $\widetilde{r}$ a sub-gradient (i.e., for all $\Delta \in \mathbb{R}^{|S|N}$, $\widetilde{r}(\cdot, \Delta)$ is a sub-gradient of $\rho(\cdot, \Pi(\Delta))$).

The sub-gradients are evaluated at the following points. (Recall that since the feedback is deterministic, $s_t = h(I_t, J_t)$.) For $t = 1, 2, \ldots$, let

$$\widehat{h}_t = \left[\widehat{h}_{i,t}\right]_{i=1,\ldots,N} = \left[\frac{\delta_{s_t}}{p_{i,t}} \mathbb{1}_{I_t=i}\right]_{i=1,\ldots,N} . \tag{6}$$

The $\widehat{h}_{i,t}$ estimate the feedbacks $H(i, J_t) = \delta_{h(i,J_t)}$ received by action i at round t. They are still conditionally unbiased estimators of the $h(i, J_t)$, and so is $\widehat{h}_t$ for $H(\cdot, J_t)$. The proposed forecaster is defined in Figure 4 and the regret bound is established in Theorem 3.

Theorem 3. *There exists a constant C only depending on r and h such that for all $\delta > 0$, $\gamma \in (0,1)$, and $\eta > 0$, the regret against any strategy of the environment is bounded, with probability at least $1 - \delta$, as*

$$R_n \leq 2NC\sqrt{\frac{2}{n\gamma} \ln \frac{2}{\delta}} + \frac{NC}{3\gamma n} \ln \frac{2}{\delta} + \frac{\ln N}{\eta n} + \frac{\eta K^2}{2} + \gamma + \sqrt{\frac{1}{2n} \ln \frac{2}{\delta}} .$$

The choice $\gamma \sim n^{-1/3}N^{2/3}$ and $\eta \sim \sqrt{(\ln N)/n}$ ensures that, with probability at least $1 - \delta$, $R_n = O\left(n^{-1/3}N^{2/3}\sqrt{\ln(1/\delta)}\right)$.

Proof. The proof is similar to the one of Theorem 2, except that we do not have to consider the grouping steps and that we do not apply the Hoeffding-Azuma inequality to the estimated feedbacks but to the estimated rewards. By the bound on r in terms of ρ and convexity (linearity) of ρ in its second argument,

$$n\, \rho(p, H(\cdot, \overline{q}_n)) - \sum_{t=1}^{n} r(p_t, J_t) \leq \sum_{t=1}^{n} \left(\rho\left(p, H(\cdot, J_t)\right) - \rho\left(p_t, H(\cdot, J_t)\right)\right) .$$

Parameters: Real numbers $\eta, \gamma > 0$.
Initialization: $\boldsymbol{w}_1 = (1, \ldots, 1)$.
For each round $t = 1, 2, \ldots$

1. choose the distribution $\boldsymbol{p}_t = (1-\gamma)\widetilde{\boldsymbol{p}}_t + \gamma\boldsymbol{u}$, where $\widetilde{\boldsymbol{p}}_t$ is defined component-wise as

$$\widetilde{p}_{k,t} = \frac{w_{k,t}}{\sum_{j=1}^{N} w_{j,t}}$$

   and $\boldsymbol{u}$ denotes the uniform distribution, $\boldsymbol{u} = (1/N, \ldots, 1/N)$; then draw an action I_t from $\{1, \ldots, N\}$ according to $\boldsymbol{p}_t$;
2. perform the update

$$w_{k,t+1} = w_{k,t}\, e^{\eta \left(\widetilde{r}(\boldsymbol{p}_t, \widehat{h}_t)\right)_k} \qquad \text{for each } k = 1, \ldots, N,$$

   where Π is the projection operator defined after the statement of Lemma 1, for all $\Delta \in \mathbb{R}^{|S|N}$, $\widetilde{r}(\cdot, \Delta)$ is a sub-gradient of $\rho(\cdot, \Pi(\Delta))$, and $\widehat{h}_t$ is defined in (6).

Fig. 4. The forecaster for deterministic feedback depending on action–outcome pair

Next we estimate

$$\rho\left(\boldsymbol{p}, H(\cdot, J_t)\right) - \rho\left(\boldsymbol{p}_t, H(\cdot, J_t)\right) \qquad \text{by} \qquad \rho\left(\boldsymbol{p}, \Pi\left(\widehat{h}_t\right)\right) - \rho\left(\boldsymbol{p}_t, \Pi\left(\widehat{h}_t\right)\right).$$

By Freedman's inequality (see, again, [4, Lemma A.1]), since $\widehat{h}_t$ is a conditionally unbiased estimator of $H(\cdot, J_t)$ and all functions at hand are linear in their second argument, we get that, with probability at least $1 - \delta/2$,

$$\sum_{t=1}^{n} \left(\rho\left(\boldsymbol{p}, H(\cdot, J_t)\right) - \rho\left(\boldsymbol{p}_t, H(\cdot, J_t)\right)\right)$$

$$= \sum_{t=1}^{n} \left(\rho\left(\boldsymbol{p}, \Pi\left(H(\cdot, J_t)\right)\right) - \rho\left(\boldsymbol{p}_t, \Pi\left(H(\cdot, J_t)\right)\right)\right)$$

$$\leq \sum_{t=1}^{n} \left(\rho\left(\boldsymbol{p}, \Pi\left(\widehat{h}_t\right)\right) - \rho\left(\boldsymbol{p}_t, \Pi\left(\widehat{h}_t\right)\right)\right) + 2NC\sqrt{2\frac{n}{\gamma}\ln\frac{2}{\delta}} + \frac{NC}{3\gamma}\ln\frac{2}{\delta}$$

where, denoting by $\boldsymbol{e}_i(\delta_{h(i,j)})$ the column vector whose i-th component is $\delta_{h(i,j)}$ and all other components equal 0,

$$C = \max_{i,j} \max_{\boldsymbol{p}} \rho\left(\boldsymbol{p}, \Pi\left[\boldsymbol{e}_i(\delta_{h(i,j)})\right]\right) < +\infty.$$

This is because for all t, the conditional variances are bounded as follows. For all $\boldsymbol{p}'$,

$$\mathbb{E}_t\left[\rho\left(\boldsymbol{p}', \Pi\left(\widehat{h}_t\right)\right)^2\right] = \sum_{i=1}^{N} p_{i,t}\, \rho\left(\boldsymbol{p}', \Pi\left[\boldsymbol{e}_i(\delta_{h(i,j)}/p_{i,t})\right]\right)^2$$

$$= \sum_{i=1}^{N} \frac{1}{p_{i,t}} \, \rho \left(p', \Pi \left[e_i (\delta_{h(i,j)} / p_{i,t}) \right] \right)^2 \le \sum_{i=1}^{N} \frac{C^2}{p_{i,t}} \le \frac{C^2 N^2}{\gamma} \; .$$

The remaining part is bounded by using the same slope inequality argument as in the previous sections (recall that $\widetilde{r}$ denotes a sub-gradient in the first argument of $\rho(\cdot, \Pi(\cdot))$, bounded between $-K$ and K),

$$\sum_{t=1}^{n} \left(\rho \left(p, \Pi \left(\widehat{h}_t \right) \right) - \rho \left(p_t, \Pi \left(\widehat{h}_t \right) \right) \right) \le \sum_{t=1}^{n} \widetilde{r} \left(p_t, \widehat{h}_t \right) \cdot (p - p_t) \; .$$

Finally, we deal with the mixing with the uniform distribution:

$$\sum_{t=1}^{n} \widetilde{r} \left(p, \widehat{h}_t \right) \cdot (p - p) \le (1 - \gamma) \sum_{t=1}^{n} \widetilde{r} \left(p_t, \widehat{h}_t \right) \cdot (p - \widetilde{p}_t) + \gamma n$$

$$\text{(since by definition } p_t = (1 - \gamma) \widetilde{p}_t + \gamma u)$$

$$\le (1 - \gamma) \left(\frac{\ln N}{\eta} + \frac{n \eta K^2}{2} \right) + \gamma n \quad \text{(by (1))}.$$

As before, the proof is concluded by the Hoeffding-Azuma inequality (2) and the union bound.

References

1. Azuma, K.: Weighted sums of certain dependent random variables. Tohoku Mathematical Journal 68, 357–367 (1967)
2. Blackwell, D.: Controlled random walks. In: Proceedings of the International Congress of Mathematicians, 1954, volume III, pp. 336–338. North-Holland (1956)
3. Cesa-Bianchi, N., Lugosi, G.: Prediction, Learning, and Games. Cambridge University Press, New York (2006)
4. Cesa-Bianchi, N., Lugosi, G., Stoltz, G.: Regret minimization under partial monitoring. Mathematics of Operations Research 31, 562–580 (2006)
5. Chen, X., White, H.: Laws of large numbers for Hilbert space-valued mixingales with applications. Econometric Theory 12(2), 284–304 (1996)
6. Freedman, D.A.: On tail probabilities for martingales. Annals of Probability 3, 100–118 (1975)
7. Hannan, J.: Approximation to Bayes risk in repeated play. Contributions to the theory of games 3, 97–139 (1957)
8. Hoeffding, W.: Probability inequalities for sums of bounded random variables. Journal of the American Statistical Association 58, 13–30 (1963)
9. Mannor, S., Shimkin, N.: On-line learning with imperfect monitoring. In: Proceedings of the 16th Annual Conference on Learning Theory, pp. 552–567. Springer, Heidelberg (2003)
10. Piccolboni, A., Schindelhauer, C.: Discrete prediction games with arbitrary feedback and loss. In: Proceedings of the 14th Annual Conference on Computational Learning Theory, pp. 208–223 (2001)
11. Rustichini, A.: Minimizing regret: The general case. Games and Economic Behavior 29, 224–243 (1999)

Bounded Parameter Markov Decision Processes with Average Reward Criterion

Ambuj Tewari[1] and Peter L. Bartlett[2]

[1] University of California, Berkeley
Division of Computer Science
544 Soda Hall # 1776
Berkeley, CA 94720-1776, USA
`ambuj@cs.berkeley.edu`
[2] University of California, Berkeley
Division of Computer Science and Department of Statistics
387 Soda Hall # 1776
Berkeley, CA 94720-1776, USA
`bartlett@cs.berkeley.edu`

Abstract. Bounded parameter Markov Decision Processes (BMDPs) address the issue of dealing with uncertainty in the parameters of a Markov Decision Process (MDP). Unlike the case of an MDP, the notion of an optimal policy for a BMDP is not entirely straightforward. We consider two notions of optimality based on optimistic and pessimistic criteria. These have been analyzed for discounted BMDPs. Here we provide results for average reward BMDPs.

We establish a fundamental relationship between the discounted and the average reward problems, prove the existence of Blackwell optimal policies and, for both notions of optimality, derive algorithms that converge to the optimal value function.

1 Introduction

Markov Decision Processes (MDPs) are a widely used tool to model decision making under uncertainty. In an MDP, the uncertainty involved in the outcome of making a decision in a certain state is represented using various probabilities. However, these probabilities themselves may not be known precisely. This can happen for a variety of reasons. The probabilities might have been obtained via an estimation process. In such a case, it is natural that confidence intervals will be associated with them. State aggregation, where groups of similar states of a large MDP are merged to form a smaller MDP, can also lead to a situation where probabilities are no longer known precisely but are only known to lie in an interval.

This paper is concerned with such higher level uncertainty, namely uncertainty about the parameters of an MDP. Bounded parameter MDPs (BMDPs) have been introduced in the literature [1] to address this problem. They use intervals (or equivalently, lower and upper bounds) to represent the set in which the

N. Bshouty and C. Gentile (Eds.): COLT 2007, LNAI 4539, pp. 263–277, 2007.

parameters of an MDP can lie. We obtain an entire family, say $\mathcal{M}$, of MDPs by taking all possible choices of parameters consistent with these intervals. For an exact MDP M and a policy μ (which is a mapping specifying the actions to take in various states), the α-discounted return from state i, $V_{\alpha,\mu,M}(i)$ and the long term average return $V_{\mu,M}(i)$ are two standard ways of measuring the quality of μ with respect to M. When we have a family $\mathcal{M}$ of MDPs, we are immediately faced with the problem of finding a way to measure the quality of a policy. An optimal policy will then be the one that maximizes the particular performance measure chosen.

We might choose to put a distribution over $\mathcal{M}$ and define the return of a policy as its average return under this distribution. In this paper, however, we will avoid taking this approach. Instead, we will consider the worst and the best MDP for each policy and accordingly define two performance measures,

$$V_{\mu}^{\mathrm{opt}}(i) := \sup_{M \in \mathcal{M}} V_{\mu,M}(i)$$

$$V_{\mu}^{\mathrm{pes}}(i) := \inf_{M \in \mathcal{M}} V_{\mu,M}(i)$$

where the superscripts denote that these are optimistic and pessimistic criteria respectively. Analogous quantities for the discounted case were defined in [1] and algorithms were given to compute them. In this paper, our aim is to analyze the average reward setting.

The optimistic criterion is motivated by the *optimism in the face of uncertainty* principle. Several learning algorithms for MDPs [2,3,4,5] proceed in the following manner. Faced with an unknown MDP, they start collecting data which yields confidence intervals for the parameters of the MDP. Then they choose a policy which is optimal in the sense of the optimistic criterion. This policy is followed for the next phase of data collection and the process repeats. In fact, the algorithm of Auer and Ortner requires, as a blackbox, an algorithm to compute the optimal (with respect to the optimistic criterion) value function for a BMDP.

The pessimistic criterion is related to research on robust control of MDPs [6]. If nature is adversarial, then once we pick a policy μ it will pick the worst possible MDP M from $\mathcal{M}$. In such a scenario, it is reasonable to choose a policy which is best in the worst case. Our work also extends this line of research to the case of the average reward criterion.

A brief outline of the paper is as follows. Notation and preliminary results are established in Section 2. Most of these results are not new but are needed later, and we provide independent, self-contained proofs in the appendix. Section 3 proves one of the key results of the paper: the existence of Blackwell optimal policies. In the exact MDP case, a Blackwell optimal policy is a policy that is optimal for an entire range of discount factors in the neighbourhood of 1. Existence of Blackwell optimal policies is an important result in the theory of MDPs. We extend this result to BMDPs. Then, in Section 4, we exploit the relationship between the discounted and average returns together with the existence of a Blackwell optimal policy to derive algorithms that converge to optimal value functions for both optimistic as well as pessimistic criteria.

2   Preliminaries

A Markov Decision Process is a tuple $\langle S, A, R, \{p_{(i,j)}(a)\}\rangle$. Here S is a finite set of states, A a finite set of actions, $R : S \mapsto [0, 1]$ is the reward function and $p_{i,j}(a)$ is the probability of moving to state j upon taking action a in state i. A policy $\mu : S \mapsto A$ is a mapping from states to actions. Any policy induces a Markov chain on the state space of a given MDP M. Let $\mathbb{E}_{\mu,M}[\cdot]$ denote expectation taken with respect to this Markov chain. For $\alpha \in [0, 1)$, define the α-discounted value function at state $i \in S$ by

$$V_{\alpha,\mu,M}(i) := (1 - \alpha)\mathbb{E}_{\mu,M}\left[\sum_{t=0}^{\infty} \alpha^t R(s_t) \,\middle|\, s_0 = i\right] .$$

The optimal value function is obtained by maximizing over policies.

$$V_{\alpha,M}^*(i) := \max_{\mu} V_{\alpha,\mu,M}(i) .$$

From the definition it is not obvious that there is a single policy achieving the maximum above for all $i \in S$. However, it is a fundamental result of the theory of MDPs that such an optimal policy exists.

Instead of considering the discounted sum, we can also consider the long term average reward. This leads us to the following definition.

$$V_{\mu,M}(i) := \lim_{T \to \infty} \frac{\mathbb{E}_{\mu,M}\left[\sum_{t=0}^{T} R(s_t) \,\middle|\, s_0 = i\right]}{T + 1}$$

The above definition assumes that the limit on the right hand side exists for every policy. This is shown in several standard texts [7]. There is an important relationship between the discounted and undiscounted value functions of a policy. For every policy μ, there is a function $h_{\mu,M} : S \mapsto \mathbb{R}$ such that

$$\forall i, \ V_{\mu,M}(i) = V_{\alpha,\mu,M}(i) + (1 - \alpha)h_{\mu,M}(i) + O\left(|1 - \alpha|^2\right) . \tag{1}$$

A bounded parameter MDP (BMDP) is a collection of MDPs specified by bounds on the parameters of the MDPs. For simplicity, we will assume that the reward function is fixed, so that the only parameters that vary are the transition probabilities. Suppose, for each state-action pair i, a, we are given lower and upper bounds, $l(i, j, a)$ and $u(i, j, a)$ respectively, on the transition probability $p_{i,j}(a)$. We assume that the bounds are legitimate, that is

$$\forall i, a, j, \ 0 \leq l(i, j, a) \leq u(i, j, a) ,$$

$$\forall i, a, \ \sum_{j} l(i, j, a) \leq 1 \ \& \ \sum_{j} u(i, j, a) \geq 1 .$$

This means that the set defined[1] by

$$\mathcal{C}_{i,a} := \{q \in \mathbb{R}_+^{|S|} \; : \; q^T \mathbf{1} = 1 \; \& \; \forall j, \; l(i,j,a) \leq q_j \leq u(i,j,a)\}$$

is non-empty for each state-action pair i, a. Finally, define the collection of MDPs

$$\mathcal{M} := \{ \; \langle S, A, R, \{p_{i,j}(a)\} \rangle \; : \; \forall i, a, \; p_{i,.}(a) \in \mathcal{C}_{i,a} \; \} \; .$$

Given a BMDP $\mathcal{M}$ and a policy μ, there are two natural choices for the value function: an optimistic and a pessimistic one,

$$V_{\alpha,\mu}^{\mathrm{opt}}(i) := \sup_{M \in \mathcal{M}} V_{\alpha,\mu,M}(i) \qquad\qquad V_{\alpha,\mu}^{\mathrm{pes}}(i) := \inf_{M \in \mathcal{M}} V_{\alpha,\mu,M}(i) \; .$$

We also define the undiscounted value functions,

$$V_{\mu}^{\mathrm{opt}}(i) := \sup_{M \in \mathcal{M}} V_{\mu,M}(i) \qquad\qquad V_{\mu}^{\mathrm{pes}}(i) := \inf_{M \in \mathcal{M}} V_{\mu,M}(i) \; .$$

Optimal value functions are defined by maximizing over policies.

$$\mathbf{V}_{\alpha}^{\mathrm{opt}}(i) := \max_{\mu} V_{\alpha,\mu}^{\mathrm{opt}}(i) \qquad\qquad \mathbf{V}_{\alpha}^{\mathrm{pes}}(i) := \max_{\mu} V_{\alpha,\mu}^{\mathrm{pes}}(i)$$

$$\mathbf{V}^{\mathrm{opt}}(i) := \max_{\mu} V_{\mu}^{\mathrm{opt}}(i) \qquad\qquad \mathbf{V}^{\mathrm{pes}}(i) := \max_{\mu} V_{\mu}^{\mathrm{pes}}(i)$$

In this paper, we are interested in computing $\mathbf{V}^{\mathrm{opt}}$ and $\mathbf{V}^{\mathrm{pes}}$. Algorithms to compute $\mathbf{V}_{\alpha}^{\mathrm{opt}}$ and $\mathbf{V}_{\alpha}^{\mathrm{pes}}$ have already been proposed in the literature. Let us review some of the results pertaining to the discounted case. We note that the results in this section, with the exception of Corollary 4, either appear or can easily be deduced from results appearing in [1]. However, we provide self-contained proofs of these in the appendix. Before we state the results, we need to introduce a few important operators. Note that, since $\mathcal{C}_{i,a}$ is a closed, convex set, the maximum (or minimum) of $q^T V$ (a linear function of q) appearing in the definitions below is achieved.

$$(T_{\alpha,\mu,M} V)(i) := (1-\alpha)R(i) + \alpha \sum_j p_{i,j}(\mu(i))V(j)$$

$$(T_{\alpha,M} V)(i) := \max_{a \in A} \left[(1-\alpha)R(i) + \alpha \sum_j p_{i,j}(a)V(j) \right]$$

$$(T_{\alpha,\mu}^{\mathrm{opt}} V)(i) := (1-\alpha)R(i) + \alpha \max_{q \in \mathcal{C}_{i,\mu(i)}} q^T V$$

$$(T_{\alpha}^{\mathrm{opt}} V)(i) := \max_{a \in A} \left[(1-\alpha)R(i) + \alpha \max_{q \in \mathcal{C}_{i,a}} q^T V \right]$$

$$(T_{\alpha,\mu}^{\mathrm{pes}} V)(i) := (1-\alpha)R(i) + \alpha \min_{q \in \mathcal{C}_{i,\mu(i)}} q^T V$$

$$(T_{\alpha}^{\mathrm{pes}} V)(i) := \max_{a \in A} \left[(1-\alpha)R(i) + \alpha \min_{q \in \mathcal{C}_{i,a}} q^T V \right]$$

---

[1] We denote the transpose of a vector q by q^T.

Recall that an operator T is a contraction mapping with respect to a norm $\|\cdot\|$ if there is an $\alpha \in [0,1)$ such that

$$\forall V_1, V_2, \ \|TV_1 - TV_2\| \le \alpha\|V_1 - V_2\| \ .$$

A contraction mapping has a unique solution to the fixed point equation $TV = V$ and the sequence $\{T^k V_0\}$ converges to that solution for any choice of V_0. It is straightforward to verify that the six operators defined above are contraction mappings (with factor α) with respect to the norm

$$\|V\|_\infty := \max_i |V(i)| \ .$$

It is well known that the fixed points of $T_{\alpha,\mu,M}$ and $T_{\alpha,M}$ are $V_{\alpha,\mu,M}$ and $V^*_{\alpha,M}$ respectively. The following theorem tells us what the fixed points of the remaining four operators are.

Theorem 1. *The fixed points of $T^{\mathrm{opt}}_{\alpha,\mu}, T^{\mathrm{opt}}_{\alpha}, T^{\mathrm{pes}}_{\alpha,\mu}$ and $T^{\mathrm{pes}}_{\alpha}$ are $V^{\mathrm{opt}}_{\alpha,\mu}, \mathbf{V}^{\mathrm{opt}}_{\alpha}, V^{\mathrm{pes}}_{\alpha,\mu}$ and $\mathbf{V}^{\mathrm{pes}}_{\alpha}$ respectively.*

Existence of optimal policies for BMDPs is established by the following theorem.

Theorem 2. *For any $\alpha \in [0,1)$, there exist optimal policies μ_1 and μ_2 such that, for all $i \in S$,*

$$V^{\mathrm{opt}}_{\alpha,\mu_1}(i) = \mathbf{V}^{\mathrm{opt}}_{\alpha}(i) \ ,$$
$$V^{\mathrm{pes}}_{\alpha,\mu_2}(i) = \mathbf{V}^{\mathrm{pes}}_{\alpha}(i) \ .$$

A very important fact is that out of the uncountably infinite set $\mathcal{M}$, only a finite set is of real interest.

Theorem 3. *There exist finite subsets $\mathcal{M}_{\mathrm{opt}}, \mathcal{M}_{\mathrm{pes}} \subset \mathcal{M}$ with the following property. For all $\alpha \in [0,1)$ and for every policy μ there exist $M_1 \in \mathcal{M}_{\mathrm{opt}}$, $M_2 \in \mathcal{M}_{\mathrm{pes}}$ such that*

$$V^{\mathrm{opt}}_{\alpha,\mu} = V_{\alpha,\mu,M_1} \ ,$$
$$V^{\mathrm{pes}}_{\alpha,\mu} = V_{\alpha,\mu,M_2} \ .$$

Corollary 4. *The optimal undiscounted value functions are limits of the optimal discounted value functions. That is, for all $i \in S$, we have*

$$\lim_{\alpha \to 1} \mathbf{V}^{\mathrm{opt}}_{\alpha}(i) = \mathbf{V}^{\mathrm{opt}}(i) \ , \tag{2}$$

$$\lim_{\alpha \to 1} \mathbf{V}^{\mathrm{pes}}_{\alpha}(i) = \mathbf{V}^{\mathrm{pes}}(i) \ . \tag{3}$$

Proof. Fix $i \in S$. We first prove (2). Using Theorem 3, we have

$$\mathbf{V}^{\mathrm{opt}}_{\alpha}(i) = \max_{\mu} \max_{M \in \mathcal{M}_{\mathrm{opt}}} V_{\alpha,\mu,M}(i) \ .$$

Therefore,

$$\lim_{\alpha \to 1} \mathbf{V}_\alpha^{\mathrm{opt}}(i) = \lim_{\alpha \to 1} \max_\mu \max_{M \in \mathcal{M}_{\mathrm{opt}}} V_{\alpha,\mu,M}(i)$$

$$= \max_\mu \max_{M \in \mathcal{M}_{\mathrm{opt}}} \lim_{\alpha \to 1} V_{\alpha,\mu,M}(i)$$

$$= \max_\mu \max_{M \in \mathcal{M}_{\mathrm{opt}}} V_{\mu,M}(i)$$

$$= \mathbf{V}^{\mathrm{opt}}(i) \ .$$

The second equality holds because lim and max over a finite set commute. Note that finiteness is crucial here since lim and sup do not commute. The third equality follows from (1).

To prove (3), one repeats the steps above with appropriate changes. In this case, one additionally uses the fact that lim and min over a finite set also commute.

3   Existence of Blackwell Optimal Policies

Theorem 5. *There exist* $\alpha_{\mathrm{opt}} \in (0,1)$, *a policy* μ_{opt} *and an MDP* $M_{\mathrm{opt}} \in \mathcal{M}_{\mathrm{opt}}$ *such that*

$$\forall \alpha \in (\alpha_{\mathrm{opt}}, 1), \ V_{\alpha,\mu_{\mathrm{opt}},M_{\mathrm{opt}}} = \mathbf{V}_\alpha^{\mathrm{opt}} \ .$$

Similarly, there exist $\alpha_{\mathrm{pes}} \in (0,1)$, *a policy* μ_{pes} *and an MDP* $M_{\mathrm{pes}} \in \mathcal{M}_{\mathrm{pes}}$ *such that*

$$\forall \alpha \in (\alpha_{\mathrm{pes}}, 1), \ V_{\alpha,\mu_{\mathrm{pes}},M_{\mathrm{pes}}} = \mathbf{V}_\alpha^{\mathrm{pes}} \ .$$

Proof. Given an MDP $M = \langle S, A, R, \{p_{i,j}(a)\} \rangle$ and a policy μ, define the associated matrix P_μ^M by

$$P_\mu^M(i,j) := p_{i,j}(\mu(i)) \ .$$

The value function $V_{\alpha,\mu,M}$ has a closed form expression.

$$V_{\alpha,\mu,M} = (1 - \alpha) \left(I - \alpha P_\mu^M \right)^{-1} R$$

Therefore, for all i, the map $\alpha \mapsto V_{\alpha,\mu,M}(i)$ is a rational function of α. Two rational functions are either identical or intersect each other at a finite number of points. Further, the number of policies and the number of MDPs in $\mathcal{M}_{\mathrm{opt}}$ is finite. Therefore, for each i, there exists $\alpha_i \in [0,1)$ such that no two functions in the set

$$\{\alpha \mapsto V_{\alpha,\mu,M}(i) \ : \ \mu : S \mapsto A, \ M \in \mathcal{M}_{\mathrm{opt}}\}$$

intersect each other in the interval $(\alpha_i, 1)$. Let $\alpha_{\mathrm{opt}} = \max_i \alpha_i$. By Theorem 2, there is an optimal policy, say μ_{opt}, such that

$$V_{\alpha_{\mathrm{opt}},\mu_{\mathrm{opt}}}^{\mathrm{opt}} = \mathbf{V}_{\alpha_{\mathrm{opt}}}^{\mathrm{opt}} \ .$$

By Theorem 3, there is an MDP, say M_{opt}, in $\mathcal{M}_{\mathrm{opt}}$ such that

$$V_{\alpha_{\mathrm{opt}},\mu_{\mathrm{opt}},M_{\mathrm{opt}}} = V_{\alpha_{\mathrm{opt}},\mu_{\mathrm{opt}}}^{\mathrm{opt}} = \mathbf{V}_{\alpha_{\mathrm{opt}}}^{\mathrm{opt}} \ . \tag{4}$$

We now claim that

$$V_{\alpha,\mu_{\mathrm{opt}},M_{\mathrm{opt}}} = \mathbf{V}^{\mathrm{opt}}_{\alpha_{\mathrm{opt}}}$$

for all $\alpha \in (\alpha_{\mathrm{opt}},1)$. If not, there is an $\alpha' \in (\alpha_{\mathrm{opt}},1)$, a policy μ' and an MDP $M' \in \mathcal{M}_{\mathrm{opt}}$ such that

$$V_{\alpha',\mu_{\mathrm{opt}},M_{\mathrm{opt}}}(i) < V_{\alpha',\mu',M'}(i)$$

for some i. But this yields a contradiction, since (4) holds and by definition of α_{opt}, the functions

$$\alpha \mapsto V_{\alpha,\mu_{\mathrm{opt}},M_{\mathrm{opt}}}(i)$$

and

$$\alpha \mapsto V_{\alpha,\mu',M'}(i)$$

cannot intersect in $(\alpha_{\mathrm{opt}},1)$.

The proof of the existence of $\alpha_{\mathrm{pes}}, \mu_{\mathrm{pes}}$ and M_{pes} is based on similar arguments.

4   Algorithms to Compute the Optimal Value Functions

4.1   Optimistic Value Function

The idea behind our algorithm (Algorithm 1) is to start with some initial vector and perform a sequence of updates while increasing the discount factor at a certain rate. The following theorem guarantees that the sequence of value functions thus generated converge to the optimal value function. Note that if we held the discount factor constant at some value, say α, the sequence would converge to $\mathbf{V}^{\mathrm{opt}}_\alpha$.

Algorithm 1. Algorithm to Compute $\mathbf{V}^{\mathrm{opt}}$

$V^{(0)} \leftarrow \mathbf{0}$
for $k = 0,1,\ldots$ **do**
   $\alpha_k \leftarrow \frac{k+1}{k+2}$
   for all $i \in S$ **do**
      $V^{(k+1)}(i) \leftarrow \max_{a \in A}\left[(1-\alpha_k)R(i) + \alpha_k \max_{q \in \mathcal{C}_{i,a}} q^T V^{(k)}\right]$
   end for
end for

Theorem 6. *Let $\{V^{(k)}\}$ be the sequence of functions generated by Algorithm 1. Then we have, for all $i \in S$,*

$$\lim_{k\to\infty} V^{(k)}(i) = \mathbf{V}^{\mathrm{opt}}(i) \,.$$

We need a few intermediate results before proving this theorem. Let α_{opt}, μ_{opt} and M_{opt} be as given by Theorem 5. To avoid too many subscripts, let μ and M denote μ_{opt} and M_{opt} respectively for the remainder of this subsection. From (1), we have that for k large enough, say $k \geq k_1$, we have,

$$\left| V_{\alpha_k, \mu, M}(i) - V_{\alpha_{k+1}, \mu, M}(i) \right| \leq K(\alpha_{k+1} - \alpha_k) \ , \tag{5}$$

where K can be taken to be $\|h_{\mu,M}\|_\infty + 1$. Since $\alpha_k \uparrow 1$, we have $\alpha_k > \alpha_{\mathrm{opt}}$ for all $k > k_2$ for some k_2. Let $k_0 = \max\{k_1, k_2\}$. Define

$$\delta_{k_0} := \|V^{(k_0)} - V_{\alpha_{k_0}, \mu, M}\|_\infty \ . \tag{6}$$

Since rewards are in $[0, 1]$, we have $\delta_{k_0} \leq 1$. For $k \geq k_0$, define δ_{k+1} recursively as

$$\delta_{k+1} := K(\alpha_{k+1} - \alpha_k) + \alpha_k \delta_k \ . \tag{7}$$

The following lemma shows that this sequence bounds the norm of the difference between $V^{(k)}$ and $V_{\alpha_k, \mu, M}$.

Lemma 7. *Let $\{V^{(k)}\}$ be the sequence of functions generated by Algorithm 1. Further, let μ, M denote $\mu_{\mathrm{opt}}, M_{\mathrm{opt}}$ mentioned in Theorem 5. Then, for $k \geq k_0$, we have*

$$\|V^{(k)} - V_{\alpha_k, \mu, M}\|_\infty \leq \delta_k \ .$$

Proof. Base case of $k = k_0$ is true by definition of δ_{k_0}. Now assume we have proved the claim till $k \geq k_0$. So we know that,

$$\max_i \left| V^{(k)}(i) - V_{\alpha_k, \mu, M}(i) \right| \leq \delta_k \ . \tag{8}$$

We wish to show

$$\max_i \left| V^{(k+1)}(i) - V_{\alpha_{k+1}, \mu, M}(i) \right| \leq \delta_{k+1} \ . \tag{9}$$

Recall that $\mathbf{V}_\alpha^{\mathrm{opt}}$ is the fixed point of T_α^{opt} by Theorem 1. We therefore have, for all i,

$$V_{\alpha_k, \mu, M}(i) = \left(T_{\alpha_k}^{\mathrm{opt}} V_{\alpha_k, \mu, M} \right)(i)$$

$$[\ \alpha_k > \alpha_{\mathrm{opt}} \text{ and } V_{\alpha, \mu, M} = \mathbf{V}_\alpha^{\mathrm{opt}} \text{ for } \alpha > \alpha_{\mathrm{opt}}\ ]$$

$$= \max_{a \in A} [\ (1 - \alpha_k) R(i) + \alpha_k \max_{q \in \mathcal{C}_{i,a}} \sum_j q(j) V_{\alpha_k, \mu, M}(j)\ ]$$

$$[\ \text{defn. of } T_{\alpha_k}^{\mathrm{opt}}]$$

$$\leq \max_{a \in A} [\ (1 - \alpha_k) R(i) + \alpha_k \max_{q \in \mathcal{C}_{i,a}} \sum_j q(j) V^{(k)}(j)\ ] + \alpha_k \delta_k$$

$$[\ (8) \text{ and } \sum_j q(j) \delta_k = \delta_k]$$

$$= V^{(k+1)}(i) + \alpha_k \delta_k \ .$$

$$[\ \text{defn. of } V^{(k+1)}(i)\ ]$$

Similarly, for all i,

$$V^{(k+1)}(i) = \max_{a \in A}[\ (1 - \alpha_k)R(i) + \alpha_k \max_{q \in \mathcal{C}_{i,a}} \sum_j q(j)V^{(k)}(j)\ ]$$

$[\ \text{defn. of } V^{(k+1)}(i)]$

$$\leq \max_{a \in A}[\ (1 - \alpha_k)R(i) + \alpha_k \max_{q \in \mathcal{C}_{i,a}} \sum_j q(j)V_{\alpha_k,\mu,M}(j)\ ] + \alpha_k\delta_k$$

$[\ (8) \text{ and } \sum_j q(j)\delta_k = \delta_k]$

$$= \left(T_{\alpha_k}^{\mathrm{opt}} V_{\alpha_k,\mu,M}\right)(i) + \alpha_k\delta_k$$

$[\ \text{defn. of } T_{\alpha_k}^{\mathrm{opt}}]$

$$= V_{\alpha_k,\mu,M}(i) + \alpha_k\delta_k\ .$$

$[\ \alpha_k > \alpha_{\mathrm{opt}} \text{ and } V_{\alpha,\mu,M} = \mathbf{V}_\alpha^{\mathrm{opt}} \text{ for } \alpha > \alpha_{\mathrm{opt}}\ ]$

Thus, for all i,

$$\left|V^{(k+1)}(i) - V_{\alpha_k,\mu,M}(i)\right| \leq \alpha_k\delta_k\ .$$

Combining this with (5) (as $k \geq k_0 \geq k_1$), we get

$$\left|V^{(k+1)}(i) - V_{\alpha_{k+1},\mu,M}(i)\right| \leq \alpha_k\delta_k + K(\alpha_{k+1} - \alpha_k)\ .$$

Thus we have shown (9).

The sequence $\{\delta_k\}$ can be shown to converge to zero using elementary arguments.

Lemma 8. *The sequence $\{\delta_k\}$ defined for $k \geq k_0$ by equations (6) and (7) converges to 0.*

Proof. Plugging $\alpha_k = \frac{k+1}{k+2}$ into the definition of δ_{k+1} we get,

$$\delta_{k+1} = K\left(\frac{k+2}{k+3} - \frac{k+1}{k+2}\right) + \frac{k+1}{k+2}\delta_k$$

$$= \frac{K}{(k+3)(k+2)} + \frac{k+1}{k+2}\delta_k\ .$$

Applying the recursion again for δ_k, we get

$$\delta_{k+1} = \frac{K}{(k+3)(k+2)} + \frac{k+1}{k+2}\left(\frac{K}{(k+2)(k+1)} + \frac{k}{k+1}\delta_{k-1}\right)$$

$$= \frac{K}{k+2}\left(\frac{1}{k+3} + \frac{1}{k+2}\right) + \frac{k}{k+2}\delta_{k-1}\ .$$

Continuing in this fashion, we get for any $j \geq 0$,

$$\delta_{k+1} = \frac{K}{k+2}\left(\frac{1}{k+3} + \frac{1}{k+2} + \dots + \frac{1}{k-j+3}\right) + \frac{k-j+1}{k+2}\delta_{k-j}\ .$$

Setting $j = k - k_0$ above, we get

$$\delta_{k+1} = \frac{K}{k+2}(H_{k+3} - H_{k_0+2}) + \frac{k_0+1}{k+2}\delta_{k_0} ,$$

where $H_n = 1 + \frac{1}{2} + \ldots + \frac{1}{n}$. This clearly tends to 0 as $k \to \infty$ since $H_n = O(\log n)$ and $\delta_{k_0} \le 1$.

We can now prove Theorem 6.

Proof. (of Theorem 6) Fix $i \in S$. We have,

$$|V^{(k)}(i) - \mathbf{V}^{\text{opt}}(i)| \le \underbrace{|V^{(k)}(i) - V_{\alpha_k,\mu,M}(i)|}_{\le \delta_k} + \underbrace{|V_{\alpha_k,\mu,M}(i) - \mathbf{V}^{\text{opt}}_{\alpha_k}(i)|}_{\epsilon_k}$$
$$+ \underbrace{|\mathbf{V}^{\text{opt}}_{\alpha_k}(i) - \mathbf{V}^{\text{opt}}(i)|}_{\zeta_k} .$$

We use Lemma 7 to bound the first summand on the right hand side by δ_k. By Lemma 8, $\delta_k \to 0$. Also, $\epsilon_k = 0$ for sufficiently large k because $\alpha_k \uparrow 1$ and $V_{\alpha,\mu,M}(i) = \mathbf{V}^{\text{opt}}_{\alpha}(i)$ for α sufficiently close to 1 (by Theorem 5). Finally, $\zeta_k \to 0$ by Corollary 4.

4.2 Pessimistic Value Function

Algorithm 2 is the same as Algorithm 1 except that the max over $\mathcal{C}_{i,a}$ appearing inside the innermost loop gets replaced by a min. The following analogue of Theorem 6 holds.

Algorithm 2. Algorithm to Compute $\mathbf{V}^{\text{pes}}$

$V^{(0)} \leftarrow \mathbf{0}$
for $k = 0, 1, \ldots$ **do**
  $\alpha_k \leftarrow \frac{k+1}{k+2}$
  for all $i \in S$ **do**
    $V^{(k+1)}(i) \leftarrow \max_{a \in A} \left[(1 - \alpha_k)R(i) + \alpha_k \min_{q \in \mathcal{C}_{i,a}} q^T V^{(k)} \right]$
  end for
end for

Theorem 9. *Let $\{V^{(k)}\}$ be the sequence of functions generated by Algorithm 2. Then we have, for all $i \in S$,*

$$\lim_{k \to \infty} V^{(k)}(i) = \mathbf{V}^{\text{pes}}(i) .$$

To prove this theorem, we repeat the argument given in the previous subsection with appropriate changes. Let α_{pes}, μ_{pes} and M_{pes} be as given by Theorem 5. For the remainder of this subsection, let μ and M denote μ_{pes} and M_{pes} respectively. Let k_1, k_2 be large enough so that, for all $k \ge k_1$,

$$|V_{\alpha_k,\mu,M}(i) - V_{\alpha_{k+1},\mu,M}(i)| \le K(\alpha_{k+1} - \alpha_k) ,$$

for some constant K (which depends on μ, M), and $\alpha_k > \alpha_{\text{pes}}$ for $k > k_2$. Set $k_0 = \max\{k_1, k_2\}$ and define the sequence $\{\delta_k\}_{k \geq k_0}$ as before (equations (6) and (7)).

The proof of the following lemma can be obtained from that of Lemma 7 by fairly straightforward changes and is therefore omitted.

Lemma 10. *Let* $\{V^{(k)}\}$ *be the sequence of functions generated by Algorithm 2. Further, let* μ, M *denote* $\mu_{\text{pes}}, M_{\text{pes}}$ *mentioned in Theorem 5. Then, for* $k \geq k_0$, *we have*

$$\|V^{(k)} - V_{\alpha_k, \mu, M}\|_\infty \leq \delta_k .$$

Theorem 9 is now proved in exactly the same fashion as Theorem 6 and we therefore omit the proof.

5 Conclusion

In this paper, we chose to represent the uncertainty in the parameters of an MDP by intervals. One can ask whether similar results can be derived for other representations. If the intervals for $p_{i,j}(a)$ are equal for all j then our representation corresponds to an L_∞ ball around a probability vector. It will be interesting to investigate other metrics and even non-metrics like relative entropy (for an example of an algorithm using sets defined by relative entropy, see [8]). Generalizing in a different direction, we can enrich the language used to express constraints on the probabilities. In this paper, constraints had the form

$$l(i, j, a) \leq p_{i,j}(a) \leq u(i, j, a) .$$

These are simple inequality constraints with two hyperparameters $l(i, j, a)$ and $u(i, j, a)$. We can permit more hyperparameters and include arbitrary semi-algebraic constraints (i.e. constraints expressible as boolean combination of polynomial equalities and inequalities). It can be shown using the Tarski-Seidenberg theorem that Blackwell optimal policies still exist in this much more general setting. However, the problem of optimizing $q^T V$ over $C_{i,a}$ now becomes more complicated.

Our last remark is regarding the convergence rate of the algorithms given in Section 4. Examining the proofs, one can verify that the number of iterations required to get to within ϵ accuracy is $O(\frac{1}{\epsilon})$. This is a pseudo-polynomial convergence rate. It might be possible to obtain algorithms where the number of iterations required to achieve ϵ-accuracy is poly$(\log \frac{1}{\epsilon})$.

Acknowledgments

We gratefully acknowledge the support of DARPA under grant FA8750-05-2-0249.

References

1. Givan, R., Leach, S., Dean, T.: Bounded-parameter Markov decision processes. Artificial Intelligence 122, 71–109 (2000)
2. Strehl, A.L., Littman, M.: A theoretical analysis of model-based interval estimation. In: Proceedings of the Twenty-Second International Conference on Machine Learning, pp. 857–864. ACM Press, New York (2005)
3. Auer, P., Ortner, R.: Logarithmic online regret bounds for undiscounted reinforcement learning. In: dvances in Neural Information Processing Systems 19, MIT Press, Cambridge (2007) (to appear)
4. Brafman, R.I., Tennenholtz, M.: R-MAX – a general polynomial time algorithm for near-optimal reinforcement learning. Journal of Machine Learning Research 3, 213–231 (2002)
5. Even-Dar, E., Mansour, Y.: Convergence of optimistic and incremental Q-learning. In: Advances in Neural Information Processing Systems 14, pp. 1499–1506. MIT Press, Cambridge (2001)
6. Nilim, A., El Ghaoui, L.: Robust control of Markov decision processes with uncertain transition matrices. Operations Research 53, 780–798 (2005)
7. Bertsekas, D.P.: Dynamic Programming and Optimal Control. Vol. 2. Athena Scientific, Belmont, MA (1995)
8. Burnetas, A.N., Katehakis, M.N.: Optimal adaptive policies for Markov decision processes. Mathematics of Operations Research 22, 222–255 (1997)

Appendix

Throughout this section, vector inequalities of the form $V_1 \leq V_2$ are to be interpreted to mean $V_1(i) \leq V_2(i)$ for all i.

Proofs of Theorems 1 and 2

Lemma 11. *If $V_1 \leq V_2$ then, for all $M \in \mathcal{M}$,*

$$T_{\alpha,\mu,M}V_1 \leq T_{\alpha,\mu}^{\mathrm{opt}}V_2 \ ,$$
$$T_{\alpha,\mu}^{\mathrm{pes}}V_1 \leq T_{\alpha,\mu,M}V_2 \ .$$

Proof. We prove the first inequality. Fix an MDP $M \in \mathcal{M}$. Let $p_{i,j}(a)$ denote transition probabilities of M. We then have,

$$(T_{\alpha,\mu,M}V_1)(i) = (1-\alpha)R(i) + \alpha \sum_j p_{i,j}(\mu(i))V_1(j)$$

$$\leq (1-\alpha)R(i) + \alpha \sum_j p_{i,j}(\mu(i))V_2(j) \qquad [\because V_1 \leq V_2]$$

$$\leq (1-\alpha)R(i) + \alpha \max_{q \in \mathcal{C}_{i,\mu(i)}} q^T V_2 \qquad [\because M \in \mathcal{M}]$$

$$= (T_{\alpha,\mu}^{\mathrm{opt}}V_2)(i) \ .$$

The proof of the second inequality is similar.

Lemma 12. *If $V_1 \leq V_2$ then, for any policy μ,*

$$T_{\alpha,\mu}^{\mathrm{opt}}V_1 \leq T_\alpha^{\mathrm{opt}}V_2 \; ,$$
$$T_{\alpha,\mu}^{\mathrm{pes}}V_1 \leq T_\alpha^{\mathrm{pes}}V_2 \; .$$

Proof. Again, we prove only the first inequality. Fix a policy μ. We then have,

$$\begin{aligned}
\left(T_{\alpha,\mu}^{\mathrm{opt}}V_1\right)(i) &= (1-\alpha)R(i) + \alpha \max_{q \in \mathcal{C}_{i,\mu(i)}} q^T V_1 \\
&\leq (1-\alpha)R(i) + \alpha \max_{q \in \mathcal{C}_{i,\mu(i)}} q^T V_2 \\
&\leq \max_{a \in A} \left[(1-\alpha)R(i) + \alpha \max_{q \in \mathcal{C}_{i,a}} q^T V_2\right] \\
&= \left(T_\alpha^{\mathrm{opt}}V_2\right)(i)
\end{aligned}$$

Proof (of Theorems 1 and 2). Let $\tilde{V}$ be the fixed point of $T_{\alpha,\mu}^{\mathrm{opt}}$. This means that for all $i \in S$,

$$\tilde{V}(i) = (1-\alpha)R(i) + \alpha \max_{q \in \mathcal{C}_{i,\mu(i)}} q^T \tilde{V} \; .$$

We wish to show that $\tilde{V} = V_{\alpha,\mu}^{\mathrm{opt}}$. Let q_i be the probability vector that achieves the maximum above. Construct an MDP $M_1 \in \mathcal{M}$ as follows. Set the transition probability vector $p_{i,.}(\mu(i))$ to be q_i. For $a \neq \mu(i)$, choose $p_{i,.}(a)$ to be any element of $\mathcal{C}_{i,a}$. It is clear that $\tilde{V}$ satisfies, for all $i \in S$,

$$\tilde{V}(i) = (1-\alpha)R(i) + \alpha \sum_j p_{i,j}(\mu(i))\tilde{V}(j) \; ,$$

and therefore $\tilde{V} = V_{\alpha,\mu,M_1} \leq V_{\alpha,\mu}^{\mathrm{opt}}$. It remains to show that $\tilde{V} \geq V_{\alpha,\mu}^{\mathrm{opt}}$. For that, fix an arbitrary MDP $M \in \mathcal{M}$. Let V_0 be any initial vector. Using Lemma 11 and straightforward induction, we get

$$\forall k \geq 0, \; (T_{\alpha,\mu,M})^k V_0 \leq (T_{\alpha,\mu}^{\mathrm{opt}})^k V_0 \; .$$

Taking limits as $k \to \infty$, we get $V_{\alpha,\mu,M} \leq \tilde{V}$. Since $M \in \mathcal{M}$ was arbitrary, for any $i \in S$,

$$V_{\alpha,\mu}^{\mathrm{opt}}(i) = \sup_{M \in \mathcal{M}} V_{\alpha,\mu,M}(i) \leq \tilde{V}(i) \; .$$

Therefore, $\tilde{V} = V_{\alpha,\mu}^{\mathrm{opt}}$.

Now let $\tilde{V}$ be the fixed point of T_α^{opt}. This means that for all $i \in S$,

$$\tilde{V}(i) = \max_{a \in A} \left[(1-\alpha)R(i) + \alpha \max_{q \in \mathcal{C}_{i,a}} q^T \tilde{V}\right] \; .$$

We wish to show that $\tilde{V} = \mathbf{V}_\alpha^{\mathrm{opt}}$. Let $\mu_1(i)$ be any action that achieves the maximum above. Since $\tilde{V}$ satisfies, for all $i \in S$,

$$\tilde{V}(i) = (1-\alpha)R(i) + \alpha \max_{q \in \mathcal{C}_{i,\mu_1(i)}} q^T \tilde{V} \; ,$$

we have $\tilde{V} = V_{\alpha,\mu_1}^{\mathrm{opt}} \leq \mathbf{V}_\alpha^{\mathrm{opt}}$. It remains to show that $\tilde{V} \geq \mathbf{V}_\alpha^{\mathrm{opt}}$. For that, fix an arbitrary policy μ. Let V_0 be any initial vector. Using Lemma 12 and straightforward induction, we get

$$\forall k \geq 0, \ (T_{\alpha,\mu}^{\mathrm{opt}})^k V_0 \leq (T_\alpha^{\mathrm{opt}})^k V_0 .$$

Taking limits as $k \to \infty$, we get $V_{\alpha,\mu}^{\mathrm{opt}} \leq \tilde{V}$. Since μ was arbitrary, for any $i \in S$,

$$\mathbf{V}_\alpha^{\mathrm{opt}}(i) = \max_\mu V_{\alpha,\mu}^{\mathrm{opt}}(i) \leq \tilde{V}(i) .$$

Therefore, $\tilde{V} = \mathbf{V}_\alpha^{\mathrm{opt}}$. Moreover, this also proves the first part of Theorem 2 since

$$V_{\alpha,\mu_1}^{\mathrm{opt}} = \tilde{V} = \mathbf{V}_\alpha^{\mathrm{opt}} .$$

The claim that the fixed points of $T_{\alpha,\mu}^{\mathrm{pes}}$ and T_α^{pes} are $V_{\alpha,\mu}^{\mathrm{pes}}$ and $\mathbf{V}_\alpha^{\mathrm{pes}}$ respectively, is proved by making a few obvious changes to the argument above. Further, as it turned out above, the argument additionally yields the proof of the second part of Theorem 2.

Proof of Theorem 3

We prove the existence of $\mathcal{M}_{\mathrm{opt}}$ only. The existence of $\mathcal{M}_{\mathrm{pes}}$ is proved in the same way. Note that in the proof presented in the previous subsection, given a policy μ, we explicitly constructed an MDP M_1 such that $V_{\alpha,\mu}^{\mathrm{opt}} = V_{\alpha,\mu,M_1}$. Further, the transition probability vector $p_{i,\cdot}(\mu(i))$ of M_1 was a vector that achieved the maximum in

$$\max_{\mathcal{C}_{i,\mu(i)}} q^T V_{\alpha,\mu}^{\mathrm{opt}} .$$

Recall that the set $\mathcal{C}_{i,\mu(i)}$ has the form

$$\{q \ : \ q^T \mathbf{1} = 1, \ \forall j \in S, \ l_j \leq q_j \leq u_j\} , \tag{10}$$

where $l_j = l(i,j,\mu(i))$, $u_j = u(i,j,\mu(i))$. Therefore, all that we require is the following lemma.

Lemma 13. *Given a set $\mathcal{C}$ of the form (10), there exists a finite set $Q = Q(\mathcal{C})$ of cardinality no more than $|S|!$ with the following property. For any vector V, there exists $\tilde{q} \in Q$ such that*

$$\tilde{q}^T V = \max_{q \in \mathcal{C}} q^T V .$$

We can then set

$$\mathcal{M}_{\mathrm{opt}} = \{ \ \langle S, A, R, \{p_{i,j}(a)\} \rangle \ : \ \forall i, a, \ p_{i,\cdot}(a) \in Q(\mathcal{C}_{i,a}) \ \} .$$

The cardinality of $\mathcal{M}_{\mathrm{opt}}$ is at most $(|S||A|)|S|!$

Proof (of Lemma 13). A simple greedy algorithm (Algorithm 3) can be used to find a maximizing $\tilde{q}$. The set $\mathcal{C}$ is specified using upper and lower bounds, denoted by u_i and l_i respectively. The algorithm uses the following idea recursively. Suppose i^* is the index of a largest component of V. It is clear that we should set $\tilde{q}(i^*)$ as large as possible. The value of $\tilde{q}(i^*)$ has to be less than u_i. Moreover, it has to be less than $1 - \sum_{i \neq i^*} l_i$. Otherwise, the remaining lower bound constraints cannot be met. So, we set $\tilde{q}(i^*)$ to be the minimum of these two quantities.

Note that the output depends only on the sorted order of the components of V. Hence, there are only $|S|!$ choices for $\tilde{q}$.

Algorithm 3. A greedy algorithm to maximize $q^T V$ over $\mathcal{C}$.

INPUTS The vector V and the set $\mathcal{C}$. The latter is specified by bounds $\{l_i\}_{i \in S}$ and $\{u_i\}_{i \in S}$ that satisfy $\forall i, 0 \leq l_i \leq u_i$ and $\sum_i l_i \leq 1 \leq \sum_i u_i$.
OUTPUT A maximizing vector $\tilde{q} \in \mathcal{C}$.

$indices \leftarrow$ **order**(V) $\triangleright$ **order**(V) gives the indices of the largest to smallest elements of V

$massLeft \leftarrow 1$
$indicesLeft \leftarrow S$
for all $i \in indices$ **do**
    $elem \leftarrow V(i)$
    $lowerBoundSum \leftarrow \sum_{j \in indicesLeft, j \neq i} l_j$
    $\tilde{q}(i) \leftarrow \min(u_i, massLeft - lowerBoundSum)$
    $massLeft \leftarrow massLeft - \tilde{q}(i)$
    $indicesLeft \leftarrow indicesLeft - \{i\}$
end for
return $\tilde{q}$

On-Line Estimation with the Multivariate Gaussian Distribution

Sanjoy Dasgupta and Daniel Hsu

University of California, San Diego
{dasgupta,djhsu}@cs.ucsd.edu

Abstract. We consider on-line density estimation with the multivariate Gaussian distribution. In each of a sequence of trials, the learner must posit a mean $\boldsymbol{\mu}$ and covariance $\boldsymbol{\Sigma}$; the learner then receives an instance $\boldsymbol{x}$ and incurs loss equal to the negative log-likelihood of $\boldsymbol{x}$ under the Gaussian density parameterized by $(\boldsymbol{\mu}, \boldsymbol{\Sigma})$. We prove bounds on the regret for the follow-the-leader strategy, which amounts to choosing the sample mean and covariance of the previously seen data.

1 Introduction

We consider an on-line learning problem based on Gaussian density estimation in $\mathbb{R}^d$. The learning task proceeds in a sequence of trials. In trial t, the learner selects a mean $\boldsymbol{\mu}_t$ and covariance $\boldsymbol{\Sigma}_t$. Then, Nature reveals an instance $\boldsymbol{x}_t$ to the learner, and the learner incurs a loss $\ell_t(\boldsymbol{\mu}_t, \boldsymbol{\Sigma}_t)$ equal to the negative log-likelihood of $\boldsymbol{x}_t$ under the Gaussian density parameterized by $(\boldsymbol{\mu}_t, \boldsymbol{\Sigma}_t)$.

We will compare the total loss incurred from selecting the $(\boldsymbol{\mu}_t, \boldsymbol{\Sigma}_t)$ in T trials to the total loss incurred using the best *fixed strategy* for the T trials. A fixed strategy is one that sets $(\boldsymbol{\mu}_t, \boldsymbol{\Sigma}_t)$ to the same $(\boldsymbol{\mu}, \boldsymbol{\Sigma})$ for each t. The difference of these total losses is the *regret* of following a strategy and not instead selecting this best-in-hindsight $(\boldsymbol{\mu}, \boldsymbol{\Sigma})$ in every trial; it is the cost of not seeing all of the data ahead of time. In this paper, we will analyze the regret of the *follow-the-leader* strategy: the strategy which chooses $(\boldsymbol{\mu}_t, \boldsymbol{\Sigma}_t)$ to be the sample mean and covariance of $\{\boldsymbol{x}_1, \boldsymbol{x}_2, \ldots, \boldsymbol{x}_{t-1}\}$.

First, we find that a naïve formulation of the learning problem suffers from degenerate cases that lead to unbounded regret. We propose a straightforward alternative that avoids these problems by incorporating an additional, hallucinated, trial at time zero. In this setting, a trivial upper bound on the regret of follow-the-leader (FTL) is $O(T^2)$ after T trials. We obtain the following bounds.

- For any $p > 1$, there are sequences $(\boldsymbol{x}_t)$ for which FTL has regret $\Omega(T^{1-1/p})$ after T trials. A similar result holds for any sublinear function of T.
- There is a linear bound on the regret of FTL that holds for all sequences.
- For any sequence, the average regret of FTL is ≤ 0 in the limit; formally,

$$\text{For any sequence } (\boldsymbol{x}_t), \ \limsup_{T \geq 1} \left\{ \frac{\text{Regret after } T \text{ trials}}{T} \right\} \leq 0.$$

N. Bshouty and C. Gentile (Eds.): COLT 2007, LNAI 4539, pp. 278–292, 2007.

On-line density estimation has been previously considered by Freund (1996), Azoury and Warmuth (2001), and Takimoto and Warmuth (2000a, 2000b). Collectively, they have considered the Bernoulli, Gamma, and fixed-covariance Gaussian distributions, as well as a general class of one-dimensional exponential families. However, on-line Gaussian density estimation with arbitrary covariance (that is, when the covariance is to be estimated) is all but unmentioned in the literature, even in the one-dimensional case. Indeed, these earlier bounds are logarithmic whereas most of ours are linear, a clear sign of a very different regime.

Learning a covariance matrix on-line is the main challenge not present in earlier analyses. Even in the univariate case, the total loss of the best fixed strategy in hindsight after T trials can lie anywhere in the range $[T - T \log T, \, T]$ (constants suppressed), while a learner that predicts a fixed variance $\sigma_t^2 \equiv c$ in every trial t will incur a total loss of at least $T \ln c$. This leaves the regret on the order of $T \log T$ in the worst case. Thus, even a linear regret bound is out of reach unless one makes an effort to estimate the variance.

Letting $\sigma^2(t)$ denote the sample variance of the first t observations, it turns out that our regret lower bounds are determined by sequences for which $\sigma^2(t) \to 0$ as t goes to infinity. On the other hand, if $\liminf \sigma^2(t) > 0$ – that is, if $\sigma^2(t)$ stays above a fixed constant for all $t > T_0$ – then it is easy to see from Lemmas 1 and 2 that the regret after T trials ($T > T_0$) is $O(T_0 + \log(T/T_0))$. Thus, our results show that the performance of FTL depends on which of these two regimes the data falls under.

1.1   Related Work

On-line density estimation is a special case of sequential prediction with expert advice, a rich and widely applicable framework with roots in information theory, learning theory, and game theory (Cesa-Bianchi and Lugosi, 2006). In on-line density estimation, the set of experts is often an uncountably-infinite set, and the experts' predictions in a trial t only depend on the outcome $\boldsymbol{x}_t$ determined by Nature. Similar in spirit to density estimation is on-line subspace tracking (Crammer, 2006; Warmuth and Kuzmin, 2006). In the setup of Warmuth and Kuzmin, experts are low-dimensional linear subspaces, and the loss is the squared distance of $\boldsymbol{x}_t$ to the subspace (as in PCA).

We already mentioned work by Freund (1996), Azoury and Warmuth (2001), and Takimoto and Warmuth (2000a, 2000b). In each of the cases they considered, the regret bound is at most logarithmic in the number of trials. For the Bernoulli distribution, Freund showed that the Bayes algorithm with Jeffrey's prior asymptotically achieves the minimax regret. For the fixed-covariance Gaussian, Takimoto and Warmuth gave a recursively-defined strategy that achieves the minimax regret of $(r^2/2)(\ln T - \ln \ln T + O(\ln \ln T / \ln T))$, where $\|\boldsymbol{x}_t\| \leq r$ for all $1 \leq t \leq T$.

Recent algorithms and frameworks for general on-line convex optimization (Zinkevich, 2003; Hazan et al, 2006; Shalev-Shwartz and Singer, 2006) are applicable to, among several other machine learning problems, many on-line density estimation tasks. However, they crucially rely on features of the loss function not enjoyed by the negative logarithm of the Gaussian density (e.g. finite minima, bounded derivatives). The follow-the-leader strategy and its variants are also applicable to many problems (Hannan, 1957; Kalai and Vempala, 2005; Zinke-vich, 2003; Hazan et al, 2006). While FTL does not guarantee sublinear regret in many settings, several of the on-line density estimation algorithms derived by Azoury and Warmuth (2001) are special cases of FTL and do have logarithmic regret bounds.

2   On-Line Univariate Gaussian Density Estimation

To build intuition, we first demonstrate our results in the one-dimensional case before showing them in the general multivariate setting.

The learning protocol is as follows.

> For trial $t = 1, 2, \ldots$
> - The learner selects $\mu_t \in \mathbb{R}$ and $\sigma_t^2 \in \mathbb{R}_{>0} \triangleq \{x \in \mathbb{R} : x > 0\}$.
> - Nature selects $x_t \in \mathbb{R}$ and reveals it to the learner.
> - The learner incurs loss $\ell_t(\mu_t, \sigma_t^2)$ (ℓ_t implicitly depends on x_t).

The loss $\ell_t(\mu, \sigma^2)$ is the negative log-likelihood of x_t under the Gaussian density with mean μ and variance σ^2 (omitting the constant 2π),

$$\ell_t(\mu, \sigma^2) \triangleq -\ln \frac{1}{\sqrt{\sigma^2}} \exp\left\{ -\frac{(x_t - \mu)^2}{2\sigma^2} \right\} = \frac{(x_t - \mu)^2}{2\sigma^2} + \frac{1}{2} \ln \sigma^2 \qquad (1)$$

Suppose, over the course of the learning task, a strategy S prescribes the sequence of means and variances $((\mu_t, \sigma_t^2) : t = 1, 2, \ldots)$. We denote by $L_T(S)$ the total loss incurred by the learner following strategy S after T trials, and by $L_T(\mu, \sigma^2)$ the total loss incurred by the learner following the fixed strategy that selects $(\mu_t, \sigma_t^2) = (\mu, \sigma^2)$ for each trial t. So, we have

$$L_T(S) \triangleq \sum_{t=1}^{T} \ell_t(\mu_t, \sigma_t^2) \quad \text{and} \quad L_T(\mu, \sigma^2) \triangleq \sum_{t=1}^{T} \ell_t(\mu, \sigma^2). \qquad (2)$$

The learner seeks to adopt a strategy so that the regret after T trials

$$R_T(S) \triangleq L_T(S) - \inf_{\mu \in \mathbb{R}, \sigma^2 \in \mathbb{R}_{>0}} L_T(\mu, \sigma^2) \qquad (3)$$

is as small as possible, even when Nature selects the x_t adversarially. Notice that, because $L_T(\mu, \sigma^2)$ is the likelihood of $\{x_1, x_2, \ldots, x_T\}$ under a single Gaussian model, the infimum in (3) is a maximum likelihood problem.

2.1   Degeneracies

Unfortunately, as the setting currently stands, the learner is doomed by two degen-eracies that lead to unbounded regret. First, since we haven't restricted the mag-nitudes of the x_t, the regret can be unbounded even after just one trial. Takimoto and Warmuth (2000b) note that this is an issue even with fixed-variance Gaussian density estimation. Their remedy is to assume all $|x_t| \le r$ for some $r \ge 0$, and we will do the same.

The second degeneracy is specific to allowing arbitrary variances and arises when the x_t are very close to each other. In fact, it stems from a standard difficulty with maximum likelihood estimation of Gaussians. To see the problem, suppose that the first few observations $x_1, x_2, \ldots, x_T$ are all the same. Then, while any reasonable learner must have set some nonzero variances σ_t^2 for $t = 1, 2, \ldots, T$ (for fear of facing an infinite penalty), the infimum of $L_T(\mu, \sigma^2)$ is $-\infty$ because the true variance of the data is 0. In fact, even if the x_t are not all the same, they can still be arbitrarily close together, leaving the infimum unbounded from below.

Our remedy is to hallucinate a zeroth trial that precludes the above degeneracy; it provides some small amount of variance, even if all the subsequent observations x_t are closely bunched together. Specifically, let $\tilde{\sigma}^2 > 0$ be some fixed constant. In the zeroth trial, we cause the learner to incur a loss of

$$\ell_0(\mu, \sigma^2) \triangleq \frac{1}{2} \sum_{x \in \{\pm\tilde{\sigma}\}} \left(\frac{(x - \mu)^2}{2\sigma^2} + \frac{1}{2} \ln \sigma^2 \right) = \frac{\mu^2 + \tilde{\sigma}^2}{2\sigma^2} + \frac{1}{2} \ln \sigma^2.$$

Essentially, we hallucinate two instances, $\tilde{\sigma}$ and $-\tilde{\sigma}$, and incur half of the usual loss on each point.[1] This can be interpreted as assuming that there is some non-negligible variation in the sequence of instances, and for convenience, that it appears up front. We need to include the zeroth trial loss in the total loss after T trials. Thus, (2) should now read

$$L_T(S) \triangleq \sum_{t=0}^{T} \ell_t(\mu_t, \sigma_t^2) \quad \text{and} \quad L_T(\mu, \sigma^2) \triangleq \sum_{t=0}^{T} \ell_t(\mu, \sigma^2).$$

It can be shown that the infimum in (3) is always finite with the redefined $L_T(\mu, \sigma^2)$. With the extra zeroth trial, the infimum is no longer the Gaussian maximum likelihood problem; nevertheless, the form of the new optimization problem is similar. We have

$$\inf_{\mu \in \mathbb{R}, \sigma^2 \in \mathbb{R}_{>0}} L_T(\mu, \sigma^2) = L_T(\overline{\mu}_T, \overline{\sigma}_T^2) = \frac{T+1}{2} + \frac{T+1}{2} \ln \overline{\sigma}_T^2 > -\infty \quad (4)$$

for any $T \ge 0$, where

$$\overline{\mu}_T = \frac{1}{T+1} \sum_{t=1}^{T} x_t \quad \text{and} \quad \overline{\sigma}_T^2 = \frac{1}{T+1} \left(\tilde{\sigma}^2 + \sum_{t=1}^{T} x_t^2 \right) - \overline{\mu}^2 \ge \frac{\tilde{\sigma}^2}{T+1}$$

(the last inequality follows from Cauchy-Schwarz).

Before continuing, we pause to recap our notation and setting.

- $(\mu_t, \sigma_t^2) \in \mathbb{R} \times \mathbb{R}_{>0}$: parameters selected by the learner in trial $t \ge 0$.
- $x_t \in [-r, r]$: instances revealed to the learner in trial $t \ge 1$.

---

[1] Or, we take the expected loss of a zero-mean random variable with variance $\tilde{\sigma}^2$.

- $\ell_t(\mu, \sigma^2)$: loss incurred for selecting (μ, σ^2) in trial $t \geq 0$.
- $L_T(S)$: total loss of strategy S after T trials $(t = 1, 2, \ldots, T)$, plus the loss incurred in the hallucinated zeroth trial $(t = 0)$.
- $R_T(S) = L_T(S) - \inf_{(\mu, \sigma^2)} L_T(\mu, \sigma^2)$: regret after T trials of strategy S.

2.2   Follow-the-Leader

Motivated by the simplicity and success of the follow-the-leader based strategies for on-line density estimation with other distributions (Azoury and Warmuth, 2001), we instantiate such a strategy for on-line Gaussian density estimation. The name suggests using, in trial t, the setting of (μ, σ^2) that minimizes $L_{t-1}(\mu, \sigma^2)$. We will denote this setting as (μ_t, σ_t^2). It is precisely the values $(\overline{\mu}_{t-1}, \overline{\sigma}_{t-1}^2)$ given above; without the benefit of foresight, FTL is always one step behind the optimal strategy.

As noted in (Azoury and Warmuth, 2001), using FTL for on-line density estimation with exponential families leads to an intuitive recursive update. For the Gaussian distribution, it is

$$\mu_{t+1} = \mu_t + \frac{1}{t+1}(x_t - \mu_t) \text{ and } \sigma_{t+1}^2 = \frac{t}{t+1}\sigma_t^2 + \frac{t}{(t+1)^2}(x_t - \mu_t)^2 \quad (5)$$

for $t \geq 1$. The loss function in the zeroth trial is fully known; so in the base cases, we have $(\mu_0, \sigma_0^2) = (0, \tilde{\sigma}^2)$ to optimize $\ell_0(\mu, \sigma^2)$, and $(\mu_1, \sigma_1^2) = (\mu_0, \sigma_0^2)$ as per FTL.

It will prove useful to derive an alternative expression for σ_t^2 by expanding the recursion in (5). We have $(t+1)\sigma_{t+1}^2 - t\sigma_t^2 = (t/(t+1)) \cdot (x_t - \mu_t)^2$ for $t \geq 1$; by telescoping,

$$\sigma_t^2 = \frac{1}{t}\left(\tilde{\sigma}^2 + \sum_{i=1}^{t-1} \Delta_i\right) \text{ where } \Delta_t \triangleq \frac{t}{t+1}(x_t - \mu_t)^2. \quad (6)$$

2.3   Regret of Following the Leader

We obtain an expression for the regret $R_T \triangleq R_T(FTL)$ after T trials by analyzing the telescoping sum of $R_t - R_{t-1}$ from $t = 1$ to T. The difference $R_t - R_{t-1}$ is the *penalty* incurred by FTL for the additional trial t. The output our analysis will allow us to extract the core contribution of additional trials to the regret. Looking ahead, we'll show lower and upper bounds on the regret by focusing on this part of $R_t - R_{t-1}$.

Lemma 1. *The regret of FTL after T trials satisfies the bounds*

$$R_T \leq \sum_{t=1}^{T} \frac{1}{4(t+1)}\left[\frac{(x_t - \mu_t)^2}{\sigma_t^2}\right]^2 + \frac{1}{4}\ln(T+1) + \frac{1}{12} \quad and$$

$$R_T \geq \sum_{t=1}^{T}\left(\frac{1}{4(t+1)}\left[\frac{(x_t - \mu_t)^2}{\sigma_t^2}\right]^2 - \frac{1}{6(t+1)^2}\left[\frac{(x_t - \mu_t)^2}{\sigma_t^2}\right]^3\right) + \frac{1}{4}\ln(T+1).$$

Proof. First, we make substitutions in $R_t - R_{t-1}$ using the FTL update rule (5) and the minimizer of $L_T(\mu, \sigma^2)$ (from (4)):

$$
\begin{aligned}
R_t - R_{t-1} &= (L_t(FTL) - L_t(\mu_{t+1}, \sigma_{t+1}^2)) - (L_{t-1}(FTL) - L_{t-1}(\mu_t, \sigma_t^2)) \\
&= (L_t(FTL) - L_{t-1}(FTL)) + (L_{t-1}(\mu_t, \sigma_t^2) - L_t(\mu_{t+1}, \sigma_{t+1}^2)) \\
&= \left(\frac{(x_t - \mu_t)^2}{2\sigma_t^2} + \frac{1}{2}\ln\sigma_t^2 \right) + \left(\frac{t}{2} + \frac{t}{2}\ln\sigma_t^2 - \frac{t+1}{2} - \frac{t+1}{2}\ln\sigma_{t+1}^2 \right) \\
&= \frac{(x_t - \mu_t)^2}{2\sigma_t^2} - \frac{t+1}{2}\ln\frac{\sigma_{t+1}^2}{\sigma_t^2} - \frac{1}{2} \\
&= \frac{(x_t - \mu_t)^2}{2\sigma_t^2} - \frac{t+1}{2}\ln\left(\frac{t}{t+1} + \frac{t}{(t+1)^2} \cdot \frac{(x_t - \mu_t)^2}{\sigma_t^2} \right) - \frac{1}{2} \\
&= \frac{(x_t - \mu_t)^2}{2\sigma_t^2} - \frac{t+1}{2}\ln\left(1 + \frac{(x_t - \mu_t)^2}{(t+1)\sigma_t^2} \right) + \frac{t+1}{2}\ln\frac{t+1}{t} - \frac{1}{2}.
\end{aligned}
$$

To deal with the first two summands, we employ Taylor expansions $z - z^2/2 + z^3/3 \geq \ln(1+z) \geq z - z^2/2$ for $z \geq 0$. To deal with the last two, we use Stirling's formula via Lemma 6 in the appendix (for a quick estimate, apply the same Taylor expansions). Finally, since the sum is telescoping and $R_0 = 0$, summing $R_t - R_{t-1}$ from $t = 1$ to T gives the bounds. $\qquad\square$

We let UB_t be the term inside the summation in the upper bound in Lemma 1, and LB_t be the corresponding term in the lower bound. Using the alternative expression for the variance (6), we get the following:

$$
\sum_{t=1}^{T} LB_t \leq R_T - \frac{1}{4}\ln(T+1) \leq \sum_{t=1}^{T} UB_t + \frac{1}{12}
$$

where

$$
UB_t \triangleq \frac{t+1}{4}\left[\frac{\Delta_t}{\tilde{\sigma}^2 + \sum_{i=1}^{t-1}\Delta_i} \right]^2 \quad \text{and} \quad LB_t \triangleq UB_t - \frac{t+1}{6}\left[\frac{\Delta_t}{\tilde{\sigma}^2 + \sum_{i=1}^{t-1}\Delta_i} \right]^3.
$$

2.4   Lower Bounds

We exhibit a sequence (x_t) that forces the regret R_T incurred by FTL after T trials to be linear in T. The idea behind the sequence is to trick the learner into being "overly confident" about its choice of the mean μ_t and to then suddenly penalize it with an observation that is far from this mean. The initial ego-building sequence causes FTL to prescribe a σ_t^2 so small that when the penalty $(x_t - \mu_t)^2 \neq 0$ finally hits, the increase in regret $R_t - R_{t-1}$ is very large. In fact, this large increase in regret happens just once, in trial T.

To make this more precise, the form of LB_t suggests "choosing" $\Delta_t = 0$ for $1 \leq t \leq T - 1$ and hitting the learner with $\Delta_T > 0$. Then, while $LB_1 = LB_2 = \cdots = LB_{T-1} = 0$, the final contribution to the regret LB_T is linear in T. The necessary Δ_t are achieved with the sequence that has $x_1 = x_2 = \ldots = x_{T-1} = 0$ and $x_T = r$, so we get the following lower bound.

Theorem 1. *Suppose $r \leq \tilde{\sigma}$. For any $T \geq 1$, there exists a sequence (x_t) such that the regret of FTL after T trials is*

$$R_T \geq \frac{1}{12} \cdot \left(\frac{r}{\tilde{\sigma}}\right)^4 \cdot \frac{T^2}{T+1} + \frac{1}{4}\ln(T+1).$$

Proof. Using the sequence described above, we have $\Delta_T = T/(T+1)$ and all other $\Delta_t = 0$. By Lemma 1, substituting these values in LB_t gives the bound.   □

While Theorem 1 says nothing about the regret after $T' > T$ trials, we can iterate the argument to give a sequence that forces FTL to incur nearly linear regret for infinitely many T. To motivate our argument, we first show one approach that doesn't work: namely, to keep penalizing the learner in successive trials after the one in trial T. That is, we set $\Delta_t = 0$ for $t < T$ and then $\Delta_T > 0$, $\Delta_{T+1} > 0$, $\Delta_{T+2} > 0$, and so on. The reason this is not too bad for the learner is that the denominator of LB_t increases significantly during $t = T+1, T+2, \ldots$; specifically, the denominator of LB_t increases quadratically, while the leading t only increases linearly. Eventually, the LB_t become more like $1/t$ instead of t.

Instead, we space out the non-zero penalties so that they strike only when FTL sets very small variances. Let $f : \mathbb{N} \to \mathbb{N}$ be an increasing function and f^{-1} be its inverse map. We will inflict the nth non-zero penalty in trial $f(n)$, so f can be thought of as the schedule of penalties. When f doles out the penalties sparingly enough, the regret after $f(n)$ trials is very close to being linear in $f(n)$.

Theorem 2. *Suppose $r \leq \tilde{\sigma}$. Let $f : \mathbb{N} \to \mathbb{N}$ be any increasing function and f^{-1} its inverse map. Then there exists a sequence (x_t) such that, for any T in the range of f, the regret of FTL after T trials is*

$$R_T \geq \frac{1}{6} \cdot \left(\frac{r}{\tilde{\sigma}}\right)^4 \cdot \frac{T+1}{(f^{-1}(T)+1)^2} + \frac{1}{4}\ln(T+1).$$

Proof. Following the discussion above, the sequence (x_t) is defined so that $\Delta_{f(n)} = r^2/2$ for all $n \geq 1$ and $\Delta_t = 0$ for all other t. Let $x_t = \mu_t - \text{sign}(\mu_t)r\sqrt{(t+1)/(2t)}$ for t in the range of f, and $x_t = \mu_t$ elsewhere. In both cases, $|x_t| \leq r$. Then, in trial $f(n)$, we have

$$\text{LB}_{f(n)} = \frac{f(n)+1}{4}\left[\frac{r^2/2}{\tilde{\sigma}^2 + (n-1)(r^2/2)}\right]^2 - \frac{f(n)+1}{6}\left[\frac{r^2/2}{\tilde{\sigma}^2 + (n-1)(r^2/2)}\right]^3$$

$$\geq \frac{f(n)+1}{6}\left[\frac{r^2/2}{\tilde{\sigma}^2 + (n-1)(r^2/2)}\right]^2$$

$$= \frac{f(n)+1}{6}\left(\frac{r^2/2}{\tilde{\sigma}^2/2}\right)^2\left[\frac{1}{2+(n-1)\frac{r^2/2}{\tilde{\sigma}^2/2}}\right]^2 \geq \frac{f(n)+1}{6}\left(\frac{r}{\tilde{\sigma}}\right)^4\frac{1}{(n+1)^2}.$$

Then, Lemma 1 conservatively gives $R_{f(n)} \geq \text{LB}_{f(n)} + (1/4)\ln(f(n)+1)$.   □

If f is a polynomial of degree $p \geq 1$, we can actually sum (integrate) the LB_t from $t = 1$ to T (as opposed to just taking the final term LB_T) and yield a tighter bound $R_T \geq c \cdot (T+1)^{1-1/p} + (1/4)\ln(T+1)$ for some positive constant c. Notice that when $f(n) = \Theta(n)$ (the schedule used in our first attempt to give the bound), the bound has only the log term. Of course, there exists penalty schedules f for which $T/(f^{-1}(T))^2 = \omega(T^{1-1/p})$ for any $p \geq 1$. For example, if the penalty schedule is $f(n) = \Theta(\exp(n^2))$, then $T/(f^{-1}(T))^2$ is $\Omega(T/\log T)$.

2.5   Upper Bounds

We show two types of upper bounds on the regret of FTL. The first shows that the regret after T trials is at most linear in T. This bound is not immediately apparent from the Taylor approximation in Lemma 1: the σ_t^2 can be as small as $\tilde{\sigma}^2/(t+1)$, so each UB_t can be linear in t, which naïvely would give a *quadratic* upper bound on R_T. But this cannot be the case for all t: after all, σ_t^2 can only be very small in trial t if earlier trials have been relatively penalty-free. The key to the analysis is the potential function argument of Lemma 2, which shows that UB_t is at most a constant on average, and allows us to conclude the following.

Theorem 3. *For any $T \geq 1$ and any sequence (x_t), the regret of FTL after T trials is*

$$R_T \leq \frac{1}{4} \cdot \left(\left(\frac{2r}{\tilde{\sigma}}\right)^4 + \left(\frac{2r}{\tilde{\sigma}}\right)^2 \right) \cdot (T+1) + \frac{1}{4}\ln(T+1) + \frac{1}{12}.$$

Proof. We have $|\mu_t| \leq r$ since it is a convex combination of real numbers in $[-r, r]$. So $|x_t - \mu_t| \leq 2r$ by the triangle inequality; the theorem follows from combining Lemma 1 and Lemma 2 (below) with $c = (2r)^2/\tilde{\sigma}^2$, $a_1 = 0$, and $a_t = \Delta_{t-1}/\tilde{\sigma}^2$ for $2 \leq t \leq T+1$.   □

Lemma 2. *For any $a_1, a_2, \ldots, a_T \in [0, c]$,*

$$\sum_{t=1}^{T} t \left[\frac{a_t}{1 + \sum_{i=1}^{t-1} a_i} \right]^2 \leq (c^2 + c) \cdot T \cdot \left(1 - \frac{1}{1 + \sum_{t=1}^{T} a_t} \right).$$

The bound in the lemma captures the fact that when $\sum_{i=1}^{t-1} a_i$ is small, a large penalty may be imminent, but when $\sum_{i=1}^{t-1} a_i$ is large, the tth penalty cannot be too large. The final parenthesized term $1 - 1/(1 + \sum_{i=1}^{T} a_i)$ is treated as 1 when we apply this lemma, but the more elaborate form is essential for the proof.

Proof. Trivial if $c = 0$. Otherwise, we proceed by induction on T. In the base case, we need to show $a_1^2 \leq (c^2 + c)(1 - 1/(1 + a_1))$; this follows because $a_1(1 + a_1) \leq c^2 + c$. For the inductive step, we assume the bound holds for $T - 1$ and show that it holds for T. Let $S_T = 1 + a_1 + \ldots a_{T-1}$. We need

$$(c^2 + c)(T-1)\left(1 - \frac{1}{S_T}\right) + T\left[\frac{a_T}{S_T}\right]^2 \leq (c^2 + c)T\left(1 - \frac{1}{S_T + a_T}\right).$$

After rearranging, this reads

$$1 + T \left(\frac{1}{S_T} - \frac{1}{S_T + a_T} \right) \geq \frac{1}{S_T} + \frac{T}{c^2 + c} \left[\frac{a_T}{S_T} \right]^2 .$$

Since $S_T \geq 1$ and $a_T \leq c$, we have $1 \geq 1/S_T$ and $1/S_T - 1/(S_T + a_T) \geq (a_T/S_T)^2/(c^2 + c)$, which suffices to give the required bound.   □

The second upper bound we show concerns the *average (per-trial) regret*, R_T/T. This quantity reflects the improvement of a strategy over time; if R_T/T tends to a positive constant or worse, the strategy can be said to either stagnate or diminish over time.

Although Theorems 1 and 3 show that the worst-case regret of FTL after T trials is proportional to T, they don't imply that the average regret tends to a positive constant. Theorem 2 exhibits a sequence (x_t) for which the regret after T trials is nearly linear in T for infinitely many T, but the average regret still tends to 0. The following theorem complements this sublinear lower bound by showing that, indeed, the average regret of FTL is at most zero in the limit.

Theorem 4. *For any sequence (x_t), the average regret of FTL after T trials R_T/T satisfies*

$$\limsup_{T \geq 1} \frac{R_T}{T} \leq 0.$$

Proof. We'll show, for any $\varepsilon > 0$ sufficiently small, that $\limsup_{T \geq 1} R_T/T \leq \varepsilon$. The idea is to partition the trials into two sets: those in which $\Delta_t \leq b_\varepsilon$, for some constant b_ε (independent of T), and those in which $\Delta_t > b_\varepsilon$. The former trials produce small penalties: the constant b_ε is chosen so that the average of these penalties is at most ε. The latter set of trials have larger deviations-from-the-mean, but therefore cause the variance to rise substantially, which means they cannot contribute too heavily to regret. To analyze the trials in this second set, we consider the penalty schedule $f : \mathbb{N} \to \mathbb{N}$ such that the nth trial in this second set is $f(n)$. Because each $\Delta_{f(n)}$ is (relatively) large, we can show that, no matter the schedule f, the cumulative penalty from these trials is $o(T)$. This then implies that the average penalty is $o(1)$. The remaining terms in the regret are at most logarithmic in T, so they contribute $o(1)$ on average, as well.

We just need to detail our handling the penalties from the two sets of trials. Let $A \triangleq \{t \in \mathbb{N} : \Delta_t \leq b_\varepsilon\}$ and $B \triangleq \{t \in \mathbb{N} : \Delta_t > b_\varepsilon\}$, where $b_\varepsilon \triangleq \tilde{\sigma}^2(\sqrt{1 + 4\varepsilon} - 1)/2$. Notice that $\tilde{\sigma}^2/b_\varepsilon \geq 1$ whenever $\varepsilon \leq 3/4$. Furthermore, let $A^t \triangleq A \cap \{1, 2, \ldots, t\}$ and $B^t \triangleq B \cap \{1, 2, \ldots, t\}$. By Lemma 2 and the choice of b_ε,

$$\frac{1}{T} \sum_{t \in A^T} \mathrm{UB}_t \leq \frac{1}{4} \left(\frac{b_\varepsilon^2}{\tilde{\sigma}^4} + \frac{b_\varepsilon}{\tilde{\sigma}^2} \right) + o(1) < \varepsilon + o(1).$$

If B is finite, then we're done. So assume B is infinite and index it with $\mathbb{N}$ by assigning the nth smallest element of B to $f(n)$. Define $f^{-1}(T) = \max\{n :$

$f(n) \le T\}$, so we have $f(f^{-1}(T)) \le T$ with equality when T is in the image of f. Then, using the fact $b_\varepsilon < \Delta_t \le (2r)^2$,

$$\frac{1}{T} \sum_{t \in B^T} \mathrm{UB}_t = \frac{1}{T} \sum_{t \in B^T} \frac{t+1}{4} \left[\frac{\Delta_t}{\tilde{\sigma}^2 + \sum_{i=1}^{t-1} \Delta_i} \right]^2$$

$$\le \frac{4r^4}{T} \sum_{t \in B^T} \frac{t+1}{(\tilde{\sigma}^2 + \sum_{i \in B^{t-1}} \Delta_i)^2} \le \frac{4r^4}{T} \sum_{n=1}^{f^{-1}(T)} \frac{f(n)+1}{(\tilde{\sigma}^2 + (n-1)b_\varepsilon)^2}$$

$$\le \frac{4r^4}{Tb_\varepsilon^2} \sum_{n=1}^{f^{-1}(T)} \frac{f(n)+1}{n^2} \le \frac{4r^4}{Tb_\varepsilon^2} \left(\mathrm{o}(f(f^{-1}(T))) + \frac{\pi^2}{6} \right) = \mathrm{o}(1),$$

where the second-to-last step follows from Lemma 3. □

The following is a consequence of the fact that $\sum_{n \ge 1} 1/n^2$ is finite.

Lemma 3. *If* $f : \mathbb{N} \to \mathbb{N}$ *is strictly increasing, then* $\sum_{k=1}^{n} f(k)/k^2 = \mathrm{o}(f(n))$.

Proof. Fix any $\varepsilon > 0$, $n_0 \in \mathbb{N}$ such that $\sum_{k=n_0+1}^{\infty} 1/k^2 \le \varepsilon/2$, and $n_1 \in \mathbb{N}$ such that $f(n_0)/f(n_1) \le 3\varepsilon/\pi^2$. Then for any $n \ge n_1$,

$$\frac{1}{f(n)} \sum_{k=1}^{n} \frac{f(k)}{k^2} = \frac{1}{f(n)} \sum_{k=1}^{n_0} \frac{f(k)}{k^2} + \frac{1}{f(n)} \sum_{k=n_0+1}^{n} \frac{f(k)}{k^2} \le \frac{f(n_0)}{f(n)} \sum_{k=1}^{n_0} \frac{1}{k^2} + \sum_{k=n_0+1}^{n} \frac{1}{k^2}$$

which, by the choices of n_0 and n_1, is at most ε. □

3   On-Line Multivariate Gaussian Density Estimation

In the d-dimensional setting, the learning protocol is generalized to the following.

> For trial $t = 1, 2, \dots$
> - The learner selects $\boldsymbol{\mu}_t \in \mathbb{R}^d$ and $\boldsymbol{\Sigma}_t \in \mathbb{S}_{\succ 0}^d \triangleq \{\boldsymbol{X} \in \mathbb{R}^{d \times d} : \boldsymbol{X} = \boldsymbol{X}^\top, \boldsymbol{X} \succ \boldsymbol{0}\}$ (the cone of symmetric positive-definite $d \times d$ matrices).
> - Nature selects $\boldsymbol{x}_t \in \mathbb{R}^d$ and reveals it to the learner.
> - The learner incurs loss $\ell_t(\boldsymbol{\mu}_t, \boldsymbol{\Sigma}_t)$.

The loss $\ell_t(\boldsymbol{\mu}, \boldsymbol{\Sigma})$ is the negative log-likelihood of $\boldsymbol{x}_t$ under the multivariate Gaussian density with mean $\boldsymbol{\mu}$ and covariance matrix $\boldsymbol{\Sigma}$ (omitting the $(2\pi)^d$),

$$\ell_t(\boldsymbol{\mu}, \boldsymbol{\Sigma}) \triangleq \frac{1}{2}(\boldsymbol{x}_t - \boldsymbol{\mu})^\top \boldsymbol{\Sigma}^{-1}(\boldsymbol{x}_t - \boldsymbol{\mu}) + \frac{1}{2} \ln |\boldsymbol{\Sigma}|$$

where $|\boldsymbol{X}|$ denotes the determinant of a matrix $\boldsymbol{X}$.

3.1   Multivariate Degeneracies

Even in the case $d = 1$, we had to amend the setting to avoid trivial conclusions. Recall, the one-dimensional degeneracies occur when (1) the $|x_t|$ are unbounded, or (2) the x_t are all (nearly) the same. For arbitrary d, the first issue becomes unbounded $\|x_t\|$; the remedy is to assume a bound $\|x_t\| \leq r$ for all t. The second issue is similar to the one-dimensional case, except now the issue can occur along any dimension, such as when the x_t lie in (or are arbitrarily close to) a $k < d$ dimensional subspace. As before, we'll hallucinate a zeroth trial to preclude singularity in the data. For a known constant $\tilde{\sigma}^2 > 0$, the loss in this trial is

$$\ell_0(\boldsymbol{\mu}, \boldsymbol{\Sigma}) \triangleq \mathbb{E}_{\boldsymbol{v}} \left(\frac{1}{2}(\boldsymbol{v} - \boldsymbol{\mu})^\top \boldsymbol{\Sigma}^{-1}(\boldsymbol{v} - \boldsymbol{\mu}) + \frac{1}{2} \ln |\boldsymbol{\Sigma}| \right)$$

where $\boldsymbol{v}$ is any zero-mean random vector with $\mathbb{E}\boldsymbol{v}\boldsymbol{v}^\top = \tilde{\sigma}^2 \boldsymbol{I}$ (for example, take $\boldsymbol{v}$ to be uniform over the the $2d$ points $\{\pm\tilde{\sigma}\sqrt{d}\boldsymbol{e}_i : i = 1, 2, \ldots, d\}$, where $\boldsymbol{e}_i$ is the ith elementary unit vector). The zeroth trial can be seen as assuming a minimal amount of full-dimensional variation in the data. Again, including the zeroth trial loss in the total loss is enough to ensure a non-trivial infimum of $L_T(\boldsymbol{\mu}, \boldsymbol{\Sigma})$ over $\boldsymbol{\mu} \in \mathbb{R}^d$ and $\boldsymbol{\Sigma} \in \mathbb{S}^d_{\succ 0}$. We have

$$\inf_{\boldsymbol{\mu} \in \mathbb{R}^d, \boldsymbol{\Sigma} \in \mathbb{S}^d_{\succ 0}} L_T(\boldsymbol{\mu}, \boldsymbol{\Sigma}) = L_T(\overline{\boldsymbol{\mu}}, \overline{\boldsymbol{\Sigma}}) = \frac{d(T+1)}{2} + \frac{T+1}{2} \ln |\overline{\boldsymbol{\Sigma}}| > -\infty \qquad (7)$$

for any $T \geq 0$, where

$$\overline{\boldsymbol{\mu}} = \frac{1}{T+1} \sum_{t=1}^T \boldsymbol{x}_t \text{ and } \overline{\boldsymbol{\Sigma}} = \frac{1}{T+1} \left(\tilde{\sigma}^2 \boldsymbol{I} + \sum_{t=1}^T \boldsymbol{x}_t \boldsymbol{x}_t^\top \right) - \overline{\boldsymbol{\mu}}\,\overline{\boldsymbol{\mu}}^\top \succeq \frac{\tilde{\sigma}^2}{T+1} \boldsymbol{I} \succ 0.$$

3.2   Multivariate Follow-the-Leader and Regret Bounds

Follow-the-leader for multivariate Gaussian density estimation admits the following recursion for its setting of $(\boldsymbol{\mu}_t, \boldsymbol{\Sigma}_t)$: for $t \geq 1$

$$\boldsymbol{\mu}_{t+1} = \boldsymbol{\mu}_t + \frac{1}{t+1}(\boldsymbol{x}_t - \boldsymbol{\mu}_t) \text{ and } (t+1)\boldsymbol{\Sigma}_{t+1} = t\boldsymbol{\Sigma}_t + \boldsymbol{\Delta}_t \qquad (8)$$

where $\boldsymbol{\Delta}_t = (\boldsymbol{x}_t - \boldsymbol{\mu}_t)(\boldsymbol{x}_t - \boldsymbol{\mu}_t)^\top t/(t+1)$; the base cases are $(\boldsymbol{\mu}_0, \boldsymbol{\Sigma}_0) = (\boldsymbol{\mu}_1, \boldsymbol{\Sigma}_1) = (\boldsymbol{0}, \tilde{\sigma}^2 \boldsymbol{I})$.

Our bounds for FTL in the univariate case generalize to the following for the multivariate setting.

Theorem 5. *Suppose $r \leq \tilde{\sigma}$. For any $T \geq d$, there exists a sequence $(\boldsymbol{x}_t)$ such that the regret of FTL after T trials is*

$$R_T \geq \frac{d}{12} \cdot \left(\frac{r}{\tilde{\sigma}} \right)^4 \cdot \left(T - \frac{d}{2} + \frac{1}{2} \right) \left(\frac{T-d+1}{T-d+2} \right) \left(1 - \frac{d-1}{(T-d+1)(T-d+2)} \right)^2$$
$$+ \frac{d}{4} \ln(T+1).$$

Theorem 6. *Suppose $r \leq \tilde{\sigma}$. For any strictly increasing $f : \mathbb{N} \to \mathbb{N}$ with $f(n) \geq dn$, there exists a sequence $(\boldsymbol{x}_t)$ such that, for any T in the range of f, the regret of FTL after T trials is*

$$R_T \geq \frac{d}{6} \cdot \left(\frac{r}{\tilde{\sigma}}\right)^4 \cdot \frac{T - (d/2) + (3/2)}{(f^{-1}(T) + 1)^2} + \frac{d}{4}\ln(T+1).$$

Theorem 7. *For any sequence $(\boldsymbol{x}_t)$ and any $T \geq 1$, the regret of FTL after T trials is*

$$R_T \leq \frac{d}{4} \cdot \left(\left(\frac{2r}{\tilde{\sigma}}\right)^4 + \left(\frac{2r}{\tilde{\sigma}}\right)^2\right) \cdot (T+1) + \frac{d}{4}\ln(T+1) + \frac{d}{12}.$$

Theorem 8. *For any sequence $(\boldsymbol{x}_t)$, the average regret of FTL after T trials R_T/T satisfies $\limsup_{T \geq 1} R_T/T \leq 0$.*

We achieve the extra factor d in the lower bounds by using the sequences from the one-dimensional bound but repeating each non-zero penalty d times – one for each orthogonal direction. Some care must be taken to ensure that $\|\boldsymbol{x}_t\| \leq r$; also, the non-zero penalties are not all of the same value because they occur in different trials. For the upper bounds, the potential function has to account for variation in all directions; thus it is now based on $\mathrm{Tr}(\boldsymbol{\Sigma}_{T+1}^{-1})$ as opposed to the variance in any single direction.

3.3   Proof Sketches

We first need to characterize the penalty of FTL for each trial.

Lemma 4. *The regret of FTL after T trials satisfies the bounds*

$$R_T \leq \sum_{t=1}^{T} \frac{((\boldsymbol{x}_t - \boldsymbol{\mu}_t)^\top \boldsymbol{\Sigma}_t^{-1}(\boldsymbol{x}_t - \boldsymbol{\mu}_t))^2}{4(t+1)} + \frac{d}{4}\ln(T+1) + \frac{d}{12} \quad and$$

$$R_T \geq \sum_{t=1}^{T} \left(\frac{((\boldsymbol{x}_t - \boldsymbol{\mu}_t)^\top \boldsymbol{\Sigma}_t^{-1}(\boldsymbol{x}_t - \boldsymbol{\mu}_t))^2}{4(t+1)}\right.$$
$$\left. - \frac{((\boldsymbol{x}_t - \boldsymbol{\mu}_t)^\top \boldsymbol{\Sigma}_t^{-1}(\boldsymbol{x}_t - \boldsymbol{\mu}_t))^3}{6(t+1)^2}\right) + \frac{d}{4}\ln(T+1).$$

Proof. We proceed as in Lemma 1, using (8) and (7) to get

$$R_t - R_{t-1} = \frac{1}{2}(\boldsymbol{x}_t - \boldsymbol{\mu}_t)^\top \boldsymbol{\Sigma}_t^{-1}(\boldsymbol{x}_t - \boldsymbol{\mu}_t) - \frac{d}{2} + \frac{d(t+1)}{2}\ln\frac{t+1}{t}$$
$$- \frac{t+1}{2}\ln\left|\boldsymbol{I} + \frac{1}{t+1}(\boldsymbol{x}_t - \boldsymbol{\mu}_t)(\boldsymbol{x}_t - \boldsymbol{\mu}_t)^\top \boldsymbol{\Sigma}_t^{-1}\right|.$$

The matrix inside the log-determinant has $d-1$ eigenvalues equal to 1 and one eigenvalue equal to $1 + (\boldsymbol{x}_t - \boldsymbol{\mu}_t)^\top \boldsymbol{\Sigma}_t^{-1}(\boldsymbol{x}_t - \boldsymbol{\mu}_t)/(t+1)$. Since the determinant of a matrix is the product of its eigenvalues, we can apply Taylor approximations $z - z^2/2 + z^3/3 \geq \ln(1+z) \geq z - z^2/2$ to the log-determinant, and Lemma 6 (in the appendix) to the other logarithm. $\square$

Once again, we'll focus on the terms inside the summation. Let UB_t be the term under the summation in the upper bound, and LB_t be the that in the lower bound. Expanding the recursion for $\boldsymbol{\Sigma}_t$ in (8), we can express UB_t and LB_t as

$$\text{UB}_t \triangleq (t+1)\text{Tr}(\boldsymbol{\Delta}_t(\tilde{\sigma}^2\boldsymbol{I} + \textstyle\sum_{i=1}^{t-1}\boldsymbol{\Delta}_i)^{-1})^2/4 \quad \text{and}$$

$$\text{LB}_t \triangleq \text{UB}_t - (t+1)\text{Tr}(\boldsymbol{\Delta}_t(\tilde{\sigma}^2\boldsymbol{I} + \textstyle\sum_{i=1}^{t-1}\boldsymbol{\Delta}_i)^{-1})^3/6$$

Lower Bounds. For Theorem 5, we want to cause non-zero penalties in orthogonal directions once the variance in these directions are small. The sequence begins with $\boldsymbol{x}_t = \boldsymbol{0}$ for $t \leq T - d$, and for $i = 1, 2, \ldots, d$, has

$$\boldsymbol{x}_{T-d+i} = \boldsymbol{\mu}_{T-d+i} + r\sqrt{1 - \frac{\|\boldsymbol{\mu}_{T-d+i}\|^2}{r^2}}\, \boldsymbol{e}_i.$$

For Theorem 6, we combine the techniques from Theorem 5 and Theorem 2. Non-zero penalties occur in trials $f(n)-d+1, f(n)-d+2, \ldots, f(n)$ with $\|\boldsymbol{\delta}_t\|^2 = r^2/2$ in these trials and $\|\boldsymbol{\delta}_t\|^2 = 0$ in other trials.

Upper Bounds. The following generalization of Lemma 2 is the key argument for our upper bounds.

Lemma 5. *For any $\boldsymbol{a}_1, \boldsymbol{a}_2, \ldots, \boldsymbol{a}_T \in \mathbb{R}^d$ with $\|\boldsymbol{a}_t\|^2 \leq c$,*

$$\sum_{t=1}^{T} t\text{Tr}\left(\boldsymbol{A}_t\left(\boldsymbol{I} + \sum_{i=1}^{t-1}\boldsymbol{A}_i\right)^{-1}\right)^2 \leq (c^2+c)\cdot T\cdot\left(d - \text{Tr}\left(\left(\boldsymbol{I}+\sum_{i=1}^{T}\boldsymbol{A}_i\right)^{-1}\right)\right)$$

where $\boldsymbol{A}_i = \boldsymbol{a}_i\boldsymbol{a}_i^\top$ for all i.

Proof. Trivial if $c = 0$. Otherwise we proceed by induction on T. In the base case, we need $d(c^2 + c) - (c^2 + c)\text{Tr}((\boldsymbol{I} + \boldsymbol{A}_1)^{-1}) - \|\boldsymbol{a}_1\|^4 \geq 0$. Using the Sherman-Morrison formula (for a matrix $\boldsymbol{M}$ and vector $\boldsymbol{v}$, $(\boldsymbol{M} + \boldsymbol{v}\boldsymbol{v}^\top)^{-1} = \boldsymbol{M}^{-1} - (\boldsymbol{M}^{-1}\boldsymbol{v}\boldsymbol{v}^\top\boldsymbol{M}^{-1})/(1 + \boldsymbol{v}^\top\boldsymbol{M}^{-1}\boldsymbol{v}))$, we have

$$(c^2+c)\text{Tr}\left((\boldsymbol{I}+\boldsymbol{A}_1)^{-1}\right) = (c^2+c)\text{Tr}\left(\boldsymbol{I} - \frac{\boldsymbol{A}_1}{1+\|\boldsymbol{a}_1\|^2}\right) = d(c^2+c) - \frac{(c^2+c)\|\boldsymbol{a}_1\|^2}{1+\|\boldsymbol{a}_1\|^2}$$

and also

$$\frac{(c^2+c)\|\boldsymbol{a}_1\|^2}{1+\|\boldsymbol{a}_1\|^2} - \|\boldsymbol{a}_1\|^4 \geq c\|\boldsymbol{a}_1\|^2 - \|\boldsymbol{a}_1\|^4 \geq 0.$$

Thus the base case follows. For the inductive step, we assume the bound holds for $T-1$ and show that it holds for T. Let $\boldsymbol{S} = \boldsymbol{I} + \boldsymbol{A}_1 + \ldots + \boldsymbol{A}_{T-1}$ and $\boldsymbol{A} = \boldsymbol{a}\boldsymbol{a}^\top = \boldsymbol{A}_T$. We need

$$(c^2+c)(T-1)\left(d - \text{Tr}\left(\boldsymbol{S}^{-1}\right)\right) + T\text{Tr}\left(\boldsymbol{A}\boldsymbol{S}^{-1}\right)^2 \leq (c^2+c)T\left(d - \text{Tr}\left((\boldsymbol{S}+\boldsymbol{A})^{-1}\right)\right),$$

which, after rearranging, reads

$$d + T \left(\mathrm{Tr} \left(\boldsymbol{S}^{-1} \right) - \mathrm{Tr} \left(\left(\boldsymbol{S} + \boldsymbol{A} \right)^{-1} \right) \right) \geq \mathrm{Tr} \left(\boldsymbol{S}^{-1} \right) + \frac{T \mathrm{Tr} \left(\boldsymbol{A} \boldsymbol{S}^{-1} \right)^2}{c^2 + c}.$$

Since $\boldsymbol{S} \succeq \boldsymbol{I}$, we have $\mathrm{Tr} \left(\boldsymbol{S}^{-1} \right) \leq d$, which takes care of the first terms on each side. For the remaining terms, first note that $\mathrm{Tr}(\boldsymbol{A} \boldsymbol{S}^{-1}) \leq \|\boldsymbol{a}\|^2 \leq c$. Then, using Sherman-Morrison again gives

$$\mathrm{Tr} \left(\boldsymbol{S}^{-1} \right) - \mathrm{Tr} \left(\left(\boldsymbol{S} + \boldsymbol{A} \right)^{-1} \right) = \mathrm{Tr} \left(\frac{\boldsymbol{S}^{-1} \boldsymbol{A} \boldsymbol{S}^{-1}}{1 + \mathrm{Tr} \left(\boldsymbol{A} \boldsymbol{S}^{-1} \right)} \right) = \frac{\|\boldsymbol{a}\|^2 \boldsymbol{a}^\top \boldsymbol{S}^{-2} \boldsymbol{a}}{\|\boldsymbol{a}\|^2 \left(1 + \mathrm{Tr} \left(\boldsymbol{A} \boldsymbol{S}^{-1} \right) \right)}.$$

The denominator is at most $c(1 + c)$, so it remains to show $\|\boldsymbol{a}\|^2 \mathrm{Tr}(\boldsymbol{a}^\top \boldsymbol{S}^{-2} \boldsymbol{a}) \geq (\boldsymbol{a}^\top \boldsymbol{S}^{-1} \boldsymbol{a})^2$. Without loss of generality, $\|\boldsymbol{a}\| = 1$ and $\boldsymbol{S}$ is diagonal with eigenvalues $\lambda_1, \ldots, \lambda_d > 0$. Then $a_1^2/\lambda_1^2 + \ldots + a_d^2/\lambda_d^2 \geq (a_1^2/\lambda_1 + \ldots + a_d^2/\lambda_d)^2$ follows from Jensen's inequality. $\qquad\square$

For Theorem 8, we proceed as in Theorem 4, but to handle the trials in B, we have to deal with each direction separately, so further partitions are needed.

4 Conclusion and Open Questions

On-line density estimation with a Gaussian distribution presents difficulties markedly different from those usually encountered in on-line learning. They appear even in the one-dimensional setting and scale up to the multivariate case as familiar issues in data analysis (e.g. unknown data scale, hidden low dimensional structure). Although the natural estimation strategy remains vulnerable to hazards after the problem is rid of degeneracies, our results suggest that it is still sensible even under adversarial conditions.

We still do not know the minimax strategy for on-line Gaussian density estimation with arbitrary covariances – a question first posed by Warmuth and Takimoto (2000b) – although our work sheds some light on the problem. While using arbitrary-covariance multivariate Gaussians is a step forward from simpler distributions like the fixed-covariance Gaussian and Bernoulli, it would also be interesting to consider on-line estimation with other statistical models, such as low-dimensional Gaussians or a mixture of Gaussians. Extending the work on on-line PCA (Warmuth and Kuzmin, 2006) may be one approach for the first.

Acknowledgements. We are grateful to the anonymous reviewers for their helpful suggestions, to the Los Alamos National Laboratory for supporting the second author with a graduate fellowship, and to the NSF for grant IIS-0347646.

References

Azoury, K., Warmuth, M.: Relative loss bounds for on-line density estimation with the exponential family of distributions. Journal of Machine Learning 43(3), 211–246 (2001)

Cesa-Bianchi, N., Lugosi, G.: Prediction, Learning, and Games. Cambridge University Press, Cambridge (2006)

Crammer, K.: Online tracking of linear subspaces. 19th Annual Conference on Learning Theory (2006)

Freund, Y.: Predicting a binary sequence almost as well as the optimal biased coin. 9th Annual Conference on Computational Learning Theory (1996)

Hannan, J.: Approximation to Bayes risk in repeated play. In: M. Dresher, A. Tucker, P. Wolfe (Eds.), Contributions to the Theory of Games, vol. III, pp. 97–139 (1957)

Hazan, E., Kalai, A., Kale, S., Agarwal, A.: Logarithmic regret algorithms for online convex optimization. 19th Annual Conference on Learning Theory (2006)

Kalai, A., Vempala, S.: Efficient algorithms for the online decision problem. 16th Annual Conference on Learning Theory (2005)

Shalev-Shwartz, S., Singer, Y.: Convex repeated games and Fenchel duality. Advances in Neural Information Processing Systems 19 (2006)

Takimoto, E., Warmuth, M.: The last-step minimax algorithm. 11th International Conference on Algorithmic Learning Theory (2000a)

Takimoto, E., Warmuth, M.: The minimax strategy for Gaussian density estimation. 13th Annual Conference on Computational Learning Theory (2000b)

Warmuth, M., Kuzmin, D.: Randomized PCA algorithms with regret bounds that are logarithmic in the dimension. Advances in Neural Information Processing Systems 19 (2006)

Zinkevich, M.: Online convex programming and generalized infinitesimal gradient ascent. In: 20th International Conference on Machine Learning (2003)

Appendix

Lemma 6. *For any $n \in \mathbb{N}$,*

$$(n+1)\ln\frac{n+1}{n} = 1 + \frac{1}{2}\ln\frac{n+1}{n} + s(n) - s(n+1)$$

where $s(n) = 1/(12n) - 1/(360n^3) + \ldots$ is (the tail of) Stirling's series.

Proof. Apply Stirling's formula: $\ln n! = n\ln n - n + (1/2)\ln(2\pi n) + s(n)$. $\qquad \square$

Generalised Entropy and Asymptotic Complexities of Languages

Yuri Kalnishkan, Vladimir Vovk, and Michael V. Vyugin

Department of Computer Science, Royal Holloway, University of London, Egham, Surrey, TW20 0EX, UK
{yura,vovk,misha}@cs.rhul.ac.uk

Abstract. In this paper the concept of asymptotic complexity of languages is introduced. This concept formalises the notion of learnability in a particular environment and generalises Lutz and Fortnow's concepts of predictability and dimension. Then asymptotic complexities in different prediction environments are compared by describing the set of all pairs of asymptotic complexities w.r.t. different environments. A geometric characterisation in terms of generalised entropies is obtained and thus the results of Lutz and Fortnow are generalised.

1 Introduction

We consider the following on-line learning problem: given a sequence of previous outcomes $x_1, x_2, \ldots, x_{n-1}$, a prediction strategy is required to output a prediction γ_n for the next outcome x_n.

We assume that outcomes belong to a finite set Ω; it may be thought of as an alphabet and sequences as words. We allow greater variation in predictions though. Predictions may be drawn from a compact set. A loss function $\lambda(\omega, \gamma)$ is used to measure the discrepancy between predictions and actual outcomes. The performance of the strategy is measured by the cumulative loss $\sum_{i=1}^{n} \lambda(x_i, \gamma_i)$. Different aspects of this prediction problem have been extensively studied; see [1] for an overview.

A loss function specifies a prediction environment. We study the notion of predictability in a particular environment. There are different approaches to formalising this intuitive notion. One is predictive complexity introduced in [2]. In this paper we introduce another formalisation, namely, asymptotic complexity.

Asymptotic complexity applies to languages, i.e., classes of sequences of outcomes. Roughly speaking, the asymptotic complexity of a language is the loss per element of the best prediction strategy. This definition can be made precise in several natural ways. We thus get several different variants. One of them, which we call lower non-uniform complexity, generalises the concepts of dimension and predictability from [3] (the conference version was presented at COLT 2002). In our framework dimension and predictability can be represented by means of complexities for two specific games.

In this paper we study the following problem. Let AC_1 be asymptotic complexity specified by a loss function λ_1 and let AC_2 be asymptotic complexity specified

N. Bshouty and C. Gentile (Eds.): COLT 2007, LNAI 4539, pp. 293–307, 2007.

by a loss function λ_2. What relations exist between them? We give a complete answer to this question by describing the set $(\mathrm{AC}_1(L), \mathrm{AC}_2(L))$, where L ranges over all languages, on the Euclidean plane. The main theorem is formulated in Sect. 4. This set turns out to have a simple geometric description in terms of so called generalised entropy. Generalised entropy is the optimal expected loss per element. In the case of the logarithmic loss function, generalised entropy coincides with Shannon entropy. Generalised entropy is discussed in [4]. In [5] connections between generalised entropy and predictive complexity are studied. We thus generalise the result from [3], where only the case of predictability and dimension is considered.

Our main result holds for all convex games. We show that this requirement cannot be omitted.

The definitions and results in this paper are formulated without any reference to computability. However all constructions in the paper are effective. All the results from the paper can therefore be reformulated in either computable or polynomial-time computable fashion provided the loss functions are computable in a sufficiently efficient way. We discuss this in more detail in Sect. 6.

2   Preliminaries

The notation $\mathbb{N}$ refers to the set of all non-negative integers $\{0, 1, 2, \ldots\}$.

2.1   Games, Strategies, and Losses

A *game* $\mathfrak{G}$ is a triple $\langle \Omega, \Gamma, \lambda \rangle$, where Ω is an *outcome space*, Γ is a *prediction space*, and $\lambda : \Omega \times \Gamma \to [0, +\infty]$ is a *loss function*.

We assume that $\Omega = \{\omega^{(0)}, \omega^{(1)}, \ldots, \omega^{(M-1)}\}$ is a finite set of cardinality $M < +\infty$. If $M = 2$, then Ω may be identified with $\mathbb{B} = \{0, 1\}$; we will call this case *binary*. We denote the set of all finite sequences of elements of Ω by Ω^* and the set of all infinite sequences by Ω^∞; bold letters x, y etc. are used to refer to both finite and infinite sequences. By $|x|$ we denote the length of a finite sequence x, i.e., the number of elements in it. The set of sequences of length n, $n = 0, 1, 2, \ldots$, is denoted by Ω^n. We will also be using the notation $\sharp_i x$ for the number of $\omega^{(i)}$s among elements of x. Clearly, $\sum_{i=0}^{M-1} \sharp_i x = |x|$ for any finite sequence x. By $x|_n$ we denote the prefix of length n of a (finite of infinite) sequence x.

We also assume that Γ is a compact topological space and λ is continuous w.r.t. the topology of the extended real line $[-\infty, +\infty]$. We treat Ω as a discrete space and thus the continuity of λ in two arguments is the same as continuity in the second argument.

In order to take some important games into account we must allow λ to attain the value $+\infty$. However, we assume that for every $\gamma_0 \in \Gamma$ such that $\lambda(\omega^*, \gamma_0) = +\infty$ for some $\omega^* \in \Omega$, there is a sequence $\gamma_1, \gamma_2, \ldots \in \Gamma$ such that $\gamma_n \to \gamma_0$ and $\lambda(\omega, \gamma_n) < +\infty$ for all $n = 1, 2, \ldots$ and all $\omega \in \Omega$ (but, by continuity, $\lambda(\omega^*, \gamma_n) \to +\infty$ as $n \to +\infty$). In other terms, we assume that every prediction γ_0 leading to infinite loss can be approximated by predictions giving finite losses.

The following are examples of binary games with $\Omega = \mathbb{B}$ and $\Gamma = [0, 1]$: the *square-loss* game with the loss function $\lambda(\omega, \gamma) = (\omega - \gamma)^2$, the *absolute-loss* game with the loss function $\lambda(\omega, \gamma) = |\omega - \gamma|$, and the *logarithmic* game with

$$\lambda(\omega, \gamma) = \begin{cases} -\log_2(1 - \gamma) & \text{if } \omega = 0 \\ -\log_2 \gamma & \text{if } \omega = 1 \end{cases} .$$

A *prediction strategy* $\mathfrak{A} : \Omega^* \to \Gamma$ maps a finite sequence of outcomes to a prediction. We say that on a finite sequence $\boldsymbol{x} = x_1 x_2 \ldots x_n \in \Omega^n$ the strategy $\mathfrak{A}$ suffers loss $\text{Loss}_{\mathfrak{A}}^{\mathfrak{G}}(\boldsymbol{x}) = \sum_{i=1}^{n} \lambda(x_i, \mathfrak{A}(x_1 x_2 \ldots x_{i-1}))$. By definition, we let $\text{Loss}_{\mathfrak{A}}^{\mathfrak{G}}(\Lambda) = 0$, where Λ is the sequence of length 0.

We need to define one important class of games. The definition is in geometric terms. An M-tuple $(s_0, s_1, \ldots, s_{M-1}) \in [0, +\infty]^M$ is a *superprediction* w.r.t. $\mathfrak{G}$ if there is a prediction $\gamma \in \Gamma$ such that $\lambda(\omega^{(i)}, \gamma) \le s_i$ for all $i = 0, 1, \ldots, M-1$. We say that the game $\mathfrak{G}$ is *convex* if the finite part of its set of superpredictions, $S \cap \mathbb{R}^M$, where S is the set of superpredictions, is convex.

It is shown in [6] that convexity is equivalent to another property called *weak mixability*. We will be using these terms as synonyms.

2.2   Generalised Entropies

Fix a game $\mathfrak{G} = \langle \Omega, \Gamma, \lambda \rangle$. Let $\mathbb{P}(\Omega)$ be the set of probability distributions on Ω. Since Ω is finite, we can identify $\mathbb{P}(\Omega)$ with the standard $(M - 1)$-simplex $\mathbb{P}_M = \{(p_0, p_1, \ldots, p_{M-1}) \in [0, 1]^M \mid \sum_{i=0}^{M-1} p_i = 1\}$.

Generalised entropy $H : \mathbb{P}(\Omega) \to \mathbb{R}$ is the infimum of expected loss over $\gamma \in \Gamma$, i.e., for $p^* = (p_0, p_1, \ldots, p_{M-1}) \in \mathbb{P}(\Omega)$

$$H(p^*) = \min_{\gamma \in \Gamma} \mathbf{E}_{p^*} \lambda(\omega, \gamma) = \min_{\gamma \in \Gamma} \sum_{i=0}^{M-1} p_i \lambda(\omega^{(i)}, \gamma) .$$

The minimum in the definition is achieved because λ is continuous and Γ compact.

Since p_i can accept the value 0 and $\lambda(\omega^{(i)}, \gamma)$ can be $+\infty$, we need to resolve the possible ambiguity. Let us assume that in this definition $0 \times (+\infty) = 0$. This is the same as replacing the minimum by the infimum over the values of $\gamma \in \Gamma$ such that $\lambda(\omega, \gamma) < +\infty$ for all $\omega \in \Omega$.

In the binary case $\Omega = \mathbb{B}$ the definition can be simplified. Let p be the probability of 1. Clearly, p fully specifies a distribution from $\mathbb{P}(\mathbb{B})$ and thus $\mathbb{P}(\mathbb{B})$ can be identified with the line segment $[0, 1]$. We get $H(p) = \min_{\gamma \in \Gamma}[(1 - p)\lambda(0, \gamma) + p\lambda(1, \gamma)]$.

If it is not clear from the context what game we are referring to, we will use subscripts for H. We will use the term $\mathfrak{G}$-*entropy* to refer to generalised entropy w.r.t. the game $\mathfrak{G}$. The notation ABS, SQ, and LOG will be used to refer to the absolute-loss, square-loss, and logarithmic games respectively, e.g., we will write 'ABS-entropy'.

3 Asymptotic Complexities

Fix a game $\mathfrak{G} = \langle \Omega, \Gamma, \lambda \rangle$. We are going to define measures of complexity for *languages*, i.e., sets of sequences. The finite and infinite sequences should be considered separately.

3.1 Finite Sequences

In this subsection we consider languages $L \subseteq \Omega^*$. We shall call the values

$$\overline{\mathrm{AC}}(L) = \inf_{\mathfrak{A}} \limsup_{n \to +\infty} \max_{x \in L \cap \Omega^n} \frac{\mathrm{Loss}_{\mathfrak{A}}(x)}{n} \ , \tag{1}$$

$$\underline{\mathrm{AC}}(L) = \inf_{\mathfrak{A}} \liminf_{n \to +\infty} \max_{x \in L \cap \Omega^n} \frac{\mathrm{Loss}_{\mathfrak{A}}(x)}{n} \tag{2}$$

upper and *lower asymptotic complexity* of L w.r.t. the game $\mathfrak{G}$. As with generalised entropies, we will use subscripts for AC to specify a particular game if it is not clear from the context.

In order to complete the definition, we must decide what to do if L contains no sequences of certain lengths at all. In this paper we are concerned only with infinite sets of finite sequences. One can say that asymptotic complexity of a finite language $L \subseteq \Omega^*$ is undefined. Let us also assume that the limits in (1) and (2) are taken over such n that $L \cap \Omega^n \neq \varnothing$. An alternative arrangement is to assume that in (1) $\max \varnothing = 0$, while in (2) $\max \varnothing = +\infty$.

3.2 Infinite Sequences

There are two natural ways to define complexities of languages $L \subseteq \Omega^\infty$.

First we can extend the notions we have just defined. Indeed, every nonempty set of infinite sequences can be identified with the set of all finite prefixes of all its sequences. The language thus obtained is infinite and has upper and lower complexities. For the resulting complexities we shall retain the notation $\overline{\mathrm{AC}}(L)$ and $\underline{\mathrm{AC}}(L)$. We shall refer to those complexities as *uniform*.

The second way is the following. Let

$$\overline{\overline{\mathrm{AC}}}(L) = \inf_{\mathfrak{A}} \sup_{x \in L} \limsup_{n \to +\infty} \frac{\mathrm{Loss}_{\mathfrak{A}}(x|_n)}{n} \text{ and } \underline{\underline{\mathrm{AC}}}(L) = \inf_{\mathfrak{A}} \sup_{x \in L} \liminf_{n \to +\infty} \frac{\mathrm{Loss}_{\mathfrak{A}}(x|_n)}{n} \ .$$

We shall refer to this complexity as *non-uniform*.

The concept of asymptotic complexity generalises certain complexity measures studied in the literature. The concepts of predictability and dimension studied in [3] can be easily reduced to asymptotic complexity: the dimension is the lower non-uniform complexity w.r.t. a multidimensional generalisation of the logarithmic game and predictability equals $1 - \underline{\mathrm{AC}}$, where $\underline{\mathrm{AC}}$ is the lower non-uniform complexity w.r.t. a multidimensional generalisation of the absolute-loss game.

3.3 Differences Between Complexities

Let us show that the complexities we have introduced are different.

First let us show that upper and lower complexities differ. For example, consider the absolute-loss game. Let $0^{(n)}$ be the sequence of n zeros and let $\Xi_n = \{0^{(n)}\} \times \mathbb{B}^n$. Consider the language $L = \prod_{i=0}^{\infty} \Xi_{2^{2i}} \subseteq \mathbb{B}^\infty$. In other terms, L consists of sequences that have alternating constant and random segments. It is easy to see that $\overline{AC}(L) = \overline{\overline{AC}}(L) = 1/2$, while $\underline{AC}(L) = \underline{\underline{AC}}(L) = 0$.

Secondly, let us show that uniform complexities differ from non-uniform. Once again, consider the absolute-loss game. Let $L \subseteq \mathbb{B}^\infty$ be the set of all sequences that have only zeros from some position on. In other terms, $L = \cup_{n=0}^{\infty}(\mathbb{B}^n \times \{0^{(\infty)}\})$, where $0^{(\infty)}$ is the infinite sequence of zeros. We have $\overline{\overline{AC}}(L) = \underline{\underline{AC}}(L) = 0$ while $\overline{AC}(L) = \underline{AC}(L) = 1/2$.

4 Main Result

Consider two games $\mathfrak{G}_1$ and $\mathfrak{G}_2$ with the same finite set of outcomes Ω. Let H_1 be $\mathfrak{G}_1$-entropy and H_2 be $\mathfrak{G}_2$-entropy. The $\mathfrak{G}_1/\mathfrak{G}_2$-*entropy set* is the set $\{(H_1(p), H_2(p)) \mid p \in \mathbb{P}(\Omega)\}$. The convex hull of the $\mathfrak{G}_1/\mathfrak{G}_2$-entropy set is called the $\mathfrak{G}_1/\mathfrak{G}_2$-*entropy hull*.

We say that a closed convex $\mathcal{S} \subseteq \mathbb{R}^2$ is a *spaceship* if for every pair of points $(x_1, y_1), (x_2, y_2) \in \mathcal{S}$ the point $(\max(x_1, x_2), \max(y_1, y_2))$ belongs to $\mathcal{S}$. The *spaceship closure* of a set $\mathcal{H} \subseteq \mathbb{R}^2$ is the smallest spaceship containing $\mathcal{H}$, i.e., the intersection of all spaceships containing $\mathcal{H}$.

We can now formulate the main result of this paper.

Theorem 1. *If games $\mathfrak{G}_1$ and $\mathfrak{G}_2$ have the same finite outcome space Ω and are convex, then the spaceship closure of the $\mathfrak{G}_1/\mathfrak{G}_2$-entropy hull coincides with the following sets, where AC_1 and AC_2 are asymptotic complexities w.r.t. $\mathfrak{G}_1$ and $\mathfrak{G}_2$:*

- $\{(\overline{AC}_1(L), \overline{AC}_2(L)) \mid L \subseteq \Omega^* \text{ and } L \text{ is infinite}\}$;
- $\{(\underline{AC}_1(L), \underline{AC}_2(L)) \mid L \subseteq \Omega^* \text{ and } L \text{ is infinite}\}$;
- $\{(\overline{AC}_1(L), \overline{AC}_2(L)) \mid L \subseteq \Omega^\infty \text{ and } L \neq \varnothing\}$;
- $\{(\underline{AC}_1(L), \underline{AC}_2(L)) \mid L \subseteq \Omega^\infty \text{ and } L \neq \varnothing\}$;
- $\{(\overline{\overline{AC}}_1(L), \overline{\overline{AC}}_2(L)) \mid L \subseteq \Omega^\infty \text{ and } L \neq \varnothing\}$;
- $\{(\underline{\underline{AC}}_1(L), \underline{\underline{AC}}_2(L)) \mid L \subseteq \Omega^\infty \text{ and } L \neq \varnothing\}$.

In other words, the spaceship closure $\mathcal{S}$ of the entropy hull contains all points $(AC_1(L), AC_2(L))$, where AC is one type of complexity, and these points fill the set $\mathcal{S}$ as L ranges over all languages that have complexity. The last item on the list covers Theorem 5.1 (Main Theorem) from [3].

Appendices A and B contain a discussion of shapes of the entropy hull and some examples. The theorem is proved in Sect. 5.

The requirement of convexity cannot be omitted. For example, consider the simple prediction game $\langle \mathbb{B}, \mathbb{B}, \lambda \rangle$, where $\lambda(\omega, \gamma)$ is 0 if $\omega = \gamma$ and 1 otherwise.

The convex hull of the set of superpredictions w.r.t. the simple prediction game coincides with the set of superpredictions w.r.t. the absolute-loss game. Geometric considerations imply that their generalised entropies coincide. Thus the maximum of the generalised entropy w.r.t. the simple prediction game is $1/2$ (see Appendix B). On the other hand, it is easy to check that $AC(\mathbb{B}^*) = 1$, where AC is any of the asymptotic complexities w.r.t. the simple prediction game.

The statement of the theorem does not apply to pairs $(\overline{AC}_1(L), \underline{AC}_2(L))$ or pairs $(\overline{\overline{AC}}_1(L), \underline{AC}_2(L))$. Indeed, let $\mathfrak{G}_1 = \mathfrak{G}_2$. Then $H_1 = H_2$ and the entropy hull with its spaceship closure are subsets of the bisector of the first quadrant. At the same time we know that upper and lower complexities differ and thus there will be pairs outside the bisector.

5   Proof of the Main Theorem

In this section we prove Theorem 1.

The following lemma proved in Appendix C allows us to 'optimise' the performance of a strategy w.r.t. two games. We shall call it *recalibration lemma*.

Lemma 1. *If $\mathfrak{G}_1$ and $\mathfrak{G}_2$ are convex games with the same finite set of outcomes Ω and $\mathcal{H}$ is the $\mathfrak{G}_1/\mathfrak{G}_2$-entropy hull, then for every prediction strategy $\mathfrak{A}$ and positive ε there are prediction strategies $\mathfrak{A}^1_\varepsilon$ and $\mathfrak{A}^2_\varepsilon$ and a function $f : \mathbb{N} \to \mathbb{R}$ such that $f(n) = o(n)$ as $n \to +\infty$ and for every sequence $\boldsymbol{x} \in \Omega^*$ there exists a point $(u_{\boldsymbol{x}}, v_{\boldsymbol{x}}) \in \mathcal{H}$ such that the following inequalities hold:*

$$u_{\boldsymbol{x}}|\boldsymbol{x}| \le \mathrm{Loss}_{\mathfrak{A}}^{\mathfrak{G}_1}(\boldsymbol{x}) + \varepsilon|\boldsymbol{x}| \; , \tag{3}$$

$$\mathrm{Loss}_{\mathfrak{A}^1_\varepsilon}^{\mathfrak{G}_1}(\boldsymbol{x}) \le |\boldsymbol{x}|(u_{\boldsymbol{x}} + \varepsilon) + f(|\boldsymbol{x}|) \; , \tag{4}$$

$$\mathrm{Loss}_{\mathfrak{A}^2_\varepsilon}^{\mathfrak{G}_2}(\boldsymbol{x}) \le |\boldsymbol{x}|(v_{\boldsymbol{x}} + \varepsilon) + f(|\boldsymbol{x}|) \; . \tag{5}$$

Below in Subsect. 5.1 we use this lemma to show that pairs of complexities belong to the spaceship closure. It remains to show that the pairs fill in the closure and it is done in Appendix D.

5.1   Every Pair of Complexities Belongs to the Spaceship Closure of the Hull

Let AC be one of the types of complexity we have introduced. Let us show that for every language L the pair $(AC_1(L), AC_2(L))$ belongs to the spaceship closure $\mathcal{S}$ of the entropy hull.

We start by showing that the pair $(AC_1(L), AC_2(L))$ belongs to the cucumber closure $\mathcal{C}$ of the $\mathfrak{G}_1/\mathfrak{G}_2$-entropy hull $\mathcal{H}$ (see Appendix A for a definition).

Let $AC_1(L) = c$. Lemma 1 implies that $c_{\min} \le c \le c_{\max}$, where $c_{\min} = \min_{p \in \mathbb{P}(\Omega)} H_1(p)$ and $c_{\max} = \max_{p \in \mathbb{P}(\Omega)} H_1(p)$.

We need to show that $c_2 \le AC_2(L) \le c_1$, where c_1 and c_2 correspond to intersections of the vertical line $x = c$ with the boundary of the cucumber as shown on Fig. 1.

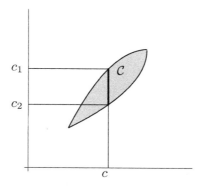

Fig. 1. A section of the cucumber hull

Let $f_1, f_2 : [c_{\min}, c_{\max}] \to \mathbb{R}$ be the non-decreasing functions that bound $\mathcal{C}$ from above and below, i.e., $\mathcal{C} = \{(x, y) \mid x \in [c_{\min}, c_{\max}] \text{ and } f_2(x) \leq y \leq f_1(x)\}$ (see Appendix A). We have $f_1(c) = c_1$ and $f_2(c) = c_2$. The function f_1 is concave and the function f_2 is convex; therefore they are continuous.

Since $\mathrm{AC}_1(L) = c$, for every $\varepsilon > 0$ there is a prediction strategy $\mathfrak{A}$ such that for certain infinite sets of finite sequences $\boldsymbol{x}$ there are functions $g : \mathbb{N} \to \mathbb{R}$ such that $g(n) = o(n)$ as $n \to +\infty$ and for all appropriate $\boldsymbol{x}$ we have

$$\mathrm{Loss}^{\mathfrak{G}_1}_{\mathfrak{A}}(\boldsymbol{x}) \leq (c + \varepsilon)|\boldsymbol{x}| + g(|\boldsymbol{x}|) \ . \tag{6}$$

Let us apply Lemma 1 to $\mathfrak{A}$ and ε. We obtain the strategies $\mathfrak{A}^1_\varepsilon$ and $\mathfrak{A}^2_\varepsilon$ and a function $f : \mathbb{N} \to \mathbb{R}$ such that $f(n) = o(n)$ as $n \to +\infty$ and for every $\boldsymbol{x}$ there exists a point $(u_{\boldsymbol{x}}, v_{\boldsymbol{x}}) \in \mathcal{H}$ such that the inequalities

$$\mathrm{Loss}^{\mathfrak{G}_1}_{\mathfrak{A}^1_\varepsilon}(\boldsymbol{x}) \leq |\boldsymbol{x}|(u_{\boldsymbol{x}} + \varepsilon) + f(|\boldsymbol{x}|) \ ,$$

$$\mathrm{Loss}^{\mathfrak{G}_2}_{\mathfrak{A}^2_\varepsilon}(\boldsymbol{x}) \leq |\boldsymbol{x}|(v_{\boldsymbol{x}} + \varepsilon) + f(|\boldsymbol{x}|) \ ,$$

$$|\boldsymbol{x}|u_{\boldsymbol{x}} \leq \mathrm{Loss}^{\mathfrak{G}_1}_{\mathfrak{A}}(\boldsymbol{x}) + \varepsilon|\boldsymbol{x}| \leq (c + 2\varepsilon)|\boldsymbol{x}| + g(|\boldsymbol{x}|)$$

hold. The last inequality implies that $u_{\boldsymbol{x}} \leq c + 2\varepsilon + o(1)$ at $|\boldsymbol{x}| \to \infty$ and thus for all sufficiently long sequences $\boldsymbol{x}$ we have $u_{\boldsymbol{x}} \leq c + 3\varepsilon$. Therefore the point $(u_{\boldsymbol{x}}, v_{\boldsymbol{x}})$ lies to the left of the line $x = c + 3\varepsilon$. This implies $v_{\boldsymbol{x}} \leq f_1(c + 3\varepsilon)$ and $\mathrm{AC}_2(L) \leq f_1(x + 3\varepsilon) + \varepsilon$. Since f_1 is continuous and $\varepsilon > 0$ is arbitrary, we get $\mathrm{AC}_2(L) \leq f_1(c) = c_1$.

Now let us prove that $\mathrm{AC}_2(L) \geq c_2$. Assume the contrary. Let $\mathrm{AC}_2(L) = c_2 - \delta_2$, where $\delta_2 > 0$. There is $\delta_1 > 0$ such that $f_2(c - \delta_1) = c_2 - \delta_2$. By applying the same argument as above to the 'swapped' situation, one can show that $\mathrm{AC}_1(L) \leq c - \delta_1$. This contradicts the assumption that $\mathrm{AC}_1(L) = c$.

In order to show that $(\mathrm{AC}_1(L), \mathrm{AC}_2(L)) \in \mathcal{S}$, it remains to prove that $(\mathrm{AC}_1(L), \mathrm{AC}_2(L)) \notin \mathcal{C} \setminus \mathcal{S}$. Let $U = \{(u, v) \in \mathbb{R}^2 \mid \exists (h_1, h_2) \in \mathcal{H} : h_1 \leq u \text{ and } h_2 \leq v\}$ be the set of points that lie 'above' the entropy set $\mathcal{H}$. Let e_i, $i = 0, 1, \ldots, M - 1$, be the vector with the i-th component equal to 1 and all other components equal to 0. Clearly, $e_i \in \mathbb{P}_M$; it represents a special degenerate distribution. We have $H_1(e_i) = \min_{\gamma \in \Gamma_1} \lambda_1(\omega^{(i)}, \gamma)$. For any prediction strategy $\mathfrak{A}$ we get

$$\mathrm{Loss}_{\mathfrak{A}}^{\mathfrak{G}_1}(\boldsymbol{x}) \geq \sum_{i=0}^{M-1} \sharp_i \boldsymbol{x} \min_{\gamma \in \Gamma_1} \lambda_1(\omega^{(i)}, \gamma) = |\boldsymbol{x}| \sum_{i=0}^{M-1} p_i H_1(e_i) \ ,$$

where $p_i = \sharp_i \boldsymbol{x} / |\boldsymbol{x}|$. The same holds for $\mathfrak{G}_2$. We thus get inequalities

$$\frac{\mathrm{Loss}_{\mathfrak{A}_1}^{\mathfrak{G}_1}(\boldsymbol{x})}{|\boldsymbol{x}|} \geq \sum_{i=0}^{M-1} p_i H_1(e_i) \quad \text{and} \quad \frac{\mathrm{Loss}_{\mathfrak{A}_2}^{\mathfrak{G}_2}(\boldsymbol{x})}{|\boldsymbol{x}|} \geq \sum_{i=0}^{M-1} p_i H_2(e_i) \ ,$$

where p_i depend only on $\boldsymbol{x}$, for all strategies $\mathfrak{A}_1$ and $\mathfrak{A}_2$. Therefore the pair $(\mathrm{Loss}_{\mathfrak{A}_1}^{\mathfrak{G}_1}(\boldsymbol{x})/|\boldsymbol{x}|, \mathrm{Loss}_{\mathfrak{A}_2}^{\mathfrak{G}_2}(\boldsymbol{x})/|\boldsymbol{x}|)$ belongs to U. Since U is closed, the same holds for every pair $(\mathrm{AC}_1(L), \mathrm{AC}_2(L))$.

6   Computability Aspects

The definition of the asymptotic complexity can be modified in the following way. The infima in definitions may be taken over a particular class of strategies. Examples of such classes are the computable strategies and polynomial-time computable strategies. This provides us with different definitions of asymptotic complexity. The theorems from this paper still hold for these modified complexities provided some straightforward adjustments are made.

If we want to take computability aspects into consideration, we need to impose computability restrictions on loss functions. If we are interested in computable strategies, it is natural to consider computable loss functions.

The definition of weak mixability needs modifying too. It is natural to require that the strategy $\mathfrak{A}$ obtained by aggregating $\mathfrak{A}_1$ and $\mathfrak{A}_2$ is computable by an algorithm that has access to oracles computing $\mathfrak{A}_1$ and $\mathfrak{A}_2$. Results from [6] still hold since strategies can be merged effectively provided λ is computable.

The recalibration procedure provides us with strategies $\mathfrak{A}_\varepsilon^1$ and $\mathfrak{A}_\varepsilon^2$ that are computable given an oracle computing $\mathfrak{A}$. The proof of the main theorem remains valid almost literally. Note that we do not require the languages L to be computable in any sense. We are only concerned with transforming some strategies into others. If the original strategies are computable, the resulting strategies will be computable too. All pairs $(\mathrm{AC}_1(L), \mathrm{AC}_2(L))$ still belong to the spaceship closure of the entropy hull and fill it.

Similar remarks can be made about polynomial-time computability.

Acknowledgements

The authors would like to thank Ivan Polikarov from the Moscow State University for his inspiring ideas on turnip and spaceships.

References

1. Cesa-Bianchi, N., Lugosi, G.: Prediction, Learning, and Games. Cambridge University Press, Cambridge (2006)
2. Vovk, V., Watkins, C.J.H.C.: Universal portfolio selection. In: Proceedings of the 11th Annual Conference on Computational Learning Theory, pp. 12–23. ACM Press, New York (1998)
3. Fortnow, L., Lutz, J.H.: Prediction and dimension. Journal of Computer and System Sciences 70(4), 570–589 (2005)
4. Grünwald, P.D., Dawid, A.P.: Game theory, maximum entropy, minimum discrepancy and robust Bayesian decision theory. The Annals of Statistics 32(4), 1367–1433 (2004)
5. Kalnishkan, Y., Vovk, V., Vyugin, M.V.: Loss functions, complexities, and the Legendre transformation. Theoretical Computer Science 313(2), 195–207 (2004)
6. Kalnishkan, Y., Vyugin, M.V.: The weak aggregating algorithm and weak mixability. In: Auer, P., Meir, R. (eds.) COLT 2005. LNCS (LNAI), vol. 3559, pp. 188–203. Springer, Heidelberg (2005)
7. Eggleston, H.G.: Convexity. Cambridge University Press, Cambridge (1958)
8. Hoeffding, W.: Probability inequalities for sums of bounded random variables. Journal of the American Statistical Association 58(301), 13–30 (1963)

Appendix A: Shapes of Entropy Hulls

In this section we discuss geometrical aspects of the statement of the main theorem in more detail.

We start with a fundamental property of entropy. The set $\mathbb{P}_M$ is convex. Therefore we can prove by direct calculation the following lemma.

Lemma 2. *If $H : \mathbb{P}_M \to \mathbb{R}$ is $\mathfrak{G}$-entropy, then H is concave.*

Note that concavity of H implies continuity of H. Therefore every entropy set is a closed set w.r.t. the standard Euclidean topology. It is also bounded. Thus the entropy hull is also bounded and closed (see, e.g., [7], Theorem 10).

We need to introduce a classification of planar convex sets. A closed convex $\mathcal{C} \subseteq \mathbb{R}^2$ is a *cucumber* if for every pair of points $(x_1, y_1), (x_2, y_2) \in \mathcal{C}$ the points $(\min(x_1, x_2), \min(y_1, y_2))$ and $(\max(x_1, x_2), \max(y_1, y_2))$ belong to $\mathcal{C}$. In other terms, a closed convex $\mathcal{C}$ is a cucumber if and only if there are nondecreasing functions $f_1, f_2 : I \to \mathbb{R}$, where I is an interval, perhaps infinite, such that $\mathcal{C} = \{(x, y) \mid x \in I \text{ and } f_1(x) \le y \le f_2(x)\}$.

If a closed convex set is not a cucumber, we call it a *turnip*.

We will formulate a criterion for $\mathcal{H}$ to be a cucumber. Let $\arg\min f$, where f is a function from I to $\mathbb{R}$, be the set of points of I where f achieves the value of its global minimum on I. If no global minimum exists, the set $\arg\min f$ is empty. The notation $\arg\max f$ is defined similarly.

Lemma 3. *If $H_1, H_2 : I \to \mathbb{R}$, where $I \subseteq \mathbb{R}^n$ is a closed bounded set, are two continuous functions, then the convex hull of the set $\{(H_1(p), H_2(p)) \mid p \in I\}$ is a cucumber if and only if the following pair of conditions hold:*

$$\arg\min H_1 \cap \arg\min H_2 \neq \varnothing$$
$$\arg\max H_1 \cap \arg\max H_2 \neq \varnothing .$$

In the binary case natural games, including the absolute-loss, square-loss and logarithmic games, are *symmetric*, i.e., their sets of superpredictions are symmetric w.r.t. the bisector of the positive quadrangle. For example, every game $\mathfrak{G} = \langle \mathbb{B}, [0,1], \lambda \rangle$ such that $\lambda(0, \gamma) = \lambda(1, 1 - \gamma)$ for all $\gamma \in [0,1]$ is symmetric. Clearly, if H is $\mathfrak{G}$-entropy w.r.t. a symmetric game $\mathfrak{G}$, then $H(p) = H(1 - p)$ for all $p \in [0,1]$. Thus H achieves its maximum at $p = 1/2$ and its minimum at $p = 0$ and $p = 1$. Therefore if H_1 and H_2 are entropies w.r.t. symmetric games $\mathfrak{G}_1$ and $\mathfrak{G}_2$, then their $\mathfrak{G}_1/\mathfrak{G}_2$-entropy hull is a cucumber.

The *cucumber closure* of a set $\mathcal{H} \subseteq \mathbb{R}^2$ is the smallest cucumber that contains $\mathcal{H}$, i.e., the intersection of all cucumbers that contain $\mathcal{H}$.

The definition of a spaceship given above uses only the upper point of the two that should belong to a cucumber. In terms of boundaries the definition is as follows. A closed convex $\mathcal{S} \subseteq \mathbb{R}^2$ is a spaceship if and only if there are functions $f_1, f_2 : I \to \mathbb{R}$, where I is an interval, perhaps infinite, such that f_2 is non-decreasing and $\mathcal{S} = \{(x, y) \mid x \in I \text{ and } f_1(x) \leq y \leq f_2(x)\}$.

Lemma 4. *If $H_1, H_2 : I \to \mathbb{R}$, where $I \subseteq \mathbb{R}$ is a closed bounded interval, are two continuous functions, then the convex hull of the set $\{(H_1(p), H_2(p)) \mid I\}$ is a spaceship if and only if the following condition holds:*

$$\arg\max H_1 \cap \arg\max H_2 \neq \varnothing . \tag{7}$$

Note that the definitions of turnips, cucumbers, and spaceships as well as of cucumber and spaceship closures are coordinate-dependent.

Appendix B: Examples of Entropy Hulls

This section contains some examples of entropy sets and hulls for the binary case.

It is easy to check by direct calculation that the ABS-entropy is given by $H^{\mathrm{ABS}}(p) = \min(p, 1 - p)$, the SQ-entropy is given by $H^{\mathrm{SQ}}(p) = p(1 - p)$, and the LOG-entropy is given by $H^{\mathrm{LOG}}(p) = -p \log_2 p - (1 - p) \log_2 (1 - p)$, and thus it coincides with Shannon entropy. The entropy hulls are shown on Figs. 2, 3, and 4; the corresponding entropy sets are represented by bold lines. Since all the three games are symmetric, the entropy hulls are cucumbers.

Let us construct an entropy hull that is a turnip. It follows from the previous section, that the example must be rather artificial. Let $\mathfrak{G}_1 = \langle \mathbb{B}, [0,1], \lambda_1 \rangle$, where $\lambda_1(0, \gamma) = \gamma$ and $\lambda_1(1, \gamma) = 1 - \frac{\gamma}{2}$ for all $\gamma \in [0,1]$, and let $\mathfrak{G}_2 = \langle \mathbb{B}, [0,1], \lambda_2 \rangle$, where $\lambda_2(0, \gamma) = 1 + \frac{\gamma}{2}$ and $\lambda_2(1, \gamma) = \frac{3}{2} - \gamma$ for all $\gamma \in [0,1]$. It is easy to evaluate

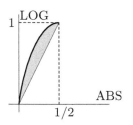

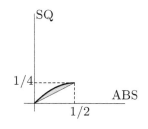

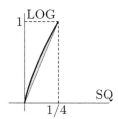

Fig. 2. The ABS/LOG-entropy set and hull

Fig. 3. The ABS/SQ-entropy set and hull

Fig. 4. The LOG/SQ-entropy set and hull

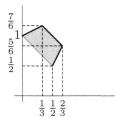

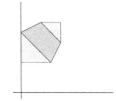

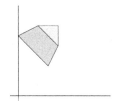

Fig. 5. The $\mathfrak{G}_1/\mathfrak{G}_2$-entropy hull (a turnip)

Fig. 6. The cucumber closure

Fig. 7. The spaceship closure

the corresponding entropies, $H_1(p) = \min(p, 1 - \frac{p}{2})$ and $H_2(p) = \min(1 + \frac{p}{2}, \frac{3}{2} - p)$. Fig. 5 shows $\mathfrak{G}_1/\mathfrak{G}_2$-entropy hull, which is a turnip. Figure 6 shows its cucumber closure, while Fig. 7 shows its spaceship closure.

Appendix C: Proof of the Recalibration Lemma

Let $\mathfrak{G}_1 = \langle \Omega, \Gamma_1, \lambda_1 \rangle$ and $\mathfrak{G}_2 = \langle \Omega, \Gamma_2, \lambda_2 \rangle$. We shall describe the procedure transforming $\mathfrak{A}$ into $\mathfrak{A}_\varepsilon^1$ and $\mathfrak{A}_\varepsilon^2$. The construction is in four stages.

First let us perform an ε-*quantisation* of $\mathfrak{A}$.

Lemma 5. *For any* $\mathfrak{G} = \langle \Omega, \Gamma, \lambda \rangle$ *and* $\varepsilon > 0$ *there is a finite set* Γ_ε *such that for any* $\gamma \in \Gamma$ *there is* $\gamma^* \in \Gamma_\varepsilon$ *such that* $\lambda(\omega, \gamma^*) \leq \lambda(\omega, \gamma) + \varepsilon$ *for every* $\omega \in \Omega$.

Lemma 2 from [6] implies that it is sufficient to consider bounded loss functions λ. If λ is bounded, the lemma follows from continuity of λ and compactness of Γ.

Let us find such finite subsets $\Gamma_\varepsilon' \subseteq \Gamma_1$ and $\Gamma_\varepsilon'' \subseteq \Gamma_2$. Without restricting the generality, one can assume that they are of the same size $|\Gamma_\varepsilon'| = |\Gamma_\varepsilon''| = N$; indeed, if this is not the case, we can add more elements to the smaller set. Let $\Gamma_\varepsilon' = \{\gamma_1, \gamma_2, \ldots, \gamma_N\}$ and $\Gamma_\varepsilon'' = \{\gamma_1'', \gamma_2'', \ldots, \gamma_N''\}$.

There is a strategy $\mathfrak{A}_\varepsilon^q$ that outputs only predictions from Γ_ε' and such that $\mathrm{Loss}_{\mathfrak{A}_\varepsilon^q}^{\mathfrak{G}_1}(\boldsymbol{x}) \leq \mathrm{Loss}_{\mathfrak{A}}^{\mathfrak{G}_1}(\boldsymbol{x}) + \varepsilon|\boldsymbol{x}|$ for all $\boldsymbol{x} \in \Omega^*$.

Secondly let us construct the table of frequencies.

Table 1. Predictions and outcomes for a given sequence x

Predictions	Number of $\omega^{(0)}$s	Number of $\omega^{(1)}$s	$\vdots$	Number of $\omega^{(M-1)}$s
γ_1	$n_1^{(0)}$	$n_1^{(1)}$		$n_1^{(M-1)}$
γ_2	$n_2^{(0)}$	$n_2^{(1)}$	$\vdots$	$n_2^{(M-1)}$
		$\ldots$		
γ_j	$n_j^{(0)}$	$n_j^{(1)}$	$\vdots$	$n_j^{(M-1)}$
		$\ldots$		
γ_N	$n_N^{(0)}$	$n_N^{(1)}$	$\vdots$	$n_N^{(M-1)}$

Given a sequence x of length n, let us count the number of times each of these predictions $\gamma_1, \gamma_2, \ldots, \gamma_N$ occurs as $\mathfrak{A}_\varepsilon^{\mathfrak{q}}$ predicts elements of x. For each $j = 1, 2, \ldots, N$ and $i = 0, 1, \ldots, M-1$ let $n_j^{(i)}$ be the number of occasions when $\mathfrak{A}_\varepsilon^{\mathfrak{q}}$ outputs the prediction γ_j just before the outcome $\omega^{(i)}$ occurs. We get Table 1, where $\sum_{j=1}^N n_j^{(i)} = \sharp_i x$ for all $i = 0, 1, \ldots, M-1$.

Thirdly we perform the recalibration and construct auxiliary 'strategies' $\widetilde{\mathfrak{A}_\varepsilon^{(1)}}$ and $\widetilde{\mathfrak{A}_\varepsilon^{(2)}}$. Formally they are not strategies because they have access to side information.

Suppose that we predict elements of x and have access to Table 1 right from the start. We can optimise the performance of $\mathfrak{A}_\varepsilon^{\mathfrak{q}}$ as follows. If on some step $\mathfrak{A}_\varepsilon^{\mathfrak{q}}$ outputs γ_j, we know that we are on the j-th line of the table. However γ_j is not necessarily the best prediction to output in this situation. Let γ_j^* be an element of Γ_ε where the minimum $\min_{\gamma \in \Gamma_\varepsilon} \sum_{i=0}^{M-1} n_j^{(i)} \lambda_1(\omega^{(i)}, \gamma)$ is attained. This minimum can be expressed though the generalised entropy H_1. Put $p_j^{(i)} = n_j^{(i)} / \sum_i n_j^{(i)}$; the M-tuple $p_j = (p_j^{(0)}, p_j^{(1)}, \ldots, p_j^{(M-1)})$ is a distribution on Ω. We have $\sum_{i=0}^{M-1} n_j^{(i)} \lambda_1(\omega^{(i)}, \gamma) = \left(\sum_i n_j^{(i)} \right) \sum_{i=0}^{M-1} p_j^{(i)} \lambda_1(\omega^{(i)}, \gamma)$ and thus

$$\left(\sum_i n_j^{(i)} \right) H_1(p_j) \leq \sum_{i=0}^{M-1} n_j^{(i)} \lambda_1(\omega^{(i)}, \gamma_j^*) \leq \left(\sum_i n_j^{(i)} \right) (H_1(p_j) + \varepsilon) . \quad (8)$$

Let us output γ_j^* each time instead of γ_j.

This is how the 'strategy' $\widetilde{\mathfrak{A}_\varepsilon^1}$ works. The loss of $\widetilde{\mathfrak{A}_\varepsilon^1}$ on x is $\mathrm{Loss}_{\widetilde{\mathfrak{A}_\varepsilon^1}}^{\mathfrak{G}_1}(x) = \sum_{j=1}^N \sum_{i=0}^{M-1} n_j^{(i)} \lambda_1(\omega^{(i)}, \gamma_j^*)$. Put $q_j = \left(\sum_{i=0}^{M-1} n_j^{(i)} \right) / n$; we have $\sum_j q_j = 1$. It follows from (8) that

$$\left| \mathrm{Loss}_{\widetilde{\mathfrak{A}_\varepsilon^1}}^{\mathfrak{G}_1}(x) - n \sum_{j=1}^N q_j H_1(p_j) \right| \leq \varepsilon n . \quad (9)$$

On the other hand, $\mathrm{Loss}^{\mathfrak{G}_1}_{\widetilde{\mathfrak{A}^1_\varepsilon}}(\boldsymbol{x}) \leq \mathrm{Loss}^{\mathfrak{G}_1}_{\mathfrak{A}^q_\varepsilon}(\boldsymbol{x}) \leq \mathrm{Loss}^{\mathfrak{G}_1}_{\mathfrak{A}}(\boldsymbol{x}) + \varepsilon n$ because $\widetilde{\mathfrak{A}^1_\varepsilon}$ attempts to minimise losses. Note that each sequence $\boldsymbol{x} \in \Omega^*$ specifies its own sets of values p and q.

The strategy $\widetilde{\mathfrak{A}^2_\varepsilon}$ works as follows. It simulates $\widetilde{\mathfrak{A}^q_\varepsilon}$ and when $\widetilde{\mathfrak{A}^q_\varepsilon}$ outputs γ_j it finds itself on the j-th line of the table and outputs $\gamma_j^{**} \in \Gamma_\varepsilon''$ such that the minimum $\min_{\gamma \in \Gamma_\varepsilon''} \sum_{i=0}^{M-1} n_j^{(i)} \lambda_2(\omega^{(i)}, \gamma)$ is attained on γ_j^{**}. We obtain

$$\left| \mathrm{Loss}^{\mathfrak{G}_2}_{\widetilde{\mathfrak{A}^2_\varepsilon}}(\boldsymbol{x}) - n \sum_{i=1}^N q_i H_2(p_i) \right| \leq \varepsilon n \ . \tag{10}$$

Finally, we should get rid of the side information; prediction strategies are not supposed to use any. There is a finite number (to be precise, N^N) of functions that map $\{1, 2, \ldots, N\}$ into itself. Every $\sigma : \{1, 2, \ldots, N\} \to \{1, 2, \ldots, N\}$ defines a strategy that works as follows. The strategy runs $\mathfrak{A}^q_\varepsilon$, and each time $\mathfrak{A}^q_\varepsilon$ outputs γ_i our strategy outputs $\gamma_{\sigma(i)}$, $i = 1, 2, \ldots, N$. For every finite sequence $\boldsymbol{x}$ there is a mapping σ such that the corresponding strategy works exactly like $\widetilde{\mathfrak{A}^1_\varepsilon}$.

Since the game $\mathfrak{G}_1$ is weakly mixable, we can obtain $\mathfrak{A}^1_\varepsilon$ that works nearly as good as each one from the final pool of strategies when the loss is measured w.r.t. the loss function λ_1. We get

$$\mathrm{Loss}^{\mathfrak{G}_1}_{\mathfrak{A}^1_\varepsilon}(\boldsymbol{x}) \leq n \sum_{i=1}^N q_i H_1(p_i) + \varepsilon n + f_1(n) \tag{11}$$

for every $\boldsymbol{x}$, where $f_1(n) = o(n)$ as $n \to +\infty$. Similarly, there is $\mathfrak{A}^2_\varepsilon$ such that

$$\mathrm{Loss}^{\mathfrak{G}_2}_{\mathfrak{A}^2_\varepsilon}(\boldsymbol{x}) \leq n \sum_{i=1}^N q_i H_2(p_i) + \varepsilon n + f_2(n) \tag{12}$$

for every $\boldsymbol{x}$, where $f_2(n) = o(n)$ as $n \to +\infty$. The lemma follows.

Appendix D: Filling in the Spaceship

We shall now construct languages $L \subseteq \Omega^\infty$ such that $\overline{\mathrm{AC}}_1(L) = \overline{\overline{\mathrm{AC}}}_1(L) = \underline{\mathrm{AC}}_1(L) = \underline{\underline{\mathrm{AC}}}_1(L)$ as well as $\overline{\mathrm{AC}}_2(L) = \overline{\overline{\mathrm{AC}}}_2(L) = \underline{\mathrm{AC}}_2(L) = \underline{\underline{\mathrm{AC}}}_2(L)$ and pairs $(\mathrm{AC}_1(L), \mathrm{AC}_2(L))$ fill the spaceship closure.

We start by constructing languages filling in the entropy set, then construct languages filling in the entropy hull and finally obtain languages filling in the spaceship closure. First let $u = H_1(p)$ and $v = H_2(p)$ for some $p \in \mathbb{P}(\Omega)$.

Lemma 6. *For every $p \in \mathbb{P}(\Omega)$ there is a set $L_p \subseteq \Omega^\infty$ such that for every game $\mathfrak{G} = \langle \Omega, \Gamma, \lambda \rangle$ we have $\overline{\mathrm{AC}}(L_p) = \overline{\overline{\mathrm{AC}}}(L_p) = \underline{\mathrm{AC}}(L_p) = \underline{\underline{\mathrm{AC}}}(L_p) = H(p)$.*

Proof (of the Lemma)
Let $p = (p_0, p_1, \ldots, p_{M-1}) \in \mathbb{P}(\Omega)$. If some of p_i are equal to 0, we can completely ignore those dimensions, or, in other words, consider the games with the sets of superpredictions that are the projection of the sets of superpredictions w.r.t. G_1 and $\mathfrak{G}_2$ to non-zero directions. So let us assume, without restricting the generality, that all $p_i \neq 0$.

Consider the set $\Xi_n^{(p)} \subseteq \Omega^n$ of sequences $\boldsymbol{x}$ of length n with the following property. For each $i = 0, 1, \ldots, M-1$ the number of $\omega^{(i)}$s among the elements of $\boldsymbol{x}$ is between the numbers $np_i - n^{3/4}$ and $np_i + n^{3/4}$, i.e., $np_i - n^{3/4} \leq \sharp_i \boldsymbol{x} \leq np_i + n^{3/4}$ for $i = 0, 1, \ldots, M-1$.

We need the Chernoff bound in Hoeffding's form (see Theorem 1 in [8]):

Proposition 1 (Chernoff bound). *If $\xi_1, \xi_2, \ldots, \xi_n$ are independent random variables with finite first and second moments and such that $0 \leq \xi_i \leq 1$ for all $i = 1, 2, \ldots, n$ then*

$$\Pr\{\overline{\xi} - \mu \geq t\} \leq e^{-2nt^2} ,$$

for all $t \in (0, 1 - \mu)$, where $\overline{\xi} = (\xi_1 + \xi_2 + \ldots + \xi_n)/n$ and $\mu = \mathbf{E}\overline{\xi}$.

Let $\xi_1^{(p)}, \xi_2^{(p)}, \ldots, \xi_n^{(p)}$ be independent random variables that accept the values $\omega^{(i)}$ with probabilities p_i, $i = 0, 1, \ldots, M-1$. The Chernoff bound implies that

$$\Pr\left\{\left|\sharp_i(\xi_1^{(p)} \xi_2^{(p)} \ldots, \xi_n^{(p)}) - p_i n\right| \geq n^{3/4}\right\} \leq 2e^{-2\sqrt{n}} \qquad (13)$$

for all $n \geq N_0$ (the constant N_0 is necessary in order to ensure that $t \leq 1 - \mu$ in the bound) and all $i = 0, 1, \ldots, M-1$. If we denote by $\Pr_p(S)$ the probability that $\xi_1^{(p)} \xi_2^{(p)} \ldots, \xi_n^{(p)} \in S$, we get $\Pr_p(\Omega^n \setminus \Xi_n^{(p)}) \leq 2M e^{-2\sqrt{n}}$.

Let $L_p = \Xi_{n_1}^{(p)} \times \Xi_{n_2}^{(p)} \times \Xi_{n_3}^{(p)} \ldots \times \Xi_{n_k}^{(p)} \times \ldots \subseteq \Omega^\infty$. In other terms, L_p consists of all infinite sequences $\boldsymbol{x}$ with the following property. For every non-negative integer k the elements of $\boldsymbol{x}$ from $\sum_{j=1}^{k-1} n_j$ to $\sum_{j=1}^{k} n_j$ form a sequence from $\Xi_{n_k}^{(p)}$. We will refer to these elements as the k-th segment of L_p. Take $n_j = N_0 + j$ so that $\sum_{j=1}^{k} n_j = kN_0 + k(k+1)/2$. We will show that L_p proves the lemma.

First let us prove that $\mathrm{AC}(L_p) \leq H(p)$. Let $\mathfrak{A}^{(p)}$ be the strategy that always outputs the same prediction $\gamma^* \in \arg\min_{\gamma \in \Gamma} \sum_{i=0}^{M-1} p_i \lambda(\omega^{(i)}, \gamma)$. Let $n = \sum_{j=1}^{k} n_j$. There is a constant $C_{\gamma^*} > 0$ such that for every $\boldsymbol{x} \in L_p$ we get

$$\mathrm{Loss}_{\mathfrak{A}^{(p)}}(\boldsymbol{x}|_n) \leq H(P)n + M C_{\gamma^*} \sum_{j=1}^{k} n_j^{3/4} .$$

We have

$$\frac{\sum_{j=1}^{k} n_j^{3/4}}{n} = \frac{\sum_{j=1}^{k}(N_0 + j)^{3/4}}{\sum_{j=1}^{k}(N_0 + j)} \sim \frac{\frac{4}{7}k^{7/4}}{\frac{1}{2}k^2} \to 0$$

as $k \to +\infty$. Therefore $\overline{\mathrm{AC}}(L_p)$ and $\underline{\mathrm{AC}}(L_p)$ do not exceed $H(p)$.

Now consider m such that $n - n_k = \sum_{j=1}^{k-1} n_j < m < \sum_{j=1}^{k} n_j = n$. It is easy to see that $|\operatorname{Loss}_{\mathfrak{A}(p)}(\boldsymbol{x}|_n) - \operatorname{Loss}_{\mathfrak{A}(p)}(\boldsymbol{x}|_m)| \leq C_{\gamma*} n_k$. We have

$$\frac{n_k}{m} \leq \frac{(N_0 + k)}{\sum_{j=1}^{k-1}(N_0 + j)} = \frac{(N_0 + k)}{N_0(k-1) + k(k-1)/2} \to 0 \tag{14}$$

and hence the upper complexities do not exceed $H(p)$ either.

Now let us prove that $\operatorname{AC}(L_p) \geq H(p)$. Consider a strategy $\mathfrak{A}$. First let us assume that λ is bounded and $D > 0$ is an upper bound on λ. We have

$$H(p)n \leq \mathbf{E}\operatorname{Loss}_{\mathfrak{A}}(\xi_1^{(p)}\xi_2^{(p)}\ldots,\xi_n^{(p)}) \leq \Pr_p(\Xi_n) \max_{\boldsymbol{x} \in \Xi_n} \operatorname{Loss}_{\mathfrak{A}}(\boldsymbol{x}) + \Pr_p(\Omega^n \setminus \Xi_n)Dn .$$

Therefore there is a sequence $\boldsymbol{x} \in \Xi_n$ such that

$$\operatorname{Loss}_{\mathfrak{A}}(\boldsymbol{x}) \geq H(p)n - \Pr_p(\Omega^n \setminus \Xi_n)Dn \geq H(p)n - 2nMDe^{-2\sqrt{n}}$$

provided $n \geq N_0$.

We construct $\boldsymbol{x} \in L_p$ from finite segments of length n_i. The series $\sum_{j=1}^{\infty}(N_0 + j)e^{-2\sqrt{N_0+j}}$ converges and thus upper complexities are at least $H(p)$. We can extend this bound to lower complexity by using (14).

Now let λ be unbounded. Take $\lambda^{(D)} = \min(\lambda, D)$, where D is a constant. It is easy to see that for sufficiently large D we get $\min_{\gamma \in \Gamma} \sum_{i=0}^{M-1} p_i\lambda(\omega^{(i)}, \gamma) = \min_{\gamma \in \Gamma} \sum_{i=0}^{M-1} p_i\lambda^{(D)}(\omega^{(i)}, \gamma)$ (recall that $p \in \mathbb{P}(\Omega)$ is fixed).

Pick such D and let $\mathfrak{G}^{(D)}$ be the game with the loss function $\lambda^{(D)}$. It is easy to see that for every strategy $\mathfrak{A}$ and every sequence $\boldsymbol{x}$ we have $\operatorname{Loss}_{\mathfrak{A}}^{\mathfrak{G}}(\boldsymbol{x}) \geq \operatorname{Loss}_{\mathfrak{A}}^{\mathfrak{G}^{(D)}}(\boldsymbol{x})$. Since the loss function $\lambda^{(D)}$ is bounded, one can apply the above argument; for every $\mathfrak{A}$ and every n there is a sequence $\boldsymbol{x} \in L_p$ such that $\operatorname{Loss}_{\mathfrak{A}}^{\mathfrak{G}^{(D)}}(\boldsymbol{x}|_n) \geq H(p)n - o(n)$. The inequality implies $\operatorname{Loss}_{\mathfrak{A}}^{\mathfrak{G}}(\boldsymbol{x}|_n) \geq H(p)n - o(n)$. This proves the lemma. $\quad\square$

Secondly let (u, v) be some point from $\mathcal{H}$. The definition of convexity implies that there are probabilities $p_1, p_2, \ldots, p_N \in \mathbb{P}(\Omega)$ and weights $q_1, q_2, \ldots, q_N \in [0, 1]$ such that $u = \sum_{j=1}^{N} q_j H_1(p_j)$ and $v = \sum_{j=1}^{N} q_j H_2(p_j)$.

Let us 'paint' all positive integers into N colours $1, 2, \ldots, N$. Number 1 is painted colour 1. Suppose that all numbers from 1 to n have been painted and there are n_1 numbers among them painted colour 1, n_2 numbers painted colour 2 etc. The values $q_j n - n_j$ are *deficiencies*. Let j_0 corresponds to the largest deficiency (if there are several largest deficiencies, we take the one with the smallest j). We paint the number $n + 1$ the colour j_0.

During the infinite construction process deficiencies never exceed N. Indeed, the value $-(q_j n - n_j)$ never exceeds 1 and the sum of all deficiencies is 0.

We now proceed to constructing $L \subseteq \Omega^\infty$ that corresponds to (u, v). The set L consists of all infinite sequences $\boldsymbol{x}$ with the following property. The subsequence of $\boldsymbol{x}$ formed by bits with numbers painted the colour j belongs to L_{p_j} from Lemma 6 for all $j = 1, 2, \ldots, N$. One can easily check that L has all the required properties.

Thirdly let $(u, v) \in \mathcal{S} \setminus \mathcal{H}$. It is easy to check that if a game $\mathfrak{G}$ is weakly mixable, then for every pair of languages L_1, L_2 constructed above we have $\operatorname{AC}(L_1 \cup L_2) = \max(\operatorname{AC}(L_1), \operatorname{AC}(L_2))$.

Q-Learning with Linear Function Approximation[*]

Francisco S. Melo[**] and M. Isabel Ribeiro

Institute for Systems and Robotics,
Instituto Superior Técnico,
Lisboa, Portugal
{fmelo,mir}@isr.ist.utl.pt

Abstract. In this paper, we analyze the convergence of Q-learning with linear function approximation. We identify a set of conditions that implies the convergence of this method with probability 1, when a fixed learning policy is used. We discuss the differences and similarities between our results and those obtained in several related works. We also discuss the applicability of this method when a changing policy is used. Finally, we describe the applicability of this approximate method in partially observable scenarios.

1 Introduction

Value-based methods such as TD-learning [1], Q-learning [2], SARSA [3] and others [4,5,6] have been exhaustively covered in the reinforcement learning (RL) literature and, under mild assumptions, have been proven to converge to the desired solution [7].

However, many such algorithms require explicit representation of the state-space, and it is often the case that the latter is unsuited for explicit representation. A common way to overcome this difficulty is to combine a suitable approximation architecture with one's favorite learning method [8,9]. Encouraging results were reported, perhaps the most spectacular of which by Tesauro's Gammon player [10]. Several other works provided formal analysis of convergence when RL algorithms are combined with function approximation. We refer the early works by Singh et al. [11], Gordon [12] and Van Roy [13]. A few other works further extended the applicability/performance of these methods, *e.g.*, [6,14,15,16].

In this paper, we analyze the convergence of Q-learning with linear function approximation. Our approach is closely related to interpolation-based Q-learning [15] and the learning algorithm by Borkar [17]. We identify conditions that ensure convergence of our method with probability 1 (w.p.1). We interpret the obtained approximation and discuss the corresponding error bounds. We conclude the

---

[*] This work was partially supported by Programa Operacional Sociedade do Conhecimento (POS_C) that includes FEDER funds.
[**] The author acknowledges the PhD grant SFRH/BD/3074/2000.

N. Bshouty and C. Gentile (Eds.): COLT 2007, LNAI 4539, pp. 308–322, 2007.

paper by addressing the applicability of our methods to partially observable scenarios. [1]

2   The Framework of Markov Decision Process

A *Markov decision process* (MDP) is a tuple $(\mathcal{X}, \mathcal{A}, \mathsf{P}, r, \gamma)$ where $\mathcal{X}$ is compact subspace of $\mathbb{R}^p$ representing the state-space and $\mathcal{A}$ is a finite set of possible actions. $\mathsf{P}_a(x, U)$ is a probability kernel determining the probability of moving from state $x \in \mathcal{X}$ to a measurable set $U \subset \mathcal{X}$ by choosing action $a \in \mathcal{A}$. The function $r : \mathcal{X} \times \mathcal{A} \times \mathcal{X} \longrightarrow \mathbb{R}$ is a deterministic function assigning a numerical reward $r(x, a, y)$ every time a transition from x to y occurs after taking action a. The use of this function r greatly simplifies the notation without introducing a great loss in generality. We further assume that there is a constant $\mathcal{R} \in \mathbb{R}$ such that $|r(x, a, y)| < \mathcal{R}$ for all $x, y \in \mathcal{X}$ and all $a \in \mathcal{A}$.[2] The constant $0 < \gamma < 1$ is a discount-factor.

The purpose of the agent is to maximize the expected total sum of discounted rewards, $\mathbb{E}\left[\sum_{t=0}^{\infty} \gamma^t R(X_t, A_t)\right]$, where $R(x, a)$ represents the random "reward" received for taking action $a \in \mathcal{A}$ in state $x \in \mathcal{X}$.[3] The *optimal value function* V^* is defined for each state $x \in \mathcal{X}$ as

$$V^*(x) = \max_{\{A_t\}} \mathbb{E}\left[\sum_{t=0}^{\infty} \gamma^t R(X_t, A_t) \mid X_0 = x\right] \tag{1}$$

and verifies

$$V^*(x) = \max_{a \in \mathcal{A}} \int_{\mathcal{X}} \left[r(x, a, y) + \gamma V^*(y)\right] \mathsf{P}_a(x, dy).$$

which is a form of the Bellman optimality equation. The optimal Q-values $Q^*(x, a)$ are defined for each state-action pair $(x, a) \in \mathcal{X} \times \mathcal{A}$ as

$$Q^*(x, a) = \int_{\mathcal{X}} \left[r(x, a, y) + \gamma V^*(y)\right] \mathsf{P}_a(x, dy). \tag{2}$$

From Q^*, the *optimal policy* is defined as a mapping $\pi^* : \mathcal{X} \longrightarrow \mathcal{A}$ verifying

$$\pi^*(x) = \arg\max_{a \in \mathcal{A}} Q^*(x, a), \qquad \text{for all } x \in \mathcal{X}.$$

Since the optimal policy π^* can be obtained from Q^*, the optimal control problem is solved once the function Q^* is known for all pairs $(x, a) \in \mathcal{X} \times \mathcal{A}$.

More generally, we define a *policy* π_t as a mapping $\pi_t : \mathcal{X} \times \mathcal{A} \longrightarrow [0, 1]$ that generates a control process $\{A_t\}$ verifying

$$\mathbb{P}\left[A_t = a \mid X_t = x\right] = \pi_t(x, a),$$

---

[1] Due to space limitations, we do not include the proof of the results in here and simply provide the general idea behind the proof. The details can be found in [18].

[2] This assumption is tantamount to the standard requirement that the rewards $R(x, a)$ have uniformly bounded variance.

[3] Notice that $R(x, a)$ is random in its dependence of the next state.

for all t. Since $\pi_t(x,\cdot)$ is a probability distribution over $\mathcal{A}$, it must satisfy $\sum_{a\in\mathcal{A}} \pi_t(x,a) = 1$, for all $x \in \mathcal{X}$. A *stationary policy* is a policy π that does not depend on t. A *deterministic policy* is a policy assigning probability 1 to a single action in each state. We denote such policy as a function $\pi_t : \mathcal{X} \longrightarrow \mathcal{A}$.

Given any function $q : \mathcal{X} \times \mathcal{A} \longrightarrow \mathbb{R}$, we can define the operator

$$(\mathbf{H}q)(x,a) = \int_{\mathcal{X}} \left[r(x,a,y) + \gamma \max_{u\in\mathcal{A}} q(y,u)\right] \mathsf{P}_a(x,dy). \qquad (3)$$

The function Q^* introduced above is a fixed-point of the operator $\mathbf{H}$. This operator is a contraction in the sup-norm and, theoretically, a fixed-point iteration could be used to determine Q^*. On the other hand, if P or r (or both) are not known, the *Q-learning algorithm* can be used, defined by the update rule

$$Q_{k+1}(x,a) = (1 - \alpha_k)Q_k(x,a) + \alpha_k\left[R(x,a) + \gamma \max_{u\in\mathcal{A}} Q_k(X(x,a),u)\right], \qquad (4)$$

where $Q_k(x,a)$ is the kth estimate of $Q^*(x,a)$, $X(x,a)$ is a $\mathcal{X}$-valued random variable obtained according to the probabilities defined by P and $\{\alpha_k\}$ is a step-size sequence. Notice that $R(x,a)$ and $X(x,a)$ can be obtained through some simulation device, not requiring the knowledge of either P or r. The estimates Q_k converge with probability 1 (w.p.1) to Q^* as long as

$$\sum_t \alpha_t = \infty \qquad\qquad \sum_t \alpha_t^2 < \infty.$$

The Q-learning algorithm was first proposed by Watkins in 1989 [2] and its convergence w.p.1 later established by several authors [19, 7].

3   *Q*-Learning with Linear Function Approximation

In this section, we establish the convergence properties of Q-learning when using linear function approximation. We identify the conditions ensuring convergence w.p.1 and derive error bounds for the obtained approximation. The results derived herein are deeply related with other approaches described in the literature, *e.g.*, [15, 17].

3.1   Combining *Q*-Learning with Linear Function Approximation

We previously suggested that a fixed-point iteration could theoretically be used to determine Q^*. This implicitly requires that the successive estimates for Q^* can be represented compactly and stored in a computer with finite memory. To solve for Q^* we can use the fixed-point iteration proposed in Section 2 or the Q-learning algorithm, if P and r are not known.

However, if $\mathcal{X}$ is an infinite set, it is no longer possible to straightforwardly apply any of the aforementioned methods. For example, the updates in (4) explicitly consider the Q-values for each individual state-action pair and there will be infinitely many such pairs if $\mathcal{X}$ is not finite. Therefore, some compact representation of either $\mathcal{X}$ or Q^* is necessary to tackle the infinite nature of $\mathcal{X}$. In our approach, we focus on compact representations for Q^*.

In our pursuit to approximate Q^*, we consider a family of functions $\mathcal{Q} = \{Q_\theta\}$ parameterized by a finite-dimensional parameter vector $\theta \in \mathbb{R}^M$. We replace the iterative procedure to find Q^* by a suitable "equivalent" procedure to find a parameter θ^* so as to best approximate Q^* by a function in $\mathcal{Q}$. We thus move from a search in an infinite dimensional function space to a search in a finite dimensional space ($\mathbb{R}^M$). This has an immediate implication: unless if $Q^* \in \mathcal{Q}$, we will not be able to determine Q^* exactly. Instead, we will determine the fixed point of a combined operator $\mathcal{P}\mathbf{H}$, where $\mathcal{P}$ is some mapping that "projects" a function defined in $\mathcal{X} \times \mathcal{A}$ to a point in $\mathcal{Q}$.

In this paper we admit the family $\mathcal{Q}$ to be linear in that if $q_1, q_2 \in \mathcal{Q}$, then so does $\alpha q_1 + q_2$ for any $\alpha \in \mathbb{R}$. Thus, $\mathcal{Q}$ is the linear span of some set of linearly independent functions $\xi_i : \mathcal{X} \times \mathcal{A} \longrightarrow \mathbb{R}$, and each $q \in \mathcal{Q}$ can be written as a linear combination of such ξ_i. Therefore, if $\Xi = \{\xi_1, \ldots, \xi_M\}$ is a set of linearly independent functions, we interchangeably use Q_θ and $Q(\theta)$ to denote the function

$$Q_\theta(x, a) = \sum_{i=1}^{M} \xi_i(x, a)\theta(i) = \xi^\top(x, a)\theta, \qquad (5)$$

where $\theta(i)$ is the ith component of the the vector $\theta \in \mathbb{R}^M$ and $\xi_i(x, a)$ is the ith component of the vector $\xi(x, a) \in \mathbb{R}^M$.

We throughout take $\Xi = \{\xi_i, i = 1, \ldots, M\}$ as a set of M bounded, linearly independent functions verifying

$$\sum_i |\xi_i(x, a)| \leq 1 \qquad (6)$$

for all $(x, a) \in \mathcal{X} \times \mathcal{A}$ and eventually introduce further restrictions on the set Ξ as needed.

3.2   Linear Approximation Using Sample-Based Projection

We now consider a sample-based approximation model that, while imposing somewhat strict conditions on the set of functions Ξ, will allow us to derive useful error bounds for the obtained approximation Q_{θ^*}. For that, we assume that the functions in Ξ verify

$$\|\xi_i\|_\infty = 1. \qquad (7)$$

Clearly, if (6) and (7) simultaneously hold, linear independence of the functions in Ξ arises as an immediate consequence. [4] We take the family $\mathcal{Q}$ as the linear span of Ξ.

For each function $\xi_i \in \Xi$ we take a point (x_i, a_i) in $\mathcal{X} \times \mathcal{A}$ such that $|\xi_i(x_i, a_i)| = 1$ and denote by I the set obtained by gathering M of such points, one for each $\xi_i \in$

---

[4] For each function $\xi_i \in \Xi$ there is a point (x, a) such that $|\xi_i(x, a)| = 1$, as $\|\xi_i\|_\infty = 1$. Then, $\xi_j(x, a) = 0$ for all $j \neq i$ and the functions in Ξ are linearly independent.

Ξ. Let $\mathcal{B}$ is the set of all (essentially) bounded functions defined on $\mathcal{X} \times \mathcal{A}$ and taking values on $\mathbb{R}$ and define the mapping $\wp : \mathcal{B} \longrightarrow \mathbb{R}^M$ as

$$(\wp f)(i) = f(x_i, a_i), \tag{8}$$

where $(\wp f)(i)$ denotes the ith component of $\wp f$ and (x_i, a_i) is the point in I corresponding to ξ_i. $\wp f$ is properly defined for every $f \in \mathcal{B}$ and verifies

$$\|\wp f\|_\infty \leq \|f\|_\infty$$
$$\wp[\alpha f_1 + f_2] = \alpha \wp f_1 + \wp f_2.$$

Our variant of Q-learning iteratively determines the point $\theta^* \in \mathbb{R}^M$ verifying the fixed-point recursion

$$\theta^* = \wp \mathbf{H} Q(\theta^*), \tag{9}$$

where $\mathbf{H}$ is the operator defined in (3). Since $\mathbf{H}$ is a contraction in the sup-norm and $\sum_i |\xi_i(x, a)| \leq 1$, the fixed point in (9) is properly and uniquely defined.

To derive the expression of the algorithm, we remark that (9) can be explicitly written as

$$\theta^*(i) = \int_{\mathcal{X}} \delta_{(x_i, a_i)}(x, a) \int_{\mathcal{X}} \left[r(x, a, y) + \gamma \max_u \xi^\top(y, u)\theta^* \right] \mathsf{P}_a(x, dy) d\mu(x, a),$$

where μ is some probability measure on $\mathcal{X} \times \mathcal{A}$ and $\delta_{(x_i, a_i)}$ is the Dirac delta centered around (x_i, a_i). Let g_ε be a smooth Dirac approximation, such that

$$\int g_\varepsilon(x, a; y, u) d\mu(y, u) = 1$$

$$\lim_{\varepsilon \to 0} \int g_\varepsilon(x, a; y, u) f(y, u) d\mu(y, u) = f(x, a).$$

Let π be a stochastic stationary policy and suppose that $\{x_t\}$, $\{a_t\}$ and $\{r_t\}$ are sampled trajectories from the MDP $(\mathcal{X}, \mathcal{A}, \mathsf{P}, r, \gamma)$ using policy π. Then, given any initial estimate θ_0, we generate a sequence $\{\theta_t\}$ according to the update rule

$$\theta_{t+1}(i) = \theta_t(i) + \alpha_t g_{\varepsilon_t}(x_i, a_i; x_t, a_t) \left[r_t + \gamma \max_{u \in \mathcal{A}} \xi^\top(x_{t+1}, u)\theta_t - \xi^\top(x_t, a_t)\theta_t \right],$$

where $\{\varepsilon_t\}$ is a sequence verifying

$$\varepsilon_{t+1} = (1 - \beta_t)\varepsilon_t.$$

More generally, we can have

$$\varepsilon_{t+1} = \varepsilon_t + \beta_t h(\varepsilon_t),$$

where h is chosen so that the ODE $\dot{x}_t = h(x_t)$ has a globally asymptotically stable equilibrium in the origin.

Under some regularity assumptions on the Markov chain $(\mathcal{X}, \mathsf{P}_\pi)$ obtained using the policy π and on the step-sizes α_t and β_t, the trajectories of the algorithm closely follow those of an associated ODE with a globally asymptotically stable equilibrium point θ^*. Therefore, the sequence $\{\theta_t\}$ will converge w.p.1 to the equilibrium point θ^* of the ODE.

We now state our main convergence result. Given a MDP $(\mathcal{X}, \mathcal{A}, \mathsf{P}, r, \gamma)$, let π be a stationary stochastic policy and $(\mathcal{X}, \mathsf{P}_\pi)$ the corresponding Markov chain with invariant probability measure μ_X. Denote by $\mathbb{E}_\pi[\cdot]$ the expectation w.r.t. the probability measure μ_π defined for every set $Z \times U \subset \mathcal{X} \times \mathcal{A}$ as

$$\mu_\pi(Z \times U) = \int_Z \sum_{a \in U} \pi(x, a) \mu_X(dx).$$

Also, define $\hat{\alpha}_t(i)$ as

$$\hat{\alpha}_t(i) = \alpha_t g_{\varepsilon_t}(x_i, a_i; x_t, a_t).$$

Theorem 1. *Let $(\mathcal{X}, \mathcal{A}, \mathsf{P}, r, \gamma)$ be a Markov decision process and assume the Markov chain $(\mathcal{X}, \mathsf{P}_\pi)$ to be geometrically ergodic with invariant probability measure μ_X. Suppose that $\pi(x, a) > 0$ for all $a \in \mathcal{A}$ and μ_X-almost all $x \in \mathcal{X}$.*

Let $\Xi = \{\xi_i, i = 1, \ldots, M\}$ be a set of M functions defined on $\mathcal{X} \times \mathcal{A}$ and taking values in $\mathbb{R}$. In particular, admit the functions in Ξ to verify $\|\xi_i\|_\infty = 1$ and $\sum_i |\xi_i(x, a)| \leq 1$.

Then, the following hold:

1. ***Convergence:** For any initial condition $\theta_0 \in \mathbb{R}^M$, the algorithm*

$$\theta_{t+1}(i) = \theta_t(i) + \alpha_t g_{\varepsilon_t}(x_i, a_i; x_t, a_t) \big[r_t + \gamma \max_{u \in \mathcal{A}} \xi^\top(x_{t+1}, u)\theta_t - \xi^\top(x_t, a_t)\theta_t \big],$$

(10a)

$$\varepsilon_{t+1} = (1 - \beta_t)\varepsilon_t.$$

(10b)

converges w.p.1 as long as the step-size sequences $\{\alpha_t\}, \{\beta_t\}$ are such that

$$\sum_t \alpha_t = \infty \qquad\qquad \sum_t \alpha_t^2 < \infty;$$

(11a)

$$\sum_t \beta_t = \infty \qquad\qquad \sum_t \beta_t^2 < \infty$$

(11b)

$\beta_t = o(\alpha_t)$ and $\{\alpha_t\}$ is built so that $\min_i \sum_t \hat{\alpha}_t(i) = \infty$.

2. ***Limit of convergence:** Under these conditions, the limit function $Q(\theta^*)$ of (10) verifies*

$$Q_{\theta^*}(x, a) = (\mathcal{P}\mathbf{H}Q_{\theta^*})(x, a),$$

(12)

where $\mathcal{P} : \mathcal{B} \to \mathcal{Q}$ denotes the operator given by

$$(\mathcal{P}Q)(x, a) = \xi^\top(x, a)\wp Q.$$

3. ***Error bounds:** Under these conditions, the limit function Q_{θ^*} verifies the bound*

$$\|Q(\theta^*) - Q^*\|_\infty \leq \frac{1}{1 - \gamma} \|\mathcal{P}Q^* - Q^*\|_\infty.$$

(13)

Proof. See [18].

3.3   Discussion

Before concluding this section, we briefly discuss the conditions of Theorem 1 and compare our results with several related works in the literature.

Convergence Conditions: In Theorem 1 we identified several conditions that guarantee convergence w.p.1 of the algorithm defined by the update rule in (10). These conditions can be classified in two main groups: *conditions on the problem* and *conditions on the algorithm*.

The fundamental condition on the model is that of *geometric ergodicity of the Markov chain* $(\mathcal{X}, \mathsf{P}_\pi)$. Geometric ergodicity ensures that the chain converges exponentially fast to stationarity and, as such, its steady-state behavior is properly captured by the sample trajectories used in the updates. This allows the analysis of convergence to be conducted in terms of a stationary "version" of it: we compare the trajectories of the algorithm with those a "mean" ODE, which is globally asymptotically stable with equilibrium point θ^*.

Moreover, geometric ergodicity also ensures that all "interesting" regions of the state-space are visited infinitely often [20]. The condition that $\pi(x, a) > 0$ for all $a \in \mathcal{A}$ and μ_X-almost every $x \in \mathcal{X}$ ensures that, in these "interesting" regions of the state-space, every action is tried infinitely often. Therefore, geometric ergodicity and the requirement that $\pi(x, a) > 0$ for all $a \in \mathcal{A}$ and μ_X-almost all $x \in \mathcal{X}$ can be interpreted as a continuous counterpart to the usual condition that all state-action pairs are visited infinitely often.

The conditions on the algorithm are those concerning the basis functions used and those concerning the step-size sequences ($\{\alpha_t\}$ and $\{\beta_t\}$). With respect to the former, we require that the functions are linearly independent. This is a simple way of guaranteeing (in a rather conservative way) that no two functions ξ_i lead to "colliding updates" as happens in the known counter-example presented by [21]. Furthermore, by requiring that $\sum |\xi_i(x, a)| \leq 1$ for all $(x, a) \in \mathcal{X} \times \mathcal{A}$, we ensure that $\|Q(\theta)\|_\infty \leq \|\theta\|_\infty$, thus making $\mathbf{H}Q(\theta)$ a contraction in θ (in the sup-norm). This fact is important, for example, to ensure the existence of θ^*.

To clarify the conditions on the step-size sequences, we start by remarking that, if ε is held fixed, the algorithm will converge to a *neighborhood of the desired point in parameter space*. We could then proceed as follows. As soon as the estimates were "sufficiently close" to this neighborhood, we could decrease ε and wait for the estimates to, once again, approach a new, smaller neighborhood of the desired point. We would then decrease ε once again, etc.

This "gross" version of our algorithm illustrates the fact that ε cannot go to zero arbitrarily fast. In particular, it is necessary to ensure that each component of the estimate vector θ_t is "sufficiently" updated as ε is decreased. This clearly depends on the smooth Dirac approximation chosen. The relation between the two referred entities (g_ε and the rate of convergence of ε_t) is stated in (11).

Such condition on the step-sizes $\{\alpha_t\}$ can be ensured in different ways (for example, defining α_t from the ε-cuts of g_ε as in [15]). As one final note, we remark that the use of "broader" Dirac approximations will probably allow faster convergence of ε_t while "narrower" Dirac approximations will probably lead to slower convergence of ε_t.

Finally, one last remark to state that since the space $\mathcal{B}$ of essentially bounded functions with the sup-norm is a Banach space (with no orthogonal projection defined), we defined a projection operator $\mathcal{P}$ that is non-expansive in the sup-norm, thus making the combined operator $\mathcal{P}\mathbf{H}$ a contraction in this norm.

Related Work: The early works by Gordon [12] and Tsitsiklis and Van Roy [13] provide convergence analysis for several variations of dynamic programming using function approximation. There is also a brief discussion on how stochastic variations of these algorithms can be used. Closely related is the soft-state aggregation approach [11]. This approach uses a "soft"-partition of the state-space (each state x belongs to region i with a probability $p_i(x)$) and an "average" Q-value $Q(i, a)$ is defined for each region-action pair. The method uses standard Q-learning updates to determine the average Q-values for each region.

In a different work, Tsitsiklis and Van Roy [16] provide a detailed analysis of temporal difference methods for policy evaluation. Given a stationary policy π whose value function V^π is to be estimated, a parameterized linear family $\mathcal{V}$ of functions is used to approximate V^π. The authors establish the the convergence of this method w.p.1 and provide an interpretation of the obtained limit point as a fixed point of a composite operator $\mathcal{P}\mathbf{T}^{(\lambda)}$, where $\mathcal{P}$ is the orthogonal projection into $\mathcal{V}$ and $\mathbf{T}^{(\lambda)}$ is the TD operator. The authors also derive error bounds on the obtained approximation. Several authors later extended these results, e.g., [6, 14, 22].

Szepesvári and Smart [15] proposed a version of Q-learning that approximates the optimal Q-values at a given set of sample points $\{(x_i, a_i), i = 1, \ldots, N\}$ and then uses interpolation to estimate Q^* at any query point. This method, dubbed *interpolation-based Q-learning* (IBQL) uses the update rule

$$\theta_{t+1}(i) = \theta_t(i) + \alpha_t(i)g_\varepsilon(x_i, a_i; x_t, a_t)\left(r_t + \max_{u \in \mathcal{A}} Q_{\theta_t}(x_{t+1}, u) - \theta_t(i)\right). \quad (14)$$

The authors establish convergence w.p.1 of the algorithm and provide an interpretation of the limit point as the fixed-point of a composite operator $\mathcal{P}\hat{\mathbf{H}}$, where $\mathcal{P}$ is a projection-like operator and $\hat{\mathbf{H}}$ can be interpreted as a modified Bellman operator.

We emphasize the similarity between the update rules in (14) and (10). The fundamental difference between these two methods lies on the fact that IBQL only makes use of the estimated Q-function to predict the value of the next state, as seen in (14). Therefore, the updates of IBQL rely on a vector $\hat{d}_t$ of modified temporal differences with ith component given by

$$\hat{d}_t(i) = r_t + \gamma \max_{u \in \mathcal{A}} Q_{\theta_t}(x_{t+1}, u) - \theta_t(i) =$$
$$= r_t + \gamma \max_{u \in \mathcal{A}} Q_{\theta_t}(x_{t+1}, u) - Q_{\theta_t}(x_i, a_i).$$

Notice that each $\hat{d}_t(i)$ is not a temporal-difference in the strict sense, since it does not provide a one-step estimation "error". This means that the information provided by $\hat{d}_t(i)$ may lead to "misleading" updates. Although not affecting the convergence of IBQL in the long-run, IBQL may exhibit slower convergence because of this. On the other hand, if IBQL is used with a vanishing ε, the effect of these misleading updates will vanish as $t \to \infty$. In the experimental results portrayed in [15], a vanishing ε was used. Nevertheless, IBQL exhibited initially slower convergence than of other methods, probably because of this reported effect.

We also remark that, in [15], the convergence result requires the underlying Markov chain to be positive Harris and aperiodic. These conditions are actually weaker than the geometric ergodicity required by our result. However, in many practical situations, the former conditions will actually imply the latter.[5] This means that the conditions on the problem required in Theorem 1 are essentially similar to those in [15] placing the results of both papers in a common line of work and, basically, leading to concordant conclusions.

Finally, we also refer the close relation between the method in Subsection 3.2 and the algorithm described in [17]. In the aforementioned work, Borkar provides a convergence analysis of what we may refer to as *functional Q-learning*. This functional Q-learning can be seen as an extension of classical Q-learning to functional spaces, and arises from the approach proposed by Baker [23] to stochastic approximation in function spaces. The update equation for this method is fundamentally similar to (10). The main difference is that, while we consider only a fixed, finite set of points $I = \{(x_1, a_1), \ldots, (x_M, a_M)\}$, the algorithm in [17] maintains a *complete representation of Q^**, each component of which is updated at each iteration. Clearly, maintaining such a representation of Q^* is computationally infeasible and the algorithm should instead maintain a complete record of the history of past events $\mathcal{H} = \{(x_0, a_0, r_0), \ldots, (x_t, a_t, r_t), \ldots\}$, used to estimate Q^* at a generic point (x, a).

4   Partially Observable Markov Decision Processes

Recall that, in a Markov decision process $(\mathcal{X}, \mathcal{A}, \mathsf{P}, r, \gamma)$, an agent acts at each time instant based on the current state of the environment and so as to maximize its expected total discounted reward. However, if the current state is unknown and the agent has available only a noisy observation of it, the elegant theory and effective algorithms developed for Markov decision processes are in general not applicable, even in the simpler case of finite $\mathcal{X}$.

Partially observable Markov decision processes (POMDPs) present a complex challenge due to the remarkable complications arising from the "simple" consideration of partial state observability. Exact solution methods for POMDPs generally consist on dynamic-programming based iterative procedures and have been found computationally too expensive for systems with more than a few dozen states [24, 25]. This has led many researchers to focus on developing approximate methods using a variety of approaches. We refer to [26, 27] for good surveys on POMDP exact and approximate methods.

---

[5] An aperiodic, positive Harris chain is geometrically ergodic as long as supp μ_X has non-empty interior.

Some approximate solution methods rely on value-based reinforcement learning algorithms such as Q-learning. Examples include the Linear-Q algorithm [28], the SPOVA-RL algorithm [29] or the Fast-RL algorithm [30]. A thorough analysis of several such methods can also be found in [26].

In this section we discuss how our results from the previous section can be applied to POMDPs. We identify a set of conditions on POMDPs that ensure the applicability of the method in Section 3. As a side-note, we remark that the Linear-Q algorithm referred above can be cast as a simple variation of the method described in Section 3. Our analysis in this section can easily be adapted to provide a formal proof of the convergence of this algorithm.

4.1   Partial Observability and Internal State

Let $(\mathcal{X}, \mathsf{P})$ be a finite state-space Markov chain. Let $\mathcal{Z}$ be a finite set of possible observations and suppose that, at each time instant, the the state X_t of the chain is unaccessible. Instead, a random measurement Z_t is "observed" which depends on the state X_t according to an observation probability given by

$$\mathbb{P}\left[Z_t = z \mid X_t = x\right] = \mathsf{O}(x, z), \tag{15}$$

A partially observable Markov chain is a 4-tuple $(\mathcal{X}, \mathcal{Z}, \mathsf{P}, \mathsf{O})$, where $\mathcal{X}$ and $\mathcal{Z}$ are, respectively, the state and observation spaces (both considered finite) and P and O are the transition and observation probability matrices.

Let b_t be a discrete probability measure on $\mathcal{X}$ conveying the probability distribution of the state X_t over the set $\mathcal{X}$ at time instant t. Since $\mathcal{X}$ is assumed finite, b_t is a vector with xth component

$$b_t(x) = \mathbb{P}\left[X_t = x \mid \mathcal{F}_t\right], \tag{16}$$

where $\mathcal{F}_t$ is the history up to time t. Suppose that at time instant t the chain is in state $x \in \mathcal{X}$ with probability $b_t(x)$ and a transition occurs, with an observation $Z_{t+1} = z$ made at instant $t+1$. Then it holds that

$$b_{t+1}(y) = \frac{\sum_{x \in \mathcal{X}} b_t(x)\mathsf{P}(x, y)\mathsf{O}(y, z)}{\sum_{x, w \in \mathcal{X}} b_t(x)\mathsf{P}(x, w)\mathsf{O}(w, x)}. \tag{17}$$

It is clear from (17) that b_{t+1} *is Markovian in its dependence of the past history*. Therefore, we define from b_t a sequence $\{B_t\}$ of random variables, each taking the value $B_t = b_t$ at time instant t. Since each b_t is a probability vector with, say, $n + 1$ components, B_t lies in the n-dimensional probability simplex $\mathbb{S}^n$.

Summarizing, for any partially observable Markov chain $(\mathcal{X}, \mathcal{Z}, \mathsf{P}, \mathsf{O})$ there is an equivalent fully-observable Markov chain $(\mathbb{S}^n, \hat{\mathsf{P}})$, where the kernel $\hat{\mathsf{P}}$ is given, for any $b \in \mathbb{S}^n$ and any measurable set $U \subset \mathbb{S}^n$, by

$$\hat{\mathsf{P}}(b, U) = \sum_z \sum_{x, y} b(x)\mathsf{P}(x, y)\mathsf{O}(y, z)\mathbb{I}_U\left(B(b, z)\right),$$

where $B(b,z)$ is the vector obtained from b using (17) with observation z and $\mathbb{I}_U$ is the indicator function for the set U. Notice that the xth coordinate of vector B_t describes the *belief* that the underlying state of the chain is $X_t = x$, and it is common to refer to the b vectors as *belief-states*.

Notice that, by considering the chain $(\mathbb{S}^n, \hat{\mathsf{P}})$ of beliefs instead of the partially observable chain $(\mathcal{X}, \mathcal{Z}, \mathsf{P}, \mathsf{O})$ we move from a finite, partially observable Markov chain with state-space $\mathcal{X}$ to an infinite, fully observable Markov chain with state-space $\mathbb{S}^n$. We now identify conditions on P and/or O that ensure the chain $(\mathbb{S}^n, \hat{\mathsf{P}})$ to be uniformly ergodic.

Theorem 2. *Let $(\mathcal{X}, \mathcal{Z}, \mathsf{P}, \mathsf{O})$ be a partially observable Markov chain, where the chain $(\mathcal{X}, \mathsf{P})$ is irreducible and aperiodic. Suppose that there is an observation $z \in \mathcal{Z}$ and a state $x^* \in \mathcal{X}$ such that, for all $y \in \mathcal{X}$, $\mathsf{O}(y,z) = \delta(x^*, y)$. Then, the Markov chain $(\mathbb{S}^n, \hat{\mathsf{P}})$ is uniformly ergodic.*

Proof. See [18]. $\quad\square$

4.2 POMDPs and Associated MDPs

A tuple $(\mathcal{X}, \mathcal{A}, \mathcal{Z}, \mathsf{P}, \mathsf{O}, r, \gamma)$ is a *partially Observable Markov Decision Process* (POMDP), where $\mathcal{X}, \mathcal{A}, \mathsf{P}, r$ and γ are as defined in Section 2, $\mathcal{Z}$ is the observation-space and O represents the (action-dependent) observation probabilities. We consider $\mathcal{X}$, $\mathcal{A}$ and $\mathcal{Z}$ to be finite sets.

Using a development entirely similar to the one presented in the previous subsection, given a POMDP $(\mathcal{X}, \mathcal{A}, \mathcal{Z}, \mathsf{P}, \mathsf{O}, r, \gamma)$ we can derive a fully observable MDP $(\mathbb{S}^n, \mathcal{A}, \hat{\mathsf{P}}, \hat{r}, \gamma)$, where, for each $a \in \mathcal{A}$, $\hat{\mathsf{P}}$ and $\hat{r}$ are defined as

$$\hat{\mathsf{P}}_a(b,U) = \sum_z \sum_{x,y} b(x)\mathsf{P}_a(x,y)\mathsf{O}_a(y,z)\mathbb{I}_U(B(b,a,z));$$
$$\hat{r}(b,a,b') = \sum_{x,y} b(x)\mathsf{P}_a(x,y)r(x,a,y),$$

where $B(b,a,z)$ is the updated probability vector given action a and observation z with yth component given by

$$B(b,a,z)_y = \frac{\sum_{x\in\mathcal{X}} b_t(x)\mathsf{P}_a(x,y)\mathsf{O}_a(y,z)}{\sum_{x,w\in\mathcal{X}} b_t(x)\mathsf{P}_a(x,w)\mathsf{O}_a(w,x)}.$$

Notice that the reward $\hat{r}(b,a,b')$ corresponds to the expected immediate reward for being in each state x with probability $b(x)$ and taking action a. As expected, it does not depend on b'.[6]

This new MDP is an infinite state-space counterpart to the partially observable Markov decision process $(\mathcal{X}, \mathcal{A}, \mathcal{Z}, \mathsf{P}, \mathsf{O}, r, \gamma)$ and we are interested in applying the methods from the previous section to this continuous-state MDP.

---

[6] Notice that the rewards do not depend on the observations and the belief b' is a function of the current belief, action and observation, so it is natural that $\hat{r}$ is independent of b'.

Notice that, even if the complete POMDP model is known, the use of a simulation-based solution may still be preferable to the computationally heavier, exact methods. On the other hand, it may happen that the reward r is unknown and, therefore, recurring to simulation-based methods is the only alternative available. Finally, we emphasize that, in order to use the methods from the previous section, the MDP $(\mathbb{S}^n, \mathcal{A}, \hat{\mathsf{P}}, \hat{r}, \gamma)$ needs to be fully observable, *i.e.*, the beliefs b_t must be computable at every time step t. This means that the agent must know the model parameters P and O.

In the new MDP $(\mathbb{S}^n, \mathcal{A}, \hat{\mathsf{P}}, \hat{r}, \gamma)$, it is straightforward to define the optimal value function $V^* : \mathbb{S}^n \longrightarrow \mathbb{R}$, verifying

$$V^*(b) = \max_{a \in \mathcal{A}} \mathbb{E}\left[\hat{r}(b, a, b') + \gamma V^\delta(b')\right],$$

and the optimal Q-function, verifying

$$Q^*(b, a) = \mathbb{E}\left[r(b, a, b') + \gamma \max_{u \in \mathcal{A}} Q^*(b', u)\right].$$

More intuitive and well-known expressions for these functions can readily be obtained by replacing $\hat{\mathsf{P}}$ and $\hat{r}$ by the corresponding definitions, yielding

$$V^*(b) = \max_{a \in \mathcal{A}} \sum_{x, y \in \mathcal{X}} b(x) \mathsf{P}_a(x, y) \left[r(x, a, y) + \gamma \sum_{z \in \mathcal{Z}} \mathsf{O}_a(y, z) V^*(b_z)\right];$$

$$Q^*(b, a) = \sum_{x, y \in \mathcal{X}} b(x) \mathsf{P}_a(x, y) \left[r(x, a, y) + \gamma \sum_{z \in \mathcal{Z}} \mathsf{O}_a(y, z) \max_{b \in \mathcal{A}} Q^*(b_z, b)\right].$$

To apply the method from Section 3 to the MDP $M = (\mathbb{S}^n, \mathcal{A}, \hat{\mathsf{P}}, \hat{r}, \gamma)$ with guaranteed convergence, we need to check if M verifies all conditions *on the problem* required in Theorem 1. This condition is concerned with the geometric ergodicity of the chain obtained with the learning policy. Combining Theorem 1 with Theorem (2), it is immediate that the Q-learning algorithm with linear function approximation analyzed in Section 3 can be applied to POMDPs with guaranteed convergence, as long as the underlying MDP is ergodic and there is a *distinguishable* state $x^* \in \mathcal{X}$. We note that ergodicity of the underlying MDP is a standard assumption in classical RL methods and, therefore, partial observability simply requires the single additional condition of a distinguishable state.

5 Conclusions and Future Work

In this paper we have analyzed the convergence of Q-learning with linear function approximation. Given a linear family $\mathcal{Q}$ of functions, we defined an update rule that "relies" on a projection operator $\mathcal{P}$ defined in the space of (essentially) bounded functions. For the algorithm thus obtained we identified the conditions

under which convergence w.p.1 is guaranteed. We also showed the limit function
to verify the fixed-point recursion

$$Q_{\theta^*}(x, a) = (\mathcal{P}\mathbf{H}Q_{\theta^*})(x, a)$$

and discussed the relation between the method and results in this paper and
those in related works such as [15, 17]. Finally, we showed that partially observable Markov decision processes can be addressed by RL algorithms using function
approximation as long as the typical convergence conditions are verified for the
underlying Markov decision process and there is, at least, one observable state.

Several important remarks are in order. First of all, the error bound in Theo-
rem 1 is given as a function of the quantity $\|\mathcal{P}Q^* - Q^*\|$. Notice that the func-
tion $\mathcal{P}Q^*$ can be interpreted as the "best" representation of Q^* in $\mathcal{Q}$. The error
bound in Theorem 1 means that the obtained approximation is, at most, "almost
as good" as $\mathcal{P}Q^*$. It also means that, this approximation may be of little use, if
the space $\mathcal{Q}$ poorly represents the desired function: the closest function in $\mathcal{Q}$ will
still be a poor approximation, and there are no guarantees on its practical usefulness (in terms of the corresponding greedy policy). Notice nevertheless that,
if $Q^* \in \mathcal{Q}$, the method will deliver the optimal function Q^*. Therefore, when
using function approximation, the space $\mathcal{Q}$ should be chosen so as to include all
available information regarding the true function to be estimated. The problem
of how to choose the basis functions is currently the target of intense research
in the RL community. Some work has been done in this area [31, 32, 33], but a
lot more can be done.

A second remark concerns the usefulness of the algorithm in Section 3 if a
fixed policy must be used during learning (instead of a policy that depends on
the estimates Q_t). Although the result described in the paper considers a fixed
learning policy, it is possible to extend this result to encompass the use of a policy
π_θ that depends continuously on θ. In particular, if the following condition holds
for every $(x, a) \in \mathcal{X} \times \mathcal{A}$

$$|\pi_\theta(x, a) - \pi_{\theta'}(x, a)| \leq C \|\theta - \theta'\|,$$

with $C > 0$, it is possible to extend the conclusions of Theorem 1 to algorithms
using θ-dependent policies. Further work can explore results on the stability of
perturbed ODEs to extend the fundamental ideas in this paper to address the
convergence of on-policy learning algorithm (*e.g.*, SARSA).

Also, the methods proposed make no use of eligibility traces. It seems likely
that the results in this paper can be modified so as to accommodate eligibility
traces and thus improve their overall performance.

Thirdly, we comment on the results presented in Section 3. In this section,
we described the use of the algorithm in Section 3 to POMDPs by considering
equivalent, fully observable MDPs. Recall that tracking the state of an associated MDP consists in tracking the belief-state b_t of the original POMDP. As
already stated, this implies that the agent must know the parameters P and
O of the POMDP. This is less general than the approach adopted in many RL
methods, where no model of the system is assumed. However, in several practical
applications (*e.g.*, robotic applications) this is a reasonable assumption.

Finally, notice that the overall conditions required to ensure convergence of the methods in Section 3 in partially observable scenarios are similar to the requirements for convergence in fully observable scenarios. Convergence in partially observable scenarios simply requires one extra condition: that at least one state is identifiable. If we consider that, in many situations, *the reinforcement function provides additional information on the underlying state of the system*, the existence of a distinguishable state may be a less stringent condition than it appears at first sight. Nevertheless, it is likely that results on the ergodic behavior of the posterior probabilities of hidden Markov models may be adapted so as to alleviate this condition.

Acknowledgements

The authors would like to acknowledge the helpful discussions with Prof. João Xavier and the many useful comments from the anonymous reviewers that helped to greatly improve the paper.

References

1. Sutton, R.: Learning to predict by the methods of temporal differences. Machine Learning 3, 9–44 (1988)
2. Watkins, C.: Learning from delayed rewards. PhD thesis, King's College, University of Cambridge (May 1989)
3. Rummery, G., Niranjan, M.: On-line *Q*-learning using connectionist systems. Technical Report CUED/F-INFENG/TR 166, Cambridge University Engineering Department (1994)
4. Sutton, R.: DYNA, an integrated architecture for learning, planning, and reacting. ACM SIGART Bulletin 2(4), 160–163 (1991)
5. Barto, A., Bradtke, S., Singh, S.: Learning to act using real-time dynamic programming. Technical Report UM-CS-1993-002, Department of Computer Science, University of Massachusetts at Amherst (1993)
6. Boyan, J.: Least-squares temporal difference learning. In: Proc. 16th Int. Conf. Machine Learning, 49–56 (1999)
7. Bertsekas, D., Tsitsiklis, J.: Neuro-Dynamic Programming. Athena Scientific (1996)
8. Sutton, R.: Generalization in reinforcement learning: Successful examples using sparse coarse coding. Advances in Neural Information Processing Systems 8, 1038–1044 (1996)
9. Boyan, J., Moore, A.: Generalization in reinforcement learning: Safely approximating the value function. Advances in Neural Information Processing Systems 7, 369–376 (1994)
10. Tesauro, G.: TD-Gammon, a self-teaching backgammon program, achieves master-level play. Neural Computation 6(2), 215–219 (1994)
11. Singh, S., Jaakkola, T., Jordan, M.: Reinforcement learning with soft state aggregation. Advances in Neural Information Processing Systems 7, 361–368 (1994)
12. Gordon, G.: Stable function approximation in dynamic programming. Technical Report CMU-CS-95-103, School of Computer Science, Carnegie Mellon University (1995)

322   F.S. Melo and M.I. Ribeiro

13. Tsitsiklis, J., Van Roy, B.: Feature-based methods for large scale dynamic programming. Machine Learning 22, 59–94 (1996)
14. Precup, D., Sutton, R., Dasgupta, S.: Off-policy temporal-difference learning with function approximation. In: Proc. 18th Int. Conf. Machine Learning, 417–424 (2001)
15. Szepesvári, C., Smart, W.: Interpolation-based Q-learning. In: Proc. 21st Int. Conf. Machine learning, 100–107 (2004)
16. Tsitsiklis, J., Van Roy, B.: An analysis of temporal-difference learning with function approximation. IEEE Transactions on Automatic Control AC-42(5), 674–690 (1996)
17. Borkar, V.: A learning algorithm for discrete-time stochastic control. Probability in the Engineering and Informational Sciences 14, 243–258 (2000)
18. Melo, F., Ribeiro, M.I.: Q-learning with linear function approximation. Technical Report RT-602-07, Institute for Systems and Robotics (March 2007)
19. Watkins, C., Dayan, P.: Technical note: Q-learning. Machine Learning 8, 279–292 (1992)
20. Meyn, S., Tweedie, R.: Markov Chains and Stochastic Stability. Springer, Heidelberg (1993)
21. Baird, L.: Residual algorithms: Reinforcement learning with function approximation. In: Proc. 12th Int. Conf. Machine Learning, 30–37 (1995)
22. Bertsekas, D., Borkar, V., Nedić, A.: 9. In: Improved temporal difference methods with linear function approximation. Wiley Publishers, 235–260 (2004)
23. Baker, W.: Learning via stochastic approximation in function space. PhD Thesis (1997)
24. Lusena, C., Goldsmith, J., Mundhenk, M.: Nonapproximability results for partially observable Markov decision processes. J. Artificial Intelligence Research 14, 83–103 (2001)
25. Papadimitriou, C., Tsitsiklis, J.: The complexity of Markov chain decision processes. Mathematics of Operations Research 12(3), 441–450 (1987)
26. Cassandra, A.: Exact and approximate algorithms for partially observable Markov decision processes. PhD thesis, Brown University (May 1998)
27. Aberdeen, D.: A (revised) survey of approximate methods for solving partially observable Markov decision processes. Technical report, National ICT Australia, Canberra, Australia (2003)
28. Littman, M., Cassandra, A., Kaelbling, L.: Learning policies for partially observable environments: Scaling up. In: Proc. 12th Int. Conf. Machine Learning, 362–370 (1995)
29. Parr, R., Russell, S.: Approximating optimal policies for partially observable stochastic domains. In: Proc. Int. Joint Conf. Artificial Intelligence, 1088–1094 (1995)
30. He, Q., Shayman, M.: Solving POMDPs by on-policy linear approximate learning algorithm. In: Proc. Conf. Information Sciences and Systems (2000)
31. Glaubius, R., Smart, W.: Manifold representations for value-function approximation in reinforcement learning. Technical Report 05-19, Department of Computer Science and Engineering, Washington University in St. Louis (2005)
32. Keller, P., Mannor, S., Precup, D.: Automatic basis function construction for approximate dynamic programming and reinforcement learning. In: Proc. 23rd Int. Conf. Machine Learning, 449–456 (2006)
33. Menache, I., Mannor, S., Shimkin, N.: Basis function adaptation in temporal difference reinforcement learning. Annals of Operations Research 134(1), 215–238 (2005)

How Good Is a Kernel When Used as a Similarity Measure?

Nathan Srebro

Toyota Technological Institute-Chicago IL, USA
IBM Haifa Research Lab, Israel
nati@uchicago.edu

Abstract. Recently, Balcan and Blum [1] suggested a theory of learning based on general similarity functions, instead of positive semi-definite kernels. We study the gap between the learning guarantees based on kernel-based learning, and those that can be obtained by using the kernel as a similarity function, which was left open by Balcan and Blum. We provide a significantly improved bound on how good a kernel function is when used as a similarity function, and extend the result also to the more practically relevant hinge-loss rather then zero-one-error-rate. Furthermore, we show that this bound is tight, and hence establish that there is in-fact a real gap between the traditional kernel-based notion of margin and the newer similarity-based notion.

1   Introduction

A common contemporary approach in machine learning is to encode prior knowledge about objects using a *kernel*, specifying the inner products between implicit high-dimensional representations of objects. Such inner products can be viewed as measuring the *similarity* between objects. In-fact, many generic kernels (e.g. Gaussian kernels), as well as very specific kernels (e.g. Fisher kernels [2] and kernels for specific structures such as [3]), describe different notions of similarity between objects, which do not correspond to any intuitive or easily interpretable high-dimensional representation. However, not every mapping of pairs of objects to "similarity values" is a valid kernel.

Recently, Balcan and Blum [1] proposed an alternative theory of learning, which is based on a more general notion of similarity functions between objects, which unlike valid kernel functions, need not be positive semi-definite. Balcan and Blum provide a definition for a separation *margin* of a classification problem under a general similarity measure and present learning methods with guarantees that parallel the familiar margin-based guarantees for kernel methods.

It is interesting to study what this alternative theory yields for similarity functions which are in-fact valid kernel functions. Does the similarity-based theory subsume the kernel-based theory without much deterioration of guarantees? Or can the kernel-based theory provide better results for functions which are in-fact positive semi-definite. To answer these questions, one must understand how a kernel-based margin translates to a similarity-based margin. Balcan and

N. Bshouty and C. Gentile (Eds.): COLT 2007, LNAI 4539, pp. 323–335, 2007.
© Springer-Verlag Berlin Heidelberg 2007

Blum showed that if an input distribution can be separated, in the kernel sense, with margin γ and error rate ϵ_0 (i.e. ϵ_0 of the inputs are allowed to violate the margin), then viewing the kernel mapping as a similarity measure, for any $\epsilon_1 > 0$, the target distribution can be separated with similarity-based margin[1] $\frac{\gamma\epsilon_1}{96/\gamma^2 - 32\log\epsilon_1} = \tilde{\Theta}(\epsilon_1\gamma^3)$ and error rate $8\epsilon_0/\gamma + \epsilon_1$. Although this does establish that good kernels can also be used as similarity measures, in the Blum and Balcan sense, there is a significant deterioration in the margin yielding a significant deterioration in the learning guarantee. The tightness of this relationship, or a possible improved bound, was left unresolved. Also, this result of Balcan and Blum refers only to a zero-one error-rate, which does not yield efficient learning algorithms. Guarantees referring to the hinge-loss are desirable.

Here, we resolve this question by providing an improved bound, with a simpler proof, and establishing its tightness. We show that:

- If an input distribution can be separated, in the kernel sense, with margin γ and error rate ϵ_0, then for any $\epsilon_1 > 0$, it can also be separated by the kernel mapping viewed as a similarity measure, with similarity-based margin $\frac{1}{2}(1 - \epsilon_0)\epsilon_1\gamma^2$ and error rate $\epsilon_0 + \epsilon_1$.
- We also obtain a similar bound in terms of the average hinge loss, instead of the margin violation error rate: If for a target distribution we can achieve, in the kernel sense, average hinge loss of ϵ_0 for margin γ, then for any $\epsilon_1 > 0$, we can also achieve average hinge loss of $\epsilon_0 + \epsilon_1$ for margin $2\epsilon_1\gamma^2$, when the kernel mapping is used as a similarity measure. A result in terms of the hinge-loss is perhaps more practical, since for computational reasons, we usually minimize the hinge-loss rather then error rate.
- The above bounds are tight, up to a factor of sixteen: We show, for any $\gamma < \frac{1}{2}$ and ϵ_1, a specific kernel function and input distribution that can be separated with margin γ and no errors in the kernel sense, but which can only be separated with margin at most $32\epsilon_1\gamma^2$ in the similarity sense, if we require hinge loss less than ϵ_1 or error-rate less than $4\epsilon_1$, when using the same kernel mapping as a similarity measure.

In the next Section we formally present the framework in which we work and remind the reader of the definitions and results of Balcan and Blum. We then state our results (Section 3) and prove them (Sections 4 and 5).

2   Setup

We briefly review the setting used by Balcan and Blum [1], which we also use here.

We consider input distributions (X, Y) over $\mathcal{X} \times \{\pm 1\}$, where $\mathcal{X}$ is some abstract object space. As in Balcan and Blum [1], we consider only *consistent* input distributions in which the label Y is a *deterministic* function of X. We can think of such input distributions as a distributions over $\mathcal{X}$ and a deterministic mapping $y(x)$.

---

[1] The $\tilde{\Theta}(\cdot)$ and $\tilde{\mathcal{O}}(\cdot)$ notations hide logarithmic factors.

A *kernel function* is a mapping $K : \mathcal{X} \times \mathcal{X} \rightarrow \mathbb{R}$ for which there exists an (implicit) feature mapping $\phi : \mathcal{X} \rightarrow \mathcal{H}$ of objects into an (implicit) Hilbert space $\mathcal{H}$ such that $K(x_1, x_2) = \langle \phi(x_1), \phi(x_2) \rangle$. See, e.g., Smola and Schölkopf [4] for a discussion on conditions for a mapping being a kernel function. Throughout this work, and without loss of generality, we will only consider kernels such that $K(x, x) \leq 1$ for all $x \in \mathcal{X}$. Kernalized large-margin classification relies on the existence of a large margin linear separator for the input distribution, in the Hilbert space implied by K. This is captured by the following definition of when a kernel function is *good* for an input distribution:

Definition 1. *A kernel K is (ϵ, γ)-**kernel-good** for an input distribution if there exists a classifier $\beta \in \mathcal{H}$, $\|\beta\| = 1$, such that $\Pr(Y\langle\beta, \phi(X)\rangle < \gamma) \leq \epsilon$. We say β has margin-γ-error-rate $\Pr(Y\langle\beta, \phi(X)\rangle < \gamma)$.*

Given a kernel that is (ϵ, γ)-kernel-good (for some unknown source distribution), a predictor with error rate at most $\epsilon + \epsilon_{\text{acc}}$ (on the source distribution) can be learned (with high probability) from a sample of $\tilde{\mathcal{O}}\big((\epsilon + \epsilon_{\text{acc}})/(\gamma^2 \epsilon_{\text{acc}}^2)\big)$ examples (drawn independently from the source distribution) by minimizing the number of margin γ violations on the sample [5]. However, minimizing the number of margin violations on the sample is a difficult optimization problem. Instead, it is common to minimize the so-called *hinge loss* relative to a margin:

Definition 2. *A kernel K is (ϵ, γ)-**kernel-good** in hinge-loss for an input distribution if there exists a classifier $\beta \in \mathcal{H}$, $\|\beta\| = 1$, such that*

$$\mathbf{E}[[1 - Y\langle\beta, \phi(X)\rangle/\gamma]_+] \leq \epsilon,$$

where $[1 - z]_+ = \max(1 - z, 0)$ is the hinge loss.

Given a kernel that is (ϵ, γ)-kernel-good in hinge-loss, a predictor with error rate at most $\epsilon + \epsilon_{\text{acc}}$ can be efficiently learned (with high probability) from a sample of $\mathcal{O}\big(1/(\gamma^2 \epsilon_{\text{acc}}^2)\big)$ examples by minimizing the average hinge loss relative to margin γ on the sample [6].

A *similarity function* is any symmetric mapping $K : \mathcal{X} \times \mathcal{X} \rightarrow [-1, +1]$. In particular, a (properly normalized) kernel function is also a similarity function. Instead of functionals in an implicit Hilbert space, similarity-based predictors are given in terms of a *weight function* $w : \mathcal{X} \rightarrow [0, 1]$. The classification margin of (x, y) is then defined as [1]:

$$\mathbf{E}_{X',Y'}[w(X')Y'K(x, X')|y = Y'] - \mathbf{E}_{X',Y'}[w(X')Y'K(x, X')|y \neq Y']$$
$$= y\mathbf{E}_{X',Y'}[w(X')Y'K(x, X')/p(Y')] \tag{1}$$

where $p(Y')$ is the marginal probability of the label, i.e. the prior. We choose here to stick with this definition used by Balcan and Blum. All our results apply (up to a factor for $1/2$) also to a weaker definition, dropping the factor $1/p(Y')$ from definition of the classification margin (1).

We are now ready to define when a similarity function is good for an input distribution:

Definition 3. *A similarity function K is (ϵ, γ)-**similarity-good** for an input distribution if there exists a mapping $w : \mathcal{X} \to [0, 1]$ such that:*

$$\Pr_{X,Y}\left(Y\mathbf{E}_{X',Y'}[w(X')Y'K(X, X')/p(Y')] < \gamma\right) \leq \epsilon.$$

Balcan and Blum showed how, given a similarity function that is (ϵ, γ)-similarity-good, a predictor with error at most $\epsilon + \epsilon_{\mathrm{acc}}$ can be learned (with high probability) from a sample of $\tilde{\mathcal{O}}\big((\epsilon + \epsilon_{\mathrm{acc}})/(\gamma^2 \epsilon_{\mathrm{acc}}^2)\big)$ examples. This is done by first using $\tilde{\mathcal{O}}(1/\gamma^2)$ positive and $\tilde{\mathcal{O}}(1/\gamma^2)$ negative examples to construct an explicit feature map ϕ which is $(\epsilon + \epsilon_{\mathrm{acc}}/2, \gamma/4)$-kernel-good (that is, the inner product in this space is a good kernel) [1, Theorem 2], and then searching for a margin $\gamma/4$ linear separator in this space minimizing the number of margin violations. As mentioned before, this last step (minimizing margin violations) is a difficult optimization problem. We can instead consider the hinge-loss:

Definition 4. *A similarity function K is (ϵ, γ)-**similarity-good in hinge loss** for an input distribution if there exists a mapping $w : \mathcal{X} \to [0, 1]$ such that:*

$$\mathbf{E}_{X,Y}[[1 - Y\mathbf{E}_{X',Y'}[w(X')Y'K(X, X')/p(Y')]/\gamma]_+] \leq \epsilon.$$

Using the same approach as above, given a similarity function that is (ϵ, γ)-similarity-good in hinge loss, a predictor with error at most $\epsilon + \epsilon_{\mathrm{acc}}$ can be efficiently learned (with high probability) from a sample of $\mathcal{O}(1/(\gamma^2 \epsilon_{\mathrm{acc}}^2))$ examples, where this time in the second stage the hinge loss, rather then the number of margin violations, is minimized.

We see, then, that very similar learning guarantees can be obtained by using mappings that are (ϵ, γ)-kernel-good or (ϵ, γ)-similarity-good. A natural question is then, whether a kernel that is (ϵ, γ)-kernel-good is also $(\epsilon, \Omega\gamma)$-similarity-good. A positive answer would indicate that learning guarantees based on similarity-goodness subsume the more restricted results based on kernel-goodness (up to constant factors). However, a negative result would indicate that for a mapping that is a valid kernel (i.e. is positive semi-definite), the theory of kernel-based learning provides stronger guarantees than those that can be established using Balcan and Blum's learning methods and guarantees based on similarity goodness (it is still possible that stronger similarity-based guarantees might be possible using a different learning approach).

3   Summary of Results

Considering the question of whether the theory of learning with similarity function subsumes the theory of learning with kernels, Balcan and Blum showed [1, Theorem 4] that a kernel that is (ϵ_0, γ)-kernel-good for a (consistent) input distribution, is also $(8\epsilon_0/\gamma + \epsilon_1, \frac{\gamma\epsilon_1}{96/\gamma^2 - 32\log\epsilon_1})$-similarity-good for the input distribution, for any $\epsilon_1 > 0$. This result applies only to margin violation goodness, and not to the more practically useful hinge-loss notion of goodness. The result still leaves a large gap even for the margin violation case, as the margin is decreased from γ to $\Theta(\epsilon_1\gamma^3)$, and the error is increased by both an additive factor of ϵ_1 and a multiplicative factor of $8/\gamma$.

First, we improve on this result, obtaining a better guarantee on similarity-goodness based on kernel-goodness, that applies both for margin-violations and for hinge-loss:

Theorem 1 (Main Result, Margin Violations). *If K is (ϵ_0, γ)-kernel-good for some (consistent) input distribution, then it is also $(\epsilon_0 + \epsilon_1, \frac{1}{2}(1 - \epsilon_0)\epsilon_1\gamma^2)$-similarity-good for the distribution, for any $\epsilon_1 > 0$.*

Note that in any useful situation $\epsilon_0 < \frac{1}{2}$, and so the guaranteed margin is at least $\frac{1}{4}\epsilon_1\gamma^2$.

Theorem 2 (Main Result, Hinge Loss). *If K is (ϵ_0, γ)-kernel-good in hinge loss for some (consistent) input distribution, then it is also $(\epsilon_0 + \epsilon_1, 2\epsilon_1\gamma^2)$-similarity-good in hinge loss for the distribution, for any $\epsilon_1 > 0$.*

These guarantees still yield a significant deterioration of the margin, when considering similarity-goodness as opposed to kernel-goodness. However, we establish that this is the best that can be hoped for by presenting examples of kernels for which these guarantees are tight (up to a small multiplicative factor):

Theorem 3 (Tightness, Margin Violations). *For any $0 < \gamma < \sqrt{1/2}$ and any $0 < \epsilon_1 < 1/2$, there exists an input distribution and a kernel function K, which is $(0, \gamma)$-kernel-good for the input distribution, but which is only $(\epsilon_1, 8\epsilon_1\gamma^2)$-similarity-good. That is, it is not (ϵ_1, γ')-similarity-good for any $\gamma' > 8\epsilon_1\gamma^2$.*

Theorem 4 (Tightness, Hinge Loss). *For any $0 < \gamma < \sqrt{1/2}$ and any $0 < \epsilon_1 < 1/2$, there exists an input distribution and a kernel function K, which is $(0, \gamma)$-kernel-good in hinge loss for the input distribution, but which is only $(\epsilon_1, 32\epsilon_1\gamma^2)$-similarity-good in hinge loss.*

4   An Improved Guarantee

We are now ready to prove Theorems 1 and 2. We will consider a kernel function that is (ϵ_0, γ)-kernel-good and show that it is also good as a similarity function. We begin, in Section 4.1, with goodness in hinge-loss, and prove Theorem 2, which can be viewed as a more general result. Then, in Section 4.2, we prove Theorem 1 in terms of the margin violation error rate, by using the hinge-loss as a bound on the error rate.

In either case, our proof is based on the representation of the optimal SVM solution in terms of the dual optimal solution.

4.1   Proof of Theorem 2: Goodness in Hinge-Loss

We consider consistent input distributions, in which Y is a deterministic function of X. For simplicity of presentation, we first consider finite discrete distributions, where:

$$\Pr(\,(X,Y) = (x_i, y_i)\,) = p_i \tag{2}$$

for $i = 1 \ldots n$, with $\sum_{i=1}^{n} p_i = 1$ and $x_i \neq x_j$ for $i \neq j$.

Let K be any kernel function that is (ϵ_0, γ)-kernel good in hinge loss for our input distribution. Let ϕ be the implied feature mapping and denote $\phi_i = \phi(x_i)$. Consider the following weighted-SVM quadratic optimization problem with regularization parameter C:

$$\text{minimize} \quad \frac{1}{2} \|\beta\|^2 + C \sum_{i=1}^{n} p_i [1 - y_i \langle \beta, \phi_i \rangle]_+ \tag{3}$$

The dual of this problem, with dual variables α_i, is:

$$\text{maximize} \quad \sum_i \alpha_i - \frac{1}{2} \sum_{ij} y_i y_j \alpha_i \alpha_j K(x_i, x_j)$$
$$\text{subject to} \quad 0 \leq \alpha_i \leq C p_i \tag{4}$$

There is no duality gap, and furthermore the primal optimum β^* can be expressed in terms of the dual optimum α^*: $\beta^* = \sum_i \alpha_i^* y_i x_i$.

Since K is (ϵ_0, γ)-kernel-good in hinge-loss, there exists a predictor $\|\beta_0\| = 1$ with average-hinge loss ϵ_0 relative to margin γ. The primal optimum β^* of (3), being the optimum solution, then satisfies:

$$\frac{1}{2} \|\beta^*\|^2 + C \sum_i p_i [1 - y_i \langle \beta^*, \phi_i \rangle]_+ \leq$$

$$\frac{1}{2} \left\| \frac{1}{\gamma} \beta_0 \right\|^2 + C \sum_i p_i [1 - y_i \langle \frac{1}{\gamma} \beta_0, \phi_i \rangle]_+$$

$$= \frac{1}{2\gamma^2} + C\mathbf{E} \left[[1 - Y \langle \frac{1}{\gamma} \beta_0, \phi(X) \rangle]_+ \right] = \frac{1}{2\gamma^2} + C\epsilon_0 \tag{5}$$

Since both terms on the left hand side are non-negative, each of them is bounded by the right hand side, and in particular:

$$C \sum_i p_i [1 - y_i \langle \beta^*, \phi_i \rangle]_+ \leq \frac{1}{2\gamma^2} + C\epsilon_0 \tag{6}$$

Dividing by C we get a bound on the average hinge-loss of the predictor β^*, relative to a margin of one:

$$\mathbf{E}[[1 - Y \langle \beta^*, \phi(X) \rangle]_+] \leq \frac{1}{2C\gamma^2} + \epsilon_0 \tag{7}$$

We now use the fact that β^* can be written as $\beta^* = \sum_i \alpha_i^* y_i \phi_i$ with $0 \leq \alpha_i^* \leq C p_i$. Using the weights

$$w_i = w(x_i) = \alpha_i^* p(y_i)/(C p_i) \leq p(y_i) \leq 1 \tag{8}$$

we have for every x, y:

$$y\mathbf{E}_{X',Y'}[w(X')Y'K(x,X')/p(Y')] = y\sum_i p_i w(x_i)y_i K(x,x_i)/p(y_i) \quad (9)$$

$$= y\sum_i p_i \alpha_i^* p(y_i)y_i K(x,x_i)/(Cp_i p(y_i))$$

$$= y\sum_i \alpha_i^* y_i \langle \phi_i, \phi(x)\rangle /C = y\langle \beta^*, \phi(x)\rangle /C$$

Multiplying by C and using (7):

$$\mathbf{E}_{X,Y}\big[[\,1 - CY\mathbf{E}_{X',Y'}[w(X')Y'K(X,X')/p(Y')]\,]_+\big]$$

$$= \mathbf{E}_{X,Y}\big[[\,1 - Y\langle \beta^*, \phi(X)\rangle\,]_+\big] \le \frac{1}{2C\gamma^2} + \epsilon_0 \quad (10)$$

This holds for any C, and describes the average hinge-loss relative to margin $1/C$. To get an average hinge-loss of $\epsilon_0 + \epsilon_1$, we set $C = 1/(2\epsilon_1\gamma^2)$ and get:

$$\mathbf{E}_{X,Y}\big[[\,1 - Y\mathbf{E}_{X',Y'}[w(X')Y'K(X,X')/p(Y')]/(2\epsilon_1\gamma^2)\,]_+\big] \le \epsilon_0 + \epsilon_1 \quad (11)$$

This establishes that K is $(\epsilon_0 + \epsilon_1, 2\epsilon_1\gamma^2)$-similarity-good in hinge-loss.

Non-discrete Input Distribution. The same arguments apply also in the general (not necessarily discrete) case, except that this time, instead of a fairly standard (weighted) SVM problem, we must deal with a variational optimization problem, where the optimization variable is a random variable (a function from the sample space to the reals). We will present the dualization in detail.

We consider the primal objective

$$\text{minimize } \frac{1}{2}\|\beta\|^2 + C\mathbf{E}_{Y,\phi}[[1 - Y\langle\beta,\phi\rangle]_+] \quad (12)$$

where the expectation is w.r.t. the input distribution, with $\phi = \phi(X)$ here and throughout the rest of this section. We will rewrite this objective using explicit slack, in the form of a random variable ξ, which will be a variational optimization variable:

$$\text{minimize } \frac{1}{2}\|\beta\|^2 + C\mathbf{E}[\xi]$$
$$\text{subject to } \Pr(\,1 - y\langle\beta,\phi\rangle - \xi \le 0\,) = 1 \quad (13)$$
$$\Pr(\,\xi \ge 0\,) = 1$$

In the rest of this section all our constraints will implicitly be required to hold with probability one. We will now introduce the dual variational optimization variable α, also a random variable over the same sample space, and write the problem as a saddle problem:

$$\min_{\beta,\xi} \max_\alpha \frac{1}{2}\|\beta\|^2 + C\mathbf{E}[\xi] + \mathbf{E}[\alpha(1 - Y\langle\beta,\phi\rangle - \xi)]$$
$$\text{subject to } \xi \ge 0 \quad \alpha \ge 0 \quad (14)$$

Note that this choice of Lagrangian is a bit different than the more standard Lagrangian leading to (4). Convexity and the existence of a feasible point in the dual interior allows us to change the order of maximization and minimization without changing the value of the problem [7]. Rearranging terms we obtaining the equivalent problem:

$$\max_\alpha \min_{\beta,\xi} \frac{1}{2}\|\beta\|^2 - \langle \mathbf{E}[\alpha Y \phi], \beta \rangle + \mathbf{E}[\xi(C-\alpha)] + \mathbf{E}[\alpha] \tag{15}$$
$$\text{subject to } \xi \geq 0, \quad \alpha \geq 0$$

Similarly to the finite case, we see that the minimum of the minimization problem is obtained when $\beta = \mathbf{E}[\alpha Y \phi]$ and that it is finite when $\alpha \leq C$ almost surely, yielding the dual:

$$\text{maximize } \mathbf{E}[\alpha] - \frac{1}{2}\mathbf{E}[\alpha Y \alpha' Y K(X,X')] \tag{16}$$
$$\text{subject to } 0 \leq \alpha \leq C$$

where (X,Y,α) and (X',Y',α') are two independent draws from the same distribution. The primal optimum can be expressed as $\beta^* = \mathbf{E}[\alpha^* Y \phi]$, where α^* is the dual optimum. We can now apply the same arguments as in (5),(6) to get (7). Using the weight mapping

$$w(x) = \mathbf{E}[\alpha^*|x]\, p(y(x)) \,/\, C \leq 1 \tag{17}$$

we have for every x, y:

$$y\mathbf{E}_{X',Y'}[w(X')Y'K(x,X')/p(Y')] = y\langle \mathbf{E}_{X',Y',\alpha'}[\alpha'Y'X'], x \rangle / C$$
$$= y\langle \beta^*, \phi(x) \rangle / C. \tag{18}$$

From here we can already get (10) and setting $C = 1/(2\epsilon_1\gamma^2)$ we get (11), which establishes Theorem 2 for any input distribution.

4.2 Proof of Theorem 1: Margin-Violation Goodness

We will now turn to guarantees on similarity-goodness with respect to the margin violation error-rate. We base these on the results for goodness in hinge loss, using the hinge loss as a bound on the margin violation error-rate. In particular, a violation of margin $\gamma/2$ implies a hinge-loss at margin γ of at least $\frac{1}{2}$. Therefore, twice the average hinge-loss at margin γ is an upper bound on the margin violation error rate at margin $\gamma/2$.

The kernel-separable case, i.e. $\epsilon_0 = 0$, is simpler, and we consider it first. Having no margin violations implies zero hinge loss. And so if a kernel K is $(0,\gamma)$-kernel-good, it is also $(0,\gamma)$-kernel-good in hinge loss, and by Theorem 2 it is $(\epsilon_1/2, 2(\epsilon_1/2)\gamma^2)$-similarity-good in hinge loss. Now, for any $\epsilon_1 > 0$, by bounding the margin $\frac{1}{2}\epsilon_1\gamma^2$ error-rate by the $\epsilon_1\gamma^2$ average hinge loss, K is $(\epsilon_1, \frac{1}{2}\epsilon_1\gamma^2)$-similarity-good, establishing Theorem 1 for the case $\epsilon_0 = 0$.

We now return to the non-separable case, and consider a kernel K that is (ϵ_0, γ)-kernel-good, with some non-zero error-rate ϵ_0. Since we cannot bound the hinge loss in terms of the margin-violations, we will instead consider a modified input distribution where the margin-violations are removed.

Since we will be modifying the input distribution, and so potentially also the label marginals, it will be simpler for us to use a definition of similarity-based margin that avoids the factor $1/p(Y')$. Therefore, in this Section, we will refer to similarity-goodness where the classification margin of (x, y) is given by:

$$y\mathbf{E}_{X',Y'}[w(X')Y'K(x, X')]. \tag{19}$$

It is easy to verify, by dropping the factor $p(y_i)$ in (8) or (17), that Theorem 2, and hence also Theorem 1 for the case $\epsilon_0 = 0$, hold also under this definition. Furthermore, if a kernel is (ϵ, γ)-good under this definition, then multiplying the label marginals into the weights establishes that it is also (ϵ, γ)-good under the definitions in Section 2.

Let β^* be the linear classifier achieving ϵ_0 margin violation error-rate with respect to margin γ, i.e. such that $\Pr(Y\langle\beta^*, X\rangle \geq \gamma) > 1 - \epsilon_0$. We will consider an input distribution which is conditioned on $Y\langle\beta^*, X\rangle \geq \gamma$. We denote this event as $\text{OK}(X)$ (recall that Y is a deterministic function of X). The kernel K is obviously $(0, \gamma)$-kernel-good, and so by the arguments above also $(\epsilon_1, \frac{1}{2}\epsilon_1\gamma^2)$-similarity-good, on the conditional distribution. Let w be the weight mapping achieving

$$\Pr_{X,Y}(Y\mathbf{E}_{X',Y'}[w(X')Y'K(X, X')|\text{OK}(X')] < \gamma_1|\text{OK}(X)) \leq \epsilon_1, \tag{20}$$

where $\gamma_1 = \frac{1}{2}\epsilon_1\gamma^2$, and set $w(x) = 0$ when $\text{OK}(X)$ does not hold. We have:

$$\Pr_{X,Y}(Y\mathbf{E}_{X',Y'}[w(X')Y'K(X, X')] < (1 - \epsilon_0)\gamma_1)$$
$$\leq \Pr(\text{not OK}(X))$$
$$\quad + \Pr(\text{OK}(X))\Pr_{X,Y}(Y\mathbf{E}_{X',Y'}[w(X')Y'K(X, X')] < (1 - \epsilon_0)\gamma_1 \mid \text{OK}(X))$$
$$= \epsilon_0$$
$$\quad + (1-\epsilon_0)\Pr_{X,Y}(Y(1-\epsilon_0)\mathbf{E}_{X',Y'}[w(X')Y'K(X, X')|\text{OK}(X)] < (1-\epsilon_0)\gamma_1|\text{OK}(X))$$
$$= \epsilon_0 + (1 - \epsilon_0)\Pr_{X,Y}(Y\mathbf{E}_{X',Y'}[w(X')Y'K(X, X')|\text{OK}(X)] < \gamma_1|\text{OK}(X))$$
$$\leq \epsilon_0 + (1 - \epsilon_0)\epsilon_1 \leq \epsilon_0 + \epsilon_1 \tag{21}$$

establishing that K is $(\epsilon_0+\epsilon_1, \gamma_1)$-similarity-good for the original (unconditioned) distribution, and yielding Theorem 1.

5 Tightness

Consider a distribution on four labeled points in $\mathbb{R}^3$, which we denote x_1, x_2, x_3, x_4:

$$p(X = x_1 = (\gamma, \gamma, \sqrt{1 - 2\gamma^2}), Y = 1) = \frac{1}{2} - \epsilon$$

$$p(X = x_2 = (\gamma, -\gamma, \sqrt{1 - 2\gamma^2}), Y = 1) = \epsilon$$

$$p(X = x_3 = (-\gamma, \gamma, \sqrt{1 - 2\gamma^2}), Y = -1) = \epsilon$$

$$p(X = x_4 = (-\gamma, -\gamma, \sqrt{1 - 2\gamma^2}), Y = -1) = \frac{1}{2} - \epsilon$$

for some (small) $0 < \gamma < \sqrt{\frac{1}{2}}$ and (small) probability $0 < \epsilon < \frac{1}{2}$. The four points are all on the unit sphere, and are clearly separated by $\beta = (1, 0, 0)$ with a margin of γ. The standard inner-product kernel is therefore $(0, \gamma)$-kernel-good on this distribution.

5.1 Margin-Violation Error-Rate

We will show that when this kernel (the standard inner product kernel in $\mathbb{R}^3$) is used as a similarity function, the best margin that can be obtained on all four points, i.e. on at least $1 - \epsilon$ probability mass of examples, is $8\epsilon\gamma^2$.

Consider the classification margin on point x_2 with weights w (denote $w_i = w(x_i)$, and note that $p(y_i) = \frac{1}{2}$ for all i):

$$\mathbf{E}[w(X)YK(x_2, X)/p(Y)]$$

$$= 2(\frac{1}{2} - \epsilon)w_1(\gamma^2 - \gamma^2 + (1 - 2\gamma^2)) + 2\epsilon w_2(2\gamma^2 + (1 - 2\gamma^2))$$

$$- 2\epsilon w_3(-2\gamma^2 + (1 - 2\gamma^2)) - 2(\frac{1}{2} - \epsilon)w_4(-\gamma^2 + \gamma^2 + (1 - 2\gamma^2))$$

$$= 2\left((\frac{1}{2} - \epsilon)(w_1 - w_4) + \epsilon(w_2 - w_3)\right)(1 - 2\gamma^2) + 4\epsilon(w_2 + w_3)\gamma^2 \qquad (22)$$

If the first term is positive, we can consider the symmetric calculation

$$- \mathbf{E}[w(X)YK(x_3, X)/p(Y)]$$

$$= -2\left((\frac{1}{2} - \epsilon)(w_1 - w_4) + \epsilon(w_2 - w_3)\right)(1 - 2\gamma^2) + 4\epsilon(w_2 + w_3)\gamma^2 \qquad (23)$$

in which the first term is negated. One of the above margins must therefore be at most

$$4\epsilon(w_2 + w_3)\gamma^2 \leq 8\epsilon\gamma^2 \qquad (24)$$

This establishes Theorem 3.

5.2 Hinge Loss

In the above example, suppose we would like to get an average hinge-loss relative to margin γ_1 of at most ϵ_1:

$$\mathbf{E}_{X,Y}[[1 - Y\mathbf{E}_{X',Y'}[w(X')Y'K(X,X')/p(Y')]/\gamma_1]_+] \leq \epsilon_1 \qquad (25)$$

Following the arguments above, equation (24) can be used to bound the hinge-loss on at least one of the points x_2 or x_3, which, multiplied by the probability ϵ of the point, is a bound on the average hinge loss:

$$\mathbf{E}_{X,Y}[[1 - Y\mathbf{E}_{X',Y'}[w(X')Y'K(X,X')/p(Y')]/\gamma_1]_+] \geq \epsilon(1 - 8\epsilon\gamma^2/\gamma_1) \qquad (26)$$

and so to get an an average hinge-loss of at most ϵ_1 we must have:

$$\gamma_1 \leq \frac{8\epsilon\gamma^2}{1 - \epsilon_1/\epsilon} \qquad (27)$$

For any target hinge-loss ϵ_1, consider a distribution with $\epsilon = 2\epsilon_1$, in which case we get that the maximum margin attaining average hinge-loss ϵ_1 is $\gamma_1 = 32\epsilon_1\gamma^2$, even though we can get a hinge loss of zero at margin γ using a kernel. This establishes Theorem 4.

6   Discussion

In this paper, we studied how tightly the similarity-based theory of learning, proposed by Balcan and Blum, captures the well-studied theory of kernel-based learning. In other words, how well does a kernel-based learning guarantee translate to a similarity-based learning guarantee. We significantly improved on the bounds presented by Balcan and Blum, providing stronger, simpler, bounds that apply also in the more practically relevant case of hinge-loss minimization. However, these bounds still leave a gap between the kernel-based learning guarantees and the learning guarantee obtained when using the kernel as a similarity measure. We show that the bounds are tight, and so there is a real gap between the similarity-based theory and the kernel-based theory.

We hope that the results presented here can help us better understand similarity-based learning, and possibly suggest revisions to the theory presented by Balcan and Blum.

The quadratic increase in the margin can perhaps be avoided by using the distances, or perhaps the square root of the kernel, rather then the inner products, as a similarity function. Consider the simplest case of two points, with opposite labels and probability half, at $(\gamma, \sqrt{1 - \gamma^2})$ and $(-\gamma, \sqrt{1 - \gamma^2})$. The geometric margin is γ. The inner product (kernel) is only $(0, \gamma^2)$-similarity-good, but the distance function, or just the square root of the inner product, is $(0, \gamma)$-similarity-good. It would be interesting to understand what guarantees can be provided on these measures as similarity functions.

However, even if distance functions are used, the dependence on ϵ in the margin cannot be avoided. Consider the input distribution:

$$p(X = x_1 = (\gamma, \sqrt{1 - 2\gamma^2}), Y = 1) = \frac{1}{2} - \epsilon$$

$$p(X = x_2 = (\gamma, -\sqrt{1 - 2\gamma^2}), Y = 1) = \epsilon$$

$$p(X = x_3 = (-\gamma, \sqrt{1 - 2\gamma^2}), Y = -1) = \frac{1}{2} - \epsilon$$

$$p(X = x_4 = (-\gamma, -\sqrt{1 - 2\gamma^2}), Y = -1) = \epsilon$$

It can be shown that the best margin that can be achieved on all four points by using the distance as a similarity is $2(\epsilon\gamma + 2\gamma^2)$.

All the results in this paper (and also the results of Balcan and Blum [1]) refer to consistent input distributions. Noisy input distributions, where some x might take either label with positive probability, are problematic when we use the definitions of Section 2: The weight $w(x)$ can depend only on x, but not on the label y, and so a positive weight yields a contribution from both labels. A point x with $\Pr(1|x)$ and $\Pr(-1|x)$ both high, cannot contribute much to the similarity-based classification margin (in the extreme case, if $\Pr(1|x) = \Pr(-1|x) = 0.5$, its contribution to the similarity-based classification margin will always be zero).

It is possible to use the results presented here also to obtain (rather messy) results for the noisy case by first removing examples with highly ambiguous labels, then applying Theorems 1 or 2, and finally correcting the weights to account for the negative contribution of the "wrong" label. The amount of this "correction", which will reduce the margin, can be bounded by the amount of allowed ambiguity, and the overall number of removed, highly ambiguous examples, can be bounded in terms of the error-rate. If the error-rate is bounded away from $\frac{1}{2}$, such an approach introduces only a multiplicative factor to both the resulting margin, and the associated margin-violations error-rate (note that in Theorem 1, for the consistent case, we only have an *additive* increase in the error-rate). However, since the hinge-loss on those examples that we removed might be extremely high, the deterioration of the hinge-loss guarantee is much worse. For this reason, a different approach might be appropriate.

We suggest changing the definition of the similarity-based classification margin, removing the effect of the label Y' and instead allowing both positive and negative weights in the range $[-1, +1]$, with the following as an alternative to the classification margin given in equation (1):

$$y\mathbf{E}_{X'}[w(X')K(x, X')]. \tag{28}$$

When the labels are balanced, i.e. $p(Y)$ is bounded away from 0, this yields strictly more flexible definitions, up to margin deterioration of $(\min_Y p(Y))$, for similarity goodness: the effect of the label can be incorporated into $w(x)$ by setting $w(x) \leftarrow w(x)\mathbf{E}_Y[Y/p(Y)|x](\min_Y p(Y))$. Nevertheless, all the learning results and methods of Balcan and Blum hold also using this revised definition of classification margin.

Under the revised definitions using (28), there is no problem handling noisy input distributions: Consider changing the weight mapping of equation (17) to

$$w(x) = \mathbf{E}[Y\alpha^*|x] / C. \tag{29}$$

We now no longer have to require that the label y is a deterministic function of x, and obtain the result of Theorems 1 and 2, with the same constants, for both consistent and noisy distributions, where the classification margin in equation (28) replaces that of equation (1) in Definitions 3 and 4. Note that the results do *not* depend on the label imbalance, and hold also when $p(y)$ is arbitrarily close to zero.

Acknowledgments

I would like to thank Avrim Blum and Nina Balcan for helpful discussions and quick responses and clarifications about their work; and Alexandre d'Aspremont for pointing me to [7]. It has been brought to my attention that the example of Section 5 was also independently constructed, and discussed in private communication, by Sanjoy Dasputa.

References

1. Balcan, M.F., Blum, A.: On a theory of learning with similarity functions. In: Proceedings of the 23rd International Conference on Machine Learning. (2006)
2. Jaakkola, T.S., Haussler, D.: Exploiting generative models in discriminative classifiers. In: Advances in Neural Information Processing Systems 11. MIT Press (1999)
3. Viswanathan, S., Smola, A.J.: Fast kernels for string and tree matching. In: Advances in Neural Information Processing Systems 15. MIT Press (2003)
4. Smola, A.J., Schölkopf, B.: Learning with Kernels. MIT Press (2002)
5. McAllester, D.: Simplified PAC-bayesian margin bounds. In: Proceedings of the 16th Annual Conference on Learning Theory. (2003)
6. Bartlett, P.L., Mendelson, S.: Rademacher and gaussian complexities: risk bounds and structural results. J. Mach. Learn. Res. **3** (2003) 463–482
7. Hettich, R., Kortanek, K.O.: Semi-infinite programming: theory, methods, and applications. SIAM Rev. **35** (1993) 380–429

Gaps in Support Vector Optimization

Nikolas List[1], Don Hush[2], Clint Scovel[2], and Ingo Steinwart[2]

[1] Lehrstuhl Mathematik und Informatik, Ruhr-University Bochum, Germany
nlist@lmi.rub.de
[2] CCS-3, Informatics Group, Los Alamos National Laboratory,
Los Alamos, New Mexico, USA
{dhush,jcs,ingo}@lanl.gov

Abstract. We show that the stopping criteria used in many support vector machine (SVM) algorithms working on the dual can be interpreted as primal optimality bounds which in turn are known to be important for the statistical analysis of SVMs. To this end we revisit the duality theory underlying the derivation of the dual and show that in many interesting cases primal optimality bounds are the same as known dual optimality bounds.

1 Introduction

Given a labeled training set $(x_1, y_1), \ldots, (x_\ell, y_\ell) \in X \times \{-1, 1\}$ on an input space X the standard $L1$-SVM for binary classification introduced by Vapnik et. al in [1] solves an optimization problem of the form

$$\arg\min_{(f,b,\xi)} \quad \mathcal{R}(f, b, \xi) := \frac{1}{2}\|f\|_{\mathcal{H}}^2 + C \sum_{i=1}^{\ell} \xi_i \tag{1}$$
$$\text{s.t.} \quad \xi_i \geq 0 \ \text{ and } \ y_i(f(x_i) + b) \geq 1 - \xi_i \ \text{ f.a. } \ i = 1, \ldots, \ell$$

where $\mathcal{H}$ is the reproducing kernel Hilbert space (RKHS) of a kernel $k : X \times X \to \mathbb{R}$ and $C > 0$ is a free regularization parameter. Instead of solving this problem directly one usually applies standard Lagrange techniques to derive the following dual problem

$$\min_{\alpha \in \mathbb{R}^\ell} \quad W(\alpha) := \frac{1}{2}\langle K\alpha, \alpha \rangle - \alpha \cdot e \tag{2}$$
$$\text{s.t.} \quad y \cdot \alpha = 0 \ \text{ and } \ 0 \leq \alpha_i \leq C \ \text{ f.a. } \ i = 1, \ldots, \ell$$

where $K := (y_i y_j k(x_i, x_j))_{1 \leq i,j \leq \ell}$ is the so-called kernel matrix, $e \in \mathbb{R}^\ell$ is the all ones vector, and $y := (y_1, \ldots, y_\ell)$. Since the kernel is symmetric and positive semi-definite (2) is a standard convex quadratic optimization problem, which is simpler to solve than the primal problem (1). The motivation for this procedure is usually given by the well known fact from Lagrangian Duality Theory, that for the special convex optimization problems (1) and (2) the strong duality

N. Bshouty and C. Gentile (Eds.): COLT 2007, LNAI 4539, pp. 336–348, 2007.

assumption holds (see for example [2, Chapter 5]) in the sense that primal and dual optimal values coincide. Therefore starting from optimal dual solutions one can calculate optimal primal solutions using a simple transformation.

However, due to the usually large and dense kernel matrix it is not easy to solve (2) directly. To address this issue several techniques based on sequentially solving small subproblems have been proposed [14,7,15,13,5,11,21]. Of course, all these methods have in common that they only produce an *approximate* solution to the dual problem (2). However, recall that in order to establish guarantees on the generalization performance of (f, b, ξ) one needs to know that $\mathcal{R}(f, b, \xi)$ approximates the minimum of (1) up to some pre-defined $\varepsilon_P > 0$ (see e.g. [20]). But unfortunately, it is not obvious why the above transformation should produce ε_P-optimal primal points from ε_D-optimal dual points. Consequently, the usual statistical analysis of SVMs does not apply to the learning machines applied in practice. This lack of theoretical guarantees has first been addressed by [6] were the authors showed that ε_D-optimal dual points can be transformed to $O(\sqrt{\epsilon_D})$-optimal primal points using specific transformations.

In this paper we will show, that certain dual optimality bounds transform directly to primal optimality bounds in the sense of $\varepsilon_P = \varepsilon_D$. Let us note, that there has already been a similar argumentation for the special case of $L1$-SVMs in [18, Sec. 10.1]. The authors there, however, ignore the influence of the offset parameter b which leads to ambiguous formulas in Proposition 10.1. Besides that the approach we describe here is far more general and promises to give a unified approach for analyzing approximate duality.

In addition, we will show, that the above dual optimality bounds coincide with the σ-gaps that are used to analyze the convergence behavior [5,11] of certain algorithms working on the dual problem (2). Because of this connection, the results of this paper make it possible to combine convergence rates for certain L1-SVM algorithms and oracle inequalities (see e.g. [20]) describing the statistical performance of the resulting classifier.

The rest of this work is organized as follows: In Section 2 we revisit duality theory[1] and introduce certain gap functions. We then illustrate the theory for convex quadratic optimization problems. In Section 3 we apply our findings to L1-SVMs. In particular, we there consider σ-gaps and a stopping criterion for maximal violating pairs algorithms.

2   Gaps in Constrained Optimization

Let U be a nonempty set and let $\varphi : U \to \mathbb{R}$ and $c_i : U \to \mathbb{R}, i = 1, \ldots, m$ be real valued functions. Let $c : U \to \mathbb{R}^m$ denote the function with components c_i. Consider the primal constrained optimization problem

$$\sup_{u \in U, c(u) \le 0} \varphi(u) \tag{3}$$

---

[1] See for example [3, Chapter XII] for a more detailed introduction.

The set $C := \{u \in U \mid c(u) \leq 0\}$ is called *feasibility region* of (3) and each $u \in C$ is called *a (primal) feasible point*. We define the Lagrangian $L : U \times \mathbb{R}^m \to \mathbb{R}$ associated with (3) by

$$L(u, \lambda) := \varphi(u) - \lambda \cdot c(u) \tag{4}$$

and write $(\mathbb{R}^+)^m := \{\lambda \in \mathbb{R}^m : \lambda \geq 0\}$. Note that although it is customary to define the Lagrangian to be ∞ when $\lambda \notin (\mathbb{R}^+)^m$ the definition (4) will be convenient when applying the subdifferential calculus. Now the *dual function* to (3) is defined by

$$\psi(\lambda) := \sup_{u \in U} L(u, \lambda) \tag{5}$$

and for fixed $\lambda \in \mathbb{R}^m$ the maximizers of $L(\cdot, \lambda)$ are denoted by

$$U_\lambda := \arg\max_{u \in U} L(u, \lambda).$$

Note that for any $u \in U_\lambda$ we have $L(u, \lambda) = \psi(\lambda)$ and $L(u, \lambda) \geq L(u', \lambda)$ for all $u' \in U$. Since the latter equation amounts to one of the two inequalities defining a saddle point we refer to any $(u, \lambda) \in U_\lambda \times \mathbb{R}^m$ as a *semi-saddle*. The following lemma attributed to Uzawa from [12, Lemma 5.3.1] provides sufficient conditions for $u \in U$ to be an optimal primal solution:

Lemma 1. *Any $u \in U$ is a primal optimal point if there exists a $\lambda \geq 0$ such that $u \in U_\lambda$,*

$$c(u) \leq 0$$

and

$$\lambda_i c_i(u) = 0 \text{ for all } i = 1, \ldots, m.$$

The second condition is the feasibility of u the third one is called complementary slackness.

The next lemma shows that without any assumptions on φ and c the dual function has some remarkable properties.

Lemma 2. *The dual $\psi : \mathbb{R}^m \to \mathbb{R} \cup \{+\infty\}$ is convex and for $u \in U_\lambda$ we have $-c(u) \in \partial\psi(\lambda)$, where $\partial\psi(\lambda)$ denotes the subdifferential of ψ at λ.*

Proof. Since ψ is a pointwise supremum of affine functions it is convex. Moreover, $U \neq \emptyset$ implies $\psi(\lambda) = \sup_{u \in U} L(u, \lambda) > -\infty$ for all λ. Finally, for $\lambda' \in \mathbb{R}^m$ and $u \in U_\lambda$ we obtain

$$\psi(\lambda') \geq L(u, \lambda') = L(u, \lambda) + \lambda \cdot c(u) - \lambda' \cdot c(u) = \psi(\lambda) - c(u) \cdot (\lambda' - \lambda). \quad \square$$

Given the Lagrangian L of the problem (3) the corresponding *dual problem* is defined by

$$\inf_{\lambda \geq 0} \psi(\lambda). \tag{6}$$

Note that this a convex optimization problem by Lemma 2. We define the feasibility region of the dual to be $(\mathbb{R}^+)^m$ and any $\lambda \geq 0$ is called a *(dual)feasible point.* Now, for any primal feasible u and any dual feasible λ we have $\varphi(u) \leq \varphi(u) - \lambda \cdot c(u) = L(u, \lambda) \leq \psi(\lambda)$ and hence we obtain

$$\psi(\lambda) - \varphi(u) \geq 0, \qquad u \in C, \ \lambda \geq 0. \qquad (7)$$

Let us write

$$\varphi^* := \sup_{u \in U, \, c(u) \leq 0} \varphi(u) \quad \text{and} \quad \psi^* := \inf_{\lambda \geq 0} \psi(\lambda)$$

for the values of the primal and dual problem, respectively. Then $\psi^* - \varphi^*$ is the smallest possible gap in (7) and is called the *duality gap*. However, in this work we also need the gap for *arbitrary* primal-dual pairs, i.e. for not necessarily feasible $u \in U$ and $\lambda \in \mathbb{R}^m$ we consider

$$\text{gap}(u, \lambda) := \psi(\lambda) - \varphi(u). \qquad (8)$$

The following lemma computes $\text{gap}(u, \lambda)$ for semi-saddles.

Lemma 3. *For all semi-saddles* $(u, \lambda) \in U_\lambda \times \mathbb{R}^m$ *we have*

$$\text{gap}(u, \lambda) = -\lambda \cdot c(u).$$

Proof. We have $\text{gap}(u, \lambda) = \psi(\lambda) - \varphi(u) = L(u, \lambda) - \varphi(u) = -\lambda \cdot c(u).$ □

Now note that for $(u, \lambda) \in (U_\lambda \cap C) \times (\mathbb{R}^+)^m$ we have $c(u) \leq 0$ and $\lambda \geq 0$ and hence Lemma 3 shows that $\text{gap}(u, \lambda) = 0$ is equivalent to the complementary slackness condition of Lemma 1. This fact leads to the following simple and natural optimality bounds:

Definition 1 (Forward Gap). *The forward gap of a feasible* $u \in U$ *is defined by*

$$\overrightarrow{G}(u) := \inf\{-\lambda \cdot c(u) \mid \lambda \geq 0, \ u \in U_\lambda\}. \qquad (9)$$

Definition 2 (Backward Gap). *The backward gap of a feasible* λ *is defined by*

$$\overleftarrow{G}(\lambda) := \inf\{-\lambda \cdot c(u) \mid u \in U_\lambda, c(u) \leq 0\}. \qquad (10)$$

Furthermore, for any feasible primal $u \in U$ we define its suboptimality to be

$$\Delta_P(u) := \varphi^* - \varphi(u)$$

and analogously for any feasible dual λ we define its suboptimality to be

$$\Delta_D(\lambda) := \psi(\lambda) - \psi^*.$$

The following simple lemma shows that the gaps control suboptimality:

Lemma 4. *Suppose that* u *and* λ *are feasible. Then we have*

$$\Delta_P(u) \leq \overrightarrow{G}(u) \quad \text{and} \quad \Delta_D(\lambda) \leq \overleftarrow{G}(\lambda).$$

Proof. Using (7) we obtain $\Delta_P(u) = \varphi^* - \varphi(u) \leq \psi(\lambda') - \varphi(u) = \text{gap}(u, \lambda')$ for all $\lambda' \geq 0$ satisfying $u \in U_{\lambda'}$. Similarly, for $u' \in U_\lambda \cap C$ we have $\Delta_D(\lambda) = \psi(\lambda) - \psi^* \leq \psi(\lambda) - \varphi(u') = \text{gap}(u', \lambda)$. By Lemma 3 we then obtain the assertion. □

2.1 Forward Gap and Dual Optimality

Let us now focus on the dual problem with the tools from above in mind. To that end we consider the dual to be our new "primal" and write (6) as a maximization problem by changing ψ to $-\psi$. The corresponding Lagrangian is then

$$L^D(\lambda, \mu) = -\psi(\lambda) + \mu \cdot \lambda.$$

Since ψ is convex we observe that $\lambda \in U_\mu := \operatorname{argmax}_{\lambda' \in \mathbb{R}^m} L^D(\lambda', \mu)$ if and only if $0 \in \partial_\lambda\left(-L^D(\lambda, \mu)\right) = \partial\psi(\lambda) - \mu$ which occurs if and only if $\mu \in \partial\psi(\lambda)$. In other words we have $U_\mu = \{\lambda \in \mathbb{R}^m : \mu \in \partial\psi(\lambda)\}$. Since this implies

$$\{\mu \geq 0 \,|\, \lambda \in U_\mu\} = \partial\psi(\lambda) \cap (\mathbb{R}^+)^m$$

we see that the forward gap of (6) can be computed by

$$\overrightarrow{G}(\lambda) = \inf\left\{\mu \cdot \lambda \mid \mu \in \partial\psi(\lambda), \ \mu \geq 0\right\} \tag{11}$$

Note, that this gap becomes trivial if ψ is differentiable at λ or is equivalent to solving a LP if $\partial\psi(\lambda)$ is a polyhedra. We will see in Section 3, that this forward gap of the dual is not only of theoretical interest, but is in fact used in analyzing dual SVM optimization problems.

The following two results establish important properties of (11).

Lemma 5. *Given a feasible $\lambda \geq 0$. Then $\overrightarrow{G}(\lambda) \geq 0$ and the minimum value $\overrightarrow{G}(\lambda)$ in (11) is finite and attained iff $\partial\psi(\lambda) \cap (\mathbb{R}^+)^m \neq \emptyset$.*

Proof. Obviously $\mu \cdot \lambda \geq 0$ for $\lambda, \mu \geq 0$. If $\partial\psi(\lambda) \cap (\mathbb{R}^+)^m = \emptyset$ the feasible region of (11) is empty and therefore $\overrightarrow{G}(\lambda) = +\infty$.

In the second case the objective function $\lambda \cdot \mu$ and the constraint set $\{\mu \geq 0 \,|\, \lambda \in U_\mu\}$ have no direction of recession in common. Moreover $\{\mu \geq 0 \,|\, \lambda \in U_\mu\} = \partial\psi(\lambda) \cap (\mathbb{R}^+)^m$ is closed and convex and hence we obtain the assertion by [16, Theorem 27.3]. □

Theorem 1. *If $\lambda \geq 0$ satisfies $\overrightarrow{G}(\lambda) = 0$, then λ is optimal for (6). On the other hand if $\lambda \geq 0$ is optimal for (6) and $\operatorname{ri}(\operatorname{dom}\psi) \cap \operatorname{ri}((\mathbb{R}^+)^m) \neq \emptyset$ then $\overrightarrow{G}(\lambda) = 0$, where $\operatorname{ri} A$ denotes the relative interior of a set A.*

Proof. The first assertion follows directly from Lemma 4. For the second suppose that $\lambda \geq 0$ is optimal for (6). We write (6) as an unconstrained maximization of the function $-\psi(\lambda) - \mathbf{1}_{(\mathbb{R}^+)^m}(\lambda)$ where we note that for $\lambda \geq 0$ we have $\partial\mathbf{1}_{(\mathbb{R}^+)^m}(\lambda) = \{\mu \leq 0 \mid \lambda_i > 0 \Rightarrow \mu_i = 0\}$. Since $\lambda \geq 0$ is optimal it follows that $0 \in \partial(\psi(\lambda) + \mathbf{1}_{(\mathbb{R}^+)^m}(\lambda))$. However, by [16, Thm. 23.8] the assumptions imply that $\partial(\psi(\lambda) + \mathbf{1}_{(\mathbb{R}^+)^m}(\lambda)) = \partial\psi(\lambda) + \partial\mathbf{1}_{(\mathbb{R}^+)^m}(\lambda)$ so that we conclude that there exists a $\mu \in \partial\psi(\lambda)$ such that $\mu \geq 0$ and $\mu_i = 0$ for all i such that $\lambda_i > 0$. This implies $\overrightarrow{G}(\lambda) = 0$. □

2.2   The Filling Property

Let us now return to the relation between primal and dual problem. Suppose we have a feasible dual variable λ and we ask for the best possible associated primal $u \in U_\lambda$. Given the backward gap $\overleftarrow{G}(\lambda)$ and Lemma 4 the answer is easy: The best possible primal $\hat{u} \in U_\lambda$ has an expected primal optimality distance of at most $\Delta_P(\hat{u}) = \varphi^* - \varphi(\hat{u}) \le \psi(\lambda) - \varphi(\hat{u}) = \text{gap}(\hat{u}, \lambda) \le \overleftarrow{G}(\lambda)$. Our main aim will be to characterize $\overleftarrow{G}(\lambda)$ solely in terms of the dual problem.

Recall therefore that Lemma 2 implies that $\{-c(u) \mid u \in U_\lambda\} \subseteq \partial\psi(\lambda)$. Since $\partial\psi(\lambda)$ is convex it then follows that

$$C_\lambda := \{c(u) \mid u \in U_\lambda\}.$$

satisfies $-\operatorname{co} C_\lambda \subseteq \partial\psi(\lambda)$, where $\operatorname{co} C_\lambda$ denotes the convex hull of C_λ. The reverse inclusion will prove to be extremely useful so we recall the following definition from [3, Def. XII.2.3.1]:

Definition 3. *We say the* filling property *holds for λ, iff*

$$-\operatorname{co} C_\lambda = \partial\psi(\lambda). \tag{12}$$

If in addition C_λ is convex we say, that the strict filling property *holds for λ.*

We will present some conditions under which the strict filling property holds in Section 2.4. To illustrate the importance of (12) we end this section by the following theorem.[2]

Theorem 2. *Assume the filling property holds for a given $\lambda \ge 0$. Then λ is an optimal dual solution iff there exist $s \le m+1$ feasible primal points $u_1, \ldots, u_s \in U_\lambda$ and $\alpha_1, \ldots, \alpha_s \ge 0$ such that $\sum_{r=1}^{s} \alpha_r = 1$,*

$$\sum_{r=1}^{s} \alpha_r c(u_r) \le 0, \qquad and \qquad \lambda_i \sum_{r=1}^{s} \alpha_r c_i(u_r) = 0 \quad for\ all\ i = 1, \ldots, m.$$

Moreover if the strict filling property holds for an optimal λ, then the duality gap $\psi^* - \varphi^*$ is 0 and the solutions of the primal problem are given by the feasible $u \in U_\lambda$, for which $\text{gap}(u, \lambda) = 0$. Since $(u, \lambda) \in U_\lambda \times (\mathbb{R}^+)^m$ the latter is equivalent to complementary slackness.

2.3   Relation Between the Gaps

Let us once again repeat the main question in this work: Given a dual feasible point λ, for which only approximate optimality can be guaranteed, how can this be translated into approximate optimality guarantees for "associated" primal points $u \in U_\lambda$?

The answer is quite simple if we use forward and backward gaps as optimality bounds as the following main theorem shows:

---

[2] Since this theorem is not needed in the following we omit its elementary proof.

Theorem 3. *Let $\lambda \geq 0$ be a dual point for which the strict filling property holds. Then we have*

$$\overleftarrow{G}(\lambda) = \overrightarrow{G}(\lambda).$$

In addition, if $\overrightarrow{G}(\lambda)$ is finite, there exists a feasible $\hat{u} \in U_\lambda$ such that $-\lambda \cdot c(\hat{u}) = \overrightarrow{G}(\lambda)$. Moreover, $\hat{u}$ is an optimal solution of

$$\sup \{\varphi(u) \mid u \in U_\lambda, c(u) \leq 0\}.$$

Proof. Since the strict filling property implies that the infima in (10) and (11) range over the same set, we obtain equality of the gaps. If $\overrightarrow{G}(\lambda) < +\infty$ Lemma 5 and the strict filling property then imply, that there exists a feasible $\hat{u} \in U_\lambda$ such that $\overrightarrow{G}(\lambda) = -\lambda \cdot c(\hat{u})$. Moreover, for $(u, \lambda) \in U_\lambda \times \mathbb{R}^m$ Lemma 3 shows $\varphi(u) - \lambda \cdot c(u) = \psi(\lambda)$. Consequently, we see that for fixed $\lambda \geq 0$ maximizing φ is equivalent to minimizing $-\lambda \cdot c(\cdot)$ and therefore $\varphi(\hat{u})$ is also the maximal value φ attains on $\{u \in U_\lambda \mid c(u) \leq 0\}$. □

2.4 Sufficient Conditions for Filling

We now show that for concave quadratic optimization problems the strict filling property holds for any feasible dual point in the effective domain of the dual function (see [19] for more general settings). To that end let U be a Hilbert space, $w \in U$, $d \in \mathbb{R}^m$, $Q : U \to U$ be a nonnegative selfadjoint operator such that $Q : \ker(Q)^\perp \to \ker(Q)^\perp$ has a continuous inverse Q^{-1} and $A : U \to \mathbb{R}^m$ be continuous and linear. Then the convex quadratic problem

$$\sup_{\substack{u \in U \\ Au - d \leq 0}} -\frac{1}{2}\langle Qu, u \rangle + \langle w, u \rangle \tag{13}$$

is of the form (3) for $\varphi(u) := -\frac{1}{2}\langle Qu, u \rangle + \langle w, u \rangle$ and $c(u) := Au - d$. The next lemma, which includes the linear programming case, shows that the strict filling property holds:

Lemma 6. *Consider the convex quadratic programming problem (13). Then the strict filling property holds for all λ in the domain of the Lagrangian dual criterion function.*

Proof. The associated Lagrangian is $L(u, \lambda) = -\frac{1}{2}\langle Qu, u \rangle + \langle w, u \rangle - \lambda \cdot (Au - d) = -\frac{1}{2}\langle Qu, u \rangle + \langle w - A^*\lambda, u \rangle + \lambda \cdot d$ and its dual criterion function is defined by (5). If $w - A^*\lambda$ is not orthogonal to $\ker Q$ then it is easy to see that $\psi(\lambda) = \infty$. Now suppose that $w - A^*\lambda \in (\ker Q)^\perp = \text{img } Q$. Then we can solve $0 = \partial_u L(u, \lambda) = -Qu + w - A^*\lambda$ for u and hence we obtain

$$U_\lambda = Q^{-1}(w - A^*\lambda) + \ker Q,$$

$$\psi(\lambda) = \frac{1}{2}\langle Q^{-1}(w - A^*\lambda), w - A^*\lambda \rangle + \lambda \cdot d$$

$$\text{dom } \psi = \{\lambda \in \mathbb{R}^m \mid w - A^*\lambda \in \text{img } Q\}. \tag{14}$$

The latter formula for $\mathrm{dom}\,\psi$ implies

$$\partial\psi(\lambda) = AQ^{-1}(A^*\lambda - w) + d + \{\mu \mid A^*\mu \in \mathrm{img}\,Q\}^\perp$$

for all $\lambda \in \mathrm{dom}\,\psi$. Moreover, for $\lambda \in \mathrm{dom}\,\psi$ we also obtain

$$\begin{aligned}
-C_\lambda &:= \{\, -c(u) \mid u \in U_\lambda \,\} \\
&= \{\, d - Au \mid u \in Q^{-1}(w - A^*\lambda) + \ker Q \} \\
&= d + AQ^{-1}(A^*\lambda - w) + A\ker Q\,.
\end{aligned}$$

From Lemma 2 it suffices to show that $(A\ker Q)^\perp \subset \{\mu \mid A^*\mu \in \mathrm{img}\,Q\}$ to complete the proof. To that end suppose that $\mu \perp A\ker Q$. Then we have $\langle A^*\mu, z\rangle = \langle \mu, Az\rangle = 0$ for all $z \in \ker Q$ which implies $A^*\mu \in \mathrm{img}\,Q$. $\square$

Let us denote the gradient of the dual criterion function (14) restricted to its domain by

$$\nabla\psi(\lambda) := AQ^{-1}(A^*\lambda - w) + d. \tag{15}$$

Using this notation the following corollary follows immediately from (15), the definition of the backward-gap and Theorem 3:

Corollary 1. *Given a dual feasible point $\lambda \in \mathrm{dom}\,\psi$, $\lambda \geq 0$, we have*

$$G_{QP}(\lambda) := \overleftarrow{G}(\lambda) = \inf_{z\in\ker Q}\{\lambda \cdot (\nabla\psi(\lambda) - Az) \mid \nabla\psi(\lambda) - Az \geq 0\}\,. \tag{16}$$

3 Applications to SVM Optimization

In this section we we apply our results to SVMs. We begin by showing, that in this case (16) is a generalization of the σ-gap which has been used in [5,11] both as stopping criterion for the dual problem and as an important quantity in the construction of algorithms which possess convergence rates. We then calculate the forward-gap for $L1$-SVMs in Subsection 3.2. Finally, in Section 3.3 we show that the stopping criteria used in MVP dual algorithms can directly be derived from this gap leading to primal optimality guarantees.

3.1 The σ-Gap

Let λ^* denote an optimal solution to the dual problem (6). From the convexity of ψ it then follows that $\psi(\lambda) - \psi(\lambda^*) \leq \partial\psi(\lambda) \cdot (\lambda - \lambda^*)$. Consequently $\sigma(\lambda) := \sup\{\partial\psi(\lambda) \cdot (\lambda - \acute{\lambda}) \mid \acute{\lambda} \in \mathrm{dom}\,\psi, \acute{\lambda} \geq 0\}$ satisfies $\psi(\lambda) - \psi(\lambda^*) \leq \sigma(\lambda)$ and hence σ can be used as a stopping criteria for the dual. For quadratic convex programs the σ-gap amounts to that defined in [11], namely

$$\sigma(\lambda) = \sup\{\nabla\psi(\lambda) \cdot (\lambda - \mu) \mid \mu \geq 0,\ w - A^*\mu \perp \ker Q\}\,. \tag{17}$$

It was shown in [5] for $L1$-SVMs that iterative schemes which choose a successor λ_{n+1} of λ_n that satisfies $\partial\psi(\lambda_n) \cdot (\lambda_n - \lambda_{n+1}) \geq \tau\sigma(\lambda_n)$ converge to optimal with a

344   N. List et al.

rate depending upon τ. This result was improved and extended to general convex quadratic programming problems in [11]. Our next results relate the σ-gap to $G_{QP}(\lambda)$:

Lemma 7. *For any feasible $\lambda \in \mathrm{dom}\,\psi$ such that $G_{QP}(\lambda) < \infty$ we have*

$$\sigma(\lambda) = G_{QP}(\lambda).$$

Proof. Lemma 6 ensures that the strict filling property holds for any dual point $\lambda \in \mathrm{dom}\,\psi = \{\lambda \mid w - A^*\lambda \perp \ker Q\}$. Let $P : \mathbb{R}^m \to A\ker Q$ denote the orthogonal projection onto $A\ker Q$. Since the duality gap for linear programming is zero (see for example [3, Cor. XII.2.3.6]) we have

$$
\begin{aligned}
G_{QP}(\lambda) &= \inf\{\lambda \cdot (\nabla\psi(\lambda) - Az) \mid z \in \ker Q,\ \nabla\psi(\lambda) - Az \geq 0\} \\
&= -\sup\{\lambda \cdot \eta \mid \eta \in \mathbb{R}^m,\ P\eta = 0,\ \eta \leq \nabla\psi(\lambda)\} + \lambda \cdot \nabla\psi(\lambda) \\
&= -\inf\{\mu \cdot \nabla\psi(\lambda) \mid \mu \geq 0,\ \nu \in \mathbb{R}^m,\ \mu + P\nu = \lambda\} + \lambda \cdot \nabla\psi(\lambda).
\end{aligned}
$$

Since $(\lambda - \mu) = P\nu$ is equivalent $w - A^*\mu \perp \ker Q$ the right hand is equivalent to the σ-gap defined in (17) and the claim follows. □

The next corollary follows directly from Theorem 3 and Lemma 7:

Corollary 2. *Let λ be feasible such that $w - A^*\lambda \perp \ker Q$ and $\sigma(\lambda) < \infty$. Let $\hat{z}$ optimize the gap $G_{QP}(\lambda)$ defined in (16). Then $\hat{u} := w - A^*\lambda + \hat{z}$ is a $\sigma(\lambda)$-optimal solution of the primal problem, i.e*

$$\Delta_P(\hat{u}) \leq \sigma(\lambda).$$

3.2 L1-SVMs

To represent the $L1$-SVM optimization problem (1) as a quadratic programming problem (13) we write $U := \mathcal{H} \times \mathbb{R} \times \mathbb{R}^\ell$ where $\mathcal{H}$ is the RKHS associated with a kernel k. Recall that the canonical feature map $\Phi : X \to \mathcal{H}$ is given by $\Phi(x) = k(x, \cdot)$, $x \in X$, and that the reproducing property states $f(x) = \langle f, \Phi(x)\rangle$, $f \in \mathcal{H}$, $x \in X$. We further write

$$
Q := \begin{pmatrix} \mathrm{Id}_\mathcal{H} & 0 & 0 \\ 0_\mathcal{H} & 0 & 0 \\ 0_\mathcal{H} & 0 & 0 \end{pmatrix}, \quad
A := \begin{pmatrix} -y_1\Phi(x_1) & -y_1 & -e_1 \\ \vdots & \vdots & \vdots \\ -y_\ell\Phi(x_\ell) & -y_\ell & -e_\ell \\ 0_\mathcal{H} & 0 & -e_1 \\ \vdots & \vdots & \vdots \\ 0_\mathcal{H} & 0 & -e_\ell \end{pmatrix}, \quad
\begin{aligned}
w &:= -C\begin{pmatrix} 0_\mathcal{H} \\ 0 \\ e \end{pmatrix}, \\
d &:= \begin{pmatrix} -e \\ 0 \end{pmatrix},
\end{aligned}
$$

where $\mathbf{0}$ denotes the zero vector in $\mathbb{R}^\ell$ and e denotes the vector of all 1's in $\mathbb{R}^\ell$. Let us solve (2) using Corollary 1. To that end let us write $\lambda = \binom{\alpha}{\beta} \in \mathbb{R}^{2\ell}$. Then elementary calculations show that the condition $w - A^*\lambda \perp \ker Q$ amounts to

$$y \cdot \alpha = 0 \quad \text{and} \quad \alpha + \beta = Ce. \tag{18}$$

For feasible λ satisfying (18) elementary calculations show that

$$\nabla\psi(\lambda) = \begin{bmatrix} \sum_{i=1}^{\ell} \alpha_i y_1 y_i k(x_i, x_1) - 1 \\ \vdots \\ \sum_{i=1}^{\ell} \alpha_i y_j y_i k(x_i, x_j) - 1 \\ \vdots \\ \sum_{i=1}^{\ell} \alpha_i y_\ell y_i k(x_i, x_\ell) - 1 \\ 0 \\ \vdots \\ 0 \end{bmatrix} = \begin{bmatrix} \nabla W(\alpha) \\ 0 \end{bmatrix} \in \mathbb{R}^{2\ell},$$

where $W(\alpha)$ is given as in (2). Since $\ker Q$ equals the last two components of $U = \mathcal{H} \times \mathbb{R} \times \mathbb{R}^\ell$ it follows from (16) that the gap $\overleftarrow{G}(\lambda)$ for the L1-SVM is

$$\inf_{(b,\xi)} \quad \alpha \cdot (\nabla W(\alpha) + b \cdot y + \xi) + \beta \cdot \xi$$

$$\text{s.t.} \quad \nabla W(\alpha) + b \cdot y + \xi \geq 0, \ \xi \geq 0.$$

For feasible $\lambda \in \operatorname{dom}\psi$ we have $\alpha_i \geq 0$ and $\beta = C - \alpha_i \geq 0$. Therefore the infimum above for fixed b is obtained by setting each $\xi_i = [-\nabla W(\alpha)_i - by_i]^+$ where $[\nu]^+ := \max(0, \nu)$. If we use the equality $\nu = [\nu]^+ - [-\nu]^+$ we conclude that $\overleftarrow{G}(\lambda) = G(\alpha)$ where

$$G(\alpha) := \inf_{-b \in \mathbb{R}} \left(\sum_{i=1}^{\ell} \alpha_i [\nabla W(\alpha)_i - by_i]^+ + (C - \alpha_i) [by_i - \nabla W(\alpha)_i]^+ \right). \quad (19)$$

Note, that $G(\alpha)$ can be computed solely in terms of the dual problem since it is the forward gap on the dual. In the form of the σ-gap it has been a main tool in deriving convergence guarantees for dual SVM-algorithms [5]. From (19) we easily see, that for every feasible α we have $G(\alpha) < \infty$ and using Theorem 3 we know that for each feasible α there exists an associated primal classifier for which we are now able to give direct primal optimality guarantees:

Corollary 3. *Let $\varepsilon_D > 0$, let $0 \leq \alpha \leq C \cdot e$ be a vector satisfying $y^\top \alpha = 0$, and let $\hat{b}$ be an optimal solution of (19). Assume that α is ε_D-optimal in the sense that $G(\alpha) = \overleftarrow{G}(\alpha) \leq \varepsilon_D$. Define $\hat{f} := \sum_{i=1}^{\ell} y_i \alpha_i \Phi(x_i)$ and $\hat{\xi}_i := [\hat{b}y_i - \nabla W(\alpha)_i]^+, i = 1,..,\ell$. Then $(\hat{f}, \hat{b}, \hat{\xi})$ is a ε_D-optimal solution of (1), i.e.*

$$\mathcal{R}(\hat{f}, \hat{b}, \hat{\xi}) - \mathcal{R}^* \leq \varepsilon_D.$$

Recall that [4, Theorem 2] only showed that $(\hat{f}, \hat{b}, \hat{\xi})$ is a $\mathcal{O}(\sqrt{\varepsilon_D})$-optimal primal solution, and consequently the above corollary substantially improves this earlier result.

3.3   Optimality Criteria and Maximal Violating Pairs

The most popular SVM algorithms are maximum-violating pair algorithms (MVP), which are implemented for example in SVM^{light} and SMO-type algorithms. Often this selection strategy has been motivated directly from Karush-Kuhn-Tucker (KKT) conditions on the dual [8,9,10], but there has been no justification in terms of primal optimality guarantees. Let us first introduce some notation to be able to formulate the stopping criterion used in MVP algorithms. To that end recall the well known top-bottom candidate definition of Joachims and Lin [7,9]:

$$\overline{I_{top}}(\alpha) := \{i \mid (\alpha_i < C, y_i = -1) \vee (\alpha_i > 0, y_i = +1)\}$$
$$\overline{I_{bot}}(\alpha) := \{i \mid (\alpha_i < C, y_i = 1) \vee (\alpha_i > 0, y_i = -1)\}. \tag{20}$$

Any pair $(i,j) \in \overline{I_{top}}(\alpha) \times \overline{I_{bot}}(\alpha)$, such that $y_i \nabla W(\alpha)_i > y_j \nabla W(\alpha)_j$ is called a *violating pair*, since it forces at least one of the summands in (19) corresponding to i or j to be non-zero for any choice of b. For the maximal violating pair define

$$\hat{t} := \max_{i \in \overline{I_{top}}(\alpha)} y_i \nabla W(\alpha)_i \quad \text{and} \quad \hat{b} := \min_{i \in \overline{I_{bot}}(\alpha)} y_i \nabla W(\alpha)_i .$$

It is well known, that whenever $\hat{t} \leq \hat{b}$ the dual variable α is optimal. This lead to the heuristic dual stopping criterion $\hat{t} - \hat{b} \leq \varepsilon$. We now show that our results do also provide primal optimality guarantees for MVP algorithms:

Lemma 8. *Given a final solution $\hat{\alpha}$ of a MVP-algorithm which terminated with accuracy ε, i.e. $\hat{t} - \hat{b} \leq \varepsilon$, then for any $b \in [\hat{b}, \hat{t}]$ the associated primal solution $(\hat{f}, b, \xi(b))$ defined by $\hat{f} := \sum_{i=1}^{\ell} \hat{\alpha}_i \Phi(x_i)$ and $\xi_i(b) := [by_i - \nabla W(\alpha)_i]^+$ is $C\ell \cdot \varepsilon$ optimal, i.e.*
$$\mathcal{R}(\hat{f}, b, \xi(b)) - \mathcal{R}^* \leq C\ell \cdot \varepsilon.$$

Proof. Using the definition (20) the gap $G(\alpha)$ given in (19) can be computed by

$$\inf_{b \in \mathbb{R}} \left(\sum_{\substack{i \in \overline{I_{top}}(\alpha) \\ y_i \nabla W(\alpha)_i > b}} \mu_i^+ [y_i \nabla W(\alpha)_i - b]^+ + \sum_{\substack{i \in \overline{I_{bot}}(\alpha) \\ y_i \nabla W(\alpha)_i < b}} \mu_i^- [b - y_i \nabla W(\alpha)_i]^+ \right), \tag{21}$$

where

$$\mu_i^+ = \begin{cases} \alpha_i & \text{if } y_i = +1 \\ C - \alpha_i & \text{else} \end{cases} \quad \text{and} \quad \mu_i^- = \begin{cases} C - \alpha_i & \text{if } y_i = +1 \\ \alpha_i & \text{else} \end{cases}.$$

Indeed note, that for any $i \in \overline{I_{top}}(\alpha)$ such that $y_i \nabla W(\alpha)_i \leq b$ we either have $i \in \overline{I_{bot}}(\alpha)$ too, and the contribution of index i is counted by the second sum, or i is a top-only candidate, i.e. $\alpha_i = 0$ and $y_i = -1$ or $\alpha_i = C$ and $y_i = 1$. In both cases the contribution of index i to (19), given by

$$\alpha_i [\nabla W(\alpha)_i - by_i]^+ + (C - \alpha_i) [by_i - \nabla W(\alpha)]^+$$

is zero. Similar arguments hold for bottom-candidates with $y_i \nabla W(\alpha)_i \geq b$.
We now try to bound the terms in (21) for arbitrary $b \in [\hat{b}, \hat{t}]$. Obviously we have

$$[y_i \nabla W(\alpha)_i - b]^+ \leq [\hat{t} - b]^+ \leq \left[\hat{t} - \hat{b}\right]^+ \qquad \text{for } i \in \overline{I_{top}}(\alpha) \quad \text{and}$$

$$[b - y_i \nabla W(\alpha)_i]^+ \leq \left[b - \hat{b}\right]^+ \leq \left[\hat{t} - \hat{b}\right]^+ \qquad \text{for } i \in \overline{I_{bot}}(\alpha).$$

Since the two sums in (21) range over disjoint index-sets and $\mu_i^{+/-} \leq C$ we
conclude for any $b \in [\hat{b}, \hat{t}]$, that

$$G(\alpha) \leq C\ell \cdot \left[\hat{t} - \hat{b}\right]^+$$

and the claim follows from Corollary 3. $\qquad\qquad\qquad\qquad\qquad\qquad\qquad\qquad\quad \Box$

Remark 1. If we count the number

$$d := \left| \left\{ i \;\middle|\; (i \in \overline{I_{top}}(\alpha) \wedge y_i \nabla W(\alpha)_i > \hat{b}) \vee (i \in \overline{I_{bot}}(\alpha) \wedge y_i \nabla W(\alpha)_i < \hat{t}) \right\} \right|$$

of indices which could indicate a violation if b is chosen in $[\hat{b}, \hat{t}]$. Then Lemma 8
can be improved so the right hand side is $Cd \cdot \varepsilon$.

4   Conclusion and Open Problems

We have presented a general framework for deriving primal optimality guarantees from dual optimality bounds. We improve the results given in [4] insofar as
we can directly transform dual in primal optimality guarantees without loosing
by an order of $\mathcal{O}(\sqrt{\varepsilon})$. In addition our results are easily extensible to more general
cases whenever the strict filling property can be proven. The main advantage in
the framework of support vector optimization is however the fact, that important
dual optimality bounds which are used in practice could directly be derived from
the abstract forward-backward gaps. This closes a main gap in analysis of support
vector machine *algorithms* since now optimality guarantees for approximately optimal dual points can be transfered to generalization guarantees for an associated
classifier using the results from statistical learning theory.

We point out, that using results from [19], the generalization of tight relation of
dual and primal problem even for approximately optimal points should be straight
forward but was beyond this work. The question if the strict filling property is also
a necessary condition for this relation is however an open question.

We leave it as an objective for future research, whether the deeper knowledge
about the optimality bounds presented here can be used to extend known convergence guarantees from quadratic optimization to more general optimization
problems.

Acknowledgments. This work was supported in part by the IST Programme of
the European Community, under the PASCAL Network of Excellence,
IST-2002-506778.

References

1. Boser, B.E., Guyon, I.M., Vapnik, V.N.: A Training Algorithm for Optimal Margin Classifiers. In: Proceedings of the 5th Annual Workshop on Computational Learning Theory, pp. 144–153. ACM Press, New York (1992)
2. Christianini, N., Shawe-Taylor, J.: An Introduction to Support Vector Machines, 5th edn. Cambridge University Press, Cambridge (2003)
3. Hiriart-Urruty, J.-B., Lemaréchal, C.: Convex Analysis and Minimization Algorithms II. Springer, Heidelberg (1993)
4. Hush, D., Kelly, P., Scovel, C., Steinwart, I.: QP Algorithms with Guaranteed Aaccuracy and Run Time for Support Vector Machines. Journal of Machine Learning Research 7, 733–769 (2006)
5. Hush, D., Scovel, C.: Polynomial-time Decomposition Algorithms for Support Vector Machines. Machine Learning 51, 51–71 (2003)
6. Hush, D., Scovel, C., Steinwart, I.: Approximate duality. Journal of Optimization Theory and Applications, to appear
7. Joachims. T.: Making Large–Scale SVM Learning Practical. In: Schölkopf et al. [17], chapter 11, pp. 169–184
8. Keerthi, S.S., Gilbert, E.G.: Convergence of a Generalized SMO Algorithm for SVM Classifier Design. Machine Learning 46, 351–360 (2002)
9. Lin, C.-J.: On the Convergence of the Decomposition Method for Support Vector Machines. IEEE Transactions on Neural Networks 12, 1288–1298 (2001)
10. List, N.: Convergence of a generalized gradient selection approach for the decomposition method. In: Proceedings of the 15th International Conference on Algorithmic Learning Theory, pp. 338–349 (2004)
11. List, N., Simon, H.U.: General Polynomial Time Decomposition Algorithms. In: Auer, P., Meir, R. (eds.) COLT 2005. LNCS (LNAI), vol. 3559, Springer, Heidelberg (2005)
12. Mangasarian, O.: Nonlinear Programming. SIAM, Philadelphia, PA (1994)
13. Mangasarian, O.L., Musicant, D.R.: Active Set Support Vector Machine Classification. In: Lee, T., Diettrich, T., Tresp, V. (eds.) Neural Information Processing Systems (NIPS) 2000, pp. 577–583. MIT Press, Cambridge (2001)
14. Osuna, E., Freund, R., Girosi, F.: An Improved Training Algorithm for Support Vector Machines. In: Principe, J., Gile, L., Morgan, N., Wilson, E., (eds.). Neural Networks for Signal Processing VII – Proceedings of the 1997 IEEE Workshop, pp. 276–285, New York (1997)
15. Platt, J. C.: Fast Training of Support Vector Machines using Sequential Minimal Optimization. In: Schölkopf et al. [17], chapter 12, pp. 185–208
16. Rockafellar, R.T.: Convex Analysis. Princeton University Press, Princeton (1970)
17. Schölkopf, B., Burges, C.J.C., Smola, A.J. (eds.): Advances in Kernel Methods – Support Vector Learning. MIT Press, Cambridge, MA (1999)
18. Schölkopf, B., Smola, A.J.: Learning with Kernels, 2nd edn. MIT Press, Cambridge, MA, London (2002)
19. Solov'ev, V.: The subdifferential and the directional derivatives of the maximum of a family of convex functions. Izvestiya: Mathematics 62(4), 807–832 (1998)
20. Steinwart, I., Hush, D., Scovel, C.: An oracle inequality for clipped regularized risk minimizers. In: Advances in Neural Information Processing Systems 19 (2007)
21. Vishwanathan, S., Smola, A.J., Murty, M.N.: Simplesvm. In: Proceedings of the Twentieth International Conference on Machine Learning (2003)

Learning Languages with Rational Kernels

Corinna Cortes[1], Leonid Kontorovich[2], and Mehryar Mohri[3,1]

[1] Google Research,
76 Ninth Avenue, New York, NY 10011
[2] Carnegie Mellon University,
5000 Forbes Avenue, Pittsburgh, PA 15213
[3] Courant Institute of Mathematical Sciences,
251 Mercer Street, New York, NY 10012

Abstract. We present a general study of learning and linear separability with rational kernels, the sequence kernels commonly used in computational biology and natural language processing. We give a characterization of the class of all languages linearly separable with rational kernels and prove several properties of the class of languages linearly separable with a fixed rational kernel. In particular, we show that for kernels with transducer values in a finite set, these languages are necessarily finite Boolean combinations of preimages by a transducer of a single sequence. We also analyze the margin properties of linear separation with rational kernels and show that kernels with transducer values in a finite set guarantee a positive margin and lead to better learning guarantees. Creating a rational kernel with values in a finite set is often non-trivial even for relatively simple cases. However, we present a novel and general algorithm, double-tape disambiguation, that takes as input a transducer mapping sequences to sequence features, and yields an associated transducer that defines a finite range rational kernel. We describe the algorithm in detail and show its application to several cases of interest.

1 Motivation

In previous work, we introduced a paradigm for learning languages that consists of mapping strings to an appropriate high-dimensional feature space and learning a separating hyperplane in that space [13]. We proved that the rich class of piecewise-testable languages [22] can be linearly separated using a high-dimensional feature mapping based on subsequences. We also showed that the positive definite kernel associated to this embedding, the *subsequence kernel*, can be efficiently computed. Support vector machines can be used in combination with this kernel to determine a separating hyperplane for piecewise-testable languages. We further proved that the languages linearly separable with this kernel are exactly the piecewise-testable languages.

The subsequence kernel is a *rational kernel* – that is, a kernel that can be represented by weighted finite-state transducers [5,12]. Most sequence kernels successfully used in computational biology and natural language processing, including mismatch kernels [15], gappy n-gram kernels [16], locality-improved

N. Bshouty and C. Gentile (Eds.): COLT 2007, LNAI 4539, pp. 349–364, 2007.
© Springer-Verlag Berlin Heidelberg 2007

kernels [25], convolutions kernels for strings [11], tree kernels [4], n-gram kernels [5], and moment kernels [6], are special instances of rational kernels. Rational kernels can be computed in quadratic time using a single general algorithm [5].

This motivates our study of learning with rational kernels, in particular the question of determining the class of languages that can be linearly separated with a given rational kernel, thereby generalizing the result relating to subsequence kernels and piecewise-testable languages, and also analyzing their generalization properties based on the margin. It is also natural to ask which languages are separable with rational kernels in general.

This paper deals with precisely these questions. We prove that the family of languages linearly separable with rational kernels is exactly that of *stochastic languages* [21], a class of languages that strictly includes regular languages and contains non-trivial context-free and context-sensitive languages. We also prove several properties of the class of languages linearly separable with a fixed rational kernel. In particular, we show that when the kernel has values in a finite set these languages are necessarily finite Boolean combinations of the preimages by a transducer of single sequences.

In previous work, we proved that linear separability with the subsequence kernel guarantees a positive margin, which helped us derive margin-based bounds for learning piecewise-testable languages [13]. This property does not hold for all rational kernels. We prove however that a positive margin is guaranteed for all rational kernels with transducer values in a finite set.

This quality and the property of the languages they separate in terms of finite Boolean combinations point out the advantages of using PDS rational kernels with transducer values in a finite set, such as the subsequence kernel used for piecewise-testable languages. However, while defining a transducer mapping sequences to the *feature sequences* of interest is typically not hard, creating one that associates to each sequence at most a predetermined finite number of instances of that feature is often non-trivial, even for relatively simple transducers.

We present a novel algorithm, *double-tape disambiguation*, precisely to address this problem. The algorithm takes as input an (unweighted) transducer mapping sequences to features and yields a transducer associating the same features to the same input sequences but at most once. The algorithm can thus help define and represent rational kernels with transducer values in a finite integer range, which offer better learning guarantees. We describe the algorithm in detail and show its application to several cases of interest.

The paper is organized as follows. Section 2 introduces the definitions and notation related to weighted transducers and probabilistic automata that are used in the remainder of the paper. Section 3 gives the proof of several characterization theorems for the classes of languages that can be linearly separated with rational kernels. The margin properties of rational kernels are studied in Section 4. Section 5 describes in detail the double-tape disambiguation algorithm which can be used to define complex finite range rational kernels and shows its application to several cases of interest.

2   Preliminaries

This section gives the standard definition and specifies the notation used for weighted transducers and briefly summarizes the definition and essential properties of probabilistic automata, which turn out to play an important role in our study of linear separability with rational kernels. In all that follows, Σ represents a finite alphabet. The length of a string $x \in \Sigma^*$ over that alphabet is denoted by $|x|$ and the complement of a subset $L \subseteq \Sigma^*$ by $\overline{L} = \Sigma^* \setminus L$. We also denote by $|x|_a$ the number of occurrences of the symbol a in x.

2.1   Weighted Transducers and Automata

Finite-state transducers are finite automata in which each transition is augmented with an output label in addition to the familiar input label [2,10]. Output labels are concatenated along a path to form an output sequence and similarly with input labels. *Weighted transducers* are finite-state transducers in which each transition carries some weight in addition to the input and output labels. The weights of the transducers considered in this paper are real values and are multiplied along the paths. The weight of a pair of input and output strings (x, y) is obtained by summing the weights of the paths labeled with (x, y). The following gives a formal definition of weighted transducers. In the following, $\mathbb{K}$ denotes either the set of real numbers $\mathbb{R}$, rational numbers $\mathbb{Q}$, or integers $\mathbb{Z}$.

Definition 1. *A weighted finite-state transducer T over $(\mathbb{K}, +, \cdot, 0, 1)$ is an 8-tuple $T = (\Sigma, \Delta, Q, I, F, E, \lambda, \rho)$ where Σ is the finite input alphabet of the transducer, Δ is the finite output alphabet, Q is a finite set of states, $I \subseteq Q$ the set of initial states, $F \subseteq Q$ the set of final states, $E \subseteq Q \times (\Sigma \cup \{\epsilon\}) \times (\Delta \cup \{\epsilon\}) \times \mathbb{K} \times Q$ a finite set of transitions, $\lambda : I \to \mathbb{K}$ the initial weight function, and $\rho : F \to \mathbb{K}$ the final weight function mapping F to $\mathbb{K}$.*

For a path π in a transducer, we denote by $p[\pi]$ the origin state of that path and by $n[\pi]$ its destination state. We also denote by $P(I, x, y, F)$ the set of paths from the initial states I to the final states F labeled with input string x and output string y. The weight of a path π is obtained by multiplying the weights of its constituent transitions and is denoted by $w[\pi]$. A transducer T is *regulated* if the output weight associated by T to any pair of strings (x, y) by:

$$T(x, y) = \sum_{\pi \in P(I, x, y, F)} \lambda(p[\pi]) \cdot w[\pi] \cdot \rho[n[\pi]] \tag{1}$$

is well-defined and in $\mathbb{K}$. $T(x, y) = 0$ when $P(I, x, y, F) = \emptyset$. If for all $q \in Q$ $\sum_{\pi \in P(q, \epsilon, \epsilon, q)} w[\pi] \in \mathbb{K}$, then T is regulated. In particular, when T does not admit any ϵ-cycle, it is regulated. The weighted transducers we will be considering in this paper will be regulated. Figure 1(a) shows an example.

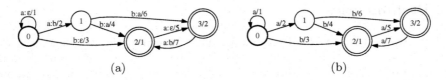

Fig. 1. (a) Example of weighted transducer T. (b) Example of weighted automaton A. A can be obtained from T by projection on the input. A bold circle indicates an initial state and a double-circle a final state. A final state carries a weight indicated after the slash symbol representing the state number. The initial weights are not indicated in all the examples in this paper since they are all equal to one.

The standard rational operations, sum $+$, product or concatenation $\cdot$, and Kleene-closure $*$ can be defined for regulated transducers [21,14]. For any pair of strings (x, y),

$$(T_1+T_2)(x, y) = T_1(x, y)+T_2(x, y) \text{ and } (T_1 \cdot T_2)(x, y) = \sum_{x_1 x_2 = x,\ y_1 y_2 = y} T_1(x_1, y_1) \cdot T_2(x_2, y_2).$$

For any transducer T, we denote by T^{-1} its *inverse*, that is the transducer obtained from T by swapping the input and output label of each transition. The *composition* of two weighted transducers T_1 and T_2 with matching input and output alphabets Σ, is a weighted transducer denoted by $T_1 \circ T_2$ when the sum:

$$(T_1 \circ T_2)(x, y) = \sum_{z \in \Sigma^*} T_1(x, z) \cdot T_2(z, y) \tag{2}$$

is well-defined and in $\mathbb{K}$ for all $x, y \in \Sigma^*$ [21,14].

Weighted automata can be defined as weighted transducers A with identical input and output labels, for any transition. Thus, only pairs of the form (x, x) can have a non-zero weight by A, which is why the weight associated by A to (x, x) is abusively denoted by $A(x)$ and identified with the *weight associated by A to x*. Similarly, in the graph representation of weighted automata, the output (or input) label is omitted. Figure 1(b) shows an example of a weighted automaton.

2.2   Probabilistic Automata

In this paper, we will consider *probabilistic automata* as originally defined by Rabin [20,19].

Definition 2. *A weighted automaton A over $\mathbb{K}$ is said to be* probabilistic *if its weights are non-negative, if it admits no ϵ-transition, and if at each state, the weights of the outgoing transitions labeled with the same symbol sum to one.*

Thus, a probabilistic automaton in this sense defines a conditional probability distribution $\Pr[q' \mid q, x]$ over all states q' that can be reached from q by reading a sequence x.[1] Probabilistic automata can be used to define languages as follows.

Definition 3 ([20]). *A language L is said to be $\mathbb{K}$-stochastic if there exist a probabilistic automaton A and $\lambda \in \mathbb{K}$, $\lambda > 0$, such that $L = \{x : A(x) > \lambda\}$. λ is then called a* cut-point.

Note that stochastic languages are not necessarily regular. They include non-trivial classes of context-free and context-sensitive languages.[2] A cut-point λ is said to be *isolated* if there exists $\delta > 0$ such that $\forall x \in \Sigma^*$, $0 < \delta \leq |A(x) - \lambda|$. Rabin [20] showed that when λ is an *isolated cut-point*, then the stochastic language defined as above is regular.

3   Properties of Linearly Separated Languages

This section analyzes the properties of the languages separated by rational kernels. It presents a characterization of the set of all languages linearly separable with rational kernels and analyzes the properties of these languages for a fixed rational kernel.

3.1   Rational Kernels

A general definition of rational kernels based on weighted transducers defined over arbitrary semirings was given in [5]. Here we consider the following simpler definition for the case of transducers defined over $(\mathbb{K}, +, \cdot, 0, 1)$.

A string kernel $K : \Sigma^* \times \Sigma^* \to \mathbb{K}$ is *rational* if it coincides with the function defined by a weighted transducer U over $(\mathbb{K}, +, \cdot, 0, 1)$, that is for all $x, y \in \Sigma^*$, $K(x, y) = U(x, y)$.

Not all rational kernels are *positive definite and symmetric* (PDS), or equivalently verify the Mercer condition, a condition that guarantees the convergence of training for discriminant classification algorithms such as SVMs. But, for any weighted transducer T over $(\mathbb{K}, +, \cdot, 0, 1)$, $U = T \circ T^{-1}$ is guaranteed to define a PDS kernel [5]. Conversely, it was conjectured that PDS rational kernels coincide with the transducers U of the form $U = T \circ T^{-1}$. A number of proofs related to closure properties favor this conjecture [5]. Furthermore, most rational kernels used in computational biology and natural language processing are of this form [15,16,25,4,6,5]. To ensure the PDS property, we will consider in what follows only rational kernels of this form.

---

[1] This definition of probabilistic automata differs from another one commonly used in language modeling and other applications (see for example [7]) where A defines a probability distribution over all strings. With that definition, A is probabilistic if for any state $q \in Q$, $\sum_{\pi \in P(q,q)} w[\pi]$, the sum of the weights of all cycles at q, is well-defined and in $\mathbb{R}_+$ and $\sum_{x \in \Sigma^*} A(x) = 1$.

[2] We are using here the original terminology of *stochastic languages* used in formal language theory [21]. Some authors have recently used the same terminology to refer to completely different families of languages [9].

Our paradigm for learning languages is based on a linear separation using PDS kernels. We will say that a language $L \subseteq \Sigma^*$ is *linearly separable by a kernel K*, if there exist $b \in \mathbb{K}$ and a finite number of strings $x_1, \ldots, x_m \in \Sigma^*$ and elements of $\mathbb{K}$, $\alpha_1, \ldots, \alpha_m \in \mathbb{K}$, such that

$$L = \{x : \sum_{i=1}^{m} \alpha_i K(x_i, x) + b > 0\}. \tag{3}$$

Lemma 1. *A language $L \subseteq \Sigma^*$ is linearly separable by a rational kernel $K = T \circ T^{-1}$ iff there exists an acyclic weighted automaton A and $b \in \mathbb{K}$ such that*

$$L = \{x : A \circ (T \circ T^{-1}) \circ M_x + b > 0\}, \tag{4}$$

where M_x is a finite (unweighted) automaton representing the string x.

Proof. When K is a rational kernel, $K = T \circ T^{-1}$, the linear combination defining the separating hyperplane can be written as:

$$\sum_{i=1}^{m} \alpha_i K(x_i, x) = \sum_{i=1}^{m} \alpha_i (T \circ T^{-1})(x_i, x) = \sum_{i=1}^{m} \alpha_i (M_{x_i} \circ T \circ T^{-1} \circ M_x) \tag{5}$$

$$= (\sum_{i=1}^{m} \alpha_i M_{x_i}) \circ T \circ T^{-1} \circ M_x, \tag{6}$$

where we used the distributivity of + over composition, that is for any three weighted transducers $(U_1 \circ U_3) + (U_2 \circ U_3) = (U_1 + U_2) \circ U_3$ (a consequence of distributivity and of + over · and the definition of composition). The result follows the observation that a weighted automaton A over $(\mathbb{K}, +, \cdot, 0, 1)$ is acyclic iff it is equivalent to $\sum_{i=1}^{m} \alpha_i M_{x_i}$ for some strings $x_1, \ldots, x_m \in \Sigma^*$ and elements of $\mathbb{K}$, $\alpha_1, \ldots, \alpha_m \in \mathbb{K}$. □

3.2   Languages Linearly Separable with Rational Kernels

This section presents a characterization of the languages linearly separable with rational kernels.

Theorem 1. *A language L is linearly separable by a PDS rational kernel $K = T \circ T^{-1}$ iff it is stochastic.*

Proof. Assume that L is linearly separable by a rational kernel and let T be a weighted transducer such that $K = T \circ T^{-1}$. By lemma 1, there exist $b \in \mathbb{K}$ and an acyclic weighted automaton A such that $L = \{x : A \circ (T \circ T^{-1}) \circ M_x + b > 0\}$. Let R denote the projection of the weighted transducer $A \circ T \circ T^{-1}$ on the output, that is the weighted automaton over $(\mathbb{K}, +, \cdot, 0, 1)$ derived from $A \circ T \circ T^{-1}$ by omitting input labels. Then, $A \circ (T \circ T^{-1}) \circ M_x = R \circ M_x = R(x)$. Let S be the weighted automaton $R + b$, then, $L = \{x : S(x) > 0\}$. By Turakainen's theorem ([23,21]), a language defined in this way is stochastic, which proves one direction of the theorem's claim.

Conversely, let R be a probabilistic automaton and $\lambda \in \mathbb{K}$, $\lambda > 0$, such $L = \{x : R(x) > \lambda\}$. We can assume $L \neq \emptyset$ since any rational kernel can be trivially used to linearly separate the empty set by using an empty acyclic automaton A. It is straightforward to construct a weighted automaton R_λ assigning weight λ to all strings in Σ^*. Let S denote the weighted automaton over $(\mathbb{K}, +, \cdot, 0, 1)$ defined by $S = R - R_\lambda$. Thus, $L = \{x : S(x) > 0\}$. Let T be the weighted transducer constructed from S by augmenting all transitions of S with the same output label ϵ. By construction, for all $x, y \in \Sigma^*$, $T(x, y) = S(x)$ if $y = \epsilon$, $T(x, y) = 0$ otherwise and

$$(T \circ T^{-1})(x, y) = \sum_{z \in \Sigma^*} T(x, z) T(y, z) = T(x, \epsilon) T(y, \epsilon) = S(x) \cdot S(y). \quad (7)$$

Since $L \neq \emptyset$, we can select an arbitrary string $x_0 \in L$, thus $S(x_0) > 0$. Let A be the acyclic automaton only accepting the string x_0 and with weight 1. Then,

$$\forall x \in \Sigma^*, \ A \circ (T \circ T^{-1}) \circ M_x = A(x_0) \cdot (T \circ T^{-1})(x_0, x) = S(x_0) \cdot S(x). \quad (8)$$

Since $S(x_0) > 0$, $A \circ (T \circ T^{-1}) \circ M_x > 0$ iff $S(x) > 0$, which proves that L can be linearly separated with a PDS rational kernel.   □

The theorem highlights the importance of stochastic languages in the question of linear separation of languages with rational kernels. The proof is constructive. Given a PDS rational kernel $K = T \circ T^{-1}$, $b \in \mathbb{K}$, and an acyclic automaton A, a probabilistic automaton B can be constructed and a cut-off $\lambda \in \mathbb{K}$ determined such that:

$$L = \{x : A \circ (T \circ T^{-1}) \circ M_x + b > 0\} = \{x : B(x) > \lambda\}, \quad (9)$$

using the weighted automaton S derived from T, b, and A as in the proof of Theorem 1, and the following result due to Turakainen [23].

Theorem 2 ([23]). *Let S be a weighted automaton over $(\mathbb{K}, +, \cdot, 0, 1)$ with n states, with $\mathbb{K} = \mathbb{R}$ or $\mathbb{K} = \mathbb{Q}$. A probabilistic automaton B over $(\mathbb{K}, +, \cdot, 0, 1)$ with $n + 3$ states can be constructed from S such that:*

$$\forall x \in \Sigma^+, \ S(x) = c^{|x|} \left(B(x) - \frac{1}{n+3} \right), \quad (10)$$

where $c \in \mathbb{K}$ is a large number.

3.3   Languages Linearly Separable with a Fixed Rational Kernel

Theorem 1 provides a characterization of the set of linearly separable languages with rational kernels. This section studies the family of languages linearly separable by a given PDS rational kernel $K = T \circ T^{-1}$.

A weighted transducer T defines an (unweighted) mapping from Σ^* to 2^{Σ^*} (a *transduction*) denoted by $\hat{T}$:

$$\forall x \in \Sigma^*, \ \hat{T}(x) = \{y : T(x, y) \neq 0\}. \quad (11)$$

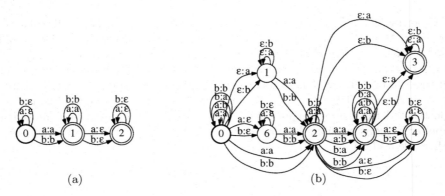

Fig. 2. (a) Weighted transducer T counting the number of occurrences of non-empty substrings of any length: for each $x \in \Sigma^*$ and any substring $y \in \Sigma^+$ of x, $T(x, y)$ gives the number of occurrences of y in x. All transition weights and final weights are equal to 1. (b) Corresponding kernel transducer $K = T \circ T^{-1}$.

For any $x \in \Sigma^*$, $\hat{T}(x)$ is a regular language that can be computed from a weighted transducer T by projecting $M_x \circ T$ on the output side, applying weighted deterministic [18], and then removing the weights.

$\hat{T}(x)$ can be viewed as the set of non-zero features y (sequences) associated to x by the kernel K, each with some weight $T(x, y)$. For example, for the kernel of Figure 2(b), $\hat{T}(x)$ associates to x the set of its substrings, that is contiguous sequences of symbols appearing in x.

For all the rational kernels we have seen in practice, the cardinality of $\hat{T}(x)$ is finite for any $x \in \Sigma^*$. $\hat{T}(x)$ may be for example the set of substrings, n-grams, or other subsequences, which in all cases are finite. Furthermore, when $\hat{T}(x)$ is not finite, then T is typically not a regulated transducer. This justifies the assumption made in the following theorem.

Theorem 3. *Let $K = T \circ T^{-1}$ be a PDS rational kernel. Assume that for each $x \in \Sigma^*$, $\hat{T}(x)$ is finite. Then, a language L linearly separable by K is necessarily of the form*

$$L = \{x : \sum_{i=1}^{n} \lambda_i T(x, z_i) + b > 0\}, \tag{12}$$

with $z_1, \ldots, z_n \in \Sigma^*$ and $\lambda_1, \ldots, \lambda_n, b \in \mathbb{K}$.

Proof. Let L be a language linearly separable by K. By Lemma 1, there exists an acyclic weighted automaton A and $b \in \mathbb{K}$ such that $L = \{x : A \circ (T \circ T^{-1}) \circ M_x + b > 0\}$, where M_x is a finite automaton representing the string x. Since $\hat{T}(x)$ is finite and A is acyclic, $\bigcup_{x:A(x)\neq 0}\{y : (A \circ T)(x, y) \neq 0\}$ is a finite set. Thus, the projection of $(A \circ T)$ on the output side is an acyclic weighted automaton and is thus equivalent to $\sum_{i=1}^{n} \lambda_i M_{z_i}$ for some $z_1, \ldots, z_n \in \Sigma^*$ and $\lambda_1, \ldots, \lambda_n, b \in \mathbb{K}$. By definition of L, $L = \{x : \sum_{i=1}^{n} \lambda_i\, M_{z_i} \circ T^{-1} \circ M_x + b\} = \{x : \sum_{i=1}^{n} \lambda_i T(x, z_i) + b > 0\}$. $\qquad \square$

Corollary 1. *Let $K = T \circ T^{-1}$ be a PDS rational kernel. Assume that for each $x \in \Sigma^*$, $\hat{T}(x)$ is finite and that $T(x,y)$ takes values in some finite set $E_T \subset \mathbb{K}$. Then, the following two properties hold:*

1. L is necessarily of the form:

$$L = \{x : \sum_{i=1}^{n} \sum_{v \in E_T} \mu_{i,v} \mathbb{1}_{\{\hat{T}_v^{-1}(z_i)\}}(x) + b > 0\}, \tag{13}$$

where $\mu_{i,v} \in \mathbb{K}$ and $\hat{T}_v(x) = \{y : T(x,y) = v\}$

2. L is a finite Boolean combination of languages $L_{z,v} = \hat{T}_v^{-1}(z)$.

Proof. Let L, λ_i, and z_i be as in Equation 12. Define the feature $\phi_{z,v} : \Sigma^* \to \{0,1\}$ by $\phi_{z,v}(x) = \mathbb{1}_{\{T(x,z)=v\}}$. Then, letting $\mu_{i,v} = v\lambda_i$, we have

$$\lambda_i T(x, z_i) = \sum_{v \in E_T} \mu_{i,v} \phi_{z_i,v(x)} = \sum_{v \in E_T} \mu_{i,v} \mathbb{1}_{\{\hat{T}_v^{-1}(z_i)\}}(x)$$

for all $x \in \Sigma^*$, which proves (13). Now define $f : \Sigma^* \to \mathbb{K}$ by

$$f(x) = b + \sum_{i=1}^{n} \sum_{v \in E_T} \mu_{i,v} \phi_{z_i,v(x)}$$

and observe that f must have a finite range $\{r_k \in \mathbb{K} : k = 1, \dots, F\}$. Let $L_r \subseteq \Sigma^*$ be defined by

$$L_r = f^{-1}(r). \tag{14}$$

A subset $I \subseteq \{1, 2, \dots, n\} \times E_T$ is said to be *r-acceptable* if $b + \sum_{(i,v) \in I} \mu_{i,v} = r$. Any such r-acceptable set corresponds to a set of strings $L_I \subseteq \Sigma^*$ such that

$$L_I = \left(\bigcap_{(i,v) \in I} \hat{T}_v^{-1}(z_i) \right) \setminus \left(\bigcup_{(i,v) \in \bar{I}} \hat{T}_v^{-1}(z_i) \right). \tag{15}$$

Each L_r is the union of finitely many r-acceptable L_I's, and L is the union of L_r for positive r. □

We will refer to kernels with finite range transducer values as *finite range kernels*. The Corollary provides some insight into the family of languages that is linearly separable with a fixed PDS finite range rational kernel $K = T \circ T^{-1}$. In practice, it is often straightforward to determine $\hat{T}_v^{-1}(x)$ for any $x \in \Sigma^*$. For example, for the subsequence kernel, $\hat{T}_1^{-1}(x) = \hat{T}^{-1}(x)$ represents the set of all sequences admitting x as a subsequence. Corollary 1 shows that any language linearly separated by K is a finite Boolean combination of these sets. This result and that of Theorem 3 apply to virtually all cases in computational biology or natural language processing where string kernels are used in combination with SVMs, since most string kernels used in practice (if not all) are rational kernels.

It was proven in [13] that in the case of the subsequence kernel, the second property of the Corollary 1 gives in fact a characterization of linearly separable languages (as the piecewise-testable ones). In general, however, the converse may not hold. There exist indeed finite boolean combinations of $\hat{T}^{-1}(x)$ that are not linearly separable when K is selected to be the n-gram kernel for example.

Corollary 1 points out an interesting property of PDS rational kernels with values in a finite set. In the following section, we will see that linear separability with such kernels also ensures useful margin properties.

4   Learning and Margin Guarantees

This section deals with the problem of learning families of languages using PDS rational kernels.

Linear separability with some rational kernels K guarantees a positive margin. In particular, as previously shown, the subsequence kernel guarantees a positive margin [13]. When this property holds, a linear separation learning technique such as support vector machines (SVMs) [3,8,24] combined with a rational kernel K can be used to learn a family of languages. Since rational kernels can be computed in quadratic time [5], the complexity of the algorithm for a sample of size m, where $x_{\max}$ is the longest string, is in $O(\mathrm{QP}(m)) + m^2 |x_{\max}|^2 |\Sigma|)$, where $\mathrm{QP}(m)$ is the cost of solving a quadratic programming problem of size m, which is at most $O(m^3)$.

We will use the standard margin bound to analyze the behavior of that algorithm when that margin property holds. Note, however, that since the VC-dimension of the typical family of languages one wishes to learn (e.g., piecewise-testable languages) is infinite, PAC-learning is not possible and we need to resort to a weaker guarantee.

Not all PDS rational kernels guarantee a positive margin (as we shall see later), but we will prove that all PDS finite range rational kernels admit this property, which further emphasizes their benefits for learning.

4.1   Margin

Let $\mathcal{S}$ be a sample extracted from a set X ($X = \Sigma^*$ when learning languages) and let the margin ρ of a hyperplane with weight vector $w \in \mathbb{K}^{\mathbb{N}}$ and offset $b \in \mathbb{K}$ over this sample be defined by:

$$\rho = \inf_{x \in \mathcal{S}} \frac{|\langle w, \Phi(x) \rangle + b|}{\|w\|}.$$

This definition also holds for infinite-size samples. For finite samples, linear separation with a hyperplane $\langle w, x \rangle + b = 0$ is equivalent to a positive margin $\rho > 0$. But, this may not hold for infinite-size samples, since points in an infinite-dimensional space may be arbitrarily close to the separating hyperplane and their infimum distance could be zero. There are in fact PDS rational kernels for which this can occur.

4.2   Example of Linear Separation with Zero Margin

Let $K = T \circ T^{-1}$ be the PDS rational defined by the weighted transducer T counting the number of occurrences of a and b when the alphabet $\Sigma = \{a, b\}$. Figure 4(c) shows the corresponding weighted transducer. $\hat{T}(x)$ is finite for all $x \in \Sigma^*$, the feature space F associated to K has dimension 2, and the points mapped by the corresponding feature mapping are those with non-negative integer coordinates. Let the sample include all non-empty sequences, $\mathcal{S} = \Sigma^+$, and let H, the hypothesis to be learned, be the hyperplane going through the point $(0, 0)$ with a positive irrational slope α. By definition, H does not cross any point with positive integer coordinates (p, q), since $\frac{p}{q} \in \mathbb{Q}$, thus it is indeed a separating hyperplane for $\mathcal{S}$. But, since $\mathbb{Q}$ is dense in $\mathbb{R}$, for any $\epsilon > 0$, there exists a rational number $\frac{p}{q}$ such that $|\frac{p}{q} - \alpha| < \epsilon$. This shows that there are points with positive integer coordinates arbitrarily close to H and thus that the margin associated to H is zero. The language separated by H is the non-regular language of non-empty sequences with α times more bs than as:[3] $L = \{x \in \Sigma^+ : |x|_b > \alpha |x|_a\}$.

The relationship between the existence of a positive margin for a PDS rational kernel and an isolated cut-off point is not straightforward. By Theorem 2, if for all $x \in \Sigma^+$, $S(x) > \rho > 0$, then there exists a probabilistic automaton B with N states such that $\forall x \in \Sigma^+$, $|B(x) - \frac{1}{N}| > \frac{\rho}{c^{|x|}}$. But, since $|x|$ can be arbitrarily large, this does not guarantee an isolated cut-point.

4.3   Positive Margin

When the values $T(x, y)$ taken by the transducer T for all pairs of sequences (x, y) are in a finite set $E_T \subset \mathbb{K}$, then linear separation with a PDS rational kernel defined by $K = T \circ T^{-1}$ guarantees a positive margin. The feature mapping Φ associated to K then also takes its values in the finite set.

Proposition 1. *Let $\Phi : X \to E_T^{\mathbb{N}}$ be mapping from a set X to a finite set $E_T \subset \mathbb{R}$ and let C be a class of concepts defined over X that is linearly separable using the mapping Φ and a weight vector $w \in \mathbb{R}^{\mathbb{N}}$.[4] Then, the margin ρ of the hyperplane defined by w is strictly positive $(\rho > 0)$.*

Proof. By assumption, the support of w is finite. For any $x \in X$, let $\Phi'(x)$ be the projection of $\Phi(x)$ on the vector space defined by the support of w, denoted by $\text{supp}(w)$. Thus, $\Phi'(x)$ is a finite-dimensional vector for any $x \in X$ with discrete coordinates in E_T. Thus, the set of $\mathcal{S} = \{\Phi'(x) : x \in X\}$ is finite. Since for any $x \in X$, $\langle w, \Phi(x) \rangle = \langle w, \Phi'(x) \rangle$, the margin can be defined over a finite set:

$$\rho = \inf_{x \in X} \frac{|\langle w, \Phi'(x) + b \rangle|}{\|w\|} = \min_{z \in \mathcal{S}} \frac{|\langle w, z \rangle + b|}{\|w\|}, \qquad (16)$$

which implies $\rho > 0$ since $|\langle w, z \rangle + b| > 0$ for all $z \in \mathcal{S}$. $\square$

---

[3] When α is a rational number, it can be shown that the margin is positive, the language L being still non-regular.

[4] As in the general case of kernels (Equation 3), our definition of linear separability assumes a weight vector with finite support.

Many of the PDS rational kernels used in practice follow these conditions. In particular, for kernels such as the subsequence kernels, the transducer T takes only values 0 or 1. When the existence of a positive margin is guaranteed as in the case of finite range rational kernels, the following theorem applies.

Theorem 4. *Let C be a finitely linearly separable concept class over X with a feature mapping $\Phi : X \to E_T^{\mathbb{N}}$. Define the class $\mathcal{F}$ of real-valued functions on the ball of radius R in $\mathbb{R}^n$ as*

$$\mathcal{F} = \{x \mapsto \langle w, \Phi(x)\rangle : \|w\| \leq 1, \|\Phi(x)\| \leq R\}. \tag{17}$$

There is a constant α_0 such that, for all distributions D over X, for any concept $c \in C$, there exists $\rho_0 > 0$ such that with probability at least $1 - \delta$ over m independently generated examples according to D, there exists a classifier $\mathrm{sgn}(f)$, with $f \in \mathcal{F}$, with margin at least ρ_0 on the training examples, and generalization error no more than

$$\frac{\alpha_0}{m}\left(\frac{R^2}{\rho_0^2}\log^2 m + \log(\frac{1}{\delta})\right). \tag{18}$$

Proof. Fix a concept $c \in C$. By assumption, c is finitely linearly separable by some hyperplane. By Proposition 1, the corresponding margin ρ_0 is strictly positive, $\rho_0 > 0$. ρ_0 is less than or equal to the margin of the optimal hyperplane ρ separating c from $X \setminus c$ based on the m examples.

Since the full sample X is linearly separable, so is any subsample of size m. Let $f \in \mathcal{F}$ be the linear function corresponding to the optimal hyperplane over a sample of size m drawn according to D. Then, the margin of f is at least as large as ρ since not all points of X are used to define f. Thus, the margin of f is greater than or equal to ρ_0 and the statement follows a standard margin bound of Bartlett and Shawe-Taylor [1]. □

Observe that in the statement of the theorem, ρ_0 depends on the particular concept c learned but does not depend on the sample size m.

5 Algorithm for Finite Range Rational Kernels

The previous section showed that PDS rational kernels with finite feature values ensure a positive margin and thus learning with the margin-based guarantees previously described.[5] However, while it is natural and often straightforward to come up with a transducer mapping input sequences to the features sequences, that transducer often cannot be readily used for the definition of the kernel. This is because it may contain multiple paths with the same output feature sequence and the same input sequence. This typically generates unbounded path multiplicity, and so the finiteness of the range does not hold.

For example, it is easy to come up with a transducer mapping each string to the set of its subsequences. Figure 4(a) shows a simple one-state transducer

---

[5] This section concentrates on kernels with just binary feature values but much of our analysis generalizes to the more general case of finite feature value.

doing that. But, when applied to the sequence $x = aba$, that transducer generates two paths with input x and output a because a appears twice in x. Instead, we need to construct a transducer that contains exactly one path with input x and output a. Figure 4(b) shows a subsequence transducer with that property.

The construction of such a transducer is not trivial even for this simple case. One may then ask if there exists a general procedure for constructing a transducer with multiplicity one from a given transducer. This section describes a novel and general algorithm that serves precisely that purpose.

The algorithm takes as input an (unweighted) transducer T and outputs a transducer T' that is unambiguous in the following way: for any pair of input and output sequence (x, y) labeling a successful path of T, T' contains exactly one successful path with that label. We will refer to our algorithm as the *double-tape disambiguation*. Note that our algorithm is distinct from the standard *disambiguation algorithm* for transducers [2] which applies only to transducers that represent a partial function mapping input sequences to output sequences and which generates a transducer with unambiguous input.

To present the algorithm, we need to introduce some standard concepts of word combinatorics [17]. To any $x \in \Sigma^*$, we associate a new element x' denoted by x^{-1} and extend string concatenation so that $xx^{-1} = x^{-1}x = \epsilon$. We denote by $(\Sigma^*)^{-1}$ the set of all these new elements. The *free group generated by Σ* denoted by $\Sigma^{(*)}$ is the set of all elements that can be written as a concatenation of elements of Σ^* and Σ^{*-1}. We say that an $x \in \Sigma^{(*)}$ of the free group is *pure* if $x \in \Sigma^* \cup \Sigma^{*-1}$ and we denote that set by $\Pi = \Sigma^* \cup \Sigma^{*-1}$.

The algorithm constructs a transducer T' whose states are pairs (p, m) where $p \in Q$ is a state of the original transducer and a m is a multiset of triplets (q, x, y) with $q \in Q$ and $x, y \in \Sigma^* \cup (\Sigma^*)^{-1}$. Each triplet (q, x, y) indicates that state q can be reached from the initial state by reading either the same input string or the same output string as what was used to reach p. x and y serve to keep track of the extra or missing suffix of the labels of the path leading to q versus the current one used to reach p.

Let (u, v) denote the input and output label of the path followed to reach p, and (u', v') the labels of the path reaching q. Then, x and y are defined by: $x = (u)^{-1}u'$ and $y = (v)^{-1}v'$. We define a partial transition function δ for triplets. For any (q, x, y) and $(a, b) \in (\Sigma \cup \{\epsilon\})^2 - \{(\epsilon, \epsilon)\}$, $\delta((q, x, y), a, b)$ is a multiset containing $(q', xa^{-1}a', yb^{-1}b')$, if $(q, a', b', q') \in E$, $xa^{-1}a \in \Pi$, and $yb^{-1}b' \in \Pi$, $\delta((q, x, y), a, b) = \emptyset$ otherwise. We further extend δ to multisets by defining $\delta(m, a, b)$ as the multiset of all $\delta((q, x, y), a, b)$ with (q, x, y) in m.

The set of initial states I' of T' are the states $(i, (i, \epsilon, \epsilon))$ with $i \in I$. Starting from an initial state, the algorithm creates new transitions of T' as follows. When $(p, a, b, p') \in E$ and when it does not generate ambiguities (as we shall see later), it creates a transition from state (p, m) to $(p', \delta(m))$ with input a and output b.

At the price of splitting final states, without loss of generality, we can assume that the transducer T does not admit two paths with the same label leading to the same final state. When there are k paths in T with the same input and output labels and leading to distinct final states $p_1, \ldots, p_k$, the algorithm must

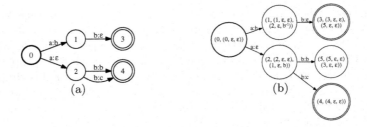

Fig. 3. Illustration of the application of the double-tape disambiguation algorithm. (a) Transducer T. (b) Equivalent double-tape unambiguous transducer T' obtained by application of the algorithm. The destination state of the transition labeled with $b:b$ is made non-final by the algorithm, which makes the result unambiguous. That state is non-coaccessible and can be later removed by a standard trimming algorithm.

disallow all but one in T'. Observe that these paths correspond to paths in T' ending at the states (p_i, m), $i \in [1, k]$, with the same multiset m, which therefore contains (ϵ, ϵ) with multiplicity k. To guarantee the result to be unambiguous, the algorithm allows only one of the states (p_i, m), $i \in [1, k]$ to be final. This preserves the mapping defined by T since it does not affect other paths leaving (p_i, m), $i \in [1, k]$. The choice of the particular state to keep final is arbitrary and does not affect the result. Different choices lead to transducers with different topologies that are all equivalent.

The algorithm described thus far, DOUBLE-TAPE-DISAMBIGUATION, can be applied to acyclic transducers since it creates at most a finite number of states in that case and since it disallows ambiguities. Figure 3 illustrates the application of the algorithm in a simple case. In the general case, the creation of infinitely many states is avoided, after disambiguation, by using a more complex condition. Due to lack of space, this case will be presented in a longer version of this paper.

Theorem 5. *Let T be an arbitrary acyclic transducer. Then, running the algorithm* DOUBLE-TAPE-DISAMBIGUATION *with input T produces an equivalent transducer T' that is double-tape unambiguous.*

Proof. We give a sketch of the proof. By definition of the condition on the finality of the states created, the output transducer T' is double-tape unambiguous. The equivalence and termination of the algorithm are clear since the destination state of e' is (p', m') and that the number of possible multisets m' is finite.   □

The input transducer T can be determinized as an acceptor defined over pairs of input-output symbols. When it is deterministic, then the transducer T' output by the algorithm is also necessarily deterministic, by construction. The application of the standard automata minimization can then help reduce the size of T'.

Figures 4(a)-(b) and Figures 4(c)-(d) show examples of applications of our algorithm to some kernels of interest after minimization. Figure 4(b) shows the subsequence transducer resulting from the application of our algorithm to the transducer of Figure 4(a) which counts subsequences with their multiplicity. Figure 4(b)

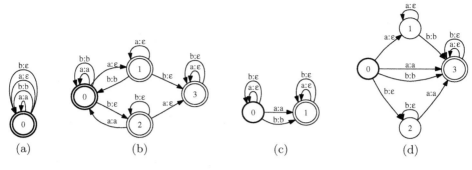

Fig. 4. Applications of the double-tape disambiguation algorithm. (a) Transducer T_0 associating to each input string $x \in \Sigma^*$ the set of its subsequences (with multiplicity) for $\Sigma = \{a, b\}$. (b) Subsequence transducer T associating to each string $x \in \Sigma^*$ the set of its subsequences with multiplicity one regardless of the number of occurrences of the subsequences in x. Unigram transducers for $\Sigma = \{a, b\}$. (c) Transducer T_0 associating to each input string $x \in \Sigma^*$ the set of its unigrams a and b (with multiplicity). (d) Unigram transducer T associating to each string its unigrams with multiplicity one.

shows the subsequence transducer obtained by applying our algorithm to the transducer of Figure 4(a) which counts unigrams with their multiplicity. In both cases, the resulting transducers are not straightforward to define even for such relatively simple examples. The double-tape disambiguation algorithm can be used as a tool to define finite range rational kernels based on such transducers.

6 Conclusion

We presented a general study of learning and linear separability with rational kernels, the sequence kernels commonly used in computational biology and natural language processing. We gave a characterization of the family of languages linearly separable with rational kernels demonstrating the central role of stochastic languages in this setting. We also pointed out several important properties of languages separable with a fixed rational kernel in terms of finite Boolean combination of languages.

Rational kernels with values in a finite set stand out as a particularly interesting family of kernels since they verify this property and guarantee a positive margin. The double-tape disambiguation algorithm we presented can be used to create efficiently such kernels from a transducer defining the mapping to feature sequences. The algorithm is of independent interest for a variety of applications in text and speech processing where such a disambiguation is beneficial.

References

1. Bartlett, P., Shawe-Taylor, J.: Generalization performance of support vector machines and other pattern classifiers. In: Advances in kernel methods: support vector learning, pp. 43–54. MIT Press, Cambridge, MA, USA (1999)

2. Berstel, J.: Transductions and Context-Free Languages. Teubner Studienbucher: Stuttgart (1979)
3. Boser, B.E., Guyon, I., Vapnik, V.N.: A training algorithm for optimal margin classifiers. In: Proceedings of COLT '92, vol. 5, ACM Press, New York (1992)
4. Collins, M., Duffy, N.: Convolution kernels for natural language. In: NIPS 14, MIT Press, Cambridge, MA (2002)
5. Cortes, C., Haffner, P., Mohri, M.: Rational Kernels: Theory and Algorithms. Journal of Machine Learning Research 5, 1035–1062 (2004)
6. Cortes, C., Mohri, M.: Moment Kernels for Regular Distributions. Machine Learning 60(1-3), 117–134 (2005)
7. Cortes, C., Mohri, M., Rastogi, A., Riley, M.: Efficient Computation of the Relative Entropy of Probabilistic Automata. In: LATIN 2006, vol. 3887, Springer, Heidelberg (2006)
8. Cortes, C., Vapnik, V.N.: Support-Vector Networks. Machine Learning 20(3), 273–297 (1995)
9. Denis, F., Esposito, Y.: Rational stochastic languages. In: Lugosi, G., Simon, H.U. (eds.) COLT 2006. LNCS (LNAI), vol. 4005, Springer, Heidelberg (2006)
10. Eilenberg, S.: Automata, Languages and Machines, vol. A–B. Academic Press, 1974–1976
11. Haussler, D.: Convolution Kernels on Discrete Structures. Technical Report UCSC-CRL-99-10, University of California at Santa Cruz (1999)
12. Kontorovich, L., Cortes, C., Mohri, M.: Kernel Methods for Learning Languages. Theoretical Computer Science (submitted) (2006)
13. Kontorovich, L., Cortes, C., Mohri, M.: Learning Linearly Separable Languages. In: Balcázar, J.L., Long, P.M., Stephan, F. (eds.) ALT 2006. LNCS (LNAI), vol. 4264, Springer, Heidelberg (2006)
14. Kuich, W., Salomaa, A.: Semirings, Automata, Languages. In: EATCS Monographs on Theoretical Computer Science, vol. 5, Springer, Heidelberg (1986)
15. Leslie, C., Eskin, E., Weston, J., Noble, W.S.: Mismatch String Kernels for SVM Protein Classification. In: NIPS 2002, MIT Press, Cambridge (2003)
16. Lodhi, H., Shawe-Taylor, J., Cristianini, N., Watkins, C.: Text classification using string kernels. In: NIPS 2000, pp. 563–569. MIT Press, Cambridge (2001)
17. Lothaire, M.: Combinatorics on Words. In: Encyclopedia of Mathematics and Its Applications. Encyclopedia of Mathematics and Its Applications, vol. 17, Addison-Wesley, London (1983)
18. Mohri, M.: Finite-State Transducers in Language and Speech Processing. Computational Linguistics 23, 2 (1997)
19. Paz, A.: Introduction to probabilistic automata. Academic Press, New York (1971)
20. Rabin, M.O.: Probabilistic automata. Information and Control, 6 (1963)
21. Salomaa, A., Soittola, M. (eds.): Automata-Theoretic Aspects of Formal Power Series. Springer, Heidelberg (1978)
22. Imre Simon. Piecewise testable events. In: Aut. Theory and Formal Lang (1975)
23. Turakainen, P.: Generalized Automata and Stochastic Languages. In: Proceedings of the American Mathematical Society, 21(2), 303–309 (1969)
24. Vapnik, V.N.: Statistical Learning Theory. John Wiley & Sons, New York (1998)
25. Zien, A., Rätsch, G., Mika, S., Schölkopf, B., Lengauer, T., Müller, K.-R.: Engineering support vector machine kernels that recognize translation initiation sites. Bioinformatics 16(9), 799–807 (2000)

Generalized SMO-Style Decomposition Algorithms

Nikolas List

Lehrstuhl Mathematik und Informatik, Ruhr-University Bochum, Germany
nlist@lmi.rub.de

Abstract. Sequential Minimal Optimization (SMO) [14] is a major tool for solving convex quadratic optimization problems induced by Support Vector Machines (SVMs). It is based on the idea to iterativley solve subproblems of size two. In this work we will give a characterization of convex quadratic optimization problems, which can be solved with the SMO technique as well. In addition we will present an efficient $1/m$-rate-certifying pair selection algorithm [8,13] leading to polynomial-time convergence rates for such problems.

1 Introduction

Throughout the paper, we will consider the following convex optimization problem with compact feasibility region:

$$\inf_x f(x) \quad \text{s.t. } Ax = b, \ l \le x \le r, \tag{1}$$

where f is a convex function, $\nabla f(x) \in \mathbb{R}^m$ is available to us, and $A \in \mathbb{R}^{k \times m}$ is a linear mapping. A special instance of (1) will be denoted by $\mathcal{P}(f, A, b, l, r)$ or simply $\mathcal{P}$ if the parameters are clear from the context. As the results we build on are mostly given for quadratic convex functions, we will always have the special case $f(x) = \frac{1}{2}x^\top Q x - w^\top x$ in mind, where $Q \in \mathbb{R}^{m \times m}$ is positive semi-definite and $w \in \mathbb{R}^m$, but most proofs will be given for the general case. With

$$\mathcal{R}\big(\mathcal{P}(f, A, b, l, r)\big) := \{x \mid Ax = b, \ l \le x \le r\}$$

we will denote the feasibility region of (1) and call any $x \in \mathcal{R}(\mathcal{P})$ feasible.

Given a feasible solution $z \in \mathcal{R}(\mathcal{P})$ and a working set $I \subseteq \{1, \ldots, m\}$ we will use the notation $\mathcal{P}_{I,z}$ for the following induced (sub-)problem of (1):

$$\inf_x f(x) \quad \text{s.t. } Ax = b, \ l \le x \le r, \ x_i = z_i, i \notin I.$$

Note, that this problem is again of the same form as (1). The decomposition algorithm then proceeds iteratively by choosing a working set I, such that the currently given point $x^{(n)}$ is not optimal in $\mathcal{P}_{I,x^{(n)}}$ and chooses the next solution

$$x^{(n+1)} \leftarrow \text{opt } \mathcal{P}_{I,x^{(n)}}$$

N. Bshouty and C. Gentile (Eds.): COLT 2007, LNAI 4539, pp. 365–377, 2007.

to be the optimum of the subproblem induced by I and $x^{(n)}$. The algorithm terminates if $x^{(n)}$ is optimal (or at least close enough). The crucial point is the selection of the working set I, such that the induced problem is simple to solve, the solution of the subproblem leads to a fast convergence to the global optimum and the set I is efficiently computable.

To motivate the task we will pursue, consider the optimization problem induced by C-SVM, which is a special case of (1):

$$\inf_x f(x) \quad \text{s.t.} \ y^\top x = 0, \ 0 \le x_i \le C, \ i = 1, \ldots, m \ , \tag{2}$$

where $y \in \{\pm 1\}^m$ and $C \in \mathbb{R}^+$. For this special setting an extreme variant of the working-set selection sketched above has been proposed by [14], where sets of size two are chosen.

Although larger working sets promise more progress in a single iteration there are some reasons to use this technique: First of all, its simplicity makes it easy to handle in practice and it is in fact implemented in many software packages for SVM-optimization [2,6]. Second, empirical results show, that the working-set size of two tends to have the overall smallest runtime for SVM-optimization problems [5]. In addition the extension of the selection heuristics based on second-order information [7,4] is easier for small working-sets. It is therefore an interesting question under which conditions such a pairwise selection strategy is possible.

This strategy is well analyzed in the special case of C-SVM [9,1,10,8], but these analysis depend on the special structure of the equality constraint $y^\top x = 0$. However there exist important learning problems with more than one equality constraints. This includes popular SVM algorithms like the ν-SVM, which solves a QP of the following form [16,3]:

$$\inf_x f(x) \quad \text{s.t.} \ y^\top x = 0, \ e^\top x = \nu, \ 0 \le x_i \le \frac{1}{m}, \ i = 1, \ldots, m. \tag{3}$$

Another example is multiclass learning in a maximal margin regression framework [18], which leads to equality constraints in the number of the dimension of the output space.

In the last years there have been efforts to extend the selection strategies in the framework of decomposition method to general quadratic problems (1) with k equality constraints [12,11,13] but they either don't give convergence rates or give only selection strategies for working sets of size at least $k + 1$. In this paper we will characterize when SMO-style selection of pairs is applicable. In addition, building on the results in [8,13], we will propose a selection algorithm for a working set $I = \{i, j\}$ of size two which is efficient and leads to a polynomial-time convergence rate.

1.1   Notational Conventions

Before we start let us introduce some notational conventions: First of all we will use the short notation $[\nu]^+$ for any $\nu \in \mathbb{R}$ to denote the maximum of 0 and ν:

$$[\nu]^+ := \max \{0, \nu\} \, .$$

Given a subset $I \subseteq \{1, \ldots, m\}$ of size $q = |I|$ and a vector $d \in \mathbb{R}^m$ we write $d_I \in \mathbb{R}^q$ to denote the vector consisting only of entries d_i for $i \in I$.

For any matrix $A \in \mathbb{R}^{k \times m}$, $A_i \in \mathbb{R}^k$ denotes the i-th column of A and, more generally, $A_I \in \mathbb{R}^{k \times q}$ denotes the matrix, whose column vectors are the A_i with $i \in I$.

2   Basic Theory

Let us start by giving a clear definition of the special class of problems, which can be decomposed using working sets of size 2.

Definition 1. *Given a problem instance* $\mathcal{P}(f, A, b, l, r)$ *of* (1). *$\mathcal{P}$ is called decomposable by pairing iff for any suboptimal feasible* $x \in \mathcal{R}(\mathcal{P})$ *there exists a working set* $I \subseteq \{1, \ldots, m\}$ *of size two, such that x is as well suboptimal for the induced subproblem* $\mathcal{P}_{I,x}$.

As guideline for the selection process and a technical tool in the proofs, we will use the technique of q-sparse witnesses introduced in [12]:

Definition 2. *Let* $(C_I(x))$, $I \subseteq \{1, \ldots, m\}$ *be a family of functions and consider the three following properties:*

(C1) *For each* $I \subseteq \{1, \ldots, m\}$ *such that* $|I| \leq q$, $C_I(x)$ *is continuous on* $R(\mathcal{P})$.
(C2) *If* $|I| \leq q$ *and x is an optimal solution for the subproblem* $\mathcal{P}_{I,x}$ *then* $C_I(x) = 0$.
(C3) *If x is not an optimal solution for* $\mathcal{P}$, *then there exists an* $I \subseteq \{1, \ldots, m\}$ *such that* $|I| \leq q$ *and* $C_I(x) > 0$.

Any family of functions satisfying conditions (C2) *and* (C3) *will be called a q-sparse witness of sub-optimality. If* $(C_I(x))$ *fulfills* (C1) *in addition we call it a continuous q-sparse witness of sub-optimality.*[1]

As shown in [12], continuous q-sparse witnesses give rise to a general selection strategy, for which the authors could prove asymptotic convergence. Lately the authors could prove, that approximate working-set selection based on continuous q-sparse witnesses is in fact equivalent to the selection of rate certifying sets [13], leading to polynomial convergence rates.

Using the properties (C2) and (C3) one can directly derive the following characterization of problems decomposable by pairing:

Lemma 1. *Given a problem instance* $\mathcal{P}(f, A, b, l, r)$ *of* (1). *$\mathcal{P}$ is decomposable by pairing iff there exists a 2-sparse witness of suboptimality.*

---

[1] Note, that this definition differs slightly from the use in [12], where the continuity property (C1) is crucial for the proof of asymptotic convergence. The authors therefore only considered as sparse-witness what we call continuous sparse-witness of suboptimality.

Proof. The existence of a 2-sparse witness $C_I(x)$ implies, that given a suboptimal $x \in \mathcal{R}(\mathcal{P})$, we can always find a $I = \{i, j\}$ such that $C_I(x) > 0$ and therefore using (C2) x is not optimal for $P_{I,x}$.

To prove the other direction, simply consider the following family of functions:

$$C_I(x) := f(x) - \operatorname{opt} P_{I,x}.$$

Obviously $C_I(x)$ fulfills condition (C2). As $\mathcal{P}$ is assumed to be pairable we conclude, that (C3) holds as well, and therefore $C_I(x)$ is a 2-sparse witness of suboptimality. □

Remark 1. If there even exists a continuous 2-sparse witness of suboptimality we will call $\mathcal{P}$ *continuously decomposable by pairing*.

The main aim of the paper will now be to show under which conditions such a 2-sparse witness of suboptimality exists. We will therefore be concerned with a special witness, the $\sigma(x|I)$ function:

$$\sigma(x|I) := \sup_{d \in \mathbb{R}^m} \left\{ \nabla f(x)_I^\top d_I \mid A_I d_I = 0, l \leq x + d \leq r \right\}$$

$$= \inf_{\lambda \in \mathbb{R}^k} \sum_{i \in I} \left\{ (x_i - l_i) \left[\nabla f(x)_i - A_i^\top \lambda \right]^+ + (r_i - x_i) \left[A_i^\top \lambda - \nabla f(x)_i \right]^+ \right\} \quad (4)$$

Note, that the two representations of this function have been independently motivated. The sup-representation can be used to guide the selection of $1/m$-rate certifying sets of size $k+1$ in each iteration leading to an ε-optimal solution in $O(\frac{m^2(k+1)}{\varepsilon})$ iterations [13]. The inf-term has been used to prove, that this function is a continuous $k+1$-sparse witness of suboptimality [12]. The equality of the two simply follows from LP-duality as shown in [13]. In the following we will use both representations given in (4) interchangeably.

It is crucial to note, that the special function $\sigma : \mathcal{R}(\mathcal{P}) \to \mathbb{R}^+$, defined by

$$\sigma(x) := \sigma(x|\{1, \ldots, m\}) = \sup_{x' \in \mathbb{R}^m} \left\{ \nabla f(x)^\top (x - x') \mid Ax' = b, l \leq x' \leq r \right\},$$

is an upper bound on the distance to optimum:[2]

$$f(x) - f(x^*) \leq \nabla f(x)^\top (x - x^*) \leq \sigma(x).$$

Using the first order optimality condition of convex optimization we can conclude, that x is optimal for $\mathcal{P}$ iff $\sigma(x) = 0$. For an arbitrary $x \in \mathcal{R}(\mathcal{P})$ we call any $I \subseteq \{1, \ldots, m\}$, such that $|I| \leq q$ and

$$\sigma(x|I) \geq f(x) - f(x^*)$$

an (α, q)-*rate certifying set* for $x \in \mathcal{R}(\mathcal{P})$.[3] If the stronger inequality

$$\sigma(x|I) \geq \alpha\sigma(x)$$

holds, we will call I a *strong* (α, q)-rate certifying set (see [13]).

---

[2] This has been the usual way to introduce $\sigma(x)$.

[3] Note, that the set I depends on x.

The σ-function given in (4) will play a two-fold role: First we will extend the results given in [12] and show, that under special conditions (see Theorem 2) $\sigma(x|I)$ is even a 2-sparse witness of suboptimality. In addition we will show, that under the same conditions a $1/m$-rate certifying pair can be derived from (4) and we will give an efficient algorithm which computes this pair in linear time.

The second use of this function is based on the observation that the $\sigma(\cdot|I)$ function restricted to the feasibility region of $\mathcal{P}_{I,x}$

$$\sigma(\cdot|I) : \mathcal{R}(\mathcal{P}_{I,x}) \to \mathbb{R}^+ .$$

plays exactly the same role for $\mathcal{P}_{I,x}$ as $\sigma(x)$ for $\mathcal{P}$. That means for any $z \in \mathcal{R}(\mathcal{P}_{I,x})$: z is an optimal solution of $\mathcal{P}_{I,x}$ iff $\sigma(z|I) = 0$. We will use this, to show, that if ever we find a feasible but suboptimal point x, such that for all possible pairwise selections $I = \{i, j\}$ we have $\sigma(x|i, j) = 0$, we cannot hope to advance any further with two-dimensional subproblems and the problem at hand can't be decomposable by pairing.

A main tool in the given analysis, introduced in [11], will be the following: Given a problem instance $\mathcal{P}(f, A, b, l, r)$ the linear equality constraint matrix induces the following equivalence relation on $\{1, \dots, m\}$:

$$i \sim j \Leftrightarrow \exists c_{i,j} \neq 0 : A_i = c_{i,j} A_j.$$

We will denote the equivalence classes for a given i by $[i] := \{j \mid j \sim i\}$. Given a set of representatives $\{i_r \mid r = 1, \dots, s\}$ we choose the subset[4]

$$\{a_r := A_{i_r} \mid r = 1, \dots, s\} \subseteq \{A_i \mid i = 1, \dots, m\}$$

whose elements represent the columns of A up to scalar multiplication. For each equivalence class we define $c_i := c_{i,i_r}$, such that for any $i \in [i_r]$ $c_i A_i = a_r$. In addition we will use the distance to the borders defined as follows

$$\mu_i^+(x) = \begin{cases} x_i - l_i & \text{if } c_i > 0 \\ x_i - r_i & \text{otherwise} \end{cases} \quad \text{and} \quad \mu_i^-(x) = \begin{cases} r_i - x_i & \text{if } c_i > 0 \\ l_i - x_i & \text{otherwise} \end{cases} .$$

Note that with these definitions we have $\frac{\mu_i^+(x)}{c_i}, \frac{\mu_i^-(x)}{c_i} \geq 0$ for all $i = 1, \dots, m$.

3   The Main Results

From the construction of the equivalence classes $[i_r], r = 1, \dots, s$ we easily see, that rank $A \leq s$. In the following we will show, that problems $\mathcal{P}(f, A, b, l, r)$ are decomposable by pairing if they have an equality constraint matrix of maximal rank, i.e. rank $A = s$.

We start by giving the following simplifications of the σ-function:

---

[4] Note, that $a_r = A_{i_r} \in \mathbb{R}^k$ is as well a column of the equality constraint matrix A. We will however use the notation a_r with small a if ever we want to emphasize, that we refer to a_r as a representative of the columns for the equivalence class $[i_r]$.

Lemma 2. *Given a set of representatives $\{i_r \mid r = 1, \dots, s\}$, then for any feasible $x \in \mathcal{R}(\mathcal{P})$ the following properties hold:*

1. *If $I \subseteq [i_r]$ for an $r \in \{1, \dots, s\}$, then*

$$\sigma(x|I) = \inf_{\nu \in \mathbb{R}} \sum_{i \in I} \left\{ \frac{\mu_i^+(x)}{c_i} [c_i \nabla f(x)_i - \nu]^+ + \frac{\mu_i^-(x)}{c_i} [\nu - c_i \nabla f(x)_i]^+ \right\}$$

2. *If $\operatorname{rank} A = s$, then for all $I \subseteq \{1, \dots, m\}$*

$$\sigma(x|I) = \sum_{r=1}^{s} \sigma(x|I \cap [i_r]).$$

Proof. To prove the first claim let us rewrite $\sigma(x|I)$ by replacing each A_i by $\frac{1}{c_i} a_r$:[5]

$$\inf_{\lambda \in \mathbb{R}^k} \sum_{i \in I} \left\{ (x_i - l_i) \left[\nabla f(x)_i - A_i^\top \lambda \right]^+ + (r_i - x_i) \left[A_i^\top \lambda - \nabla f(x)_i \right]^+ \right\}$$

$$= \inf_{\lambda \in \mathbb{R}^k} \sum_{i \in I} \left\{ \frac{\mu_i^+(x)}{c_i} \left[c_i \nabla f(x)_i - a_r^\top \lambda \right]^+ + \frac{\mu_i^-(x)}{c_i} \left[a_r^\top \lambda - c_i \nabla f(x)_i \right]^+ \right\}$$

$$= \inf_{\nu \in \mathbb{R}} \sum_{i \in I} \left\{ \frac{\mu_i^+(x)}{c_i} \left[c_i \nabla f(x)_i - \nu \right]^+ + \frac{\mu_i^-(x)}{c_i} \left[\nu - c_i \nabla f(x)_i \right]^+ \right\}.$$

The second claim is proven with a similar calculation:

$$\sigma(x|I) = \inf_{\lambda \in \mathbb{R}^k} \sum_{r=1}^{s} \sum_{i \in I \cap [i_r]} \left\{ \frac{\mu_i^+(x)}{c_i} \left[c_i \nabla f(x)_i - a_r^\top \lambda \right]^+ \right.$$

$$\left. + \frac{\mu_i^-(x)}{c_i} \left[a_r^\top \lambda - c_i \nabla f(x)_i \right]^+ \right\}$$

$$\geq \sum_{r=1}^{s} \inf_{\beta_r \in \mathbb{R}} \sum_{i \in I \cap [i_r]} \left\{ \frac{\mu_i^+(x)}{c_i} \left[c_i \nabla f(x)_i - \beta_r \right]^+ + \frac{\mu_i^-(x)}{c_i} \left[\beta_r - c_i \nabla f(x)_i \right]^+ \right\}$$

$$= \sum_{r=1}^{s} \sigma(x|I \cap [i_r]).$$

By assumption $\operatorname{rank} A = s$ and therefore $(a_1, \dots, a_s)^\top \in \mathbb{R}^{s \times k}$ is surjective. This implies, that for any $\beta \in \mathbb{R}^s$ we can find a $\lambda \in \mathbb{R}^k$ solving all equations $a_r^\top \lambda = \beta_r$ simultaneously. We conclude that the inequality holds in the reverse direction as well and the claim follows.   □

As already pointed out it is well known, that one can construct sets I of size $q \ll m$ for which the function $\sigma(x|I)$ achieves at least a fraction of the overall forward

---

[5] Note, that for the first equality the terms are effectively swapped if $c_i < 0$.

gap $\sigma(x)$. List and Simon [13] could prove, that such sets can be constructed with a size $q \geq k + 1$ achieving the fraction $\frac{1}{m}$ of $\sigma(x)$. For problems where rank $A = s$ this can be extended. Let us start with the special case $I \subseteq [i_r]$:

Lemma 3. *Given a problem instance $\mathcal{P}(f, A, b, l, r)$, where rank $A = s$ and a set of representatives $\{i_r \mid r = 1, \ldots, s\}$. For any feasible $x \in \mathcal{R}(\mathcal{P})$ and any $I \subseteq [i_r]$, there exists a pair $\{i, j\} \subseteq I$, such that*

$$\sigma(x|i, j) \geq \frac{1}{q} \sigma(x|I),$$

where $q := |I|$ is the size of the working set.

Proof. As already pointed out, $\sigma(x|I)$ is the σ-function of the q-dimensional subproblem $\mathcal{P}_{I,x}$. The assumption $I \subseteq [i_r]$ implies, that the equality constraints of this problem have rank one and we conclude from [13, Theorem 4], that there exists a strong $1/q$-rate certificate of size 2 for problem $\mathcal{P}_{I,x}$ and the claim follows. $\qquad\square$

We are now in the position to give a central result of this section:

Theorem 1. *Given a problem instance $\mathcal{P}(f, A, b, l, r)$, where rank $A = s$. Then for any feasible $x \in \mathcal{R}(\mathcal{P})$ there exists a strong $\frac{1}{m}$-rate certifying pair (i, j) such that*

$$\sigma(x|i, j) \geq \frac{1}{m} \sigma(x).$$

Proof. For each $r \in \{1, \ldots, s\}$ consider the fractions $0 \leq \alpha_r \leq 1$ of $\sigma(x)$ which can be achieved restricting the working set to $[i_r]$:

$$\alpha_r \sigma(x) = \sigma(x|[i_r]).$$

From Lemma 2 we conclude, that $\sum_{r=1}^{s} \alpha_r = 1$. In addition we know from Lemma 3, that for each $r \in \{1, \ldots, s\}$ there exists a pair $\hat{i}_r, \hat{j}_r \in [i_r]$ such that

$$\sigma(x|[i_r]) \leq q_r \sigma\left(x \,\middle|\, \hat{i}_r, \hat{j}_r\right),$$

where $q_r := |[i_r]|$ denotes the size of the equivalence class $[i_r]$. As $\sum_{r=1}^{s} q_r = m$, we see, that for each r we have

$$\frac{\alpha_r}{q_r} \sigma(x) \leq \sigma\left(x \,\middle|\, \hat{i}_r, \hat{j}_r\right).$$

For sake of contradiction let us then assume, that for each $r \in \{1, \ldots, s\}$ we have $\frac{\alpha_r}{q_r} < \frac{1}{m}$. This would imply $m\alpha_r < q_r$ and therefore

$$m = \sum_{r=1}^{s} m\alpha_r < \sum_{r=1}^{s} q_r = m.$$

Consequently, there exists at least one r such that

$$\sigma\left(x \,\middle|\, \hat{i}_r, \hat{j}_r\right) \geq \frac{\alpha_r}{q_r}\sigma(x) \geq \frac{1}{m}\sigma(x).$$

$\square$

With the help of Theorem 1 we can now answer the main question:

Theorem 2. *For any problem $\mathcal{P}(f, A, b, l, r)$ such that rank $A = s$, where s is the number of equivalence classes induced by A, the family $(\sigma(x|I))_{I \subseteq \{1,\ldots,m\}}$ is a (continuous) 2-sparse-witness of suboptimality. Any such problem therefore is (continuously) decomposable by pairing.*

Proof. The conditions (C1) and (C2) are obviously fulfilled. As $\sigma(x) = 0$ iff x is an optimal solution of $\mathcal{P}$, condition (C3) follows from Theorem 1. $\square$

The next theorem will show, that for quadratic optimization problems the rank condition rank $A = s$ is in some sense a necessary condition as well:

Theorem 3. *Given an equality constraint matrix A, where rank $A < s$. Then there exist choices of $l, r \in \mathbb{R}^m$, such that for any strictly convex quadratic objective $f(x) = \frac{1}{2}x^\top Q x - w^\top x$ and any $b \in \mathbb{R}^k$ the instance $\mathcal{P}(f, A, b, l, r)$ is not decomposable by pairing.*

Proof. Consider the set

$$\mathcal{U} := \{g \in \mathbb{R}^m \mid \forall i \sim j : c_i g_i = c_j g_j\} \subseteq \mathbb{R}^m,$$

which we will call the set of *unpairable points*. From Lemma 2 we directly see, that for any x, such that $\nabla f(x) \in \mathcal{U}$ we have $\sigma(x|i,j) = 0$ for any pair $\{i,j\} \subseteq \{1,\ldots,m\}$. We will now construct a suboptimal x, such that $\nabla f(x) \in \mathcal{U}$, which will prove the claim.

Observe, that $\mathcal{U}$ is a linear subspace of $\mathbb{R}^m$ and $\dim \mathcal{U} = s$. By the construction of the equivalence classes we can conclude, that img $A^\top \subseteq \mathcal{U}$. rank $A < s$ then implies, that there exists a point $g \in \mathcal{U} \setminus \text{img } A^\top$ and as Q is of full-rank we can therefore find $x \in \mathbb{R}^m$, such that $\nabla f(x) = g$.

Now choose arbitrary $l, r \in \mathbb{R}^m$ such that $l < x < r$. As therefore x is an interior point of the box-constraints, x is optimal for $\mathcal{P}$ iff $\nabla f(x) \perp \text{kern } A$. As by construction $\nabla f(x) \notin \text{img } A^\top$ we conclude, that x cannot be optimal for $\mathcal{P}$. $\square$

4   An Efficient Selection Algorithm

In the last section it was shown, that a pair chosen from one equivalence class can constitute a rate certificate. We will now show, that such a pair can be computed in linear time. To this purpose we extend the fast rate certifying pair algorithm introduced by Simon for C-support vector optimization problems [17] to the more general setting of problems decomposable by pairing. Let us therefore assume throughout this section, that rank $A = s$. The following notion will be helpful:

Definition 3. *Let* $\{i_r \mid r = 1, \ldots, s\}$ *be a set of representatives. For any* $r = 1, \ldots, s$ *and any feasible* x *we define*

$$\overline{I_{top,r}}(x) := \left\{ j \in [i_r] \;\middle|\; \frac{\mu_j^+(x)}{c_j} > 0 \right\},$$

$$\overline{I_{bot,r}}(x) := \left\{ j \in [i_r] \;\middle|\; \frac{\mu_j^-(x)}{c_j} > 0 \right\}.$$

Such indexes are called (r)-*top/bottom-candidates.*[6] *Any pair* $(i, j) \in \overline{I_{top,r}}(x) \times \overline{I_{bot,r}}(x)$ *such that* $c_i \nabla f(x)_i > c_j \nabla f(x)_j$ *is called an* (r)-*violating pair.*

Lemma 4. *For any* $i, j \in \{1, \ldots, m\}$, $i \neq j$, *the following holds:* $\sigma(x|i, j) > 0$ *iff* (i, j) *is a violating pair. If this is the case, we have*

$$\sigma(x|i, j) = (c_i \nabla f(x)_i - c_j \nabla f(x)_j) \min \left\{ \frac{\mu_i^+(x)}{c_i}, \frac{\mu_j^-(x)}{c_j} \right\}.$$

Proof. From Lemma 2 we see, that

$$\sigma(x|i, j) = \sigma(x|i) + \sigma(x|j) = 0$$

if $i \not\sim j$. Let us therefore assume, that $i \sim j$ and $i, j \in [i_r]$. Again with Lemma 2 we have

$$\sigma(x|i, j) = \inf_{\nu \in \mathbb{R}} \left\{ \frac{\mu_i^+(x)}{c_i} [c_i \nabla f(x)_i - \nu]^+ + \frac{\mu_i^-(x)}{c_i} [\nu - c_i \nabla f(x)_i]^+ \right.$$
$$\left. + \frac{\mu_j^+(x)}{c_j} [c_j \nabla f(x)_j - \nu]^+ + \mu_j^-(x) [\nu - c_j \nabla f(x)_j]^+ \right\}$$

From this formulation we can see, that $\sigma(x|i, j) = 0$ if either[7] $\mu_i^+(x) = \mu_j^+(x) = 0$ or $\mu_i^-(x) = \mu_j^-(x) = 0$ or $c_i \nabla f(x)_i = c_j \nabla f(x)_j$. In all other cases left, (i, j) is a violating pair and we can assume wlg $c_i \nabla f(x)_i > c_j \nabla f(x)_j$. For any $\nu \in (c_j \nabla f(x)_j, c_i \nabla f(x)_i)$ the σ-function (depending on ν) reads

$$\sigma_\nu(x|i, j) = \frac{\mu_i^+(x)}{c_i} [c_i \nabla f(x)_i - \nu]^+ + \frac{\mu_j^-(x)}{c_j} [\nu - c_j \nabla f(x)_j]^+.$$

It is therefore optimal to choose either $\nu = c_i \nabla f(x)_i$ if $\frac{\mu_i^+(x)}{c_i} \geq \frac{\mu_j^-(x)}{c_j}$ or $\nu = c_j \nabla f(x)_j$ otherwise. This proves the claim. □

---

[6] Using the definitions of $\mu_i^{+/-}(x)$ one can check, that this definition is a generalization of the definition given in [10,11].

[7] Note, that in the first two cases the variables are at the border, i.e. they are either bottom-only or top-only-candidates and we can choose ν to be the maximum (or minimum respectively) of $c_i \nabla f(x)_i$ and $c_j \nabla f(x)_j$, which implies $\sigma(x|i, j) = 0$.

In the following we will extend the fast rate-certifying pair algorithm from [17] to the case of problems decomposable by pairing.

Corollary 1. *Let $[i_r], r = 1, \ldots, s$ be a set of representatives, then consider for any r the set $M_r := \left\{ \frac{\mu_i^+(x)}{c_i}, \frac{\mu_i^-(x)}{c_i} \mid i \in [i_r] \right\}$ and define*

$$\sigma_{\mu,r}(x) := \max_{i \in [i_r]: \frac{\mu_i^+(x)}{c_i} \geq \mu} c_i \nabla f(x_i) - \min_{j \in [i_r]: \frac{\mu_j^-(x)}{c_j} \geq \mu} c_j \nabla f(x_j).$$

Then the following relation holds for each $r = 1, \ldots, s$

$$\max_{\mu \in M_r} \sigma_{\mu,r}(x) \cdot \mu = \max_{\substack{(i,j) \in \\ \overline{I_{top,r}}(x) \times \overline{I_{bot,r}}(x)}} \sigma(x|i,j).$$

Proof. Let[8] us first prove, that for each $r = 1, \ldots, s$

$$\max_{\mu \in M_r} \sigma_{\mu,r}(x) \cdot \mu \geq \max_{\substack{(i,j) \in \\ \overline{I_{top,r}}(x) \times \overline{I_{bot,r}}(x)}} \sigma(x|i,j).$$

We therefore choose $i^*, j^* \in [i_r]$ such that

$$\max_{\substack{(i,j) \in \\ \overline{I_{top,r}}(x) \times \overline{I_{bot,r}}(x)}} \sigma(x|i,j) = (c_{i^*} \nabla f(x)_{i^*} - c_{j^*} \nabla f(x)_{j^*}) \mu^*.$$

where $\mu^* := \min \left\{ \frac{\mu_{i^*}^+(x)}{c_{i^*}}, \frac{\mu_{j^*}^-(x)}{c_{j^*}} \right\}$. As μ^*, i^*, j^* are possible choices in the maximization $\max_{\mu \in M_r} \sigma_{\mu,r}(x) \cdot \mu$ the first inequality follows. To prove the reverse inequality

$$\max_{\mu \in M_r} \sigma_{\mu,r}(x) \cdot \mu \leq \max_{\substack{(i,j) \in \\ \overline{I_{top,r}}(x) \times \overline{I_{bot,r}}(x)}} \sigma(x|i,j),$$

let us choose μ^*, i^*, j^* such that $\frac{\mu_{i^*}^+(x)}{c_{i^*}} \geq \mu^*$, $\frac{\mu_{j^*}^-(x)}{c_{j^*}} \geq \mu^*$ and

$$\max_{\mu \in M_r} \sigma_{\mu,r}(x) \cdot \mu = (c_{i^*} \nabla f(x)_{i^*} - c_{j^*} \nabla f(x)_{j^*}) \mu^*.$$

We conclude

$$\max_{\mu \in M_r} \sigma_{\mu,r}(x) \cdot \mu \leq (c_{i^*} \nabla f(x)_{i^*} - c_{j^*} \nabla f(x)_{j^*}) \min \left\{ \frac{\mu_{i^*}^+(x)}{c_{i^*}}, \frac{\mu_{j^*}^-(x)}{c_{j^*}} \right\}$$

$$\leq \max_{\substack{(i,j) \in \\ \overline{I_{top,r}}(x) \times \overline{I_{bot,r}}(x)}} \sigma(x|i,j),$$

---

[8] The proof given here is similar to the proof of Claim 2 in [17].

where the last inequality follows from the fact, that either $\mu^* = 0$ and the inequality is trivial or $\mu^* > 0$ and therefore $(i^*, j^*) \in \overline{I_{top,r}}(x) \times \overline{I_{bot,r}}(x)$. This proves the claim.   □

To compute a pair

$$\left(\hat{i}, \hat{j}\right) = \arg\max_{(i,j)} \sigma(x|i,j)$$

we can now proceed as follows (compare [17]): For each equivalence class consider the $\mu \in M_r$ in decreasing order and keep track of the index $i_r(\mu)$ that maximizes $c_i \nabla f(x)_i$ subject to $i \in [i_r]$ and $\frac{\mu_i^+(x)}{c_i} \geq \mu$ and $j_r(\mu)$ minimizing $c_j \nabla f(x)_j$ subject to $j \in [i_r]$ and $\frac{\mu_j^-(x)}{c_j} \geq \mu$. Finally pick the μ^* that maximizes $\sigma_{\mu_r,r} \cdot \mu_r$ for any $\mu_r \in M_r$ and $r = 1, \dots, s$. Following the arguments in [17] one can show, that this can be done in $O(m)$ steps provided, that we maintain two sorted lists $\left(i, \frac{\mu_i^+(x)}{c_i}\right)$ and $\left(i, \frac{\mu_i^-(x)}{c_i}\right)$ for each equivalence class. Note, that the sorting can be updated efficiently, as two subsequent solutions only differ in two components.

5   Conclusions

The selection algorithm presented above leads to a $\left(\frac{1}{m}, 2\right)$-certifying algorithm in the sense of [13]. For any problem instance $\mathcal{P}(f, A, b, l, r)$ with quadratic objective function and "maximal rank" equality constraint matrix, i.e. rank $A = s$. We can therefore implement a decomposition method with polynomial runtime. This result will be stated in the following theorem:

Theorem 4. *Given an instance $\mathcal{P}(f, A, b, l, r)$ with quadratic objective equivalent constraint matrix A such that* rank $A = s$, *where s is the number of equivalence classes of the columns of A. Then an SMO-decomposition algorithm using the working set*

$$I^{(n)} = \arg \max_{\substack{(i,j) \in \\ \overline{I_{top,r}}(x) \times \overline{I_{bot,r}}(x)}} \sigma\left(x^{(n)}\Big| i, j\right)$$

in iteration n, is within ε of optimality after at most $O\left(\frac{m^3}{\varepsilon}\right)$ steps.[9]

Proof. As each update step in the SMO-technique can be done in constant time, each iteration is dominated by the selection procedure taking $O(m)$ steps. From Theorem 1 and [13, Theorem 4] we conclude, that we need at most $O\left(\frac{m^2}{\varepsilon}\right)$ iterations and the claim follows.   □

The following two lemma show, that Theorem 4 applies to ν-support vector classification (3) and regression:

---

[9] This holds for a Random Access Machine model with unit cost for an arithmetic operation over the reals.

Lemma 5. *The dual optimization problem induced by the ν-SVC (3) has maximal rank equality constraints* $\operatorname{rank} A = s$.

Proof. The equality constraint matrix of (3) is given by $A = \left(\begin{smallmatrix} y_1 & \cdots & y_m \\ 1 & \cdots & 1 \end{smallmatrix} \right)$, where $y_i = \pm 1$. Thus either $\operatorname{rank} A = 1$ if all labels are the same and we therefore have $s = 1$ as well or $\operatorname{rank} A = 2$ In this case the equivalence classes are given by $\left[\left(\begin{smallmatrix} 1 \\ 1 \end{smallmatrix} \right) \right]$ and $\left[\left(\begin{smallmatrix} -1 \\ 1 \end{smallmatrix} \right) \right]$ and we conclude $\operatorname{rank} A = s = 2$. □

Lemma 6. *For any $\nu \in [0,1]$ there exists a dual formulation of the ν-support vector regression problem[10] of the general form (1) such that* $\operatorname{rank} A = s$.

Proof. Consider the dual optimization problem of ν-SVR which is given by

$$\inf_{x,x^*} f\left(x^* - x\right) \quad \text{s.t. } e^\top \left(x - x^*\right) = 0, \ e^\top \left(x + x^*\right) \le C \cdot \nu,$$

$$0 \le x_i, x_i^* \le \frac{C}{m}, \ i = 1, \ldots, m,$$

where $x, x^* \in \mathbb{R}^m$, f is quadratic and $C > 0$ is a regularization parameter. In the following we will prove, that there exists an optimal solution where $e^\top (x + x^*) = C \cdot \nu$ and therefore we can as well solve a problem of the general form (1) with $b = \left(\begin{smallmatrix} 0 \\ C \cdot \nu \end{smallmatrix} \right) \in \mathbb{R}^2$ and $A = \left(\begin{smallmatrix} 1 & \cdots & 1 & -1 & \cdots & -1 \\ 1 & \cdots & 1 & 1 & \cdots & 1 \end{smallmatrix} \right) \in \mathbb{R}^{2 \times 2m}$, where again $\operatorname{rank} A = 2 = s$.

To show $e^\top (x + x^*) = C \cdot \nu$ for at least one optimal (x, x^*) choose among all optimal points one, that achieves the maximal value of $e^\top (x + x^*)$. Let as denote such a solution as $(\hat{x}, \hat{x}^*)$. For sake of contradiction assume $e^\top (\hat{x} + \hat{x}^*) < C \cdot \nu < 2C$. Thus, there exists at least one $j \in \{1, \ldots, m\}$ such that $\hat{x}_j \le \hat{x}_j^* < \frac{C}{m}$ or $\hat{x}_j \le \hat{x}_j^* < \frac{C}{m}$. In both cases we are able to shift the solutions $\hat{x}_j, \hat{x}_j^*$ without changing their difference, but improve the value of $e^\top (x + x^*)$. □

The results given above therefore extend (or unify) known results in the following sense: It was known, that problems of the type above could be solved by extended maximal-violating pair algorithms [3,11] but no convergence rate could be guaranteed for such selection procedures. On the other hand the selection strategy proposed by [13] required larger working-set sizes (e.g. $q = 3$ for ν-SVM). Let us note, that using the presented selection algorithm based on [17] has the additional benefit, that extending the results from [7] should be straight forward.

In addition we presented a simple algebraic criterion which is sufficient and (to some extent) necessary for a given quadratic convex optimization problem to be decomposable by pairing and showed, that under this condition a fast and simple working set selection algorithm exists.

Acknowledgments. This work was supported in part by the IST Programme of the European Community, under the PASCAL Network of Excellence, IST-2002-506778. This publication only reflects the authors' views.

---

[10] See for example Chapter 9.3 in [15].

References

1. Chang, C.-C., Hsu, C.-W., Lin, C.-J.: The Analysis of Decomposition Methods for Support Vector Machines. IEEE Transaction on Neural Networks 11(4), 1003–1008 (2000)
2. Chang, C.-C., Lin, C.-J.: LIBSVM: A Library for Support Vector Machines, (2001)Software available at http://www.csie.ntu.edu.tw/~cjlin/libsvm
3. Chang, C.-C., Lin, C.-J.: Training ν- Support Vector Classifiers: Theory and Algorithms. Neural Computation 10(9), 2119–2147 (2001)
4. Chen, P.-H., Fan, R.-E., Lin, C.-J.: A study on SMO-type Decomposition Methods for Support Vector Machines. IEEE Transactions on Neural Networks 17, 893–908 (2006)
5. Collobert, R.: Large Scale Machine Learning. PhD thesis, Université de Paris VI, LIP6 (2004)
6. Collobert, R., Bengio, S.: SVMTorch: Support Vector Machines for Large-Scale Regression Problems. Journal of Machine Learning Research 1, 143–160 (2001)
7. Hush, D., Kelly, P., Scovel, C., Steinwart, I.: QP Algorithms with Guaranteed Aaccuracy and Run Time for Support Vector Machines. Journal of Machine Learning Research 7, 733–769 (2006)
8. Hush, D., Scovel, C.: Polynomial-time Decomposition Algorithms for Support Vector Machines. Machine Learning 51, 51–71 (2003)
9. Keerthi, S.S., Gilbert, E.G.: Convergence of a Generalized SMO Algorithm for SVM Classifier Design. Machine Learning 46, 351–360 (2002)
10. Lin, C.-J.: On the Convergence of the Decomposition Method for Support Vector Machines. IEEE Transactions on Neural Networks 12, 1288–1298 (2001)
11. List, N.: Convergence of a generalized gradient selection approach for the decomposition method. In: Proceedings of the 15th International Conference on Algorithmic Learning Theory, pp. 338–349 (2004)
12. List, N., Simon, H.U.: A General Convergence Theorem for the Decomposition Method. In: Proceedings of the 17th Annual Conference on Learning Theory, COLT 2004, pp. 363–377 (2004)
13. List, N., Simon, H.U.: General Polynomial Time Decomposition Algorithms. Journal of Machine Learning Research 8, 303–321 (2006)
14. Platt, J.C.: Fast Training of Support Vector Machines using Sequential Minimal Optimization. In: Schölkopf, B., Burges, C.J.C., Smola, A. J., (eds.). Advances in Kernel Methods – Support Vector Learning. Cambridge, MA (1999)
15. Schölkopf, B., Smola, A.J.: Learning with Kernels, 2nd edn. MIT Press, Cambridge, MA, London (2002)
16. Schölkopf, B., Smola, A.J., Williamson, R., Bartlett, P.: New Support Vector Algorithms. Neural Computation 12(5), 1207–1245 (2000)
17. Simon, H.U.: On the Complexity of Working Set Selection. In: Proceedings of the 15th International Conference on Algorithmic Learning Theory, pp. 324–337. Springer, Heidelberg (2004)
18. Szedmak, S., Shawe-Taylor, J., Parado-Hernandez, E.: Learning via Linear Operators: Maximum Margin Regression. Technical report (2006), available at http://eprints.pascal-network.org/archive/00001765/

Learning Nested Halfspaces and Uphill Decision Trees

Adam Tauman Kalai*

Georgia Tech
http://www.cc.gatech.edu/~atk

Abstract. Predicting class probabilities and other real-valued quantities is often more useful than binary classification, but comparatively
little work in PAC-style learning addresses this issue. We show that two
rich classes of real-valued functions are learnable in the probabilistic-
concept framework of Kearns and Schapire.

Let X be a subset of Euclidean space and f be a real-valued function
on X. We say f is a *nested halfspace function* if, for each real threshold t,
the set $\{x \in X | f(x) \le t\}$, is a halfspace. This broad class of functions in-
cludes binary halfspaces with a margin (e.g., SVMs) as a special case. We
give an efficient algorithm that provably learns (Lipschitz-continuous)
nested halfspace functions on the unit ball. The sample complexity is
independent of the number of dimensions.

We also introduce the class of *uphill decision trees*, which are real-
valued decision trees (sometimes called *regression trees*) in which the
sequence of leaf values is non-decreasing. We give an efficient algorithm
for provably learning uphill decision trees whose sample complexity is
polynomial in the number of dimensions but independent of the size of
the tree (which may be exponential). Both of our algorithms employ a
real-valued extension of Mansour and McAllester's boosting algorithm.

1   Introduction

Consider the problem of predicting whether a patient will develop diabetes ($y \in \{0, 1\}$) given n real valued attributes ($x \in \mathbb{R}^n$). A real prediction of $\Pr[y = 1 | x]$ is
much more informative than the binary prediction of whether $\Pr[y = 1 | x] > 1/2$
or not. Hence, learning probabilities and, more generally, real-valued functions
has become a central problem in machine learning.

This paper introduces algorithms for learning two classes of real-valued functions. The first is the class of *nested halfspace functions* (NHFs), and the second is that of *uphill decision trees*. These are real-valued classes of functions
which naturally generalize halfspaces and decision lists, respectively. We believe
that these classes of functions are much richer than their binary classification
counterparts.

---

* Supported in part by NSF award SES-527656. Part of this work was done while the
author was visiting the Weizmann Institute.

N. Bshouty and C. Gentile (Eds.): COLT 2007, LNAI 4539, pp. 378–392, 2007.

Kearns and Schapire give a rigorous definition of learning such probabilistic concepts [5] in which there is a set X, and a distribution $\mathcal{D}$ over $(x, y) \in X \times \{0, 1\}$. The learner's goal is to predict $f(x) = \Pr_{\mathcal{D}}[y = 1|x]$ as accurately as possible. Roughly speaking, a learning algorithm *learns* a family $\mathcal{C}$ of *concepts* $c : X \to [0, 1]$ if, for **any** distribution $\mathcal{D}$ such that $f(x) = \Pr_{(x,y)\sim\mathcal{D}}[y = 1|x] \in \mathcal{C}$, with high probability it outputs an *hypothesis* $h : X \to [0, 1]$ such that,

$$\mathrm{E}_{\mathcal{D}}[(h(x) - f(x))^2] \leq \epsilon. \tag{1}$$

The algorithm should be computationally efficient and use only $\mathrm{poly}(1/\epsilon)$ independent samples from $\mathcal{D}$.

Remark 1. Two remarks from [5] elucidate the power of their probabilistic learning model. First of all, without loss of generality one can allow $y \in [0, 1]$ (the generalization to any interval $[a, b]$ is straightforward) as long as $f \in \mathcal{C}$ where now $f(x) = \mathrm{E}[y|x]$. The reason is that, one can *randomly round* any example in $(x, y) \in X \times [0, 1]$ to be in $X \times \{0, 1\}$ by choosing $(x, 1)$ with probability y and $(x, 0)$ with probability $1 - y$. This does not change $\mathrm{E}[y|x]$ and converts a distribution over $X \times [0, 1]$ to be over $X \times \{0, 1\}$. Such a setting models real-valued prediction, e.g., estimating the value of a used car from attributes.[1]

Remark 2. In expanding $\mathrm{E}[(h(x) - f(x) + f(x) - y)^2]$, for $f(x) = \mathrm{E}[y|x]$ and any hypothesis h, the cross-term $\mathrm{E}[(h(x) - f(x))(f(x) - y)] = 0$ cancels. So,

$$\mathrm{E}_{(x,y)\sim\mathcal{D}}[(h(x) - y)^2] = \mathrm{E}[(h(x) - f(x))^2] + \mathrm{E}[(f(x) - y)^2]. \tag{2}$$

Hence, a hypothesis meeting (1) not only makes predictions $h(x)$ that are close to the *truth* $f(x)$, but also has expected *squared error* $\mathrm{E}[(h(x) - y)^2]$ within ϵ of the minimal squared error that could achieve knowing f.

1.1   Nested Halfspace Functions and Uphill Decision Trees

Let $X \subseteq \mathbb{R}^n$ and define a function $f : X \to \mathbb{R}$ to be an NHF if for every $t \in \mathbb{R}$, the set of x such that $f(x) \leq t$ is a halfspace. More formally, for all $t \in \mathbb{R}$, there must exist $w \in \mathbb{R}^n, \theta \in \mathbb{R}$ such that

$$\{x \in X \mid f(x) \leq t\} = \{x \in X \mid x \cdot w \leq \theta\}.$$

We call this a *nested* halfspace function because for thresholds $t < t'$, the set $H_t = \{x \in X \mid f(x) \leq t\}$ must be contained in $H_{t'} = \{x \in X \mid f(x) \leq t'\}$ and both must be halfspaces.

When $X = \mathbb{R}^n$, the NHFs reduce[2] to the class of *generalized linear models* where it is required that $f(x) = u(w \cdot x)$ where $w \in \mathbb{R}^n$ and $u : \mathbb{R} \to \mathbb{R}$ is a

---

[1] Note that the learner does not directly get samples $(x, f(x))$. If $y = f(x)$ always was the case (a special distribution), then learning nested halfspaces would be trivial, as the learner could learn $f(x) \leq t$ for each t himself by thresholding the data to see which $y \geq t$ and then running a standard halfspace learning algorithm.

[2] Technically we need to also permit the set $\{x \in X \mid f(X) \leq t\}$ to be an open halfspace $\{x \in X \mid x \cdot w < \theta\}$, but for simplicity, we consider only closed halfspaces.

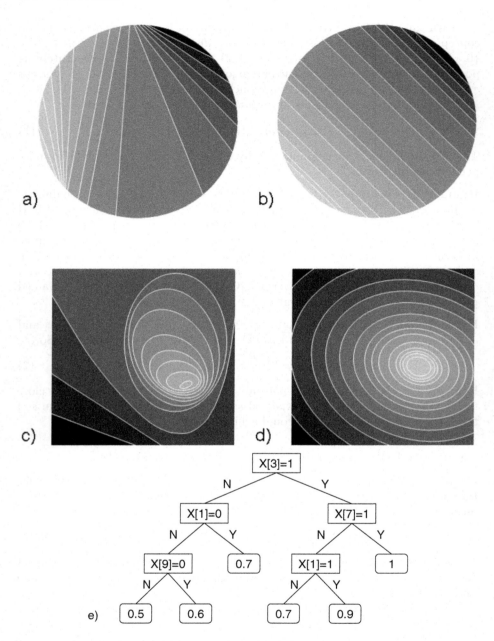

Fig. 1. a-d) Illustrations of NHFs. Whiter=larger function value. a) An NHF on a ball. b) A generalized linear model, where all halfspaces must be parallel. c) An NHF with a degree-2 polynomial kernel. The function can be a potpourri of ellipses, parabolas, etc., at varying orientations. d) A generalized linear model with a degree-2 polynomial kernel. The objects must be concentric, of the same type and same orientation. e) An uphill decision tree.

nondecreasing function. Generalized linear models include halfspaces as well as linear and logistic regression as special cases.

For general $X \subseteq \mathbb{R}^n$, the NHFs have much more flexibility. Figure 1 illustrates NHFs overs the unit ball, and kernelized NHFs with a degree 2 polynomial kernel. There are several additional characterizations of NHFs. For example, an NHF has the property that the restriction of the function to any line is either nondecreasing or nonincreasing.

In Section 3, we give an algorithm for learning continuous NHFs over the unit ball $B = \{x \in \mathbb{R}^n \mid \|x\| \leq 1\}$. A function $f : X \to \mathbb{R}$ is said to be L-*Lipschitz* continuous if,

$$\forall x, x' \in X \quad |f(x) - f(x')| \leq L\|x - x'\|.$$

(For differentiable f and convex X, this is equivalent to requiring $\|\nabla f(x)\| \leq L$ for all $x \in X$). Formally, the class of functions we learn is,

$$\mathrm{NHF}_L = \{f : B \to [0, 1] \mid f \text{ is } L\text{-Lipschitz and an NHF}\}.$$

Result 1. *The class* NHF_L *for any dimension* n *can be learned to error* $\leq \epsilon$ *using a computationally efficient algorithm and* $poly(1/\epsilon, L)$ *data.*

Notice that the amount of data does not depend on n, and the algorithm can be naturally Kernelized. In this sense, the parameter L plays the analogous role to a margin parameter of $1/L$.

1.2 Uphill Decision Trees

In this case, let $X = \{0, 1\}^n$. A decision tree with real values at the leaves (sometimes called a regression tree) is called an uphill decision tree if the values on the leaves are nondecreasing in order from left to right. Formally, this means that there should be some depth-first traversal of the tree in which the values encountered at the leaves occur in nondecreasing order. An example of an uphill decision tree is given in Figure 1e). Note that uphill (or downhill) decision trees differ from the notion of *monotonic decision trees* (see, e.g., [10]), which require that changing any single attribute from 0 to 1 can only increase (or decrease) the function. The example in Figure 1e) demonstrates that an uphill decision tree need not be monotonic: changing $x[1]$ from 0 to 1 may increase or decrease the value, depending on the other attributes.

Result 2. *The class of uphill decision trees (of any size) in any dimension* n *can be learned to error* $\leq \epsilon$ *using a computationally efficient algorithm and* $poly(n, 1/\epsilon)$ *data.*

We note that the set of uphill decision trees with $\{0, 1\}$ leaf values is exactly the same as the set of binary decision lists. Similarly, thresholding an uphill decision tree gives a binary decision list. Hence uphill decision trees are in fact a special case of NHFs. However, we cannot use our result (or algorithm) from the previous section here because it has incompatible conditions.

It is also worth defining Kearns and Schapire's notion of a Probabilistic decision list [5]. This is a decision list with real values in the leaves. However, there is the additional restriction that the real values have to be an interleaving of two sequences: one nonincreasing and the other nondecreasing up until some common value θ. This seemingly strange condition actually makes them a special case of uphill decision trees.

2   Preliminaries: Real-Valued Learning

Concept class of real functions	Binary $\{0, 1\}$ special case
Monotonic functions of a single variable [5]	1-dimensional threshold functions
Functions of (const.) k relevant variables [5]	Binary functions of k relevant variables
Probabilistic decision lists [5]	Decision lists
(Lipschitz) Generalized Linear Models [3,8]	Halfspaces(+margin)
(Lipschitz) Generalized Additive Models [3,2]	Additive threshold functions(+margin)
(Lipschitz) NHFs	Halfspaces(+margin)
Uphill decision trees	Decision lists

Following Kearns and Schapire [5], we assume that we have a set X, a probability distribution $\mathcal{D}$ over $X \times [0, 1]$, and a family $\mathcal{C}$ of *concepts* $f : X \to [0, 1]$ such that $f(x) = \mathrm{E}_{(x,y) \sim \mathcal{D}}[y|x] \in \mathcal{C}$.[3] An example oracle $EX = EX_{\mathcal{D}}$ is an oracle that, each time called, returns an independent draw (x, y) from distribution $\mathcal{D}$. That is, if the algorithm calls the oracle m times, it receives samples $(x_1, y_1), \ldots, (x_m, y_m)$ which are i.i.d. from $\mathcal{D}$. In the case where $X \subseteq \mathbb{R}^n$, we denote the ith attribute $x[i] \in \mathbb{R}$.

Definition 1 (Polynomial learning in the real-valued setting). *A (possibly randomized) learning algorithm L takes as input $\epsilon, \delta > 0$ and EX and outputs a function $h : X \to [0, 1]$. L polynomially learns $(X, \mathcal{C})$ if there exists a polynomial $p(\cdot, \cdot)$ such that: for any $\epsilon, \delta > 0$ and any distribution $\mathcal{D}$ over $X \times [0, 1]$ whose $f(x) = \mathrm{E}_{(x,y) \sim \mathcal{D}}[y|x] \in \mathcal{C}$, with probability $1 - \delta$ over the samples returned by EX (and its internal randomization), it outputs $h : X \to [0, 1]$ such that, $\mathrm{E}_{(x,y) \sim \mathcal{D}}[(h(x) - f(x))^2] \leq \epsilon$ and with probability 1, the runtime of the algorithm (hence number of calls to EX as well) and the runtime of h on any $x \in X$, are at most $p(1/\epsilon, 1/\delta)$.*

Remark. Often times we are interested in the asymptotic behavior of an algorithm on sequence of learning problems $(X_n, \mathcal{C}_n)$ for $n = 1, 2, \ldots$. In this case, n is an input to the learning algorithm as well, and the above requirement must hold for any $n \geq 1$ and learning problem $(X_n, \mathcal{C}_n)$, and the runtime may grow with n but must be polynomial in n as well. In this case we say the algorithm polynomially learns $\{(X_n, \mathcal{C}_n)\}$.

---

[3] This means $f(z) = E[y|x = z]$ if we think of (x, y) as joint random variables drawn according to $\mathcal{D}$. For x not in the support of $\mathcal{D}$, $f(x) \in [0, 1]$ may be chosen arbitrarily so that $f \in \mathcal{C}$.

2.1   Covariance and Correlation

While $\{0, 1\}$ error rate is often the most useful metric in designing binary classification algorithms, in the real-valued setting notions of variance, covariance and correlation often prove useful.

For random variables $A, B \in \mathbb{R}$, define the *covariance* to be,

$$\text{cov}(A, B) = \text{E}[AB] - \text{E}[A]\text{E}[B] = \text{E}[(A - \mu_A)(B - \mu_B)] = \text{E}[(A - \mu_A)B],$$

where $\mu_A = \text{E}[A]$ denotes the expectation of random variable A. We note that for any constant $c \in \mathbb{R}$, $\text{cov}(A+c, B) = \text{cov}(A, B)$. Also, covariance is symmetric ($\text{cov}(A, B) = \text{cov}(B, A)$) and bilinear (for any random variables $A_1, A_2, B \in \mathbb{R}$ and constants $c_1, c_2 \in \mathbb{R}$, $\text{cov}(c_1 A_1 + c_2 A_2, B) = c_1 \text{cov}(A_1, B) + c_2 \text{cov}(A_2, B)$). Define the *variance* of A to be

$$\text{var}(A) = \text{cov}(A, A) = \text{E}[A^2] - \text{E}[A]^2 = \text{E}[(A - \mu_A)^2].$$

We assume that we have some distribution $\mathcal{D}$ over $X \times [0, 1]$. For functions $g, h : X \to \mathbb{R}$, we define

$$\text{cov}(g(x), h(x)) = \text{E}_{(x,y)\sim\mathcal{D}}[g(x)h(x)] - \text{E}[g(x)]\text{E}[h(x)] = \text{E}[(g(x) - \mu_g)h(x)],$$

where $\mu_g = \text{E}[g(x)]$. Similarly, define $\text{var}(g(x)) = \text{E}[g^2(x)] - \text{E}[g(x)]^2$. Note that $\text{var}(f(x)) = 0$ has special meaning. It means that $f(x) = \text{E}[y|x]$ is constant for all x in the support of $\mathcal{D}$, hence the most accurate hypothesis to output is this constant function and no better learning is possible.

Note that for f and any $h : X \to \mathbb{R}$ we also have

$$\text{cov}(f(x), h(x)) = \text{E}[f(x)h(x)] - \text{E}[f(x)]\text{E}[h(x)] = \text{E}[yh(x)] - \mu_f \text{E}[h(x)].$$

Hence we have the useful relation, for any $h : X \to \mathbb{R}$:

$$\text{cov}(f(x), h(x)) = \text{E}[yh(x)] - \text{E}[y]\text{E}[h(x)] = \text{cov}(y, h(x)). \tag{3}$$

We also refer to $\text{cov}(y, h(x))$ as the *true* covariance of h in analogy to the *true error* (also called *generalization error*) of an algorithm outputting $h : X \to \mathbb{R}$. For such an algorithm, we refer to the *expected covariance* $\text{E}[\text{cov}(y, h(x))]$, where the expectation is over draws of the training set $\mathcal{Z}_m = (x_1, y_1), \ldots, (x_m, y_m)$ drawn i.i.d. from $\mathcal{D}$, and we are talking about the expectation, over datasets of the true covariance. In particular, this is, $\text{E}_{\mathcal{Z}_m \sim \mathcal{D}^m}[\text{cov}(y, h(x))]$ and is not to be confused with the *empirical covariance* $\widehat{\text{cov}}(y, h(x))$ defined as follows.

$$\widehat{\text{cov}}(y, h(x)) = \frac{1}{m}\sum_{i=1}^{m} y_i h(x_i) - \frac{1}{m}\sum_{i=1}^{m} y_i \frac{1}{m}\sum_{i=1}^{m} h(x_i) = \frac{1}{m}\sum_{i=1}^{m}(y_i - \hat{\mu}_f)h(x_i),$$

where we define $\hat{\mu}_f = \frac{1}{m}\sum_{i=1}^{m} y_i$.

Finally, for random variables A, B, we define the *correlation coefficient*,

$$\text{cor}(A, B) = \frac{\text{cov}(A, B)}{\sqrt{\text{var}(A)\text{var}(B)}} \in [-1, 1].$$

Note that $\text{cor}(c_1 A + c_2, B) = \text{cor}(A, B)$ for constants $c_1 > 0, c_2 \in \mathbb{R}$. Similarly for $g, h : X \to \mathbb{R}$, we define $\text{cor}(g(x), h(x)) = \text{cov}(g(x), h(x))/\sqrt{\text{var}(h(x))\text{var}(g(x))}$.

2.2   Real Boosting

Classification boosting [11] is an extremely useful tool for designing provably efficient learning algorithms. In order to learn real-valued functions, we need to use the real-valued analog of boosting. In [3], it was shown that the boosting by branching programs algorithm of Mansour and McAllester [7] (building on work of Kearns and Mansour [4]) can be adapted to the real-valued setting.

In classification boosting, a weak learner was defined [6] to be an algorithm whose output had error strictly less than $1/2$ ($\leq 1/2 - \gamma$ for $\gamma > 0$). In the real-valued setting, this definition does not make sense. Instead, the definition we use requires positive correlation rather than error less than $1/2$. Note that in the real-valued setting, our definition of a weak learner is complicated by the fact that when $\mathrm{var}(f(x)) = 0$, it is impossible to have positive covariance (or positive correlation), i.e., $\mathrm{cov}(h(x), y) = 0$ for all $h : X \to \mathbb{R}$.

Definition 2 (Weak correlator [3]). *Let* $\rho : [0,1] \to [0,1]$ *be a nondecreasing function. A* ρ-*weak correlator for* $(X, \mathcal{C})$ *is a learning algorithm that takes input* $\epsilon, \delta > 0$ *and* EX *such that, for any* $\epsilon, \delta > 0$, *and any distribution* $\mathcal{D}$ *over* $X \times [0,1]$ *where* $f(x) = \mathrm{E}[y|x] \in \mathcal{C}$ *and* $\mathrm{var}(f(x)) \geq \epsilon$, *with probability* $1 - \delta$, *it outputs* $h : X \to \mathbb{R}$ *such that* $\mathrm{cor}(h(x), f(x)) \geq \rho(\epsilon)$.

A weak correlator is said to be *efficient* if its runtime (hence number of calls to EX) and the runtime of evaluating h, are polynomial in $1/\epsilon, 1/\delta$ and if $1/\rho(\epsilon)$ is polynomial in $1/\epsilon$ as well. In the case where we consider a sequence of learning problems $\{(X_n, \mathcal{C}_n)\}$, the runtime and $1/\rho$ must grow polynomially in n as well.

The following is shown:

Theorem 1 (Real-valued boosting [3]). *There is a boosting algorithm that, given any black-box efficient* ρ-*correlator for* $(X, \mathcal{C})$, *polynomially learns* $(X, \mathcal{C})$ *in the real-valued setting.*

A somewhat simpler notion of weak learner in the real-valued setting can be given, making analysis simpler. We define a simplified weak learner as follows.

Definition 3 (Simplified real weak learner). *Let* $\sigma : [0,1] \to [0,1]$ *be a nondecreasing function such that* $1/\sigma(\epsilon)$ *is polynomial in* $1/\epsilon$ *and let* $q(\cdot)$ *be a polynomial. The simplified real weak learner for* $(X, \mathcal{C})$ *is a learning algorithm that takes input* $m \geq 1$ *and training set* $\mathcal{Z}_m = (x_1, y_1), \ldots, (x_m, y_m)$ *drawn i.i.d. from* $\mathcal{D}$ *such that, for any* $\epsilon > 0$ *and any* $m \geq q(1/\epsilon)$, *and any distribution* $\mathcal{D}$ *over* $X \times [0,1]$ *where* $f(x) = \mathrm{E}[y|x] \in \mathcal{C}$ *and* $\mathrm{var}(f(x)) \geq \epsilon$, *it outputs* $h : X \to [-1,1]$ *such that* $\mathrm{E}_{\mathcal{Z}_m \sim \mathcal{D}^m}\big[|\mathrm{cov}(h(x), y)|\big] \geq \sigma(\epsilon)$ *and the runtime of the weak learner and* h *on any inputs in* $(X \times [0,1])^m$ *must be polynomial in* m.

We call this definition "simplified," because it involves covariance rather than correlation, and because it is arguably more natural to view a learning algorithm as taking a training set as input rather than desired accuracy and confidence parameters. In this way, we also avoid explicit dependence on $1/\delta$.

Again, in the case of a sequence of learning problems $\{(X_n, \mathcal{C}_n)\}$, the above guarantee must hold for any $n \geq 1$, but $1/\rho$, p, and the runtimes are allowed to be polynomial in n as well. Using standard techniques, given a simplified real weak learner for $\{X_n, C_n\}_{n \geq 1}$, we can construct a efficient ρ-weak learner and hence polynomially learn the family.

Lemma 1. *Given a simplified weak learner for (X, C), one can construct an efficient weak correlator (and hence a polynomial learner) for (X, C).*

Proof (Sketch). Notice that for any $h : X \to [-1, 1]$, $\mathrm{var}(h(x)) \leq 1$. Since $f : X \to [0, 1]$, we have $\mathrm{var}(f(x)) \leq 1/4$. Hence,

$$\mathrm{cor}(h(x), f(x)) = \frac{\mathrm{cov}(h(x), y)}{\sqrt{\mathrm{var}(h(x))\mathrm{var}(f(x))}} \geq 2\mathrm{cov}(h(x), y).$$

Hence, to achieve $\geq \rho$ correlation, it suffices to output hypothesis $h : X \to [-1, 1]$ with $\mathrm{cov}(h(x), y) \geq \rho/2$.

We take $\rho(\epsilon) = \sigma(\epsilon)$. Given $\epsilon, \delta > 0$, we run the simplified weak learner $T = O(\log(1/\delta)/\epsilon)$ times on fresh data. For each run $t = 1, \ldots, T$, we have an output $h_t : X \to [0, 1]$. We use $O(\log(1/\delta)/\sigma^2(\epsilon))$ fresh random samples to estimate the covariance on a fresh set of held-out data set, and return $h(x) = h_t(x)$ or $h(x) = -h_t(x)$ of maximal empirical covariance. Since $\mathrm{cov}(-h_t(x)) = -\mathrm{cov}(h_t(x))$ and we are considering both possibilities for each t, WLOG we can assume that $cov(h_t(x), y) \geq 0$.

Now, for each $1 \leq t \leq T$, we have $\mathrm{E}_{\mathcal{Z}_m}[1 - \mathrm{cov}(h_t(x), y)] \leq 1 - \sigma(\epsilon)$ and also $\mathrm{cov}(h_t(x), y) \in [0, 1]$ since $h_t(x), f(x) \leq 1$. By Markov's inequality on $1 - \mathrm{cov}(h_t(x), y) \geq 0$, we have,

$$\mathrm{Pr}_{\mathcal{Z}_m \sim \mathcal{D}^m}[1 - \mathrm{cov}(h_t(x), y) \geq 1 - (3/4)\sigma(\epsilon)] \leq \frac{1 - \sigma(\epsilon)}{1 - (3/4)\sigma(\epsilon)} \leq 1 - \sigma(\epsilon)/4.$$

In other words, with probability $\geq \sigma(\epsilon)/4$, $\mathrm{cov}(h_t(x), y) \geq (3/4)\sigma(\epsilon)$. Thus, after $T = O(\log(1/\delta)/\sigma(\epsilon))$ repetitions of the algorithm, with probability $\geq 1 - \delta/2$, at least one of them will have $\mathrm{cov}(h_t(x), y) = \mathrm{cov}(h_t(x), f(x)) \geq (3/4)\sigma(\epsilon)$. If we measure the empirical covariance $\widehat{\mathrm{cov}}(h_t(x), y)$ of each on a test set of size $O(\log(1/\delta)/\sigma^2(\epsilon))$, with probability $\geq 1 - \delta/2$, all of them (including both $h_t(x)$ and $-h_t(x)$ will have empirical covariance within $\sigma(\epsilon)/8$ of their true covariance. Hence, by the union bound, with probability $\geq 1 - \delta$, we will output $h : X \to [-1, 1]$ with $\mathrm{cov}(h(x), y) \geq \sigma(\epsilon)/2 = \rho(\epsilon)/2$. $\qquad\square$

The same lemma holds for $\{(X_n, C_n)\}$ as the polynomial dependence on n trivially carries through the above reduction.

3   Learning Continuous NHFs

In this section we take $X = B = \{x \in \mathbb{R}^n \mid \|x\| \leq 1\}$ to be the unit ball, and we consider NHFs $f : B \to [0, 1]$ that are L-Lipschitz-continuous, for some value $L > 0$.

The idea is to use a linear $h(x) = w \cdot x$ weak learner that maximizes the empirical covariance with y on the data. This is easy to compute, as follows. Define $\hat{\mu}_f = \frac{1}{m} \sum_{i=1}^{m} y_i$, and $v, \hat{v} \in \mathbb{R}^n$ by,

$$v = \mathrm{E}_{(x,y)\sim\mathcal{D}}[(y - \mu_f)x]$$

$$\hat{v} = \frac{1}{m} \sum_{i=1}^{m} (y_i - \hat{\mu}_f)x_i.$$

For any $w \in \mathbb{R}^n$, we have,

$$\mathrm{cov}(y, w \cdot x) = \mathrm{E}[(y - \mu_f)(w \cdot x)] = w \cdot \mathrm{E}[(y - \mu_f)x] = w \cdot v. \qquad (4)$$

Similarly,

$$\widehat{\mathrm{cov}}(y, w \cdot x) = \frac{1}{m} \sum_{i=1}^{m} (y_i - \hat{\mu}_f)(w \cdot x_i) = w \cdot \frac{1}{m} \sum_{i=1}^{m} (y_i - \hat{\mu}_f)x_i = w \cdot \hat{v}. \qquad (5)$$

Thus the vectors $u, \hat{u} \in B$ that maximize $\mathrm{cov}(y, u \cdot x)$ and $\widehat{\mathrm{cov}}(y, \hat{u} \cdot x)$ are $u = \frac{v}{\|v\|}$ and $\hat{u} = \frac{\hat{v}}{\|\hat{v}\|}$, respectively[4].

The main result of this section is that the (trivially efficient) algorithm that outputs hypothesis $h(x) = \hat{u} \cdot x$ is a simplified real weak learner. This directly implies Result 1, through Lemma 1.

Theorem 2. *For any $\epsilon > 0$ distribution $\mathcal{D}$ over $B \times \{0, 1\}$ such that $f \in \mathrm{NHF}_L$ and $\mathrm{var}(f) \geq \epsilon$, given $m \geq 100L^2/\epsilon^4$ examples, the vector $\hat{u} = \frac{\hat{v}}{\|\hat{v}\|}$ defined by $\hat{v} = \frac{1}{m} \sum_{i=1}^{m} (y_i - \hat{\mu}_f)x_i$ yields,*

$$\mathrm{E}_{\mathcal{Z}_m}[\mathrm{cov}(y, u \cdot x)] \geq \frac{1}{5L}\epsilon^2.$$

To prove this, we begin by claiming that there is some vector $w \in B$ such that $(w \cdot x)$ has relatively large covariance with respect to y.

Lemma 2. *Suppose $f \in \mathrm{NHF}_L$. Then there exists some vector $w \in B$ such that,*

$$\mathrm{cov}(y, w \cdot x) = \mathrm{cov}(f(x), w \cdot x) \geq \frac{4}{5L} \left(\mathrm{var}(f(x)) \right)^2.$$

We will prove this lemma in Section 3.1. Finally, we also use the following generalization bound for covariance.

Lemma 3. *For any distribution $\mathcal{D}$ over $B \times [0, 1]$, any $\epsilon, \delta > 0$, and m samples iid from $\mathcal{D}$,*

$$\mathrm{E}\left[\sup_{w \in B} |\widehat{\mathrm{cov}}(y, w \cdot x) - \mathrm{cov}(y, w \cdot x)| \right] \leq \frac{3}{\sqrt{m}}.$$

---

[4] If v (or $\hat{v}$) is 0, we take $u = 0$ (resp. $\hat{u} = 0$).

Proof. By equations (4) and (5), we have for any $w \in B$,

$$|\widehat{\text{cov}}(y, w \cdot x) - \text{cov}(y, w \cdot x)| = |w \cdot (\hat{v} - v)| \leq \|\hat{v} - v\|.$$

Thus it suffices to show that $\text{E}\left[\|\hat{v} - v\|^2\right] \leq 9/m$ because $\text{E}[|Z|] \leq \sqrt{\text{E}[Z^2]}$ for any random variable $Z \in \mathbb{R}$.

Note that $\text{E}[\hat{v}] = v$. Also note that $\hat{v}$, which is a function of the training data $(x_1, y_1), \ldots, (x_m, y_m)$ is *stable* in the following sense. If we change only one training example $(x_i, y_i) \in B \times [0, 1]$, this can move $\hat{v}$ by a vector of magnitude at most $3/m$. To see this, note that $(1/m)(y_i - \hat{\mu}_f)x_i$ is a vector of magnitude $\leq 1/m$ and hence changing (x_i, y_i) changes this by a vector of magnitude at most $2/m$. Also, changing (x_i, y_i) moves $(1/m)(y_j - \hat{\mu}_f)x_j$ (for $j \neq i$) by a vector of at most $1/m^2$ because $\hat{\mu}_f$ changes by at most $1/m$ and $(x_j, y_j) \in B \times [0, 1]$ do not change. Hence the magnitude of the total change is at most $2/m + (m - 1)/m^2 \leq 3/m$. (For those who are familiar with McDiarmid's inequality [9], we remark that we do something similar for the vector $\hat{v}$, though it is much simpler since we are only looking for a bound in expectation and not with high probability.).

Define vector-valued random variables $V_1, V_2, \ldots, V_m \in \mathbb{R}^n$ to be,

$$V_i = V_i(x_1, y_1, \ldots, x_i, y_i) = \text{E}\left[\hat{v}|x_1, y_1, \ldots, x_i, y_i\right] - \text{E}\left[\hat{v}|x_1, y_1, \ldots, x_{i-1}, y_{i-1}\right].$$

Hence, we have

$$\hat{v} - v = \sum_{i=1}^{m} V_i(x_1, y_1, \ldots, x_i, y_i).$$

It is also not difficult to see that $\text{E}[V_i] = 0$ and even $\text{E}[V_i|x_1, y_1, \ldots, x_{i-1}, y_{i-1}] = 0$, and hence $\text{E}[V_i|V_j] = 0$ for $i > j$. Thus we also have $\text{E}[V_i \cdot V_j] = 0$ for $i \neq j$. Also, note that $\|V_i\| \leq 3/m$ since changing (or fixing) (x_i, y_i) changes $\hat{v}$ by a vector of magnitude at most $3/m$. Finally,

$$\text{E}\left[(\hat{v} - v)^2\right] = \text{E}\left[(V_1 + \ldots + V_m)^2\right] = \sum_i \text{E}\left[V_i^2\right] + 2\sum_{i>j} \text{E}[V_i \cdot V_j].$$

The above is $\leq m \left(\frac{3}{m}\right)^2 = \frac{9}{m}$. □

We can now prove Theorem 2.

Proof (of Theorem 2). The proof is straightforward given what we have shown already. We know by Lemma 2 that there is some vector $w \in B$ of covariance at least $\frac{4}{5L}\epsilon^2$. If every vector has true covariance within δ of its empirical covariance, then by outputting the vector of maximal empirical covariance, we achieve a true covariance $\geq \frac{4}{5L}\epsilon^2 - 2\delta$. By Lemma 3, we have $\text{E}[\delta] \leq \frac{3}{\sqrt{m}}$. By our choice of $m = 100L^2/\epsilon^4$, the expected true covariance is $\geq \frac{4}{5L}\epsilon^2 - 2(3\epsilon^2/10L) = \frac{1}{5L}\epsilon^2$. □

388   A.T. Kalai

3.1   Proof of Lemma 2

In order to prove Lemma 2, the following geometric lemma is helpful:

Lemma 4. *Suppose $f : B \to \mathbb{R}$ is an L-Lipschitz function, $w \in \mathbb{R}^n$, $\|w\| = 1$, $t \in \mathbb{R}$, and $\{x \in B \mid f(x) \le t\} = \{x \in B \mid w \cdot x \le \theta\}$. (a) If $\theta \ge 0$ then $|f(x) - t| \le L|w \cdot x - \theta|$ for all $x \in B$ such that $w \cdot x > \theta$. (b) If $\theta \le 0$ then $|f(x) - t| \le L|w \cdot x - \theta|$ for all $x \in B$ such that $w \cdot x < \theta$.*

In other words, we have a Lipschitz-bound on $f(x)$ based on the projection onto the vector w, but it only holds on side of the hyperplane $w \cdot x = \theta$ (the side that has the smaller intersection with the ball).

Proof. For any $x \in B$ such that $(w \cdot x - \theta)\theta \ge 0$ (note that this includes both cases $\theta \ge 0 \wedge w \cdot x - \theta > 0$ and $\theta < 0 \wedge w \cdot x - \theta < 0$), consider the point $x' = x - w(w \cdot x - \theta)$. Note that we have chosen x' so that $w \cdot x' = \theta$ and $x' \in B$. To see that $x' \in B$, notice that $\|w\| = 1$ implies,

$$\begin{aligned}
\|x\|^2 - \|x'\|^2 &= 2x \cdot w(w \cdot x - \theta) - w^2(w \cdot x - \theta)^2 \\
&= (w \cdot x - \theta) \cdot (2w \cdot x - (w \cdot x - \theta)) \\
&= (w \cdot x - \theta) \cdot (w \cdot x + \theta) \\
&= (w \cdot x - \theta)^2 + 2(w \cdot x - \theta)\theta \ge 0
\end{aligned}$$

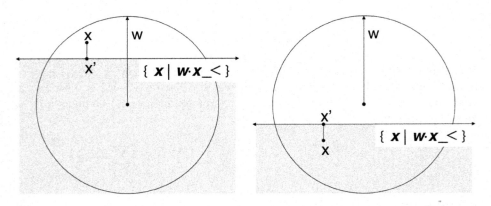

Fig. 2. On the left, we illustrate the case $\theta > 0$ and, on the right, $\theta < 0$. In either case, the lemma only applies to the part of the ball that has less than $1/2$ the volume. Not shown are the cases $\theta \ge 1$ ($\{x \in B | w \cdot x \le \theta\} = B$) and $\theta < -1$ ($\{x \in B | w \cdot x \le \theta\} = \emptyset$).

Hence $\|x'\| \le \|x\|$, so $x' \in B$. This is more easily seen geometrically from Figure 2. Now, using the Lipschitz property with the points x, x', we have

$$|f(x) - f(x')| \le L\|x - x'\| = L|w \cdot x - \theta|.$$

Case 1: $|\theta| \ge 1$. In this case, the lemma holds vacuously because there can be no point $x \in B$ meeting the conditions of the lemma. **Case 2:** $\theta \in (-1, 1)$. Since

$x \cdot w = \theta$, we have $f(x') \leq t$. On the other hand, the continuity of f and the fact that $\{x \in B | w \cdot x > \theta\} = \{x \in B | f(x) > t\}$ is non-empty implies that $f(x') = t$. This combined with the displayed equation above gives the lemma.   □

We also use the following probabilistic lemma. It states that the variance of a random variable can be broken into two parts, based on whether the variable is greater or smaller than its mean, and both parts can be lower-bounded with respect to the variance of the original variable.

Lemma 5. *Let $X \in [0,1]$ be a random variable with expectation μ and variance $V = \mathrm{E}\left[(X - \mu)^2\right]$. Then $\mathrm{E}\left[(X - \mu)^2 I(X > \mu)\right] \geq \frac{4}{5}V^2$ and similarly $\mathrm{E}\left[(X - \mu)^2 I(X < \mu)\right] \geq \frac{4}{5}V^2$.*

Here the indicator function $I(P) = 1$ if predicate P holds and 0, otherwise. The proof of this lemma is in the appendix.

Proof (of Lemma 2). Take $w \in \mathbb{R}^n$, $\theta \in \mathbb{R}$ such that $\{x \in B \mid f(x) \leq \mu_f\} = \{x \in B \mid w \cdot x \leq \theta\}$. WLOG we assume $\|w\| = 1$ (if $w = 0$ then $\mathrm{var}(f(x)) = 0$ and the lemma holds trivially). Note that $(f(x) - \mu_f)(w \cdot x - \theta) \geq 0$ for all x, be we would like to lower-bound the expectation of this quantity, i.e., $\mathrm{cov}(f(x), w \cdot x)$.
Case 1: $\theta \geq 0$. Lemma 5 implies that

$$\mathrm{E}[(f(x) - \mu_f)^2 I(w \cdot x > \theta)] \geq \frac{4}{5}\mathrm{var}^2(f).$$

However, whenever $I(w \cdot x > \theta) = 1$, we have $f(x) > \mu_f$ and $f(x) - \mu_f \leq L(w \cdot x - \theta)$. Hence, we have,

$$\begin{aligned}
\frac{4}{5}\mathrm{var}^2(f) &\leq \mathrm{E}[(f(x) - \mu_f)^2 I(w \cdot x > \theta)] \\
&\leq \mathrm{E}[(f(x) - \mu_f)L(w \cdot x - \theta)I(w \cdot x \geq \theta)] \\
&\leq \mathrm{E}[(f(x) - \mu_f)L(w \cdot x - \theta)] \\
&= \mathrm{cov}(f(x), w \cdot x)L.
\end{aligned}$$

The last equality holds by the definition of covariance and the fact that it remains unchanged under additive shifts, i.e., $\mathrm{cov}(A, B) = \mathrm{cov}(A, B + \theta)$ for any constant $\theta \in \mathbb{R}$. **Case 2:** $\theta \leq 0$. This follows in an entirely similar manner to case 1.   □

4   Learning Uphill Decision Trees

In this case $X = \{0,1\}^n$. Our algorithm here again uses boosting. The weak learner here is quite similar to the (strong) learner used by Kearns and Schapire for learning Probabilistic Decision Lists.

The following simple probabilistic lemma will be helpful.

Lemma 6. *Let $\mathcal{G}$ be a finite family of binary functions $g : X \to \{0,1\}$ and let $\mathcal{D}$ be an arbitrary probability distribution over $X \times [0,1]$. Then, for any $\epsilon > 0$*

1. Let dataset $\mathcal{Z} := \mathcal{Z}_m$.
2. Let $P := \emptyset, N := \emptyset$.
3. If there is an attribute $x[j]$ such that the number of examples in $\mathcal{Z}$ with $x[j] = 0$ is $\leq 6m^{7/8} \ln(n+3)$, then:
   (a) Let $P := P \cup \{j\}$.
   (b) Remove all examples from $\mathcal{Z}$ such that $x[j] = 0$.
   (c) Goto 3.
4. If there is an attribute $x[j]$ such that the number of examples in $\mathcal{Z}$ with $x[j] = 1$ is $\leq 6m^{7/8} \ln(n+3)$, then:
   (a) Let $N := N \cup \{j\}$.
   (b) Remove all examples from $\mathcal{Z}$ such that $x[j] = 1$.
   (c) Goto 3.
5. OUTPUT $h(x) := (x[j^*] = b^*) \bigwedge_{j \in P}(x[j] = 1) \bigwedge_{j \in N}(x[j] = 0)$ where $j^* \in [n], b^* \in \{0, 1\}$ are chosen to maximize $|\widehat{\mathrm{cov}}(h(x), y)|$ (over the original $\mathcal{Z}_m$).

Fig. 3. A weak learner for uphill decision trees

and $m \geq 1$, for a random dataset $\mathcal{Z}_m$ of m examples,

$$\Pr_{\mathcal{Z}_m \sim \mathcal{D}^m}\left[\max_{g \in \mathcal{G}} |\hat{\mu}_g - \mu_g| \geq \sqrt{\frac{\ln(2|\mathcal{G}|/\delta)}{2m}}\right] \leq \delta$$

$$\Pr_{\mathcal{Z}_m \sim \mathcal{D}^m}\left[\max_{g \in \mathcal{G}} |\widehat{\mathrm{cov}}(g(x), y) - \mathrm{cov}(g(x), y)| \geq \sqrt{\frac{2\ln(4|\mathcal{G}|/\delta)}{m}}\right] \leq \delta.$$

The proof of this lemma is in the appendix. The following lemma shows that the algorithm of Figure 3 is a weak learner for Uphill decision trees. This implies Result 2, through Lemma 1.

Lemma 7. For any $\epsilon > 0$ and distribution μ over $\{0, 1\}^n \times \{0, 1\}$ such var$(f(x)) \geq \epsilon$, given $m \geq (12n \ln(n+3)/\epsilon)^4$ examples, the algorithm of Figure 3 returns $h(x)$ such that,

$$E\left[|cov(h(x), y)|\right] \geq \frac{\epsilon^4}{250}.$$

The proof is available in the full version of the paper on the author's web page.

5   Conclusions and Future Work

We have introduced NHFs, a natural generalization of generalized linear models, halfspaces, and decision lists. We have given computationally and statistically efficient learning algorithms for two classes of real valued functions that are special cases of NHFs. Our algorithms are efficient in the sense that their runtime and sample complexity are polynomial in the sizes of the problems. In one case the size corresponds to the Lipschitz constant, analogous to a margin. In the second, discrete case, the size corresponds to the number of variables (interestingly with no dependence on the size of the tree).

Our algorithms and analyses are almost certainly not the best possible. It would be very interesting to improve on the present results. Also, it would be interesting to generalize the types of NHFs that one can learn. It seems like a difficult problem to remove the Lipschitz requirement for NHFs over a ball in n dimensions. It does not seem that one can easily generalize the techniques used by Blum et al. [1] for removing the margin constraint in learning halfspaces with random classification noise, which are another special case of NHFs.

Lastly, classification Boosting has received much attention in the machine learning community, and elegant characterizations are known about what is possible to learn theoretically via boosting. Real-valued boosting seems, at present, much more complex. It would be interesting to come up with simpler models and a deeper understanding of what is provably possible to learn using real-valued boosting.

References

1. Blum, A., Frieze, A., Kannan, R., Vempala, S.: A polynomial time algorithm for learning noisy linear threshold functions. Algorithmica 22(1/2), 35–52 (1997)
2. Hastie, T.J., Tibshirani, R.J.: Generalized Additive Models, London: Chapman and Hall (1990)
3. Kalai, A.: Learning Monotonic Linear Functions. Lecture Notes in Computer Science: Proceedings of the 17th Annual Conference on Learning Theory 3120, 487–501 (2004)
4. Kearns, M., Mansour, Y.: On the boosting ability of top-down decision tree learning algorithms. Journal of Computer and System Sciences 58, 109–128 (1999)
5. Kearns, M., Schapire, R.: Efficient distribution-free learning of probabilistic concepts. Journal of Computer and Systems Sciences 48, 464–497 (1994)
6. Kearns, M., Valiant, L.: Learning boolean formulae or finite automata is as hard as factoring. Technical Report TR-14-88, Harvard University Aiken Computation Laboratory (1988)
7. Mansour, Y., McAllester, D.: Boosting using branching programs. Journal of Computer and System Sciences 64, 103–112 (2002)
8. McCullagh, P., Nelder, J.: Generalized Linear Models, Chapman and Hall, London (1989)
9. McDiarmid, C.: On the method of bounded differences. In: J Siemons, (ed.), Surveys in Combinatorics. London Math Society (1989)
10. O'Donnell, R., Servedio, R.: Learning Monotone Decision Trees in Polynomial Time. In: Proceedings of the 21st Annual Conference on Computational Complexity (CCC), pp. 213–225 (2006)
11. Schapire, R.: The strength of weak learnability. Machine Learning 5, 197–227 (1990)

A   Additional Proofs

Proof (of Lemma 5). Let $p = \Pr[X \geq \mu]$ and $q = \Pr[X < \mu] = 1 - p$. Let $a = \mathrm{E}[X - \mu | X \geq \mu]$ and $b = \mathrm{E}[\mu - X | X < \mu]$. Since $\mu = \mathrm{E}[X]$, $pa = qb$. Finally, let $V_1 = \mathrm{E}[(X - \mu)^2 | X \geq \mu]$ and $V_2 = \mathrm{E}[(X - \mu)^2 | X < \mu]$ so $V = pV_1 + qV_2$. We assume $V \in (0, 1/4]$ (variance $V \leq 1/4$ for any random variable $X \in [0,1]$ and if $V = 0$ the lemma follows trivially) which implies that $0 < p, q, a, b, V_1, V_2 < 1$.

Since $\mathrm{E}[Y^2] \geq \mathrm{E}[Y]^2$ for any random variable Y, we have that that $V_1 \geq a^2$ (by letting $Y = X - \mu$ conditioned on $X \geq \mu$). We can upper-bound V_2 by noting,

$$V_2 = \mathrm{E}[(\mu - X)^2 | X < \mu] \leq \mathrm{E}[\mu - X | X < \mu] = b.$$

In the above we have used the fact that $x^2 \leq x$ for any real $x \in [0,1]$.

Now, since $V \leq 1/4$, in our notation it suffices to show the stronger inequality that $\mathrm{E}[(\mu - X)^2 | X > \mu] = pV_1 \geq V^2/(1+V)$ (the case $X < \mu$ follows by symmetry). In order to complete the lemma, it thus suffices to show that,

$$pV_1 \geq \frac{V^2}{1+V} \Leftrightarrow$$
$$pV_1 \geq (V - pV_1)V = qV_2(pV_1 + qV_2) \Leftrightarrow$$
$$pV_1 \geq \frac{(qV_2)^2}{1 - qV_2}$$

However, we have already shown that $V_1 \geq a^2$ and $V_2 \leq b$. This implies that $pV_1 \geq pa^2$ and $(qV_2)^2 \leq (qb)^2 = (pa)^2$. We also have $1 - qV_2 \geq 1 - qb \geq 1 - q = p$, using $b \in [0,1]$ since $X \in [0,1]$. Hence $(qV_2)^2/(1 - qV_2) \leq (pa)^2/p = pa^2 \leq pV_1$, which is what we needed for the last displayed equation. $\square$

Proof (of Lemma 6). For the first part of the lemma, we have by Hoeffding bounds that for any single g, $\Pr[|\hat{\mu}_g - \mu_g| \geq \epsilon] \leq 2e^{-2m\epsilon^2}$. By the union bound, this happens for any $g \in \mathcal{G}$ with probability $\leq 2e^{-2m\epsilon^2}|\mathcal{G}|$. For the stated value of ϵ in the first part of the theorem, this probability is $\leq \delta$.

The second part follows from the fact that, for any $g : X \to reals$,

$$|\widehat{\mathrm{cov}}(g(x), y) - \mathrm{cov}(g(x), y)| = \left| \frac{1}{m} \sum_{i=1}^{m} (y_i - \hat{\mu}_f)g(x_i) - \mathrm{E}[(y - \mu_f)g(x)] \right|.$$

The above is at most

$$\leq \left| \frac{1}{m} \sum_{i=1}^{m} (y_i - \mu_f)g(x_i) - \mathrm{E}[(y - \mu_f)g(x)] \right| + \left| \frac{1}{m} \sum_{i=1}^{m} (\mu_f - \hat{\mu}_f)g(x_i) \right|.$$

By Chernoff bounds, for any $g : X \to \{0, 1\}$, the probability that the term on the left is $\geq \epsilon/2$ is at most $2e^{-m\epsilon^2/2}$. Similarly, $\Pr[|\mu_f - \hat{\mu}_f| \geq \epsilon] \leq 2e^{-m\epsilon^2/2}$. (Note that $\frac{1}{m}|\sum(\mu_f - \hat{\mu}_f)g(x_i)| \leq |\mu_f - \hat{\mu}_f|$.) The probability any of these events happen for any $g \in \mathcal{G}$ or f is $\leq 2e^{-m\epsilon^2/2}(|\mathcal{G}| + 1) \leq 4e^{-m\epsilon^2/2}|\mathcal{G}|$, which is $\leq \delta$ for the value of ϵ used in the second part of the lemma. If none of these events happens, then we have that the left and right terms are at most $\epsilon/2$ for all $g \in \mathcal{G}$ and hence the empirical and true covariance differ by at most ϵ.

An Efficient Re-scaled Perceptron Algorithm for Conic Systems

Alexandre Belloni[1,2], Robert M. Freund[1], and Santosh S. Vempala[1,3]

[1] MIT
[2] IBM
[3] Georgia Tech
belloni@mit.edu, rfreund@mit.edu, vempala@cc.gatech.edu

Abstract. The classical perceptron algorithm is an elementary algorithm for solving a homogeneous linear inequality system $Ax > 0$, with many important applications in learning theory (e.g., [11,8]). A natural condition measure associated with this algorithm is the Euclidean width τ of the cone of feasible solutions, and the iteration complexity of the perceptron algorithm is bounded by $1/\tau^2$. Dunagan and Vempala [5] have developed a re-scaled version of the perceptron algorithm with an improved complexity of $O(n \ln(1/\tau))$ iterations (with high probability), which is theoretically efficient in τ, and in particular is polynomial-time in the bit-length model. We explore extensions of the concepts of these perceptron methods to the general homogeneous conic system $Ax \in \mathbf{int}\ K$ where K is a regular convex cone. We provide a conic extension of the re-scaled perceptron algorithm based on the notion of a *deep-separation oracle* of a cone, which essentially computes a certificate of strong separation. We give a general condition under which the re-scaled perceptron algorithm is theoretically efficient, i.e., polynomial-time; this includes the cases when K is the cross-product of half-spaces, second-order cones, and the positive semi-definite cone.

1 Introduction

We consider the problem of computing a solution of the following conic system

$$\begin{cases} Ax \in \mathbf{int}\ K \\ x \in X \end{cases} \tag{1}$$

where X and Y are n- and m-dimensional Euclidean subspaces, respectively, $A : X \to Y$ is a linear operator and $K \subset Y$ is a regular closed convex cone. We refer to this problem as the "conic inclusion" problem, we call K the *inclusion cone* and we call $\mathcal{F} := \{x \in X : Ax \in K\}$ the *feasibility cone*. The goal is to compute an interior element of the feasibility cone $\mathcal{F}$. Important special cases of this format include feasibility problem instances for linear programming (LP), second-order cone programming (SOCP) and positive semi-definite programming (SDP). These problems are often encountered in learning theory, e.g., to learn threshold functions and in support vector machines, to mention two well-known examples.

N. Bshouty and C. Gentile (Eds.): COLT 2007, LNAI 4539, pp. 393–408, 2007.

The ellipsoid method ([10]), the random walk method ([2]), and interior-point methods (IPMs) ([9], [12]) are examples of methods which solve (1) in polynomial-time. These methods differ substantially in their representation requirement as well as in their practical performance. For example, a membership oracle suffices for the ellipsoid method and the random walk method, while a special barrier function for K is required to implement an IPM. The latter is by far the most successful algorithm for conic programming in practice: for example, applications of SDP range over several fields including optimal control, eigenvalue optimization, combinatorial optimization and many others, see [18].

For the important special case of linear inequalities, when $X = \mathbb{R}^n$ and $K = \mathbb{R}^m_+$, an alternative method is the perceptron algorithm [17,13], developed primarily in learning theory. It is well-known that this simple method terminates after a finite number of iterations which can be bounded by the square of the inverse of the *width* τ of the feasibility cone $\mathcal{F}$. Although attractive due to its simplicity and its noise-tolerance [4,3], the perceptron algorithm is not considered theoretically efficient since the width τ can be exponentially small in the size of the instance in the bit-length model. Dunagan and Vempala ([5]) combined the perceptron algorithm with a sequence of re-scalings constructed from near-feasible solutions. These re-scalings gradually increase τ on average and the resulting re-scaled perceptron algorithm has complexity $O(n \ln(1/\tau))$ iterations (with high probability), which is theoretically efficient.

Here we extend the re-scaled perceptron algorithm proposed in [5] to the conic setting of (1). Although the probabilistic analysis is similar, this is not the case for the remainder of the analysis. In particular, we observe that the improvement obtained in [5] arises from a clever use of a *deep-separation oracle* (see Def. 3), which is stronger than the usual separation oracle used in the classical perceptron algorithm. In the case of a system of linear inequalities studied in [5], there is no difference between the implementation of both oracles. However, this difference is quite significant for more general cones.

We investigate, in detail, ways to construct a deep-separation oracle for several classes of cones, since it is the driving force of the re-scaled perceptron algorithm. We establish important properties of the deep-separation oracle and its implementation for several classes. Our main technical result is a general scheme that yields a polynomial-time deep-separation oracle using only a deep-separation oracle for the dual cone of K (which is readily available for many cones of interest such as the cone of positive semi-definite matrices). This implies that the re-scaled perceptron algorithm runs in polynomial time for any conic program, provided we have a suitable deep separation oracle. This captures the important cases of linear programs, second-order cone programs and semidefinite programs[1] and thus conveys the benefits of the perceptron algorithm to these problems.

We start in Section 2 with properties of convex cones, oracles, and the definition of a deep-separation oracle. Section 3 generalizes the classical perceptron

---

[1] There have been earlier attempts to extend the algorithm of [5], to SDPs in particular, but unfortunately these have turned out to be erroneous.

algorithm to the conic setting, and Section 4 extends the re-scaled perceptron algorithm of [5] to the conic setting. Section 5 contains the probabilistic and complexity analysis of the re-scaled perceptron algorithm, which reviews some material from [5] for completeness. Section 6 is devoted to methods for constructing a deep-separation oracle for both specific and general cones. We conclude the introduction with an informal discussion of the main ideas and technical difficulties encountered in obtaining our results.

The perceptron algorithm is a greedy procedure that updates the current proposed solution by using any violated inequality. The number of iterations is finite but can be exponential. The modified perceptron algorithm (proposed in [3], used in [5]) is a similar updating procedure that only uses inequalities that are violated by at least some fixed threshold. Although this procedure is not guaranteed to find a feasible solution, it finds a near-feasible solution with the guarantee that no constraint is violated by more than the threshold and the number of steps to convergence is proportional to the inverse square of the threshold, independent of the conditioning of the initial system. The key idea in [5] is that such a near-feasible solution can be used to improve the width of the original system by a multiplicative factor. As we show in this paper, this analysis extends naturally to the full generality of conic systems.

The main difficulty is in identifying a constraint that is violated by more than a fixed threshold by the current proposed solution, precisely what we call a deep-separation oracle. This is not an issue in the linear setting (one simply checks each constraint). For conic systems, the deep-separation itself is a conic feasibility problem! It has the form: find $w \in K^*$, the dual of the original inclusion cone, such that w satisfies a single second-order conic constraint. Our idea is to apply the re-scaled percepron algorithm to this system which is considerably simpler than $\mathcal{F}$. For many interesting inclusion cones, including the cone of positive semi-definite matrices, a suitable oracle is available.

2   Preliminaries

Let X and Y denote Euclidean spaces with finite dimension n and m, respectively. Denote by $\| \cdot \|$ their Euclidean norms, and $\langle \cdot, \cdot \rangle$ their Euclidean inner products. For $\bar{x} \in X$, $B(\bar{x}, r)$ will denote the ball centered at $\bar{x}$ with radius r, and analogously for Y. Let $A : X \to Y$ denote a linear operator, and $A^* : Y \to X$ denote the adjoint operator associated with A.

2.1   Convex Cones

Let C be a convex cone. The dual cone of C is defined as

$$C^* = \{d : \langle x, d \rangle \geq 0, \text{ for all } x \in C\} \tag{2}$$

and $\mathbf{ext}C$ denote the set of extreme rays of C. A cone is pointed if it contains no lines. We say that C is a *regular* cone if C is a pointed closed convex cone with non-empty interior. It is elementary to show that C is regular if and only if C^* is regular. Given a regular convex cone C, we use the following geometric (condition) measure:

Definition 1. *If C is a regular cone in X, the* width *of C is given by*

$$\tau_C \triangleq \max_{x,r} \left\{ \frac{r}{\|x\|} : B(x,r) \subset C \right\} .$$

Furthermore the center *of C is any vector $\bar{z}$ that attains the above maximum, normalized so that $\|\bar{z}\| = 1$.*

We will be particularly interested in the following three classes of cones: the non-negative orthant $\mathbb{R}_+^m := \{x \in \mathbb{R}^m : x \geq 0\}$, the second order cone denoted by $Q^n := \{x \in \mathbb{R}^n : \|(x_1, x_2, \ldots, x_{n-1})\| \leq x_n\}$, and the cone of positive semidefinite matrices $S_+^{p \times p} := \{X \in S^{p \times p} : \langle v, Xv \rangle \geq 0 \text{ for all } v \in \mathbb{R}^p\}$ where $S^{p \times p} := \{X \in \mathbb{R}^{p \times p} : X = X^T\}$. These three cones are self-dual and their widths are $1/\sqrt{m}$, $1/\sqrt{2}$, and $1/\sqrt{p}$, respectively.

The following characterization will be used in our analysis.

Lemma 1. *Let $\mathcal{G} = \{x : Mx \in C\}$ and Let $T = \{M^*\lambda : \lambda \in C^*\}$. Then $\mathcal{G}^* = \text{cl} (T)$.*

Proof. ($\subseteq$) Let $\lambda \in C^*$. Then for every x satisfying $Mx \in C$, $\langle x, M^*\lambda \rangle = \langle Mx, \lambda \rangle \geq 0$, since $Mx \in C$ and $\lambda \in C^*$. Thus, $\text{cl} (T) \subseteq \mathcal{G}^*$ since $\mathcal{G}^*$ is closed.

($\supseteq$) Assume that there exists $y \in \mathcal{G}^* \backslash \text{cl} (T)$. Thus there exists $h \neq 0$ satisfying $\langle h, y \rangle < 0$ and $\langle h, w \rangle \geq 0$ for all $w \in \text{cl} (T)$. Notice that $\langle h, M^*\lambda \rangle \geq 0$ for all $\lambda \in C^*$, which implies that $Mh \in C$ and so $h \in \mathcal{G}$. On the other hand, since $y \in \mathcal{G}^*$, it follows that $\langle h, y \rangle \geq 0$, contradicting $\langle h, y \rangle < 0$.

The question of sets of the form T being closed has been recently studied by Pataki [14]. Necessary and sufficient conditions for T to be a closed set are given in [14] when C^* belongs to a class called "nice cones," a class which includes polyhedra and self-scaled cones. Nonetheless, the set T may fail to be closed even in simple cases.

The following property of convex cones is well-known.

Lemma 2. *$B(z,r) \subseteq C$ if and only if $\langle d, z \rangle \geq r\|d\|$ for all $d \in C^*$.*

2.2   Oracles

In our algorithms and analysis we will distinguish two different types of oracles.

Definition 2. *An* interior separation oracle *for a convex set $S \subset \mathbb{R}^n$ is a subroutine that given a point $x \in \mathbb{R}^n$, identifies if $x \in \text{int } S$ or returns a vector $d \in \mathbb{R}^n$, $\|d\| = 1$, such that*

$$\langle d, x \rangle \leq \langle d, y \rangle \text{ for all } y \in S .$$

Definition 3. *For a fixed positive scalar t, a* deep-separation oracle *for a cone $C \subset \mathbb{R}^n$ is a subroutine that given a non-zero point $x \in \mathbb{R}^n$, either*

(I) correctly identifies that $\dfrac{\langle d, x \rangle}{\|d\|\|x\|} \geq -t$ for all $d \in \mathbf{ext}C^*$ or

(II) returns a vector $d \in C^*$, $\|d\| = 1$ satisfying $\dfrac{\langle d, x \rangle}{\|d\|\|x\|} \leq -t$.

Definition 2 is standard in the literature, whereas Definition 3 is new as far as we know. Our motivation for this definition arises from a relaxation of the orthogonality characterization of a convex cone. For $d, x \neq 0$ let $\cos(d, x)$ denote the cosine of the angle between d and x, i.e., $\cos(d, x) = \frac{\langle d, x \rangle}{\|d\|\|x\|}$. Notice that $x \in C$ if and only if $\cos(d, x) \geq 0$ for all $d \in C^*$ if and only if $\cos(d, x) \geq 0$ for all $d \in \mathbf{ext}C^*$. The latter characterization states that $\frac{\langle d, x \rangle}{\|d\|\|x\|} \geq 0$ for all $d \in \mathbf{ext}C^*$. Condition (I) of the deep-separation oracle relaxes the cosine condition from 0 to $-t$. The following example illustrates that the perceptron improvement algorithm described in [5] corresponds to a deep-separation oracle for a linear inequality system.

Example 1. Let $C = \{x \in \mathbb{R}^n : Mx \geq 0\}$ where M is an $m \times n$ matrix none of whose rows are zero. Notice that $C^* = \{M^*\lambda : \lambda \geq 0\}$ is the conic hull of the rows of M, and the extreme rays of C^* are a subset of the rows of M. Therefore a deep-separation oracle for C can be constructed by identifying for a given $x \neq 0$ if there is an index $i \in \{1, \ldots, m\}$ for which M_i (the ith-row of the matrix M) satisfies $\frac{\langle M_i, x \rangle}{\|M_i\|\|x\|} \leq -t$ and returning $M_i/\|M_i\|$ in such a case. Notice that we do not need to know which vectors M_i are extreme rays of C^*; if m is not excessively large it is sufficient to simply check the aforementioned inequality for every row index i.

3   Perceptron Algorithm for a Conic System

The classical perception algorithm was proposed to solve a homogeneous system of linear inequalities (1) with $K = \mathbb{R}^m_+$. It is well-known that the algorithm has finite termination in at most $\lfloor 1/\tau_{\mathcal{F}}^2 \rfloor$ iterations, see Rosenblatt 1962 [17]. This complexity bound can be exponential in the bit-model.

   Our starting point herein is to show that the classical perceptron algorithm can be easily extended to the case of a conic system of the form (1).

Perceptron Algorithm for a Conic System
(a) Let x be the origin in X. Repeat:
(b) If $Ax \in \mathbf{int} \, K$, Stop. Otherwise, call interior separation oracle for $\mathcal{F}$ at x, returning $d \in \mathcal{F}^*$, $\|d\| = 1$, such that $\langle d, x \rangle \leq 0$, and set $x \leftarrow x + d$.

This algorithm presupposes the availability of a separation oracle for the feasibility cone $\mathcal{F}$. In the typical case when the inclusion cone K has an interior separation oracle, this oracle can be used to construct an interior separation oracle for $\mathcal{F}$: if $x \notin \textbf{int } \mathcal{F}$, then $Ax \notin \textbf{int } K$ and there exists $\lambda \in K^*$ satisfying $\langle \lambda, Ax \rangle \leq 0$, whereby $d = A^*\lambda/\|A^*\lambda\|$ satisfies $\langle d, x \rangle \leq 0$, $d \in \mathcal{F}^*$, and $\|d\| = 1$.

Exactly as in the case of linear inequalities, we have the following guarantee. It's proof is identical, via the potential function $\pi(x) = \langle x, \bar{z} \rangle /\|x\|$.

Lemma 3. *The perceptron algorithm for a conic system will compute a solution of (1) in at most $\lfloor 1/\tau_{\mathcal{F}}^2 \rfloor$ iterations.*

4   Re-scaled Conic Perceptron Algorithm

In this section we construct a version of the perceptron algorithm whose complexity depends only logarithmically on $1/\tau_{\mathcal{F}}$. To accomplish this we will systematically re-scale the system (1) using a linear transformation related to a suitably constructed random vector that approximates the center $\bar{z}$ of $\mathcal{F}$. The linear transformation we use was first proposed in [5] for the case of linear inequality systems (i.e., $K = \mathbb{R}_+^m$). Here we extend these ideas to the conic setting. Table 1 contains a description of our algorithm, which is a structural extension of the algorithm in [5].

Note that the perceptron improvement phase requires a deep-separation oracle for $\mathcal{F}$ instead of the interior separation oracle for $\mathcal{F}$ as required by the perceptron algorithm. For the remainder of this section we presuppose that a deep-separation for $\mathcal{F}$ is indeed available. In Section 6 we will show that for most standard cones K a deep-separation oracle for $\mathcal{F}$ can be efficiently constructed.

We begin the analysis with the following lemma that quantifies the impact of the re-scaling (Step 6) on the width of the feasibility cone $\mathcal{F}$.

Lemma 4. *Let $\bar{z}$ denote the center of the feasibility cone $\mathcal{F}$, normalized so that $\|\bar{z}\| = 1$. Let A, $\hat{A}$ denote the linear operators and $\tau_{\mathcal{F}}$, $\tau_{\hat{\mathcal{F}}}$ denote the widths of the feasibility cones $\mathcal{F}$, $\hat{\mathcal{F}}$ of two consecutive iterations of the re-scaled perception algorithm. Then*

$$\tau_{\hat{\mathcal{F}}} \geq \frac{(1 - \sigma)}{\sqrt{1 + 3\sigma^2}\|\hat{z}\|}\tau_{\mathcal{F}}$$

where $\hat{z} = \bar{z} + \frac{1}{2}\left(\tau_{\mathcal{F}} - \left\langle \frac{x}{\|x\|}, \bar{z} \right\rangle\right)\frac{x}{\|x\|}$, and x is the output of the perceptron improvement phase.

Proof. At the end of the perception improvement phase, we have a vector x satisfying

$$\frac{\langle d, x \rangle}{\|d\|\|x\|} \geq -\sigma \text{ for all } d \in \textbf{ext}\mathcal{F}^*.$$

Table 1. One iteration of the re-scaled perceptron algorithm is one pass of **Steps 2-6**

Re-scaled Perceptron Algorithm for a Conic System

Step 1 Initialization. Set $B = I$ and $\sigma = 1/(32n)$.

Step 2 Perceptron Algorithm for a Conic System.
(a) Let x be the origin in X. Repeat at most $\lfloor (1/\sigma^2) \rfloor$ times:
   (b) If $Ax \in \operatorname{int} K$, Stop. Otherwise, call interior separation oracle for $\mathcal{F}$ at x,
     returning $d \in \mathcal{F}^*$, $\|d\| = 1$, such that $\langle d, x \rangle \leq 0$, and set $x \leftarrow x + d$.

Step 3 Stopping Criteria. If $Ax \in \operatorname{int} K$ then output Bx and **Stop**.

Step 4 Perceptron Improvement Phase.
(a) Let x be a random unit vector in X. Repeat at most $\lfloor (1/\sigma^2) \ln(n) \rfloor$ times:
   (b) Call deep-separation oracle for $\mathcal{F}$ at x with $t = \sigma$.
     If $\langle d, x \rangle \geq -\sigma \|d\|\|x\|$ for all $d \in \operatorname{ext}\mathcal{F}^*$ (condition I), End Step 4.
     Otherwise, oracle returns $d \in \mathcal{F}^*$, $\|d\| = 1$, such that $\langle d, x \rangle \leq -\sigma \|d\|\|x\|$
     (condition II), and set $x \leftarrow x - \langle d, x \rangle d$.
     If $x = 0$ restart at (a).
(c) Call deep-separation oracle for $\mathcal{F}$ at x with $t = \sigma$.
   If oracle returns condition (II), restart at (a).

Step 5 Stopping Criteria. If $Ax \in \operatorname{int} K$ then output Bx and **Stop**.

Step 6 Re-scaling. $A \leftarrow A \circ \left(I + \dfrac{xx^T}{\langle x, x \rangle} \right)$, $B \leftarrow B \circ \left(I + \dfrac{xx^T}{\langle x, x \rangle} \right)$,
   and Goto **Step 2**.

Let $\bar{x} = x/\|x\|$. Then $\langle d, \bar{x} \rangle \geq -\sigma \|d\|$ for all $d \in \operatorname{ext}\mathcal{F}^*$. From Lemma 2, it holds that

$$\frac{\langle d, \bar{z} \rangle}{\|d\|\|\bar{z}\|} = \frac{\langle d, \bar{z} \rangle}{\|d\|} \geq \tau_{\mathcal{F}} \quad \text{for all } d \in \mathcal{F}^*,$$

i.e. $\langle d, \bar{z} \rangle \geq \tau_{\mathcal{F}} \|d\|$ for all $d \in \mathcal{F}^*$.

From Lemma 1 it therefore holds that

$$\langle \lambda, A\bar{z} \rangle = \langle A^*\lambda, \bar{z} \rangle \geq \tau_{\mathcal{F}} \|A^*\lambda\| \quad \text{for all } \lambda \in K^*.$$

Note that $\hat{z} = \bar{z} + \frac{1}{2}(\tau_{\mathcal{F}} - \langle \bar{x}, \bar{z} \rangle)\bar{x}$, and let $\hat{\tau} := \frac{(1-\sigma)}{\sqrt{1+3\sigma^2}} \tau_{\mathcal{F}}$. We want to show that

$$\langle v, \hat{z} \rangle \geq \hat{\tau} \|v\| \quad \text{for all } v \in \operatorname{ext}\mathcal{F}^*. \tag{3}$$

If (3) is true, then by convexity of the function $f(v) = \hat{\tau}\|v\| - \langle v, \hat{z} \rangle$ it will also be true that $\langle v, \hat{z} \rangle \geq \hat{\tau}\|v\|$ for any $v \in \mathcal{F}^*$. Then from Lemma 2 it would follow that $B(\hat{z}, \hat{\tau}) \subset \mathcal{F}$, whereby $\tau_{\hat{\mathcal{F}}} \geq \frac{\hat{\tau}}{\|\hat{z}\|}$ as desired.

Let v be an extreme ray of $\mathcal{F}^*$. Using Lemma 1, there exist a sequence $\{\lambda^i\}_{i\geq1}$, $\lambda^i \in K^*$, $A^*\lambda^i \to v$ as $i \to \infty$. Since (3) is trivially true for $v = 0$, we can assume that $v \neq 0$ and hence $A^*\lambda^i \neq 0$ for i large enough. Next note that

$$\|\hat{A}^*\lambda^i\|^2 = \|A^*\lambda^i\|^2 + 2\left\langle A^*\lambda^i, \bar{x}\right\rangle^2 + \langle \bar{x}, \bar{x}\rangle \left\langle A^*\lambda^i, \bar{x}\right\rangle^2$$
$$= \|A^*\lambda^i\|^2 \left(1 + 3\left(\frac{\langle A^*\lambda^i, \bar{x}\rangle}{\|A^*\lambda^i\|}\right)^2\right)$$

and $\left\langle \hat{A}^*\lambda^i, \hat{z}\right\rangle = \left\langle A^*\lambda^i, \hat{z}\right\rangle + \langle \bar{x}, \hat{z}\rangle \left\langle A^*\lambda^i, \bar{x}\right\rangle$
$$= \left\langle A^*\lambda^i, \bar{z}\right\rangle + (\tau_{\mathcal{F}} - \langle \bar{x}, \bar{z}\rangle)\left\langle A^*\lambda^i, \bar{x}\right\rangle + \langle \bar{x}, \bar{z}\rangle \left\langle A^*\lambda^i, \bar{x}\right\rangle$$
$$\geq \tau_{\mathcal{F}}\|A^*\lambda^i\| + \tau_{\mathcal{F}}\left\langle A^*\lambda^i, \bar{x}\right\rangle \qquad (4)$$
$$= \tau_{\mathcal{F}}\left(1 + \frac{\langle A^*\lambda^i, \bar{x}\rangle}{\|A^*\lambda^i\|}\right)\|A^*\lambda^i\|.$$

Therefore $\dfrac{\left\langle \hat{A}^*\lambda^i, \hat{z}\right\rangle}{\|\hat{A}^*\lambda^i\|} \geq \tau_{\mathcal{F}}\dfrac{1 + t_i}{\sqrt{1 + 3t_i^2}}$ where $t_i = \dfrac{\langle A^*\lambda^i, \bar{x}\rangle}{\|A^*\lambda^i\|}$. Note that $t_i \leq 1$ and $\langle v, \bar{x}\rangle \geq -\sigma\|v\|$ since $v \in \mathbf{ext}\mathcal{F}^*$, and so $\dfrac{\langle v, \bar{x}\rangle}{\|v\|} \geq -\sigma$. By continuity, for any $\varepsilon > 0$ it holds that $t_i \geq -\sigma - \varepsilon$ for i sufficiently large. Thus, $t_i \in [-\sigma - \varepsilon, 1]$ for i large enough.

For $t \in [0, 1]$, we have $\frac{1+t}{\sqrt{1+3t^2}} \geq \frac{1+t}{\sqrt{1+2t+t^2}} = 1$, and for $t \in [-\sigma - \varepsilon, 0]$, the function $g(t) = \frac{1+t}{\sqrt{1+3t^2}} \geq \frac{1-\sigma-\varepsilon}{\sqrt{1+3(\sigma+\varepsilon)^2}}$ since $\frac{dg(t)}{dt} = \frac{1-3t}{(1+3t^2)^{3/2}} \geq 0$ for $t \in [-\sigma - \varepsilon, 0]$, that is, $g(t)$ is increasing on $[-\sigma - \varepsilon, 0]$. Therefore, for i large enough we have

$$\frac{\left\langle \hat{A}\lambda^i, \hat{z}\right\rangle}{\|\hat{A}^*\lambda^i\|} \geq \tau_{\mathcal{F}}\frac{(1-\sigma-\varepsilon)}{\sqrt{1+3(\sigma+\varepsilon)^2}}.$$

Passing to the limit as $\lambda^i \to v$ obtain

$$\frac{\langle v, \hat{z}\rangle}{\|v\|} \geq \tau_{\mathcal{F}}\frac{(1-\sigma-\varepsilon)}{\sqrt{1+3(\sigma+\varepsilon)^2}} \quad \text{whereby} \quad \frac{\langle v, \hat{z}\rangle}{\|v\|} \geq \tau_{\mathcal{F}}\frac{(1-\sigma)}{\sqrt{1+3\sigma^2}} = \hat{\tau}.$$

5 Probabilistic Analysis

As mentioned before, the probabilistic analysis of our conic framework is similar to the analysis with linear inequalities in [5]. We state the main lemmas of the analysis without proof. Our exposition intentionally separates the probabilistic analysis from the remaining sections.

The first lemma of this section was established in [3] for the case of linear inequalities, and here is generalized to the conic framework. Roughly speaking, it shows that the perceptron improvement phase generates near-feasible solutions if started at a good initial point, which happens with at least a fixed probability $p = 1/8$.

Lemma 5. *Let z be a feasible solution of (1) of unit norm. With probability at least $\frac{1}{8}$, the perception improvement phase returns a vector x satisfying:*

(i) $\langle d, x \rangle \geq -\sigma\|x\|$ *for every* $d \in \text{ext}\mathcal{F}^*$, $\|d\| = 1$, *and*
(ii) $\langle z, x/\|x\| \rangle \geq \frac{1}{\sqrt{n}}$.

Lemma 5 establishes that points obtained after the perceptron improvement phase are near-feasible for the current conic system. The next lemma clarifies the implications of using these near-feasible points to re-scale the conic system.

Lemma 6. *Suppose that $n \geq 2$, $\tau_\mathcal{F}, \sigma \leq 1/32n$ and A is the linear operator of the current iteration. Let $\hat{A}$ be the linear operator obtained after one iteration of the perceptron improvement phase. Let $\tau_{\hat{\mathcal{F}}}$ denote the width of the cone of feasible solutions $\hat{\mathcal{F}}$ of the updated conic system associated with $\hat{A}$. Then*

(i) $\tau_{\hat{\mathcal{F}}} \geq \left(1 - \dfrac{1}{32n} - \dfrac{1}{512n^2} \right) \tau_\mathcal{F}$;

(ii) *With probability at least $\frac{1}{8}$,* $\tau_{\hat{\mathcal{F}}} \geq \left(1 + \dfrac{1}{3.02n} \right) \tau_\mathcal{F}$.

Finally, the following theorem bounds the number of overall iterations and the number of oracle calls made by the algorithm.

Theorem 1. *Suppose that $n \geq 2$. If (1) has a solution, the re-scaled perceptron algorithm will compute a solution in at most*

$$T = \max\left\{ 4096 \ln\left(\frac{1}{\delta}\right), 139n \ln\left(\frac{1}{32n\tau_\mathcal{F}}\right) \right\} = O\left(n \ln\left(\frac{1}{\tau_\mathcal{F}}\right) + \ln\left(\frac{1}{\delta}\right) \right)$$

iterations, with probability at least $1 - \delta$. Moreover, the algorithm makes at most $O(T\, n^2 \, \ln(n))$ calls of a deep-separation oracle for $\mathcal{F}$ and at most $O(T\, n^2)$ calls of a separation oracle for $\mathcal{F}$ with probability at least $1 - \delta$.

It will useful to amend Definition 3 of the deep-separation oracle as follows:

Definition 4. *For a fixed positive scalar σ, a* half-deep-separation oracle *for a cone $C \subset \mathbb{R}^n$ is a subroutine that given a non-zero point $x \in \mathbb{R}^n$, either*

(I) *correctly identifies that* $\dfrac{\langle d, x \rangle}{\|d\|\|x\|} \geq -\sigma$ *for all* $d \in \text{ext}C^*$ *or*

(II) *returns a vector* $d \in C^*$, $\|d\| = 1$ *satisfying* $\dfrac{\langle d, x \rangle}{\|d\|\|x\|} \leq -\sigma/2$.

Remark 1. Definition 4 only differs from Definition 3 in the inequality in condition (II), where now $\sigma/2$ is used instead of σ. This minor change only affects the iteration bound in Step 4 of the re-scaled perceptron algorithm, which needs to be changed to $\lfloor (4/\sigma^2) \ln(n) \rfloor$; all other analysis in this Section remains valid.

6 Deep-Separation Oracles

The re-scaled perceptron algorithm needs a deep-separation oracle for the feasibility cone $\mathcal{F}$. Herein we show that such a deep-separation oracle is fairly easy to construct when (1) has the format:

$$\begin{cases} A_L x \in \text{int } \mathbb{R}^m_+ \\ A_i x \in \text{int } Q^{n_i} \quad i = 1, \ldots, q \\ x_s \in \text{int } S^{p \times p}_+ , \end{cases} \tag{5}$$

where x is composed as the cartesian product $x = (x_s, x_p)$. Note that (5) is an instance of (1) for $K = \mathbb{R}^m_+ \times Q^{n_1} \times \cdots \times Q^{n_q} \times S^{p \times p}_+$ and the only special structure on A is that the semi-definite inclusion is of the simple format "$I x_s \in S^{p \times p}_+$." In Section 6.4 we show how to construct a deep-separation oracle for more general problems that also include the semi-definite inclusion "$A_s x \in S^{p \times p}_+$," but this construction takes more work.

The starting point of our analysis is a simple observation about intersections of feasibility cones. Suppose we have available deep-separation oracles for each of the feasibility cones $\mathcal{F}_1$ and $\mathcal{F}_2$ of instances:

$$\begin{cases} A_1 x \in \text{int } K_1 \\ x \in X \end{cases} \quad \text{and} \quad \begin{cases} A_2 x \in \text{int } K_2 \\ x \in X \end{cases} \tag{6}$$

and consider the problem of finding a point that simultaneously satisfies both conic inclusions:

$$\begin{cases} A_1 x \in \text{int } K_1 \\ A_2 x \in \text{int } K_2 \\ x \in X . \end{cases} \tag{7}$$

Let $\mathcal{F} = \{x : A_1 x \in K_1, A_2 x \in K_2\} = \{x : Ax \in K\}$ where $K = K_1 \times K_2$ and A is defined analogously. Then $\mathcal{F} = \mathcal{F}_1 \cap \mathcal{F}_2$ where $\mathcal{F}_i = \{x : A_i x \in K_i\}$ for $i = 1, 2$. It follows from the calculus of convex cones that $\mathcal{F}^* = \mathcal{F}_1^* + \mathcal{F}_2^*$, and therefore

$$\text{ext}\mathcal{F}^* \subset (\text{ext}\mathcal{F}_1^* \cup \text{ext}\mathcal{F}_2^*) . \tag{8}$$

This observation leads to an easy construction of a deep-separation oracle for $\mathcal{F}_1 \cap \mathcal{F}_2$ if one has available deep-separation oracles for $\mathcal{F}_1$ and $\mathcal{F}_2$:

Deep-separation Oracle for $\mathcal{F}_1 \cap \mathcal{F}_2$
Given: scalar $t > 0$ and $x \neq 0$, call deep-separation oracles for $\mathcal{F}_1$ and $\mathcal{F}_2$ at x.
   If both oracles report Condition I, return Condition I.
   Otherwise at least one oracle reports Condition II and provides
   $d \in \mathcal{F}_i^* \subset \mathcal{F}^*$, $\|d\| = 1$, such that $\langle d, x \rangle \leq -t\|d\|\|x\|$; return d and Stop.

Remark 2. If deep-separation oracles for $\mathcal{F}_i$ are available and their efficiency is $O(T_i)$ operations for $i = 1, 2$, then the deep-separation oracle for $\mathcal{F}_1 \cap \mathcal{F}_2$ given above is valid and its efficiency is $O(T_1 + T_2)$ operations.

Utilizing Remark 2, in order to construct a deep-separation oracle for the feasibility cone of (5) it will suffice to construct deep-separation oracles for each of the conic inclusions therein, which is what we now examine.

6.1   Deep-Separation Oracle for $\mathcal{F}$ When $K = \mathbb{R}^m_+$

We consider $\mathcal{F} = \{x : Ax \in \mathbb{R}^m_+\}$. Example 1 has already described a deep-separation oracle for $\mathcal{F}$ when the inclusion cone is $\mathbb{R}^m_+$. It is easy to see that this oracle can be implemented in $O(mn)$ operations.

6.2   Deep-Separation Oracle for $\mathcal{F}$ When $K = Q^k$

In this section we develop the deep-separation oracle for the second-order cone case which allows this method to be used to solve support vector machines problems. For convenience we amend our notation so that $\mathcal{F} = \{x : \|Mx\| \leq g^T x\}$ for a given real $(k-1) \times n$ matrix M and a real n-vector g, so that $\mathcal{F} = \{x : Ax \in Q^k\}$ where the linear operator A is specified by $Ax := \begin{bmatrix} Mx \\ g^T x \end{bmatrix}$.

We will construct an efficient half-deep-separation oracle (Definition 4) by considering the following optimization problem:

$$t^* \quad := \quad \min_d d^T x$$

$$\text{s.t. } \|d\| = 1 \tag{9}$$
$$d \in \mathcal{F}^* \ .$$

If $x \in \mathcal{F}$, then $t^* \geq 0$ and clearly condition I of Definition 4 is satisfied. If $x \notin \mathcal{F}$, then $t^* < 0$ and we can replace the equality constraint in (9) with an inequality constraint. We obtain the following primal/dual pair of convex problems with common optimal objective function value t^*:

$$t^* := \min_d x^T d \qquad = \qquad \max_y -\|y - x\|$$

$$\begin{array}{ll} \text{s.t. } \|d\| \leq 1 & \quad \text{s.t. } y \in \mathcal{F} \\ d \in \mathcal{F}^* & \end{array} \tag{10}$$

Now consider the following half-deep-separation oracle for $\mathcal{F}$ when $K = Q^k$.

Half-Deep-Separation Oracle for $\mathcal{F}$
when $K = Q^k$, for $x \neq 0$ and relaxation parameter $\sigma > 0$
If $\|Mx\| \leq g^T x$, return Condition I, and Stop.
Solve (10) for feasible primal and dual solutions $\bar{d}, \bar{y}$ with duality gap $\bar{g}$
satisfying $\bar{g}/\|x\| \leq \sigma/2$
 If $x^T \bar{d}/\|x\| \geq -\sigma/2$, report Condition (I), and Stop.
 If $x^T \bar{d}/\|x\| \leq -\sigma/2$, then return $d = \bar{d}$, report Condition (II), and Stop.

To see the validity of this method, note that if $\|Mx\| \leq g^T x$, then $x \in \mathcal{F}$ and clearly Condition (I) of Definition 4 is satisfied. Next, suppose that $x^T \bar{d}/\|x\| \geq$

404   A. Belloni, R.M. Freund, and S.S. Vempala

$-\sigma/2$, then $t^* \geq -\|\bar{y} - x\| = x^T \bar{d} - \bar{g} \geq -\|x\|\sigma/2 - \|x\|\sigma/2 = -\|x\|\sigma$. Therefore $\frac{x^T d}{\|x\|\|d\|} \geq -\sigma$ for all $d \in \mathcal{F}^*$, and it follows that Condition (I) of Definition 4 is satisfied. Finally, if $x^T \bar{d}/\|x\| \leq -\sigma/2$, then $\frac{\bar{d}^T x}{\|\bar{d}\|\|x\|} \leq -\sigma/2$ and $\bar{d} \in \mathcal{F}^*$, whereby Condition (II) of Definition 4 is satisfied using $\bar{d}$.

The computational efficiency of this deep-separation oracle depends on the ability to efficiently solve (10) for feasible primal/dual solutions with duality gap $\bar{g} \leq \sigma\|x\|/2$. For the case when $K = Q^k$, it is shown in [1] that (10) can be solved very efficiently to this desired duality gap, namely in $O(n^3 + n \ln \ln(1/\sigma) + n \ln \ln(1/\min\{\tau_\mathcal{F}, \tau_{\mathcal{F}^*}\}))$ operations in practice, using a combination of Newton's method and binary search. Using $\sigma = 1/(32n)$ this is $O(n^3 + n \ln \ln(1/\min\{\tau_\mathcal{F}, \tau_{\mathcal{F}^*}\}))$ operations for the relaxation parameter σ needed by the re-scaled perceptron algorithm.

6.3   Deep-Separation Oracle for $S_+^{p \times p}$

Let $C = S_+^{p \times p}$, and for convenience we alter our notation herein so that $X \in S^{p \times p}$ is a point under consideration. A deep-separation oracle for C at $X \neq 0$ for the scalar $t > 0$ is constructed by simply checking the condition "$X + t\|X\|I \succeq 0$." If $X + t\|X\|I \succeq 0$, then condition I of the deep-separation oracle is satisfied. This is true because the extreme rays of C are the collection of rank-1 matrices vv^T, and

$$\frac{\langle vv^T, X \rangle}{\|X\|\|vv^T\|} = \frac{v^T X v}{\|X\|\|vv^T\|} \geq \frac{-t\|X\|v^T v}{\|X\|\|vv^T\|} = -t$$

for any $v \neq 0$. On the other hand, if $X + t\|X\|I \nsucceq 0$, then compute any nonzero v satisfying $v^T X v + t\|X\|v^T v \leq 0$, and return $D = vv^T/v^T v$, which will satisfy

$$\frac{\langle D, X \rangle}{\|X\|\|D\|} = \frac{v^T X v}{\|X\|v^T v} \leq -t \ ,$$

thus satisfying condition II. Notice that the work per oracle call is simply to check the eigenvalue condition $X \succeq -t\|X\|I$ and possibly to compute an appropriate vector v, which is typically $O(p^3)$ operations in practice.

6.4   Deep-Separation Oracle for $\mathcal{F}$ When $K = S_+^{p \times p}$

We know from the results in Section 6.3 and the self-duality of $S_+^{p \times p}$ ($(S_+^{p \times p})^* = S_+^{p \times p}$) that K^* has an efficiently computable maximum violation separation oracle when $K = S_+^{p \times p}$. Furthermore, we have $\tau_K = \tau_{K^*} = 1/\sqrt{p}$.

The complexity analysis that we develop in this subsection uses the data-perturbation condition measure model of Renegar [15], which we now briefly review. Considering (1) as a system with fixed cone K and fixed spaces X and Y, let $\mathcal{M}$ denote those operators $A : X \to Y$ for which (1) has a solution. For $A \in \mathcal{M}$, let $\rho(A)$ denote the "distance to infeasibility" for (1), namely:

$$\rho(A) := \min_{\Delta A} \{\|\Delta A\| : A + \Delta A \notin \mathcal{M}\} \ .$$

Then $\rho(A)$ denotes the smallest perturbation of our given operator A which would render the system (1) infeasible. Next let $\mathcal{C}(A)$ denote the *condition measure* of (1), namely $\mathcal{C}(A) = \|A\|/\rho(A)$, which is a scale-invariant reciprocal of the distance to infeasibility. $\ln(\mathcal{C}(A))$ is tied to the complexity of interior-point methods and the ellipsoid method for computing a solution of (1), see [16] and [6].

Given the inclusion cone $K = S_+^{p \times p}$, the feasibility cone for (1) is $\mathcal{F} = \{x : Ax \in K\}$. Given the relaxation parameter $t > 0$ and a non-zero vector $x \in \mathbb{R}^n$, consider the following conic feasibility system in the variable d:

$$(S_{t,x}) : \quad \begin{cases} \frac{\langle x,d \rangle}{\|x\|\|d\|} < -t \\ \\ d \in \mathcal{F}^* \end{cases} \tag{11}$$

It follows from Definition 3 that if d is feasible for $(S_{t,x})$, then Condition II of Definition 3 is satisfied; however, if $(S_{t,x})$ has no solution, then Condition I is satisfied. Utilizing Lemma 1 and rearranging terms yields the equivalent system in variables w:

$$(S_{t,x}) : \quad \begin{cases} t\|x\|\|A^*w\| + \langle w, Ax \rangle < 0 \\ \\ w \in \operatorname{int} K^* \end{cases} \tag{12}$$

Note that if $\tilde{w}$ solves (12), then $\tilde{d} = A^*\tilde{w}$ solves (11) from Lemma 1. This leads to the following approach to constructing a deep-separation oracle for $\mathcal{F}$:

> given $x \neq 0$ and $t := \sigma$, compute a solution $\tilde{w}$ of (12) or certify that no solution exists. If (12) has no solution, report Condition I and Stop; otherwise (12) has a solution $\tilde{w}$, return $d := A^*\tilde{w}/\|A^*\tilde{w}\|$, report Condition II, and Stop.

In order to implement this deep-separation oracle we need to be able to compute a solution $\tilde{w}$ of (12) if such a solution exists, or be able to provide a certificate of infeasibility of (12) if no solution exists. Now notice that (12) is a homogeneous conic feasibility problem of the form (5), as it is comprised of a single second-order cone inclusion constraint ($Mw := (t\|x\|A^*w, \langle w, -Ax \rangle) \in Q^{n+1}$) plus a constraint that the variable w must lie in K^*. This suggests that we attempt to solve (12) itself using the re-scaled perceptron algorithm. Using this strategy, let $\bar{w}_1, \bar{w}_2, \ldots, \bar{w}_{k+1}$ denote the sequence of normalized ($\|\bar{w}_i\| = 1$) output vectors w at the end of Step 4 of Table 1, yielding the re-scaling matrices $B_0 = I, B_1, B_2, \ldots, B_k$, where $B_i = (I + \bar{w}_1\bar{w}_1') \circ (I + \bar{w}_2\bar{w}_2') \circ \cdots \circ (I + \bar{w}_i\bar{w}_i')$. After the kth update the current system is:

$$(S_{t,x}) : \quad \begin{cases} MB_kw \in Q^{n+1} \\ \\ B_kw \in \operatorname{int} K^* \end{cases} \tag{13}$$

In the case when (12) (and hence (13)) has a solution, we develop a slight modification of the re-scaled perceptron algorithm for solving (13) in Section

6.5. However, in the case when (12) does not have a solution, it will be necessary to develop a means to certify this infeasibility. To do so, we first analyze its feasibility cone, denoted as $\tilde{\mathcal{F}}_{(t,x)} := \{w : t\|x\|\|A^*w\| + \langle w, Ax\rangle \le 0, \ w \in K^*\}$. We have:

Proposition 1. *For a given $\sigma \in (0, 1/2)$ and $x \ne 0$, suppose that $S_{(\sigma,x)}$ has a solution and let $t \in (0, \sigma)$. Then*

$$\tau_{\tilde{\mathcal{F}}_{(t,x)}} \ge \frac{\tau_{K^*}(\sigma - t)}{3\mathcal{C}(A)} \ .$$

Now consider the following half-deep-separation oracle for $\mathcal{F}$ (recall Definition 4) which takes as input an estimate L of $\mathcal{C}(A)$:

Probabilistic Half-deep-separation Oracle for $\mathcal{F}$, for $x \ne 0$, relaxation parameter σ, failure probability δ, and estimate L
Set $t := \sigma/2$, and run the re-scaled perceptron algorithm to compute a solution $\tilde{w}$ of (12) for at most $\hat{T} := \max\left\{4096 \ln\left(\frac{1}{\delta}\right), 139n \ln\left(\frac{6L}{\tau_{K^*}}\right)\right\}$ iterations.
   If a solution $\tilde{w}$ of (12) is computed, return $d := A^*\tilde{w}/\|A^*\tilde{w}\|$,
      report Condition II, and Stop.
   If no solution is computed within $\hat{T}$ iterations, report
      "either Condition I is satisfied, or $L < \mathcal{C}(A)$," and Stop.

The following states the correctness of the above oracle:

Theorem 2. *Using the iteration count $\hat{T}$ above, with probability at least $1 - \delta$ the output of the probabilistic oracle is correct.*

We note that the above-outlined method for constructing a deep-separation oracle is inelegant in many respects. Nevertheless, it is theoretically efficient, i.e., it is polynomial-time in n, $\ln(1/\tau_{K^*})$, $\ln(L)$, and $\ln(1/\delta)$. It is an interesting and open question whether, in the case of $K = S_+^{p \times p}$, a more straightforward and more efficient deep-separation oracle for $\mathcal{F}$ can be constructed.

Finally, it follows from Theorem 7 of [7] that the width of $\mathcal{F}$ can be lower-bounded by Renegar's condition measure:

$$\tau_{\mathcal{F}} \ge \frac{\tau_K}{\mathcal{C}(A)} \ . \tag{14}$$

This can be used in combination with binary search (for bounding $\mathcal{C}(A)$) and the half-deep-separation oracle above to produce a complexity bound for computing a solution of (1) in time polynomial in n, $\ln(\mathcal{C}(A))$, $\ln(1/\delta)$, $\ln(1/\tau_K)$, and $\ln(1/\tau_{K^*})$.

6.5 Solving (13) Via a Modified Re-scaled Perceptron Algorithm

Herein we show how the re-scaled perceptron algorithm can be slightly modified to efficiently solve (13) when a solution exists. To motivate our approach, let $\bar{w}_1, \bar{w}_2, \ldots, \bar{w}_{k+1}$ denote the sequence of normalized $(\|\bar{w}_i\| = 1)$ output vectors w at the end of Step 4 of Table 1, yielding the re-scaling matrices $B_0 = I, B_1, B_2, \ldots, B_k$, where $B_i = (I + \bar{w}_1 \bar{w}_1') \circ (I + \bar{w}_2 \bar{w}_2') \circ \cdots \circ (I + \bar{w}_i \bar{w}_i')$, $i = 1, \ldots, k$. Here $\bar{w}_{k+1}$ is the output based on the re-scaling matrix B_k. From the perceptron improvement phase, we have no guarantee that $B_k \bar{w}_{k+1} \in K^*$. However, if such is the case, we have the following result which will be useful algorithmically:

Lemma 7. *Suppose that K is self-dual, and that $B_i \bar{w}_{i+1} \in K^*$ and $\|\bar{w}_i\| = 1$ for $i = 0, \ldots, k$. Then $B_i B_i^* d \in K^*$ for all $d \in K$ and $i = 0, \ldots, k+1$.*

Proof. We proceed by induction on i. Since $B_0 = B_0^* = I$ the statement trivially holds for $i = 0$ due to the self-duality of K. Next assume it holds for an arbitrary $i \leq k$. Therefore we have

$$B_{i+1} B_{i+1}^* d = B_i (I + \bar{w}_{i+1} \bar{w}_{i+1}')(I + \bar{w}_{i+1} \bar{w}_{i+1}') B_i^* d$$
$$= B_i B_i^* d + 3 B_i \bar{w}_{i+1} \bar{w}_{i+1}' B_i^* d \in K^*$$

by the induction assumption and the hypothesis that $B_i \bar{w}_{i+1} \in K^*$.

In order to take advantage of Lemma 7, we now show how to modify the perceptron improvement methodology of Step 4 of Table 1 to guarantee that $B_i \bar{w}_{i+1} \in K^*$ for all i. With probability at least $1/8$ the starting vector w of Step 4 satisfies $\langle z^k, w \rangle / \|w\| \geq 1/8 > 0$, where z^k is the center of the feasibility cone of (13). Now suppose that w is an iterate of the Step 4. If $B_k w \notin K^*$, and specifying to the case when $K = K^* = S_+^{p \times p}$, we let $d = vv' \in K$ where v is an eigenvector of a negative eigenvalue of $B_k w$, and replace

$$w^+ \leftarrow w + \theta B_k^* d \tag{15}$$

for $\theta := - \langle d, B_k w \rangle / \|B_k^* d\|^2$. It then follows that

$$\langle w^+, z^k \rangle = \langle w, z^k \rangle + \theta \langle B_k^* d, z^k \rangle \geq \langle w, z^k \rangle$$

since $\langle d, B_k z^k \rangle \geq 0$. Furthermore, from the particular choice of θ we have

$$\|w^+\|^2 = \|w\|^2 + 2\theta \langle w, B_k^* d \rangle + \theta^2 \|B_k^* d\|^2 \leq \|w\|^2 ,$$

and hence the potential function $\langle z^k, w \rangle / \|w\|$ is non-decreasing if we replace w by w^+. If all previous iterates satisfied $B_i w_{i+1} \in K^*$ we have from Lemma 7 that

$$B_k w^+ - B_k w = B_k B_k^* d \in K^*$$

and furthermore from the choice of θ we have

$$v'(B_k w^+) v = v'(B_k w + \theta B_k B_k^* d) v = \langle B_k w + \theta B_k B_k^* d, vv' \rangle$$
$$= \langle B_k w + \theta B_k B_k^* d, d \rangle = 0 .$$

Therefore $B_k w^+ \succeq B_k w$ and $B_k w^+$ has at least one fewer negative eigenvalue than $B_k w$. Therefore after repeating the replacement at most p times we ensure that the final replacement iterate satisfies $B_k w^+ \in K^*$. Inductively this shows that the process yields replacement iterates that satisfy $B_k w^+ \in K^*$ whose potential function value for the perceptron improvement methodology is improved. Therefore the iteration bound on the perceptron improvement methodology is left unchanged.

References

1. Belloni, A., Freund, R.M.: Characterization of second-order cone inclusion, and efficient projection, Technical Report, MIT Operations Research Center, OR-380-06 (2006)
2. Bertsimas, D., Vempala, S.: Solving convex programs by random walks. Journal of the ACM 51(4), 540–556 (2004)
3. Blum, A., Frieze, A., Kannan, R., Vempala, S.: A polynomial-time algorithm for learning noisy linear threshold functions. Algorithmica 22(1), 35–52 (1998)
4. Bylander, T.: Learning linear threshold functions in the presence of classification noise, Proceedings of the Seventh Annual Workshop on Computational Learning Theory, pp. 340–347 (1994)
5. Dunagan, J., Vempala, S.: A simple polynomial-time rescaling algorithm for solving linear programs, to appear in Mathemathical Programming (2007)
6. Freund, R.M., Vera, J.R.: Condition-based complexity of convex optimization in conic linear form via the ellipsoid algorithm. SIAM Journal on Optimization 10(1), 155–176 (1999)
7. Some characterizations and properties of the distance to ill-posedness and the condition measure of a conic linear system, Mathematical Programming 86(2) , 225–260. (1999)
8. Freund, Y., Schapire, R.E.: Large margin classification using the perceptron algorithm. Machine Learning 37(3), 297–336 (1999)
9. Karmarkar, N.: A new polynomial-time algorithm for linear programming. Combinatorica 4(4), 373–395 (1984)
10. Khachiyan, L.G.: A polynomial algorithm in linear programming. Soviet Math. Dokl. 20(1), 191–194 (1979)
11. Minsky, M., Papert, S.: Perceptrons: An introduction to computational geometry. MIT Press, Cambridge (1969)
12. Nesterov, Y., Nemirovskii, A.: Interior-point polynomial algorithms in convex programming, Society for Industrial and Applied Mathematics (SIAM), Philadelphia (1993)
13. Novikoff, A.B.J.: On convergence proofs on perceptrons. In: Proceedings of the Symposium on the Mathematical Theory of Automata X11, 615–622 (1962)
14. Pataki, G.: On the closedness of the linear image of a closed convex cone, Technical Report, University of North Carolina, TR-02-3 Department of Operations Research (1992)
15. Renegar, J.: Some perturbation theory for linear programming. Mathematical Programming 65(1), 73–91 (1994)
16. Linear programming, complexity theory, and elementary functional analysis Mathematical Programming 70(3) 279–351 (1995)
17. Rosenblatt, F.: Principles of neurodynamics, Spartan Books, Washington, DC (1962)
18. Wolkowicz, H., Saigal, R., Vandenberghe, L.: Handbook of Semidefinite Programming. Kluwer Academic Publishers, Boston, MA (2000)

A Lower Bound for Agnostically Learning Disjunctions

Adam R. Klivans and Alexander A. Sherstov

The University of Texas at Austin
Department of Computer Sciences
Austin, TX 78712 USA
{klivans,sherstov}@cs.utexas.edu

Abstract. We prove that the concept class of disjunctions cannot be pointwise approximated by linear combinations of any small set of *arbitrary* real-valued functions. That is, suppose there exist functions $\phi_1, \ldots, \phi_r : \{-1, 1\}^n \to \mathbb{R}$ with the property that every disjunction f on n variables has $\|f - \sum_{i=1}^r \alpha_i \phi_i\|_\infty \leqslant 1/3$ for some reals $\alpha_1, \ldots, \alpha_r$. We prove that then $r \geqslant 2^{\Omega(\sqrt{n})}$. This lower bound is tight. We prove an incomparable lower bound for the concept class of linear-size DNF formulas. For the concept class of majority functions, we obtain a lower bound of $\Omega(2^n/n)$, which almost meets the trivial upper bound of 2^n for *any* concept class.

These lower bounds substantially strengthen and generalize the polynomial approximation lower bounds of Paturi and show that the regression-based agnostic learning algorithm of Kalai et al. is optimal. Our techniques involve a careful application of results in communication complexity due to Razborov and Buhrman et al.

1 Introduction

Approximating Boolean functions by linear combinations of small sets of features is a fundamental area of study in machine learning. Well-known algorithms such as linear regression, support vector machines, and boosting attempt to learn concepts as linear functions or thresholds over a fixed set of real-valued features.

In particular, much work in learning theory has centered around approximating various concept classes, with respect to a variety of distributions and metrics, by *low-degree polynomials* [21, 26, 18, 17, 28, 3, 10, 19]. In this case, the features mentioned above are simply monomials. For example, Linial et al. [21] gave a celebrated uniform-distribution algorithm for learning constant-depth circuits by proving that any such circuit can be approximated by a low-degree Fourier polynomial, with respect to the uniform distribution and ℓ_2 norm.

A more recent application of this polynomial technique is due to Kalai et al. [11], who considered the well-studied problem of agnostically learning disjunctions [27, 6, 14, 34]. Kalai et al. recalled a result of Paturi [29] that a disjunction on n variables can be approximated pointwise by a degree-$\tilde{O}(\sqrt{n})$ polynomial. They then used linear regression to obtain the first subexponential ($2^{\tilde{O}(\sqrt{n})}$-time) algorithm for *agnostically* learning disjunctions with respect to *any* distribution [11, Thm. 2]. More generally, Kalai et al. used ℓ_∞-norm approximation to formulate the first, and so far only, approach

N. Bshouty and C. Gentile (Eds.): COLT 2007, LNAI 4539, pp. 409–423, 2007.

to distribution-free agnostic learning. One goal of this paper is to show the fundamental limits of this approximation-based paradigm.

1.1 Key Definitions

Before stating our results formally, we briefly describe our notation. A Boolean function is a mapping $f : \{-1, 1\}^n \to \{-1, 1\}$, where -1 corresponds to "true." A *feature* is any function $\phi : \{-1, 1\}^n \to \mathbb{R}$. We say that ϕ *approximates* f *pointwise within* ε, denoted

$$\|f - \phi\|_\infty \leqslant \varepsilon,$$

if $|f(x) - \phi(x)| \leqslant \varepsilon$ for all x. We say that *a linear combination of features* $\phi_1, \dots, \phi_r$ *approximates* f *pointwise within* ε if $\|f - \sum_{i=1}^r \alpha_i \phi_i\|_\infty \leqslant \varepsilon$ for some reals $\alpha_1, \dots, \alpha_r$.

1.2 Our Results

Let $\mathscr{C}$ be a concept class. Suppose that $\phi_1, \dots, \phi_r$ are features whose linear combinations can pointwise approximate every function in $\mathscr{C}$. We first observe that the algorithm of Kalai et al.—assuming that $\phi_1, \dots, \phi_r$ can be evaluated efficiently—learns $\mathscr{C}$ agnostically under any distribution in time $\mathrm{poly}(n, r)$. As far as we are aware, this is the only known method for developing provably efficient, distribution-free agnostic learning algorithms. To determine the limits of this paradigm, our paper focuses on lower bounds on r for an *arbitrary* choice of features.

We start with the concept class of disjunctions.

Theorem 1 (Disjunctions). *Let* $\mathscr{C} = \{\bigvee_{i \in S} x_i : S \subseteq [n]\}$ *be the concept class of disjunctions. Let* $\phi_1, \dots, \phi_r : \{-1, 1\}^n \to \mathbb{R}$ *be arbitrary functions whose linear combinations can pointwise approximate every* $f \in \mathscr{C}$ *within* $\varepsilon = 1/3$. *Then* $r \geqslant 2^{\Omega(\sqrt{n})}$.

Theorem 1 obviously also holds for the concept class of *conjunctions*.

Theorem 1 shows the optimality of using monomials as features for approximating disjunctions. In particular, it rules out the possibility of using the algorithm of Kalai et al. with other, cleverly constructed features to obtain an improved agnostic learning result for disjunctions.

We obtain an incomparable result against linear-size DNF formulas.

Theorem 2 (DNF formulas). *Let* $\mathscr{C}$ *be the concept class of DNF formulas of linear size. Let* $\phi_1, \dots, \phi_r : \{-1, 1\}^n \to \mathbb{R}$ *be arbitrary functions whose linear combinations can pointwise approximate every* $f \in \mathscr{C}$ *within* $\varepsilon = 1 - 2^{-cn^{1/3}}$, *where* $c > 0$ *is a sufficiently small absolute constant. Then* $r \geqslant 2^{\Omega(n^{1/3})}$.

Theorems 1 and 2 both give exponential lower bounds on r. Comparing the two, we see that Theorem 1 gives a better bound on r against a simpler concept class. On the other hand, Theorem 2 remains valid for a particularly weak success criterion: when the approximation quality is exponentially close to trivial ($\varepsilon = 1$).

The last concept class we study is that of majority functions. Here we prove our best lower bound, $r = \Omega(2^n/n)$, that essentially meets the trivial upper bound of 2^n for any concept class. Put differently, we show that the concept class of majorities is essentially as hard to approximate as *any* concept class at all. In particular, this shows that the Kalai et al. paradigm cannot yield any nontrivial ($2^{o(n)}$-time) distribution-free algorithm for agnostically learning majority functions.

Theorem 3 (Majority functions). *Let $\mathscr{C} = \{\mathrm{MAJ}(\pm x_1, \ldots, \pm x_n)\}$ be the concept class of majority functions. Let $\phi_1, \ldots, \phi_r : \{-1, 1\}^n \to \mathbb{R}$ be arbitrary functions whose linear combinations can pointwise approximate every $f \in \mathscr{C}$ within $\varepsilon = c/\sqrt{n}$, where c is a sufficiently small absolute constant. Then $r \geqslant \Omega(2^n/n)$. For approximation to within $\varepsilon = 1/3$, we obtain $r \geqslant 2^{\Omega(n/\log n)}$.*

We also relate our inapproximability results to the fundamental notions of *dimension complexity* and *SQ dimension* (Sections 5–7). Among other things, we show that the types of approximation lower bounds we study are prerequisites for lower bounds on dimension complexity and the SQ dimension. It is a hard open problem [32] to prove exponential lower bounds on the dimension complexity and SQ dimension of polynomial-size DNF formulas, or even AC^0 circuits.

Optimality of polynomial-based approximation. The preceding discussion has emphasized the implications of Theorems 1–3 in learning theory. Our results also have interesting consequences in approximation theory. Paturi [29] constructs polynomials of degree $\tilde{\Theta}(\sqrt{n})$ and $\Theta(n)$ that pointwise approximate disjunctions and majority functions, respectively. He also shows that these *degree* results are optimal for polynomials. This, of course, does not exclude polynomials that are *sparse*, i.e., contain few monomials. Our lower bounds strengthen Paturi's result by showing that the approximating polynomials cannot be sparse. In addition, our analysis remains valid when monomials are replaced by *arbitrary* features. As anticipated, our techniques differ significantly from Paturi's.

1.3 Our Techniques

To prove our approximation lower bounds, we need to use various techniques from matrix analysis, communication complexity, and Fourier analysis. We obtain our main theorems in two steps. First, we show how to place a lower bound on the quantity of interest (the size of feature sets that pointwise approximate a concept class $\mathscr{C}$) using the *discrepancy* and the *ε-approximate trace norm* of the characteristic matrix of $\mathscr{C}$. The latter two quantities have been extensively studied. In particular, the discrepancy estimate that we need is a recent result of Buhrman et al. [5]. For estimates of the ε-approximate trace norm, we turn to the pioneering work of Razborov [30] on quantum communication complexity, as well as a recent construction of Linial and Shraibman [24].

2 Preliminaries

The notation $[n]$ stands for the set $\{1, 2, \ldots, n\}$, and $\binom{[n]}{k}$ stands for the family of all k-element subsets of $[n] = \{1, 2, \ldots, n\}$. The symbol $\mathbb{R}^{n \times m}$ refers to the family of all $m \times n$ matrices with real entries. The (i, j)th entry of a matrix A is denoted by A_{ij} or

$A(i,j)$. We frequently use "generic-entry" notation to specify a matrix succinctly: we write $A = [F(i,j)]_{i,j}$ to mean that that the (i,j)th entry of A is given by the expression $F(i,j)$.

A *concept class* $\mathscr{C}$ is any set of Boolean functions $f : \{-1,1\}^n \to \{-1,1\}$. The *characteristic matrix* of $\mathscr{C}$ is the matrix $M = [f(x)]_{f\in\mathscr{C}, x\in\{-1,1\}^n}$. In words, the rows of M are indexed by functions $f \in \mathscr{C}$, the columns are indexed by inputs $x \in \{-1,1\}^n$, and the entries are given by $M_{f,x} = f(x)$.

2.1 Agnostic Learning

The agnostic learning model was defined by Kearns et al. [15]. It gives the learner access to arbitrary example-label pairs with the requirement that the learner output a hypothesis competitive with the best hypothesis from some fixed concept class. Specifically, let D be a distribution on $\{-1,1\}^n \times \{-1,1\}$ and let $\mathscr{C}$ be a concept class. For a Boolean function f, define its *error* as $\mathrm{err}(f) = \mathrm{Pr}_{(x,y)\sim D}[f(x) \neq y]$. Define the *optimal error* of $\mathscr{C}$ as $\mathrm{opt} = \min_{f\in\mathscr{C}} \mathrm{err}(f)$.

A concept class $\mathscr{C}$ is *agnostically learnable* if there exists an algorithm which takes as input δ, ε, and access to an example oracle $\mathrm{EX}(D)$, and outputs with probability at least $1 - \delta$ a hypothesis $h : \{-1,1\}^n \to \{-1,1\}$ such that $\mathrm{err}(h) \leqslant \mathrm{opt} + \varepsilon$. We say $\mathscr{C}$ is agnostically learnable in time t if its running time (including calls to the example oracle) is bounded by $t(\varepsilon, \delta, n)$.

The following proposition relates pointwise approximation by linear combinations of features to efficient agnostic learning.

Proposition 1. *Fix $\varepsilon > 0$ and a concept class $\mathscr{C}$. Assume there are functions $\phi_1, \ldots, \phi_r : \{-1,1\}^n \to \mathbb{R}$ whose linear combinations can pointwise approximate every $f \in \mathscr{C}$. Assume further that each $\phi_i(x)$ is computable in polynomial time. Then $\mathscr{C}$ is agnostically learnable to accuracy ε in time $\mathrm{poly}(r,n)$.*

We defer a proof of Proposition 1 to the full version. The needed simulation is a straightforward generalization of the ℓ_1 polynomial regression algorithm from Kalai et al. [11].

2.2 Fourier Transform

Consider the vector space of functions $\{-1,1\}^n \to \mathbb{R}$, equipped with the inner product $\langle f,g \rangle = 2^{-n}\sum_{x\in\{-1,1\}^n} f(x)g(x)$. The parity functions $\chi_S(x) = \prod_{i\in S} x_i$, where $S \subseteq [n]$, form an orthonormal basis for this inner product space. As a result, every Boolean function f can be uniquely written as

$$f = \sum_{S\subseteq[n]} \hat{f}(S)\chi_S,$$

where $\hat{f}(S) = \langle f, \chi_S \rangle$. The f-specific reals $\hat{f}(S)$ are called the *Fourier coefficients* of f. We denote

$$\|\hat{f}\|_1 = \sum_{S\subseteq[n]} |\hat{f}(S)|.$$

2.3 Matrix Analysis

We draw freely on basic notions from matrix analysis; a standard reference on the subject is [9]. This section only reviews the notation and the more substantial results.

Let $A \in \mathbb{R}^{m \times n}$. We let $\|A\|_\infty \stackrel{\text{def}}{=} \max_{ij} |A_{ij}|$, the largest absolute value of an entry of A. We denote the singular values of A by $\sigma_1(A) \geqslant \sigma_2(A) \geqslant \ldots \geqslant \sigma_{\min\{m,n\}}(A) \geqslant 0$. Recall that $\|A\|_\Sigma = \sum_{i=1}^{\min\{m,n\}} \sigma_i(A)$ and $\|A\|_F = \sqrt{\sum_{i=1}^m \sum_{j=1}^n A_{ij}^2}$ are the trace norm and Frobenius norm of A. We will also need the ε-approximate trace norm, defined as

$$\|A\|_\Sigma^\varepsilon = \min\{\|B\|_\Sigma : \|A - B\|_\infty \leqslant \varepsilon\}.$$

The well-known Hoffman-Wielandt inequality plays an important role in our analysis. In words, it states that small perturbations to the entries of a matrix result in small perturbations to its singular values. This inequality has seen numerous uses in the literature [12, 25, 8].

Theorem 4 (Hoffman-Wielandt inequality [9, Thm. 8.6.4]). *Let* $A, B \in \mathbb{R}^{m \times n}$. *Then* $\sum_{i=1}^{\min\{m,n\}} (\sigma_i(A) - \sigma_i(B))^2 \leqslant \|A - B\|_F^2$. *In particular, if* $\text{rank}(B) = k$ *then* $\sum_{i \geqslant k+1} \sigma_i(A)^2 \leqslant \|A - B\|_F^2$.

The Hoffman-Wielandt inequality is central to the following lemma, which allows us to easily construct matrices with high $\|\cdot\|_\Sigma^\varepsilon$ norm.

Lemma 1 (Linial and Shraibman [24], implicit). *Let* $M = [f(x \oplus y)]_{x,y}$, *where* $f : \{-1,1\}^n \to \{-1,1\}$ *is arbitrary. Then for all* $\varepsilon \geqslant 0$,

$$\|M\|_\Sigma^\varepsilon \geqslant 2^n (\|\hat{f}\|_1 - \varepsilon 2^{n/2}).$$

Proof (adapted from Linial and Shraibman [24]). Let $N = 2^n$ be the order of M. Consider an arbitrary matrix A with $\|A - M\|_\infty \leqslant \varepsilon$. We have:

$$N^2 \varepsilon^2 \geqslant \|A - M\|_F^2 \overset{\text{Thm. 4}}{\geqslant} \sum_{i=1}^N (\sigma_i(A) - \sigma_i(M))^2 \geqslant \frac{1}{N} (\|A\|_\Sigma - \|M\|_\Sigma)^2,$$

so that $\|A\|_\Sigma \geqslant \|M\|_\Sigma - N^{3/2} \varepsilon$. Since the choice of A was arbitrary, we conclude that

$$\|M\|_\Sigma^\varepsilon \geqslant \|M\|_\Sigma - N^{3/2} \varepsilon. \tag{1}$$

It remains to analyze $\|M\|_\Sigma$. Let $Q = N^{-1/2} [\chi_S(x)]_{x,S}$. It is easy to check that Q is orthogonal. On the other hand,

$$M = [f(x \oplus y)]_{x,y} = \left[\sum_{S \subseteq [n]} \hat{f}(S) \chi_S(x) \chi_S(y) \right]_{x,y} = Q \begin{bmatrix} N\hat{f}(\emptyset) & & \\ & \ddots & \\ & & N\hat{f}([n]) \end{bmatrix} Q^{\mathsf{T}}.$$

The last equation reveals the singular values of M. In particular, $\|M\|_\Sigma = N\|\hat{f}\|_1$. Together with (1), this completes the proof. $\square$

A *sign matrix* is any matrix with ± 1 entries.

2.4 Communication Complexity

We consider functions $f : X \times Y \to \{-1, 1\}$. Typically $X = Y = \{-1, 1\}^n$, but we also allow X and Y to be arbitrary sets, possibly of unequal cardinality. A *rectangle* of $X \times Y$ is any set $R = A \times B$ with $A \subseteq X$ and $B \subseteq Y$. For a fixed distribution μ over $X \times Y$, the *discrepancy* of f is defined as

$$\mathrm{disc}_\mu(f) = \max_R \left| \sum_{(x,y) \in R} \mu(x,y) f(x,y) \right|,$$

where the maximum is taken over all rectangles R. We define $\mathrm{disc}(f) = \min_\mu \{\mathrm{disc}_\mu(f)\}$. We identify the function f with its *communication matrix* $M = [f(x,y)]_{x,y}$ and define $\mathrm{disc}_\mu(M) = \mathrm{disc}_\mu(f)$.

Discrepancy is a powerful quantity with various applications. In particular, it immediately yields lower bounds in various models of communication complexity, as well as circuit lower bounds for depth-2 majority circuits [20, 33, 24]. This paper shows yet another application of discrepancy. A definitive resource for further details on communication complexity is the book of Kushilevitz and Nisan [20].

2.5 SQ Dimension

The statistical query (SQ) model of learning, due to Kearns [13], is a restriction of Valiant's PAC model. See [16] for a comprehensive treatment. The SQ model is recognized as a powerful abstraction of learning and plays a major role in learning theory. The *SQ dimension* of $\mathscr{C}$ under μ, denoted $\mathrm{sqdim}_\mu(\mathscr{C})$, is the largest d for which there are d functions $f_1, \ldots, f_d \in \mathscr{C}$ with

$$\left| \mathop{\mathbf{E}}_{x \sim \mu} [f_i(x) \cdot f_j(x)] \right| \leqslant \frac{1}{d}$$

for all $i \neq j$. We denote

$$\mathrm{sqdim}(\mathscr{C}) = \max_\mu \{\mathrm{sqdim}_\mu(\mathscr{C})\}.$$

The SQ dimension is a tight measure [13] of the learning complexity of a given concept class $\mathscr{C}$ in the SQ model. In addition, the SQ dimension is strongly related to complexity theory [32].

3 Approximation Rank: Definition and Properties

For a real matrix A, its ε-*approximation rank* is defined as

$$\mathrm{rank}_\varepsilon(A) = \min_B \{\mathrm{rank}(B) : B \text{ real}, \|A - B\|_\infty \leqslant \varepsilon\}.$$

This notion is a natural one and has been studied before. In particular, Buhrman and de Wolf [4] show that the approximation rank of a matrix implies lower bounds on its quantum communication complexity (in the bounded-error model without entanglement). In Section 6, we survey two other related concepts: matrix rigidity and dimension complexity.

We define the ε-*approximation rank* of a concept class $\mathscr{C}$ as

$$\text{rank}_\varepsilon(\mathscr{C}) = \text{rank}_\varepsilon(M),$$

where M is the characteristic matrix of $\mathscr{C}$. For example, $\text{rank}_0(\mathscr{C}) = \text{rank}(M)$ and $\text{rank}_1(\mathscr{C}) = 0$. It is thus the behavior of $\text{rank}_\varepsilon(\mathscr{C})$ for intermediate values of ε that is of primary interest. The following proposition follows trivially from our definitions.

Proposition 2 (Approximation rank reinterpreted). *Let $\mathscr{C}$ be a concept class. Then* $\text{rank}_\varepsilon(\mathscr{C})$ *is the smallest integer r such that there exist real functions $\phi_1, \ldots, \phi_r :$* $\{-1, 1\}^n \to \mathbb{R}$ *with the property that each $f \in \mathscr{C}$ has $\|f - \sum_{i=1}^r \alpha_i \phi_i\|_\infty \leqslant \varepsilon$ for some reals $\alpha_1, \ldots, \alpha_r$.*

3.1   Improving the Quality of the Approximation

We now take a closer look at $\text{rank}_\varepsilon(M)$ as a function of ε. Suppose we have an estimate of $\text{rank}_E(M)$ for some $0 < E < 1$. Can we use this information to obtain a nontrivial upper bound on $\text{rank}_\varepsilon(M)$, where $0 < \varepsilon < E$? It turns out that we can. We first recall that the sign function can be approximated well by a real polynomial:

Fact 1. *Let $0 < E < 1$ be given. Then for each integer $d \geqslant 1$, there exists a degree-d real univariate polynomial $p(t)$ such that*

$$|p(t) - \text{sign}(t)| \leqslant 8\sqrt{d}\left(1 - \frac{(1-E)^2}{16}\right)^d \qquad (1 - E \leqslant |t| \leqslant 1 + E).$$

Fact 1 can be extracted with little effort from Rudin's proof [31, Thm. 7.26] of the Weierstrass approximation theorem. Subtler, improved versions of Fact 1 can be readily found in the approximation literature.

Theorem 5. *Let M be a sign matrix, and let $0 < \varepsilon < E < 1$. Then*

$$\text{rank}_\varepsilon(M) \leqslant \text{rank}_E(M)^d,$$

where d is any positive integer with $8\sqrt{d}(1 - (1-E)^2/16)^d \leqslant \varepsilon$.

Proof. Let d be as stated. By Fact 1, there is a degree-d polynomial $p(t)$ with

$$|p(t) - \text{sign}(t)| \leqslant \varepsilon \qquad (1 - E \leqslant |t| \leqslant 1 + E).$$

Let A be a real matrix with $\|A - M\|_\infty \leqslant E$ and $\text{rank}(A) = \text{rank}_E(M)$. Then the matrix $B = [p(A_{ij})]_{i,j}$ approximates M to the desired accuracy: $\|B - M\|_\infty \leqslant \varepsilon$. Since p is a polynomial of degree d, elementary linear algebra shows that $\text{rank}(B) \leqslant \text{rank}(A)^d$. $\square$

Note. The key idea in the proof of Theorem 5 is to improve the quality of the approximating matrix by applying a suitable polynomial to its entries. This idea is not new. For example, Alon [1] uses the same method in the simpler setting of *one-sided* errors.

We will mainly need the following immediate consequences of Theorem 5.

Corollary 1. *Let M be a sign matrix. Let* ε, E *be constants with* $0 < \varepsilon < E < 1$. *Then* $\text{rank}_\varepsilon(M) \leqslant \text{rank}_E(M)^c$, *where* $c = c(\varepsilon, E)$ *is a constant.*

Corollary 2. *Let M be a sign matrix. Let* ε *be a constant with* $0 < \varepsilon < 1$. *Then* $\text{rank}_{1/n^c}(M) \leqslant \text{rank}_\varepsilon(M)^{O(\log n)}$ *for every constant* $c > 0$.

By Corollary 1, the choice of the constant ε affects $\text{rank}_\varepsilon(M)$ by at most a polynomial factor. When such factors are unimportant, we will adopt $\varepsilon = 1/3$ as a canonical setting.

3.2   Estimating the Approximation Rank

We will use two methods to estimate the approximation rank. The first uses the ε-approximate trace norm of the same matrix, and the second uses its discrepancy.

Lemma 2 (Lower bound via approximate trace norm). *Let* $M \in \{-1, 1\}^{N \times N}$. *Then*

$$\text{rank}_\varepsilon(M) \geqslant \left(\frac{\|M\|_\Sigma^\varepsilon}{(1+\varepsilon)N} \right)^2.$$

Proof. Let A be an arbitrary matrix with $\|M - A\|_\infty \leqslant \varepsilon$. We have:

$$(\|M\|_\Sigma^\varepsilon)^2 \leqslant (\|A\|_\Sigma)^2 = \left(\sum_{i=1}^{\text{rank}(A)} \sigma_i(A) \right)^2 \leqslant \left(\sum_{i=1}^{\text{rank}(A)} \sigma_i(A)^2 \right) \text{rank}(A)$$

$$= (\|A\|_F)^2 \text{rank}(A) \leqslant (1+\varepsilon)^2 N^2 \text{rank}(A). \qquad \square$$

Our second method is as follows.

Lemma 3 (Lower bound via discrepancy). *Let M be a sign matrix and* $0 \leqslant \varepsilon < 1$. *Then*

$$\text{rank}_\varepsilon(M) \geqslant \frac{1-\varepsilon}{1+\varepsilon} \cdot \frac{1}{64 \, \text{disc}(M)^2}.$$

The proof of Lemma 3 requires several definitions and facts that we do not use elsewhere in this paper. For this reason, we defer it to Appendix A.

4   Approximation Rank of Specific Concept Classes

We proceed to prove our main results (Theorems 1–3), restated here as Theorems 7, 9, and 10.

4.1 Disjunctions

We recall a breakthrough result of Razborov [30] on the quantum communication complexity of disjointness. The crux of that work is the following theorem.

Theorem 6 (Razborov [30, Sec. 5.3]). *Let M be the $\binom{n}{n/4} \times \binom{n}{n/4}$ matrix whose rows and columns are indexed by sets in $\binom{[n]}{n/4}$ and entries given by*

$$M_{S,T} = \begin{cases} 1 & \text{if } S \cap T = \emptyset, \\ 0 & \text{otherwise.} \end{cases}$$

Then $\|M\|_{\Sigma}^{1/4} = 2^{\Omega(\sqrt{n})} \binom{n}{n/4}$.

We can now prove an exponential lower bound on the approximation rank of disjunctions, a particularly simple concept class.

Theorem 7 (Approximation rank of disjunctions). *Let $\mathscr{C} = \{\bigvee_{i \in S} x_i : S \subseteq [n]\}$ be the concept class of disjunctions. Then $\operatorname{rank}_{1/3}(\mathscr{C}) = 2^{\Omega(\sqrt{n})}$.*

Proof. One easily verifies that the characteristic matrix of $\mathscr{C}$ is $M_{\mathscr{C}} = [\bigvee_{i=1}^{n} (x_i \wedge y_i)]_{x,y}$. We can equivalently view $M_{\mathscr{C}}$ as the $2^n \times 2^n$ sign matrix whose rows and columns indexed by sets in $[n]$ and entries given by:

$$M_{\mathscr{C}}(S,T) = \begin{cases} 1 & \text{if } S \cap T = \emptyset, \\ -1 & \text{otherwise.} \end{cases}$$

Now let A be a real matrix with $\|M_{\mathscr{C}} - A\|_{\infty} \leqslant 1/3$. Let $Z_{\mathscr{C}} = \frac{1}{2}(M_{\mathscr{C}} + J)$, where J is the all-ones matrix. We immediately have $\|Z_{\mathscr{C}} - \frac{1}{2}(A+J)\|_{\infty} \leqslant 1/6$, and thus

$$\operatorname{rank}_{1/6}(Z_{\mathscr{C}}) \leqslant \operatorname{rank}\left(\tfrac{1}{2}(A+J)\right) \leqslant \operatorname{rank}(A) + 1. \tag{2}$$

However, $Z_{\mathscr{C}}$ contains as a submatrix the matrix M from Theorem 6. Therefore,

$$\operatorname{rank}_{1/6}(Z_{\mathscr{C}}) \;\overset{\text{Lem. 2}}{\geqslant}\; \operatorname{rank}_{1/6}(M) \;\geqslant\; \left(\frac{\|M\|_{\Sigma}^{1/4}}{(1+1/4)\binom{n}{n/4}}\right)^2 \;\overset{\text{Thm. 6}}{\geqslant}\; 2^{\Omega(\sqrt{n})}. \tag{3}$$

The theorem follows immediately from (2) and (3). $\qquad\qquad\square$

4.2 DNF Formulas

The centerpiece of our proof is the following recent result of Buhrman et al. [5].

Theorem 8 (Buhrman, Vereshchagin, and de Wolf [5, Sec. 3]). *There is a function $f : \{-1,1\}^n \times \{-1,1\}^n \to \{-1,1\}$ in $\mathsf{AC}^{0,3}$ such that $\operatorname{disc}(f) = 2^{-\Omega(n^{1/3})}$. Moreover, for each fixed y, the function $f_y(x) = f(x,y)$ is a DNF formula of linear size.*

We can now analyze the approximation rank of linear-size DNF formulas.

Theorem 9 (Approximation rank of DNF). *Let $\mathscr{C}$ denote the concept class of functions $f : \{-1,1\}^n \to \{-1,1\}$ computable by DNF formulas of linear size. Then $\mathrm{rank}_\varepsilon(\mathscr{C}) = 2^{\Omega(n^{1/3})}$ for $0 \leqslant \varepsilon \leqslant 1 - 2^{-cn^{1/3}}$, where $c > 0$ is a sufficiently small absolute constant.*

Proof. Let M be the characteristic matrix of $\mathscr{C}$, and let $f(x,y)$ be the function from Theorem 8. Since $[f(x,y)]_{y,x}$ is a submatrix of M, we have $\mathrm{rank}_\varepsilon(M) \geqslant \mathrm{rank}_\varepsilon([f(x,y)]_{y,x})$. The claim is now immediate from Lemma 3. $\qquad\square$

Comparing the results of Theorems 7 and 9 for small constant ε, we see that Theorem 7 is stronger in that it gives a better lower bound against a simpler concept class. On the other hand, Theorem 9 is stronger in that it remains valid for the broad range $0 \leqslant \varepsilon \leqslant 1 - 2^{-\Theta(n^{1/3})}$, whereas the ε-approximation rank in Theorem 7 is easily seen to be at most n for all $\varepsilon \geqslant 1 - \frac{1}{2n}$.

4.3 Majority Functions

As a final application, we consider the concept class $\mathscr{C}$ of majority functions. Here we prove a lower bound of $\Omega(2^n/n)$ on the approximation rank, which is the best of our three constructions.

Theorem 10 (Approximation rank of majority functions). *Let $\mathscr{C}$ denote the concept class of majority functions, $\mathscr{C} = \{\mathrm{MAJ}(\pm x_1,\ldots,\pm x_n)\}$. Then $\mathrm{rank}_{c/\sqrt{n}}(\mathscr{C}) \geqslant \Omega(2^n/n)$ for a sufficiently small absolute constant $c > 0$. Also, $\mathrm{rank}_{1/3}(\mathscr{C}) = 2^{\Omega(n/\log n)}$.*

Proof. The characteristic matrix of $\mathscr{C}$ is $M = [\mathrm{MAJ}(x \oplus y)]_{x,y}$. The Fourier spectrum of the majority function has been extensively studied by various authors. In particular, it is well known that

$$\|\widehat{\mathrm{MAJ}}\|_1 = \Omega\left(\frac{2^{n/2}}{\sqrt{n}}\right). \tag{4}$$

(See, e.g., [22, Sec. 7] for a self-contained calculation.) Taking $\varepsilon = c/\sqrt{n}$ for a suitably small constant $c > 0$, we obtain:

$$\mathrm{rank}_{c/\sqrt{n}}(M) \overset{\text{Lem. 2}}{\geqslant} \left(\frac{\|M\|_\Sigma^{c/\sqrt{n}}}{(1+c/\sqrt{n})2^n}\right)^2 \overset{\text{Lem. 1}}{\geqslant} \frac{1}{4}\left(\|\widehat{\mathrm{MAJ}}\|_1 - \frac{c2^{n/2}}{\sqrt{n}}\right)^2 \overset{(4)}{\geqslant} \Omega\left(\frac{2^n}{n}\right).$$

Finally, $\mathrm{rank}_{1/3}(\mathscr{C}) \geqslant [\mathrm{rank}_{c/\sqrt{n}}(\mathscr{C})]^{1/O(\log n)} \geqslant 2^{\Omega(n/\log n)}$ by Corollary 2. $\qquad\square$

5 Approximation Rank vs. SQ Dimension

This section relates the approximation rank of a concept class $\mathscr{C}$ to its SQ dimension, a fundamental quantity in learning theory. In short, we prove that (1) the SQ dimension is a lower bound on the approximation rank, and that (2) the gap between the two quantities can be exponential. A starting point in our analysis is the relationship between the SQ dimension of $\mathscr{C}$ and ℓ_2-norm approximation of $\mathscr{C}$, which is also of some independent interest.

Theorem 11 (SQ dimension and ℓ_2 approximation). *Let $\mathscr{C}$ be a concept class, and let μ be a distribution over $\{-1,1\}^n$. Suppose there exist functions $\phi_1,\ldots,\phi_r : \{-1,1\}^n \to \mathbb{R}$ such that each $f \in \mathscr{C}$ has $\mathbf{E}_{x\sim\mu}\left[(f(x) - \sum_{i=1}^r \alpha_i \phi_i(x))^2\right] \leqslant \varepsilon$ for some reals $\alpha_1,\ldots,\alpha_r$. Then*

$$r \geqslant (1-\varepsilon)d - \sqrt{d},$$

where $d = \mathrm{sqdim}_\mu(\mathscr{C})$.

Proof. By the definition of the SQ dimension, there exist functions $f_1,\ldots,f_d \in \mathscr{C}$ with $|\mathbf{E}_\mu[f_i \cdot f_j]| \leqslant 1/d$ for all $i \neq j$. For simplicity, assume that μ is a distribution with rational weights (extension to the general case is straightforward). Then there is an integer $k \geqslant 1$ such that each $\mu(x)$ is an integral multiple of $1/k$. Construct the $d \times k$ sign matrix

$$M = [f_i(x)]_{i,x},$$

whose rows are indexed by the functions $f_1,\ldots,f_d$ and whose columns are indexed by inputs $x \in \{-1,1\}^n$ (a given input x indexes exactly $k\mu(x)$ columns). It is easy to verify that $MM^\mathsf{T} = [k\mathbf{E}_\mu[f_i \cdot f_j]]_{i,j}$, and thus

$$\|MM^\mathsf{T} - k \cdot I\|_F < k. \tag{5}$$

The existence of $\phi_1,\ldots,\phi_r$ implies the existence of a rank-r real matrix A with $\|M - A\|_F^2 \leqslant \varepsilon kd$. On the other hand, the Hoffman-Wielandt inequality (Theorem 4) guarantees that $\|M - A\|_F^2 \geqslant \sum_{i=r+1}^d \sigma_i(M)^2$. Combining these two inequalities yields:

$$\varepsilon kd \geqslant \sum_{i=r+1}^d \sigma_i(M)^2 = \sum_{i=r+1}^d \sigma_i(MM^\mathsf{T})$$

$$\geqslant k(d-r) - \sum_{i=r+1}^d |\sigma_i(MM^\mathsf{T}) - k|$$

$$\geqslant k(d-r) - \sqrt{\sum_{i=r+1}^d (\sigma_i(MM^\mathsf{T}) - k)^2} \sqrt{d-r} \qquad \text{by Cauchy-Swartz}$$

$$\geqslant k(d-r) - \|MM^\mathsf{T} - k \cdot I\|_F \sqrt{d-r} \qquad \text{by Hoffman-Wielandt}$$

$$\geqslant k(d-r) - k\sqrt{d} \qquad \text{by (5).}$$

We have shown that $\varepsilon d \geqslant (d-r) - \sqrt{d}$, which is precisely what the theorem claims. To extend the proof to irrational distributions μ, one considers a rational distribution $\tilde{\mu}$ suitably close to μ and repeats the above analysis. We omit these simple details. $\square$

We are now in a position to relate the SQ dimension to the approximation rank.

Theorem 12 (SQ dimension vs. approximation rank). *Let $\mathscr{C}$ be a concept class. Then for $0 \leqslant \varepsilon < 1$,*

$$\mathrm{rank}_\varepsilon(\mathscr{C}) \geqslant (1-\varepsilon^2)\mathrm{sqdim}(\mathscr{C}) - \sqrt{\mathrm{sqdim}(\mathscr{C})}. \tag{6}$$

Moreover, there exists a concept class $\mathscr{A}$ with

$$\text{sqdim}(\mathscr{A}) \leqslant O(n^2) \qquad and \qquad \text{rank}_{1/3}(\mathscr{A}) \geqslant 2^{\Omega(n/\log n)}.$$

Proof. Let $r = \text{rank}_\varepsilon(\mathscr{C})$. Then there are functions $\phi_1, \ldots, \phi_r$ such that each $f \in \mathscr{C}$ has $\|f - \sum_{i=1}^r \alpha_i \phi_i\|_\infty \leqslant \varepsilon$ for some reals $\alpha_1, \ldots, \alpha_r$. As a result,

$$\mathbf{E}_\mu \left[(f - \sum_{i=1}^r \alpha_i \phi_i)^2 \right] \leqslant \varepsilon^2$$

for every distribution μ. By Theorem 11, $r \geqslant (1 - \varepsilon^2) \text{sqdim}_\mu(\mathscr{C}) - \sqrt{\text{sqdim}_\mu(\mathscr{C})}$. Maximizing this over μ establishes (6).

To prove the second part, let $\mathscr{A} = \{\text{MAJ}(\pm x_1, \ldots, \pm x_n)\}$. Theorem 10 shows that $\mathscr{A}$ has the stated approximation rank. To bound its SQ dimension, note that each function in $\mathscr{A}$ can be pointwise approximated within error $1 - 1/n$ by a linear combination of the functions $x_1, \ldots, x_n$. Therefore, (6) implies that $\text{sqdim}(\mathscr{A}) \leqslant O(n^2)$. $\square$

6 Related Work

Approximation rank and dimension complexity. Dimension complexity is a fundamental and well-studied notion [7, 8, 22]. It is defined for a sign matrix M as

$$\text{dc}(M) = \min_A \{\text{rank}(A) : A \text{ real}, A_{ij} M_{ij} > 0 \text{ for all } i, j\}.$$

In words, the dimension complexity of M is the smallest rank of a real matrix A that has the same sign pattern as M. Thus, $\text{rank}_\varepsilon(M) \geqslant \text{dc}(M)$ for each sign matrix M and $0 \leqslant \varepsilon < 1$.

Ben-David et al. [2] showed that almost all concept classes with constant VC dimension have dimension complexity $2^{\Omega(n)}$; recall that $\text{dc}(\mathscr{C}) \leqslant 2^n$ always. Forster [7] later developed a powerful tool for lower-bounding the dimension complexity of explicit concept classes. His method has since seen several refinements.

However, this rich body of work is not readily applicable to our problem. Two of the three matrices we study have trivial dimension complexity, and we derive lower bounds on the approximation rank that are exponentially larger. Furthermore, in Theorem 3 we are able to exhibit an explicit concept class with approximation rank $\Omega(2^n/n)$, whereas the highest dimension complexity proved for any explicit concept class is Forster's lower bound of $2^{n/2}$. The key to our results is to bring out, through a variety of techniques, the additional structure in approximation that is not present in sign-representation.

Approximation rank and rigidity. Approximation rank is also closely related to ε-*rigidity*, a variant of matrix rigidity introduced by Lokam [25]. For a fixed real matrix A, its ε-rigidity function is defined as

$$R_A(r, \varepsilon) = \min_B \{\text{weight}(A - B) : \text{rank}(B) \leqslant r, \|A - B\|_\infty \leqslant \varepsilon\},$$

where weight$(A - B)$ stands for the number of nonzero entries in $A - B$. In words, $R_A(r, \varepsilon)$ is the minimum number of entries of A that must be perturbed to reduce its rank to r, provided that the perturbation to any single entry is at most ε. We immediately have:

$$\text{rank}_\varepsilon(A) = \min\{r : R_A(r, \varepsilon) \leqslant mn\} \qquad (A \in \mathbb{R}^{m \times n}).$$

As a result, lower bounds on ε-rigidity translate into lower bounds on approximation rank. In particular, ε-rigidity is a more complicated and nuanced quantity. Nontrivial lower bounds on ε-rigidity are known for some special matrix families, most notably the Hadamard matrices [25, 12]. Unfortunately, these results are not applicable to the matrices in our work (see Section 4). To obtain near-optimal lower bounds on approximation rank, we use specialized techniques that target approximation rank without attacking the harder problem of ε-rigidity.

7   Conclusions and Open Problems

This paper studies the ε-approximation rank of a concept class $\mathscr{C}$, defined as the minimum size of a set of features whose linear combinations can pointwise approximate each $f \in \mathscr{C}$ within ε. Our main results give exponential lower bounds on $\text{rank}_\varepsilon(\mathscr{C})$ even for the simplest concept classes. These in turn establish exponential lower bounds on the running time of the known algorithms for distribution-free agnostic learning. An obvious open problem is to develop an approach to agnostic learning that does not rely on pointwise approximation by a small set of features.

Another major open problem is to prove strong lower bounds on the dimension complexity and SQ dimension of natural concept classes. We have shown that

$$\text{rank}_{1/3}(\mathscr{C}) \geqslant \frac{1}{2}\text{sqdim}(\mathscr{C}) - O(1) \qquad \text{and} \qquad \text{rank}_\varepsilon(\mathscr{C}) \geqslant \text{dc}(\mathscr{C}),$$

for each concept class $\mathscr{C}$. In this sense, lower bounds on approximation rank are prerequisites for lower bounds on dimension complexity and the SQ dimension. Of particular interest in this respect are polynomial-size DNF formulas and, more broadly, AC^0 circuits. While this paper obtains strong lower bounds on their approximation rank, it remains a hard open problem to prove an exponential lower bound on their dimension complexity and SQ dimension.

References

1. Alon, N.: Problems and results in extremal combinatorics, Part I. Discrete Mathematics 273(1-3), 31–53 (2003)
2. Ben-David, S., Eiron, N., Simon, H.U.: Limitations of learning via embeddings in Euclidean half spaces. J. Mach. Learn. Res 3, 441–461 (2003)
3. Bshouty, N.H., Tamon, C.: On the Fourier spectrum of monotone functions. J. ACM 43(4), 747–770 (1996)
4. Buhrman, H., de Wolf, R.: Communication complexity lower bounds by polynomials. In: Conference on Computational Complexity (CCC), pp. 120–130 (2001)

5. Buhrman, H., Vereshchagin, N.K., de Wolf, R.: On computation and communication with small bias. In: 22nd IEEE Conference on Computational Complexity (2007)
6. Decatur, S.E.: Statistical queries and faulty PAC oracles. In: COLT, pp. 262–268 (1993)
7. Forster, J.: A linear lower bound on the unbounded error probabilistic communication complexity. J. Comput. Syst. Sci. 65(4), 612–625 (2002)
8. Forster, J., Simon, H.U.: On the smallest possible dimension and the largest possible margin of linear arrangements representing given concept classes. Theor. Comput. Sci. 350(1), 40–48 (2006)
9. Golub, G.H., Loan, C.F.V.: Matrix computations, 3rd edn. Johns Hopkins University Press, Baltimore, MD, USA (1996)
10. Jackson, J.C.: The harmonic sieve: A novel application of Fourier analysis to machine learning theory and practice. PhD thesis, Carnegie Mellon University (1995)
11. Kalai, A., Klivans, A., Mansour, Y., Servedio, R.: Agnostically learning halfspaces. In: FOCS: IEEE Symposium on Foundations of Computer Science (FOCS) (2005)
12. Kashin, B., Razborov, A.A.: Improved lower bounds on the rigidity of Hadamard matrices (In Russian). Matematicheskie zamet 63(4), 535–540 (1998)
13. Kearns, M.: Efficient noise-tolerant learning from statistical queries. In: STOC '93: Proceedings of the twenty-fifth annual ACM symposium on theory of computing, pp. 392–401. ACM Press, New York (1993)
14. Kearns, M., Li, M.: Learning in the presence of malicious errors. SIAM Journal on Computing 22(4), 807–837 (1993)
15. Kearns, M.J., Shapire, R.E., Sellie, L.M.: Toward efficient agnostic learning. Machine Learning 17(2–3), 115–141 (1994)
16. Kearns, M.J., Vazirani, U.V.: An Introduction to Computational Learning Theory. MIT Press, Cambridge, MA, USA (1994)
17. Klivans, A.R., O'Donnell, R., Servedio, R.A.: Learning intersections and thresholds of halfspaces. J. Comput. Syst. Sci. 68(4), 808–840 (2004)
18. Klivans, A.R., Servedio, R.: Learning DNF in time $2^{\tilde{O}(n^{1/3})}$. In: STOC '01: Proceedings of the thirty-third annual ACM symposium on Theory of computing, pp. 258–265. ACM Press, New York (2001)
19. Kushilevitz, E., Mansour, Y.: Learning decision trees using the Fourier spectrum. SIAM J. Comput. 22(6), 1331–1348 (1993)
20. Kushilevitz, E., Nisan, N.: Communication complexity. Cambridge University Press, Cambridge (1997)
21. Linial, N., Mansour, Y., Nisan, N.: Constant depth circuits, Fourier transform, and learnability. J. ACM 40(3), 607–620 (1993)
22. Linial, N., Mendelson, S., Schechtman, G., Shraibman, A.: Complexity measures of sign matrices. Combinatorica, (2006) To appear, Manuscript at http://www.cs.huji.ac.il/~nati/PAPERS/complexity_matrices.ps.gz
23. Linial, N., Shraibman, A.: Learning complexity vs. communication complexity. (December 2006) Manuscript at http://www.cs.huji.ac.il/~nati/PAPERS/lcc.pdf
24. Linial, N., Shraibman, A.: Lower bounds in communication complexity based on factorization norms. (December 2006) Manuscript at http://www.cs.huji.ac.il/~nati/PAPERS/ccfn.pdf
25. Lokam, S.V.: Spectral methods for matrix rigidity with applications to size-depth trade-offs and communication complexity. J. Comput. Syst. Sci. 63(3), 449–473 (2001)
26. Mansour, Y.: An $O(n^{\log \log n})$ learning algorithm for DNF under the uniform distribution. In: COLT '92: Proceedings of the Fifth Annual Workshop on Computational Learning Theory, pp. 53–61. ACM Press, New York, USA (1992)

27. Mansour, Y., Parnas, M.: On learning conjunctions with malicious noise. In: ISTCS, pp. 170–175 (1996)
28. O'Donnell, R., Servedio, R.A.: Extremal properties of polynomial threshold functions. In: IEEE Conference on Computational Complexity, pp. 3–12 (2003)
29. Paturi, R.: On the degree of polynomials that approximate symmetric Boolean functions. In: STOC: ACM Symposium on Theory of Computing (STOC) (1992)
30. Razborov, A.A.: Quantum communication complexity of symmetric predicates. Izvestiya of the Russian Academy of Science, Mathematics 67, 145–159 (2002)
31. Rudin, W.: Principles of Mathematical Analysis, 3rd edn. McGraw-Hill, New York (1976)
32. Sherstov, A.A.: Halfspace matrices. In: Proc. of the 22nd Conference on Computational Complexity (CCC) (2007)
33. Sherstov, A.A.: Separating AC^0 from depth-2 majority circuits. In: Proc. of the 39th Symposium on Theory of Computing (STOC) (2007)
34. Valiant, L.G.: Learning disjunctions of conjunctions. California 1, 560–566 (1985)

A   Discrepancy and Approximation Rank

The purpose of this section is to prove the relationship between discrepancy and approximation rank needed in Section 4. We start with several definitions and auxiliary results due to Linial et al. [22, 24, 23].

For a real matrix A, let $\|A\|_{1\to 2}$ denote the largest Euclidean norm of a column of A, and let $\|A\|_{2\to\infty}$ denote the largest Euclidean norm of a row of A. Define

$$\gamma_2(A) = \min_{XY=A} \|X\|_{2\to\infty}\|Y\|_{1\to 2}.$$

For a sign matrix M, its *margin complexity* is defined as

$$\mathrm{mc}(M) = \min\{\gamma_2(A) : A \text{ real, } A_{ij}M_{ij} \geq 1 \text{ for all } i,j\}.$$

Lemma 4 (Linial et al. [22, Lem. 9]). *Let A be a real matrix. Then $\gamma_2(A) \leq \sqrt{\mathrm{rank}(A) \cdot \|A\|_\infty}$.*

Theorem 13 (Linial and Shraibman [23]). *Let M be a sign matrix. Then $\mathrm{mc}(M) \geq 1/(8\,\mathrm{disc}(M))$.*

Putting these pieces together yields our desired result:

Lemma 3 (Restated from Sec. 3.2). *Let M be a sign matrix and $0 \leq \varepsilon < 1$. Then*

$$\mathrm{rank}_\varepsilon(M) \geq \frac{1-\varepsilon}{1+\varepsilon} \cdot \frac{1}{64\,\mathrm{disc}(M)^2}.$$

Proof. Let A be any real matrix with $\|A-M\|_\infty \leq \varepsilon$. Put $B = \frac{1}{1-\varepsilon}A$. We have:

$$\mathrm{rank}(A) = \mathrm{rank}(B) \overset{\text{Lem. 4}}{\geq} \frac{\gamma_2(B)^2}{\|B\|_\infty} \geq \frac{\mathrm{mc}(M)^2}{\|B\|_\infty} \overset{\text{Thm. 13}}{\geq} \frac{1}{\|B\|_\infty} \cdot \frac{1}{64\,\mathrm{disc}(M)^2}$$

$$\geq \frac{1-\varepsilon}{1+\varepsilon} \cdot \frac{1}{64\,\mathrm{disc}(M)^2}. \qquad \square$$

Sketching Information Divergences

Sudipto Guha[1,*], Piotr Indyk[2], and Andrew McGregor[3]

[1] University of Pennsylvania
sudipto@cis.upenn.edu
[2] Massachusetts Institute of Technology
indyk@theory.lcs.mit.edu
[3] University of California, San Diego
andrewm@ucsd.edu

Abstract. When comparing discrete probability distributions, natural measures of similarity are not ℓ_p distances but rather are information-divergences such as Kullback-Leibler and Hellinger. This paper considers some of the issues related to constructing small-space *sketches* of distributions, a concept related to dimensionality-reduction, such that these measures can be approximately computed from the sketches. Related problems for ℓ_p distances are reasonably well understood via a series of results including Johnson, Lindenstrauss [27,18], Alon, Matias, Szegedy [1], Indyk [24], and Brinkman, Charikar [8]. In contrast, almost no analogous results are known to date about constructing sketches for the information-divergences used in statistics and learning theory.

1 Introduction

Which distances can be sketched in sub-linear space? In recent years, streaming algorithms have received significant attention in an attempt to cope with massive datasets [23,1,20]. A streaming computation is a sublinear space algorithm that reads the input in sequential order and any item not explicitly remembered is inaccessible. A fundamental problem in the model is the estimation of distances between two objects that are determined by the stream, e.g., the network traffic matrices at two routers. Estimation of distances allows us to construct approximate representations, e.g., histograms, wavelets, Fourier summaries, or equivalently, find models of the input stream, since this problem reduces to finding the "closest" representation in a suitable class. In this paper, the objects of interest are probability distributions defined by a stream of updates as follows.

Definition 1. *Given a data stream $S = \langle a_1, \ldots, a_m \rangle$ with each data item $a_i \in \{p, q\} \times [n]$ we define $S(p) = \langle a_1^p, \ldots, a_{m(p)}^p \rangle$ to be the sub-stream consisting of data items of the form $\langle p, \cdot \rangle$. $S(p)$ defines a distribution $(p_1, \ldots, p_n)$ where $p_i = m(p)_i / m(p)$ and $m(p)_i = |\{j : a_j^p = \langle p, i \rangle\}|$. Similarly define $S(q)$ and q_i.*

* This research was supported by in part by an Alfred P. Sloan Research Fellowship and by NSF Awards CCF-0430376, and CCF-0644119.

N. Bshouty and C. Gentile (Eds.): COLT 2007, LNAI 4539, pp. 424–438, 2007.
© Springer-Verlag Berlin Heidelberg 2007

One of the cornerstones in the theory of data stream algorithms has been the result of Alon, Matias, and Szegedy [1]. They showed that it is possible to compute a $(1 + \epsilon)$-approximation of $\ell_2(p, q)$ using only $\text{poly}(\epsilon^{-1}, \log n)$ space. The algorithm can be viewed as a partial de-randomization of the famous embedding result of Johnson and Lindenstrauss [27,18]. This result implies that for any two vectors p and q and an $n \times k$ matrix A whose entries are independent $N(0, 1)$ random variables, then, with constant probability,

$$(1 - \epsilon)\ell_2(p, q) \leq nk^{-1}\ell_2(Ap, Aq) \leq (1 + \epsilon)\ell_2(p, q)$$

for some $k = \text{poly}(\epsilon^{-1}, \log n)$. Alon, Matias, and Szegedy demonstrated that an "effective" A can be stored in small space and can be used to maintain a small-space, update-able summary, or *sketch*, of p and q. The ℓ_2 distance between p and q can then be estimated using only the sketches of p and q. While Brinkman and Charikar [8] proved that there was no analogy of the Johnson-Lindenstrauss result for ℓ_1, Indyk [24] demonstrated that $\ell_1(p, q)$ could also be estimated in $\text{poly}(\epsilon^{-1}, \log n)$ space using Cauchy$(0, 1)$ random variables rather than $N(0, 1)$ random variables. The results extended to all ℓ_p-measures with $0 < p \leq 2$ using stable distributions. Over a sequence of papers [36,11,25,4,14], ℓ_p and Hamming distances have become well understood. In parallel, several methods of creating summary representations of streams have been proposed for a variety of applications [9,12,15]; in terms of distances they can be adapted to compute the Jaccard coefficient (symmetric difference over union) for two sets. One of the principal motivations of this work is to characterize the distances that can be sketched.

The Information Divergences. Applications in pattern matching, image analysis, statistical learning, etc., use distances which are not ℓ_p norms. Several distances[1] such as the Kullback-Leibler and Hellinger divergences are central to estimating the distances between distributions, and have had a long history of study in statistics and information theory literature. We will discuss two broad classes of distance measures (1) f-divergences, which are central to statistical tests and (2) Bregman Divergences which are central to finding optimal models using mathematical programming.

Definition 2 (f-Divergences). *Given two distributions $p = (p_1, \ldots, p_n)$ and $q = (q_1, \ldots, q_n)$ these distances are given by, $\mathcal{D}_f(p, q) = \sum_i p_i f(q_i/p_i)$, for any function f that is convex over $(0, \infty)$ and satisfies $f(1) = 0$. We define $0f(0/0) = 0$, and $0f(a/0) = \lim_{t \to 0} t f(a/t) = a \lim_{u \to \infty} f(u)/u$.*

The quantity q_i/p_i is the "likelihood ratio" and a fundamental aspect of these measures is that these divergences are tied to "ratio tests" in Neyman-Pearson style hypothesis testing [16]. Several of these divergences appear as exponents of error probabilities for optimal classifiers, e.g., in Stein's Lemma. Results of Csiszár [17], Liese and Vajda [31], and Amari [2,3] show that f-divergences are

---

[1] Several of the "distances" used are not metric, and a more appropriate reference is divergence; we will refer to them as divergences for the rest of the paper.

the unique class of distances on distributions that arise from a fairly simple set of axioms, e.g., permutation invariance, non-decreasing local projections, and certain direct sum theorems. In many ways these divergences are "natural" to distributions and statistics, in much the same way that ℓ_2 is a natural measure for points in $\mathbb{R}^n$. Given streams $S(p)$ and $S(q)$, it is natural to ask whether these streams are alike or given a prior model of the data, how well does either conform to the prior? These are scenarios where estimation of f-divergences is the most natural problem at hand. Notably, ℓ_1 distance is an f-divergence, $f(u) = |u-1|$, referred to as the Variational distance. However, ℓ_1 distances do not capture the "marginal" utilities of evidence and in innumerable cases Kullback–Leibler $(f(u) = -\log(u))$, Hellinger $(f(u) = (\sqrt{u} - 1)^2)$, and Jensen–Shannon divergences $(f(u) = -(u+1)\log\frac{1+u}{2} + u\log u)$ are preferred. An important "smooth" subclass of the f-divergences are the α-divergences where $f(u) = 1 - u^{(1+\alpha)/2}$.

A major reason for investigating these f-divergences lies in loss functions used in statistical learning. The ℓ_1 distance captures the "hinge loss" and the other divergences are geared towards non-linear losses. To understand the connection better, we need to also discuss the connections between f-divergences and Bregman divergences. The general family of "arcing" [7] and "AnyBoost" [32] family of algorithms fall into a constrained convex programming framework introduced earlier by Bregman [6]. Friedman, Hastie and Tibshirani [26] established the connection between boosting algorithms and logistic loss, and subsequently over a series of papers [30,29,28,13], the study of Bregman divergences and information geometry has become the method of choice for studying exponential loss functions. The connection between loss functions and f-divergences are investigated more recently by Nguyen, Wainright, and Jordan [34].

Definition 3 (Decomposable Bregman Divergences). *Given two distributions $p = (p_1, \ldots, p_n)$ and $q = (q_1, \ldots, q_n)$, the Bregman divergence between p and q is $\mathcal{B}_F(p, q) = \sum_i [F(p_i) - F(q_i) - (p_i - q_i)F'(q_i)]$ for any strictly convex function F.*

Perhaps the most familiar Bregman divergence is ℓ_2^2 with $F(z) = z^2$. The Kullback–Leibler divergence is also a Bregman divergence with $F(z) = z \log z$, and the Itakura–Saito divergence $F(z) = -\log z$. Lafferty et al. [30] suggest $F(z) = -z^\alpha + \alpha z - \alpha + 1$ for $\alpha \in (0, 1)$, $F(z) = z^\alpha - \alpha z + \alpha - 1$ for $\alpha < 0$.

The fundamental use of Bregman divergences is in finding optimal models. Given a distribution q we are interested in finding a p that best matches the data, and this is posed as a convex optimization problem $\min_p \mathcal{B}_F(p, q)$. It is easy to verify that any positive linear combination of Bregman divergences is a Bregman divergence and that the Bregman balls are convex in the first argument but often not in the second. This is the particular appeal of the technique, that the divergence depends on the data naturally and the divergences have come to be known as Information Geometry techniques. Furthermore there is a natural convex duality between the optimum representation p^* under $\mathcal{B}_F$, and the divergence $\mathcal{B}_F$. This connection to convex optimization is one of the many reasons for the emerging heavy use of Bregman divergences in the learning literature.

Given that we can estimate ℓ_1 and ℓ_2 distances between two streams in small space, it is natural to ask which other f-divergences and Bregman-divergences are sketchable?

Our Contributions: In this paper we take several steps towards a characterization of the distances that can be sketched. Our first results are negative and help us understand why the ℓ_1 and ℓ_2 distances are special among the f and Bregman divergences.

- We prove the *Shift Invariant Theorem* that characterizes a large family of distances that are not estimable in the streaming model. This theorem pertains to decomposable distances, i.e., distances $d : \mathbb{R}^n \times \mathbb{R}^n \to \mathbb{R}^+$ for which there exists a $\phi : \mathbb{R} \times \mathbb{R} \to \mathbb{R}^+$ such that $d(x,y) = \sum_{i \in [n]} \phi(x_i, y_i)$. The theorem suggest that unless $\phi(x_i, y_i)$ is a function of $x_i - y_i$ then the measure d cannot be sketched.
- For all f-divergence where f is twice differentiable and f'' is strictly positive, no polynomial factor approximation of $\mathcal{D}_f(p,q)$ is possible in sub-linear space. Note that for ℓ_1, which can be sketched, the function $f(\zeta) = |\zeta - 1|$ and therefore f'' is not defined at 1.
- For all Bregman divergences $\mathcal{B}_F$ where F is twice differentiable and there exists $\rho, z_0 > 0$ such that,

$$\forall\, 0 \leq z_2 \leq z_1 \leq z_0, \frac{F''(z_1)}{F''(z_2)} \geq \left(\frac{z_1}{z_2}\right)^\rho \text{ or } \forall\, 0 \leq z_2 \leq z_1 \leq z_0, \frac{F''(z_1)}{F''(z_2)} \leq \left(\frac{z_2}{z_1}\right)^\rho$$

then no polynomial factor approximation of $\mathcal{B}_F$ is possible in sub-linear space. This condition effectively states that $F''(z)$ vanishes or diverges monotonically, and polynomially fast, as z approaches zero. Note that for ℓ_2^2, which can be sketched, the function $F(z) = z^2$ and F'' is constant everywhere.

Given the lower bounds, we ask the question of finding additive bounds in sublinear space. We say an algorithm returns an (ϵ, δ)-additive-approximation for a real number Q if it outputs a value $\hat{Q}$ such that $|\hat{Q} - Q| \leq \epsilon$ with probability at least $(1 - \delta)$ over its internal coin tosses. Some results for two pass algorithms were presented in [22]. In this paper we show sharp characterizations about what can be achieved in a single pass.

- Any $(\epsilon, 1/4)$-additive-approximation of an unbounded $\mathcal{D}_f$ requires $\Omega(n)$-space for any constant ϵ. Alternatively if $\mathcal{D}_f$ is bounded then we can (ϵ, δ)-additive-approximate $\mathcal{D}_f$ in $O_\epsilon(\sqrt{n} \log n \log \delta^{-1})$ space[2]. The space bound can be improved for the Jensen-Shannon divergence. Also, for all bounded symmetric f-divergences, we can approximate $\mathcal{D}_f(p,q)$ up to an additive ϵ in $O(\epsilon^{-2} \log \delta^{-1} \log n)$ space if one of p or q is known in advance.
- If $F(0)$ or $F'(0)$ is unbounded, then any $(\epsilon, 1/4)$-additive-approximation of $\mathcal{B}_F$ requires $\Omega(n)$ space for any constant ϵ. Alternatively, if $F(0), F'(0)$ and $F'(1)$ exist, we can approximate $\mathcal{B}_F(p,q)$ in $O_\epsilon(\log n \log \delta^{-1})$ space.

---

[2] The notation $O_\epsilon(\cdot)$ treats ϵ as if constant

2   Geometry of $\mathcal{D}_f$ and $\mathcal{B}_F$

In this section we first present some simple geometric results that will allow us to make certain useful assumptions about an f or F defining an f–divergence or Bregman divergence.

We start by defining a *conjugate* $f^*(u) = uf(\frac{1}{u})$. We can then write any f-Divergence as,

$$D_f(p,q) = \sum_{i:p_i>q_i} p_i f(q_i/p_i) + \sum_{i:q_i>p_i} q_i f^*(p_i/q_i) \ .$$

The following lemma that demonstrates that we may assume that $f(u) \in [0, f(0)]$ and $f^*(u) \in [0, f^*(0)]$ for $u \in [0,1]$ where both $f(0) = \lim_{u\to 0} f(u)$ and $f^*(0) = \lim_{u\to 0} f^*(u)$ exist if f is bounded.

Lemma 1. *Let f be a real-valued function that is convex on $(0,\infty)$ and satisfies $f(1) = 0$. Then there exists a real-valued function g that is convex on $(0,\infty)$ and satisfies $g(1) = 0$ such that*

1. $\mathcal{D}_f(p,q) = \mathcal{D}_g(p,q)$ *for all distributions p and q.*
2. *g is decreasing in the range $(0,1]$ and increasing in the range $[1,\infty)$. In particular, if f is differentiable at 1 then $g'(1) = 0$.*

Furthermore, if $\mathcal{D}_f$ is bounded then

3. *$g(0) = \lim_{u\to 0} g(u)$ and $g^*(0) = \lim_{u\to 0} g^*(u)$ exists.*

For example, the Hellinger divergence can be realized by either $f(u) = (\sqrt{u} - 1)^2$ or $f(u) = 2 - 2\sqrt{u}$. The next lemma will be important when bounding the error terms in our algorithms.

Lemma 2. *For any function f that is positive and convex on $(0,1]$ with $f(1) = 0$, for all $0 < a < b < c \le 1$, $|f(c) - f(b)| \le \frac{c-b}{c-a} f(a)$.*

Similar to Lemma 1, the following lemma demonstrates that, without loss of generality, we may make various assumptions about the F that defines a Bregman divergence.

Lemma 3. *Let F be a differentiable, real valued function that is strictly convex on $(0,1]$ such that $\lim_{u\to 0+} F(u)$ and $\lim_{u\to 0+} F'(u)$ exist. Then there exists a differentiable, real valued function G that is strictly convex on $(0,1]$ and,*

1. $\mathcal{B}_F(p,q) = \mathcal{B}_G(p,q)$ *for all distributions p and q.*
2. *$G(z) \ge 0$ for $x \in (0,1]$ and G is increasing in the range $(0,1]$.*
3. $\lim_{u\to 0+} G'(u) = 0$ and $\lim_{u\to 0+} G(u) = 0$.

3   Techniques

In this section we summarize some of the sketching and sampling techniques that we will use in the algorithms in the subsequent sections. We then review the general approach for proving lower bounds in the data stream model.

AMS-Sketches: A size-k AMS-Sketch of the stream $S(p) = \langle a_1^p, \ldots, a_{m(p)}^p \rangle$ consists of k independent, identically distributed random variables $X_1, \ldots, X_k$. Each X_i is determined by $X_i = |\{j : a_j^p = a_J^p, J \leq j \leq m(p)\}|$ where J is chosen uniformly at random from $[m(p)]$. This sketch is useful for estimating quantities of the form $m(p)^{-1} \sum_{i \in [n]} f(m(p)_i)$ because, if $f(0) = 0$ then

$$E\left[f(X_i) - f(X_i - 1)\right] = m(p)^{-1} \sum_{i \in [n]} f(m(p)_i) \ .$$

It can be constructed by a streaming computation using only $O(k)$ counters [1].

MG-Sketches: A size-k MG-Sketch of the stream $S(p)$ is a deterministic construction that consists of estimates $(\tilde{p}_i)_{i \in [n]}$ for the probability distribution $(p_i)_{i \in [n]}$. These estimates satisfy $p_i - 1/k \leq \tilde{p}_i \leq p_i$ for all $i \in [n]$. Also, at most k values of $\tilde{p}_i$ are non-zero and hence a size k MG-Sketch can be stored with $O(k)$ counters. Furthermore, the sketch can be constructed by a streaming computation using only $O(k)$ counters [33,5,19].

Universe-Sampling: A size-k Universe-Sample of $S(p)$ consists of the exact values of p_i for k randomly chosen $i \in [n]$. It can be trivially constructed by a streaming computation using only $O(k)$ counters.

Lower Bounds: A component of the lower bounds we prove in this paper is a reduction from the communication complexity of SET-DISJOINTNESS. An instance of this problem consists of two binary strings, $x, y \in \mathbb{F}_2^n$ such that $\sum_i x_i = \sum_i y_i = n/4$. Alice knows the string x and Bob knows the string y. Alice and Bob take turns to send messages to each other with the goal of determining if x and y are disjoint, i.e. $x.y = 0$. Determining if $x.y = 0$ with probability at least $3/4$ requires $\Omega(n)$ bits to be communicated [35].

Our lower bound proofs use the following template. We suppose that there exists a streaming algorithm $\mathcal{A}$ that takes P passes over a stream and uses W working memory to approximate some quantity. We then show how Alice and Bob can construct a set of stream elements $S_A(x)$ and $S_B(y)$ such that the value returned by $\mathcal{A}$ on the stream containing $S_A(x) \cup S_B(y)$ determines whether $x.y = 0$. Alice and Bob can then emulate $\mathcal{A}$: Alice runs $\mathcal{A}$ on $S_A(x)$, communicates the memory state of $\mathcal{A}$, Bob runs $\mathcal{A}$ initiated with this memory state on $S_B(x)$ and communicates the memory state of $\mathcal{A}$ to Alice and so on. This protocol transmits $(2P-1)W$ bits and hence if $P = O(1)$, we deduce that $W = \Omega(n)$.

It should be noted that such a style of proof has been used widely. The novelty of our lower bound proofs is in using the geometry of $\mathcal{D}_f$ and $\mathcal{B}_F$ to construct suitable $S_A(x)$ and $S_B(y)$.

4   Multiplicative Approximations

We start with the central theorem of this section, the *Shift Invariance Theorem*. This theorem characterizes a large class of divergences that are not sketchable.

Theorem 1 (Shift Invariance Theorem). *Let* $\phi : [0,1] \times [0,1] \to \mathbb{R}^+$ *satisfy* $\phi(x,x) = 0$ *for all* $x \in [0,1]$ *and there exists* $n_0, a, b, c \in \mathbb{N}$ *such that for all* $n \geq n_0,$

$$\max\left(\phi\left(\frac{a}{m}, \frac{a+c}{m}\right), \phi\left(\frac{a+c}{m}, \frac{a}{m}\right)\right) > \frac{\alpha^2 n}{4}\left(\phi\left(\frac{b+c}{m}, \frac{b}{m}\right) + \phi\left(\frac{b}{m}, \frac{b+c}{m}\right)\right)$$

where $m = an/4 + bn + cn/2$. *Then any algorithm that returns an* α *approximation of* $d(p,q) = \sum_{i \in [5n/4]} \phi(p_i, q_i)$ *with probability at least* $3/4$ *where* p *and* q *are defined by a stream of length* $O((a+b+c)n)$ *over* $[5n/4]$ *requires* $\Omega(n)$ *space.*

Proof. We refer the reader to the lower bounds template discussed in Section 3. Assume that n is divisible by 4 and $n > n_0$. Let $(x, y) \in \mathbb{F}_2^n \times \mathbb{F}_2^n$ be an instance of SET-DISJOINTNESS where $\sum_i x_i = \sum_i y_i = n/4$. Alice and Bob determine the prefix of a stream $S_A(x)$ and the suffix $S_B(y)$ respectively. We first assume that $\phi(a/m, (a+c)/m) \geq \phi((a+c)/m, a/m)$.

$$S_A(x) = \bigcup_{i \in [n]} \{ax_i + b(1 - x_i) \text{ copies of } \langle p, i \rangle \text{ and } \langle q, i \rangle\}$$

$$\cup \bigcup_{i \in [n/4]} \{b \text{ copies of } \langle p, i+n \rangle \text{ and } \langle q, i+n \rangle\}$$

$$S_B(y) = \bigcup_{i \in [n]} \{cy_i \text{ copies of } \langle q, i \rangle\} \cup \bigcup_{i \in [n/4]} \{c \text{ copies of } \langle p, i+n \rangle\}$$

Observe that $m(p) = m(q) = an/4 + bn + cn/2$ and

$$\mathcal{D}_f(p,q) = (x.y)\phi\left(\frac{a}{m}, \frac{a+c}{m}\right) + (n/4 - x.y)\phi\left(\frac{b}{m}, \frac{b+c}{m}\right) + (n/4)\phi\left(\frac{b+c}{m}, \frac{b}{m}\right) .$$

Therefore,

$$x.y = 0 \Leftrightarrow \mathcal{D}_f(p,q) = (n/4)(\phi(b/m, (b+c)/m) + \phi((b+c)/m, b/m))$$
$$x.y = 1 \Leftrightarrow \mathcal{D}_f(p,q) \geq \alpha^2(n/4)(\phi(b/m, (b+c)/m) + \phi((b+c)/m, b/m))$$

Therefore any α-approximation would determine the value of $x.y$ and hence an α-approximation requires $\Omega(n)$ space [35]. If $\phi(a/m, (a+c)/m) \leq \phi((a+c)/m, a/m)$ then the proof follows by reversing the roles of p and q.

The above theorem suggests that unless $\phi(x_i, y_i)$ is some function of $x_i - y_i$ then the distance is not sketchable. The result holds even if the algorithm may take a constant number of passes over the data. We also mention a simpler result that can be proved using similar ideas to those employed above. This states that if there exist $a, b, c \in \mathbb{N}$ such that

$$\max\left(\frac{\phi(a+c, a)}{\phi(b+c, b)}, \frac{\phi(a, a+c)}{\phi(b, b+c)}\right) > \alpha^2 ,$$

then any single-pass α-approximation of $\sum_{i\in[n]} \phi(m(p)_i, m(q)_i)$ requires $\Omega(n)$ space.

We next present two corollaries of Theorem 1. These characterize the f-divergences and Bregman divergences that can be not be sketched. Note that ℓ_1 and ℓ_2^2, which can be sketched, are the only commonly used divergences that do not satisfy the relevant conditions.

Corollary 1 (f-Divergences). *Given an f-divergence $\mathcal{D}_f$, if f is twice differentiable and f'' is strictly positive, then no polynomial factor approximation of $\mathcal{D}_f$ is possible in sub-linear space.*

Proof. We first note that by Lemma 1 we may assume $f(1) = f'(1) = 0$. Let $a = c = 1$ and $b = \alpha^2 n(f''(1) + 1)/(8f(2))$ where α is an arbitrary polynomial in n. Note that $f(2) > 0$ because f is strictly convex.

We start by observing that,

$$\phi(b/m, (b+c)/m) = (b/m)f(1 + 1/b) = (b/m)\left[f(1) + \frac{1}{b}f'(1) + \frac{1}{2!b^2}f''(1+\gamma)\right]$$

for some $\gamma \in [0, 1/b]$ by Taylor's Theorem. Since $f(1) = f'(1) = 0$ and $f''(t)$ is continuous at $t = 1$ this implies that for sufficiently large n, $f''(1+\gamma) \leq f''(1)+1$ and so,

$$\phi(b/m, (b+c)/m) \leq \frac{f''(1)+1}{2mb} = \frac{f''(1)+1}{2f(2)b}m^{-1}f(2) \leq \frac{8}{\alpha^2 n}\phi(a/m, (a+c)/m) \ .$$

Similarly we can show that for sufficiently large n,

$$\phi((b+c)/m, b/m) \leq \frac{8}{\alpha^2 n}\phi(a/m, (a+c)/m) \ .$$

Then appealing to Theorem 1 we get the required result.

Corollary 2 (Bregman Divergences). *Given a Bregman divergences $\mathcal{B}_F$, if F is twice differentiable and there exists $\rho, z_0 > 0$ such that,*

$$\forall\, 0 \leq z_2 \leq z_1 \leq z_0,\ \frac{F''(z_1)}{F''(z_2)} \geq \left(\frac{z_1}{z_2}\right)^\rho \ or \ \forall\, 0 \leq z_2 \leq z_1 \leq z_0,\ \frac{F''(z_1)}{F''(z_2)} \leq \left(\frac{z_2}{z_1}\right)^\rho$$

then no polynomial factor approximation of $\mathcal{B}_F$ is possible in sub-linear space.

This condition effectively states that $F''(z)$ vanishes or diverges monotonically, and polynomially fast, as $z \to 0$.

Proof. By the Mean-Value Theorem, for any $m, r \in \mathbb{N}$, there exists $\gamma(r) \in [0, 1]$ such that, $\phi(r/m, (r + 1)/m) + \phi((r + 1)/m, r/m) = m^{-2}F''((r + \gamma(r))/m)$. Therefore, for any $a, b \in \mathbb{N}, c = 1$ and $m = an/4 + bn + n/2$,

$$\frac{\max\left(\phi\left(\frac{a}{m}, \frac{a+c}{m}\right), \phi\left(\frac{a+c}{m}, \frac{a}{m}\right)\right)}{\phi\left(\frac{b+c}{m}, \frac{b}{m}\right) + \phi\left(\frac{b}{m}, \frac{b+c}{m}\right)} \geq \frac{1}{2}\frac{F''((a+\gamma(a))/m)}{F''((b+\gamma(b))/m)} \ .$$

If $\forall\ 0 \leq z_2 \leq z_1 \leq z_0$, $F''(z_1)/F''(z_2) \geq (z_1/z_2)^\rho$ then set $a = (\alpha^2 n)^{1/\rho}$ and $b = 1$ where α is an arbitrary polynomial in n. If $\forall\ 0 \leq z_2 \leq z_1 \leq z_0$, $F''(z_1)/F''(z_2) \geq (z_2/z_1)^\rho$ then set $a = 1$ and $b = (\alpha n)^{1/\rho}$. In both cases we deduce that the RHS of Eqn. 1 is greater than $\alpha^2 n/4$. Hence, appealing to Theorem 1, we get the required result.

5   Additive Approximations

In this section we focus on additive approximations. As mentioned earlier, the probability of misclassification using ratio tests is often bounded by $2^{-\mathcal{D}_f}$, for certain $\mathcal{D}_f$. Hence, an additive ϵ approximation translates to a multiplicative 2^ϵ factor for computing the error probability. Our goal is the characterization of divergences that can be approximated additively.

5.1   Lower Bound for f-Divergences

In this section we show that to additively approximate $\mathcal{D}_f(p,q)$ up to any additive $\epsilon > 0$, $\mathcal{D}_f$ must be bounded.

Theorem 2. *Any $(\epsilon, 1/4)$-additive-approximation of an unbounded $\mathcal{D}_f$ requires $\Omega(n)$ space. This applies even if one of the distributions is known to be uniform.*

Proof. We refer the reader to the template for lower bounds discussed in Section 3. Let $(x, y) \in \mathbb{F}_2^n \times \mathbb{F}_2^n$ be an instance of SET-DISJOINTNESS. Then define q be the following stream elements.

$$S_A(x) = \{1 - x_i \text{ copies of } \langle q, i \rangle \text{ for } i \in [n]\}$$
$$S_B(y) = \{1 - y_i \text{ copies of } \langle q, i \rangle \text{ for } i \in [n]\}$$

Let p be the uniform distribution. If $\lim_{u \to 0} f(u)$ is unbounded then $\mathcal{D}_f(p, q)$ is finite iff $x.y = 0$. If $\lim_{u \to \infty} \frac{1}{u} f(u)$ is unbounded then $\mathcal{D}_f(q, p)$ is finite iff $x.y = 0$.

5.2   Upper Bounds for f-Divergences

In this section we show an additive approximation that complements the lower bound in the previous section. Note that since for any f–divergence, a function $af(\cdot)$ for $a > 0$ gives another f–divergence, the best we can hope for is an approximation which is dependent on $\max\{\lim_{u \to 0} f(u), \lim_{u \to \infty} \frac{1}{u} f(u)\}$. In what follows we assume that this value is 1. The idea behind the algorithm is a combination of Universe-Sampling and MG-Sketching. With MG-Sketches we can identify all $i \in [n]$ such that either p_i or q_i is larger than some threshold. For the remaining i it is possible to show that $p_i f(q_i/p_i)$ is small enough such that estimating the contribution of these terms by Universe-Sampling yields the required result. See Figure 1 for a detailed description of the algorithm.

The algorithm f-Est(p,q): Let ϵ be a user-specified value in the range $(0,1)$. Let $\gamma(\epsilon) < \epsilon/16$ be such that

$$\forall u \leq \gamma, |f(u) - \lim_{u \to 0} f(u)| \leq \epsilon/16 \quad \text{and} \quad \forall u \geq \frac{1}{\gamma}, \left|\frac{1}{u}f(u) - \lim_{u \to \infty} \frac{1}{u}f(u)\right| \leq \epsilon/16 .$$

1. Use Universe-Sampling to compute p_i, q_i for $i \in S$ where S is a random subset of $[n]$ of size $3\epsilon^{-2}n(\rho + \gamma^2\rho)\ln(2\delta^{-1})$ where $\rho = 1/\sqrt{n}$.
2. Use MG-Sketches to compute $(\tilde{p}_i)_{i \in [n]}$ and $(\tilde{q}_i)_{i \in [n]}$ such that

$$p_i - \gamma^2\rho \leq \tilde{p}_i \leq p_i \quad \text{and} \quad q_i - \gamma^2\rho \leq \tilde{q}_i \leq q_i .$$

3. Return,

$$\sum_{i \in T} \tilde{p}_i f(\tilde{q}_i/\tilde{p}_i) + \frac{n}{|S|}\sum_{i \in S \setminus T} p_i f(q_i/p_i)$$

where $T = \{i : \max\{\tilde{p}_i, \tilde{q}_i\} \geq \rho\}$.

Fig. 1. Additive Approximation of Some f-Divergences

Lemma 4. $\max\{p_i, q_i\} \leq \rho + \gamma^2\rho$ for $i \notin T$ and $\max\{p_i, q_i\} \geq \rho$ for $i \in T$. Furthermore,

$$\left|\sum_{i \in T} p_i f(q_i/p_i) - \sum_{i \in T} \tilde{p}_i f(\tilde{q}_i/\tilde{p}_i)\right| \geq \epsilon/2.$$

Proof. The first part of the lemma follows from the properties of the MG-Sketch discussed in Section 3. Let $\Delta(p_i)$, $\Delta(q_i/p_i)$, $\Delta(f(q_i/p_i))$, and $\Delta(q_i)$ be the absolute errors in $p_i, q_i/p_i, f(q_i/p_i), q_i$ respectively and note that,

$$|\tilde{p}_i f(\tilde{q}_i/\tilde{p}_i) - p_i f(q_i/p_i)| \leq f(q_i/p_i)\Delta(p_i) + p_i\Delta(f(q_i/p_i)) + \Delta(p_i)\Delta(f(q_i/p_i)) .$$

There are four cases to consider.

1. $p_i \geq \rho$ and $q_i \leq \gamma\rho/2$. Then $\Delta(f(q_i/p_i)) \leq \epsilon/8$ since $q_i/p_i, \tilde{q}_i/\tilde{p}_i \leq \gamma$ and f is non-increasing in the range $(0,1)$. Therefore,

$$|\tilde{p}_i f(\tilde{q}_i/\tilde{p}_i) - p_i f(q_i/p_i)| \leq \gamma^2\rho f(q_i/p_i) + \epsilon p_i/16 + \gamma^2\rho\epsilon/16+ \leq \epsilon p_i/8 .$$

2. $q_i \geq \rho$ and $p_i \leq \gamma\rho/2$. Similar to case 1.
3. $p_i \geq \rho$, $q_i \geq \gamma\rho/2$ and $p_i > q_i$. First note that $\Delta(q_i/p_i) \leq (2\gamma + \gamma^2)q_i/p_i$.

$$|\tilde{p}_i f(\tilde{q}_i/\tilde{p}_i) - p_i f(q_i/p_i)| \leq \gamma^2 p_i + p_i(2\gamma + \gamma^2)q_i/p_i + \gamma^2 p_i(2\gamma + \gamma^2)q_i/p_i$$
$$\leq \epsilon p_i/16 + \epsilon q_i/8 .$$

4. $q_i \geq \rho$, $p \geq \gamma\rho/2$, and $p_i < q_i$. Similar to case 3.

Therefore summarizing all cases, the additive error per-term is at most $\epsilon(q_i + p_i)/4$. Summing over all $i \in T$ establishes the second part of the lemma.

Theorem 3. *There exists an (ϵ, δ)-additive-approximation for any bounded f-divergence using $O_\epsilon(\sqrt{n}\log n \log \delta^{-1})$ space.*

Proof. The space use is immediate from the algorithm. The main observation to prove correctness is that for each $i \notin T$, $p_i, q_i \le \rho + \gamma^2\rho$, and hence $p_i f(q_i/p_i) \le \rho + 2\gamma^2\rho$. Hence, by an application of the Chernoff bound,

$$\Pr\left[\left|\frac{n}{|S|}\sum_{i\in S\backslash T} p_i f\left(\frac{q_i}{p_i}\right) - \sum_{i\in[n]\backslash T} p_i f\left(\frac{q_i}{p_i}\right)\right| \ge \epsilon/2\right] \le 2\exp\left(-\frac{|S|\epsilon^2}{3n(\rho + 2\gamma^2\rho)}\right).$$

This is at most δ for our value of $|S|$. Appealing to Lemma 4 yields the result.

Some f-divergences can be additively approximated in significantly smaller space. For example, the Jensen–Shannon divergence can be rewritten as

$$JS(p,q) = \ln 2\left(2H\left(\frac{p+q}{2}\right) - H(p) - H(q)\right),$$

where H is the entropy. There exists a single-pass (ϵ, δ)-additive-approximation of entropy in the streaming model [10]. This yields the following theorem.

Theorem 4. *There exists a single-pass (ϵ, δ)-additive-approximation of the JS-divergence using $O(\epsilon^{-2}\log^2 n \log^2 m \log \delta^{-1})$ space.*

Finally in this section we show that the space bound of $O_\epsilon(\sqrt{n}\log n \log \delta^{-1})$ can be improved if we knew one of the distributions, e.g., if we had a prior distribution and were trying to estimate a fit.

Theorem 5. *We can (ϵ, δ)-additively-approximate any f-divergence $\mathcal{D}_f(p,q)$ in space $O(\epsilon^{-2}\log n \log \delta^{-1})$ if $\mathcal{D}_f$ is bounded and one of p or q is known in advance.*

Proof. Let p be the known distribution and let q be defined by the stream. We may assume that $f(1) = f'(1) = 0$. Therefore,

$$\mathcal{D}_f(p,q) = \sum_{q_i<p_i} p_i f\left(\frac{q_i}{p_i}\right) + \sum_{q_i>p_i} q_i f^*\left(\frac{p_i}{q_i}\right).$$

We consider each term separately. To approximate the first term the algorithm picks i with respect to the known distribution p and then computes q_i. The basic estimator is

$$g(i) = \begin{cases} 0 & \text{if } q_i > p_i \\ f(q_i/p_i) & \text{if } q_i \le p_i \end{cases}.$$

Note that $E[g(i)] = \sum_{i:q_i<p_i} p_i f(q_i/p_i)$ and $0 \le g(i) \le f(0)$. Hence, applying Chernoff bounds we can $(\epsilon/2, \delta/2)$-additively-approximate $E[g(i)]$ with $O(\epsilon^{-2}\log \delta^{-1})$ basic estimators.

To approximate the second term we use an AMS-Sketch. Specifically, the algorithm picks a random i in the stream q and computes, r_i, the number of times i occurs after it was picked. The basic estimator is,

$$h(r_i) = \begin{cases} 0 & \text{if } p_i \geq r_i/m \\ f^*(0) & \text{if } p_i = 0 \\ r_i f^*(\frac{mp_i}{r_i}) - (r_i - 1)f^*(\frac{mp_i}{r_i-1}) & \text{otherwise} \end{cases}.$$

Note that $E[h(r_i)] = \sum_{i:q_i>p_i} q_i f(\frac{p_i}{q_i})$ and $0 \leq h(i) \leq f^*(0)$ by Lemma 2. Hence, applying Chernoff bounds we can $(\epsilon/2, \delta/2)$-additively-approximate $E[g(i)]$ with $O(\epsilon^{-2} \log \delta^{-1})$ basic estimators.

5.3   Lower Bound for Bregman Divergences

Theorem 6. *If* $\max\{\lim_{u\to 0} F(u), \lim_{u\to 0} F'(u)\}$ *is unbounded then* $(\epsilon, 1/4)$-*additive-approximation of* $\mathcal{B}_F$ *requires* $\Omega(n)$ *space. This applies even if one of the distributions is known to be uniform.*

Proof. We refer the reader to the lower bounds template discussed in Section 3. Let $(x, y) \in \mathbb{F}_2^n \times \mathbb{F}_2^n$ be an instance of SET-DISJOINTNESS. Let q be determined by Alice and Bob as in Theorem 2. and let p be the uniform distribution. If $\lim_{u\to 0} F(u)$ is unbounded then $\mathcal{B}_F(q, p)$ is finite iff $x.y = 0$. If $\lim_{u\to 0} F(u)$ is bounded but $\lim_{u\to 0} F'(u)$ is unbounded then $\mathcal{B}_F(p, q)$ is finite iff $x.y = 0$.

5.4   Upper Bound for Bregman Divergences

In this section we show the matching upper bounds to Theorem 6. In the section we assume that $F(0), F'(0)$ and $F'(1)$ are defined. Recall from Lemma 3 that we may assume that $F(0) = F'(0) = 0$. This makes F monotone increasing over $[0, 1]$. Note that this transformation preserves $F'(1)$ to be a constant. As with the f-divergences, any multiple of an Bregman divergence is another Bregman divergence and hence the best we can hope for is an approximation which is dependent on $F'(1)$. In what follows we assume that this value is 1.

Theorem 7. *Assuming* $F(0), F'(0), F'(1)$ *exist we can approximate* $\mathcal{B}_F(p, q)$ *for any two unknown streams* p, q *upto additive* ϵ *in* $O_\epsilon(\log n \log \delta^{-1})$ *space.*

Proof. Write $\mathcal{B}_F$ as $\mathcal{B}_F(p, q) = \sum_i F(p_i) - \sum_i F(q_i) - \sum_i p_i F'(q_i) + \sum_i q_i F'(q_i)$. We show how to estimate each term with probability at least $1 - \delta/4$ up to an additive $\epsilon/4$ term. Because $0 \leq m(p)[F(X_j/m(p)) - F((X_j - 1)/m(p))] \leq F'(1) = 1$,

$$\Pr\left[\left|\sum_i \widetilde{F(p_i)} - \sum_i F(p_i)\right| > \epsilon/4\right] \leq 2\exp(-|S|\epsilon^2/48) \leq \delta/4 .$$

> *Algorithm $\mathcal{B}$-Est(p,q):* Let $\epsilon_2 = \epsilon/12$. Let $\gamma(\epsilon_2) \leq \epsilon_2$ be such that, $\forall u \in$ $(0, 1]$, $|F'(u + \gamma) - F'(u)| \leq \epsilon_2$ and let $\epsilon_1 = \gamma \epsilon_2$.
>
> 1. Use AMS-Sketches to estimate $\sum_i F(p_i)$: Choose a random subset of $S \subset$ $[m(p)]$ of size $48 \epsilon^{-2} \ln(4\delta^{-1})$. For each $j \in S$,
>   (a) Let $e(j) = i$ where $a_j^p = \langle p, i \rangle$.
>   (b) Let $X_j = |\{k : a_k = a_j, k \geq j\}|$
>   Let
> $$\widetilde{\sum_i F(p_i)} = \frac{m(p)}{|S|} \sum_j [F\left(\frac{X_j}{m(p)}\right) - F\left(\frac{X_j - 1}{m(p)}\right)]$$
>   and define $\widetilde{\sum_i F(q_i)}$ analogously.
> 2. Use MG-Sketches to compute $(\tilde{p}_i)_{i \in [n]}$ and $(\tilde{q}_i)_{i \in [n]}$ such that
> $$p_i - \epsilon_1 \leq \tilde{p}_i \leq p_i \quad \text{and} \quad q_i - \epsilon_2 \leq \tilde{q}_i \leq q_i .$$
> 3. Return,
> $$\widetilde{\sum_i F(p_i)} - \widetilde{\sum_i F(q_i)} - \sum_i (\tilde{p}_i - \tilde{q}_i) F'(\tilde{q}_i) .$$

Fig. 2. Additive Approximation of Some Bregman Divergences

The calculation for the second term is similar. To bound the remaining terms, since $p_i \geq \tilde{p}_i \geq \max\{p_i - \epsilon_1, 0\}$ and $q_i \geq \tilde{q}_i \geq \max\{q_i - \epsilon_1, 0\}$, we get that $F'(q_i) \geq F'(\tilde{q}_i) \geq \max\{F'(q_i) - \epsilon_2, 0\}$ and $\sum_i p_i F'(q_i) \geq \sum_i \tilde{p}_i F'(\tilde{q}_i)$. Hence,

$$\sum_i \tilde{p}_i F'(\tilde{q}_i) \geq \sum_i \max\{p_i - \epsilon_1, 0\} \max\{F'(q_i) - \epsilon_2, 0\}$$

$$\geq \sum_i p_i F'(q_i) - \sum_{i:\epsilon_1 < p_i, q_i < \gamma} \epsilon_1 F'(q_i) - \sum_{i:\epsilon_1 < p_i, q_i \geq \gamma} \epsilon_1 F'(q_i) - \epsilon_2$$

$$\geq \sum_i p_i F'(q_i) - \epsilon_2 - \frac{\epsilon_1}{\gamma} - \epsilon_2$$

$$\geq \sum_i p_i F'(q_i) - 3\epsilon_2 \geq \sum_i p_i F'(q_i) - \epsilon/4 .$$

The calculation for the fourth term is entirely similar.

6   Conclusions and Open Questions

We presented a partial characterization of the information divergences that can be multiplicatively approximated in the data stream model. This characterization was based on a general result that suggests that any distance that is sketchable has certain "norm-like" properties.

We then considered additive-approximation of f-divergences and Bregman divergences. In particular, we showed that all bounded f-divergences can be approximated up to an additive ϵ term in a single pass using $O_\epsilon(\sqrt{n}\,\text{polylog}\,n)$

space. In two passes, $O(\text{polylog}\,n)$-space is known to be sufficient [22]. As was noted, there does exists a single-pass, $O_\epsilon(\text{polylog}\,n)$-space additive approximation for the Jensen-Shannon divergence. This begs the question whether there exist single-pass $O_\epsilon(\text{polylog}\,n)$-space algorithms for all bounded f-divergences?

A final open question relates to multiplicative approximation of information divergences in the *aggregate data stream model* in which all elements of the form $\langle p, \cdot \rangle$ appear consecutively. It is easy to $(1 + \epsilon)$ multiplicatively approximate the Hellinger divergence in this aggregate model using $O(\epsilon^{-2}\,\text{polylog}\,n)$ space by exploiting the connection between the Hellinger divergence and the L_2 distance. The Jensen-Shannon divergence is constant factor related to Hellinger and therefore there exists a constant factor approximation to Jensen-Shannon in $O(\text{polylog}\,n)$ space. How much space is required to find an $(1+\epsilon)$-approximation?

References

1. Alon, N., Matias, Y., Szegedy, M.: The space complexity of approximating the frequency moments. Journal of Computer and System Sciences 58(1), 137–147 (1999)
2. Amari, S.-I.: Differential-geometrical methods in statistics. Springer-Verlag, New York (1985)
3. Amari, S.-I., Nagaoka, H.: Methods of Information Geometry. Oxford University and AMS Translations of Mathematical Monographs (2000)
4. Bhuvanagiri, L., Ganguly, S., Kesh, D., Saha, C.: Simpler algorithm for estimating frequency moments of data streams. In: ACM-SIAM Symposium on Discrete Algorithms, pp. 708–713 (2006)
5. Bose, P., Kranakis, E., Morin, P., Tang, Y.: Bounds for frequency estimation of packet streams. In: SIROCCO, pp. 33–42 (2003)
6. Bregman, L.M.: The relaxation method of finding the common point of convex sets and its application to the solution of problems in convex programming. U.S.S.R. Computational Mathematics and Mathematical Physics 7(1), 200–217 (1967)
7. Breiman, L.: Prediction games and arcing algorithms. Neural Computation 11(7), 1493–1517 (1999)
8. B. Brinkman and M. Charikar. On the impossibility of dimension reduction in l_1. In IEEE Symposium on Foundations of Computer Science, pages 514–523, 2003.
9. Broder, A.Z., Charikar, M., Frieze, A.M., Mitzenmacher, M.: Min-wise independent permutations. J. Comput. Syst. Sci. 60(3), 630–659 (2000)
10. Chakrabarti, A., Cormode, G., McGregor, A.: A near-optimal algorithm for computing the entropy of a stream. In: ACM-SIAM Symposium on Discrete Algorithms (2007)
11. Chakrabarti, A., Khot, S., Sun, X.: Near-optimal lower bounds on the multi-party communication complexity of set disjointness. In: IEEE Conference on Computational Complexity, pp. 107–117 (2003)
12. Charikar, M., Chen, K., Farach-Colton, M.: Finding frequent items in data streams. In: International Colloquium on Automata, Languages and Programming, pp. 693–703 (2002)
13. Collins, M., Schapire, R.E., Singer, Y.: Logistic regression, Adaboost and Bregman distances. Machine Learning 48(1-3), 253–285 (2002)

14. Cormode, G., Datar, M., Indyk, P., Muthukrishnan, S.: Comparing data streams using Hamming norms (how to zero in). IEEE Trans. Knowl. Data Eng. 15(3), 529–540 (2003)
15. Cormode, G., Muthukrishnan, S.: An improved data stream summary: the count-min sketch and its applications. J. Algorithms 55(1), 58–75 (2005)
16. Cover, T.M., Thomas, J.A.: Elements of Information Theory. Wiley Series in Telecommunications. John Wiley & Sons, New York, NY, USA (1991)
17. Csiszár, I.: Why least squares and maximum entropy? an axiomatic approach to inference for linear inverse problems. Ann. Statist. pp. 2032–2056 (1991)
18. Dasgupta, S., Gupta, A.: An elementary proof of a theorem of johnson and lindenstrauss. Random Struct. Algorithms 22(1), 60–65 (2003)
19. Demaine, E.D., López-Ortiz, A., Munro, J.I.: Frequency estimation of internet packet streams with limited space. In: ESA, pp. 348–360 (2002)
20. Feigenbaum, J., Kannan, S., Strauss, M., Viswanathan, M.: An approximate L^1 difference algorithm for massive data streams. SIAM Journal on Computing 32(1), 131–151 (2002)
21. Guha, S., McGregor, A.: Space-efficient sampling. In: AISTATS, pp. 169–176 (2007)
22. Guha, S., McGregor, A., Venkatasubramanian, S.: Streaming and sublinear approximation of entropy and information distances. In: ACM-SIAM Symposium on Discrete Algorithms, pp. 733–742 (2006)
23. Henzinger, M.R., Raghavan, P., Rajagopalan, S.: Computing on data streams. External memory algorithms, pp. 107–118 (1999)
24. Indyk, P.: Stable distributions, pseudorandom generators, embeddings and data stream computation. IEEE Symposium on Foundations of Computer Science, pp. 189–197 (2000)
25. Indyk, P., Woodruff, D.P.: Optimal approximations of the frequency moments of data streams. In: ACM Symposium on Theory of Computing, pp. 202–208 (2005)
26. Jerome Friedman, R.T., Hastie, T.: Additive logistic regression: a statistical view of boosting. Annals of Statistics 28, 337–407 (2000)
27. Johnson, W.B., Lindenstrauss, J.: Extensions of Lipshitz mapping into Hilbert Space. Contemporary Mathematics 26, 189–206, May (1984)
28. Kivinen, J., Warmuth, M.K.: Boosting as entropy projection. In: COLT, pp. 134–144 (1999)
29. Lafferty, J.D.: Additive models, boosting, and inference for generalized divergences. In: COLT, pp. 125–133 (1999)
30. Lafferty, J.D., Pietra, S.D., Pietra, V.J.D.: Statistical learning algorithms based on bregman distances. In: Canadian Workshop on Information Theory (1997)
31. Liese, F., Vajda, F.: Convex statistical distances. Teubner-Texte zur Mathematik, Band 95, Leipzig (1987)
32. Mason, L., Baxter, J., Bartlett, P., Frean, M.: Functional gradient techniques for combining hypotheses. In: Advances in Large Margin Classifiers, MIT Press, Cambridge (1999)
33. Misra, J., Gries, D.: Finding repeated elements. Sci. Comput. Program. 2(2), 143–152 (1982)
34. Nguyen, X., Wainwright, M.J., Jordan, M.I.: Divergences, surrogate loss functions and experimental design. In: Proceedings of NIPS (2005)
35. Razborov, A.A.: On the distributional complexity of disjointness. Theor. Comput. Sci. 106(2), 385–390 (1992)
36. Saks, M.E., Sun, X.: Space lower bounds for distance approximation in the data stream model. ACM Symposium on Theory of Computing, pp. 360–369 (2002)

Competing with Stationary Prediction Strategies

Vladimir Vovk

Computer Learning Research Centre, Department of Computer Science
Royal Holloway, University of London, Egham, Surrey TW20 0EX, UK
vovk@cs.rhul.ac.uk

Abstract. This paper introduces the class of stationary prediction strategies and constructs a prediction algorithm that asymptotically performs as well as the best continuous stationary strategy. We make mild compactness assumptions but no stochastic assumptions about the environment. In particular, no assumption of stationarity is made about the environment, and the stationarity of the considered strategies only means that they do not depend explicitly on time; it is natural to consider only stationary strategies for many non-stationary environments.

1 Introduction

In universal prediction of individual sequences, one starts with a benchmark class of prediction strategies and tries to design a prediction algorithm competitive with the strategies in the class. One noticeable trend in this area has been an increase in the size and flexibility of the considered benchmark classes.

In Hannan's and Blackwell's pioneering papers [1,2] the benchmark class consisted of the constant prediction strategies, i.e., strategies always recommending the same prediction. In later work (see, e.g., [3,4,5], or the recent review [6]) attention shifted to competing with classes of arbitrary prediction strategies.

An important class of prediction strategies consists of "prediction rules", i.e., prediction strategies whose prediction for the next observation y_n is only based on the environment's signal x_n (see the next section for the precise prediction protocol). Standard methods developed in this area allow one to construct a prediction algorithm competitive with the continuous prediction rules (such methods were developed in, e.g., [7], [8], and, especially, [9], Section 3.2; for an explicit statement see [10]). This paper constructs a prediction algorithm competitive with a much wider class of prediction strategies, namely, with the continuous strategies not depending on the choice of the origin of time.

The main technical tool used in the paper is Kalnishkan and Vyugin's Weak Aggregating Algorithm (WAA) [11]; it is, however, possible that some of the other known techniques could be used instead. The WAA provides strong loss bounds for non-negative loss functions, but our main results will be stated in an asymptotic fashion without giving explicit loss bounds; this is discussed further in Section 7.

In Section 2 we give the main definitions and state our main results, Propositions 1–2 and Theorems 1–2; their proofs are given in Sections 3–6. The proofs

N. Bshouty and C. Gentile (Eds.): COLT 2007, LNAI 4539, pp. 439–453, 2007.

of Propositions 1–2 are rather routine, essentially combining well-known ideas. For further details and discussions, see [12].

2   Main Results

The *game of prediction* between Predictor and Environment is played according to the following protocol (of *perfect information*, in the sense that either player can see the other player's moves made so far).

GAME OF PREDICTION

Environment announces $(\ldots, x_{-1}, y_{-1}, x_0, y_0) \in (\mathbf{X} \times \mathbf{Y})^\infty$.
FOR $n = 1, 2, \ldots$:
    Environment announces $x_n \in \mathbf{X}$.
    Predictor announces $\gamma_n \in \Gamma$.
    Environment announces $y_n \in \mathbf{Y}$.
END FOR.

After Environment's first move the game proceeds in rounds numbered by the positive integers n. At the beginning of each round $n = 1, 2, \ldots$ Predictor is given some signal x_n relevant to predicting the following observation y_n. The signal is taken from the *signal space* $\mathbf{X}$ and the observation from the *observation space* $\mathbf{Y}$. Predictor then announces his prediction γ_n, taken from the *prediction space* Γ, and the prediction's quality in light of the actual observation is measured by a *loss function* $\lambda : \Gamma \times \mathbf{Y} \to \mathbb{R}$. At the beginning of the game Environment chooses the infinite past, (x_n, y_n) for all $n \leq 0$.

In the games of prediction traditionally considered in machine learning there is no infinite past. This situation is modeled in our framework by extending the signal space and observation space by new elements $? \in \mathbf{X}$ and $? \in \mathbf{Y}$, defining $\lambda(\gamma, ?)$ arbitrarily, and making Environment announce the infinite past $(\ldots, x_{-1}, y_{-1}, x_0, y_0) = (\ldots, ?, ?, ?, ?)$ and refrain from announcing $x_n = ?$ or $y_n = ?$ afterwards (intuitively, $?$ corresponds to "no feedback from Environment").

We will always assume that the signal space $\mathbf{X}$, the prediction space Γ, and the observation space $\mathbf{Y}$ are non-empty topological spaces and that the loss function λ is continuous. Moreover, we are mainly interested in the case where $\mathbf{X}$, Γ, and $\mathbf{Y}$ are locally compact metric spaces, the prime examples being Euclidean spaces and their open and closed subsets. Our first results will be stated for the case where all three spaces $\mathbf{X}$, Γ, and $\mathbf{Y}$ are compact.

Remark. Our results can be easily extended to the case where the loss on the nth round is allowed to depend, in addition to γ_n and y_n, on the past $\ldots, x_{n-1}, y_{n-1}, x_n$. This would, however, complicate the notation.

Predictor's strategies in the game of prediction will be called *prediction strategies* (or *prediction algorithms*, when they are defined explicitly and we want to emphasize this). Mathematically such a strategy is a function $D : (\mathbf{X} \times \mathbf{Y})^\infty \times \mathbf{X} \times$

$\{1, 2, \ldots\} \to \Gamma$; it maps each history $(\ldots, x_{n-1}, y_{n-1}, x_n)$ and the current time n to the chosen prediction. In this paper we will only be interested in continuous prediction strategies D. An especially natural class of strategies is formed by the *stationary prediction strategies* $D : (\mathbf{X} \times \mathbf{Y})^\infty \times \mathbf{X} \to \Gamma$, which do not depend on time explicitly; since the origin of time is usually chosen arbitrarily, this appears a reasonable restriction.

Universal Prediction Strategies: Compact Deterministic Case

In this and next subsections we will assume that the spaces $\mathbf{X}, \Gamma, \mathbf{Y}$ are all compact. A prediction strategy is *CS universal* for a loss function λ if its predictions γ_n satisfy

$$\limsup_{N \to \infty} \left(\frac{1}{N} \sum_{n=1}^N \lambda(\gamma_n, y_n) - \frac{1}{N} \sum_{n=1}^N \lambda\big(D(\ldots, x_{n-1}, y_{n-1}, x_n), y_n\big) \right) \leq 0 \quad (1)$$

for any continuous stationary prediction strategy D and any biinfinite sequence $\ldots, x_{-1}, y_{-1}, x_0, y_0, x_1, y_1, \ldots$. ("CS" refers to the continuity and stationarity of the prediction strategies we are competing with).

Proposition 1. *Suppose $\mathbf{X}$ and $\mathbf{Y}$ are compact metric spaces, Γ is a compact convex subset of a Banach space, and the loss function $\lambda(\gamma, y)$ is continuous in (γ, y) and convex in the variable $\gamma \in \Gamma$. There exists a CS universal prediction algorithm.*

Remark. Simplest examples show that it is impossible to compete, in the sense of (1), with the class of all continuous prediction strategies: we can set $D(\ldots, x_{n-1}, y_{n-1}, x_n) := f_n(x_n)$, and there need not be any connection whatsoever between f_n for different n. Our solution was to restrict attention to stationary prediction strategies, which, in the absence of stochastic assumptions about the environment, required the unusual feature of having an infinite past.

Universal Prediction Strategies: Compact Randomized Case

When the loss function $\lambda(\gamma, y)$ is not convex in γ, two difficulties appear:

- the conclusion of Proposition 1 becomes false if the convexity requirement is removed ([11], Theorem 2);
- in some cases the notion of a continuous prediction strategy becomes vacuous: e.g., there are no non-constant continuous stationary prediction strategies when $\Gamma = \{0, 1\}$ and $(\mathbf{X} \times \mathbf{Y})^\infty \times \mathbf{X}$ is connected (the latter condition is equivalent to $\mathbf{X}$ and $\mathbf{Y}$ being connected—see [13], Theorem 6.1.15).

To overcome these difficulties, we follow the standard practice and consider randomized prediction strategies. The proof of Proposition 1 will give a universal, in a natural sense, randomized prediction algorithm; on the other hand, there will be a vast supply of continuous stationary prediction strategies.

Remark. In fact, the second difficulty is more apparent than real: for example, in the binary case ($\mathbf{Y} = \{0, 1\}$) there are many non-trivial continuous prediction strategies in the canonical form (as defined in [5]) of the prediction game with the prediction space redefined as the boundary of the set of superpredictions (as defined in [11]).

A *randomized prediction strategy* is a function $D : (\mathbf{X} \times \mathbf{Y})^\infty \times \mathbf{X} \times \{1, 2, \ldots\} \to \mathcal{P}(\Gamma)$ mapping the past complemented by the current time to the probability measures on the prediction space; $\mathcal{P}(\Gamma)$ is always equipped with the topology of weak convergence ([14], Appendix III). In other words, this is a prediction strategy in the extended game of prediction with the prediction space $\mathcal{P}(\Gamma)$. Analogously, a *stationary randomized prediction strategy* is a function $D : (\mathbf{X} \times \mathbf{Y})^\infty \times \mathbf{X} \to \mathcal{P}(\Gamma)$.

Let us say that a randomized prediction strategy outputting γ_n is *CS universal* for a loss function λ if, for any continuous stationary randomized prediction strategy D and any biinfinite $\ldots, x_{-1}, y_{-1}, x_0, y_0, x_1, y_1, \ldots$,

$$\limsup_{N \to \infty} \left(\frac{1}{N} \sum_{n=1}^N \lambda(g_n, y_n) - \frac{1}{N} \sum_{n=1}^N \lambda(d_n, y_n) \right) \le 0 \text{ a.s.,} \tag{2}$$

where $g_1, g_2, \ldots, d_1, d_2, \ldots$ are independent random variables distributed as

$$g_n \sim \gamma_n, \tag{3}$$
$$d_n \sim D(\ldots, x_{n-1}, y_{n-1}, x_n), \tag{4}$$

$n = 1, 2, \ldots$. Intuitively, the "a.s." in (2) refers to the prediction strategies' internal randomization; the environment is not modeled stochastically.

Proposition 2. *Let* $\mathbf{X}$, Γ, *and* $\mathbf{Y}$ *be compact metric spaces and* λ *be a continuous loss function. There exists a CS universal randomized prediction algorithm.*

Universal Prediction Strategies: Deterministic Case

Let us say that a set in a topological space is *precompact* if its closure is compact. In Euclidean spaces, precompactness means boundedness. In this and next subsections we drop the assumption of compactness of $\mathbf{X}$, Γ, and $\mathbf{Y}$, and so we have to redefine the notion of CS universality.

A prediction strategy outputting $\gamma_n \in \Gamma$ is *CS universal* for a loss function λ if, for any continuous stationary prediction strategy D and for any biinfinite $\ldots, x_{-1}, y_{-1}, x_0, y_0, x_1, y_1, \ldots$,

$(\{\ldots, x_{-1}, x_0, x_1, \ldots\}$ and $\{\ldots, y_{-1}, y_0, y_1, \ldots\}$ are precompact)

$$\implies \limsup_{N \to \infty} \left(\frac{1}{N} \sum_{n=1}^N \lambda(\gamma_n, y_n) - \frac{1}{N} \sum_{n=1}^N \lambda\big(D(\ldots, x_{n-1}, y_{n-1}, x_n), y_n\big) \right) \le 0. \tag{5}$$

The intuition behind the antecedent of (5), in the Euclidean case, is that the predictor knows that $\|x_n\|$ and $\|y_n\|$ are bounded but does not know an upper bound in advance.

Let us say that the loss function λ is *large at infinity* if, for all $y^* \in \mathbf{Y}$,

$$\lim_{\substack{y \to y^* \\ \gamma \to \infty}} \lambda(\gamma, y) = \infty$$

(in the sense that for each constant M there exists a neighborhood $O_{y^*} \ni y^*$ and compact $C \subseteq \Gamma$ such that $\lambda(\Gamma \setminus C, O_{y^*}) \subseteq (M, \infty)$). Intuitively, we require that faraway $\gamma \in \Gamma$ should be poor predictions for nearby $y \in \mathbf{Y}$. This assumption is satisfied for most of the usual loss functions used in universal prediction.

Theorem 1. *Suppose $\mathbf{X}$ and $\mathbf{Y}$ are locally compact metric spaces, Γ is a convex subset of a Banach space, and the loss function $\lambda(\gamma, y)$ is continuous, large at infinity, and convex in the variable $\gamma \in \Gamma$. There exists a CS universal prediction algorithm.*

To have a specific example in mind, the reader might check that $\mathbf{X} = \mathbb{R}^K$, $\Gamma = \mathbf{Y} = \mathbb{R}^L$, and $\lambda(\gamma, y) := \|y - \gamma\|$ satisfy the conditions of the theorem.

Universal Prediction Strategies: Randomized Case

We say that a randomized prediction strategy outputting randomized predictions $\gamma_n \in \mathcal{P}(\Gamma)$ is *CS universal* if, for any continuous stationary randomized prediction strategy D and for any biinfinite $\ldots, x_{-1}, y_{-1}, x_0, y_0, x_1, y_1, \ldots,$

$$(\{\ldots, x_{-1}, x_0, x_1, \ldots\} \text{ and } \{\ldots, y_{-1}, y_0, y_1, \ldots\} \text{ are precompact})$$

$$\implies \left(\limsup_{N \to \infty} \left(\frac{1}{N} \sum_{n=1}^{N} \lambda(g_n, y_n) - \frac{1}{N} \sum_{n=1}^{N} \lambda(d_n, y_n) \right) \leq 0 \text{ a.s.} \right), \quad (6)$$

where $g_1, g_2, \ldots, d_1, d_2, \ldots$ are independent random variables distributed according to (3)–(4).

Theorem 2. *Let $\mathbf{X}$ and $\mathbf{Y}$ be locally compact metric spaces, Γ be a metric space, and λ be a continuous and large at infinity loss function. There exists a CS universal randomized prediction algorithm.*

It is clear that Theorems 1 and 2 contain Propositions 1 and 2, respectively, as special cases: in the compact case the condition that the loss function should be large at infinity is satisfied automatically.

3   Proof of Proposition 1

In the rest of the paper we will be using the notation Σ for $(\mathbf{X} \times \mathbf{Y})^\infty \times \mathbf{X}$. By the Tikhonov theorem ([13], Theorem 3.2.4) this is a compact space; it is also metrizable ([13], Theorem 4.2.2). Another standard piece of notation throughout the rest of the paper will be $\sigma_n := (\ldots, x_{n-1}, y_{n-1}, x_n) \in \Sigma$. Remember that λ, as a continuous function on a compact set, is bounded below and above ([13], Theorem 3.10.6).

Let Γ^Σ be the set of all continuous functions from Σ to Γ with the *topology of uniform convergence*, generated by the metric

$$\hat{\rho}(D_1, D_2) := \sup_{\sigma \in \Sigma} \rho\big(D_1(\sigma), D_2(\sigma)\big),$$

ρ being the metric in Γ (induced by the norm in the containing Banach space). Since the topological space Γ^Σ is separable ([13], Corollary 4.2.18 in combination with Theorem 4.2.8), we can choose a dense sequence $D_1, D_2, \ldots$ in Γ^Σ.

Remark. The topology in Γ^Σ is defined via a metric, and this is one of the very few places in this paper where we need a specific metric (for brevity we often talk about "metric spaces", but this can always be replaced by "metrizable topological spaces"). Without using the metric, we could say that the topology in Γ^Σ is the compact-open topology ([13], Section 3.4). Since Σ is compact, the compact-open topology on Γ^Σ coincides with the topology of uniform convergence ([13], Theorem 4.2.17). The separability of Γ^Σ now follows from [13], Theorem 3.4.16 in combination with Theorem 4.2.8.

The next step is to apply Kalnishkan and Vyugin's [11] Weak Aggregating Algorithm (WAA) to this sequence. (The WAA is similar to Kivinen and Warmuth's [15] Weighted Average Algorithm but has variable learning rate and is coupled with a novel and ingenious performance analysis.) We cannot just refer to [11] and will have to redo their derivation of the WAA's main property since Kalnishkan and Vyugin only consider the case of finitely many "experts" D_k and finite $\mathbf{Y}$. (Although in other respects we will not need their algorithm in full generality and so slightly simplify it.).

Let $q_1, q_2, \ldots$ be a sequence of positive numbers summing to 1, $\sum_{k=1}^\infty q_k = 1$. Define

$$\ell_n^{(k)} := \lambda\left(D_k(\sigma_n), y_n\right), \quad L_N^{(k)} := \sum_{n=1}^N \ell_n^{(k)}$$

to be the instantaneous loss of the kth expert D_k on the nth round and his cumulative loss over the first N rounds. For all $n, k = 1, 2, \ldots$ define

$$w_n^{(k)} := q_k \beta_n^{L_{n-1}^{(k)}}, \quad \beta_n := \exp\left(-\frac{1}{\sqrt{n}}\right)$$

($w_n^{(k)}$ are the weights of the experts to use on round n) and

$$p_n^{(k)} := \frac{w_n^{(k)}}{\sum_{k=1}^\infty w_n^{(k)}}$$

(the normalized weights; it is obvious that the denominator is positive and finite). The WAA's prediction on round n is

$$\gamma_n := \sum_{k=1}^\infty p_n^{(k)} D_k(\sigma_n) \tag{7}$$

(the series is convergent in the Banach space since the compactness of Γ implies $\sup_{\gamma \in \Gamma} \|\gamma\| < \infty$; and $\gamma_n \in \Gamma$ since Γ is convex and

$$
\gamma_n - \sum_{k=1}^{K} \frac{p_n^{(k)}}{\sum_{k=1}^{K} p_n^{(k)}} D_k(\sigma_n)
$$

$$
= \sum_{k=1}^{K} \left(1 - \frac{1}{\sum_{k=1}^{K} p_n^{(k)}} \right) p_n^{(k)} D_k(\sigma_n) + \sum_{k=K+1}^{\infty} p_n^{(k)} D_k(\sigma_n) \to 0 \quad (8)
$$

as $K \to \infty$).

Let $\ell_n := \lambda(\gamma_n, y_n)$ be the WAA's loss on round n and $L_N := \sum_{n=1}^{N} \ell_n$ be its cumulative loss over the first N rounds.

Lemma 1 (cf. [11], Lemma 3). *The WAA guarantees that, for all N,*

$$
L_N \leq \sum_{n=1}^{N} \sum_{k=1}^{\infty} p_n^{(k)} \ell_n^{(k)} - \sum_{n=1}^{N} \log_{\beta_n} \sum_{k=1}^{\infty} p_n^{(k)} \beta_n^{\ell_n^{(k)}} + \log_{\beta_N} \sum_{k=1}^{\infty} q_k \beta_N^{L_N^{(k)}}. \quad (9)
$$

The first two terms on the right-hand side of (9) are sums over the first N rounds of different kinds of mean of the experts' losses (see, e.g., [16], Chapter III, for a general definition of the mean); we will see later that they nearly cancel each other out. If those two terms are ignored, the remaining part of (9) is identical (except that β now depends on n) to the main property of the "Aggregating Algorithm" (see, e.g., [17], Lemma 1). All infinite series in (9) are trivially convergent.

Proof of Lemma 1. Inequality (9) can be obtained from the conjunction of

$$
L_N \leq \sum_{n=1}^{N} \sum_{k=1}^{\infty} p_n^{(k)} \ell_n^{(k)} \quad (10)
$$

and

$$
\sum_{n=1}^{N} \log_{\beta_n} \sum_{k=1}^{\infty} p_n^{(k)} \beta_n^{\ell_n^{(k)}} \leq \log_{\beta_N} \sum_{k=1}^{\infty} q_k \beta_N^{L_N^{(k)}}. \quad (11)
$$

The first of these inequalities, (10), follows from the "countable convexity" $\ell_n \leq \sum_{k=1}^{\infty} p_n^{(k)} \ell_n^{(k)}$, which in turn follows from (8), the continuity of λ, and

$$
\lambda \left(\sum_{k=1}^{K} \frac{p_n^{(k)}}{\sum_{k=1}^{K} p_n^{(k)}} D_k(\sigma_n), y_n \right) \leq \sum_{k=1}^{K} \frac{p_n^{(k)}}{\sum_{k=1}^{K} p_n^{(k)}} \lambda \left(D_k(\sigma_n), y_n \right)
$$

if we let $K \to \infty$. The second inequality, (11), is obtained by summing

$$
\log_{\beta_n} \sum_{k=1}^{\infty} p_n^{(k)} \beta_n^{\ell_n^{(k)}} \leq \log_{\beta_n} \sum_{k=1}^{\infty} q_k \beta_n^{L_n^{(k)}} - \log_{\beta_{n-1}} \sum_{k=1}^{\infty} q_k \beta_{n-1}^{L_{n-1}^{(k)}} \quad (12)
$$

over $n = 1, \ldots, N$ (the subtrahend on the right-hand side of (12) is interpreted as 0 when $n = 1$). Since (12) is trivial for $n = 1$, we will prove it assuming $n \geq 2$. By the definition of $p_n^{(k)}$, (12) can be rewritten as

$$\log_{\beta_n} \frac{\sum_{k=1}^{\infty} q_k \beta_n^{L_{n-1}^{(k)}} \beta_n^{\ell_n^{(k)}}}{\sum_{k=1}^{\infty} q_k \beta_n^{L_{n-1}^{(k)}}} \leq \log_{\beta_n} \sum_{k=1}^{\infty} q_k \beta_n^{L_n^{(k)}} - \log_{\beta_{n-1}} \sum_{k=1}^{\infty} q_k \beta_{n-1}^{L_{n-1}^{(k)}},$$

which after cancellation becomes

$$\log_{\beta_{n-1}} \sum_{k=1}^{\infty} q_k \beta_{n-1}^{L_{n-1}^{(k)}} \leq \log_{\beta_n} \sum_{k=1}^{\infty} q_k \beta_n^{L_{n-1}^{(k)}}. \tag{13}$$

The last inequality follows from a general result about comparison of different means ([16], Theorem 85), but we can also check it directly (following [11]). Let $\beta_n = \beta_{n-1}^a$, where $0 < a < 1$. Then (13) can be rewritten as

$$\left(\sum_{k=1}^{\infty} q_k \beta_{n-1}^{L_{n-1}^{(k)}} \right)^a \geq \sum_{k=1}^{\infty} q_k \beta_{n-1}^{a L_{n-1}^{(k)}},$$

and the last inequality follows from the concavity of the function $t \mapsto t^a$.   ∎

Lemma 2 (cf. [11], Lemma 1). *Let L be an upper bound on $|\lambda|$. The WAA guarantees that, for all N and K,*

$$L_N \leq L_N^{(K)} + \left(L^2 e^L + \ln \frac{1}{q_K} \right) \sqrt{N}. \tag{14}$$

(There is no term e^L in [11] since it only considers non-negative loss functions.)

Proof. From (9), we obtain:

$$L_N \leq \sum_{n=1}^{N} \sum_{k=1}^{\infty} p_n^{(k)} \ell_n^{(k)} + \sum_{n=1}^{N} \sqrt{n} \ln \sum_{k=1}^{\infty} p_n^{(k)} \exp\left(-\frac{\ell_n^{(k)}}{\sqrt{n}} \right) + \log_{\beta_N} q_K + L_N^{(K)}$$

$$\leq \sum_{n=1}^{N} \sum_{k=1}^{\infty} p_n^{(k)} \ell_n^{(k)} + \sum_{n=1}^{N} \sqrt{n} \left(\sum_{k=1}^{\infty} p_n^{(k)} \left(1 - \frac{\ell_n^{(k)}}{\sqrt{n}} + \frac{\left(\ell_n^{(k)} \right)^2}{2n} e^L \right) - 1 \right)$$

$$+ \log_{\beta_N} q_K + L_N^{(K)}$$

$$= L_N^{(K)} + \frac{1}{2} \sum_{n=1}^{N} \frac{1}{\sqrt{n}} \sum_{k=1}^{\infty} p_n^{(k)} \left(\ell_n^{(k)} \right)^2 e^L + \sqrt{N} \ln \frac{1}{q_K}$$

$$\leq L_N^{(K)} + \frac{L^2 e^L}{2} \sum_{n=1}^{N} \frac{1}{\sqrt{n}} + \sqrt{N} \ln \frac{1}{q_K} \leq L_N^{(K)} + \frac{L^2 e^L}{2} \int_0^N \frac{dt}{\sqrt{t}} + \sqrt{N} \ln \frac{1}{q_K}$$

$$= L_N^{(K)} + L^2 e^L \sqrt{N} + \sqrt{N} \ln \frac{1}{q_K}$$

(in the second "$\leq$" we used the inequalities $e^t \leq 1 + t + \frac{t^2}{2} e^{|t|}$ and $\ln t \leq t - 1$).   ∎

Now it is easy to prove Proposition 1. Let γ_n be the predictions output by the WAA. Consider any continuous stationary prediction strategy D. Since every continuous function on a metric compact is uniformly continuous ([13], Theorem 4.3.32), for any $\epsilon > 0$ we can find $\delta > 0$ such that $|\lambda(\gamma_1, y) - \lambda(\gamma_2, y)| < \epsilon$ whenever $\rho(\gamma_1, \gamma_2) < \delta$. We can further find K such that $\hat{\rho}(D_K, D) < \delta$, and (14) then gives, for all biinfinite $\ldots, x_{-1}, y_{-1}, x_0, y_0, x_1, y_1, \ldots$,

$$\limsup_{N \to \infty} \left(\frac{1}{N} \sum_{n=1}^{N} \lambda(\gamma_n, y_n) - \frac{1}{N} \sum_{n=1}^{N} \lambda(D(\sigma_n), y_n) \right)$$

$$\leq \limsup_{N \to \infty} \left(\frac{1}{N} \sum_{n=1}^{N} \lambda(\gamma_n, y_n) - \frac{1}{N} \sum_{n=1}^{N} \lambda(D_K(\sigma_n), y_n) \right) + \epsilon$$

$$\leq \limsup_{N \to \infty} \left(L^2 e^L + \ln \frac{1}{q_K} \right) \frac{1}{\sqrt{N}} + \epsilon = \epsilon;$$

since ϵ can be arbitrarily small, the WAA is CS universal.

4   Proof of Proposition 2

Since Γ is compact, $\mathcal{P}(\Gamma)$ is also compact (this is a special case of Prokhorov's theorem, [14], Appendix III, Theorem 6). Since Γ is a metric compact, $\mathcal{P}(\Gamma)$ is metrizable (e.g., by the well-known Prokhorov metric: [14], Appendix III, Theorem 6).

Define

$$\lambda(\gamma, y) := \int_{\Gamma} \lambda(g, y) \gamma(dg), \tag{15}$$

where γ is a probability measure on Γ. This is the loss function in the new game of prediction with the prediction space $\mathcal{P}(\Gamma)$; it is convex in γ.

Let us check that the loss function (15) is continuous. If $\gamma_n \to \gamma$ and $y_n \to y$ for some $(\gamma, y) \in \mathcal{P}(\Gamma) \times \mathbf{Y}$,

$$|\lambda(\gamma_n, y_n) - \lambda(\gamma, y)| \leq |\lambda(\gamma_n, y_n) - \lambda(\gamma_n, y)| + |\lambda(\gamma_n, y) - \lambda(\gamma, y)| \to 0$$

(the first addend tends to zero because of the uniform continuity of $\lambda : \Gamma \times \mathbf{Y} \to \mathbb{R}$ and the second addend by the definition of the topology of weak convergence).

Unfortunately, Proposition 1 cannot be applied to the new game of prediction directly since it assumes that the prediction space is a subset of a Banach space. (It is true that $\mathcal{P}(\Gamma)$ is a subspace of the dual, equipped with the weak* topology, to the space $C(\Gamma)$ of continuous functions on Γ with the topology of uniform convergence. However, since $C(\Gamma)$ is typically infinite-dimensional, the dual may fail to be even metrizable: see [18], 3.16.) The proof of Proposition 1, however, still works for the new game.

Since $(\mathcal{P}(\Gamma))^{\Sigma}$ is separable (for the same reasons as Γ^{Σ} in the previous section), we can choose a dense sequence $D_1, D_2, \ldots$ in it. It is clear that the mixture (7) is a probability measure. The result of the previous section is still true, and the randomized prediction strategy (7) produces $\gamma_n \in \mathcal{P}(\Gamma)$ that are guaranteed to satisfy

$$\limsup_{N \to \infty} \left(\frac{1}{N} \sum_{n=1}^{N} \lambda(\gamma_n, y_n) - \frac{1}{N} \sum_{n=1}^{N} \lambda(D(\sigma_n), y_n) \right) \leq 0, \tag{16}$$

for any continuous stationary randomized prediction strategy D. The loss function is bounded in absolute value by a constant L, and so the law of the iterated logarithm (see, e.g., [19], (5.8)) implies that

$$\limsup_{N \to \infty} \frac{\left| \sum_{n=1}^{N} \left(\lambda(g_n, y_n) - \lambda(\gamma_n, y_n) \right) \right|}{\sqrt{2L^2 N \ln \ln N}} \leq 1,$$

$$\limsup_{N \to \infty} \frac{\left| \sum_{n=1}^{N} \left(\lambda(d_n, y_n) - \lambda(D(\sigma_n), y_n) \right) \right|}{\sqrt{2L^2 N \ln \ln N}} \leq 1$$

with probability one. Combining the last two inequalities with (16) gives

$$\limsup_{N \to \infty} \left(\frac{1}{N} \sum_{n=1}^{N} \lambda(g_n, y_n) - \frac{1}{N} \sum_{n=1}^{N} \lambda(d_n, y_n) \right) \leq 0 \text{ a.s.}$$

Therefore, the WAA (applied to $D_1, D_2, \ldots$) is a CS universal continuous randomized prediction strategy.

5   Proof of Theorem 1

In view of Proposition 1, we only need to get rid of the assumption of compactness of $\mathbf{X}$, Γ, and $\mathbf{Y}$.

Game of Removal

The proofs of Theorems 1 and 2 will be based on the following game (an abstract version of the "doubling trick", [6]) played in a topological space X:

GAME OF REMOVAL $G(X)$

FOR $n = 1, 2, \ldots$:
    Remover announces compact $K_n \subseteq X$.
    Evader announces $p_n \notin K_n$.
END FOR.

Winner: Evader if the set $\{p_1, p_2, \ldots\}$ is precompact; Remover otherwise.

Intuitively, the goal of Evader is to avoid being removed to the infinity. Without loss of generality we will assume that Remover always announces a nondecreasing sequence of compact sets: $K_1 \subseteq K_2 \subseteq \cdots$.

Lemma 3 (Gruenhage). *Remover has a winning strategy in $G(X)$ if X is a locally compact and paracompact space.*

Proof. We will follow the proof of Theorem 4.1 in [20] (the easy direction). If X is locally compact and σ-compact, there exists a non-decreasing sequence $K_1 \subseteq K_2 \subseteq \cdots$ of compact sets covering X, and each K_n can be extended to compact K_n^* so that $\operatorname{Int} K_n^* \supseteq K_n$ ([13], Theorem 3.3.2). Remover will obviously win $G(X)$ choosing $K_1^*, K_2^*, \ldots$ as his moves.

If X is the sum of locally compact σ-compact spaces X_s, $s \in S$, Remover plays, for each $s \in S$, the strategy described in the previous paragraph on the subsequence of Evader's moves belonging to X_s. If Evader chooses $p_n \in X_s$ for infinitely many X_s, those X_s will form an open cover of the closure of $\{p_1, p_2, \ldots\}$ without a finite subcover. If x_n are chosen from only finitely many X_s, there will be infinitely many x_n chosen from some X_s, and the result of the previous paragraph can be applied. It remains to remember that each locally compact paracompact space can be represented as the sum of its locally compact σ-compact subsets ([13], the proof of Theorem 5.1.27). ∎

Large at Infinity Loss Functions

We will need the following useful property of large at infinity loss functions.

Lemma 4. *Let λ be a loss function that is large at infinity. For each compact set $B \subseteq \mathbf{Y}$ and each constant M there exists a compact set $C \subseteq \Gamma$ such that*

$$\forall \gamma \notin C, y \in B: \quad \lambda(\gamma, y) > M. \tag{17}$$

Proof. For each point $y^* \in B$ fix an open neighborhood $O_{y^*} \ni y^*$ and a compact set $C(y^*) \subseteq \Gamma$ such that $\lambda(\Gamma \setminus C(y^*), O_{y^*}) \subseteq (M, \infty)$. Since the sets O_{y^*} form an open cover of B, we can find this cover's finite subcover $\{O_{y_1^*}, \ldots, O_{y_n^*}\}$. It is clear that $C := \bigcup_{j=1,\ldots,n} C\left(y_j^*\right)$ satisfies (17). ∎

In fact, the only property of large at infinity loss functions that we will be using is that in the conclusion of Lemma 4. In particular, it implies the following lemma.

Lemma 5. *Under the conditions of Theorem 1, for each compact set $B \subseteq \mathbf{Y}$ there exists a compact convex set $C = C(B) \subseteq \Gamma$ such that for each continuous stationary prediction strategy $D : \Sigma \to \Gamma$ there exists a continuous stationary prediction strategy $D' : \Sigma \to C$ that dominates D in the sense*

$$\forall \sigma \in \Sigma, y \in B: \quad \lambda(D'(\sigma), y) \leq \lambda(D(\sigma), y). \tag{18}$$

Proof. Without loss of generality B is assumed non-empty. Fix any $\gamma_0 \in \Gamma$. Let

$$M_1 := \sup_{y \in B} \lambda(\gamma_0, y),$$

let $C_1 \subseteq \Gamma$ be a compact set such that

$$\forall \gamma \notin C_1, y \in B: \quad \lambda(\gamma, y) > M_1 + 1,$$

let

$$M_2 := \sup_{(\gamma,y)\in C_1\times B} \lambda(\gamma,y),$$

and let $C_2 \subseteq \Gamma$ be a compact set such that

$$\forall \gamma \notin C_2, y \in B: \quad \lambda(\gamma,y) > M_2 + 1.$$

It is obvious that $M_1 \leq M_2$ and $\gamma_0 \in C_1 \subseteq C_2$. We can and will assume C_2 convex (see [18], Theorem 3.20(c)).

Let us now check that C_1 lies inside the interior of C_2. Indeed, for any fixed $y \in B$ and $\gamma \in C_1$, we have $\lambda(\gamma,y) \leq M_2$; since $\lambda(\gamma',y) > M_2 + 1$ for all $\gamma' \notin C_2$, some neighborhood of γ will lie completely in C_2.

Let $D : \Sigma \to \Gamma$ be a continuous stationary prediction strategy. We will show that (18) holds for some continuous stationary prediction strategy D' taking values in the compact convex set $C(B) := C_2$. Namely, we define

$$D'(\sigma) :=$$
$$\begin{cases} D(\sigma) & \text{if } D(\sigma) \in C_1 \\ \frac{\rho(D(\sigma),\Gamma\setminus C_2)}{\rho(D(\sigma),C_1)+\rho(D(\sigma),\Gamma\setminus C_2)}D(\sigma) + \frac{\rho(D(\sigma),C_1)}{\rho(D(\sigma),C_1)+\rho(D(\sigma),\Gamma\setminus C_2)}\gamma_0 & \text{if } D(\sigma) \in C_2 \setminus C_1 \\ \gamma_0 & \text{if } D(\sigma) \in \Gamma \setminus C_2 \end{cases}$$

where ρ is the metric in Γ; the denominator $\rho(D(\sigma),C_1) + \rho(D(\sigma),\Gamma \setminus C_2)$ is positive since already $\rho(D(\sigma),C_1)$ is positive. Since C_2 is convex, we can see that D' indeed takes values in C_2. The only points σ at which the continuity of D' is not obvious are those for which $D(\sigma)$ lies on the boundary of C_1 or C_2: in this case one has to use the fact that C_1 is covered by the interior of C_2.

It remains to check (18); the only non-trivial case is $D(\sigma) \in C_2 \setminus C_1$. By the convexity of $\lambda(\gamma,y)$ in γ, the inequality in (18) will follow from

$$\frac{\rho(D(\sigma),\Gamma\setminus C_2)}{\rho(D(\sigma),C_1)+\rho(D(\sigma),\Gamma\setminus C_2)}\lambda(D(\sigma),y)$$
$$+ \frac{\rho(D(\sigma),C_1)}{\rho(D(\sigma),C_1)+\rho(D(\sigma),\Gamma\setminus C_2)}\lambda(\gamma_0,y) \leq \lambda(D(\sigma),y),$$

i.e.,

$$\lambda(\gamma_0,y) \leq \lambda(D(\sigma),y).$$

Since the left-hand side of the last inequality is at most M_1 and its right-hand side exceeds $M_1 + 1$, it holds true.   ∎

The Proof

For each compact $B \subseteq \mathbf{Y}$ fix a compact convex $C(B) \subseteq \Gamma$ as in Lemma 5. Predictor's strategy ensuring (5) is constructed from Remover's winning strategy in $G(\mathbf{X} \times \mathbf{Y})$ (see Lemma 3; metric spaces are paracompact by the Stone theorem, [13], Theorem 5.1.3) and from Predictor's strategies $\mathcal{S}(A, B)$ outputting predictions

$$\gamma_n \in C(B) \qquad (19)$$

and ensuring the consequent of (5) for all continuous

$$D : (A \times B)^\infty \times A \to C(B) \qquad (20)$$

under the assumption that $(x_n, y_n) \in A \times B$ for given compact $A \subseteq \mathbf{X}$ and $B \subseteq \mathbf{Y}$ (the existence of such $\mathcal{S}(A, B)$ is asserted in Proposition 1). Remover's moves are assumed to be of the form $A \times B$ for compact $A \subseteq \mathbf{X}$ and $B \subseteq \mathbf{Y}$. Predictor is simultaneously playing the game of removal $G(\mathbf{X} \times \mathbf{Y})$ as Evader.

At the beginning of the game of prediction Predictor asks Remover to make his first move $A_1 \times B_1$ in the game of removal; without loss of generality we assume that $A_1 \times B_1$ contains all (x_n, y_n), $n \leq 0$ (there is nothing to prove if $\{(x_n, y_n) \mid n \leq 0\}$ is not precompact). Predictor then plays the game of prediction using the strategy $\mathcal{S}(A_1, B_1)$ until Environment chooses $(x_n, y_n) \notin A_1 \times B_1$ (forever if Environment never chooses such (x_n, y_n)). As soon as such (x_n, y_n) is chosen, Predictor announces (x_n, y_n) in the game of removal and notes Remover's response (A_2, B_2). He then continues playing the game of prediction using the strategy $\mathcal{S}(A_2, B_2)$ until Environment chooses $(x_n, y_n) \notin A_2 \times B_2$, etc.

Let us check that this strategy for Predictor will always ensure (5). If Environment chooses (x_n, y_n) outside Predictor's current $A_k \times B_k$ finitely often, the consequent of (5) will be satisfied for all continuous stationary $D : \Sigma \to C(B_K)$ (B_K being the second component of Remover's last move (A_K, B_K)) and so, by Lemma 5, for all continuous stationary $D : \Sigma \to \Gamma$. If Environment chooses (x_n, y_n) outside Predictor's current $A_k \times B_k$ infinitely often, the set of (x_n, y_n), $n = 1, 2, \ldots$, will not be precompact, and so the antecedent of (5) will be violated.

6   Proof of Theorem 2

We will prove that the prediction strategy of the previous section with (19) replaced by $\gamma_n \in \mathcal{P}(C(B))$, (20) replaced by

$$D : (A \times B)^\infty \times A \to \mathcal{P}(C(B)),$$

and Proposition 1 replaced by Proposition 2 is CS universal. Let $D : \Sigma \to \mathcal{P}(\Gamma)$ be a continuous stationary randomized prediction strategy, i.e., a continuous stationary prediction strategy in the new game of prediction with loss function (15), and let (A_K, B_K) be Remover's last move (if Remover makes infinitely many moves, the antecedent of (6) is false, and there is nothing to prove).

Define a continuous stationary randomized prediction strategy $D' : \Sigma \to \mathcal{P}(C(B_K))$ as follows. First define γ_0, M_1, C_1, M_2, and C_2 as in the proof of Lemma 5, with $B := B_K$. Fix a continuous function $f : \Gamma \to [0, 1]$ such that $f = 0$ on C_1 and $f = 1$ on $\Gamma \setminus C_2$ (such an f exists by the Tietze–Uryson theorem, [13], Theorem 2.1.8, and the fact that C_1 lies in the interior of C_2). The randomized prediction $D'(\sigma_n) \in \mathcal{P}(\Gamma)$ generates the actual prediction $d'_n \in \Gamma$ in two steps: first d_n is generated from $D(\sigma_n)$, and then it is replaced by γ_0 with probability $f(d_n)$ (independently of everything else). Notice that when a replacement is made, the loss decreases:

$$\lambda(d'_n, y) \le M_1 < M_1 + 1 < \lambda(d_n, y),$$

assuming $y \in B$. It is clear that the stationary randomized prediction strategy D' defined in this way is continuous (in the topology of weak convergence, as usual) and takes values in $\mathcal{P}(C_2)$. Remembering that γ_n were chosen to satisfy the condition of universality in Proposition 2, we now obtain

$$\limsup_{N \to \infty} \left(\frac{1}{N} \sum_{n=1}^{N} \lambda(g_n, y_n) - \frac{1}{N} \sum_{n=1}^{N} \lambda(d_n, y_n) \right)$$

$$\le \limsup_{N \to \infty} \left(\frac{1}{N} \sum_{n=1}^{N} \lambda(g_n, y_n) - \frac{1}{N} \sum_{n=1}^{N} \lambda(d'_n, y_n) \right) \le 0 \text{ a.s.;}$$

it remains to compare this with (6).

7   Conclusion

An interesting direction of further research is to obtain non-asymptotic versions of our results. If the benchmark class of continuous stationary prediction strategies is compact, loss bounds can be given in terms of ϵ-entropy. In general, one can give loss bounds in terms of a nested family of compact sets whose union is dense in the set of continuous stationary prediction strategies (in analogy with Vapnik and Chervonenkis's principle of structural risk minimization [21]).

Acknowledgments

I am grateful to Yura Kalnishkan, Ilia Nouretdinov, and COLT'2007 anonymous reviewers for useful comments; in particular, the reviewers' comments have led to a radical revision of the paper. The construction of CS universal prediction strategies uses Gábor Lugosi's and Alex Smola's suggestions. This work was partially supported by MRC (grant G0301107).

References

1. Hannan, J.F.: Approximation to Bayes risk in repeated play. In: Dresher, M., Tucker, A.W., Wolfe, P. (eds.) Contribution to the Theory of Games, III. Annals of Mathematics Studies, vol. 39, pp. 97–139. Princeton University Press, Princeton (1957)
2. Blackwell, D.: Controlled random walks. In: Proceedings of the International Congress of Mathematicians, Vol. 3, Amsterdam, North-Holland (1954) 336–338 (1956)

3. DeSantis, A., Markowsky, G., Wegman, M.N.: Learning probabilistic prediction functions. In: Proceedings of the Twenty Ninth Annual IEEE Symposium on Foundations of Computer Science, pp. 110–119. IEEE Computer Society Press, Los Alamitos, CA (1988)
4. Littlestone, N., Warmuth, M.K.: The Weighted Majority Algorithm. (The conference version appeared in the FOCS'1989 Proceedings). Information and Computation 108, 212–261 (1994)
5. Vovk, V.: Aggregating strategies. In: Fulk, M., Case, J. (eds.) Proceedings of the Third Annual Workshop on Computational Learning Theory, pp. 371–383. Morgan Kaufmann, San Mateo, CA (1990)
6. Cesa-Bianchi, N., Lugosi, G.: Prediction, Learning, and Games. Cambridge University Press, Cambridge (2006)
7. Cesa-Bianchi, N., Long, P.M., Warmuth, M.K.: Worst-case quadratic loss bounds for on-line prediction of linear functions by gradient descent. IEEE Transactions on Neural Networks 7, 604–619 (1996)
8. Kivinen, J., Warmuth, M.K.: Exponentiated Gradient versus Gradient Descent for linear predictors. Information and Computation 132, 1–63 (1997)
9. Auer, P., Cesa-Bianchi, N., Gentile, C.: Adaptive and self-confident on-line learning algorithms. Journal of Computer and System Sciences 64, 48–75 (2002)
10. Vovk, V.: On-line regression competitive with reproducing kernel Hilbert spaces. In: Cai, J.-Y., Cooper, S.B., Li, A. (eds.) TAMC 2006. LNCS, vol. 3959, Springer, Heidelberg (2006)
11. Kalnishkan, Y., Vyugin, M.V.: The Weak Aggregating Algorithm and weak mixability. In: Auer, P., Meir, R. (eds.) COLT 2005. LNCS (LNAI), vol. 3559, pp. 188–203. Springer, Heidelberg (2005)
12. Vovk, V.: Competing with stationary prediction strategies. Technical Report arXiv:cs.LG/0607067, arXiv.org e-Print archive (first posted in July 2006)
13. Engelking, R.: General Topology. Second edition. Volume 6 of Sigma Series in Pure Mathematics. Heldermann, Berlin (1989)
14. Billingsley, P.: Convergence of Probability Measures. Wiley, New York (1968)
15. Kivinen, J., Warmuth, M.K.: Averaging expert predictions. In: Fischer, P., Simon, H.U. (eds.) EuroCOLT 1999. LNCS (LNAI), vol. 1572, pp. 153–167. Springer, Heidelberg (1999)
16. Hardy, G.H., Littlewood, J.E., Pólya, G.: Inequalities, 2nd edition. Cambridge University Press, Cambridge, England (1952)
17. Vovk, V.: Competitive on-line statistics. International Statistical Review 69, 213–248 (2001)
18. Rudin, W.: Functional Analysis. 2nd edition. International Series in Pure and Applied Mathematics. McGraw-Hill, Boston (1991)
19. Shafer, G., Vovk, V.: Probability and Finance: It's Only a Game! Wiley, New York (2001)
20. Gruenhage, G.: The story of a topological game. Rocky Mountain Journal of Mathematics 36, 1885–1914 (2006)
21. Vapnik, V.N.: Statistical Learning Theory. Wiley, New York (1998)

Improved Rates for the Stochastic Continuum-Armed Bandit Problem

Peter Auer[1], Ronald Ortner[1], and Csaba Szepesvári[2]

[1] University of Leoben, A-8700 Leoben, Austria
auer@unileoben.ac.at, ronald.ortner@unileoben.ac.at
[2] University of Alberta, Edmonton T6G 2E8, Canada
szepesva@cs.ualberta.ca

Abstract. Considering one-dimensional continuum-armed bandit problems, we propose an improvement of an algorithm of Kleinberg and a new set of conditions which give rise to improved rates. In particular, we introduce a novel assumption that is complementary to the previous smoothness conditions, while at the same time smoothness of the mean payoff function is required only at the maxima. Under these new assumptions new bounds on the expected regret are derived. In particular, we show that apart from logarithmic factors, the expected regret scales with the square-root of the number of trials, provided that the mean payoff function has finitely many maxima and its second derivatives are continuous and non-vanishing at the maxima. This improves a previous result of Cope by weakening the assumptions on the function. We also derive matching lower bounds. To complement the bounds on the expected regret, we provide high probability bounds which exhibit similar scaling.

1 Introduction

We consider continuum-armed bandit problems defined by some unknown distribution-family $P(\cdot|x)$, indexed by $x \in [0,1]$. In each trial $t = 1, 2, \ldots$ the learner chooses $X_t \in [0,1]$ and receives return $Y_t \sim P(\cdot|X_t)$. We assume that Y_t is independent of $\mathcal{F}_{t-1} = \sigma(X_1, Y_1, \ldots, X_{t-1}, Y_{t-1})$ given X_t. Furthermore, the returns are assumed to be uniformly bounded, say $Y_t \in [0,1]$.

The goal of the learner is to maximize her expected return. Let the mean return at x be

$$b(x) \triangleq \mathbb{E}\left[Y_1 \mid X_1 = x\right],$$

where we assume that $b : [0,1] \to [0,1]$ is measurable. Let $b^* \triangleq \sup_{x \in [0,1]} b(x)$ be the best possible return. Since P is unknown, in every trial the learner suffers a loss of $b^* - Y_t$, so that after T trials the learner's regret is

$$R_T \triangleq T\, b^* - \sum_{t=1}^{T} Y_t.$$

With this, return-maximization is the same as regret minimization.

N. Bshouty and C. Gentile (Eds.): COLT 2007, LNAI 4539, pp. 454–468, 2007.

In general, the domain of the decision or action variable X_t can be multi-dimensional. Here we restrict our attention to the one-dimensional case as this shares many of the difficulties of the full multi-dimensional problem, while it allows a simplified presentation of the main ideas.

The continuum-armed bandit problem has many applications (for references see e.g. [1]) and has been studied by a number of authors (e.g., [2,1,3]). It turns out that the continuum-armed bandit problem is much harder than finite-armed bandit problems. For the latter, it is known that logarithmic regret is achievable (see e.g. [4] and the references therein), while for the continuum-armed bandit the regret in typical cases will be polynomial. Concerning results on one-dimensional decision spaces, Kleinberg has derived upper and lower bounds on the regret under the assumption that the mean payoff function is uniformly locally Lipschitz with some exponent $0 < \alpha \leq 1$. Functions in this class satisfy the requirement that there exists some neighborhood size $\delta > 0$ and constant $L \geq 0$ such that for any $x, x' \in [0, 1]$ which are δ-close to each other, $|b(x) - b(x')| \leq L|x - x'|^\alpha$ holds. Kleinberg proposed a natural discretization-based algorithm that divides the domain into subintervals of equal lengths and plays a finite-armed bandit problem over the discretized problem. When choosing an interval, Kleinberg's algorithm samples its midpoint. He proves that this algorithm achieves an expected regret of $\tilde{O}\left(T^{2/3}\right)$ over T steps, along with a lower bound of $\Omega(T^{2/3})$ that matches the upper bound apart from a logarithmic factor. If the exponent α is known, the algorithm is shown to achieve expected regret of size $\tilde{O}\left(T^{(1+\alpha)/(1+2\alpha)}\right)$.

In another recent work Cope [3] studies a modified Kiefer-Wolfowitz algorithm (the modification concerns the learning rates). He shows an expected regret bound of size $O(T^{1/2})$ if b is unimodal, three times continuously differentiable, and its derivative is well behaved at its maxima x^* in the sense that $c_1|x - x^*|^2 \leq (x - x^*)b'(x)$ and $|b'(x)| \leq c_2|x - x^*|$ hold for some $c_1, c_2 > 0$.

In this paper, we provide a refined performance characterization for the following modification of Kleinberg's algorithm: While Kleinberg suggested to pick the midpoints of the intervals, we propose to sample actions uniformly at random within the interval. The key underlying idea is the following. There are two sources of the loss in the algorithm: the loss coming from the discretization of the continuous action space (the approximation loss) and the loss for selecting suboptimal arms (cost of learning). A bound on the approximation loss is controlled by the smoothness of the function at its maxima. The cost of learning, on the other hand, is controlled by the gap between the payoffs of suboptimal intervals and the optimal payoff. These gaps are easier to control if one samples uniformly from an interval than if one samples only the midpoint of the interval. Our analysis overcomes another limitation of Kleinberg's analysis which is incapable of capturing higher order smoothness: If b is uniformly locally Lipschitz with coefficient $\alpha > 1$ then it must be constant. We avoid this problem by demanding continuity only at the maxima of the mean payoff function.

A careful analysis then leads to a number of improved bounds. In particular, the modified algorithm achieves expected regret of $\tilde{O}\left(T^{1/2}\right)$ if b has finitely many maxima and non-vanishing, continuous second derivatives at all maxima.

Compared with the result of Cope, the regret is within a logarithmic factor, while our conditions on the payoff function are much weaker. Our upper bounds on the expected regret are complemented by a matching lower bound and a high-probability bound.

2 Problem Setup and Algorithm

In this section we state our assumptions on the mean payoff function, give our algorithm and an outline of the rest of the paper.

Our first assumption is a continuity condition. Without such a condition the regret may grow linearly with T, as it is hard to find maxima of a function, which are obtained at a sharp peak. We propose to capture this difficulty by the degree of continuity at the maxima:

Assumption 1. *There exist constants $L \geq 0$, $\alpha > 0$ such that for any point $x^* \in [0, 1]$ with $\limsup_{x \to x^*} b(x) = b^* \triangleq \sup_{x \in [0,1]} b(x)$, and all $x \in [0, 1]$*

$$b(x^*) - b(x) \leq L|x^* - x|^\alpha.$$

Define the loss function $d_{x^*}(x) \triangleq b(x^*) - b(x)$. Under Assumption 1, $0 \leq d_{x^*}(x) \leq L|x^* - x|^\alpha$. Hence d_{x^*} is Hölder continuous at x^* with exponent α, and so is b. In particular, $d_{x^*}(x^*) = 0$ and thus $b(x^*) = b^*$. Note that since we do not require this condition to hold at all points in the domain of b, we may allow $\alpha > 1$ without restricting the set of admissible functions to the set of constant functions.

Finding the maximum is also hard, if there are many candidates for the maximum, i.e., if for many x the value of b is close to b^*. This difficulty is captured by the measure of points with value close to the maximum:

Assumption 2. *There exist constants $M \geq 0$, $\beta > 0$ such that for all $\varepsilon > 0$,*

$$m(\{\, x \,:\, b^* - \varepsilon < b(x) \leq b^* \,\}) \leq M\varepsilon^\beta$$

holds, where m denotes the Lebesgue measure.

In terms of the loss function $d(x) \triangleq b^* - b(x)$ the condition states that $m(\{\, x \,:\, d(x) \geq \epsilon \,\}) \geq 1 - M\varepsilon^\beta$. For large β and $\epsilon > 0$, $m(\{\, x \,:\, d(x) \geq \epsilon \,\}) \approx 1$. Hence the maxima of the function do not have strong competitors. In fact, Assumptions 1 and 2 are complementary to each other in the sense that $\alpha\beta \leq 1$ holds for most functions. In particular, an elementary argument shows that under these assumptions $\alpha\beta \leq 1$ holds if b is measurable, all maxima of b are in $(0, 1)$ and b is not constant in the vicinity of any of its maxima.

Assumptions 1 and 2 put global constraints on the function. We will also consider the following assumption which relaxes this requirement:

Assumption 3. *Let X^* be the set of maxima of b. Then $X^* \subset (0, 1)$ and there exist $\rho > 0, \nu > 0, \alpha > 0, \beta > 0, L \geq 0, M \geq 0$ such that for any maximum $x^* \in X^*$, Assumptions 1 and 2 hold when x is restricted to the intervals $(x^* - 2\rho, x^* + 2\rho) \subset [0, 1]$. Further, it holds that whenever $x \in [0, 1] \setminus \bigcup_{x^* \in X^*}(x^* - \rho, x^* + \rho)$ then $b(x) \leq b^* - \nu$.*

Parameter: n

Initialization: Divide $[0,1]$ into n subintervals I_k with $I_k = [\frac{k-1}{n}, \frac{k}{n})$ $(1 \le k < n)$ and $I_n = [\frac{n-1}{n}, 1]$.

Execute UCB on the set of intervals:

- **Initialization:** Choose from each interval I_k a point uniformly at random.
- **Loop:**
  - Choose the interval I_k that maximizes $\hat{b}_k + \sqrt{\frac{2 \ln t}{t_k}}$, where $\hat{b}_k$ is the average return obtained from points in interval I_k, t_k is the number of times interval I_k was chosen, and t is the overall number of steps taken so far.
  - Choose a point uniformly at random from the chosen interval I_k.

Fig. 1. The **UCBC** algorithm with the number of intervals as parameter

This assumption requires that the function is well behaved in the vicinity of its well separated maxima.

As discussed before, we use a discretization-based algorithm that divides the domain into subintervals of equal lengths. Within each subinterval the algorithm chooses the actions uniformly at random. The problem is then to set the number of intervals n and to decide which interval to sample from. While we leave the choice of n open at the moment (n is a parameter of the algorithm, and a central theme of the paper is to find the "right" value of n), for the latter part, just like Kleinberg, we use the UCB algorithm (i.e. UCB1 from [4]). UCB is a finite-armed bandit algorithm that uses upper confidence bounds on the arms' sample-means and achieves optimal logarithmic regret-rates [4]. A more formal description of our UCBC (UCB for continuous bandits) algorithm is given in Figure 1.

Under Assumptions 1 and 2, in Section 3.1 we prove a generic result that gives a bound on the expected regret in terms of the number of subintervals n and the length T of the trial. As will be shown in Section 3.2, this result also holds under Assumption 3. We then give a high probability bound in Section 4. In Section 5, we show that without any knowledge of β, we get the same bounds as Kleinberg. However, for known β we get an improved bound of $\tilde{O}(T^{\frac{1+\alpha-\alpha\beta}{1+2\alpha-\alpha\beta}})$. In particular, if b has finitely many maxima and a non-vanishing, continuous second derivative at all maxima, then we prove $\mathbb{E}[R_T] = \tilde{O}(\sqrt{T})$. We also present lower bounds on the regret under Assumptions 1 and 2 in Section 6. These lower bounds essentially match our upper bound, hence showing that the algorithm's performance is optimal if α, β are known.

3   Bounds on the Expected Regret

3.1   Bounds Under Assumptions 1 and 2

In this section we analyze the regret of UCBC under Assumptions 1 and 2. We use the following result that can be extracted from the analysis of UCB (in particular, from the proof of Theorem 1 in [4]):

Lemma 1. *Consider UCB applied to a multi-armed bandit problem with payoffs in $[0, 1]$. Let $\tau_i(T)$ denote number of times an arm is chosen up to (and including) time step T, and let d_i be the expected loss when playing arm i instead of an optimal arm. If i is the index of a suboptimal arm then*

$$\mathbb{E}\left[\tau_i(T)\right] \leq \frac{A\ln(T)}{d_i^2} + B \tag{1}$$

for some constants A, B. In particular, one may select $A = 8$ and $B = 1 + \pi^2/3$.

Analysis of the Regret of UCBC: Our analysis will follow the idea described earlier, bounding separately the loss resulting from the discretization, and the cost of learning which interval is the best. According to Lemma 1, for the latter we need to lower bound the gap between the best arm's payoff and the suboptimal arms' payoffs. This is the critical part of the proof.

For $k = 1, 2, \ldots, n$ let I_k denote the k-th interval, i.e. $I_k \triangleq [(k-1)/n, k/n)$ if $1 \leq k < n$ and $I_n \triangleq [(n-1)/n, 1]$. Let the choice of UCB be $U_t \in \{1, \ldots, n\}$, the choice of UCBC be X_t and the received payoff Y_t. Let $\tau_i(T) \triangleq \sum_{t=1}^{T} \mathbb{I}_{\{U_t=i\}}$ be the number of times UCBC selects arm i in the first T trials.

Denote by $\bar{b}_k \triangleq n \int_{I_k} b(x)dx$ the expected payoff when the algorithm selects to sample from the k-th subinterval. Let $b_1 \leq b_2 \leq \ldots \leq b_n$ be the ordering of $(\bar{b}_k)_k$, and let π be the permutation that gives this ordering, i.e. $b_{\pi(k)} = \bar{b}_k$. Set $\tau_i'(T) \triangleq \tau_{\pi^{-1}(i)}(T)$. Finally, let $d_i^* \triangleq b^* - b_i$, and $d_i \triangleq b_n - b_i$.

By Wald's identity, the expected regret of UCBC can be expressed via the sampling times $\tau_k(T)$, alternatively using $\tau_k'(T)$, as follows:

$$\mathbb{E}\left[R_T\right] = \sum_{k=1}^{n}(b^* - \bar{b}_k)\mathbb{E}\left[\tau_k(T)\right] = \sum_{i=1}^{n} d_i^* \mathbb{E}\left[\tau_i'(T)\right].$$

In what follows, we analyze $\tilde{R}_T \triangleq \sum_{i=1}^{n} d_i^* \bar{\tau}_i'(T)$, where $\bar{\tau}_i'(T) \triangleq \mathbb{E}\left[\tau_i'(T)\right]$. We start with a simple observation that follows immediately from Assumption 1:

$$d_n^* \triangleq b^* - b_n \leq Ln^{-\alpha}. \tag{2}$$

To see that this holds pick any maximum x^* of b and let k^* be the index of the interval containing x^*: $x^* \in I_{k^*}$. Let $i^* \triangleq \pi(k^*)$. Then $b^* - b_n \leq b^* - b_{i^*} = b(x^*) - n \int_{I_{i^*}} b(x)dx = n \int_{I_{i^*}} (b(x^*) - b(x))dx \leq nL \int_0^{1/n} z^\alpha dz \leq nL(1/n)^{\alpha+1}/(\alpha+1) \leq Ln^{-\alpha}$ as promised.

We split the set of arms into two parts. Let $\gamma \geq 1$ be a real-valued number to be selected later and define

$$S \triangleq \{i : d_i^* > \gamma Ln^{-\alpha}\}.$$

By design, S contains the indices of "strongly" suboptimal intervals.

We split the regret based on if the payoff in an interval is "strongly" suboptimal:

$$\sum_{i=1}^{n} d_i^* \bar{\tau}_i'(T) \leq \sum_{i \notin S} d_i^* \bar{\tau}_i'(T) + \sum_{i \in S} d_i^* \bar{\tau}_i'(T) \triangleq \tilde{R}_{T,1} + \tilde{R}_{T,2}.$$

Bounding $\tilde{R}_{T,1}$: $\tilde{R}_{T,1}$ is controlled by the resolution of the discretization: By the choice of S, $d_i^* \leq \gamma Ln^{-\alpha}$ whenever $i \notin S$. Hence

$$\tilde{R}_{T,1} \leq \gamma Ln^{-\alpha} \sum_{i \notin S} \overline{\tau}_i'(T) \leq \gamma Ln^{-\alpha}T. \tag{3}$$

Bounding $\tilde{R}_{T,2}$: The idea here is to "sort" intervals with index in S according to the size of the "gaps" d_i into different buckets and then argue that the number of indices in a bucket with small gaps cannot be too large. Within each bucket we use Lemma 1 to bound the regret.

First, let us note that when $n^\alpha \leq \gamma L$ then $S = \emptyset$, hence $\tilde{R}_{T,2} = 0$. Thus, in what follows we assume that $n^\alpha > \gamma L$ or $\gamma Ln^{-\alpha} < 1$.

Observe that S does not contain any interval with an optimal response: if $b_i = b_n$, then $i \notin S$. Indeed, by (2) $d_n^* \leq Ln^{-\alpha} \leq \gamma Ln^{-\alpha}$. Therefore, we may use Lemma 1 to bound $\overline{\tau}_i'(T)$ for $i \in S$. By (2), $d_i^* = b^* - b_i \leq b_n - b_i + Ln^{-\alpha} = d_i + Ln^{-\alpha}$ and hence using (1) we get

$$\tilde{R}_{T,2} \leq A\ln(T) \sum_{i \in S} \left(\frac{1}{d_i} + \frac{Ln^{-\alpha}}{d_i^2} \right) + B|S|. \tag{4}$$

Let $\Delta_k \triangleq 2^{-k}$, $k = 0,1,2,\ldots$ so that $1 = \Delta_0 > \Delta_1 > \Delta_2 > \ldots$. Let

$$S_k \triangleq \{ i \in S : \Delta_k \leq d_i^* < \Delta_{k-1} \}, \quad k = 0,1,2,\ldots.$$

Note that if $\Delta_{k-1} \leq \gamma Ln^{-\alpha}$ then $S_k = \emptyset$. Hence, if we define K to be the unique index such that $\gamma Ln^{-\alpha} \in [\Delta_K, \Delta_{K-1})$, then $S = \bigcup_{k=0}^{K} S_k$. (The existence of K is guaranteed since by assumption $\gamma Ln^{-\alpha} < 1$.) Note that $K = \lceil \ln_2(n^\alpha/(\gamma L)) \rceil$, and if $k \leq K$, then $\Delta_{k-1} > \gamma Ln^{-\alpha}$. Now set $\gamma \triangleq 4$. By (2), $d_i \triangleq b_n - b_i \geq b^* - Ln^{-\alpha} - b_i = d_i^* - Ln^{-\alpha}$, hence for $i \in S_k$, $k = 0,1,\ldots,K$,

$$d_i \geq \Delta_k - Ln^{-\alpha} = \Delta_k(1 - Ln^{-\alpha}/\Delta_k) > \Delta_k/2. \tag{5}$$

Here in the last step we used that $\Delta_k = (1/2)\Delta_{k-1} > (1/2)\gamma Ln^{-\alpha} = 2Ln^{-\alpha}$. Using (5) we get

$$\sum_{i \in S} \left(\frac{1}{d_i} + \frac{Ln^{-\alpha}}{d_i^2} \right) = \sum_{k=0}^{K} \sum_{i \in S_k} \left(\frac{1}{d_i} + \frac{Ln^{-\alpha}}{d_i^2} \right) \leq \sum_{k=0}^{K} \left(\frac{2}{\Delta_k} + \frac{4Ln^{-\alpha}}{\Delta_k^2} \right) |S_k|. \tag{6}$$

A Bound on $|S_k|$: Let $U_i(\varepsilon) \triangleq \{ x \in I_i : b^* - b(x) \geq \varepsilon \}$ with some $\varepsilon > 0$. Note that $b^* - b(x) \geq 0$ and hence by Markov's inequality, $m(U_i(\varepsilon)) \leq (1/\varepsilon) \int_{I_i} (b^* - b(x))dx = (b^* - b_i)m(I_i)/\varepsilon = d_i^* m(I_i)/\varepsilon$ and thus for $\overline{U}_i(\varepsilon) = I_i \setminus U_i(\varepsilon)$, $m(\overline{U}_i(\varepsilon)) \geq (1 - d_i^*/\varepsilon) m(I_i)$. Assume that $i \in S_k$. By the definition of S_k, $\Delta_{k-1} > d_i^*$ and hence $m(\overline{U}_i(\varepsilon)) \geq (1 - \Delta_{k-1}/\varepsilon) m(I_i)$. Set $\varepsilon = 2\Delta_{k-1}$ so that $m(\overline{U}_i(2\Delta_{k-1})) \geq 1/2 \, m(I_i)$. Therefore,

$$|S_k|m(I_1) = \sum_{i \in S_k} m(I_i) \leq 2 \sum_{i \in S_k} m(\overline{U}_i(2\Delta_{k-1})) = 2\, m(\cup_{i \in S_k}^* \overline{U}_i(2\Delta_{k-1})), \tag{7}$$

where the disjointness follows since $\overline{U}_i(2\Delta_{k-1}) \subset I_i$. Since $\overline{U}_i(2\Delta_{k-1}) = \{ x \in I_i : b^* - b(x) \le 2\Delta_{k-1} \} = \{ x \in I_i : b(x) \ge b^* - \Delta_{k-2} \}$, the union of these sets is contained in $\{ x \in [0,1] : b(x) \ge b^* - \Delta_{k-2} \}$ and therefore by Assumption 2, $m(\bigcup_{i \in S_k}^* \overline{U}_i(2\Delta_{k-1})) \le M (4\,\Delta_k)^\beta$. Combined with (7), this gives $|S_k| m(I_1) \le 2M (4\,\Delta_k)^\beta$ and hence $|S_k| \le 2\,Mn\,(4\,\Delta_k)^\beta$.

Putting Things Together: The bound on $|S_k|$ together with (6) and (4) yields

$$\tilde{R}_{T,2} \le 2AMn\ln(T) \left(\sum_{k=0}^{K} (4\,\Delta_k)^\beta \left(\frac{2}{\Delta_k} + \frac{4Ln^{-\alpha}}{\Delta_k^2} \right) \right) + B\,n$$

$$= 4^{\beta+1} AMn\ln(T) \left(\sum_{k=0}^{K} 2^{(1-\beta)k} + 2Ln^{-\alpha} \sum_{k=0}^{K} 2^{(2-\beta)k} \right) + B\,n. \quad (8)$$

Assuming that $\beta \notin \{0,1,2\}$ and exploiting that $2^{K+1} \le n^\alpha/L$ (this follows from $K - 1 \le \ln_2(1/(\gamma Ln^{-\alpha}))$ and $\gamma = 4$), we get

$$\tilde{R}_{T,2} \le 4^{\beta+1} AMn\ln(T) \left(\frac{(n^\alpha/L)^{1-\beta} - 1}{2^{1-\beta} - 1} + 2Ln^{-\alpha} \frac{(n^\alpha/L)^{2-\beta} - 1}{2^{2-\beta} - 1} \right) + Bn. \quad (9)$$

Considering β:

- If $\beta < 1$, from (9) we get via some tedious calculations,

$$\tilde{R}_{T,2} \le \frac{3 \cdot 4^{\beta+1} AML^{\beta-1}}{2^{1-\beta} - 1} n^{1+\alpha-\alpha\beta} \ln(T) + Bn.$$

- $\beta = 1$: Since by our earlier remark we assume that $n^\alpha > \gamma L = 4L$, working directly from (8) gives

$$\tilde{R}_{T,2} \le \frac{4^{\beta+1} AM\alpha}{\ln 2} n \ln n \ln T + 4^{\beta+1} AM(3 + \ln_2(2/L)) n \ln(T) + Bn.$$

- $1 < \beta < 2$: Using (9) and $n^\alpha > \gamma L > L$ we get

$$\tilde{R}_{T,2} \le \frac{4^{\beta+1} AM}{1 - 2^{1-\beta}} n \ln T + \frac{2\,4^{\beta+1} AML^{\beta-1}}{2^{2-\beta} - 1} n^{1+\alpha-\alpha\beta} \ln T + Bn.$$

- If $\beta = 2$, from (8) using $\ln x/x \le 1/e$ we get

$$\tilde{R}_{T,2} \le 2\,4^{\beta+1} \left(1 + \frac{1}{4e\ln 2} \right) AMn \ln T + 2\,4^{\beta+1} AMLn^{1-\alpha} \ln T + Bn.$$

- If $\beta > 2$, using again (9),

$$\tilde{R}_{T,2} \le \frac{4^{\beta+1} AM}{1 - 2^{1-\beta}} n \ln T + \frac{2\,4^{\beta+1} AML}{1 - 2^{2-\beta}} n^{1-\alpha} \ln T + Bn.$$

Lemma 5. *Under the assumptions of Lemma 1, with probability at least $1 - n\delta_0$, simultaneously for all suboptimal arms i,*

$$\tau_i(T) \le \frac{A' \ln(T/\delta_0)}{d_i^2} + B'$$

for some constants A', B'.

Setting $\delta_0 \triangleq \delta/(2n)$ in UCBC(δ_0), we get that $\tau_i(T) \le A' \ln(2Tn/\delta)/d_i^2 + B'$ holds for all suboptimal arms simultaneously with probability at least $1 - \delta/2$. Hence, with probability at least $1 - \delta$,

$$R_T \le 4Ln^{-\alpha}T + \sum_{i \in S} d_i^* \tau_i(T) + H_T(\delta/2)$$

$$\le 4Ln^{-\alpha}T + A' \ln(2Tn/\delta)\Big(\sum_{i \in S} d_i^* d_i^{-2}\Big) + nB' + H_T(\delta/2).$$

Continuing as in Section 3, we obtain the following result:

Lemma 6. *Let $\delta > 0$. Consider UCBC with n intervals and confidence sequence $c_{t,s}(\delta/(2n))$ applied to a continuum-armed bandit problem, where the payoffs are in the range $[0,1]$ and the mean payoff function satisfies Assumptions 1 and 2 with some constants L, α, M, β. If $n^\alpha \le 4L$, then the regret satisfies $R_T \le 4Ln^{-\alpha}T + H_T(\delta/2)$ with probability $1 - \delta$, while for $n^\alpha > 4L$ it holds with probability at least $1 - \delta$ that*

$$R_T \le 4Ln^{-\alpha}T + 4^{\beta+1}A'MnR_T' \ln(2Tn/\delta) + B'n + H_T(\delta/2).$$

Using the reasoning of Section 3.2, this result can be extended to the localized version of Assumptions 1 and 2 (Assumption 3). We omit the details.

5   Choice of the Parameters

First note that according to Lemma 2 we have for $0 \le \beta < 1$ and a suitable constant c

$$\mathbb{E}[R_T] \le 4L\frac{T}{n^\alpha} + \frac{c\,4^\beta\,ML^{\beta-1}}{2^{1-\beta} - 1}n^{1+\alpha-\alpha\beta} \ln T. \tag{11}$$

5.1   Results Without Assumption 2

With $\beta = 0$ and $M = 1$ Assumption 2 trivially holds true. From (11) we get

$$\mathbb{E}[R_T] \le 4L\frac{T}{n^\alpha} + \frac{c}{L}n^{1+\alpha} \ln T.$$

Corollary 1. *If α is known, setting $n \triangleq \left(\frac{T}{\ln T}\right)^{\frac{1}{1+2\alpha}}$ gives*

$$\mathbb{E}[R_T] \leq \left(4L + \frac{c}{L}\right) T^{\frac{1+\alpha}{1+2\alpha}} (\ln T)^{\frac{\alpha}{1+2\alpha}}, \tag{12}$$

while if α is unknown, setting $n \triangleq \left(\frac{T}{\ln T}\right)^{\frac{1}{3}}$ gives for sufficiently large T

$$\mathbb{E}[R_T] \leq 4L \cdot T^{\max\{1-\frac{\alpha}{3},\frac{2}{3}\}} (\ln T)^{\frac{1}{3}} + \frac{c}{L} \cdot T^{\frac{2}{3}} (\ln T)^{\frac{2}{3}}. \tag{13}$$

Proof. (12) is straightforward. Concerning (13), first note that for our choice of n and $\alpha \leq 1$ we have

$$\mathbb{E}[R_T] \leq 4L \cdot T^{1-\frac{\alpha}{3}} (\ln T)^{\frac{1}{3}} + \frac{c}{L} \cdot T^{\frac{2}{3}} (\ln T)^{\frac{2-\alpha}{3}}. \tag{14}$$

On the other hand, if $\alpha > 1$, then $Ln^{-\alpha} \leq L\sqrt{nT^{-1}\ln T}$ for $n = \left(\frac{T}{\ln T}\right)^{1/3}$. Then $\mathbb{E}[R_T] \leq \left(4L + \frac{c}{L}\right) T^{\frac{2}{3}} (\ln T)^{\frac{1}{3}}$. Combining this with (14) gives (13). $\square$

5.2   Results Using Assumption 2

The most interesting case is $\beta < 1$. For known α and β, we set $n \triangleq \left(\frac{T}{\ln T}\right)^{\frac{1}{1+2\alpha-\alpha\beta}}$ and get from (11), $\mathbb{E}[R_T] \leq \left(4L + \frac{4cML^{\beta-1}}{2^{1-\beta}-1}\right) \cdot T^{\frac{1+\alpha-\alpha\beta}{1+2\alpha-\alpha\beta}} (\ln T)^{\frac{\alpha}{1+2\alpha-\alpha\beta}}$.

As noted before, comparing Assumptions 1 and 2 we find that for most functions b we have $\alpha\beta \leq 1$, the only exception being when b is constant in the vicinity of the maximum. Making the optimistic assumption that $\alpha\beta = 1$, we may set $n \triangleq \left(\frac{T}{\ln T}\right)^{\frac{1}{2\alpha}}$ and get

$$\mathbb{E}[R_T] \leq \left(4L + \frac{4cML^{\beta-1}}{2^{1-\beta}-1}\right) \cdot \sqrt{T \ln T}. \tag{15}$$

If the function b has continuous second derivatives, then Assumptions 1 and 2 are satisfied with $\alpha = 2$ and $\beta = 1/2$:

Theorem 1. *If b has a finite number of maxima x^* with $\limsup_{x \to x^*} b(x) = b^*$, and continuous second derivatives $\neq 0$ at all these x^*, then our algorithm with $n \triangleq \left(\frac{T}{\ln T}\right)^{\frac{1}{4}}$ achieves*

$$\mathbb{E}[R_T] \leq O\left(\sqrt{T \ln T}\right).$$

Proof. By assumption, $b'(x^*) = 0$ and $b''(x^*) \neq 0$ for any maximum x^*. Using Taylor series expansion we find

$$b(x^*) - L_1(x^* - x)^2 \leq b(x) \leq b(x^*) - L_2(x^* - x)^2 + L_3|x^* - x|^3$$

for suitable constants $L_1, L_2, L_3 > 0$, any maximum x^*, and any $x \in [0, 1]$. Hence, Assumption 1 is satisfied with $\alpha = 2$.

Furthermore, there are $\varepsilon_0 > 0$ and $0 < \delta_0 < L_2/(2L_3)$ such that $b(x) \leq b^* - \varepsilon_0$ for all x with $\min_{x^*} |x - x^*| \geq \delta_0$. Thus $b(x) > b(x^*) - \varepsilon$ for $\varepsilon < \varepsilon_0$ implies $\min_{x^*} |x - x^*| < \delta_0$ and $b(x^*) - \varepsilon < b(x) \leq b(x^*) - L_2(x^* - x)^2 + L_3|x^* - x|^3 = b(x^*) - (x^* - x)^2(L_2 - L_3|x^* - x|) \leq b(x^*) - L_2(x^* - x)^2/2$ such that $|x - x^*| < \sqrt{2\varepsilon/L_2}$ for some maximum x^* (out of the finitely many). For $\varepsilon \geq \varepsilon_0$ we have $|x - x^*| \leq 1 \leq \sqrt{\varepsilon/\varepsilon_0}$. Hence, Assumption 2 is satisfied with $\beta = 1/2$. The theorem follows from (15).
$\hfill\square$

5.3   When the Number of Steps T Is Unknown

If unlike in the previous sections the total number of steps T is unknown, then a simple application of the doubling trick gives the same bounds with somewhat worse constants. That is, UCBC is executed for 2^k steps in rounds $k = 1, 2, \ldots$. Then after T steps at most $K = 1 + \lceil \ln_2 T \rceil$ rounds have been played. Thus the total regret can be obtained by summing up over all rounds $\sum_{k=1}^{K} (2^k)^a (\ln(2^k))^b = O\left((2^K)^a (\ln(2^K))^b\right) = O\left(T^a (\ln T)^b\right)$.

6   Lower Bounds on the Regret

In this section we extend the lower bound result of Kleinberg [1] and show that our upper bounds on the regret are tight (apart from a logarithmic factor).

Theorem 2. *For any $\alpha > 0, \beta \geq 0, \alpha\beta \leq 1$, and any learning algorithm, there is a function b satisfying Assumptions 1 and 2 such that for any $\gamma < \frac{1+\alpha-\alpha\beta}{1+2\alpha-\alpha\beta}$,*

$$\limsup_{T \to \infty} \frac{\mathbb{E}[R_T]}{T^\gamma} \to \infty.$$

In [1] this theorem was proven for $\beta = 0$. We extend the construction of [1] to consider also $\beta > 0$.

Proof. We define function b as

$$b(x) \triangleq \sum_{k=k_0}^{\infty} [\phi_k(x) + \psi_k(x)]$$

for an appropriate k_0 and functions ϕ_k and ψ_k. We set $c_{k_0-1} = 0$ and $d_{k_0-1} = 1$ and iteratively define intervals $[c_k, d_k]$ at random. The functions ϕ_k and ψ_k are defined in respect to these random intervals. As such, the function b is constructed by a random process. We will argue, that for any learning algorithm the average regret in respect to this random process is large, which will imply the theorem.

The functions ϕ_k and ψ_k are continuous, non-negative, and positive only within a part of the interval $[c_{k-1}, d_{k-1}]$. The main part of these functions is a plateau where they remain constant, and they rise to and fall from this plateau governed by a function $f : [0, 1] \mapsto [0, 1]$ where $f(x) \triangleq 1 - (1 - x)^\alpha$, such that $f(0) = 0$ and $f(1) = 1$. The lengths δ_k of the intervals $[c_k, d_k]$ are very rapidly decreasing. We are also using sub-intervals $[c'_k, d'_k]$ with the property $[c_k, d_k] \subset [c'_{k-1}, d'_{k-1}] \subset [c_{k-1}, d_{k-1}]$. Let

$$\delta_k \triangleq 2^{-k!}, \qquad \Delta_k \triangleq \frac{1}{5}\delta_{k-1}^{1/(\alpha\beta)}, \qquad L_k \triangleq \max\left\{2, \left\lfloor \tfrac{1}{5}\delta_k^{\alpha\beta-1}\delta_{k-1} \right\rfloor\right\},$$

$$c'_{k-1} \triangleq c_{k-1} + \Delta_k, \quad \text{and} \quad d'_{k-1} \triangleq c_{k-1} + \Delta_k + 3L_k\delta_k,$$

and

$$\phi_k(x) \triangleq \begin{cases} 0 & \text{for} & x \le c_{k-1} \\ \Delta_k^\alpha f\!\left(\frac{x-c_{k-1}}{\Delta_k}\right) & \text{for} & c_{k-1} \le x \le c'_{k-1} \\ \Delta_k^\alpha & \text{for} & c'_{k-1} \le x \le d'_{k-1} \\ \Delta_k^\alpha f\!\left(1 - \frac{x-d'_{k-1}}{\Delta_k}\right) & \text{for} & d'_{k-1} \le x \le d'_{k-1} + \Delta_k \\ 0 & \text{for } d'_{k-1} + \Delta_k \le x \end{cases}.$$

Observe that

$$d'_{k-1} + \Delta_k \le c_{k-1} + 2\Delta_k + 3L_k\delta_k \le c_{k-1} + \frac{2}{5}\delta_{k-1}^{1/(\alpha\beta)} + \max\left\{6\delta_k, \frac{3}{5}\delta_k^{\alpha\beta}\delta_{k-1}\right\}$$

$$\le c_{k-1} + \frac{2}{5}\delta_{k-1} + \frac{3}{5}\delta_{k-1} \le c_{k-1} + \delta_{k-1}.$$

Let $\ell_k \in \{0, \ldots, L_k - 1\}$ be chosen uniformly at random and set

$$c_k \triangleq c'_{k-1} + (L_k + \ell_k)\delta_k, \quad d_k \triangleq c_k + \delta_k,$$

and

$$\psi_k(x) \triangleq \begin{cases} 0 & \text{for} & x \le c_k - \delta_k \\ \delta_k^\alpha f\!\left(\frac{x-c_k+\delta_k}{\delta_k}\right) & \text{for} & c_k - \delta_k \le x \le c_k \\ \delta_k^\alpha & \text{for} & c_k \le x \le d_k \\ \delta_k^\alpha f\!\left(1 - \frac{x-d_k}{\delta_k}\right) & \text{for} & d_k \le x \le d_k + \delta_k \\ 0 & \text{for } d_k + \delta_k \le x \end{cases}.$$

Then any fixed b has a unique maximum at $x^* = \lim_k c_k = \lim_k d_k$. The intuition of the construction is the following: the slope of function f is responsible for matching Assumption 1 tightly (this is rather obvious), whereas the length $3L_k\delta_k$ of $[c'_{k-1}, d'_{k-1}]$ is responsible for matching Assumption 2 tightly. This can be seen from the fact that the peak of function b on top of the plateau $[c'_k, d'_k]$ is approximately of size $\varepsilon = \delta_k^\alpha$, such that $L_k\delta_k \approx \delta_k^{\alpha\beta}\delta_{k-1} \approx \varepsilon^\beta$. ($\delta_{k-1}$ is very large compared to δ_k and can be ignored.).

The heights of functions ϕ_k and ψ_k are chosen such that Assumptions 1 and 2 are satisfied. We first check that function b satisfies Assumption 1. For any $x \in [0, 1]$, $x \ne x^*$, there is a $k \ge 1$ such that $x \in [c_{k-1}, d_{k-1}] \setminus [c_k, d_k]$. We assume without loss of generality that $x < c_k < x^*$. Then $b(x^*) - b(x) = b(x^*) - b(c_k) + b(c_k) - b(x)$ and

$$b(x^*) - b(c_k) \le \sum_{i=k+1}^\infty (\Delta_i^\alpha + \delta_i^\alpha) \le 2(\Delta_{k+1}^\alpha + \delta_{k+1}^\alpha) \le 4(x^* - c_k)^\alpha,$$

since $x^* - c_k > \Delta_{k+1} + \delta_{k+1}$. To bound $b(c_k) - b(x)$ consider the following cases:

a) If $c_k - \delta_k \le x < c_k$, then $b(c_k) - b(x) = \delta_k^\alpha - \delta_k^\alpha f\left(\frac{x-c_k+\delta_k}{\delta_k}\right) = \delta_k^\alpha - \delta_k^\alpha (1 - (1 - \frac{x-c_k+\delta_k}{\delta_k})^\alpha) = (c_k - x)^\alpha$.

b) If $c'_{k-1} \le x \le c_k - \delta_k$, then $b(c_k) - b(x) \le \delta_k^\alpha \le (c_k - x)^\alpha$.

c) If $c_{k-1} \le x \le c'_{k-1}$, then $b(c_k) - b(x) = \delta_k^\alpha + \Delta_k^\alpha [1 - f(\frac{x-c_{k-1}}{\Delta_k})] = \delta_k^\alpha + \Delta_k^\alpha [1 - \frac{x-c_{k-1}}{\Delta_k}]^\alpha = \delta_k^\alpha + \Delta_k^\alpha [\frac{c'_{k-1}-x}{\Delta_k}]^\alpha \le 2(c_k - x)^\alpha$.

Since $4(x^* - c_k)^\alpha + 2(c_k - x)^\alpha \le 6(x^* - x)^\alpha$, Assumption 1 is satisfied.

For checking Assumption 2, let $x \in [0,1]$ be such that $b(x^*) - b(x) < \varepsilon$. We distinguish two cases, $\delta_k^\alpha \le \varepsilon < \Delta_k^\alpha$ and $\Delta_k^\alpha \le \varepsilon < \delta_{k-1}^\alpha$ for some $k \ge k_0$.

a) If $\delta_k^\alpha \le \varepsilon < \Delta_k^\alpha$, then $\phi_k(x) \ge \Delta_k^\alpha + \delta_k^\alpha - \varepsilon$, which by definition of ϕ_k and f holds if $x \in [c'_{k-1} - (\varepsilon - \delta_k^\alpha)^{1/\alpha}, d'_{k-1} + (\varepsilon - \delta_k^\alpha)^{1/\alpha}]$. As $(\varepsilon - \delta_k^\alpha)^{1/\alpha} < \varepsilon^{1/\alpha} \le \varepsilon^\beta$ and $d'_{k-1} - c'_{k-1} = 3L_k\delta_k \le \frac{3}{5}\delta_k^{\alpha\beta}\delta_{k-1} \le \delta_k^{\alpha\beta} \le \varepsilon^\beta$, the length of this interval does not exceed $3\varepsilon^\beta$.

b) On the other hand, if $\Delta_k^\alpha \le \varepsilon < \delta_{k-1}^\alpha$, then $\psi_{k-1}(x) \ge \Delta_k^\alpha + \delta_{k-1}^\alpha - \varepsilon$, which by definition of ψ_{k-1} and f holds, if $x \in [c_{k-1} - (\varepsilon - \Delta_k^\alpha)^{1/\alpha}, d_{k-1} + (\varepsilon - \Delta_k^\alpha)^{1/\alpha}]$. The length of this interval is smaller than $7\varepsilon^\beta$, since $(\varepsilon - \Delta_k^\alpha)^{1/\alpha} < \varepsilon^\beta$ and $d_{k-1} - c_{k-1} = \delta_{k-1} = 5\Delta_k^{\alpha\beta} \le 5\varepsilon^\beta$.

Thus Assumption 2 is satisfied, too.

Finally we show that for $T_k \triangleq \lfloor \frac{1}{2} L_k \delta_k^{-2\alpha} \rfloor = \Theta(\delta_k^{\alpha\beta-1-2\alpha}\delta_{k-1})$, and any $\gamma < \frac{1+\alpha-\alpha\beta}{1+2\alpha-\alpha\beta}$

$$\lim_{k\to\infty} \frac{\mathbb{E}[R_{T_k}]}{T_k^\gamma} \to \infty .$$

For any $x_1, x_2 \in [c'_{k-1}, d'_{k-1}]$, the Kullback-Leibler distance between the bandits x_1 and x_2 is $O(\delta_k^{2\alpha})$ and it is 0 if both $x_1, x_2 \notin [c_k, d_k]$. Therefore, to identify $[c_k, d_k]$ with probability $\Omega(1)$, at least half of the intervals $[c'_{k-1} + (L_k + \ell_k)\delta_k, c'_{k-1} + (L_k + \ell_k + 1)\delta_k]$, $\ell_k \in 0, \ldots, L_k - 1$, need to be probed $\lceil \delta_k^{-2\alpha} \rceil$ times. Since $b(x^*) - b(x) \ge \delta_k^\alpha$ for $x \notin [c_k, d_k]$, we find

$$\mathbb{E}[R_{T_k}] = \Omega(T_k \delta_k^\alpha) = \Omega\left(\delta_k^{\alpha\beta-1-\alpha}\delta_{k-1}\right)$$
$$= \Omega\left(T_k^{\frac{\alpha\beta-1-\alpha}{\alpha\beta-1-2\alpha}}\delta_{k-1}^{1-\frac{\alpha\beta-1-\alpha}{\alpha\beta-1-2\alpha}}\right) = \Omega\left(T_k^{\frac{1+\alpha-\alpha\beta}{1+2\alpha-\alpha\beta}}\delta_{k-1}^{\frac{\alpha}{1+2\alpha-\alpha\beta}}\right) .$$

Since $\lim_{k\to\infty} \delta_{k-1}^{\gamma_1}/\delta_k^{\gamma_2} \to \infty$ for any $\gamma_1, \gamma_2 > 0$, this proves the theorem.   □

7   Conclusions and Future Work

We have shown that by changing the algorithm of Kleinberg, it is possible to get improved regret bounds under a wide range of conditions. In particular, the uniform local Lipschitz condition is replaced with a smoothness condition that is localized to the set of maxima of the payoff function. A complementary condition ensures that the maxima do not have many strong competitors. These two conditions allow us to get improved bounds compared to the bounds of Kleinberg [1]. Moreover, the new algorithm is shown to match the performance of the Kiefer-Wolfowitz algorithm [3], but under substantially weaker conditions.

One limitation of the presented results is that in order to get the best possible rates, the user must know the exponents α, β of Assumptions 1 and 2. It is an open question, if it is possible to achieve the optimal rates when this knowledge is not available, possibly by restricting the payoff function in some other reasonable way. In connection to this, we could recently show that a two-phase algorithm achieves regret of $\tilde{O}\left(T^{1/2}\right)$ for functions with well separated maxima, provided that in a small neighborhood of the maxima the functions are unimodal and satisfy a not too strong rate-condition (which holds e.g. for locally strictly convex functions). There is also room for improvement regarding the high probability bounds. Thus, a better bound on the inferior sampling time for UCB would immediately lead to better bounds for our algorithm.

We have not considered d-dimensional action spaces in this paper, though we believe that our results can be extended to this case. Previous lower bounds show that in the worst-case, the regret would scale exponentially with the dimension d. An interesting open question is if there exists an algorithm that scales better when the mean payoff function depends only on some unknown subset of the variables.

Finally, let us remark that if UCB is replaced with UCB-tuned [4] and there is no observation noise, i.e. $Y_t = b(X_t)$, then the analysis presented can be used to prove the improved rate $\tilde{O}\left(T^{1/(1+\alpha)}\right)$, i.e. $\tilde{O}\left(T^{1/2}\right)$ for $\alpha = 1$. Hence, the cost of control-learning is substantially less when there is no observation noise present.

Acknowledgements. Csaba Szepesvári greatly acknowledges the support received through the Alberta Ingenuity Center for Machine Learning (AICML) and the Computer and Automation Research Institute of the Hungarian Academy of Sciences. This work was supported in part by the the Austrian Science Fund FWF (S9104-N04 SP4) and the IST Programme of the European Community, under the PASCAL Network of Excellence, IST-2002-506778. We also acknowledge support by the PASCAL pump priming projects "Sequential Forecasting" and "Online Performance of Reinforcement Learning with Internal Reward Functions". This publication only reflects the authors' views.

References

1. Kleinberg, R.: Nearly tight bounds for the continuum-armed bandit problem. In: Advances in Neural Information Processing Systems 17 NIPS, 697–704 (2004)
2. Agrawal, R.: The continuum-armed bandit problem. SIAM J. Control Optim. 33, 1926–1951 (1995)
3. Cope, E.: Regret and convergence bounds for a class of continuum-armed bandit problems. submitted (2006)
4. Auer, P., Cesa-Bianchi, N., Fischer, P.: Finite-time analysis of the multi-armed bandit problem. Mach. Learn. 47, 235–256 (2002)
5. Cesa-Bianchi, N., Lugosi, G., Stoltz, G.: Minimizing regret with label efficient prediction. IEEE Trans. Inform. Theory 51, 2152–2162 (2004)

Learning Permutations with Exponential Weights

David P. Helmbold and Manfred K. Warmuth[*]

Computer Science Department
University of California, Santa Cruz
{dph|manfred}@cse.ucsc.edu

Abstract. We give an algorithm for learning a permutation on-line. The algorithm maintains its uncertainty about the target permutation as a doubly stochastic matrix. This matrix is updated by multiplying the current matrix entries by exponential factors. These factors destroy the doubly stochastic property of the matrix and an iterative procedure is needed to re-normalize the rows and columns. Even though the result of the normalization procedure does not have a closed form, we can still bound the additional loss of our algorithm over the loss of the best permutation chosen in hindsight.

1 Introduction

Finding a good permutation is a key aspect of many problems such as the ranking of search results or matching workers to tasks. In this paper we present an efficient and effective algorithm for learning permutations in the on-line setting called PermELearn. In each trial, the algorithm probabilistically chooses a permutation and incurs a loss based on how appropriate the permutation was for that trial. The goal of the algorithm is to have low total expected loss compared to the best permutation chosen in hindsight for the whole sequence of trials.

Since there are $n!$ permutations on n elements, it is infeasible to simply treat each permutation as an expert and apply Weighted Majority or another expert algorithm. Our solution is to implicitly represent the weights of the $n!$ permutations with a more concise representation. This approach has been successful before where exponentially many experts have a suitable combinatorial structure (see e.g. [HS97, TW03, WK06] for examples).

We encode a permutation of n elements as an $n \times n$ permutation matrix Π: $\Pi_{i,j} = 1$ if the permutation maps i to j and $\Pi_{i,j} = 0$ otherwise. The uncertainty of the algorithm about which permutation is the target is represented as a mixture of permutation matrices, i.e. a doubly stochastic weight matrix[1] W. The entry $W_{i,j}$ represents the algorithm's belief that the target permutation maps

---

[*] Manfred K. Warmuth acknowledges the support of NSF grant CCR 9821087.
[1] Recall that a doubly stochastic matrix has non-negative entries and the property that every row and column sums to 1.

N. Bshouty and C. Gentile (Eds.): COLT 2007, LNAI 4539, pp. 469–483, 2007.

element i to position j. Every doubly stochastic matrix is the convex combination of at most $n^2 - 2n + 2$ permutations (see e.g. [Bha97]). We present a simple matching-based algorithm that efficiently decomposes the weight matrix into a slightly larger than necessary convex combination. Our algorithm PermELearn samples a permutation from this convex combination to produce its prediction.

As the algorithm is randomly selecting its permutation, an adversary simultaneously selects a loss matrix $L \in [0, 1]^{n \times n}$ for the trial. The adversary is allowed to see the algorithm's doubly stochastic matrix, but not its random choice of permutation. The loss matrix has the interpretation that $L_{i,j}$ is the loss for mapping element i to j and the loss of a whole permutation is the sum of the losses of the permutation's mappings. This linear decomposition of the loss is necessary to make the algorithm efficient and fits nicely with the algorithm's weight matrix representation. Section 3 shows how a variety of intuitive loss motifs can be expressed in this matrix form.

Before the next trial, algorithm PermELearn makes a weighted-majority style update to its weight matrix: each entry $W_{i,j}$ is multiplied by $e^{-\eta L_{i,j}}$ where η is a learning rate in $[0, 1]$. After this update, the weight matrix no longer has the doubly stochastic property, and the weight matrix must be projected back into the space of doubly stochastic matrices (called "Sinkhorn Balancing", see Section 4) before the next prediction can be made. Our method based on Sinkhorn Balancing bypasses a potential issue: if the probability of each permutation Π is proportional to $\prod_i W_{i,\Pi(i)}$ then the normalization constant is the permanent of W, and calculating the permanent is a known #P-complete problem.

We bound (Theorem 1) the expected loss of PermELearn over any sequence of trials by

$$\frac{n \ln n + \eta \mathcal{L}_{\text{best}}}{1 - e^{-\eta}}, \tag{1}$$

where η is the learning rate and $\mathcal{L}_{\text{best}}$ is the loss of the best permutation on the entire sequence. If an upper bound $\mathcal{L}_{\text{est}} \geq \mathcal{L}_{\text{best}}$ is known, then η can be tuned (as in [FS97]) and the bound becomes

$$\mathcal{L}_{\text{best}} + \sqrt{2\mathcal{L}_{\text{est}} n \ln n} + n \ln n. \tag{2}$$

Since $\ln n! \approx n \ln n - n$, this is close to the loss bound when Weighted Majority is run over the $n!$ permutations. We also can show (omitted) a lower bound of $\mathcal{L}_{\text{best}} + \Omega(\sqrt{\mathcal{L}_{\text{best}} n \ln n} + n \ln n)$.

The Exponentiated Gradient family of learning algorithms uses probability vectors as their weight vectors. In this case the normalization is straightforward and is folded directly into the update. PermELearn's hypothesis is a doubly stochastic matrix. Its update step first multiplies the entries of the matrix by exponential factors and then uses Sinkhorn re-balancing to iteratively re-normalize the rows and columns. We are able to prove bounds for our algorithm despite the fact the re-normalization does not have a closed form solution. We show that the multiplicative update minimizes a tradeoff between the loss and a relative entropy between non-negative matrices. This multiplicative update takes the matrix outside of the set of doubly stochastic matrices. Luckily this un-normalized update already makes enough progress (towards the best permutation) for the loss bound quoted above. We interpret the iterations of Sinkhorn balancing as projections w.r.t. the same relative entropy. Finally, using Bregman projection methods one can show these projections only increase the progress and thus don't hurt the analysis.

Our new insight of splitting the update into an un-normalized step followed by a normalization step also leads to a streamlined proof of the loss bound of the randomized weighted majority algorithm that is interesting in its own right. On the other hand, the bounds for the expert algorithms can be proven in many different ways, including potential based methods (see e.g. [KW99, CBL06]). We were not able to find a potential based proof for learning permutations with doubly stochastic matrices, since there is no closed form solution for Sinkhorn Balancing. Finally, Kalai and Vempala's "Follow the Perturbed Leader" [KV05] approach can easily be applied to our problem, but it leads to worse bounds.

We introduce our notation in the next section. Section 3 presents the permutation learning model and gives several intuitive examples of appropriate loss motifs. Section 4 describes the details of the PermELearn algorithm, while Section 5 contains the proof of its relative mistake bound and uses the same methodology in an alternate analysis of the Weighted Majority algorithm. In Section 6, we apply the "Follow the Perturbed Leader" algorithm to learning permutations. The concluding section describes extensions and further work.

2   Notation

All matrices will be $n \times n$, and $\mathbf{1}$ and $\mathbf{0}$ denote the all all ones and all zero matrices. For a matrix A, $A_{i,j}$ is the element of A in row i, and column j. We use $A \bullet B$ to denote the dot product between matrices A and B, i.e. $\sum_{i,j} A_{i,j} B_{i,j}$. We use single subscripts (e.g. A_k) to identify matrices/permutations from a sequence.

Permutations on n elements are frequently represented in two ways: as a vector, and as a matrix. We use the notation Π (and $\widehat{\Pi}$) to represent a permutation of elements $\{1, \ldots, n\}$ into positions $\{1, \ldots, n\}$ in either format, using the context to indicate the appropriate representation. Thus, for each $i \in \{1, \ldots, n\}$, we use $\Pi(i)$ to denote the position that the ith element is mapped to by permutation Π, and matrix element $\Pi_{i,j} = 1$ if $\Pi(i) = j$ and 0 otherwise.

If L is a matrix with n rows then the product ΠL permutes the rows of L:

$$\Pi = \begin{pmatrix} 0\ 1\ 0\ 0 \\ 0\ 0\ 0\ 1 \\ 0\ 0\ 1\ 0 \\ 1\ 0\ 0\ 0 \end{pmatrix} \qquad L = \begin{pmatrix} 11\ 12\ 13\ 14 \\ 21\ 22\ 23\ 24 \\ 31\ 32\ 33\ 34 \\ 41\ 42\ 43\ 44 \end{pmatrix} \qquad \Pi L = \begin{pmatrix} 21\ 22\ 23\ 24 \\ 41\ 42\ 43\ 44 \\ 31\ 32\ 33\ 34 \\ 11\ 12\ 13\ 14 \end{pmatrix}$$

Matrix for $\Pi = (2,4,3,1)$ An arbitrary matrix   Permuting the rows

Our algorithm will have some uncertainty about which permutation to predict with. Therefore it maintains a probability distribution over permutations in the form of a $n \times n$ doubly stochastic matrix W as its data structure.

3   The On-Line Protocol

We are interested in learning permutations in the on-line setting, where learning proceeds in a series of trials. We assume the losses are generated by an (adversarial) process that we will call "nature". In each trial:

- The learner (probabilistically) chooses a permutation $\widehat{\Pi}$.
- Nature simultaneously chooses a loss matrix $L \in [0..1]^{n \times n}$ for the trial with the interpretation that $L_{i,j}$ is the loss for mapping element i to position j, and the loss of a permutation is the sum of the losses of its mappings, i.e. $\sum_i L_{i,\widehat{\Pi}(i)} = \widehat{\Pi} \bullet L$.
- At the end of the trial the algorithm is given L so that it can adjust its future predictions.

The expected loss incurred by the algorithm on the trial is $\mathbb{E}[\widehat{\Pi} \bullet L]$, where the expectation is over the algorithm's random choice of $\widehat{\Pi}$.

Since the dot product is linear, $\mathbb{E}[\widehat{\Pi} \bullet L] = W \bullet L$, where $W = \mathbb{E}(\widehat{\Pi})$. The entry $W_{i,j}$ is the probability that the learner chooses a permutation $\widehat{\Pi}$ such that $\widehat{\Pi}(i) = j$. Since permutation matrices are doubly stochastic, the convex combination W is so as well.

It is worth emphasizing that the W matrix is a convenient *summary* of the distribution over permutations used by any algorithm (it doesn't indicate which permutations have non-zero probability, for example). However, this summary is *sufficient* to determine the algorithm's expected loss.

Although our algorithm is capable of handling arbitrary sequences of loss matrices L, nature is usually significantly more restricted. Most applications have a loss motif M that is known to the algorithm and nature is constrained to choose (row) permutations of M as its loss matrix L. In effect, at each trial nature chooses a "correct" permutation Π and uses the loss matrix $L = \Pi M$. Note that the permutation left-multiplies the loss motif, and thus permutes the rows of M. If nature chooses the identity permutation then the loss matrix L is the motif M itself. When M is known to the algorithm, it suffices to give the algorithm only the permutation Π at the end of the trial, rather than L itself.

Figure 1 gives examples of loss motifs. The last loss in the table is associated with the competitive analysis of adaptive list structures where the cost is the number of links traversed to find the desired element[2]. Blum, Chawla, and Kalai [BCK03] give very efficient algorithms for this special case. In our notation, their bound has the same form as ours (1) but with the $n \ln n$ replaced by $O(n)$. However, our lower bound shows that the $\ln n$ factors in (2) are necessary in the general permutation setting.

Note that many compositions of loss motifs are possible. For example, given two motifs with their associated losses, any convex combination of the motifs creates a new motif for the (same) convex combination of the associated losses. Other component-wise combinations of two motifs (such as product or max) can

---

[2] In the adaptive list problem the searched element can be moved forward in the list for free, but other reorderings of the elements incur a cost not modeled here.

loss $\mathcal{L}(\widehat{\Pi}, \Pi)$	motif M
the number of elements i where $\widehat{\Pi}(i) \neq \Pi$	$\begin{pmatrix} 0 & 1 & 1 & 1 \\ 1 & 0 & 1 & 1 \\ 1 & 1 & 0 & 1 \\ 1 & 1 & 1 & 0 \end{pmatrix}$
$\frac{1}{n-1}\sum_{i=1}^{n} \|\widehat{\Pi}(i) - \Pi(i)\|$, how far the elements are from there "correct" positions (division by $n-1$ ensures that the entries of M are in $[0,1]$.)	$\frac{1}{3}\begin{pmatrix} 0 & 1 & 2 & 3 \\ 1 & 0 & 1 & 2 \\ 2 & 1 & 0 & 1 \\ 3 & 2 & 1 & 0 \end{pmatrix}$
$\frac{1}{n-1}\sum_{i=1}^{n} \frac{\|\widehat{\Pi}(i) - \Pi(i)\|}{\Pi(i)}$, a position weighted version of the above emphasizing the early positions in Π	$\frac{1}{3}\begin{pmatrix} 0 & 1 & 2 & 3 \\ 1/2 & 0 & 1/2 & 1 \\ 2/3 & 1/3 & 0 & 1/3 \\ 3/4 & 1/2 & 1/4 & 0 \end{pmatrix}$
the number of elements mapped to the first half by Π but the second half by $\widehat{\Pi}$, or vice versa	$\begin{pmatrix} 0 & 0 & 1 & 1 \\ 0 & 0 & 1 & 1 \\ 1 & 1 & 0 & 0 \\ 1 & 1 & 0 & 0 \end{pmatrix}$
the number of elements mapped to the first two positions by Π that fail to appear in the top three position of $\widehat{\Pi}$	$\begin{pmatrix} 0 & 0 & 0 & 1 & 1 \\ 0 & 0 & 0 & 1 & 1 \\ 0 & 0 & 0 & 0 & 0 \\ 0 & 0 & 0 & 0 & 0 \\ 0 & 0 & 0 & 0 & 0 \end{pmatrix}$
the number of links traversed to find the first element of Π in a list ordered by $\widehat{\Pi}$	$\frac{1}{3}\begin{pmatrix} 0 & 1 & 2 & 3 \\ 0 & 0 & 0 & 0 \\ 0 & 0 & 0 & 0 \\ 0 & 0 & 0 & 0 \end{pmatrix}$

Fig. 1. Loss motifs

also produce interesting loss motifs, but the combination usually cannot be distributed across the matrix dot-product calculation, and so cannot be expressed as a simple function of the original losses.

4 Algorithm

Our permutation learning algorithm uses exponenential weights and we call it PermELearn. It maintains an $n \times n$ dimensional doubly stochastic W as its main data structure, where $W_{i,j}$ is the probability that PermELearn predicts with a permutation mapping element i to position j. In the absence of prior information it is natural to start with the uniform prior, i.e. the matrix $\frac{1}{n}$ in each entry.

In each iteration PermELearn must do two things:

1. Choose a permutation $\widehat{\Pi}$ from some distribution s.t. $\mathbb{E}[\widehat{\Pi}] = W$.
2. Create a new doubly stochastic matrix $\widetilde{W}$ for use in the next trial based on the current W and the loss matrix L.

The first step is described in Algorithm 1. The algorithm greedily decomposes W into a convex combination of at most $n^2 - n + 1$ permutations, and then randomly selects one of these permutations for the prediction.[3] By Birkhoff's theorem (see [Bha97]), every doubly stochastic matrix A is a convex combination

---

[3] The decomposition is not unique and the implementation may have a bias as to exactly which convex combination is chosen.

Algorithm 1. PermELearn: Selecting a permutation

Require: a doubly stochastic $n \times n$ matrix W
   $A := W$;
   for $\ell = 1$ to $n^2 - n + 1$ **do**
      Find permutation Π_ℓ such that each $A_{i,\Pi_\ell(i)}$ is positive
      $\alpha_\ell := \min_i A_{i,\Pi(i)}$
      $A := A - \alpha_\ell \Pi_\ell$
      Exit loop if all entries of A are zero
   end for   {at end of loop $W = \sum_{k=1}^{\ell} \alpha_k \Pi_k$}
   Randomly select $\Pi_k \in \{\Pi_1, \ldots, \Pi_\ell\}$ using probabilities α_k and return it.

Algorithm 2. PermELearn: Weight Matrix Update

Require: learning rate η, non-negative loss matrix L, and doubly stochastic weight
   matrix W
   for each entry i, j of W **do**
      Create W' where each $W'_{i,j} = W_{i,j} e^{-\eta L_{i,j}}$
   end for
   Create doubly stochastic $\widetilde{W}$ by re-scaling the rows and columns of W' (Sinkhorn
   balancing) and update W to $\widetilde{W}$.

---

of permutation matrices. In addition, one can find a permutation Π where each $A_{i,\Pi(i)} > 0$ by finding a perfect matching on the $n \times n$ bipartite graph containing the edge (i, j) whenever $A_{i,j} > 0$. Given a permutation Π where each $A_{i,\Pi(i)} > 0$ we form the new matrix $A' = A - \alpha \Pi$ where $\alpha = \min_i A_{i,\Pi(i)}$. Matrix A' has non-negative entries and A' has more zeros than A. Furthermore, each row and column of A' sum to $1 - \alpha$, so A' is $1 - \alpha$ times a doubly stochastic matrix (and thus $1 - \alpha$ times a convex combination of permutations).

After at most $n^2 - n$ iterations we arrive at a matrix A' with exactly n non-zero entries. Since the row and column sums of A' are the same, A' is just a constant times a permutation matrix. Therefore, we have found a way to express the original doubly stochastic matrix as the convex combination of (at most) $n^2 - n + 1$ permutation matrices (see Algorithm 1).

There are several improvements possible. In particular, we need not compute each perfect matching from scratch. If only q entries are zeroed by a permutation, then that permutation still represents a matching of size $n - q$ in the graph for the new matrix. Thus we need to find only q augmenting paths to complete the perfect matching. The whole process requires finding $O(n^2)$ augmenting paths at a cost of $O(n^2)$ each, for a total cost of $O(n^4)$ to decompose W into a convex combination of permutations.

The second step first multiplies the $W_{i,j}$ entries of the loss matrix by the factors $e^{-\eta L_{i,j}}$. These factors destroy the row and column normalization, so the matrix must be re-normalized to restore the doubly-stochastic property. There is no closed form for the normalization step. The standard iterative re-normalization method for non-negative matrices is called *Sinkhorn Balancing*.

This method first normalizes the rows of the matrix to sum to one, and then normalizes the columns. Since normalizing the columns typically destroys the row normalization, the process must be iterated until convergence [Sin64].

Normalizing the rows corresponds to pre-multiplying by a diagonal matrix. The product of these diagonal matrices thus represents the combined effect of the multiple row normalization steps. Similarly, the combined effect of the column normalization steps can be represented by post-multiplying the matrix by a diagonal matrix. Therefore Sinkhorn balancing a matrix A results in a doubly stochastic matrix RAC where R and C are diagonal matrices. Each entry $R_{i,i}$ is the positive multiplier applied to row i, and each entry $C_{j,j}$ is the positive multiplier of column j in order to convert A into a doubly stochastic matrix.

Convergence: There has been much written on the scaling of matrices, and we briefly describe only a few of the results here. Sinkhorn showed that this procedure converges and that the RAC conversion of any matrix A is unique if it exists[4] (up to canceling multiples of R and C) [Sin64].

A number of authors consider scaling a matrix A so that the row and column sums are $1 \pm \epsilon$. Franklin and Lorenz [FL89] show that $O(\text{length}(A)/\epsilon)$ Sinkhorn iterations suffice, where $\text{length}(A)$ is the bit-length of matrix A's binary representation. Kalantari and Khachiyan [KK96] show that $O(n^4 \ln \frac{n}{\epsilon} \ln \frac{1}{\min A_{i,j}})$ operations suffice using an interior point method. Linial, Samorodnitsky, and Widgerson [LSW00] give a preprocessing step after which only $O((n/\epsilon)^2)$ Sinkhorn iterations suffice. They also present a strongly polynomial time iterative procedure requiring $\tilde{O}(n^7 \log(1/\epsilon))$ iterations. Balakrishan, Hwang, and Tomlin [BHT04] give an interior point method with complexity $O(n^6 \log(n/\epsilon))$. Finally, Fürer [Fur04] shows that if the row and column sums of A are $1 \pm \epsilon$ then every matrix entry changes by at most $\pm n\epsilon$ when A is scaled to a doubly stochastic matrix.

We defer further analysis of the imprecision in $\widetilde{W}$ to the full paper, and continue assuming that the algorithm produces a doubly stochastic $\widetilde{W}$.

5   Bounds for PermELearn

Our analysis of PermELearn follows the entropy-based analysis of the exponentiated gradient family of algorithms [KW97]. This style of analysis first shows a per-trial progress bound using relative entropy to a comparator as a measure of progress, and then sums this invariant over the trials to obtain an expected total loss of the algorithm. As with the exponentiated gradient family of algorithms, we show that PermELearn's weight update is the solution to a relative entropy-regularized minimization problem.

Recall that the expected loss of PermELearn on a trial is a linear function of its W weight matrix. Therefore the gradient of the loss is independent of

---

[4] Some non-negative matrices, like $\left(\begin{smallmatrix} 1 & 1 & 0 \\ 0 & 1 & 0 \\ 0 & 1 & 1 \end{smallmatrix}\right)$, cannot be converted into doubly stochastic matrices because of their pattern of zeros. The weight matrices we deal with have strictly positive entries, and thus can always be made doubly stochastic with an RAC conversion.

the current value of W. This property of the loss greatly simplifies the analysis. Our analysis for this relatively simple setting provides a good foundation for learning permutation matrices and lays the groundwork for the future study of more complicated permutation loss functions.

We start our analysis with an attempt to mimic the standard analysis [KW97] for the exponentiated gradient family updates which multiply by exponential factors and re-normalize. Unfortunately, the lack of a closed form for the normalization causes difficulties. Our solution is to break PermELearn's update (Algorithm 2) into two steps, and use only the progress made to the intermediate un-normalized matrix in our per-trial bound (7). After showing that the normalization to a doubly stochastic matrix only increases the progress, we can sum the per-trial bound to obtain our main theorem.

The per-trial invariant used to analyze the exponentiated gradient family bounds (for every weight vector U) the decrease in relative entropy from a (normalized) U to the algorithm's weight vector by a linear combination of the algorithm's loss and the loss of U on the trial. In our case the weight vectors are matrices and we use the following (un-normalized) relative entropy between matrices A and B with non-negative entries:

$$\Delta(A, B) = \sum_{i,j} A_{i,j} \ln \frac{A_{i,j}}{B_{i,j}} + B_{i,j} - A_{i,j} \ .$$

Note that this is just the sum of the relative entropies between the corresponding rows (or equivalently, between the corresponding columns):

$$\Delta(A, B) = \sum_i \Delta(A_{i,\star}, B_{i,\star}) = \sum_j \Delta(A_{\star,j}, B_{\star,j}) \ .$$

A Dead End: In each trial, PermELearn multiplies each entry of its weight matrix by an exponential factor, and the rows and columns are normalized using one additional factor per row and column (Algorithm 2):

$$\widetilde{W}_{i,j} := \frac{W_{i,j} e^{-\eta L_{i,j}}}{r_i c_j}, \tag{3}$$

where r_i, c_j are chosen so that row i and column j of the matrix $\widetilde{W}$ sum to one.

PermELearn's update (3) solves the the following minimization problem:

$$\operatorname*{argmin}_{\substack{\forall i : \sum_j A_{i,j} = 1 \\ \forall j : \sum_i A_{i,j} = 1}} (\Delta(A, W) + \eta (A \bullet L)). \tag{4}$$

Lemma 1. *PermELearn's updated weight matrix $\widetilde{W}$ (3) is the solution of (4).*

Proof. We form a Lagrangian for the optimization problem:

$$l(A, \rho, \gamma) = \Delta(A, W) + \eta (A \bullet L) + \sum_i \rho_i (1 - \sum_j A_{i,j}) + \sum_j \gamma_j (1 - \sum_i A_{i,j}).$$

Setting the derivative with respect to $A_{i,j}$ to 0 yields $A_{i,j} = W_{i,j}e^{-\eta L_{i,j}}e^{\rho_i}e^{\gamma_j}$ and shows that the normalization factors r_i and c_j are exponentials of the Lagrange multipliers. □

Since the linear constraints are feasible and the divergence is strictly convex, there always is a unique solution, even though the solution does not have a closed form.

We now examine the progress $\Delta(U, W) - \Delta(U, \widetilde{W})$ towards an arbitrary stochastic matrix U. Using Equation (3) and noting that all three matrices are doubly stochastic (so their entries sum to n), we see that

$$\Delta(U, W) - \Delta(U, \widetilde{W}) = -\eta\, U \bullet L + \sum_i \ln r_i + \sum_j \ln c_j.$$

Making this a useful invariant requires lower bounding the sums on the rhs by a constant times $W \bullet L$, the loss of the algorithm. Unfortunately we are stuck because the normalization factors don't even have a closed form.

Successful Analysis: We split the update (3) into two steps:

$$W'_{i,j} := W_{i,j}e^{-\eta L_{i,j}} \quad \text{and} \quad \widetilde{W}_{i,j} := \frac{W'_{i,j}}{r_i c_j}, \tag{5}$$

where r_i and c_j are chosen so that row i and column j of the matrix $\widetilde{W}$ sum to one, respectively. Using the Lagrangian (as in the proof of Lemma 1), it is easy to see that these steps solve the following minimization problems:

$$W' = \operatorname*{argmin}_{A}\left(\Delta(A, W) + \eta\,(A \bullet L)\right) \text{ and } \widetilde{W} := \operatorname*{argmin}_{\substack{\forall i: \sum_j A_{i,j} = 1 \\ \forall j: \sum_i A_{i,j} = 1}} \Delta(A, W'). \tag{6}$$

The second problem shows that the doubly stochastic matrix $\widetilde{W}$ is the projection of W' onto to the linear row and column sum constraints. The strict convexity of the relative entropy between non-negative matrices and the feasibility of the linear constraints ensure that the solutions for both steps are unique.

We now lower bound the progress $\Delta(U, W) - \Delta(U, W')$ in the following lemma to get our per-trial invariant.

Lemma 2. *For any η, any doubly stochastic matrices U and W and any trial with loss matrix L,*

$$\Delta(U, W) - \Delta(U, W') \geq (1 - e^{\eta})(W \bullet L) - \eta(U \bullet L),$$

where W' is the intermediate matrix (6) constructed by PermELearn from W.

Proof. The proof manipulates the difference of relative entropies and applies the inequality $e^{-\eta x} \leq 1 - (1 - e^{-\eta})x$, which holds for any $x \in [0,1]$ any η:

$$
\begin{aligned}
\Delta(U,W) - \Delta(U,W') &= \sum_{i,j} \left(U_{i,j} \ln \frac{W'_{i,j}}{W_{i,j}} + W_{i,j} - W'_{i,j} \right) \\
&= \sum_{i,j} \left(U_{i,j} \ln(e^{-\eta L_{i,j}}) + W_{i,j} - W_{i,j} e^{-\eta L_{i,j}} \right) \\
&\geq \sum_{i,j} \left(-\eta L_{i,j} U_{i,j} + W_{i,j} - W_{i,j}(1 - (1 - e^{-\eta})L_{i,j}) \right) \\
&= -\eta(U \bullet L) + (1 - e^{-\eta})(W \bullet L). \quad\square
\end{aligned}
$$

The relative entropy is a Bregman divergence and $\widetilde{W}$ is the relative entropy projection of W' w.r.t. linear constraints. Therefore, since U satisfies the constraints, we have by the Generalized Pythagorean Theorem (see e.g. [HW01])

$$\Delta(U,W') - \Delta(U,\widetilde{W}) = \Delta(\widetilde{W},W') \geq 0.$$

Combining this with the inequality of Lemma 2 gives the critical per-trial invariant:

$$\Delta(U,W) - \Delta(U,\widetilde{W}) \geq (1 - e^{-\eta})(W \bullet L) - \eta(U \bullet L) . \tag{7}$$

Before presenting our main theorem we introduce some notation to deal with sequences of trials. With respect to a sequence of T trials, define W_t and $\widetilde{W}_t$ to be the initial and updated weight matrices at each trial $t \in \{1,\ldots,T\}$ so that $\widetilde{W}_t = W_{t+1}$ for $1 \leq t \leq T$. We now bound $\sum_{t=1}^T W_t \bullet L_t$, the total expected loss of PermELearn over the entire sequence of trials.

Theorem 1. *For any learning rate η, any doubly stochastic matrices U and initial W_1, and any sequence of T trials with loss matrices $L_t \in [0,1]^{n \times n}$ (for $1 \leq t \leq T$), the loss of PermELearn is bounded by:*

$$\sum_{t=1}^T W_t \bullet L_t \leq \frac{\Delta(U,W_1) - \Delta(U,W_{T+1}) + \eta \sum_{t=1}^T U \bullet L_t}{1 - e^{-\eta}} .$$

Proof. Summing Equation (7) over the trials gives

$$\Delta(U,W_1) - \Delta(U,W_{T+1}) \geq (1 - e^{-\eta}) \sum_{t=1}^T W_t \bullet L_t - \eta \sum_{t=1}^T U \bullet L_t.$$

The bound then follows by solving for the loss of the algorithm. $\square$

When the entries of W_1 are all initialized to $\frac{1}{n}$ and U is a permutation then $\Delta(U,W_1) \leq n \ln n$. Note that the loss $\sum_{t=1}^T U \bullet L$ is minimized when U is a single permutation. If $\mathcal{L}_{\text{best}}$ denotes the loss of such a permutation, then the bound of Theorem 1 implies that the total loss of the algorithm is bounded by

$$\frac{n \ln n + \eta \mathcal{L}_{\text{best}}}{1 - e^{-\eta}}.$$

If an upper $\mathcal{L}_{\text{est}} \geq \mathcal{L}_{\text{best}}$ is known, then η can be tuned as done by Freund and Schapire [FS97] and the above bound becomes

$$\mathcal{L}_{\text{best}} + \sqrt{2\mathcal{L}_{\text{est}} n \ln n} + n \ln n.$$

Splitting the Analysis of Weighted Majority: Perhaps the simplest case where the loss is linear in the parameter vector is the "decision theoretic" setting of [FS97]. There are N experts and the algorithm keeps a probability distribution $\boldsymbol{w}$ over the experts. In each trial the algorithm picks expert i with probability w_i and then gets a loss vector $\boldsymbol{\ell} \in [0,1]^N$. Each expert i incurs loss ℓ_i and the algorithm's expected loss is $\boldsymbol{w} \cdot \boldsymbol{\ell}$. Finally $\boldsymbol{w}$ is updated to $\widetilde{\boldsymbol{w}}$ for the next trial.

The (Randomized) Weighted Majority algorithm [LW94] or Hedge algorithm [FS97] in this setting updates $\widetilde{w}_i = \frac{w_i e^{-\eta \ell_i}}{\sum_j w_j e^{-\eta \ell_j}}$. This update is motivated by a tradeoff between the un-normalized relative entropy and expected loss [KW99] :

$$\widetilde{\boldsymbol{w}} := \underset{\sum_i \widehat{w}_i = 1}{\operatorname{argmin}} \left(\Delta(\widehat{\boldsymbol{w}}, \boldsymbol{w}) + \eta \, \widehat{\boldsymbol{w}} \cdot \boldsymbol{\ell} \right).$$

As in the permutation case, we can split this update (and motivation) into two steps: setting each $w_i' = w_i e^{-\eta \ell_i}$ then $\widetilde{\boldsymbol{w}} = \boldsymbol{w}'/\sum_i w_i'$. These correspond to:

$$\boldsymbol{w}' := \underset{\widehat{\boldsymbol{w}}}{\operatorname{argmin}} \left(\Delta(\widehat{\boldsymbol{w}}, \boldsymbol{w}) + \eta \, \widehat{\boldsymbol{w}} \cdot \boldsymbol{\ell} \right) \quad \text{and} \quad \widetilde{\boldsymbol{w}} := \underset{\sum_i \widehat{w}_i = 1}{\operatorname{argmin}} \Delta(\widehat{\boldsymbol{w}}, \boldsymbol{w}').$$

The following lower bound has been shown on the progress towards any probability vector $\boldsymbol{u}$ serving as a comparator [LW94, FS97, KW99]:

$$\Delta(\boldsymbol{u}, \boldsymbol{w}) - \Delta(\boldsymbol{u}, \widetilde{\boldsymbol{w}}) \geq \boldsymbol{w} \cdot \boldsymbol{\ell} \, (1 - e^{-\eta}) - \eta \, \boldsymbol{u} \cdot \boldsymbol{\ell} . \tag{8}$$

Surprisingly the same inequality already holds for the un-normalized update[5]:

$$\Delta(\boldsymbol{u}, \boldsymbol{w}) - \Delta(\boldsymbol{u}, \boldsymbol{w}') = -\eta \, \boldsymbol{u} \cdot \boldsymbol{\ell} + \sum_i w_i (1 - e^{-\eta \ell_i}) \geq \boldsymbol{w} \cdot \boldsymbol{\ell} \, (1 - e^{-\eta}) - \eta \, \boldsymbol{u} \cdot \boldsymbol{\ell},$$

where the last inequality uses $e^{-\eta x} \leq 1 - (1 - e^{-\eta})x$, for any $x \in [0,1]$. Since the normalization is a projection w.r.t. a Bregman divergence onto a linear constraint satisfied by the comparator $\boldsymbol{u}$, $\Delta(\boldsymbol{u}, \boldsymbol{w}') - \Delta(\boldsymbol{u}, \widetilde{\boldsymbol{w}}) \geq 0$ by the Generalized Pythagorean Theorem [HW01]. The total progress for both steps is again (8).

When to Normalize? Probably the most surprising aspect about the proof methodology is the flexibility about how and when to project onto the constraints. Instead of projecting a nonnegative matrix onto all $2n$ constraints at once (as in optimization problem (6)), we could mimic the Sinkhorn balancing algorithm and iteratively project onto the n row and n column constraints until convergence. The Generalized Pythagorean Theorem shows that projecting

---

[5] Note that if the algorithm does not normalize the weights then $\boldsymbol{w}$ is no longer a distribution. When $\sum_i w_i < 1$, the loss $\boldsymbol{w} \cdot L$ amounts to abstaining (incurring 0 loss) with probability $1 - \sum_i w_i$, and predicting as expert i with probability w_i.

onto *any* convex constraint that is satisfied by the comparator class of doubly stochastic matrices brings the weight matrix closer to *every* doubly stochastic matrix[6]. Therefore our bound on $\sum_t W_t \bullet L_t$ (Theorem 1) holds if the exponential updates are interleaved with any sequence of projections to some subsets of the constraints. However, if the normalization constraint are not enforced then W is no longer a convex combination of permutations, and W can approach $\mathbf{0}$ (so $W \bullet L \approx 0$ for all L).

There is a direct argument that shows that the same final doubly stochastic matrix is reached if we interleave the exponential updates with projections to any of the constraints as long as all $2n$ hold at the end. To see this we partition the class of matrices with positive entries into equivalence classes. Call two such matrices A and B *equivalent* if there are diagonal matrices R and C with positive diagonal entries such that $B = RAC$. Note that $[RAC]_{i,j} = R_{i,i}A_{i,j}C_{j,j}$ so B is just a rescaled version of A. Projecting onto any row (and/or column) sum constraints amounts to pre- (and/or post-) multiplying the matrix by some positive diagonal matrix R (and/or C). Therefore if matrices A and B are equivalent then either projecting one onto a set of row/column sum constraints or multiplying their corresponding entries by the same factor results in matrices that are still equivalent. This means that any two runs from equivalent initial matrices that involve the same exponential updates end with equivalent final matrices even if they use different projections at different times. Finally, for any two equivalent matrices A and RAC, where the entries of A and the diagonal entries of R and C are positive, we have (from the Lagrangians):

$$\begin{array}{cc} \operatorname*{argmin}_{\substack{\forall i\,:\,\sum_j \widehat{A}_{i,j} = 1 \\ \forall j\,:\,\sum_i \widehat{A}_{i,j} = 1}} \Delta(\widehat{A}, A) & = & \operatorname*{argmin}_{\substack{\forall i\,:\,\sum_j \widehat{A}_{i,j} = 1 \\ \forall j\,:\,\sum_i \widehat{A}_{i,j} = 1}} \Delta(\widehat{A}, RAC). \end{array}$$

Since the relative entropy is strictly convex, both minimization problems have the same unique minimum. Curiously enough the same phenomenon already happens in the weighted majority case: Two non-negative vectors $\boldsymbol{a}$ and $\boldsymbol{b}$ are *equivalent* if $\boldsymbol{a} = c\boldsymbol{b}$, where c is any nonnegative scalar, and again each equivalence class has exactly one normalized weight vector.

6   Follow the Perturbed Leader

Kalai and Vempala [KV05] describe and bound "follow the perturbed leader" (FPL) algorithms for on-line prediction in a very general setting. Their FPL* algorithm has bounds closely related to WM and other multiplicative weight algorithms. However, despite the apparent similarity between our representations and the general formulation of FPL*, the bounds we were able to obtain for FPL* are weaker than the bounds derived using the relative entropies.

---

[6] There is a large body of work on finding a solution subject to constraints via iterated Bregman projections (See e.g. [CL81]).

The FPL setting has an abstract k-dimensional decision space used to encode predictors as well as a k-dimensional state space used to represent the losses of the predictors. At any trial, the current loss of a particular predictor is the dot product between that predictor's representation in the decision space and the state-space vector for the trial. This general setting can explicitly represent each permutation and its loss when $k = n!$. The FPL setting also easily handles the encodings of permutations and losses used by PermELearn by representing each permutation matrix Π and loss matrix L as n^2-dimensional vectors.

The FPL* algorithm [KV05] takes a parameter ϵ and maintains a cumulative loss matrix C (initially C is the zero matrix) At each trial, FPL*:

1. Generates a random perturbation matrix P where each $P_{i,j}$ is proportional to $\pm r_{i,j}$ where $r_{i,j}$ is drawn from the standard exponential distribution.
2. Predicts with a permutation Π minimizing $\Pi \bullet (C + P)$.
3. After getting the loss matrix L, updates C to $C + L$.

Note that FPL* is more computationally efficient that PermELearn. It takes only $O(n^3)$ time to make its prediction (the time to compute a minimum weight bipartite matching) and only $O(n^2)$ time to update C. Unfortunately the generic FPL* loss bounds are not as good as the bounds on PermELearn. In particular, they show that the loss of FPL* on any sequence of trials is at most[7]

$$(1 + \epsilon)\mathcal{L}_{\text{best}} + \frac{8n^3(1 + \ln n)}{\epsilon}$$

where ϵ is a parameter of the algorithm. When the loss of the best expert is known ahead of time, ϵ can be tuned and the bound becomes

$$\mathcal{L}_{\text{best}} + 4\sqrt{2\mathcal{L}_{\text{best}} n^3(1 + \ln n)} + 8n^3(1 + \ln n) \ .$$

Although FPL* gets the same $\mathcal{L}_{\text{best}}$ leading term, the excess loss over the best permutation grows as $n^3 \ln n$ rather the $n \ln n$ growth of PermELearn's bound. Of course, PermELearn pays for the improved bound by requiring more time.

It is important to note that Kalai and Vempala also present a refined analysis of FPL* when the perturbed leader changes only rarely. This analysis leads to bounds on weighted majority that are similar to the bounds given by the entropic analysis (although the constant on the square-root term is not quite as good). However, this refined analysis cannot be directly applied with the efficient representations of permutations because the total perturbations associated with different permutations are no longer independent exponentials. We leave the adaptation of the refined analysis to the permutation case as an open problem.

7 Conclusions and Further Work

The main technical insight in our analysis of PermELearn is that the per-trial progress bound already holds for the un-normalized update and that the

---

[7] The n^3 terms in the bounds for FPL are n times the sum of the entries in the loss motif. So if the loss motif's entries sum to only n, then the n^3 factors become n^2.

normalization step only helps. This finesses the difficulty of accounting for the normalization (which does not have a closed form) in the analysis. The same thing already happens in the Weighted Majority setting.

As our main contribution we showed that the problem of learning a permutation is amenable to the same techniques as learning in the expert setting. This means that all techniques from that line of research are likely to carry over: lower bounding the weights when the comparator is shifting, long-term memory when shifting between a small set of comparators [BW02], capping the weights from the top if the goal is to be close to the best set of comparators [WK06], adapting the updates to the multi-armed bandit setting when less feedback is provided [ACBFS02], PAC Bayes analysis of the exponential updates [McA03].

Our analysis techniques rely on Bregman projection methods. This means that the bounds remain unchanged if we add convex side constraints on the parameter matrix because as long as the comparator satisfies the side constraints, we can always project onto these constraints without hurting the analysis [HW01]. With the side constraints we can enforce relationships between the parameters, such as $W_{i,j} \geq W_{i,k}$ (i is more likely mapped to j than k).

We also applied the "Follow the Perturbed Leader" techniques to our permutation problem. This algorithm adds randomness to the total losses and then predicts with a minimum weighted matching which costs $O(n^3)$ whereas our more complicated algorithm is at least $O(n^4)$ and has precision issues. However the bounds provable for FPL are much worse than for the WM style analysis used here. The key open problem is whether we can have the best of both worlds: add randomness to the loss matrix so that the expected minimum weighted matching is the stochastic matrix produced by the PermELearn update (3). This would mean that we could use the faster algorithm together with our tighter analysis. In the simpler weighted majority setting this has been done already [KW05, Kal05]. However we do not yet know how to simulate the PermELearn update this way.

Acknowledgments. We thank David DesJardins, Jake Abernethy, Dimitris Achlioptas, Dima Kuzmin, and the anonymous referees for helpful feedback.

References

[ACBFS02] Auer, P., Cesa-Bianchi, N., Freund, Y., Schapire, R.E.: The nonstochastic multiarmed bandit problem. SIAM Journal on Computing 32(1), 48–77 (2002)

[BCK03] Blum, A., Chawla, S., Kalai, A.: Static optimality and dynamic search-optimality in lists and trees. Algorithmica 36, 249–260 (2003)

[Bha97] Bhatia, R.: Matrix Analysis. Springer, Heidelberg (1997)

[BHT04] Balakrishnan, H., Hwang, I., Tomlin, C.: Polynomial approximation algorithms for belief matrix maintenance in identity management. In: 43rd IEEE Conference on Decision and Control, pp. 4874–4879 (December 2004)

[BW02] Bousquet, O., Warmuth, M.K.: Tracking a small set of experts by mixing past posteriors. Journal of Machine Learning Research 3, 363–396 (2002)

[CBL06]   Cesa-Bianchi, N., Lugosi, G.: Prediction, Learning, and Games. Cambridge University Press, Cambridge (2006)
[CL81]   Censor, Y., Lent, A.: An iterative row-action method for interval convex programming. Journal of Optimization Theory and Applications 34(3), 321–353 (1981)
[FL89]   Franklin, J., Lorenz, J.: On the scaling of multidimensional matrices. Linear Algebra and its applications, 114/115, 717–735 (1989)
[FS97]   Freund, Y., Schapire, R.E.: A decision-theoretic generalization of on-line learning and an application to boosting. Journal of Computer and System Sciences 55(1), 119–139 (1997)
[Fur04]   Martin Furer. Quadratic convergence for scaling of matrices. In: Proceedings of ALENEX/ANALCO, pp. 216–223. SIAM (2004)
[HS97]   Helmbold, D.P., Schapire, R.E.: Predicting nearly as well as the best pruning of a decision tree. Machine Learning 27(01), 51–68 (1997)
[HW01]   Herbster, M., Warmuth, M.K.: Tracking the best linear predictor. Journal of Machine Learning Research 1, 281–309 (2001)
[Kal05]   Kalai, A.: Simulating weighted majority with FPL. Private communication (2005)
[KK96]   Kalantari, B., Khachiyan, L.: On the complexity of nonnegative-matrix scaling. Linear Algebra and its applications 240, 87–103 (1996)
[KV05]   Kalai, A., Vempala, S.: Efficient algorithms for online decision problems (Special issue Learning Theory 2003). J. Comput. Syst. Sci. 71(3), 291–307 (2003)
[KW97]   Kivinen, J., Warmuth, M.K.: Additive versus exponentiated gradient updates for linear prediction. Information and Computation 132(1), 1–64 (1997)
[KW99]   Kivinen, J., Warmuth, M.K.: Averaging expert predictions. In: Fischer, P., Simon, H.U. (eds.) EuroCOLT 1999. LNCS (LNAI), vol. 1572, pp. 153–167. Springer, Heidelberg (1999)
[KW05]   Kuzmin, D., Warmuth, M.K.: Optimum follow the leader algorithm (Open problem). In: Auer, P., Meir, R. (eds.) COLT 2005. LNCS (LNAI), vol. 3559, pp. 684–686. Springer, Heidelberg (2005)
[LSW00]   Linial, N., Samorodnitsky, A., Wigderson, A.: A deterministic strongly polynomial algorithm for matrix scaling and approximate permanents. Combinatorica 20(4), 545–568 (2000)
[LW94]   Littlestone, N., Warmuth, M.K.: The weighted majority algorithm. Inform. Comput. 108(2), 212–261 (1994)
[McA03]   McAllester, D.: PAC-Bayesian stochastic model selection. Machine Learning 51(1), 5–21 (2003)
[Sin64]   Sinkhorn, R.: A relationship between arbitrary positive matrices and doubly stochastic matrices. The. Annals of Mathematical Staticstics 35(2), 876–879 (1964)
[TW03]   Takimoto, E., Warmuth, M.K.: Path kernels and multiplicative updates. Journal of Machine Learning Research 4, 773–818 (2003)
[WK06]   Warmuth, M.K., Kuzmin, D.: Randomized PCA algorithms with regret bounds that are logarithmic in the dimension. In: Advances in Neural Information Processing Systems 19 (NIPS 06), MIT Press, Cambridge (2006)

Multitask Learning with Expert Advice

Jacob Abernethy[1], Peter Bartlett[1,2], and Alexander Rakhlin[1]

[1] Department of Computer Science, UC Berkeley
[2] Department of Statistics, UC Berkeley
{jake,bartlett,rakhlin}@cs.berkeley.edu

Abstract. We consider the problem of prediction with expert advice in the setting where a forecaster is presented with several online prediction tasks. Instead of competing against the best expert separately on each task, we assume the tasks are related, and thus we expect that a few experts will perform well on the entire set of tasks. That is, our forecaster would like, on each task, to compete against the best expert *chosen from a small set of experts*. While we describe the "ideal" algorithm and its performance bound, we show that the computation required for this algorithm is as hard as computation of a matrix permanent. We present an efficient algorithm based on mixing priors, and prove a bound that is nearly as good for the sequential task presentation case. We also consider a harder case where the task may change arbitrarily from round to round, and we develop an efficient approximate randomized algorithm based on Markov chain Monte Carlo techniques.

1 Introduction

A general model of sequential prediction with expert advice is the following. A *forecaster* is given the following *task*: make a sequence of predictions given access to a number of *experts*, where each expert makes its own prediction at every round. The forecaster combines the predictions of the experts to form its own prediction, taking into account each expert's past performance. He then learns the true outcome and suffers some loss based on the difference between the true outcome and its prediction. The goal of the forecaster, in the cumulative sense, is to predict not much worse than the single best expert. This sequence prediction problem has been widely studied in recent years. We refer the reader to the excellent book of Cesa-Bianchi and Lugosi [1] for a comprehensive treatment of the subject.

We consider an extension of this framework where a forecaster is presented with several prediction tasks. The most basic formulation, which we call the *sequential multitask problem* is the following: the forecaster is asked to make a sequence of predictions for task one, then another sequence of predictions for task two, and so on, and receives predictions from a constant set of experts on every round. A more general formulation, which we consider later in the paper, is the *shifting multitask problem*: on every round, the forecaster is asked to make a prediction for some task, and while the task is known to the forecaster, it may change arbitrarily from round to round.

N. Bshouty and C. Gentile (Eds.): COLT 2007, LNAI 4539, pp. 484–498, 2007.

The multitask learning problem is fundamentally a sequence prediction problem, yet we provide the forecaster with extra information for each prediction, namely the task to which this round belongs. This extra knowledge could be quite valuable. In particular, the forecaster may have observed that certain experts have performed well on this task while poorly on others. Consider, for example, an investor that, on each day, would like to make a sequence of trades for a particular stock, and has a selection of trading strategies available to him. We may consider each day a separate prediction task. The behavior of the stock will be quite related from one day to the next, even though the optimal trading strategy may change. How can the investor perform as well as possible on each day, while still leveraging information from previous days?

As the above example suggests, we would like to take advantage of *task relatedness*. This idea is quite general and in the literature several such frameworks have been explored [2,3,4,5,6,7]. In this paper, we attempt to capture the following intuitive notion of relatedness: experts that perform well on one task are more likely to perform well on others. Of course, if the same best expert is shared across several tasks, then we should not expect to find so many best experts. We thus consider the following problem: given a "small" m, design a multitask forecaster that performs well relative to the best m-sized subset of experts.

The contribution of this paper is the following. We first introduce a novel multitask learning framework within the "prediction with expert advice" model. We then show how techniques developed by Bousquet and Warmuth [8] can be applied in this new setting. Finally, we develop a randomized prediction algorithm, based on an approximate Markov chain Monte Carlo method, that overcomes the hardness of the corresponding exact problem, and demonstrate empirically that the Markov chain mixes rapidly.

We begin in Section 2 by defining the online multitask prediction problem and notation. In Section 3 we provide a reduction from the multitask setting to the single task setting, yet we also show that computing the prediction is as hard as computing a matrix permanent. In Section 4, however, we provide an efficient solution for the *sequential multitask problem*. We attack the more general *shifting multitask problem* in Section 5, and we present the MCMC algorithm and its analysis.

2   Formal Setting

First, we describe the "prediction with expert advice" setting. A *forecaster* must make a sequence of predictions for every round $t = 1, 2, 3, \ldots, T$. This forecaster is given access to a set of N "experts". At every round t, expert i makes prediction $f_i^t \in [0, 1]$. The forecaster is given access to $\boldsymbol{f}^t := (f_1^t, \ldots, f_N^t)$ and then makes a prediction $\hat{p}^t \in [0, 1]$. Finally, the outcome $y^t \in \{0, 1\}$ is revealed, expert i suffers $\ell_i^t := \ell(f_i^t, y^t)$, and the forecaster suffers $\ell(\hat{p}^t, y^t)$, where ℓ is a loss function that is convex in its first argument. We consider the cumulative loss of the forecaster, $\hat{L}^T := \sum_{t \leq T} \ell(\hat{p}^t, y^t)$, relative to the cumulative loss of each expert, $L_i^T := \sum_{t \leq T} \ell(f_i^t, y^t)$.

In the multitask setting we have additional structure on the order of the sequence. We now assume that the set of rounds is partitioned into K "tasks" and the forecaster knows K in advance. On round t, in addition to learning the predictions $\boldsymbol{f}^t$, the forecaster also learns the *task number* $\kappa(t) \in [K] :=$ $\{1, 2, \ldots, K\}$. For convenience, we also define $\tau(k) = \{t \in [T] : \kappa(t) = k\}$, the set of rounds where the task number is k. After T rounds we record the cumulative loss, $L_{k,i}^T$ of expert i for task k, defined as $L_{k,i}^T := \sum_{t \in \tau(k)} \ell_i^t$.

As described in the introduction, we are interested in the *sequential multitask problem*, where we assume that the subsequences $\tau(k)$ are contiguous. We also consider the more general case, the *shifting multitask problem*, where the task may change arbitrarily from round to round. For the remainder of Section 2 and section 3, however, we need not make any assumptions about the sequence of tasks presented.

2.1   The Multitask Comparator Class

We now pose the following question: what should be the goal of the forecaster in this multitask setting? Typically, in the single task expert setting, we compare the performance of the forecaster relative to that of the *best* expert in our class. This is quite natural: we should expect the forecaster to predict only as well as the best information available. Thus, the forecaster's goal is to minimize *regret*, $\hat{L}^T - \min_{i=1}^N L_i^T$. We will call the quantity $L_*^T := \min_i L_i^T$ the *comparator*, since it is with respect to this that we measure the performance of the forecaster.

Following this, we might propose the following as a multitask comparator, which we will call the *unrelated* comparator: $L_*^T := \sum_{k=1}^K \min_i L_{k,i}^T$. Here, the forecaster's goal is to minimize loss relative to the best expert on task one, plus loss relative to the best expert on task two, and so on. However, by minimizing the sum over tasks, the forecaster may as well minimize each separately, thus considering every task as independent of the rest.

Alternatively, we might propose another comparator, which we will call *fully related*: $L_*^T := \min_i \sum_{k=1}^K L_{k,i}^T$. Here, the forecaster competes against the best expert on all tasks, that is, the single best expert. The forecaster can simply ignore the task number and predict as though there were only one task.

These two potential definitions represent ends of a spectrum. By employing the unrelated comparator, we are inherently expecting that each task will have a different best expert. With the fully related comparator, we expect that one expert should perform well on all tasks. In this paper, we would like to choose a comparator which captures the more general notion of "partial relatedness" across tasks. We propose the following: the goal of the forecaster is to perform as well as the best choice of experts from a *small set*. More precisely, given a positive integer $m \leq N$ as a parameter, letting $\mathcal{S}_m := \{S \subset [N] : |S| = m\}$ be the set of m-sized subsets of experts, we define our comparator as

$$L_*^T := \min_{S \in \mathcal{S}_m} \sum_{k=1}^K \min_{i \in S} L_{k,i}^T. \tag{1}$$

Notice that, for the choice $m = N$, we obtain the unrelated comparator as described above; for the choice $m = 1$, we obtain the fully related comparator.

2.2 Taking Advantage of Task Relatedness

There is a benefit in competing against the constrained comparator described in (1). We are interested in the case when m is substantially smaller than K. By searching for only the m best experts, rather than K, the forecaster may learn faster by leveraging information from other tasks. For example, even when the forecaster arrives at a task for which it has seen no examples, it already has some knowledge about which experts are likely to be amongst the best $S \in \mathcal{S}_m$.

In this paper, we are interested in designing forecasters whose performance bound has the following form,

$$\hat{L}^T \leq c_1 \left(\min_{S \in \mathcal{S}_m} \sum_{k=1}^{K} \min_{i \in S} L_{k,i}^T \right) + c_2 \left(K \log m + m \log \frac{N}{m} \right), \qquad (2)$$

where c_1 and c_2 are constants. This bound has two parts, the loss term on the left and the complexity term on the right, and there is an inherent trade-off between these two terms given a choice of m. Notice, for $m = 1$, the complexity term is only $c_2 \log N$, although there may not be a single good expert. On the other hand, when $m = N$, the loss term will be as small as possible, while we pay $c_2 K \log N$ to find the best expert separately for each task. Intermediate choices of m result in a better trade-off between the two terms whenever the tasks are related, which implies a smaller bound.

3 A Reduction to the Single Task Setting

Perhaps the most well-known prediction algorithm in the single-task experts setting, as described at the beginning of Section 2, is the (Exponentially) Weighted Average Forecaster, also known as Randomized Weighted Majority. On round t, the forecaster has a table of cumulative losses of the experts, $L_1^t, \ldots, L_N^t$, a learning parameter η, and receives the predictions $\boldsymbol{f}^t$. The forecaster computes a weight $w_i^t := e^{-\eta L_i^t}$ for each i, and predicts $\hat{p}^t := \frac{\sum_i w_i^t f_i^t}{\sum_i w_i^t}$. He receives the outcome y^t, suffers loss $\ell(\hat{p}^t, y^t)$, and updates $L_i^{t+1} \leftarrow L_i^t + \ell(f_i^t, y^t)$ for each i.

This simple yet elegant algorithm has the following bound,

$$\hat{L}^T \leq c_\eta \left(\min_i L_i^T + \eta^{-1} \log N \right), \qquad (3)$$

where[1] $c_\eta = \frac{\eta}{1 - e^{-\eta}}$ tends to 1 as $\eta \to 0$. The curious reader can find more details of the Weighted Average Forecaster and relative loss bounds in [1]. We will appeal to this algorithm and its loss bound throughout the paper.

---

[1] Depending on the loss function, tighter bounds can be obtained.

3.1   Weighted Average Forecaster on "Hyperexperts"

We now define a reduction from the multitask experts problem to the single task setting and we immediately get an algorithm and a bound. Unfortunately, as we will see, this reduction gives rise to a computationally infeasible algorithm, and in later sections we will discuss ways of overcoming this difficulty.

We will now be more precise about how we define our comparator class. In Section 2.1, we described our comparator by choosing the best subset $S \in \mathcal{S}_m$ and then, for each task, choosing the best expert in this subset. However, this is equivalent to assigning the set of tasks to the set of experts such that at most m experts are used. In particular, we are interested in maps $\pi : [K] \to [N]$ such that $\mathrm{img}(\pi) := \{\pi(k) : k \in [K]\}$ has size $\leq m$. Define

$$\mathcal{H}_m := \{\pi : [K] \to [N] \text{ s.t. } \mathrm{img}(\pi) \leq m\}.$$

Given this new definition, we can now rewrite our comparator,

$$L_*^T = \min_{S \in \mathcal{S}_m} \sum_{k=1}^{K} \min_{i \in S} L_{k,i}^T = \min_{\pi \in \mathcal{H}_m} \sum_{k=1}^{K} L_{k,\pi(k)}^T. \qquad (4)$$

More importantly, this new set $\mathcal{H}_m$ can now be realized as itself a set of experts. For each $\pi \in \mathcal{H}_m$, we can associate a "hyperexpert" to π. So as not to be confused, we now also use the term "base expert" for our original class of experts. On round t, we define the prediction of hyperexpert π to be $f_{\pi(\kappa(t))}^t$, and thus the loss of this hyperexpert is exactly $\ell_{\pi(\kappa(t))}^t$. We can define the cumulative loss of this hyperexpert in the natural way,

$$L_\pi^T := \sum_{t=1}^{T} \ell_{\pi(\kappa(t))}^t = \sum_{k=1}^{K} L_{k,\pi(k)}^T.$$

We may now apply the Weighted Average Forecaster using, as our set of experts, the class $\mathcal{H}_m$. Assume we are given a learning parameter $\eta > 0$. We maintain a $K \times N$ matrix of weights $[w_{k,i}^t]$ for each base expert and each task. For $i \in [N]$ and $k \in [K]$, let $w_{k,i}^t := \exp(-\eta L_{k,i}^t)$. We now define weight v_π^t of a hyperexpert π at time t to be $v_\pi^t := \exp(-\eta L_\pi^t) = \prod_{k=1}^{K} w_{k,\pi(k)}^t$. This gives an explicit formula for the prediction of the algorithm at time t,

$$\hat{p}^t = \frac{\sum_{\pi \in \mathcal{H}_m} v_\pi^t f_{\pi(\kappa(t))}^t}{\sum_{\pi \in \mathcal{H}_m} v_\pi^t} = \frac{\sum_{\pi \in \mathcal{H}_m} \left(\prod_{k=1}^{K} w_{k,\pi(k)}^t \right) f_{\pi(\kappa(t))}^t}{\sum_{\pi \in \mathcal{H}_m} \prod_{k'=1}^{K} w_{k',\pi(k')}^t}. \qquad (5)$$

The prediction f_i^t will be repeated many times, and thus we can factor out the terms where $\pi(\kappa(t)) = i$. Let $\mathcal{H}_m^{k,i} \subset \mathcal{H}_m$ be the assignments π such that $\pi(k) = i$, and note that, for any k, $\bigcup_{i=1}^{N} \mathcal{H}_m^{k,i} = \mathcal{H}_m$. Letting

$$u_{k,i}^t := \frac{\sum_{\pi \in \mathcal{H}_m^{k,i}} \prod_{k'=1}^{K} w_{k',\pi(k')}^t}{\sum_{\pi \in \mathcal{H}_m} \prod_{k'=1}^{K} w_{k',\pi(k')}^t} \qquad \text{gives} \qquad \hat{p}^t = \sum_{i=1}^{N} u_{\kappa(t),i}^t \cdot f_i^t.$$

We now have an exponentially weighted average forecaster that predicts given the set of hyperexperts $\mathcal{H}_m$. In order to obtain a bound on this algorithm we still need to determine the size of $\mathcal{H}_m$. The proof of the next lemma is omitted.

Lemma 1. *Given $m < K$, it holds that $\binom{N}{m}m^{K-m}m! \leq |\mathcal{H}_m| \leq \binom{N}{m}m^K$, and therefore $log|\mathcal{H}_m| = \Theta\left(\log\binom{N}{m} + K\log m\right) = \Theta\left(m\log\frac{N}{m} + K\log m\right)$.*

We now have the following bound for our forecaster, which follows from (3).

Theorem 1. *Given a convex loss function ℓ, for any sequence of predictions $\boldsymbol{f}^t$ and outcomes y^t, where $t = 1, 2, \ldots, T$,*

$$\frac{\hat{L}^T}{c_\eta} \leq \min_{\pi \in \mathcal{H}_m} L_\pi^T + \frac{\log|\mathcal{H}_m|}{\eta} \leq \min_{S \in \mathcal{S}_m} \sum_{k=1}^K \min_{i \in S} L_{k,i}^T + \frac{m\log\frac{N}{m} + K\log m}{\eta}.$$

3.2   An Alternative Set of Hyperexperts

We now consider a slightly different description of a hyperexpert. This alternative representation, while not as natural as that described above, will be useful in Section 5. Formally, we define the class

$$\bar{\mathcal{H}}_m := \{(S, \phi) \text{ for every } S \in \mathcal{S}_m \text{ and } \phi : [K] \to [m]\}.$$

Notice, the pair (S, ϕ) induces a map $\pi \in \mathcal{H}_m$ in the natural way: if $S = \{i_1, \ldots, i_m\}$, with $i_1 < \ldots < i_m$, then π is defined as the mapping $k \mapsto i_{\phi(k)}$. For convenience, write $\Psi(S, \phi, k) := i_{\phi(k)} = \pi(k)$. Then the prediction of the hyperexpert (S, ϕ) on round t is exactly the prediction of π, that is f_i^t where $i = \Psi(S, \phi, \kappa(t))$. Similarly, we define the weight of a hyperexpert $(S, \phi) \in \bar{\mathcal{H}}_m$ simply as $v_{S,\phi}^t := \prod_{k=1}^K w_{k,\Psi(S,\phi,k)}^t = v_\pi^t$. Thus, the prediction of the Weighted Average Forecaster with access to the set of hyperexperts $\bar{\mathcal{H}}_m$ is

$$\hat{q}^t = \frac{\sum_{(S,\phi)\in\bar{\mathcal{H}}_m} v_{S,\phi}^t f_{\Psi(S,\phi,\kappa(t))}^t}{\sum_{(S',\phi')\in\bar{\mathcal{H}}_m} v_{S',\phi'}^t}. \tag{6}$$

We note that any $\pi \in \mathcal{H}_m$ can be described by some (S, ϕ), and so we have a surjection $\bar{\mathcal{H}}_m \to \mathcal{H}_m$, yet this is not an injection. Indeed, maps π for which $\text{img}(\pi) < m$ will be represented by more than one pair (S, ϕ). In other words, we have "overcounted" our comparators a bit, and so the prediction $\hat{q}^t$ will differ from $\hat{p}^t$. However, Theorem 1 will also hold for the weighted average forecaster given access to the expert class $\bar{\mathcal{H}}_m$. Notice, the set $\bar{\mathcal{H}}_m$ has size exactly $\binom{N}{m}m^K$, and thus Lemma 1 tells us that $\log|\mathcal{H}_m|$ and $\log|\bar{\mathcal{H}}_m|$ are of the same order.

3.3   Hardness Results

Unfortunately, the algorithm for computing either $\hat{p}^t$ or $\hat{q}^t$ described above requires performing a computation in which we sum over an exponentially large number of subsets. One might hope for a simplification but, as the following lemmas suggest, we cannot hope for such a result. For this section, we let $W^t := [w_{k,i}^t]_{k,i}$, an arbitrary nonnegative matrix, and $\phi_m(W^t) := \sum_{\pi\in\mathcal{H}_m} \prod_{k=1}^K w_{k,\pi(k)}^t$.

Lemma 2. *Computing $\hat{p}^t$ as in (5) for an arbitrary nonnegative matrix W^t and arbitrary prediction vector $\boldsymbol{f}^t$ is as hard as computing $\phi_m(W^t)$.*

Proof. Because $\boldsymbol{f}^t$ is arbitrary, computing $\hat{p}^t$ is equivalent to computing the weights $u_{k,i} = \frac{1}{\phi_m(W^t)} \sum_{\pi \in \mathcal{H}_m^{k,i}} \prod_{k'=1}^{K} w_{k',\pi(k')}^t$. However, this also implies that we could compute $\frac{\phi_{m-1}(W^t)}{\phi_m(W^t)}$. To see this, augment W^t as follows. Let $\hat{W}^t :=$ $\left[\begin{smallmatrix} & W^t & 0 \\ 1 & \cdots & 1 \end{smallmatrix}\right]$. If we could compute the weights $u_{k,i}$ for this larger matrix $\hat{W}^t$ then, in particular, we could compute $u_{K+1,N+1}$. However, it can be checked that $u_{K+1,N+1} = \frac{\phi_{m-1}(W^t)}{\phi_m(W^t)}$ given the construction of $\hat{W}^t$.

Furthermore, if we compute $\frac{\phi_{m-1}(W^t)}{\phi_m(W^t)}$ for each m, then we could compute $\prod_{l=1}^{m-1} \frac{\phi_l(W^t)}{\phi_{l+1}(W^t)} = \frac{\phi_1(W^t)}{\phi_m(W^t)}$. But the quantity $\phi_1(W^t) = \sum_{i=1}^{N} \prod_{k=1}^{K} w_{k,i}^t$ can be computed efficiently, giving us $\phi_m(W^t) = \phi_1(W^t) \left(\frac{\phi_1(W^t)}{\phi_m(W^t)} \right)^{-1}$.

Lemma 3. *Assuming $K = N$, computing $\phi_m(W^t)$ for any nonnegative W^t and any m is as hard as computing $\text{Perm}(W^t)$, the permanent of a nonnegative matrix W^t.*

Proof. The permanent $\text{Perm}(W)$ is defined as $\sum_{\pi \in \text{Sym}_N} \prod w_{k,\pi(k)}^t$. This expression is similar to $\phi_N(W)$, yet this sum is taken over only permutations $\pi \in \text{Sym}_N$, the symmetric group on N, rather than all functions from $[N] \to [N]$. However, the set of permutations on $[N]$ is exactly the set of all functions on $[N]$ minus those functions π for which $|\text{img}(\pi)| \leq N - 1$. Thus, we see that $\text{Perm}(W) = \phi_N(W) - \phi_{N-1}(W)$.

Theorem 2. *Computing either $\hat{p}^t$ or $\hat{q}^t$, as in (5) or (6) respectively, is hard.*

Proof. Combining Lemmas 2 and 3, we see that computing the prediction $\hat{p}^t$ is at least as hard as computing the permanent of any matrix with positive entries, which is known to be a hard problem. While we omit it, the same analysis can be used for computing $\hat{q}^t$, i.e. when our expert class is $\tilde{\mathcal{H}}_m$.

As an aside, it is tempting to consider utilizing the Follow the Perturbed Leader algorithm of Kalai and Vempala [9]. However, the curious reader can also check that not only is it hard to compute the prediction, it is even hard to find the best hyperexpert and thus the perturbed leader.

4   Deterministic Mixing Algorithm

While the reduction to a single-task setting, discussed in the previous section, is natural, computing the predictions $\hat{p}^t$ or $\hat{q}^t$ directly proves to be infeasible. Somewhat surprisingly, we can solve the *sequential multitask problem* without computing these quantities.

The problem of multitask learning, as presented in this paper, can be viewed as a problem of competing against comparators which shift within a pool of size m, a problem analyzed extensively in Bousquet and Warmuth [8]. However, there are a few important differences. On the positive side, we have the extra information that no shifting of comparators occurs when staying within the same task. First, this allows us to design a truly online algorithm which has to keep only K weight vectors, instead of a complete history (or its approximation) as for the Decaying Past scheme in [8]. Second, the extra information allows us to obtain a bound which is independent of time: it only depends on the number of switches between the tasks. On the down side, in the case of the *shifting multitask problem*, tasks and comparators can change at every time step.

In this section, we show how the mixing algorithm of [8] can be adapted to our setting. We design the mixing scheme to obtain the bounds of Theorem 1 for the *sequential multitask problem*, and prove a bound for the *shifting multitask problem* in terms of the number of shifts, but independent of the time horizon.

Algorithm 1. Multitask Mixing Algorithm

1: Input: η
2: Initialize $\tilde{\mathbf{w}}_k^0 = \frac{1}{N}\mathbf{1}$ for all $k \in [K]$
3: **for** $t = 1$ to T **do**
4:     Let $k = \kappa(t)$, the current task
5:     Choose a distribution β_t over tasks
6:     Set $\tilde{\mathbf{z}}^t = \sum_{k'=1}^{K} \beta_t(k')\tilde{\mathbf{w}}_{k'}^{t-1}$
7:     Predict $\hat{p}^t = \tilde{\mathbf{z}}^t \cdot \mathbf{f}^t$
8:     Update $\tilde{w}_{k,i}^t = \left(\tilde{z}_i^t e^{-\eta\ell_i^t}\right) / \left(\sum_{i=1}^{N} \tilde{z}_i^t e^{-\eta\ell_i^t}\right)$ for all $i \in [N]$
9:     Set $\tilde{\mathbf{w}}_{k'}^t = \tilde{\mathbf{w}}_{k'}^{t-1}$ for any $k' \neq k$.
10: **end for**

The above algorithm keeps normalized weights $\tilde{\mathbf{w}}_k^t \in \mathbb{R}^N$ over experts for each task $k \in [K]$ and mixes $\tilde{\mathbf{w}}_k^t$'s together with an appropriate mixing distribution β_t over tasks to form a prediction. It is precisely by choosing β_t correctly that one can pass information from one task to another through sharing of weights. The mixture of weights across tasks is then updated according to the usual exponential weighted average update. The new normalized distribution becomes the new weight vector for the current task. It is important to note that $\tilde{\mathbf{w}}_k^t$ is updated *only* when $k = \kappa(t)$. [2] The following per-step bound holds for our algorithm, similarly to Lemma 4 in [8]. For any $\tilde{\mathbf{u}}_t$ and $k' \in [K]$,

$$\hat{\ell}^t \leq c_\eta \left(\tilde{\mathbf{u}}_t \cdot \boldsymbol{\ell}^t + \frac{1}{\eta}\triangle\left(\tilde{\mathbf{u}}_t, \tilde{\mathbf{w}}_{k'}^{t-1}\right) - \frac{1}{\eta}\triangle\left(\tilde{\mathbf{u}}_t, \tilde{\mathbf{w}}_{\kappa(t)}^t\right) + \frac{1}{\eta}\ln\frac{1}{\beta_t(k')} \right) \quad (7)$$

where the relative entropy is $\triangle(\boldsymbol{u}, \boldsymbol{v}) = \sum_{i=1}^{N} u_i \ln\frac{u_i}{v_i}$ for normalized $\boldsymbol{u}, \boldsymbol{v} \in \mathbb{R}^N$ (see Appendix A for the proof). If the loss function ℓ is η-exp-concave (see [1]), the constant c_η disappears from the bound.

---

[2] Referring to $\tilde{\mathbf{w}}_k^q$, where q is the last time the task k was performed, is somewhat cumbersome. Hence, we set $\tilde{\mathbf{w}}_{k'}^t = \tilde{\mathbf{w}}_{k'}^{t-1}$ for any $k' \neq k$ and avoid referring to time steps before $t - 1$.

We first show that a simple choice of β_t leads to the trivial case of unrelated tasks. Intuitively, if no mixing occurs, i.e. β_t puts all the weight on the current task at the previous step, the tasks are uncoupled. This is exhibited by the next proposition, whose proof is straightforward, and is omitted.

Proposition 1. *If we choose $\beta_t(k) = 1$ if $k = \kappa(t)$ and 0 otherwise, then Algorithm 1 yields*

$$\hat{L}^T \leq c_\eta \min_{S \in \mathcal{S}_m} \sum_{k=1}^{K} \min_{i \in S} L_{k,i}^T + \frac{c_\eta}{\eta} K \ln N.$$

Of course, if we are to gain information from the other tasks, we should mix the weights instead of concentrating on the current task. The next definition is needed to quantify which tasks appeared more recently: they will be given more weight by our algorithm.

Definition 1. *If, at time t, tasks are ordered according to the most recent appearance, we let the rank $\rho_t(k) \in [K] \cup \{\infty\}$ be the position of task k in this ordered list. If k has not appeared yet, set $\rho_t(k) = \infty$.*

Theorem 3. *Suppose the tasks are presented in an arbitrary order, but necessarily switching at every time step. If we choose $\beta_t(\kappa(t)) = \alpha$ and for any $k \neq \kappa(t)$ set $\beta_t(k) = (1 - \alpha) \cdot \frac{1}{\rho_t(k)^2} \frac{1}{Z_t}$ then Algorithm 1 yields*

$$\hat{L}^T \leq c_\eta \min_{S \in \mathcal{S}_m} \sum_{k=1}^{K} \min_{i \in S} L_{k,i}^T + \frac{c_\eta}{\eta} \left(m \ln \frac{N}{m-2} + 3T \ln m \right).$$

Here, $Z_t = \sum_{k \in [K], k \neq \kappa(t)} \frac{1}{\rho_t(k)^2} < 2$, $\alpha = 1 - \frac{2}{m}$, and $m > 2$. It is understood that we set $\beta_t(k) = 0$ when $\rho_t(k) = \infty$.

In the theorem above, the number of switches n between the tasks is $T - 1$. Now, consider an arbitrary sequence of task presentations. The proof of the above theorem, given in the appendix, reveals that the complexity term in the bound only depends on the number n of switches between the tasks, and not on the time horizon T. Indeed, when continuously performing the same task, we exploit the information that the comparator does not change and put all the weight β_t on the current task, losing nothing in the complexity term. This improves the bound of [8] by removing the $\ln T$ term, as the next corollary shows.

Corollary 1. *Let $\beta_t(k)$ be defined as in Theorem 3 whenever a switch between tasks occurs and let $\beta_t(\kappa(t)) = 1$ whenever no switch occurs. Then for the shifting multitask problem, Algorithm 1 yields*

$$\hat{L}^T \leq c_\eta \min_{S \in \mathcal{S}_m} \sum_{k=1}^{K} \min_{i \in S} L_{k,i}^T + \frac{c_\eta}{\eta} \left(m \ln \frac{N}{m-2} + 3n \ln m \right).$$

where n is the number of switches between the tasks.

Corollary 2. *With the same choice of β_t as in Corollary 1, for the* sequential multitask problem, *Algorithm 1 yields*

$$\hat{L}^T \leq c_\eta \min_{S \in \mathcal{S}_m} \sum_{k=1}^{K} \min_{i \in S} L_{k,i}^T + \frac{c_\eta}{\eta} \left(m \ln \frac{N}{m-2} + 3K \ln m \right).$$

Up to a constant factor, this is the bound of Theorem 1. Additionally to removing the $\ln T$ term, we obtained a space and time-efficient algorithm. Indeed, the storage requirement is only KN, which does not depend on T.

5 Predicting with a Random Walk

In the previous section we exhibited an efficient algorithm which attains the bound of Theorem 1 for the *sequential multitask problem*. Unfortunately, for the more general case of the *shifting multitask problem*, the bound degrades with the number of switches between the tasks. Encouraged by the fact that it is possible to design online algorithms even if the prediction is provably hard to compute, we look for a different algorithm for the *shifting multitask problem*.

Fortunately, the hardness of computing the weights exactly, as shown in Section 3.3, does not immediately imply that *sampling* according to these weights is necessarily difficult. In this section we provide a randomized algorithm based on a Markov chain Monte Carlo method. In particular, we show how to sample a random variable $X^t \in [0, 1]$ such that $\mathbb{E}X^t = \hat{q}^t$, where $\hat{q}^t$ is the prediction defined in (6).

Algorithm 2. Randomized prediction

1: Input: Round t; Number R_1 of iterations; Parameter $m < N$; $K \times N$ matrix $[w_{k,i}^t]$
2: **for** $j = 1$ to R_1 **do**

3:    Sample $S \in \mathcal{S}_m$ according to $P(S) = \left(\prod_{k=1}^{K} \sum_{i \in S} w_{k,i}^t \right) / \left(\sum_{S' \in \mathcal{S}_m} \prod_{k=1}^{K} \sum_{i \in S'} w_{k,i}^t \right)$

4:    Order $S = \{i_1, \ldots, i_m\}$

5:    Sample $\phi : [K] \to [m]$ according to $P(\phi|S) = \left(\prod_{k=1}^{K} w_{k,i_{\phi(k)}}^t \right) / \left(\prod_{k=1}^{K} \sum_{i \in S} w_{k,i}^t \right)$

6:    Set $X_j^t = f_{\Psi(S,\phi,\kappa(t))}^t$
7: **end for**
8: Predict with $\bar{X}^t = \frac{1}{R_1} \sum_{j=1}^{R_1} X_j^t$

Algorithm 2 samples a subset of m experts $S = \{i_1, \ldots, i_m\}$, and then samples a map ϕ from the set of tasks to this subset of experts. If the current task is k, the algorithm returns the prediction of expert $i_{\phi(k)} = \Psi(S, \phi, k)$. We have,

$$P(S, \phi) = P(S)P(\phi|S) = \frac{\prod_{k=1}^{K} w_{k,\Psi(S,\phi,k)}^t}{\sum_{S' \in \mathcal{S}_m} \prod_{k=1}^{K} \sum_{i \in S'} w_{k,i}^t} = \frac{v_{S,\phi}}{\sum_{(S',\phi')} v_{S',\phi'}}.$$

Note that $\hat{q}^t = \sum_{(S,\phi) \in \bar{\mathcal{H}}_m} P(S, \phi) f_{\Psi(S,\phi,k)}^t$, and it follows that $\mathbb{E}X^t = \hat{q}^t$.

Notice that, in the above algorithm, every step can be computed efficiently except for step 2. Indeed, sampling ϕ given a set S can be done by independently sampling assignments $\phi(k)$ for all k. In step 2, however, we must sample a subset S whose weight we define as $\prod_{k=1}^{K} \sum_{i \in S} w_{k,i}^t$. Computing the weights for all subsets is implausible, but it turns out that we can apply a Markov Chain Monte Carlo technique known as the Metropolis-Hastings algorithm. This process begins with subset S of size m and swaps experts in and out of S according to a random process. At the end of R_2 rounds, we will have an *induced* distribution Q_{R_2} on the collection of m-subsets $\mathcal{S}_m$ which will approximate the distribution P defined in step 3 of Algorithm 2.

More formally, the process of sampling S is as follows.

Algorithm 3. Sampling a set of m experts

1: Input: Matrix of $w_{k,i}^t$, $i \in [N]$, $k \in [K]$, and number of rounds R_2
2: Start with some $S_0 \in \mathcal{S}_m$, an initial set of m experts
3: **for** $r = 0$ to $R_2 - 1$ **do**
4:     Uniformly at random, choose $i \in [N] \setminus S_r$ and $j \in S_r$. Let $S_r' = S_r \cup i \setminus j$.
5:     Calculate $\omega(S_r) = \prod_{k=1}^{K} \sum_{i \in S_r} w_{k,i}^t$ and $\omega(S_r') = \prod_{k=1}^{K} \sum_{i \in S_r'} w_{k,i}^t$
6:     With probability $\min\left\{1, \frac{\omega(S_r')}{\omega(S_r)}\right\}$, set $S_{r+1} \leftarrow S_r'$, otherwise $S_{r+1} \leftarrow S_r$
7: **end for**
8: Output: S_{R_2}

Definition 2. *Given two probability distributions P_1 and P_2 on a space X, we define the total variation distance $\|P_1 - P_2\| = \frac{1}{2}\sum_{x \in X} |P_1(x) - P_2(x)|$.*

It can be shown that the distance $\|Q_{R_2} - P\| \to 0$ as $R_2 \to \infty$. While we omit the details of this argument, it follows from the fact that P is the stationary distribution of the Markov chain described in Algorithm 3. More information can be found in any introduction to the Metropolis-Hastings algorithm.

Theorem 4. *If a forecaster predicts according to algorithm 2 with the sampling step 2 approximated by Algorithm 3, then with probability at least $1 - \delta$,*

$$\hat{L}^T \leq c_\eta \min_{\pi \in \mathcal{H}_m} \sum_{k=1}^{K} L_{k,\pi(k)}^T + \frac{c_\eta}{\eta}\left(m \log \frac{N}{m} + K \log m\right) + CT\epsilon + CT\sqrt{\frac{\ln \frac{2T}{\delta}}{2R_1}},$$

where R_1 is the number of times we sample the predictions, C is the Lipschitz constant of ℓ, and R_2 is chosen such that $\|Q_{R_2} - P\| \leq \epsilon/2$. The last two terms can be made arbitrarily small by choosing large enough R_1 and R_2.

A key ingredient of this theorem is our ability to choose R_2 such that $\|Q_{R_2} - P\| < \epsilon$. In general, since ϵ must depend on T, we would hope that $R_2 = poly(1/\epsilon)$. In other words, we would like to show that our Markov chain has a fast *mixing time*. In some special cases, one can prove a useful bound on the mixing time, yet such results are scarce and typically quite difficult to prove. On the other hand, this does not imply that the mixing time is prohibitively large. In the next section, we provide empirical evidence that, in fact, our Markov chain mixes extremely quickly.

5.1 Experiments

For small K and N and some matrix $[w_{k,i}^t]_{k,i}$ we can compute the true distribution P on $\mathcal{S}_m$, and we can compare that to the distribution Q_{R_2} induced by the random walk described in Algorithm 3. The graphs in Figure 1 show that, in fact, Q_{R_2} approaches P very quickly even after only a few rounds R_2.

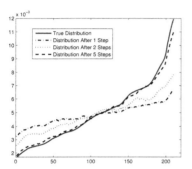
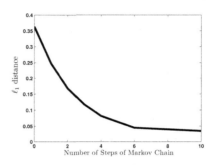

Fig. 1. We generate a random $K \times N$ matrix $[w_{k,i}^t]_{k,i}$, where $K = 5$, $N = 10$, and we consider the distribution on $\mathcal{S}_m$ described in algorithm 2. In the first graph we compare this "true distribution" P, sorted by $P(S)$, to the induced distribution Q_{R_2} for the values $R_2 = 1, 2, 5$. In the second graph we see how quickly the total variation distance $\|P - Q_{R_2}\|$ shrinks relative to the number of steps R_2.

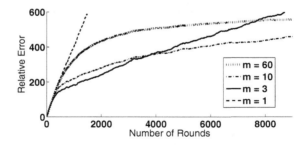

Fig. 2. The performance of Algorithm 2 on a toy example. Large values of m have good long-term performance yet are "slow" to find the best expert. On the other hand, the algorithm learns very quickly with small values of m, but pays a price in the long run. In this example, $m = 10$ appears to be a good choice.

Figure 2 demonstrates the performance of Algorithm 2, for various choices of m, on the following problem. We used $R_1 = 5$ and we employ Algorithm 3 to sample $S \in \mathcal{S}_m$ with $R_2 = 700$. On each round, we draw a random $x_t \in X = \mathbf{R}^d$, where in this case $d = 4$, and this x_t is used to generate the outcome and the predictions of the experts. We have $K = 60$ tasks, where each task f_k is a linear classifier on X. If $k = \kappa(t)$, the outcome for round t is $I(f_k \cdot x_t > 0)$. We choose 70 "bad" experts, who predict randomly, and 30 "good" experts which are, themselves, randomly chosen linear classifiers e_i on X: on round t expert i predicts $I(e_i \cdot x_t > 0)$ with 30% label noise. In the plots below, we compare the performance of the algorithm for all values of m to the comparator $\sum_k \min_i L^t_{k,i}$. It is quite interesting to see the tradeoff between short and long-term performance for various values of m.

6   Conclusion

We conclude by stating some open problems.

Recall that in Section 3.3 we show a crucial relationship between computing the forecaster's prediction and a matrix permanent. Interestingly, in very recent work, Jerrum et al [10] exhibit a Markov chain, and a bound on the mixing time, that can be used to efficiently approximate the permanent of an arbitrary square matrix with nonnegative entries. Could such techniques be employed to provide a randomized prediction algorithm with provably fast convergence?

Is it possible to develop a version of the Multitask Mixing Algorithm for the *shifting multitask problem* and prove that performance does not degrade with the number of shifts between the tasks? Are there reasonable assumptions under which Φ in the proof of Theorem 3 depends sublinearly on the number of shifts?

Acknowledgments. We would like to thank Manfred Warmuth for his knowledge of prediction algorithms and helpful discussions on mixing priors. We would like to thank Alistair Sinclair for his expertise on the MCMC methods. Thanks to Madhur Tulsiani for helpful suggestions on the hardness proof. We gratefully acknowledge the support of DARPA under grant FA8750-05-20249.

References

1. Cesa-Bianch, N., Lugosi, G.: Prediction, Learning, and Games. Cambridge University Press, Cambridge (2006)
2. Evgeniou, T., Micchelli, C.A., Pontil, M.: Learning multiple tasks with kernel methods. JMLR 6, 615–637 (2005)
3. Ando, R.K., Zhang, T.: A framework for learning predictive structures from multiple tasks and unlabeled data. JMLR 6, 1817–1853 (2005)
4. Caruana, R.: Multitask learning. Machine Learning 28(1), 41–75 (1997)
5. Dekel, O., Singer, Y., Long, P.: Online multitask learning. In: Lugosi, G., Simon, H.U. (eds.) COLT 2006. LNCS (LNAI), vol. 4005, Springer, Heidelberg (2006)
6. Baxter, J.: A model of inductive bias learning. JAIR 12, 149–198 (2000)
7. Ben-David, S., Schuller, R.: Exploiting task relatedness for mulitple task learning. In: COLT 2003, pp. 567–580. Springer, Heidelberg (2003)
8. Bousquet, O., Warmuth, M.K.: Tracking a small set of experts by mixing past posteriors. JMLR 3, 363–396 (2002)

9. Kalai, A., Vempala, S.: Efficient algorithms for online decision problems. J. Comput. Syst. Sci. 71(3), 291–307 (2005)
10. Jerrum, M., Sinclair, A., Vigoda, E.: A polynomial-time approximation algorithm for the permanent of a matrix with non-negative entries. In: STOC '01

A   Proofs

Proof (of Inequality (7)). The details of this proof can be found in [8,1].

$$\hat{\ell}^t/c_\eta \le \ell(\tilde{z}^t \cdot f^t, y^t)/c_\eta \le c_\eta^{-1} \sum_{i=1}^{N} \tilde{z}_i^t \ell_i^t \le -\frac{1}{\eta} \ln \sum_{i=1}^{N} \tilde{z}_i^t e^{-\eta \ell_i^t}$$

$$= \tilde{u}_t \cdot \ell^t + \frac{1}{\eta} \sum_{i=1}^{N} u_{t,i} \ln e^{-\eta \ell_i^t} - \frac{1}{\eta} \ln \sum_{i=1}^{N} \tilde{z}_i^t e^{-\eta \ell_i^t}$$

$$= \tilde{u}_t \cdot \ell^t + \frac{1}{\eta} \triangle \left(\tilde{u}_t, \tilde{z}^t\right) - \frac{1}{\eta} \triangle \left(\tilde{u}_t, \tilde{w}_{\kappa(t)}^t\right)$$

$$\le \tilde{u}_t \cdot \ell^t + \frac{1}{\eta} \triangle \left(\tilde{u}_t, \tilde{w}_{k'}^{t-1}\right) - \frac{1}{\eta} \triangle \left(\tilde{u}_t, \tilde{w}_{\kappa(t)}^t\right) + \frac{1}{\eta} \ln \frac{1}{\beta_t(k')}$$

Proof (of Theorem 3). The proof is an adaptation of the proof of Corollary 9 in [8], taking into account the task information. Let $\tilde{u}_1, \ldots, \tilde{u}_m$ be m arbitrary comparators. For any $\pi : [K] \mapsto [m]$, $\tilde{u}_{\pi(k)}$ is the comparator used by the environment for task k (known only in the hindsight). For any t,

$$\hat{\ell}^t/c_\eta \le \tilde{u}_{\pi(k)} \cdot \ell^t + \frac{1}{\eta} \left(\triangle \left(\tilde{u}_{\pi(k)}, \tilde{z}^t\right) - \triangle \left(\tilde{u}_{\pi(k)}, \tilde{w}_k^t\right)\right),$$

where $k = \kappa(t)$. There are m time points when a task k begins and it is the first task being compared to the comparator $\tilde{u}_{\pi(k)}$. For these m time steps,

$$\hat{\ell}^t/c_\eta \le \tilde{u}_{\pi(k)} \cdot \ell^t + \frac{1}{\eta} \left(\triangle \left(\tilde{u}_{\pi(k)}, \tilde{w}_k^{t-1}\right) - \triangle \left(\tilde{u}_{\pi(k)}, \tilde{w}_k^t\right) + \ln \frac{1}{\alpha}\right),$$

where $\tilde{w}_k^{t-1} = \tilde{w}_k^0$, as it has not been modified yet. Otherwise,

$$\hat{\ell}^t/c_\eta \le \tilde{u}_{\pi(k)} \cdot \ell^t + \frac{1}{\eta} \left(\triangle \left(\tilde{u}_{\pi(k)}, \tilde{w}_{k'}^{t-1}\right) - \triangle \left(\tilde{u}_{\pi(k)}, \tilde{w}_k^t\right) + \ln \frac{\rho_t(k')^2 Z_t}{1 - \alpha}\right),$$

where k' is the most recent task played against the comparator $\tilde{u}_{\pi(k)}$ (this is still true in the case k is the only task for the comparator $\tilde{u}_{\pi(k)}$ because $\alpha > \frac{1-\alpha}{\rho_t(k)^2 Z_t}$ with the choice of α below). We upper bound

$$\hat{\ell}^t/c_\eta \le \tilde{u}_{\pi(k)} \cdot \ell^t + \frac{1}{\eta} \left(\triangle \left(\tilde{u}_{\pi(k)}, \tilde{w}_{k'}^{t-1}\right) - \triangle \left(\tilde{u}_{\pi(k)}, \tilde{w}_k^t\right) + \ln \rho_t(k')^2 + \ln \frac{2}{1 - \alpha}\right).$$

We note that for each comparator $\tilde{u}_j$, the relative entropy terms telescope. Recall that $\tilde{w}_k^0 = \frac{1}{N}\mathbf{1}$ and $\triangle\left(\tilde{u}_j, \frac{1}{N}\mathbf{1}\right) \leq \ln N$. Summing over $t = 1,\ldots,T$,

$$\hat{L}^T/c_\eta \leq \sum_{k=1}^{K} \sum_{t \in \tau(k)} \tilde{u}_{\pi(k)} \cdot \ell^t + \frac{1}{\eta}\left(m \ln N + m \ln \frac{1}{\alpha} + (T-m)\ln\frac{2}{1-\alpha} + 2\Phi\right),$$

where $\Phi = \sum_{t=1}^{T} \ln \rho_t(k')$ and k' is the task previous to $\kappa(t)$ which used the same comparator. We now upper-bound Φ by noting that $\rho_t(k')$ is smaller than the number of time steps δ_t that elapsed since task k' was performed. Note that $\sum_{t=1}^{T} \delta_t \leq mT$ as there are m subsequences summing to at most T each. Hence, $\ln \prod_{t=1}^{T} \delta_t$ is maximized when all the terms δ_t are equal (i.e. at most m), resulting in $\Phi \leq T \ln m$. Note that Φ, which depends on the sequence of task presentations, is potentially much smaller than $T \ln m$.

Choosing, for instance, $\alpha = 1 - \frac{2}{m}$ whenever $m > 2$,

$$\hat{L}^T/c_\eta \leq \sum_{k=1}^{K} \sum_{t \in \tau(k)} \tilde{u}_{\pi(k)} \cdot \ell^t + \frac{1}{\eta}\left(m \ln \frac{N}{m-2} + 3T \ln m\right).$$

The constant 3 can be optimized by choosing a non-quadratic power decay for β_t at the expense of having an extra $T \ln K$ term. Setting the comparators $\tilde{u}_1,\ldots,\tilde{u}_m$ to be unit vectors amounts to finding the best m-subset of N experts. The minimum over the assignment π of tasks to experts then amounts to choosing the best expert out of m possibilities for each task.

Proof (of Theorem 4). Let $\tilde{P}(S,\phi) = Q_{R_2}(S)P(\phi|S)$, the induced distribution on the (S,ϕ) pairs when the MCMC Algorithm 3 is used for sampling. Let X^t now stand for the random choices f_i^t according to this induced distribution $\tilde{P}$, which is close to P. Then $\mathbb{E}X^t = \sum_{(S,\phi)\in\bar{\mathcal{H}}_m} f_{\Psi(S,\phi,k)}^t \tilde{P}(S,\phi)$. Hence,

$$|\hat{q}^t - \mathbb{E}X^t| = \left| \sum_{(S,\phi)\in\bar{\mathcal{H}}_m} f_{\Psi(S,\phi,k)}^t \left(P(\phi,S) - \tilde{P}(\phi,S) \right) \right|$$

$$\leq \sum_{(S,\phi)\in\bar{\mathcal{H}}_m} f_{\Psi(S,\phi,k)}^t P(\phi|S)\, |P(S) - Q_{R_2}(S)| \leq 2\|Q_{R_2} - P\| \leq \epsilon.$$

Since we sample X^t independently R_1 times, standard concentration inequalities ensure that $P\left(|\bar{X}^t - \mathbb{E}X^t| \geq \sqrt{\left(\ln \frac{2T}{\delta}\right)/(2R_1)}\right) \leq \frac{\delta}{T}$. Combining with the above result, $P\left(|\bar{X}^t - \hat{q}^t| \geq \epsilon + \sqrt{\left(\ln \frac{2T}{\delta}\right)/(2R_1)}\right) \leq \frac{\delta}{T}$. Since ℓ is Lipschitz, $|\ell(\bar{X}^t, y^t) - \ell(\hat{q}^t, y^t)| \leq C\epsilon + C\sqrt{\left(\ln \frac{2T}{\delta}\right)/(2R_1)}$ with probability at least $1 - \delta/T$. By the union-bound, with probability at least $1 - \delta$,

$$\left| \sum_{t=1}^{T} \ell(\bar{X}^t, y^t) - \sum_{t=1}^{T} \ell(\hat{q}^t, y^t) \right| \leq T \cdot C\epsilon + T \cdot C\sqrt{\frac{\ln \frac{2T}{\delta}}{2R_1}}.$$

Combining with the bound of Theorem 1 (for $\bar{\mathcal{H}}_m$), we obtain the desired result.

Online Learning with Prior Knowledge

Elad Hazan and Nimrod Megiddo

IBM Almaden Research Center
{hazan,megiddo}@us.ibm.com

Abstract. The standard so-called experts algorithms are methods for utilizing a given set of "experts" to make good choices in a sequential decision-making problem. In the standard setting of experts algorithms, the decision maker chooses repeatedly in the same "state" based on information about how the different experts would have performed if chosen to be followed. In this paper we seek to extend this framework by introducing state information. More precisely, we extend the framework by allowing an experts algorithm to rely on state information, namely, partial information about the cost function, which is revealed to the decision maker before the latter chooses an action. This extension is very natural in prediction problems. For illustration, an experts algorithm, which is supposed to predict whether the next day will be rainy, can be extended to predicting the same given the current temperature.

We introduce new algorithms, which attain optimal performance in the new framework, and apply to more general settings than variants of regression that have been considered in the statistics literature.

1 Introduction

Consider the following standard "experts problem": an online player attempts to predict whether it will rain or not the next day, given advices of various experts. Numerous "experts algorithms" are known, which make predictions based on previous observations and expert advice. These algorithms guarantee that after many iterations the number of mistakes that the algorithm makes is approximately at least as good as that of the best expert in retrospect.

In this paper we address the question of how to utilize prior "state information" in online learning. In the prediction example, suppose that the online predictor has access to various measurements, e.g., temperature and cloud location. Intuitively, this information can potentially improve the performance of the online predictor.

It is not clear a priori how to model prior information in the online learning framework. The information (e.g., temperature) may or may not be correlated with the actual observations (e.g., whether or not it later rains). Even more so, it is conceivable that the state information may be strongly correlated with the observations, but this correlation is very hard to extract. For example, the prior knowledge could be encoded as a solution to a computationally hard problem or even an uncomputable one.

N. Bshouty and C. Gentile (Eds.): COLT 2007, LNAI 4539, pp. 499–513, 2007.

Various previous approaches attempted to learn the correlation between the given information and the observable data. By the above argument, we think such an approach is not robust.

Another approach could be to associate different experts with different decision states and then use standard expert algorithms. The problem here is that the number of states grows exponentially with the dimension of the state space. Therefore, this approach quickly becomes infeasible even for a modest amount of prior information. Other difficulties with this approach arise when the domain of the attributes is infinite.

Perhaps the previous work that is most similar to our approach is the model for portfolio management with side information by Cover and Ordentlich [CO96]. Their approach handles discrete side information, and amounts to handling different side information values as separate problem instances. The measure of performance in their model is standard regret, which must increase in proportion to the available side information.

We propose a framework which does not assume anything about the distribution of the data, prior information, or correlation between the two. The measure of performance is comparative, i.e., based on an extension of the concept of regret. However, unlike [CO96], our model allows the learner to correlate between different states. Our model takes into account the geometric structure of the available information space. As such, it is more similar to the statistical framework of nonparametric regression.

We propose and analyze algorithms which achieve near optimal performance in this framework. Our performance guarantees are valid in both adversarial and stochastic scenarios, and apply to the most general prediction setting, as opposed to previous methods such as nonparametric regression, which apply only to the stochastic scenario and to a more restrictive prediction setting.

We begin with an example of an instance of online learning with state information, in which the information need not be correlated with the observed outcomes. We prove, however, a surprising gain in performance (measured by the standard measure of *regret*) of algorithms that exploit the state information, compared to those that ignore it.

Following this proof of concept, in section 4 we precisely define our model and the measure of performance. We give algorithms and analyze them according to the new performance measure. In section 5 we prove nearly tight lower bounds on the performance of the algorithms, and compare our framework to the well-studied statistical problem of nonparametric regression.

2   Preliminaries

The *online convex optimization* (OCO) problem is defined as follows. The *feasible domain* of the problem is a given convex compact set $\mathcal{P} \subset \mathbb{R}^n$. An adversary picks a sequence of T convex functions $f_t : \mathcal{P} \to \mathbb{R}$, $t = 1, 2, \ldots, T$. The adversary is not restricted otherwise. At time t, $(t = 1, 2, \ldots)$, the decision maker knows only the functions $f_1, \ldots, f_{t-1}$ and has to pick a point $\mathbf{x}_t \in \mathcal{P}$. The decision maker also recalls his previous choices $\mathbf{x}_1 \ldots, \mathbf{x}_{t-1}$. The decision maker is subsequently informed in full about the function f_t, and incurs a cost of $f_t(\mathbf{x}_t)$.

We denote the gradient (resp., Hessian) of a mapping $f : \mathcal{P} \mapsto \mathbb{R}$ at $\mathbf{x} \in \mathcal{P}$ by $\nabla f(\mathbf{x})$ (resp., $\nabla^2 f(\mathbf{x})$). For a family of loss functions $\{f_t(\cdot) : t \in [T]\}$ (henceforth we denote $[n] \triangleq \{1, ..., n\}$) and an underlying convex set $\mathcal{P}$, we denote by $G = \max\{\|\nabla f_t(\mathbf{x})\|_2 : t \in [T], \mathbf{x} \in \mathcal{P}\}$ an upper bound on the ℓ_2-norm of the gradients, and by G_∞ an upper bound on the ℓ_∞-norm.

Minimizing Regret. The *regret* of the decision maker after T steps is defined as the difference between the total cost that the decision maker has actually incurred and the minimum cost that the decision maker could have incurred by choosing a certain point repeatedly throughout. More precisely, the regret is equal to

$$R = R(\mathbf{x}_1, \ldots, \mathbf{x}_T ; f_1, \ldots, f_T) \triangleq \sum_{t=1}^{T} f_t(\mathbf{x}_t) - \min_{\mathbf{x} \in \mathcal{P}} \sum_{t=1}^{T} f_t(\mathbf{x}) .$$

Denote by $\mathcal{A}$ the *algorithm* that is used by the decision maker to make the sequential choices. Thus, $\mathcal{A}$ is sequence of mappings $(\mathcal{A}_t : t = 1, 2, \ldots)$ so that $\mathbf{x}_t = \mathcal{A}_t(f_1, \ldots, f_{t-1})$. For brevity, denote $\mathbf{x}^T = (\mathbf{x}_1, \ldots, \mathbf{x}_T)$, $f^T = (f_1, \ldots, f_T)$ and $\mathbf{x}^T = \mathcal{A}(f^{T-1})$. The worst-case regret from an algorithm $\mathcal{A}$ at time T can be defined as

$$\text{Regret}_T(\mathcal{A}) \triangleq \sup_{f^T} R(\mathcal{A}(f^{T-1}), f^T) .$$

In other words,

$$\text{Regret}_T(\mathcal{A}) = \sup_{f_1, \ldots, f_T} \left\{ \sum_{t=1}^{T} f_t(\mathbf{x}_t) - \min_{\mathbf{x} \in \mathcal{P}} \sum_{t=1}^{T} f_t(\mathbf{x}) \right\}$$

The traditional approach to the OCO problem seeks algorithms that minimize the worst-case regret.

Online convex optimization with state information. In this paper we extend the common OCO problem to situations where the decision maker has some information about the "state" prior to his choosing of $\mathbf{x}_t$. We consider specific situations where some state information is revealed to the decision maker. A precise definition is given in section 4.

3   A "Proof of Concept"

In this section we consider the basic online convex optimization setting over the Euclidean ball $\mathbb{B}_n = \{\mathbf{x} \in \mathbb{R}^n : \|\mathbf{x}\|_2 \leq 1\}$. We assume that each payoff function f_t is linear, i.e., $f_t(\mathbf{x}) = \mathbf{c}_t^\top \mathbf{x}$ for some $\mathbf{c} \in \mathbb{R}^n$ (see see [Zin03] for a reduction from the general OCO problem to the case of linear cost functions). Furthermore, we consider here the case where $\mathbf{c}_t \in [-1, 1]^n$, and assume that only c_{t1}, the first coordinate of $\mathbf{c}_t$, is revealed to the decision maker as state information prior to the choosing of $\mathbf{x}_t \in \mathbb{B}_n$.

The following lower bound is well known for the case where c_{t1} is not revealed to the decision maker prior to choosing $\mathbf{x}_t$ (a similar bound was given in [CBFH+93]; see Appendix for proof):

Lemma 1 (Folk). *For the Online Convex Optimization problem over the Euclidean ball with $\mathbf{c}_t \in [-1,1]^n$ (or even $\mathbf{c}_t \in \{-1,1\}^n$) with no state information, every algorithm has a worst-case regret of at least $\Omega(\sqrt{nT})$.*

We first prove a surprising result that the decision maker can do much better when c_{t1} is known, even if there is no dependency between c_{t1} and the rest of the coordinates of $\mathbf{c}_t$.

Theorem 2. *For the OCO problem over the Euclidean ball with $\mathbf{c}_t \in [-1,1]^n$, in which c_{t1} is bounded away from zero and is revealed to the decision maker as state information prior to the choosing of $\mathbf{x}_t$, there exists an algorithm with a worst-case regret of $O(n^2 \log T)$.*

The condition that c_{t1} is bounded away from zero is intuitively necessary in order to have non-vanishing state information. It is also easy to show that for state information that is identically zero, the lower bound of Lemma 1 holds.

We now analyze the case with prior information, specifically where the decision maker is informed of c_{t1} prior to choosing $\mathbf{x}_t$. The basic idea is to reformulate the OCO problem with state information as an equivalent OCO problem without state information. In our particular case, this can be done by modifying the convex cost function as follows. Suppose the coordinates of $\mathbf{y}_t \equiv (x_{t2}, \ldots, x_{t,n})^\top$ have been fixed so that $\|\mathbf{y}_t\|^2 \leq 1$. Then, the optimal choice of x_{t1}, subject to the constraint $\|\mathbf{x}_t\|^2 \leq 1$, is

$$x_{t1} = \begin{cases} \sqrt{1 - \|\mathbf{y}_t\|^2} & \text{if } c_{t1} < 0 \\ -\sqrt{1 - \|\mathbf{y}_t\|^2} & \text{if } c_{t1} \geq 0 . \end{cases}$$

In other words,

$$x_{t1} = -\operatorname{sgn}(c_{t1}) \cdot \sqrt{1 - \|\mathbf{y}_t\|^2} .$$

It turns out that the cost of choosing $\mathbf{y}_t$ and completing it with an optimal choice of x_{t1} is

$$g_t(\mathbf{y}_t) = c_{t2}x_{t2} + \cdots + c_{tn}x_{tn} - |c_{t1}|\sqrt{1 - \|\mathbf{y}_t\|^2} = \mathbf{u}_t^\top \mathbf{y}_t - |c_{t1}|\sqrt{1 - \|\mathbf{y}_t\|^2} ,$$

where

$$\mathbf{u}_t \equiv (c_{t2}, \ldots, c_{tn})^\top .$$

Thus, our problem is equivalent to an OCO problem where the decision maker has to choose vector $\mathbf{y}_t$, and the adversary picks cost functions of the form of g_t where c_{t1} is known to the decision maker.

The following algorithm chooses vectors based on weights, which are updated in a multiplicative fashion. Let

$$w_t(\mathbf{y}) = \exp\left\{-\alpha \sum_{\tau=1}^{t-1} g_\tau(\mathbf{y})\right\} .$$

Thus,
$$w_t(\mathbf{y}) = w_{t-1}(\mathbf{y}) \cdot \exp\left\{-\alpha\, g_{t-1}(\mathbf{y})\right\}\ .$$
The weight function $w_t(\cdot)$ determines the choice of $\mathbf{y}_t$ as follows, where $\mathcal{P} = \mathbb{B}_{n-1}$.

$$\mathbf{y}_t = \frac{\int_{\mathcal{P}} \mathbf{y} \cdot w_t(\mathbf{y})\, d\mathbf{y}}{\int_{\mathcal{P}} w_t(\mathbf{y})\, d\mathbf{y}} \in \mathcal{P}\ .$$

Note that $\mathbf{y}_t$ is a convex combination of points in $\mathcal{P}$ and hence $\mathbf{y}_t \in \mathcal{P}$. The corresponding vector $\mathbf{x}_t$ in the OCO problem with state information is the following:

$$(x_{t2}, \ldots, x_{tn})^\top = \mathbf{y}_t$$
$$x_{t1} = \begin{cases} \sqrt{1 - \|\mathbf{y}_t\|^2} & \text{if } c_{t1} < 0 \\ -\sqrt{1 - \|\mathbf{y}_t\|^2} & \text{if } c_{t1} \geq 0 \end{cases}$$

We refer to the above-stated algorithm as $\textsc{Alg1}$. Denote $\rho = \min\{|c_{t1}|\ :\ t = 1, \ldots, T\}$.

Lemma 3. *The worst-case regret of* $\textsc{Alg1}$ *is at most* $(4n^2/\rho) \cdot \log T$.

The proof of this Lemma is given in the appendix. Briefly, $\textsc{Alg1}$ belongs to a family of well studied "exponential weighting" algorithms, which can exploit the curvature of the functions $g(\mathbf{y})$, and hence obtain a logarithmic regret. Theorem 2 follows.

Algorithm $\textsc{Alg1}$ can be implemented in time polynomial in n and T, in a way similar to the implementation of Cover's algorithm [Cov91] by Blum and Kalai [BK97].

4 The General Case

To capture state information, we revise the online convex optimization framework as defined in section 2 as follows. We model state information by a vector in a metric space $\mathcal{I}$, which we also call the *information space*. In iteration t, an online algorithm $\mathcal{A}$ accepts besides f^{t-1} and $\mathbf{x}^{t-1}$ also a state vector $\mathbf{k}_t \in \mathcal{I}$ as well as all previous state vector $\mathbf{k}_1, \ldots, \mathbf{k}_{t-1}$.

Henceforth we consider the information space $\mathcal{I}$ as a subset of d-dimensional Euclidean space, even though it makes sense to consider general metric spaces so as to allow the representation of both scalar quantities (e.g., temperature) and problem-specific quanta (e.g., board configurations in the game of chess). The space should at least be metric since the main point of our algorithms is to take advantage of similarity between consecutive state vectors, which is measured according to some distance function. Note that ignoring the similarity between states is equivalent to employing disjoint sets of experts in different states. We also refer to the intrinsic dimensionality of the space, denoted d. For Euclidean space this is the standard dimension, but more generally the notion of *box dimension* [Cla06] is suitable for our applications.

The new performance measure we propose is a strict generalization of the game-theoretic concept of regret as follows.

Definition 1. *For $L > 0$,*

(i) *Denote by X_L the family of mappings $\mathbf{x} : \mathcal{I} \mapsto \mathcal{P}$, from the information space to the underlying convex set $\mathcal{P}$, with Lipschitz-constant L, i.e., for all $\mathbf{k}_1, \mathbf{k}_2 \in \mathcal{I}$,*

$$\|\mathbf{x}(\mathbf{k}_1) - \mathbf{x}(\mathbf{k}_2)\| \leq L \cdot \|\mathbf{k}_1 - \mathbf{k}_2\| .$$

(ii) *The L-regret from a sequence of choices $\mathbf{x}_1, ..., \mathbf{x}_T$ is defined as*

$$\sum_{t=1}^{T} f_t(\mathbf{x}_t) - \min_{\mathbf{x} \in X_L} \sum_{t=1}^{T} f_t(\mathbf{x}(\mathbf{k}_t))$$

When L and $\mathbf{k}_1, \ldots, \mathbf{k}_T$ have been fixed, we denote by $\mathbf{x}^*(\cdot)$ a minimizer of $\sum_{t=1}^{T} f_t(\mathbf{x}(\mathbf{k}_t))$ over X_L.

Thus, the actual costs are compared with the costs that could be incurred by the best experts in a family of experts with Lipschitz-constant L. Note that this definition reduces to the standard regret when $L = 0$. If $L = \infty$, then L-regret is the "competitive ratio" studied in competitive analysis of online algorithms. Our model for prior information allows for algorithms which attain sublinear L-regret for $0 < L < \infty$.

4.1   An Algorithm for Minimizing L-Regret

To describe the first algorithm which attains a non-trivial worst-case L-regret, we recall the geometric notion of an ε-net.

Definition 2. *A subset $\mathcal{N} \subseteq \mathcal{I}$ of points in a metric space $\mathcal{I}$ with distance function Δ is called an ε-net for the set $S \subseteq \mathcal{I}$ if for every $x \in S$, $\Delta(x, \mathcal{N}) \equiv \inf\{\Delta(x, y) | y \in \mathcal{N}\} \leq \varepsilon$, and in addition $\forall x, y \in \mathcal{N} . \Delta(x, y) \geq \varepsilon$.*

The first algorithm, ALG2, which attains a non-trivial worst-case L-regret, constructs an ε-net of the observed data points, denoted $\mathcal{N}$, according to the online greedy algorithm (see [Cla06, KL04]). We also maintain a mapping, denoted $\mathcal{M}$, from all points in $\mathcal{N}$ to the decision space $\mathcal{P}$. Let D denote the diameter of $\mathcal{P}$ and W denote the diameter of the information space $\mathcal{I}$. The algorithm relies on the Lipschitz-constant L and the number of time periods T.

Algorithm ALG2 (L,T)
Set $\varepsilon = W (D/L)^{2/(d+2)} T^{-1/(d+2)}$ and $\mathcal{N} = \emptyset$.

 - Given $\mathbf{k}_t \in [0,1]^d$, let $\tilde{\mathbf{k}}_t$ be the state that is closest to $\mathbf{k}_t$ among all state vectors in $\mathcal{N}$, i.e., $\tilde{\mathbf{k}}_t = \arg\min\{\|\mathbf{k} - \mathbf{k}_t\| : \mathbf{k} \in \mathcal{N}\}$.
 - Set $\mathbf{x}_t \leftarrow \mathcal{M}(\tilde{\mathbf{k}}_t)$ or, if $t = 0$, then set $\mathbf{x}_0$ arbitrarily.
 - Denote by $\prod_{\mathcal{P}}$ the projection operator into the convex set $\mathcal{P}$. Set

$$\mathbf{y} \leftarrow \prod_{\mathcal{P}} \left(\mathcal{M}(\tilde{\mathbf{k}}_t) - \tfrac{1}{\sqrt{T}} \nabla f_t(\mathcal{M}(\tilde{\mathbf{k}}_t)) \right)$$

– If $\|\tilde{\mathbf{k}}_t - \mathbf{k}_t\| \le \varepsilon$, then update $\mathcal{M}(\tilde{\mathbf{k}}_t) \leftarrow \mathbf{y}$ (the size of $\mathcal{N}$ does not increase); else, add $\mathbf{k}_t$ to $\mathcal{N}$ and set $\mathcal{M}(\mathbf{k}_t) \leftarrow \mathbf{y}$.

Theorem 4. *Given L, $\mathcal{P}$, and T,*

$$L\text{-regret}(\text{ALG2}) = O\left(W\,G\,L^{1-\frac{2}{d+2}}\,D^{\frac{2}{d+2}} \cdot T^{1-\frac{1}{d+2}}\right)$$

The theorem is proved by independently summing up the L-regret over the "representative" points in the set $\mathcal{N}$. For each such representative point, the optimal strategy in hindsight is almost fixed by diameter considerations. In addition, the total number of such representatives is not too large because the set $\mathcal{N}$ is an ε-net of the observed set of state vectors.

Proof. Summing up the L-regret over the "representative" points in the set $\mathcal{N}$:

$$L\text{-regret}(\text{ALG2}) = \sum_{t=1}^{T}[f_t(\mathbf{x}_t) - f_t(\mathbf{x}^*(\mathbf{k}_t))] = \sum_{\mathbf{k}\in\mathcal{N}}\sum_{t:\tilde{\mathbf{k}}_t=\mathbf{k}}[f_t(\mathbf{x}_t) - f_t(\mathbf{x}^*(\mathbf{k}_t))]\ .$$

Let $T_{\mathbf{k}} = |\{t \in [T] \mid \tilde{\mathbf{k}}_t = \mathbf{k}\}|$ be the number of iterations during which the prior knowledge $\mathbf{k}_t$ is equal to the representative vector $\mathbf{k} \in \mathcal{N}$. By the properties of the gradient-descent algorithm (Theorem 1 in [Zin03]), for each set of time periods $T_{\mathbf{k}}$, the 0-regret can be bounded as follows.

$$\sum_{t\in T_{\mathbf{k}}} f_t(\mathbf{x}_t) - \min_{\mathbf{x}\in\mathcal{P}}\sum_{t\in T_{\mathbf{k}}} f_t(\mathbf{x}) = \sum_{t\in T_{\mathbf{k}}}[f_t(\mathbf{x}_t) - f_t(\mathbf{x}_{\mathbf{k}}^*)] \le 2GD\sqrt{T_{\mathbf{k}}}\ , \qquad (1)$$

where $\mathbf{x}_{\mathbf{k}}^* = \arg\min\sum_{t\in T_{\mathbf{k}}} f_t(\mathbf{x})$. Also, since for each time period during which $\tilde{\mathbf{k}}_t = \mathbf{k}$ the distance between state vectors is bounded by (using the triangle inequality for the norm),

$$\|\mathbf{x}^*(\mathbf{k}_1) - \mathbf{x}^*(\mathbf{k}_2)\| \le L \cdot \|\mathbf{k}_1 - \mathbf{k}_2\| \le L \cdot (\|\mathbf{k}_1 - \mathbf{k}\| + \|\mathbf{k}_2 - \mathbf{k}\|) \le 2L\varepsilon\ , \quad (2)$$

combining (1) and (2) we get for every $\mathbf{k}$,

$$\sum\nolimits_{t\in T_{\mathbf{k}}}[f_t(\mathbf{x}_t) - f_t(\mathbf{x}^*(\mathbf{k}_t))]$$

$$= \sum_{t\in T_{\mathbf{k}}}[f_t(\mathbf{x}_t) - f_t(\mathbf{x}_{\mathbf{k}}^*)] + \sum_{t\in T_{\mathbf{k}}}[f_t(\mathbf{x}_{\mathbf{k}}^*) - f_t(\mathbf{x}^*(\mathbf{k}_t))]$$

$$\le 2GD\sqrt{T_{\mathbf{k}}} + \sum_{t\in T_{\mathbf{k}}}\nabla f_t(\mathbf{x}^*(\mathbf{k}_t))(\mathbf{x}_{\mathbf{k}}^* - \mathbf{x}^*(\mathbf{k}_t))$$

$$\le 2GD\sqrt{T_{\mathbf{k}}} + \sum_{t\in T_{\mathbf{k}}}\|\nabla f_t(\mathbf{x}^*(\mathbf{k}_t))\| \cdot \|\mathbf{x}^*(\mathbf{k}_1) - \mathbf{x}^*(\mathbf{k}_t)\|$$

$$\le 2GD\sqrt{T_{\mathbf{k}}} + GT_{\mathbf{k}} \cdot \varepsilon L\ .$$

Thus, the total regret is bounded by (using concavity of the square root function)

$$\sum_{t=1}^{T}[f_t(\mathbf{x}_t) - f_t(\mathbf{x}^*(\mathbf{k}_t))] \le \sum_{\mathbf{k}\in\mathcal{N}}[2GD\sqrt{T_{\mathbf{k}}} + G\varepsilon LT_{\mathbf{k}}] \le |\mathcal{N}|\cdot 2GD\sqrt{T/|\mathcal{N}|} + G\varepsilon LT\ .$$

It remains to bound the size of $\mathcal{N}$, which is standard for a greedy construction of an ε-net. Since the distance between every two distinct vectors $\mathbf{k}_1, \mathbf{k}_2 \in \mathcal{N}$ is at least ε, by volume arguments and the fact that the information space $\mathcal{I}$ has (box) dimension d, we have $|\mathcal{N}| \leq (W/\varepsilon)^d$. Thus,

$$L\text{-regret}(\text{ALG2}) = O\left((W/\varepsilon)^{d/2} GD\sqrt{T} + G\varepsilon LT\right)$$

By choosing $\varepsilon = W(D/L)^{2/(d+2)}T^{-1/(d+2)}$, we obtain the result.

Remark 1. Algorithm ALG2 receives as input the number of iterations T. This dependence can be removed by the standard "doubling trick" as follows. Apply the algorithm with $t_1 = 100$. Recursively, if the number of iterations exceeds t_{j-1}, then apply ALG2 with $t_j = 2t_{j-1}$ from iteration t_j onwards. The overall regret is

$$\sum_{j=1}^{\log T} WGL^{1-\frac{2}{d+2}} D^{\frac{2}{d+2}} \cdot t_j^{1-\frac{1}{d+2}} \leq \log T \cdot WGL^{1-\frac{2}{d+2}} D^{\frac{2}{d+2}} \cdot T^{1-\frac{1}{d+2}}.$$

The same remark shall apply to all consequent variants. For simplicity, we assume henceforth that T is known in advance.

Implementation and running time. It is straightforward to implement ALG2 in time linear in T, n, and d, apart from the projection operator onto the convex set $\mathcal{P}$. This projection is a convex program and can be computed in polynomial time (for various special cases faster algorithms are known).

The performance guarantee of ALG2 decreases exponentially with the dimension of the information space, denoted d. As we show in the next section, this "curse of dimensionality" is inherent in the model, and the bounds are asymptotically tight. Next, we describe an approach to deal with this difficulty.

4.2   Extensions to the Basic Algorithm

Exploiting Low Dimensionality of Data. If the state vectors originate from a lower-dimensional subspace of the information space, the algorithm of the preceding section can be adapted to attain bounds that are proportional to the dimension of the subspace rather than the dimension of the entire information space.

Corollary 5. *Suppose that the prior knowledge vectors* $\mathbf{k}_t$ *originate from an r-dimensional subspace of* $\mathcal{I}$. *Then setting* $\varepsilon = W(\frac{D}{L})^{2/(r+2)} T^{-1/(r+2)}$ *in* ALG2 *we obtain*

$$L\text{-regret}(\text{ALG2}) = O(WGL^{1-\frac{2}{r+2}} D^{\frac{2}{r+2}} \cdot T^{1-\frac{1}{r+2}})$$

This corollary follows from the fact that the constructed ε-net in an r-dimensional subspace has size $(W/\varepsilon)^r$ rather than $(W/\varepsilon)^d$.

Specialization to Other Online Convex Optimization Variants. It is possible to modify ALG2 by replacing the online gradient descent step inside the main loop by any other online convex optimization algorithm update. In certain cases this may lead to more efficient algorithms. For example, if the underlying convex set $\mathcal{P}$ is the n-dimensional simplex, then using the ubiquitous Multiplicative-Weights online algorithm (introduced to the learning community by Littlestone and Warmuth [LW94]; see survey [AHK05]) we can obtain the following regret bound

$$L\text{-regret}(\text{MW-ALG2}) = O(WG_\infty L^{1-\frac{2}{d+2}} D^{\frac{2}{d+2}} \cdot T^{1-\frac{1}{d+2}} \sqrt{\log n}) \ .$$

Another possible variant applies a Newton-type update rather than a gradient update. Such second-order algorithms are known to achieve substantial lower regret when the cost functions are exp-convex [HKKA06]. It is also possible to plug in "bandit" algorithms such as [FKM05].

Better ε-Nets. The metric embedding literature is rich with sophisticated data structures for constructing ε-nets and computing nearest neighbors over these nets - exactly the geometrical tasks performed by algorithm ALG2. Specifically, it is possible to use the techniques in [KL04] and related papers to obtain algorithms with much better running times.

5   Limitations of Learning with Prior Knowledge

In this section we discuss the limitations of our model for learning with prior knowledge. As a first step, we give lower bounds on the achievable L-regret, which are asymptotically tight up to constant factors.

Following that, we discuss a well-studied statistical methodology, called non-parametric regression, and show that our model generalizes that methodology. As a consequence, the lower bounds proved in the statistics literature apply to our framework and imply lower bounds on the achievable L-regret. These lower bounds are tight in the sense that the algorithms we described in the previous sections attain these bounds up to constant factors.

5.1   Simple Lower Bounds for L-Regret

We begin with a simple lower bound, which shows that the L-regret of any online algorithm with prior information deteriorates exponentially as the dimension grows. Compared to Theorem 4 the bounds are tight up to constant factors.

Lemma 6. *For $\mathcal{P} = [-1, 1]$, $d > 1$, and every $L \geq 0$, the L-regret of any online algorithm is at least $\Omega(GLT^{1-\frac{1}{d}})$.*

Proof. Partition the hypercube $[0, 1]^d$ into $T = \delta^{-d}$ small cubes of edge-length δ. Consider loss functions $f_t(x)$ and prior knowledge vectors $\mathbf{k}_t$ as follows. The sequence of prior knowledge vectors $(\mathbf{k}_1, \ldots, \mathbf{k}_T)$ consists of all centers of the small cubes. Note that for every $i \neq j$, $\|\mathbf{k}_i - \mathbf{k}_j\| \geq \delta$. For each t, independently, pick $f_t = f_t(x)$ to be either Gx or $-Gx$ with equal probability. Note that $\|\nabla f(x)\| = |f'(x)| = G$. Obviously, the expected loss of any algorithm that picks x_t without knowing $f_t(x)$ is zero; thus,

$$\mathbf{E}_{f_1,\ldots,f_t}\left[\sum_{t=1}^{T} f_t(x_t)\right] = 0.$$

Now, define the following function:

$$x^*(\mathbf{k}_t) \triangleq \begin{cases} -\frac{1}{2}L\delta & \text{if } f_t(x) \equiv Gx \\ +\frac{1}{2}L\delta & \text{if } f_t(x) \equiv -Gx . \end{cases}$$

The function $x^*(\cdot)$ is in X_L because for every $\mathbf{k}_1$ and $\mathbf{k}_2$,

$$|x^*(\mathbf{k}_1) - x^*(\mathbf{k}_2)| \leq L\delta \leq L \cdot \|\mathbf{k}_1 - \mathbf{k}_2\| .$$

Also, the minimum possible total cost using an optimal strategy x^* is

$$\sum_{t=1}^{T} -\frac{1}{2}L\delta \cdot G = -T \cdot \frac{1}{2}L\delta G = -\frac{1}{2}GLT^{1-\frac{1}{d}}$$

where the last equality follows since $T = \delta^{-d}$ and hence $\delta = T^{-\frac{1}{d}}$. Therefore, the expected regret of *any* online algorithm is as claimed.

The previous Lemma does not cover the case of $d = 1$, so for completeness we prove the following lemma.

Lemma 7. *For* $d = 1$, *prior knowledge space* $K = [0,1]$, $\mathcal{P} = [-1,1]$, *and any* $L \geq 0$, *the* L-*regret of any online algorithm is at least* $\Omega(G\sqrt{T(\lfloor L \rfloor + 1)})$

Proof (sketch). Without loss of generality, assume L is an integer. If $L \leq 1$, then this lemma follows from Lemma 1; otherwise, divide the real line $[0,1]$ into L segments, each of length $\frac{1}{L}$.

The online sequence is as follows. The prior knowledge vectors will be all $L+1$ points $\{k_1, \ldots, k_{L+1}\}$ which divide the segment $[0,1]$ into L smaller segments. For each such point we have a sequence of $T/(L+1)$ loss functions $f_t(x)$, each chosen at random, independently, to be either Gx or $-Gx$.

Obviously, the expected payoff of any online algorithm is zero. Now, to define the optimal strategy in hindsight, for each sequence of random functions corresponding to one of the points $\{k_1, \ldots, k_{L+1}\}$, with very high probability, the standard deviation is $O(\sqrt{T/(L+1)})$. Let $x^*(k_i)$ be either $\frac{1}{4}$ or $-\frac{1}{4}$ according to the direction of the deviation. We claim $x^* \in X_L$ since $|k_1 - k_2| \geq 1/L$ and for all k_1 and k_2,

$$|x^*(k_1) - x^*(k_2)| \leq \frac{1}{2} \leq L \cdot |k_1 - k_2| .$$

The loss obtained by x^* is

$$(L+1) \cdot \frac{1}{4}\sqrt{\frac{T}{L+1}} = \frac{1}{4}\sqrt{T(L+1)} .$$

This completes the proof.

5.2   The Relation to Nonparametric Regression

Nonparametric regression is the following well-studied problem which can be described as follows. There exists a distribution Ψ on $K \times X$, where that $K \subseteq \mathbb{R}^d$ and $X \subseteq \mathbb{R}$. We are given t samples, $\{(\mathbf{k}_1, x_1), \ldots, (\mathbf{k}_t, x_t)\}$, from this distribution, which we denote by $\mathbf{z}^t = \{\mathbf{z}_1, \ldots, \mathbf{z}_t\}$ ($\mathbf{z}_i = (\mathbf{k}_i, x_i)$). The problem is to come up with an estimator for x, given $\mathbf{k} \in \mathbb{R}^d$. An estimator for X which has seen t samples $\mathbf{z}^t$ from the distribution Ψ is denoted by $\theta_t : K \mapsto X$. The goal is to come up with an estimator which is as close as possible to the "optimal" Bayes estimator $\theta(\mathbf{k}) = E[x \mid \mathbf{k}]$.

Various distance metrics are considered in the literature for measuring the distance of an estimator from the Bayes estimator. For our purposes it is most convenient to use the L_2-error given by

$$\mathbf{Perf}(\theta_t) \triangleq \mathbf{E}_{(\mathbf{k}, x)} \left[(\theta_t(\mathbf{k}) - \theta(\mathbf{k}))^2 \right] .$$

The online framework we consider is more general than nonparametric regression in the following sense: an algorithm for online convex optimization with prior information is also an estimator for non-parametric regression, as we show below.

Recall that an algorithm for online optimization $\mathcal{A}$ takes as input the history of cost functions $f_1, \ldots, f_{t-1}$ as well as historical and current state information $\mathbf{k}_1, \ldots, \mathbf{k}_{t-1}, \mathbf{k}_t$, and produces a point in the underlying convex set $x_t = \mathcal{A}(f_1, \ldots, f_{t-1} ; \mathbf{k}_1, \ldots, \mathbf{k}_t)$. Given an instance of nonparametric regression (K, X), and t samples $\{(\mathbf{k}_i, x_i)\}$, define t cost functions as

$$f_i(x) \triangleq (x - \theta(\mathbf{k}_i))^2 .$$

Note that these cost functions are continuous and convex (although not differentiable). Motivated by results on *online-to-batch algorithm conversion*, let the hypothesis of online algorithm $\mathcal{A}$ at iteration t be

$$h_t^{\mathcal{A}}(\mathbf{k}) \triangleq \mathcal{A}(f_1, \ldots, f_{t-1} ; \mathbf{k}_1, \ldots, \mathbf{k}_{t-1}, \mathbf{k}) .$$

Now, define the estimator corresponding to $\mathcal{A}$ by

$$\theta_t^{\mathcal{A}}(\mathbf{k}) \triangleq \tfrac{1}{t} \sum_{\tau=1}^{t} h_\tau^{\mathcal{A}}.$$

Standard techniques imply a bound on the performance of this estimator as a function of the L-regret achievable by $\mathcal{A}$:

Lemma 8. *Let L be the Lipschitz constant of the function $\theta : K \mapsto X$. Then,*

$$\lim_{T \mapsto \infty} \Pr_{\mathbf{z}^T \sim \Psi^T} \left[\mathbf{Perf}(\theta_T^{\mathcal{A}}) \leq \frac{1}{T} L\text{-regret}_T(\mathcal{A}) + O\left(\frac{\log T}{\sqrt{T}} \right) \right] = 1 .$$

Proof. Standard results of converting online algorithms to batch algorithms, in particular Theorem 2 from [CBCG04], rephrased in our notation, reduces to:

$$\Pr_{\mathbf{z}^t \sim \Psi} \left[\mathbf{E}_{(\mathbf{k}, x) \sim \Psi}[f(\theta_t^{\mathcal{A}}(k))] \leq \frac{1}{t} \sum_{\tau=1}^{t-1} f_\tau(h_\tau^{\mathcal{A}}(k_\tau)) + O\left(\frac{1}{\sqrt{t}} \log \frac{1}{\delta} \right) \right] \geq 1 - \delta .$$

Since for every τ, $f_\tau(\theta(\mathbf{k}_\tau)) = 0$, we obtain

$$
1 - \delta \leq \Pr_{\mathbf{z}^t \sim \Psi} \left[\mathbf{E}_{(\mathbf{k},x)\sim\Psi}[f(\theta_t^{\mathcal{A}}(\mathbf{k}))] \leq \frac{1}{t} \sum_{\tau=1}^{t-1} f_\tau(h_\tau^{\mathcal{A}}(\mathbf{k}_\tau)) + O\left(\frac{1}{\sqrt{t}} \log \frac{1}{\delta}\right) \right]
$$

$$
= \Pr_{\mathbf{z}^t \sim \Psi} \left[\mathbf{Perf}(\theta_t^{\mathcal{A}}) \leq \frac{1}{t} \left[\sum_{\tau=1}^{t-1} f_\tau(h_\tau^{\mathcal{A}}(\mathbf{k}_\tau)) - f_\tau(\theta(\mathbf{k}_\tau)) \right] + O\left(\frac{1}{\sqrt{t}} \log \frac{1}{\delta}\right) \right]
$$

$$
\leq \Pr_{\mathbf{z}^t \sim \Psi} \left[\mathbf{Perf}(\theta_t^{\mathcal{A}}) \leq \frac{1}{t} [L\text{-regret}_T(\mathcal{A})] + O\left(\frac{1}{\sqrt{t}} \log \frac{1}{\delta}\right) \right]
$$

where the equality follows from the definition of $\mathbf{Perf}(\theta_t)$, and in the last inequality we use the fact that $\theta \in X_L$ by our assumption on the Lipschitz constant of θ.

By choosing $\delta = \frac{1}{t}$, with probability approaching 1 we have

$$
\mathbf{Perf}(\theta_t^{\mathcal{A}}) \leq \frac{1}{t} [L\text{-regret}_T(\mathcal{A})] + O\left(\frac{\log t}{\sqrt{t}}\right) .
$$

Hence, online algorithm with non-trivial L-regret guarantee automatically give a method for producing estimators for nonparameteric regression. In addition, the numerous lower bounds for nonparametric regression that appear in the literature apply to online learning with prior information. In particular, the lower bounds of [Sto82] and [AGK00] show that the exponential dependence of the L-regret is inherent and necessary even for the easier problem of nonparametric regression. It appears that Stone's lower bound [Sto82] has exactly the same asymptotic behavior as achieved in Theorem 4. Closing the gap between the convergence rate $1 - \frac{1}{d+2}$ and our lower bound of $1 - \frac{1}{d}$ is left as an open question.

Acknowledgements

We thank Ken Clarkson and Robi Krauthgamer for useful comments and references on ε-nets and nearest neighbor algorithms.

References

[AGK00] Antos, A., Györfi, L., Kohler, M.: Lower bounds on the rate of convergence of nonparametric regression estimates. Journal of Statistical Planning and Inference 83(1), 91–100 (2000)

[AHK05] Arora, S., Hazan, E., Kale, S.: The multiplicative weights update method: a meta algorithm and applications. Manuscript (2005)

[BK97] Blum, A., Kalai, A.: Universal portfolios with and without transaction costs. In: COLT '97: Proceedings of the tenth annual conference on Computational learning theory, pp. 309–313. ACM Press, New York, USA (1997)

[CBCG04]   Cesa-Bianchi, N., Conconi, A., Gentile, C.: On the generalization ability
            of on-line learning algorithms. IEEE Transactions on Information Theory
            (2004)
[CBFH⁺93]   Cesa-Bianchi, N., Freund, Y., Helmbold, D.P., Haussler, D., Schapire,
            R.E., Warmuth, M.K.: How to use expert advice. In: STOC '93: Proceed-
            ings of the twenty-fifth annual ACM symposium on Theory of computing,
            pp. 382–391. ACM Press, New York, NY, USA (1993)
[CBL06]   Cesa-Bianchi, N., Lugosi, G.: Prediction, Learning, and Games. Cam-
            bridge University Press, New York, USA (2006)
[Cla06]   Clarkson, K.L.: Nearest-neighbor searching and metric space dimensions.
            In: Shakhnarovich, G., Darrell, T., Indyk, P. (eds.) Nearest-Neighbor
            Methods for Learning and Vision: Theory and Practice, pp. 15–59. MIT
            Press, Cambridge (2006)
[CO96]   Cover, T.M., Ordentlich, E.: Universal portfolios with side information.
            42, 348–363 (1996)
[Cov91]   Cover, T.: Universal portfolios. Math. Finance 1, 1–19 (1991)
[FKM05]   Flaxman, A., Kalai, A.T., McMahan, H.B.: Online convex optimization
            in the bandit setting: gradient descent without a gradient. In: Proceedings
            of 16th SODA, pp. 385–394 (2005)
[HKKA06]   Hazan, E., Kalai, A., Kale, S.: A.t Agarwal. Logarithmic regret algo-
            rithms for online convex optimization. In: COLT '06: Proceedings of the
            19'th annual conference on Computational learning theory (2006)
[KL04]   Krauthgamer, R., Lee, J.R.: Navigating nets: Simple algorithms for prox-
            imity search. In: 15th Annual ACM-SIAM Symposium on Discrete Algo-
            rithms, pp. 791–801 (January 2004)
[KW99]   Kivinen, J., Warmuth, M.K.: Averaging expert predictions. In: Euro-
            COLT '99: Proceedings of the 4th European Conference on Computa-
            tional Learning Theory, London, UK, pp. 153–167. Springer, Heidelberg
            (1999)
[LW94]   Littlestone, N., Warmuth, M.K.: The weighted majority algorithm. In-
            formation and Computation 108(2), 212–261 (1994)
[Sto82]   Stone, C.J.: Optimal global rates of convergence for nonparametric re-
            gression. Annals of Statistics 10, 1040–1053 (1982)
[Zin03]   Zinkevich, M.: Online convex programming and generalized infinitesimal
            gradient ascent. In: Proceedings of the Twentieth International Confer-
            ence (ICML), pp. 928–936 (2003)

A   Proof of Lemma 1

Proof. Suppose the adversary picks each of the coordinates of $\mathbf{c}_1, \ldots, \mathbf{c}_T$ independently at random from $\{-1, 1\}$. Then, for every algorithm, the expected cost to
the decision maker is zero. Given $(\mathbf{c}_1, \ldots, \mathbf{c}_T)$, consider the vector $\mathbf{v} \equiv \sum_{t=1}^{T} \mathbf{c}_t$.
The best vector $\mathbf{x}^* \in \mathbb{B}_n$ with respect to $\mathbf{v}$ is obtained by minimizing $\mathbf{v}^\top \mathbf{x}$ over
all $\mathbf{x} \in \mathbb{B}_n$. Obviously, $\mathbf{x}^* = -\mathbf{v}/\|\mathbf{v}\|$ and $\mathbf{v}^\top \mathbf{x}^* = -\mathbf{v}^\top \mathbf{v}/\|\mathbf{v}\| = -\|\mathbf{v}\|$. Thus,
the *expected* regret is $\mathbf{E}[\|\mathbf{v}\|]$. By the central limit theorem, each coordinate v_j is
distributed approximately as normal with expectation 0 and variance T. It fol-
lows that the expected regret is $\mathbf{E}[\|\mathbf{v}\|] = \Omega(\sqrt{nT})$ and hence also the worst-case
regret is $\Omega(\sqrt{nT})$.

B   Proof of Lemma 3

Proof. Recall that by definition of $g_t(\cdot)$ and the construction of $\mathbf{x}_t$,

$$\mathbf{c}_t^\top \mathbf{x}_t = g_t(\mathbf{y}_t) . \tag{3}$$

Let $\mathbf{x}^*$ be the minimizer of $\sum_{t=1}^T \mathbf{c}_t^\top \mathbf{x}$ over $\mathbf{x} \in \mathbb{B}_n$. Recall that

$$\mathbf{v} = \mathbf{c}_1 + \cdots + \mathbf{c}_T$$

and $\mathbf{x}^* = -\mathbf{v}/\|\mathbf{v}\|$. Denote $\mathbf{y}^* = (x_2^*, \ldots, x_n^*)^\top$. It follows that

$$x_1^* = \begin{cases} \sqrt{1 - \|\mathbf{y}^*\|^2} & \text{if } v_1 < 0 \\ -\sqrt{1 - \|\mathbf{y}^*\|^2} & \text{if } v_1 \geq 0 \end{cases}$$

i.e.,

$$x_1^* = -\operatorname{sgn}(v_1)\sqrt{1 - \|\mathbf{y}^*\|^2} .$$

Recall that for every $\mathbf{y}$,

$$g_t(\mathbf{y}) = \sum_{j=1}^n c_{tj} y_j - |c_{t1}|\sqrt{1 - \|\mathbf{y}\|^2} = \mathbf{u}^\top \mathbf{y} - |c_{t1}|\sqrt{1 - \|\mathbf{y}\|^2} .$$

Therefore, for every t,

$$\mathbf{c}_t^\top \mathbf{x}^* = c_{t1} x_1^* + \mathbf{u}^\top \mathbf{y}^* = -c_{t1} \cdot \operatorname{sgn}(v_1)\sqrt{1 - \|\mathbf{y}^*\|^2} + \mathbf{u}^\top \mathbf{y}^* \geq g_t(\mathbf{y}^*) . \tag{4}$$

From (3) and (4) we have

$$\operatorname{Regret}_T(\text{ALG1}) = \sum_{t=1}^T \mathbf{c}_t^\top \mathbf{x}_t - \sum_{t=1}^T \mathbf{c}_t^\top \mathbf{x}^*$$

$$= \sum_{t=1}^T \mathbf{c}_t^\top \mathbf{x}_t - \mathbf{v}^\top \mathbf{x}^* \leq \sum_{t=1}^T g_t(\mathbf{y}_t) - \sum_{t=1}^T g_t(\mathbf{y}^*).$$

Therefore, we proceed to bound the latter difference. The following notion of convexity called "α-exp-concavity" was introduced by Kivinen and Warmuth [KW99] (see also [CBL06])

Definition 3. (*i*) *For square matrices of the same order* $\mathbf{P}$ *and* $\mathbf{Q}$*, the notation* $\mathbf{P} \succeq \mathbf{Q}$ *means that* $\mathbf{P} - \mathbf{Q}$ *is positive semidefinite. In other words, for every vector* $\mathbf{x}$*,* $\mathbf{x}^\top \mathbf{P}\mathbf{x} \geq \mathbf{x}^\top \mathbf{Q}\mathbf{x}$*.*
(*ii*) *For* $\alpha > 0$*, a twice-differentiable mapping* $f : \mathcal{P} \to \mathbb{R}$ *is said to be* α*-exp-concave if the mapping* $h(\mathbf{x}) \triangleq e^{-\alpha \cdot f(\mathbf{x})}$ *is concave.*

Proposition 1. *For* $f : \mathbb{R}^n \mapsto \mathbb{R}$*,* $e : \mathbb{R} \mapsto \mathbb{R}$*, and* $h = e \circ f$*, it holds that* $\nabla h(\mathbf{x}) = e'(f(\mathbf{x}))\nabla f(\mathbf{x})$ *and hence*

$$\nabla^2 h(\mathbf{x}) = e''(f(\mathbf{x}))\nabla f(\mathbf{x})(\nabla f(\mathbf{x}))^\top + e'(f(\mathbf{x}))\nabla^2 f(\mathbf{x}) .$$

The following proposition is proved in [HKKA06].

Proposition 2. *A mapping $f : \mathcal{P} \to \mathbb{R}$ is α-exp-concave if and only if for all $\mathbf{x} \in \mathcal{P}$,*

$$\nabla^2 f(\mathbf{x}) \succeq \alpha \cdot \nabla f(\mathbf{x})(\nabla f(\mathbf{x}))^\top .$$

Proposition 3. *The mapping $g_t(\mathbf{y}) = \mathbf{u}_t^\top \mathbf{y} - |c_{t1}|\sqrt{1 - \|\mathbf{y}\|^2}$ is $\frac{\rho}{2n}$-exp-concave.*

Proof. Assume $\rho > 0$ (else the statement is trivially correct). The gradient of g_t is

$$\nabla g_t(\mathbf{y}) = \mathbf{u}_t + \frac{|c_{t1}|}{\sqrt{1 - \|\mathbf{y}\|^2)}}\, \mathbf{y} ,$$

hence the Hessian is

$$\nabla^2 g_t(\mathbf{y}) = \frac{|c_{t1}|}{(1 - \|\mathbf{y}\|^2)^{3/2}}\, \mathbf{y}\mathbf{y}^\top + \frac{|c_{t1}|}{\sqrt{1 - \|\mathbf{y}\|^2}}\, \mathbf{I}_{n-1} .$$

For the proof we rely on the following relation:

$$(\mathbf{a} + \mathbf{b})(\mathbf{a} + \mathbf{b})^\top \preceq 2(\mathbf{a}\mathbf{a}^\top + \mathbf{b}\mathbf{b}^\top) , \tag{5}$$

which is true because for every vector $\mathbf{w}$,

$$\mathbf{w}^\top(\mathbf{a} + \mathbf{b})(\mathbf{a} + \mathbf{b})^\top \mathbf{w} = (\mathbf{w}^\top \mathbf{a} + \mathbf{w}^\top \mathbf{b})^2$$
$$\leq 2[(\mathbf{w}^\top \mathbf{a})^2 + (\mathbf{w}^\top \mathbf{b})^2] = \mathbf{w}^\top[2\mathbf{a}\mathbf{a}^\top + 2\mathbf{b}\mathbf{b}^\top]\mathbf{w}$$

since $(x + y)^2 \leq 2(x^2 + y^2)$ for all real x and y. Denoting $\nabla_t = \nabla g_t(\mathbf{y})$, and $\mathbf{u}_t = (c_{t2}, \ldots, c_{tn})^\top$, it follows from (5) that

$$\nabla_t \nabla_t^\top \preceq 2\mathbf{u}_t\mathbf{u}_t^\top + \frac{2c_{t1}^2}{1 - \|\mathbf{y}\|^2}\, \mathbf{y}\mathbf{y}^\top .$$

Since $\|\mathbf{u}_t\|^2 \leq n - 1$, it follows that

$$\mathbf{u}_t\mathbf{u}_t^\top \preceq (n - 1)\,\mathbf{I}_{n-1} \preceq \frac{n-1}{|c_{t1}|}\, \nabla^2 g_t(\mathbf{y}) .$$

Also, since $\sqrt{1 - \|\mathbf{y}\|^2} \leq 1$ and $|c_{t1}| \leq 1$,

$$\frac{c_{t1}^2 \cdot \mathbf{y}\mathbf{y}^\top}{1 - \|\mathbf{y}\|^2} \preceq \frac{|c_{t1}| \cdot \mathbf{y}\mathbf{y}^\top}{(1 - \|\mathbf{y}\|^2)^{3/2}} \preceq \nabla^2 g_t(\mathbf{y}) .$$

Combining the above relations,

$$\nabla_t \nabla_t^\top \preceq 2\left(1 + \frac{n-1}{|c_1|}\right) \nabla^2 g_t(\mathbf{y}) \preceq \frac{2n}{\rho}\nabla^2 g_t(\mathbf{y}) .$$

The remainder of the proof follows from the analysis of regret bounds of the EWOO algorithm of [HKKA06], following Blum and Kalai [BK97].

Nonlinear Estimators and Tail Bounds for Dimension Reduction in l_1 Using Cauchy Random Projections

Ping Li[1], Trevor J. Hastie[1], and Kenneth W. Church[2]

[1] Department of Statistics, Stanford University, Stanford CA 94305, USA
{pingli,hastie}@stat.stanford.edu
[2] Microsoft Research, One Microsoft Way, Redmond WA 98052, USA
church@microsoft.com

Abstract. For dimension reduction in l_1, one can multiply a data matrix $\mathbf{A} \in \mathbb{R}^{n \times D}$ by $\mathbf{R} \in \mathbb{R}^{D \times k}$ ($k \ll D$) whose entries are i.i.d. samples of Cauchy. The impossibility result says one can not recover the pairwise l_1 distances in $\mathbf{A}$ from $\mathbf{B} = \mathbf{AR} \in \mathbb{R}^{n \times k}$, using linear estimators. However, nonlinear estimators are still useful for certain applications in data stream computations, information retrieval, learning, and data mining.

We propose three types of nonlinear estimators: the bias-corrected sample median estimator, the bias-corrected geometric mean estimator, and the bias-corrected maximum likelihood estimator. We derive tail bounds for the geometric mean estimator and establish that $k = O\left(\frac{\log n}{\epsilon^2}\right)$ suffices with the constants explicitly given. Asymptotically (as $k \to \infty$), both the sample median estimator and the geometric mean estimator are about 80% efficient compared to the maximum likelihood estimator (MLE). We analyze the moments of the MLE and propose approximating the distribution of the MLE by an inverse Gaussian.

1 Introduction

There has been considerable interest in the l_1 norm in machine learning, as the l_1 distance is far more robust than the l_2 distance against "outliers." Success stories include Lasso, 1-norm SVM [1], and Laplacian basis kernel [2].

This paper focuses on dimension reduction in l_1 using *Cauchy random projections*, a special case of *linear (stable) random projections*. The idea is to multiply a data matrix $\mathbf{A} \in \mathbb{R}^{n \times D}$ by a random matrix $\mathbf{R} \in \mathbb{R}^{D \times k}$, resulting in $\mathbf{B} = \mathbf{AR} \in \mathbb{R}^{n \times k}$. If $k \ll D$, then it should be much more efficient to compute certain summary statistics (e.g., pairwise distances) from $\mathbf{B}$ as opposed to $\mathbf{A}$. Moreover, $\mathbf{B}$ may be small enough to reside in physical memory while $\mathbf{A}$ is often too large to fit in the main memory.

For dimension reduction in l_p ($0 < p \le 2$), one could construct $\mathbf{R}$ from i.i.d. samples of p-stable distributions[3,4]. In the stable distribution family[5], normal is 2-stable and Cauchy is 1-stable. Thus, we will call random projections for l_2 and l_1, *normal random projections* and *Cauchy random projections*, respectively.

N. Bshouty and C. Gentile (Eds.): COLT 2007, LNAI 4539, pp. 514–529, 2007.

For *normal random projections* [6], we can estimate the original pairwise l_2 distances in $\mathbf{A}$ directly using the corresponding l_2 distances in $\mathbf{B}$. Furthermore, the Johnson-Lindenstrauss (JL) Lemma [7] provides the performance guarantees.

For *Cauchy random projections*, however, one shall not use the l_1 distance in $\mathbf{B}$ to approximate the l_1 distance in $\mathbf{A}$, as Cauchy does not have a finite expectation. The impossibility result [8,9] says one can not recover the l_1 distance using linear projections and linear estimators, without incurring large errors.

We provide three types of nonlinear estimators: the bias-corrected sample median estimator, the bias-corrected geometric mean estimator, and the bias-corrected maximum likelihood estimator (MLE). The sample median and the geometric mean estimators are asymptotically equivalent (i.e., both are about 80% efficient as the MLE), but the latter is more accurate at small sample size k. Furthermore, we derive explicit tail bounds for the bias-corrected geometric mean estimator and establish an analog of the JL Lemma for l_1, which is weaker than the classical JL Lemma for l_2, because the geometric mean is not convex.

Nonlinear estimators may be useful in the following important scenarios:

- **Estimating l_1 distances online.**   The data matrix $\mathbf{A} \in \mathbb{R}^{n \times D}$ requires $O(nD)$ storage and all pairwise distances in $\mathbf{A}$ requires $O(n^2)$ storage; both may be too large for physical memory. To avoid page faults, it is more efficient to estimate the distances *on the fly* from the projected data $\mathbf{B}$ in the memory.
- **Computing all pairwise l_1 distances.**   In distance-based clustering, classification, and kernels, we need to compute all pairwise distances in $\mathbf{A}$, at the cost $O(n^2 D)$. Using *Cauchy random projections*, the cost is reduced to $O(nDk + n^2 k)$.
- **Linear scan nearest neighbor searching**.   Nearest neighbor searching is notorious for being inefficient, especially when the data matrix $\mathbf{A}$ is too large for the memory. Searching for the nearest neighbors from the projected data matrix $\mathbf{B}$ becomes much more efficient, even by linear scans.
- **Data stream computations.**   See [3,10].

We briefly comment on *random coordinate sampling*. One can randomly sample k columns from $\mathbf{A} \in \mathbb{R}^{n \times D}$ and estimate the summary statistics (including l_1 and l_2 distances). Despite its simplicity, this strategy has two major disadvantages. First, in heavy-tailed data, we may have to choose k very large in order to achieve a sufficient accuracy. Second, large datasets are often highly sparse. For sparse data, [11,12,13] provide an alternative coordinate sampling strategy, called *Conditional Random Sampling (CRS)*. For non-sparse data, however, methods based on *linear (stable) random projections* are superior.

2   Introduction to Linear (Stable) Random Projections

Assume a data matrix $\mathbf{A} \in \mathbb{R}^{n \times D}$. Let $\{u_i^{\mathrm{T}}\}_{i=1}^n \in \mathbb{R}^D$ be the ith row of $\mathbf{A}$. Let $\mathbf{R} \in \mathbb{R}^{D \times k}$ be a random matrix and denote the entries of $\mathbf{R}$ by $\{r_{ij}\}_{i=1}^D {}_{j=1}^k$. The projected data matrix $\mathbf{B} = \mathbf{AR} \in \mathbb{R}^{n \times k}$. Let $\{v_i^{\mathrm{T}}\}_{i=1}^n \in \mathbb{R}^k$ be the ith row of $\mathbf{B}$, i.e., $v_i = \mathbf{R}^T u_i$. For simplicity, we focus on the leading two rows, u_1 and u_2, in $\mathbf{A}$, and the leading two rows, v_1 and v_2, in $\mathbf{B}$. Define $\{x_j\}_{j=1}^k$ to be

$$x_j = v_{1,j} - v_{2,j} = \sum_{i=1}^{D} r_{ij}(u_{1,i} - u_{2,i}), \qquad j = 1, 2, ..., k. \tag{1}$$

2.1 Normal Random Projections

When r_{ij} is sampled from the standard normal, i.e., $r_{ij} \sim N(0,1)$, i.i.d., then

$$x_j = \sum_{i=1}^{D} r_{ij}(u_{1,i} - u_{2,i}) \sim N\left(0, \sum_{i=1}^{D} |u_{1,i} - u_{2,i}|^2\right), \qquad j = 1, 2, ..., k. \tag{2}$$

The squared l_2 distance, $d_{l_2} = \sum_{i=1}^{D} |u_{1,i} - u_{2,i}|^2$, can be estimated from the sample squared l_2 distance: $\hat{d}_{l_2} = \frac{1}{k}\sum_{j=1}^{k} x_j^2$. It is easy to show that [6,14,15,16]

$$\mathrm{E}\left(\hat{d}_{l_2}\right) = d_{l_2}, \qquad \mathrm{Var}\left(\hat{d}_{l_2}\right) = \frac{2}{k}d_{l_2}^2, \tag{3}$$

$$\mathbf{Pr}\left(\left|\hat{d}_{l_2} - d_{l_2}\right| \geq \epsilon d_{l_2}\right) \leq 2\exp\left(-\frac{k}{4}\epsilon^2 + \frac{k}{6}\epsilon^3\right), \quad 0 < \epsilon < 1 \tag{4}$$

We need to bound the error probability $\mathbf{Pr}\left(\left|\hat{d}_{l_2} - d_{l_2}\right| \geq \epsilon d_{l_2}\right)$ by δ, simultaneously for all $\frac{n(n-1)}{2}$ pairs of distances among n data points. By the Bonferroni union bound, it suffices if

$$k \geq \frac{2\log n - \log \delta}{\epsilon^2/4 - \epsilon^3/6}, \tag{5}$$

from which one version of the Johnson-Lindenstrauss (JL) Lemma follows:
If $k \geq \frac{2\log n - \log \delta}{\epsilon^2/4 - \epsilon^3/6}$, then with probability at least $1 - \delta$, the squared l_2 distance between any pair of data points (among n points) can be approximated within a $1 \pm \epsilon$ factor, using the squared l_2 distance of the projected data.

2.2 Cauchy Random Projections

For *Cauchy random projections*, we sample r_{ij} i.i.d. from the standard Cauchy distribution, i.e., $r_{ij} \sim C(0,1)$. By the 1-stability of Cauchy [5], we know that

$$x_j = v_{1,j} - v_{2,j} \sim C\left(0, \sum_{i=1}^{D} |u_{1,i} - u_{2,i}|\right). \tag{6}$$

That is, the projected differences $x_j = v_{1,j} - v_{2,j}$ are also Cauchy with the scale parameter being the original l_1 distance, $d = \sum_{i=1}^{D} |u_{1,i} - u_{2,i}|$. The problem boils down to estimating the Cauchy scale parameter of $C(0,d)$ from k i.i.d. samples $x_j \sim C(0,d)$. Unfortunately, unlike in *normal random projections*, we can no longer estimate d from the sample mean $(\frac{1}{k}\sum_{j=1}^{k} |x_j|)$ because $\mathrm{E}(x_j) = \infty$.

3   Main Results

Three types of nonlinear estimators are summarized as follows.

3.1   The Bias-Corrected Sample Median Estimator

Denoted by $\hat{d}_{me,c}$, the bias-corrected sample median estimator is

$$\hat{d}_{me,c} = \frac{\text{median}(|x_j|, j = 1, 2, ..., k)}{b_{me}}, \tag{7}$$

$$b_{me} = \int_0^1 \frac{(2m+1)!}{(m!)^2} \tan\left(\frac{\pi}{2}t\right)(t - t^2)^m \, dt, \quad k = 2m + 1 \tag{8}$$

Here, for convenience, we only consider $k = 2m + 1$, $m = 1, 2, 3, ...$

- $\mathrm{E}\left(\hat{d}_{me,c}\right) = d$, i.e, $\hat{d}_{me,c}$ is unbiased.
- When $k \geq 5$, the variance of $\hat{d}_{me,c}$ is

$$\mathrm{Var}\left(\hat{d}_{me,c}\right) = d^2 \left(\frac{(m!)^2}{(2m+1)!} \frac{\int_0^1 \tan^2\left(\frac{\pi}{2}t\right)(t - t^2)^m \, dt}{\left(\int_0^1 \tan\left(\frac{\pi}{2}t\right)(t - t^2)^m \, dt\right)^2} - 1\right). \tag{9}$$

- As $k \to \infty$, $\hat{d}_{me,c}$ converges to a normal in distribution

$$\sqrt{k}\left(\hat{d}_{me,c} - d\right) \xrightarrow{D} N\left(0, \frac{\pi^2}{4}d^2\right). \tag{10}$$

3.2   The Bias-Corrected Geometric Mean Estimator

Denoted by $\hat{d}_{gm,c}$, the bias-corrected geometric mean estimator is

$$\hat{d}_{gm,c} = \cos^k\left(\frac{\pi}{2k}\right) \prod_{j=1}^k |x_j|^{1/k}, \quad k > 1 \tag{11}$$

- It is unbiased, i.e., $\mathrm{E}\left(\hat{d}_{gm,c}\right) = d$.
- Its variance is (for $k > 2$)

$$\mathrm{Var}\left(\hat{d}_{gm,c}\right) = d^2 \left(\frac{\cos^{2k}\left(\frac{\pi}{2k}\right)}{\cos^k\left(\frac{\pi}{k}\right)} - 1\right) = \frac{\pi^2}{4} \frac{d^2}{k} + \frac{\pi^4}{32} \frac{d^2}{k^2} + O\left(\frac{1}{k^3}\right). \tag{12}$$

- For $0 \leq \epsilon \leq 1$, its tail bounds can be represented in exponential forms

$$\mathbf{Pr}\left(\left|\hat{d}_{gm,c} - d\right| > \epsilon d\right) \leq 2\exp\left(-k\left(\frac{\epsilon^2}{8(1+\epsilon)}\right)\right), \quad k \geq \frac{\pi^2}{1.5\epsilon} \tag{13}$$

- An analog of the JL Lemma for dimension reduction in l_1:
  If $k \geq \frac{8(2\log n - \log \delta)}{\epsilon^2/(1+\epsilon)} \geq \frac{\pi^2}{1.5\epsilon}$, then with probability at least $1 - \delta$, one can recover the original l_1 distance between any pair of data points (among all n data points) within $1 \pm \epsilon$ ($0 \leq \epsilon \leq 1$) fraction of the truth, using $\hat{d}_{gm,c}$.

3.3   The Bias-Corrected Maximum Likelihood Estimator

Denoted by $\hat{d}_{MLE,c}$, the bias-corrected maximum likelihood estimator (MLE) is

$$\hat{d}_{MLE,c} = \hat{d}_{MLE} \left(1 - \frac{1}{k} \right), \tag{14}$$

where $\hat{d}_{MLE}$ solves a nonlinear MLE equation

$$-\frac{k}{\hat{d}_{MLE}} + \sum_{j=1}^{k} \frac{2\hat{d}_{MLE}}{x_j^2 + \hat{d}_{MLE}^2} = 0. \tag{15}$$

- It is nearly unbiased, $E\left(\hat{d}_{MLE,c}\right) = d + O\left(\frac{1}{k^2}\right)$.
- Its asymptotic variance is

$$\text{Var}\left(\hat{d}_{MLE,c}\right) = \frac{2d^2}{k} + \frac{3d^2}{k^2} + O\left(\frac{1}{k^3}\right), \tag{16}$$

i.e., $\frac{\text{Var}(\hat{d}_{MLE,c})}{\text{Var}(\hat{d}_{me,c})} \to \frac{8}{\pi^2}$, $\frac{\text{Var}(\hat{d}_{MLE,c})}{\text{Var}(\hat{d}_{gm,c})} \to \frac{8}{\pi^2}$, as $k \to \infty$. ($\frac{8}{\pi^2} \approx 80\%$)

- Its distribution can be accurately approximated by an inverse Gaussian, from which the following approximate tail bound follows

$$\mathbf{Pr}\left(\left| \hat{d}_{MLE,c} - d \right| \geq \epsilon d \right) \overset{\sim}{\leq} 2\exp\left(-\frac{\epsilon^2/(1+\epsilon)}{2\left(\frac{2}{k} + \frac{3}{k^2}\right)} \right), \quad 0 \leq \epsilon \leq 1. \tag{17}$$

4   The Sample Median Estimators

Recall in Cauchy random projections, the problem boils down to estimating the l_1 distance $d = \sum_{i=1}^{D} |u_{1,i} - u_{2,i}|$ from $\{x_j\}_{j=1}^{k}$, $x_j = v_{1,j} - v_{2,j} \sim C(0, d)$, i.i.d. The sample median estimator, suggested in [3],

$$\hat{d}_{me} = \text{median}\{|x_j|, j = 1, 2, ..., k\}, \tag{18}$$

is a special case of sample quantile estimators [17].

Lemma 1 follows from known statistical properties of the sample quantiles.

Lemma 1. *The sample median estimator, $\hat{d}_{me}$, is asymptotically (as $k \to \infty$) unbiased and normal*

$$\sqrt{k}\left(\hat{d}_{me} - d\right) \overset{D}{\Longrightarrow} N\left(0, \frac{\pi^2}{4}d^2\right) \tag{19}$$

When $k = 2m + 1$, $m = 1, 2, 3, ...$, the rth moment of $\hat{d}_{me}$ would be

$$E\left(\hat{d}_{me}\right)^r = d^r \left(\int_0^1 \frac{(2m+1)!}{(m!)^2} \tan^r\left(\frac{\pi}{2}t\right) \left(t - t^2\right)^m dt \right), \quad m \geq r \tag{20}$$

If $m < r$, then $E\left(\hat{d}_{me}\right)^r = \infty$.

For simplicity, we only consider $k = 2m+1$ when evaluating $E\left(\hat{d}_{me}\right)^r$. Once we know $E\left(\hat{d}_{me}\right)$, we can remove the bias of $\hat{d}_{me}$ using

$$\hat{d}_{me,c} = \frac{\hat{d}_{me}}{b_{me}}, \tag{21}$$

where b_{me}, which can be numerically evaluated and tabulated, is

$$b_{me} = \frac{E\left(\hat{d}_{me}\right)}{d} = \int_0^1 \frac{(2m+1)!}{(m!)^2} \tan\left(\frac{\pi}{2}t\right) \left(t - t^2\right)^m dt. \tag{22}$$

Therefore, $\hat{d}_{me,c}$ is unbiased, i.e., $E\left(\hat{d}_{me,c}\right) = d$. Its variance would be

$$\mathrm{Var}\left(\hat{d}_{me,c}\right) = d^2 \left(\frac{(m!)^2}{(2m+1)!} \frac{\int_0^1 \tan^2\left(\frac{\pi}{2}t\right) \left(t - t^2\right)^m dt}{\left(\int_0^1 \tan\left(\frac{\pi}{2}t\right) \left(t - t^2\right)^m dt\right)^2} - 1 \right). \tag{23}$$

5   The Geometric Mean Estimators

The estimators based on the geometric mean are more accurate than the sample median estimators and allow us to derive tail bounds in explicit forms.

Lemma 2. *Assume* $x \sim C(0,d)$. *Then*

$$E\left(|x|^\lambda\right) = \frac{d^\lambda}{\cos(\lambda\pi/2)}, \qquad |\lambda| < 1. \tag{24}$$

Proof. Assume $x \sim C(0,d)$. *Using the integral tables [18, 3.221.1, page 337],*

$$E\left(|x|^\lambda\right) = \frac{2d}{\pi} \int_0^\infty \frac{y^\lambda}{y^2 + d^2} dy = \frac{d^\lambda}{\pi} \int_0^\infty \frac{y^{\frac{\lambda-1}{2}}}{y+1} dy = \frac{d^\lambda}{\cos(\lambda\pi/2)}. \tag{25}$$

From Lemma 2, by taking $\lambda = \frac{1}{k}$, we obtain an unbiased estimator based on the geometric mean in the next Lemma, proved in Appendix A.

Lemma 3

$$\hat{d}_{gm,c} = \cos^k\left(\frac{\pi}{2k}\right) \prod_{j=1}^k |x_j|^{1/k}, \quad k > 1 \tag{26}$$

is unbiased, with the variance (valid when $k > 2$)

$$\mathrm{Var}\left(\hat{d}_{gm,c}\right) = d^2 \left(\frac{\cos^{2k}\left(\frac{\pi}{2k}\right)}{\cos^k\left(\frac{\pi}{k}\right)} - 1 \right) = \frac{d^2}{k} \frac{\pi^2}{4} + \frac{\pi^4}{32} \frac{d^2}{k^2} + O\left(\frac{1}{k^3}\right). \tag{27}$$

The third and fourth central moments are (for $k > 3$ and $k > 4$, respectively)

$$E\left(\hat{d}_{gm,c} - E\left(\hat{d}_{gm,c}\right)\right)^3 = \frac{3\pi^4}{16}\frac{d^3}{k^2} + O\left(\frac{1}{k^3}\right) \tag{28}$$

$$E\left(\hat{d}_{gm,c} - E\left(\hat{d}_{gm,c}\right)\right)^4 = \frac{3\pi^4}{16}\frac{d^4}{k^2} + O\left(\frac{1}{k^3}\right). \tag{29}$$

The higher (third or fourth) moments may be useful for approximating the distribution of $\hat{d}_{gm,c}$. In Section 6, we approximate the distribution of the maximum likelihood estimator by matching the first four moments. We could apply the similar technique to approximate $\hat{d}_{gm,c}$. Fortunately, we are able to derive the tail bounds of $\hat{d}_{gm,c}$ in Lemma 4, proved in Appendix B.

Lemma 4

$$\mathbf{Pr}\left(\hat{d}_{gm,c} \geq (1+\epsilon)d\right) \leq \frac{\cos^{kt_1^*}\left(\frac{\pi}{2k}\right)}{\cos^k\left(\frac{\pi t_1^*}{2k}\right)(1+\epsilon)^{t_1^*}}, \qquad \epsilon \geq 0 \tag{30}$$

$$t_1^* = \frac{2k}{\pi}\tan^{-1}\left(\left(\log(1+\epsilon) - k\log\cos\left(\frac{\pi}{2k}\right)\right)\frac{2}{\pi}\right). \tag{31}$$

$$\mathbf{Pr}\left(\hat{d}_{gm,c} \leq (1-\epsilon)d\right) \leq \frac{(1-\epsilon)^{t_2^*}}{\cos^k\left(\frac{\pi t_2^*}{2k}\right)\cos^{kt_2^*}\left(\frac{\pi}{2k}\right)}, \qquad 0 \leq \epsilon \leq 1, \quad k \geq \frac{\pi^2}{8\epsilon} \tag{32}$$

$$t_2^* = \frac{2k}{\pi}\tan^{-1}\left(\left(-\log(1-\epsilon) + k\log\cos\left(\frac{\pi}{2k}\right)\right)\frac{2}{\pi}\right). \tag{33}$$

By restricting $0 \leq \epsilon \leq 1$, the tail bounds can be written in exponential forms:

$$\mathbf{Pr}\left(\hat{d}_{gm,c} \geq (1+\epsilon)d\right) \leq \exp\left(-k\frac{\epsilon^2}{8(1+\epsilon)}\right) \tag{34}$$

$$\mathbf{Pr}\left(\hat{d}_{gm,c} \leq (1-\epsilon)d\right) \leq \exp\left(-k\frac{\epsilon^2}{8(1+\epsilon)}\right), \qquad k \geq \frac{\pi^2}{1.5\epsilon} \tag{35}$$

An analog of the JL bound for l_1 follows directly from (34)(35).

Lemma 5. *Using $\hat{d}_{gm,c}$ with $k \geq \frac{8(2\log n - \log \delta)}{\epsilon^2/(1+\epsilon)} \geq \frac{\pi^2}{1.5\epsilon}$, then with probability at least $1 - \delta$, the l_1 distance, d, between any pair of data points (among n data points), can be estimated with errors bounded by $\pm\epsilon d$, i.e., $|\hat{d}_{gm,c} - d| \leq \epsilon d$.*

Figure 1 compares $\hat{d}_{gm,c}$ with the sample median estimators $\hat{d}_{me}$ and $\hat{d}_{me,c}$, in terms of the mean square errors (MSE). $\hat{d}_{gm,c}$ is considerably more accurate than $\hat{d}_{me}$ at small k. The bias correction significantly reduces the mean square errors of $\hat{d}_{me}$.

6   The Maximum Likelihood Estimators

The maximum likelihood estimators (MLE) are asymptotically optimum (in term of the variance), while the sample median and geometric mean estimators

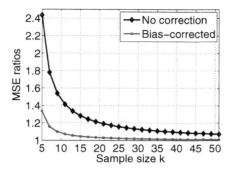

Fig. 1. The ratios of the mean square errors (MSE), $\frac{\mathrm{MSE}(\hat{d}_{me})}{\mathrm{MSE}(\hat{d}_{gm,c})}$ and $\frac{\mathrm{MSE}(\hat{d}_{me,c})}{\mathrm{MSE}(\hat{d}_{gm,c})}$, demonstrate that the bias-corrected geometric mean estimator $\hat{d}_{gm,c}$ is considerably more accurate than the sample median estimator $\hat{d}_{me}$. The bias correction on $\hat{d}_{me}$ considerably reduces the MSE.

are not. The method of maximum likelihood is widely used. For example, [15] applied the maximum likelihood method to improve *normal random projections*.

Given k i.i.d. samples $x_j \sim C(0, d), j = 1, 2, ..., k$, it is easy to show that the maximum likelihood estimator of d, denoted by $\hat{d}_{MLE}$, is the solution to

$$-\frac{k}{\hat{d}_{MLE}} + \sum_{j=1}^{k} \frac{2\hat{d}_{MLE}}{x_j^2 + \hat{d}_{MLE}^2} = 0. \tag{36}$$

For better accuracy, we recommend the following bias-corrected estimator:

$$\hat{d}_{MLE,c} = \hat{d}_{MLE}\left(1 - \frac{1}{k}\right). \tag{37}$$

Lemma 6 concerns the asymptotic moments $\hat{d}_{MLE,c}$, proved in Appendix C.

Lemma 6. *The first four moments of* $\hat{d}_{MLE,c}$ *are*

$$E\left(\hat{d}_{MLE,c} - d\right) = O\left(\frac{1}{k^2}\right) \tag{38}$$

$$Var\left(\hat{d}_{MLE,c}\right) = \frac{2d^2}{k} + \frac{3d^2}{k^2} + O\left(\frac{1}{k^3}\right) \tag{39}$$

$$E\left(\hat{d}_{MLE,c} - E(\hat{d}_{MLE,c})\right)^3 = \frac{12d^3}{k^2} + O\left(\frac{1}{k^3}\right) \tag{40}$$

$$E\left(\hat{d}_{MLE,c} - E(\hat{d}_{MLE,c})\right)^4 = \frac{12d^4}{k^2} + \frac{186d^4}{k^3} + O\left(\frac{1}{k^4}\right). \tag{41}$$

6.1   The Inverse Gaussian Approximation

Theoretical analysis on the exact distribution of the MLE is difficult. The standard approach is to assume normality, which, of course, is quite inaccurate. The

Edgeworth expansion improves the normal approximation by matching higher moments, which, however, is sophisticated and not accurate at the tails. The approximate probability may have values below zero. Also, Edgeworth expansions consider the support to be $(-\infty, \infty)$, while $\hat{d}_{MLE,c}$ is non-negative.

We propose approximating the distributions of $\hat{d}_{MLE,c}$ by a *generalized gamma distribution*, which allows us to match the support $[0, \infty)$ and the first three (asymptotic) moments of $\hat{d}_{MLE,c}$. Interestingly, in this case, the generalized gamma approximation turns out to be an inverse Gaussian, which also (almost) matches the fourth central moment of $\hat{d}_{MLE,c}$. By simulations, the inverse Gaussian approximation is highly accurate. As the related work, [19] applied generalized gamma approximations to model the performance measure distribution in some wireless communication channels.

The generalized gamma distribution [19] is denoted by $GG(\alpha, \beta, \eta)$. (The usual gamma distribution is a special case with $\eta = 1$.) If $z \sim GG(\alpha, \beta, \eta)$, then

$$\mathrm{E}(z) = \alpha\beta, \quad \mathrm{Var}(z) = \alpha\beta^2, \quad \mathrm{E}\left(z - \mathrm{E}(z)\right)^3 = \alpha\beta^3(1 + \eta). \quad (42)$$

We approximate the distribution of $\hat{d}_{MLE,c}$ by matching the first three moments,

$$\alpha\beta = d, \quad \alpha\beta^2 = \frac{2d^2}{k} + \frac{3d^2}{k^2}, \quad \alpha\beta^3(1 + \eta) = \frac{12d^3}{k^2}, \quad (43)$$

from which we obtain

$$\alpha = \frac{1}{\frac{2}{k} + \frac{3}{k^2}}, \quad \beta = \frac{2d}{k} + \frac{3d}{k^2}, \quad \eta = 2 + O\left(\frac{1}{k}\right). \quad (44)$$

Taking the leading term, the generalized gamma approximation $GG(\alpha, \beta, \eta = 2)$ is an inverse Gaussian (IG) distribution. Assuming $\hat{d}_{MLE,c} \sim IG(\alpha, \beta)$, with parameters α and β defined in (44), the moment generating function (MGF) and cumulative density function (CDF) would be [20, Chapter 2] [19]

$$\mathrm{E}\left(\exp(\hat{d}_{MLE,c}t)\right) \stackrel{\sim}{=} \exp\left(\alpha\left(1 - (1 - 2\beta t)^{1/2}\right)\right), \quad (45)$$

$$\mathbf{Pr}\left(\hat{d}_{MLE,c} \leq y\right) \stackrel{\sim}{=} \Phi\left(\sqrt{\frac{\alpha d}{y}}\left(\frac{y}{d} - 1\right)\right) + e^{2\alpha}\Phi\left(-\sqrt{\frac{\alpha d}{y}}\left(\frac{y}{d} + 1\right)\right), \quad (46)$$

where $\Phi(.)$ is the standard normal CDF. Here we use $\stackrel{\sim}{=}$ to indicate that these equalities are based on an approximate distribution.

Assuming $\hat{d}_{MLE,c} \sim IG(\alpha, \beta)$, the fourth central moment should be

$$\mathrm{E}\left(\hat{d}_{MLE,c} - \mathrm{E}\left(\hat{d}_{MLE,c}\right)\right)^4 \stackrel{\sim}{=} 15\alpha\beta^4 + 3\left(\alpha\beta^2\right)^2 = \frac{12d^4}{k^2} + \frac{156d^4}{k^3} + O\left(\frac{1}{k^4}\right), \quad (47)$$

which matches not only the leading term, $\frac{12d^4}{k^2}$, but also almost the higher order term, $\frac{186d^4}{k^3}$, of the true asymptotic fourth moment of $\hat{d}_{MLE,c}$ in Lemma 6.

Assuming $\hat{d}_{MLE,c} \sim IG(\alpha, \beta)$, the tail probability of $\hat{d}_{MLE,c}$ would be

$$\mathbf{Pr}\left(\hat{d}_{MLE,c} \geq (1+\epsilon)d\right) \cong \Phi\left(-\epsilon\sqrt{\frac{\alpha}{1+\epsilon}}\right) - e^{2\alpha}\Phi\left(-(2+\epsilon)\sqrt{\frac{\alpha}{1+\epsilon}}\right), \quad \epsilon \geq 0 \quad (48)$$

$$\mathbf{Pr}\left(\hat{d}_{MLE,c} \leq (1-\epsilon)d\right) \cong \Phi\left(-\epsilon\sqrt{\frac{\alpha}{1-\epsilon}}\right) + e^{2\alpha}\Phi\left(-(2-\epsilon)\sqrt{\frac{\alpha}{1-\epsilon}}\right), \quad 0 \leq \epsilon < 1. \quad (49)$$

Assuming $\hat{d}_{MLE,c} \sim IG(\alpha, \beta)$, it is easy to show the Chernoff bounds:

$$\mathbf{Pr}\left(\hat{d}_{MLE,c} \geq (1+\epsilon)d\right) \overset{\sim}{\leq} \exp\left(-\frac{\alpha\epsilon^2}{2(1+\epsilon)}\right), \quad \epsilon \geq 0 \quad (50)$$

$$\mathbf{Pr}\left(\hat{d}_{MLE,c} \leq (1-\epsilon)d\right) \overset{\sim}{\leq} \exp\left(-\frac{\alpha\epsilon^2}{2(1-\epsilon)}\right), \quad 0 \leq \epsilon < 1. \quad (51)$$

Combining (50) and (51) yields a symmetric bound

$$\mathbf{Pr}\left(|\hat{d}_{MLE,c} - d| \geq \epsilon d\right) \overset{\sim}{\leq} 2\exp\left(-\frac{\epsilon^2/(1+\epsilon)}{2\left(\frac{2}{k} + \frac{3}{k^2}\right)}\right), \quad 0 \leq \epsilon \leq 1 \quad (52)$$

Figure 2 compares the inverse Gaussian approximation with simulations, indicating that the approximation is highly accurate. The upper bounds (50) + (51) are always reliable in our simulation range (the tail probability $\geq 10^{-10}$).

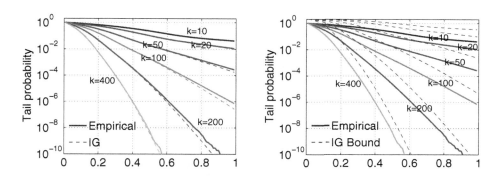

Fig. 2. Verify the inverse Gaussian approximation by simulations. The left panel compares the empirical tail probabilities with the inverse Gaussian tail probabilities, indicating that the approximation is highly accurate. The right panel compares the empirical tail probabilities with the inverse Gaussian upper bound (50)+(51). The upper bounds are all above the corresponding empirical curves, indicating that our proposed bounds are reliable at least in our simulation range.

7   Conclusion

Dimension reduction in the l_1 norm has been proved *impossible* if we use *linear projections* and *linear estimators*. We propose three types of nonlinear estimators for *Cauchy random projections*. The bias-corrected sample median estimator and the bias-corrected geometric mean estimator are asymptotically equivalent but the latter is more accurate at small sample size. We have derived explicit tail bounds for the bias-corrected geometric mean estimator in exponential forms and have established an analog of the Johnson-Lindenstrauss (JL) Lemma for dimension reduction in l_1, which is weaker than the classical JL Lemma for dimension reduction in l_2.

Both the sample median estimator and the geometric mean estimator are about 80% efficient as the bias-corrected maximum likelihood estimator (MLE). We propose approximating the distribution of the MLE by an inverse Gaussian, which has the same support and matches the leading terms of the first four moments of the MLE. Approximate tail bounds have been provided, which, as verified by simulations, hold at least in the $\geq 10^{-10}$ tail probability range.

Although these nonlinear estimators are not metrics, they are useful for certain applications in (e.g.,) data stream computation, information retrieval, learning and data mining, whenever the goal is to compute the l_1 distances efficiently using a small space.

Recently, [4] extended the geometric mean estimator to the stable distribution family, for dimension reduction in l_p ($0 < p \leq 2$). [4] also proposed a *harmonic mean* estimator for $p \to 0+$, useful for approximating the Hamming distances. In addition, [4] suggested *very sparse stable random projections* to considerably simplify sampling from $\mathbf{R}$ and to significantly speed up computing $\mathbf{A} \times \mathbf{R}$.

Acknowledgment

We are grateful to Piotr Indyk and Assaf Naor. We thank the local chair of COLT2006 for letting us present the main results of this paper in the Impromptu Session. We also thank the four anonymous reviewers for their helpful comments.

References

1. Zhu, J., Rosset, S., Hastie, T., Tibshirani, R.: 1-norm support vector machines. In: NIPS, Vancouver, BC, Canada (2003)
2. Chapelle, O., Haffner, P., Vapnik, V.N.: Support vector machines for histogram-based image classification. IEEE Trans. Neural Networks 10, 1055–1064 (1999)
3. Indyk, P.: Stable distributions, pseudorandom generators, embeddings, and data stream computation. Journal of ACM 53, 307–323 (2006)
4. Li, P.: Very sparse stable random projections, estimators and tail bounds for stable random projections. Technical report, http://arxiv.org/PS_cache/cs/pdf/0611/0611114.pdf (2006)
5. Zolotarev, V.M.: One-dimensional Stable Distributions. American Mathematical Society, Providence, RI (1986)

6. Vempala, S.: The Random Projection Method. American Mathematical Society, Providence, RI (2004)
7. Johnson, W.B., Lindenstrauss, J.: Extensions of Lipschitz mapping into Hilbert space. Contemporary Mathematics 26, 189–206 (1984)
8. Lee, J.R., Naor, A.: Embedding the diamond graph in l_p and dimension reduction in l_1. Geometric And. Functional Analysis 14, 745–747 (2004)
9. Brinkman, B., Charikar, M.: On the impossibility of dimension reduction in l_1. Journal of ACM 52, 766–788 (2005)
10. Babcock, B., Babu, S., Datar, M., Motwani, R., Widom, J.: Models and issues in data stream systems. In: PODS, Madison, WI, pp. 1–16 (2002)
11. Li, P., Church, K.W.: Using sketches to estimate associations. In: HLT/EMNLP, Vancouver, BC, Canada, pp. 708–715 ((2005)
12. Li, P., Church, K.W., Hastie, T.J.: Conditional random sampling: A sketch-based sampling technique for sparse data. In: NIPS, Vancouver, BC, Canada (2007)
13. Li, P., Church, K.W.: A sketch algorithm for estimating two-way and multi-way associations. Computational Linguistics, To Appear (2007)
14. Achlioptas, D.: Database-friendly random projections: Johnson-Lindenstrauss with binary coins. Journal of Computer and System Sciences 66, 671–687 (2003)
15. Li, P., Hastie, T.J., Church, K.W.: Improving random projections using marginal information. In: COLT, Pittsburgh, PA, pp. 635–649 (2006)
16. Arriaga, R., Vempala, S.: An algorithmic theory of learning: Robust concepts and random projection. Machine Learning 63, 161–182 (2006)
17. Fama, E.F., Roll, R.: Parameter estimates for symmetric stable distributions. Journal of the American Statistical Association 66, 331–338 (1971)
18. Gradshteyn, I.S., Ryzhik, I.M.: Table of Integrals, Series, and Products, 5th edn. Academic Press, London (1994)
19. Li, P., Paul, D., Narasimhan, R., Cioffi, J.: On the distribution of SINR for the MMSE MIMO receiver and performance analysis. IEEE Trans. Inform. Theory 52, 271–286 (2006)
20. Seshadri, V.: The Inverse Gaussian Distribution: A Case Study in Exponential Families. Oxford University Press, New York (1993)
21. Philips, T.K., Nelson, R.: The moment bound is tighter than Chernoff's bound for positive tail probabilities. The American Statistician 49, 175–178 (1995)
22. Lugosi, G.: Concentration-of-measure inequalities. Lecture Notes (2004)
23. Shenton, L.R., Bowman, K.: Higher moments of a maximum-likelihood estimate. Journal of Royal Statistical Society B 25, 305–317 (1963)

A   Proof of Lemma 3

Assume that x_1, x_2, ..., x_k, are i.i.d. $C(0, d)$. The estimator, $\hat{d}_{gm,c}$, expressed as

$$\hat{d}_{gm,c} = \cos^k \left(\frac{\pi}{2k} \right) \prod_{j=1}^{k} |x_j|^{1/k},$$

is unbiased, because, from Lemma 2,

$$\mathrm{E}\left(\hat{d}_{gm,c} \right) = \cos^k \left(\frac{\pi}{2k} \right) \prod_{j=1}^{k} \mathrm{E}\left(|x_j|^{1/k} \right) = \cos^k \left(\frac{\pi}{2k} \right) \prod_{j=1}^{k} \left(\frac{d^{1/k}}{\cos \left(\frac{\pi}{2k} \right)} \right) = d.$$

The variance is

$$\mathrm{Var}\left(\hat{d}_{gm,c}\right) = \cos^{2k}\left(\frac{\pi}{2k}\right)\prod_{j=1}^{k}\mathrm{E}\left(|x_j|^{2/k}\right) - d^2$$

$$= d^2\left(\frac{\cos^{2k}\left(\frac{\pi}{2k}\right)}{\cos^{k}\left(\frac{\pi}{k}\right)} - 1\right) = \frac{\pi^2}{4}\frac{d^2}{k} + \frac{\pi^4}{32}\frac{d^2}{k^2} + O\left(\frac{1}{k^3}\right),$$

because

$$\frac{\cos^{2k}\left(\frac{\pi}{2k}\right)}{\cos^{k}\left(\frac{\pi}{k}\right)} = \left(\frac{1}{2}+\frac{1}{2}\left(\frac{1}{\cos(\pi/k)}\right)\right)^k = \left(1+\frac{1}{4}\frac{\pi^2}{k^2}+\frac{5}{48}\frac{\pi^4}{k^4}+O\left(\frac{1}{k^6}\right)\right)^k$$

$$= 1 + k\left(\frac{1}{4}\frac{\pi^2}{k^2}+\frac{5}{48}\frac{\pi^4}{k^4}\right) + \frac{k(k-1)}{2}\left(\frac{1}{4}\frac{\pi^2}{k^2}+\frac{5}{48}\frac{\pi^4}{k^4}\right)^2 + \dots$$

$$= 1 + \frac{\pi^2}{4}\frac{1}{k}+\frac{\pi^4}{32}\frac{1}{k^2}+O\left(\frac{1}{k^3}\right).$$

Some more algebra can similarly show the third and fourth central moments:

$$\mathrm{E}\left(\hat{d}_{gm,c}-\mathrm{E}\left(\hat{d}_{gm,c}\right)\right)^3 = \frac{3\pi^4}{16}\frac{d^3}{k^2}+O\left(\frac{1}{k^3}\right)$$

$$\mathrm{E}\left(\hat{d}_{gm,c}-\mathrm{E}\left(\hat{d}_{gm,c}\right)\right)^4 = \frac{3\pi^4}{16}\frac{d^4}{k^2}+O\left(\frac{1}{k^3}\right).$$

B   Proof of Lemma 4

As $\hat{d}_{gm,c}$ does not have a bounded moment generating function, we will use the Markov moment bound.[1] For $\epsilon \geq 0$ and $0 \leq t < k$, the Markov inequality says

$$\mathbf{Pr}\left(\hat{d}_{gm,c}\geq(1+\epsilon)d\right) \leq \frac{\mathrm{E}\left(\hat{d}_{gm,c}\right)^t}{(1+\epsilon)^t d^t} = \frac{\cos^{kt}\left(\frac{\pi}{2k}\right)}{\cos^k\left(\frac{\pi t}{2k}\right)(1+\epsilon)^t},$$

which can be minimized by choosing the optimum $t = t_1^*$, where

$$t_1^* = \frac{2k}{\pi}\tan^{-1}\left(\left(\log(1+\epsilon)-k\log\cos\left(\frac{\pi}{2k}\right)\right)\frac{2}{\pi}\right).$$

By Taylor expansions, t_1^* can be well approximated by $t_1^* \approx \frac{4k\epsilon}{\pi^2}+\frac{1}{2} \approx \frac{4k\epsilon}{\pi^2} = t_1^{**}$, at small ϵ. Therefore, for $0 \leq \epsilon \leq 1$, taking $t = t_1^{**} = \frac{4k\epsilon}{\pi^2}$, the tail bound becomes

$$\mathbf{Pr}\left(\hat{d}_{gm,c}\geq(1+\epsilon)d\right)$$

$$\leq \frac{\cos^{kt_1^{**}}\left(\frac{\pi}{2k}\right)}{\cos^k\left(\frac{\pi t_1^{**}}{2k}\right)(1+\epsilon)^{t_1^{**}}} = \left(\frac{\cos^{t_1^{**}}\left(\frac{\pi}{2k}\right)}{\cos\left(\frac{2\epsilon}{\pi}\right)(1+\epsilon)^{4\epsilon/\pi^2}}\right)^k \leq \left(\frac{1}{\cos\left(\frac{2\epsilon}{\pi}\right)(1+\epsilon)^{4\epsilon/\pi^2}}\right)^k$$

$$= \exp\left(-k\left(\log\left(\cos\left(\frac{2\epsilon}{\pi}\right)\right)+\frac{4\epsilon}{\pi^2}\log(1+\epsilon)\right)\right) \leq \exp\left(-k\frac{\epsilon^2}{8(1+\epsilon)}\right). \qquad (53)$$

---

[1] When the moment generating function does exist, for any positive random variable, the Markov moment bound is always sharper than the Chernoff bound. See [21,22].

The last step in (53) needs some explanations. First, by the Taylor expansion,

$$\log\left(\cos\left(\frac{2\epsilon}{\pi}\right)\right) + \frac{4\epsilon}{\pi^2}\log(1+\epsilon)$$

$$= \left(-\frac{2\epsilon^2}{\pi^2} - \frac{4}{3}\frac{\epsilon^4}{\pi^4} + ...\right) + \frac{4\epsilon}{\pi^2}\left(\epsilon - \frac{1}{2}\epsilon^2 + ...\right) = \frac{2\epsilon^2}{\pi^2}(1 - \epsilon + ...)$$

Therefore, we can seek the smallest constant γ_1 so that

$$\log\left(\cos\left(\frac{2\epsilon}{\pi}\right)\right) + \frac{4\epsilon}{\pi^2}\log(1+\epsilon) \geq \frac{\epsilon^2}{\gamma_1(1+\epsilon)} = \frac{\epsilon^2}{\gamma_1}(1 - \epsilon + ...)$$

Figure 3(a) illustrates that $\gamma_1 = 8$ suffices, which can be numerically verified.

Now we need to show the other tail bound $\mathbf{Pr}\left(\hat{d}_{gm,c} \leq (1-\epsilon)d\right)$:

$$\mathbf{Pr}\left(\hat{d}_{gm,c} \leq (1-\epsilon)d\right) = \mathbf{Pr}\left(\cos\left(\frac{\pi}{2k}\right)^k \prod_{j=1}^{k}|x_j|^{1/k} \leq (1-\epsilon)d\right)$$

$$= \mathbf{Pr}\left(\sum_{j=1}^{k}\log\left(|x_j|^{1/k}\right) \leq \log\left(\frac{(1-\epsilon)d}{\cos^k\left(\frac{\pi}{2k}\right)}\right)\right)$$

$$= \mathbf{Pr}\left(\exp\left(\sum_{j=1}^{k}\log\left(|x_j|^{-t/k}\right)\right) \geq \exp\left(-t\log\left(\frac{(1-\epsilon)d}{\cos^k\left(\frac{\pi}{2k}\right)}\right)\right)\right), \qquad 0 \leq t < k$$

$$\leq \left(\frac{(1-\epsilon)}{\cos^k\left(\frac{\pi}{2k}\right)}\right)^t \frac{1}{\cos^k\left(\frac{\pi t}{2k}\right)},$$

which is minimized at $t = t_2^*$ (provided $k \geq \frac{\pi^2}{8\epsilon}$)

$$t_2^* = \frac{2k}{\pi}\tan^{-1}\left(\left(-\log(1-\epsilon) + k\log\cos\left(\frac{\pi}{2k}\right)\right)\frac{2}{\pi}\right).$$

Again, t_2^* can be replaced by its approximation $t_2^* \approx t_2^{**} = \frac{4k\epsilon}{\pi^2}$. Thus,

$$\mathbf{Pr}\left(\hat{d}_{gm,c} \leq (1-\epsilon)d\right) \leq \left(\frac{(1-\epsilon)}{\cos^k\left(\frac{\pi}{2k}\right)}\right)^{t_2^{**}} \frac{1}{\cos^k\left(\frac{\pi t_2^{**}}{2k}\right)}$$

$$= \exp\left(-k\left(\log\left(\cos\frac{2\epsilon}{\pi}\right) - \frac{4\epsilon}{\pi^2}\log(1-\epsilon) + \frac{4k\epsilon}{\pi^2}\log\left(\cos\frac{\pi}{2k}\right)\right)\right).$$

We bound $\frac{4k\epsilon}{\pi^2}\log\left(\cos\frac{\pi}{2k}\right)$ by restricting k. To attain $\mathbf{Pr}\left(\hat{d}_{gm,c} \leq (1-\epsilon)d\right) \leq \exp\left(-k\left(\frac{\epsilon^2}{8(1+\epsilon)}\right)\right)$, we have to restrict k to be larger than a certain value. We find $k \geq \frac{\pi^2}{1.5\epsilon}$ suffices. If $k \geq \frac{\pi^2}{1.5\epsilon}$, then $\frac{4k\epsilon}{\pi^2}\log\left(\cos\frac{\pi}{2k}\right) \geq \frac{8}{3}\log\left(\cos\frac{\epsilon}{3\pi}\right)$. Thus,

$$\mathbf{Pr}\left(\hat{d}_{gm,c} \leq (1-\epsilon)d\right) \leq \exp\left(-k\left(\log\left(\cos\frac{2\epsilon}{\pi}\right) - \frac{4\epsilon}{\pi^2}\log(1-\epsilon) + \frac{8}{3}\log\left(\cos\frac{\epsilon}{3\pi}\right)\right)\right)$$

$$\leq \exp\left(-k\frac{\epsilon^2}{8(1+\epsilon)}\right), \qquad \left(k \geq \frac{\pi^2}{1.5\epsilon}\right) \tag{54}$$

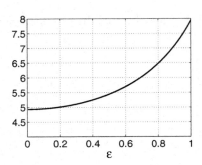 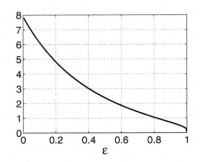

Fig. 3. Left: $\dfrac{\epsilon^2/(1+\epsilon)}{\log\left(\cos\left(\frac{2\epsilon}{\pi}\right)\right)+\frac{4\epsilon}{\pi^2}\log(1+\epsilon)}$ v.s. ϵ. Right: $\dfrac{\epsilon^2/(1+\epsilon)}{\log\left(\cos\frac{2\epsilon}{\pi}\right)-\frac{4\epsilon}{\pi^2}\log(1-\epsilon)+\frac{8}{3}\log\left(\cos\frac{\epsilon}{3\pi}\right)}$
v.s. ϵ. It suffices to use a constant 8 in (53) and (54). The optimal constant will be
different for different ϵ. For example, if $\epsilon = 0.2$, we could replace the constant 8 by 5.

C   Proof of Lemma 6

Assume $x \sim C(0, d)$. The log likelihood $l(x; d)$ and its first three derivatives are

$$l(x; d) = \log(d) - \log(\pi) - \log(x^2 + d^2), \qquad l'(d) = \frac{1}{d} - \frac{2d}{x^2 + d^2}$$

$$l''(d) = -\frac{1}{d^2} - \frac{2x^2 - 2d^2}{(x^2 + d^2)^2}, \qquad l'''(d) = \frac{2}{d^3} + \frac{4d}{(x^2 + d^2)^2} + \frac{8d(x^2 - d^2)}{(x^2 + d^2)^3}.$$

For the bias and higher moments of the MLE, we need to evaluate [23, 16a-16d]:

$$\mathrm{E}\left(\hat{d}_{MLE}\right) = d - \frac{[12]}{2kI^2} + O\left(\frac{1}{k^2}\right)$$

$$\mathrm{Var}\left(\hat{d}_{MLE}\right) = \frac{1}{kI} + \frac{1}{k^2}\left(-\frac{1}{I} + \frac{[1^4] - [1^22] - [13]}{I^3} + \frac{3.5[12]^2 - [1^3]^2}{I^4}\right) + O\left(\frac{1}{k^3}\right)$$

$$\mathrm{E}\left(\hat{d}_{MLE} - \mathrm{E}\left(\hat{d}_{MLE}\right)\right)^3 = \frac{[1^3] - 3[12]}{k^2I^2} + O\left(\frac{1}{k^3}\right)$$

$$\mathrm{E}\left(\hat{d}_{MLE} - \mathrm{E}\left(\hat{d}_{MLE}\right)\right)^4 = \frac{3}{k^2I^2} + \frac{1}{k^3}\left(-\frac{9}{I^2} + \frac{7[1^4] - 6[1^22] - 10[13]}{I^4}\right)$$
$$+ \frac{1}{k^3}\left(\frac{-6[1^3]^2 - 12[1^3][12] + 45[12]^2}{I^5}\right) + O\left(\frac{1}{k^4}\right),$$

where

$$[12] = \mathrm{E}(l')^3 + \mathrm{E}(l'l''), \qquad [1^4] = \mathrm{E}(l')^4, \qquad [1^22] = \mathrm{E}(l''(l')^2) + \mathrm{E}(l')^4,$$

$$[13] = \mathrm{E}(l')^4 + 3\mathrm{E}(l''(l')^2) + \mathrm{E}(l'l'''), \qquad [1^3] = \mathrm{E}(l')^3.$$

Without giving the detail, we report

$$\mathrm{E}\left(l'\right)^3 = 0, \qquad \mathrm{E}\left(l'l''\right) = -\frac{1}{2}\frac{1}{d^3}, \qquad \mathrm{E}\left(l'\right)^4 = \frac{3}{8}\frac{1}{d^4},$$

$$\mathrm{E}(l''(l')^2) = -\frac{1}{8}\frac{1}{d^4}, \qquad \mathrm{E}\left(l'l'''\right) = \frac{3}{4}\frac{1}{d^4}.$$

$$[12] = -\frac{1}{2}\frac{1}{d^3}, \qquad [1^4] = \frac{3}{8}\frac{1}{d^4}, \qquad [1^22] = \frac{1}{4}\frac{1}{d^4}, \qquad [13] = \frac{3}{4}\frac{1}{d^4}, \qquad [1^3] = 0.$$

Thus, we obtain

$$E\left(\hat{d}_{MLE}\right) = d + \frac{d}{k} + O\left(\frac{1}{k^2}\right)$$

$$\text{Var}\left(\hat{d}_{MLE}\right) = \frac{2d^2}{k} + \frac{7d^2}{k^2} + O\left(\frac{1}{k^3}\right)$$

$$E\left(\hat{d}_{MLE} - E\left(\hat{d}_{MLE}\right)\right)^3 = \frac{12d^3}{k^2} + O\left(\frac{1}{k^3}\right)$$

$$E\left(\hat{d}_{MLE} - E\left(\hat{d}_{MLE}\right)\right)^4 = \frac{12d^4}{k^2} + \frac{222d^4}{k^3} + O\left(\frac{1}{k^4}\right).$$

Because $\hat{d}_{MLE}$ has $O\left(\frac{1}{k}\right)$ bias, we recommend $\hat{d}_{MLE,c} = \hat{d}_{MLE}\left(1 - \frac{1}{k}\right)$, whose first four moments are, after some algebra,

$$E\left(\hat{d}_{MLE,c}\right) = d + O\left(\frac{1}{k^2}\right)$$

$$\text{Var}\left(\hat{d}_{MLE,c}\right) = \frac{2d^2}{k} + \frac{3d^2}{k^2} + O\left(\frac{1}{k^3}\right)$$

$$E\left(\hat{d}_{MLE,c} - E\left(\hat{d}_{MLE,c}\right)\right)^3 = \frac{12d^3}{k^2} + O\left(\frac{1}{k^3}\right)$$

$$E\left(\hat{d}_{MLE,c} - E\left(\hat{d}_{MLE,c}\right)\right)^4 = \frac{12d^4}{k^2} + \frac{186d^4}{k^3} + O\left(\frac{1}{k^4}\right).$$

Sparse Density Estimation with ℓ_1 Penalties*

Florentina Bunea[1], Alexandre B. Tsybakov[2], and Marten H. Wegkamp[1]

[1] Florida State University, Tallahassee FL 32306, USA
flori@stat.fsu.edu, wegkamp@stat.fsu.edu
[2] Laboratoire de Probabilités et Modèles Aléatoires, Université Paris VI, France
tsybakov@ccr.jussieu.fr

Abstract. This paper studies oracle properties of ℓ_1-penalized estimators of a probability density. We show that the penalized least squares estimator satisfies sparsity oracle inequalities, i.e., bounds in terms of the number of non-zero components of the oracle vector. The results are valid even when the dimension of the model is (much) larger than the sample size. They are applied to estimation in sparse high-dimensional mixture models, to nonparametric adaptive density estimation and to the problem of aggregation of density estimators.

1 Introduction

Let $X_1, \ldots, X_n$ be independent random variables with common unknown density f in $\mathbb{R}^d$. Let $\{f_1, \ldots, f_M\}$ be a finite set of functions with $f_j \in L_2(\mathbb{R}^d), j = 1, \ldots, M$, called a dictionary. We consider estimators of f that belong to the linear span of $\{f_1, \ldots, f_M\}$. We will be particularly interested in the case where $M \gg n$, where n is the sample size. Denote by f_λ the linear combinations

$$\mathsf{f}_\lambda(x) = \sum_{j=1}^{M} \lambda_j f_j(x), \quad \lambda = (\lambda_1, \ldots, \lambda_M) \in \mathbb{R}^M.$$

We provide below a number of examples where such estimates are of importance.

- *Estimation in sparse mixture models.* Assume that the density f can be represented as a finite mixture $f = \mathsf{f}_{\lambda^*}$ where f_j are known probability densities and λ^* is a vector of mixture probabilities. The number M can be very large, much larger than the sample size n, but we believe that the representation is sparse, i.e., that very few coordinates of λ^* are non-zero. Our goal is to estimate λ^* by a vector $\tilde{\lambda}$ that adapts to this unknown sparsity.
- *Adaptive nonparametric density estimation.* Assume that the density f is a smooth function, and $\{f_1, \ldots, f_M\}$ are the first M functions from a basis in $L_2(\mathbb{R}^d)$. If the basis is orthonormal, a natural idea is to estimate f by an orthogonal series estimator which has the form $\mathsf{f}_{\tilde{\lambda}}$ with $\tilde{\lambda}$ having the coordinates $\tilde{\lambda}_j = n^{-1} \sum_{i=1}^{n} f_j(X_i)$. However, it is well known that such

---

* Research of F. Bunea and M. Wegkamp is supported in part by NSF grant DMS 0406049.

N. Bshouty and C. Gentile (Eds.): COLT 2007, LNAI 4539, pp. 530–543, 2007.

estimators are very sensitive to the choice of M, and a data-driven selection of M or thresholding is needed to achieve adaptivity (cf., e.g., [25,17,3,15]); moreover these methods have been applied with $M \leq n$. We would like to cover more general problems where the system $\{f_j\}$ is not necessarily orthonormal, even not necessarily a basis, M is not necessarily smaller than n, but an estimate of the form $f_{\widehat{\lambda}}$ still achieves, adaptively, the optimal rates of convergence.

– *Aggregation of density estimators.* Assume now that $f_1, \ldots, f_M$ are some preliminary estimators of f constructed from a training sample independent of $(X_1, \ldots, X_n)$, and we would like to aggregate $f_1, \ldots, f_M$. This means that we would like to construct a new estimator, the aggregate, which is approximately as good as the best among $f_1, \ldots, f_M$ or approximately as good as the best linear or convex combination of $f_1, \ldots, f_M$. Our aggregates will be of the form $f_{\widehat{\lambda}}$ with suitably chosen weights $\widehat{\lambda} = \widehat{\lambda}(X_1, \ldots, X_n) \in \mathbb{R}^M$.

In this paper, we suggest a data-driven choice of $\widehat{\lambda}$ that can be used in all the examples mentioned above and also more generally. We define $\widehat{\lambda}$ as a minimizer of an ℓ_1-penalized criterion, that we call SPADES (SPArse Density EStimation). The idea of ℓ_1-penalized estimation is widely used in the statistical literature, mainly in linear regression where it is usually referred to as the Lasso criterion [26,7,11,10,14,21]. For Gaussian sequence models or for regression with orthogonal design matrix the Lasso is equivalent to soft thresholding [9,20]. Recently, Lasso methods have been extended to nonparametric regression with general fixed or random design [4,5,6], as well as to some classification and other more general prediction type models [18,19,29].

We prove below oracle inequalities for the L_2-risk of the proposed SPADES estimator, and we obtain as corollaries some sparsity or optimality properties of this estimator for the three above mentioned examples.

2   Definition of SPADES

Consider the $L_2(\mathbb{R}^d)$ norm

$$\|g\| = \left(\int_{\mathbb{R}^d} g^2(x) \, \mathrm{d}x \right)^{1/2}$$

associated with the inner product

$$< g, h > = \int_{\mathbb{R}^d} g(x) h(x) \, \mathrm{d}x$$

for $g, h \in L_2(\mathbb{R}^d)$. Note that if the density f belongs to $L_2(\mathbb{R}^d)$ and X has the same distribution as X_i, we have, for any $g \in L_2$,

$$< g, f > = \mathbb{E} g(X),$$

where the expectation is taken under f. Moreover

$$\|f - g\|^2 = \|f\|^2 + \|g\|^2 - 2 < g, f > = \|f\|^2 + \|g\|^2 - 2\mathbb{E}g(X). \qquad (1)$$

In view of identity (1), minimizing $\|f_\lambda - f\|^2$ in λ is the same as minimizing

$$\gamma(\lambda) = -2\mathbb{E}f_\lambda(X) + \|f_\lambda\|^2.$$

The function $\gamma(\lambda)$ depends on f but can be approximated by its empirical counterpart

$$\widehat{\gamma}(\lambda) = -\frac{2}{n} \sum_{i=1}^{n} f_\lambda(X_i) + \|f_\lambda\|^2.$$

This motivates the use of $\widehat{\gamma} = \widehat{\gamma}(\lambda)$ as the empirical criterion, see, for instance, [3,25,30].

Let $0 < \delta < 1/2$ be a small tuning parameter. We define the penalty

$$\text{pen}(\lambda) = 2 \sum_{j=1}^{M} \omega_j |\lambda_j| \quad \text{with} \quad \omega_j = 2 \sup_{x \in \mathbb{R}^d} |f_j(x)| \sqrt{\frac{2 \log(M/\delta)}{n}} \qquad (2)$$

and we propose the following data-driven choice of λ:

$$\widehat{\lambda} = \underset{\lambda \in \mathbb{R}^M}{\arg\min} \left\{ \widehat{\gamma}(\lambda) + \text{pen}(\lambda) \right\}$$

$$= \underset{\lambda \in \mathbb{R}^M}{\arg\min} \left\{ -\frac{2}{n} \sum_{i=1}^{n} f_\lambda(X_i) + \|f_\lambda\|^2 + 2 \sum_{j=1}^{M} \omega_j |\lambda_j| \right\}.$$

The estimator of the density f, henceforth called the *SPADES estimator*, is defined by

$$f^\spadesuit(x) = f_{\widehat{\lambda}}(x), \ \forall x \in \mathbb{R}^d.$$

Our estimate can be computed easily even if $M \gg n$ and retains the desirable theoretical properties of other density estimators the computation of which may become problematic in such case. We refer to [30] for optimal bandwidth selection for kernel density estimators using the same empirical criterion as ours, to [8] for a thorough overview on combinatorial methods in density estimation, and to [2,28] for density estimation using penalization by the dimension over a sequence of models.

3   Oracle Inequalities for SPADES

For any $\lambda \in \mathbb{R}^M$, let

$$J(\lambda) = \{j \in \{1, \ldots, M\} : \lambda_j \neq 0\}$$

be the set of non-zero indices of λ and

$$M(\lambda) = |J(\lambda)| = \sum_{j=1}^{M} I\{\lambda_j \neq 0\}$$

its cardinality. Here $I\{\cdot\}$ denotes the indicator function. Set $L_j = \|f_j\|_\infty$ for $1 \le j \le M$ where $\|\cdot\|_\infty$ is the L_∞ norm on $\mathbb{R}^d$. We begin with following preliminary lemma.

Lemma 1. *Assume that $L_j < \infty$ for $j = 1,\ldots,M$. For all $n \ge 1$ and $\lambda \in \mathbb{R}^M$ we have*

$$\|f^{\spadesuit} - f\|^2 + \sum_{j=1}^{M} \omega_j |\widehat{\lambda}_j - \lambda_j| \le \|f_\lambda - f\|^2 + 4 \sum_{j \in J(\lambda)} \omega_j |\widehat{\lambda}_j - \lambda_j| \tag{3}$$

with probability at least $1 - 2\delta$, for any $0 < \delta < 1/2$.

Proof. By the definition of $\widehat{\lambda}$,

$$-\frac{2}{n}\sum_{i=1}^{n} f_{\widehat{\lambda}}(X_i) + \|f_{\widehat{\lambda}}\|^2 + 2\sum_{j=1}^{M}\omega_j|\widehat{\lambda}_j| \le -\frac{2}{n}\sum_{i=1}^{n} f_\lambda(X_i) + \|f_\lambda\|^2 + 2\sum_{j=1}^{M}\omega_j|\lambda_j|$$

for all $\lambda \in \mathbb{R}^M$. We rewrite this inequality as

$$\|f^{\spadesuit} - f\|^2 \le \|f_\lambda - f\|^2 + 2\sum_{j=1}^{M}\left(\frac{1}{n}\sum_{i=1}^{n} f_j(X_i) - \mathbb{E}f_j(X_i)\right)(\widehat{\lambda}_j - \lambda_j)$$

$$+ 2\sum_{j=1}^{M}\omega_j|\lambda_j| - 2\sum_{j=1}^{M}\omega_j|\widehat{\lambda}_j|.$$

Define the random variables

$$V_j = \frac{1}{n}\sum_{i=1}^{n}\{f_j(X_i) - \mathbb{E}f_j(X_i)\}.$$

By Hoeffding's inequality, it follows that the probability of the event

$$A = \bigcap_{j=1}^{M}\{2|V_j| \le \omega_j\}$$

exceeds

$$1 - 2\sum_{j=1}^{M}\exp\left(-\frac{n\omega_j^2}{8L_j^2}\right) = 1 - 2\delta.$$

Then, on the event A,

$$\|f^{\spadesuit} - f\|^2 \le \|f_\lambda - f\|^2 + \sum_{j=1}^{M}\omega_j|\widehat{\lambda}_j - \lambda_j| + 2\sum_{j=1}^{M}\omega_j|\lambda_j| - 2\sum_{j=1}^{M}\omega_j|\widehat{\lambda}_j|.$$

Add $\sum_j \omega_j |\widehat{\lambda}_j - \lambda_j|$ to both sides of the inequality to obtain

$$\|f^\spadesuit - f\|^2 + \sum_{j=1}^M \omega_j |\widehat{\lambda}_j - \lambda_j|$$

$$\leq \|f_\lambda - f\|^2 + 2\sum_{j=1}^M \omega_j |\widehat{\lambda}_j - \lambda_j| + 2\sum_{j=1}^M \omega_j |\lambda_j| - 2\sum_{j=1}^M \omega_j |\widehat{\lambda}_j|$$

$$\leq \|f_\lambda - f\|^2 + 2\sum_{j\in J(\lambda)} \omega_j |\widehat{\lambda}_j - \lambda_j| + 2\sum_{j=1}^M \omega_j |\lambda_j| - 2\sum_{j\in J(\lambda)} \omega_j |\widehat{\lambda}_j|$$

$$\leq \|f_\lambda - f\|^2 + 4\sum_{j\in J(\lambda)} \omega_j |\widehat{\lambda}_j - \lambda_j|$$

where we used that $\lambda_j = 0$ for $j \notin J(\lambda)$ and the triangle inequality. ∎

For any fixed integer $M \geq 2$ we introduce the following notation. We denote by $\Psi_M = (<f_i, f_j>)_{1\leq i,j\leq M}$ the Gram matrix associated with $f_1,\ldots,f_M$ and by I_M the $M \times M$ identity matrix. The next theorem will be shown under the following assumption.

ASSUMPTION (I). *There exists $\kappa_M > 0$ such that $\Psi_M - \kappa_M I_M$ is positive semi-definite.*

Theorem 1. *Let Assumption (I) hold and let $L_j < \infty$ for $1 \leq j \leq M$. Then, for all $n \geq 1$, $\alpha > 1$ and all $\lambda \in \mathbb{R}^M$, we have with probability at least $1 - 2\delta$,*

$$\|f^\spadesuit - f\|^2 + \frac{\alpha}{\alpha-1}\sum_{j=1}^M \omega_j |\widehat{\lambda}_j - \lambda_j| \leq \frac{\alpha+1}{\alpha-1}\|f_\lambda - f\|^2 + \frac{64\alpha^2}{\alpha-1}\frac{G(\lambda)\log\frac{M}{\delta}}{n\,\kappa_M} \quad (4)$$

where $G(\lambda) \triangleq \sum_{j\in J(\lambda)} L_j^2$.

Proof. By Assumption (I) we have

$$\|f_\lambda\|^2 = \sum_{1\leq i,j\leq M}\lambda_i\lambda_j \int_{\mathbb{R}^d} f_i(x)f_j(x)\,dx \geq \kappa_M \sum_{j\in J(\lambda)}\lambda_j^2.$$

By the definition of ω_j and the Cauchy-Schwarz inequality, we find

$$4\sum_{j\in J(\lambda)}\omega_j|\widehat{\lambda}_j - \lambda_j| \leq 4\sqrt{\frac{8\log(M/\delta)}{n}}\sum_{j\in J(\lambda)}L_j|\widehat{\lambda}_j - \lambda_j|$$

$$\leq 8\sqrt{\frac{2G(\lambda)\log(M/\delta)}{n\kappa_M}}\|f^\spadesuit - f_\lambda\|.$$

Combination with Lemma 1 yields that with probability greater than $1 - 2\delta$,

$$\|f^\spadesuit - f\|^2 + \sum_{j=1}^{M} \omega_j |\widehat{\lambda}_j - \lambda_j| \le \|f_\lambda - f\|^2 + 8\sqrt{\frac{2G(\lambda)\log(M/\delta)}{n\kappa_M}} \|f^\spadesuit - f_\lambda\| \quad (5)$$

$$\le \|f_\lambda - f\|^2 + b\Big(\|f^\spadesuit - f\| + \|f_\lambda - f\|\Big)$$

where $b = 8\sqrt{2G(\lambda)\log(M/\delta)}/\sqrt{n\kappa_M}$. This inequality is of the form $v^2 + d \le c^2 + vb + cb$ with

$$v = \|f^\spadesuit - f\|, \quad c = \|f_\lambda - f\|, \quad d = \sum_{j=1}^{M} \omega_j |\widehat{\lambda}_j - \lambda_j|.$$

After applying the inequality $2xy \le x^2/\alpha + \alpha y^2$ $(x, y \in \mathbb{R}, \ \alpha > 1)$ twice, we easily find

$$v^2 + d \le v^2/(2\alpha) + \alpha\, b^2 + (2\alpha + 1)/(2\alpha)\, c^2,$$

whence

$$v^2 + d\{\alpha/(\alpha - 1)\} \le \alpha/(\alpha - 1)\{b^2(\alpha/2) + c^2(\alpha + 1)/\alpha\}. \quad (6)$$

The claim of the theorem follows from (5) and (6).

4   Oracle Inequalities for SPADES: The Local Mutual Coherence Assumption

When the dictionary $\{f_1, \dots, f_M\}$ is over-complete (see, e.g., discussion in [10]) Assumption (I) may not be satisfied. Nevertheless, as discussed in [10], for many interesting dictionaries the Gram matrices satisfy the mutual coherence property, that is the correlations

$$\rho_M(i,j) = \frac{< f_i, f_j >}{\|f_i\| \|f_j\|}, \quad i, j = 1, \dots, M,$$

admit a uniform (small) upper bound for all $i \ne j$. It can be shown that if this bound, called coherence, is relatively small, namely of the order $O(1/M(\lambda))$ for some λ, then the oracle inequalities of the previous section remain valid for such λ. The assumption that the correlations are small for all $i \ne j$ may still be too stringent a requirement in many situations. We relax this here by only imposing bounds on $\rho_M(i,j)$ with $j \in J(\lambda)$ and $i \ne j$. In our setting the correlations $\rho_M(i,j)$ with $i, j \notin J(\lambda)$ can be arbitrarily close to 1 or to -1. Note that such $\rho_M(i,j)$ constitute the overwhelming majority of the elements of the correlation matrix if $J(\lambda)$ is a set of small cardinality: $M(\lambda) \ll M$.

For $\lambda \in \mathbb{R}^M$, we define our first local coherence number (called *maximal local coherence*) by

$$\rho(\lambda) = \max_{i \in J(\lambda)} \max_{j \ne i} |\rho_M(i,j)|,$$

and we also define

$$F(\lambda) = \max_{j \in J(\lambda)} \frac{\|f_j\|_\infty}{\|f_j\|}.$$

Theorem 2. *Assume that $L_j < \infty$ for $1 \le j \le M$. Then, with probability at least $1 - 2\delta$, for all $n \ge 1$, $\alpha > 1$ and $\lambda \in \mathbb{R}^M$ that satisfy*

$$32F(\lambda)\rho(\lambda)M(\lambda) \le 1, \tag{7}$$

we have the following oracle inequality:

$$\|f^\spadesuit - f\|^2 + \frac{1}{2}\frac{\alpha}{\alpha - 1}\sum_{j=1}^M \omega_j|\widehat{\lambda}_j - \lambda_j|$$

$$\le \frac{\alpha + 1}{\alpha - 1}\|f_\lambda - f\|^2 + \frac{\alpha^2}{\alpha - 1}\{8F(\lambda)\}^2 M(\lambda)\frac{\log(M/\delta)}{n}.$$

Proof. In view of Lemma 1, we need to bound $\sum_{j \in J(\lambda)} \omega_j|\widehat{\lambda}_j - \lambda_j|$. Set

$$u_j = \widehat{\lambda}_j - \lambda_j, \quad U(\lambda) = \sum_{j \in J(\lambda)} |u_j| \|f_j\|, \quad U = \sum_{j=1}^M |u_j| \|f_j\|.$$

Then, by the definition of ω_j and $F(\lambda)$ we obtain

$$\sum_{j \in J(\lambda)} \omega_j|\widehat{\lambda}_j - \lambda_j| \le 2\sqrt{\frac{2\log(M/\delta)}{n}}F(\lambda)U(\lambda).$$

Clearly

$$\sum_{i,j \notin J(\lambda)}\sum <f_i, f_j> u_iu_j \ge 0$$

and so we obtain

$$\sum_{j \in J(\lambda)} u_j^2\|f_j\|^2 = \|f^\spadesuit - f_\lambda\|^2 - \sum_{i,j \notin J(\lambda)}\sum u_iu_j <f_i, f_j>$$

$$-2\sum_{i \notin J(\lambda)}\sum_{j \in J(\lambda)} u_iu_j <f_i, f_j> - \sum_{i,j \in J(\lambda),\ i \ne j}\sum u_iu_j <f_i, f_j>$$

$$\le \|f^\spadesuit - f_\lambda\|^2 + 2\rho(\lambda)\sum_{i \notin J(\lambda)} |u_i| \|f_i\| \sum_{j \in J(\lambda)} |u_j| \|f_j\|$$

$$+\rho(\lambda)\sum_{i,j \in J(\lambda)}\sum |u_i||u_j| \|f_i\| \|f_j\|$$

$$= \|f^\spadesuit - f_\lambda\|^2 + 2\rho(\lambda)U(\lambda)U - \rho(\lambda)U^2(\lambda). \tag{8}$$

The left-hand side can be bounded by $\sum_{j \in J(\lambda)} u_j^2\|f_j\|^2 \ge U^2(\lambda)/M(\lambda)$ using the Cauchy-Schwarz inequality, and we obtain that

$$U^2(\lambda) \le \|f^\spadesuit - f_\lambda\|^2 M(\lambda) + 2\rho(\lambda)M(\lambda)U(\lambda)U$$

and, using the properties of a function of degree two in $U(\lambda)$, we further obtain

$$U(\lambda) \leq 2\rho(\lambda)M(\lambda)U + \sqrt{M(\lambda)}\|f^\spadesuit - f_\lambda\|. \tag{9}$$

Hence, by Lemma 1, we have with probability at least $1 - 2\delta$,

$$\|f^\spadesuit - f\|^2 + \sum_{j=1}^{M} \omega_j |\widehat{\lambda}_j - \lambda_j|$$

$$\leq \|f_\lambda - f\|^2 + 4 \sum_{j \in J(\lambda)} \omega_j |\widehat{\lambda}_j - \lambda_j|$$

$$\leq \|f_\lambda - f\|^2 + 8\sqrt{\frac{2\log(M/\delta)}{n}} F(\lambda)U(\lambda)$$

$$\leq \|f_\lambda - f\|^2 + 8\sqrt{\frac{2\log(M/\delta)}{n}} F(\lambda)\left\{2\rho(\lambda)M(\lambda)U + \sqrt{M(\lambda)}\|f^\spadesuit - f_\lambda\|\right\}$$

$$\leq \|f_\lambda - f\|^2 + 16F(\lambda)\rho(\lambda)M(\lambda) \sum_{j=1}^{M} \omega_j |\widehat{\lambda}_j - \lambda_j|$$

$$+ 8F(\lambda)\sqrt{\frac{2\log(M/\delta)}{n}} \sqrt{M(\lambda)}\|f^\spadesuit - f_\lambda\|.$$

For all $\lambda \in \mathbb{R}^M$ that satisfy relation (7), we find that with probability exceeding $1 - 2\delta$,

$$\|f^\spadesuit - f\|^2 + \frac{1}{2}\sum_{j=1}^{M} \omega_j |\widehat{\lambda}_j - \lambda_j|$$

$$\leq \|f_\lambda - f\|^2 + 8F(\lambda)\sqrt{\frac{2\log(M/\delta)}{n}} \sqrt{M(\lambda)}\|f^\spadesuit - f_\lambda\|.$$

This inequality is of the same form as (5), and we use (6) to conclude the proof.

Note that only a condition on the local coherence (7) is required to obtain the result of Theorem 2. However, even this weak condition can be too strong, because the bound on correlations is *uniform* over $j \in J(\lambda), i \neq j$, cf. definition of $\rho(\lambda)$. This excludes, for instance, the cases where the correlations can be relatively large for a small number of pairs (i, j) and almost zero otherwise. A possible solution is to require that the *cumulative local coherence*, rather than the maximal local coherence, be bounded, where the cumulative local coherence is defined as

$$\rho_*(\lambda) = \sum_{i \in J(\lambda)} \sum_{j > i} |\rho_M(i, j)|.$$

Theorem 3. *Assume that $L_j < \infty$ for $1 \leq j \leq M$. Then, with probability at least $1 - 2\delta$, for all $n \geq 1$, $\alpha > 1$ and $\lambda \in \mathbb{R}^M$ that satisfy*

$$32F(\lambda)\rho_*(\lambda)\sqrt{M(\lambda)} \leq 1, \tag{10}$$

we have the following oracle inequality:

$$\|f^{\spadesuit} - f\|^2 + \frac{1}{2}\frac{\alpha}{\alpha - 1}\sum_{j=1}^{M}\omega_j|\widehat{\lambda}_j - \lambda_j|$$

$$\leq \frac{\alpha + 1}{\alpha - 1}\|f_\lambda - f\|^2 + \frac{\alpha^2}{\alpha - 1}\{8F(\lambda)\}^2 M(\lambda)\frac{\log(M/\delta)}{n}.$$

Proof. The proof is similar to that of Theorem 2. With

$$U_*(\lambda) = \sqrt{\sum_{j\in J(\lambda)} u_j^2 \|f_j\|^2}$$

we obtain now the following analogue of (8):

$$U_*^2(\lambda) \leq \|f^{\spadesuit} - f_\lambda\|^2 + 2\rho_*(\lambda)\max_{i\in J(\lambda), j>i}|u_i|\|f_i\||u_j|\|f_j\|$$

$$\leq \|f^{\spadesuit} - f_\lambda\|^2 + 2\rho_*(\lambda)U_*(\lambda)\sum_{j=1}^{M}|u_j|\|f_j\|$$

$$= \|f^{\spadesuit} - f_\lambda\|^2 + 2\rho_*(\lambda)U_*(\lambda)U.$$

Hence, as in the proof of Theorem 2, we have

$$U_*(\lambda) \leq 2\rho_*(\lambda)U + \|f^{\spadesuit} - f_\lambda\|,$$

and using the inequality $U_*(\lambda) \geq U(\lambda)/\sqrt{M(\lambda)}$ we find

$$U(\lambda) \leq 2\rho_*(\lambda)\sqrt{M(\lambda)}U + \sqrt{M(\lambda)}\|f^{\spadesuit} - f_\lambda\|. \tag{11}$$

Note that (11) differs from (9) only in the fact that the factor $2\rho(\lambda)M(\lambda)$ on the right hand side is now replaced by $2\rho_*(\lambda)\sqrt{M(\lambda)}$. The rest of the proof is identical to that of Theorem 2.

Theorem 3 is useful when we deal with sparse Gram matrices Ψ_M, i.e., matrices having only a small number N of non-zero off-diagonal entries. This number will be called a *sparsity index* of matrix Ψ_M, and is formally defined as

$$N = |\{(i,j) : i,j \in \{1,\ldots,M\}, i > j \text{ and } \psi_M(i,j) \neq 0\}|,$$

where $\psi_M(i,j)$ is the (i,j)th entry of Ψ_M and $|A|$ denotes the cardinality of a set A. Clearly, $N < M(M+1)/2$. We get then the following immediate corollary of Theorem 3.

Corollary 1. *Let Ψ_M be a sparse matrix with sparsity index N. Then Theorem 3 continues to hold with condition (10) replaced by*

$$32F(\lambda)N\sqrt{M(\lambda)} \leq 1. \tag{12}$$

5   Sparse Estimation in Mixture Models

In this section we assume that the true density f can be represented as a finite mixture

$$f(x) = \sum_{j=1}^{M} \lambda_j^* f_j(x), \tag{13}$$

for some $\lambda^* \in \Lambda^M$ where Λ^M is a simplex in $\mathbb{R}^M$:

$$\Lambda^M = \{\lambda \in \mathbb{R}^M : \lambda_j \geq 0, \sum_{j=1}^{M} \lambda_j = 1\}$$

and f_j are known probability densities. The number M can be very large, much larger than the sample size n, but we believe that the representation (13) is sparse, i.e., there are very few non-zero coefficients λ_j^*, in other words $M(\lambda^*) \ll M$. If the representation (13) is not unique, we consider λ^* corresponding to the most parsimonious representation, i.e., such that $M(\lambda^*) = \min \left\{ \sum_{j=1}^{M} I_{\{\lambda_j \neq 0\}} : f = \sum_{j=1}^{M} \lambda_j f_j \right\}$.

From Theorems 1 and 2, using that $\min_{\alpha>1} \alpha^2/(\alpha - 1) = 4$, we easily get the following result.

Theorem 4. *(i) Let (13) and Assumption (I) hold and let $L_j < \infty$ for $1 \leq j \leq M$. Then, for all $n \geq 1$, we have with probability at least $1 - 2\delta$,*

$$\|f^\spadesuit - f\|^2 \leq \frac{256\, G(\lambda^*) \log(M/\delta)}{n\, \kappa_M}. \tag{14}$$

(ii) Let (13) hold, $L_j < \infty$ for $1 \leq j \leq M$, and let $\lambda^* \in \mathbb{R}^M$ satisfy

$$32F(\lambda^*)\rho(\lambda^*)M(\lambda^*) \leq 1. \tag{15}$$

Then, for all $n \geq 1$, we have with probability at least $1 - 2\delta$,

$$\|f^\spadesuit - f\|^2 \leq 256\, F^2(\lambda^*)M(\lambda^*)\frac{\log(M/\delta)}{n}. \tag{16}$$

Example. Let f_j's be Gaussian densities in $\mathbb{R}^d$ with means μ_j and unit covariance matrices, such that $|\mu_j - \mu_k| \geq \tau > 0$, $k \neq j$, where $|\cdot|$ stands for the Euclidean distance. Then, for all λ, the mutual coherence satisfies $\rho(\lambda) \leq \exp(-\tau^2/4)$, and also $F(\lambda) \equiv 2^{-d/2}\pi^{-d/4}$. So, for τ large enough (15) is satisfied, and we can apply Theorem 4. It is interesting that the dimension "helps" here: the larger is d, the smaller is $F(\lambda)$. The large constant 256 in (16) is compensated by the small value of $F(\lambda)$ when the dimension is sufficiently high, say $d \geq 8$.

6   SPADES for Adaptive Nonparametric Density Estimation

We assume in this section that the density f is defined on $[0, 1]$. Let $f_1, \ldots, f_M$ be the first M functions of of the Fourier basis $\{f_j\}_{j=0}^{\infty}$ in $L_2[0, 1]$ defined by $f_1(x) \equiv 1$, $f_{2k}(x) = \sqrt{2}\cos(2\pi k x)$, $f_{2k+1}(x) = \sqrt{2}\sin(2\pi k x)$ for $k = 1, 2, \ldots$, $x \in [0, 1]$. Then $f^{\spadesuit}$ is a nonparametric estimator of density f. The following oracle inequality is a direct consequence of Theorem 1.

Theorem 5. *Let $f_1, \ldots, f_M$ be as defined above, and set $\omega_j \equiv 4\sqrt{\frac{\log(M/\delta)}{n}}$ for some $0 < \delta < 1/2$. Then for all $n \geq 1$, $\varepsilon > 0$ and all $\lambda \in \mathbb{R}^M$, we have with probability at least $1 - 2\delta$,*

$$\|f^{\spadesuit} - f\|^2 \leq (1 + \varepsilon)\|f_\lambda - f\|^2 + C(\varepsilon)\frac{M(\lambda)\log(M/\delta)}{n} \qquad (17)$$

where $C(\varepsilon) > 0$ is a constant depending only on ε.

This is a very general inequality that allows one to show that the estimator $f^{\spadesuit}$ attains minimax rates of convergence, up to a logarithmic factor simultaneously on various functional classes. In fact, since (17) holds with arbitrary λ, we may use (17) with λ such that $\lambda_j = 0$ if $j \geq n^{1/(2\beta+1)}$, for some $\beta > 0$, and thus show in a standard way that $f^{\spadesuit}$ attains the minimax rate, up to logarithms, on usual smoothness classes of densities, such as Sobolev or Hölder classes with smoothness index β. Since the rates are attained on one and the same estimator $f^{\spadesuit}$ which does not depend on β, this means adaptivity of $f^{\spadesuit}$ on the corresponding scales of classes. Results of such type, and even more pointed (without extra logarithmic factors in the rate and sometimes with exact asymptotic minimax constants) are known for various other adaptive density estimators, see, e.g., [3,12,15,16,17,23,24] and the references therein.

Although Theorem 5 is somewhat less precise than the benchmarks for these standard classes of densities, it can be used to show adaptivity of $f^{\spadesuit}$ on a wider scale of classes than those traditionally considered. In particular, Theorem 5 holds for unbounded densities f, and even for densities $f \notin L_2[0, 1]$.

For example, let f belong to a subset of $L_2[0, 1]$ containing possibly unbounded densities and such that $\|f_{\lambda^*(k)} - f\| \leq a_k, \forall k \leq M$, for some sequence a_k tending to 0 very slowly, where $\lambda^*(k)$ is the vector with components $\lambda_1 = <f, f_1>, \ldots, \lambda_k = <f, f_k>, \lambda_j = 0, j > k$. Then choosing k^* as a solution of $a_k \sim (k \log M)/n$ and using (17) with $\lambda = \lambda^*(k^*)$ we get that our estimator $f^{\spadesuit}$ achieves some (slow) convergence rates even for such "bad" classes of unbounded densities.

Another example is given by the $\mathcal{L}_0$-classes. Assume that f belongs to one of the classes

$$\mathcal{L}_0(k)$$
$$= \left\{ f : [0, 1] \to \mathbb{R} : f \text{ is a probability density and } |\{j : <f, f_j> \neq 0\}| \leq k \right\}$$

where $k \leq M$ is an unknown integer and $|A|$ denotes the cardinality of a set A. We have the following minimax adaptive result.

Corollary 2. *Let the assumptions of Theorem 5 hold with $\delta = n^{-2}$ and $M \leq n^s$ for some $s > 0$. Then*

$$\sup_{f \in \mathcal{L}_0(k)} \mathbb{P}\left\{\|f^\spadesuit - f\|^2 \geq b(s)\left(\frac{k \log n}{n}\right)\right\} \leq 2n^{-2}, \quad \forall\, k \leq M, \qquad (18)$$

where $b(s) > 0$ is a constant depending on s only.

This can be viewed as an extension to density estimation problem of the adaptive minimax results for $\mathcal{L}_0$-classes obtained in the Gaussian sequence space model [1,13] and in random design regression model [6].

7   SPADES for Aggregation of Density Estimators

In this section we assume that $f_1, \ldots, f_M$ are density estimators constructed from a preliminary sample that will be considered as frozen in further discussion.

The aim of aggregation is to construct a new estimator, called aggregate, which is approximately as good as the best among $f_1, \ldots, f_M$ (model selection, or MS-aggregation) or approximately as good as the best linear or convex combination of $f_1, \ldots, f_M$ (L-aggregation and C-aggregation respectively) or approximately as good as the best linear combination of $D \leq M$ estimators among $f_1, \ldots, f_M$ (subset selection, or S-aggregation). We refer to [4,22,23,24,27] for discussion of aggregation methods. Each type of aggregation corresponds to a particular set H^M where the weights λ are allowed to lie. The set H^M is either the whole $\mathbb{R}^M$ (for L-aggregation), or the simplex Λ^M (for C-aggregation), or the set of all vertices of Λ^M, except the vertex $(0, \ldots, 0) \in \mathbb{R}^M$ (for MS-aggregation). For subset selection, or S-aggregation we put $H^M = \Lambda^{M,D}$, where $\Lambda^{M,D}$ denotes the set of all $\lambda \in \mathbb{R}^M$ having at most D non-zero coordinates. The corresponding oracles are the values of λ minimizing the risk on these sets.

Using Theorem 1 we obtain the following oracle inequalities for these four types of aggregation.

Theorem 6. *Let Assumption (I) be satisfied and $L_j \leq L < \infty$ for $1 \leq j \leq M$. Let $f^\spadesuit$ be the SPADES estimator with $\delta = (Mn)^{-1}$. Then for all $\varepsilon > 0$ there exists a constant $C_\epsilon = C(\epsilon, L, \kappa_M) > 0$ such that for all integers $n \geq 1$, $M \geq 2$ and $1 \leq D \leq M$ we have, with probability greater than $1 - 2\delta$,*

$$\|f^\spadesuit - f\|^2 \leq (1 + \varepsilon) \inf_{1 \leq j \leq M} \|f_j - f\|^2 + C_\epsilon \frac{\log(Mn)}{n}. \qquad (19)$$

$$\|f^\spadesuit - f\|^2 \leq (1 + \varepsilon) \inf_{\lambda \in \Lambda^{M,D}} \|f_\lambda - f\|^2 + C_\epsilon \frac{D \log(Mn)}{n}. \qquad (20)$$

$$\|f^\spadesuit - f\|^2 \leq (1 + \varepsilon) \inf_{\lambda \in \mathbb{R}^M} \|f_\lambda - f\|^2 + C_\epsilon \frac{M \log(Mn)}{n}. \qquad (21)$$

$$\|f^\spadesuit - f\|^2 \leq (1 + \varepsilon) \inf_{\lambda \in \Lambda^M} \|f_\lambda - f\|^2 + C_\epsilon \overline{\psi}_n^C(M), \qquad (22)$$

where

$$\overline{\psi}_n^C(M) = \begin{cases} (M\log n)/n & \text{if } M \le \sqrt{n}, \\ \sqrt{(\log M)/n} & \text{if } M > \sqrt{n}. \end{cases}$$

This theorem follows from Theorem 1 via arguments analogous to those used in the regression estimation context in [4], proof of Corollary 3.2. For brevity we do not repeat the proof here.

The remainder terms on the right hand side of inequalities (19), (21) and (22) in Theorem 6 are optimal up to logarithmic factors. This follows from the corresponding lower bounds and the expressions optimal rates of aggregation [24,23]. We conjecture that the remainder term in (21) is optimal as well, and that this can be shown by a technique similar to that of [4].

In conclusion, SPADES is obtained via one procedure and achieves near optimal aggregation of all four types: model selection, subset selection, convex and linear aggregation.

References

1. Abramovich, F., Benjamini, Y., Donoho, D.L., Johnstone, I.M: Adapting to unknown sparsity by controlling the False Discovery Rate. Annals of Statistics 34, 584–653 (2006)
2. Barron, A., Birgé, L., Massart, P.: Risk bounds for model selection via penalization. Probability Theory and Related Fields 113, 301–413 (1999)
3. Birgé, L., Massart, P.: From model selection to adaptive estimation. Festschrift for Lucien LeCam. In: Pollard, D., Torgersen, E., Yang, G. (eds.) Research Papers in Probability and Statistics, pp. 55–87. Springer, New York (1997)
4. Bunea, F., Tsybakov, A.B., Wegkamp, M.H.: Aggregation for Gaussian regression. Preprint Department of Statistics, Florida State University. Annals of Statistics, to appear (2005)
5. Bunea, F., Tsybakov, A.B., Wegkamp, M.H.: Aggregation and sparsity via ℓ_1-penalized least squares. In: Lugosi, G., Simon, H.U. (eds.) COLT 2006. LNCS (LNAI), vol. 4005, pp. 379–391. Springer, Heidelberg (2006a)
6. Bunea, F., Tsybakov, A.B., Wegkamp, M.H: b). Sparsity oracle inequalities for the Lasso. Submitted (2006)
7. Chen, S., Donoho, D., Saunders, M.: Atomic decomposition by basis pursuit. SIAM Review 43, 129–159 (2001)
8. Devroye, L., Lugosi, G.: Combinatorial Methods in density estimation. Springer, Heidelberg (2000)
9. Donoho, D.L.: Denoising via soft-thresholding. IEEE Trans. Info. Theory 41, 613–627 (1995)
10. Donoho, D.L., Elad, M., Temlyakov, V.: Stable Recovery of Sparse Overcomplete Representations in the Presence of Noise. Manuscript (2004)
11. Donoho, D.L., Huo, X.: Uncertainty principles and ideal atomic decomposition. IEEE Transactions Inform. Theory 47, 2845–2862 (2001)
12. Golubev, G.K.: Nonparametric estimation of smooth probability densties in L_2. Problems of Information Transmission 28, 44–54 (1992)

13. Golubev, G.K.: Reconstruction of sparse vectors in white Gaussian noise. Problems of Information Transmission 38, 65–79 (2002)
14. Greenshtein, E., Ritov, Y.: Persistency in high dimensional linear predictor-selection and the virtue of over-parametrization. Bernoulli 10, 971–988 (2004)
15. Hall, P., Kerkyacharian, G., Picard, D.: Block threshold rules for curve estimation using kernel and wavelet methods. Annals of Statistics 26, 922–942 (1998)
16. Härdle, W., Kerkyacharian, G., Picard, D., Tsybakov, A.: Wavelets, Approximation and Statistical Applications. Lecture Notes in Statistics, vol. 129, Springer, New York (1998)
17. Kerkyacharian, G., Picard, D., Tribouley, K.: L^p adaptive density estimation. Bernoulli 2, 229–247 (1996)
18. Koltchinskii, V.: Model selection and aggregation in sparse classification problems. Oberwolfach Reports. Mathematisches Forschungsinstitut Oberwolfach. 2, 2663–2667 (2005)
19. Koltchinskii, V.: Sparsity in penalized empirical risk minimization. Submitted (2006)
20. Loubes, J.– M., van de Geer, S.A.: Adaptive estimation in regression, using soft thresholding type penalties. Statistica Neerlandica 56, 453–478 (2002)
21. Meinshausen, N., Bühlmann, P.: High-dimensional graphs and variable selection with the Lasso. Annals of Statistics 34, 1436–1462 (2006)
22. Nemirovski, A.: Topics in non-parametric statistics. In: Bernard, P. (ed.) Ecole d'Eté de Probabilités de Saint-Flour 1998. Lecture Notes in Mathematics, vol. XXVIII, Springer, New York (2000)
23. Rigollet, Ph.: Inégalités d'oracle, agrégation et adaptation. PhD thesis, University of Paris 6 (2006)
24. Rigollet, Ph.,Tsybakov, A. B.: Linear and convex aggregation of density estimators. (2004), `https://hal.ccsd.cnrs.fr/ccsd-00068216`.
25. Rudemo, M.: Empirical choice of histograms and kernel density estimato. Scandinavian Journal of Statistics 9, 65–78 (1982)
26. Tibshirani, R.: Regression shrinkage and selection via the Lasso. Journal of the Royal Statistical Society, Series B 58, 267–288 (1996)
27. Tsybakov, A.B.: Optimal rates of aggregation. In: Schölkopf, B., Warmuth, M.K. (eds.) COLT/Kernel 2003. LNCS (LNAI), vol. 2777, Springer, Heidelberg (2003)
28. Vapnik, V.N.: Statistical Learning Theory. Wiley, New York (1998)
29. van de Geer, S.A.: High dimensional generalized linear models and the Lasso. Research report No.133. Seminar für Statistik, ETH, Zürich (2006)
30. Wegkamp, M.H.: Quasi-Universal Bandwidth Selection for Kernel Density Estimators. Canadian Journal of Statistics 27, 409–420 (1999)

ℓ_1 Regularization in Infinite Dimensional Feature Spaces

Saharon Rosset[1], Grzegorz Swirszcz[1], Nathan Srebro[2], and Ji Zhu[3]

[1] IBM T.J. Watson Research Center, Yorktown Heights, NY 10549, USA
{srosset,swirszcz}@us.ibm.com
[2] IBM Haifa Research Lab, Haifa, Israel and Toyota Technological Institute,
Chicago, IL 60637, USA
[3] University of Michigan, Ann Arbor, MI 48109, USA

Abstract. In this paper we discuss the problem of fitting ℓ_1 regularized prediction models in infinite (possibly non-countable) dimensional feature spaces. Our main contributions are: a. Deriving a generalization of ℓ_1 regularization based on measures which can be applied in non-countable feature spaces; b. Proving that the sparsity property of ℓ_1 regularization is maintained in infinite dimensions; c. Devising a path-following algorithm that can generate the set of regularized solutions in "nice" feature spaces; and d. Presenting an example of penalized spline models where this path following algorithm is computationally feasible, and gives encouraging empirical results.

1 Introduction

Given a data sample $(x_i, y_i)_{i=1}^n$ (with $x_i \in \mathbb{R}^p$ and $y_i \in \mathbb{R}$ for regression, $y_i \in \{\pm 1\}$ for classification), the "non-linear" regularized optimization problem calls for fitting models to the data, embedded into a high dimensional feature space, while controlling complexity, by solving a penalized fitting problem:

$$\hat{\beta}(\lambda) = \arg\min_\beta \sum_i L(y_i, \beta^\mathsf{T}\phi(x_i)) + \lambda J(\beta) \qquad (1)$$

where L is a convex loss function; J is a convex model complexity penalty (typically taken to be the ℓ_q norm of β, with $q \geq 1$); $\phi(x_i) \in \mathbb{R}^\Omega$ is an embedding of x_i into the feature space indexed by Ω; and $\beta \in \mathbb{R}^\Omega$ is the parameter vector describing model fit. This formulation is at the heart of many successful modern data analysis tools.

Kernel Support Vector Machines (Schöelkopf and Smola 12) and other kernel methods, fit ℓ_2 regularized models in high (often infinite) dimensional reproducing kernel Hilbert spaces (RKHS). The key observation which allows us to solve these problems is that the optimal solution in fact lies in an n-dimensional sub-space spanned by the embedded data. When we move away from ℓ_2 regularization, the nice algebra of kernel methods no longer applies, and the prevalent view is that exact very high dimensional fitting becomes practically impossible.

Boosting (Freund and Schapire 4), is a popular and successful *committee* method, which builds prediction models as linear combinations of *weak learners* (usually small decision trees), which we can think of as features in a high dimensional

N. Bshouty and C. Gentile (Eds.): COLT 2007, LNAI 4539, pp. 544–558, 2007.

feature space. As shown in Rosset et al. (9) and references therein, boosting approximately and incrementally fits ℓ_1 regularized models in high dimensional spaces — typically the space of all trees with a given number of terminal nodes.

Fitting ℓ_1-regularized models in very high (finite) dimension is known to be attractive because of their "primal" sparsity property:

> Every ℓ_1 regularized problem has an optimal solution with at most n non-zero coefficients, no matter how high the dimension of the feature space used. Under mild conditions, this solution is unique.

This result is a simple consequence of Caratheodory's convex hull theorem. It is proven, for example, in Rosset et al. (9).

Thus, the success of boosting (approximate ℓ_1 regularization under embedding) and the attractiveness of the ℓ_1 sparsity property, lead us to the two main questions we address in this paper:

1. Can we generalize ℓ_1 regularization to infinite dimension in a consistent way, and will the sparsity property still hold?
2. Can we solve the resulting regularized problems despite the fact that they are infinite dimensional?

We answer the first question in Sections 2 and 3. In Section 2 we offer a formulation of ℓ_1 regularization based on measure rather than norm, which naturally generalized to infinite non-countable dimension. We then show (Section 3) that the sparsity property extends to infinite dimensional fitting, and even to non-countable dimensions, when using this definition. However, this property is contingent on the existence of the solution (which is not guaranteed in non-countable dimension), and we present sufficient conditions for this existence. We also formulate a simple, testable criterion for optimality of finite-dimensional solutions to infinite dimensional problems.

Armed with these results, in Section 4 we offer an answer to our second question, and present an algorithm that can provably generate these solutions, if they exist, which is based on a generalization of path-following algorithms previously devised for the Lasso and its extensions (Efron et al. 3, Zhu et al. 16).

We then describe in Section 5 an embedding problem — of fitting penalized splines to low dimensional data — where our algorithm is practical, and demonstrate its application on several datasets.

Throughout this paper we denote the index set of the functions in our feature space by Ω. The notation we use in this feature space is: $\phi(x) \in \mathbb{R}^\Omega$ is the embedding of x, $\phi_A(x) \in \mathbb{R}^A$ with $A \subset \Omega$ is the subset of coordinates of this embedding indexed by A (in particular, $\phi_\omega(x) \in \mathbb{R}$ is the "ω coordinate" of $\phi(x)$ for $\omega \in \Omega$), while $\phi_A(X) \in \mathbb{R}^{n \times A}$ is a matrix of the empirical partial embedding of all observations. We also assume throughout that $\sup_{\omega,x} |\phi_\omega(x)| < \infty$, i.e., that embedded coordinates are uniformly bounded.

Remark: Throughout the first part of this paper we also assume no intercept (or bias), i.e., that all features in Ω participate in the norm being penalized. This is done for simplicity of exposition, but we note that all our results hold and are easily generalized to the case that contains intercept (or even multi-dimensional intercept, like the spline basis in Section 5).

2 ℓ_1 Regularization in Finite and Infinite Dimensions

The standard ℓ_1-penalized problem in Eq. (1) has $J(\beta) = \|\beta\|_1 = \sum_{\omega \in \Omega} |\beta_\omega|$. The alternative "constrained" formulation, which is equivalent under convexity of L, is:

$$\hat{\beta}(C) = \arg \min_\beta \sum_i L(y_i, \beta^\mathsf{T} \phi(x_i)) \text{ s.t. } \|\beta\|_1 \leq C \tag{2}$$

This definition works fine when $|\Omega| \leq \aleph_0$, i.e., when the feature space is finite or countably infinite. We now generalize it to the non-countable case. First, we replace the ℓ_1 norm by a sum with a positivity constraint, by the well known trick of "doubling" the dimension of the feature space. We define $\tilde{\Omega} = \Omega \times \{-1, 1\}$ and for every $\tilde{\omega} \in \tilde{\Omega}$, $\tilde{\omega} = \{\omega, s\}$ define $\tilde{\phi}_{\tilde{\omega}}(x) = s\phi_\omega(x)$. Our new feature space is: $\tilde{\phi}(x) \in \mathbb{R}^{|\tilde{\Omega}|}$. It is well known and very easy to prove that any optimal solution $\hat{\beta}$ of Eq. (2) corresponds to one (or more) optimal solutions of a positive constrained problem

$$\hat{\tilde{\beta}}(C) = \arg \min_{\tilde{\beta}} \sum_i L(y_i, \tilde{\beta}^\mathsf{T} \tilde{\phi}(x_i)) \text{ s.t. } \|\tilde{\beta}\|_1 \leq C, \ \tilde{\beta} \succeq 0. \tag{3}$$

Through the transformation,

$$\hat{\beta}_\omega = \hat{\tilde{\beta}}_{\omega,1} - \hat{\tilde{\beta}}_{\omega,-1}.$$

Thus without loss of generality we can limit ourselves to only formulation Eq. (3) with positive coefficients and drop $\sim$ from our notation.

Given the positivity constraint, we next replace the coefficient vector β by a positive measure on Ω. Let (Ω, Σ) be a measurable space, where we require $\Sigma \supset \{\{\omega\} : \omega \in \Omega\}$, i.e., the sigma algebra Σ contains all singletons (this is a very mild assumption, which holds for example for the "standard" Borel sigma algebra). Let $\mathcal{P}$ be the set of positive measures on this space. Then we generalize (3) as:

$$\hat{P}_C = \arg \min_{P \in \mathcal{P}} \sum_i L\left(y_i, \int_\Omega \phi_\omega(x_i) dP(\omega)\right) \text{ s.t. } P(\Omega) \leq C \tag{4}$$

For finite or infinite countable Ω we will always get $\Sigma = 2^\Omega$ (which is the only possible choice given our singleton-containment requirement above), and recover exactly the formulation of (3) since $P(\Omega) = \|\beta\|_1$, but the problem definition in (4) also covers the non-countable case.

3 Existence and Sparsity of ℓ_1 Regularized Solutions in Infinite Dimensions

In this section we show that using the formulation (4), we can generalize the sparsity property of ℓ_1 regularized solutions to infinite dimensions, assuming an optimal solution exists. We then formulate a sufficient condition for existence of optimal solutions, and a testable criterion for optimality of a sparse solution.

3.1 Sparsity Result

Theorem 1. *Assume that an optimal solution of the problem (4) exists, then there exists an optimal solution $\hat{P}_C$ supported on at most $n + 1$ features in Ω.*

To understand this result and its proof let us define the set $D = \{\phi_\omega(X) : \omega \in \Omega\} \subset \mathbb{R}^n$ as the collection of *feature columns* in $\mathbb{R}^n$. Then the sparsity property simply states that any (scaled) convex combination of points in D can be described as an (identically scaled) convex combination of no more than $n + 1$ points in D. For this finite case, this is simply Caratheodory's convex hull theorem. For the infinite case, we need to generalize this result, as follows:

Theorem 2. *Let μ be a positive measure supported on a bounded subset D of $\mathbb{R}^n$. Then there exists a measure ν whose support is a finite subset of D, $\{z_1, \ldots, z_k\}$, $k \le n+1$, such that*

$$\int_D z d\mu(z) = \sum_{i=1}^{k} z_i d\nu(z_i).$$

We postpone the proof of Theorem 2 to Appendix A, and use it to prove Theorem (1). For simplicity we assume that $\mu(D) = C$, or equivalently, that $P_C(\Omega) = C$ in (4). If this is not the case and $\hat{P}_C(\Omega) = C' < C$ then we can simply apply Theorem 1 to $\hat{P}_{C'}$ for which equality holds, and the resulting sparse solution will also be optimal for constraint value C, i.e. $\hat{P}_C = \hat{P}_{C'}$.

Proof (of Theorem 1). Let $\hat{P}_C$ be an optimal solution of (4). We define a measure μ on $\mathbb{R}^n$ as a push–forward of $\hat{P}$, i.e. $\mu(B) = P(\{\omega : \phi_\omega(X) \in B\})$. Let D (as previously defined) be the image of Ω under mapping $\phi_.(X)$. The measure μ is supported on D, and by our assumption from Section 1, D is bounded. We apply Theorem 2 to set D and measure μ. Each $z_i \in D$, so the preimage of z_i under the mapping $\phi_.(X)$ is nonempty. For each i we pick any ω_i such that $\phi_{\omega_i}(X) = z_i$. Then $\sum_{i=1}^{k} \nu(z_i) \cdot \phi_{\omega_i}(\cdot)$ is an optimal solution of (4) supported on at most $n + 1$ features.

3.2 Sufficient Conditions for Existence of Solution of (4)

Theorem 3. *If the set $D = \{\phi_\omega(X) : \omega \in \Omega\} \subset \mathbb{R}^n$ is compact, then the problem (4) has an optimal solution*

Proof of Theorem 3 uses the following result:

Proposition 1. *The convex hull of a compact set in $\mathbb{R}^n$ is compact*

Proof of Proposition 1 is provided in Appendix A.

Proof (of Theorem 3). We consider the set $C \cdot D = \{C \cdot \phi_\omega(X) : \omega \in \Omega\} \subset \mathbb{R}^n$, where C is the (scalar) constraint from (4). By Proposition 1, the convex hull $co(C \cdot D)$ is also a compact set. By Weierstraß Theorem the continuous function $\sum_i L(y_i, z_i)$, $(z_1, \ldots, z_n)^T \in \mathbb{R}^n$ obtains its minimum at some point $\hat{z} = (\hat{z}_1, \ldots, \hat{z}_n)^T \in co(C \cdot D)$. By Caratheodory's Convex Hull Theorem 6 there exist points $z^1, \ldots, z^k \in D, k \le n+1$ and $b_i > 0$, $\sum_{i=1}^{k} b_i z^i = z$. For each z^i we pick any ω_i such that $C \cdot \phi_{\omega_i}(X) = z^i$. The measure $\mu = C \sum_i b_i \delta_{\omega_i}$ on Ω solves the problem (4).

The condition for existence of an optimal solution of the problem (4) provided in Theorem 3 can be difficult to check in practice. The following corollary provides us with much simpler and elegant criterion

Corollary 1. *If the set Ω is compact and the mapping $\phi_.(X) : \Omega \to \mathbb{R}^n$ is continuous, then the problem (4) has an optimal solution.*

Proof. It is an immediate consequence of the fact that the continuous image of a compact set is compact.

3.3 Simple Criterion for Optimality

Given our results here, we can now devise a simple criterion for optimality of a finite solution to an infinite dimensional problem:

Theorem 4. *If an optimal solution to the regularized problem exists, and we are presented with a finite-support candidate solution of (3) $\tilde{P}$ such that $\exists A \subset \Omega$, $|A| < \infty$, $supp(\tilde{P}) = A$, we can test its optimality using the following criterion:*
$\tilde{P}$ *is optimal solution of (3)* $\Leftrightarrow$ $\forall B$ *s.t.* $A \subseteq B$, $|B| < \infty$, $\tilde{P}$ *is optimal solution for:*

$$\min_{P \in \mathcal{P}_B} \sum_i C(y_i, \int_B \phi_w(x_i)dP(\omega)) \ s.t. \ P(B) \leq C$$

Proof
$\Rightarrow$:$\tilde{P}$ is the optimal solution in the whole (infinite) space, so it is the optimal solution in any subspace containing its support.

$\Leftarrow$: Assume by contradiction that $\tilde{P}$ is not optimal. We know a finite-support optimal solution exists from Theorem 1, mark this by $\hat{P}$. Set $B = supp(\tilde{P}) \cup supp(\hat{P})$. Then $|B| < \infty$ and $A \subseteq B$ obviously, and $\hat{P}$ is also better than $\tilde{P}$ in B.

This theorem implies that in order to prove that a finite solution is optimal for the *infinite* problem, it is sufficient to show that it is optimal for any *finite* sub-problem containing it. We will use it in the next section to prove that our proposed algorithm does indeed generate the optimal solutions to the infinite problem, if they exist.

4   Algorithms to Generate the Full Solution Paths

In this section, we are assuming that the optimal solution to the problem (4) exists for every C (possibly because the feature space complies with the required sufficient conditions of Theorem 3 or Corollary 1).

We now show how we can devise and implement a "path-following" algorithm, which generates this full solution path at a manageable computational cost. We describe this construction for the case of Lasso, i.e., when the loss is quadratic, and note that a similar algorithm can be devised for ℓ_1 regularized hinge loss (AKA ℓ_1-SVM) (Zhu et al. 16).

Efron et al. (3) have shown how an incremental homotopy algorithm can be used to generate the full regularized path at the cost of approximately one least square calculation on the full data set, for a finite feature set. Their algorithm is geometrically motivated and derived. For our purposes, we prefer to derive and analyze it from an optimization perspective, through the Karush-Kuhn-Tucker (KKT) conditions for optimality of solutions to (3). See Rosset and Zhu (10) for details of the KKT conditions and their implications. The resulting algorithm, in our parameterized basis notation, and with our space-doubling, non-negativity trick of Section 2:

Algorithm 1. *LAR-Lasso with parameterized feature space* [4]

1. *Initialize:*
   Set $\beta = 0$ (Starting from empty model)
   $\mathcal{A} = \arg\min_\omega \phi_\omega(X)^\mathsf{T}\mathbf{y}$ *(initial set of active variables)*
   $\mathbf{r} = \mathbf{y}$ *(residual vector)*
   $\gamma_\mathcal{A} = -(\phi_\mathcal{A}(X)^\mathsf{T}\phi_\mathcal{A}(X))^{-1}sgn(\phi_\mathcal{A}(X)^\mathsf{T}\mathbf{y})$, $\gamma_{\mathcal{A}^c} = 0$ *(direction of model change)*
2. *While* $(\min_\omega \phi_\omega(X)^\mathsf{T}\mathbf{r} < 0)$
   (a) $d_1 = \min\{d > 0 : \phi_\omega(X)^\mathsf{T}(\mathbf{r} - d\phi_\mathcal{A}(X)\gamma_\mathcal{A}) = \phi_{\omega'}(X)^\mathsf{T}(\mathbf{r} - d\phi_\mathcal{A}(X)\gamma_\mathcal{A}), \omega \notin \mathcal{A}, \omega' \in \mathcal{A}\}$
   (b) $d_2 = \min\{d > 0 : \beta_\omega + d\gamma_\omega = 0, \omega \in \mathcal{A}\}$ *(hit 0)*
   (c) $d = \min(d_1, d_2)$
   (d) *Update:*
       $\beta \leftarrow \beta + d\gamma$
       $\mathbf{r} = \mathbf{y} - \phi_\mathcal{A}(X)\beta_\mathcal{A}$
       If $d = d_1$ then add feature attaining equality at d to $\mathcal{A}$.
       If $d = d_2$ then remove feature attaining 0 at d from $\mathcal{A}$.
       $\gamma_\mathcal{A} = -(\phi_\mathcal{A}(X)^\mathsf{T}\phi_\mathcal{A}(X))^{-1}sgn(\phi_\mathcal{A}(X)^\mathsf{T}\mathbf{r})$
       $\gamma_{\mathcal{A}^c} = 0$

This algorithm generates the full regularized solution path for (3), i.e., for a

Theorem 5. *At any iteration of Algorithm 1, assume we are after step 2(c), and let $l \leq d$, where d is given by step 2(c). Then the finitely-supported measure P_l with atoms at $\mathcal{A}$ of size $\beta_\mathcal{A} + l\gamma_\mathcal{A}$ is an optimal solution to (3) with $C = \|\beta_\mathcal{A}\|_1 + l$.*

Proof. For finite Ω this algorithm is equivalent to LARS-Lasso of Efron et al.(3), and hence is known to generate the solution path.

For infinite Ω, Theorem 4 and the finite Ω result combined complete the proof, since for any finite $\mathcal{B}$ such that $\mathcal{A} \subseteq \mathcal{B} \subset \Omega$, the finite feature set result implies optimality of the finite-support measure $\hat{P}(C)$, generated by the algorithm, in the feature set $\mathcal{B}$.

The key computational observation regarding Algorithm 1 is that the only step where the size of the feature space comes into play is step 2(a). All other steps only consider the set of (at most $n+1$) features included in the current solution. So the key to applying this algorithm in very high dimension lies in being able to do the search in step 2(a) efficiently over the whole non active feature space. Denote:

$$\lambda(\beta) = -\phi_{\omega'}(X)^\mathsf{T}\mathbf{r}$$

---

[4] For simplicity, our description does not include a non-penalized constant. Including the constant (or constants, as we do in Section 5) complicates the notation but does not cause any difficulty.

where $\mathbf{r}$, β, and $\omega' \in \mathcal{A}$ are as in step 2(a). We can then re-write 2(a) as:

$$d_1 = \min\{d > 0 : -\phi_\omega(X)^\mathsf{T}(\mathbf{r} - d\phi_\mathcal{A}(X)\gamma_\mathcal{A}) = \lambda(\beta) - d, \text{ for some } \omega \notin \mathcal{A}\}$$

If we fix $\omega \notin \mathcal{A}$, we can find the value $l(\omega)$ at which we would attain equality. Denote:

$$l(\omega) = \frac{\phi_\omega(X)^\mathsf{T}\mathbf{r} + \lambda(\beta)}{\phi_\omega(X)^\mathsf{T}\phi_\mathcal{A}(X)\gamma_\mathcal{A} + 1} \tag{5}$$

and let:

$$d(\omega) = \begin{cases} l(\omega) \text{ if } l(\omega)) \geq 0 \\ \infty \quad \text{if } l(\omega)) < 0 \end{cases} \tag{6}$$

then our search problem in 2(a) becomes one of finding:

$$\omega^* = \arg\min_{\omega \notin \mathcal{A}} d(\omega) \tag{7}$$

Now, feature spaces in which our algorithm would be applicable are ones that allow a minimization of $d(\omega)$ over the infinite feature space, e.g., by analytically solving the problem (7) using a parametrization of Ω.

4.1 Computational Cost

Efron et al. (3) argue that for the algorithm we present, the number of pieces of the regularized path, and hence the number of iterations is "typically" $O(n)$, with a finite number of features. The switch to infinite dimension does not change the fundamental setting: the sparsity property we prove in Section 3 implies that, once we have $n + 1$ features included in our solution, we do not have to consider other features anymore (except if a "drop" event happens, which reduces the number of active features).

Assuming $O(n)$ iterations, the cost hinges on the complexity of the step length / next feature search. For the lasso spline example below, the step length calculation for each iteration is $O(n^2 p)$ (where p, the dimension of the original data, is typically very small), and the direction calculation is $O(n^2)$ (using an updating formula) for an overall iteration complexity of $O(n^2 p)$. The total complexity thus comes to $O(n^3 p)$ under the assumption on the number of iterations. In our experiments, this assumption seemed to hold.

5   Example: Additive Splines with Total Variation Penalty

In this Section, we illustrate the power of infinite-dimensional ℓ_1-regularized learning by considering a regression problem on functions in $[0, 1] \to \mathbb{R}$. We will suggest a specific (infinite) feature space, and show that ℓ_1-regularization under this feature space corresponds closely to bounding the kth total variation for the predictor function, recovering at the optimum a kth order polynomial spline (i.e., a piecewise degree $k - 1$ polynomial function with $k - 2$ continuous derivatives). We focus here on quadratic loss, but our results can be easily generalized to other loss functions.

For a given order k, let $\Omega = \{(a, s) | a \in [0, 1], s \in \pm 1\}$ and consider the features:

$$\phi_{a,s}(x) = s(x - a)_+^{k-1}$$

We also allow k additional unregularized features ("intercepts"):

$$\phi_r(x) = x^r$$

for $r = 0, \ldots, k - 1$. For observations $(x_i, y_i), i = 1, \ldots, n$, our optimization problem is then given by:

$$\text{minimize} \quad \sum_{i=1}^{n}(y_i - f_{P,\beta}(x_i))^2 \text{ s.t. } P(\Omega) \leq C \tag{8}$$

where P is a measure over Ω, $\beta \in \mathbb{R}^k$ and

$$f_{P,\beta}(x) = \int_{(a,s)} \phi_{a,s}(x)dP(a,s) + \sum_r \beta_r \phi_r(x) \tag{9}$$

is the fitted function corresponding to (P, β). From Theorem 1 and Corollary 1 we know that a sparse optimal solution to problem (8) exists. This will be a k-th order spline.

We note that with the above features we can approximate any function arbitrary well, and can exactly match any finite number of (consistent) observations. The key to this specific choice of basis for functions is the regularization cost (i.e. $P(\Omega)$) that applies to some predictor $f_{P,\beta}$. This is a familiar situation in learning with infinite-dimensional feature spaces, which we are used to encountering in kernel-based methods, where the choice of kernel (implicitly specifying a feature space) defines the regularization cost of predictor, rather than the space of available predictors.

In our case the ℓ_1 regularization cost, $P(\Omega)$, using our feature space, corresponds to the kth total variation (the total variation of the $(k-1)$th derivative). We can demonstrate that on our sparse spline solution

Proposition 2. *For an optimal solution that is a polynomial spline $f_{\hat{P},\hat{\beta}}$ with m knots at $(a_1, s_1), \ldots (a_m, s_m)$, and for which $\hat{P}(\Omega) = C$ (i.e., the constraint in (8) is tight) we have:*

$$TV(f_{\hat{P},\hat{\beta}}^{(k-1)}) = (k-1)!\hat{P}(\Omega)$$

Proof. We first observe:

$$f_{\hat{P},\hat{\beta}}^{(k-1)}(x) = (k-1)! \sum_{a_i < x} s_i \hat{P}(a_i, s_i)$$

Assume we have some i, j such that $a_i = a_j$ and $s_i \neq s_j$, and assume wlog that $s_i = 1$ and $\hat{P}(a_i, 1) > \hat{P}(a_i, -1)$. We can now define $\tilde{P}$ by $\tilde{P}(a_i, 1) = \hat{P}(a_i, 1) - \hat{P}(a_i, -1)$, $\hat{P}(a_i, -1) = 0$ and $\tilde{P} = \hat{P}$ everywhere else. Then $\tilde{P}(\Omega) < \hat{P}(\Omega)$ and $f_{\tilde{P},\hat{\beta}} = f_{\hat{P},\hat{\beta}}$ and we get a contradiction to optimality

Thus we have no knot with both positive and negative coefficient, and it follows that:

$$TV(f_{\hat{P},\hat{\beta}}^{(k-1)}) = (k-1)! \sum_i |s_i \hat{P}(a_i, s_i)| = (k-1)!\hat{P}(\Omega)$$

For motivation and discussion of total variation penalties, we refer the reader to Mammen and van de Geer (7) and refrences therein. Intuitively, by imposing a total variation constraint on a (very) large family of functions, we are forcing the resulting solution to be *smooth* (by limiting wiggliness of the $(k-1)$th derivative).

It has previously been shown that minimizing a quadratic loss subject to a constraint on the kth total variation yields a kth order spline (Mammen and van de Geer 7). It follows immediately that our sparse spline solution is indeed the optimal solution, not only of our ℓ_1 regularized problem, but also of the fully non-parametric regression problem, where a total-variation penalty is applied.

5.1 Practical Implementation and the Feature Search Problem

Looking back at Algorithm 1 and the next feature search problem, we observe that at each iteration of the path following algorithm we have a set $\mathcal{A}$ of indices of active functions with indexes in Ω_{pen}, characterized by their knots:

$$\omega \in \mathcal{A} \Rightarrow (x-\omega)_+^{k-1} \text{ has non-0 coefficient in the solution.}$$

In the search criterion for the next basis function in (5), $l(\omega)$ comprises a ratio of polynomials of degree $k-1$ in ω. The coefficients of these polynomials are fixed as long as ω does not cross a data point or a current knot in $\mathcal{A}$ (since both of these events change the parametric form of ϕ_ω, due to the positive-part function $(\cdot)_+$).

Investigating these polynomials we observe that for $k \in \{1,2\}$ we get in (5) ratios of constant or linear functions, respectively. It is easy to show that the extrema of such functions on closed intervals are always at the end points. Thus, the chosen knots will always be at the data points (this was first observed by Mammen and van de Geer 7). Interestingly, we get here a situation that is analogous to the RKHS case: we have identified an $n + k$ dimensional sub-space of the feature space such that the solution path lies fully within this sub-space. If $k \geq 3$, however, then we get ratios of higher degree polynomials in (5), and their extrema are not guaranteed to be at the ends of the intervals. Hence, knots can fall outside data points and we are really facing an optimization problem in infinite dimensional space.

As a concrete example, we now concentrate on the case $k = 3$ and the lasso modeling problem. The ratio of quadratics we get in (5) can be optimized analytically within each segment (flanked by two points which are either existing knots or data points), and once we do this for all such segments (there are at most $2n$ per dimension, or a maximum of $2np$ for the additive model), we can find ω^* — the global minimizer of $d(\omega)$ in (6) — which will be the next knot.

We demonstrate this on a 2-dimensional simulation example. For $x \in [0,1]$, let:

$$g(x) = 0.125 - 0.125x - x^2 + 2(x-0.25)_+^2 - 2(x-0.5)_+^2 + 2(x-0.75)_+^2.$$

a quadratic spline with knots at $0.25, 0.5, 0.75$. Our target function, drawn in the upper left box of Figure 1, is $f(x_1, x_2) = g(x_1) + g(x_2)$.

We draw 100 training samples uniformly in $[0,1] \times [0,1]$ with gaussian noise:

$$y_i = f(x_{i1}, x_{i2}) + \epsilon_i, \quad \epsilon_i \overset{\text{i.i.d}}{\sim} N(0, 0.03)$$

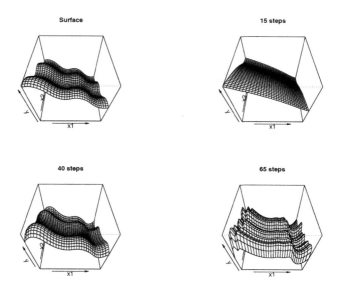

Fig. 1. True model (top left) and models generated in 15,40 and 65 steps of Algorithm 1

We then apply our quadratic spline algorithm. The results can be seen in Figure 1. Initially the data is clearly under-fitted, but in about 40 iterations of Algorithm 1 we get a reasonable estimate of the true surface. After that, the fit deteriorates as over-fitting occurs and we are mostly fitting the noise.

5.2   Real Data Examples: Boston and California Housing Datasets

We briefly describe application of our additive spline algorithm with $k = 3$ to the Boston Housing dataset (Blake and Merz 2) (13 features, 506 observations, of them 455 used for fitting, the rest held out for evaluation) and the California Housing dataset (Pace and Barry 8) (8 features, 20640 observations, of them 1000 used for fitting). Figure 2 shows the performance on holdout data, as a function of the number of iterations of the path following algorithm (an indication of model complexity). We observe that for both datasets, increased complexity through additive spline fitting does seem to significantly improve the predictive performance (although the small size of the holdout set for the Boston Housing dataset implies we should take these results with some caution). For both datasets, the performance still seems to be improving after about 200 iterations, when the additive spline model already contains 10 knots across all original variables for the Boston Housing dataset and 15 knots for the California Housing dataset. Overall performance improvement due to the use of splines was 10% (California) and 15% (Boston) in MSE compared to quadratic regression and 17% (California) and 45% (Boston) compared to simple linear regression.

Remark 1. *We were not able to run the algorithm beyond about 200 iterations for Boston Housing and about 250 iterations for California Housing due to accumulation of numerical inaccuracies in our R implementation (caused by operations like squared*

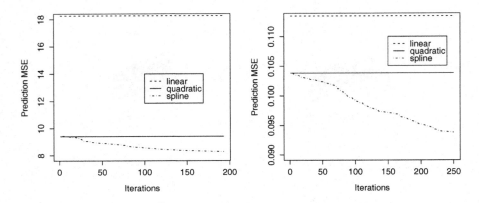

Fig. 2. Results of running additive spline algorithm on Boston (left) and California (right) Housing datasets. For comparison, both plots show the holdout MSE of regular linear regression (dashed) and quadratic regression (solid), compared to the improved performance from the additive splines. See text for details.

root performed in finding ω^*). So the knots selected are not exactly where they should be and these tiny errors accumulate as the algorithm proceeds, eventually leading it astray.

6 Discussion

In this paper we have addressed some of the theoretical and practical aspects of fitting ℓ_1 regularized models in infinite dimensional embedding feature spaces. In Section 3 we described some of the important mathematical and statistical properties of the solutions: existence, sparsity, and optimality testing. In Section 4 we developed an algorithm which can practically find the solutions, if the feature spaces facilitate the next feature search problem we defined in Eq. (7). We demonstrated in Section 5 that this indeed leads to a practical and useful modeling tool in the case of penalized regression splines.

While our results combine together to give a coherent picture of a theoretically attractive and practically applicable methodology, there are clearly a few additional questions that should be addressed to fully understand the potential of ℓ_1 regularization in infinite dimensions.

First and foremost is the question of learning performance, both practical and theoretical — can ℓ_1 regularized embeddings really offer a useful learning tool? From the practical side, we have evidence in the success of boosting, basis pursuit and other ℓ_1-type methods in high dimension. We can also add our spline example and the promising performance it demonstrates.

From the learning theory perspective, learning with ℓ_2 regularization in infinite-dimensional spaces enjoys strong learning guarantees which depend only on the ℓ_2 norm of the classifier and the ℓ_2 norm of the feature vector (i.e. the the kernel values).

Unfortunately, the situation is not as favorable in the case of ℓ_1 regularized learning in infinite dimensional spaces. Learning guarantees based on the ℓ_1-norm of the classifier and on $\sup_{\omega,x} |\phi_\omega(x)|$ (i.e. the ℓ_∞-norm of the feature vectors) also depend logarithmically on the dimensionality (Zhang 15). In fact, it can easily be seen that bounding $\sup_{\omega,x} |\phi_\omega(x)|$ alone is not enough to guarantee learning in infinite dimensional spaces: consider a space with a feature w_B for each finite set $B \subset \Omega$ such that $\phi_B(x) = 1$ iff $x \in B$. Any finite sample can be perfectly fitted with a classifier of ℓ_1-norm 1 without attaining any generalization.

However, learning can be assured if the space of feature mappings $\{\phi_w : x \to \mathbb{R} | w \in \Omega\}$ is of low-complexity, e.g. low VC-dimension, low Rademacher complexity, or having a low covering numbers. In this case, we can view a bounded ℓ_1-classifier as a convex combination of (scaled) base-predictors, and apply results for combined classifiers (Koltchinski and Panchenko 6).

It is interesting whether more general learning guarantees can also be obtained based on analytic properties of the features $\phi_\omega(x)$. Zhang (15) has already provided guarantees on infinite-dimensional learning with a bound on $\sup_{\omega,x} |\phi_\omega(x)|$ and on the ℓ_1-norm of the classifier, by also requiring the *entropy* of the classifier to be high. This requirement precludes sparse classifiers and so is disappointing from our perspective. However, perhaps it is possible to require some sort of "dual" constraint on the features instead, precluding them from being overly sparse or disjoint. Another possibility is obtaining guarantees in terms of smoothness or topological proprieties of the features, especially when there is a natural parametrization of the features, as in spline example of Section 5.

A second important question relates to deriving a general characterization of the "interesting" feature spaces where the feature search problem can be solved. We have seen in Section 5 that for the spline example, for $k < 2$ the problem is trivial, and for $k > 3$ it cannot easily be solved analytically. The case where the full power of our methodology was deployed was when $k = 3$ (quadratic splines): on the one hand, solving the truly infinite dimensional problem would not be possible without Algorithm 1, and on the other the feature search problem admits an analytic solution. We have some preliminary results about the properties of the feature spaces and their parametrization through Ω that facilitate such analytic solutions, but that is a topic for future work.

Our spline regression example has interesting connections to recent work on use of the ℓ_1 penalty for multiple kernel and multiple component learning (Bach et al. 1, Zhang and Lin 14). These works employ the ℓ_1 penalty *between components or kernels* to get sparsity in these objects (note that if they have less than n objects no sparsity is guaranteed). Within kernels or components the ℓ_2 penalty is still used. Our approach gives sparsity in the original feature space, and when it has several components (like the two dimensions x_1, x_2 in the simulated multivariate spline example), our methods control the total number of features used across all components combined. Another important difference is that our approach leads to simple, efficient, algorithms for generating the full regularized path, while Bach et al. (1) and Zhang and Lin (14) require complex optimization approaches to solve for a single regularization setting.

References

Bach, F., Lanckriet, G. & Jordan, M.: Multiple Kernel Learning, Conic Duality, and the SMO Algorithm. ICML-04

Blake, C.L., Merz, C.J.: UCI Repository of machine learning databases. (1998) http://www.ics.uci.edu/~mlearn/MLRepository.html

Efron, B., Hastie, T., Johnstone, I., Tibshirani, R.: Least Angle Regression (with discussion). The Annals of Statistics 32, 407–499 (2004)

Freund, Y., Schapire, R.: A decision-theoretic generalization of on-line learning and an application to boosting. Journal of Computer and System Sciences 55(1), 119–139 (1997)

Hastie, T., Tibshirani, R.: Generalized Additive Models. Chapman and Hall (1990)

Koltchinski, V., Panchenko, D.: Empirical margin distributions and bounding the generalization error of combined classifiers. Annals of Statistics, vol. 30(1) (2002)

Mammen, E., Van de Geer, S.: Locally Adaptive Regression Splines. The Annals of Statistics 25(1), 387–413 (1997)

Pace, R.K., Barry, R.: Sparse Spatial Autoregressions. Stat. and Prob. Let. 33, 291–297 (1997)

Rosset, S., Zhu, J., Hastie, T.: Boosting as a regularized path to a maximum margin classifier. Journal of Machine Learning Research 5, 941–973 (2004)

Rosset, S., Zhu, J.: Piecewise linear regularized solution paths. Annals of Statistics, to appear (2006) www-stat.stanford.edu/~saharon/papers/piecewise-revised.pdf

Rudin, W.: Functional Analysis, 2nd edn. McGraw-Hill, Inc, New York (1991)

Schöelkopf, B., Smola, A.J.: Learning with Kernels. MIT Press, Cambridge (2002)

Tibshirani, R.: Regression shrinkage and selection via the lasso. Journlal of the Royal Statistical Society B 58(1), 267–288 (1996)

Zhang, H.H., Lin, Y.: Component Selection and Smoothing for Nonparametric Regression in Exponential Families. Statistica Sinica 16, 1021–1041 (2006)

Zhang, T.: Covering number bounds of certain regularized linear function classes. Journal of Machine Learning Research 2, 527–550 (2002)

Zhu, J., Rosset, S., Hastie, T., Tibshirani, R.: 1-norm support vector machines. Neural Information Processing Systems, vol. 16 (2004)

A   Proofs of Convexity and Measure Results

Appendix A is organized as follows. First we present necessary definitions and facts about measures and convex sets. Then we prove Theorem 2.

Definition 1. *We define $co(A)$ as the intersection of all convex sets B containing A,*

$$co(A) = \bigcap_{\substack{A \subset B \\ B - \text{convex}}} B.$$

Analogously $\overline{co}(A)$ will denote the closure of $co(A)$.

Another natural way to define a $co(A)$ is to define it as the set of all convex combinations of finite subsets of A. Next lemma states that both those definitions are equivalent.

Lemma 1. *For a set A let $co'(A) = \{x : x = \sum_{i=1}^{n} a_i x_i, x_i \in A, \sum_{i=1}^{n} a_i = 1, a_i > 0\}$. Then $co(A) = co'(A)$.*

This is a very well known fact, but the proof is easy so we provide it.

Proof (of Lemma 1). The inclusion $co'(A) \subset co(A)$ is obvious, as every convex set containing A contains all convex combinations of points of A.

It remains to prove that $co'(A) \supset co(A)$. We shall show that $co'(A)$ is a convex set. Indeed, let $x, y \in co'(A)$. By definition $x = \sum_{i=1}^{n} \alpha_i x_i, y = \sum_{i=1}^{k} \beta_i y_i, x_i, y_i \in A, \sum_{i=1}^{n} \alpha_i = 1, \sum_{i=1}^{k} \beta_i = 1, \alpha_i, \beta_i > 0$. Then for every $t \in [0, 1]$

$$tx + (1-t)y = t \sum_{i=1}^{n} \alpha_i x_i + (1-t) \sum_{i=1}^{k} \beta_i y_i$$

is a convex combination of points $x_1, \ldots, x_n, y_1, \ldots, y_k$, so it is an element of $co'(A)$. Trivially $A \subset co'(A)$, so $co'(A)$ is a convex set containing A, and thus it contains $co(A)$.

We are going to need the following classical result:

Theorem 6 (Caratheodory's Convex Hull Theorem). *Let A be a finite set of points in $\mathbb{R}^n$. Then every $x \in co(A)$ can be expressed as a convex combination of at most $n+1$ points of A.*

A corollary of Caratheodory's Convex Hull Theorem is Proposition 1, the classical fact which is essential for our considerations (see also Rudin (11), Theorem 3.20.).

Proof (of Proposition 1 from Section 3.2)
By Caratheodory's Convex Hull Theorem and Lemma 1 $co(A)$ is the image of a mapping $\{a_1, \ldots, a_{n+1}, z_1, \ldots, z_{n+1}\} \mapsto \sum_{i=1}^{n+1} a_i z_i$. This is a continuous mapping on a compact domain $\{\sum_{i=1}^{n+1} a_i, a_i \geq 0\} \times A^n$, so its image is compact.

Now we need to connect the theory of convex sets with measures on bounded subsets of $\mathbb{R}^n$. Lemma 2 provides such a link.

Lemma 2. *Let A be a bounded subset of $\mathbb{R}^n$. Then for any probability measure μ with $supp(\mu) \subset A$ there holds*

$$\int_A x d\mu(x) \in co(A).$$

Remark 2. *This result does not generalize to the non-Euclidean case .*

If A is a subset of a topological vector space V such that V^{*} [5] separates the points of V and if $\overline{co}(A)$ is a compact set then it is always true that $\int_A x d\mu(x) \in \overline{co}(A)$. Compare (Rudin 11, Theorem 3.27).

However, even if A is a bounded subset of a a Hilbert space and coA is not closed, $\int_A x d\mu(x)$ might not be contained in coA.

---

[5] For a topological space V we are using a V^* symbol to denote a dual space of V–the space of all continuous linear functionals on V. In case of $\mathbb{R}^n$ this space is of course isometric to $\mathbb{R}^n$ itself. In particular $\varphi \in (\mathbb{R}^n)^*, \|\varphi\| = 1$ can be identified with a set of all vectors of length 1.

For every bounded subset A of $\mathbb{R}^n$ and $C \in \mathbb{R}$ we define $\mathcal{D}_C(A)$ to be a set of all $\varphi \in (\mathbb{R}^n)^*$, $\|\varphi\| = 1$ such that $\varphi(x) \leq C$ for every $x \in A$.

For the proof of Lemma 2 we shall need the following two propositions. Proposition 3 states that $\overline{co}(A)$ is an intersection of all halfspaces containing A.

Proposition 3. *Let A be a bounded subset of $\mathbb{R}^n$. Then $\overline{co}A$ is an intersection of all sets of the form $\{x : \varphi(x) \leq C, \varphi \in \mathcal{D}_C(A)\}$.*

Proof. This is an immediate corollary of a much stronger results - the Separation Theorem for topological vector space, see Rudin (11, Theorem 3.21).

The next proposition states that every point on a boundary of a convex hull of A has a "supporting plane".

Proposition 4. *For every $z \in \overline{co}(A) \setminus co(A)$ there exist $C \in \mathbb{R}$ and $\Lambda \in \mathcal{D}_C(A)$ such that $\Lambda(z) - C = 0$.*

Proof. Let $z \in \overline{co}(A) \setminus co(A)$. Then there exists a convex set W containing A such that $z \notin W$ and $z \in \overline{W}$. Let $c = \sup\limits_{C \in \mathbb{R}, \Lambda \in \mathcal{D}_C(W)} \Lambda(z) - C$. As $z \in \overline{W}$, for every $\Lambda \in \mathcal{D}_C(\omega)$ there holds $\Lambda(z) - c \leq 0$. By continuity of linear operators in $\mathbb{R}^n$ there holds $c \leq 0$. Due to compactness arguments there exist C_0 and $\Lambda_0 \in \mathcal{D}_{C_0}(W)$ such that $c = \Lambda_0(z) - C_0$. Thus for every point $z' \in B(z, -c)$ and every $\Lambda \in \mathcal{D}_C(W)$ for some C there holds $\Lambda(z') - C = \Lambda(z' - z) + \Lambda(z) - C \leq \Lambda(z' - z) - c \leq 0$ as $|\Lambda(z' - z)| < -c$ because $\|\Lambda\| = 1$. Thus $B(z, -c) \subset \overline{W}$. Let us suppose that $c \neq 0$. Let I be any diameter of $B(z, -c)$. The intersection $I \cap W$ is a convex set, it is a subinterval of I. Moreover, as $\overline{W} \cap I = \overline{W \cap I}$, only the endpoints of I can be not contained in W. As z is a midpoint of I, this is a contradiction with an assumption $z \notin W$, so there must be $c = 0$. Thus $\Lambda_0(z) - C_0 = 0$. As $\mathcal{D}_C(W) \subset \mathcal{D}_C(A)$, the proposition follows.

Proof (of Lemma 2). The proof is by induction on n, the dimension of the space. For $n = 0$, $\mathbb{R}^n$ consists of a single point and the theorem is trivially true.

Let us assume that the assertion holds for n and let A be a bounded subset of $\mathbb{R}^{n+1}$. We will denote $y = \int\limits_A x d\mu(x)$. Let Λ be a linear functional on $\mathbb{R}^{n+1}$. We have (by linearity of an integral)

$$\Lambda(y) = \int\limits_A \Lambda(x) d\mu(x)$$

and therefore if $\Lambda \in \mathcal{D}_C(A)$, then $\Lambda(y) \leq C$. By Proposition 3 $y \in \overline{co}(A)$. By Proposition 4 either $y \in co(A)$ and our assertion is true, or there exist C and $\Lambda \in \mathcal{D}_C(A)$ such that $\Lambda(y) = C$. In the second case $\mu(A \setminus \{x : \Lambda(x) = C\}) = 0$, and therefore $supp(\mu) \subset \mu(A \cap \{x : \Lambda(x) = C\})$. The later set is a convex subset of n-dimensional hyperplane, and by inductive assumption $y \in A \cap \{x : \Lambda(x) = C\} \subset A$.

Now we are ready to prove Theorem 2.

Proof (of Theorem 2 from Section 3.1). Is is an immediate consequence of Lemma 2 and Caratheodory's convex hull theorem .

Prediction by Categorical Features: Generalization Properties and Application to Feature Ranking

Sivan Sabato[1] and Shai Shalev-Shwartz[1,2]

[1] IBM Research Laboratory in Haifa, Haifa 31905, Israel
[2] School of Computer Sci. & Eng., The Hebrew University, Jerusalem 91904, Israel

Abstract. We describe and analyze a new approach for feature ranking in the presence of categorical features with a large number of possible values. It is shown that popular ranking criteria, such as the Gini index and the misclassification error, can be interpreted as the training error of a predictor that is deduced from the training set. It is then argued that using the *generalization* error is a more adequate ranking criterion. We propose a modification of the Gini index criterion, based on a robust estimation of the generalization error of a predictor associated with the Gini index. The properties of this new estimator are analyzed, showing that for most training sets, it produces an accurate estimation of the true generalization error. We then address the question of finding the optimal predictor that is based on a single categorical feature. It is shown that the predictor associated with the misclassification error criterion has the minimal expected generalization error. We bound the bias of this predictor with respect to the generalization error of the Bayes optimal predictor, and analyze its concentration properties.

1 Introduction

Filter methods for supervised feature selection rank a given set of features according to their relevance for predicting the label. As in other supervised learning methods, the ranking of the features is generated based on an input training set. Examples of widely used filter ranking criteria are the Gini index, the misclassification error, and the cross-entropy [6]. In this paper we address the problem of feature ranking in the presence of *categorical* features. We show that a direct application of existing ranking criteria might lead to poor results in the presence of categorical features that can take many values. We propose an adaptation of existing filter criteria that copes with these difficulties.

Many feature ranking methods can be viewed as a two-phase process: First, each individual feature is used to construct a predictor of the label. Then, the features are ranked based on the errors of these predictors. The training set is used both for constructing each predictor and for evaluating its error. Most current filters use the error over the training set as the ranking criterion. In contrast, we argue that the *generalization* error of each predictor is a more adequate ranking criterion. When dealing with binary features, the training error is likely to be close to the generalization error, and therefore the ranking generated by current filters works rather well. However, this is not the case when dealing with categorical features that can take a large number of values. To illustrate this fact, consider the problem of predicting whether someone is unemployed, based on their social security number (SSN). A predictor constructed using

N. Bshouty and C. Gentile (Eds.): COLT 2007, LNAI 4539, pp. 559–573, 2007.

any finite training set would have zero error on the training set but a large generalization error. The first contribution of this paper is an estimator for the generalization error of the predictor associated with the Gini index. This estimator can be calculated from the training set and we propose to use it instead of the original Gini index criterion in the presence of categorical features. We prove that regardless of the underlying distribution, our estimation is close to the true value of the generalization error for most training sets.

Based on our perspective of ranking criteria as estimators of the generalization error of a certain predictor, a natural question that arises is which predictor to use. Among all predictors that are based on a single feature, we ultimately would like to use the one whose generalization error is minimal. We prove that the best predictor in this sense is the predictor associated with the misclassification error criterion. We analyze the difference between the expected generalization error of this predictor and the error of the Bayes optimal hypothesis. Finally, we show a concentration result for the generalization error of this predictor.

Filter methods have been extensively studied in the context of decision trees [10,7,12]. The failure of existing filter ranking criteria in the presence of categorical features with a large number of possible values has been previously discussed in [12,11]. Quinlan suggested the Information Gain Ratio as a correction to the cross-entropy (a.k.a. Information Gain) criterion. In a broader context, information-theoretic measures are commonly used for feature ranking (see for example [14] and the references therein). One justification for their use is the existence of bounds on the Bayes optimal error that are based on these measures [14]. However, obtaining estimators for the entropy or mutual information seems to be difficult in the general case [2]. Another ranking criterion designed to address the above difficulty is a distance-based measure introduced by [3].

The problem we address shares some similarities with the problem of estimating the missing mass of a sample, typically encountered in language modeling [5,8,4]. The missing mass of a sample is the total probability mass of the values not occurring in the sample. Indeed, in the aforementioned example of the SSN feature, the value of the missing mass will be close to one. In some of our proofs we borrow ideas from [8,4]. However, our problem is more involved, as even for a value that we do observe in the sample, if it appears only a small number of times then the training error is likely to diverge from the generalization error. Finally, we would like to note that classical VC theory for bounding the difference between the training error and the generalization error is not applicable here. This is because the VC dimension grows with the number of values a categorical feature may take, and in our framework this number is unbounded.

2   Problem Setting

In this section we establish the notation used throughout the paper and formally describe our problem setting. In the supervised feature selection setting we are provided with k categorical features and with a label. Each categorical feature is a random variable that takes values from a finite set. We denote by X_i the i'th feature and by V_i the set of values X_i can take. We make no assumptions on the identity of V_i nor on its size. The label is a binary random variable, denoted Y, that takes values from $\{0,1\}$.

Generally speaking, the goal of supervised feature selection is to find a subset of the features that can be used later for constructing an accurate classification rule. We focus on the filter approach in which we rank *individual* features according to their "relevance" to the label. Different filters employ different criteria for assessing the relevance of a feature to the label. Since we are dealing with individual features, let us ignore the fact that we have k features and from now on focus on defining a relevance measure for a single feature X (and denote by V the set of values X can take). To simplify our notation we denote $p_v \stackrel{\Delta}{=} \Pr[X = v]$ and $q_v \stackrel{\Delta}{=} \Pr[Y = 1 | X = v]$.

In practice, the probabilities $\{p_v\}$ and $\{q_v\}$ are unknown. Instead, it is assumed that we have a training set $S = \{(x_i, y_i)\}_{i=1}^m$, which is sampled i.i.d. according to the joint probability distribution $\Pr[X, Y]$. Based on S, the probabilities $\{p_v\}$ and $\{q_v\}$ are usually estimated as follows. Let $c_v = |\{i : x_i = v\}|$ be the number of examples in S for which the feature takes the value v and let $c_v^+ = |\{i : x_i = v \wedge y_i = 1\}|$ be the number of examples in which the value of the feature is v and the label is 1. Then $\{p_v\}$ and $\{q_v\}$ are estimated as follows:

$$\hat{p}_v \stackrel{\Delta}{=} \frac{c_v}{m} \quad \text{and} \quad \hat{q}_v \stackrel{\Delta}{=} \begin{cases} \frac{c_v^+}{c_v} & c_v > 0 \\ \frac{1}{2} & c_v = 0 \end{cases} \tag{1}$$

Note that $\hat{p}_v$ and $\hat{q}_v$ are implicit functions of the training set S.

Two popular filters used for feature selection [6] are the misclassification error

$$\sum_{v \in V} \hat{p}_v \, \min\{\hat{q}_v, (1 - \hat{q}_v)\}, \tag{2}$$

and the Gini index

$$2 \sum_{v \in V} \hat{p}_v \, \hat{q}_v (1 - \hat{q}_v). \tag{3}$$

In these filters, smaller values indicate more relevant features.

Both the misclassification error and the Gini index were found to work rather well in practice when $|V|$ is small. However, for categorical features with a large number of possible values, we might end up with a poor feature ranking criterion. As an example (see also [11]), suppose that Y indicates whether a person is unemployed and we have two features: X_1 is the person's SSN and X_2 is 1 if the person has a mortgage and 0 otherwise. For the first feature, V is the set of all the SSNs. Because the SSN alone determines the target label, we have that $\hat{q}_v$ is either 0 or 1 for any v such that $\hat{p}_v > 0$. Thus, both the misclassification error and the Gini index are zero for this feature. For the second feature, it can be shown that with high probability over the choice of the training set, the two criteria mentioned above take positive values. Therefore, both criteria prefer the first feature over the second. In contrast, for our purposes X_2 is much better than X_1. This is because X_2 can be used later for learning a reasonable classification rule based on a finite training set, while X_1 will suffer from over-fitting.

It would have been natural to attribute the failure of the filter criteria to the fact that we use estimated probabilities instead of the true (unknown) probabilities. However, note that in the above example, the same problem would arise even if we used $\{p_v\}$ and $\{q_v\}$ in Eq. (2) and Eq. (3). The aforementioned problem was previously underscored in the context of the Information Gain filter [12,3,11]. In that context, Quinlan [12] suggested an adaptation of the Information Gain, called Information Gain Ratio, which was found rather effective in practice.

In this paper, we take a different approach, and propose to interpret a filter's criterion as the generalization error of a classification rule that can be inferred from the training set. To do so, let us first introduce some additional notation. A probabilistic hypothesis is a function $h : V \to [0, 1]$, where $h(v)$ is the probability to predict the label 1 given the value v. The generalization error of h is the probability to wrongly predict the label,

$$\ell(h) \stackrel{\Delta}{=} \sum_{v \in V} p_v \left(q_v \left(1 - h(v) \right) + \left(1 - q_v \right) h(v) \right) . \tag{4}$$

We now define two hypotheses based on the training set S. The first one is

$$h_S^{\text{Gini}}(v) = \hat{q}_v . \tag{5}$$

As its name indicates, h_S^{Gini} is closely related to the Gini index filter given in Eq. (3). To see this, we note that the generalization error of h_S^{Gini} is

$$\ell(h_S^{\text{Gini}}) = \sum_{v \in V} p_v \left(q_v \left(1 - \hat{q}_v \right) + \left(1 - q_v \right) \hat{q}_v \right) . \tag{6}$$

If the estimated probabilities $\{\hat{p}_v\}$ and $\{\hat{q}_v\}$ coincide with the true probabilities $\{p_v\}$ and $\{q_v\}$, then $\ell(h_S^{\text{Gini}})$ is identical to the Gini index defined in Eq. (3). This will be approximately true, for example, when $m \gg |V|$. In contrast, when the training set is small, using $\ell(h_S^{\text{Gini}})$ is preferable to using the Gini index given in Eq. (3), because $\ell(h_S^{\text{Gini}})$ takes into account the fact that the estimated probabilities might be skewed.

The second hypothesis we define is

$$h_S^{\text{Bayes}}(v) = \begin{cases} 1 & \hat{q}_v > \frac{1}{2} \\ 0 & \hat{q}_v < \frac{1}{2} \\ \frac{1}{2} & \hat{q}_v = \frac{1}{2} \end{cases} . \tag{7}$$

Note that if $\{\hat{q}_v\}$ coincide with $\{q_v\}$ then h_S^{Bayes} is the Bayes optimal classifier, which we denote by h_∞^{Bayes}. If in addition $\{\hat{p}_v\}$ and $\{p_v\}$ are the same, then $\ell(h_S^{\text{Bayes}})$ is identical to the misclassification error defined in Eq. (2). Here again, the misclassification error might differ from $\ell(h_S^{\text{Bayes}})$ for small training sets.

To illustrate the advantage of $\ell(h_S^{\text{Gini}})$ and $\ell(h_S^{\text{Bayes}})$ over their counterparts given in Eq. (3) and Eq. (2), we return to the example mentioned above. For the SSN feature we have $\ell(h_S^{\text{Gini}}) = \ell(h_S^{\text{Bayes}}) = \frac{1}{2} M_0$, where $M_0 \stackrel{\Delta}{=} \sum_{v:c_v=0} p_v$. In general, we denote

$$M_k \stackrel{\Delta}{=} \sum_{v:c_v=k} p_v . \tag{8}$$

The quantity M_0 is known as the missing mass [5,8] and for the SSN feature, $M_0 \geq (|V| - m)/|V|$. Therefore, the generalization error of both h_S^{Gini} and h_S^{Bayes} would be close to 1 for a reasonable m. On the other hand, for the second feature (having a mortgage), it can be verified that both $\ell(h_S^{\text{Bayes}})$ and $\ell(h_S^{\text{Gini}})$ are likely to be small. Therefore, using $\ell(h_S^{\text{Gini}})$ or $\ell(h_S^{\text{Bayes}})$ yields a correct ranking for this naive example.

We have proposed a modification of the Gini index and the misclassification error that uses the generalization error and therefore is suitable even when m is smaller than

$|V|$. In practice, however, we cannot directly use the generalization error criterion since it depends on the unknown probabilities $\{p_v\}$ and $\{q_v\}$. To overcome this obstacle, we must derive estimators for the generalization error that can be calculated from the training set. In the next section we discuss the problem of estimating $\ell(h_S^{\text{Gini}})$ and $\ell(h_S^{\text{Bayes}})$ based on the training set. Additionally, we analyze the difference between $\ell(h_S^{\text{Bayes}})$ and the error of the Bayes optimal hypothesis.

3   Main Results

We start this section with a derivation of an estimator for $\ell(h_S^{\text{Gini}})$, which can serve as a new feature ranking criterion. We show that for most training sets, this estimator will be close to the true value of $\ell(h_S^{\text{Gini}})$. We then shift our attention to $\ell(h_S^{\text{Bayes}})$. First, we prove that among all predictors with no prior knowledge on the distribution $\Pr[X, Y]$, the generalization error of h_S^{Bayes} is smallest in expectation. Next, we bound the difference between the generalization error of h_S^{Bayes} and the error of the Bayes optimal hypothesis. Finally, we prove a concentration bound for $\ell(h_S^{\text{Bayes}})$. Regretfully, we could not find a good estimator for $\ell(h_S^{\text{Bayes}})$. Nevertheless, we believe that our concentration results can be utilized for finding such an estimator. This task is left for future research.

We propose the following estimator for the generalization error of h_S^{Gini}:

$$\hat{\ell} \triangleq \frac{|\{v : c_v = 1\}|}{2m} + \sum_{v:c_v>1} \frac{2c_v}{c_v - 1} \hat{p}_v \hat{q}_v (1 - \hat{q}_v) \ . \tag{9}$$

In the next section, we derive this estimator based on a conditional cross-validation technique. We suggest to use the estimation of $\ell(h_S^{\text{Gini}})$ given in Eq. (9) rather than the original Gini index given in Eq. (3) as a feature ranking criterion. Let us compare these two criteria: First, for values v that appear many times in the training set we have that $\frac{c_v}{c_v-1} \approx 1$. If for all $v \in V$ we have that the size of the training set is much larger than $1/p_v$, then all values in V are likely to appear many times in the training set and thus the definitions in Eq. (9) and Eq. (3) consolidate. The two definitions differ when there are values that appear rarely in the training set. For such values, the correction term is larger than 1. Special consideration is given to values that appear exactly once in the training set. For such values we estimate the generalization error to be $\frac{1}{2}$, which is the highest possible error. Intuitively, since one example provides us with no information as to the variance of the label Y given $X = v$, we cannot have a more accurate estimation for the contribution of this value to the total generalization error. Furthermore, the fraction of values that appear exactly once in the training set is an estimator for the probability mass of those values that do not appear at all in the training set (see also [5,8]).

We now turn to analyze the quality of the proposed estimator. We first show (Thm. 1 below) that the bias of this estimator is small. Then, in Thm. 2, we prove a concentration bound for the estimator, which holds for any joint distribution of $\Pr[X, Y]$ and does not depend on the size of V. Specifically, we show that for any $\delta \in (0, 1)$, in a fraction of at least $1 - \delta$ of the training sets the error of the estimator is $O(\frac{\ln(m/\delta)}{\sqrt{m}})$.

Theorem 1. *Let S be a set of m examples sampled i.i.d. according to the probability measure* $\Pr[X, Y]$. *Let h_S^{Gini} be the Gini hypothesis given in Eq. (5) and let $\ell(h_S^{\text{Gini}})$ be* *the generalization error of h_S^{Gini}, where ℓ is as defined in Eq. (4). Let $\hat{\ell}$ be the estimation of $\ell(h_S^{Gini})$ as given in Eq. (9). Then, $\left| \mathbb{E}[\ell(h_S^{Gini})] - \mathbb{E}[\hat{\ell}] \right| \leq \frac{1}{2m}$, where expectation is taken over all sets S of m examples.*

The next theorem shows that for most training sets, our estimator is close to the true generalization error of h_S^{Gini}.

Theorem 2. *Under the same assumptions as in Thm. 1, let δ be an arbitrary scalar in $(0, 1)$. Then, with probability of at least $1 - \delta$ over the choice of S, we have*

$$\left| \ell(h_S^{Gini}) - \hat{\ell} \right| \leq O\left(\frac{\ln(m/\delta)\sqrt{\ln(1/\delta)}}{\sqrt{m}} \right) .$$

Based on the above theorem, $\hat{\ell}$ can be used as a filter criterion. The convergence rate shown can be used to establish confidence intervals on the true Gini generalization error. The proofs of Thm. 1 and Thm. 2 are given in the next section.

So far we have derived an estimator for the generalization error of the Gini hypothesis and shown that it is close to the true Gini error. The Gini hypothesis has the advantage of being highly concentrated around its mean. This is important especially when the sample size is fairly small. However, the Gini hypothesis does not produce the lowest generalization error in expectation. We now turn to show that the hypothesis h_S^{Bayes} defined in Eq. (7) is optimal in this respect, but that its concentration is weaker. These two facts are characteristic of the well known bias-variance tradeoff commonly found in estimation and prediction tasks.

Had we known the underlying distribution of our data, we could have used the Bayes optimal hypothesis, h_∞^{Bayes}, that achieves the smallest possible generalization error. When the underlying distribution is unknown, the training set is used to construct the hypothesis. Thm. 3 below shows that among all hypotheses that can be learned from a finite training set, h_S^{Bayes} achieves the smallest generalization error in expectation. More precisely, h_S^{Bayes} is optimal among all the hypotheses that are symmetric with respect to both $|V|$ and the label values. This symmetry requirement limits the examined hypotheses to those that do not exploit prior knowledge on the underlying distribution $\Pr[X, Y]$. Formally, let H_S be the set of all hypotheses that can be written as $h(v) = f_h(c_v(S), c_v^+(S))$ where $f_h : \mathbb{N} \times \mathbb{N} \to [0, 1]$ is a function such that $f_h(n_1, n_2) = 1 - f_h(n_1, n_1 - n_2)$ for all $n_1, n_2 \in \mathbb{N}$. The following theorem establishes the optimality of h_S^{Bayes} and bounds the difference between the Bayes optimal error and the error achieved by h_S^{Bayes}.

Theorem 3. *Let S be a set of m examples sampled i.i.d. according to the probability measure $\Pr[X, Y]$. For any hypothesis h, let $\ell(h)$ be the generalization error of h, as defined in Eq. (4). Let h_S^{Bayes} be the hypothesis given in Eq. (7) and let h_∞^{Bayes} be the Bayes optimal hypothesis. Let H_S be the set of symmetric hypotheses. Then $\mathbb{E}[\ell(h_S^{Bayes})] = \min_{h \in H_S} \mathbb{E}[\ell(h)]$, and*

$$\mathbb{E}[\ell(h_S^{Bayes})] - \ell(h_\infty^{Bayes}) \leq \tfrac{1}{2} \mathbb{E}[M_0] + \tfrac{1}{8} \mathbb{E}[M_1] + \tfrac{1}{8} \mathbb{E}[M_2] + \sum_{k=3}^m \tfrac{1}{\sqrt{ek}} \mathbb{E}[M_k],$$

where M_k is as defined in Eq. (8).

Note that the first term in the difference between $\mathbb{E}[\ell(h_S^{\text{Bayes}})]$ and $\ell(h_\infty^{\text{Bayes}})$ is exactly half the expectation of the missing mass. This is expected, because we cannot improve our prediction over the baseline error of $\frac{1}{2}$ for values not seen in the training set, as exemplified in the SSN example described in the previous section. Subsequent terms in the bound can be attributed to the fact that even for values observed in the training set, a wrong prediction might be generated if there is a small number of examples.

We have shown that h_S^{Bayes} has the smallest generalization error in expectation, but this does not guarantee a small generalization error on a given sample. Thm. 4 below bounds the concentration of $\ell(h_S^{\text{Bayes}})$. This concentration along with Thm. 3 provides us with a bound on the difference between h_S^{Bayes} and the Bayes optimal error that is true for most samples.

Theorem 4. *Under the same assumptions of Thm. 3, assume that $m \geq 8$ and let δ be an arbitrary scalar in $(0, 1)$. Then, with probability of at least $1 - \delta$ over the choice of S, we have*

$$|\ell(h_S^{\text{Bayes}}) - \mathbb{E}[\ell(h_S^{\text{Bayes}})]| \leq O\left(\frac{\ln(m/\delta) \sqrt{\ln(1/\delta)}}{m^{1/6}}\right).$$

The concentration bound for $\ell(h_S^{\text{Bayes}})$ is worse than the concentration bound for $\ell(h_S^{\text{Gini}})$, suggesting that indeed the choice between h_S^{Gini} and h_S^{Bayes} is not trivial. To use $\ell(h_S^{\text{Bayes}})$ as a filter criterion, an estimator for this quantity is needed. However, at this point we cannot provide such an estimator. We conjecture that based on Thm. 4 an estimator with a small bias but a weak concentration can be constructed. We leave this task to further work. Finally, we would like to note that Antos et al. [1] have shown that the Bayes optimal error cannot be estimated based on a finite training set. Finding an estimator for $\ell(h_S^{\text{Bayes}})$ would allow us to approximate the Bayes optimal error up to the bias term quantified in Thm. 3.

4   Proofs of Main Results

In this section the results presented in the previous section are proved. Due to the lack of space, some of the proofs are omitted and can be found in [13].

In the previous section, an estimator for the generalization error of the Gini hypothesis was presented. We stated that for most training sets this estimation is reliable. In this section, we first derive the estimator $\hat{\ell}$ given in Eq. (9) using a conditional cross-validation technique, and then utilize this interpretation of $\hat{\ell}$ to prove Thm. 1 and Thm. 2.

To derive the estimator given in Eq. (9), let us first rewrite $\ell(h_S^{\text{Gini}})$ as the sum $\sum_v \ell_v(h_S^{\text{Gini}})$, where $\ell_v(h_S^{\text{Gini}})$ is the amount of error due to value v and is formally defined as

$$\ell_v(h) \stackrel{\Delta}{=} \Pr[X = v] \Pr[h(X) \neq Y \mid X = v] = p_v \left(q_v \left(1 - h(v)\right) + \left(1 - q_v\right) h(v)\right).$$

We now estimate the two factors $\Pr[X = v]$ and $\Pr[h_S^{\text{Gini}}(X) \neq Y \mid X = v]$ independently. Later on we multiply the two estimations. The resulting local estimator of $\ell_v(h)$ is denoted $\hat{\ell}_v$ and our global estimator is $\hat{\ell} \stackrel{\Delta}{=} \sum_v \hat{\ell}_v$.

To estimate $\Pr[X = v]$, we use the straightforward estimator $\hat{p}_v$. Turning to the estimation of $\Pr[h_S^{\mathrm{Gini}}(X) \neq Y \mid X = v]$, recall that h_S^{Gini}, defined in Eq. (5), is a probabilistic hypothesis where $\hat{q}_v$ is the probability to return the label 1 given that the value of X is v. Equivalently, we can think of the label that $h_S^{\mathrm{Gini}}(v)$ returns as being generated based on the following process: Let $S(v)$ be the set of those indices in the training set in which the feature takes the value v, namely, $S(v) = \{i : x_i = v\}$. Then, to set the label $h_S^{\mathrm{Gini}}(v)$ we randomly choose an index $i \in S(v)$ and return the label y_i. Based on this interpretation, a natural path for estimating $\Pr[h_S^{\mathrm{Gini}}(X) \neq Y \mid X = v]$ is through cross-validation: Select an $i \in S(v)$ to determine $h_S^{\mathrm{Gini}}(v)$, and estimate the generalization error to be the fraction of the examples whose label is different from the label of the selected example. That is, the estimation is $\frac{1}{c_v-1} \sum_{j \in S(v): j \neq i} \mathbf{1}_{y_i \neq y_j}$. Obviously, this procedure cannot be used if $c_v = 1$. We handle this case separately later on. To reduce the variance of this estimation, this process can be repeated, selecting each single example from $S(v)$ in turn and validating each time using the rest of the examples in $S(v)$. It is then possible to average over all the choices of the examples. The resulting estimation therefore becomes

$$\sum_{i \in S(v)} \frac{1}{c_v} \left(\frac{1}{c_v - 1} \sum_{j \in S(v): j \neq i} \mathbf{1}_{y_i \neq y_j} \right) = \frac{1}{c_v(c_v - 1)} \sum_{i,j \in S(v): i \neq j} \mathbf{1}_{y_i \neq y_j} .$$

Thus, we estimate $\Pr[h_S^{\mathrm{Gini}}(X) \neq Y \mid X = v]$ based on the fraction of differently-labeled pairs of examples in $S(v)$. Multiplying this estimator by $\hat{p}_v$ we obtain the following estimator for $\ell_v(h_S^{\mathrm{Gini}})$,

$$\hat{\ell}_v = \hat{p}_v \frac{1}{c_v(c_v - 1)} \sum_{i,j \in S(v), i \neq j} \mathbf{1}_{y_i \neq y_j} \tag{10}$$

$$= \hat{p}_v \frac{2c_v^+(c_v - c_v^+)}{c_v(c_v - 1)} = \hat{p}_v \frac{2c_v^2 \hat{q}_v(1 - \hat{q}_v)}{c_v(c_v - 1)} = \hat{p}_v \cdot \frac{2c_v}{c_v - 1} \hat{q}_v(1 - \hat{q}_v).$$

Finally, for values v that appear only once in the training set, the above cross-validation procedure cannot be applied, and we therefore estimate their generalization error to be $\frac{1}{2}$, the highest possible error. The full definition of $\hat{\ell}_v$ is thus:

$$\hat{\ell}_v = \begin{cases} \hat{p}_v \cdot \frac{1}{2} & c_v \leq 1 \\ \hat{p}_v \cdot \frac{2c_v}{c_v - 1} \hat{q}_v(1 - \hat{q}_v) & c_v \geq 2 \end{cases} \tag{11}$$

The resulting estimator $\hat{\ell}$ defined in Eq. (9) is exactly the sum $\sum_v \hat{\ell}_v$.

Based on the above derivation of $\hat{\ell}_v$, we now turn to prove Thm. 1, in which it is shown that the expectations of our estimator and of the true generalization error of the Gini hypothesis are close. To do so, we first inspect each of these expectations separately, starting with $\mathbb{E}[\hat{\ell}_v]$. The following lemma calculates the expectation of $\hat{\ell}_v$ over those training sets with exactly k appearances of the value v.

Lemma 1. *For k such that $1 < k \leq m$, $\mathbb{E}[\hat{\ell}_v \mid c_v(S) = k] = \frac{k}{m} \cdot 2q_v(1 - q_v)$.*

Proof. If $c_v = k$, then $\hat{p}_v = \frac{k}{m}$. Therefore, based on Eq. (10), we have

$$\mathbb{E}[\hat{\ell}_v \mid c_v(S) = k] = \frac{k}{m} \frac{1}{k(k-1)} \mathbb{E}\Big[\sum_{i,j \in S(v), i \neq j} \mathbf{1}_{y_i \neq y_j} \mid c_v(S) = k\Big]. \quad (12)$$

Let $Z_1, \dots, Z_k$ be independent binary random variables with $\Pr[Z_i = 1] = q_v$ for all $i \in [k]$. The conditional expectation on the right-hand side of Eq. (12) equals to

$$\mathbb{E}\Big[\sum_{i \neq j} \mathbf{1}_{Z_i \neq Z_j}\Big] = \sum_{i \neq j} \mathbb{E}[\mathbf{1}_{Z_i \neq Z_j}] = \sum_{i \neq j} 2\,q_v\,(1-q_v) = k(k-1) \cdot 2\,q_v\,(1-q_v) .$$

Combining the above with Eq. (12) concludes the proof. □

Based on the above lemma, we are now ready to calculate $\mathbb{E}[\hat{\ell}_v]$. We have

$$\mathbb{E}[\hat{\ell}_v] = \sum_{S} \Pr[S]\,\mathbb{E}[\hat{\ell}_v] = \sum_{k=0}^{m} \sum_{S : c_v(S) = k} \Pr[S] \cdot \mathbb{E}[\hat{\ell}_v \mid c_v(S) = k]. \quad (13)$$

From the definition of $\hat{\ell}$, we have $\mathbb{E}[\hat{\ell}_v \mid c_v(S) = 1] = \frac{1}{2m}$ and $\mathbb{E}[\hat{\ell}_v \mid c_v(S) = 0] = 0$. Combining this with Lemma 1 and Eq. (13), we get

$$E[\hat{\ell}_v] = \Pr[c_v = 1] \cdot \frac{1}{2m} + \sum_{k=2}^{m} \Pr[c_v = k] \cdot \frac{k}{m} \cdot 2q_v(1-q_v)$$

$$= \frac{1}{m}\left(\frac{1}{2} - 2q_v(1-q_v)\right)\Pr[c_v = 1] + 2q_v(1-q_v)\sum_{k=0}^{m}\Pr[c_v = k] \cdot \frac{k}{m}$$

$$= \frac{1}{m}\left(\frac{1}{2} - 2q_v(1-q_v)\right)\Pr[c_v = 1] + p_v \cdot 2q_v(1-q_v) , \quad (14)$$

where the last equality follows from the fact that $\sum_{k=0}^{m}\Pr[c_v = k]\frac{k}{m} = \mathbb{E}[\hat{p}_v] = p_v$. Having calculated the expectation of $\hat{\ell}_v$ we now calculate the expectation of $\ell_v(h_S^{\mathrm{Gini}})$. The proof of the following lemma can be found in [13].

Lemma 2. $\mathbb{E}[\ell_v(h_S^{\mathrm{Gini}})] = p_v(\frac{1}{2} - 2q_v(1-q_v))\Pr[c_v = 0] + p_v \cdot 2q_v(1-q_v).$

Equipped with the expectation of $\hat{\ell}_v$ given in Eq. (14) and the expectation of $\ell_v(h_S^{\mathrm{Gini}})$ given in Lemma 2, we are now ready to prove Thm. 1.

Proof (of Thm. 1). Using the definitions of $\ell(h_S^{\mathrm{Gini}})$ and $\hat{\ell}$ we have that

$$\mathbb{E}[\hat{\ell}] - \mathbb{E}[\ell(h_S^{\mathrm{Gini}})] = \mathbb{E}\Big[\sum_{v}\hat{\ell}_v\Big] - \mathbb{E}\Big[\sum_{v}\ell_v(h_S^{\mathrm{Gini}})\Big] = \sum_{v}\big(\mathbb{E}[\hat{\ell}_v] - \mathbb{E}[\ell_v(h_S^{\mathrm{Gini}})]\big) . \quad (15)$$

Fix some $v \in V$. From Eq. (14) and Lemma 2 we have

$$\mathbb{E}[\hat{\ell}_v] - \mathbb{E}[\ell_v(h_S^{\mathrm{Gini}})] = \left(\frac{1}{2} - 2q_v(1-q_v)\right)\left(\frac{1}{m}\Pr[c_v = 1] - p_v \Pr[c_v = 0]\right) . \quad (16)$$

Also, it is easy to see that $\frac{1}{m}\Pr[c_v = 1] - p_v\Pr[c_v = 0] = \frac{p_v}{m}\Pr[c_v = 1]$. Plugging this into Eq. (16) we obtain: $\mathbb{E}[\hat{\ell}_v] - \mathbb{E}[\ell_v(h_S^{\text{Gini}})] = (\frac{1}{2} - 2q_v(1 - q_v))\frac{1}{m}p_v\Pr[c_v = 1]$. For any q_v we have that $0 \le 2q_v(1 - q_v) \le \frac{1}{2}$, which implies the following inequality: $0 \le \mathbb{E}[\hat{\ell}_v] - \mathbb{E}[\ell_v(h_S^{\text{Gini}})] \le \frac{1}{2m}p_v\Pr[c_v = 1] \le \frac{p_v}{2m}$. Summing this over v and using Eq. (15) we conclude that $0 \le \mathbb{E}[\hat{\ell}] - \mathbb{E}[\ell(h_S^{\text{Gini}})] \le \sum_v \frac{p_v}{2m} = \frac{1}{2m}$.   □

We now turn to prove Thm. 2 in which we argue that with high confidence on the choice of S, the value of our estimator is close to the actual generalization error of h_S^{Gini}. To do this, we show that both our estimator and the true generalization error of h_S^{Gini} are concentrated around their mean. Then, based on Thm. 1, we can easily prove Thm. 2.

We start by showing that our estimator $\hat{\ell}$ is concentrated around its expectation. The concentration of $\hat{\ell}$ follows relatively easily by application of McDiarmid's Theorem [9]. To simplify our notation, we will henceforth use the shorthand $\forall^\delta S \quad \pi[S, \delta]$ to indicate that the predicate $\pi[S, \delta]$ holds with probability of at least $1 - \delta$ over the choice of S.

Lemma 3. Let $\delta \in (0, 1)$. Then, $\forall^\delta S \quad \left|\hat{\ell} - \mathbb{E}[\hat{\ell}]\right| \le 12\sqrt{\frac{\ln(\frac{2}{\delta})}{2m}}$.

The proof of this lemma can be found in [13]. We now turn to show a concentration bound on the true generalization error $\ell(h_S^{\text{Gini}})$. Here we cannot directly use McDiarmid's Theorem since the bounded differences property does not hold for $\ell(h_S^{\text{Gini}})$. To see this, suppose that $V = \{0, 1\}$, $p_0 = p_1 = \frac{1}{2}$, $q_0 = 0.99$ and $q_1 = 1$. Assume in addition that $|S(0)| = 1$; namely, there is only a single example in S for which the feature takes the value 0, an unlikely but possible scenario. In this case, if the single example in $S(0)$ is labeled 1, then $\ell(h_S^{\text{Gini}}) = 0.01$, but if this example is labeled 0, then $\ell(h_S^{\text{Gini}}) = 0.99$. That is, a change of a single example might have a dramatic effect on $\ell(h_S^{\text{Gini}})$. This problem can intuitively be attributed to the fact that S is an atypical sample of the underlying distribution $\{p_v\}$. To circumvent this obstacle, we define a new hypothesis h_S^δ that depends both on the sample S and on the desired confidence parameter δ. This hypothesis would 'compensate' for atypical samples. For h_S^δ we show that the following properties hold:

$$\forall^\delta S \quad \ell(h_S^\delta) = \ell(h_S^{\text{Gini}}) \tag{17}$$

$$\left|\mathbb{E}[\ell(h_S^\delta)] - \mathbb{E}[\ell(h_S^{\text{Gini}})]\right| \le 1/m \tag{18}$$

$$\forall^\delta S \quad \left|\ell(h_S^\delta) - \mathbb{E}[\ell(h_S^\delta)]\right| \le O\left(\ln(m/\delta)/\sqrt{m}\right). \tag{19}$$

Eq. (17) states that with high confidence, the generalization error of the new hypothesis h_S^δ is exactly equal to the error of h_S^{Gini}. Eq. (18) states that the expectations of the generalization errors of the two hypotheses are close. Finally, Eq. (19) states that the generalization error of h_S^δ is concentrated around its expectation. Combining these three properties and using the triangle inequality, we will be able to bound $|\ell(h_S^{\text{Gini}}) - \mathbb{E}[\ell(h_S^{\text{Gini}})]|$ with high confidence.

We construct a hypothesis h_S^δ that satisfies the three requirements given in Eqs. (17-19) based on Lemma 4 below. This lemma states that except for values with small probabilities, we can assure that with high confidence, $c_v(S)$ grows with p_v. This means that as long as p_v is not too small, a change of a single example in $c_v(S)$ does not change $h_S^\delta(v)$

too much. On the other hand, if p_v is small then the value v has little effect on the error to begin with. Therefore, regardless of the probability p_v, the error $\ell(h_S^\delta)$ cannot be changed too much by a single change of example in S. This would allow us to prove a concentration bound on $\ell(h_S^\delta)$ using McDiardmid's theorem. Let us first introduce a new notation. Given a confidence parameter $\delta > 0$, a probability $p \in [0, 1]$, and a sample size m, we define

$$\rho(\delta, p, m) \overset{\Delta}{=} mp - \sqrt{mp \cdot 3\ln(2/\delta)}. \tag{20}$$

Lemma 4 below states that $c_v(S)$ is likely to be at least $\rho(\delta/m, p_v, m)$ for all values with non-negligible probabilities.

Lemma 4. *Let $\delta \in (0, 1)$ be a confidence parameter. Then,*

$$\forall^\delta S \quad \forall v \in V : \ p_v \geq \tfrac{6\ln(\frac{2m}{\delta})}{m} \quad \Rightarrow \quad c_v(S) \geq \rho(\delta/m, p_v, m) > 1.$$

The proof is based on lemma 44 from [4] and can be found in [13]. Based on the bound given in the above lemma, we define h_S^δ to be

$$h_S^\delta(v) \overset{\Delta}{=} \begin{cases} h_S^{\text{Gini}}(v) & p_v < \tfrac{6\ln(\frac{2m}{\delta})}{m} \text{ or } c_v \geq \rho(\tfrac{\delta}{m}, p_v, m) \\ \frac{c_v^+ + q_v(\lceil \rho(\frac{\delta}{m}, p_v, m)\rceil - c_v)}{\lceil \rho(\frac{\delta}{m}, p_v, m)\rceil} & \text{otherwise} \end{cases}$$

That is, $h_S^\delta(v)$ is equal to $h_S^{\text{Gini}}(v)$ if either p_v is negligible or if there are enough representatives of v in the sample. If this is not the case, then S is not a typical sample and thus we "force" it to be typical by adding $\lceil \rho(\tfrac{\delta}{m}, p_v, m)\rceil - c_v$ 'pseudo-examples' to S with the value v and with labels that are distributed according to q_v. Therefore, except for values with negligible probability p_v, the hypothesis $h_S^\delta(v)$ is determined by at least $\lceil \rho(\tfrac{\delta}{m}, p_v, m)\rceil$ 'examples'. As a direct result of this construction we obtain that a single example from S has a small effect on the value of $\ell(h_S^\delta)$.

We can now show that each of the properties in (17-19) hold. From the definition of h_S^δ and Lemma 4 it is clear that Eq. (17) holds. Lemma 5 and Lemma 6 below state that Eq. (18) and Eq. (19) hold. Lemma 7 that follows bounds the concentration of $\ell(h_S^{\text{Gini}})$ using the three properties. The proofs of these three lemmas can be found in [13].

Lemma 5. $\left| \mathbb{E}[\ell(h_S^{\text{Gini}})] - \mathbb{E}[\ell(h_S^\delta)] \right| \leq \tfrac{1}{m}.$

Lemma 6. $\forall \delta > 0 \quad \forall^\delta S \quad \left| \ell(h_S^\delta) - \mathbb{E}[\ell(h_S^\delta)] \right| \leq \frac{12\ln(\frac{2m}{\delta})\sqrt{\ln(\frac{2}{\delta})}}{\sqrt{2m}}.$

Lemma 7. *For all $\delta > 0$ we have* $\forall^\delta S \quad \left| \ell(h_S^{\text{Gini}}) - \mathbb{E}[\ell(h_S^{\text{Gini}})] \right| \leq \tfrac{1}{m} + \frac{12\ln(\frac{4m}{\delta})\sqrt{\ln(\frac{4}{\delta})}}{\sqrt{2m}}.$

Thm. 2 states that with high confidence, the estimator $\hat{\ell}$ is close to the true generalization error of the Gini hypothesis, $\ell(h_S^{\text{Gini}})$. We conclude the analysis of the Gini estimator by proving this theorem.

Proof (of Thm. 2). Substituting $\tfrac{\delta}{2}$ for δ and applying a union bound, we have that all three properties stated in Lemma 7, Thm. 1 and Lemma 3 hold with probability of at least $1 - \delta$. We therefore conclude that with probability of at least $1 - \delta$,

$$\left|\ell(h_S^{\text{Gini}}) - \hat{\ell}\right| \leq |\ell(h_S^{\text{Gini}}) - \mathbb{E}[\ell(h_S^{\text{Gini}})]| + \left|\mathbb{E}[\ell(h_S^{\text{Gini}})] - \mathbb{E}[\hat{\ell}]\right| + \left|\mathbb{E}[\hat{\ell}] - \hat{\ell}\right|$$

$$\leq \frac{2}{m} + \frac{12 \ln\left(\frac{8m}{\delta}\right)\sqrt{\ln\left(\frac{8}{\delta}\right)}}{\sqrt{2m}} + 12\sqrt{\frac{\ln(\frac{4}{\delta})}{2m}} = O\left(\frac{\ln(\frac{m}{\delta})\sqrt{\ln(\frac{1}{\delta})}}{\sqrt{m}}\right).$$

□

Due to lack of space, we omit the proof of Thm. 3 and refer the reader to [13]. To prove Thm. 4, we first introduce some additional notation. Let $\delta \in (0,1)$ be a confidence parameter. Let V_1^δ, V_2^δ, and V_3^δ be three sets that partition V according to the values of the probabilities p_v:

$$V_1^\delta = \{v \mid p_v \leq 6 \ln(2m/\delta)\, m^{-\frac{2}{3}}\}$$
$$V_2^\delta = \{v \mid 6 \ln(2m/\delta)\, m^{-\frac{2}{3}} < p_v \leq 6 \ln(2m/\delta)\, m^{-\frac{1}{2}}\}$$
$$V_3^\delta = \{v \mid 6 \ln(2m/\delta)\, m^{-\frac{1}{2}} < p_v\}$$

We denote the contribution of each set to $\ell(h_S^{\text{Bayes}})$ by $\ell_i^\delta(S) \triangleq \sum_{v \in V_i^\delta} \ell_v(h_S^{\text{Bayes}})$. Additionally, given two samples S and S', let $\kappa(S, S')$ be the predicate that gets the value "true" if for all $v \in V$ we have $c_v(S) = c_v(S')$.

Using the above definitions and the triangle inequality, we can bound $|\ell(h_S^{\text{Bayes}}) - \mathbb{E}[\ell(h_S^{\text{Bayes}})]|$ as follows:

$$|\ell(h_S^{\text{Bayes}}) - \mathbb{E}[\ell(h_S^{\text{Bayes}})]| = |\sum_{i=1}^{3} (\ell_i^\delta(S) - \mathbb{E}[\ell_i^\delta])| \leq A_1 + A_2 + A_3 + A_4 \quad, \text{where}$$

$$A_1 = |\ell_1^\delta(S) - \mathbb{E}[\ell_1^\delta]|$$
$$A_2 = |\ell_2^\delta(S) - \mathbb{E}[\ell_2^\delta(S') \mid \kappa(S, S')]| \qquad\qquad (21)$$
$$A_3 = |\ell_3^\delta(S) - \mathbb{E}[\ell_3^\delta(S') \mid \kappa(S, S')]|$$
$$A_4 = |\mathbb{E}[\ell_2^\delta(S') + \ell_3^\delta(S') \mid \kappa(S, S')] - \mathbb{E}[\ell_2^\delta + \ell_3^\delta]|\ .$$

To prove Thm. 4 we bound each of the above terms as follows: First, to bound A_1 (Lemma 8 below), we use the fact that for each $v \in V_1^\delta$ the probability p_v is small. Thus, a single change of an example in S has a moderate effect on the error and we can use McDiarmid's theorem. To bound A_2 (Lemma 9 below) we note that the expectation is taken with respect to those samples S' in which $c_v(S') = c_v(S)$ for all v. Therefore, the variables $\ell_v(h_S^{\text{Bayes}})$ are independent. We show in addition that each of these variables is bounded in $[0, p_v]$ and thus we can apply Hoeffding's bound. Next, to bound A_3 (Lemma 12 below), we use the fact that in a typical sample, $c_v(S)$ is large for all $v \in V_3^\delta$. Thus, we bound the difference between $\ell_v(h_S^{\text{Bayes}})$ and $\mathbb{E}[\ell_v(S') \mid \kappa(S, S')]$ for each value in V_3^δ separately. Then, we apply a union bound to show that for all of these values the above difference is small. Finally, we use the same technique to bound A_4 (Lemma 13 below). The proof of the first lemma, stated below, is omitted.

Lemma 8. $\forall \delta > 0 \quad \forall^\delta S \quad |\ell_1^\delta(S) - \mathbb{E}[\ell_1^\delta]| \leq \frac{12\ln\left(\frac{2m}{\delta}\right)}{m^{1/6}}\sqrt{\frac{1}{2}\ln\left(\frac{2}{\delta}\right)}.$

Lemma 9. $\forall \delta > 0 \quad \forall^\delta S \quad |\ell_2^\delta(S) - \mathbb{E}[\ell_2^\delta(S') \mid \kappa(S,S')]| \leq \frac{\sqrt{3\ln(2m/\delta)\ln(2/\delta)}}{m^{1/4}}.$

Proof. Since the expectation is taken over samples S' for which $c_v(S') = c_v(S)$, for each $v \in V$ we get that $\ell_2^\delta(S) = \sum_{v \in V_2^\delta} \ell_v(h_S^{\mathrm{Bayes}})$ is a sum of independent random variables and the expectation of this sum is $\mathbb{E}[\ell_2^\delta(S') \mid \kappa(S,S')]$. In addition, it is trivial to show that $\ell_v(h_S^{\mathrm{Bayes}}) \in [0, p_v]$ for all v. Thus, by Hoeffding's inequality,

$$\Pr[|\ell_2^\delta(S) - \mathbb{E}[\ell_2^\delta(S') \mid \kappa(S,S')]| \geq t] \leq 2e^{-2t^2/\sum_{v \in V_2^\delta} p_v^2}. \tag{22}$$

Using the fact that for v in V_2^δ, $p_v \leq 6\ln(2m/\delta)/\sqrt{m}$ we obtain that

$$\sum_{v \in V_2^\delta} p_v^2 \leq \max_{v \in V_2^\delta}\{p_v\} \cdot \sum_{v \in V_2^\delta} p_v \leq 6\ln(2m/\delta)/\sqrt{m}.$$

Plugging the above into Eq. (22) we get that

$$\Pr[|\ell_2^\delta(S) - \mathbb{E}[\ell_2^\delta(S') \mid \kappa(S,S')]| \geq t] \leq 2e^{-2t^2\sqrt{m}/(6\ln(2m/\delta))}.$$

Setting the right-hand side to δ and solving for t, we conclude our proof. $\qquad\square$

So far, we have bounded the terms A_1 and A_2. In both of these cases, we utilized the fact that p_v is small for all $v \in V_1^\delta \cup V_2^\delta$. We now turn to bound the term A_3. In this case, the probabilities p_v are no longer negligible. Therefore, we use a different technique whereby we analyze the probability of $h_S^{\mathrm{Bayes}}(v)$ to be 'wrong', i.e. to return the less probable label. Since p_v is no longer small, we expect c_v to be relatively large. The following key lemma bounds the probability of $h_S^{\mathrm{Bayes}}(v)$ to be wrong given that c_v is large. The resulting bound depends on the difference between q_v and $1/2$ and becomes vacuous whenever q_v is close to $1/2$. On the other hand, if q_v is close to $1/2$, the price we pay for a wrong prediction is small. In the second part of this lemma, we balance these two terms and end up with a bound that does not depend on q_v.

Lemma 10. *Let* $\bar{Z} = (Z_1, \ldots, Z_k)$ *be a sequence of i.i.d. binary random variables where* $\Pr[Z_i = 1] = q$ *for all* i, *and assume that* $q \geq \frac{1}{2}$. *Then,*

$$\Pr[\sum_i Z_i \leq k/2] \leq e^{-2(q-\frac{1}{2})^2 k} \quad and \quad (2q-1)\Pr[\sum_i Z_i \leq k/2] \leq \frac{1}{\sqrt{ek}}.$$

Proof. The first inequality is a direct application of Hoeffding's inequality. Multiplying both sides by $2q - 1$ we get that the left-hand side of the second inequality is bounded above by $(2q-1)e^{-2(q-\frac{1}{2})^2 k}$. We now let $x = q - \frac{1}{2}$ and utilize the inequality $2xe^{-2x^2 k} \leq 1/\sqrt{ek}$, which holds for all $x \geq 0$ and $k > 0$. $\qquad\square$

Based on the above lemma, we now bound A_3. First, we show that if $c_v(S)$ is large then $\ell_v(S)$ is likely to be close to the expectation of ℓ_v over samples S' in which $c_v(S) = c_v(S')$. This is equivalent to the claim of the following lemma.

Lemma 11. *Under the same assumptions of Lemma 10. Let $f(\bar{Z})$ be the function*

$$f(\bar{Z}) = \begin{cases} (1-q) & \text{if } \sum_i Z_i > k/2 \\ q & \text{if } \sum_i Z_i < k/2 \\ \frac{1}{2} & \text{if } \sum_i Z_i = k/2 \end{cases}.$$

Then, for all $\delta \in (0, e^{-1/2}]$ we have $\forall^\delta \bar{Z}$ $|f(\bar{Z}) - \mathbb{E}[f]| \leq \sqrt{\frac{2\ln(1/\delta)}{ek}}$.

Proof. To simplify our notation, denote $\alpha = \Pr[\sum_i Z_i > k/2]$, $\beta = \Pr[\sum_i Z_i < k/2]$, and $\gamma = \Pr[\sum_i Z_i = k/2]$. A straightforward calculation shows that

$$|f(\bar{Z}) - \mathbb{E}[f(\bar{Z})]| = \begin{cases} (2q-1)\,(\beta + \gamma/2) & \text{with probability } \alpha \\ (2q-1)\,(\alpha + \gamma/2) & \text{with probability } \beta \\ (2q-1)\,(\alpha - \beta) & \text{with probability } \gamma \end{cases}.$$

Using the fact that (α, β, γ) is in the probability simplex we immediately obtain that $|f(\bar{z}) - \mathbb{E}[f(\bar{Z})]| \leq (2q-1)$. If $2q-1 \leq \sqrt{2\ln(1/\delta)/k}$ then the bound in the lemma clearly holds. Therefore, from now on we assume that $2q-1 > \sqrt{2\ln(1/\delta)/k}$. In this case, using the first inequality of Lemma 10 we have that $\beta + \gamma \leq e^{-2(q-\frac{1}{2})^2 k} \leq \delta$. Therefore, $1 - \delta < \alpha$, and so with probability of at least $1 - \delta$ we have that

$$|f(\bar{Z}) - \mathbb{E}[f(\bar{Z})]| = (2q-1)\,(\beta + \gamma/2) \leq (2q-1)\,(\beta + \gamma) .$$

Applying the second inequality of Lemma 10 on the right-hand side of the above inequality we get that $|f(\bar{Z}) - \mathbb{E}[f(\bar{Z})]| \leq \sqrt{1/ek} \leq \sqrt{2\ln(1/\delta)/ek}$, where the last inequality holds since we assume that $\delta \leq e^{-1/2}$. $\qquad\square$

Equipped with the above lemma we are now ready to bound A_3.

Lemma 12. *If $m \geq 4$ then* $\quad \forall^{(2\delta)} S \quad |\ell_3^\delta(S) - \mathbb{E}[\ell_3^\delta(S') \mid \kappa(S, S')]| \leq 1/m^{\frac{1}{4}}$.

Proof. Recall that $\ell_3^\delta(S) = \sum_{v \in V_3^\delta} \ell_v(S)$. $m \geq 4$, hence $\delta/m \leq 1/m \leq e^{-1/2}$. Choose $v \in V_3^\delta$ and without loss of generality assume that $q_v \geq 1/2$. Thus, from Lemma 11 and the definition of $\ell_v(S)$ we get that with probability of at least $1 - \delta/m$ over the choice of the labels in $S(v)$: $|\ell_v(S) - \mathbb{E}[\ell_v(S')|\kappa(S, S')]| \leq p_v \sqrt{\frac{2\ln(m/\delta)}{e \cdot c_v(S)}}$. By the definition of V_3^δ and Lemma 4, $\forall^\delta S$, $\forall v \in V_3^\delta$, $c_v(S) \geq \rho(\delta/m, p_v, m)$. Using the fact that ρ is monotonically increasing with respect to p_v it is possible to show (see [13]) that $\rho(\delta/m, p_v, m) \geq 2\ln(m/\delta)\,m^{1/2}$ for all $v \in V_3^\delta$ for $m \geq 4$. Therefore, $|\ell_v(S) - \mathbb{E}[\ell_v(S')|\kappa(S, S')]| \leq p_v\, m^{-1/4}$. Using a union bound, we obtain that $\forall^{(2\delta)} S \quad \forall v \in V_3^\delta \quad |\ell_v(S) - \mathbb{E}[\ell_v(S')|\kappa(S, S')]| \leq p_v\, m^{-1/4}$. Summing over $v \in V_3^\delta$, using the triangle inequality, and using the fact that $\sum_v p_v = 1$ we conclude the proof. $\qquad\square$

Lastly, we bound A_4 in the next lemma. See [13] for the proof.

Lemma 13. *For $m \geq 8$,*

$$\forall^\delta S \quad |\mathbb{E}[\ell_2^\delta(S') + \ell_3^\delta(S') \mid \kappa(S, S')] - \mathbb{E}[\ell_2^\delta(S') + \ell_3^\delta(S')]| \leq \tfrac{1}{m} + \tfrac{1}{m^{1/6}}.$$

5   Discussion

In this paper, a new approach for feature ranking is proposed, based on a direct estimation of the true generalization error of predictors that are deduced from the training set. We focused on two specific predictors, namely h_S^{Gini} and h_S^{Bayes}. An estimator for the generalization error of h_S^{Gini} was proposed and its convergence was analyzed. We showed that the expected error of h_S^{Bayes} is optimal and that its concentration is weaker than that of h_S^{Gini}. Constructing an estimator for h_S^{Bayes} is left for future work.

There are various extensions for this work that we did not pursue. First, it is interesting to analyze the number of categorical features one can rank while avoiding overfitting. This is especially important when ranking groups of categorical features. Second, our view of a ranking criterion as an estimator for the generalization error of a predictor can be used for constructing new ranking criteria by defining other predictors. Finally, understanding the relationship between this view and information theoretic measures is also an interesting future direction.

Acknowledgments

We would like to thank Yishay Mansour for helpful discussions.

References

1. Antos, A., Devroye, L., Gyorfi, L.: Lower bounds for bayes error estimation. IEEE Trans. Pattern Anal. Mach. Intell. 21(7) (1999)
2. Antos, A., Kontoyiannis, I.: Convergence properties of functional estimates for discrete distributions. Random Struct. Algorithms, 19(3-4) (2001)
3. Lopez de Mantaras, R.: A distance-based attribute selection measure for decision tree induction. Machine Learning Journal (1991)
4. Drukh, E., Mansour, Y.: Concentration bounds for unigrams language model. JMLR (2005)
5. Good, I.J.: The population frequencies of species and the estimation of pulation parameters. Biometrika (1953)
6. Hastie, T., Tibshirani, R., Friedman, J.: The Elements of Statistical Learning. Springer, Heidelberg (2001)
7. Kearns, M., Mansour, Y.: On the boosting ability of top-down decision tree learning algorithms. In: STOC (1996)
8. McAllester, D.A., Schapire, R.E.: On the convergence rate of good-turing estimators. In: COLT (2000)
9. McDiarmid, C.: On the method of bounded differences. Surveys in Combinatorics, pp. 148–188 (1989)
10. Mingers, J.: An empirical comparison of selection measures for decision-tree induction. Machine Learning (1989)
11. Mitchell, T.M.: Machine Learning. McGraw-Hill, New York (1997)
12. Quinlan, J.R.: C4.5: Programs for Machine Learning. Morgan Kaufmann, San Francisco (1993)
13. Sabato, S., Shalev-Shwartz, S.: Prediction by categorical features. Technical report (2007)
14. Torkkola, K.: Feature Extraction, Foundations and Applications. In: chapter Information-Theoretic Methods, Springer, Heidelberg (2006)

Observational Learning in Random Networks

Julian Lorenz, Martin Marciniszyn, and Angelika Steger

Institute of Theoretical Computer Science, ETH Zurich
8092 Zurich, Switzerland
{jlorenz,mmarcini,steger}@inf.ethz.ch

Abstract. In the standard model of observational learning, n agents sequentially decide between two alternatives a or b, one of which is objectively superior. Their choice is based on a stochastic private signal and the decisions of others. Assuming a rational behavior, it is known that informational cascades arise, which cause an overwhelming fraction of the population to make the same choice, either correct or false. Assuming that each agent is able to observe the actions of *all predecessors*, it was shown by Bikhchandani, Hirshleifer, and Welch [1,2] that, independently of the population size, false informational cascades are quite likely.

In a more realistic setting, agents observe just a *subset of their predecessors*, modeled by a random network of acquaintanceships. We show that the probability of false informational cascades depends on the edge probability p of the underlying network. As in the standard model, the emergence of false cascades is quite likely if p does not depend on n. In contrast to that, false cascades are very unlikely if $p = p(n)$ is a sequence that decreases with n. Provided the decay of p is not too fast, correct cascades emerge almost surely, benefiting the entire population.

1 Introduction

In recent years, there has been growing interest in modeling and analyzing processes of observational learning, first introduced by Banerjee [3] and Bikhchandani, Hirshleifer, and Welch [1,2]. In the model of [1,2], individuals make a once-in-a-lifetime choice between two alternatives sequentially. Each individual has access to private information, which is hidden to other individuals, and also observes the choices made by his predecessors. Since each action taken provides an information externality, individuals may start to imitate their predecessors so as to maximize their objective. Although such *herding behavior* is a locally optimal strategy for each individual, it might not be beneficial for the population as a whole. In the models of [3] and [1,2], imitation may cause an informational cascade such that all subsequent individuals make the same decision, regardless of their private information. One of the main results in [3] and [1,2] states that the probability of a cascade that leads most members of the population into the false decision is constant, independently of the population size.

This result seems counterintuitive to our every day experience since at many occasions taking the choice of others into account is wise and beneficial for the

N. Bshouty and C. Gentile (Eds.): COLT 2007, LNAI 4539, pp. 574–588, 2007.

entire society. In fact, imitation has been recognized as an important manifestation of intelligence and social learning. For instance, in his popular bestseller "The Wisdom of Crowds" [4], Surowiecki praises the superior judgment of large groups of people over an elite few. This became evident, for example, when Google launched their web search engine, at that time offering a superior service quality. Encouraged by their acquaintances, more and more users adopted Google as their primary index to the web. Moreover, the Google search engine itself leverages the wisdom of crowds by ranking their search results with the PageRank algorithm [5].

The reason that herding could be rather harmful in the model studied in [1,2] is that each individual has unlimited observational power over the actions taken by *all predecessors*. In a more realistic model, information disseminates not perfectly so that individuals typically observe merely a *small subset of their predecessors*. In this paper, we propose a generalization of the sequential learning model of [1,2]. Suppose the population has size n. For each individual $i \in \{1, \ldots, n\}$, a set of acquaintances $\Gamma(i)$ among all predecessors $j < i$ is selected, where each member of $\Gamma(i)$ is chosen with probability $p = p(n)$, $0 \leq p \leq 1$, independently of all other members. Only the actions taken by members of $\Gamma(i)$ are revealed to the individual i, all other actions remain unknown to i. Thus, the underlying social network is a random graph according to the model of Erdős and Rényi [6]. Setting $p = 1$ resembles the model of [1,2].

Extending the result of [1,2], we show that if p is a constant, the probability that a false informational cascade occurs during the decision process is constant, i.e., independent of the population size n. On the other hand, if $p = p(n)$ is a function that decays with n arbitrarily slowly, the probability of a false informational cascade tends to 0 as n tends to infinity. Informally speaking, almost all members of fairly large, moderately linked social networks make the correct choice with probability very close to 1, which is in accordance with our every day experience.

1.1   Model of Sequential Observational Learning in Networks

We consider the following framework of sequential learning in social networks that naturally generalizes the setting in [1,2]. There are n individuals (or equivalently, *agents* or *decision-makers* in the following), $V = \{v_1, \ldots, v_n\}$, facing a once-in-a-lifetime decision between two alternatives a and b. Decisions are made sequentially in the order of the labeling of V. One of the two choices is objectively superior, but which one that is remains unknown to all individuals throughout. Let $\theta \in \{a, b\}$ denote that superior choice. The a-priori probabilities of being the superior choice are

$$\mathbb{P}\left[\theta = a\right] = \mathbb{P}\left[\theta = b\right] = \frac{1}{2} \ .$$

Each agent $v_i \in V$ makes his choice $ch(v_i) \in \{a, b\}$ based on two sources of information: a private signal $s(v_i) \in \{a, b\}$ and public information. The private signal $s(v_i)$ is only observed by the individual v_i. All private signals are identically and independently distributed, satisfying $\mathbb{P}\left[s(v_i) = \theta\right] = \alpha$. That is, α

is the probability that a private signal correctly recommends the superior choice. The value of α remains unchanged throughout the entire process and is known to all agents. We assume that $1/2 < \alpha < 1$, excluding the trivial case $\alpha = 1$.

The actions $\{\mathrm{ch}(v_i) \mid 1 \leq i \leq n\}$ are public information, but an individual v_i can only observe the actions of a subset $\Gamma_i \subseteq V_{i-1} = \{v_1, \ldots, v_{i-1}\}$ of acquaintances. For all agents v_i, $2 \leq i \leq n$, each of the possible acquaintances $v_j \in V_{i-1}$ is included with probability $0 \leq p = p(n) \leq 1$ into Γ_i, independently of all other elements in V_{i-1}. Equivalently, the underlying social network can be represented as a labeled, undirected random graph $G = G_{n,p}$ on the vertex set V, where each possible edge is included with probability p, independently of all other edges. Then the set of acquaintances Γ_i of agent v_i is given by $\Gamma_G(v_i) \cap V_{i-1}$, where $\Gamma_G(v_i)$ denotes the neighborhood of v_i in G. It is easily seen that both representations are equivalent [7,8] and yield a random graph in the classical model of Erdős and Rényi [6]. We shall assume throughout this paper that the social network is exogenously determined before all decisions take place and represented in form of a random graph $G = G_{n,p}$.

Various models of social networks were proposed in the literature (see e.g. [9]). The classical random graph model of Erdős and Rényi is analytically well understood and, despite its idealistic assumptions, powerful enough to explain essential features of sequential social learning well. Moreover, it naturally generalizes the model proposed in [1,2], which is captured in the case $p = 1$.

1.2 Main Result

All agents employ the following deterministic rule for making decisions, which is a slight variation of the decision rule in [1,2].

Definition 1 (Decision rule). *Suppose individual v_i has received the private signal $s(v_i)$, and, among his acquaintances $\Gamma(i)$, m_a chose option a and m_b chose option b. Then we have*

$$\mathrm{ch}(v_i) = \begin{cases} a & \text{if } m_a - m_b \geq 2 \ , \\ b & \text{if } m_b - m_a \geq 2 \ , \\ s(v_i) & \text{otherwise} \ . \end{cases}$$

One can show that on a complete graph this strategy is locally optimal for each individual assuming that the actions of acquaintances are given in an aggregated form, that is, agent v_i merely observes how many times either of the options a and b was chosen before.

For any two sequences a_n and b_n, $n \in \mathbb{N}$, we write $a_n \ll b_n$ if

$$\lim_{n \to \infty} \frac{a_n}{b_n} = 0 \ .$$

Then our result reads as follows.

Theorem 1. *Suppose a social network with n agents $V = \{v_1, \ldots, v_n\}$ is given as a random graph $G = G_{n,p}$ with vertex set V and edge probability $p = p(n)$. Assume that private signals are correct with probability $1/2 < \alpha < 1$ and each agent applies the decision rule in Definition 1. Let $c_{\alpha,p}(n)$ be a random variable counting the number of agents that make the correct choice.*

(i) If $n^{-1} \ll p \ll 1$, we have

$$\lim_{n \to \infty} \mathbb{P}\left[c_{\alpha,p}(n) = (1 - o(1))n\right] = 1 \ . \tag{1}$$

(ii) If $0 \leq p \leq 1$ is a constant, then there exists a constant $\varrho = \varrho(\alpha, p) > 0$ such that

$$\lim_{n \to \infty} \mathbb{P}\left[c_{\alpha,p}(n) = o(n)\right] \geq \varrho \ . \tag{2}$$

In moderately linked social networks as in (i), the entire society benefits from learning. Note that if agents ignored the actions of others completely, typically a $(1 - \alpha)$-fraction of the population would make the false decision. On the other hand, if each individual has very many acquaintances on average as in (ii), incorrect informational cascades that lead almost the entire population into the false decision are quite likely.

In very sparse random networks with $p \leq c/n$ for some constant $c > 0$, no significant herding will arise since those networks typically contain γn isolated vertices for some constant $\gamma = \gamma(c) > 0$ [7,8]. These agents make their decision independently of all other agents and, hence, we expect that both groups of agents, choosing a and b respectively, contain a linear fraction of the population.

The crucial difference between the model of [1,2], which assumes that the underlying graph of the social network is complete, and our model is that in the former the probability of a false informational cascade primarily depends on the decision of very few agents at the beginning of the process. For instance, with constant probability the first three agents make the false decision, no matter which decision rule they apply. Since in a complete graph each subsequent agent observes these actions, locally optimal imitation will trick the entire population into the false decision. In contrast to that, information accumulates locally in the beginning if the underlying network is sparse as in (i). During a relatively long phase of the process, individuals make an independent decision because none of their acquaintances has decided yet. Hence, after that phase typically a fraction very close to α of these agents made the correct choice, creating a bias towards it. In later phases of the process, agents observe this bias among their acquaintances and, trusting the majority, make the correct decision, thereby increasing the bias even more. In the end, almost all agents are on the correct side.

Before presenting the proof of Theorem 1, let us make these ideas more precise. For any j, $1 \leq j \leq n$, let $V_j = \{v_1, \ldots, v_j\}$ denote the set of the first j agents. Recall that $\theta \in \{a, b\}$ denotes the objectively superior choice between a and b. For any set of agents $V' \subseteq V$, let

$$C(V') = \{v \in V' : \mathrm{ch}(v) = \theta\}$$

be the subset of agents in V' who made the correct decision. We denote the cardinality of $C(V')$ by $c(V')$. Suppose that in the first group of $j \geq 1$ agents approximately an α-fraction made the correct decision. The first important observation is that the subsequent agent v_{j+1} makes the correct choice with probability at least α if v_{j+1} obeys the decision rule in Definition 1.

Lemma 1. *Suppose the underlying social network is a random graph $G_{n,p}$ with edge probability $0 \leq p \leq 1$. Let $1/2 < \alpha < 1$ be fixed. Then there exists $\varepsilon > 0$ such that setting $\bar{\alpha} = (1 - \varepsilon)\alpha$, for all $1 \leq j \leq n - 1$, we have*

$$\mathbb{P}\left[\mathrm{ch}(v_{j+1}) = \theta \mid c(V_j) \geq \bar{\alpha}j\right] \geq \alpha ,$$

provided agent v_{j+1} obeys the decision rule in Definition 1.

So basically, following the majority and using the private signal only to break ties does not decrease the chances of any agent even if his acquaintances are randomly selected, provided that there is a bias among all predecessors towards the right direction. This enables us to show that, throughout the first stage, a bias of $\bar{\alpha} > 1/2$ remains stable in the group of decided agents. Once this group has reached a critical mass, new agents adopt the correct choice with very high probability since the bias among their acquaintances is so evident. More specifically, we can show the following "herding" lemma .

Lemma 2. *Suppose the underlying social network is a random graph $G_{n,p}$ with edge probability $1 \ll p \leq 1$. Let $1/2 < \bar{\alpha} < 1$ be fixed. Then there exists a constant $\delta > 0$ and $j_0 \geq 1$ satisfying $j_0 = \mathcal{O}(p^{-1})$ such that for all $j_0 \leq j \leq n-1$, we have*

$$\mathbb{P}\left[\mathrm{ch}(v_{j+1}) = \theta \mid c(V_j) \geq \bar{\alpha}j\right] \geq 1 - \mathrm{e}^{-\delta pj} ,$$

provided agent v_{j+1} obeys the decision rule in Definition 1.

Thus, most agents opt for θ with probability very close to 1 in the second stage. What makes the crucial difference between parts (i) and (ii) of Theorem 1 is that if p is a constant, the assumption $c(V_j) \geq \bar{\alpha}j$ in Lemmas 1 and 2 is met in the process only with probability bounded away from 1. Then it is quite likely that agents experience a bias towards the false direction among their acquaintances, and the same herding behavior as before evokes a false informational cascade.

1.3   Related Results

As already mentioned, Bikhchandani, Hirshleifer, and Welch [1,2] consider the case when the social network is a complete graph. Here informational cascades arise quickly, and it is quite likely that they are false. The authors of [1,2] consider a decision rule that is slightly different from the one in Definition 1. Both rules are locally optimal. However, one can show that false informational cascades are more likely with the rule in [1,2] (proof omitted due to space restrictions).

Models of observational learning processes were investigated in several papers. Banerjee [3] analyzes a model of sequential decision making that provokes herding behavior; as before, each decision-maker can observe the actions taken by *all* of his predecessors. In the model of Çelen and Kariv [10], decision-makers can only observe the action of their *immediate* predecessor. Banerjee and Fudenberg [11] consider the model in which each agent can observe the actions of a sample of his predecessors. This is comparable to our model with an underlying random network $G_{n,p}$. However, their model of making decisions is different; at each point in time, a proportion of the entire population leaves and is replaced by newcomers, who simultaneously make their decision. Similarly to our result, the authors of [11] show that, under certain assumptions, informational cascade are correct in the long run. In the learning process studied by Gale and Kariv [12], agents make decisions simultaneously rather than in a sequential order, but they may repeatedly revise their choice. Watts [13] studies random social networks, in which agents can either adopt or not. Starting with no adopters, in each round all agents update their state according to some rule depending on the state of their neighbors. In this model, the emergence of global informational cascades also depends on the density of the underlying random network.

1.4   Organization of the Paper

The paper is organized as follows. In Sect. 2 we present the proof of Theorem 1(i). An outline of this proof is contained in Sect. 2.1, where we also state a series of technical lemmas, which are proved in Sect. 2.2. The proof of Theorem 1(ii) is omitted due to space restrictions and will appear elsewhere. We conclude with experimental results in Sect. 3.

2   Proof of Theorem 1(i)

Suppose $n^{-1} \ll p \ll 1$ is given as in the theorem, and consider a random graph $G = G_{n,p}$ on the vertex set V with edge set E. For any set $V' \subseteq V$, let $E(V')$ denote the set of edges induced by V' in G. Recall that $C(V')$ denotes the subset of agents in V' who made the correct decision. Let $\bar{C}(V') = V' \backslash C(V')$ be its complement and set $c(V') = |C(V')|$ and $\bar{c}(V') = |\bar{C}(V')|$. The binomial distribution with mean np is denoted by $\mathrm{Bin}(n,p)$.

2.1   Outline of the Proof

The proof of of Theorem 1(i) is based on a series of lemmas that we state here. The proofs are deferred to Sect. 2.2. We will distinguish three phases as follows:

  Phase I: Agents $V_I = \{v_1, \ldots, v_{k_0}\}$.
  Phase II: Agents $V_{II} = \{v_{k_0+1}, \ldots, v_{k_1}\}$.
  Phase III: Agents $V_{III} = \{v_{k_1+1}, \ldots, v_n\}$.

We will specify $1 \le k_0 < k_1 \le n$ below as functions of n. In *Phase I*, the phase of the *early adopters*, most decision-makers have no more than one neighbor who already decided, and will follow their private signal according to the decision rule in Definition 1. Therefore, almost all agents make their decisions based solely on their private signal, which yields approximately an α-fraction of individuals who opted for θ. More specifically, we can establish the following lemma.

Lemma 3. *Let $\omega = \omega(n)$ be a sequence satisfying $1 \ll \omega \ll n$. Let $1/2 < \alpha < 1$, $0 < p \leq 1/\omega$ and $k_0 = p^{-1}\omega^{-1/2}$ be given. Then we have*

$$\mathbb{P}\left[c(V_{k_0}) \geq \left(1 - k_0^{-1/9}\right)\alpha k_0\right] = 1 - o(1) \ .$$

Note that if $0 < p \leq 1$ is a constant independent of n, Phase I breaks down; there is no $k_0 \geq 1$ such that the number of correctly decided agents in V_{k_0} is roughly k_0 with probability $1 - o(1)$. That is exactly what makes the situation in part (ii) of Theorem 1 different.

In *Phase II*, more and more agents face decisions of their acquaintances. As stated in Lemma 1, everybody makes a correct choice with probability at least α assuming that roughly an α-fraction of the preceding agents took the right action. The following lemma asserts that approximately this fraction of correct decisions is maintained throughout the second phase.

Lemma 4. *Let $\omega = \omega(n)$ be a sequence satisfying $1 \ll \omega \ll n$. Let $1/2 < \alpha < 1$, $0 < p \leq 1/\omega$ and $k_0 = p^{-1}\omega^{-1/2}$ and $k_1 = p^{-1}\omega^{1/2}$ be given. Then we have*

$$\mathbb{P}\left[c(V_{k_1}) \geq \left(1 - k_0^{-1/18}\right)\alpha k_1 \ \middle| \ c(V_{k_0}) \geq \left(1 - k_0^{-1/9}\right)\alpha k_0\right] = 1 - o(1) \ .$$

At the beginning of *Phase III*, every agent v_i has $\mathbb{E}[|\Gamma_i|] \geq pk_1 \gg 1$ decided neighbors on average. With high probability v_i disregards the private signal and follows the majority vote among its acquaintances, thereby making the correct choice.

Lemma 5. *Let $p > 0$, $\bar{\alpha} > 1/2$ and $k \geq 1$ be given. Then, for all $i > k$, we have*

$$\mathbb{P}\left[c(\Gamma_i \cap V_k) - \bar{c}(\Gamma_i \cap V_k) \geq \frac{2\bar{\alpha} - 1}{3}pk \ \middle| \ c(V_k) \geq \bar{\alpha}k\right] \geq 1 - 2\exp\left(-pkC\right) \ .$$

where $C = (2\bar{\alpha} - 1)^2/(18\bar{\alpha})$. Furthermore, if $p \geq \omega/n$ and $k \geq k_1 = p^{-1}\omega^{1/2}$ hold for some sequence $\omega = \omega(n)$ with $1 \ll \omega \ll n$, then for all $i > k$ we have

$$\mathbb{P}\left[c(\Gamma_i \cap V_k) - \bar{c}(\Gamma_i \cap V_k) \geq \omega^{1/3} \ \middle| \ c(V_k) \geq \bar{\alpha}k\right] \geq 1 - e^{-\omega^{1/3}} \ . \tag{3}$$

Using this strong probability bound, we can prove that with high probability actually almost all agents make the correct choice in Phase III.

Lemma 6. *Let $\omega = \omega(n)$ be a sequence satisfying $1 \ll \omega \ll n$. Let $1/2 < \alpha < 1$, $\omega/n \leq p \leq 1/\omega$, $k_0 = p^{-1}\omega^{-1/2}$ and $k_1 = p^{-1}\omega^{1/2}$ be given. Then we have*

$$\mathbb{P}\left[c(V_n) \geq \left(1 - \omega^{-1/20}\right)n \ \middle| \ c(V_{k_1}) \geq \left(1 - k_0^{-1/18}\right)\alpha k_1\right] = 1 - o(1) \ .$$

Combining Lemmas 3, 4 and 6, Theorem 1 follows immediately.

Proof (of Theorem 1 (i)). We consider the following three events

$$E_1: \quad c(V_{k_0}) \geq \left(1 - k_0^{-1/9}\right)\alpha k_0 \ ,$$

$$E_2: \quad c(V_{k_1}) \geq \left(1 - k_0^{-1/18}\right)\alpha k_1 \ ,$$

$$E_3: \quad c(V_n) \geq \left(1 - \omega^{-1/20}\right)n \ .$$

By Lemmas 3, 4 and 6, we have

$$\mathbb{P}\left[\overline{E}_3\right] \le \mathbb{P}\left[\overline{E}_3 \mid E_2\right] + \mathbb{P}\left[\overline{E}_2 \mid E_1\right] + \mathbb{P}\left[\overline{E}_1\right] = o(1) \ . \qquad \square$$

2.2   Proofs of Auxiliary Lemmas

Here we present the proofs of Lemmas 3, 4, 5, and 6 that were stated in the previous section. We will frequently make use of the following Chernoff tail bounds. The reader is referred to standard textbooks, e.g. [7,8], for proofs.

Lemma 7. *Let $X_1, \ldots, X_n$ be independent Bernoulli trials with $\mathbb{P}\left[X_i = 1\right] = p_i$. Let $X = \sum_{i=1}^{n} X_i$ and $\mu = \mathbb{E}\left[X\right] = \sum_{i=1}^{n} p_i$. Then we have*

(a) $\mathbb{P}\left[X \ge (1 + \delta)\mu\right] \le e^{-\mu\delta^2/3} \qquad$ *for all $\quad 0 < \delta \le 1$,*
(b) $\mathbb{P}\left[X \le (1 - \delta)\mu\right] \le e^{-\mu\delta^2/2} \qquad$ *for all $\quad 0 < \delta \le 1$,*
(c) $\mathbb{P}\left[X \ge t\right] \le e^{-t} \qquad\qquad\quad$ *for all $\quad t \ge 7\mu \quad$ and*
(d) $\mathbb{P}\left[X \ge \mu + t\right] \le e^{-\frac{t^2}{2(\mu + t/3)}} \qquad$ *for all $\quad t \ge 0$.*

We first give the proof of Lemma 3, which makes an assertion on the number of correct decision-makers in Phase I.

Proof (of Lemma 3). For all $2 \le i < k_0$, we have

$$\mathbb{P}\left[|\Gamma_{i+1}| \ge 2\right] = \sum_{j=2}^{i} \binom{i}{j} p^j (1 - p)^j \le \sum_{j=2}^{i} (ip)^j \tag{4}$$

$$\le k_0 p^2 \sum_{j=0}^{\infty} (k_0 p)^j \le \frac{k_0^2 p^2}{1 - k_0 p} \ .$$

Let $A = \{v_i : |\Gamma_i| \le 1, \ 2 \le i \le k_0\}$, and $B = V_{k_0} \setminus A$ its complement. Note that all individuals in the set A make their decision solely based on their private signals. For individuals in B we don't know whether they have observed an imbalance $|\Delta| \ge 2$ in the actions of their neighbors and chosen to follow the majority, disregarding their private signals. But because of (4) and the definition of k_0 we have

$$\mathbb{E}\left[|B|\right] = \sum_{i=1}^{k_0} \mathbb{P}\left[|\Gamma_{i+1}| \ge 2\right] \le \frac{k_0^3 p^2}{1 - k_0 p} = k_0^3 p^2 \cdot (1 + o(1)) \ .$$

Let $\mathcal{E}$ denote the event that $|B| < k_0^3 p^2 \omega^{2/3} = k_0 \omega^{-1/3}$. As $\omega \to \infty$ we can apply Lemma 7 (c) and deduce that

$$\mathbb{P}\left[\overline{\mathcal{E}}\right] = \mathbb{P}\left[|B| \ge k_0^3 p^2 \omega^{2/3}\right] \le e^{-k_0^3 p^2 \omega^{2/3}} = e^{-k_0 \omega^{-1/3}} = o(1) \tag{5}$$

by definition of k_0. Since by the decision rule in Definition 1 all individuals $v_i \in A_{k_0}$ follow their private signals, we have $\mathbb{E}\left[\bar{c}(A)\right] = (1 - \alpha)|A|$. Clearly, we have $|A| \le k_0$, and conditional on $\mathcal{E}$, we have $|A| \ge k_0 \left(1 - \omega^{-1/3}\right)$. Therefore,

$$(1 - \alpha) k_0 \left(1 - \omega^{-1/3}\right) \le \mathbb{E}\left[\bar{c}(A) \mid \mathcal{E}\right] \le (1 - \alpha) k_0 \ .$$

Using $k_0 \geq \omega^{1/2}$, Chernoff bounds imply

$$\mathbb{P}\left[c(A) \leq \left(1 - k_0^{-1/9}\right)\alpha k_0 \,\middle|\, \mathcal{E}\right] = \mathbb{P}\left[\bar{c}(A) \geq |A| - \left(1 - k_0^{-1/9}\right)\alpha k_0 \,\middle|\, \mathcal{E}\right]$$

$$\leq \mathbb{P}\left[\bar{c}(A) \geq \left(1 + \frac{\alpha\, k_0^{-1/9}}{1-\alpha}\right)\mathbb{E}\left[\bar{c}(A)|\mathcal{E}\right] \,\middle|\, \mathcal{E}\right]$$

$$\leq e^{-\frac{\alpha^2 k_0^{-2/9}}{3(1-\alpha)^2}\mathbb{E}[\bar{c}(A)|\mathcal{E}]} = e^{-\Theta\left(k_0^{7/9}\right)} = o(1) \ .$$

Thus, we have

$$\mathbb{P}\left[c(V_{k_0}) \geq \left(1 - k_0^{-1/9}\right)\alpha k_0 \,\middle|\, \mathcal{E}\right] \geq \mathbb{P}\left[c(A) \geq \left(1 - k_0^{-1/9}\right)\alpha k_0 \,\middle|\, \mathcal{E}\right] = 1-o(1) \ .$$

Since

$$\mathbb{P}\left[c(V_{k_0}) \geq \left(1 - k_0^{-1/9}\right)\alpha k_0\right] \geq \mathbb{P}\left[c(V_{k_0}) \geq \left(1 - k_0^{-1/9}\right)\alpha k_0 \,\middle|\, \mathcal{E}\right] \cdot \mathbb{P}\left[\mathcal{E}\right] \ ,$$

we conclude with (5) $\mathbb{P}\left[c(V_{k_0}) \geq \left(1 - k_0^{-1/9}\right)\alpha k_0\right] = 1 - o(1)$. $\qquad\square$

Before we proceed with the proof of Lemma 4, we need to state and prove a slightly stronger version of Lemma 1 in Sect. 1.2.

Lemma 8. *For every $1/2 < \alpha < 1$ there exists an $\varepsilon > 0$ such that if we have $c(V_k) \geq (1 - \varepsilon)\alpha k$ for $k \geq 1$, then for all $i > k$ with $\Gamma_i \subseteq V_k$ we have*

$$\mathbb{P}\left[\mathrm{ch}(v_i) = \theta\right] \geq \alpha \ .$$

Proof (of Lemma 8). Let $c(V_k) = \bar{\alpha}k$ for some constant $\bar{\alpha} > 0$. Furthermore, let

$$\Delta = c(V_k \cap \Gamma_i) - \bar{c}(V_k \cap \Gamma_i)$$

be the difference in the number of neighbors of agent i in $C(V_k)$ and in $\overline{C}(V_k)$, and let $p_j = \mathbb{P}\left[\Delta = j\right]$ denote the probability that this difference is exactly j. Let $\ell_1 = \min\{\bar{\alpha}k, (1 - \bar{\alpha})k + j\}$ and $\ell_2 = (1 - \bar{\alpha})k \leq \ell_1$. Then for all $j \geq 2$, we have

$$p_j = \sum_{s=j}^{\ell_1} \binom{\bar{\alpha}k}{s}\binom{(1-\bar{\alpha})k}{s-j}p^{2s-j}(1-p)^{k-(2s-j)}$$

and

$$p_{-j} = \sum_{s=j}^{\ell_2} \binom{(1-\bar{\alpha})k}{s}\binom{\bar{\alpha}k}{s-j}p^{2s-j}(1-p)^{k-(2s-j)} \ .$$

For $r \geq s \geq 1$, let $r^{\underline{s}} = r(r-1)\ldots(r-s+1)$ be the falling factorial. For all $j \geq 1$ and $j \leq s \leq \ell_2$, we have

$$\binom{\bar{\alpha}k}{s}\binom{(1-\bar{\alpha})k}{s-j} = \frac{(\bar{\alpha}k)^{\underline{s}}((1-\bar{\alpha})k)^{\underline{s-j}}}{s!(s-j)!}$$

$$= \frac{(\bar{\alpha}k)^{\underline{s-j}}((1-\bar{\alpha})k)^{\underline{s}}}{s!(s-j)!} \cdot \prod_{t=0}^{j-1}\frac{\bar{\alpha}k - s + j - t}{(1-\bar{\alpha})k - s + j - t}$$

$$\geq \binom{(1-\bar{\alpha})k}{s}\binom{\bar{\alpha}k}{s-j} \cdot \left(\frac{\bar{\alpha}}{1-\bar{\alpha}}\right)^j \ .$$

Therefore we have

$$p_j \geq \left(\frac{\bar{\alpha}}{1-\bar{\alpha}}\right)^2 p_{-j} \qquad \forall j \geq 2 \ ,$$

and

$$\mathbb{P}\left[\Delta \geq 2\right] \geq \left(\frac{\bar{\alpha}}{1-\bar{\alpha}}\right)^2 \mathbb{P}\left[\Delta \leq -2\right]$$

$$= \left(\frac{\bar{\alpha}}{1-\bar{\alpha}}\right)^2 \left(1 - \mathbb{P}\left[-1 \leq \Delta \leq 1\right] - \mathbb{P}\left[\Delta \geq 2\right]\right) \ .$$

Thus, we have

$$\mathbb{P}\left[\Delta \geq 2\right] \geq \frac{1}{1+\left(\frac{1-\bar{\alpha}}{\bar{\alpha}}\right)^2} \left(1 - \mathbb{P}\left[-1 \leq \Delta \leq 1\right]\right) \ . \tag{6}$$

Let $\varepsilon < \frac{2(\alpha-1)+\sqrt{\alpha^{-1}-1}}{2\alpha-1}$. A straightforward calculation shows that

$$\frac{1}{1+\left(\frac{1-\bar{\alpha}}{\bar{\alpha}}\right)^2} \geq \alpha \qquad \forall \, \bar{\alpha} \geq (1-\varepsilon)\alpha \ . \tag{7}$$

Because of the decision rule given in Definition 1, using (6) and (7) we have

$$\mathbb{P}\left[\mathrm{ch}(v_i) = \theta\right] = \alpha \mathbb{P}\left[-1 \leq \Delta \leq 1\right] + \mathbb{P}\left[\Delta \geq 2\right] \geq \alpha$$

for all $\bar{\alpha} \geq (1-\varepsilon)\alpha$. $\square$

Note that Lemma 1 follows immediately from Lemma 8. Using Lemma 8, we now present the proof of Lemma 4, which asserts that roughly an α-fraction of correct decision-makers is maintained throughout Phase II.

Proof (of Lemma 4). We consider groups W_i of $m = p^{-1/3}\omega^{-1/4} \geq \omega^{1/12}$ individuals, resulting in $\ell = (k_1 - k_0)/m \leq k_1/m \leq k_1 p^{1/3}\omega^{1/4}$ groups between individuals k_0 and k_1. Let $\mathcal{E}_i$ be the event that there is at most one individual in W_i that has a neighbor in W_i, i.e. $|E(W_i)| \leq 1$. Let $\mathcal{E} = \mathcal{E}_1 \wedge \cdots \wedge \mathcal{E}_\ell$. Since $m^2 p = o(1)$, for n sufficiently large, we have

$$\mathbb{P}\left[\overline{\mathcal{E}_i}\right] \leq \sum_{j=2}^{\binom{m}{2}} \binom{\binom{m}{2}}{j} p^j \leq \sum_{j=2}^{\binom{m}{2}} m^{2j} p^j \leq m^4 p^2 \sum_{j=0}^{\infty} m^{2j} p^j$$

$$\leq \frac{m^4 p^2}{1 - m^2 p} \leq 2 m^4 p^2 \ , \tag{8}$$

and

$$\mathbb{P}\left[\overline{\mathcal{E}}\right] \leq \ell \cdot \mathbb{P}\left[\overline{\mathcal{E}_i}\right] \leq 2 m^4 p^2 \ell \leq 2\, p k_1 \omega^{-3/4} = 2\, \omega^{-1/4} \ . \tag{9}$$

We have

$$\mathbb{P}\left[c(V_{k_1}) < \left(1 - k_0^{-1/18}\right)\alpha k_1\right] \leq \mathbb{P}\left[c(V_{k_1}) < \left(1 - k_0^{-1/18}\right)\alpha k_1 \,\Big|\, \mathcal{E}\right] + \mathbb{P}\left[\overline{\mathcal{E}}\right] \ ,$$

and defining $\mathcal{A}_i$ as the event that $c(W_i) \geq \alpha \left(1 - k_0^{-1/18}\right) m$,

$$\mathbb{P}\left[c(V_{k_1}) < \left(1 - k_0^{-1/18}\right)\alpha k_1 \,\Big|\, \mathcal{E}\right] \leq$$
$$\mathbb{P}\left[c(V_{k_1}) < \left(1 - k_0^{-1/18}\right)\alpha k_1 \,\Big|\, \mathcal{E} \wedge \mathcal{A}_1 \wedge \cdots \wedge \mathcal{A}_\ell\right] +$$
$$\sum_{j=0}^{\ell-1} \mathbb{P}\left[\overline{\mathcal{A}}_j \,|\, \mathcal{E} \wedge \mathcal{A}_1 \wedge \cdots \wedge \mathcal{A}_j\right] \ .$$

Since $\mathcal{E} \wedge \mathcal{A}_1 \wedge \cdots \wedge \mathcal{A}_\ell$ implies $c(V_{k_1}) \geq \left(1 - k_0^{-1/18}\right)\alpha k_1$, we conclude

$$\mathbb{P}\left[c(V_{k_1}) < \left(1 - k_0^{-1/18}\right)\alpha k_1\right] \leq \sum_{j=0}^{\ell-1} \mathbb{P}\left[\overline{\mathcal{A}}_j \,|\, \mathcal{E} \wedge \mathcal{A}_1 \wedge \cdots \wedge \mathcal{A}_j\right] + \mathbb{P}\left[\overline{\mathcal{E}}\right] \ . \quad (10)$$

Let $\bar{\alpha} = \left(1 - k_0^{-1/18}\right)\alpha$. The event $\mathcal{E} \wedge \mathcal{A}_1 \wedge \cdots \wedge \mathcal{A}_{j-1}$ means that before the individuals in group W_j have to make a decision, we have

$$c(V_{k_0+(j-1)m}) \geq \bar{\alpha}(k_0 + (j-1)m) \ ,$$

and there is at most one individual $w_j \in W_j$ with a neighbor in W_j that made his decision before w_j. Let $\widehat{W}_j = W_j \setminus w_j$ and $\hat{m} = m - 1$. Lemma 8 asserts, that there is an $\varepsilon > 0$ and $\bar{k} \geq 1$ (which both depend only on α), such that for all $k \geq \bar{k}$ we have $\mathbb{P}\left[\text{ch}(v) = \theta\right] \geq \alpha$ for all $v \in \widehat{W}_j$, if $1 - k_0^{-1/18} < \varepsilon$. But since $k_0 \geq \omega$, for n sufficiently large we certainly have $k_0 \geq \bar{k}$ and $\bar{\alpha} \geq (1-\varepsilon)\alpha$. Hence, we have $\mathbb{E}\left[c(\widehat{W}_j)\right] \geq \alpha \hat{m}$. Chernoff bounds imply

$$\mathbb{P}\left[c(\widehat{W}_j) \leq \left(1 - 2\,k_0^{-1/18}\right)\alpha \hat{m}\right] \leq e^{-2\,\alpha \hat{m} k_0^{-1/9}} \leq e^{-\alpha m k_0^{-1/9}} \ .$$

Since for n sufficiently large we have

$$\mathbb{P}\left[\overline{\mathcal{A}}_j \,|\, \mathcal{E} \wedge \mathcal{A}_1 \wedge \cdots \wedge \mathcal{A}_{j-1}\right] = \mathbb{P}\left[c(W_j) \leq \left(1 - k_0^{-1/18}\right)\alpha m\right]$$
$$\leq \mathbb{P}\left[c(\widehat{W}_j) \leq \left(1 - 2\,k_0^{-1/18}\right)\alpha \hat{m}\right] \ ,$$

we also have

$$\mathbb{P}\left[\overline{\mathcal{A}}_j \,|\, \mathcal{E} \wedge \mathcal{A}_1 \wedge \cdots \wedge \mathcal{A}_{j-1}\right] \leq e^{-\alpha m k_0^{-1/9}} = e^{-\alpha p^{-2/9}\omega^{-7/36}} \ .$$

Furthermore, since $\ell \leq p^{-2/3}\omega^{3/4}$, we have

$$\sum_{j=1}^{\ell} \mathbb{P}\left[\overline{\mathcal{A}}_j \,|\, G \wedge \mathcal{A}_1 \wedge \cdots \wedge \mathcal{A}_{j-1}\right] \leq \ell\, e^{-\alpha p^{-\frac{2}{9}}\omega^{-\frac{7}{36}}} = o(1) \ . \quad (11)$$

Thus, because of (9), (10) and (11) we can conclude

$$\mathbb{P}\left[c(V_{k_1}) \geq \left(1 - k_0^{-\frac{1}{18}}\right)\alpha k_1\right] = 1 - o(1) \ . \qquad \square$$

We continue with the proof of Lemma 5, which is a slightly stronger version than Lemma 2 in Sect. 1.2.

Proof (of Lemma 5). Let $N_g = C(\Gamma_i \cap V_k)$ and $N_b = \overline{C}(\Gamma_i \cap V_k)$ be the neighbors of i in V_k who made the correct (respectively false) decision, and $n_g = |N_g|$. Let $n_b = |N_b|$. We have $n_g \sim \mathrm{Bin}(c(V_k), p)$ and $n_b \sim \mathrm{Bin}(k - c(V_k), p)$. Let $\mu_g = p\,\bar{a}\,k$ and $\mu_b = p\,(1 - \bar{a})\,k$. Then we have $\mathbb{E}\,[n_g] \geq \mu_g$ and $\mathbb{E}\,[n_b] \leq \mu_b$. Define

$$\delta = \frac{1}{3} - \frac{\mu_b}{3\mu_g} = \frac{2\,\bar{a} - 1}{3\,\bar{a}} \ . \tag{12}$$

We have

$$\begin{aligned}
\mathbb{P}\,[n_g - n_b < \delta\mu_g] &= \mathbb{P}\,[n_g - (1 - \delta)\mu_g < n_b - (1 - 2\delta)\mu_g] \\
&\leq \mathbb{P}\left[n_g - (1 - \delta)\mu_g < n_b - (1 - 2\delta)\mu_g \,\Big|\, n_g \geq (1 - \delta)\mu_g\right] + \\
&\quad \mathbb{P}\left[n_g < (1 - \delta)\mu_g\right] \ ,
\end{aligned}$$

and thus

$$\mathbb{P}\,[n_g - n_b < \delta\mu_g] \leq \mathbb{P}\,[n_b > (1 - 2\delta)\mu_g] + \mathbb{P}\,[n_g < (1 - \delta)\mu_g] \ . \tag{13}$$

The Chernoff bound in Lemma 7 (b) implies that

$$\mathbb{P}\,[n_g < (1 - \delta)\mu_g] \leq \mathbb{P}\,[n_g < (1 - \delta)\mathbb{E}\,[n_g]] \leq \mathrm{e}^{-\mathbb{E}[n_g]\delta^2/2} \leq \mathrm{e}^{-\mu_g\delta^2/2} \ , \tag{14}$$

and since $1 - 2\delta - \mu_b/\mu_g = \delta$ by (12), we have

$$\begin{aligned}
\mathbb{P}\,[n_b > (1 - 2\delta)\mu_g] &= \mathbb{P}\,[n_b > \mathbb{E}\,[n_b] + (1 - 2\delta - \mathbb{E}\,[n_b]/\mu_g)\,\mu_g] \\
&\leq \mathbb{P}\,[n_b > \mathbb{E}\,[n_b] + (1 - 2\delta - \mu_b/\mu_g)\,\mu_g] \\
&= \mathbb{P}\,[n_b > \mathbb{E}\,[n_b] + \delta\mu_g] \ .
\end{aligned}$$

Thus, using the Chernoff bound in Lemma 7 (d), we obtain

$$\mathbb{P}\,[n_b > (1 - 2\delta)\mu_g] \leq \exp\left(-\frac{\delta^2\mu_g^2}{2(\mathbb{E}\,[n_b] + \delta\mu_g/3)}\right) \leq \exp\left(-\frac{\delta^2\mu_g^2}{2(\mu_b + \delta\mu_g/3)}\right) \ .$$

Because of (12) we have $\mu_b + \delta\mu_g/3 \leq \mu_g$, and thus

$$\mathbb{P}\,[n_b > (1 - 2\delta)\mu_g] \leq \mathrm{e}^{-\mu_g\delta^2/2} \ . \tag{15}$$

Because of (13) - (15) and $\delta\mu_g = (2\bar{a} - 1)pk/3$, we conclude

$$\mathbb{P}\left[|C(\Gamma_i \cap V_k)| - |\overline{C}(\Gamma_i \cap V_k)| < \frac{2\bar{a} - 1}{3}pk\right] \leq 2\,\exp\left(-pk\frac{(2\bar{a} - 1)^2}{18\bar{a}}\right) \ ,$$

and since $pk \geq \omega^{1/2}$, for n sufficiently large we have

$$\mathbb{P}\left[|C(\Gamma_i \cap V_k)| - |\overline{C}(\Gamma_i \cap V_k)| \geq \omega^{1/3}\right] \geq 1 - \mathrm{e}^{-\omega^{1/3}} \ . \qquad \square$$

Note that Lemma 2 is a straightforward corollary of Lemma 5; we omit the proof due to space restrictions. It remains to prove Lemma 6, which relies on the following lemma.

Lemma 9. *Let $\omega = \omega(n)$ be a sequence satisfying $1 \ll \omega \ll n$. Let $\frac{1}{2} < \bar{\alpha} < 1$, $\omega/n \leq p \leq 1/\omega$ and $k \geq k_1 = p^{-1}\omega^{1/2}$. Suppose we have*

$$c(V_k) \geq \bar{\alpha}k . \tag{16}$$

Then we have

$$\mathbb{P}\left[c(V_{2k} \setminus V_k) = \left(1 - \omega^{-1/19}\right)k\right] \geq 1 - e^{-kp} .$$

The proof of Lemma 9 is omitted due to space restrictions and will appear elsewhere. Now we are ready to prove Lemma 6.

Proof (of Lemma 6). We consider subphases of increasing length. More precisely, the first subphase lasts to individual $2k_1$. The second subphase then lasts until individual $4k_1$. Thus, in general subphase j lasts from individual $k_1 2^{j-1}$ until $k_1 2^j$. We will have at most $\log(n - k_1) \leq \log n$ such subphases.

Inductively, for n sufficiently large we can employ Lemma 9 for each subphase, as assumption (16) iteratively holds. We obtain

$$\mathbb{P}\left[\frac{c(V_n \setminus V_{k_1})}{n - k_1} < 1 - \omega^{-1/19}\right] \leq \sum_{j=0}^{\log n} e^{-pk_1 2^j} = e^{-pk_1} \sum_{j=0}^{\log n} e^{-pk_1(2^j - 1)}$$

$$\leq e^{-pk_1} \sum_{j=0}^{\infty} e^{-pk_1 j} = \frac{e^{-pk_1}}{1 - e^{-pk_1}} = o(1) .$$

Since $k_1 \leq n\omega^{-1/2}$, note that $c(V_n \setminus V_{k_1}) \geq (n - k_1)\left(1 - \omega^{-1/19}\right)$ implies

$$c(V_n) \geq \left(1 - k_1/n\right)\left(1 - \omega^{-1/19}\right)n \geq \left(1 - \omega^{-1/20}\right)n$$

for n sufficiently large. Thus, we conclude

$$\mathbb{P}\left[c(V_n) \geq \left(1 - \omega^{-1/20}\right)n\right] = 1 - o(1) . \qquad \square$$

3   Numerical Experiments

The statements in Theorem 1 are asymptotic, asserting the emergence of informational cascades in the limit. As our numerical experiments show, these phenomena can be observed even with moderately small populations.

We conducted experiments with varying population size n and edge probability $p = p(n)$. For each value of n and p, we sampled $N = 2000$ instances of random graphs $G = G_{n,p}$ and of private signals $s(v_i)$, $v_i \in V(G)$. The sequential decision

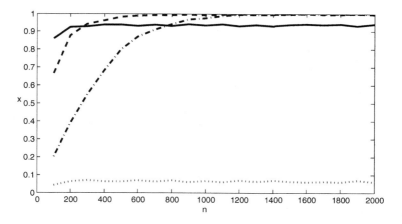

Fig. 1. Simulation results for $\alpha = 0.75$. The plot shows the relative frequencies of correct cascades for different values of the edge probability p as a function of n: $p = 0.5$ (solid line), $p = 1/\log n$ (dashed line), and $p = n^{-1/2}$ (dash-dotted line). The dotted line represents the relative frequency of incorrect cascades for $p = 0.5$.

process was evaluated on each of those instances following the decision rule in Definition 1. We identified an informational cascade in such an experiment if at least 95% of all agents opted for the same choice. We computed the relative frequency of informational cascades among the N samples for each value of n and p.

We ran the simulation for $\alpha = 0.75$, $n \in \{100 \cdot i : 1 \leq i \leq 20\}$, and three distinct sequences p. The results are plotted in Fig. 1. The solid and the dotted line represent the relative frequencies of correct and false cascades, respectively, for constant $p = 0.5$. In accordance with Theorem 1(ii), both events occur with constant frequency independent of the population size. The dashed and the dash-dotted line represent the relative frequencies of correct cascades for $p = 1/\log n$ and $p = n^{-1/2}$, respectively. Confirming Theorem 1(i) those plots approach 1 as n grows.

Acknowledgment

Julian Lorenz was partially supported by UBS AG. We would like to thank Konstantinos Panagiotou and Florian Jug for helpful discussions.

References

1. Bikhchandani, S., Hirshleifer, D., Welch, I.: A theory of fads, fashion, custom, and cultural change in informational cascades. Journal of Political Economy 100(5), 992–1026 (1992)
2. Bikhchandani, S., Hirshleifer, D., Welch, I.: Learning from the behavior of others: Conformity, fads, and informational cascades. The. Journal of Economic Perspectives 12(3), 151–170 (1998)

3. Banerjee, A.V.: A simple model of herd behavior. The Quarterly Journal of Economics 107(3), 797–817 (1992)
4. Surowiecki, J.: The Wisdom of Crowds. Anchor (2005)
5. Brin, S., Page, L.: The anatomy of a large-scale hypertextual Web search engine. Computer Networks and ISDN Systems 30(1–7), 107–117 (1998)
6. Erdős, P., Rényi, A.: On random graphs. Publ. Math. Debrecen 6, 290–297 (1959)
7. Bollobás, B.: Random graphs, 2nd edn. Cambridge Studies in Advanced Mathematics, vol. 73. Cambridge University Press, Cambridge (2001)
8. Janson, S., Łuczak, T., Rucinski, A.: Random graphs. In: Wiley-Interscience Series in Discrete Mathematics and Optimization, Wiley-Interscience, New York (2000)
9. Barabási, A.L., Albert, R.: Emergence of scaling in random networks. Science 286(5439), 509–512 (1999)
10. Çelen, B., Kariv, S.: Observational learning under imperfect information. Games Econom. Behav. 47(1), 72–86 (2004)
11. Banerjee, A., Fudenberg, D.: Word-of-mouth learning. Games Econom. Behav. 46(1), 1–22 (2004)
12. Gale, D., Kariv, S.: Bayesian learning in social networks. Games Econom. Behav. 45(2), 329–346, Special issue in honor of Rosenthal, R. W. (2003)
13. Watts, D.J.: A simple model of global cascades on random networks. In: Proc. Natl. Acad. Sci. USA 99(9), 5766–5771(electronic) (2002)

The Loss Rank Principle for Model Selection

Marcus Hutter

RSISE @ ANU and SML @ NICTA
Canberra, ACT, 0200, Australia
marcus@hutter1.net
www.hutter1.net

Abstract. A key issue in statistics and machine learning is to automatically select the "right" model complexity, e.g. the number of neighbors to be averaged over in k nearest neighbor (kNN) regression or the polynomial degree in regression with polynomials. We suggest a novel principle (LoRP) for model selection in regression and classification. It is based on the loss rank, which counts how many other (fictitious) data would be fitted better. LoRP selects the model that has minimal loss rank. Unlike most penalized maximum likelihood variants (AIC,BIC,MDL), LoRP only depends on the regression functions and the loss function. It works without a stochastic noise model, and is directly applicable to any non-parametric regressor, like kNN.

1 Introduction

Regression. Consider a regression or classification problem in which we want to determine the functional relationship $y_i \approx f_{true}(x_i)$ from data $D = \{(x_1,y_1),...,(x_n,y_n)\} \in \mathcal{D}$, i.e. we seek a function f_D such that $f_D(x)$ is close to the unknown $f_{true}(x)$ for all x. One may define regressor f_D directly, e.g. 'average the y values of the k nearest neighbors (kNN) of x in D', or select the f from a class of functions $\mathcal{F}$ that has smallest (training) error on D. If the class $\mathcal{F}$ is not too large, e.g. the polynomials of fixed reasonable degree d, this often works well.

Model selection. What remains is to select the right model complexity c, like k or d. This selection cannot be based on the training error, since the more complex the model (large d, small k) the better the fit on D (perfect for $d = n$ and $k = 1$). This problem is called overfitting, for which various remedies have been suggested:

We will not discuss empirical test set methods like cross-validation, but only training set based methods. See e.g. [Mac92] for a comparison of cross-validation with Bayesian model selection. Training set based model selection methods allow using all data D for regression. The most popular ones can be regarded as penalized versions of Maximum Likelihood (ML). In addition to the function class $\mathcal{F}$, one has to specify a sampling model $P(D|f)$, e.g. that the y_i have independent Gaussian distribution with mean $f(x_i)$. ML chooses $\hat{f}_D^c = \text{argmax}_{f \in \mathcal{F}_c} P(D|f)$, Penalized ML (PML) then chooses $\hat{c} = \text{argmin}_c\{-\log P(D|\hat{f}_D^c) + \text{Penalty}(c)\}$, where the penalty depends on the used approach (MDL [Ris78], BIC [Sch78],

N. Bshouty and C. Gentile (Eds.): COLT 2007, LNAI 4539, pp. 589–603, 2007.

AIC [Aka73]). In particular, modern MDL [Grü04] has sound exact foundations and works very well in practice. All PML variants rely on a proper sampling model (which may be difficult to establish), ignore (or at least do not tell how to incorporate) a potentially given loss function, and are typically limited to (semi)parametric models.

Main idea. The main goal of the paper is to establish a criterion for selecting the "best" model complexity c based on regressors $\hat{f}_D^c$ given as a black box without insight into the origin or inner structure of $\hat{f}_D^c$, that does not depend on things often not given (like a stochastic noise model), and that exploits what is given (like the loss function). The key observation we exploit is that large classes $\mathcal{F}_c$ or more flexible regressors $\hat{f}_D^c$ can fit more data $D' \in \mathcal{D}$ well than more rigid ones, e.g. many D' can be fit well with high order polynomials. We define the *loss rank* of $\hat{f}_D^c$ as the number of other (fictitious) data $D' \in \mathcal{D}$ that are fitted better by $\hat{f}_{D'}^c$ than D is fitted by $\hat{f}_D^c$, as measured by some loss function. The loss rank is large for regressors fitting D not well *and* for too flexible regressors (in both cases the regressor fits many other D' better). The loss rank has a minimum for not too flexible regressors which fit D not too bad. We claim that minimizing the loss rank is a suitable model selection criterion, since it trades off the quality of fit with the flexibility of the model. Unlike PML, our new Loss Rank Principle (LoRP) works without a noise (stochastic sampling) model, and is directly applicable to any non-parametric regressor, like kNN.

Contents. In Section 2, after giving a brief introduction to regression, we formally state LoRP for model selection. To make it applicable to real problems, we have to generalize it to continuous spaces and regularize infinite loss ranks. In Section 3 we derive explicit expressions for the loss rank for the important class of linear regressors, which includes kNN, polynomial, linear basis function (LBFR), Kernel, and projective regression. In Section 4 we compare linear LoRP to Bayesian model selection for linear regression with Gaussian noise and prior, and in Section 5 to PML, in particular MDL, BIC, AIC, and MacKay's [Mac92] and Hastie's et al. [HTF01] trace formulas for the effective dimension. In this paper we just scratch at the surface of LoRP. Section 6 contains further considerations, to be elaborated on in the future.

2   The Loss Rank Principle (LoRP)

After giving a brief introduction to regression, classification, model selection, overfitting, and some reoccurring examples (polynomial regression Example 1 and kNN Example 2), we state our novel Loss Rank Principle for model selection. We first state it for classification (Principle 3 for discrete values), and then generalize it for regression (Principle 5 for continuous values), and exemplify it on two (over-simplistic) artificial Examples 4 and 6. Thereafter we show how to regularize LoRP for realistic regression problems.

Setup. We assume data $D = (\boldsymbol{x}, \boldsymbol{y}) := \{(x_1, y_1), ..., (x_n, y_n)\} \in (\mathcal{X} \times \mathcal{Y})^n =: \mathcal{D}$ has been observed. We think of the y as having an approximate functional dependence on

x, i.e. $y_i \approx f_{true}(x_i)$, where $\approx$ means that the y_i are distorted by noise or otherwise from the unknown "true" values $f_{true}(x_i)$.

Regression and classification. In regression problems $\mathcal{Y}$ is typically (a subset of) the real numbers $\mathbb{R}$ or some more general measurable space like $\mathbb{R}^m$. In classification, $\mathcal{Y}$ is a finite set or at least discrete. We impose no restrictions on $\mathcal{X}$. Indeed, x will essentially be fixed and plays only a spectator role, so we will often notationally suppress dependencies on x. The goal of regression is to find a function $f_D \in \mathcal{F} \subset \mathcal{X} \to \mathcal{Y}$ "close" to f_{true} based on the past observations D. Or phrased in another way: we are interested in a regression function $r : \mathcal{D} \to \mathcal{F}$ such that $\hat{y} := r(x|D) \equiv r(D)(x) \equiv f_D(x) \approx f_{true}(x)$ for all $x \in \mathcal{X}$.

Notation. We will write (x,y) or (x_0,y_0) for generic data points, use vector notation $\boldsymbol{x} = (x_1,...,x_n)^\top$ and $\boldsymbol{y} = (y_1,...,y_n)^\top$, and $D' = (\boldsymbol{x}',\boldsymbol{y}')$ for generic (fictitious) data of size n.

Example 1 (polynomial regression). For $\mathcal{X} = \mathcal{Y} = \mathbb{R}$, consider the set $\mathcal{F}_d := \{f_{\boldsymbol{w}}(x) = w_d x^{d-1} + ... w_2 x + w_1 : \boldsymbol{w} \in \mathbb{R}^d\}$ of polynomials of degree $d-1$. Fitting the polynomial to data D, e.g. by least squares regression, we estimate $\boldsymbol{w}$ with $\hat{\boldsymbol{w}}_D$. The regression function $\hat{y} = r_d(x|D) = f_{\hat{\boldsymbol{w}}_D}(x)$ can be written down in closed form (see Example 9). $\qquad \diamond$

Example 2 (k nearest neighbors, kNN). Let $\mathcal{Y}$ be some vector space like $\mathbb{R}$ and $\mathcal{X}$ be a metric space like $\mathbb{R}^m$ with some (e.g. Euclidian) metric $d(\cdot,\cdot)$. kNN estimates $f_{true}(x)$ by averaging the y values of the k nearest neighbors $\mathcal{N}_k(x)$ of x in D, i.e. $r_k(x|D) = \frac{1}{k}\sum_{i \in \mathcal{N}_k(x)} y_i$ with $|\mathcal{N}_k(x)| = k$ such that $d(x,x_i) \le d(x,x_j)$ for all $i \in \mathcal{N}_k(x)$ and $j \notin \mathcal{N}_k(x)$. $\qquad \diamond$

Parametric versus non-parametric regression. Polynomial regression is an example of parametric regression in the sense that $r_d(D)$ is the optimal function from a family of functions $\mathcal{F}_d$ indexed by $d < \infty$ real parameters $(\boldsymbol{w})$. In contrast, the kNN regressor r_k is directly given and is not based on a finite-dimensional family of functions. In general, r may be given either directly or be the result of an optimization process.

Loss function. The quality of fit to the data is usually measured by a loss function $\text{Loss}(\boldsymbol{y},\hat{\boldsymbol{y}})$, where $\hat{y}_i = \hat{f}_D(x_i)$ is an estimate of y_i. Often the loss is additive: $\text{Loss}(\boldsymbol{y},\hat{\boldsymbol{y}}) = \sum_{i=1}^n \text{Loss}(y_i,\hat{y}_i)$. If the class $\mathcal{F}$ is not too large, good regressors r can be found by minimizing the loss w.r.t. all $f \in \mathcal{F}$. For instance, $r_d(D) = \text{argmin}_{f \in \mathcal{F}_d} \sum_{i=1}^n (y_i - f(x_i))^2$ and $\hat{y} = r_d(x|D)$ in Example 1.

Regression class and loss. In the following we assume a (typically countable) class of regressors $\mathcal{R}$ (whatever their origin), e.g. the kNN regressors $\{r_k : k \in \mathbb{N}\}$ or the least squares polynomial regressors $\{r_d : d \in \mathbb{N}_0\}$. Note that unlike $f \in \mathcal{F}$, regressors $r \in \mathcal{R}$ are not functions of x alone but depend on all observations D, in particular on $\boldsymbol{y}$. Like for functions f, we can compute the empirical loss of each regressor $r \in \mathcal{R}$:

$$\text{Loss}_r(D) \equiv \text{Loss}_r(\boldsymbol{y}|\boldsymbol{x}) := \text{Loss}(\boldsymbol{y},\hat{\boldsymbol{y}}) = \sum_{i=1}^n \text{Loss}(y_i, r(x_i|\boldsymbol{x},\boldsymbol{y}))$$

where $\hat{y}_i = r(x_i|D)$ in the third expression, and the last expression holds in case of additive loss.

Overfitting. Unfortunately, minimizing Loss_r w.r.t. r will typically *not* select the "best" overall regressor. This is the well-known overfitting problem. In case of polynomials, the classes $\mathcal{F}_d \subset \mathcal{F}_{d+1}$ are nested, hence Loss_{r_d} is monotone decreasing in d with $\mathrm{Loss}_{r_n} \equiv 0$ perfectly fitting the data. In case of kNN, Loss_{r_k} is more or less an increasing function in k with perfect regression on D for $k=1$, since no averaging takes place. In general, $\mathcal{R}$ is often indexed by a "flexibility" or smoothness or complexity parameter, which has to be properly determined. More flexible r can closer fit the data and hence have smaller empirical loss, but are not necessarily better, since they have higher variance. Clearly, too inflexible r also lead to a bad fit ("high bias").

Main goal. The main goal of the paper is to establish a selection criterion for the "best" regressor $r \in \mathcal{R}$

- based on r given as a black box that does not require insight into the origin or inner structure of r,
- that does not depend on things often not given (like a stochastic noise model),
- that exploits what is given (like the loss function).

While for parametric (e.g. polynomial) regression, MDL and Bayesian methods work well (effectively the number of parameters serve as complexity penalty), their use is seriously limited for non-parametric black box r like kNN or if a stochastic/coding model is hard to establish (see Section 4 for a detailed comparison).

Main idea: loss rank. The key observation we exploit is that a more flexible r can fit more data $D' \in \mathcal{D}$ well than a more rigid one. For instance, r_d can perfectly fit all D' for $d = n$, all D' that lie on a parabola for $d = 3$, but only linear D' for $d = 2$. We consider discrete $\mathcal{Y}$ i.e. classification first, and fix $\boldsymbol{x}$. $\boldsymbol{y}$ is the observed data and $\boldsymbol{y}'$ are fictitious others.

Instead of minimizing the unsuitable $\mathrm{Loss}_r(\boldsymbol{y}|\boldsymbol{x})$ w.r.t. r, we could ask how many $\boldsymbol{y}' \in \mathcal{Y}^n$ lead to smaller Loss_r than $\boldsymbol{y}$. Many $\boldsymbol{y}'$ have small loss for flexible r, and so smallness of Loss_r is less significant than if $\boldsymbol{y}$ is among very few other $\boldsymbol{y}'$ with small Loss_r. We claim that the loss rank of $\boldsymbol{y}$ among all $\boldsymbol{y}' \in \mathcal{Y}^n$ is a suitable measure of fit. We define the rank of $\boldsymbol{y}$ under r as the number of $\boldsymbol{y}' \in \mathcal{Y}^n$ with smaller or equal empirical loss than $\boldsymbol{y}$:

$$\mathrm{Rank}_r(\boldsymbol{y}|\boldsymbol{x}) \equiv \mathrm{Rank}_r(L) := \#\{\boldsymbol{y}' \in \mathcal{Y}^n : \mathrm{Loss}_r(\boldsymbol{y}'|\boldsymbol{x}) \leq L\} \text{ with } L := \mathrm{Loss}_r(\boldsymbol{y}|\boldsymbol{x}) \quad (1)$$

For this to make sense, we have to assume (and will later assure) that $\mathrm{Rank}_r(L) < \infty$, i.e. there are only finitely many $\boldsymbol{y}' \in \mathcal{Y}^n$ having loss smaller than L. In a sense, $\rho = \mathrm{Rank}_r(\boldsymbol{y}|\boldsymbol{x})$ measures how compatible $\boldsymbol{y}$ is with r; $\boldsymbol{y}$ is the ρth most compatible with r.

Since the logarithm is a strictly monotone increasing function, we can also consider the logarithmic rank $\mathrm{LR}_r(\boldsymbol{y}|\boldsymbol{x}) := \log\mathrm{Rank}_r(\boldsymbol{y}|\boldsymbol{x})$, which will be more convenient.

Principle 3 (loss rank principle (LoRP) for classification). *For discrete* $\mathcal{Y}$, *the best classifier/regressor* $r : \mathcal{D} \times \mathcal{X} \to \mathcal{Y}$ *in some class* $\mathcal{R}$ *for data* $D = (\boldsymbol{x}, \boldsymbol{y})$ *is the one of smallest loss rank:*

$$r^{best} \;=\; \arg\min_{r \in \mathcal{R}} \mathrm{LR}_r(\boldsymbol{y}|\boldsymbol{x}) \;\equiv\; \arg\min_{r \in \mathcal{R}} \mathrm{Rank}_r(\boldsymbol{y}|\boldsymbol{x}) \tag{2}$$

where Rank_r *is defined in (1).*

We give a simple example for which we can compute all ranks by hand to help better grasping how the principle works, but the example is too simplistic to allow any conclusion on whether the principle is appropriate.

Example 4 (simple discrete). Consider $\mathcal{X} = \{1,2\}$, $\mathcal{Y} = \{0,1,2\}$, and two points $D = \{(1,1),(2,2)\}$ lying on the diagonal $x = y$, with polynomial (zero, constant, linear) least squares regression $\mathcal{R} = \{r_0, r_1, r_2\}$ (see Ex.1). r_0 is simply 0, r_1 the y-average, and r_2 the line through points $(1,y_1)$ and $(2,y_2)$. This, together with the quadratic Loss for generic $\boldsymbol{y}'$ and observed $\boldsymbol{y} = (1,2)$ (and fixed $\boldsymbol{x} = (1,2)$), is summarized in the following table

d	$r_d(x\|\boldsymbol{x}, \boldsymbol{y}')$	$\mathrm{Loss}_d(\boldsymbol{y}'\|\boldsymbol{x})$	$\mathrm{Loss}_d(D)$
0	0	$y_1'^2 + y_2'^2$	5
1	$\frac{1}{2}(y_1' + y_2')$	$\frac{1}{2}(y_2' - y_1')^2$	$\frac{1}{2}$
2	$(y_2' - y_1')(x-1) + y_1'$	0	0

From the Loss we can easily compute the Rank for all nine $\boldsymbol{y}' \in \{0,1,2\}^2$. Equal rank due to equal loss is indicated by a $=$ in the table below. Whole equality groups are actually assigned the rank of their right-most member, e.g. for $d = 1$ the ranks of $(y_1', y_2') = (0,1),(1,0),(2,1),(1,2)$ are all 7 (and not 4,5,6,7).

	$\mathrm{Rank}_{r_d}(y_1' y_2' \| 12)$									
d	1	2	3	4	5	6	7	8	9	$\mathrm{Rank}_{r_d}(D)$
0	$y_1'y_2' = 00$	< 01	$= 10$	< 11	< 02	$= 20$	< 21	$= \mathbf{12}$	< 22	8
1	$y_1'y_2' = 00$	$= 11$	$= 22$	< 01	$= 10$	$= 21$	$= \mathbf{12}$	< 02	$= 20$	7
2	$y_1'y_2' = 00$	$= 01$	$= 02$	$= 10$	$= 11$	$= 20$	$= 21$	$= 22$	$= \mathbf{12}$	9

So LoRP selects r_1 as best regressor, since it has minimal rank on D. r_0 fits D too badly and r_2 is too flexible (perfectly fits all D'). $\diamond$

LoRP for continuous $\mathcal{Y}$. We now consider the case of continuous or measurable spaces $\mathcal{Y}$, i.e. normal regression problems. We assume $\mathcal{Y} = \mathbb{R}$ in the following exposition, but the idea and resulting principle hold for more general measurable spaces like $\mathbb{R}^m$. We simply reduce the model selection problem to the discrete case by considering the discretized space $\mathcal{Y}_\varepsilon = \varepsilon \mathbb{Z}$ for small $\varepsilon > 0$ and discretize $\boldsymbol{y} \rightsquigarrow \boldsymbol{y}_\varepsilon \in \varepsilon \mathbb{Z}^n$. Then $\mathrm{Rank}_r^\varepsilon(L) := \#\{\boldsymbol{y}_\varepsilon' \in \mathcal{Y}_\varepsilon^n : \mathrm{Loss}_r(\boldsymbol{y}_\varepsilon'|\boldsymbol{x}) \leq L\}$ with $L = \mathrm{Loss}_r(\boldsymbol{y}_\varepsilon|\boldsymbol{x})$ counts the number of ε-grid points in the set

$$V_r(L) \;:=\; \{\boldsymbol{y}' \in \mathcal{Y}^n : \mathrm{Loss}_r(\boldsymbol{y}'|\boldsymbol{x}) \leq L\} \tag{3}$$

which we assume (and later assure) to be finite, analogous to the discrete case. Hence $\mathrm{Rank}_r^\varepsilon(L) \cdot \varepsilon^n$ is an approximation of the *loss volume* $|V_r(L)|$ of set $V_r(L)$, and typically $\text{Rank}_r^\varepsilon(L)\cdot\varepsilon^n=|V_r(L)|\cdot(1+O(\varepsilon))\to|V_r(L)|$ for $\varepsilon\to 0$. Taking the logarithm we get $\text{LR}_r^\varepsilon(\boldsymbol{y}|\boldsymbol{x})=\log\text{Rank}_r^\varepsilon(L)=\log|V_r(L)|-n\log\varepsilon+O(\varepsilon)$. Since $n\log\varepsilon$ is independent of r, we can drop it in comparisons like (2). So for $\varepsilon\to 0$ we can define the log-loss "rank" simply as the log-volume

$$\text{LR}_r(\boldsymbol{y}|\boldsymbol{x}) := \log|V_r(L)|, \quad \text{where} \quad L := \text{Loss}_r(\boldsymbol{y}|\boldsymbol{x}) \tag{4}$$

Principle 5 (loss rank principle for regression). *For measurable $\mathcal{Y}$, the best regressor $r:\mathcal{D}\times\mathcal{X}\to\mathcal{Y}$ in some class $\mathcal{R}$ for data $D=(\boldsymbol{x},\boldsymbol{y})$ is the one of smallest loss volume:*

$$r^{best} = \arg\min_{r\in\mathcal{R}}\text{LR}_r(\boldsymbol{y}|\boldsymbol{x}) \equiv \arg\min_{r\in\mathcal{R}}|V_r(L)|$$

where LR, V_r, *and* L *are defined in (3) and (4), and* $|V_r(L)|$ *is the volume of* $V_r(L)\subseteq\mathcal{Y}^n$.

For discrete $\mathcal{Y}$ with counting measure we recover the discrete Loss Rank Principle 3.

Example 6 (simple continuous). Consider Example 4 but with interval $\mathcal{Y}=[0,2]$. The first table remains unchanged, while the second table becomes

d	$V_d(L)=\{\boldsymbol{y}'\in[0,2]^2:...\}$	$\|V_d(L)\|$	$\|V_d(\text{Loss}_d(D))\|$
0	$y_1'^2+y_2'^2\le L$	$2\sqrt{\max\{L-4,0\}}+$ $L(\frac{\pi}{4}-\cos^{-1}(\min\{\frac{2}{\sqrt{L}},1\}))$	≈ 3.6
1	$\frac{1}{2}(y_2'-y_1')^2\le L$	$4\sqrt{2L}-2L$	3
2	$0\le L$	4	4

So LoRP again selects r_1 as best regressor, since it has smallest loss volume on D. $\diamond$

Infinite rank or volume. Often the loss rank/volume will be infinite, e.g. if we had chosen $\mathcal{Y}=\mathbb{Z}$ in Ex.4 or $\mathcal{Y}=\mathbb{R}$ in Ex.6. We will encounter such infinities in Section 3. There are various potential remedies. We could modify (a) the regressor r or (b) the Loss to make LR_r finite, (c) the Loss Rank Principle itself, or (d) find problem-specific solutions. Regressors r with infinite rank might be rejected for philosophical or pragmatic reasons. We will briefly consider (a) for linear regression later, but to fiddle around with r in a generic (blackbox way) seems difficult. We have no good idea how to tinker with LoRP (c), and also a patched LoRP may be less attractive. For kNN on a grid we later use remedy (d). While in (decision) theory, the application's goal determines the loss, in practice the loss is often more determined by convenience or rules of thumb. So the Loss (b) seems the most inviting place to tinker with. A very simple modification is to add a small penalty term to the loss.

$$\text{Loss}_r(\boldsymbol{y}|\boldsymbol{x}) \rightsquigarrow \text{Loss}_r^\alpha(\boldsymbol{y}|\boldsymbol{x}) := \text{Loss}_r(\boldsymbol{y}|\boldsymbol{x})+\alpha||\boldsymbol{y}||^2, \quad \alpha>0 \text{ "small"} \tag{5}$$

The Euclidian norm $||\boldsymbol{y}||^2:=\sum_{i=1}^n y_i^2$ is default, but other (non)norm regularizes are possible. The regularized $\text{LR}_r^\alpha(\boldsymbol{y}|\boldsymbol{x})$ based on Loss_r^α is always finite, since

$\{\boldsymbol{y}:||\boldsymbol{y}||^2 \leq L\}$ has finite volume. An alternative penalty $\alpha\hat{\boldsymbol{y}}^\top\hat{\boldsymbol{y}}$, quadratic in the regression estimates $\hat{y}_i = r(x_i|\boldsymbol{x},\boldsymbol{y})$ is possible if r is unbounded in every $\boldsymbol{y} \to \infty$ direction.

A scheme trying to determine a single (flexibility) parameter (like d and k in the above examples) would be of no use if it depended on one (or more) other unknown parameters (α), since varying through the unknown parameter leads to any (non)desired result. Since LoRP seeks the r of smallest rank, it is natural to also determine α by minimizing LR_r^α w.r.t. α. The good news is that this leads to meaningful results.

3   LoRP for Linear Models

In this section we consider the important class of linear regressors with quadratic loss function. Since linearity is only assumed in y and the dependence on x can be arbitrary, this class is richer than it may appear. It includes kNN (Example 7), kernel (Example 8), and many other regressors. For linear regression and $\mathcal{Y} = I\!\!R$, the loss rank is the volume of an n-dimensional ellipsoid, which can efficiently be computed in time $O(n^3)$ (Theorem 10). For the special case of projective regression, e.g. linear basis function regression (Example 9), we can even determine the regularization parameter α analytically (Theorem 11).

Linear regression. We assume $\mathcal{Y} = I\!\!R$ in this section; generalization to $I\!\!R^m$ is straightforward. A linear regressor r can be written in the form

$$\hat{y} = r(x|\boldsymbol{x},\boldsymbol{y}) = \sum_{j=1}^n m_j(x,\boldsymbol{x})y_j \quad \forall x \in \mathcal{X} \quad \text{and some} \quad m_j : \mathcal{X} \times \mathcal{X}^n \to I\!\!R \quad (6)$$

Particularly interesting is r for $x = x_1,...,x_n$.

$$\hat{y}_i = r(x_i|\boldsymbol{x},\boldsymbol{y}) = \sum_j M_{ij}(\boldsymbol{x})y_j \quad \text{with} \quad M : \mathcal{X}^n \to I\!\!R^{n \times n} \quad (7)$$

where matrix $M_{ij}(\boldsymbol{x}) = m_j(x_i,\boldsymbol{x})$. Since LoRP needs r only on the training data $\boldsymbol{x}$, we only need M.

Example 7 (kNN ctd.). For kNN of Ex.2 we have $m_j(x,\boldsymbol{x}) = \frac{1}{k}$ if $j \in \mathcal{N}_k(x)$ and 0 else, and $M_{ij}(\boldsymbol{x}) = \frac{1}{k}$ if $j \in \mathcal{N}_k(x_i)$ and 0 else. $\diamondsuit$

Example 8 (kernel regression). Kernel regression takes a weighted average over $\boldsymbol{y}$, where the weight of y_j to y is proportional to the similarity of x_j to x, measured by a kernel $K(x,x_j)$, i.e. $m_j(x,\boldsymbol{x}) = K(x,x_j)/\sum_{j=1}^n K(x,x_j)$. For example the Gaussian kernel for $\mathcal{X} = I\!\!R^m$ is $K(x,x_j) = \mathrm{e}^{-||x-x_j||_2^2/2\sigma^2}$. The width σ controls the smoothness of the kernel regressor, and LoRP selects the real-valued "complexity" parameter σ. $\diamondsuit$

Example 9 (linear basis function regression, LBFR). Let $\phi_1(x),...,\phi_d(x)$ be a set or vector of "basis" functions often called "features". We place no restrictions on $\mathcal{X}$ or $\boldsymbol{\phi}:\mathcal{X} \to I\!\!R^d$. Consider the class of functions linear in $\boldsymbol{\phi}$:

$$\mathcal{F}_d = \{f_{\boldsymbol{w}}(x) = \sum_{a=1}^d w_a\phi_a(x) = \boldsymbol{w}^\top\boldsymbol{\phi}(x) : \boldsymbol{w} \in I\!\!R^d\}$$

For instance, for $\mathcal{X} = \mathbb{R}$ and $\phi_a(x) = x^{a-1}$ we would recover the polynomial regression Example 1. For quadratic loss function $\mathrm{Loss}(y_i, \hat{y}_i) = (y_i - \hat{y}_i)^2$ we have

$$\mathrm{Loss}_{\boldsymbol{w}}(\boldsymbol{y}|\boldsymbol{\phi}) \; := \; \textstyle\sum_{i=1}^{n}(y_i - f_{\boldsymbol{w}}(x_i))^2 \; = \; \boldsymbol{y}^{\top}\boldsymbol{y} - 2\boldsymbol{y}^{\top}\boldsymbol{\Phi}\boldsymbol{w} + \boldsymbol{w}^{\top}B\boldsymbol{w}$$

where matrix $\boldsymbol{\Phi}$ is defined by $\boldsymbol{\Phi}_{ia} = \phi_a(x_i)$ and B is a symmetric matrix with $B_{ab} = \sum_{i=1}^{n}\phi_a(x_i)\phi_b(x_i) = [\boldsymbol{\Phi}^{\top}\boldsymbol{\Phi}]_{ab}$. The loss is quadratic in $\boldsymbol{w}$ with minimum at $\boldsymbol{w} = B^{-1}\boldsymbol{\Phi}^{\top}\boldsymbol{y}$. So the least squares regressor is $\hat{y} = \boldsymbol{y}^{\top}\boldsymbol{\Phi}B^{-1}\boldsymbol{\phi}(x)$, hence $m_j(x, \boldsymbol{x}) = (\boldsymbol{\Phi}B^{-1}\boldsymbol{\phi}(x))_j$ and $M(\boldsymbol{x}) = \boldsymbol{\Phi}B^{-1}\boldsymbol{\Phi}^{\top}$. $\qquad\qquad\qquad\qquad\qquad\qquad\qquad\qquad \diamond$

Consider now a general linear regressor M with quadratic loss and quadratic penalty

$$\mathrm{Loss}_{M}^{\alpha}(\boldsymbol{y}|\boldsymbol{x}) = \textstyle\sum_{i=1}^{n}\left(y_i - \sum_{j=1}^{n}M_{ij}y_j\right)^2 + \alpha||\boldsymbol{y}||^2 \; = \; \boldsymbol{y}^{\top}S_{\alpha}\boldsymbol{y},$$

$$\text{where}^1 \quad S_{\alpha} = (\mathbb{1} - M)^{\top}(\mathbb{1} - M) + \alpha\mathbb{1} \qquad\qquad\qquad (8)$$

($\mathbb{1}$ is the identity matrix). S_{α} is a symmetric matrix. For $\alpha > 0$ it is positive definite and for $\alpha = 0$ positive semidefinite. If $\lambda_1, ... \lambda_n \geq 0$ are the eigenvalues of S_0, then $\lambda_i + \alpha$ are the eigenvalues of S_{α}. $V(L) = \{\boldsymbol{y}' \in \mathbb{R}^n : \boldsymbol{y}'^{\top}S_{\alpha}\boldsymbol{y}' \leq L\}$ is an ellipsoid with the eigenvectors of S_{α} being the main axes and $\sqrt{L/(\lambda_i + \alpha)}$ being their length. Hence the volume is

$$|V(L)| \; = \; v_n\prod_{i=1}^{n}\sqrt{\frac{L}{\lambda_i + \alpha}} \; = \; \frac{v_n L^{n/2}}{\sqrt{\det S_{\alpha}}}$$

where $v_n = \pi^{n/2}/\frac{n}{2}!$ is the volume of the n-dimensional unit sphere, $z! := \Gamma(z+1)$, and det is the determinant. Taking the logarithm we get

$$\mathrm{LR}_{M}^{\alpha}(\boldsymbol{y}|\boldsymbol{x}) \; = \; \log|V(\mathrm{Loss}_{M}^{\alpha}(\boldsymbol{y}|\boldsymbol{x}))| \; = \; \tfrac{n}{2}\log(\boldsymbol{y}^{\top}S_{\alpha}\boldsymbol{y}) - \tfrac{1}{2}\log\det S_{\alpha} + \log v_n \quad (9)$$

Consider now a *class* of linear regressors $\mathcal{M} = \{M\}$, e.g. the kNN regressors $\{M_k : k \in \mathbb{N}\}$ or the d-dimensional linear basis function regressors $\{M_d : d \in \mathbb{N}_0\}$.

Theorem 10 (LoRP for linear regression). *For $\mathcal{Y} = \mathbb{R}$, the best linear regressor $M : \mathcal{X}^n \to \mathbb{R}^{n \times n}$ in some class $\mathcal{M}$ for data $D = (\boldsymbol{x}, \boldsymbol{y})$ is*

$$M^{best} \; = \; \operatorname*{arg\,min}_{M \in \mathcal{M}, \alpha \geq 0}\left\{\tfrac{n}{2}\log(\boldsymbol{y}^{\top}S_{\alpha}\boldsymbol{y}) - \tfrac{1}{2}\log\det S_{\alpha}\right\} \; = \; \operatorname*{arg\,min}_{M \in \mathcal{M}, \alpha \geq 0}\left\{\frac{\boldsymbol{y}^{\top}S_{\alpha}\boldsymbol{y}}{(\det S_{\alpha})^{1/n}}\right\}$$
$$(10)$$

where S_{α} is defined in (8).

Since v_n is independent of α and M it was possible to drop v_n. The last expression shows that linear LoRP minimizes the Loss times the geometric average of the squared axes lengths of ellipsoid $V(1)$. Note that M^{best} depends on $\boldsymbol{y}$ unlike the $M \in \mathcal{M}$.

Nullspace of S_0. If M has an eigenvalue 1, then $S_0 = (\mathbb{1} - M)^{\top}(\mathbb{1} - M)$ has a zero eigenvalue and $\alpha > 0$ is necessary, since $\det S_0 = 0$. Actually this is true for

---

[1] The mentioned alternative penalty $\alpha||\hat{\boldsymbol{y}}||^2$ would lead to $S_{\alpha} = (\mathbb{1} - M)^{\top}(\mathbb{1} - M) + \alpha M^{\top}M$. For LBFR, penalty $\alpha||\hat{\boldsymbol{w}}||^2$ is popular (ridge regression). Apart from being limited to parametric regression, it has the disadvantage of not being reparametrization invariant. For instance, scaling $\phi_a(x) \rightsquigarrow \gamma_a\phi_a(x)$ doesn't change the class $\mathcal{F}_d$, but changes the ridge regressor.

most practical M. Nearly all linear regressors are invariant under a constant shift of $\boldsymbol{y}$, i.e. $r(y_i + c|D) = r(y_i|D) + c$, which implies that M has eigenvector $(1,...,1)^\top$ with eigenvalue 1. This can easily be checked for kNN (Ex.2), Kernel (Ex.8), and LBFR (Ex.9). Such a generic 1-eigenvector effecting all $M \in \mathcal{M}$ could easily and maybe should be filtered out by considering only the orthogonal space or dropping these $\lambda_i = 0$ when computing $\det S_0$. The 1-eigenvectors that depend on M are the ones where we really need a regularizer $\alpha > 0$ for. For instance, M_d in LBFR has d eigenvalues 1, and M_{kNN} has as many eigenvalues 1 as there are disjoint components in the graph determined by the edges $M_{ij} > 0$. In general we need to find the optimal α numerically. If M is a projection we can find α_{min} analytically.

Projective regression. Consider a projection matrix $M = P = P^2$ with $d = \text{tr}P$ eigenvalues 1, and $n - d$ zero eigenvalues. For instance, $M = \boldsymbol{\Phi} B^{-1} \boldsymbol{\Phi}^\top$ of LBFR Ex.9 is such a matrix, since $M\boldsymbol{\Phi} = \boldsymbol{\Phi}$ and $M\boldsymbol{\Psi} = 0$ for $\boldsymbol{\Psi}$ such that $\boldsymbol{\Phi}^\top \boldsymbol{\Psi} = 0$. This implies that S_α has d eigenvalues α and $n - d$ eigenvalues $1 + \alpha$. Hence

$$\det S_\alpha = \alpha^d (1+\alpha)^{n-d}, \quad \text{where} \quad S_\alpha = S_0 + \alpha\mathbb{1} = \mathbb{1} - P + \alpha\mathbb{1}$$
$$\boldsymbol{y}^\top S_\alpha \boldsymbol{y} = (\rho + \alpha)\boldsymbol{y}^\top \boldsymbol{y}, \quad \text{where} \quad \rho := \frac{\boldsymbol{y}^\top S_0 \boldsymbol{y}}{\boldsymbol{y}^\top \boldsymbol{y}} = 1 - \frac{\boldsymbol{y}^\top P \boldsymbol{y}}{\boldsymbol{y}^\top \boldsymbol{y}}$$
$$\Rightarrow \quad \text{LR}_P^\alpha = \tfrac{n}{2}\log \boldsymbol{y}^\top \boldsymbol{y} + \tfrac{n}{2}\log(\rho + \alpha) - \tfrac{d}{2}\log\alpha - \tfrac{n-d}{2}\log(1+\alpha) \tag{11}$$

The first term is independent of α. Consider $1 - \rho > \frac{d}{n}$, the reasonable region in practice. Solving $\partial \text{LR}_P^\alpha / \partial \alpha = 0$ w.r.t. α we get a minimum at $\alpha = \alpha_{min} := \frac{\rho d}{(1-\rho)n - d}$. After some algebra we get

$$\text{LR}_P^{\alpha_{min}} = \tfrac{n}{2}\log\boldsymbol{y}^\top\boldsymbol{y} - \tfrac{n}{2}\text{KL}(\tfrac{d}{n}||1-\rho), \quad \text{where} \quad \text{KL}(p||q) = p\log\tfrac{p}{q} + (1-p)\log\tfrac{1-p}{1-q} \tag{12}$$

is the relative entropy or Kullback-Leibler divergence. Minimizing $\text{LR}_P^{\alpha_{min}}$ w.r.t. M is equivalent to maximizing $\text{KL}(\tfrac{d}{n}||1-\rho)$. This is an unusual task, since one mostly encounters KL minimizations. For fixed d, $\text{LR}_P^{\alpha_{min}}$ is monotone increasing in ρ. Since $\text{Loss}_P^\alpha \propto \rho + \alpha$, LoRP suggests to minimize Loss for fixed model dimension d. For fixed ρ, $\text{LR}_P^{\alpha_{min}}$ is monotone increasing in d, i.e. LoRP suggests to minimize model dimension d for fixed Loss. Normally there is a tradeoff between minimizing d and ρ, and LoRP suggests that the optimal choice is the one that maximizes KL.

Theorem 11 (LoRP for projective regression). *The best projective regressor* $P : \mathcal{X}^n \to I\!\!R^{n \times n}$ *with* $P = P^2$ *in some projective class* $\mathcal{P}$ *for data* $D = (\boldsymbol{x}, \boldsymbol{y})$ *is*

$$P^{best} = \arg\max_{P \in \mathcal{P}} \text{KL}(\tfrac{\text{tr}P(x)}{n}||\tfrac{\boldsymbol{y}^\top P(x)\boldsymbol{y}}{\boldsymbol{y}^\top \boldsymbol{y}}), \quad provided \quad \tfrac{\text{tr}P}{n} < \tfrac{\boldsymbol{y}^\top P \boldsymbol{y}}{\boldsymbol{y}^\top \boldsymbol{y}}$$

4   Comparison to Gaussian Bayesian Linear Regression

We now consider linear basis function regression (LBFR) from a Bayesian perspective with Gaussian noise and prior, and compare it to LoRP. In addition to the noise model as in PML, one also has to specify a prior. Bayesian model selection (BMS) proceeds by selecting the model that has largest evidence. In the special case of LBFR with Gaussian noise and prior and an ML-II estimate for the noise variance, the expression for the evidence has a similar structure as the expression of the loss rank.

Gaussian Bayesian LBFR / MAP. Recall from Sec.3 Ex.9 that $\mathcal{F}_d$ is the class of functions $f_{\boldsymbol{w}}(x) = \boldsymbol{w}^\top \boldsymbol{\phi}(x)$ $(\boldsymbol{w} \in I\!\!R^d)$ that are linear in feature vector $\boldsymbol{\phi}$. Let

$$\text{Gauss}_N(\boldsymbol{z}|\boldsymbol{\mu}, \Sigma) := \frac{\exp(-\frac{1}{2}(\boldsymbol{z} - \boldsymbol{\mu})^\top \Sigma^{-1}(\boldsymbol{z} - \boldsymbol{\mu}))}{(2\pi)^{N/2}\sqrt{\det \Sigma}} \tag{13}$$

denote a general N-dimensional Gaussian distribution with mean $\boldsymbol{\mu}$ and covariance matrix Σ. We assume that observations y are perturbed from $f_{\boldsymbol{w}}(x)$ by independent additive Gaussian noise with variance β^{-1} and zero mean, i.e. the likelihood of $\boldsymbol{y}$ under model $\boldsymbol{w}$ is $\text{P}(\boldsymbol{y}|\boldsymbol{w}) = \text{Gauss}_n(\boldsymbol{y}|\boldsymbol{\Phi}\boldsymbol{w}, \beta^{-1}\mathbb{1})$, where $\boldsymbol{\Phi}_{ia} = \phi_a(x_i)$. A Bayesian assumes a prior (before seeing $\boldsymbol{y}$) distribution on $\boldsymbol{w}$. We assume a centered Gaussian with covariance matrix $(\alpha C)^{-1}$, i.e. $\text{P}(\boldsymbol{w}) = \text{Gauss}_d(\boldsymbol{w}|\boldsymbol{0}, \alpha^{-1}C^{-1})$. From the prior and the likelihood one can compute the evidence and the posterior

Evidence: $\text{P}(\boldsymbol{y}) = \int \text{P}(\boldsymbol{y}|\boldsymbol{w})\text{P}(\boldsymbol{w})d\boldsymbol{w} = \text{Gauss}_n(\boldsymbol{y}|\boldsymbol{0}, \beta^{-1}S^{-1})$ (14)

Posterior: $\text{P}(\boldsymbol{w}|\boldsymbol{y}) = \text{P}(\boldsymbol{y}|\boldsymbol{w})\text{P}(\boldsymbol{w})/P(\boldsymbol{y}) = \text{Gauss}_d(\boldsymbol{w}|\hat{\boldsymbol{w}}, A^{-1})$

$B := \boldsymbol{\Phi}^\top\boldsymbol{\Phi}, \quad A := \alpha C + \beta B, \quad M := \beta\boldsymbol{\Phi}A^{-1}\boldsymbol{\Phi}^\top,$ (15)

$S := \mathbb{1} - M, \quad \hat{\boldsymbol{w}} := \beta A^{-1}\boldsymbol{\Phi}^\top\boldsymbol{y}, \quad \hat{\boldsymbol{y}} := \boldsymbol{\Phi}\hat{\boldsymbol{w}} = M\boldsymbol{y}$

A standard Bayesian point estimate for $\boldsymbol{w}$ for fixed d is the one that maximizes the posterior (MAP) (which in the Gaussian case coincides with the mean) $\hat{\boldsymbol{w}} = \text{argmax}_{\boldsymbol{w}}\text{P}(\boldsymbol{w}|\boldsymbol{y}) = \beta A^{-1}\boldsymbol{\Phi}^\top\boldsymbol{y}$. For $\alpha \to 0$, MAP reduces to Maximum Likelihood (ML), which in the Gaussian case coincides with the least squares regression of Ex.9. For $\alpha > 0$, the regression matrix M is not a projection anymore.

Bayesian model selection. Consider now a family of models $\{\mathcal{F}_1, \mathcal{F}_2, ...\}$. Here the $\mathcal{F}_d$ are the linear regressors with d basis functions, but in general they could be completely different model classes. All quantities in the previous paragraph implicitly depend on the choice of $\mathcal{F}$, which we now explicate with an index. In particular, the evidence for model class $\mathcal{F}$ is $\text{P}_{\mathcal{F}}(\boldsymbol{y})$. Bayesian Model Selection (BMS) chooses the model class (here d) $\mathcal{F}$ of highest evidence:

$$\mathcal{F}^{\text{BMS}} = \arg\max_{\mathcal{F}} \text{P}_{\mathcal{F}}(\boldsymbol{y})$$

Once the model class $\mathcal{F}^{\text{BMS}}$ is determined, the MAP (or other) regression function $f_{\boldsymbol{w}_{\mathcal{F}^{\text{BMS}}}}$ or $M_{\mathcal{F}^{\text{BMS}}}$ are chosen. The data variance β^{-1} may be known or estimated from the data, C is often chosen $\mathbb{1}$, and α has to be chosen somehow. Note that while $\alpha \to 0$ leads to a reasonable MAP=ML regressor for fixed d, this limit cannot be used for BMS.

Comparison to LoRP. Inserting (13) into (14) and taking the logarithm we see that BMS minimizes

$$-\log \text{P}_{\mathcal{F}}(\boldsymbol{y}) = \frac{\beta}{2}\boldsymbol{y}^\top S\boldsymbol{y} - \frac{1}{2}\log\det S - \frac{n}{2}\log\frac{\beta}{2\pi} \tag{16}$$

w.r.t. $\mathcal{F}$. Let us estimate β by ML: We assume a broad prior $\alpha \ll \beta$ so that $\beta \frac{\partial S}{\partial \beta} = O(\frac{\alpha}{\beta})$ can be neglected. Then $\frac{\partial \log \mathrm{P}_{\mathcal{F}}(\boldsymbol{y})}{\partial \beta} = \frac{1}{2}\boldsymbol{y}^\top S\boldsymbol{y} - \frac{n}{2\beta} + O(\frac{\alpha}{\beta}n) = 0 \Leftrightarrow$ $\beta \approx \hat{\beta} := n/(\boldsymbol{y}^\top S\boldsymbol{y})$. Inserting $\hat{\beta}$ into (16) we get

$$- \log \mathrm{P}_{\mathcal{F}}(\boldsymbol{y}) \;=\; \tfrac{n}{2}\log \boldsymbol{y}^\top S\boldsymbol{y} - \tfrac{1}{2}\log \det S - \tfrac{n}{2}\log \tfrac{n}{2\pi e} \qquad (17)$$

Taking an improper prior $\mathrm{P}(\beta) \propto \beta^{-1}$ and integrating out β leads for small α to a similar result. The last term in (17) is a constant independent of $\mathcal{F}$ and can be ignored. The first two terms have the same structure as in linear LoRP (10), but the matrix S is different. In both cases, α act as regularizers, so we may minimize over α in BMS like in LoRP. For $\alpha = 0$ (which neither makes sense in BMS nor in LoRP), M in BMS coincides with M of Ex.9, but still the S_0 in LoRP is the square of the S in BMS. For $\alpha > 0$, M of BMS may be regarded as a regularized regressor as suggested in Sec.2 (a), rather than a regularized loss function (b) used in LoRP. Note also that BMS is limited to (semi)parametric regression, i.e. does not cover the non-parametric kNN Ex.2 and Kernel Ex.8, unlike LoRP.

Since B only depends on $\boldsymbol{x}$ (and not on $\boldsymbol{y}$), and all P are implicitly conditioned on $\boldsymbol{x}$, one could choose $C = B$. In this case, $M = \gamma \boldsymbol{\Phi} B^{-1} \boldsymbol{\Phi}^\top$, with $\gamma = \frac{\beta}{\alpha + \beta} < 1$ for $\alpha > 0$, is a simple multiplicative regularization of projection $\boldsymbol{\Phi} B^{-1} \boldsymbol{\Phi}^\top$, and (17) coincides with (11) for suitable α, apart from an irrelevant additive constant, hence minimizing (17) over α also leads to (12).

5   Comparison to Other Model Selection Schemes

In this section we give a brief introduction to Penalized Maximum Likelihood (PML) for (semi)parametric regression, and its major instantiations, the Akaike and the Bayesian Information Criterion (AIC and BIC), and the Minimum Description Length (MDL) principle, whose penalty terms are all proportional to the number of parameters d. The *effective* number of parameters is often much smaller than d, e.g. if there are soft constraints like in ridge regression. We compare MacKay's [Mac92] trace formula for Gaussian Bayesian LBFR and Hastie's et al. [HTF01] trace formula for general linear regression with LoRP.

Penalized ML (AIC, BIC, MDL). Consider a d-dimensional stochastic model class like the Gaussian Bayesian linear regression example of Section 4. Let $\mathrm{P}_d(\boldsymbol{y}|\boldsymbol{w})$ be the data likelihood under d-dimensional model $\boldsymbol{w} \in I\!\!R^d$. The maximum likelihood (ML) estimator for fixed d is

$$\hat{\boldsymbol{w}} \;=\; \arg\max_{\boldsymbol{w}} \mathrm{P}_d(\boldsymbol{y}|\boldsymbol{w}) \;=\; \arg\min_{\boldsymbol{w}}\{- \log \mathrm{P}_d(\boldsymbol{y}|\boldsymbol{w})\}$$

Since $-\log \mathrm{P}_d(\boldsymbol{y}|\boldsymbol{w})$ decreases with d, we cannot find the model dimension by simply minimizing over d (overfitting). Penalized ML adds a complexity term to get reasonable results

$$\hat{d} \;=\; \arg\min_{d}\{- \log \mathrm{P}_d(\boldsymbol{y}|\hat{\boldsymbol{w}}) + \mathrm{Penalty}(d)\}$$

The penalty introduces a tradeoff between the first and second term with a minimum at $\hat{d} < \infty$. Various penalties have been suggested: The Akaike Information Criterion (AIC) [Aka73] uses d, the Bayesian Information Criterion (BIC) [Sch78] and the (crude) Minimum Description Length (MDL) principle use $\frac{d}{2}\log n$ [Ris78, Grü04] for Penalty(d). There are at least *three important conceptual differences* to LoRP:

- In order to apply PML one needs to specify not only a class of regression functions, but a full probabilistic model $P_d(\boldsymbol{y}|\boldsymbol{w})$,
- PML ignores or at least does not tell how to incorporate a potentially given loss-function,
- PML (AIC,BIC,MDL) is mostly limited to (semi)parametric models (with d "true" parameters).

We discuss two approaches to the last item in the remainder of this section: AIC, BIC, and MDL are not directly applicable (a) for non-parametric models like kNN or Kernel regression, or (b) if d does not reflect the "true" complexity of the model. For instance, ridge regression can work even for d larger than n, because a penalty pulls most parameters towards (but not exactly to) zero. MacKay [Mac92] suggests an expression for the effective number of parameters d_{eff} as a substitute for d in case of (b), and Hastie et al. [HTF01] more generally also for (a).

The trace penalty for parametric Gaussian LBFR. We continue with the Gaussian Bayesian linear regression example (see Section 4 for details and notation). Performing the integration in (14), MacKay [Mac92, Eq.(21)] derives the following expression for the Bayesian evidence for $C = \mathbb{1}$

$$-\log P(\boldsymbol{y}) = (\alpha \hat{E}_W + \beta \hat{E}_D) + (\tfrac{1}{2}\log\det A - \tfrac{d}{2}\log\alpha) - \tfrac{n}{2}\log\tfrac{\beta}{2\pi} \qquad (18)$$
$$\hat{E}_D = \tfrac{1}{2}||\boldsymbol{\Phi}\hat{\boldsymbol{w}} - \boldsymbol{y}||_2^2, \quad \hat{E}_W = \tfrac{1}{2}||\hat{\boldsymbol{w}}||_2^2$$

(the first bracket in (18) equals $\frac{\beta}{2}\boldsymbol{y}^{\top}S\boldsymbol{y}$ and the second equals $-\frac{1}{2}\log\det S$, cf. (16)). Minimizing (18) w.r.t. α leads to the following relation:

$$0 = \frac{-\partial \log P(\boldsymbol{y})}{\partial\alpha} = \hat{E}_W + \tfrac{1}{2}\mathrm{tr}A^{-1} - \tfrac{d}{2\alpha} \qquad (\tfrac{\partial}{\partial\alpha}\log\det A = \mathrm{tr}A^{-1})$$

He argues that $\alpha||\hat{\boldsymbol{w}}||_2^2$ corresponds to the effective number of parameters, hence

$$d_{eff}^{\mathrm{McK}} := \alpha||\hat{\boldsymbol{w}}||_2^2 = 2\alpha\hat{E}_W = d - \alpha\,\mathrm{tr}A^{-1} \qquad (19)$$

The trace penalty for general linear models. We now return to general linear regression $\hat{\boldsymbol{y}} = M(\boldsymbol{x})\boldsymbol{y}$ (7). LBFR is a special case of a projection matrix $M = M^2$ with rank $d = \mathrm{tr}M$ being the number of basis functions. M leaves d directions untouched and projects all other $n-d$ directions to zero. For general M, Hastie et al. [HTF01, Sec.5.4.1] argue to regard a direction that is only somewhat shrunken, say by a factor of $0 < \beta < 1$, as a fractional parameter (β degrees of freedom). If $\beta_1,...,\beta_n$ are the shrinkages = eigenvalues of M, the effective number of parameters could be defined as [HTF01, Sec.7.6]

$$d_{eff}^{\mathrm{HTF}} := \sum_{i=1}^{n} \beta_i = \mathrm{tr}M$$

which generalizes the relation $d = \mathrm{tr} M$ beyond projections. For MacKay's M (15), $\mathrm{tr} M = d - \mathrm{tr} A^{-1}$, i.e. d_{eff}^{HTF} is consistent with and generalizes d_{eff}^{McK}.

Problems. Though nicely motivated, the trace formula is not without problems. First, since for projections, $M = M^2$, one could equally well have argued for $d_{eff}^{\mathrm{HTF}} = \mathrm{tr} M^2$. Second, for kNN we have $\mathrm{tr} M = \frac{n}{k}$ (since M is $\frac{1}{k}$ on the diagonal), which does not look unreasonable. Consider now kNN' where we average over the k nearest neighbors *excluding* the closest neighbor. For sufficiently smooth functions, kNN' for suitable k is still a reasonable regressor, but $\mathrm{tr} M = 0$ (since M is zero on the diagonal). So $d_{eff}^{\mathrm{HTF}} = 0$ for kNN', which makes no sense and would lead one to always select the $k = 1$ model.

Relation to LoRP. In the case of kNN', $\mathrm{tr} M^2$ would be a better estimate for the effective dimension. In linear LoRP, $-\log\det S_\alpha$ serves as complexity penalty. Ignoring the nullspace of $S_0 = (\mathbb{1} - M)^\top (\mathbb{1} - M)$ (8), we can Taylor expand $-\frac{1}{2}\log\det S_0$ in M

$$-\tfrac{1}{2}\log\det S_0 \;=\; -\mathrm{tr}\log(\mathbb{1} - M) \;=\; \sum_{s=1}^{\infty} \tfrac{1}{s}\mathrm{tr}(M^s) \;=\; \mathrm{tr} M + \tfrac{1}{2}\mathrm{tr} M^2 + \ldots$$

For BMS (17) with $S = \mathbb{1} - M$ (15) we get half of this value. So the trace penalty may be regarded as a leading order approximation to LoRP. The higher order terms prevent peculiarities like in kNN'.

Coding/MDL interpretation of LoRP. If all loss values are different, i.e. if $\mathrm{Loss}_r(\boldsymbol{y}'|\boldsymbol{x}) \neq \mathrm{Loss}_r(\boldsymbol{y}''|\boldsymbol{x})$ for $\boldsymbol{y}' \neq \boldsymbol{y}''$ (adding infinitesimal random noise to Loss_r easily ensures this), then $\mathrm{Rank}_r(\cdot|\boldsymbol{x}) : \mathcal{Y}^n \to I\!\!N$ is an order preserving bijection, i.e. $\mathrm{Rank}_r(\boldsymbol{y}'|\boldsymbol{x}) < \mathrm{Rank}_r(\boldsymbol{y}''|\boldsymbol{x})$ iff $\mathrm{Loss}_r(\boldsymbol{y}'|\boldsymbol{x}) < \mathrm{Loss}_r(\boldsymbol{y}''|\boldsymbol{x})$ with no gaps in the range of $\mathrm{Rank}_r(\cdot|\boldsymbol{x})$. Phrased differently, $\mathrm{Rank}_r(\cdot|\boldsymbol{x})$ codes each $\boldsymbol{y}' \in \mathcal{Y}^n$ as a natural number m in increasing loss-order. The natural number m can itself be coded in $\log_2 m = \mathrm{LR}_r(\boldsymbol{y}'|\boldsymbol{x})$ bits. Among all codes this is the shortest loss-order preserving code. From this perspective, LoRP is just a different (non-stochastic, non-parametric, loss-based) incarnation of MDL: both select the model/regressor with the shortest code. The MDL philosophy provides a justification of LoRP (2), its regularization (5), and loss function selection (Section 6). This identification should also allow to apply or adapt the various consistency results of MDL, implying that LoRP is consistent under some mild conditions.

6 Outlook

So far we have only scratched at the surface of the Loss Rank Principle. LoRP seems to be a promising principle with a lot of potential, leading to a rich field. In the following we briefly summarize miscellaneous considerations, some of them are elaborated on in the extended version of the paper: Experiments, Monte Carlo estimates for non-linear LoRP, numerical approximation of $\det S_\alpha$, LoRP for classification, self-consistent regression, explicit expressions for kNN on a grid, loss function selection, and others.

Experiments. Preliminary experiments on selecting k in kNN regression confirm that LoRP selects a "good" k. (Even on artificial data we cannot determine whether the "right" k is selected, since kNN is not a generative model). LoRP for LBFR seems to be consistent with rapid convergence.

Monte Carlo estimates for non-linear LoRP. For non-linear regression we did not present an efficient algorithm for the loss rank/volume $LR_r(\boldsymbol{y}|\boldsymbol{x})$. The high-dimensional volume $|V_r(L)|$ (3) may be computed by Monte Carlo algorithms. Normally $V_r(L)$ constitutes a small part of $\mathcal{Y}^n$, and uniform sampling over $\mathcal{Y}^n$ is not feasible. Instead one should consider two competing regressors r and r' and compute $|V \cap V'|/|V|$ and $|V \cap V'|/|V'|$ by uniformly sampling from V and V' respectively e.g. with a Metropolis-type algorithm. Taking the ratio we get $|V'|/|V|$ and hence the loss rank difference $LR_r - LR_{r'}$, which is sufficient for LoRP. The usual tricks and problems with sampling apply here too.

Numerical approximation of $\det S_\alpha$. Even for linear regression, a Monte Carlo algorithm may be faster than the naive $O(n^3)$ algorithm [BFG96]. Often M is a very sparse matrix (like in kNN) or can be well approximated by a sparse matrix (like for Kernel regression), which allows to approximate $\det S_\alpha$, sometimes in linear time [Reu02].

LoRP for classification. A classification problem is or can be regarded as a regression problem in which $\mathcal{Y}$ is finite. This implies that we need to compute (count) LR_r for non-linear r somehow, e.g. approximately by Monte Carlo.

Self-consistent regression. So far we have considered only "on-data" regression. LoRP only depends on the regressor r on data D and not on $x \notin \{x_1,...,x_n\}$. One can construct canonical regressors for off-data x from regressors given only on-data in the following way: We add a virtual data point (x,y) to D, where x is the off-data point of interest. If we knew y we could estimate $\hat{y} = r(x|\{(x,y)\} \cup D)$, but we don't know y. But if we require consistency, namely that $\hat{y} = y$, we get a canonical estimate for $\hat{y}$. First, this bootstrap may ease the specification of the regression models, second, it is a canonical way for interpolation (LoRP can't distinguish between r that are identical on D), and third, many standard regressors (kNN, Kernel, LBFR) are self-consistent in the sense that they are canonical.

Explicit expressions for kNN on a grid. In order to get more insight into LoRP, a case that allows an analytic solution is useful. For k nearest neighbors classification with $\boldsymbol{x}$ lying on a hypercube of the regular grid $\mathcal{X} = \mathbb{Z}^d$ one can derive explicit expressions for the loss rank as a function of k, n, and d. For $n \gg k \gg 3^d$, the penalty $-\frac{1}{2}\log \det S$ is proportional to $\mathrm{tr} M$ with proportionality constant decreasing from about 3.2 for $d=1$ to 1.5 for $d \to \infty$.

LoRP for hybrid model classes. LoRP is not restricted to model classes indexed by a single integral "complexity" parameter, but may be applied more generally to selecting among some (typically discrete) class of models/regressors. For instance, the class could contain kNN *and* polynomial regressors, and LoRP selects the complexity *and* type of regressor (non-parametric kNN versus parametric polynomials).

General additive loss. Linear LoRP $\hat{\boldsymbol{y}} = M(\boldsymbol{x})\boldsymbol{y}$ of Section 3 can easily be generalized from quadratic to ρ-norm $\mathrm{Loss}_M(\boldsymbol{y}|\boldsymbol{x}) = ||\boldsymbol{y} - \hat{\boldsymbol{y}}||_\rho^p$ (any p). For $\alpha = 0$,

$\boldsymbol{y}^{\top}S_0\boldsymbol{y}$ in (9) becomes $||\boldsymbol{y} - \hat{\boldsymbol{y}}||_\rho^2$ and v_ρ the volume of the unit d-dimensional ρ-norm "ball". Useful expressions for general additive $\mathrm{Loss}_N = \sum_i h(y_i - \hat{y}_i)$ can also be derived. Regularization may be performed by $M \rightsquigarrow \gamma M$ with optimization over $\gamma < 1$.

Loss-function selection. In principle, the loss function should be part of the problem specification, since it characterizes the ultimate goal. In reality, though, having to specify the loss function can be a nuisance. We could interpret the regularized loss (5) as a class of loss functions parameterized by α, and $\mathrm{argmin}_\alpha \mathrm{LR}_r^a$ as a loss function optimization or selection. This suggests to choose in general the loss function that has minimal loss rank. This leads to sensible results if the considered class of loss functions is not too large (e.g. all ρ-norm losses in the previous paragraph). So LoRP can be used not only for model selection, but also for loss function selection.

Other ideas that count. There are various other ideas in machine learning that somehow count fictitious data $\boldsymbol{y}'$. In normalized maximum likelihood (NML) [Grü04], the complexity of a stochastic model class is defined as the log sum over all $\boldsymbol{y}'$ of all maximum likelihood probabilities. In the luckiness framework for classification, the loss rank is related to the level of a hypothesis, if the empirical loss is used as an unluckiness function. The empirical Rademacher complexity averages over all possible data labels. Finally, instead of considering all $\boldsymbol{y}' \in \mathcal{Y}^n$ one could consider only the set of all permutations of $\{y_1, ..., y_n\}$, like in permutation tests. The test statistic would here be the empirical loss.

References

[Aka73]   Akaike, H.: Information theory and an extension of the maximum likelihood principle. In: Proc. 2nd International Symposium on Information Theory, pp. 267–281, Budapest, Hungary, Akademiai Kaidó (1973)

[BFG96]   Bai, Z., Fahey, M., Golub, G.: Some large-scale matrix computation problems. Jrnl of Comp. and Applied Math. 74(1–2), 71–89 (1996)

[Grü04]   Grünwald, P. D.: Tutorial on minimum description length. In: Minimum Description Length: recent advances in theory and practice, page Chapters 1 and 2. MIT Press, Cambridge (2004) `http://www.cwi.nl/~pdg/ftp/mdlintro.pdf`

[HTF01]   Hastie, T., Tibshirani, R., Friedman, J.H.: The Elements of Statistical Learning. Springer, Heidelberg (2001)

[Mac92]   MacKay, D.J.C.: Bayesian interpolation. Neural Comp. 4(3), 415–447 (1992)

[Reu02]   Reusken, A.: Approximation of the determinant of large sparse symmetric positive definite matrices. SIAM Journal on Matrix Analysis and Applications 23(3), 799–818 (2002)

[Ris78]   Rissanen, J.J.: Modeling by shortest data description. Automatica 14(5), 465–471 (1978)

[Sch78]   Schwarz, G.: Estimating the dimension of a model. Annals of Statistics 6(2), 461–464 (1978)

Robust Reductions from Ranking to Classification

Maria-Florina Balcan[1], Nikhil Bansal[2], Alina Beygelzimer[2],
Don Coppersmith[3], John Langford[4], and Gregory B. Sorkin[2]

[1] Carnegie Melon University, Pittsburgh, PA
ninamf@cs.cmu.edu
[2] IBM Thomas J. Watson Research Center, Yorktown Heights + Hawthorne, NY
{bansal,beygel,sorkin}@us.ibm.com
[3] IDA Center for Communications Research, Princeton, NJ
dcopper@idaccr.org
[4] Yahoo Research, New York, NY
jl@yahoo-inc.com

Abstract. We reduce ranking, as measured by the Area Under the Receiver Operating Characteristic Curve (AUC), to binary classification. The core theorem shows that a binary classification regret of r on the induced binary problem implies an AUC regret of at most $2r$. This is a large improvement over approaches such as ordering according to regressed scores, which have a regret transform of $r \mapsto nr$ where n is the number of elements.

1 Introduction

We consider the problem of ranking a set of instances. In the most basic version, we are given a set of unlabeled instances belonging to two classes, 0 and 1, and the goal is to rank all instances from class 0 before any instance from class 1. A common measure of success for a ranking algorithm is the area under the ROC curve (AUC). The associated loss, $1 - \text{AUC}$, measures how many pairs of neighboring instances would have to be swapped to repair the ranking, normalized by the number of 0s times the number of 1s. The loss is zero precisely when all 0s precede all 1s; one when all 1s precede all 0s. It is greater for mistakes at the beginning and the end of an ordering, which satisfies the intuition that an unwanted item placed at the top of a recommendation list should have a higher associated loss than when placed in the middle.

The classification problem is simply predicting whether a label is 0 or 1 with success measured according to the error rate, i.e., the probability of a misprediction.

These two problems appear quite different. For the classification loss function, a misclassified instance incurs the same loss independently of how other instances are classified. The AUC loss, on the other hand, depends on the whole (ranked) sequence of instances. It is natural to ask whether we need fundamentally different algorithms to optimize these two loss functions. This paper shows that, in some precise sense, the answer is no. We prove that the problem of optimizing

N. Bshouty and C. Gentile (Eds.): COLT 2007, LNAI 4539, pp. 604–619, 2007.

the AUC can be reduced to classification in such a way that good performance on the classification problem implies good performance on the AUC problem. We call a pair of instances *mixed* if they have different labels. The classification problem is to predict, given a random mixed pair of instances in the test set, whether the first instance should be ordered before the second. We show that there is a robust mechanism for translating any binary classifier learning algorithm into a ranking algorithm.

Several observations should help understand the setting and the result better.

Relation to Regression and Classification: A common way to generate a ranking is to order examples according to a regressed score or estimated conditional class probability. The problem with this approach is that it is not robust (see, however, a discussion in Section 6). The fundamental difficulty is exhibited by highly unbalanced test sets. If we have one 1 and many 0s, a pointwise (i.e., regression or classification) loss on the 1 with a perfect prediction for the 0s can greatly harm the AUC while only slightly affecting the pointwise loss with respect to the induced distribution. This observation implies that such schemes transform pointwise loss l to AUC loss nl, where n is the number of elements in the test set. (In the example above, classification loss of $1/n$ induces AUC loss of 1 if ties are broken against us.).

A similar observation holds for regrets in place of losses: pointwise regret r translates into AUC regret nr. *Regret* is the difference between the incurred loss and the lowest achievable loss on the problem. The motivation for regret analysis is to separate avoidable loss from noise intrinsic to the problem, to give bounds that apply nontrivially even for problems with large intrinsic noise.

Our core theorem (Theorem 1) shows that a pairwise classifier with regret r implies an AUC regret of at most $2r$, for arbitrary distributions over instances. Thus, for example, if the binary error rate is 20% due to inherent noise and 5% due to errors made by the classifier, then AUC regret is at most 10%, i.e., only the 5% would be at most doubled.

Section 5 shows that this is the best possible. The theorem is a large improvement over the approaches discussed above, which have a dependence on n. For comparison, the relationship of ranking to classification is functionally tighter than has been proven for regression to binary classification $(r \mapsto \sqrt{r})$ [?].

Relation to the Feedback Arc Set Problem: Let U be the set of unlabeled examples we want to rank. There is a hidden bipartition of U into a set of 0s (called "winners") and a set of 1s (called "losers"), drawn from the underlying conditional distribution of label sequences given U.

Consider running a tournament on U. Every element (or "player" or "instance") of U plays all other elements, and the outcome of each play is determined by a classifier c trained to predict which of the two given elements should be ordered first. What is the best way to rank the players in U so that all winners are ordered before all losers?

The tournament induced by c on U does not have to be consistent with any linear ordering, while a ranking algorithm must predict an ordering. A natural objective, dating back to Slater [Sla61], is to find an ordering which agrees with the tournament on as many player pairs as possible, i.e., minimizes the number of inconsistent pairs where a higher-ranked player (one ordered closer to the beginning of the list) lost to a lower-ranked player. This is the NP-hard "minimum feedback arc set problem in tournaments". (Although the hardness was conjectured for a long time, it was proved only recently; see [A06].).

A *mistake* is defined as a winner–loser pair where the loser beats (i.e., is preferred to) the winner. Section 4 proves that a solution to the feedback arc set problem satisfies a basic guarantee: If the classifier c makes at most k mistakes on U, then the algorithm minimizing the number of inconsistent pairs produces an ordering, or equivalently a transitive tournament, with at most $2k$ mistakes on U. Section 5 exhibits a tournament matching this bound.

Instead of solving feedback arc set, another natural way to break cycles is to rank instances according to their number of wins in the tournament produced by c. The way ties are broken is inessential; for definiteness, let us say they are broken against us. Coppersmith, Fleischer, and Rudra [CFR06] proved that this algorithm provides a 5-approximation for the feedback arc set problem. An approximation, however, does not generally imply any finite regret transform for the AUC problem. For example, c may make no mistakes (i.e., make correct predictions on all winner–loser pairs) while inducing a non-transitive tournament on the winners or the losers, so an approximation that does not know the labeling can incur a non-zero number of mistakes.

We prove, however, that the algorithm that simply orders the elements by their number of wins, transforms classification regret k into AUC regret at most $2k$. That is, ordering by the number of wins has the *same* regret and loss transform as an optimal solution to the (NP-hard) feedback arc set problem. (Again, Section 5 shows that solving feedback arc set does no better.).

Relation to Generalization Bounds: A number of papers analyze generalization properties of ranking algorithms (see, e.g., [FIS+03,AHR05,AN05,RCM +05]). These results analyze ranking directly by estimating the rate of convergence of empirical estimates of the ranking loss to its expectation. The bounds typically involve some complexity parameter of the class of functions searched by the algorithms (which serves as a regularizer), and some additional quantities considered relevant for the analysis. The examples are assumed to be drawn independently from some fixed distribution.

The type of results in this paper is different. We bound the realized AUC performance in terms of the realized classification performance. Since the analysis is relative, it does not have to rely on any assumptions about the way the world produces data. In particular, the bounds apply when there are arbitrary high-order dependencies between examples. This seems important in a number of applications where ranking is of interest.

By itself, our analysis does not say anything about the number of samples needed to achieve a certain level of performance. Instead it says that achieved performance can be robustly *transferred* from classification to ranking. Thus any generalization result for the induced classification problem implies, via the reduction, a generalization result for the AUC problem. For example, Clémençon, Lugosi, and Vayatis [CLV05] derive bounds on the performance of empirical risk minimization for the classification problem of ranking two instances (under the assumption that instances are independent and identically distributed). By composing these bounds with our result, one can derive bounds for ranking n independent instances (instead of just two), without introducing a dependence on n.

2   Preliminaries

Classification: A *binary classification problem* is defined by a distribution P over $X \times \{0,1\}$, where X is some observable feature space and $\{0,1\}$ is the binary label space. The goal is to find a classifier $c : X \to \{0,1\}$ minimizing the *classification loss* on P given by

$$e(c, P) = \mathbf{Pr}_{(x,y)\sim P}[c(x) \neq y].$$

The *classification regret* of c on P is defined as

$$r(c, P) = e(c, P) - \min_{c^*} e(c^*, P),$$

where the minimum is taken over all classifiers $c^* : X \to \{0,1\}$. The results clearly hold for any constrained class of functions that contains a Bayes optimal classifier for the induced binary problem.[1]

Ranking: Where $X^{(2)}$ denotes the set of ordered pairs of distinct elements of X, let $\pi : X^{(2)} \to \{0,1\}$ be a *preference function* (called a *ranking rule* in [CLV05]): $\pi(x, x') = 1$ if π "prefers" x to x', and 0 otherwise (so $\pi(x, x') = 1 - \pi(x', x)$). If π is consistent with some linear ordering of a set of examples, we call π itself an *ordering* on this set. The *AUC loss* of an ordering π on a set $S = (x_1, y_1), \dots, (x_n, y_n)$ is defined as

$$l(\pi, S) = \frac{\sum_{i \neq j} \mathbf{1}(y_i > y_j)\pi(x_i, x_j)}{\sum_{i<j} \mathbf{1}(y_i \neq y_j)}.$$

(Indices i and j in the summations range from 1 to n, and $\mathbf{1}(\cdot)$ is the indicator function which is 1 if its argument is true, and 0 otherwise.) By convention, 0s should be ordered ahead of 1s, so any pair where a 1 is ordered before a 0 contributes to the loss.

A pair of examples $(x_1, y_1), (x_2, y_2)$ is called *mixed* if $y_1 \neq y_2$.

An *AUC problem* is defined by a distribution D over $(X \times \{0,1\})^*$. The goal is to find an ordering $\pi : X^{(2)} \to \{0,1\}$ minimizing the expected AUC loss on D, given by

$$l(\pi, D) = \mathbf{E}_{S\sim D} l(\pi, S).$$

---

[1] Any such optimal classifier can be represented in the form $c(x, x') = \mathbf{1}(s(x) \geq s(x'))$ for some *scoring* function $s : X \to \mathbf{R}$. Thus the results hold for any class of functions that contains all classifiers defined by scoring functions.

Algorithm 1. AUC-TRAIN (labeled set S, binary learning algorithm A)

1. Let $S' = \{\langle (x_1, x_2), \mathbf{1}(y_1 < y_2)\rangle : (x_1, y_1), (x_2, y_2) \in S \text{ and } y_1 \neq y_2\}$
2. return $c = A(S')$.

Algorithm 2. DEGREE (unlabeled set U, pairwise classifier c)

1. For $x \in U$, let $\deg(x) = |\{x' : c(x, x') = 1, x' \in U\}|$.
2. Sort U in descending order of $\deg(x)$, breaking ties arbitrarily.

As an example, consider the internet search problem, where there is some underlying distribution of queries, each yielding a set of search results. This process generates a distribution over subsets; whether or not the subsets have the same size is inessential for the analysis. Note that D is allowed to encode arbitrary dependencies between examples.

The *AUC regret* of π on D is given by $r_{\text{AUC}}(\pi, D) = l(\pi, D) - \min_{\pi^*} l(\pi^*, D)$, where the minimum is taken over all preference functions π^* (transitive on any subset in the support of D). Since our goal is to upper bound the AUC regret, the fact that the minimum is taken over all such functions makes the result only stronger.

Tournaments: A *tournament* is a complete graph with no self-loops, in which each edge is directed one way or the other, so that for every pair of vertices $i \neq j$, either $i \rightarrow j$ is an edge or $j \rightarrow i$ is an edge, but not both. The edge $i \rightarrow j$ says that i *beats* j ("i is preferred to j"); edges point from winners to losers. Since we adopt the convention that 0s should be ordered ahead of 1s, ideally 0s should beat 1s. We write $\deg(i)$ for the *outdegree* of vertex i, so $\deg(i) = \sum_j \mathbf{1}(i \rightarrow j)$, where the indicator function $\mathbf{1}(i \rightarrow j)$ is 1 if $i \rightarrow j$ is an edge and 0 otherwise. Thus we generally expect 0s to have large outdegree and 1s small outdegree; however, we allow and analyze arbitrary tournaments.

3   Ordering by the Number of Wins

In this section, we describe the reduction and prove the main result.

The reduction consists of two components. The training part, AUC-TRAIN (Algorithm 1), takes a set S of labeled examples of type $X \times \{0, 1\}$ and transforms all mixed pairs in S into binary examples for the oracle learning algorithm. The binary classification problem induced by the reduction is to predict, given a random mixed pair of examples in S, whether the first example should be ordered before the second. For any process D generating datasets S, we can define the induced distribution over $(X \times X) \times \{0, 1\}$ by first drawing S from D, and then drawing a random mixed pair from S. We denote this induced distribution by AUC-TRAIN(D), admittedly overloading the notation.

The test part, DEGREE (Algorithm 2), uses the pairwise classifier c learned in Algorithm 1 to run a tournament on a test set U, and then ranks the elements of U in decreasing order of their number of wins in the tournament, breaking ties arbitrarily. Recall that we expect 0s to beat 1s, and thus have larger outdegree.

For the analysis, it is best to think of the classifier c as an adversary playing against the ranking algorithm DEGREE. The goal of c is to pay little in classification regret while making DEGREE$(\cdot, c)$ pay a lot in AUC regret.

The regret problem can be reduced to the following combinatorial problem. Given a set U with each element labeled either 0 or 1, the adversary c starts with a tournament of its choice where every 0 beats every 1. Then c can choose to invert the outcome of any game between a 0 and a 1, and she is charged for each such "mistake". Again, c can choose any (not necessarily transitive) subtournaments on the 0s and on the 1s for free. The resulting tournament is shown to the algorithm.

Without seeing the labels, the algorithm needs to approximate c's tournament with a transitive tournament (or equivalently, a linear order). The goal of the algorithm is to minimize the number of mistakes it makes (i.e., pairs where a 1 precedes a 0 in the order). If c were itself consistent with a linear order, the algorithm could simply output that, at a cost in mistakes identical to the adversary's. In general it is not, and we would expect the cost of the more-constrained linear order to be higher. Our goal is to show that the reduction is robust in the sense that c cannot cause DEGREE to make many mistakes without making many mistakes itself. More precisely, DEGREE never makes more than twice as many mistakes as c. This combinatorial result (Theorem 2) is invoked $(n-1)$ times in the proof of the main theorem below.

Theorem 1. *For all distributions D and all pairwise classifiers c,*

$$r_{\text{AUC}}(\text{DEGREE}(\cdot, c), D) \leq 2r(c, \text{AUC-TRAIN}(D)). \tag{1}$$

Note the quantification in the above theorem: it applies to *all* settings where Algorithms 1 and 2 are used; in particular, D may encode arbitrary dependences between examples.

Proof. Given an unlabeled test set $U \in X^n$, the joint distribution D induces a conditional distribution $D(Y_1, \ldots, Y_n \mid U)$ over the set of label sequences $\{0, 1\}^n$. In the remainder of the paper, let Q denote this conditional distribution. We identify U with $\{1, \ldots, n\}$. We prove the theorem by fixing U, taking the expectation over the draw of U at the end.

Our goal is to rewrite both sides of (1) as sums of pairwise regrets. A *pairwise loss* is defined by

$$l_Q(i, j) = \mathbf{E}_{y^n \sim Q} \frac{\mathbf{1}(y_i > y_j)}{\sum_{u < v} \mathbf{1}(y_u \neq y_v)}.$$

It is the loss of ordering i before j. If $l_Q(i, j) < l_Q(j, i)$, the *regret* $r_Q(i, j)$ of ordering i before j is 0; otherwise, $r_Q(i, j) = l_Q(i, j) - l_Q(j, i)$.

We can assume without loss of generality that the ordering minimizing the AUC loss (thus having zero AUC regret) is $\langle 1, 2, \ldots, n \rangle$. Lemma 2 in Section A shows that all regret-zero pairwise predictions must be consistent with the ordering: $r_Q(i,j) = 0$ for all $i < j$.

Lemma 1 in Appendix A establishes a basic property of pairwise regrets. Applied repeatedly, the lemma says that for any pair $i < j$, the regret $r_Q(j,i)$ can be decomposed as

$$r_Q(j,i) = \sum_{k=i}^{j-1} r_Q(k+1,k).$$

This allows us to decompose the AUC regret of π on Q as a sum of pairwise regrets (where $\langle U, y^n \rangle$ denotes the unlabeled sample U labeled with y^n):

$$r_{\text{AUC}}(\pi, Q) = l(\pi, Q) - \min_{\pi^*} l(\pi^*, Q)$$

$$= \mathbf{E}_{y^n \sim Q}[l(\pi, \langle U, y^n \rangle)] - \min_{\pi^*} \mathbf{E}_{y^n \sim Q}[l(\pi^*, \langle U, y^n \rangle)]$$

$$= \mathbf{E}_{y^n \sim Q} \frac{\sum_{i,j} \mathbf{1}(y_i > y_j)\pi(i,j)}{\sum_{u<v} \mathbf{1}(y_u \neq y_v)} - \min_{\pi^*} \mathbf{E}_{y^n \sim Q} \frac{\sum_{i,j} \mathbf{1}(y_i > y_j)\pi^*(i,j)}{\sum_{u<v} \mathbf{1}(y_u \neq y_v)}$$

$$= \max_{\pi^*} \mathbf{E}_{y^n \sim Q} \frac{\sum_{i,j}[\mathbf{1}(y_i > y_j)\pi(i,j) - \mathbf{1}(y_i > y_j)\pi^*(i,j)]}{\sum_{u<v} \mathbf{1}(y_u \neq y_v)}$$

$$= \sum_{i<j:\pi(j,i)=1} r_Q(j,i) = \sum_{k=1}^{n-1} |\{i \leq k < j : \pi(j,i) = 1\}| \cdot r_Q(k+1,k).$$

The last equality follows by repeated application of Lemma 1.

The classification regret can also be written in terms of pairwise regrets:

$$r(c, \text{AUC-TRAIN}(Q)) = e(c, \text{AUC-TRAIN}(Q)) - \min_{c^*} e(c^*, \text{AUC-TRAIN}(Q))$$

$$= \max_{c^*} \mathbf{E}_{y^n \sim Q} \left[\frac{\sum_{i,j}[\mathbf{1}(y_i > y_j)c(i,j) - \mathbf{1}(y_i > y_j)c^*(i,j)]}{\sum_{u<v} \mathbf{1}(y_u \neq y_v)} \right]$$

$$= \sum_{i<j:c(j,i)=1} r_Q(j,i) = \sum_{k=1}^{n-1} |\{i \leq k < j : c(j,i) = 1\}| \cdot r_Q(k+1,k).$$

Let g_k and f_k denote the coefficients with which the term $r_Q(k+1,k)$ appears in the above decompositions of $r_{\text{AUC}}(\pi, Q)$ and $r(c, \text{AUC-TRAIN}(Q))$ respectively. To complete the proof it suffices to show that $g_k \leq 2f_k$ for each k.

Fix k and consider a bipartition of U into a set $\{1, \ldots, k\}$ of "winners" and a set $\{k+1, \ldots, n\}$ of "losers". In this terminology, g_k is the number of winner–loser pairs where the loser has at least as many wins as the winner, and f_k is the number of winner–loser pairs where the loser beats the winner (in the tournament induced by c on U). Theorem 2 below shows that $g_k \leq 2f_k$, completing this proof. ∎

Let T be a tournament and let the vertices of T be arbitrarily partitioned into a set W of "winners" and a set L of "losers". Call the triple (T, W, L) a winner–loser partitioned tournament, and denote it by $\mathbf{T}$. We will show that for any $\mathbf{T}$, the number of winner–loser pairs where the loser's degree is larger than or equal to the winner's, is at most twice the number of winner–loser pairs where the loser beats the winner. Formally, define two measures:

$$g(\mathbf{T}) = \sum_{\ell \in L} \sum_{w \in W} \mathbf{1}(\deg(\ell) \geq \deg(w)),$$

$$f(\mathbf{T}) = \sum_{\ell \in L} \sum_{w \in W} \mathbf{1}(\ell \to w).$$

Theorem 2. *For any winner–loser partitioned tournament* $\mathbf{T}$, $g(\mathbf{T}) \leq 2f(\mathbf{T})$.

Since the number of edges from L to W is equal to the total number of edges out of L minus the number of edges from L to L, we can rewrite

$$f(\mathbf{T}) = \sum_{\ell \in L} \sum_{w \in W} \mathbf{1}(\ell \to w) = \sum_{\ell \in L} \deg(\ell) - \binom{|L|}{2}.$$

Both $f(\mathbf{T})$ and $g(\mathbf{T})$ depend only on the degrees of the vertices of T, so rather than working with a (labeled) tournament, a relatively complex object, we can work with a (labeled) degree sequence.

Landau's theorem [Lan53] says that there exists a tournament with outdegree sequence $d_1 \leq d_2 \leq \cdots \leq d_n$ if and only if, for all $1 \leq i \leq n$, $\sum_{j=1}^{i} d_j \geq \sum_{j=1}^{i}(j-1)$, with equality for $i = n$.

Recall that a sequence $\langle a_1, \ldots, a_n \rangle$ is *majorized* by $\langle b_1, \ldots, b_n \rangle$ if the two sums are equal and if, when each sequence is sorted in non-increasing order, the prefix sums of the b sequence are at least as large as (dominate) those of the a sequence. (For a comprehensive treatment of majorization, see [?].) Landau's condition is precisely that $\langle d_1, \ldots, d_n \rangle$ is majorized by $\langle 0, \ldots, n-1 \rangle$. (With the sequences sorted in increasing order, Landau's condition is that prefix sums of the degree sequence dominate those of the progression, which is the same as saying that the suffix sums of the degree sequence are dominated by the suffix sums of the progression.) This allows us to take advantage of well-known properties of majorization, notably that if A' is obtained by averaging together any elements of A, then A majorizes A'.

This allows us to restate Theorem 2 in terms of a sequence and majorization, rather than a tournament, but first we relax the constraints. First, where the original statement requires elements of the degree sequence to be non-negative integers, we allow them to be non-negative reals. Second, the original statement requires that we attach a winner/loser label to each element of the degree sequence. Instead, we aggregate equal elements of the degree sequence, and for a degree d_i of (integral) multiplicity m_i, assign arbitrary non-negative (but not necessarily integral) portions to winners and losers: $w_i + \ell_i = m_i$.

Let $\mathbf{D} = (D, W, L)$ be such a generalized "winner–loser labeled compressed sequence". Note that the majorization condition applies only to the values $\{d_i, m_i\}$, not the labeling. The definitions of f and g above are easily extended to this broader domain: $g(\mathbf{D}) = \sum_i \sum_{j \leq i} l_i w_j$, $f(\mathbf{D}) = \sum_i l_i d_i - \binom{\sum_j l_i}{2}$, where we define $\binom{x}{2} = x(x-1)/2$ for all x (not just integers). If we prove $g \leq 2f$ over this larger domain, the inequality holds in particular for plain winner–loser labeled degree sequences (the case where all weights happen to be integral). That is, Theorem 3, below, implies Theorem 2.

Theorem 3. *For any winner–loser labeled compressed sequence* $\mathbf{D} = (D, W, L)$ *where D is majorized by* $\langle 0, \ldots, n-1 \rangle$, $g(\mathbf{D}) \leq 2f(\mathbf{D})$.

Proof. We begin with an outline of the proof. Define a compressed sequence $\mathbf{D}$ as being *canonical* if it consists of at most three degrees: a smallest degree d_1 having only losers ($w_1 = 0$), a middle degree d_2 potentially with both winners and losers ($w_2, \ell_2 \geq 0$), and a largest degree d_3 having only winners ($\ell_3 = 0$). We first establish that any canonical sequence has $g(\mathbf{D}) - 2f(\mathbf{D}) \leq 0$. We then show how to transform *any* degree sequence to a canonical one with a larger (or equal) value of $g - 2f$, which completes the argument.

We first show that a canonical sequence $\mathbf{D}$ has $g - 2f \leq 0$. For the canonical configuration, $g = w_2 \ell_2$ and $f = \ell_1 d_1 + \ell_2 d_2 - \binom{\ell_1 + \ell_2}{2}$, and hence our goal is to show that

$$\ell_1 d_1 + \ell_2 d_2 \geq (\ell_1 + \ell_2)(\ell_1 + \ell_2 - 1)/2 + w_2 \ell_2 / 2 \tag{2}$$

By Landau's condition applied to ℓ_1 and $\ell_1 + w_2 + \ell_2$, we have the following two relations:

$$\ell_1 d_1 \geq \binom{\ell_1}{2} \tag{3}$$

and

$$\ell_1 d_1 + (\ell_2 + w_2) d_2 \geq \binom{\ell_1 + w_2 + \ell_2}{2}. \tag{4}$$

Multiplying (3) by $w_2/(\ell_2 + w_2)$ and (4) by $\ell_2/(\ell_2 + w_2)$ and adding them, we obtain that

$$\ell_1 d_1 + \ell_2 d_2 \geq \frac{1}{\ell_2 + w_2} \left(w_2 \binom{\ell_1}{2} + \ell_2 \binom{\ell_1 + \ell_2 + w_2}{2} \right). \tag{5}$$

A simple calculation shows that the right side of inequality (5) is exactly equal to the right hand side of (2). This proves that $g \leq 2f$ for a canonical sequence.

If a sequence is not canonical then there are two consecutive degrees d_i and d_j ($j = i + 1$) such that one of the cases 1a, 1b, or 2 (described below) holds. In each case we apply a transformation producing from the degree sequence $\mathbf{D}$ a new degree sequence $\mathbf{D}'$, where:

- the total weight of winners in $\mathbf{D}'$ is equal to that of $\mathbf{D}$; similarly for losers, and thus for the total weight; furthermore, the total weight on each degree remains integral;
- $\mathbf{D}'$ maintains the majorization needed for Landau's theorem;
- the value of $g - 2f$ is at least as large for $\mathbf{D}'$ as for $\mathbf{D}$; and
- either the number of nonzero values w_i and ℓ_i or the number of distinct degrees d_i is strictly smaller for $\mathbf{D}'$ than for $\mathbf{D}$, and the other is no larger for $\mathbf{D}'$ than for $\mathbf{D}$.

We first sketch the cases and then detail the transformations.

Case 1a d_i has only winners ($l_i = 0$).
Apply Transformation 1a, combining the two degrees into one.

Case 1b d_j has only losers ($w_j = 0$).
Apply Transformation 1b, combining the two degrees into one.

Case 2 All of w_i, l_i, w_j and l_j are nonzero.
Apply Transformation 2, leaving the degrees the same but transforming the weights so that one of them is equal to 0 and one of the preceding cases applies, or the weights obey an equality allowing application of Transformation 3, which combines the two degrees into one.

Either there is some pair i, j to which one of the cases applies, or the sequence is canonical. We argue this by showing that if there is no pair i, j for which Cases 1a or 1b apply, then either the sequence is canonical, or there is a pair to which Case 2 applies. First, note that for any $i \neq n$, $l_i > 0$ (else Case 1a applies to $i, i+1$) and for any $i \neq 1$, $w_i > 0$ (else Case 1b applies to $i-1, i$). In particular, for any $1 < i < n$, both $l_i, w_i > 0$. If $n \geq 4$ this implies immediately that Case 2 applies to the pair 2, 3. If $n = 1$, $\mathbf{D}$ is automatically canonical. If $n = 2$ and $l_2 = 0$ or $w_1 = 0$ then $\mathbf{D}$ is canonical, while if both $l_2, w_1 > 0$ we may apply Case 2 (since, as we first argued, $l_1, w_2 > 0$). Finally, if $n = 3$, we know $l_1, l_2, w_2, w_3 > 0$. If $w_1 = l_3 = 0$ then $\mathbf{D}$ is canonical, and otherwise Case 2 applies.

Transformation 1a: In Case 1a, where d_i has only winners, change $\mathbf{D}$ to a new sequence $\mathbf{D}'$ by replacing the pair $(d_i, w_i, 0)$, (d_j, w_j, l_j) by their "average": the single degree (d', w', l'), where

$$w' = w_i + w_j, \quad l' = l_j, \quad d' = \frac{w_i d_i + (w_j + l_j) d_j}{w_i + w_j + l_j}.$$

The stated conditions on a transformation are easily checked. The total weight of winners is clearly preserved, as is the total weight of losers and the total degree (out-edges). Summing weights preserves integrality. The number of distinct degrees is reduced by one, and the number of nonzero weights may be decreased by one or may remain unchanged. The Landau majorization condition holds because $\mathbf{D}'$, as an averaging of $\mathbf{D}$, is majorized by it, and majorization is transitive. The only non-trivial condition is the non-decrease in $g - 2f$. The number of loser–winner pairs where the loser outranks the winner remains the same, so $g(\mathbf{D}) = g(\mathbf{D}')$. Also, f depends only on the total weight of losers (which is unchanged) and on the average degree of losers. This average degree would be unchanged if w_i were 0; since $w_i \geq 0$, the average degree may decrease. Thus $f(\mathbf{D}) \geq f(\mathbf{D}')$, and $(g - 2f)(\mathbf{D}) \leq (g - 2f)(\mathbf{D}')$, as desired.

Transformation 1b: Symmetrically to Transformation 1a, obtain $\mathbf{D}'$ by replacing the pair of labeled weighted degrees (d_i, w_i, l_i) and $(d_j, 0, l_j)$ with a single one (d', w', l'), where $w' = w_i$, $l' = l_i + l_j$, and $d' = [(l_i + w_i)d_i + l_j d_j]/(l_i + w_i + l_j)$.

Transformation 2: Where w_i, l_i, w_j and l_j are all nonzero, we begin with one case, which leads to one other. In the usual case, we transform $\mathbf{D}$ to $\mathbf{D}'$ by replacing the pair (d_i, w_i, l_i), (d_j, w_j, l_j) with (d_i, w_i+x, l_i-x), (d_j, w_j-x, l_j+x), for some value of x (positive or negative) to be determined. This affects only the labeling, not the weighted degree sequence itself, and is therefore legitimate as long as the four quantities $w_i + x$, $l_i - x$, $w_j - x$ and $l_j + x$ are all non-negative.

Defining $\Delta = (g-2f)(\mathbf{D}') - (g-2f)(\mathbf{D})$, we wish to choose x to make $\Delta > 0$.

$$\Delta = \left\{ \left[(l_j + x)(w_i + x + w_j - x) + (l_i - x)(w_i + x) \right] - \left[l_j(w_i + w_j) + l_i w_i \right] \right\}$$
$$- 2\left\{ \left[(l_i - x)d_i + (l_j + x)d_j \right] - \left[l_i d_i + l_j d_j \right] \right\}$$
$$= x(w_j + l_i - 2(d_j - d_i) - x) = x(a - x),$$

where $a = w_j + l_i - 2(d_j - d_i)$. This is a simple quadratic expression with negative coefficient on x^2, so its value increases monotonically as x is varied from 0 to $a/2$, where the maximum is obtained. (Note that a may be negative.) If $a = 0$ then we do not use this transformation but Transformation 3, below. Otherwise, vary x from 0 to $a/2$ stopping when x reaches $a/2$ or when any of $w_i + x$, $l_i - x$, $w_j - x$ and $l_j + x$ becomes 0. Call this value $x^\star$, and use it to define the transformation.

If any of $w_i + x$, $l_i - x$, $w_j - x$ and $l_j + x$ is 0 then the number of nonzero weights is decreased (while the number of distinct degees is unchanged). Otherwise, $x^\star = a/2$. In that case, the new $\mathbf{D}'$ has $a = 0$ (the optimal "weight shift" has already been performed). With $a = 0$ we apply Transformation 3, which reduces the number of nonzero weights.

Transformation 3: Similar to Cases 1a and 1b, transform $\mathbf{D}$ to $\mathbf{D}'$ by replacing the pair (d_i, w_i, l_i), (d_j, w_j, l_j) with a single degree (d', w', l') that is their weighted average,

$$w' = w_i + w_j, \quad l' = l_i + l_j, \quad d' = \frac{(w_i + l_i)d_i + (w_j + l_j)d_j}{w_i + l_i + w_j + l_j}.$$

This gives

$$\Delta = (g - 2f)(\mathbf{D}') - (g - 2f)(\mathbf{D})$$
$$= (l_i w_j) - 2(l_i d' + l_j d' - l_i d_i - l_j d_j)$$
$$= l_i w_j + \frac{2(d_j - d_i)(w_i l_j - w_j l_i)}{w_i + l_i + w_j + l_j}.$$

We apply this transformation only in the case where Transformation 2 fails to give any improvement because its "a" expression is equal to 0, i.e., $d_j - d_i = (w_j + l_i)/2$. Making the corresponding substitution gives

$$\Delta = l_i w_j + \frac{(w_j + l_i)(w_i l_j - w_j l_i)}{w_i + l_i + w_j + l_j}$$
$$= \frac{(l_i w_j)(l_j + w_i) + (l_j w_i)(l_i + w_j)}{w_i + l_i + w_j + l_j} > 0.$$

This reduces the number of distinct degrees by one, without increasing the number of nonzero weights.

Concluding the argument, we have shown that any non-canonical configuration $\mathbf{D}$ can be replaced by a configuration with a strictly smaller total of distinct degrees and nonzero weights, and at least as large a value of $g - 2f$. Since $\mathbf{D}$ had at most n distinct degrees and $2n$ nonzero weights originally, a canonical configuration $\mathbf{D}^\star$ is reached after at most $3n - 1$ transformations. (All that is important is that the number of transformations is finite: that a canonical configuration is eventually reached.) Then, $(g - 2f)(\mathbf{D}) \leq (g - 2f)(\mathbf{D}^\star) \leq 0$. ∎

A further generalization of Theorem 3 may be found in [BCS06].

4   An Upper Bound for Minimum Feedback Arc Set

This section shows an analog of Theorem 2 for an optimal solution to the feedback arc set problem. (The decomposition argument in Theorem 1 is algorithm-independent and applies here as well.) For a tournament T and an ordering π, a *back edge* is an edge $i \rightarrow j$ in T such that j is ordered before i in π. Let $\text{back}(T, \pi)$ denote the number of back edges induced by π in T.

For a winner–loser partitioned tournament $\mathbf{T} = (T, W, L)$ and any minimum feedback arc set ordering π of T, let $g'(\mathbf{T}, \pi)$ be the number of winner–loser pairs where the loser comes before the winner in π, and as before let

$$f(\mathbf{T}) = \sum_{\ell \in L} \sum_{w \in W} \mathbf{1}(\ell \rightarrow w)$$

be the number of winner–loser pairs where the loser beats the winner.

Theorem 4. *For any winner–loser partitioned tournament* $\mathbf{T} = (T, W, L)$ *and any minimum feedback arc set ordering* π *of* T, $g'(\mathbf{T}, \pi) \leq 2f(\mathbf{T})$.

Proof. Let k_w be the smallest possible number of back edges in the subtournament induced by W. Define k_l similarly for the subtournament induced by L. Let k_w^π and k_l^π be the number of back edges in π that go from W to W and from L to L, respectively. Denote the number of remaining (i.e., winner–loser or loser–winner) back edges in π by k_o^π.

Consider another ordering σ where all winners are ordered before all losers, and both the winners and the losers are ordered optimally among themselves, i.e., with k_w and k_l back edges respectively. The number of back edges in σ is $\text{back}(\mathbf{T}, \sigma) = k_w + k_l + f(\mathbf{T})$. But we also have $\text{back}(\mathbf{T}, \sigma) \geq \text{back}(\mathbf{T}, \pi)$ since π minimizes the number of back edges, and thus $k_w + k_l + f(\mathbf{T}) \geq k_w^\pi + k_l^\pi + k_o^\pi$. Since $k_w \leq k_w^\pi$ and $k_l \leq k_l^\pi$ by definition of k_w and k_l, we have $f(\mathbf{T}) \geq k_o^\pi$.

Consider any winner–loser pair with the loser ordered before the winner. If $w \rightarrow l$ is the edge, it is a back edge in π and thus is counted by k_o^π. If $l \rightarrow w$ is the edge instead, it is counted by $f(\mathbf{T})$. Thus $g'(\mathbf{T}, \pi)$ is at most $k_o^\pi + f(\mathbf{T})$. Since $f(\mathbf{T}) \geq k_o^\pi$, this number is never more than $2f(\mathbf{T})$, which implies $g'(\mathbf{T}, \pi) \leq 2f(\mathbf{T})$. ∎

5   Lower Bounds

We first show that Theorem 2 is best possible: the DEGREE ranking really can make twice as many mistakes as the adversary. Recall that f denotes the number of winner–loser pairs where the loser beats the winner, and g the number of winner–loser pairs where the loser outranks the winner. The example below generates an infinite family of tournaments with $g = 2f$.

Example 1.   With n odd, let every vertex have degree $(n-1)/2$; note that the degree sequence $\langle \frac{n-1}{2}, \ldots, \frac{n-1}{2} \rangle$ does indeed respect Landau's condition, so it is realizable as a tournament. Label $(n-1)/2$ of the vertices as winners and $(n+1)/2$ as losers. With ties broken against us, all winners are ordered after all losers. This gives $f = \frac{n+1}{2} \cdot \frac{n-1}{2} - \binom{(n+1)/2}{2} = (n+1)(n-1)/8$, while $g = \frac{n+1}{2} \cdot \frac{n-1}{2} = (n+1)(n-1)/4 = 2f$. (A similar example gives a lower bound of $2 - O(1/n)$ with ties broken optimally.) ∎

Theorem 4 is also essentially best possible. The next construction gives an infinite family of tournaments for which an optimal solution to the feedback arc set problem has $g \geq (2 - \epsilon)f$, for any $\epsilon > 0$.

Example 2.   Set $\delta = \frac{\epsilon}{1-\epsilon}$, and let the set of vertices be partitioned into three components, V_1, V_2, and V_3, with $|V_1| = \delta n^2$, $|V_2| = 2n^2$, and $|V_3| = n$, for a sufficiently large n. The vertices in $V_1 \cup V_2$ are the winners, the vertices in V_3 are the losers.

The edges within each of the three components form acyclic tournaments. The cross-component edges are defined as follows: All edges between V_3 and V_1 point from V_3 to V_1, and all edges between V_1 and V_2 point from V_1 to V_2. To define the edges between V_2 and V_3, divide V_2 into $2n$ consecutive blocks $B_1, \ldots, B_{2n}$ of n vertices each, such that edges point from B_i to B_j where $1 \leq i < j \leq 2n$. If i is odd, all edges from B_i point to V_3; otherwise all edges from V_3 point to B_i.

We have $f = (1 + \delta)n^3$. What is the value of g induced by an ordering minimizing the number of back edges? Any such ordering must put V_1 before V_2; otherwise we would have $\Omega(n^4)$ back edges while an optimal ordering does not need to have more than $O(n^3)$ such edges. Now, the tournament induced by $V_2 \cup V_3$ has n^3 edge-disjoint cycles of length 3 since there are n^2 such cycles for every pair of blocks in V_2 (and there are n disjoint pairs). There has to be at least one back edge for every such cycle, so any ordering must have at least n^3 back edges. The ordering that puts V_3 before V_2 is thus optimal since it has exactly n^3 back edges. Thus the ordering $\{V_3, V_1, V_2\}$ minimizes the number of back edges. This ordering has $(2 + \delta)n^3$ pairs where the loser is ordered before the winner, implying the bound $g \geq (2 - \frac{\delta}{1+\delta})f = (2 - \epsilon)f$. ∎

6   Practicality and Relation to Other Work

The reduction analysis is representation independent, which means that it works for any representation. Naturally, some representations are more computationally efficient than others. If, for example, $c(x_i, x_j) = \mathbf{1}(s(x_i) \geq s(x_j))$ for some learned scoring function $s : X \to [0, 1]$, the complexity of test-time evaluation is linear rather than quadratic in the number of elements. Note that s is not trained as a simple regressor, because what we want to optimize is the pairwise ordering of elements. If c is a scoring function, the tournament it labels is transitive and the reduction just outputs the linear ordering consistent with the tournament, so the corresponding regret transform is $r \mapsto r$.

It would be interesting to consider other efficient representations describing more general classes of preference functions, as well as extend the results to partial tournaments and other ranking loss functions.

Cohen, Schapire, and Singer [CSS99], similarly, use a two-stage approach to ranking: They first learn a preference function that takes a pair of instances and returns a score predicting how certain it is that the first instance should be ranked before the second. The learned function is then evaluated on all pairs of instances in the test set and an ordering approximating the largest possible l_1 agreement with the predictions is created, using a variant of the degree-based algorithm. One of the results they show is that the agreement achieved by an optimal feedback arc set ordering is at most twice the agreement obtained by their algorithm. To translate this result into the language of losses, let MFA be the AUC loss of the minimum feedback arc set ordering and APPROX be the AUC loss of the approximation. Then the result says that $1 - \text{APPROX} \geq \frac{1}{2}(1 - \text{MFA})$ or $\text{APPROX} \leq \frac{1}{2} + \text{MFA}/2$. The result is difficult to compare with the results given here, as the settings are different. A very rough comparison requires specializations and yields a bound that is weaker than ours: As we have seen in Section 4, $\text{MFA} \leq 2 \text{BIN}$, where BIN is the loss of the pairwise predictor, so the result of [CSS99] roughly says that $\text{APPROX} \leq \frac{1}{2} + \text{BIN}$, while we show that $\text{APPROX} \leq 2 \text{BIN}$ (modulo the slight differences in the approximation algorithm and the binary problem).

Cortes and Mohri [CM04] analyzed the relationship between the AUC and the error rate on the same classification problem, treating the two as different loss functions. They derived expressions for the expected value and the standard deviation of the AUC over all classifications with a fixed number of errors, under the assumption that all such classifications are equiprobable (i.e., the classifier is as likely to err on any one example as on any other). There is no direct connection with the present work.

Acknowledgement. We would like to thank the reviewers for their helpful comments and suggestions.

References

[AHR05]   Agarwal, S., Har-Peled, S., Roth, D.: A uniform convergence bound for the area under the ROC curve. In: Proceedings of the 10th International Workshop on Artificial Intelligence and Statistics (2005)

[AN05]   Agarwal, S., Niyogi, P.: Stability and generalization of bipartite ranking algorithms. In: Auer, P., Meir, R. (eds.) COLT 2005. LNCS (LNAI), vol. 3559, pp. 32–47. Springer, Heidelberg (2005)

[A06]   Alon, N.: Ranking tournaments. SIAM Journal on Discrete Mathematics 20, 137–142 (2006)
[BCS06]   Bansal, N., Coppersmith, D., Sorkin, G.B.: A winner–loser labeled tournament has at most twice as many outdegree misrankings as pair misrankings, IBM Research Report RC24107 (November 2006)
[CLV05]   Clémençon, S., Lugosi, G., Vayatis, N.: Ranking and scoring using empirical risk minimization. In: Auer, P., Meir, R. (eds.) COLT 2005. LNCS (LNAI), vol. 3559, pp. 1–15. Springer, Heidelberg (2005)
[CSS99]   Cohen, W., Schapire, R., Singer, Y.: Learning to order things. Journal of Artificial Intelligence Research 10, 243–270 (1999)
[CFR06]   Coppersmith, D., Fleischer, L., Rudra, A.: Ordering by weighted number of wins gives a good ranking for weighted tournaments. In: Proceeding of the 17th Annual Symposium on Discrete Algorithms (SODA), pp. 776–782 (2006)
[CM04]   Cortes, C., Mohri, M.: AUC optimization versus error rate minimization, Advances in Neural Information Processing Systems (NIPS) (2004)
[FIS+03]   Freund, Y., Iyer, R., Schapire, R., Singer, Y.: An efficient boosting algorithm for combining preferences. J. of Machine Learning Research 4, 933–969 (2003)
[Lan53]   Landau, H.: On dominance relations and the structure of animal societies: III. The condition for a score structure. Bull. Math. Biophys. 15, 143–148 (1953)
[RCM+05]   Rudin, C., Cortes, C., Mohri, M., Schapire, R.: Margin-based ranking meets Boosting in the middle. In: Auer, P., Meir, R. (eds.) COLT 2005. LNCS (LNAI), vol. 3559, Springer, Heidelberg (2005)
[Sla61]   Slater, P.: Inconsistencies in a schedule of paired comparisons. Biometrika 48, 303–312 (1961)

A   Supporting Lemmas

The proof of Theorem 1 used two simple lemmas which we prove here.

Recall that Q denotes the distribution of label sequences $\{0,1\}^n$ of an unlabeled set $\{1, \ldots, n\}$. Call regret $r_Q(i,j)$ proper if $l_Q(i,j) - l_Q(j,i) \geq 0$. Notice that if $r_Q(i,j)$ is proper, then $r_Q(j,i) = 0$.

Lemma 1. *For any i, j, and k in $\{1, \ldots, n\}$, if $r_Q(i,j)$ and $r_Q(j,k)$ are proper,*

$$r_Q(i,k) = r_Q(i,j) + r_Q(j,k).$$

Proof. Let p be a shorthand for the restriction of Q to indices $\{i,j,k\}$ (so p is a distribution over $\{0,1\}^3$ obtained by summing over all label indices other than i, j, and k). A simple algebraic manipulation verifies the claim.

$$r_Q(i,j) + r_Q(j,k) =$$
$$p(100) + p(101) - p(010) - p(011) + p(010) + p(110) - p(001) - p(101) =$$
$$p(100) + p(110) - p(001) - p(011) = r_Q(i,k).$$

Notice that all label assignments above have exactly two mixed pairs, so the factor of $1/2$ is cancelled throughout.   ∎

Lemma 2. *If with respect to Q, the ordering $\langle 1, 2, \ldots, n \rangle$ has zero AUC regret, then all regret-zero pairwise predictions must be consistent with the ordering: $r_Q(i, j) = 0$ for all $1 \leq i < j \leq n$.*

Proof. All regrets $r_Q(i, i+1)$ must be 0, since swapping i and $i+1$ does not affect other pairwise regrets and would thus decrease the overall regret, contradicting the assumption that $\langle 1, 2, \ldots, n \rangle$ is regret minimizing. Consequently, all $r_Q(i+1, i)$ are proper. Repeated application of Lemma 1 implies that, for any $j > i$, $r_Q(j, i)$ is proper, which in turn implies that $r_Q(i, j) = 0$, concluding the proof.   ∎

Rademacher Margin Complexity

Liwei Wang and Jufu Feng

State Key Laboratory on Machine Perception,
School of Electronics Engineering and Computer Sciences, Peking University,
100871 Beijing, China
{wanglw,fjf}@cis.pku.edu.cn

The Rademacher complexity [1] of a function class F is defined as

$$R_n(F) = \mathop{E}_{\substack{x_1,\ldots x_n \\ \sigma_1,\ldots \sigma_n}} \left[\sup_{f \in F} \left| \frac{1}{n} \sum_{i=1}^{n} \sigma_i f(x_i) \right| \right]$$

where $\sigma_1, \ldots \sigma_n$ are iid Rademacher random variables. $R_n(F)$ characterizes the extent to which the functions in F can be best correlated with a Rademacher noise sequence. A number of generalization error bounds have been proposed based on Rademacher complexity [1,2].

In this open problem, we introduce a new complexity measure for function classes. We focus on function classes F that is the convex hull of a base function class H, which consists of indicator functions. Hence each $f \in F$ is a voting classifier of the form

$$f(x) = \sum \alpha_i h_i(x), \qquad \sum \alpha_i = 1, \quad \alpha_i \geq 0, \quad h_i \in H.$$

Since $h_i(x) \in \{-1, 1\}$, then $f(x) \in [-1, 1]$. We assume that H is symmetric: if $h \in H$, then $-h \in H$. The measure presented is referred to as Rademacher margin complexity, defined as:

$$RM_n(F, \theta) = \mathop{E}_{\substack{x_1,\ldots x_n \\ \sigma_1,\ldots \sigma_n}} \left[\sup_{f \in F} \frac{1}{n} \sum_{i=1}^{n} sgn \left[\sigma_i f(x_i) - \theta \right] \right], \qquad 0 < \theta \leq 1$$

Rademacher margin complexity quantifies the extent to which the functions in F can be best correlated, at least at margin θ, with a Rademacher noise sequence. Intuitively, Rademacher margin complexity is more suitable for characterizing the function class on its ability of producing large margin classifiers.

Our first open problem is a conjecture on a margin bound of voting classifiers in terms of the Rademacher margin complexity.

Conjecture: With probabiltiy at least $1 - \delta$, for all $f \in F$ satisfies

$$P_D(y \cdot f(x) \leq 0) \leq P_S(y \cdot f(x) \leq \theta) + k \cdot RM_n(F, \theta) + \varepsilon(n, \delta) \tag{1}$$

where P_D is the probability when the example is chosen according to the underlying distribution D of the problem. P_S is the probability with respect to the empirical distribution on the training examples. k is some universal constant. ε depends on n and δ, and is typically of the form $O((\frac{1}{n} \ln(1/\delta))^{1/2})$.

N. Bshouty and C. Gentile (Eds.): COLT 2007, LNAI 4539, pp. 620–621, 2007.

We next consider the properties of the Rademacher margin complexity. It is easy to check that if H is symmetric, then:

1. $RM_n(H, \theta) = R_n(H)$, $0 \leq \theta \leq 1$.

That is, the Rademacher margin complexity of an indicator function class reduces to its Rademacher complexity.

2. $RM_n(F, \theta)$ is monotonic decreasing with respect to θ for $0 \leq \theta \leq 1$ and

$$RM_n(F, 1) = RM_n(H, 1) = R_n(H).$$

Now our second problem. Is there a upper bound of $RM_n(F, \theta)$ in terms of $R_n(H)$ and θ ? In particular, whether the following inequality holds:

$$RM_n(F, \theta) \leq k \cdot R_n(H) \cdot \theta^{-1}, \quad 0 < \theta \leq 1 \tag{2}$$

where k is a constant.

Note that if Eq.(1) and Eq.(2) are both true, we recover a margin bound given in [2].

Monetary Rewards:
RMB 250 for each problem. Either prove it or give a counter example.

Acknowledgments. Supported by Program for New Century Excellent Talents in University and NSFC(60575002, 60635030) and NKBRPC(2004CB318000).

References

1. Bartlett, P., Mendelson, S.: Rademacher and Gaussian Complexities: Risk Bounds and Structural Resuls. J. Mach. Learn. Res. 3, 463–482 (2002)
2. Koltchinskii, V., Panchenko, D.: Empirical Margin Distributions and Bounding the Generalization Error of Combined Classifiers. Ann. Stat. 30, 1–50 (2002)

Open Problems in Efficient Semi-supervised PAC Learning

Avrim Blum* and Maria-Florina Balcan*

Carnegie Mellon University

1 Introduction

The standard PAC model focuses on learning a class of functions from labeled examples, where the two critical resources are the number of examples needed and running time. In many natural learning problems, however, unlabeled data can be obtained much more cheaply than labeled data. This has motivated the notion of semi-supervised learning, in which algorithms attempt to use this cheap unlabeled data in a way that (hopefully) reduces the number of labeled examples needed for learning [4]. For instance, semi-supervised and transductive SVM [2,5] and co-training [3] are two examples of semi-supervised learning algorithms. In [1], a semi-supervised PAC model is introduced that provides a common framework for the kinds of assumptions these algorithms make; however, most of the results in [1] deal with sample complexity rather than computational efficiency, or are only computationally efficient under strong assumptions on the underlying distribution. This note poses several questions related to developing computationally efficient algorithms in this semi-supervised PAC model.

2 The Model

The high-level idea of the semi-supervised PAC model of [1] is that rather than talking of learning a concept class C, one talks of learning a class C under a compatibility notion χ. Given a hypothesis h and distribution D, $\chi(h, D)$ is a score in $[0, 1]$ indicating how compatible h is with D. For example, if we believe data should be separable by a large margin, then χ would give a low score to separators that slice through dense regions under D and high score to those that do not. Or, if data has two "views" and one believes that either view should be sufficient for classification (as in co-training) then χ can give a low score to hypothesis pairs that disagree on a large probability mass of examples and a high score to those that tend to agree. Formally, in order to ensure that compatibility can be estimated from a finite sample, one requires that (overloading notation) $\chi(h, D) \equiv \mathbf{E}_{x \sim D}[\chi(h, x)]$ where $\chi(h, x) \in [0, 1]$. The quantity $1 - \chi(h, D)$ can be viewed as a notion of unlabeled error rate. For example, if we define $\chi(h, x) = 0$ if x is within distance γ of hyperplane h and

* Supported in part by National Science Foundation grant CCF-0514922 and a Google Research Grant.

N. Bshouty and C. Gentile (Eds.): COLT 2007, LNAI 4539, pp. 622–624, 2007.

$\chi(h, x) = 1$ otherwise, then the unlabeled error rate $1 - \chi(h, D)$ is the probability mass within distance γ of h. The analog to the standard PAC "realizable case" assumption that the target function lies in C is an assumption that furthermore the target is perfectly compatible (i.e., it has both zero true error and zero unlabeled error). In such a case, unlabeled data from D can allow one to reduce the space of plausible functions from the set of all functions in C (which are all potential candidates before any unlabeled data is seen) to just those that happen to be highly compatible with the distribution D (once enough unlabeled data has been seen to uniformly estimate compatibilities of all functions in C).

3 The Question

For a given class C, compatibility notion χ, and distribution D, define $C_{D,\chi}(\epsilon) = \{h \in C : 1 - \chi(h, D) \le \epsilon\}$. Under the assumption that the target belongs to C and is fully compatible, then given enough unlabeled data we can in principle reduce our search space from C down to $C_{D,\chi}(\epsilon)$. Thus, we should in principle need at most $O(\frac{1}{\epsilon}(\log |C_{D,\chi}(\epsilon)| + \log \frac{1}{\delta}))$ labeled examples to learn well.[1] Furthermore, if the distribution D is helpful, then $|C_{D,\chi}(\epsilon)|$ may be much smaller than $|C|$. The high-level question is whether for interesting classes C and notions of compatibility χ, one can learn with this many (or polynomial in this many) labeled examples by *efficient* algorithms. If so, we say that such an algorithm is an efficient semi-supervised learning algorithm for the pair (C, χ). We now instantiate this high-level question with a few specific classes and compatibility notions.

3.1 A Simple Non-open Problem

Before presenting open problems, here is a simple example from [1] of a (C, χ) pair for which efficient semi-supervised learning is easy. Let C be the class of monotone disjunctions over $\{0, 1\}^n$. Now, suppose we say an example x is compatible with function h if either all variables set to 1 in x are relevant variables of h or none of them are. This is a very strong notion of "margin": it says, in essence, that every variable is either a positive indicator or a negative indicator, and no example should contain both positive and negative indicators.

In this case efficient semi-supervised learning is easy. Just draw a large set of unlabeled examples and create a graph with n vertices, one for each variable. Put an edge between two vertices if any example has both variables set to 1. Under the compatibility assumption, all variables in the same connected component of this graph must either all be positive indicators or all be negative indicators. So, if we have k components, we only need $O(\frac{1}{\epsilon}[k + \log \frac{1}{\delta}])$ labeled examples to achieve a PAC guarantee. Furthermore, as long as we created the graph using enough unlabeled data we can be confident that $k \le \lg |C_{D,\chi}(\epsilon)|$. Note that in this context, a "helpful" distribution is one that produces a small number of components.

---

[1] Or even less depending on the structure of C. For example, we would ideally use an ϵ-cover bound here. Note that we have overloaded "ϵ" for both labeled and unlabeled error bounds for simplicity.

3.2 Specific Open Problems

Two-sided disjunctions: This is a generalization of the example above where we now allow variables to be positive indicators, negative indicators, or irrelevant. Specifically, define a "two-sided disjunction" h to be a pair of disjunctions (h_+, h_-) where only h_+ is used for classification, but h is compatible with D iff for all examples x, $h_+(x) = -h_-(x)$. That is, D is such that both the positive and negative classes can be described by OR-functions.

Two-sided majority with margins: As a different generalization of the problem from Section 3.1, suppose that again every variable is either a positive or negative indicator, but we relax the margin condition a bit. In particular, say we require that x either contain at least 60% of the positive indicators and at most 40% of the negative indicators (for positive examples) or vice versa (for negative examples).

Co-training with disjunctions: This is the "inverse" of the two-sided disjunction problem. Let C be the class of disjunctions, but an example x is a *pair* of points (x_1, x_2) in $\{0, 1\}^n$. Define $h(x) = h(x_1)$ but say that h is compatible with x iff $h(x_1) = h(x_2)$. That is, under our compatibility assumption, each unlabeled example is either a pair of positive examples or a pair of negative examples. Note that D is now a distribution over pairs.

Co-training with linear separators: A generalization of the above problem is the case that h is a linear separator. It is known that the consistency problem is NP-hard [A. Flaxman, personal communication], however efficient algorithms are known for the special case that the elements x_1 and x_2 of the pair are drawn independently given their label [3,1]. Even if one cannot solve the problem efficiently in general, a natural question is whether one can at least weaken the independence-given-the-label assumption in a nontrivial way and still get an efficient algorithm for this class.

Monetary rewards: $300 for a positive solution to any of the above questions. More generally, it would be interesting to consider other classes and notions of compatibility as well.

References

1. Balcan, M.-F., Blum, A.: A PAC-style model for learning from labeled and unlabeled data. In: Proc. 18th Annual Conference on Learning Theory (2005)
2. Bennett, K. P., Demiriz, A.: Semi-supervised support vector machines. In: NIPS, pp. 368–374 (1998)
3. Blum, A., Mitchell, T.M.: Combining labeled and unlabeled data with co-training. In: Proc. 11th Annual Conference on Learning Theory, pp. 92–100 (1998)
4. Chapelle, O., Schölkopf, B., Zien, A. (eds.): Semi-Supervised Learning. MIT Press, Cambridge (2006)
5. Joachims, T.: Transductive inference for text classification using support vector machines. In: Proc. ICML, pp. 200–209 (1999)

Resource-Bounded Information Gathering for Correlation Clustering

Pallika Kanani and Andrew McCallum

University of Massachusetts, Amherst

Abstract. We present a new class of problems, called *resource-bounded information gathering for correlation clustering*. Our goal is to perform correlation clustering under circumstances in which accuracy may be improved by augmenting the given graph with additional information. This information is obtained by querying an external source under resource constraints. The problem is to develop the most effective query selection strategy to minimize some loss function on the resulting partitioning. We motivate the problem using an entity resolution task.

1 Problem Definition

The standard correlation clustering problem on a graph with real-valued edge weights is as follows: there exists a fully connected graph $G(V, E)$ with n nodes and edge weights, $w_{ij} \in [-1, +1]$. The goal is to partition the vertices in V by minimizing the inconsistencies with the edge weights [1]. That is, we want to find a partitioning that maximizes the objective function $\mathcal{F} = \sum_{ij} w_{ij} f(i, j)$, where $f(i, j) = 1$ when v_i and v_j are in the same partition and -1 otherwise.

Now consider a case in which there exists some "true" partitioning $\mathcal{P}$, and the edge weights $w_{ij} \in [-\infty, +\infty]$ are drawn from a random distribution (noise model) that is correlated with whether or not edge $e_{ij} \in E$ is cut by a partition boundary. The goal is to find an approximate partitioning, $\mathcal{P}_a$, of V into an unknown number of k partitions, such that $\mathcal{P}_a$ is as 'close' to $\mathcal{P}$ as possible. There are many different possible measures of closeness to choose from. Let $\mathcal{L}(\mathcal{P}, \mathcal{P}_a)$ be some arbitrary loss function. If no additional information is available, then we could simply find a partitioning that optimizes $\mathcal{F}$ on the given weights.

In this paper, we consider settings in which we may issue queries for additional information to help us reduce loss $\mathcal{L}$. Let $G_0(V_0, E_0)$ be the original graph. Let $\mathcal{F}_0$ be the objective function defined over G_0. Our goal is to perform correlation clustering and optimize $\mathcal{F}_0$ with respect to the true partitioning of G_0. We can augment the graph with additional information using two alternative methods: (1) updating the weight on an existing edge, (2) adding a new vertex and edges connecting it to existing vertices. We can obtain this additional information by querying a (possibly adversarial) oracle using two different types of queries. In the first method, we use query of type Q1, which takes as input edge e_{ij} and returns a new edge weight w'_{ij}, where w'_{ij} is drawn from a different distribution that has higher correlation with the true partitioning $\mathcal{P}$.

N. Bshouty and C. Gentile (Eds.): COLT 2007, LNAI 4539, pp. 625–627, 2007.

In the second method, we can expand the graph G_0, by adding a new set of vertices, V_1 and the corresponding new set of edges, E_1 to create a larger, fully connected graph, G'. Although we are not interested in partitioning V_1, we hypothesize that partitioning G' would improve the optimization of $\mathcal{F}$, on G_0 due to transitivity of partition membership. In this case, given resource constraints, we must select $V_s' \subset V_1$ to add to the graph. These can be obtained by second type of query, Q2, which takes as input (V_0, E_0) and returns a subset $V_s' \subset V_1$. Note that the additional nodes obtained as a result of the queries of type Q2 help by inducing a new, and presumably more accurate partitioning on the nodes of G_0. Fig. 1 illustrates the result of these queries.

However, there exist many possible queries of type Q1 and Q2, each with an associated cost. There is also a cost for performing computation on the additional information. Hence, we need an efficient way to select and order queries under the given resource constraints.

Formally, we define the problem of *resource-bounded information gathering for correlation clustering* as follows. Let $c(q)$ be the cost associated with a query $q \in Q1 \cup Q2$. Let b be the total budget on queries and computation. Find distinct queries $q_1, q_2, ...q_m \in Q1 \cup Q2$ and $\mathcal{P}_a$, to minimize $\mathcal{L}(\mathcal{P}, \mathcal{P}_a)$, s.t. $\sum_{q_i} c(q_i) \leq b$.

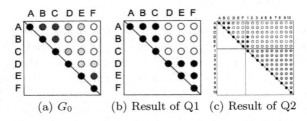

(a) G_0 (b) Result of Q1   (c) Result of Q2

Fig. 1. Results of the two kinds of queries. (a) The adjacency matrix of G_0 where darker circles represent edges with higher weight. (b) The new edge weights w'_{ij} after issuing the queries from Q1. (c) The graph expanded after issuing queries from Q2. The upper left corner of the matrix corresponds to G_0 and the remaining rows and columns correspond to the nodes in V_1.

2   Example Application and Related Work

The problem described above is inspired by our work in author coreference. Here we are given a set of citations that mention similar author names, and must partition them by the true identity of the author. As in our previous work [2], we build a graph in which nodes represent author mentions. The edge weights indicate the strength of our belief that two mentions refer to the same real author, and are estimated by a binary logistic regression classifier that uses features such as title, co-author overlap, etc. Note that, each partition should represent the set of mentions that correspond to the same real author.

Experimentally, we have shown significant accuracy improvement by making queries of type Q1 and Q2. In our case, we issue the queries to the web. We incorporate the results of the queries either as additional features or as additional nodes in the graph. For example, we can form a query by joining the titles of two citations and issuing it to a search engine API. A hit indicates the presence of a document on the web that contains both of these citations and hence provides some evidence that they are authored by the same person. The result of the query is translated into a binary input feature to our classifier and is used to update the weight on the corresponding edge. The problem is resource bounded because for a fully connected graph, obtaining additional feature value for every pair of mentions is prohibitively expensive.

Similarly, we can add nodes corresponding to documents obtained by web queries. Note that these web documents represent author mentions and help improve accuracy by transitivity. For example, the additional node could be the list of publications or CV of one of the authors and would show strong affinity towards several nodes in the original graph. Hence, by transitivity, applying graph partitioning on this expanded graph leads to improvement in accuracy. However, since the web is too large to incorporate all its data, we need an efficient procedure for selecting a subset of web queries and resulting documents.

In [2], we propose an approach to resource bounded information gathering based on expected entropy, in which we use web information as an additional feature. We also propose centroid-based methods in which we add nodes to the graph.

Learning and inference under resource limitations has been studied in various forms, including resource-bounded reasoning and the value of information [5], budgeted learning, [4], and active learning, for example, [3].

Acknowledgments

We thank Avrim Blum, Katrina Ligett, Chris Pal, Sridhar Mahadevan, Arnold Rosenberg, Gideon Mann, Siddharth Srivastava and Aron Culotta for useful discussions. Supported in part by the CIIR, CIA, NSA and NSF under grant #IIS-0326249 and in part by DoD contract #HM1582-06-1-2013.

References

1. Bansal, N., Chawla, S., Blum, A.: Correlation Clustering. In: Proc. of 43rd FOCS (2002)
2. Kanani, P., McCallum, A., Pal, C.: Improving Author Coreference by Resource-bounded Information Gathering from the Web. In: Proc. of IJCAI (2007)
3. Roy, N., McCallum, A.: Toward Optimal Active Learning through Sampling Estimation of Error Reduction. In: Proc. of 18th ICML (2001)
4. Kapoor, A., Greiner, R.: Learning and Classifying Under Hard Budgets, ECML (2005)
5. Grass, J., Zilberstein, S.: A Value-Driven System for Autonomous Information Gathering, JIIS, 14 (2000)

Are There Local Maxima in the Infinite-Sample Likelihood of Gaussian Mixture Estimation?

Nathan Srebro

Toyota Technological Institute-Chicago IL, USA
nati@uchicago.edu

Consider the problem of estimating the centers $\boldsymbol{\mu} = (\mu_1, \ldots, \mu_k)$ of a uniform mixture of unit-variance spherical Gaussians in $\mathbb{R}^d$,

$$f_{(\mu_1,\mu_2,\ldots,\mu_k)}(x) = \sum_{i=1}^{k} \frac{1}{k} \frac{1}{(2\pi)^{d/2}} e^{|x-\mu_i|^2/2}, \tag{1}$$

from i.i.d. samples $x_1, \ldots, x_m$ drawn from this distribution. This can be done by maximizing the (average log) likelihood $L_{(x_1,\ldots,x_m)}(\boldsymbol{\mu}) = \frac{1}{m} \sum_i \log f_{\boldsymbol{\mu}}(x_i)$. Maximizing the likelihood is guaranteed to recover the correct centers, in the large-sample limit, for any mixture model of the form (1). Unfortunately, maximizing the likelihood is hard in the worst case, and we usually revert to local search heuristics such as Expectation Maximization (EM) which can get trapped in the many local minima the likelihood function might have.

Despite this, a string of results establishes that the centers *can* be tractably recovered, given enough data sampled from a well-separated mixture, using projection-based methods [1,2,3], and even using EM [4].

These results require a large separation between centers. In practice, even with a much smaller separation, given enough data and proper initialization, EM converges to the global ML solution and allows recovery of the centers [5]. It seems that when data is plentiful, the local minima disappear.

Although the likelihood function for finite data sets may admit many local minima, the conjecture proposed here is that in the infinite sample limit, for data sampled from a distribution of the form (1), with *any* true centers $\boldsymbol{\mu}^0 = (\mu_1^0, \ldots, \mu_k^0)$, the only local maxima are the global maxima, given by permutations of the true centers $\mu_1^0, \ldots, \mu_k^0$.

At the infinite sample limit, the likelihood is given by the KL-divergence between mixture models: $L(\boldsymbol{\mu}) \xrightarrow{m \to \infty} \mathbf{E}_{X \sim f_{\mu^0}}[\log f_{\boldsymbol{\mu}}(X)] = -D\left(\boldsymbol{\mu}^0 \| \boldsymbol{\mu}\right) - H(\boldsymbol{\mu}^0)$, where the entropy $H(\boldsymbol{\mu}^0)$ of f_{μ^0} is constant. Maxima of the infinite-sample likelihood are thus exactly minima of the KL-divergence $D\left(\boldsymbol{\mu}^0 \| \boldsymbol{\mu}\right) = \mathbf{E}_{f_{\mu^0}}\left[\log \frac{f_{\mu^0}}{f_{\boldsymbol{\mu}}}\right]$. The KL-divergence is non-negative and zero only when $f_{\boldsymbol{\mu}} = f_{\mu^0}$. This happens iff $\mu_1, \ldots, \mu_k$ are a permutation of $\mu_1^0, \ldots, \mu_k^0$, and so these are the only global minima of the KL-divergence. Our conjecture can therefore be equivalently stated as: **for any set of centers $\boldsymbol{\mu}^0$, the only local minima of $D\left(\boldsymbol{\mu}^0 \| \boldsymbol{\mu}\right)$, with respect to $\boldsymbol{\mu}$, are the global minima obtained at permutations of $\boldsymbol{\mu}^0$.**

The KL-divergence has many stable points which are not local minima, but rather saddle points. For example, such a saddle point arises when two centers

N. Bshouty and C. Gentile (Eds.): COLT 2007, LNAI 4539, pp. 628–629, 2007.
© Springer-Verlag Berlin Heidelberg 2007

coincide in $\boldsymbol{\mu}$ (but not in $\boldsymbol{\mu}^0$). There are also several different basins, one for each permutation of the centers, separated by non-convex ridges and near-plateaus. When only a finite data set is considered, local minima easily arise in these near-plateaus. Even in the infinite-sample limit, EM, or other local-search methods, might take a very large number of steps to traverse these near-plateaus and converge. For this reason the conjecture does not directly imply tractability.

The conjecture *does* imply that no minimum separation is required in order to establish convergence to the global minimum at the infinite sample limit— if it is true, what remains is to study the relationship between the speed of convergence, the sample size and the separation. Moreover, the conjecture implies that local search (e.g. EM) will converge to the correct model *regardless of initialization* (except for a measure zero set of "ridge manifolds" between the attraction basins of different permutations of the correct centers). Empirical simulations with "infinite sample" EM (working directly on the KL-divergence) on three centers in two dimensions confirm this by showing eventual convergence to the global likelihood, even when initialized with two nearby centers. Current large-separation results require careful initialization ensuring at least one initial center from the vicinity of each true center [4,6].

Of course, the real quantity of interest is the probability P_m, under some specific random initialization scheme, of being in the basin of attraction of the global maximum of the likelihood given a random sample of finite size m. In fact, our interest in the problem stemmed from study of the probability P_m for some reasonable initialization schemes. The conjecture can be equivalently stated as $P_m \to 1$ for any initialization scheme, and can thus be seen as a prerequisite to understanding P_m.

Clarification: The KL-divergence $D(p\|\boldsymbol{\mu})$ between a fixed arbitrary distribution p and mixture models (1), may have non-global local minima. The conjecture only applies when p itself is a mixture model of the form (1). In particular, if p is a mixture of more than k Gaussians, and we are trying to fit it with a mixture of only k Gaussians, non-global local minima can arise.

References

1. Dasgupta, S.: Learning mixtures of gaussians. In: Proc. of the 40th Ann. Symp. on Foundations of Computer Science (1999)
2. Arora, S., Kannan, R.: Learning mixtures of arbitrary gaussians. In: Proceedings of the thirty-third annual ACM symposium on Theory of computing (2001)
3. Vempala, S., Wang, G.: A spectral algorithm for learning mixture models. J. Comput. Syst. Sci. 68, 841–860 (2004)
4. Dasgupta, S., Schulman, L.: A two-round variant of em for gaussian mixtures. In: Proc. of the 16th Ann. Conf. on Uncertainty in Artificial Intelligence (2000)
5. Srebro, N., Shakhnarovich, G., Roweis, S.: An investigation of computational and informational limits in gaussian mixture clustering. In: Proceedings of the 23rd International Conference on Machine learning (ICML) (2006)
6. Ostrovsky, R., Rabani, Y., Schulman, L.J., Swamy, C.: The effectiveness of lloyd-type methods for the k-means problem. In: Proceedings of the 47th Annual IEEE Symposium on Foundations of Computer Science (FOCS'06), pp. 165–176 (2006)

When Is There a Free Matrix Lunch?

Manfred K. Warmuth

University of California - Santa Cruz

The "no-free lunch theorems" essentially say that for any two algorithms A and B, there are "as many" targets (or priors over targets) for which A has lower expected loss than B as vice-versa. This can be made precise for certain loss functions [WM97]. This note concerns itself with cases where seemingly harder matrix versions of the algorithms have the same on-line loss bounds as the corresponding vector versions. So it seems that you get a free "matrix lunch" (Our title is however not meant to imply that we have a technical refutation of the no-free lunch theorems).

The simplest case of this phenomenon occurs in the so-called *expert setting*. We have n experts. In each trial the algorithm proposes a probability vector $\mathbf{w}^t$ over the n experts, receives a loss vector $\boldsymbol{\ell}^t \in [0,1]^n$ for the experts and incurs an expected loss $\mathbf{w}^t \cdot \boldsymbol{\ell}^t$. The Weighted Majority or Hedge algorithm uses exponential weights $w_i^t \sim w_i^1 e^{-\eta \sum_{t=1}^{t-1} \ell_i^t}$ and has the following expected loss bound [FS97]:

$$\sum_{t=1}^{T} \mathbf{w}^t \cdot \boldsymbol{\ell}^t \;\leq\; \ell^* + \sqrt{2\ell^* \ln n} + \ln n,$$

when η is tuned as a function of n and the best loss $\ell^* = \inf_i \sum_{t=1}^{T} \ell_i^t$.

Recently a matrix version of this algorithm has been developed in parallel by a number of researchers [WK06b, AK07]. Now the experts are outer products or *dyads* $\mathbf{u}\mathbf{u}^\top$, where $\mathbf{u}$ is a unit vector in $\mathbb{R}^n$, and there are continuously many such dyads (one for each pair $\pm\mathbf{u}$). The uncertainty of the algorithm about which dyad is good is expressed as a mixture of dyads (or density matrix) $\mathbf{W}^t$.

The loss vector $\boldsymbol{\ell}^t$ at trial t is replaced by a covariance matrix $\mathbf{L}^t$ whose eigenvalues must lie in the interval $[0,1]$. The symmetric matrix $\mathbf{L}^t$ specifies the loss for all dyads $\mathbf{u}\mathbf{u}^\top$ at trial t via the formula $(\mathbf{u}\mathbf{u}^\top) \bullet \mathbf{L}^t = \mathbf{u}^\top \mathbf{L}^t \mathbf{u}$ which is the variance at trial t in direction $\mathbf{u}$. The algorithm is charged by the expected variance $\mathbf{W}^t \bullet \mathbf{L}^t = \sum_{i,j} W_{i,j}^t L_{i,j}^t$ and its total expected variance is bounded as

$$\sum_{t=1}^{T} \mathbf{W}^t \bullet \mathbf{L}^t \;\leq\; L^* + \sqrt{2L^* \ln n} + \ln n,$$

when η is tuned as a function of n and $L^* = \inf_{\mathbf{u}} \sum_{t=1}^{T} \mathbf{u}^\top \mathbf{L}^t \mathbf{u}$. The algorithm that achieves this is a matrix generalization of the weighted majority algorithm defined using the matrix exponential (See [WK06b, AK07] for details).

Curiously enough, if the initial density matrix is uniform and we let $\mathbf{L}^t = \mathrm{diag}(\boldsymbol{\ell}^t)$, then the matrix version of the algorithm and bound specialize to the original vector version. That is, the original Weighted Majority algorithm is

N. Bshouty and C. Gentile (Eds.): COLT 2007, LNAI 4539, pp. 630–632, 2007.

retained as a special case when all instance/loss matrices $\mathbf{L}^t$ have the identity matrix as an eigensystem. The same phenomenon happens for linear regression w.r.t. square loss: The bounds proven for matrix version of the exponentiated gradient algorithm [TRW05] are identical to the original bounds [KW97] when the instances are diagonal matrices. The same happens for Boosting [TRW05] and the matrix version of the Winnow algorithm [War07]. There is even a Bayes rule for density matrices that has the standard Bayes rule and its bounds as a special case when the priors and data likelihoods are diagonal matrices [WK06a].

Note that this phenomenon is also really puzzling from an information theoretic point of view. It takes $\ln n$ nats to encode the identity of one of the n experts. However it should take more than $\ln n$ nats to encode an arbitrary direction/dyad in n dimensions. **What properties are required for an on-line algorithm and its bound for solving a problem with symmetric matrix instances so that the worst-case of the bound is attained when the instances are diagonal (i.e. have the identity matrix as an eigensystem), thus allowing us to get the matrix case for free?** So far, all cases where this has been shown is for algorithms that are motivated by some kind of relative entropy regularized optimization problem. Does this phenomenon occur for other families of updates as well that are motivated by different divergences?

Ideally, we would like the characterization be defined i.t.o. some spectral invariance of the regularization and loss function (see e.g. [WV05] for an example where a family of updates is characterized by a notion of rotation invariance).

Acknowledgement. Thanks to Dima Kuzmin for helpful discussions.

References

[AK07]   Arora, S., Kale, S.: A combinatorial primal-dual approach to semidefinite programs. In: Proc. 39th Annual ACM Symposium on Theory of Computing,To appear, ACM, New York (2007)

[FS97]   Freund, Y., Schapire, R.E.: A decision-theoretic generalization of on-line learning and an application to Boosting. Journal of Computer and System Sciences 55(1), 119–139 (1997)

[KW97]   Kivinen, J., Warmuth, M.K.: Additive versus exponentiated gradient updates for linear prediction. Information and Computation 132(1), 1–64 (1997)

[TRW05] Tsuda, K., Rätsch, G., Warmuth, M.K.: Matrix exponentiated gradient updates for on-line learning and Bregman projections. Journal of Machine Learning Research 6, 995–1018 (2005)

[War07]   Warmuth, M.K.: Winnowing subspaces. Unpublished manuscript (February 2007)

[WK06a] Warmuth, M., Kuzmin, D.: A Bayesian probability calculus for density matrices. In: Proceedings of the 22nd Conference on Uncertainty in Artificial Intelligence UAI06, Springer, Heidelberg (2006)

[WK06b] Warmuth, M.K., Kuzmin, D.: Online variance minimization. In: Lugosi, G., Simon, H.U. (eds.) COLT 2006. LNCS (LNAI), vol. 4005, Springer, Heidelberg (2006)

[WM97]   Wolpert, D.H., Macready, W.G.: No free lunch theorems for optimization. IEEE Transaction for Evolutionary Computation, 1(67) (1997)
[WV05]   Warmuth, M.K., Vishwanathan, S.V.N.: Leaving the span. In: Auer, P., Meir, R. (eds.) COLT 2005. LNCS (LNAI), vol. 3559, Springer, Heidelberg (2005) Journal version: http://www.cse.ucsc.edu/~manfred/pubs/span.pdf

Author Index

Lecture Notes in Artificial Intelligence (LNAI)